Lecture Notes in Electrical Engineering

Volume 211

For further volumes:
http://www.springer.com/series/7818

Lecture Notes in Electrical Engineering

Volume 21

Wei Lu · Guoqiang Cai
Weibin Liu · Weiwei Xing
Editors

Proceedings of the 2012 International Conference on Information Technology and Software Engineering

Information Technology & Computing Intelligence

 Springer

Editors
Wei Lu
Beijing Jiaotong University
Beijing
People's Republic of China

Guoqiang Cai
Beijing Jiaotong University
Beijing
People's Republic of China

Weibin Liu
Beijing Jiaotong University
Beijing
People's Republic of China

Weiwei Xing
Beijing Jiaotong University
Beijing
People's Republic of China

ISSN 1876-1100 ISSN 1876-1119 (electronic)
ISBN 978-3-662-51185-5 ISBN 978-3-642-34522-7 (eBook)
DOI 10.1007/978-3-642-34522-7
Springer Heidelberg New York Dordrecht London

Committees

Honorary Chair
Yaoxue Zhang, Central South University, China

General Chairs
Wei Lu, Beijing Jiaotong University, China
Jianhua Ma, Hosei University, Japan

Steering Committee Chairs
Zengqi Sun, Tsinghua University, China
Shi-Kuo Chang, University of Pittsburgh, Knowledge Systems Institute, USA
Mirko Novak, Institute of Computer Science, Czech Academy of Sciences, Czech Republic

Program Committee Chairs
Guoqiang Cai, Beijing Jiaotong University, China
Weibin Liu, Beijing Jiaotong University, China

Organizing Committee Chairs
Weiwei Xing, Beijing Jiaotong University, China
Qingshan Jiang, Shenzhen Institute of Advanced Technology, Chinese Academy of Science, China
Kin Fun Li, University of Victoria, Canada
Tole Sutikno, Ahmad Dahlan University, Indonesia

Technical Program Committee Members
Bin Luo, Nanjing University, China
Charles Clarke, University of Waterloo, Canada
Chih Lai, University of St.Thomas, USA
Chris Price, Aberystwyth University, England
David Levy, University of Sydney, Australia
Hong-Chuan Yang, University of Victoria, Canada

Preface

The 2012 International Conference on Information Technology and Software Engineering (ITSE2012) was held by Beijing Jiaotong University in Beijing on December 8–10, 2012. The objective of ITSE2012 was to provide a platform for researchers, engineers, academicians as well as industrial professionals from all over the world to present their research results and development activities in Information Technology and Software Engineering. This conference provided opportunities for the delegates to exchange new ideas and application experiences face-to-face, to establish research or business relations and to find global partners for future collaboration.

We have received more than 1,300 papers covering most of the aspects in Information Technology, Software Engineering, Computing Intelligence, Digital Media Technology, Visual Languages and Computing, etc. All submitted papers have been subject to a strict peer-review process; about 300 of them were selected for presentation at the conference and included in the ITSE2012 Proceedings. We believe the proceedings can provide the readers a broad overview of the latest advances in the fields of Information Technology and Software Engineering.

ITSE2012 has been supported by many professors (see the name list of the committees); we would like to take this opportunity to express our sincere gratitude and highest respect to them. At the same time, we also express our sincere thanks for the support of every delegate.

Wei Lu
Chair of ITSE2012

Contents

Part I
Information Technology

Chapter 1
Discovering Core Architecture Classes to Assist Initial Program Comprehension

Muhammad Kamran, Farooque Azam and Aasia Khanum

Abstract Before making modifications to an unfamiliar software system, the new programmer needs to gain some knowledge about that system. The core classes that constitute the system architecture can reveal important structural properties of the system. Hence these core classes can be used to catch an initial glimpse of the system during initial stages of program comprehension. We propose an efficient technique that pinpoints the core architecture classes of the system with the help of our own conceived variant of a dynamic coupling metric. The results are compared with the already performed experiments of similar nature on the same software system. There is a noticeable improvement in the performance with our approach while the precision and recall contest with the best results obtained in other analogous experiments.

Keywords Dynamic analysis · Program comprehension · Dynamic coupling

M. Kamran (✉) · F. Azam · A. Khanum
Department of Computer Engineering, College of Electrical and Mechanical Engineering, National University of Sciences and Technology (NUST), Islamabad, Pakistan
e-mail: kamran_1259@yahoo.com

F. Azam
e-mail: farooq@ceme.nust.edu.pk

A. Khanum
e-mail: aasia@ceme.nust.edu.pk

W. Lu et al. (eds.), *Proceedings of the 2012 International Conference on Information Technology and Software Engineering*, Lecture Notes in Electrical Engineering 211, DOI: 10.1007/978-3-642-34522-7_1, © Springer-Verlag Berlin Heidelberg 2013

1.1 Introduction

The continuous modification of software systems, the increasing size of the software and the expensive development process are the factors that are responsible for the increase in the amount of the effort that is being expended on the maintenance phase. Mostly each maintenance cycle is performed to achieve a specific goal, for instance improving the efficiency of a procedure, provision of new application features, assembling existing components into the new software and so on [1]. A programmer will not be able to achieve any of the above goals unless he understands the particular software at a sufficient level of detail that allows him to implement the desired change in the system. The process of exploring the software and its associated artifacts with the aim to gain knowledge about the inner workings of the system for carrying out the necessary changes in the system is termed as program comprehension [2].

The process of building an understanding of the system is time consuming and takes around 40 % of the allocated time for a maintenance task [3]. How a new software developer proceeds to build an initial acquaintance with the software differs a lot and depends on a number of factors like the experience of the individual, the size and type of the software, the level of detail required to modify the system and so on [4–6].

It has been observed during experiments that the programmer's general awareness and domain knowledge about the specific program are the main factors that affect the success of building useful cognitive models by program decomposition [7]. A large number of models have been recognized for the cognitive process which can be placed into one of the following categories: (1) top-down conception (2) bottom-up conception (3) hybrid of the two preceding models [8]. The programmers familiar with the source code of the system usually follow the top-down model. Domain knowledge is utilized by the programmers to effectively map the code with the requirements of the system. In case, the programmers have little or no acquaintance with the source code of the system, they usually start with the bottom-up model [9]. They make use of their knowledge about the programming to assess the source code and construct the cognitive models to understand the system [2].

Full automation of the process of developing an understanding of the program is not possible since it involves human learning activity. Therefore, it has been suggested that the specialized tools should help the programmer discover the software freely [10]. The segments of the program that can be attractive from the comprehension viewpoint must be brought into the notice of the programmer by the exploration tools [11].

In this paper we have proposed a heuristic approach for pinpointing the core classes of the system using a variation of the dynamic coupling metric proposed in the literature [12]. Our approach can be placed in the dynamic analysis category. We have demonstrated the proposed approach using the open source case study, namely Apache Ant. The results have shown that our variant of the dynamic coupling metric is certainly a good indication for pinpointing the core classes of the software and is far more efficient than the already proposed approaches [13, 14].

1.2 Dynamic Coupling and Program Comprehension

We aim to present a miniature and targeted number of starting points to the programmer, which can be used to gain familiarity with the unknown system and subsequent dependency analysis of the program structure. We have used dynamic coupling for the identification of these initial points of significance for program understanding.

Mostly the coupling metrics have been estimated statically through the source code (or any other static model of program structure) by analyzing the dependencies that exist among various program elements. The precision of coupling metrics that are estimated statically declines quickly in the presence of dead code, dynamic binding and inheritance. This loss of precision has compelled for the search of more accurate alternatives like dynamic coupling measures, a research area in software engineering that is developing [12].

In his work on dynamic coupling, a total of twelve metrics have been defined by Arisholm et al. We have used the definition of one metric from his work and made a slight variation of this metric to meet our objective of finding the core classes of the system. We will now discuss the metric from [12] and then discuss our variation.

1.2.1 Distinct Method Invocations

This metric is a numeric score that is obtained by calculating the unique method invocations being originated from every method in each object. It must be noticed that each distinct method is counted only once which is dissimilar from counting all method invocations (that may include recurrence of method call). The score is calculated for each object and to obtain the score for a class, the sum of the scores for all the objects of that class is used. One metric from [12] that counts distinct methods at class level and belongs to import category of coupling is called IC_CM. All methods calls that come under the definition of cohesion are not included in the score.

The detailed discussion of the definitions in Table 1.1 is beyond the scope of this paper. We assume that the reader is familiar with the concept of dynamic coupling metrics. The reader is encouraged to consult [12] to understand the definitions in Table 1.1.

Table 1.1 Dynamic coupling measures [12]

Definitions	
C	Set of classes in the system
M	Set of methods in the system
R_{MC}	$R_{MC} \subseteq M \times C$ The set of all methods that are actually defined in a class
IV	$IV \subseteq M \times C \times M \times C$ The set of possible method invocations in the system
$IC\_CM (c_1)$	$\|\{(m_1, c_1, m_2, c_2) \mid (\exists (m_1, c_1),(m_2, c_2) \in R_{MC}) \wedge c_1 \neq c_2 \wedge (m_1, c_1, m_2, c_2) \in IV\}\|$

1.2.2 Our Variant of IC_CM

We have made a variation of the IC_CM metric with the inclusion of a new numeric parameter that is initialized with a value of zero and is incremented each time an object of a distinct class is initialized. We name this parameter as "loading_order". Whenever a constructor of any class is called during the execution of program, we first check if the constructor of this class is being called for the first time? If yes, we say that this class is being loaded for the first time in the application so we add this class to the list of distinct classes that have already been loaded. The numeric parameter (loading_order) is incremented by one and is stored along with the other information like source/target of method/class.

We have built an analogy from civil engineering structures like bridge/buildings that the core part of the structure is laid first and the rest of the structure is based on that core part. So we proposed that the classes loaded during the start up that have strong coupling with other classes are prime candidates for early program comprehension.

1.3 Implementation

Our approach consists of three steps. This section provides an overview of the steps involved in our approach.

1.3.1 Start the System Using AspectJ Library

We have used AspectJ for dynamic analysis of the system. AspectJ supports load-time weaving of applications. While using load-time weaving, the application is treated as a black-box, since any application can be monitored/traced using AspectJ library without modifying the application code. This implies that our technique is non-invasive; the source code of the application is not a pre-requisite for our approach. Instead the technique can be applied to the deployed application without modifying/re-compiling the source code. The only requirement of our approach is the addition of our custom built aspect library to the application class-path and the launch of the system with load-time aspect weaving enabled.

1.3.2 Run the Instrumented System and Calculate Metrics

When we run the instrumented System, AspectJ allows us to intercept each and every method call and provides us with the relevant information like the name of the class, name of the method, method signature, line number of code etc. System classes and class libraries can be excluded easily to filter unwanted classes. It can also be specified that only specified classes of the application should be intercepted. Inclusion/exclusion of classes is at the programmer's discretion. We have built our approach around on-line analysis of the application, since we calculate the metrics in parallel to program execution. This is opposite to off-line analysis approach in which the system is executed first and after the execution is finished the execution traces are analyzed to extract the information. As the system gets executed, we record relevant information in a linked list like data-structure.

1.3.3 Rank the Results

At the end of the execution, we rank the results according to their metric value and display the top fifteen percent results to the user.

1.4 Experimental Setup, Baseline and Results

We have demonstrated the potential of our technique using an open source case study named Apache Ant. The reason behind choosing Apache Ant as a case study was that the results of similar experiments using Apache Ant were readily available in [13, 14], which are used perform the comparison with our approach. At the time of writing, the latest release of Apache Ant is 1.8.3. To compare the results of our implementation with the approach presented in [13, 14], we have used the same version (i.e. 1.6.1) and the identical execution scenario (i.e. build the source code of Ant 1.6.1 using the Ant 1.6.1 binary release) for the experiment.

To evaluate the accuracy of our heuristic, we have used as baseline the most important classes, extracted and provided by [13, 14] (from design documents of Apache Ant 1.6.1) in their experiment of finding key classes of a software system.

The top 15 % classes identified by our approach are presented in Table 1.2. The 15 % mark is set by the authors in [14]; they argue that the documentation of Apache Ant mentions about 10 % of the total classes that are deemed important by the original authors of Apache Ant. Hence the 15 % mark is quite reasonable. Also the 15 % mark keeps a fair balance between the precision and recall.

The precision and recall percentage mentioned in Table 1.3 for our approach is calculated with the help of Table 1.2. Whereas the results for the other approaches in Table 1.3 like IC_CM, ICC_CC, IC_CC' and so on are taken from [13, 14].

Table 1.2 Classes identified by our approach (top 15 %)

Our identified classes	Baseline classes [13, 14]
Project	Project
UnknownElement	UnknownElement
AntTypeDefinition	
ComponentHelper	
Main	Main
ElementHandler	ElementHandler
IntrospectionHelper	IntrospectionHelper
Property	
FileUtils	
ProjectHelper2	
PropertyHelper	
DefaultLogger	
ProjectHelper	ProjectHelper
ProjectHandler	
RuntimeConfigurable	RuntimeConfigurable
TargetHandler	
RootHandler	
Task	Task
Target	Target
	TaskContainer

The precision and recall of our approach competes with the best performing metric of the experiment conducted by [14] as shown in Table 1.3.

It can easily be noticed that there is a remarkable increase in the performance with our approach as shown in Table 1.3. The original execution time for the execution scenario (i.e. build the source code of Ant 1.6.1 using the Ant 1.6.1 binary release) was 23 s [13]. But when tracing was enabled for dynamic analysis, the same execution scenario took 60 min for trace collection plus 45 min for metric calculation [14]. Clearly there is a huge overhead involved in the approach mentioned in [13, 14] that increased the execution time from 23 s to 105 min. In our approach, the original execution time to build the source code of Apache Ant

Table 1.3 Comparison of our approach with [14]

Approach	Recall (%)	Precision (%)	Execution time of approach (min)	Original execution time (s)
IC_CM	40	21	105	23
IC_CC	70	37	105	23
IC_CC'	70	37	105	23
IC_CM + HITS	60	32	105	23
IC_CC + HITS	80	42	105	23
IC_CC' + HITS	90	47	105	23
Our approach	90	47	6	15

1.6.1 was 15 s on a machine whose specifications were very close to the one that was used in [14]. When the tracing was enabled in our approach using AspectJ, the same execution scenario took 6 min. It is evident that our approach is adding relatively less overhead to the original execution time, while calculating the metrics with similar level of accuracy as in [14]. The performance boost comes at the cost of the online analysis that uses extra memory space during program execution. The extra cycle of reading large trace file is avoided that saves a major portion of the time spent on calculations.

1.5 Related Work

In [13], the application of webmining principles has been proposed on the runtime information produced by the system. This could reveal the important classes in the system which can be explored for further understanding of the system. The technique is demonstrated using two open source case studies. In continuation of their work in [14], the same authors have presented the use of dynamic coupling metrics in combination with webmining to determine the most important classes of the system. The use of run-time information to gain acquaintance with the system is again exercised in [15]. A technique to aid program comprehension is proposed that discover the critical components of the guinea pig system. They have introduced the concept of dynamic Fan-in and Fan-out Metrics and provided a mechanism to instrument the system and calculate these dynamic metrics. A tool named InsECT is introduced in [16]. It is capable of measuring wide range of run-time information through execution of the instrumented system. It provides a mechanism to specify the entities of interest for instrumentation purpose and enables to gather the particular piece of information about those entities.

1.6 Conclusion

In this paper, we have proposed a variation of the dynamic coupling metric by introducing a new parameter for the metric IC_CM. We have demonstrated that our parameter is effective for pinpointing the core classes that constitute the system architecture. The ranking of the classes with respect to their significance in the architecture is certainly helpful in the early program comprehension. A substantial amount of time can be saved if the programmer is provided with a targeted set of core classes when he is starting to build his understanding of the system.

References

1. Stroulia E, Systä T (2002) Dynamic analysis for reverse engineering and program understanding. SIGAPP Appl Comput Rev 10(1):8–17
2. Ng D, Kaeli DR, Kojarski S, Lorenz DH (2004) Program comprehension using aspects. In: ICSE 2004 workshop WoDiSEE'2004
3. Corbi T (1990) Program understanding: challenge for the 90 s. IBM Syst J 28(2):294–306
4. Lakhotia A (1993) Understanding someone else's code: analysis of experiences. J Syst Softw 23:269–275
5. Zayour I, Lethbridge TC (2001) Adoption of reverse engineering tools: a cognitive perspective and methodology. In: Proceedings of the 9th international workshop on program comprehension, pp 245–255
6. Storey M-AD, Wong K, Müller HA (2000) How do program understanding tools affect how programmers understand programs? Sci Comput Program 36(2–3):183–207
7. von Mayrhauser A, Marie Vans A (1995) Program comprehension during software maintenance and evolution. Computer 10(8):44–55
8. Pennington N (1987) Comprehension strategies in programming. In: Empirical studies of programmers: second workshop, Ablex Publishing Corp, Norwood pp 100–113
9. Demeyer S, Ducasse S, Nierstrasz O (2003) Object-oriented reengineering patterns. Morgan Kaufmann, San Francisco
10. Eisenbarth T, Koschke R, Simon D (2001) Aiding program comprehension by static and dynamic feature analysis. In: ICSM, pp 602–611
11. Jahnke JH, Walenstein A (2000) Reverse engineering tools as media for imperfect knowledge. In: Proceedings of the seventh working conference on reverse engineering, IEEE, pp 22–31
12. Arisholm E, Briand L, Foyen A (2004) Dynamic coupling measurement for object-oriented software. IEEE Trans Softw Eng 30(8):491–506
13. Zaidman A, Calders T, Demeyer S, Paredaens J (2005) Applying webmining techniques to execution traces to support the program comprehension process. In: Proceedings of the European conference on software maintenance and reengineering (CSMR), IEEE Computer Society, Los Alamitos, CA, pp 134–142
14. Zaidman A, Demeyer S (2008) Automatic identification of key classes in a software system using webmining techniques. J Softw Maint Evol Res Pract 20(6):387–417
15. Yuying W, Qingshan L, Ping C, Chunde R (2005) Dynamic fan-in and fan-out metrics for program comprehension. 1st Workshop on program comprehension through dynamic analysis (PCODA 2005) Co-located with the 12th WCRE, 10 November 2005, Pittsburgh, Pennsylvania, http://lore.ua.ac.be.Events/PCODA2005/PCODA2005proceedings.pdf
16. Chawla A, Orso A (2004) A generic instrumentation framework for collecting dynamic information. Sigsoft software engineering notes, section: workshop on empirical research in software testing, vol 29(5). ACM Press, New York, pp 1–4

Chapter 2
Frequency Estimation on Power System Using Recursive-Least-Squares Approach

Liangliang Li, Wei Xia, Dongyuan Shi and Jianzhuang Li

Abstract An approach based on recursive-least-squares (RLS) algorithm is applied to the frequency estimation of the instantaneous power system. The three-phase voltage signal is transformed to a complex form which is easy to be handled by the proposed approach. When compared with other algorithms, the RLS algorithm is more suitable for online frequency estimation due to its rapid convergence rate. An arccosine function-free technique is applied to the frequency estimation approach to reduce computational complexity. The effect of noise, convergence rate, harmonics and dynamic frequency variation on the performance of the approach is discussed.

Keywords Frequency estimation · Power system · Recursive-least-squares

2.1 Introduction

In a power system, frequency is a quite important parameter that its fast and precise estimation is vitally necessary. The rapid development of signal processing technology makes modern frequency measurement flourishing, and many approaches have been applied to it [1–3]. The Least Mean Square (LMS) algorithm is a typical representative of an adaptive algorithm. Its inherent disadvantage is slow convergence rate. The LS algorithm is also widely used for frequency

L. Li (✉) · W. Xia · D. Shi · J. Li
School of Electronic Engineering, University of Electronic Science and Technology of China, Qingshuihe Campus:No.2006, Xiyuan Ave, West Hi-Tech Zone, Chengdu, Sichuan, People's Republic of China
e-mail: liliangliang98765@163.com

W. Lu et al. (eds.), *Proceedings of the 2012 International Conference on Information Technology and Software Engineering*, Lecture Notes in Electrical Engineering 211, DOI: 10.1007/978-3-642-34522-7_2, © Springer-Verlag Berlin Heidelberg 2013

estimation while it must re-compute every time. To solve these problems, the Recursive-Least-Squares (RLS) algorithm is applied to frequency estimation.

The RLS algorithm is used extensively in signal processing area. It is an algorithm which recursively finds the coefficients that minimize a weighted linear least squares cost function related to the input signals [4]. When compared with other algorithms, the RLS algorithm exhibits the feature of rapid convergence rate. However, this benefit comes at the cost of high computational complexity. In this paper, an arccosine function-free technique is applied to the frequency estimation to reduce the burden of computation with little decline in frequency estimation accuracy. Moreover, a complex signal model derived from the three-phase voltage signal with the transform [5] is also suitable for RLS algorithm. With its fast convergence and good robustness, the algorithm is fit for online frequency estimation.

This paper is organized as follows. In Sect. 2.2, we present the RLS algorithm (one-phase case). In Sect. 2.3, inspired by the algorithm of one-phase case, we extend it to three-phase case. In Sect. 2.4, the performances of these approaches in different situations are discussed. Finally, in Sect. 2.5, we conclude this paper.

2.2 Proposed Algorithm

In this section, we present the RLS algorithm for online frequency estimation. A power system signal is sampled by an Analog to Digital Converter (ADC). Hence, the voltage signal can be described in discrete form as follows:

$$v(n) = A\cos(\omega t_n + \varphi_0) = A\cos(\omega n T_s + \varphi_0) \tag{2.1}$$

where A is the amplitude of fundamental component, ω is the actual angular frequency, φ_0 is the initial phase, t_n is the time, and T_s is the sampling clock period.

Similarly, $v(n-1)$ and $v(n+1)$ can be described as follows:

$$v(n-1) = A\cos(\omega(n-1)T_s + \varphi_0)$$
$$v(n+1) = A\cos(\omega(n+1)T_s + \varphi_0) \tag{2.2}$$

Then

$$v(n-1) + v(n+1) = 2A\cos(\omega n T_s + \varphi_0)\cos(\omega T_s) = 2v(n)\cos(\omega T_s) = \eta v(n) \tag{2.3}$$

where $\eta = 2\cos(\omega T_s)$. The actual frequency f can be directly estimated with the relationship below.

$$\hat{f} = \frac{\arccos\left(\frac{\eta}{2}\right)}{2\pi T_s} \tag{2.4}$$

Although this frequency estimation approach frequently presents high precision and speed, it is still unreliable because of two deficiencies. First, derivation of equation of this algorithm does not take noise effect into account. Second, when $v(n)$ is around zero, the precision of the approach would become poor. Given $v(n) = 0$, the frequency f cannot be obtained from Eq. (2.3) [6]. Therefore, the algorithm must be modified to improve the performance. The recursive-least-squares (RLS) algorithm can be applied to Eq. (2.3) to estimate η and calculate the frequency f by Eq. (2.4). In Eq. (2.3), $v(n)$ is regarded as the input vector, and $v(n-1) + v(n+1)$ is the desired signal, and $\eta(n)$ is the weight vector.

Based on above discussion, the RLS algorithm for frequency estimation can be described as

Initialization:

$$\eta(1) = 0 \qquad P(1) = \delta^{-1}I = \delta^{-1} \tag{2.5}$$

Computation: for $n = 2, 3, \ldots$

$$
\begin{aligned}
k(n) &= \frac{P(n-1)v(n)}{\lambda + v^2(n)P(n-1)} \\
\xi(n) &= v(n) + v(n-2) - \eta(n-1)v(n) \\
\eta(n) &= \eta(n-1) + k(n)\xi(n) \\
P(n) &= \lambda^{-1}P(n-1) - \lambda^{-1}k(n)v(n)P(n-1)
\end{aligned}
\tag{2.6}
$$

where λ is forgetting factor, δ is the value to initialize $P(1)$. The frequency is obtained by the Eq. (2.4).

In this algorithm above, there is a high computational complexity so that it will have a negative effect on the speed of online frequency estimation. Especially, the arccosine is a transcendental function which needs a time-consuming computation. Therefore, the arccosine function should be modified for speed as

$$
\begin{aligned}
v(n-1) + v(n+1) &= 2v(n)\cos(\omega T_s) = 2v(n)\cos((\omega_0 + \Delta\omega)T_s) \\
&= 2v(n)\cos(\omega_0 T_s)\cos(\Delta\omega T_s) - 2v(n)\sin(\omega_0 T_s)\sin(\Delta\omega T_s)
\end{aligned}
\tag{2.7}
$$

where ω_0 is the normal frequency, $\Delta\omega$ is the frequency drift. As we know, the frequency drift is small in a real power system. And the sampling time interval T_s is also small. Consequently, $\Delta\omega T_s$ can be regarded as a number that approaches to zero.

Then

$$v(n-1) + v(n+1) \approx 2v(n)\cos(\omega_0 T_s) - 2v(n)\sin(\omega_0 T_s)\Delta\omega T_s \tag{2.8}$$

Using the relationship of $\omega_0 = 2\pi f_0$, $T_s = 1/f_s$, $\Delta\omega = 2\pi\Delta f$, $f_s = Nf_0$, we can obtain

$$v(n)\Delta f = \frac{2\cos\left(\frac{2\pi}{N}\right)v(n) - v(n+1) - v(n-1)}{4\pi T_s \sin\left(\frac{2\pi}{N}\right)} \tag{2.9}$$

Similarly, the RLS algorithm can be applied to Eq. (2.9), just like Eq. (2.3). We recursively find the frequency drift. Finally, the estimated frequency is equal to

$$f(n) = f_0 + \Delta f(n) \tag{2.10}$$

So by this method the arccosine function is removed from the algorithm. Moreover, in Eq. (2.9) $4\pi T_s \sin(2\pi/N)$ and $2\cos(2\pi/N)$ can be calculated offline. It effectively reduces the computational complexity and improves the speed of the algorithm.

2.3 Three-Phase Case

In Sect. 2.2, we have discussed the proposed algorithm in one-phase case of a power system. Now, inspired by [7], we extend the algorithm to three-phase case. Similarly, the three-phase signal of a power system can be described as follows:

$$
\begin{aligned}
v_a(n) &= A\cos(\omega t_n + \varphi_0) \\
v_b(n) &= A\cos(\omega t_n - \frac{2\pi}{3} + \varphi_0) \\
v_c(n) &= A\cos(\omega t_n + \frac{2\pi}{3} + \varphi_0)
\end{aligned} \tag{2.11}
$$

Then we apply the $\alpha\beta$ transform to Eq. (2.11).

$$\begin{bmatrix} v_\alpha(n) \\ v_\beta(n) \end{bmatrix} = \sqrt{\frac{2}{3}} \begin{bmatrix} 1 & -1/2 & -1/2 \\ 0 & \sqrt{3}/2 & -\sqrt{3}/2 \end{bmatrix} [v_a(n) \quad v_b(n) \quad v_c(n)]^T \tag{2.12}$$

Finally, a complex voltage $V(n)$ can be obtained

$$V(n) = v_\alpha(n) + iv_\beta(n) \tag{2.13}$$

Equation (2.3) is a classical relationship that is suitable for sinusoidal signal. Therefore, it can be proved that Eq. (2.3) is also suitable for the complex signal $V(n)$.

$$V(n-1) + V(n+1) = 2V(n)\cos(\omega T_s) \tag{2.14}$$

With the same principle as one-phase signal, the RLS algorithm can be applied to a complex form based on Eq. (2.14). The complex form of RLS algorithm for frequency estimation is described as

Initialization:

$$\eta(1) = 0 \qquad P(1) = \delta^{-1}I = \delta^{-1} \qquad (2.15)$$

Computation: for $n = 2, 3, \ldots$

$$
\begin{aligned}
k(n) &= \frac{P(n-1)V(n)}{\lambda + V^*(n)P(n-1)V(n)} \\
\xi(n) &= V(n) + V(n-2) - \eta^*(n-1)V(n) \\
\eta(n) &= \eta(n-1) + k(n)\xi^*(n) \\
P(n) &= \lambda^{-1}P(n-1) - \lambda^{-1}k(n)V^*(n)P(n-1)
\end{aligned}
\qquad (2.16)
$$

Moreover, due to Eq. (2.14), we can also obtain the complex form of frequency drift as follows:

$$V(n)\Delta f = \frac{2\cos\left(\frac{2\pi}{N}\right)V(n) - V(n+1) - V(n-1)}{4\pi T_s \sin\left(\frac{2\pi}{N}\right)} \qquad (2.17)$$

The RLS algorithm similarly can be applied to this equation to estimate the frequency drift Δf, and the unknown frequency can be obtained in Eq. (2.10).

2.4 Simulation Results

In this paper, four approaches for frequency estimation are proposed, i.e., one-phase arccosine, one-phase arccosine free, three-phase arccosine and three-phase arccosine free. In this section, we discuss the effect of noise, convergence rate, harmonics and dynamic frequency variation on the performance of the proposed approaches. In the simulation, the sampling rate is 1 KHz and the normal frequency is 50 Hz. By default, the parameters of the RLS algorithm in this paper are $\delta = 0.01$ and $\lambda = 0.98$. Zero-mean Gaussian noise is added to the normal frequency signal to simulate a power system.

Case 1 Noise effect: We study the performance of these approaches by adding zero-mean Gaussian noise to the fundamental signal. As an index of accuracy, we use normalized mean square error (MSE), which is define as $\sum_n (f - \hat{f}_n)^2 / (f^2 \sum_n 1)$, where f is the exact and $\hat{f}_n$ the estimated frequency at time t_n [2]. In this simulation, the real frequency is 49.5 Hz. The initial weight vector of the arccosine approach is $\eta(1) = 2\cos(2\pi \times 50 \times T_s)$, while that of the arccosine free approach is $\eta(1) = 0$. Figure 2.1 shows the relationship between SNRs and the MSE. It shows that the performance of these approaches badly declines in highly noisy environment. This is an inherent defect of many algorithms, which are not inherently filter based [2]. Moreover, the arccosine-free approach can decrease the computation complexity at the cost of little increasing in the mean of square error of frequency estimation.

Fig. 2.1 MSE of different
SNRs

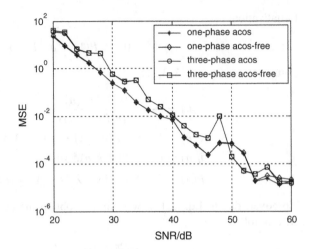

Case 2 Convergence rate: When compared with the LMS algorithm, the RLS algorithm shows its good convergence rate. Figure 2.2 describes the comparison. In this simulation, the SNR of the input signal is 40 dB and the initial weight vectors of both algorithms are zeros. The step size of the LMS algorithm is 0.1.

Case 3 Harmonics effect: In our simulation, the fundamental signal, the SNR and the initial weight vectors are the same as Case 2. We compare the performance of the harmonics signal and the filtered signal with the one-phase arccosine-use approach. The harmonics signal contains 10 % third harmonics, 5 % fifth harmonic, and 3 % seventh harmonic besides the fundamental signal. A three-order low-pass Butterworth filter with a cut-off frequency of 100 Hz is performed. It is observed from Fig. 2.3 that the estimated frequency is quite close to the fundamental frequency after pre-filtering.

Fig. 2.2 Convergence rate of
LMS and RLS

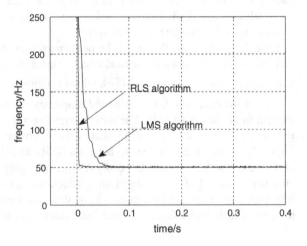

Fig. 2.3 Harmonics effect

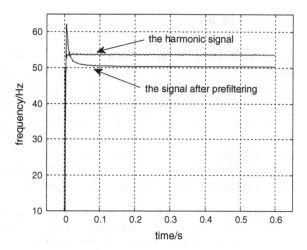

Fig. 2.4 Estimation during dynamic variation

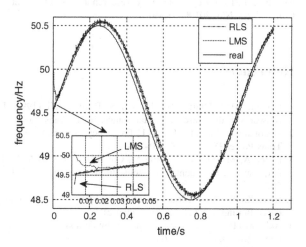

Case 4 Dynamic frequency estimation: Voltage signal with ± 1 Hz frequency oscillation starting from 49.5 Hz are exposed to the first proposed approach. In this simulation, the SNR is 40 dB, the forgetting factor is $\lambda = 0.95$, The step size of the LMS algorithm is 0.1 and the initial weight vector of both algorithms is $2\cos(2\pi \times 50 \times T_s)$. We learn from Fig. 2.4 that the estimated frequency which is calculated in real time is the same as real frequency. Moreover, the performance of the RLS algorithm is better than that of the LMS algorithm in [6] because of its faster convergence rate.

2.5 Conclusion

A new frequency estimating approach based on the RLS algorithm is proposed in this paper. The approach is derived from a classical formula which holds for every three consecutive samples. An arccosine-free version of the approach is proposed for reducing the computational complexity. Moreover, we extend the three-phase signal to a complex form, and apply the RLS algorithm to it. Simulation results show that the accuracy and speed of estimation is satisfactory even in the presence of noise, harmonics, and frequency variation. When compared with other approaches, this approach shows rapid convergence rate. Therefore, the proposed approach is suitable for application in online frequency estimation.

Acknowledgments This work is supported in part by National Natural Science Foundation of China (Grant NO. 61101173), the Fundamental Research Funds for the Central Universities (Grant NO. ZYGX2010J020), Guangdong-Hongkong Technology Cooperation Funding (Grant NO. 2009205133), Key Technology Research and Development Program of Sichuan Province of China (Grant NO. 2010GZ0149).

References

1. Begovic MM, Djuric PM, Dunlap S, Phadke AG (1993) Frequency Tracking in Power Networks in the Presence of Harmonics. IEEE Trans Power Delivery 8:480–486
2. Abdollahi A, Matinfar F (2011) Frequency estimation: a least-squares new approach. IEEE Trans Power Delivery 26:790–798
3. Lopez A, Montao JC, Castilla M, Gutierrez J, Borras MD, Bravo JC (2008) Power system frequency measurement under nonstationary situations. IEEE Trans Power Delivery 23:562–567
4. He Z, Xia W (2009) Modern digital signal processing and its applications. Tsinghua university press, Beijing, pp 223–227 (in Chinese)
5. Akke M (1997) frequency estimation by demodulation of two complex signals. IEEE Trans Power Delivery 12:157–163
6. Qing WJ (2009) Disturbance rejection through disturbance observer with adaptive frequency estimation. IEEE Trans Mag 45:2675–2678
7. Pradhan AK, Routray A, Basak A (2005) Power system frequency estimation using least mean square technique. IEEE Trans Power Delivery 20:1812–1816

Chapter 3
GNSS Integrity Monitoring Based on the Robust Positioning Solution

Haibo Tong, Jing Peng, Guozhu Zhang and Gang Ou

Abstract The receiver autonomous integrity monitoring (RAIM) is the straight-forward way to handle the outlier, but the protection levels are vulnerable to the satellite geometry. A robust protection level is proposed. Firstly, a robust positioning solution based on MM-estimation is introduced. Then the protection level of the robust solution is presented. Finally, the experiments with actual GPS data demonstrate that the robust protection levels are less affected by the geometry. Moreover, the robust protection levels are more stringent to bound the maximum error than the conventional protection levels.

Keywords GNSS · Integrity · Robust positioning · Protection level

3.1 Introduction

To reduce the risk caused by the outliers in the global navigation satellite system (GNSS), there are always two methods. A straightforward and efficient method is RAIM, which performs a consistency check in the range or position domains to detect and exclude a single outlier. The conventional RAIM has been well used for many years during the en route and terminal phases of flight [1–3], whose protection levels are always several hundreds of meters. In recent years, the GNSS is a rapidly developing field. More than 100 satellites will be operational in the next decade. More stringent applications, such as aircraft takeoff, approach and landing

H. Tong (✉) · J. Peng · G. Zhang · G. Ou
Satellite Navigation R&D Centre, School of Electronic Science and Engineering,
National University of Defense Technology, Changsha 410073 Hunan, China
e-mail: hho.tong@gmail.com

W. Lu et al. (eds.), *Proceedings of the 2012 International Conference on Information Technology and Software Engineering*, Lecture Notes in Electrical Engineering 211, DOI: 10.1007/978-3-642-34522-7_3, © Springer-Verlag Berlin Heidelberg 2013

operations are expected to be realized by the GNSS signals. The challenge is to provide reliable position estimates in smaller protection levels when more measurements and outliers coexist. The conventional RAIM has been generalized to handle multiple outliers [4], but the protection levels increase dramatically with the number of outliers. More recently, many papers focus on the modifications of the RAIM algorithms to handle multiple outliers with optimized protection levels, which are still under development and required to be standardized [5–7].

The alternative method to handle outliers is based on robust estimation, which aims at deriving reliable estimation of the data following the assumed distribution exactly or the actual distribution with heavy tails. The fundamental work of John Tukey, Peter Huber and Frank Hampel constructs the basic theory of the robust M-estimation [8, 9]. As the electronic hardware develop fast nowadays, the applicability of the different robust schemes enlightened by the M-estimation becomes possible [10–14]. The main ideal of the robust estimators is using the inconsistent residuals to estimate the non-uniform weights for restraining the influence of the erroneous measurements, while the weight factors are uniform in the LS estimation. In order to improve the reliability of the static positioning results, different weighting schemes are proposed to account for the actual measurement errors [15–17]. Similarly, the M-estimators are used to obtain the weights for the innovations in Kalman filter so that the small weighting factors will greatly reduce the influence of the outliers in kinematic positioning [18]. More recently, the quantitive analysis of the two M-estimation schemes, i.e., Huber and IGGIII, shows that up to four outliers can be effectively mitigated in the scenario with 14 satellites [19]. Furthermore, numerous robust estimators are compared with the outlier test in GPS positioning [20], then the simulated results show that the MM-estimation and L_1-norm have the greatest ability to correctly exclude the multiple outliers.

Compared with the traditional RAIM-based method, numerous results of the robust estimation are more promising and encouraging to handle the multiple outliers in the GPS positioning. However, the robustness of the M-estimation with the leverage measurements will be worse [21]. Therefore, how to monitor the integrity of the robust GNSS solution is an interesting problem.

3.2 The Robust Positioning Scheme Based on MM-Estimate

First proposed by Yohai [12], the MM-estimators have become increasingly popular and widely applied in statistics. For example, the default robust regression estimators in S-PLUS are the MM-estimators. The MM-estimation simultaneously has high BP and high efficiency under normal errors. MM-estimation is quite effective when the number of samples is large enough. However, the ranging measurements only can be seen as small samples. If we directly use the MM-estimation to compute the user position, the solution always converges to the unsatisfactory value with a large bias.

In this paper, we modify the estimation in the first stage to avoid the bad solution for the GPS positioning [22]. The initial estimate in the first stage of MM-estimation is usually computed by the S-estimation, which is defined by [11]

$$\hat{\mathbf{x}} = \arg \min_{\mathbf{x}} s(\mathbf{y} - \mathbf{H}\mathbf{x}), \qquad (3.1)$$

where $s(\cdot)$ is the robust scale estimate satisfying

$$\frac{1}{n} \sum_{i=1}^{n} \rho \left(\frac{\Delta \mathbf{r}_{(i)}}{s(\Delta \mathbf{r}_{(i)})} \right) = b, \qquad (3.2)$$

where b is the constant that can be obtained by

$$b = \int_{-\infty}^{+\infty} \rho(x) \frac{1}{\sqrt{2\pi}} e^{x^2/2} dx. \qquad (3.3)$$

The breakdown point of S-estimation is equal to b, and b is always taken as 0.5. For the pseudorange measurements, the breakdown point is less than 0.5 and is dependant on the number of measurements. We know that the finite breakdown point ε_n^* satisfies [12]

$$\varepsilon_n^* = \frac{[n/2] - p + 2}{n}, \qquad (3.4)$$

where $[x]$ returns the nearest integer less than or equal to x, n is the number of the available measurements, p is the parameters number and equal to 4 here.

The main procedures of the proposed robust positioning scheme for solving (3.1) can be summarized as follows

1. Calculate breakdown point in (3.4) with the measurements number.
2. Make the b equal to ε_n^*, then obtain k_0 from the inverse function of the (3.3).
3. Compute the initial estimate $\hat{\mathbf{x}}_0$ using the S-estimation with $\rho_{k_0}(\cdot)$, and obtain the robust scale $\hat{\sigma}$ of $\hat{\mathbf{x}}_0$ simultaneously.
4. Perform the M-estimation starting at $\hat{\mathbf{x}}_0$ for the final $\hat{\mathbf{x}}$ with the constant $k_1 = 4.680$ in the ρ function.

Similar to M-estimation, MM-estimation is not optimal estimation either. Though MM-estimation performs better with outliers, the accuracy is worse than LS at the normal distribution. Generally, we care about how degraded the accuracy will be in the positioning. In robust statistics, this degraded performance is described by two terms: efficiency and maximum bias.

The first term "efficiency" measures how similar the variance of MM-estimation is to LS at the normal. The asymptotic efficiency of $\hat{\mathbf{x}}$ is defined by [21]

$$Eff = \min \frac{\text{var}(\hat{\mathbf{x}}_{LS})}{\text{var}(\hat{\mathbf{x}}_{MM})}, \qquad (3.5)$$

where $\text{var}(\hat{\mathbf{x}})$ is the variance matrix of the estimate $\hat{\mathbf{x}}$. When the number of observations is large enough, the asymptotic (co)variance of the MM-estimate is given by [12]

$$\text{var}(\hat{\mathbf{x}}_{MM}) = a \cdot \hat{\sigma} \cdot (\mathbf{H}^T \mathbf{H})^{-1}, \tag{3.6}$$

where $\hat{\sigma}$ is the robust scale estimate and a satisfies

$$a = \frac{E\psi^2(x)}{(E\psi'(x))^2}. \tag{3.7}$$

It is easy to show that

$$\text{var}(\hat{\mathbf{x}}_{LS}) = \sigma \cdot (\mathbf{H}^T \mathbf{H})^{-1}, \tag{3.8}$$

where σ is the user equivalent range error and equals to $\hat{\sigma}$ at the normal distribution. Then the efficiency with many enough measurements is simply $1/a$.

However, the measurement matrix $\mathbf{H}$ is rather restricted because the available satellites are finite and all above the receiver. The positioning accuracy is also remarkably affected by the geometry. This geometry factor is evaluated by the dilution of precision (DOP) in the LS solution. The DOP is vulnerable to the weights. The M-estimate can be treated as the generalized LS with weight matrix and iteration. So the variance of $\hat{\mathbf{x}}_{MM}$ can not ignore the DOP fluctuation caused by the weight matrix. Accordingly, variance in (3.5) can be modified as

$$\text{var}(\hat{\mathbf{x}}_{MM}) = a \cdot (\mathbf{H}^T \mathbf{W} \mathbf{H})^{-1}, \tag{3.9}$$

where $\mathbf{W}$ is the weight matrix used in the last iterative step of the MM-estimator. Then asymptotic efficiency for finite measurements is

$$Eff = \min \frac{\hat{\sigma}(\mathbf{H}^T \mathbf{H})^{-1}}{a\hat{\sigma}(\mathbf{H}^T \mathbf{W} \mathbf{H})^{-1}} = \frac{\hat{\sigma}}{a} g\left((\mathbf{H}^T \mathbf{W} \mathbf{H})^{-1} \mathbf{H}^T \mathbf{H}\right), \tag{3.10}$$

where $g(\mathbf{M})$ denotes the largest eigenvalue of the matrix $\mathbf{M}$. The horizontal and vertical accuracy are always concerned, we introduce the horizontal efficiency Eff_H and vertical efficiency Eff_V defined by

$$Eff_H = \frac{\sigma^2 \cdot HDOP^2}{a \cdot \hat{\sigma} \cdot HDOP_w^2}, \tag{3.11}$$

$$Eff_V = \frac{\sigma^2 \cdot VDOP^2}{a \cdot \hat{\sigma} \cdot VDOP_w^2}, \tag{3.12}$$

where $HDOP$ and $VDOP$ are horizontal and vertical DOP respectively. $HDOP_w$ and $VDOP_w$ satisfy

$$HDOP_w^2 = (\mathbf{H}^T \mathbf{W} \mathbf{H})^{-1}_{(1,1)} + (\mathbf{H}^T \mathbf{W} \mathbf{H})^{-1}_{(2,2)}, \tag{3.13}$$

$$VDOP_w^2 = \left(\mathbf{H}^T\mathbf{W}\mathbf{H}\right)_{(3,3)}^{-1}, \tag{3.14}$$

where $\mathbf{W}$ is the same as the weight matrix in (3.9).

The second term "maximum bias (maxbias)" measures the maximum possible bias of an estimate under ε-contamination. The MM-estimation is biased estimation when the measurements are contaminated by outliers.

The MM-estimator does not reduce the maximum bias of the initial S-estimator, but it can greatly improve upon the efficiency of the initial S-estimator with an appropriately chosen $\rho_{k_1}(\cdot)$ function. The maxbias of the MM-estimator over the contamination neighborhood is given by [14]

$$MB(\delta, \varepsilon) = \sqrt{\left(\frac{h^{-1}\left(\frac{\delta}{1-\varepsilon}\right)}{h^{-1}\left(\frac{\delta-\varepsilon}{1-\varepsilon}\right)}\right)^2 - 1}, \tag{3.15}$$

where $h(\lambda) = E\rho(\lambda x)$ with $u \sim N(0, 1)$. The inverse function $h^{-1}(\lambda)$ can be obtained numerically if the analytic expression of $h(\lambda)$ is given. We derive $h(\lambda)$ with bisquare function as follow

$$h(\lambda) = 1 - \left(2\tau - 8\tau^3 + 30\tau^5\right) \cdot \mathrm{erf}(\tau) - \left(1 - 3\tau^2 + 9\tau^4 - 15\tau^6\right) \cdot \mathrm{erf}\left(\frac{\tau}{\sqrt{2}}\right) \tag{3.16}$$

where $\tau = k/\lambda$ and k is the constant value specified by the MM-estimator.

3.3 The Protection Levels Computation

In this section, we first review the protection levels in the RAIM algorithm for classical LS solution. Then the robust protection levels to bound the worst-case error for the robust positioning scheme are proposed.

3.3.1 Conventional RAIM Protection Levels

To guarantee the integrity of the non-robust LS results, the RAIM-based protection levels have been designed to allow the receiver to protect the positioning results from the abnormal situation. The RAIM protection levels like those of [2] are designed to protect against the outlier, which exist in one ranging measurement. Many researchers have studied and further developed the RAIM algorithms. Most of them are motivated by those of [2] and [23]. Since the protection levels of Brown are more conservative than that of Walter [4, 24], we adopt the formula of the horizontal protection level (HPL) and vertical protection level (VPL) given by [23]

$$HPL_{LS} = \max_i \{Hslope_i\} \cdot T(n, P_{fa}) + k(P_{md}) \cdot \sigma_H, \qquad (3.17)$$

$$VPL_{LS} = \max_i \{Vslope_i\} \cdot T(n, P_{fa}) + k(P_{md}) \cdot \sigma_V, \qquad (3.18)$$

where $T(n, P_{fa})$ and $k(P_{md})$ are the thresholds determined by the specified probabilities of false alert and miss detection. The vertical standard deviation σ_V and horizontal σ_H satisfy

$$\sigma_H = HDOP \cdot \sigma = \sqrt{\left(\mathbf{H}^T\mathbf{H}\right)^{-1}_{(1,1)} + \left(\mathbf{H}^T\mathbf{H}\right)^{-1}_{(2,2)}} \cdot \sigma, \qquad (3.19)$$

$$\sigma_H = VDOP \cdot \sigma = \sqrt{\left(\mathbf{H}^T\mathbf{H}\right)^{-1}_{(3,3)}} \cdot \sigma, \qquad (3.20)$$

where σ is user equivalent range error, and the slope of the satellite is given by

$$Vslope_i = \frac{\left|\mathbf{H}_{(3,i)}\right|}{\sqrt{\mathbf{P}_{(i,i)}}} \cdot \sigma, \quad 1 \le i \le n, \qquad (3.21)$$

and $\mathbf{P}$ is defined by

$$\mathbf{P} = \mathbf{I}_n - \mathbf{H}(\mathbf{H}^T\mathbf{H})^{-1}\mathbf{H}^T. \qquad (3.22)$$

As shown in (3.17) and (3.18), the first terms denote the maximum accepted bias caused by the geometry with the worst case, and the second term describes the confidence bound of the position error at normal situation. Additionally, we note that conventional RAIM protection levels are based on the maximum slope, which means that the conventional HPL and VPL are vulnerable to the geometry of the available satellites.

3.3.2 Robust Protection Levels

In order to bound the error in position domain, the robust protection levels for the robust positioning scheme are introduced. Just like protection levels for LS solution in (3.17) and (3.18), the first terms are used to protect for biases in measurements, and the second terms are used to protect for noises. In the robust positioning scheme, the maxbias and efficiency indicate the similar meanings of the first term and the second one respectively. Therefore, the robust protection levels for horizontal and vertical error are suggested as follows

$$HPL_{MM} = MB(\delta, \varepsilon) \cdot \hat{\sigma} + \frac{k(P_{md}) \cdot HDOP_w}{\sqrt{a}}, \qquad (3.23)$$

$$VPL_{MM} = MB(\delta, \varepsilon) \cdot \hat{\sigma} + \frac{k(P_{md}) \cdot VDOP_w}{\sqrt{a}}, \qquad (3.24)$$

where a is defined in (3.7), $MB(\delta, \varepsilon)$ is maximum bias as shown in (3.15), and $\hat{\sigma}$ is the robust scale obtained from the MM-estimate.

Comparing with conventional RAIM protection levels in (3.17) and (3.18), robust protection levels are not based on maximum slope any more, which means that they may be less vulnerable to the geometry.

3.4 Experiment with Actual GPS Measurements

The proposed scheme is applied with actual GPS data in National Satellite Test Bed (NSTB) format downloaded from the FTP site, then the Stanford GPS matlab platform (SGMP) is used for the LS solution [24]. Replacing LS with the robust scheme, we obtain the robust solution. Besides, we compare the robust protection levels with the conventional protection levels. To check the robust performance, the bias of the failure satellite increases from 0 to 300 m.

The position results of the LS and the robust scheme for original GPS data are shown in Fig. 3.1. The mean values of the positions in the earth-centered earth-fixed (ECEF) coordinate are listed in the upper panels of the subfigures. The horizontal errors are evaluated by circular error probable (CEP) in Fig. 3.1, and CEP95 is defined as the radius of a circle that contains 95 % of the error distributions when centered at the correct location. Comparing Fig. 3.1a with b, the CEP95 of the LS results increases greatly from 1.376 to 67728.145 m. If the mean values of the LS position shown in Fig. 3.1a are assumed to be the true location, the LS estimates are badly affected by the outliers. Contrastly, the CEP95 of the proposed scheme results increases slightly from 1.950 to 2.177 m shown in Fig. 3.1c and d, and the biases of the mean values are less than 1 m in every direction.

When the outliers exist, Fig. 3.1b and d shows the remarkable difference between LS and the robust scheme. The LS position error increases rapidly to thousands of meters, while the CEP95 of the robust position error is invulnerable to the outliers. It is easy to find that the proposed scheme is better to resist outliers than the LS solution.

Additionally, the comparison of the protection levels for the LS and the robust scheme are shown in Fig. 3.2. The assumed P_{fa} equals to 3.333e-7, and P_{md} is 0.001. Figure 3.2a shows the horizontal position errors (HPE) and HPLs, while Fig. 3.2b shows the vertical position error (VPE) and VPLs. The measurements are contaminated by an artificial outlier, so the LS position error becomes too large and does not appear in the figure. As shown in Fig. 3.2, the HPE and VPE of the robust scheme are well bounded by HPL and VPL respectively. It is also clear to see that the robust protection levels are smaller than those of the slope-based RAIM, especially the robust VPL is almost 1/3 of the RAIM-based VPL.

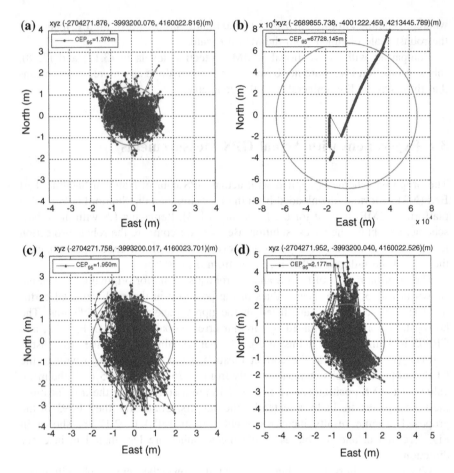

Fig. 3.1 Comparison in the horizontal position errors. **a** LS without outliers. **b** LS with 1 outlier. **c** MM-estimation without outliers. **d** MM-estimation with 1 outlier

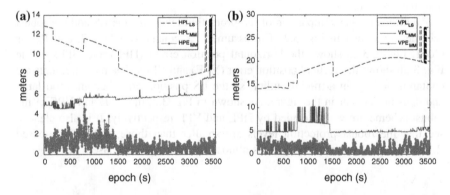

Fig. 3.2 Comparison in the protection levels. **a** Horizontal protection levels. **b** Vertical protection levels

3.5 Conclusion

The improved performance of the proposed scheme is obtained at the expense of the solution accuracy. However, the slight accuracy loss is exactly bound and acceptable. The positioning results of GPS measurements show that the scheme provides better performance in robustness and more stringent protection levels than those of the classical LS. Furthermore, the results verify that the efficiency and maxbias are plausible to describe the performance of the proposed scheme. The performance with multiple outliers need to be analyzed further.

References

1. Graas FV, Farrell JL (1992) Baseline fault detection and exclusion algorithm. In: Proceedings of the annual meeting—institute of navigation, pp 413–420
2. Brown RG (1992) A baseline GPS RAIM scheme and a note on the equivalence of three RAIM methods. Navig J Inst Navig 39(3):301–316
3. Walter T, Enge P, Blanch J, Pervan B (2008) Worldwide vertical guidance of aircraft based on modernized GPS and new integrity augmentations. Proc IEEE 96(12):1918–1935
4. Angus JE (2006) RAIM with multiple faults. Navig J Inst Navig 53(4):249–257
5. Milner CD (2009) Weighted RAIM for APV: an optimised protection level. In: ION GNSS 22nd international meeting of the satellite division, pp 1646–1652
6. Bruckner D, Graas FV, Skidmore T (2011) Approximations to composite GPS protection levels for aircraft precision approach and landing. GPS Solut 15(4):333–344
7. Phase II of the GNSS evolutionary architecture study. Technical report, GEAS Panel (2010)
8. Huber P (1981) Robust statistics. Wiley, New York
9. Hampel F, Ronchetti E, Rousseeuw P, Stahel W (1986) Robust statistics: the approach based on influence functions. Wiley, New York
10. Rousseeuw PJ, Leroy AM (1987) Robust regression and outlier detection. Wiley, New York
11. Yohai VJ (1987) High breakdown point and high efficiency robust estimates for regression. Ann Stat 15(2):642–656
12. Gervini D, Yohai VJ (2002) A class of robust and fully efficient regression estimators. Ann Stat 30(2):583–616
13. Berrendero JR, Mendes BVM, Tyler DE (2007) On the maximum bias functions of MM-estimates and constrained M-estimates of regression. Ann Stat 35(1):13–40
14. Wieser A, Fritz KB (2002) Short static GPS sessions: robust estimation results. GPS Solut 5(3):70–79
15. Yang Y, Song L, Xu T (2002) Robust estimator for correlated observations based on bifactor equivalent weights. J Geodesy 76:353–358
16. Chang XW, Guo Y (2005) Huber's M-estimation in relative GPS positioning: computational aspects. J Geodesy 79:351–362
17. Yang Y, He H, Xu G (2001) Adaptively robust filtering for kinematic geodetic positioning. J Geodesy 75:109–116
18. Wang J, Wang J (2007) Mitigating the effect of multiple outliers on GNSS navigation with M-estimation schemes. In: IGNSS symposium 2007, pp 1–9
19. Knight NL, Wang J (2009) A comparison of outlier detection procedures and robust estimation methods in GPS positioning. J Navig 62:699–709
20. Maronna RA, Martin RD, Yohai VJ (2006) Robust statistics theory and method. Wiley, Chichester

21. Tong H-B, Zhang G-Z, Ou G (2012) Iterative reweighted recursive least squares for robust positioning. Electron Lett 48(13):789–791
22. Walter T, Enge P (1995) Weighted RAIM for precision approach. In: ION GPS, pp 1995–2004
23. Tong H, Zhang G, Ou G (2011) GNSS RAIM availability assessment for worldwide precision approaches. In: 2011 International workshop on multi-platform/multi-sensor remote sensing and mapping (M2RSM), pp 1–4
24. Do J (2012) GPS/GNSS matlab platform. http://waas.stanford.edu/sgmp/sgmp.htm. Accessed 1 May 2012

Chapter 4
Carrier-Aided Smoothing for Real-Time Beidou Positioning

Dengyun Lei, Weijun Lu, Xiaoxin Cui and Dunshan Yu

Abstract In general, phase smoothing pseudorange is employed to improve the positioning accuracy. When cycle slip happened, the phase smoothing pseudorange is evidently distorted. In this paper, a new algorithm of adaptive Kalman filter is proposed. Moreover, a suitable covariance algorithm is introduced to decrease the impact of cycle slip. The covariance of carrier phase is determined by phase measurement and predicted deviation. The method has been evaluated in static real-time situation. Our results demonstrate that the proposed filter performs better than Hatch filter.

Keywords Kalman filter · Pseudorange smoothing · Beidou system

4.1 Introduction

Beidou Navigation Satellite System is an independent system offering regional position and timing service now. The Beidou receiver needs to trace at least four satellites and measure the pseudoranges. Then the receiver position and clock error can be realized with four pseudoranges. So the measurement of pseudorange is the key point of Beidou receiver. Pseudoranges can be determined by code or carrier measurements. The precision of code measurement is lower by 2–3 magnitudes than that of carrier. However, due to the ambiguity of cycle numbers between the satellites and receiver, the carrier measurement is biased.

In order to obtain high precision positioning results, Hatch Filter [1] is widely used to smooth the pseudorange by the precise carrier phase. Because of temporary

D. Lei · W. Lu (✉) · X. Cui · D. Yu
Institute of Microelectronics, Peking University, No. 5 Yiheyuan Road,
Beijing, Haidian District, China
e-mail: luwj@pku.edu.cn

W. Lu et al. (eds.), *Proceedings of the 2012 International Conference on Information Technology and Software Engineering*, Lecture Notes in Electrical Engineering 211, DOI: 10.1007/978-3-642-34522-7_4, © Springer-Verlag Berlin Heidelberg 2013

loss-of-lock in PLL, the cycle measurement is not continuous which may cause cycle slip. The cycle slip make the carrier phase measurement contain a deviation. Without cycle slip detection, the carrier smoothing pseudorange is distorted. So, Hatch filter need reinitialize frequently (e.g. [2, 3]) in order to reduce the errors in the results.

The reason of cycle slip can be distinguished as follow: (1) Failure of signal trace caused by obstruction such as buildings and trees; (2) Low signal-to-noise ratio (SNR) decreasing the signal distinguishability; (3) The receiver counter errors from hardware or software. The characteristic of discontinuity which is caused by cycle slip is utilized in cycle slip detection method. In this paper, Kalman filter technique is used to smooth pseudorange. The weight between code and carrier measurement is progressively modified according to the covariance and recursive times.

In the following sections, firstly brief overview of Hatch filter is described. Then a Kalman filter for smoothing pseudorange is established with cycle slip detection method. Finally Numerical examples and discussions are given.

4.2 Pseudorange and Carrier-Phase Model

The B1 signal radio (channel I) from Beidou satellite [4] can be given as

$$S_{B1i}(t) = \sqrt{2P_c}D_i(t - t_i)C_i(t - t_i)\cos[2\pi f_i(t - t_i) + \theta_i] + n_i(t) \qquad (4.1)$$

where i is the satellite number, S_{B1i} is the B1 signal received from satellite i, P_c is the ranging code power, $D_i(t)$ is the navigation data, f_i is carrier frequency, $C_i(t)$ is the pseudorandom noise spreading sequence ranging code, t_i is the propagation delay, θ_i is unknown phase, and $n_i(t)$ is noise.

From formula (4.1), the signal transmitting delay can be got from the difference of code or carrier measurements. When the code delay measurements are used to determine pseudorange, the pseudorange is expressed as [5]:

$$\rho_i(t) = c\tau_i(t) + c\delta_i(t) + I_i(t) + T_i(t) + \varepsilon_{p,i}(t) \qquad (4.2)$$

where $\rho_i(t)$ is the pseudorange of satellite i, c is velocity of light, $\tau_i(t)$ is the geometric distance between satellite i and receiver, $\delta_i(t)$ is the clock error, $I_i(t)$ is ionosphere delay, $T_i(t)$ is troposphere delay, and $\varepsilon_{p,i}(t)$ is the measurement noise.

While the carrier observation to confirm the pseudorange can be expressed as:

$$\lambda\Phi_i(t) = c\tau_i(t) + \lambda N_i + c\delta_i(t) - I_i(t) + T_i(t) + \varepsilon_{\Phi,i}(t) \qquad (4.3)$$

where $\Phi_i(t)$ is the difference phase between satellite i and receiver, N_i is the carrier cycle ambiguity, λ is the carrier wavelength, and $\varepsilon_{\Phi,i}(t)$ is measurement noise.

Taking the code measurement at time t subtracts that of time t−1, the change of pseudoranges in adjacent sample interval can be expressed.

$$\Delta\rho_i(t, t-1) = c\Delta\tau_i(t) + c\Delta\delta_i(t) + \Delta I_i(t) + \Delta T_i(t) + \Delta\varepsilon_{p,i}(t) \quad (4.4)$$

where Δ is the 1-time difference in adjacent sample interval.

Without cycle slip, the carrier cycle ambiguities are same in adjacent sample interval. The carrier observation difference in adjacent sample interval is

$$\lambda\Delta\Phi_i(t) = c\Delta\tau_i(t) + c\Delta\delta_i(t) - \Delta I_i(t) + \Delta T_i(t) + \Delta\varepsilon_{\Phi,i}(t) \quad (4.5)$$

If formula (4.4) is substituted into formula (4.5), the relationship of carrier difference and code difference is as follow:

$$\lambda\Delta\Phi_i(t) - \Delta\rho_i(t) = \Delta\varepsilon_{p,i}(t) - \Delta\varepsilon_{\Phi,i}(t) - 2\Delta I_i(t) \quad (4.6)$$

$\Delta I_i(t)$ can be ignored because the ionosphere is steady in a small time interval. $\Delta\varepsilon_{\Phi,i}(t)$, $\Delta\varepsilon_{p,i}(t)$ are white noise distributed. So, the expectation of formula (4.6) is

$$E[\lambda\Delta\Phi_i(t) - \Delta\rho_i(t)] = E[\Delta\varepsilon_{p,i}(t)] - E[\Delta\varepsilon_{\Phi,i}(t)] = 0 \quad (4.7)$$

The rate of ranging code is 2.046 Mcps and the frequency of carrier is 1561.098 MHz, so the accuracy of pseudorange (ε_p) is generally worse than carrier phase (ε_Φ). The carrier phase measurement probably is a good substitute for the pseudorange. However, the carrier cycle ambiguity N_i is not determined. Hatch filter is introduced to solve this problem [6].

The phase-smoothed pseudorange at time t is

$$\hat{\rho}_i(t) = W_{p,i}(t)\rho_i(t) + W_{\Phi,i}(t)[\hat{\rho}_i(t-1) + \lambda\Delta\Phi_i(t)] \quad (4.8)$$

where $\hat{\rho}_i(t)$ is smoothed pseudorange, $W_{p,i}(t)$ is the weight factor of pseudorange, $W_{\Phi,i}(t)$ is the weight factor of carrier phase observation, and $\Delta\Phi_i(t)$ is the carrier phase difference.

$$\Delta\Phi_i(t) = \Phi_i(t) - \Phi_i(t-1) \quad (4.9)$$

The covariance of $\Delta\varepsilon_\Phi(t)$ is small than that of $\Delta\varepsilon_p(t)$, so $\lambda\Delta\Phi_i(t)$ is used to smooth $\Delta\rho_i(t)$. The Hatch filer progressively increases the weight on carrier phase measurement 0.

The weight factors are changed as follow:

$$W_{p,i}(t) = W_{p,i}(t-1) - 0.01 \quad (0.01 \leq W_{p,i}(t-1) \leq 1.00) \quad (4.10)$$

$$W_{\Phi,i}(t) = W_{\Phi,i}(t-1) + 0.01 \quad (0.01 \leq W_{\Phi,i}(t-1) \leq 0.99) \quad (4.11)$$

with initial $W_{p,i}(0)$ as 1.0 and $W_{\Phi,i}(0)$ as 0.0.

When cycle slip occurs, the carrier cycle ambiguities between adjacent sample intervals are not equal. The formula (4.5) is changed and expressed as follow:

$$\lambda\Delta\Phi_i(t) = c\Delta\tau_i(t) + \lambda\Delta N_i + c\Delta\delta_i(t) - \Delta I_i(t) + \Delta T_i(t) + \Delta\varepsilon_{\Phi,i} \quad (4.12)$$

So the expectation $(E[\lambda\Delta\Phi_i(t) - \Delta\rho_i(t)])$ is no equal to zero. The phase smoothing pseudorange is evidently distorted which leads the position result in error. Without cycle slip detection, Hatch filter need reinitialize frequently in order to reduce the errors in results. For weakening the influences of cycle slip, an adaptive Kalman filter is developed.

4.3 Kalman Filter for Real-Time Positioning

Kalman filter can filter measurement noise and predict next state for a uniform sampling period [7]. Kalman filter firstly predict the current state upon the previous statement. Then the predicted state is updated using the pseudorange measurement.

In order to detect cycle slip, 2-time difference of carrier phase ($\Delta^2\Phi_i(t)$) is introduced.

$$\Delta^2\Phi_i(t) = \Delta\Phi_i(t) - \Delta\Phi_i(t - 1) \tag{4.13}$$

Assuming that the distance between the satellite and receiver changes at a constant velocity, the predicted $\Delta\hat{\Phi}_i(t)$ is

$$\Delta\hat{\Phi}_i(t) = \Delta\Phi_i(t - 1) + \Delta^2\Phi_i(t) \tag{4.14}$$

If the difference of $\Delta\Phi_i(t)$ and $\Delta\hat{\Phi}_i(t)$ is less than a threshold (N), the cycle slip did not happen. The covariance ($Q_i(t)$) is.

$$Q_i(t) = \varepsilon_{\Phi,i}(t) * \varepsilon_{\Phi,i}(t) \tag{4.15}$$

Otherwise, the cycle slip occurs and the $Q_i(t)$ is

$$Q_i(t) = \left(\varepsilon_{\Phi,i}(t) * \varepsilon_{\Phi,i}(t)\right) * \exp\left\{\left|\Delta\Phi_i(t) - \Delta\hat{\Phi}_i(t)\right|\right\} \tag{4.16}$$

The covariance increases with difference of $\Delta\Phi_i(t)$ and $\Delta\hat{\Phi}_i(t)$, so the accuracy of carrier measurement decreases. We can adjust the filter gain to weaken the impact of cycle slip.

In state transition stage, as Hatch filter, the predicted pseudorange ($\hat{\rho}_i^-(t)$) equals to the carrier phase difference plus the last optimal pseudorange ($\hat{\rho}_i(t - 1)$).

$$\hat{\rho}_i^-(t) = \hat{\rho}_i(t - 1) + \Delta\Phi_i(t) \tag{4.17}$$

The state covariance ($P_i^-(t)$) is predicted as follow:

$$P_i^-(t) = P_i(t - 1) + Q_i(t) \tag{4.18}$$

Then the filter gain is given:

$$K_i(t) = P_i^-(t)\left[P_i^-(t) + R_i(t)\right]^{-1} \tag{4.19}$$

where $R_i(t)$ is pseudorange measurement covariance.

$$R_i(t) = \varepsilon_{p,i}(t) * \varepsilon_{p,i}(t) \tag{4.20}$$

In the filtering stage, the pseudorange is constructed by the predicted pseudorange and code measurements. The optimal measurement update as follow:

$$\hat{\rho}_i(t) = \hat{\rho}_i^-(t) + K_i(t) * \left(\rho_i(t) - \hat{\rho}_i^-(t)\right) \tag{4.21}$$

Then update the state covariance:

$$P_i(t) = (I - K_i(t))P_i^-(t) \tag{4.22}$$

Therefore, the adaptive Kalman filter can offer an effective and continuous approach to smooth pseudorange.

4.4 Testing and Analysis

To demonstrate the performance, the proposed Kalman filter has been investigated using Beidou date under static real-time condition. In this section, the detail of experiments is introduced.

The platform (Fig. 4.1) is built with GPS/BD2 chip named BD-ZS3121 which is designed by lab of SoC, Peking University.

During the entire measurement campaign, six Beidou satellites were captured with a cut-off elevation angel of 10°. Time interval of an epoch is 1 s, and 1,000 continuous points are collected for each method.

Comparing the calculated position with the standard static position, the deviations in 3D are drawn in Fig. 4.2. The means and variances are shown in Table 4.1.

The result shows that the carrier phase-smoothed pseudoranges reduce the variances, even in the presence of cycle slip. The Kalman filter accelerates the

Fig. 4.1 Test platform

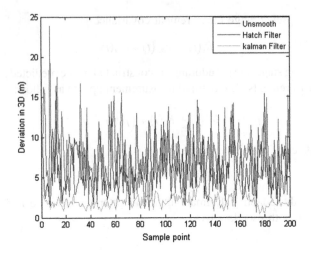

Fig. 4.2 Deviations in −130 dBm (200 samples)

Table 4.1 Mean and variance in −130 dBm

Model	X direction		Y direction		Z direction		Slip count
	Mean	Variance	Mean	Variance	Mean	Variance	
Unsmooth	−0.012	2.869	0.365	6.157	−1.513	3.833	3
Hatch filter	0.261	1.469	0.392	2.815	−1.070	1.493	7
Kalman filter	−0.029	0.534	0.750	1.298	−1.611	0.642	11

Table 4.2 Mean and variance in −140 dBm

Model	X Direction		Y direction		Z direction		Slip count
	Mean	Variance	Mean	Variance	Mean	Variance	
Unsmooth	0.218	14.428	−0.267	28.399	−1.457	15.021	231
Hatch filter	0.753	11.888	−0.546	21.261	−1.538	13.422	247
Kalman filter	−0.230	3.492	1.514	8.514	−0.435	4.572	219

recursive process by adopting the covariance of measurements. In consequence, the variance of Kalman filter is smaller than that of Hatch filter.

In order to further verify the cycle slip effect on smoothing progress, additional tests are included in which the signal power is attenuated extra 10 dB.

In Table 4.2 and Fig. 4.3, the variance of Hatch filter immensely increases with the increasing cycle slip times. In each time of cycle slip, the weight factors of Hatch filter are reset and the accuracy of results decrease. The proposed Kalman filter does not face this problem and is suitable for the cycle slip situation.

Fig. 4.3 Deviations in −140 dBm (200 samples)

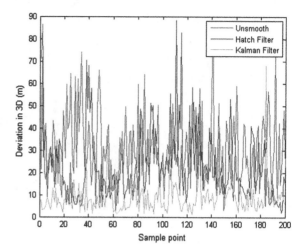

4.5 Conclusions

One of the main contributions of this paper is an adaptive Kalman filter. This filter combines the advantages of both code and carrier measurement. Meanwhile, two-time difference of carrier measurement can predict next state to judge the deviation of adjacent sample interval for cycle slip detection. The most notable merit is that the adaptive covariance of carrier measurement can weaken the impact of cycle slip and improve the consecutiveness.

References

1. Hatch R (1983) The synergism of GPS code and carrier measurements. In: Proceedings 3rd international geodetic symposium on satellite doppler positioning, pp 1213–1231
2. Lachapelle G, Falkenberg W, Neufledt D, and Kielland P (1989) Marine DGPS using code and carrier in a multipath environment. In: Proceedings of ION GPS-89, pp 343–347
3. Lachapelle G, Falkenberg W, Casey M (1987) Use of phase data for accurate differential GPS kinematic positioning. J Geodesy 61(4):367–377
4. China Satellite Navigation Office (2011) BeiDou navigation satellite system signal in space interface control document. http://www.beidou.gov.cn/. Accessed 15 Sept 2012
5. Tsui JBY (2001) Fundamentals of global positioning system receivers: a software approach. Weily, New York
6. Cheng P (1999) Remarks on Doppler-aided smoothing of code ranges. J Geodesy 73(1999):23–28
7. Brown RG, Huang PYC (1997) Introduction to random signals and applied kalman filtering. Weily, New York, pp 242–285

Chapter 5
Life Feature Extraction Based on Hilbert Marginal Spectrum Entropy for ADT Vibration

Fengjin Wang, Xiaoyang Li and Tongmin Jiang

Abstract Vibration is one of the most common condition monitoring data types for electromechanical products. Aiming at life feature extraction from vibration data and considering the advantages of Shannon information entropy in measuring product uncertainty as well as Hilbert-Huang Transform (HHT) in vibration data processing, a life feature extraction method based on Hilbert marginal spectrum entropy was proposed. Hilbert marginal spectrum entropy was taken as the life feature that could characterize product degradation. The computing way of Hilbert marginal spectrum entropy for Accelerated Degradation Testing (ADT) vibration data was presented. Finally, this method was applied to motor ADT vibration data. By quantifying metrics such as monotonicity, prognosability, trendability, and fitness of Hilbert marginal spectrum entropy feature, the analysis result shows that this life feature extraction method is effective and engineering practicable.

Keywords Hilbert marginal spectrum entropy · Life feature extraction · Accelerated degradation testing · Vibration

5.1 Introduction

The performance degradation data of a product contains a lot of life information. The study of life prediction based on performance degradation has become a hot spot, mainly including life prediction based on Accelerated Degradation Testing

F. Wang (✉) · X. Li · T. Jiang
School of Reliability and System Engineering, Beihang University, No 37 Xueyuan Road, Haidian District, Beijing, China
e-mail: fjwang@dse.buaa.edu.cn

W. Lu et al. (eds.), *Proceedings of the 2012 International Conference on Information Technology and Software Engineering*, Lecture Notes in Electrical Engineering 211, DOI: 10.1007/978-3-642-34522-7_5, © Springer-Verlag Berlin Heidelberg 2013

(ADT) and online monitoring. Nowadays, ADT is mainly applied in electronic products, and usually monitors performance parameters that have obvious change trend over time, such as power gain [1] and output optical power [2]. However, for electromechanical products, the performance degradation is usually accompanied by the emergence and development of wear, corrosion and fatigue crack, which can not be directly measured, but cause changes in vibration. Thus, some vibration-related parameters could be utilized to monitor the change in product performance. This makes vibration one of the most commonly used condition monitoring data. Vibration signal is relatively complicated, so it needs to be processed to show the trend of degradation through life feature extraction method, which is key to life prediction and affects the accuracy of life prediction. Meanwhile, ADT can obtain more monitoring data within relatively short time, which facilitates the realization of life prediction. Therefore, it is necessary to study the life feature extraction method from ADT vibration data. This paper focuses on the life prediction technique based on data-driven, not technique based on physical model.

As an index evaluating the uncertainty of signal, Shannon information entropy is introduced to time, frequency and time–frequency domain, and respectively develops to singular value entropy, power spectrum entropy, wavelet entropy, EMD entropy [3], and etc., which have been widely applied to the feature extraction in fault diagnosis [4]. Most of mechanical vibration signals are nonlinear and non-stationary. As an adaptive time–frequency analysis method without any requirement for priori knowledge, Hilbert-Huang Transform (HHT) is very suitable for processing nonlinear and non-stationary signals [5, 6]. Consequently, a life feature extraction method using Hilbert marginal spectrum entropy for ADT vibration data was proposed. The method was applied to certain motor ADT vibration data to extract life feature and predict the life under normal stress.

5.2 ADT and Hilbert Marginal Spectrum Entropy

5.2.1 Accelerated Degradation Testing

ADT is an accelerated test method that accelerates product performance degradation through high (accelerated) stress and uses the collected data to predict the product life under normal stress. The performance degradation data of product contains more life information relative to failure time data. Utilizing performance degradation information to predict the product life can save testing time and costs. Due to high stress, ADT can acquire more performance degradation data with the same time and cost. This contributes to the realization of life prediction.

5.2.2 Hilbert-Huang Transform

Hilbert-Huang transform composes of Empirical Mode Decomposition (EMD) and Hilbert transform (HT). The EMD involves the decomposition of a complex signal into a finite number of Intrinsic Mode Function (IMF) components through the sifting process, with each one having a distinct time scale. The result of the sifting is that a given signal $x(t)$ will be decomposed into n IMF components $c_1, c_2, \ldots, c_n$ and a residual r_n given by

$$x(t) = \sum_{j=1}^{n} c_j(t) + r_n(t) \tag{5.1}$$

After performing HT on each IMF component and computing instantaneous frequency and amplitude, we can get the Hilbert spectrum in the following form:

$$H(f, t) = \text{Re} \sum_{j=1}^{n} a_j(t) e^{i \int 2\pi f_j(t) dt} \tag{5.2}$$

In Eq. (5.2) the amplitude can be contoured on the frequency-time plane. The Hilbert marginal spectrum can also be defined as

$$h(f) = \int_0^T H(f, t) dt \tag{5.3}$$

With high resolution, the Hilbert marginal spectrum offers a measure of total amplitude contribution from each frequency value, the frequency in which has a totally different meaning from the Fourier spectral analysis.

5.2.3 Hilbert Marginal Spectrum Entropy

Shannon information entropy is a quantitative evaluation of system uncertainty. $X = \{x_j, j = 1, 2, \ldots, m\}$ is a signal with m-state, and the probability of each state is expressed as $P = \{p_j, j = 1, 2, \ldots, m\}$, then the information entropy of X is given by

$$H_n(x) = -\sum_{j=1}^{m} p_j \log_2 p_j \tag{5.4}$$

Hilbert marginal spectrum is a division of the original signal in frequency domain. Consequently, the Hilbert marginal spectrum entropy [7, 8] is defined by:

$$\widehat{HMSE} = -\sum_{k=1}^{m} p_k \log_2 p_k \tag{5.5}$$

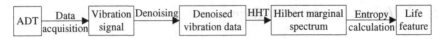

Fig. 5.1 Life feature extraction based on Hilbert marginal spectrum entropy

where $p_k = h(k) \Big/ \sum_{k=1}^{m} h(k)$, $\sum_{k=1}^{m} p_k = 1$, m is the number of frequency components.
The entropy is normalized to avoid the influence of data length, as follows:

$$HMSE = \widehat{HMSE} \Big/ \log_2 m \qquad (5.6)$$

Normalized spectrum entropy takes the minimum value 0 when the spectrum only has single frequency component, and takes the maximum value 1 when each frequency component is equal. Its value only depends on the frequency distribution of the signal, and is independence to signal intensity.

5.3 Life Feature Extraction Approach

If a product comes to failure, the amplitude of vibration signal will change over time and frequency distribution. Thus, when the product is under normal, degradation and fault state, the Hilbert marginal spectral entropy should be different. Its changes over time can describe the performance degradation of product, and life prediction can be made through its change trend.

For a product, we assume that the sampling number is n and corresponding vibration signal acquired is s_i ($i = 1, 2,..., n$) during the ADT. The extraction steps of Hilbert marginal spectrum entropy are shown as following:

1. Construct filter to perform denoising preprocessing on s_i, and x_i is the denoised signal, for $i = 1, 2,..., n$.
2. Perform HHT on x_i, for $i = 1, 2,..., n$, then respectively calculate Hilbert spectrum using Eq. (5.2) and Hilbert marginal spectrum using Eq. (5.3).
3. Compute Hilbert marginal spectrum entropy of x_i, for $i = 1, 2,..., n$.

The flow chart of the life extraction approach is shown in Fig. 5.1.

5.4 Case Study

The constant stress ADT vibration dataset of brush-permanent magnetism DC motor mentioned in [9] is used to test the proposed life feature extraction method. The wearout failure of motor is the wear between brush and commutator. The nominal voltage of motor is 3.0 V. The accelerated stress is voltage at 3.5, 4 and 6 V. There are three motors running to failure at each stress level. The sampling interval is 15 min, and the sampling frequency is 3,000 Hz.

5.4.1 Hilbert Marginal Spectrum Entropy Feature Extraction

The vibration data of one motor at 3.5 V is taken as an instance to verify the suggested life feature extraction approach. Due to the noise in the signal, useless frequency components will not only increase the decomposition levels but also decline the timeliness of EMD. Excessive decomposition levels will result in the accumulation of boundary error, even making EMD lose physical meaning [10].

Firstly, the vibration signal is preprocessed by nonlinear morphology filter combining open-closing and close-opening operations to reduce the noise. The sinusoid structure element, with its width $L_s \approx 4$ and height $A_s = 0.22A_{max}$, is selected, where A_{max} is the maximum amplitude in the signal. The denoising effect of the vibration data at 35 h is shown in Fig. 5.2. The number of decomposition levels after signal denoised reduces from 11 to 9. The interference brought by noise is eliminated to some degree.

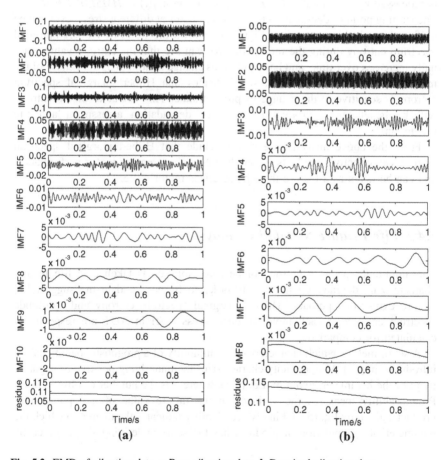

Fig. 5.2 EMD of vibration data. **a** Raw vibration data. **b** Denoised vibration data

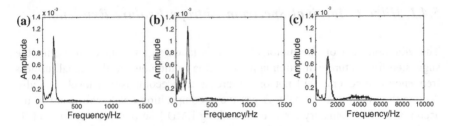

Fig. 5.3 Hilbert marginal spectrum during motor life. **a** at 5 h, **b** at 30 h, **c** at 40 h

Figure 5.3 shows the Hilbert marginal spectrum of the motor at 5, 30 and 40 h. We can see that the frequency components of vibration increase and the signal energy disperses to other frequency components when the motor from normal to failure. Thus, the Hilbert marginal spectrum entropy will gradually increase.

The value of Hilbert marginal spectrum entropy of motor at different moments is processed by the initial value $HMSE_0$, as follows: $y(t) = HMSE(t)/HMSE_0 - 1$. The starting point of degradation path of each motor at different stress level can be unified through this processing. Figure 5.4 shows the trend of Hilbert marginal spectrum entropy during the motor life. We can see that the entropy value gradually increases over time, and has an obvious change at around 33 h because of the motor running to failure. The result indicates that Hilbert marginal spectrum entropy is sensitive to the change of product state. This character of the entropy will be beneficial to product performance degradation assessment and life prediction.

From the above analysis, we can conclude that Hilbert marginal spectrum entropy can effectively reflects the gradual changing trend of motor performance, and can be taken as a feature that characterizes motor's life.

5.4.2 Life Feature Suitability Analysis

The amplitude spectrum entropy of bearing vibration is taken as a life feature characterizing degradation in [11]. In order to further validate the suggest life feature extraction approach, Hilbert marginal spectrum entropy and amplitude spectrum entropy of each motor at each stress level in ADT are respectively calculated for comparison.

A set of metrics which characterize the suitability of a prognostic parameter are introduced in [12]. Monotonicity characterizes the underlying positive or negative trend of the parameter, given by Eq. (5.7), where n is the number of observations. Prognosability measures the variance in the failure value of a population of products, given by Eq. (5.8). Finally, trendability indicates the degree to which the parameter of a population of products has the same underlying shape, given by

Fig. 5.4 The change of Hilbert marginal spectrum entropy during motor's life

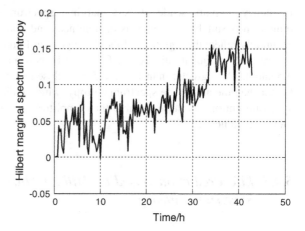

Eq. (5.9). These metrics would each range from zero to one, one indicating a very high score on that metric.

$$M = mean\left(\left|\left(\#pos^d/dx\right) - \left(\#neg^d/dx\right)\right|\Big/(n-1)\right) \qquad (5.7)$$

$$P = \exp\left(-\frac{std(failurevalues)}{mean(|failurevalue - startingvalue|)}\right) \qquad (5.8)$$

$$T = \text{Min}\left(-|corrcoef_{ij}|\right) \qquad (5.9)$$

By defining a fitness function as a weighted sum of the three metrics,

$$fitness = w_m \cdot M + w_p \cdot P + w_t \cdot T \qquad (5.10)$$

two prognostic parameters can be compared to determine the more suitable one. The constants w_m, w_p, and w_t control how important each metric. Each constant is identically given one in this paper. Table 5.1 gives the suitability computing result of Hilbert marginal spectrum entropy and amplitude spectrum entropy of all motors in ADT.

Qualitatively, amplitude spectrum based on Fourier transform is suitable for analysis of stationary signal, and can only give the statistical average result in

Table 5.1 Suitability of Hilbert marginal spectrum entropy and amplitude spectrum entropy

Stress (V)	Feature	M	P	T	fitness
3.5	Hilbert marginal spectrum entropy	0.60	0.41	0.67	1.68
	Amplitude spectrum entropy	0.20	0.95	0.52	1.67
4.0	Hilbert marginal spectrum entropy	1.00	0.93	0.66	2.58
	Amplitude spectrum entropy	0.50	0.98	0.19	1.67
6.0	Hilbert marginal spectrum entropy	0.33	0.77	0.37	1.47
	Amplitude spectrum entropy	0.33	0.65	0.03	1.01

frequency domain, while Hilbert marginal spectrum based on Hilbert-Huang transform is suitable for analysis of nonlinear and non-stationary signal, and can accurately reflect the signal amplitude change over frequency with higher accuracy and resolution. Quantitatively, the fitness of Hilbert marginal spectrum entropy at 3.5 and 4.0 V is greater than 1.5, at 3.5 V is close to 1.5, and at each stress level is higher than the amplitude spectrum entropy, which indicates that Hilbert marginal spectrum entropy is more suitable than amplitude spectrum entropy to be a prediction parameter.

5.4.3 Life Prediction Based on Hilbert Marginal Spectrum Entropy

Take the Hilbert marginal spectrum entropy extracted through the proposed method as motor's performance parameter, and use drifting Brownian motion to fit [2]

$$Y(t) = \sigma B(t) + d(s) \cdot t + y_0 \tag{5.11}$$

where $Y(t)$ is product performance, here, is Hilbert marginal spectrum entropy; y_0 is performance initial value; $B(t)$ is standard Brownian motion, $B(t) \sim N(0, t)$; σ is diffusion coefficient; $d(s)$ is accelerated model only related to stress. The accelerated stress is voltage in ADT, thus the accelerated model can select inverse power law model

$$\ln d(s) = a + b \ln s \tag{5.12}$$

where s is voltage. Through least squares method combined with maximum likelihood method introduced in [2], we can get the estimation value of unknown parameters: $a = -8.2731$, $b = 2.1268$ and $\sigma^2 = 0.0051$. The fitting results of motor degradation path at each stress level are shown in Fig. 5.5.

Fig. 5.5 Degradation path of motor

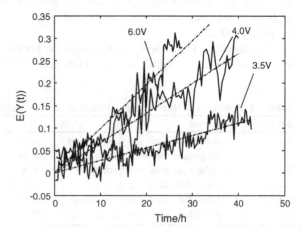

Fig. 5.6 Reliability curve of motor

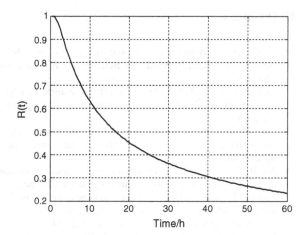

According to Nelson's cumulative failure theory, we can conclude that the failure threshold is independence to stress level. The average failure value of Hilbert marginal spectrum entropy of all motors in ADT is 0.22. Take 0.22 as the failure threshold of motor in this prediction, then the reliability of motor under normal stress (3.0 V) can be obtained by equation

$$R(t) = \Phi\left[\frac{c - y_0 - d(s)t}{\sigma\sqrt{t}}\right] - \exp\left[\frac{2d(s)(c - y_0)}{\sigma^2}\right]\Phi\left[-\frac{c - y_0 + d(s)t}{\sigma\sqrt{t}}\right] \quad (5.13)$$

Figure 5.6 shows the reliability curve. When the reliability is 0.5, the corresponding life of motor under normal using condition is 16.5 h.

5.5 Conclusion

A life feature extraction method based on Hilbert marginal spectrum entropy for ADT vibration is proposed. A case of motor is presented as a verification of the method. In conclusion, Hilbert marginal spectrum entropy is sensitive to product performance state changes. As product performance degradation developing, the entropy has a trend change and can be taken as product life feature. Hilbert marginal spectrum entropy is more suitable than amplitude spectrum entropy to be a prediction parameter. Life prediction of a product can be achieved by using the life feature parameter obtained through the presented method. The effectiveness and engineering practicability of the proposed life feature extraction method are validated.

References

1. Li X, Jiang T, Huang T et al (2008) Storage life and reliability evaluation of microwave electronical product by SSADT. J Beijing Univ Aeronaut Astronaut 34(10):1135–1138 (in Chinese)
2. Li X, Jiang T, Ma J et al (2008) CSADT and statistical analysis of SLD. In: 11th conference proceedings of CSAA reliability engineering professional committee. pp 293–298 (in Chinese)
3. Tavakkoli F, Teshnehlab M (2007) A ball bearing fault diagnosis method based on wavelet and EMD energy entropy mean. International Conference on Intelligent and Advanced Systems (ICIAS), pp 1210–1212
4. Xie P (2006) Study on information entropy feature extraction and fusion methods in fault diagnosis. Yanshan University, Qinhuangdao (in Chinese)
5. Huang NE, Shen Z, Long SR et al (1998) The empirical mode decomposition and the Hilbert spectrum for nonlinear and non-stationary time series analysis. Proceedings of the Royal Society of London. Ser A Math Phys Eng Sci 454:903–995
6. Huang NE, Wu MLC, Long SR et al (2003) A confidence limit for the empirical mode decomposition and Hilbert spectral analysis. In: Proceedings of the royal society of London. Series A: Mathematical, Physical and Engineering Sciences, vol 459, pp 2317–2345
7. Li X, Li D, Liang Z et al (2008) Analysis of depth of anesthesia with Hilbert-Huang spectral entropy. Clin Neurophysiol 119(11):2465–2475
8. Dong H, Qiu T, Zhang A et al (2010) The analysis method of heart rate variability signal based on the HHT marginal spectrum entropy and energy spectrum entropy. Chin J Biomed Eng 29(3):336–344 (in Chinese)
9. Wang L (2011) Life prediction technology for accelerated degradation testing based on time series analysis. Beihang University, Beijing (in Chinese)
10. Dai G, Liu B (2007) Instantaneous parameters extraction based on wavelet denoising and EMD. Acta Metrologica Sinica 28(2):158–162 (in Chinese)
11. Zhu Y (2009) Research on CHMM based equipment performance degradation assessment. Shanghai Jiaotong University, Shanghai (in Chinese)
12. Coble JB (2010) Merging data sources to predict remaining useful life-an automated method to identify prognostic parameters. University of Tennessee

Chapter 6
The Study of Emergency Response Dynamic Geographical Process Simulation Based On the Multi-Agent

Wensheng Zhou, Qiang Li, Jianxi Huang and Lihua Wang

Abstract Combining the Multi-Agent system (MAS) and GIS to simulate the human activity's dynamic geography process is a hotspot in currently research. High frequency of disasters has made the public safety emergency become the focus of attention. Modeling and simulation of emergency response can help people understand the dynamic complex process of it, and effectiveness and feasibility of emergency planning. But emergency response process involves many factors, so the model design and simulation system development face many difficulties. In this paper, through an experimental model we carried out the simulation to the large-scale emergency response. Based on the Repast and ArcGIS the simulation system prototype platform was established and more than 5,000 agents' interactions were analyzed. Experimental results show that multi-agent-based simulation is an effective way to assist emergency management, emergency planning and emergency response decision-making.

Keywords Multi-agent system · Emergency response · Simulation · GIS · Repast

W. Zhou (✉)
School of Architecture, Tsinghua University, 100084 Beijing, China
e-mail: zwsbj@163.com

Q. Li (✉)
295847 Department of PLA, 100120 Beijing, China
e-mail: liqiang06@mails.tsinghua.edu.cn

J. Huang
China Agricultural University, 100086 Beijing, China
e-mail: jxhuang@mail.tsinghua.edu.cn

L. Wang
Department of Computer Science and Technology, Tsinghua University, 100084 Beijing, China
e-mail: jinziye@sina.com

W. Lu et al. (eds.), *Proceedings of the 2012 International Conference on Information Technology and Software Engineering*, Lecture Notes in Electrical Engineering 211, DOI: 10.1007/978-3-642-34522-7_6, © Springer-Verlag Berlin Heidelberg 2013

6.1 Introduction

With the rapid population growth and the large quantities consumption of re-source, human living environment has deteriorated in recent years. With the frequent occurrence of major natural disasters or terrorism, the human is suffering the threat of catastrophes more and more heavily. If the disaster was occurred in a small area, the government or administration can mobilize its rescue forces to carry out rescue timely and effectively. But if disaster happened in a large-scale such as the above cases, how to we carry out the res-cue? How to respond to the incidents? How the hospital to adopt rescue methods in face of so many wounded people and how to save people's lives? About these questions, managers have no any experience, and it also beyond the ability of traditional model analysis tools.

Multi-agent system (MAS) is an effective method of using computer simulation to study Complex System. The essential idea of MAS is that many phenomena, even more complex ones, can be understood well as systems of autonomous agents that are simple and follow relatively simple rules for interaction [1]. MAS provided a framework for developing experimental platform that detailed assumptions about the behaviors and interactions of agents can be varied and the overall dynamics of the whole system will emerge. Nowadays an important development direction of MAS is to combine with Geographic Information System (GIS). The real geography spatial data were used in the simulation, and spatial analysis tools provided by GIS were used to analyze the simulation process and simulation results, thus enables the Multi-agent simulation to approach the real social situation.

In the field of emergency management, several multi-agent models have been developed to simulate emergency response. DrillSim is an example of evacuation model to simulate the evacuation plans of a limited number of agents restricted to a floor of a building [2]. Dan Guo et al. have presented an architecture which integrates ABM with GIS, and developed a generic model for emergency response planning against catastrophes, which applied to an urban firefighting simulation in Foshan city [3]. PLANC of NYC is a platform for urban disaster simulation and emergency planning features a variety of reality-based agents interacting on a realistic city map and can simulate the complex dynamics of emergency responses in different large mass casualty incident scenarios. Policy for hospital operation can be test and explored [4]. But these models or were limited to building or neighborhood scale, or agent types and quantities were less, simulation cannot truly reflect the complex dynamics of geographical processes. In this paper, taking Beijing as study areas and an imaginary emergency event as the background, carried out a simulation to the large-scale emergency response, established an emergency response simulation model framework based on the MAS and GIS, and proposed a technology framework of model implement. Under the platform, more than 5,000 agents' interaction processes were analyzed. The experiments have verified the operability of the model framework and the feasibility of technology framework.

6.2 Method

6.2.1 Framework of Model

Emergency response is an organized activity of residents and rescue forces in a certain period, space and social backgrounds. In the emergency response process, the residents affected by the disaster and the rescue forces are the basic bodies of implementation of emergency response, entitled as the 'emergency unit'. The space and social background that they are in is the natural and social environment of emergency response; they are collectively referred to as 'emergency environment'.

Emergency response simulation is the forecast or reappearance of the emergency response process of emergency event has occurred or may occur in a certain spatial extent and conditions. And it is the emulation of residents and rescue forces' behaviors during the emergency response process, as well as the statistical analysis to the emulation results. The prerequisites of simulation and the statistical analysis to the simulation results can be described and expressed by emergency response model parameters.

So synthesizing above analysis, Public Safety Emergency Response Multi-Agent Model can be defined as a four-element:

<Disaster model, Response-Agent, Environment model, Model parameters>

The Disaster model is a simulation program of a type of disaster like fire, explosion or toxic gas diffusion, that can provide the disaster spreading data over time and describe the effect to the population. The Environment model provides the real geographic space information, such as roads and buildings, as the environment of the emergency scenarios. The Response-Agent is the core of the model. Numbers of different kinds of agents are deployed in the simulation environment to simulate the human behaviors and interactions. The Model parameters included control parameter and observation parameter using to control the model running and analyzing results. The model is flexible, new disaster models and agent models can be plugged in, and the disaster dynamics and agent behaviors in different scenarios can be observed.

6.2.2 The Generic Architecture of Response-Agent

Agent model structure, there are three basic forms [5], the reactive agent, the cognitive agent (deliberative agent) and hybrid agent. The Response-Agent has the reactive behavior, such as according to their own or environment state changes to take different actions. At same time it has cognitive behavior, such as residents based on the road network information to determine their own course of action, so the Response-Agent is actually a hybrid agent.

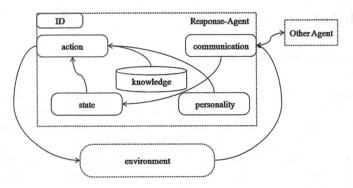

Fig. 6.1 The generic architecture of Response-Agent

Based on the analysis to the emergency response process, this paper designed the Response-Agent structure that suitable for emergency response simulation as shown in Fig. 6.1.

Every Response-Agent has the same six-component architecture: ID, State, Knowledge, Personality, Communication and Action. ID is an identification of every agent. State is the properties collection of an agent, including information about the status of the agent and all the information an agent knows about the world, like current location, degree of health or rescue capacities. Knowledge is some rules and intelligent algorithms stored in the agent. It contains all the knowledge for making decisions, like the triage of hospitals and route finding algorithm for persons. Personality is unique individuality parameter of different type Response-Agent. Communication is the interface for an agent to receive data about the environment and exchange information with other agents. Action is what an agent can do according to its role, like move along the roads or rescue people. These actions will be performed during the simulations time steps.

6.3 Experiment

6.3.1 Simulation Platform

Model design is a critical step of using multi-agent to study complex systems. But only have a simulation model is not enough, you also need a complete simulation platform. Researchers can use this platform to change the system structure, individual attributes, behavior modes, interactive methods and so on, through the graphical representation, statistics, analysis and comparison of scenarios to explore the system's inherent laws.

Agent-based modeling in the past, such as biological and economic field, the Multi-Agent activity space is abstract grid space mostly. In the studies of pedestrian travel rules, emergency evacuation and other issues combined with GIS,

Multi-Agent activity space is generally more concentrated in the building or neighborhood scale. Carrying Multi-Agent modeling and simulation in a city scale is still in its infancy. And on the other hand the emergency response process is involved in a number of factors, including a large number of individuals, so that the model implementation and simulation system development all facing many difficulties.

Through in-depth comparison [6], a simulation system prototype platform based on Repast and ArcGIS Engine was established.

6.3.2 Experiment Model Design

Experiment assumed that an emergency event occurred in a crowded place in Beijing, which resulting in a large number of casualties, the experiment model simulated the emergency response process that after the incident taking place.

Agent involved in the simulation included four categories: Person; Hospital; Onsite-Responder; and Emergency vehicle. Emergency vehicle included furthermore Police, Fire engine, Ambulance. The main parameters for each type of Agent are defined in Table 6.1.

6.3.3 Experiment

We conducted simulation experiments as follows:

1. Different person numbers effect on the mortality.
2. Different topology of hospitals effect on the mortality.

Part of the simulation diagram was shown in Figs. 6.2 and 6.3. In the simulation, we can find some results as same as the expected results, such as the number of deaths and mortality increasing with the number of person agent increase, as seen in Fig. 6.2. But there are also counter-intuitive phenomena, such as after removing three nearest hospitals to the incident location, the mortality decreased on the contrary, as seen in Fig. 6.3. To this phenomena the reason may be that after removing the three nearest hospitals, the distribution of persons were more reasonable, avoid persons crowded in the same hospital, thereby increasing the treatment rate. This result showed that the distribution of the existing hospital may not be optimal for a specific disaster scene.

Table 6.1 Agents' main parameters

Agent	Parameters		
		Name	Values
Person	ID		[0, PersonNum]
	State	Health-level	$h_l \in [0,1]$
		Destination	Home, workplace or hospital
		Treated	Yes or no
	Knowledge	Route finding	Short path algorithm to destination
	Personality	Degree of worry	$w_l \in [0,1]$
		Level of obedience	$o_l \in [0,1]$
		Level of distress	$d = w_l *(1- h_l)$
	Communication	Probability of communication device	Yes or no
	Action	Go to original destination	
		Go to hospital	
		Waiting for rescue	
Hospital	ID		[0,31]
	State	Operating mode	Available, critical, full
		Resource level	$r_l \in [0, ResourceNum]$
		Person-agents arrived	Person agent list
		Person-agents treated 1	Person agent list
		Person- agents waiting for treated	Person agent list
	Knowledge	Triage	Treating rules for all arrived persons
	Personality	Critical health level	$ch_l = 0.2$
		Non-critical health level	$nh_l = 0.5$
		Dischargeable health level	$dh_l = 0.8$
	Communication	Available of communication device	yes or no
	Action	Change operating mode	
		Treat person	
		Discharge person	
On-site responder	ID		[0,ResponderNum]
	State	Start location	[0,MaxResidentNum]
		Alert time	$[0,\infty]$
		Operating mode	Available, critical, full
		Resource level	$r_l \in [0, ResourceNum]$
		Person-agents arrived	Person agent list
		Person-agents treated	Person agent list
		Person- agents waiting for treated	Person agent list
	Knowledge	Route finding	Short path algorithm to destination
		Triage	Processing rules for all arrived persons
	Personality	Critical health level	$ch_l = 0.2$
		Dischargeable health level	$nh_l = 0.5$
	Communication	Available of communication device	Yes or no
	Action	Go to start place	
		Change operating mode	
		Treat person	
		Discharge person	
Emergency vehicle	ID		[0,vehicleragentNum]
	State	Start location	[0,MaxResidentNum]
		Alert time	$[0,\infty]$
		Speed	[0, evenspeed $\pm$ 10 %]
	Knowledge	Route finding	Coordinates of short path to start location
	Personality	None	
	Communication	None	
	Action	Go to start place	

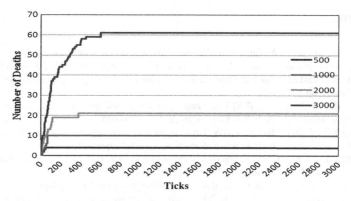

Fig. 6.2 Evolution curves of death number for different person number

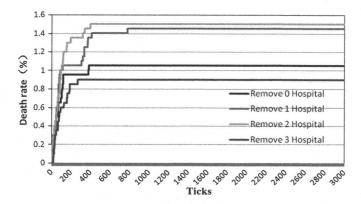

Fig. 6.3 Evolution curves of death rate for remove different nearest hospitals

6.4 Conclusions

From above simulation analysis, we can find that some important issues in the emergency response, such as: Under what circumstances should go to the hospital, when to allow patients to leave the hospital, the needs of the amount of resources, the importance of public awareness and law's sanction, the dissemination of medical information, etc., all of them can be analyzed through repeated simulations. Meanwhile, the amount of resources, and the scale and spatial topology that emergency planners concerned can also be evaluated and optimized through the models, which indicates that the model can play the important roles in the emergency decision-making, response planning, and resources allocation scheme, etc.

Acknowledgments This work was supported by the National Science Foundation of China (No. 51178236).

References

1. Wooldridge M (2002) An introduction to multi-agent systems. Wiley, Chichester
2. Massaguer D, Balasubramanian V, Mehrotra S, Venkatasubramanian N (2006) Multi-agent simulation of disaster response. First international workshop on agent technology for disaster management, pp 124–130
3. Guo D, Ren B, Wang C (2008) Integrated agent-based modeling with GIS for large scale emergency simulation. Proc Adv Comput Intell 5370:618–625
4. NYU-CCPR (2008) Planning with large agent-networks against catastrophes (plan-C) [EB\OL], [2008-2-2]. http://www.bioinformatics.nyu.edu/Projects/planc
5. Li X, Ye J, Liu X et al (2007) Geographical simulation system: cell automatics and multi-agent system. Science Press, Beijing, pp 250–260 (in chinese)
6. Castle CE (2006) Using repast to develop a prototype agent-based pedestrian evacuation model. In: Proceedings of the agent 2006 conference on social agents: results and prospects, Chicago, USA

Chapter 7
What on Earth Drive the Propagation of Tweets on Chinese MicroBlog Network

Jing Wang, Bingqiang Wang, Ke Zhu, Juan Shen and Jing Yu

Abstract This paper studies and analyses the main reasons for the propagation of tweets on Chinese MicroBlog network. We collected a large dataset from Sina-Weibo API and present an in-depth analyse on data we've got. We studied the distribution of the number of retweets for one tweet. We define the popular tweet as the tweet retweeted for more than 500 times. Then we investigated the influence of the top 2000 popular tweets' authors. Finally we focused on the contents of popular tweets. We make several interesting observation. First, the distribution of the number of retweets for one tweet is a non-power-law distribution indicating that only very small number of tweets can be retweeted for thousands of times. Second, the retweeting action does not correlate to the author's influence directly. The influential's tweets are not absolutely retweeted for more times. Third, the mention, the image and the url link are the main factors for tweets' spreading, especially the mention. We believe that these findings can help us to correct some fallacies about Chinese MicroBlog network.

Keywords SinaWeibo · Propagation of tweet · Influence of users · Contents of tweets

7.1 Introduction

The MicroBlog is an emerging social media recently all over the world. Unlike traditional media, each user in MicroBlogs can be a news producer even the ordinary persons. So the messages' contents are more timely and grassroot [1].

J. Wang (✉) · B. Wang · K. Zhu · J. Shen · J. Yu
National Digital Switching System Engineering and Technology Center,
450002 Zhengzhou, China
e-mail: zhuwangzilz@163.com

W. Lu et al. (eds.), *Proceedings of the 2012 International Conference on Information Technology and Software Engineering*, Lecture Notes in Electrical Engineering 211, DOI: 10.1007/978-3-642-34522-7_7, © Springer-Verlag Berlin Heidelberg 2013

Also the messages can be propagated at unprecedented scale and frequency due to the large size of users. MicroBlogs have made tremendous impact on our daily life. A tweet can even result in some political events. We can see that the influence of tweets is becoming more and more important. A lot of research has been done on the spreading of tweets and the influence of messages. In some western MicroBlog networks such as Twitter [2–4]. How exactly does information spread in the MicroBlog? Retweeting is the most effective method [5]. The content and topical information of messages, graph structural properties of users affect the messages' retweets [2].

In china, MicroBlogs also play an important role in news production and propagation. It has challenged the authority of the mainstream media [6]. People prefer believing in those user_generated contents in tweets to other information. The audience size of one popular tweets can even be millions. What on earth drive the propagation of messages in Chinese MicroBlogs? Is the propagation affected by the same factors as on the Twitter or not? In this regard, the goal of this work is to study the main reasons why a tweet can be spread to a large scope in Chinese MicroBlogs.

In this paper, we present an empirical analysis of why tweets can be retweeted. We use a large amount of data gathered from Sina Weibo, a famous Chinese MicroBlog network. We begin with the study of the distribution of retweets' number of one tweet. Then we select top 1000 tweets by the number of retweets for one tweet from the verified user's dataset, extract the authors of these tweets. Next we rank these users by three different measures: the number of followers, max number of retweets for one tweet in a user's tweets set within the top 1000 tweets, the percentage of a user's tweets' number in the top 1000 tweets. Then we try to find the correlation of these three different ranks. Finally, We extract the contents of the top 1000 tweets and try to find out the main elements affecting the retweeting. The result shows that users like to retweet messages including images and mentions.

7.2 Dataset

We choose Sina Weibo to do our research. Sina Weibo is one of the famous Chinese MicroBlog networks. It has more than 50 million active users per day, and 10 million newly registered users per month. So the data from Sina Weibo is typical.

SinaWeibo has offered an API since 2010 that facilitate the crawling data. We use the API to crawl and collect data on it. The data we gathered include user's profile and tweets. We launched our crawlers in August 2011 using 20 machines with different IPs. In order to gather plenty information, we gather the users profile and tweets by breadth-first search algorithm along the direction of followers and followings. Meanwhile we capture the tweets of trending topics and these authors' profiles. The user's profile we collected includes userID, username, sex, age, verified_flag, the number of followers, the number of followings and the number of tweets. The tweets information includes the full text, the written time, the messageID, the author's userID and the number of retweets.

In order to get rid of the spams, we removed the users who have not been on Sina Weibo for at least 1 day. Then we get our final dataset including 515,075 users' profile and 2,250,546 tweets. The users can be classified into verified-users and unverified-users. Among the unverified-users' dataset, we divide users into three subsets: 70hou's dataset including 4,855 users (users born between 1970 and 1979), 80hou's dataset including 19,632 users (users born between 1980 and 1989) and 90hou's dataset including 9,776 users (users born between 1990 and 2000). We believe that the datasets are representative. Our research work is deployed on the dataset.

7.3   Are the Influentials' Tweets Retweeted More?

Here we focus on whether the influence of users can affect the tweets' propagation. First we need to find out the characteristic of the tweets' propagation. We use the number of retweets for one tweet to discribe the tweets' propagation. The more the number of retweets for one tweet is, the more the influence of the tweet gets. Here we define the popular tweet as the tweet be retweeted for more than 500 times.

7.3.1   The Distribution of the Number of Retweets for One Tweet

In this section we present a quantitative analysis of retweeting action in Sina-Weibo. The tweets are spread through the path of followers and the retweeting is the most effective method to spread messages on MicroBlogs. To find the truth of the tweets' propagation, we try to find the property of the number of retweets for a certain tweet.

We analyze the tweets in the verified-users' dataset, 70hou's dataset, 80hou's dataset and 90hou's dataset separately. Figure 7.1 displays the distribution of the number of retweets for one tweet in four different user groups. The Y-axis represents complementary cumulative distribution function (CCDF). The plots show an almost line on a log–log plot up to $x = 1000$. It means that the distribution of the number of retweets for one tweet has power-law characteristics while $x \leq 1000$. But the data points in four lines beyond $x = 1000$ are below the power-law curve. These represent the tweets which are retweeted more times than the power-law distribution predicts. The power-law distribution indicates the fact that the popular tweets can be retweeted disproportionately for more times than the majority of tweets. That is to say only a small number of tweets can be retweeted frequently and most of tweets will not be retweeted. The deviation of power-law distribution indicate while the number of retweets is beyond 1000, the tweets' number will be much fewer than the power-law predict. The most retweeted tweets are very few.

Fig. 7.1 The CCDF of the
number of retweets for one
tweet

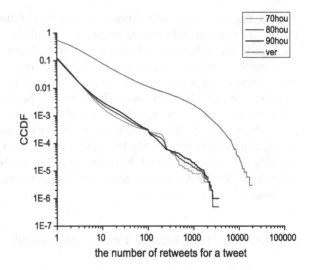

From Fig. 7.1, we can see the 3 lines representing 70hou, 80hou and 90hou are very similar and the verified-users' line is high above them. It shows the probability of retweeting written by the verified-users is higher than the unverified-users. Among the verified-users' dataset, 48.54 % is not retweeted at all and 41.74 % is retweeted once. Only 2.26 % is retweeted more than 20 times. Figure 7.2 displays the statistic result. The result consists with the distribution we analyzed above.

7.3.2 The Methodology for Analyzing the Correlation Between the Influence of Users and the Retweeting

Based on the above result, we draw a conclusion that verified-users' tweets have more number of retweets for a tweet than unverified-users' tweets. So we try to investigate the property of verified-users' tweets. Dose the retweeting action correlate to the users' influence.

In order to find the correlation between the users' influence and the retweeting action, we extract the top 2000 tweets ranked by the number of retweets for a tweet. Meanwhile we extract the authors' information of the top 2000 tweets. We totally get 147 users information. Than we rank the 147 users by three different method.

Firstly we rank the users by the users influence and get R_u. We use the number of followers N_f and the number of tweets N_{tw} as the measure of user's influence. We get two ranks by the two measures in the first step and then calculate the final user's rank $R_{u(i)}$ according to the function 1. $R_{Nf(i)}$ is the user's rank by N_f, and $R_{Ntw(i)}$ is the user's rank by N_{tw}. We use the different weight coefficient to indicate the effect of two measures [2, 7].

Fig. 7.2 Proportion of tweets according to the retweets' number in verified-users' dataset

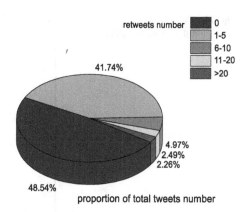

$$R_{u(i)} = 0.3 \times R_{Nf(i)} + 0.7 \times R_{Ntw(i)} \qquad (7.1)$$

Then we rank the users by the maximal number of retweets for one tweet (R_{Ntw}) and the proportion of popular tweets (R_{Ptw}). The proportion of popular tweets means the percentage of one user's tweets in top 2000 tweets dataset. If the proportions of popular tweets for different users are equal, we rank this user by the maximal number of retweets for one tweet. The two ranks can reflect the popularity of one user's tweets. Finally we compare the three ranks and plot the correlation function diagram in Fig. 7.3. Figure 7.3 shows that both the blue data and the orange data are separate. The results indicate that the retweeting action dose not correlate to the user's influence directly.

In order to prove the result, we enlarge the dataset. We extract the top 5000 and the top 10000 tweets from the verified-users' dataset. Then we collected the authors' information of these tweets and got 386 and 547 users. Using the same method mentioned above, we get the R_u, R_{Ntw} and R_{Ptw} of the two user groups. Then we use the Spearman's rank correlation coefficient [8]:

$$\rho = 1 - \frac{6 \sum (x_i - y_i)^2}{N^3 - N} \qquad (7.2)$$

as a measure of the strength of the association between different rank sets. x_i and y_i are the ranks of users based on different measures. N is the size of users. The Spearman's rank correlation coefficient indicates whether X and Y are correlate or independent. The closer the absolute value of ρ is to 1, the stronger the correlation is. If ρ is 0, the two ranks are independent. Table 7.1 lists the Spearman's rank correlation coefficients of $R_u vs R_{Ntw}$ and $R_u vs R_{Ntw}$ in three datasets.

We can see that in three dataset ρ is close to 0. That indicates the rank based on user's influence and the ranks based on the tweets influence are almost independent. The result is consistent to what Fig. 7.3 shows. So we conclude that the retweeting action does not correlate to the author's influence directly. The influentials' tweets are not absolutely retweeted for more times.

Fig. 7.3 Correlation
between different users' ranks

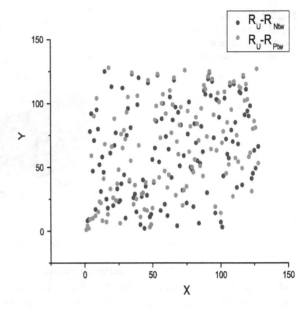

Table 7.1 Spearman's rank
correlation coefficients in
different datasets

Correlation	Top1000	Top 5000	Top 10000
$R_u vs R_{Ntw}$	0.126	0.247	0.194
$R_u vs R_{Ntw}$	0.132	0.173	0.185

7.4 The Contents of Tweets VS the Retweeting

Since the author's influence does not directly affect the spreading of tweets on
SinaWeibo, what is the main reason for the retweeting? We begin to investigate
the contents of tweets.

7.4.1 The Contents of the Popular Tweets

We start our research work on the verified-users' dataset because the popular
tweets (tweets have large amount of retweets number) are almost written by the
verified-users. We extract the top 1000 tweets based on the number of retweets for
one tweet. The last tweet in the top 1000 dataset is retweeted for 814 times. So the
top 1000 tweets are all popular tweets.

We focus on the content of these popular tweets. In order to get the complete
content of tweets, we analyze not only the text but also other information in the
content. Here we chose 5 kinds of information in tweets to extract: the image, the

Table 7.2 The contents of top 10 tweets, the author name is pingyin

Rank	Author name	Image	Videos	Url	@	##
1	Xiena	1	0	1	0	0
2	Fangxiang	1	0	0	0	0
3	Xiena	0	0	0	0	0
4	Xiena	1	0	0	1	0
5	Yebia	0	0	0	0	1
6	Xiena	1	0	0	1	0
7	Xiena	1	0	0	0	0
8	Xiena	1	0	0	1	0
9	Wangzhixin	1	0	0	0	0
10	Yechangbaoan	1	0	0	0	1

url links, the videos, the symbol of mention @ and the symbol of topical information ##. In this paper, we call this information as content element. These 5 different content elements in a tweet can represent different reasons for retweeting. The image, the video and the url link represent the style of tweets' content. The @ symbol represents the name value in the tweets [3]. The ## symbol represents the content's relationship with the current global events or social news. In the following, we analyze these 5 elements in the tweets deeply.

7.4.2 The Main Reasons for the Retweeting

Here we list the content elements of the top 10 tweets in Table 7.2.

If the tweet has one element mentioned above, the value in the Table 7.2 is 1. Otherwise the value is 0. We can see that most tweets in Table 7.2 include images, url links, the symbol @ and the symbol ##. Only the third tweet in Table 7.2 has none elements.

In order to investigate which content element is the most important one, we analyze the contents of top 1000 tweets in-depth. We calculate the number of tweets including each content element mentioned in Sect. 4.2. The statistic results are showed in Fig. 7.4.

Among the top 1000 tweets, there are 586 tweets including image and 710 tweets including mention symbol. The number of tweets containing url link follows. The proportion of tweets having other two elements is very small. The result indicates that the tweets having images is more likely to be retweeted than the tweets only having texts. Also the mention is an important factor for retweeting. This shows the name's value for spreading tweets. We find that the topic element seems not important. It is very different from the Twitter on which the popular tweets have more to do with global event and news.

We focus on the three important elements. Then we plot Venn diagram of the top 1000 tweets across the three important content elements in Fig. 7.5. And we normalize the chart so that the total is 1.

Fig. 7.4 The tweets' number including different content elements in top 1000 popular tweets

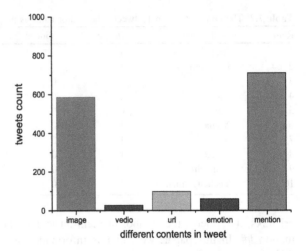

Fig. 7.5 Venn diagram of the top 1000 tweets across the three mention, url and image

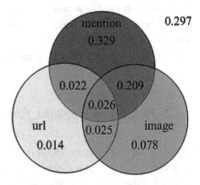

The chart tells the truth that the symbol of mention is the most important factor for retweeting. The image follows. In Fig. 7.5, the overlaps represent the tweets have more than one elements. We can see that the portion of overlap is big, especially the overlap of mention and image. This tells us that multi-element in one tweet may has more influence on retweeting than only one element. Our finding shows proper using the content elements can increase the number of retweets for one tweet.

7.5 Conclusion

This paper analyzes the propagation of tweets on SinaWeibo and trys to discover what are the reasons for retweeting. Firstly we focus on the distribution of the retweets' number for one tweet. We find that the distribution is a non-power-law distribution. While $x \leq 1000$, the distribution of the retweets' number for one tweet accords with the power-law distribution, which indicates the fact that the popular tweets can be retweeted disproportionately for more times than the majority of tweets. The data points beyond $x = 1000$ deviate from power-law distribution curve, which indicate while the number of retweets is too large, the tweets' number will be much fewer than the power-low predicts. Then we rank the authors of the top 2000 tweets in verified-users' dataset by three different measures and try to find the correlation between them. These three ranks represent users' influence and the retweeting action. We find the retweeting action does not correlate to the author's influence directly. The influential's tweets are not likely to be retweeted more. Finally, we investigate the contents of popular tweets. The conclusion we drew is that the mention, the image and the url link are the main factors for tweets' spreading, especially the mention. We can produce popular tweets by proper using the content elements.

References

1. Wu S, Hofman JM, Mason WA, Watts DJ (2011) Who says what to whom on twitter, proceeding of the 20th international conference on world wide web, pp 705–714
2. Hong L, Dan O, Davison BD (2011) Predicting popular messages in twitter, proceeding of the international conference on World Wide Web, pp 57–58
3. Suh B, Hong L, Pirolli P, Chi EH (2010) Want to be Retweeted? Large scale analytics on factors impacting retweet in twitter network, proceeding of the 2010 IEEE second international conference on social computing, pp 177–184
4. Romero DM, Galuba W, Asur S, Huberman BA (2011) Influence and passivity in social media, proceeding of the 20th international world wide web conference, pp 113–114
5. Kwak H, Lee CH, Park H, Moon S (2010) What is Twitter, a social network or a news media? Proceeding of the 19th international conference on world wide web (Raleigh, North Carolina, USA) pp 1772690–1772751
6. Yu L, Asur S, Huberman BA (2011) What trends in chinese social media, proceeding of the 5th ACM work shop on social network mining and analysis. ACM, New York
7. Agarwal N, Liu H, Ang LT, Yu PS (2008) Identifying the influential bloggers in a community, proceeding of the international conference on Web search and web data mining, pp 207–218
8. Cha M, Haddadi H, Benevenuto F, Gummad KP (2010) Measuring user influence on twitter: the million follower fallacy, proceeding of the fourth international AAAI conference on weblogs and social media, Washington DC, pp 10–17

Chapter 8
Tracking Control and Generalized Projective Synchronization of a Fourth-Order Circuit's Hyperchaotic System with Unknown Parameter and Disturbance

Xuanbing Yang

Abstract In this paper, the issue of tracking control and generalized projective synchronization for a fourth-order circuit's hyperchaotic system is investigated. Based on the LaSalle's invariant set theorem, a robust controller is contrived to acquire tracking control and generalized projective synchronization and parameter identification. It is proved theoretically that the proposed scheme can allow us to drive this hyperchaotic system to any desired reference signals, including chaotic or hyperchaotic signals, periodic orbits or fixed value by the given scaling factor. The presented simulation results further demonstrate that the proposed method is effective and robust.

Keywords Generalized projective synchronization · Tracking control · Unknown parameter · Disturbance

8.1 Introduction

The investigation of chaos control and synchronization have received a great deal of attention over the last decades because of the wide-scope potential applications in many disciplines [1–3]. Among them, tracking control is the most commonly discussed problem in the domain of chaos control. It can be explained that, for the arbitrary given reference signal, a controller is designed to cause the output of the chaotic system to follow the given reference signal asymptotically. Especially, if

X. Yang (✉)
School of Information and Communication Engineering, Hunan Institute
of Science and Technology, Yueyang, China
e-mail: Yangxb12@126.com

W. Lu et al. (eds.), *Proceedings of the 2012 International Conference on Information Technology and Software Engineering*, Lecture Notes in Electrical Engineering 211, DOI: 10.1007/978-3-642-34522-7_8, © Springer-Verlag Berlin Heidelberg 2013

the reference signal is produced by the chaotic or hyperchaotic system, the tracking control evolve into synchronization. There are many studies on the tracking control in the literature, see in [4, 5]. Nearly a decade research in chaos synchronization has focused on the concept of generalized projective synchronization which can expand the mode for encoding data and achieve communication rapidly [6, 7].

Recently, Min [8] have combined tracking control with generalized projective synchronization ingeniously and formed a kind of program called tracking generalized projective synchronization which would have a strong anti-crack ability when used for secure communication. But the proposed technique assumes that the involved systems are free from unknown parameters and external perturbations. However, in practice we may not have this scenario, and have to take parameter unknown and external disturbances into account. The effect of these uncertainties will destroy the performance of synchronization and control and even break it. Therefore, it is important to study tracking control and generalized projective synchronization in such systems with unknown parameters and disturbances.

In this paper, we propose a novel tracking control and generalized projective synchronization scheme for a Fourth-order Circuit's hyperchaotic system with unknown parameters and disturbances based on the Lyapunov's stability theory and LaSalle's invariant set theorem. It is proved theoretically that the proposed scheme can allow us to drive this hyperchaotic system to any desired reference signals, including chaotic or hyperchaotic signals, periodic orbits or fixed value with the given scaling factor, and can identify the unknown parameters simultaneously. Simulation results are presented to further demonstrate the effectiveness and robustness of the proposed method.

8.2 System Model and Problem Descriptions

A class of fourth-order circuit's hyperchaotic system considered here can be described by the following equations in dimensionless form [9],

$$
\begin{cases}
\dot{x}_1 = ax_1 - x_2 - x_3 \\
\dot{x}_2 = x_1 \\
\dot{x}_3 = b(x_1 - x_4) \\
\dot{x}_4 = cx_3 - g(x_4 - 1)H(x_4 - 1)
\end{cases}
\tag{8.1}
$$

where $H(v) = sign(v)$. The circuit will exhibit hyperchaotic under $a = 0.7, b = 3$, $c = 3, g = 30$.

Now, we present the dynamics of system (8.1) in the following form,

$$
\dot{x} = f(x) + F(x)\vartheta
\tag{8.2}
$$

where

$$x = \begin{bmatrix} x_1 \\ x_2 \\ x_3 \\ x_4 \end{bmatrix}, f(x) = \begin{bmatrix} -x_2 - x_3 \\ x_1 \\ 0 \\ 0 \end{bmatrix},$$

$$F(x) = \begin{bmatrix} x_1 & 0 & 0 & 0 \\ 0 & 0 & 0 & 0 \\ 0 & x_1 - x_4 & 0 & 0 \\ 0 & 0 & x_3 & -(x_4 - 1)H(x_4 - 1) \end{bmatrix}, \quad \vartheta = \begin{bmatrix} a \\ b \\ c \\ g \end{bmatrix}$$

Let's suppose that the parameters ϑ are unknown and the hyperchaotic system is disturbed by the exotic perturbation $\xi(t) \in R^4$ which satisfy the bounded condition $\|\xi(t)\| \leq k < \infty$ for all t, where k is not necessary to be known previously.

Then the controlled hyperchaotic system with disturbance can be described in the following form,

$$\dot{x} = f(x) + F(x)\vartheta + \xi(t) + u \tag{8.3}$$

$u \in R^4$ is the controller to be designed, ϑ are the unknown parameters, $\xi(t)$ are the disturbances.

Let $r = (r_1, r_2, r_3, r_4)^T$ be an arbitrary given reference signal with first derivative. The synchronization error between system (8.3) and the reference signal is defined as $e = x - pr$, where $p = diag(p_1, p_2, p_3, p_4)$ is called the scaling factor. Our aim is that, according to the designed controller, the all corresponding variables of system (8.3) follow the reference signal r proportionally. That is $\lim_{t \to \infty} \|e\| = \lim_{t \to \infty} \|x - pr\| = 0$, where $\|\cdot\|$ denotes a 2-norm in R^4.

8.3 Design of Adaptive Control Scheme

Theorem 8.1 *For the drive system* (8.3) *and the arbitrary reference signal, if the controller u is designed as*

$$u = p\dot{r} - Le - f(x) - F(x)\hat{\vartheta} - \hat{k}e/\|e\| \tag{8.4}$$

where $L > 0$ is the feedback strength and $\hat{\vartheta} = (\hat{a}, \hat{b}, \hat{c}, \hat{g})^T$ is the estimate of ϑ which satisfy the following updated algorithm

$$\dot{\hat{\vartheta}} = [F(x)]^T e, \tag{8.5}$$

and $\hat{k}$ complies with the following algorithm

$$\dot{\hat{k}} = \|e\|, \tag{8.6}$$

then all the corresponding variables of system (8.3) will approach the reference signal r ultimately according to the scaling factor, and all the unknown parameters ϑ can be estimated by $\hat{\vartheta}$ asymptotically.

Proof Let $\tilde{\vartheta} = \vartheta - \hat{\vartheta}, \tilde{k} = k - \hat{k}$ and the Lyapunov function of system (8.3) is constructed as

$$V = \frac{1}{2}e^T e + \frac{1}{2}\tilde{\vartheta}^T \tilde{\vartheta} + \frac{1}{2}\tilde{k}^T \tilde{k}$$

Taking the time derivative of V along the generalized projective synchronization error and applying the renewal algorithm (8.5) and (8.6) yields

$$\begin{aligned}
\dot{V} &= (f(x) + F(x)\vartheta(t) + \xi(t) + u - p\dot{r})^T e \\
&\quad - \tilde{\vartheta}^T([F(x)]^T e) - \tilde{k}^T \|e\| \\
&\leq (f(x) + F(x)\vartheta(t) + u - p\dot{r})^T e + \|\xi(t)\| \cdot \|e\| \\
&\quad - \tilde{\vartheta}^T([F(x)]^T e) - \tilde{k}^T \|e\| \\
&\leq (f(x) + F(x)\vartheta(t) + u - p\dot{r})^T e + k\|e\| \\
&\quad - \tilde{\vartheta}^T([F(x)]^T e) - \tilde{k}^T \|e\| \\
&= (f(x) + F(x)\vartheta(t) + u - p\dot{r})^T e + \hat{k}\|e\| - \tilde{\vartheta}^T([F(x)]^T e) \\
&= (F(x)\vartheta(t) - Le - F(x)\hat{\vartheta})^T e - \tilde{\vartheta}^T([F(x)]^T e) \\
&= -Le^T e \leq 0
\end{aligned}$$

It is obvious that the set $M = \{e = 0, \tilde{\vartheta} = 0, \tilde{k} = 0\}$ is the largest invariant set which is contained in the set $E = \{e | \dot{V} = 0, e \in R^4, \tilde{\vartheta} \in R^4\}$. So, according to the LaSalle's invariant set theorem, the all corresponding variables of system (8.3) will follow the reference signal r asymptotically according to the scaling factor, and the parameters ϑ can be estimated by $\hat{\vartheta}$ ultimately.

8.4 Simulation Results

In this section, some numerical simulations are presented to demonstrate and verify the effectiveness and the robustness of the proposed approach. In all the process of simulation, the fourth-order Runge–Kutta method is used with time step 0.001, the initial states of the fourth-order circuit's hyperchaotic system are taken as $x_1(0) = 0.2, x_2(0) = 0.5$, $x_3(0) = 0.5$, $x_4(0) = 0.8$, and the exotic disturbance $\zeta(t) = [n_1, n_2, n_3, n_4]^T$, n_1, n_2, n_3, n_4 are stochastic number of $(0, 1)$.

8.4.1 Tracking the Periodic Signal and Fixed Value

Firstly, we choose the sinusoidal signal and fixed value as the reference signal, that is, $r = (\cos 2t, \sin 3t + \cos 2t, \sin 3t, -3)^T$, and $p = diag(0.5, 1, -2, 1)$, $L = 1.5$. The simulation results are shown in Fig. 8.1. Figure 8.1a–d represent the time evolution of variable x and reference signal r, the solid line is the variable and the dot line is the corresponding reference signal r. Figure 8.1e shows the time evolution of synchronization errors. Figure 8.1f–i exhibit the time histories of adaptive parameters. As we can see that the system (8.3) has tracked the periodic signal and fixed value ultimately according to the scaling factor, and all the unknown parameters ϑ can be estimated by $\hat{\vartheta}$ asymptotically.

8.4.2 Tracking the Hyperchaotic System

In this section, projective synchronization of two different hyperchaotic systems will be discussed with the aid of the tracking control. And we take the all variables of the four-variable LC oscillator system as reference signals, i.e. $r = (y_1, y_2, y_3, y_4)^T$. The four-variable LC oscillator is completely different from the system (8.1) and can be described as

$$\begin{cases} \dot{y}_1 = a_1 y_1 - y_2 - y_3 \\ \dot{y}_2 = y_1 - b_1 y_2 \\ \mu \dot{y}_3 = y_1 - c_1 y_3 - y_4 \\ \varepsilon \dot{y}_4 = y_3 - d_1(y_4 - 1)H(y_4 - 1) \end{cases} \tag{8.7}$$

where $H(v) = sign(v)$, when the parameters are set equal to $a_1 = 0.6, b_1 = 0.05, c_1 = 0.015, d_1 = 10, \varepsilon = 0.33, \mu = 0.3$, the system will exhibit a hyperchaotic behavior, and the two positive Lyapunov exponents are 0.11 and 0.06 respectively.

The initial conditions of system (8.7) are $y_1(0) = 0.01, y_2(0) = 0.01, y_3(0) = 0.02, y_4(0) = -0.1$. And let $p = diag(2, -2, 0.5, 1), L = 1.8$. The simulation results are shown in Fig. 8.2. Figure 8.2a–d represent the time evolution of variable x and reference signal r, the solid line is the variable and the dot line is the corresponding reference signal r. Figure 8.2e displays the time evolution of synchronization errors. And the time evolutions of adaptive parameters are exhibited Fig. 8.2f–i. As we can see that the system (8.3) and the LC oscillator have achieved generalized projective synchronization ultimately, and all the unknown parameters ϑ are estimated by $\hat{\vartheta}$ asymptotically.

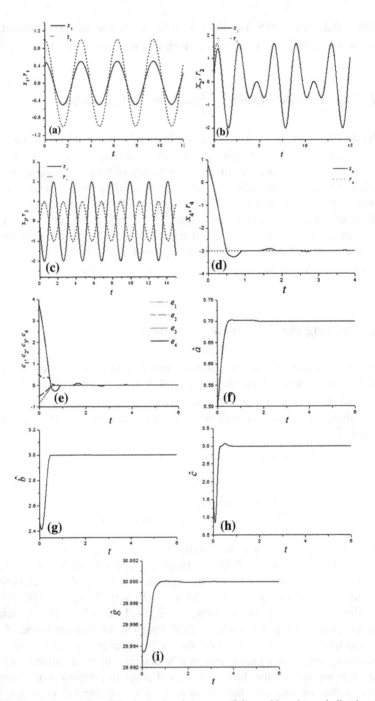

Fig. 8.1 Simulation results of the hyperchaotic system (8.3) tracking the periodic signal and fixed value: **a–d** time evolution of x and r; **e** synchronization errors e_1, e_2, e_3 and e_4; **f–i** time evolution of the estimated parameters

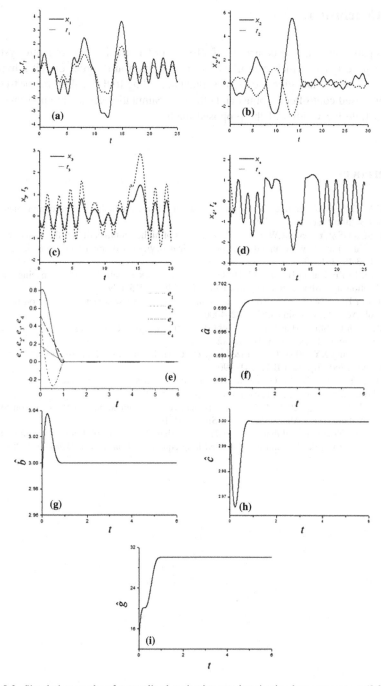

Fig. 8.2 Simulation results of generalized projective synchronization between system (8.3) and (8.7): **a–d** time evolution of x and r; **e** synchronization errors e_1, e_2, e_3 and e_4; **f–i** time evolution of the estimated parameters

8.5 Conclusion

In this paper, an adaptive controller of a fourth-order circuit's hyperchaotic system has been designed, which can allow us to drive the fourth-order circuit's hyperchaotic system to any given reference signal according to the scaling factor freely. The proposed controller is robust and effective. Simulation results are presented to demonstrate the validity of the proposed method.

References

1. Feki M (2003) An adaptive chaos synchronization scheme applied to secure communication. Chaos Soliton Fract 18:141–149
2. Ngueuteu GSM,Yamapi R,Woafo P (2008) Effects of higher nonlinearity on the dynamics and synchronization of two coupled electromechanical devices. Commun Nonlinear Sci Numer Simul 13:1213–1240
3. Cao ZJ, Li PF, Zhang H, Xie FG, Hu G (2007) Turbulence control with local pacing and its implication in cardiac defibrillation. Chaos 17:0151071–0151079
4. Li J, Lin H, Li N (2006) Chaotic synchronization with diverse structures based on tracking control. Acta Physica Sinica 55:3992–4000
5. Li Z, Chen G, Shi S, Han C (2003) Robust adaptive tracking control for a class of uncertain chaotic systems. Phys Lett A 310:40–42
6. Meng J, Wang XY (2008) Generalized projective synchronization of a class of delayed neural networks. Mod Phys Lett B 22:181–190
7. Li CP, Yan JP (2006) Generalized projective synchronization of chaos: the cascade synchronization approach. Chaos Soliton Fract 30:140–145
8. Min FH, Wang ZQ (2008) Generalized projective synchronization and tracking control of complex dynamous systems. Acta Phys Sin 57:0031–0035
9. Susuki Y, Yokoi Y, Hikihara T (2007) Energy-based analysis of frequency entrainment described by van der Pol and phase-locked loop equations. Chaos 17:0231081–0231088

Chapter 9
A New Three-Dimensional Chaotic System with Different Wing

Xuanbing Yang

Abstract This paper proposes a new 3D autonomous chaotic system which displays complicated dynamical behavior over a large range of parameters. This new chaotic system has five equilibrium points. Interestingly, this new system can generate two coexisting one-wing attractors with different initial conditions. Besides, this system can generate two-wing and four-wing chaotic attractors with variation of only one parameter. Some basic dynamical behaviors of the proposed chaotic system, such as equilibrium points, bifurcation diagram and Lyapunov exponents are investigated.

Keywords Chaotic system · Dynamical behavior · Lyapunov exponent

9.1 Introduction

Chaos is an interesting phenomenon in nonlinear dynamical systems, and has been intensively studied in the past four decades. A chaotic system is a nonlinear deterministic system that displays a complex and unpredictable behavior. The sensitive dependence on the initial conditions is a prominent characteristic of chaotic behavior. In the investigation of chaos theory and applications, it is very important to generate new chaotic systems or enhance complex dynamics and topological structure. Since Lorenz found the first chaotic attractor [1] in 1963, chaos has been intensively studied by many scholars in the last three decades [2–5]. Based on the Lorenz system, others chaotic systems were proposed in

X. Yang (✉)
School of Information and Communication Engineering, Hunan Institute of Science and Technology, Yueyang, China
e-mail: Yangxb12@126.com

W. Lu et al. (eds.), *Proceedings of the 2012 International Conference on Information Technology and Software Engineering*, Lecture Notes in Electrical Engineering 211, DOI: 10.1007/978-3-642-34522-7_9, © Springer-Verlag Berlin Heidelberg 2013

succession: Chen system [2], Lü system [3, 4], Liu system [5], etc. These chaotic systems only have three equilibrium points and two-wing chaotic attractors.

Because of simple circuit implementation, it's meaningful and challenging to constuct smooth autonomous systems with different wing attractors in both theory and engineering applications. However, there are very rare works on generating different wing chaotic attractor in a smooth system.

In this paper, a novel 3D autonomous chaotic system with five equilibria is introduced. This system has been found to has many interesting complex dynamical behaviors, including chaos, period-doubling bifurcations, etc. This new system can generate two coexisting one-wing attractors with different initial conditions. Besides, this system can generate two-wing and four-wing chaotic attractors with variation of only one parameter. Therefore, it can be concluded that this chaotic system has a complicated topological structure and dynamics. Basic dynamical behaviors of the proposed chaotic system, such as equilibrium points, bifurcation diagram and Lyapunov exponents are investigated. Simulations demonstrate the brief theoretical derivations.

9.2 New 3D Chaotic System

In this paper, a novel chaotic attractor is generated by the following simple three-dimensional autonomous system:

$$\begin{cases} \dot{x}_1 = -ax_1 + ex_2x_3 \\ \dot{x}_2 = bx_2 - x_1x_3 - fx_3 \\ \dot{x}_3 = -dx_3 + cx_1x_2 - hx_1x_3 \end{cases} \tag{9.1}$$

here x_1, x_2, x_3 are the state variables, and a, b, c, d, h, e, f are the positive constant parameters of system (9.1).

9.2.1 Dissipativity and Existence of Attractor

To ensure the existence of attractor in system (9.1), the general condition of dissipativity should be considered, i.e.

$$\nabla V = \frac{\partial \dot{x}_1}{x_1} + \frac{\partial \dot{x}_2}{x_2} + \frac{\partial \dot{x}_3}{x_3} = -a + b - d \tag{9.2}$$

So, the system (9.1) is dissipative when $a - b + d > 0$, and will exponentially converges to a subset of measure zero volume: $dV/dt = e^{-a+b-d}$, this means that for an initial volume V_0, the volume will become $V(0)e^{-(a-b+d)t}$ at time t through the flow generated by the system. So, there exists an attractor in system (9.1).

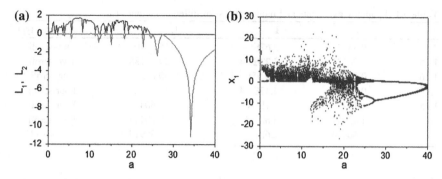

Fig. 9.1 Lyapunov exponents spectrum and bifurcation diagram of system (9.1) versus parameter a: **a** Lyapunov exponents spectrum; **b** bifurcation diagram

9.2.2 Equilibrium

By calculating, we can obtain that $O(0,0,0)$ is one of equilibrium of system (9.1). Let's suppose

$$A = \frac{c^2 e}{ah^2}, \; B = b - \frac{cf}{h} + 2\frac{cd}{h^2}, \; C = \frac{ad^2}{h^2 e} - \frac{adf}{he} \tag{9.3}$$

Then, if $AC > 0$, the other four equilibria are:

$$\begin{cases} \left(-\frac{d}{h} + \frac{ce}{ah}\Lambda_1, \; \sqrt{\Lambda_1}, \; -\frac{ad}{he\sqrt{\Lambda_1}} + \frac{c}{h}\sqrt{\Lambda_1} \right) \\ \left(-\frac{d}{h} + \frac{ce}{ah}\Lambda_1, \; -\sqrt{\Lambda_1}, \; \frac{ad}{he\sqrt{\Lambda_1}} - \frac{c}{h}\sqrt{\Lambda_1} \right) \\ \left(-\frac{d}{h} + \frac{ce}{ah}\Lambda_2, \; \sqrt{\Lambda_2}, \; -\frac{ad}{he\sqrt{\Lambda_2}} + \frac{c}{h}\sqrt{\Lambda_2} \right) \\ \left(-\frac{d}{h} + \frac{ce}{ah}\Lambda_2, \; -\sqrt{\Lambda_2}, \; \frac{ad}{he\sqrt{\Lambda_2}} - \frac{c}{h}\sqrt{\Lambda_2} \right) \end{cases} \tag{9.4}$$

where

$$\Lambda_1 = \frac{B + \sqrt{B^2 - 4AC}}{2A}, \; \Lambda_2 = \frac{B - \sqrt{B^2 - 4AC}}{2A} \tag{9.5}$$

When $AC \leq 0$, system (9.1) has only three equilibria, and the other two equilibria are

$$\begin{cases} \left(-\frac{d}{h} + \frac{ce}{ah}\Lambda_1, \; \sqrt{\Lambda_1}, \; -\frac{ad}{he\sqrt{\Lambda_1}} + \frac{c}{h}\sqrt{\Lambda_1} \right) \\ \left(-\frac{d}{h} + \frac{ce}{ah}\Lambda_1, \; -\sqrt{\Lambda_1}, \; \frac{ad}{he\sqrt{\Lambda_1}} - \frac{c}{h}\sqrt{\Lambda_1} \right) \end{cases} \tag{9.6}$$

Table 9.1 Lyapinov exponents and motion types for different parameter a

a	L_1	L_2	L_3	Attractor type
4	0.53322	3.67E−4	−15.45102	Two-scroll
11.5	0.76421	3.23E−4	−29.95138	Two-scroll
12.6	0.71211	−3.55E−4	−30.07294	One-scroll
13.8	0.844	4.47E−4	−32.15129	Four-scroll
14.5	1.1379	−1E−6	−33.60436	Four-scroll
18	1.42647	3.6E−4	−38.50137	Four-scroll
23.5	0.60424	2.6E−4	−45.35917	One-scroll

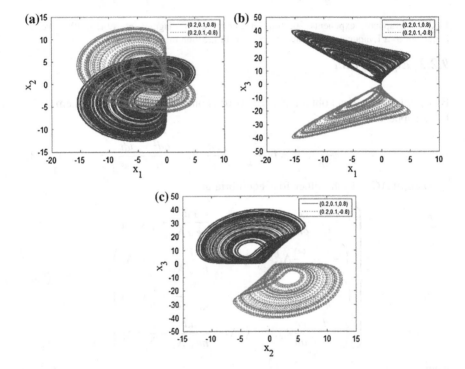

Fig. 9.2 One-wing chaotic attractors of system (1) when a = 23.5. **a** x_1−x_2 plane; **b** x_1− x_3 plane; **c** x_2− x_3 plane

9.3 Observation of Dynamics

The system (9.1) has been found to exhibit rich dynamical behaviors in a wide range of parameters, and can generate one-wing, two-wing and four-wing chaotic attractors with variation of only one parameter a or d.

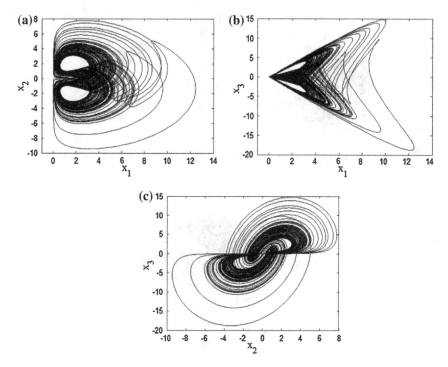

Fig. 9.3 Two-wing chaotic attractors of system (9.1) when a = 4. **a** x_1-x_2 plane; **b** x_1-x_3 plane; **c** x_2-x_3 plane

9.3.1 Dynamics of System (9.1) When a Varies

In all the numerical simulations, we fix parameters $b = 3, c = 8, d = 11, h = 0.5$, $e = 2.1, f = 2$, while let a varies. The larger two Lyapunov exponent spectrum and bifurcation diagram for system (9.1) are plotted in Fig. 9.1 with the parameter a varying in the region [0,40].

This system has been found to has many interesting complex dynamical behaviors, including chaos, period and period-doubling bifurcations, etc.

Some typical values of parameter a determining the Lyapunov exponents are chosen, as is shown in Table 9.1. The corresponding phase diagrams are shown as Figs. 9.2, 9.3, and 9.4. From Table 9.1 and Figs. 9.2–9.4, we can see that, with the varying of parameter a, the state of system (9.1) will evolve from one-wing, two-wing and four-wing chaotic attractors. And system (9.1) can display two coexisting one-wing chaotic attractors with different initial conditions.

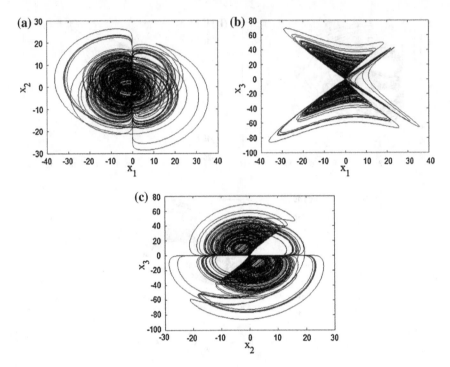

Fig. 9.4 Four-wing chaotic attractors of system (9.1) when a = 18. **a** x_1–x_2 plane; **b** x_1– x_3 plane; **c** x_2– x_3 plane

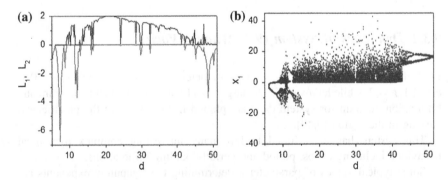

Fig. 9.5 Lyapunov exponents spectrum and bifurcation diagram of system (9.1) versus parameter d: **a** Lyapunov exponents spectrum; **b** bifurcation diagram

9.3.2 Dynamics of System (9.1) When d Varies

Now, we fix parameters $a = 17.2, b = 3, c = 8, h = 0.5, e = 2.1, f = 2$ while let d varies. And the larger two Lyapunov exponent spectrum and bifurcation diagram for system (9.1) are plotted in Fig. 9.5 with the parameter d varying in the region

Table 9.2 Lyapinov exponents and motion types for different parameter d

d	L_1	L_2	L_3	Attractor type
9.5	0.68414	5.44E−4	−33.86727	One-scroll
10	0.91786	2.41E−4	−35.0736	One-scroll
11	1.35839	5.51E−4	−37.37573	Four-scroll
15	1.40487	−0.0013	−43.71328	Four-scroll
20	2.0047	−2.38E−4	−52.49133	Two-scroll
25	1.79481	3.69E−4	−59.54259	Two-scroll
35	1.24966	1.9E−5	−73.45882	Two-scroll
40	1.05164	−6.92E−4	−80.34418	Four-scroll

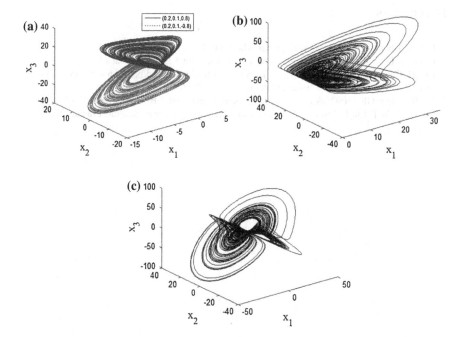

Fig. 9.6 Different-wing chaotic attractors of system (9.1) when d varies. **a** one-wing; **b** two-wing; **c** four-wing

[5, 52]. Similarly, with the varies of d, system (9.1) has been found to display complex dynamical behaviors, including chaos, period and period-doubling bifurcations, etc.

Some typical values of parameter d determining the Lyapunov exponents are chosen, as is shown in Table 9.2. The corresponding phase diagrams are shown in Fig. 9.6. From Table 9.2 and Fig. 9.6, we can see that, with the varying of parameter d, the state of system (9.1) will also evolve from one-wing, two-wing and four-wing chaotic attractors. And system (9.1) can display two coexisting one-wing chaotic attractors with different initial conditions.

9.4 Conclusion

In this paper, we proposes a new 3D autonomous chaotic system which displays complicated dynamical behavior over a large range of parameters. Interestingly, this new system can generate two coexisting one-wing attractors with different initial conditions. Besides, this system can generate two-wing and four-wing chaotic attractors with variation of only one parameter. Some basic dynamical behaviors of the proposed chaotic system, such as equilibrium points, bifurcation diagram and Lyapunov exponents are investigated.

References

1. Lorenz EN (1963) Deterministic nonperiodic flow. J Atmos Sci 20:130–141
2. Chen G, Ueta T (1999) Yet another chaotic attractor. Int J Bifurcat Chaos 9:1465–1470
3. Lü JH, Chen GR, Cheng DZ, Celikovsky S (2002) Bridge the gap between the Lorenz system and the Chen system. Int J Bifurcat Chaos 12:2917–2926
4. Lü JH, Chen GR (2002) A new chaotic attractor coined. Int J Bifurcat Chaos 12:659–661
5. Liu CX, Liu T, Liu L, Liu K (2004) A new chaotic attractor. Chaos Solitons Fractals 22:1031–1038

Chapter 10
Geochemistry Records of Palaeoenvironment from Sanfangwan Neolithic Site in Jianghan Plain, Central China

Li Wu, Feng Li, Cheng Zhu, Wei Sun, Bing Li, Huaping Meng, Hui Liu, Tongbin Xu and Suyuan Li

Abstract The culture of Qujialing (5100-4500 cal. a BP) is a representative of Chinese civilization in the Jianghan Plain, middle reaches of the Yangtze River. Nevertheless, limited geochemical data are available on this prehistoric culture in relation to environment in this region. In this study, geochemical records on TOC, TN, C/N ratio and $\delta^{13}C$ extracted from sludge sediments of unit T1610 profile at the Sanfangwan Neolithic site of late Qujialing period (4800-4500 cal. a BP) were integrated to clarify the palaeoenvironment, palaeoecology and human activities during the late Holocene in the Jianghan Plain. The results suggest that palaeo-environment changes in the Sanfangwan site went through three stages (i.e. warm and humid → mild and slightly wet → relatively warm and humid) during the late Qujialing period. C_3 plants occupied most parts around the studied area. An overall warm and humid climate around the Sanfangwan site resulted in the establishment of a more stable and predominantly C_3 plant forest ecosystems, which have provided effective protections against human impact and climate change and substantively push the development of agriculture that led to the Qujialing culture flourishing. During this period, the emergence of rammed earthen walls and moats of the Sanfangwan site might mark the inception of the Chinese civilization in the Jianghan Plain, middle reaches of the Yangtze River. The geochemical records of palaeoenvironment evolution from the Sanfangwan Neolithic site are in good

L. Wu · F. Li · C. Zhu (✉) · W. Sun · B. Li
School of Geographic and Oceanographic Sciences, Nanjing University,
No 22 Hankou Road, 210093 Nanjing, China
e-mail: zhuchengnj@yahoo.com.cn

H. Meng · H. Liu · T. Xu
Hubei Provincial Institute of Cultural Relics and Archaeology, No 156 Donghu Road
430077 Wuhan, China

S. Li
School of History, Nanjing University, No 22 Hankou Road 210093 Nanjing, China

W. Lu et al. (eds.), *Proceedings of the 2012 International Conference on Information Technology and Software Engineering*, Lecture Notes in Electrical Engineering 211, DOI: 10.1007/978-3-642-34522-7_10, © Springer-Verlag Berlin Heidelberg 2013

accordance with those of adjacent area. It responded to regional environmental change of the middle Yangtze River.

Keywords Sanfangwan Neolithic site · Palaeoenvironment · Geochemistry

10.1 Introduction

The $\delta^{13}C$ in organic matters from sludge or lacustrine sediments varies with many factors including aquatic plants, vegetation types in the catchment, atmospheric CO_2 concentration, climate, and properties of water, etc. [1–4], reflecting different material sources. Now it has been widely used to reconstruct changes over time in the relative proportions of plants using C_3, C_4 and CAM photosynthetic pathways, based on the differences in discrimination against ^{13}C that occurs when atmospheric CO_2 is fixed by these 3 pathways [4–6]. However, palaeoenvironment reconstruction of vegetation changes by using stable carbon isotopic composition in the archaeological stratum has rarely been undertaken. Therefore, $\delta^{13}C$ in the sludge or lacustrine sediments in archaeological stratum, combined with TOC, TN and C/N indexes, can provide useful information on palaeoenvironment and palaeoecology of prehistoric period in the Neolithic site.

10.2 Materials and Methods

The Sanfangwan Neolithic site (30°46′26.47″N, 113°05′15.55″E) is located north of the Shihe Town, the Tianmen City in Hubei Province. The excavation unit T1610 is situated in the south-central of the site area. The west profile of unit T1610 was chosen for this study. The depth of the profile is 426 cm and divided into four units (Fig. 10.1): 0–33 cm is the modern disturbed unit from 1st to 3rd layers; 33–223 cm is the Shijiahe cultural unit from 4th to 11th layers; 223–330 cm, the 12th layer is the Shijiahe city wall; and the basal 330–426 cm is the sludge unit from 13th to 15th layers belonging to the late Qujialing period (4800–4500 cal. a BP). A total of 48 samples were collected at 2 cm interval for the basal sludge sediments between 330 and 426 cm which is long-term submerged limnetic facies. This study attempts to reconstruct the vegetation, palaeoenvironment and human activities based on the $\delta^{13}C$, TOC, TN and C/N ratio analyses in sludge sediments of the late Qujialing period, and explores the effect of natural environment on the development of Neolithic culture in the Jianghan Plain.

For $\delta^{13}C$ analysis in sludge sediments, the samples were dried at 50 °C for 24 h, about 5 g of each ground sample was treated with HCl (2 mol/L) for 24 h at room temperature to remove carbonates. Then, the samples were brought to pH = 7 with distilled water and dried at 50 °C. Subsamples of about 0.1 g were

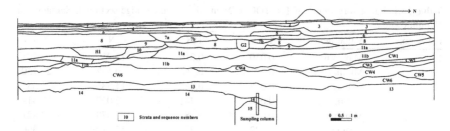

Fig. 10.1 Drawing of the western wall profile of the Unit T1610 of the Sanfangwan site. "H" means pit during the Shijiahe period, "G" means ancient channel, and "CW" means city wall relics

used for carbon isotopic analysis. The samples were combusted for 4 h at 900 °C in an evacuated sealed quartz tube in the presence of silver foil and cupric oxide. The purified carbon oxide was then analyzed for carbon isotopes using a Finnigan Delta-plus Gas Mass Spectrometer with dual inlet system. Isotopic ratios in samples are expressed as per mil deviations relative to a VPDB standard with a precision better than 0.1 ‰. A state standard specimen (in GBW04408) is added to every 5 samples during experiment.

After the same pre-treatment stated above for removing inorganic carbonates, samples were weighed up according to the content of organic carbon and nitrogen, and enwrapped them tightly with tinfoil. Following the total organic carbon (TOC) and total nitrogen (TN) contents were determined directly by a Leeman CE440 Elemental Analyzer. C/N ratios can be later calculated. The above two laboratory analyses were finished at State Key Laboratory of Lake Science and Environment, Nanjing Institute of Geography and Limnology, Chinese Academy of Sciences.

10.3 Results and Discussion

Previous studies have shown that the $\delta^{13}C$ values of C_3 plants range globally from -20 to -32 ‰, averaging around -27.0 ‰; while C_4 plants have $\delta^{13}C$ values between -10 and -17 ‰, with a mean value of -14.0 ‰ [4–8]. When plant-sourced organic carbon was added to sludge sediments, this large contrast in $\delta^{13}C$ was preserved, despite minor additional fractionation when plant debris material was decomposed in sediments [8]. The $\delta^{13}C$ values of the profile range between -19.77 and -25.81 ‰, with an average value of -21.22 ‰ (Table 10.1). That is all the three sludge layers have low $\delta^{13}C$ values, belonging to C_3 plants with higher plants as the main organic matter source. The C_3 plants tend to thrive in areas where sunlight intensity and temperature are moderate, and ground water is plentiful, but cannot grow in hot areas [9, 10]. Therefore, the $\delta^{13}C$ values of the sludge sediments in Sanfangwan profile are positively correlated to temperature and precipitation.

The content of TOC and TN in sludge or lacustrine sediments can reflect the primary productivity and biomass of the period [11, 12]. C/N ratios can be used to

Table 10.1 Laboratory values of TN, TOC, C/N and $\delta^{13}C$ in the sludge section of Sanfangwan Neolithic site

Layer no.	Value items	TN (%)	TOC (%)	C/N	$\delta^{13}C$ (‰)
13	Maximum	0.030	0.316	12.857	−20.401
	Minimum	0.021	0.261	9.567	−23.750
	Average	0.025	0.285	11.581	−22.083
14	Maximum	0.025	0.441	22.050	−20.419
	Minimum	0.019	0.182	9.579	−22.821
	Average	0.022	0.258	12.019	−21.390
15	Maximum	0.039	0.601	26.130	−19.765
	Minimum	0.020	0.254	10.889	−25.809
	Average	0.030	0.447	15.113	−20.727

All the results of the table are keeping three decimal places

infer the organic matter sourced proportion of autochthonous and allochthonous plants [13]. The C/N ratios of aquatic plants and lacustrine plankton is only 5–12, generally less than 10, while that of terrestrial plants is 20–30 and can reach up to 45–50 [1, 14, 15]. The average value of C/N ratios of the Sanfangwan sludge sediments indicates that the organic matter mainly from exogenous terrestrial plants (Table 10.1). Organic matter of terrestrial plants is transported to deposit center mainly by rain wash or surface runoff. Therefore, the value of C/N ratios increases with higher precipitation.

Based on multi−proxy geochemical analysis of TOC, TN, C/N and $\delta^{13}C$ (Table 10.1 and Fig. 10.2), palaeoenvironment changes of the Sanfangwan Neolithic site during the late Qujialing period can be interpreted as follows.

10.3.1 Early Stage of Late Qujialing Period (426–384 cm)

The $\delta^{13}C$ value is relatively higher between −19.77 and −25.81 ‰ in the average of −20.73 ‰, mainly falling into the range of C_3 plants, which is different from those in modern surface soils of the study site. Also the TOC and TN contents are higher than the average of the whole profile. The TOC contents range between 0.25 and 0.60 % with an average of 0.45 %; and the TN contents range between 0.020 and 0.039 % with an average of 0.030 %. The C/N ratios range between 10.89 and 26.13 with an average of 15.11. Such results suggest that the organic matter is mainly from allochthonous terrestrial plants. Combined with above $\delta^{13}C$ analysis, it can be considered that the climatic condition was warm and humid, and C_3 plants were the main vegetation landscape during this period. On the top of this layer (384–386 cm), rapid increase of TOC and C/N along with fast decrease of $\delta^{13}C$ value indicates that the proportion of terrestrial plant debris imported into the sludge reaching its maximum value, and the environment changed abruptly. For the TN content is lower, this abrupt event might be caused by a proximal flood rather than by intensive human activities such as the slash-and-burn cultivation, etc.

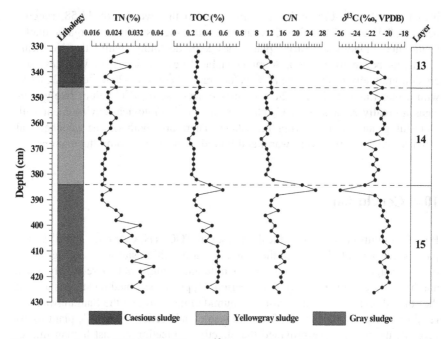

Fig. 10.2 Variations of TN, TOC, C/N and $\delta^{13}C$ values of organic carbon in the sludge section of the Sanfangwan Neolithic site

10.3.2 Middle Stage of Late Qujialing Period (384–346 cm)

The $\delta^{13}C$ values decline in the average of −21.39 %, and range between −20.42 and −22.82 %, marking the expansion of C_3 plants in the site's biological system. TOC contents range between 0.18 and 0.44 % with an average of 0.26 %; TN contents range between 0.019 and 0.025 % with an average of 0.022 %. The primary productivity and possibly water temperature decrease is revealed by the decrease of TOC and TN contents. The decrease of C/N ratios further proves the above results with an average of 12.02, ranging between 9.58 and 22.05, which indicates the reduction of allochthonous organic matter from terrestrial plants. All proxies' responses suggest a decreasing effective moisture and temperature process during this stage, but the climatic condition was still generally mild and slightly wet.

10.3.3 Late Stage of Late Qujialing Period (346–330 cm)

The TOC contents range between 0.26 and 0.32 % with an average of 0.29 %; and the TN contents range between 0.021 and 0.030 % with an average of 0.025 %. Apparently, both the contents are higher than the middle stage, but still lower than the early stage, suggesting a rise in temperature. Above 340 cm the TN markedly increases, whereas C/N ratios remain lower to the average of 11.58, ranging between 9.57 and 12.86. This C/N ratio response suggests that the organic matter from allochthonous terrestrial plants has kept declining, while the lacustrine sediments began to develop. A rather stable forest environment with less soil erosion gradually formed. The $\delta^{13}C$ values range between -20.42 and -22.82 % with a mean of -21.39 %. The progressive decrease of $\delta^{13}C$ values likely indicates a greatly expansion of C_3 plants in the site's biological environment with plentiful ground water during this stage. Therefore, both of the geochemical proxies indicate a relatively warm and humid climate with some fluctuations.

10.4 Conclusions

Based on multi-proxy geochemical analyses of TOC, TN, C/N ratio and $\delta^{13}C$, the palaeoenvironment changes in the Sanfangwan Neolithic site went through three obvious stages (i.e. warm and humid → mild and slightly wet → relatively warm and humid) during the late Qujialing period. C_3 plants occupied most parts around the studied area. An overall warm and humid climate around the Sanfangwan site resulted in the establishment of a more stable and predominantly C_3 plant forest ecosystems, which have provided the effective protection against human impact and climate change, and were suitable for the development of agriculture, that led to the Qujialing culture flourishing. During this period, the emergence of rammed earthen walls and moats of the Sanfangwan site might mark the inception of the Chinese civilization in the Jianghan Plain, middle reaches of the Yangtze River. These results are in good accordance with those of adjacent areas. Further researches are needed to understand the effect of the natural environment on the development of Neolithic culture in the study area.

Acknowledgments We thank Dr. Enlou Zhang and Yilan Liu for their help in laboratory work. This work was jointly funded by the National Natural Science Foundation of China (Grant Nos. 40971115, and 41171163), Scientific Research Foundation of Graduate School of Nanjing University, Project 985 (Grant No. 2011CL11), Major Program of National Social Science Foundation of China (Grant No. 11&ZD183), National Key Technology R&D Program of China (Grant No. 2010BAK67B02), Interdisciplinary Research Program of Nanjing University (Grant No. NJUDC2012002).

References

1. Stuiver M (1975) Climate versus changes in ^{13}C content of the organic component of lake sediments during the Late Quaternary. Quat Res 5(2):251–262
2. Boutton TW, Archer SR, Midwood AJ, Zitzer SF (1998) $\delta^{13}C$ values of soil organic carbon and their use in documenting vegetation change in a subtropical savanna ecosystem. Geoderma 82(1–3):5–41

3. Shen J, Wang Y, Liu XQ, Matsumoto R (2006) A 16 ka climate record deduced from δ^{13}C and C/N ratio in Qinghai Lake sediments, northeastern Tibetan Plateau. Chin J Oceanol Limnol 24(2):103–110

4. Lu HY, Zhou YL, Liu WG, Mason J (2012) Organic stable carbon isotopic composition reveals late Quaternary vegetation changes in the dune fields of northern China. Quat Res 77(3):433–444

5. Cerling TE, Quade J, Wang Y, Bowman JR (1989) Carbon isotopes in soils and palaeosols as ecology and palaeoecology indicators. Nature 341:138–139

6. Zhong W, Xue JB, Cao JX, Zheng YM, Ma QH, Ouyang J, Cai Y, Zeng ZG, Liu W (2010) Bulk organic carbon isotopic record of lacustrine sediments in Dahu Swamp, eastern Nanling Mountains in South China: implication for catchment environmental and climatic changes in the last 16,000 years. J Asian Earth Sci 38:162–169

7. Zhou B, Zheng HB, Yang WG, Wei GJ, Li L, Wang H (2011) Organic carbon records since the last glacial period in the Northern South China Sea sediments: implications for vegetation and environmental changes. Quat Sci 31(3):498–505

8. Zhou B, Shen CD, Zheng HB, Zhao MX, Sun YM (2009) Vegetation evolution on the central Chinese Loess Plateau since late Quaternary evidenced by elemental carbon isotopic composition. Chin Sci Bull 54(12):2082–2089

9. Hogan CM (2011) Respiration. In: McGinley M (ed) Encyclopedia of earth. National Council for Science and the Environment, Washington

10. Ma CM, Zhu C, Zheng CG, Wu CL, Guan Y, Zhao ZP, Huang LY, Huang R (2008) High-resolution geochemistry records of climate changes since late-glacial from Dajiuhu peat in Shennongjia Mountains, Central China. Chin Sci Bull 53(Supp. I):28–41

11. Shen J, Liu XQ, Matsumoto R, Wang SM, Yang XD (2005) A high-resolution climatic change since the Late Glacial Age inferred from multi-proxy of sediments in Qinghai Lake. Sci China, Ser D Earth Sci 48(6):742–751

12. Jiang QF, Shen J, Liu XQ, Zhang EL, Xiao XY (2007) A high-resolution climatic change since Holocene inferred from multi-proxy of lake sediment in westerly area of China. Chin Sci Bull 52(14):1970–1979

13. Shen J, Liu XQ, Wang SM, Matsumoto R (2005) Palaeoclimatic changes in the Qinghai Lake area during the last 18,000 years. Quatern Int 136(1):131–140

14. Krishnamurthy RV, Bhattacharya SK, Kusumgar S (1986) Palaeoclimatic changes deduced from ^{13}C/^{12}C and C/N ratios of Karewa lake sediments, India. Nature 323:150–152

15. Meyers PA, Ishiwatari R (1993) Lacustrine organic geochemistry-an overview of indicators of organic matter sources and diagenesis in lake sediments. Org Geochem 20(7):867–900

Chapter 11
Three Dimensional DNA Graph Structure Solution to Maximum Clique Problem

Xiaoling Ren and Xiyu Liu

Abstract In this paper, the 3-dimensional DNA graph structures model is used to solve the maximum clique problem. Based on the fact that the induced graph of a clique is complete, vertices building blocks are designed by k-armed DNA molecules and hairpin structures and the connecting structures are presented by 2-armed DNA structures so that they can spontaneously form into a 3-dimensional DNA graph structure with no cleaved ends if a clique were formed right by these vertices. Therefore the maximum clique is detected by finding the biggest complete graph. Theoretically, the algorithm designed here can generate initial data pool within polynomial steps and it takes constant number of steps to find the maximum clique.

Keywords 3D DNA graph structure · Maximum clique · k-armed DNA molecule · Complete graph

11.1 Introduction

k-armed DNA structures can serve to perform computations at molecular level. And they indeed exist in nature, like intermediates called Holliday in the process of homologous recombination of *E. coli* [1]. Actually, specially designed k-armed DNA structures, particularly 3-armed and 4-armed ones can be made stably and

X. Ren (✉) · X. Liu
College of Management Science and Engineering, Shandong
Normal University, Jinan, China
e-mail: heaventallxiaozhu@gmail.com; 851171287@qq.com

X. Liu
e-mail: sdxyliu@163.com

W. Lu et al. (eds.), *Proceedings of the 2012 International Conference on Information Technology and Software Engineering*, Lecture Notes in Electrical Engineering 211, DOI: 10.1007/978-3-642-34522-7_11, © Springer-Verlag Berlin Heidelberg 2013

furthermore, under certain conditions 8-armed and 12-armed ones also can be obtained [2]. In 1999, Jonoska and his partners put forward 3-dimensional DNA structures [3] integrated of k-armed DNA moleculars to solve 3-SAT problem and 3-VCP. In that design, the k-armed structure was used to present the corresponding vertex of k degree, called vertex building blocks. And then they can form intuitionisticly the desired graph structures. Next, in 2002, Seeman and others constructed the 3D graphs using k-armed moleculars [4] and in 2006, Fang Gang and others solved the edge-connectivity problem by 3D DNA graph structures [5] and proposed an improved algorithm by introducing evolutionary algorithm in 2007 [6], which could avoid theoretically the trouble of exponential increase of solution space in traditional DNA computations. The good point is that it takes constant number of laboratory steps to solve NPC or NP-hard problems regardless of the scale of graphs.

Maximum Clique Problem (MCP) is a classic combinatorial optimization problem of graph theory, and also a NPC problem [7]. It has some vital applications in the fields of artificial intelligence, cluster analysis, signal transmission, coding theory, mobile computing, fault detection and etc. And in recent years, many scholars have made some beneficial attempts in solving MCP using DNA computing. For example the literature [8] combined linear DNA molecules with genetic algorithm to solve MCP. Literature [9] presented an algorithm using pruning strategy on foundation of Adelman model to solve MCP, and literature [10] came up with an idea by sticker model to work out that. In this paper, we propose theoretically a solution to solve the MCP using 3D DNA graph structure, taking the advantage of its good nature of reflecting graph structures intuitively, the simple procedure and the huge parallelism of DNA computing.

The rest of this paper is organised as follows. In Sect. 11.2, the MCP is introduced and the details of how we work out all the desired vertex building blocks are given. Section 11.3 introduces a DNA algorithm for MCP by the model of 3D DNA graph structures. Section 11.4 shows an instance of MCP solved by the procedures in last section. Discussions and conclusions are drawn in Sects. 11.5 and 11.6.

11.2 The Maximum Clique Problem

11.2.1 Definition of MCP

Maximum clique problem is a graph-based NP-complete problem which is defined as follows: given an undirected graph $G = (V, E)$, a clique in it is a subset of the vertices set $C \subseteq V$, such that for every two vertices in C, there exists an edge connecting this two. And out of all its cliques, a maximum clique is the one that has the largest numbers of vertices. From this definition, we can sense that the subgraph induced by C is complete. Thus, finding the maximum clique is equal to find the biggest induced complete subgraph of the given graph.

Fig. 11.1 DNA molecules
of 2-armed, 3-armed and
4-armed

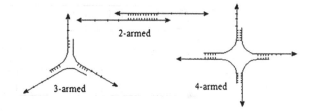

Let $V = \{v_1, v_2,..., v_n\}$ be the vertices set of G, k_i be the degree of the vertex v_i in graph G, $\omega(C)$ be the number of vertices in clique C. If v_i is in clique C, that means $\omega \leq k_i$-1. In another word, the number of vertices plus *one* in a clique can't be more than the degree of any one vertex within this clique. And we are going to use this rule to construct the vertex building blocks.

11.2.2 Design of Vertex Building Blocks

Before showing the algorithm to find the maximum clique, we must show how to get the special designed vertex building blocks so that we could use the idea of getting the biggest induced and complete subgraph.

As always, k-armed DNA molecules are used to represent the vertices of k degree. And against k_i-armed DNA molecules of v_i, single-stranded parts are labeled with edge variables adjacent to this vertex and the double-stranded parts are encoded with the same vertex variable. So, the corresponding single parts of two vertices connected by an edge are labeled in the same way. The common DNA molecules of 2-armed, 3-armed, 4-armed with cleaved ends are shown in Fig. 11.1.

The hairpin structures depicted in Fig. 11.2 are introduced here to cover some extended cleaved ends of k-armed DNA structures so that these ends can be closed. To achieve that, single-stranded parts of hairpin structures are encoded with accordingly complementary sequences of edge variables. So, n kinds of different k-armed DNA molecules and m kinds of hairpin structures (if there are m edges) are needed respectively to construct the vertex building blocks.

Since the number of vertices connected with vertice v_i of k_i degree cannot be more than k_i, if we assume that the clique to be found contains 3 vertices at least, against vertice v_i the number of different vertex building blocks needed is k_i-1. And the following DNA algorithm in Fig. 11.3 is proposed to get all the vertex building blocks. And 3 basic operations list here:

- $Split(T, T_1, T_2)$: split molecules in T into two tubes: T_1 and T_2.
- $Merge(T_1, T_2)$: this operation combines T_1, T_2 in one tube.
- $Ligase(T, cap)$: use the *cap* to cap off some cleaved end of arms in tube T.

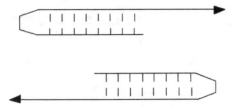

Fig. 11.2 Hairpin structures to make some ends to be closed

```
1  for  i ← 1  to  n  do
2      for  j ← 1  to  kᵢ  do
3          Split (Tᵢ, Tᵢ₁, Tᵢ₂)
4          Ligase (Tᵢ₁, capⱼ)
5          Tᵢ ← Merge (Tᵢ₁, Tᵢ₂)
6      end
7  end
```

Output: $T_1,\ldots,T_n$, where the tube T_i holds the vertex building blocks we need and differs from the original input ones.

Fig. 11.3 Procedure to produce vertex building blocks

Fig. 11.4 An undirected graph of six vertices and nine edges and its corresponding DNA graph structure

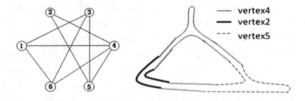

Input: $T_1,\ldots,T_n$ and m kinds of *cap*, where the first part represents n kinds of test tubes and each of them holds one kind of k-armed DNA molecules of vertice v_i. And the second part is the corresponding hairpin structures named *cap*.

Note that $(cap_1, cap_2,\ldots,capk_j)$ in line 4 represents corresponding k_j kinds of hairpin structures of v_j. After this procedure, only the arms which still hold cleaved ends can realize the hybridization reaction. For example of vertex labeled number 4 in Fig. 11.4, we need a 4-armed DNA structure with one edge closed to see if it can be in some clique with four vertices. If it was this case, the rest three arms would be closed. But if not, some of the rest arms would be still cleaved.

11.3 Solving the Maximum Clique Problem

Before introducing the algorithm, 2-armed DNA structures are necessary to be introduced here. 2-armed DNA molecules are treated as the connecting edge, with two single-stranded ends encoded with the complementary sequences of corresponding edge variables so that these can join two vertices together and avoid the forming the self-loop. And two restriction enzyme sites are added to the double-stranded sequences. As a result we can know the largest complete structure by the quantity of the parts cut down. Since there are m edges, m kinds of 2-armed DNA structures are needed.

11.3.1 Basic Algorithm

The basic algorithm is as following:

Step1. Combine all the vertex building blocks in n tubes constructed in Sect. 11.2.2 and enough 2-armed DNA molecules decipited above into a single tube. Allow them to hybridize and then be ligased.
Step2. Make a separation of potential solutions which have no open parts from the "incomplete" ones.
Step3. Find the one with most edges, that corresponding to the biggest complete graph.
Step4. Detect the constitution of 3D DNA graph structure found in Step3 and that's the result.

11.3.2 Biological Procedure

Step1. Encode n kinds of k-armed DNA structures according to vertex variables and their neighboring edges, and also encode the corresponding hairpin structures and 2-armed structures. Make sufficient of them. In addition, in order to detect the final solution, encode n kinds of vertex probes and mark them with different sizes of metal nanoparticles [11].
Step2. Use the procedure in Fig. 11.3 to get the vertex building blocks we need. That is the initial data pool we need.
Step3. Combine multiple copies of all kinds of k-armed DNA molecules and 2-armed DNA structures into a single tube with buffer solution and DNA connected enzyme to hybridize and ligate. So the 3D DNA graph structures with those vertices that can interconnect into a clique would be totally closed. In another word, those structures have no cleaved ends and they are complete.
Step4. Remove those 3-dimensional DNA graph structures which are partly formed, not fully matched and have open ends and also remove redundant hairpin structures by using an exonuclease enzyme. And then purify the solution.

Step5. Remove by gel electrophoresis the covering graphs that are larger than the original graphs formed in the above steps. The details about covering graph are explained in literature [3].

Step6. Separate the complete graphs by different kinds of structures using gel electrophoresis into different tubes. And cut those different kinds of 3D DNA graph structures with restriction enzyme to get the DNA strands between two sites. Then we can know the structures with most edges by detecting the fluorescence intensity using fluorescently labeled probes to detect the sequences cut down. And that is the biggest complete vertex-included graph structure.

Step7. Denature the 3D DNA graph structures known in Step6, and then amplified by PCR.

Step8. Because nanoparticles of different sizes can be stimulated to show the different colors by a single wavelength of light, and the colors are of high stability and not easily degradable, fluorescence analysis can be used to detect marked probes. Firstly, hybrid the amplified products with probes marked by different size of metal nanoparticles on the slide under certain conditions. Secondly, illuminate the product by fiber-optic illuminator to identify the formation of scattered colors. And by that the final vertices subset of MCP can be read.

11.4 Example

An example of a graph of six vertices and its corresponding one possible DNA graph structure of one kind of maximum clique with three vertices are given in Fig. 11.4. The maximum clique is of three vertices and here in the figure of the DNA graph structure, one possible solution is given and the vertices are represented by different kinds of lines. The lines in blue represent the 2-armed connecting structures.

The degree of each of the vertices in the graph is:

$$[d(1), d(2), d(3), d(4), d(5), d(6)] = [3, 2, 3, 4, 3, 3]$$

So, we should start to encode 6 kinds of k-armed DNA structures according to their degrees and vertex variable, the double-stranded parts encoded with vertex variables and the cleaved single-strand parts the edge variables. Then, encode 9 kinds of the hairpin structures to be complement to the cleaved parts of k-armed molecules. Also, encode nine kinds of 2-armed connecting structures with the cleaved single-stranded parts labeled with sequences complement to edge variables. Additionally, the vertex probes sequences are encoded too.

According to procedure in Fig. 11.3 to make all the vertex building blocks, and then by Step3 and Step4 to mix all of them with connecting structures to get the 3D DNA graph structures with no open ends. Next, we separate the closed graph structures from the others and detect the ones with most edges, because the biggest complete graph definitely with the most edges. For the graph in Fig. 11.4 there are three kinds of DNA graph having three connecting edges. They are (1,4,6), (1,3,6) and (2,4,5) respectively, where the numbers in bracket pairs represent corresponding vertices labels in the given graph. At last, using fluorescence analysis in Step8 the final results can be obtained. It would the same as above. And certainly, the possible DNA graph structure of one result as (2,4,5) is shown in Fig. 11.4.

11.5 Discussion

11.5.1 Space Complexity

The procedure that produces the most DNA molecules is the making of vertex building blocks. With regard to a graph of n points, the gross vertex building blocks to be constructed is $\sum_{i=1}^{n} \sum_{j=2}^{k_i} \binom{k_i}{j}$. So the worst of all, when this graph itself is complete, the complexity of average quantity of vertex building blocks of each vertex is $O(2^{n-1})$, and in the best, that is $O(1)$. Under simulation of general cases, the expectation of average complexity is $O(n^3)$. (The simulation result is in Fig. 11.5)

That means that for problem sizes larger than some value, the number of required initial strands might exceed a practical generatable number. Thus, it's vital to know the proposed algorithms can be applied on the moderate and small graph cases. And also, the technical difficulty [2] to make k-armed DNA molecules having more arms is another reason limiting this algorithm in large graphs.

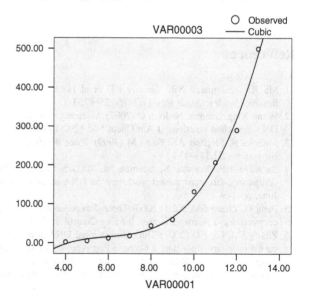

Fig. 11.5 The simulation result about the general cases, with the horizontal axis representing the number of vertices and the vertical axis the quantity expectation

11.5.2 Operational Complexity

In Fig. 11.3, it can be calculated that the number of steps to make all the vertex building blocks is 6 m if we treat operations of *Split*, *Ligase* and *Merge* as one procedure respectively. In the worst case, when graph complete, this operational complexity is $O(n^2)$, because under this special condition m equals $n(n-1)/2$.

After making the vertex building blocks, the procedure, from Step3 to Step8 in Sect. 11.3.2, to solve to MCP requires constant number of laboratory steps. It's exciting because this algorithm here just needs constant number of steps to check the solutions regardless of the size of graph while in many other platforms, the check operation must be down in polynomial steps. Therefore, using 3D DNA graph structures to compute is a model using less steps and relatively intuitive. At the same time, we don't have specific experimental results, therefore, are unable to discuss the feasibility of procedure above. However, we have used limited number of operations which can be easily implemented in the laboratory.

11.6 Conclusion

Regardless of above, we are encouraged by the progress of DNA computing and the rapid development of biological technologies. In this paper we proposed to use 3D DNA graph structures to MCP for the first time in DNA computing.

Acknowledgments This work was supported by National Natural Science Foundation of China (61170038), Shandong Province Natural Science Foundation (ZR2011FM001), Humanities and Social Sciences project of Ministry of Education (12YJA630152).

References

1. Ma RI, Kallenbach NR, Sheardy RD et al (1996) Three-arm nucleic acid junctions are flexible. Nucleic Acids Res 14(24):9725–9753
2. Wang Xing, Seeman Nadrian C (2007) Assembly and characterization of 8-arm and 12-arm DNA branched junctions. J Am Chem Soc 129:8169–8176
3. Jonoska N, Stephen AK, Saito M (1999) Three dimensional DNA structure in computing. Biosystems 52:143–153
4. Sa-ardye NP, Jonoska N, Seeman NC (2002). Self-assembling DNA graphs. In: DNA computing, 8th international workshop on DNA-based computers 8 Sapporo, Japan, 10–13 June, pp 1–9
5. Fang G, Zhang SM, Xu J (2006) Three dimensional DNA graph structure solution to edge-connectivity. J Aerosp Electron Inf Eng Control 28(1):119–121 (in Chinese)
6. Zhang SM, Fang G (2007) Three dimensional DNA structure solution to connectivity based on evolutionary algorithm. J Comput Eng Appl 43(7):41–44 (in Chinese)
7. Karp RM (1972) Reducibility among combinatorial problems[C]. In: Proceedings of complexity of computer computations. Plenum Press, New York, pp 85–103

 8. Li Y, Chen F, Qi O (2004) Genetic algorithm in DNA computing: a solution to the maximal clique problem. Chin Sci Bull 49(9):967–971
 9. Li K, Xu Z, Zou S (2008). Improved volume molecular solutions for the maximum clique problem on DNA-based supercomputing. Chin J Comput 31(12):2173–2181
10. Zhou K, Liu S, Qin L et al (2010) Sticker model based DNA algorithm of maximum clique problem. J Huazhong Univ Sci Tech (Natural Science Edition) 38(9):89–92 (in Chinese)
11. Sun W, You JY, Jiang H et al (2005) Preparation and detection application of nanoparticle tagging DNA probe. J Health Lab Technol 15:1008 (in Chinese)

Chapter 12
Technique for In-flight Calibrating Installation Errors in Multi-IMU Redundancy System

Jinliang Zhang, Yongyuan Qin and Feng Wu

Abstract An in-flight calibration algorithm is proposed to estimate installation errors between IMUs in a multi-IMU redundancy system, where more than two IMUs are installed parallel to each other. One IMU deeply integrated with GPS pseudo-range and pseudo-range rate is chosen as installation reference, and its attitude is improved through a series of aircraft maneuver before calibration to provide precise reference. At the beginning of calibration, the IMU sends real-time navigation parameters to other IMUs which will then run attitude update procedure but the velocity and position is still provided by the reference. Then a Kalman filter is designed through SINS attitude error model and measurements are attitude differences to the reference. Simulation result shows that the proposed algorithm can precisely estimate the calibration errors just through rough roll and turning maneuver, and the precision can achieve arc second level.

Keywords Multi-IMU · Redundancy system · Deep integration · Installation errors · In-flight calibration

12.1 Introduction

Integrated navigation system composed of core SINS and other instruments can significantly improve navigation precision and reliability, thus has become the ideal navigation scheme in aviation field [1–3]. Along with the development of national aviation technology especially the large transport and passenger airplane,

J. Zhang (✉) · Y. Qin · F. Wu
College of Automation, Northwestern Polytechnical University, 710072 Xi'an, China
e-mail: zhangjl84@163.com

W. Lu et al. (eds.), *Proceedings of the 2012 International Conference on Information Technology and Software Engineering*, Lecture Notes in Electrical Engineering 211, DOI: 10.1007/978-3-642-34522-7_12, © Springer-Verlag Berlin Heidelberg 2013

modern navigation has put forward a higher requirement for SINS reliability. However under current industrial condition, the effective way to improve SINS reliability is the redundancy design, which means integrating redundant inertial sensors in one IMU or simply adopting more IMUs—the former is called sensor-grade redundancy while the latter is called system-grade redundancy [4, 5]. Sensor-grade redundancy has a complicate internal structure that leads to a longer design cycle and an even longer maintenance cycle when some fault occurs. As a result, SINS in aviation by far still refers to the system-grade redundancy, such as the civil SINS LTN251 and the Boeing 757/767. LTN251 used in more than one hundred international airlines is composed of two independent IMUs and the Boeing 757/767 adopts three parallel isolate IMUs. One major problem of system-grade redundancy is the installation error between IMUs generated when the system is installed in the aircraft. The installation errors will cause difference in original signals including angular rate and specific force measured by each IMU. The difference grows with aircraft's maneuver. The difference that grows with aircraft maneuver does not affect navigation precision of each IMU; however, when these IMUs are viewed as a whole in fault detection, the small difference will cause erroneous detection result, and further degrade system reliability.

Based on above analysis, an algorithm for in-flight calibrating installation error in a multi-IMU redundancy system is proposed in this paper, which taking one IMU as installation reference and integrated with GPS pseudo range and range rate to provide precise attitude reference, then an attitude matching Kalman filter is designed to estimate installation error between the reference and other IMUs.

12.2 SINS Navigation Error Model

Navigation error model of the IMU is composed of three parts [6] as follows:

(1) Attitude error (ϕ) equation:

$$\dot{\phi} = -\omega_{in}^n \times \phi + \delta\omega_{in}^n - C_b^n \delta\omega_{ib}^b \tag{12.1}$$

(2) Velocity error (δv^n) equation:

$$\delta\dot{v}^n = -\phi \times f^n - \left(2\omega_{ie}^n + \omega_{en}^n\right) \times \delta v^n - \left(2\delta\omega_{ie}^n + \delta\omega_{en}^n\right) \times v^n + C_b^n \delta f^b \tag{12.2}$$

(3) Position error (δp) equation:

$$\delta\dot{p} = \begin{bmatrix} \delta\dot{L} \\ \delta\dot{\lambda} \\ \delta\dot{h} \end{bmatrix} = \begin{bmatrix} \dfrac{\delta v_N}{R_{Mh}} - \dfrac{v_N}{R_{Mh}^2}\delta h \\ \dfrac{\delta v_E}{R_{Nh}\cos L} + \dfrac{v_E\sin L\delta L}{R_{Nh}\cos^2 L} - \dfrac{v_E\delta h}{R_{Nh}\cos^2 L} \\ \delta v_U \end{bmatrix} \tag{12.3}$$

In formula (12.1)–(12.3), δ represents for the error of the parameter. ω_{ab}^c represents for the projection of angular rate to c frame that implies frame b rotates around a frame. C_b^n is the transformation matrix from body b frame to navigation n frame. f is the specific force. R_N and R_M represent for radius in earth prime vertical circle and in meridian circle, and $R_{Nh} = R_N + h$, $R_{Mh} = R_N + h$ for ranges from aircraft to earth center. L, λ, h represents for latitude, longitude and height of aircraft's position. $\delta\omega_{ib}^b$ and δf^b represent for measurement error of the gyro and accelerometer.

Suppose that gyro error $\delta\omega_{ib}^b$ is composed of scale factor error dK_g, zero bias ε^b, and white noise w_g^b:

$$\begin{cases} \delta\omega_{ib}^b = \varepsilon^b + w_g^b + [\omega_{ib}^b]dK_g \\ \dot{\varepsilon}^b = 0, \quad d\dot{K}_g = 0 \end{cases} \tag{12.4}$$

where $[\omega_{ib}^b]$ is a diagonal matrix constructed by ω_{ibx}^b, ω_{iby}^b, ω_{ibz}^b.

Similarly suppose that accelerometer error δf^b is composed of zero-offset ∇^b and white noise w_a^b:

$$\delta f^b = \nabla^b + w_a^b, \quad \dot{\nabla}^b = 0 \tag{12.5}$$

Formula (12.1)–(12.5) together forms the navigation error model of the SINS.

12.3 Deep Integration of SINS and GPS

In ECEF Cartesian coordinate, position of the ith satellite and the aircraft are denoted as $p_{si} = [x_{si} \ y_{si} \ z_{si}]^T$ and $p_v = [x_v \ y_v \ z_v]^T$.

So the vector and its change rate from aircraft to satellite can be expressed as:

$$\begin{cases} r_i = p_{si} - p_v = [x_{si} - x_v \ y_{si} - y_v \ z_{si} - z_v]^T \\ \dot{r}_i = \dot{p}_{si} - \dot{p}_v = [\dot{x}_{si} - \dot{x}_v \ \dot{y}_{si} - \dot{y}_v \ \dot{z}_{si} - \dot{z}_v]^T \end{cases}$$

where $\dot{x}_v$, $\dot{y}_v$, $\dot{z}_v$ are components of aircraft velocity v_v^e in ECEF, and $\dot{x}_{si}$, $\dot{y}_{si}$, $\dot{z}_{si}$ are velocity component of the ith satellite, v_s, in ECEF.

The corresponding range d_i and range rate $\dot{d}_i$ are computed as:

$$d_i = \|r_i\|, \quad \dot{d}_i = d_i^{-1} \cdot (r_i^T \dot{r}_i) \tag{12.6}$$

For GPS [7, 8], there is an inevitable range error because of the clock error t_u between the receiver and satellite clock, denoted as $\delta l = ct_u$, where c is the light speed. As a result, the range computed from receiver is academically called pseudo range, while the range rate from receiver called pseudo range rate, respectively denoted as $\rho_{gps,i}$ and $\dot{\rho}_{gps,i}$:

$$\begin{cases} \rho_{gps,i} = d_i + l = \|r_i\| + \delta l \\ \dot{\rho}_{gps,i} = \dot{d}_i + \dot{l} = d_i^{-1} \cdot (r_i^T \dot{r}_i) + \delta l_r \end{cases} \tag{12.7}$$

the error model of δl and δl_r are set as

$$\begin{cases} \dot{\delta l} = \delta l_r + w_l(t) \\ \dot{\delta l}_r = \dfrac{1}{\tau} \delta l_r + w_u(t) \end{cases} \tag{12.8}$$

Aircraft position computed from SINS is in earth sphere coordinate (L, λ, h). Using the coordinate transformation relationship between Cartesian coordinate and the sphere coordinate, the position in ECEF can be calculated as $p_{ins,v}$:

$$p_{ins,v} = \begin{bmatrix} x_{ins,v} \\ y_{ins,v} \\ z_{ins,v} \end{bmatrix} = \begin{bmatrix} (R_N + h)\cos L \cos \lambda \\ (R_N + h)\cos L \sin \lambda \\ [R_N(1 - e)^2 + h]\sin L \end{bmatrix} \tag{12.9}$$

Similarly, velocity $v_{ins,v}^n$ can be converted into ECEF frame as $v_{ins,v}^e$ by C_n^e [2]:

$$v_{ins,v}^e = [\dot{x}_{ins,v} \ \dot{y}_{ins,v} \ \dot{z}_{ins,v}]^T = C_n^e v_{ins,v}^n \tag{12.10}$$

Partially differentiate formula (12.8) can we get the relationship between position errors ($\delta x_{ins,v}$ $\delta y_{ins,v}$ $\delta z_{ins,v}$) and (δL $\delta \lambda$ δh), separately denoted as:

$$[\delta x_{ins,v} \ {}_{ins,v} \ \delta z_{ins,v}]^T = C_{err}[\delta L \ \delta \lambda \ \delta h]^T \tag{12.11}$$

where C_{err} is calculated as

$$\begin{bmatrix} -R_{Nh}\sin L \cos \lambda & -R_{Nh}\cos L \sin \lambda & \cos L \cos \lambda \\ -R_{Nh}\sin L \sin \lambda & R_{Nh}\cos L \cos \lambda & \cos L \sin \lambda \\ [R_N(1 - e)^2 + h]\cos L & 0 & \sin L \end{bmatrix}$$

Similarly, by partially differentiating formula (12.10), we got the relationship between velocity error in ECEF and sphere frame, which is

$$\delta v_{ins,v}^e = C_n^e \delta v_{ins,v}^n \tag{12.12}$$

The vector from aircraft to the ith satellite and its rate can be calculated as:

$$r_{ins,i} = p_{si} - p_{ins,v}, \quad \dot{r}_{ins,i} = \dot{p}_{si} - \dot{p}_{ins,v}$$

Further, the calculated range and range rate from SINS [9] are calculated as:

$$\rho_{ins,i} = \|r_{ins,i}\|, \quad \dot{\rho}_{ins,i} = \rho_{ins,i}^{-1}\left(r_{ins,i}^T \dot{r}_{ins,i}\right) \tag{12.13}$$

Expanding $\rho_{gps,i}$ and $\dot{\rho}_{gps,i}$ by Taylor expansion algorithm at the point $X_p = p_{ins,v}$ and $X_v = v_{ins,v}^e$, we get

$$\begin{cases} \rho_{gps,i} = \rho_{ins,i} + M_i \delta X_p + \delta l \\ \dot{\rho}_{gps,i} = \dot{\rho}_{ins,i} + G_i \delta X_p + H_i \delta X_v + \delta l_r \end{cases} \tag{12.14}$$

where

$$M_i = \frac{\partial \rho_{gps,i}}{\partial X_p}\bigg|_{underscorep_{ins,v}} = -\rho_{ins,i}^{-1} r_{ins,i}^T$$

$$H_i = \frac{\partial \dot{\rho}_{gps,i}}{\partial X_v}\bigg|_{underscorep_{ins,v}, v_{ins,v}^e} = -\rho_{ins,i}^{-1} r_{ins,i}^T$$

$$G_i = \frac{\partial \dot{\rho}_{gps,i}}{\partial X_p}\bigg|_{underscorep_{ins,v}, v_{ins,v}^e} = \frac{r_{ins,i}^T \dot{r}_{ins,i}}{\rho_{ins,i}^3} \cdot r_{ins,v}^T - \frac{\dot{r}_{ins,i}^T}{\rho_{ins,i}}$$

Based on above SINS error model and GPS error model, a deep integration Kalman filter is designed and the states are chosen as

$$x = \begin{bmatrix} \phi^T & \delta v^{nT} & \delta p^T & \varepsilon^{bT} & \nabla^{bT} & \delta l & \delta l_r \end{bmatrix}^T$$

According to formula (12.1)–(12.5) and formula (12.8), the system equation can be constructed as follows:

$$\dot{x}(t) = F(t)x(t) + \Gamma(t)w(t) \tag{12.15}$$

Taking the difference of $\rho_{ins,i}$ and $\rho_{gps,i}$, together with the difference of $\dot{\rho}_{ins,i}$ and $\dot{\rho}_{gps,i}$, and supposing that there are m effective satellites at time t_k, then the measurements of the filter, z_k can be shown as

$$z_k = \begin{bmatrix} \delta \rho_1 \\ \delta \rho_2 \\ \vdots \\ \delta \rho_m \\ \delta \dot{\rho}_1 \\ \delta \dot{\rho}_2 \\ \vdots \\ \delta \dot{\rho}_m \end{bmatrix} = \begin{bmatrix} \rho_{ins,1} - \rho_{gps,1} \\ \rho_{ins,2} - \rho_{gps,2} \\ \vdots \\ \rho_{ins,m} - \rho_{gps,m} \\ \dot{\rho}_{ins,1} - \dot{\rho}_{gps,1} \\ \dot{\rho}_{ins,2} - \dot{\rho}_{gps,2} \\ \vdots \\ \dot{\rho}_{ins,m} - \dot{\rho}_{gps,m} \end{bmatrix} = H_k x_k + v_k \tag{12.16}$$

In formula (12.16), the measurement noise v_k is mainly composed of GPS noise in pseudo range and pseudo range rate, with some small error components in linearization in formula (12.14). All these errors are processed as white noise with mean value 0 and covariance R_k, and H_k is constructed through formula (12.11), (12.12) and (12.14).

Above formula (12.15) and (12.16) together compose the Kalman filter of SINS/GPS deep integration, which is used to provide attitude reference of the aircraft.

12.4 In-flight Calibration of Installation Error

Deep integration of reference IMU and GPS provides attitude, velocity and position of the in-flight aircraft. To improve parameters precision especially the attitude, the aircraft is suggested to do a series of maneuvers, including acceleration, hover and climbing [10].

Then at the beginning of calibration, reference parameters are set to the IMU to calibrate. Then, the IMU begin to update its attitude based on its own measurements but velocity and position are from reference.

Suppose the real attitude matrix of the reference IMU is C_{b1}^n, and its calculated value is $\widehat{C}_{b1}^n$, then the misalignment angles can be represent as ϕ_1, which is related to C_{b1}^n and $\widehat{C}_{b1}^n$ as

$$\widehat{C}_{b1}^n = [I - (\phi_1 \times)]C_{b1}^n \tag{12.17}$$

Suppose the real attitude matrix of the IMU to be calibrated is C_{b2}^n, and its calculated value $\widehat{C}_{b2}^n$, then its misalignment angle represents as ϕ_2, which is related to C_{b2}^n and $\widehat{C}_{b2}^n$, as

$$\widehat{C}_{b2}^n = [I - (\phi_2 \times)]C_{b2}^n \tag{12.18}$$

Eiminating velocity error and position error in formula (12.1), we can got the simplified attitude error as

$$\dot{\phi}_2 = \phi_2 \times \omega_{in}^n - C_b^n \varepsilon^b \tag{12.19}$$

Setting gyro error as formula (12.4), states of the calibration filter are chosen as

$$x = [\phi_2^T \ \varepsilon_b^{bT} \ \delta^T \ dK_g^T]$$

Then the system equation is as follows:

$$\dot{x} = \begin{bmatrix} -\omega_{in}^n & -C_b^n & 0 & [\omega_{ib}^n] \\ 0 & 0 & 0 & 0 \\ 0 & 0 & 0 & 0 \\ 0 & 0 & 0 & 0 \end{bmatrix} x + \begin{bmatrix} C_b^n \varepsilon_w^b \\ 0 \\ 0 \\ 0 \end{bmatrix} \tag{12.20}$$

Denote the installation error as $\delta = [\delta_x \ \delta_y \ \delta_z]^T$.

Under assumption that the installation error δ is a small quantity, we get

$$C_{b2}^{b1} = I + (\delta \times) \tag{12.21}$$

Constructing filter measurements through the calculated $\widehat{C}_{b1}^n$ and $\widehat{C}_{b2}^n$, we get

$$
\begin{aligned}
z_C &= \widehat{C}_{b1}^n (\widehat{C}_{b2}^n)^T \\
&= [I - (\phi_1 \times)] C_{b1}^n C_{b1}^{b2} C_n^{b1} [I + (\phi_2 \times)] \\
&= [I - (\phi_1 \times)] C_{b1}^n [I - (\delta \times)] C_n^{b1} [I + (\phi_2 \times)] \\
&= [I - (\phi_1 \times)][I - (C_{b1}^n \delta) \times][I + (\phi_2 \times)]
\end{aligned} \tag{12.22}
$$

In formula (12.22) the real C_{b1}^n is unavailable, so it should be replaced by $\widehat{C}_{b1}^n$, as

$$C_{b1}^n \delta = [I + (\phi_1 \times)] \widehat{C}_{b1}^n \delta \tag{12.23}$$

Substitute formula (12.23) into (12.22) and eliminate high order minority error, and we finally get

$$z_C = I + [(\phi_2 - \widehat{C}_{b1}^n \delta - \phi_1) \times] \tag{12.24}$$

Based on formula (12.24), the angle error measurement z_ϕ can be shown as

$$z_\phi = \phi_2 - \widehat{C}_{b1}^n \delta - \phi_1 \tag{12.25}$$

In formula (12.25), ϕ_1 is so small that it can be thrown into measurement noise. So the formula can be arranged as

$$z_\phi = Hx + V \tag{12.26}$$

where $H = [\, I_3 \quad 0_{3 \times 3} \quad -\widehat{C}_{b1}^n \quad 0_{3 \times 3} \,]$, and V is the measurement noise.

Formula (12.20) together with formula (12.26) forms the in-flight calibration Kalman filter. The whole algorithm flow can be described as Fig. 12.1.

12.5 Simulation

Simulation is carried out to verify efficiency of the proposed algorithm. Reference IMU is set the same precision as the IMU to be calibrated. Gyro bias is set to $0.01°/h$, angle random walk $0.001°/\sqrt{h}$, and scale factor error $100\,\text{ppm}$. Accelerometer offset is set to $100\,\mu g$, and random walk $10\,\mu g/\sqrt{Hz}$. Output frequency of the IMU is set to $200\,\text{Hz}$.

Reference IMU is firstly deep integrated with GPS. STD of GPS pseudo range noise is set to $10\,\text{m}$, while STD of GPS pseudo range rate is set to $0.1\,\text{m/s}$. Clock error of GPS receiver t_u is set to $1\,\text{ms}$, while its change rate is set to obey normal distribution, which is $\dot{t}_u \sim N(0, 0.1\,\text{ms})$. Initial attitude of the aircraft is set to pitch $0°$, roll $0°$, and azimuth $0°$. Initial velocity is set to $100\,\text{m/s}$. Initial position is set to

Fig. 12.1 In-flight
calibration algorithm

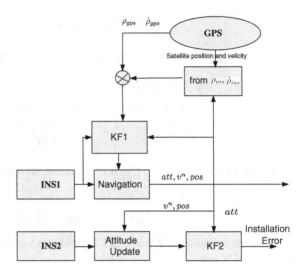

latitude 34°, longitude 108°, and height 5000 m. For the reference IMU, initial
attitude error is set to $\phi_0 = \begin{bmatrix} 10' & 10' & 20' \end{bmatrix}^T$, initial velocity error is set to 0.5 m/s
in east, north and up direction, and initial position error is set to 100 m in each
direction.

Maneuvers in-flight are set as follows:

150−170 s: Accelerate to 200 m/s with an acceleration of 5 m/s².

200−235 s: Tilt 15°, hover with an angular velocity of 2°/s, and change
horizontal at last.

250−300 s: Lift the head to 15°, climb and change horizontal at last.

380−400 s: Roll the aircraft back and forth with an angular velocity of 5°/s,
and at last change to horizontal.

405−455 s: Tilt 15°, hover with an angular velocity of 2°/s, and change horizontal at last.

480−520 s: Lift the head to 15°, climb and change horizontal at last.

550−570 s: Roll the aircraft back and forth with an angular velocity of 5°/s,
and at last change to horizontal.

Based on above maneuvers, attitude error of the deep integration is shown as
Fig. 12.2.

From the figure, we can see that after the former three maneuvers including
acceleration, hover and climbing, precision of the reference attitude has already
higher than 1′, especially after 350 s, horizon attitude error is less than 0.1′, while
azimuth error is less than 0.3′, which is high enough to be used as installation
reference to in-flight calibrate installation error.

Set the installation error of the second IMU to be $\delta = \begin{bmatrix} 10' & 15' & 20' \end{bmatrix}^T$. At
time 350 s, binding attitude, velocity and position of the reference to the IMU, and
after then the IMU begins to conduct attitude update procedure with the velocity

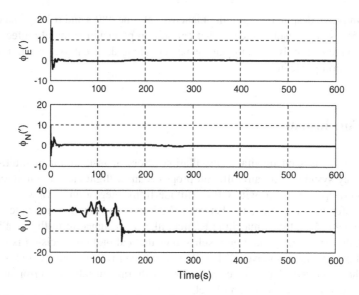

Fig. 12.2   Attitude error of the deep integration

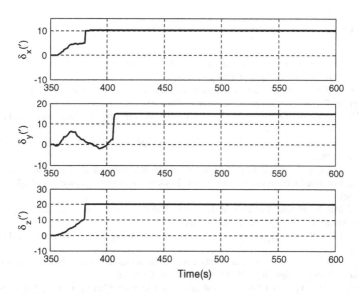

Fig. 12.3   Calibration result of the installation error

and position provided by reference. Using the in-flight calibration algorithm
proposed above to calibrate the installation error, the result is shown as Fig. 12.3.

From Fig. 12.3, we can see that at 380 s δ_x and δ_z can be estimated during the
rolling maneuver, and at time 405 s δ_y can be estimated during the hover
maneuver, and the precision is higher than $5''$. After then, the precision can not

further improve despite the climbing maneuver at time 480 s and rolling maneuver at time 550 s. The result indicates that calibration precision is mainly affected by aircraft maneuver, only two angular maneuvers along different axes are in need in the calibration procedure.

12.6 Conclusion

The paper focuses on inevitable installation errors in installation of multi-IMU redundancy system on an aircraft, and proposes an in-flight calibration algorithm based on deep integration with GPS. Attitude from integration is viewed as calibration reference, attitude error between IMU and the reference is made as the measurement. An attitude matching Kalman filter is designed to in-flight calibrate the installation error. Simulation result shows that calibration precision is mainly affected by angular maneuver. When the aircraft can rotate along two axis of its body, the proposed algorithm can precisely calibrate installation error and the precision can achieve arc second level.

References

1. Gaylor DE, B.S, M.S (2003) Integrated GPS/INS navigation system design for autonomous spacecraft rendezvous. The University of Texas at Austin, Austin
2. Qin Y (1998) Kalman filter and integrated navigation principle. Northwest Industry University Publishing Company, Xinan (in Chinese)
3. Ma YF (2006) SINS/GPS integrated navigation system and its data fusion technology. Southeast University, Nanjing
4. Gilmore JP, McKern RA (1972) A redundant strapdown inertial reference unit (SIRU). Spacecraft 9(1):39–47
5. Zhang T, Wang B, Han Z-G (2003) Study on redundancy technique in double strapdown inertial integrated navigation system. J Proj Rockets Missiles Guidance 23(4): 116–118 (in Chinese)
6. Grewal MS, Weill LR, Andrews AP (2007) Global positioning systems, inertial navigation, and integration. Wiley Interscience, Hoboken
7. Kaplan ED (2002) GPS theory and application. Publishing House of Electronic Industry, Beijing
8. Li Y, Wang J-L (2006) Low-cost tightly coupled GPS/INS integration based on a nonlinear Kalman filtering design. ION NTM, Monterey (in Chinese)
9. Lin M, Fang J, Gao G (2003) A new composed kalman filtering method for GPS/SINS integrated navigation system. J Chin Inert Technol 11(3):29–33 (in Chinese)
10. Cho SY, Park CG (2004) Calibration of a redundant IMU. AIAA guidance, navigation, and control conference and exhibit, providence, Rhode Island, AIAA, pp 5104–5123

Chapter 13
An Effective Energy-Saving Approach for Ferry Routing in Opportunistic Networks

Zhi Ren, Cai-mei Liu, Hong-jiang Lei and Ji-bi Li

Abstract In opportunistic networks, it is difficult to know in advance how a node moves and holds a poor connectivity. It has been shown that using the ferry-initialed message ferrying (FIMF) scheme can effectively improve the delivery rate of data packets. However, we found that it has the following there problems: (1) the hello message broadcast by ferry includes redundant contents (2) the ordinary node periodically broadcasts hello messages, so that node has redundant communication overhead, and (3) the ordinary node unify uses a single long range radio which consumes too much energy. To address these problems, we propose in this paper an improved algorithm called advanced ferry-initialed message ferrying (AFIMF). AFIMF uses the RSSI and power control technologies to reduce the transmit power for nodes to disperse location information, and deletes the location information in hello messages broadcast by the ferry. In addition, AFIMF sends hello messages in an on-demand way based on cross-layer information sharing. Theoretical analysis and simulation results show that AFIMF reduces energy consumption, enlarges the network lifetime, and decreases the network overhead.

Keywords Opportunistic networks · Message ferrying · Transmit power · Energy saving

Z. Ren (✉) · C. Liu (✉) · H. Lei · J. Li
Chongqing Key Lab of Mobile Communications Technology, Chongqing University of Posts and Telecommunications, 400065 Chongqing, China
e-mail: renzhi@cqupt.edu.cn

C. Liu
e-mail: liu_caimei@126.com

W. Lu et al. (eds.), *Proceedings of the 2012 International Conference on Information Technology and Software Engineering*, Lecture Notes in Electrical Engineering 211, DOI: 10.1007/978-3-642-34522-7_13, © Springer-Verlag Berlin Heidelberg 2013

13.1 Introduction

In opportunistic networks [1] it is difficult to know in advance how a node moves and holds a poor connectivity. When a node wants to deliver messages, it needs to passively wait for nodes randomly to move and establish the connection. Clearly, the traditional Internet routing algorithm (such as RIP [2]) and MANET routing algorithms (such as AODV [3]) do not apply to the opportunistic networks, for the premise of those routing protocols is to establish end-to-end connectivity between the source node and destination node. In the current reactive routing protocols (such as Epidemic routing protocol [4]) which are adapted to the opportunistic networks, nodes rely on its own movement to create a route. In order to improve the delivery success rate and reduce the transmission delay, in reactive routing protocols, nodes choose to copy a large number of copies and spread the message frequently in the network. This dramatically increases the buffer occupancy as well as energy consumption.

In order to alleviate the node energy consumption, reduce message delay, and overcome the communication disconnect in highly intermittent network, active-movement-based Routing protocol (such as Message Ferrying routing protocol [5]) introduces a particular node named ferry to opportunistic networks. For convenience, in the following paper, the common node in the network is referred to as node. It has made some progress in terms of the design and optimization of ferry route.

The optimization of ferry route is one of the study keys of message ferrying method. According to the published literature mentioned above, Zhao et al. [6] adopted the algorithm of solving the Traveling Salesman Problems (TSP) to calculate the Hamilton circuit which contains all the requests of the service nodes as the path of active movement of ferry. However, the TSP is a typical non-deterministic polynomial-time hard (NP-Hard) problem.

Authors in [7] propose a ferry-based Mobile Space Self Local (MSSL) routing scheme. The basic design about the scheme is as follows. Network is divided into several small areas. According to the probability of the node appearing in a regional, we can calculate the probability pi of the regional appearing nodes and select the regional centers which probability pi is greater than a certain threshold P as the ferry's path nodes. Polat et al. [8] bring message ferrying schemes into opportunistic networks of no specialized mobile facilities. They take advantage of the inherent nature of the node in the wireless mobile network, the message ferrying capacity, to make some ordinary nodes act as ferries in the network. Authors in [9] make nodes in the network cluster and introduce the principle of Shortest Process Time First (SPTF) in Job Shop Scheduling Problem (JSP) to optimize the function of average message delivery delay and select the residence location of ferry, dynamically optimizing the ferry route, thus it helps to reduce the latency of message delivery.

However, we find that the protocols which are based on Message Ferrying have redundant communication and storage overhead when node spreads *control* messages (such as the service request message). Besides, ferry route of active movement still can be done some optimization. These issues have an important impact on the performance of the message ferrying mechanism, so it is necessary to further research to address these issues.

The remainder of this paper is organized as follows. The network model and the improved approaches are described in Sect. 13.2. Section 13.3 shows the comparison of the two schemes under extensive network settings. Finally, Sect. 13.4 presents our conclusions.

13.2 Networks Model and Improved Methods

13.2.1 Network Model Review

This review is followed by an introduction. This paper uses the FIMF network model shown in Fig. 13.1. The network area A is a flat square of size $D \times D$. Nodes are randomly and uniformly distributed in the area. The area is averagely divided into four small square grids. The default route of ferry is the square L which vertices are the centers of each grid. Let R be the long-distance communication radius. If R takes a certain value which is not less than $\frac{\sqrt{2}}{4} D$, ferry communication range will cover the whole network with it running a circle on the closed line L.

At the beginning of network running, ferry moves along a pre-set route which is across all disconnected area and periodically broadcasts the hello messages which contains its own current position information. When node S receives a hello message broadcast by ferry, it extracts the location information from the hello message to calculate the distance d between itself and the ferry. When d < Rth and it meets the other requirements defined by Node Control Mechanism [7], the node will send a service_request message which contains the nodes' current location to ferry. In order to ensure successful transmission of Service_Request message, we take Rth < R in this paper. The process above is shown in Fig. 13.1a.

What is shown in Fig. 13.1b is that once ferry receives service_request messages of nodes, it will rely on the coordinates in the messages to change its route to meet the nodes.

When a node meets ferry, namely entering the range of both short-distance communication range with communication radius being r, the node and ferry will exchange messages by a wireless short-range communication. That all is shown in Fig. 13.1c.

After the data massages exchanging between ferry and the node finishes, ferry will return the default route. As shown in Fig. 13.1d.

At any time, ferry and the node will carry out data interaction as long as they move into each other's short-distance communication range.

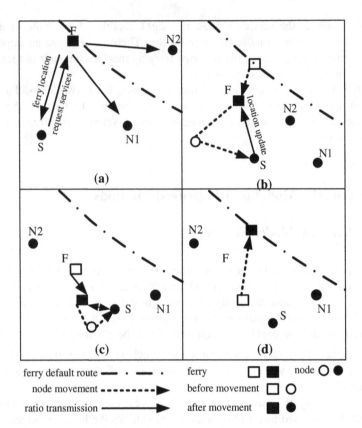

Fig. 13.1 An example of FIMF operations

13.2.2 Drawback Analysis and Improved Methods

In this paper, node is based on RSSI ranging technology to analyze the drawbacks of FIMF model. RSSI ranging technology does not require additional devices and energy consumption, and its cost and complexity are relatively low. What's more, it's generally used in a variety of wireless Multi-Hop networks, so we can use it in routing algorithm. We find three defects in FIMF and propose three advanced mechanisms which will be described in detail in the following.

13.2.2.1 Ferry Cancels the Location Information in Hello Message of Ferry

Problem Description: In the original proposals, the node needs to know the distance between itself and ferry before deciding to send a service_request message to ferry. The node can only use the location information in hello message received from ferry to calculate the distance.

Improved Method: The node adopts RSSI technology in MAC layer to detect the distance of the Signal of hello messages broadcast by ferry and informs the network layer of the distance by cross-layer information sharing.

Beneficial Effect: This mechanism shortens the size of hello message of ferry. It not only saves energy and occupation cache of node, but also reduces the complexity of the algorithm.

13.2.2.2 Nodes Broadcast Hello Messages On-Demand by Being Based on the Cross-Layer Information Sharing Way

Problem Description: The flowing three events will be taken place by the node. Assume the event A is that physical layer of node detects signals from other nodes. The event B is that there are data packets in the node cache. Event C is that the node sends hello messages. Events A, B, and C are independent of each other, and the node can independently control the occurrence of the event C. In original FIMF scheme, node periodically broadcasts hello messages. However, we find that when the event A and event B do not occur simultaneously, the event C does not work in the data transmission.

Improved Method: Only when at least one of the event A and B has occur, node makes the event C occur.

Beneficial Effect: In this mechanism, the node reduces the number of times of hello message sending, so that the node reduces the overhead of network communication control and saves energy of nodes.

Proof: If there are N nodes in a square network of size $D \times D$, the node degree is $n = \frac{N \times r^2}{D \times D}$ and the probability p of occurrence of the event A is equal to n. That we take the probability namely q of event B occurring is equal to 1/2. The probability of occurrence of events A and B at the same time is $(1 - n)/2$. The node degree of opportunistic networks is less than 1, so $(1 - n)/2$ is greater than zero. For example, in a network, if $N = 100$, $r = 250$ m, $D = 5$ km, we can obtain $n = 0.25$, thus the improved method of this mechanism can reduce in theory about 37.5 percents of the hello message of node. Therefore, the improved method of this mechanism is feasible and can achieve the beneficial effects we expected.

13.2.2.3 Node Adaptively Adjust the Power of Sending Service_Request Message and Location_Update Message

Problem Description: In original program, the node unify uses a single long-distance radio which communication radius is R to send service_request message and location_update message to ferry. The operation above will be taken place

Table 13.1 The distribution law of Y and P

y	1	2	...	i	...	k
P	P1	P2	...	Pi	...	Pk
p	p1	p2	...	pi	...	pk

after the node receives a hello message of ferry, so the distance between the node and ferry is not more than R. In general, transmit power for distance d is proportional to d^m, where m is the path loss exponent. When d is less than Rth, it can exponentially reduce the transmit power to save energy effectively.

Improved Method: Node based on the RSSI ranging technology uses its MAC layer to save the latest received distance of hello message of ferry. According to the distance, the node adaptively adjusts a suitable minimum transmit power when the MAC layer of node wants to send the service_request message or location update_message, both of which come from the routing layer.

Beneficial Effect: In this mechanism, nodes largely reduce the power of launching a service_request message or location_update message, so it saves the energy of nodes.

Proof: Set the current position of ferry as the center, and the distance between the node which wants to send a service request message or location update message and ferry is x, where, $0 < x \leq R$. Distance R is divided into k ($k = \lfloor \frac{R}{r} \rfloor$) sub-intervals, where the ith ($1 \leq i \leq k-1$) sub-interval is $((i-1)r, ir]$ and the kth sub-interval is $((k-1)r, R]$. Each sub-interval corresponds to a minimum transmission power Pi. Let y $\left(y = \lfloor \frac{x}{r} \rfloor\right)$ mean that x falls on the ith ($1 \leq i \leq k$) sub-interval, where y is a random variable, thus the corresponding transmit power P is also a random variable. The distribution law of Y and P is shown in the Table 13.1:

Set the mean value of variable P as $\overline{P}$, for $\forall i \in \{1, 2, \ldots k - 1\}$ has pi < Pk, obtains:

$$\overline{P} = \sum_{i=1}^{k} \text{pi}Pi < \sum_{i=1}^{k} \text{pi}Pk = Pk$$

Therefore, in the same network conditions, this mechanism can reduce the energy consumption of nodes.

13.3 Performance Evaluation

In this paper we use the OPNET14.5 simulation software. There are five scenarios. Each scenario has N nodes that are randomly uniformly distributed in a 5000×5000 m area $N \in \{40, 60, 80, 100, 120\}$. There is one ferry running in each scenario. Nodes move in the area according to the random-waypoint model

Table 13.2 Default
parameter settings

Transmission range of nodes' long range radio (R)	2000 m
Distance threshold for request transmission (Rth)	1800 m
Transmission range of nodes' short range radio (r)	250 m

Fig. 13.2 Total energy
consumption

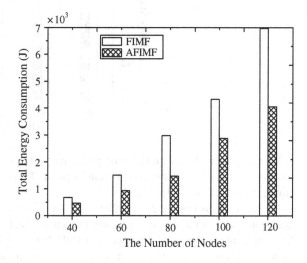

Fig. 13.3 Network overhead

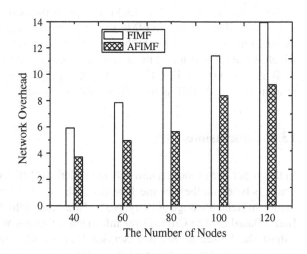

with a maximum speed 5 m/s. The ferry speed is 20 m/s. The default ferry route follows a rectangle with (1250, 1250) and (3750, 3750) as diagonal points (we use a 2×2 grid in computing the default route for AFIMF). The other default settings are shown in Table 13.2.

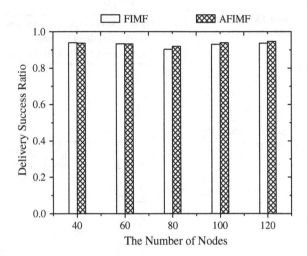

Fig. 13.4 Delivery success ratio of messages transmission

We compare and analyze the two approaches in terms of delivery success ratio, network overhead and total energy consumption. These performance metrics are shown from Figs. 13.2, 13.3, and 13.4.

As is shown in Fig. 13.2, in different network scenarios in the same network condition nodes in the AFIMF consume less energy and enhance the robustness of the routing algorithm than nodes in the FIMF. It is mainly because nodes largely reduce the power of launching a service_request message or location_update message.

What we can see from Fig. 13.3 is that the network overhead in AFIMF in each scene is smaller than that in FIMF respectively. It is mainly because node reduces the hello messages sending. In this paper, network overhead is defined as a value which is the ratio of total bits of control messages and data messages.

What's shown in Fig. 13.4 is that the delivery success ratio of messages transmission of AFIMF is over 90 % and that is almost the same as FIMF.

13.4 Conclusions

In this paper, we propose a new scheme called AFIMF for opportunistic networks, which is based on the new mechanisms such as Ferry Cancels the Location Information in Hello Message of Ferry, Nodes Broadcast Hello Messages On- demand by Being Based on The Cross-Layer Information Sharing Way and Node Adaptively Adjust the Power of Sending Service_Request Message and Location_Update Message. From the simulation results and analysis mentioned above, we can see that compared with FIMF, AFIMF with new mechanisms has better performance in terms of comprehensive performance including network overhead and total energy consumption. Meanwhile, the delivery success ratio of both schemes is close to the theoretical value.

Acknowledgments This work was supported in part by National Natural Science Foundation of China under Grant No. 60972068, the Science Research Project of Education Committee of Chongqing under Grant No. KJ120510, the open project of Emergency Communication Laboratory of Chongqing under Grant No. 201201, and the transformation project of excellent achievement of Chongqing Municipal Education Commission (Kjzh11206).

References

1. Lilien L, Kamal ZH, Gupta A (2006) Opportunistic networks. Department of Computer Science Western Michigan University
2. Hedrick C (1988) Routing information protocol, RFC 1058, Rutgers University, June
3. Perkins CE, Royer EM (1999) Ad-hoc on-demand distance vector routing. In: Proceedings of ninety-ninth mobile computing systems and applications, 25–26 Febr, pp 90–100
4. Vahdat A, Becke D (2000) Epidemic routing for partially connected ad hoc networks. Technical Report CS-2000-06, Department of Computer Science, Duke University, Durham
5. Zhao W-R, Ammar M (2003) Message ferrying: proactive routing in highly-partitioned wireless ad hoc networks. In: The ninth IEEE workshop on future trends of distributed computing systems, 28–30 May, pp 308–314
6. Zhao W-R, Ammar M, Zegura E (2004) A message ferrying approach for data delivery in sparse mobile ad hoc networks. In: Proceedings of the fifth ACM international symposium on mobile ad hoc networking and computing, pp 187–198
7. Zhang Y, Wei P, Wang R-C (2009) Research on ferry node MSSL routing algorithms in DTN. Comput Technol Dev 19(5):107–110 (in Chinese)
8. Polat BK, Sachdeva P, Ammar MH (2011) Message ferries as generalized dominating sets intermittently connected mobile networks. Pervasive Mobile Comput 7(2):189–205
9. Wang T, Low CP (2010) Dynamic message ferry route (DMFR) for partitioned MANETs. In: International conference on communications and mobile computing, April, pp 447–451

Chapter 14
Design of Nonuniform Quantizer in Satellite Navigation Receivers

Xianghua Zeng, Shaojie Ni, Rui Ge and Feixue Wang

Abstract Based on the correlation properties of the pseudo-random code in spread spectrum receivers, a novel and unified quantizer model was established, which was suitable for both uniform and nonuniform quantization. Statistical signal processing technique and extreme value theory were employed to obtain the analytical formulas of the optimal quantization value and corresponding quantization losses. Numerical results of uniform quantization, nonuniform quantization and theoretically optimal quantization are achieved using genetic algorithm and Monte Carlo simulation, which can be used to guide the engineering design of the GNSS receivers.

Keywords Uniform · Nonuniform · Quantizer · DSSS · Genetic

14.1 Introduction

Analog to Digital Converter (ADC) is a basic component of digital receivers. Properly designing the quantizer, thus minimizing the Signal-to-Noise Ratio (SNR) loss introduced by finite word length effect, is one of the basic issues in engineering design of digital receiver. As for satellite navigation receiver, the received signal is extremely weak when it reached the antenna aperture. Each component of the receiver must be carefully designed to reduce the SNR loss. In addition, in the GPS modernization plan and the signal system design of the 2nd generation of COMPASS

X. Zeng (✉) · S. Ni · R. Ge · F. Wang
College of Electronic Science and Engineering, National University of Defense Technology, Hunan, Changsha 410073, China
e-mail: 16047868@qq.com

W. Lu et al. (eds.), *Proceedings of the 2012 International Conference on Information Technology and Software Engineering*, Lecture Notes in Electrical Engineering 211, DOI: 10.1007/978-3-642-34522-7_14, © Springer-Verlag Berlin Heidelberg 2013

satellite navigation system, increasing the signal bandwidth are put forward to improve the positioning accuracy. Increasing the signal bandwidth means the increment of complexity of the receiver. Accordingly, the hardware scale will be doubled. Therefore, minimizing the quantization word length can greatly reduce the back-end hardware requirements for signal processing, which is crucial for reducing the cost and power consumption of receivers.

On the optimal quantization problem in spread spectrum receivers, extensive literature focused on the distribution characteristics of the quantization noise [1–8], and the optimal quantization is obtained on the assumptions that uniform quantization is used [9–13]. Chang [13] systematically studied the effect of the pre-sampling filter, sampling rate and quantization parameters in the non-zero Pulse-Code Modulation (PCM) receivers. Due to some similarity between PCM digital receivers and DSSS receivers in signal processing flow, some important conclusions of the former have been widely quoted [14]. However, some of the assumptions in the PCM receivers is still not applicable in DSSS receivers [15], such as the sampling rate is much larger than the signal bandwidth and inter-symbol interference can be neglected, etc.

The aforementioned researches are all based on the precondition that the quantizer is uniformly layered and the quantization noise is white Gaussian. One of the reasons is that the uniform quantizer is widely used. On the other hand, it is easier to obtain the analytical results. In fact, nonuniform quantizer is also applied in many fields, such as μ-law compression curve and A-law compression curve in speech transmission field.

In this paper, based on the correlation characteristics of PN code in spread spectrum receivers, a new and unified quantization model is established, which is suitable to both uniform and nonuniform quantizers. The analytical formulas of optimal quantization are derived using statistical signal analysis method and extreme value theory, and then numerical results of nonuniform quantization and uniform quantization are given by genetic algorithm and Monte Carlo simulation method respectively.

14.2 Signal Model

14.2.1 Received Signal

A typical signal model of satellite navigation receivers is shown in Fig. 14.1. We assume that the carrier frequency, phase and relative delay of the received signal can be accurately estimated, and other quantization effects beside the ADC are ignored.

Fig. 14.1 The simplified DSSS signal model

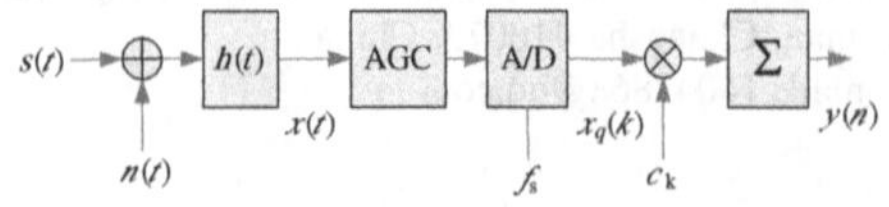

The received signal is given by

$$r(t) = s(t) + n(t) = Ad(t)\sum_i c_i u(t - iT_c) + n(t) \tag{14.1}$$

where A is the signal amplitude; $d(t)$ is information bit, which is a constant with the value 1; c_i is the pseudo-code sequence with the value +1 or -1; $n(t)$ is additive white Gaussian noise, whose unilateral power spectral density is $N_0/2$; $u(t)$ is unit square wave; and $h(t)$ is an ideal low-pass filter whose bandwidth is B. The AGC gain is a constant 1.

Let the received signal pass a low-pass filter, we obtain

$$x(t) = r(t) * h(t) = A\sum_i c_i s_h(t - iT_c) + n_h(t) \tag{14.2}$$

$$s_h(t) = u(t) * h(t) = 2B\int_{t-T_c}^{t} \sin c(2Bu)du \tag{14.3}$$

where $n_h(t)$ is band limited Gaussian noise with mean 0 and variance N_0B.

14.2.2 Quantizer

The ADC can be treated as a two-stage module consisting of sampling and quantization. The main parameters of ADC are sampling rate f_s, word length m, quantification layers $M = 2^{m-1}$ (even layered), and the limit level V.

The sampled signal has the form

$$x(k) = A\sum_i c_i s_h(kT_s - iT_c) + n_h(kT_s) = s'(k) + n'(k) \tag{14.4}$$

The quantized signal is given by

$$x_q(k) = Q[x(k)] \tag{14.5}$$

where quantization function is defined as

$$Q(x) = \begin{cases} W_M, & G_{M-1} \leq x < G_M \\ W_i, & G_{i-1} \leq x < G_i, \quad i = 2,\dots,M-2 \\ W_1, & G_0 \leq x < G_1 \\ W_{-1}, & G_{-1} \leq x < G_0 \\ W_{-i}, & G_{-i} \leq x < G_{-i+1}, \quad i = 2,\dots,M-2 \\ W_{-M}, & G_{-M} \leq x < G_{-M+1} \end{cases} \tag{14.6}$$

where $G_M = +\infty$, $G_{-M} = -\infty$, $G_0 = 0$, W_i is a real number (not necessarily a natural number), the probability distribution function of $x_q(k)$ is

$$P_i = \begin{cases} P\{x_q(k) = W_i\} = P\{G_{i-1} \leq x(k) < G_i\} \\ \quad = \Phi(\frac{s'(k)-G_i}{\sigma}) - \Phi(\frac{s'(k)-G_{i-1}}{\sigma}) & i = 1,\ldots,M \\ P\{x_q(k) = W_i\} = P\{G_{i-1} \leq x(k) < G_i\} \\ \quad = \Phi(\frac{s'(k)-G_i}{\sigma}) - \Phi(\frac{s'(k)-G_{i+1}}{\sigma}) & i = -1,\ldots,-M \end{cases} \quad (14.7)$$

$$\Phi(x) = \frac{1}{\sqrt{2\pi}} \int_{-\infty}^{x} e^{-u^2/2} du \quad (14.8)$$

14.2.3 Correlator Output

If the correlator length is N, then the output signal is computed as

$$y(n) = \sum_{k=0}^{N-1} c_k x_q(k+n) = \sum_{k=0}^{N-1} A_k \quad (14.9)$$

where

$$A_k = c_k x_q(k+n) \quad (14.10)$$

14.2.4 Calculation of Quantization Losses

The influence of pre-filter $h(t)$ on quantization had been analyzed in a former paper of the author, in which it is proved that the effect of the pre-filter and ADC can be separated under certain condition.

Ignoring the effect of the pre-filter (i.e., $h(t) = \delta(t)$), therefore there is no inter-symbol interference and a simpler quantitative formula can be derived. The probability distribution function of $x_q(k)$ can be written as

$$P_i = \begin{cases} P\{x_q(k) = W_i | c_k = 1\} = P\{x_q(k) = -W_i | c_k = -1\} \\ \quad = \Phi(\frac{A-G_i}{\sigma}) - \Phi(\frac{A-G_{i-1}}{\sigma}) & i = 1,\ldots,M \\ P\{x_q(k) = W_i | c_k = -1\} = P\{x_q(k) = -W_i | c_k = 1\} \\ \quad = \Phi(\frac{A-G_i}{\sigma}) - \Phi(\frac{A-G_{i+1}}{\sigma}) & i = -1,\ldots,-M \end{cases}$$

$$(14.11)$$

$$A_k = c_k x_q(k+n) = c_k \cdot Q[A c_{k+n} + n_h(k+n)] \quad (14.12)$$

According to the value of c_k and c_{k+n}, A_k can be divided into two sets:

Set 1: $c_k \cdot c_{k+n} = 1$, then

$$P\{A_k = W_i\} = P_i, \quad P\{A_k = -W_i\} = P_{-i}, \quad i = 1,2,\ldots,M \quad (14.13)$$

Set 2: $c_k \cdot c_{k+n} = -1$, then

$$P\{A_k = W_i\} = P_{-i}, \quad P\{A_k = -W_i\} = P_i, \quad i = 1, 2, \ldots, M \qquad (14.14)$$

Denote the elements number of these two sets as N_1 and N_2 respectively, then $N_1 + N_2 = N$.

Redistribute $\{A_k\}_{k=0}^{N-1}$ into two subsets, which are denoted as $\{B_k\}_{k=0}^{N_1-1}$ and $\{C_k\}_{k=0}^{N_2-1}$ respectively, then the correlation function can be given by

$$y(n) = \sum_{k=0}^{N_1-1} B_k + \sum_{k=0}^{N_2-1} C_k \qquad (14.15)$$

The mean and variance of correlation function are:

$$m_y = E[y(n)] = (N_1 - N_2)E[B_k] \qquad (14.16)$$

$$D_y = D[y(n)] = ND[B_k] \qquad (14.17)$$

As for the correlation peak, $N_1 = N$, $N_2 = 0$, so $m_y = NE[B_k]$; as for the side lobe, $N_1 \approx N_2$, so $m_y \approx 0$.

Therefore, the output SNR is

$$SNR_q = \frac{m_y^2}{D_y} = \frac{N(E[B_k])^2}{E[B_k^2] - (E[B_k])^2} = \frac{N}{\frac{E[B_k^2]}{(E[B_k])^2} - 1} \qquad (14.18)$$

$$SNR_{loss} = \frac{SNR_0}{SNR_q} = \frac{A^2}{\sigma^2}\left(\frac{E[B_k^2]}{(E[B_k])^2} - 1\right) \qquad (14.19)$$

To minimize SNR_{loss}, we should minimize $\frac{E[B_k^2]}{(E[B_k])^2}$

Denote $f = \frac{E[B_k^2]}{(E[B_k])^2}$, according to extreme value theory, let

$$\frac{\partial f}{\partial W_i} = \frac{2(E[B_k])^2 W_i(P_i + P_{-i}) - 2E[B_k^2] \cdot E[B_k](P_i - P_{-i})}{(E[B_k])^4} = 0 \qquad (14.20)$$

We obtain the optimal weight

$$\frac{W_i}{W_1} = \frac{P_1 + P_{-1}}{P_1 - P_{-1}} \cdot \frac{P_i - P_{-i}}{P_i + P_{-i}}, \quad i = 2, \ldots, M \qquad (14.21)$$

It is easy to see that the optimal weight value is not unique. If W_1 is set to 1, then the weight value is uniquely determined, namely the normalized weight.

When $\sum_{i=1}^{M} \frac{(P_i - P_{-i})}{P_i + P_{-i}}$ is maximum, we can obtain the expression of optimal quantization losses

$$SNR_{loss} = \frac{A^2}{\sigma^2} \left\{ \left[\sum_{i=1}^{M} \frac{(P_i - P_{-i})^2}{P_i + P_{-i}} \right]^{-1} - 1 \right\} \tag{22}$$

Some explanations of the above work are listed below:

(1) Equations (14.6–14.8) represent the general quantization model (the threshold value G_i and quantization value W_i can be arbitrary value), which is suitable to the uniform quantization, non uniform quantization and non-monotonic quantization. This is consistent with Andrzej's quantizer model [16].

(2) As for ADC input signal, the DC component is typically 0 (sometimes by removing the DC component), therefore the decision threshold is symmetric in amplitude, i.e. $W_{-i} = -W_i, G_{-i} = -G_i$.

(3) If $G_i - G_{i-1} \equiv \Delta$, $M_i - M_{i-1} = 1$, $i = 1, \ldots M$, the above formulas degenerate to the common uniform quantizer model.

(4) The above analysis method is easily extended to the odd-layered quantizer.

(5) Statistical characteristics of the PN code are used in the analysis. Correlation value is maximal when PN code synchronization is obtained; otherwise it is 0, which is appropriate for all kinds of spread spectrum receivers. The numerical simulation results also confirmed this.

14.3 Numerical Analysis

14.3.1 Parameter Setting

The signal parameters used during the numerical analysis come from the COMPASS-2 satellite navigation system. PN code is C/A code on B1 frequency of No.1 satellite (code period equals to 2046), the bandwidth is 2.046 MHz, suppose the typical value of CNR is 40 dBHz; and word length varies from 1 to 5 bits.

14.3.2 Performance Analysis of Uniform Quantizer

The uniform quantizer is widely used the ADC chips, which has equally spaced quantization thresholds and natural quantitation values. Figure 14.2 shows the relationship between SNR loss and the ADC limit level when ignoring the pre-filter, in which solid lines represent the theoretical calculation results while the dotted lines are achieved from 10^6 times Monte-Carlo simulation.

Table 14.1 shows the comprehensive effect by the ADC pre-filter bandwidth and quantization word length on the SNR after correlation, in which filter bandwidth is 1–5 times the bit rate and quantization word length is 1–5 bits. When the filter bandwidth is positive infinity, it is equivalent to ignoring the pre-filter.

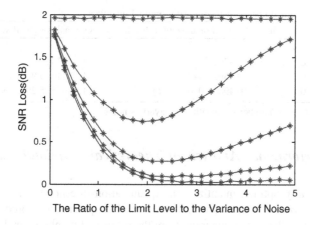

The Ratio of the Limit Level to the Variance of Noise

Fig. 14.2 Curve of SNR loss versus ADC limit level without pre-filter(*solid lines* denote theoretical results and *dashed lines* denote simulated results)

Table 14.1 Numerical results of uniform quantizer (in dB, the values in brackets are corresponding optimal quantization level V/σ)

m(bit) B/T$_c$	1	2	3	4	5
1	2.395	1.183(2.0)	0.700(2.3)	0.524(2.6)	0.464(2.9)
2	2.180	0.967(2.0)	0.486(2.3)	0.311(2.6)	0.251(2.9)
3	2.105	0.893(2.0)	0.412(2.3)	0.236(2.6)	0.177(2.9)
4	2.068	0.856(2.0)	0.374(2.3)	0.199(2.6)	0.140(2.9)
5	2.045	0.833(2.0)	0.352(2.3)	0.176(2.6)	0.117(2.9)
+ ∞	1.961	0.748(2.0)	0.265(2.3)	0.088(2.6)	0.028(2.9)

14.3.3 Performance Analysis of Nonuniform Quantizer

For nonuniform quantizer, the quantization thresholds are real number and the quantization values are natural number. Genetic algorithm is employed to analyze the non-uniform quantizer.

Table 14.2 lists numerical results of nonuniform quantizer with the bit length varying from 1–4 bits.

Table 14.2 Numerical results of nonuniform quantizer

m(bit)	2^N	Loss (dB)	Optimal quantization thresholds	Weighted values
1	2	1.955	–	–
2	4	0.742	0.975	{1, 2}
3	8	0.238	{0.686, 1.145, 1.607}	{1, 2, 3, 4}
4	16	0.069	{0.434, 0.723, 1.014, 1.306, 1.598, 1.890, 2.189}	{1, 2, 3, 4, 5, 6, 7, 8}

Table 14.3 Numerical results of theoretically optimal quantizer

m(bit)	2^N	Loss (dB)	Optimal quantization thresholds	Optimal weighted values
1	2	1.955	–	–
2	4	0.539	{0.979}	{1, 3.328}
*	6	0.257	{0.656, 1.442}	{1, 3.146, 5.941}
3	8	0.151	{0.498, 1.046, 1.741}	{1, 3.055, 5.296, 7.956, 11.691}

Notes: * indicates the number of quantitative layers is not 2^N

14.3.4 Performance Analysis of Theoretically Optimal Quantizer

For theoretically optimal quantizer, the quantization thresholds are real number and the quantization values are real number. The quantization process can be regarded as a mathematical mapping from the set of real numbers (analog signals) to the set of limited numbers (digital signals) [16]. Genetic algorithm is used to analyze the theoretically optimal quantizer.

Table 14.3 lists numerical results of the theoretically optimal quantizer.

14.3.5 Influence of Input SNR on Quantizer

Analyses of Sect. 14.3.2 to Sect. 14.3.4 are based on a typical CNR 40 dBHz. Figure 14.3 gives quantization losses versus input SNR (in order to show clearly, only results of 3 bits are given). The results show that, with the increase of SNR, quantization losses gradually decreases, but the optimal quantization level is almost unchanged.

Based on the analysis above, we can summarize as follows:

(1) Quantization losses decrease rapidly with the increase of quantization word length. The quantization loss is 1.96 dB for 1-bit quantizer while only

Fig. 14.3 Curve of SNR loss versus ADC limit level (word length is 3 bits)

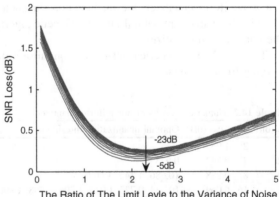

0.265 dB for 3-bit quantizer. Commercial GPS chips usually use 1-bit or 2-bit quantizer to reduce cost; in more advanced GPS receivers, 4-bit quantizers are usually adopted.

(2) Comparing Tables 14.1–14.3, it is shows that in spread spectrum receiver, performance of uniform and nonuniform quantization are almost the same, theoretical optimal quantization of 2 bit and 3 bit can respectively reduce quantization losses about 0.2 and 0.1 dB respectively. Therefore, during satellite navigation chip designing engineers can adopt uniform quantizer which has lower complexity.

(3) SNR loss is relevant to input SNR, while the optimal quantization level is irrelevant to input SNR. Effect of input SNR upon the optimal quantization level can be ignored in the receiver design.

(4) The minimum quantization loss has certain robustness, which changes little in certain quantization level range. The lager the word length, the smaller effects the quantization level has upon quantization loss. For digital receiver with 2–3 bits, quantization level should be accurately selected; for digital receiver with larger length, it usually take the three times of noise variance. In general engineering applications, ADC input level usually takes 0 dBm. Due to the ADC level and input impedance is not the same for different components, there will result in some more engineering errors when the quantization word length is small.

14.4 Conclusions

In this paper, we established a unified ADC quantization analysis model, which is suitable for the performance analysis of both uniform and nonuniform quantizer. Based on this model, the theoretical formulas of optimal quantization values and optimal quantization losses are derived.

Further More, the quantization model and formulas in this paper can be extended to quantitation analysis under interference condition. The numerical results can be employed effectively to the design of spread spectrum receivers.

References

1. Widrow B, Kollar I, Liu MC (1996) Statistical theory of quantization. IEEE Trans Instrum Meas 453:353–361
2. Sripad B, Snyder DL (1917) A necessary and sufficient condition for quantization errors to be uniform and white. IEEE Trans Acoust Speech Signal Process 25:442–448
3. Gray RM (1990) Quantization noise spectra. IEEE Trans Inf Theory 36:1220–1244
4. Kushner HB, Meisnerand M, Levy AV (1991) Almost uniformity of quantization errors. IEEE Trans Instrum Meas 40:682–687

5. Wagdy MF, Ng WM (1989) Validity of uniform quantization error model for sinusoidal signals without and with dither. IEEE Trans Instrum Meas 38:718–722

6. Gray G, Zeoli G (1971) Quantization and saturation noise due to analog-to-digital conversion. IEEE Trans Aerosp Electron Syst 222–223

7. Matteo BN, Claudio et al (1989) A noise model for digitized data. IEEE Trans Instrum Meas 49:83–86

8. Gray RM, Stockharn TG (1993) Dithered quantizers. IEEE Trans Inf Theory 39:805–812

9. Yasukawa K, Milstein L (1997) Finite word length effects on the performance of MMSE receiver for DS-CDMA systems. Proceedings of PIMRC'97, pp 724–728

10. Ouvry L, Boulanger C et al (1998) Quantization effects on a DS-CDMA Signal. Proceedings of spread spectrum techniques and applications, pp 234–238

11. Yagyu M, Kinjo S et al (1999) Analysis and minimization of loss of process gain and A/D conversion in DS-CDMA. Proceedings of vehicular technology conference, pp 2476–2480

12. Betz JW, Shnidman NR (2007) Receiver processing losses with band limiting and one-bit quantization. Proceedings of the 20th international technical meeting of the satellite division of the Institute of Navigation ION/GNSS, pp 1244–1256

13. Chang H (1982) Presampling filtering, sampling and quantisation effects on digital matched filter performance. Proceedings of the international telemetering conference, pp 889–915

14. Michael SB, Van Dierendonck AJ (1999) GPS receiver architecture and measurements. Proc IEEE 87:48–84

15. Curran JT, Borioand D et al (2009) Front-end filtering and quantisation effects on GNSS signal processing. Proceedings of IEEE conference on wireless communications. Vehicular technology information theory and aerospace and electronic systems technology, pp 227–231

16. Andrzej P, Konrad H (1998) Analog-to-digital converters: towards a generalization of widrow's theorem. IEEE instrumentation and measurement technology conference, pp 18–21

Chapter 15
A New Security Problem of USB: Monitoring Cable Attack and Countermeasures

An Wang, Zheng Li, Xianwen Yang and Boang Feng

Abstract USB interface is one of the most frequently used communication interfaces of computer, whose security problems come to appear gradually nowadays. However, people usually pay much more attention to the secure store and authenticated access rather than the security of USB cable. In this paper, a new attack approach on USB cable is proposed and a USB cable monitor is designed. Based on FPGA environment, practical monitoring experiments on common USB devices such as flash disk are made. Accordingly, some strategies against the monitoring USB cable attack are given based on cryptography.

Keywords Information security · Universal serial bus · Data communication · Monitoring cable attack

15.1 Introduction

Nowadays, there are many kinds of USB [1] devices such as keyboard, mouse, mobile storage device, printer, and so on. With widely application of them, it has become increasingly important to consider the security problems. Accordingly,

A. Wang (✉)
Institute for Advanced Study, Tsinghua University, 100084 Beijing, China
e-mail: wanganl@tsinghua.edu.cn

Z. Li · X. Yang
Department of Electronic Technology, Information Science and Technology Institute, 450004 Zhengzhou, China

B. Feng
Electronic and Information Engineering, Beihang University, 100191 Beijing, China

W. Lu et al. (eds.), *Proceedings of the 2012 International Conference on Information Technology and Software Engineering*, Lecture Notes in Electrical Engineering 211, DOI: 10.1007/978-3-642-34522-7_15, © Springer-Verlag Berlin Heidelberg 2013

Fig. 15.1 The common
attacks on the system of USB
flash disk

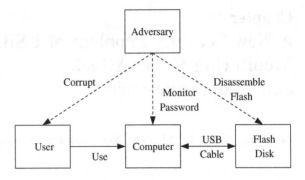

Fig. 15.1 The common attacks on the system of USB flash disk

many security USB devices are designed: security flash disk, for instance. People usually pay more attention to the memory and software of USB devices, but the potential safety hazard from USB cable is always neglected.

USB port behind a mainframe-box (in fact it's a part of mainboard) is usually connected directly to the USB connector of device. May this channel reveal some information? Surprisingly, the answer is yes and we will make some experiments to prove it. According to statistics, 99 % of desk computers have some front USB port, 60 % of computer users often adopt a USB extension cable of mini-b type to connect computer to some portable equipment such as MP3, cell phone, digital camera, 30 % of users employ a USB hub or a common USB extension cable. However, most of the front USB port, USB extension cable, and USB hub have poor quality whose manufacturer is unknown by users. An SoC (System on a Chip) can be tiny enough to be hidden into a USB cable.

15.2 Related Work

In recent years, attacks on a USB product can be divided into two classes (described in Fig. 15.1): one is illegally getting information stored in the memory such as nonvolatile memory [2] (Even if the authentication technology can be employed to protect it, the memory chip can still be disassembled and read by special device), the other is unauthorized interception of the access password which can be stolen by Trojan Horse program or corruption. Accordingly, all kinds of countermeasures are proposed against these attacks.

The security mechanisms in USB products are usually implemented by ways of software, hardware, and fingerprint identification. In 2004, FreeOTFE development group designed a management system of removable storage device which can encrypt the data in memory unit and control the access of information [3]. However, this software encounters some security problems because of the inherent shortcoming of windows user-mode. Fingerprint identification is a new technology in recent years, for example, Sony Company applies it to develop an authenticated USB storage system [4]. Unfortunately, its official document still points out the defects: when using, temperature, humidity, and physical damage bring it serious influence. The hardware technology is to carry out key management, encryption/decryption, and authentication by a chip, which is low cost and has a higher security. CE-Infosys Ltd. designed a secure personal removable storage solution named CompuSec Mobile [5], which adopts hardware approach to implement storage encryption and signature. Moreover, some ATM pin pads [6] employ some schemes of key code confusion and peeped protection against some attacks.

15.3 A Practical Attack: USB Cable Monitor

The system architecture of USB cable monitor is given in Fig. 15.2. It includes two parts: the monitor collects and sends the data transmitted through USB cable; and the receiver saves the data received and submits it to adversary. After processing the data by software, original information can be restored and an attack finishes.

15.3.1 Data Acquisition and SIE

The major component of data acquisition is USB transceiver, which converts an analog differential signal coming from D+ and D− into a digital signal. For reducing design difficulty; the PDIUSBP11AD transceiver chip [7] is employed.

After an A/D conversion, three digital signals of RCV, VM, and VP can be generated, which indicate the bit stream received and two differential signals. During the A/D conversion, we have two tries for information acquisition. One is connecting the signals directly, which brings a lot of noise. In order to decrease the error signals, two comparators are employed for the regulating circuit. The result

Fig. 15.2 System architecture of monitor device and its accessories

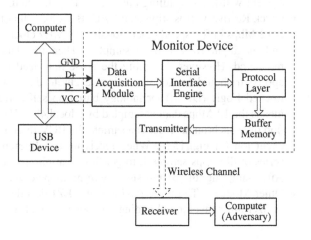

Fig. 15.3 The data
acquisition circuit for
eliminating noise

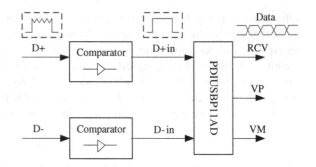

shows clear voltage traces and little glitches. The other is using P6563A electro-magnetic probe for signal measurement, which shows more sensitive data, smaller size, and lower noise. However, this method often results in misjudgments of signals. We choose the first method, which is described in Fig. 15.3.

In our practical tests, the bit error rate is less than 10^{-5}. When the monitor is connected with the USB bus, the power consumption of monitor doesn't have influence on the usual data transmission. Our tests show that the data acquisition module has low power consumption, low bit error rate, and small areas, which can satisfy the requirement of monitor. SIE which can process the bit stream initially consists of bus detection, synchronizing detection, clock recovery, NRZI decoder, bit unstuffing, and deserializer, described in Fig. 15.4.

- Bus Detection. The change of state value K/J/SE0 can be detected by this module to trigger the receiving packets stage. Meanwhile, the speed mode can be determined as well. In low speed mode, J and K are indicated by 0 and 1 respectively, which is just the opposite in full speed mode.
- Synchronizing Detection. Since all the data is transmitted in pockets, the start of packet (SOP) should be detected first. Each pocket begins with the synchroni-zation field whose NRZI code is "KJKJKJKK". The last two bits indicate end of the synchronization field, which mean start of packet identifier (PID) as well. System will keep on idling until an SOP is detected.
- Clock Recovery. It is stipulated by USB protocol that the speed of transmission is 12 Mbps in full speed mode. Ideally, 48 MHz clock can be divided frequency, and the input RCV can be sampled. Then the data from computer can be recovered. However, in reality the noise may lead to edge jitter, so effective approach should be adopted to get accurate data. We employ a Data Phase Locked Logic (DPLL) technology based on self-correcting mechanism which means the 12 Mbps data is sampled by a local 48 MHz clock. A rising edge flip-flop of asynchronous reset can sample the RCV three times to remove the phase excursion (in Fig. 15.5). When receiving the differential input signal RCV, a series of flip-flops sample it to get three sampling values dsp1, dsp2, and dsp3. After sampling, the output signal will be in sync with the local clock.
- Other Modules. The three modules of NRZI decoder, bit unstuffing, and dese-rializer are conventional coding component which we can refer to [1].

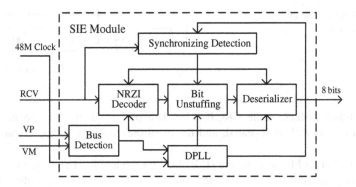

Fig. 15.4 Process of bit stream in serial interface engine module

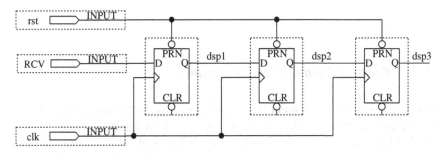

Fig. 15.5 Sampling from serial flip-flop circuit

15.3.2 Protocol Layer

Protocol layer includes three modules: packet engine, packet decoder, and internal direct memory access (IDMA), which analyzes, extracts, and checks valid data.

- Packet Engine. When the monitored USB device is plugged into a computer, some configuration, state, and property has determined and been saved into corresponding registers of SIE. Packet engine is the key control unit of protocol layer. The major functions of packet engine are:

  - Dealing with the IN, OUT, and SETUP affairs;
  - Determining the task of current transfer affair;
  - Responding to each pocket and managing the data;
  - Implementing the self-recovery mechanism of USB protocol.

- Packet Decoder. Packets can be decoded by this module so that PID, endpoint address, device address, and valid data are restored. State machine should be adopted to control the whole module. During decoding, CRC5 check (its generator polynomial, $G(X) = X^5 + X^2 + 1$, is implemented as Fig. 15.6) is made

Fig. 15.6 CRC5 circuit for
error detection

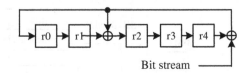

Bit stream

to a token pocket, while CRC16 to a data pocket. If an error appears, this
transmission will be repeated, and the monitored data should be discarded as
well.

- Internal Direct Memory Access (IMDA). This module has two major functions:
  one is generating a write enable signal of buffer memory according to the
  progress rate of receiving a pocket, which can control the writing of buffer
  memory. The other is feeding back current state to the protocol engine.

15.3.3 Wireless Communication Module

The data treated by the protocol layer is saved into the buffer memory which is a
first in first out (FIFO) buffer. When the quantity of accumulated data is up to a
threshold, transmitter is triggered and the data will be sent out wirelessly. Because
of the distinction of speed, power, and distance, Wi-Fi, ZigBee, and Bluetooth
technology can be employed to design the transmitter and the receiver.

Our tests show that the USB bus cannot supply enough power such that Wi-Fi
signals can be transmitted across 50 m. So we employ a sophisticated wide-band
operational amplifier, a high-pass filter, and a comparator for modifying the circuit
of Wi-Fi receiver, which is described in Fig. 15.7. The actual transmission distance is up to 80 m. To meet the speed requirement of USB protocol version 1.1,
we adopt EMB-380 Wi-Fi module to make a wireless transmission experiment.
TCP/IP protocol stack is embedded into the chip, which supports the common
protocols such as IP, TCP, and UDP. Therefore, data can be transmitted easily just
as classical UART and SPI. This module can pack data into frames.

15.3.4 Implementation and Test

The monitor can be described in Verilog and synthesized in Quartus II. Cyclone II
EP2C35F672C6 made in Altera Company is employed to test it, which has 33216
logic elements, 4 PLLs, and adequate RAM. In the synthesis report of monitor IP
core it occupies 676 LEs and its clock frequency can reach up to 116.73 MHz. We
adopt two USB connectors, a cable, data acquisition circuit, FPGA (including the
monitor IP core), and transmitter circuit to make up an USB extension cable which

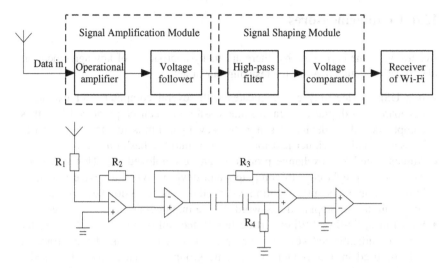

Fig. 15.7 Circuit of modified Wi-Fi receiver

Fig. 15.8 Monitoring experiment of keyboard and flash disk

embedded a monitor. With the help of the receiver and driver, the monitored data can be sent to adversary's computer. After analyzed by software, the original data will be restored. During our experiment, the USB cable monitor is applied to connect a flash disk to a computer. When a bmp picture (left of Fig. 15.8) is saved into the flash disk, the monitor will capture the transmitted data and send it to the adversary's computer. After analyzed by special software the original picture will be restored (right of Fig. 15.8).

15.4 Countermeasures

According to the cryptography, there are many approaches of key agreement and identification authentication for resisting our attack.

- If a USB device only communicates with several computers, for example a keyboard or a digital camera, a same session key can be preplaced into these computers and the device. A symmetric key algorithm is adopted to encrypt the messages, and the cipher text may be saved into the flash directly.
- Authenticated key exchange protocols can be employed [8]. That's to say, a password is preplaced into computers and devices. When a device is plugged into a computer, an authentication is carried out and a session key is established according to the preplaced password. While unplugging, the key expired.
- Sometimes, ID-Based [9] or certificate [10] technology can be applied together with an authenticated key exchange protocols. A flash disk of this group can only be used in a computer of the same group. In such a case, ID-Based or certificate technology can ensure the validity of a public key, so that a cryptographic protocol can be finished easily.

15.5 Conclusions

In this paper a new attack aiming at the USB cable is presented. We design and implement a USB cable monitor IP core and make practical experiments on keyboard and flash disk. Meanwhile, some alternative countermeasures are advised against this attack. Our monitoring attack belongs to "passive attack", whose ability is not ideal for an adversary. In the future, we will aim at a special USB device and design an active attack device named "man-in-the-middle attacker" which can break the cryptographic protocol being performed in the USB device.

References

1. Compaq, Hewlett-Packard, Intel, Lucent, Microsoft, NEC, Philips (2000) Universal serial bus specification revision 2.0, http://www.usb.org/developers/docs
2. Handschuh H, Trichina E (2007) Securing flash technology. In: Proceeding IEEE Symposium workshop on fault diagnosis and tolerance in cryptography. IEEE Press pp 3–17
3. FreeOTFE Develop Group (2009) FreeOTFE user manual. http://www.freeotfe.org/user_man-ual.html
4. Sony Corporation (2005) Sony USB storage media with fingerprint access. http://www.sony.com.cn/products/rme/b2c/flash/download/fingerprint/2550330612.pdf
5. CE-Infosys (2009) Data sheet of CompuSec mobile hardware security for notebooks. http://www.ce-infosys.com.sg/english/pdf/datasheets/CompuSec_Mobile.pdf

6. SUNZone TEC CO. Ltd. (2009) Data sheet of SUZP168x 3DES PINPad, http://www.sunzone.com.tw/PDF/PINPad_POS_Terminals/PINPad/SUZP168x_3DES/SUZCRP 168-MA10.pdf
7. Philips Semiconductor (2001) Data sheet of PDIUSBP11A universal serial bus transceiver. http://www.semiconductors.philips.com/documents/data_sheet/PDIUSBP11A_3.pdf
8. Bellovin SM, Merritt M (1992) Encrypted key exchange: password-based protocols secure against dictionary attacks. In:Proceedings of the IEEE symposium on research in security and privacy. pp 72–84
9. Shamir A (1985) Identity-based cryptosystems and signature schemes, Advances in Cryptology—Crypto 1984, LNCS vol 196, Springer, Heidelberg pp 47–53
10. Adams C, Farrell S (1999) Internet X.509 public key infrastructure: certificate management protocols, RFC 2510. March 1999

Chapter 16
BeiDou-1 Signal Simulation for Passive Location

Jianwei Zhan, Yong Wang, Jing Pang, Guozhu Zhang and Gang Ou

Abstract As BeiDou-1 (BD-1) receivers are widely applied in communication, power and defense construction areas nowadays, the technology of assessing receivers based on simulators attracts more attention. However, due to the particular retransmission characteristics in BD-1 and the lagging research on relatively signal simulator, the simulator without ephemeris and errors model simulation function is unable to meet the needs of assessing the receiver's positioning arithmetic. Therefore, it is an urgence to design a simulator with the functions of debugging and research support using simulation models. Firstly, the principle of BD-1 passive location is elaborated. Then the requirements of the dynamic navigation signal simulation are analyzed. Finally, four mathematical models are established to simulate the error corrections and the signals arriving at the receiver antenna phase center, which are: the target trajectory calculation model, the transmitting (retransmitting) time model, the satellite ephemeris parameter calculation model, and the signal propagation error model. The results show that the BD-1 signal simulator can provide a high-fidelity test environment, and satisfy passive location receiver's test requirements.

Keywords Satellite navigation · BeiDou-1 · Simulator · Simulation model · Receiver test · Chebyshev polynomials fitting

J. Zhan (✉) · Y. Wang · J. Pang · G. Zhang · G. Ou
Satellite Navigation R&D Center, School of Electronic Science and Engineering,
National University of Defense Technology, Changsha, 410073 Hunan, China
e-mail: sophy_zjw@nudt.edu.cn

W. Lu et al. (eds.), *Proceedings of the 2012 International Conference on Information Technology and Software Engineering*, Lecture Notes in Electrical Engineering 211, DOI: 10.1007/978-3-642-34522-7_16, © Springer-Verlag Berlin Heidelberg 2013

16.1 Introduction

The BeiDou-1 (BD-1) passive location receivers are designed to provide passive location and timing services. Compared to active location, the passive positioning system will have the advantages of large capacity, low power, high economic and military values. When the receiver determines its position, it receives signals retransmitted by BD-1 geosynchronous satellites (GEOs), demodulates outbound information data, and measures the pseudorange from Measuring and Control Center (MCC) to the receiver simultaneously and the altitude with the barometric altimeter. Because the signals are transmitted from MCC on the ground to the satellite's transponder (outbound channel uplink) then retransmitted to the receiver (outbound channel downlink), they suffer from a variety of propagation errors inevitably, such as the ephemeris errors, the atmospheric delays, the Sagnac effect, and the device processing value. Therefore, the pseudorange should be corrected by the outbound information and the measurements errors.

Although meeting the functional test requirements, the BD-1 simulator designed and implemented in [1] cannot satisfy test requirements because of the fact that it does not establish the ephemeris parameter calculation model, signal propagation error model, or Sagnac, etc. If the receiver corrects the pseudorange measurements according to the signal transmitted by the functional simulator, additional errors will be induced, which will affect positioning accuracy. While the satellite clock model established in [2] does not conform to the practical system.

By analyzing and establishing the key models such as the transmitting (retransmitting) time model, the ephemeris parameter calculation model, and the signal propagation error model, we design and implement a kind of simulator which can simulate BD-1 satellite dynamic signals arriving at the antenna phase center. Compared with the traditional simulator, it has the capabilities of simulation. Besides, the designed simulator can assess the impact of various errors on positioning accuracy, which will overcome the difficult separation of the system errors in real conditions. This paper focuses on the simulation modeling and analyzing its impact on the positioning.

16.2 Passive Position Determination

The basic measurement of the receiver is to determine the pseudorange of the receiver from MCC. So three BD-1 GEOs can provide three pseudorange measurements of the receiver. If altitude is known through altimeter, receiver's position, including longitude and latitude, can be resolved from Eq. (16.1). The Fig. 16.1 shows an position determination geometry [3].

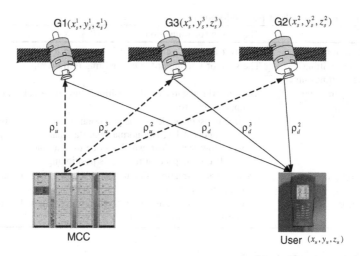

Fig. 16.1 Passive location geometry

$$\begin{cases} \rho^k = \rho_{up}^k + {}_d^k + c(\tau_t^k + \tau_{IT}^k + \delta t^k) + \varepsilon^k \\ \vdots \\ (x_u^2 + y_u^2)(a + h)^{1/2} + (x_u^2 + y_u^2)(b + h)^{1/2} = 1 \end{cases} \quad (16.1)$$

where,

$$r_d^k = \sqrt{(x_s^k - x_u)^2 + (y_s^k - y_u)^2 + (z_s^k - z_u)^2} \quad (16.2)$$

where k is the number of satellites, $k = 1, 2, 3$, ρ^ks the pseudorange measurement from MCC, ρ_{up}^k is the delay from MCC to the satellite k, r_d^k is the geometric distance from satellite k to the receiver, τ_t^k is the delay of the satellite k's transponder, τ_{IT}^k represents the atmospheric delay from satellite k to the receiver; δt^k is the bias between the receiver clock and BDT, c is the speed of light, ε^k is the model error and unknown factor, h is the height, a is the semimajor axis and b is the semiminor axis.

In the determination process, ρ_{up}^k and τ_t^k can be obtained by demodulating outbound information directly, τ_{IT}^k can be calculated by models using outbound information parameters, h can be measured by barometric altimeter with little error. Combining the four equation in (16.1) can resolve the position (x_u, y_u, z_u) and the receiver clock bias δt^k.

Table 16.1 Error models of passive location

Model	The reason for simulation
Target trajectory	Receiver position, velocity, acceleration and jerk
Satellite transmitting (retransmitting) time	The state of satellite at the transmitting (retransmitting) time
Ephemeris parameter calculation	Satellite orbit parameter: the position, velocity, acceleration, ephemeris errors
	Satellite transponder delay: the pseudorange corrections due to the transponder delay, is a normal non-stationary random process with slow mean drift, which can be used a constant model to simulate its impact on receiver's positioning
Signal propagation errors	Pseudorange corrections due to ionosphere troposphere and relativistic effects
Device error	Pseudorange corrections due to system processing value, can be considered as the receiver clock error

16.3 Simulation Model

As stated earlier, in order to assess the impacts of the various errors on positioning accuracy, the simulator needs to establish the following models, as described in Table 16.1.

Table 16.1 briefly summarizes five models: the target trajectory calculation model, satellite transmitting (retransmitting) time model, ephemeris parameter calculation model, signal propagation delay mode and device processing delay model. Thus, the signal can be simulated to provide a platform for receiver assessments. Each model has an open architecture, which is convenient for users to change models to reduce or increase errors. In the following sections, the detailed analysis of the first to the fourth models will be given.

16.3.1 Target Trajectory Calculation Model

In order to measure the performance of the receiver in motion, satellite simulators should have the capability of simulating multiple target trajectories. But there are so many factors affecting the receiver motion that the computational complexity of describing the accurate motion is high. To avoid this problem, the simplified model which can reflects the characteristic of the target trajectories is usually adopted when the simulator works.

According to the application area of the satellite navigation, the type of the receiver carrier can be divided into the following categories: stationary targets, planes, ships cars, and missile. Simulators can choose appropriate common forms of motion for simulation (uniform linear motion, linear acceleration, uniform acceleration, turning, climbing, etc.) based on the characteristics of each type of carrier [4]. And the track file with position and velocity information is also a good type which is helpful to enhance the system compatibility.

16.3.2 Signal Transmitting (Retransmitting) Time Calculation Model

According to the passive location principle, the signal received by the receiver is retransmitted by satellite at the time $t_s(t_s = t - \tau_{down})$ and transmitting by MCC at the time $t_t = t_s - \tau_{up}$, where τ_{down} is the downlink propagation delay, τ_{up} is the uplink propagation delay. In order to simulate the signal appropriately, the satellite position, the uplink and the downlink delay should be calculated iteratively at the time t_s. Therefore, the time when the signal transmitted by MCC and the one when the GEO satellite retransmits the signal are the key points during the simulation. As an example of how to use the model to calculate time, the process of calculating t_t is given, as follows.

Assuming that the signal retransmitted by the satellite at the time t_s expressed in BDT is transmitted by MCC at the time t_t, also in BDT. r is the geometric satellite-to-receiver distance. c is the speed of light in vacuum. Then the transmitting time is calculated as

$$t_t = t_s - \frac{r}{c} - \tau_{ion} - \tau_{trop} - \tau_{sagnac} \qquad (16.3)$$

where τ_{ion} is the ionospheric delay, τ_{trop} is the tropospheric delay, and τ_{sagnac} is the delay caused by the earth rotation. r is defined by the following equation

$$r = r(t_t, t_s) \qquad (16.4)$$

Given the satellite position at the retransmitting time t_s, and the MCC position at the time t_t, the geometric range r is computed in the BJ-54 coordinate system according to (16.7). $t_s(k + 1)$ is the transmitting time calculated iteratively by $k + 1$ times. The initial value is $t_s = t$ and the iteration finishes when the formula (16.8) condition is satisfied.

$$r(t_t(k + 1), t_s) = \sqrt{\Delta X(k)^2 + \Delta Y(k)^2 + \Delta Z(k)^2} \qquad (16.5)$$

where $\Delta X(k)$, $\Delta Y(k)$, $\Delta Z(k)$ are the position coordinates component difference between the MCC and the satellite.

$$|r(t_s(k + 1)) - r(t_s(k))| < \varepsilon \qquad (16.6)$$

ε denotes the precision, and it is always equal to or less than 10e−10. Simulation shows that in the condition of $\varepsilon = 1e - 10$, the calculation will converge in 3–4 iterative times, and $t_s(k + 1)$ in $r(t_s(k + 1))$ is the signal transmitting time from MCC.

As is known that the time of the propagation error is related to the satellite position and transmitting time, recalculation of the delay is strictly necessary after the satellite position and the transmitting time updating. However, the satellites in BD-1 are GEOs, and they are almost still during the signal propagation. Also the

receiver's dynamic is always not high. So the delays of the ionosphere and troposphere are assumed to be invariable and calculated only one time during the
iterative process.

16.3.3 Ephemeris Parameter Calculation Model

As stated above, a BD-1 passive user needs accurate information about the positions of the BD-1 satellites in order to determine its position. And the ephemeris
error will be an error source. It is defined by the formula

$$\Delta\rho_k = \frac{x_s^k - x_u}{r_d^k}\delta x_s + \frac{y_s^k - y_u}{r_d^k}\delta y_s + \frac{z_s^k - z_u}{r_d^k}\delta z_s \tag{16.7}$$
$$= l_u^k\delta x_s^k + m_u^k\delta y_s^k + n_u^k\delta z_s^k$$

Assume that the satellite k's ephemeris mean square error (MSE) is $(\sigma_{xs}, \sigma_{ys}, \sigma_{zs})$
(for convenience, k is omitted), then the pseudorange MSE is given by

$$\sigma_{\rho_k} = \sqrt{\left(l_u^k\sigma_{x_s}\right)^2 + \left(m_u^k\sigma_{y_s}\right)^2 + \left(n_u^k\sigma_{z_s}\right)^2} \tag{16.8}$$

where $(\delta_{xs}, \delta_{ys}, \delta_{zs})$ is the satellite k's position error, $(\sigma_{xs}, \sigma_{ys}, \sigma_{zs})$ is the satellite k's
ephemeris MSE, $\Delta\rho$ is the pseudorange error induced by the ephemeris MSE, and σ_{ρ_k}
is the MSE of $\Delta\rho$. Generally, the 3–5 m position can cause a pseudorange measurement error at the level of approximately 2 m [5]. Therefore it is important to
model the practical ephemeris accurately.

In real conditions, due to the orbital perturbations, the position of a geosta-
tionary satellite is not perfectly fixed with respect to the observer on Earth. A small
periodic motion with a daily period occurs around a central position [6]. Through
the observation of 42 h, we got the ephemeris data of the BD-1 west satellite. The
observation started at 22:08, 5 January, 2011. Figure 16.2 shows the orbit and the
relative motion decompose respectively. From the figures we can see that
the satellite runs as sinusoids in three-dimensional with the 24-h cycle and the
fluctuating ranges are about 135181, 84183, and 501586 m, respectively.

Without releasing the precise ephemeris, one effective method to ensure the
authenticity of simulated ephemeris parameters is updating the outbound information per minute by using the discrete observation data, including satellite
position, satellite velocity. But the signal parameter generation rate Δt (at the level
of 1 ms) is much smaller than the broadcast updating period T.

So in order to get the high-precision ephemeris parameters data at random time
in the interval, math methods are necessary. In practice the interpolation and fitting
algorithms are used for approximating orbit. And the Chebyshev orthogonal
polynomial algorithm has the best performance among polynomial fitting algorithms, even at the two ends of the time interval [7].

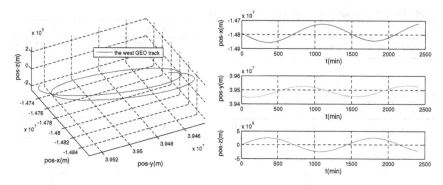

Fig. 16.2 Track and three-dimensional motion decompose of the GEO

For a detailed description of the Chebyshev polynomial fitting principle, refer to [7–9]. The Chebyshev polynomial fitting function is defined by the formula as follows when we transformed the time interval as $\tau \in [-1, 1]$.

$$f(t) = \sum_{i=0}^{n} C_i T_i(\tau) \tag{16.9}$$

where n is the order of Chebyshev polynomial, C_i is the fitting coefficient, $T_i(\tau)$ is the orthogonal polynomial, τ is the normalized fitting time. And the fitting precision denoted as σ_x, is evaluated by the formula

$$\sigma_x = \sqrt{\frac{\sum_{i=1}^{m} (x_i - f(\tau_i))}{m}} \tag{16.10}$$

At first, to get the compared standard data, the 1 min interval observation data is subdivided into two 2 min interval observation data, denoted as A and B. Then, A is used for orbit fitting to get the function $f(t)$. Another is developed as the standard. Finally, the fitting result is compared with B to evaluate the precision of fitting.

With 2 and 1 h observation data, X component of the satellite position is fitted with Chebyshev polynomial fitting at different orders. The fitting precision varying with orders is given in Tables 16.2 and 16.3, and the fitting errors at the order with the highest fitting precision are shown in Figs. 16.3 and 16.4.

From Table 16.2 and Fig. 16.3 for 2 h data length, the number of discrete data points used for fitting is 61, and the highest fitting precision is 0.519 m at the order 26, whereas 1 h data length with 31 discrete data points for fitting, the highest fitting precision is 0.438 m at the order 11, from Table 16.3 and Fig. 16.4.

So the results indicate that the fitting error is relevant to the fitting order and the sampling points. When the number of sampling points is constant, the fitting error decreases when the fitting order increases in the range, but the data fitting result

Table 16.2 Two hours fitting precision of different orders

Order	3	7–29	30–38	49 ∼
2 h data	300.0	0.5–0.9	1.3–789730.3	Morbidity

Table 16.3 One hour fitting precision of different orders

Order	2–3	4–22	23–31	32 ∼
1 h data	3.8–3.9	0.4–0.8	8.3–64087.1	Morbidity

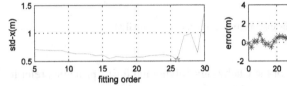 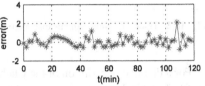

Fig. 16.3 Fitting precision of different orders and the fitting error at the highest precision (2 h)

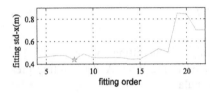 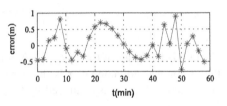

Fig. 16.4 Fitting precision of different orders and the fitting error at the highest precision (1 h)

will be poor dramatically, even cannot converge when the fitting order exceeds the range. Therefore, the fitting order and the sampling points should be selected appropriately to ensure the fitting precision.

Similarly, the satellite position Y component and Z component can also be fitted with Chebyshev polynomials. Assuming that the fitting error of satellite position is equal in the three directions, then $\sigma_{xs} = \sigma_{ys} = \sigma_{zs}$. Thus, it is obvious that the fitting precision in the fitting interval is about 0.43 m, which is two order-of-magnitude greater than BD-1's ephemeris precision. Therefore, the Chebyshev polynomial fitting algorithms is a simple and effective mean.

16.3.4 Signal Propagation Error Model

Besides ephemeris errors, the error sources related to position accuracy include the propagation error (e.g., ionosphere and troposphere delays errors) and the Sagnac effects.

From the perspective of the simulator, the propagation error models of the uplink and downlink are different due to BD-1's retransmission principle.

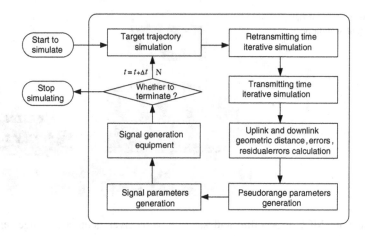

Fig. 16.5 Flow chart of simulating

The downlink troposphere and ionosphere delay can be corrected together with atmospheric correct parameters obtained from the outbound information [10]. While the uplink errors above should be corrected with classical models, for example, Hopfield model and Black model for tropospheric delay correction, Klobuchar model for ionospheric error correction. For the BD-1 conditions, the models above should be effectively accurate to about meter order or better.

Similarly, the relativistic effects are also pseudorange error sources. As known, the BD-1 atomic clocks are in MCC. Therefore, the relativistic effects related to satellite atomic clocks in satellite such as special, general and periodic relativity relativistic corrections are neglectable. And the discussion will focus on the Sagnac effect. However the residual Sagnac error is at the centimeter level, so it can be considered neglectable. For a detailed description of the correction method, refer to [11].

16.4 Simulation Model

After establishing the models in the previous chapters, Fig. 16.5 illustrates the simulation steps, where Δt with a level of 1 ms is the simulation step-size.

(1) Configure test scenes, start to simulate.
(2) Get the user position at the time t.
(3) Calculate the retransmitting time t_s based on the transmitting time iterative model, then get the satellite position at the time t_s.
(4) Calculate the transmitting time t_t based on the retransmitting time iterative model and t_s, then get the pseudorange corrections due to Sagnac.

Fig. 16.6 Picture of the
BD-1 signal simulator

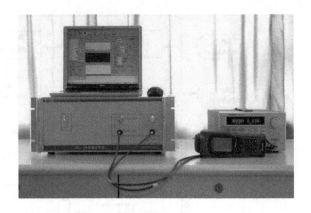

(5) Calculate MCC-to-satellite and satellite-to-receiver geometric range, errors, residual errors and other signal parameters, then get the total pseudorange delay.

(6) Generate the signal parameters at the time t.

(7) Send the signal parameters at the time t to the signal generation equipment, and let $t = t + \Delta t$, return to the step (2). If terminate, go to (8).

(8) Simulation terminates. Exits.

16.5 Implementation and Performance Analysis

Considering the passive location receiver test requirements, the simulator is designed and implemented, which is depended on the analysis of the key technology, such as the transmitting(retransmitting) time iterative model, the ephemeris parameter calculation model, the signal propagation error model, and so on. The BD-1 simulator's integrity performance is sufficient for test requirements (shown in Fig. 16.6).

- Pseudorange Accuracy: ± 0.003 m.
- Rate of Pseudorange Accuracy Change Rate: ± 0.0005 m/s.
- Channel Delay Stability: 0.5 ns RMS.

Because of the simulator's good performance, the impact on the positioning accuracy could be negligible. Therefore, ephemeris error is the primary factor that affects the accuracy. Table 16.4 presents the test data with the eligible passive receiver. In order to show more effective bits, the pseudoranges and the position component errors are shown in Table 16.4 with G1 and G3 minus the one of G2.

It is assumed that the receiver starts to determine its position when it has received the broadcast parameters, and the position of standard point is ($28°\ 13'\ 16.5''$, $112°\ 59'\ 21.9''$, 83.089). From Table 16.4, following points are made.

(1) Under the condition of no residual errors, the errors induced by ionospheres effects, troposphere delays, the system device processing value and the Sagnac

Table 16.4 The location result

Pseudorange and coordinate	No residual errors (m)	Residuals errors (m)
G2	0.00000	0.00000
G1	347269.83489	347275.659241
G3	−684843.17208	−684842.756252
X	−0.87375	−50.485
Y	0.247925	19.912
Z	0.90825	54.269

effects can be almost eliminate. And the error of point positioning is the same order-of-magnitude with ephemeris errors.

(2) The position accuracy is lower when the residual errors increase.
(3) It is important to establish the appropriate error correction models for enhancing the BD-1 position accuracy.

16.6 Conclusions

In this paper, the error models are proposed and analyzed based on the passive location process and test requirements. The discussion here focuses on the transmitting (retransmitting) time iterative model, the ephemeris parameter calculation model and the ways to improve model accuracy. Finally the implementation of the simulator is given, the level of accuracy of which is the same with ephemeris errors, about 0.4 m or better. Compared with the existing functional simulator, the BD-1 simulator has simulation function, which can simulate the signal arriving at the receiver's antenna phase center and provide a simulation platform to assess the impact of the errors on positioning. The test results indicate that the simulator design completely meet the test requirements.

References

1. Zhang GH, Sun CY (2005) Simulation and implementation of BD-1 dynamic navigation signals. J Syst Simul 17(11):2731–2733 (in Chinese)
2. Li LQ, Zhi L, Qi XY, Quan BZ (2006) Modeling and simulation in RDSS system. J Syst Simul 18(5):1199–1203
3. Briskman RD (1990) Radio determination satellite service. Proc IEEE 78(7):1096–1105
4. Lv ZC (2006) The research of the high dynamic satellite signal simulator's software. National University of Defense Technology, Changsha (in Chinese)
5. Xie G (2009) Principles of GPS and receiver design. Publishing House of Electronics Industry, Beijing (in Chinese)
6. Bauch A, Piester D, Fujieda M, Lewandowski W (2011) Directive for operational use and data handling in two-way satellite time and frequency transfer (TWSTFT), Bureau International des Poids et Mesures, Rapport BIPM-2011/01

7. Hu H, Yuan C, Fang L (2009) Extrapolation and fitting algorithms for GLONASS satellite orbit. IEEE Proc IITA. doi:10.1109/IITA.2009.484

8. Li QY, Wang NC, Yi DY (2006) Numerical analysis. HuaZhong University of Science & Technology Press, Beijing (in Chinese)

9. Lee WJ, Ronald DR (1982) Numerical analysis. Addison-Wesley Publishing Company, Reading

10. Hua Y, Hu YH (2007) The research of combined time service receiver base on the Beidou and Glonass. In: Proceedings of national time and frequency conference, pp 401–403 (in Chinese)

11. Kaplan ED, Hegarty C (2006) Understanding GPS: principle and application, 2nd edn. Artech House, Inc, Boston

Chapter 17
A Hybrid Approach of Fault Inference and Fault Identification for Aircraft Fault Diagnosis

Xianhui Liu and Zhijuan Liu

Abstract Logical inference based on a cockpit instruments fault tree (FT) sometimes cannot give a correct diagnosis of failures. In addition, in flight control systems (FCS), a fault identification method based on the multiple-model (MM) estimator cannot find the basic fault cause. To deal with these problems, a hybrid approach which is capable of integrating inference and fault identification is proposed. In this approach, the event nodes of the FT which have correlations to the FCS are separated into modules. Each module corresponds to a fault mode. To use these correlations, the inference and MM method can share fault information. Simulation results show that the proposed diagnosis approach is helpful in detecting the root cause of failure and is more correct than single fault inference method.

Keywords Hybrid · Fault diagnosis · Cockpit instrumentation · Logical inference · Multiple-model

17.1 Introduction

The cockpit instrumentation system plays an important role in human operation because it provides information with which the pilots operate the aircraft [1]. Therefore, an accurate fault diagnosis method in cockpit instrumentation systems

X. Liu (✉)
CAD Research Center, Tongji University, 200092 Shanghai, China
e-mail: liu_xian_hui@163.com

Z. Liu (✉)
Department of Automation, Tsinghua University, 100084 Beijing, China
e-mail: liuzhijuan6512@163.com

W. Lu et al. (eds.), *Proceedings of the 2012 International Conference on Information Technology and Software Engineering*, Lecture Notes in Electrical Engineering 211, DOI: 10.1007/978-3-642-34522-7_17, © Springer-Verlag Berlin Heidelberg 2013

is necessity for modern aircrafts. The fault tree (FT) [2] and intelligence inference [3] method are always used in cockpit instrumentation systems. Inferences based on FT sometimes cannot determine the faults. For instance, when the logical gate between the upper and lower nodes is "OR" in the FT, there is the possibility that the events in the lower node may all happen or the possibility that only one will happens if the event in the upper node happens. To ensure more correct diagnosis results, one has to use other information such as of the flight control system (FCS) fault information.

In this paper, a hybrid fault diagnosis method is proposed which integrates cockpit instruments FT inference with the multiple-model (MM) [4] diagnosis method in FCS. MM method employs a bank of Kalman filters, each based on a failure model. A general aviation aircraft cockpit instrumentation system is given in NASA report [5, 6]. The MM method and the logical inference run simultaneously. The MM estimator can obtain the fault mode of FCS while the fault tree can obtain fault events. The fault modes of the MM estimator may have corresponding events in the cockpit instruments fault tree. Therefore, they can contact each other based on these event nodes and share fault information with each other.

17.2 Hybrid Fault Diagnosis Scheme

17.2.1 Framework of the Diagnosis Scheme

In this paper, aircraft fault diagnosis focuses on the cockpit instrumentation system and FCS. In the cockpit instrumentation system, the fault diagnosis method is based on FT; however, it is based on MM estimator in FCS. The framework of the proposed fault diagnosis scheme is shown in Fig. 17.1.

In Fig. 17.1, the diagnosis method used in the cockpit instruments is "top to bottom" inference based on the FT. And the MM fault diagnosis method is used in FCS. The MM method employs a series of parallel filters, each based on a model representing a particular fault mode. For instance, suppose the actual system at any time can be modeled as:

$$
\begin{aligned}
x(k+1) &= F(k)x(k) + G(k)u(k) + w(k) \\
y(k) &= H_i(k)x(k) + v(k)
\end{aligned}
\tag{17.1}
$$

where $\mathbf{x}$ is the state vector, $\mathbf{y}$ is the measurement vector, $\mathbf{F}$, $\mathbf{G}$, and $\mathbf{H}$ are coefficient matrices, $\mathbf{w}$ is the system noise and $\mathbf{v}$ is the measurement noise.

Fault modes can be described by multiple models. They can be written as:

$$
\begin{aligned}
x(k+1) &= F_i(k)x(k) + G_i(k)u(k) + w_i(k) \\
y(k) &= H_i(k)x(k) + v_i(k)
\end{aligned}
\tag{17.2}
$$

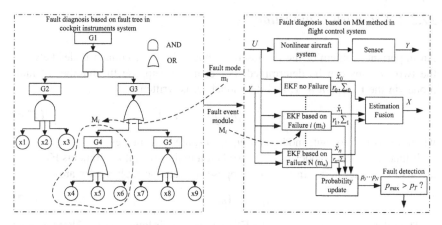

Fig. 17.1 Framework of the hybrid fault diagnosis scheme

where i represents fault mode i.

The model sequence can be described as a Markov chain. Fault occurrences can be described by the transitions among these models. Under the Gaussian assumption, the probabilities of these models are calculated as $p_0,\ldots,p_n$. The model with the highest probability is the one closest to the actual fault mode. The details of the MM method are not discussed in this paper.

In the proposed scheme, the two diagnosis systems run simultaneously and provide each other with fault information. They make contact with each other via event nodes of the fault tree. In order to combine the FT and the FCS fault information, the failure rates should be modified. If the event node Gi is a contact node corresponding to fault mode m_i, the failure rate can be written as:

$$h_i^*(t) = \begin{cases} 0 & p_i(t) \neq \max_j\{p_j(t)\} \\ 1 & p_i(t) = \max_j\{p_j(t)\} \end{cases} \tag{17.3}$$

where $h_i^*(t)$ is the modified failure rate of Gi at time t, and $p_i(t)$ is the probability of fault mode i determined by the MM method.

If the event node Gi is not a contact node, the failure rate keeps invariant:

$$h_i^*(t) = h_i(t) \tag{17.4}$$

Using the modified failure rates $h_i^*(t)$ as transition probabilities, the fault inference can be carried out. For instance, when the event G3 happens and the lower logical gate is "OR", the next inference step is made as follows.

$$\begin{cases} h_{G4}^* > h_{G5}^* & \text{event } G4 \text{ occurs} \\ h_{G4}^* < h_{G5}^* & \text{event } G5 \text{ occurs} \end{cases} \tag{17.5}$$

17.2.2 Establish Connections

An important problem of the proposed method is how the contact nodes between the two systems can be determined. For example, suppose the number of fault modes in the FCS is $n + 1$, and the model set is written as:

$$M_{FCS} = \{m_0, m_1, \ldots, m_n\} \tag{17.6}$$

where m_0 is the no-fault mode, and $m_1, \ldots, m_n$ are fault modes.

If there are r fault modes having correlation to the cockpit instruments FT, there are also r contact nodes in the FT. Suppose the relative fault modes are:

$$M_{FCS}^* = \{m_1, \ldots, m_r\} \tag{17.7}$$

The relative contact nodes in the FT may have their lower nodes. These contact nodes and their lower nodes all have correlations to the FCS. For example, nodes $\{G4, x4, x5, x6\}$ have relations to fault mode m_i. They can be divided into modules and separated from other nodes of the FT. According to this modular method, the FT can be divided into modules. The event nodes besides these relative nodes are included in a big module M_0. Then the FT is divided into $r + 1$ modules.

$$M_{FT} = \{M_0, M_1, \ldots, M_r\} \tag{17.8}$$

The correlations between modules of the FT and the fault modes can be defined as mapping.

$$\begin{aligned} FCS : M_{FCS}^* &= \{m_1, \ldots, m_r\} \quad i = 1, 2, \ldots r \\ FT : M_{FT}^* &= \{M_1, \ldots, M_r\} \end{aligned} \tag{17.9}$$

$$f : M_{FT}^* \to M_{FCS}^* \tag{17.10}$$

where f describes the mapping relationship between the subsets M_{FT}^* and M_{FCS}^*.

17.3 Cockpit Instruments Fault Tree and Inference

In the general aviation cockpit, there are six information categories. Each information categories has its sub-trees which are described in report [5, 6]. Take the sub-tree of "Loss of Airspeed Information" as an example which is shown in Fig. 17.2 [5].

The event "Loss of Pitot Static System" is a contact node which has relations to FCS fault modes. When the inference meets the contact node, it can use the modified failure rate which uses the fault information from FCS. Besides, the inference also can use nodes relations among the whole cockpit instruments fault

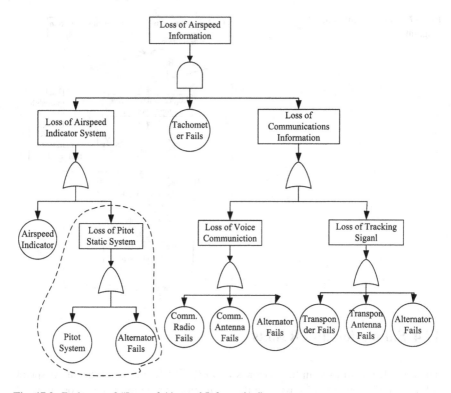

Fig. 17.2 Fault tree of "Loss of Airspeed Information"

Table 17.1 Related events of "Alternator Fails"

The related events
Loss of advisory panel information
Loss of altitude information
Loss of navigation information
Loss of communications information

tree. For instance, the event "Alternator Fails" is a minimal cut set of the events in Table 17.1 which are other sub-tree top events in the cockpit instruments system.

When there is an information error in the cockpit instruments, the "top to bottom" inference method is used to find the basic events. The fault inference process can be summarized as Fig. 17.3.

Fig. 17.3 Logical inference diagram

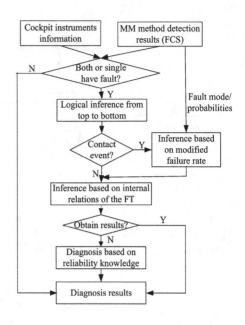

17.4 Simulation and Results

The aircraft model used in this paper is F16 [7]. The failure of "Loss of Airspeed Information" is mainly discussed in the simulation. Three fault scenarios are used to test and verify the proposed hybrid approach.

Scenario 1: The cockpit instrumentation system loses the airspeed information and the FCS does not detect airspeed fault. The diagnosis result is shown in Fig. 17.4. It can be detected that the basic events are airspeed indicator and radio failure. The red nodes are the failure influence path. The Pitot static system is normal because the FCS do not detect airspeed fault.

Scenario 2: The cockpit instrumentation system loses the airspeed information and the FCS detects airspeed fault. In addition, at least one event in Table 17.1 has not occurred. The diagnosis result is own in Fig. 17.5.

Comparing Figs. 17.4 with 17.5, one can see that when FCS detects airspeed fault, the basic failure component is Pitot system, that because the Pitot system failure will affect FCS while the airspeed indicator has no correlation to FCS. Furthermore, the events in Table 17.1 do not occur which illustrate that the alternator is normal. Therefore, the root failure causes are Pitot failure and radio failure.

Scenario 3: The cockpit instrumentation system loses the airspeed information and the FCS detects airspeed fault. All of the events in Table 17.1 occur. In this scenario, it cannot determine whether Pitot has failed or the alternator failed. The reliability method is used. The diagnosis result is shown in Fig. 17.6, which is in accordance with the logical inference result.

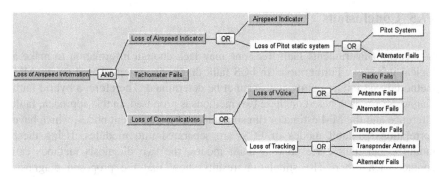

Fig. 17.4 Fault diagnosis result for scenario 1

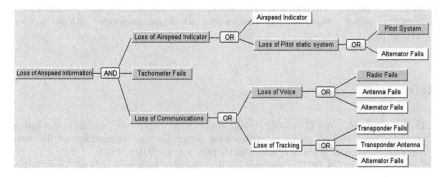

Fig. 17.5 Fault diagnosis result for scenario 2

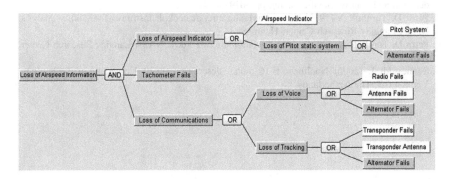

Fig. 17.6 Fault diagnosis result for scenario 3

17.5 Conclusions

In a cockpit instruments fault tree, one may lack enough information to make a logical inference. Furthermore, in FCS fault diagnosis systems based on the MM method, basic failure components cannot be determined. Therefore, a hybrid fault diagnosis approach based on these two methods is proposed. In this approach, fault inference and the MM estimator run simultaneously. The event nodes, which have correlations to fault modes of FCS, are separated into modules. Using these modules and their corresponding fault modes, the two diagnosis methods can contact each other. The simulation results show that the proposed diagnosis approach makes the fault inference more exact and can find the root causes of failures.

Acknowledgments This paper was supported by the Shanghai Municipal Science &Technology Commission's project "The study and application of civil aircraft integrated product design collaborative system based on the configurable 3D digital prototype" [Grant number 11dz1120702].

References

1. Li WC, Chen HC, Wu FE (2000) Human errors in the cockpit and accidents prevention strategies from cockpit resources management perspective. In: Proceedings of the 19th conference on digital avionics system, Philadelphia, PA, pp 5D1/1-5D1/7
2. Lapp SA, Powers GA (1977) Computer-aided synthesis of fault trees. J IEEE Trans Reliab 26(1):2–13
3. Yao YH, Lin GYP, Amy JC (2006) Using knowledge-based intelligent reasoning to support dynamic equipment diagnosis and maintenance. Int J Enterp Inf Syst 2(1):17–29
4. Rupp D, Ducard G, Shafai E, Geering HP (2005) Extended multiple model adaptive estimation for the detection of sensor and actuator faults. In: Proceedings of the 44th IEEE conference on decision and control, Seville, Spain, pp 3079–3084
5. Pettit D, Turnbull A (1997) General aviation aircraft cockpit instrument reliability analysis. NASA Langley Research Center, Hampton
6. Pettit D, Turnbull A (2001) General aviation aircraft study. NASA Langley Research Center, Hampton
7. Sonneveldt L (2006) Nonlinear F-16 model description, Delft University of Technology, Version 0.3, The Netherlands

Chapter 18
Division of Beijing Road Based on the Driving Pattern

Jingjing Chi, Jian Huang, Bowen Du and Zepeng Mao

Abstract Congestion is the main feature of traffic in megacities, which has led to severe problems for energy and the environment. At the same time, moving vehicles as the traffic participants can real-time feedback fundamental traffic parameter information such as the interval velocity, average energy consumption and so on. This paper does research on the division of Beijing road which is the basis to calculate the link energy consumption of Beijing. The paper firstly defined the driving pattern and put forward a clustering model of Beijing road link based on the vehicle-specific power (VSP) distribution. Then, by associating the clustering result and other link attributes, a link-based driving pattern classifier is established. At the end of the paper, some experiments are taken to verify that this method made a great classification accuracy of 86 %.

Keywords Driving pattern · Division of road link · Energy consumption

J. Chi (✉) · J. Huang · B. Du · Z. Mao
State Key Laboratory of Software Development Environment, Beihang University, Beijing, China
e-mail: chijingjing@nlsde.buaa.edu.cn

J. Huang
e-mail: huangjian@buaa.edu.cn

B. Du
e-mail: du_bowen@nlsde.buaa.edu.cn

Z. Mao
e-mail: maozepeng@nlsde.buaa.edu.cn

W. Lu et al. (eds.), *Proceedings of the 2012 International Conference on Information Technology and Software Engineering*, Lecture Notes in Electrical Engineering 211, DOI: 10.1007/978-3-642-34522-7_18, © Springer-Verlag Berlin Heidelberg 2013

18.1 Introduction

With increasing public attention to the energy consumption and pollution of the vehicles, lots of calculation model of vehicle energy consumption has been brought up by scholars at home and abroad. Such as the international vehicle emissions model (IVE) [1] and the comprehensive modal emissions model (CMEM) [2] taken up by the University of California, the Moves [3] model taken up by U.S. Environmental Protection Agency. However, the existed vehicle energy consumption's calculation model requires accurate input of vehicle speed and acceleration. Considering the communications technology, privacy protection and the operating costs, it's difficult to achieve large-scale real-time driving data of vehicles, and therefore can't directly apply the existing vehicle model to road energy consumption model.

In order to calculate the energy consumption based on road link, firstly take out the driving pattern of vehicle at all of the road link based on the road condition, including the road grade, road width, traffic flow and so on, then calculate the energy consumption when the vehicle driving by the road link based on the relating parameters of vehicle. Response to this demand, this paper based on the driving data of vehicle, analyzed the driving characteristics of vehicles at different types of roads, and clustered the roads through its driving pattern, then established a classifier which decides the vehicle-specific power (VSP) distribution of road link by its attribution. All above provide technical reserves for the further calculation of energy consumption.

18.2 Related Work

The concept of VSP is a concept used in the evaluation of vehicle emissions. The idea was at first developed by Jiménez at the Massachusetts Institute of Technology [4–6]. Informally, it is the sum of the loads resulting from aerodynamic drag, acceleration, rolling resistance, and hill climbing, all divided by the mass of the vehicle. Conventionally, it is reported in kilowatts per ton, the instantaneous power demand of the vehicle divided by its mass. VSP, combined with dynamometer and remote-sensing measurements, can be used to determine vehicle emissions. VSP can be represented by several mathematical formula. Haibo Zhai of North Carolina State University provides the following formula:

$$\text{VSP} = v * [1.1a + 9.81(\text{atan}(\sin(\text{grade}))) + 0.132] + 0.000302v^3 \qquad (18.1)$$

where: v indicates the vehicle speed (m/s); a indicates the vehicle acceleration (m/s^2).

Table 18.1 Cutpoints used in PRM index calculations

Speed cutpoints (m/s)		Power cutpoints (kW/ton)		Speed divider (s/m)
Min	Max	Min	Max	
0.0	5.4	−20	400	3
5.4	8.5	−20	16	5
5.4	8.5	16	400	3
8.5	12.5	−20	16	7
8.5	12.5	16	400	5
12.5	50	−20	16	13
12.5	50	16	400	5

18.2.1 Engine Stress

Engine Stress (ES) describes the engine operating state, calculated through the VSP over the past seconds and implied engine PRM [4] (Eq. 18.2; Table 18.1).

$$ES = \text{PRM-Index} + (0.08 \text{ ton/kW}) * \text{Pre-average-Power}$$
$$\text{Pre-average-Power} = \text{Average}(VSP_{t=-5 \text{ to } -25s})$$
$$\text{PRM-Index} = \text{Velocity}_{t=0}/\text{Speed-Divider} \tag{18.2}$$

where: PRM-Index indicates the speed index of the engine, Speed-Divider indicates the speed factor, it varies at different speed-VSP intervals (see Table 18.1), Pre-average-Power indicated the current average engine power.

In general, the low engine stress indicates low acceleration in the last 20 s while high engine stress indicates high speed and acceleration of the vehicle.

18.2.2 Driving Pattern

Taking the road link as a basic unit, VSP and Engine Stress are applied to define the driving pattern.

To consist with IVE model, the VSP is divided into 20 intervals, and the engine stress is divided into three intervals: (−1.6, 3.1), (3.1, 7.8), (7.8, 12.6). So a total of 60 VSP/stress categories are used, and each driving pattern is represented by a distribution of VSP/engine stress categories. Table 18.2 shows the demarcation of VSP bins in low-stress mode. Bin 1–11 corresponds to the driving condition of deceleration or going down an incline, Bin 12 corresponds to idling, while Bin 13 and above correspond to driving under a constant speed, acceleration, or, going up an incline.

Finally, driving pattern is defined as the ration of the 60 interval divided by

$$\text{VSP and ES:DP} = \{Per1, Per2, \dots, Per60\} \tag{18.3}$$

Table 18.2 VSP bins and stress modes

Low stress (−1.6 to 3.1)							
Bin	0	1	2	3	4	5	6
VSP cut point	−80	−44	−39.9	−35.8	−31.7	−27.6	−23.4
Bin	7	8	9	10	11	12	13
VSP cut point	−19.3	−15.2	−11.1	−7.0	−2.9	1.2	5.3
Bin	14	15	16	17	18	19	
VSP cut point	9.4	13.6	17.7	21.8	25.9	30	

where: Per1 indicates the ratio of bin 0 at the specific road link. Per2 indicates the ratio of bin 1 at the specific road link.

18.3 Methods

This section introduces the following three parts of work. The first one is to calculate the driving patterns at road link by analyzing the driving data collected in few days; the second one is to clustering the road link based on the similarity of the driving pattern at different road link; the third part of work is to construct the link-based classifier that will be used to determine which kind of driving pattern a vehicle on a specific link behaves in.

18.3.1 Calculate the Driving pattern

In this part, through the following three procedures, obtain the driving pattern of road links at which high-accurate driving data had been collected by GPS devices.

(1) Map Matching: Because of the positioning failure of GPS, the driving data contain some abnormal values. All of the data beyond the normal speed range or the geography scope are filtered out from the database. Besides, since the positioning offset of GPS, many driving records do not fall on the road, but the record trajectory's direction remains almost correct. Map matching means to find the nearest link on which the particular vehicle is driving and ensure that the vehicle is driving on the coherent direction. The input of the map matching program is the original data which is collected by GPS devices, including fields like time, longitude, latitude, speed, accelerate and so on. While the output of the program is the data which is organized as the following format: (road link ID, speed, accelerate).

(2) Calculate the VSP and ES: Based on the driving records collected (including speed, acceleration per second and position information), using Eqs. (18.1) and (18.2), calculate the value of VSP and ES per second of the road link which the vehicle drive at.

Fig. 18.1 Structure of
clustering feature tree

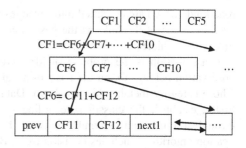

(3) Obtain the driving pattern: As mentioned above, this paper used the Eq. (18.3)
to calculate the link-based driving pattern based on the division of VSP-ES
distribution.

18.3.2 Driving Patterns Cluster

All of the driving data are split into groups according to the link they matched to.
Clustering is the task of assigning a set of objects into groups (called clusters) so
that the objects in the same cluster are more similar to each other than to those in
other clusters. Typical cluster algorithms includes hierarchical clustering, centroid-
based clustering, distribution-based clustering and density-based clustering.

This paper combines the hierarchical clustering and centroid-based clustering,
uses the leaf nodes of the clustering feature tree as the input of the centroid-based
clustering, classify the road links into several typical driving patterns. The total
structure of clustering feature tree is showed in Fig. 18.1. The leaf nodes represent
the cluster consisted of the similar driving pattern, the cluster diameter is defined
as the average distance between the driving pattern in the same cluster, the distance between clusters is defined as the average distance of the driving pattern in
the two clusters.

18.3.3 Link-Based Classifier

Since it should take high cost to acquire driving data of vehicle, it's difficult to
achieve the goal of vehicle tests on all the road links. This paper took advantage of
the limited driving data which have been collected, calculated the driving pattern
of the road link which vehicle had tested on, and then speculated the VSP-ES
distribution on the remaining road which is the foundation of energy consumption
calculation. Link attributes, including road construction, road surface quality,
intersection density and traffic condition, will influence the driving pattern of
vehicles. To some extent, the more attributes a training dataset has, the more
accurate the classifier will be. But many attributes of the links are too difficult to
acquire. Therefore, this paper took the available road link attributes (including

road kinds which are classified into seven levels, length, width, fee (toll states) and average speed of the link) as the basis, decided the driving pattern of each road link when vehicles go through.

Classification is the problem of identifying which a set of categories a new observation belongs to, on the basis of a training set of data containing instances whose category membership is known. Data classification is a two-step process, firstly, establish the classifier according to the classify rule which is obtained through training data. Secondly, classify the unknown instances. Typical classification algorithms includes decision trees, Bayesian and Rule-based algorithm.

In this paper, the classification take results of clustering as training data, link attributes as condition attributes, link categories as decision attribute, use PART algorithm to construct link-based classifier so that determine the link attribute to link category mapping. Therefore road links are classified on the basis of link attribute, and moreover, obtain the driving pattern of the road link.

The PART algorithm builds a partial C4.5 decision tree in its each iteration and makes the best leaf into a rule to constitute the final decision list. And C4.5, developed by Quinlan in 1993, is well known for its simplicity and accuracy. It use the concept of information entropy. At each node of the tree, C4.5 chooses one attribute of the data that most effectively splits its set of samples into subsets enriched in one class or the other. Its criterion is the normalized information gain that results from choosing an attribute for splitting the data. The attribute with the highest normalized information gain is chosen to make the decision.

18.4 Experiment Result

18.4.1 Calculation

In this part, firstly second by second driving data (including location information, speed, acceleration) is acquired by about 240 h test. Through data cleaning, road matching and driving pattern calculation, this paper obtained driving pattern of 3655 road links. Then, this paper cluster the 3655 link-based driving patterns into six categories. Taking the center data (VSP-ES distribution) of each cluster as the delegates of the driving pattern of the road links in its cluster so that six typical driving pattern have obtained to describe the driving pattern of the whole road link in Beijing, see in Fig. 18.2. In the first driving pattern, slowly and idle running state accounted for 70 % proportions, indicates slowly driving state under traffic jam condition. In the second and third pattern, the proportion of slow driving state is reduced, represents a relatively higher running speed and acceleration. In the fourth and fifth driving pattern low speed rate is reduced more, deceleration and acceleration ratio increased, representing a moderate speed, and the running speed is more volatile. While the coverage of the six driving pattern has been extended to the middle ES area, moreover, the proportion of high-speed and low-speed has significantly increased, representing the high-speed state of vehicle.

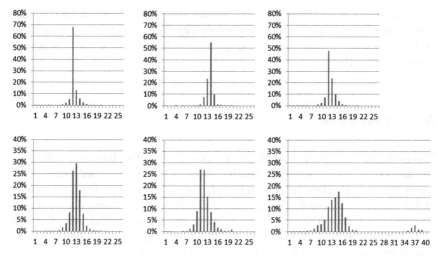

Fig. 18.2 Six typical driving patterns

Table 18.3 Training data of classifier

Link kind	Width	Toll states	Height	Average speed	Class of driving pattern
Express way	130	Free part in toll road	0.09	13.85	3
Country way	55	Toll	0.126	7.26	2
Urban freeway	55	Free part in toll road	0.798	16.53	4
...	...	...	...	...	...

Fig. 18.3 Spatial
distribution of road link class

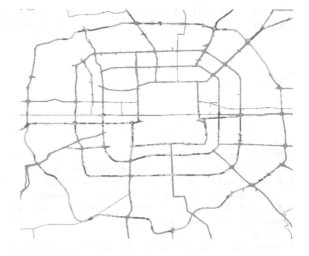

Secondly, based on the results of clustering, this paper organized the data into form shown in Table 18.3 as the classifier training data, predict the driving pattern of the unknown road link. Finally, the spatial distribution of road link category is showed in Fig. 18.3.

18.4.2 Evaluation

This paper mainly tests the classification accuracy of the link-based classifier with the method of cross-validation, specific procedures are described below. The training data of the classifier were randomly divided into ten portions, select nine of the portions as the training data set of the classifier, the remaining one as the test data set, and then test the classifier accuracy; the above process was taken ten times, and the average value of the results is taken as the classifier accuracy. Finally the paper gets the result of 86 % classification accuracy.

18.5 Conclusions

In this paper, driving patterns were at first quantified (60 VSP-ES interval distribution), and then the paper design and implement a clustering algorithm based on the driving pattern and a link-based classifier. At the end of the paper, cross-validation was used to rectify the accuracy of the classification.

Acknowledgments This research was supported by Megalopolis Advanced Transportation Operate Coordinate Command Platform Program (No. 2010ZX01045-001-009-1).

References

1. Davis N, Lents J, Osses M (2005) Development and application of an international vehicle emissions model. In: 81st annual meeting of the transportation research board, Washington, DC
2. Barth M, An F, Younglove T (2000) Comprehensive modal emissions model(CMEM), version 2.0, User's guide. University of California, Riverside
3. Koupal J, Michaels H, Cumberworth M et al (2002) EPA's plan for MOVES: a comprehensive mobile source emissions model. US EPA documentation
4. Jiménez-Palacios JL (1999) Understanding and quantifying moto vehicle emissions and vehicle specific power and TILDAS remote sensing. Ph.D thesis, Massachusetts Institute of Technology , Massachusetts
5. International Sustainable Systems Research Center, Characterizing emission variations due to driving behavior from onroad vehicles. http://www.issrc.org/ive/
6. Zhang T, Ramakrishnan R, Livny M (1996) BIRCH: an efficient data clustering method for very large databases. SIGMOD, pp 103–114

Chapter 19
The Influence of Turbulence Scintillation on The BER of THz Wireless Communication

Lianwei Bao, Hengkai Zhao, Guoxin Zheng and Weiwei Zhao

Abstract Atmospheric turbulence causes random fluctuation of terahertz beam, therefore results in bit error for data transmission. This paper studies the influence of turbulence scintillation on the Bit-Error-Rate (BER) of THz wireless communication system, gives the relationship between effective transmission distance and frequency under different BER performance. Research shows that the BER of spherical wave is less than that of plane wave in the same conditions; frequency and transmission distance causes important influence on the perfomance of BER; the effective transmission distance decreases along with frequency increasing in the case of a certain BER, and the effective transmission distance of spherical wave is longer than the effective transmission distance of plane wave under the same conditions.

Keywords THz · Turbulence · Scintillation · BER · Structure constant

19.1 Introduction

Free space THz wireless transmission technology is a means of communication which employs the terahertz beam as an information carrier in the atmospheric channel. The influence of the atmosphere on the propagation of THz waves is an essential area of research for the emerging field of THz telecommunications. There are two main factors which affect the quality of atmospheric channel, that is

L. Bao · H. Zhao (✉) · G. Zheng · W. Zhao
Key Laboratory of Specialty Fiber Optics and Optical Access Networks,
School of Communication and Information Engineering,
Shanghai University, Shanghai 200072, China
e-mail: hkzhao@staff.shu.edu.cn

W. Lu et al. (eds.), *Proceedings of the 2012 International Conference on Information Technology and Software Engineering*, Lecture Notes in Electrical Engineering 211, DOI: 10.1007/978-3-642-34522-7_19, © Springer-Verlag Berlin Heidelberg 2013

atmospheric extinction and atmospheric turbulence. So far, several literatures have done some study about the effect of atmospheric extinction. It is still a lack of study for THz band even though there have been some literatures discussed the effect of atmospheric turbulence in optical band [1]. The atmospheric turbulence would cause random fluctuation of the refractive index commonly. It will led to the strength random fluctuation and the phase random fluctuation of the received beam in time and space, that is scintillation of atmospheric turbulence [2]. The effect of scintillation is equivalent to superimposing the atmospheric turbulence noise on the basis of the original signal. It will lead to the ratio of signal to noise on receiver becoming lower and cause the bit error rate increasing [3], which will affect the stability and reliability of THz wireless communication seriously. Therefore, it is necessary to study the relationship between the system bit error rate and the scintillation of the terahertz wave caused by atmospheric turbulence.

19.2 Basic Theory

In 2001, ITU-R formally adopted the optical wave band atmospheric refractive index structure constant model [4], that is

$$
\begin{aligned}
C_n^2 = {} & 8.148 \times 10^{-56} v_{rms}^2 h^{10} \exp(-h/1000) \\
& + 2.7 \times 10^{-16} \exp(-h/1500) + C_0 \exp(-h/100)
\end{aligned}
\tag{19.1}
$$

where h is the height from the ground, $C_0 = 1.7 \times 10^{-14}\,\mathrm{m}^{-2/3}$ is the nominal value of C_n^2 at the ground, v_{rms} is the root-mean-square wind velocity along the vertical path and given by $v_{rms} = \sqrt{v_g^2 + 30.69 v_g + 348.91}\,(\mathrm{m/s})$, where v_g is the near-surface wind speed. v_g can be taken as approximate when the wind velocity of near-surface is unknown. Then we can get $v_{rms} = 21\,\mathrm{m/s}$.

The relationship between the atmospheric refractive index structure constant of optical wave and temperature structure constant is given by [2]

$$
C_n^2 = \left(\frac{79p}{T^2} \times 10^{-6}\right)^2 C_T^2
\tag{19.2}
$$

where C_T^2 is temperature structure constant, p is atmospheric pressure in mbar, T is temperature in degrees Kelvin.

However, the influence on the refractive index structure constant from humidity and temperature is significant, so the atmospheric refractive index structure constant can be approximated by the following formula [5]

$$
C_{n,T,Q}^2 = A_T^2 \frac{C_T^2}{\langle T \rangle^2} + A_Q^2 \frac{C_Q^2}{\langle Q \rangle^2} + 2A_T A_Q \frac{C_{TQ}}{\langle T \rangle \langle Q \rangle}
\tag{19.3}
$$

where C_Q^2 is humidity structure constant, C_{TQ} is the joint structure constant of temperature and humidity, Q is the concentration of water vapor in molecules$/\text{cm}^3$, $\langle T \rangle \approx T$, A_T and A_Q are the coefficients relate to atmospheric environment.

In the atmospheric surface layer, $\frac{C_T^2}{\langle T \rangle^2}$, $\frac{C_Q^2}{\langle Q \rangle^2}$ and $\frac{C_{TQ}}{\langle T \rangle \langle Q \rangle}$ meet the following relationship approximately [6]

$$\frac{C_Q^2}{\langle Q \rangle^2} = 10^4 \frac{C_T^2}{\langle T \rangle^2}, \quad \frac{C_{TQ}}{\langle T \rangle \langle Q \rangle} = \pm \left(\frac{C_Q^2}{\langle Q \rangle^2} \frac{C_T^2}{\langle T \rangle^2} \right)^{1/2} \tag{19.4}$$

The positive sign is usually found during the day and the negative sign during the night, due to change in the direction of the temperature gradient near the ground.

Atmospheric turbulence will causes the logarithmic amplitude fluctuation and phase fluctuation of terahertz beam when transmitting in the atmosphere channel. According to the Rytov theory [7, 8], the expression of logarithmic amplitude fluctuation is

$$\chi = \ln \left(\frac{A(r)}{A_0(r)} \right) \tag{19.5}$$

where $A_0(r)$ is the average amplitude of received signal on the receiving end, $A(r)$ is the amplitude of received signal on the receiving end.

For digital communication systems, when the receiver receives the signal, the BER of the wireless communications system is given by [9]

$$BER = \frac{1}{2} erfc \left(\frac{Q}{\sqrt{2}} \right) \tag{19.6}$$

where $erfc()$ is complementary error function, $Q = \frac{I_1 - I_0}{i_1 - i_0}$, I_1 and I_0 are the average light intensity corresponding to bits 1 and 0, i_1 and i_0 are the root mean square of light intensity caused by noise corresponding to bits 1 and 0 respectively.

In the case of zero-inner-scale model, according to the modified Rytov method, the scintillation indexes of plane wave and spherical wave are given by [8, 10]

$$\sigma_{I,p}^2 = \exp \left[\frac{0.54\sigma_{I,p}^2}{\left(1 + 1.22\sigma_{I,p}^{12/5} \right)^{7/6}} + \frac{0.509\sigma_{I,p}^2}{\left(1 + 0.69\sigma_{I,p}^{12/5} \right)^{5/6}} \right] - 1 \quad \left(0 \leq \sigma_{I,p}^2 < \infty \right) \tag{19.7}$$

$$\sigma_{I,s}^2 = \exp \left[\frac{0.17\sigma_{I,s}^2}{\left(1 + 0.167\sigma_{I,s}^{12/5} \right)^{7/6}} + \frac{0.225\sigma_{I,s}^2}{\left(1 + 0.259\sigma_{I,s}^{12/5} \right)^{7/6}} \right] - 1 \quad \left(0 \leq \sigma_{I,s}^2 < \infty \right) \tag{19.8}$$

where $\sigma_{l,p}^2 = 1.23C_n^2k^{7/6}L^{11/6}$, $\sigma_{l,s}^2 = 0.5C_n^2k^{7/6}L^{11/6}$, $k = \frac{2\pi f}{c}$ is wave number, and L is the propagation path length between transmitter and receiver.

19.3 The Impact of Atmospheric Turbulence on the THz Wireless Communication

For terahertz band, we can get an expression of near-ground atmospheric refractive index structure constant for THz band, that is

$$C_{n,THz}^2 = \frac{C_T^2}{\langle T \rangle^2}\left(A_T^2 + 10^4A_Q^2 \pm 2 \times 10^2A_TA_Q\right) \qquad (19.9)$$

Here, we only consider the noise caused by atmospheric turbulence, then the expression of logarithmic amplitude can be rewritten as

$$\chi = \ln(1 + \varepsilon) \qquad (19.10)$$

where $\varepsilon = \frac{A_i(r)}{A_0(r)}$ is the amplitude ratio of the noise and the original signal, $A_i(r)$ is the amplitude of the noise caused by atmospheric turbulence.

Under normal circumstances, the light intensity corresponding to bit 0 can be considered as $I_0 = 0$, and the noise corresponding to bit 0 caused by atmospheric turbulence can also be considered as $i_0 = 0$, Using Taylor series for function $\varepsilon^2 = (e^\chi - 1)^2$, we can get

$$BER = \frac{1}{2}erfc\left(\frac{1}{\sqrt{2}\alpha\langle \chi^2 \rangle}\right) \qquad (19.11)$$

where $1 \leq \alpha \leq 2$ represents the strength of scintillation.

When $\sigma_I^2 \leq 1$, scintillation probability distribution meets the lognormal distribution [2]. Ignoring those high order infinitesimal items such as χ^5, χ^6 etc., we can get $\alpha = 1 + (21/12)\langle \chi^2 \rangle$.

When $1 < \sigma_I^2 < 4$, scintillation probability distribution meets the K-distribution [11], we can get the probability density function of χ, which can be written as

$$f(\chi) = \frac{4m^{\frac{m+1}{2}}}{\Gamma(m)}\exp(\chi(m + 1))K_{m-1}\left[2\sqrt{m}\exp(\chi)\right] \qquad (19.12)$$

where $m = \frac{2}{\sigma_I^2 - 1}$.

19.4 Analysis and Discussion

According to the relationship between effective transmission distance and frequency above, we simulate the relationship between the system BER and various parameters. Under mean circumstances, we can choose $\langle Q \rangle = 6.82 \times 10^{17}$ molecules$/$cm^3, $\langle T \rangle = 300$ K, and $\langle P \rangle = 1.0$ atm during the day. For propagation 4 m above the ground, where $A_T \approx -0.402 \times 10^{-3}$, $A_Q \approx 0.15 \times 10^{-3}$ approximately.

In Fig. 19.1 we plot the terahertz band bit error rate caused by scintillation as a function of the logarithmic amplitude variance. It can be seen from Fig. 19.1 that the bit error rate correspondingly increase along with logarithmic amplitude variance increasing. The larger the value of α, the greater the BER.

Figures 19.2 and 19.3 show the terahertz band BER caused by the atmospheric refractive index structure constant and the transmission distance respectively. The value of $\sigma_{I,p}^2$ greater than 1 when the $C_{n,THz}^2 \geq 8.1 \times 10^{-11}$ in the case of $f = 0.35\,THz$, $L = 1500$ m (the red solid line with solid point in Fig. 19.2) or the $C_{n,THz}^2 \geq 6.7 \times 10^{-11}$ in the case of $f = 0.41\,THz$, $L = 1500$ m (the blue solid line with star point in Fig. 19.2). The $\sigma_{I,p}^2 > 1$ when the $L \geq 1291$ m in the case of $f = 0.67\,THz$ (the blue solid line maked in Fig. 19.3). It can be seen from Figs. 19.2 and 19.3 that the BER correspondingly increases along with atmospheric refractive index structure constant or transmission distance increasing. The bit error rate of spherical wave is less than the bit error rate of plane wave in the same conditions. Besides, the BER of weak atmosphere turbulence and moderate atmosphere turbulence are in good consistency.

Due to the ITU ruling the basic requirements of error rate for the third generation mobile communication: For sound and video images services, the BER should be less than or equal to 10^{-3}; for data services, the BER of wireless access

Fig. 19.1 The relationship between the BER and logarithmic amplitude variance

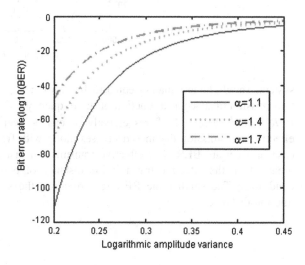

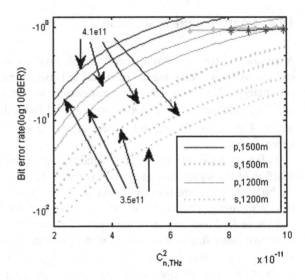

Fig. 19.2 The relationship between the BER and atmospheric refractive index structure constant

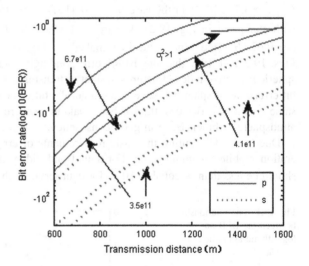

Fig. 19.3 The relationship between the BER and transmission distance

systems should be less than or equal to 10^{-6}. So in Fig. 19.4 we plot the effective transmission distance as a function of the frequency $f = c/\lambda$, adopting the case of $BER = 10^{-3}$, $BER = 10^{-6}$ respectively. It can be seen from Fig. 19.4 that the effective transmission distance decreases along with frequency increasing in the case of a certain BER. The effective transmission distance of spherical wave is greater than the effective transmission distance of plane wave under the same conditions; The smaller the BER requirements, the shorter the effective transmission distance.

Fig. 19.4 The relationship between the effective transmission distance and frequency

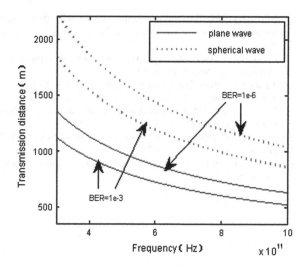

19.5 Conclusion

This paper shows that scintillation affects the transmission distance and the BER of communication system. Contributions of turbulence scintillation cannot be negligible for the practical THz wireless communication. Owing to THz wireless communication applying to line of sight transmission, we only study the transmission characteristics in free space with no obstruction. However, there are still much work need to be done for the practical application of THz wireless communication system.

Acknowledgments This work was supported by Shanghai Leading Academic Discipline Project S30108, NSFC 61132003 and NSFC 61171086, and Shanghai University Postgraduate Innovation Fund (SHUCX120146).

References

1. Rachmani R, Zilberman A, Arnon S (2012) Computer backplane with free space optical links: air turbulence effects. J Lightwave Technol 30(1):156–162
2. Zhang Y, Chi Z (1997) The transmission and imaging of the light wave in random medium. National Defence Industry Press, Beijing (in Chinese)
3. Uysal M, Li JT, Yu M (2006) Error rate performance analysis of coded free-space optical links over gamma–gamma atmospheric turbulence channel. IEEE Trans Wirel Commun 5(6):1229–1233
4. ITU Radio communication Study Groups (2001) Document 3J/Temp/312E 5
5. Hill RJ, Clifford SF, Lawrence RS (1980) Refractive-index and absorption fluctuations in the infrared caused by temperature, humidity, and pressure fluctuations. Opt Soc Am 70(10):1192–1205

6. Hill RJ (1978) Spectra of fluctuations in refractivity, temperature, humidity, and the temperature–humidity cospectrum in the inertial and dissipation ranges. Radio Sci 13:953–961

7. Chernov LA (1960) Wave propagation in a random medium (translated from the Russian). McGraw-Hill, New York, p 19604

8. Tatarski VI (1978) Wave propagation in a turbulent Medium (Wen Jingsong, Song Zhenfang, Zeng Zongyong et al.). Science Press, Beijing (in Chinese)

9. Yang Xianglin (2000) Optical Fiber Communication System, National Defence Industry Press, Beijing. (in Chinese)

10. Andrews LC, Phillips RL, Hopen CY, Al-Habash MA (1999) Theory of optical scintillation. Opt Soc Am 16(6):1417–1429

11. Parry G, Pusey PN (1979) K distributions in atmospheric propagation of laser light. J Opt Soc Am 69(5):796–798

Chapter 20
A Loosely-Coupled Platform for Urban Traffic Strategic Noise Mapping

Wensheng Xu and Nan Li

Abstract Excessive traffic noise is a major environmental complaint in residential areas. This paper investigates an SOA based loosely-coupled platform for urban traffic strategic noise mapping. Service-Oriented Computing Environment (SORCER) is employed to build the highly flexible distributed platform. After that, the platform architecture and the hierarchical services structure of this noise mapping system are presented. For platform functions implementation, the task scheduler service, prediction service and noise propagation calculation service are introduced in detail. At last, a real traffic noise mapping project is introduced to demonstrate the mechanism and the system. This platform can facilitate flexible generation process of noise mapping with ease of distributed services invoking, reduced computing cost, and improved resolution quality.

Keywords Computer aided noise mapping · Traffic noise prediction · Service oriented architecture · Distributed computing

W. Xu (✉)
School of Mechanical, Electronic and Control Engineering, Beijing Jiaotong University, Beijing, China
e-mail: wshxu@bjtu.edu.cn

N. Li
School of Material and Mechanical Engineering, Beijing Technology and Business University, Beijing, China
e-mail: linan@btbu.edu.cn

W. Lu et al. (eds.), *Proceedings of the 2012 International Conference on Information Technology and Software Engineering*, Lecture Notes in Electrical Engineering 211, DOI: 10.1007/978-3-642-34522-7_20, © Springer-Verlag Berlin Heidelberg 2013

20.1 Introduction

Excessive traffic noise is a major environmental complaint in residential areas. Noise disturbance significantly impacts many areas with high population density and affects the inhabitants in their daily life. More and more petitions to reduce noise in big cities indicate that noise problems are very serious in these metropolitan areas.

In the constituting process of noise control policies, traffic strategic noise maps are needed to survey existing distributions of noise levels, examine noise level regulations and identify primary noise sources [1] or to predict noise levels for specific areas. Therefore, computer aided noise mapping systems are extremely necessary.

Nowadays, the evolution of computer aided tools has made the road traffic noise mapping more precise and less difficult. There currently exist a number of commercial tools (like CadnaA [2] and SoundPlan [3]) which may be used to develop strategic noise maps in an effort to satisfy the requirements of different kind of users.

A noise mapping system should generate traffic strategic noise maps for different purposes [4]: (1) quantify main sources of noise; (2) clearly illustrate environmental noise exposure to provide a reference for noise-control policy makers; (3) facilitate the development of policies for controlling noise and enforcing the control of noise; (4) draft a cost-benefit plan to assist districts desiring to reduce noise levels; (5) adopt theories to examine the effects of environmental improvement plans; (6) improve the enforcement of regional or national plans to decrease new noise sources as well as to protect new noise-sensitive and tranquility-needed areas; (7) monitor noise reduction schemes and their effectiveness during the enforcement process; (8) monitor changing trends in environmental noise; (9) provide a research platform for studying the effects of noise on the human body.

Due to the purposes mentioned above, different kinds of software, such as Geographical Information Systems (GIS), statistics software or data visualization package, are usually used to work along with the noise mapping system together. Therefore, it is a big challenge to integrate all useful software tools as a loosely-coupled system that are extensible, flexible and fit well with existing legacy systems. Service Oriented Architecture (SOA) [5] is widely considered to be the best practice when solving the problems mentioned above. In this paper, we present an SOA based loosely-coupled platform for urban traffic strategic noise mapping. The wrapper mechanism and procedure of services will be discussed. Then, a real traffic noise mapping project will be introduced to demonstrate the platform.

20.2 SOA Based Noise Mapping Platform

20.2.1 Service-Oriented Computing Environment

Transparent services in the noise mapping platform can be achieved with SOA architecture. One of the first SOA applications in engineering was developed under the sponsorship of the National Institute for Standards and Technology (NIST)—the Federated Intelligent Product Environment (FIPER) [6]. The Service-Oriented Computing Environment (SORCER) [5] builds on top of FIPER to introduce a meta computing operating system with all basic services necessary, including a federated file system, to support service-oriented programming. It provides an integrated solution for complex meta computing systems.

20.2.2 Platform Architecture

Based on SORCER technology, a loosely-coupled platform for urban traffic strategic noise mapping is introduced, as shown in Fig. 20.1. The technology details of the service registry, service lookup and service employ will be hidden by SORCER. Our platform only needs to deal with noise mapping services building, services management and mapping process control.

The design targets of our platform include:

- To implement a sound objects modeling editor. In our platform, some traffic noise propagation associated data objects will be defined, including noise receivers, point sources, roads, buildings, barriers, line sources, calculation areas, auxiliaries, ground contours, ground absorption areas etc.
- To import, export and convert general data. Different kinds of data, including GIS data, measure data and noise mapping result data, need to be recognized and processed in our platform. The urban traffic information must be converted into sound objects and employed by the noise prediction module.
- A flexible traffic noise prediction algorithm library. The prediction algorithm library can supply a general template to match different prediction models.
- Noise propagation calculation model. In our platform, all of the noise propagation attenuation terms will be calculated from the method outlined in ISO 9613-2 [7], which include geometrical divergence, atmospheric absorption, diffraction, ground effect etc.
- Grid calculation and visualization for noise mapping. A large area is divided into a group of small grid areas and each grid area is carrying out the calculation and visualization and the final results are integrated together accordingly, so the grid calculation for traffic noise attenuation is the foundation of the whole noise mapping visualization.

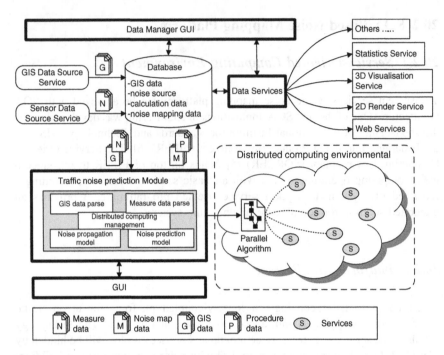

Fig. 20.1 Platform architecture for urban traffic strategic noise mapping

20.2.3 Hierarchical Services Structure for Noise Mapping

Figure 20.2 illustrates the hierarchical services structure of noise mapping. Users can play two roles in our platform: service provider and service requestor. As a service provider, a user should supply the target area with the geography information and traffic information (the geography information service and the traffic information service shown in Fig. 20.3), so the geographic map and noise sources can be modeled. To be a service requestor, a user can initiate and monitor the whole calculation process and get the final noise mapping result. Every service is autonomous and can call other services in the platform. The employer service does not need to care about what happen in the employee services, even though the employee services may call other services iteratively as well.

As shown in Fig. 20.2, the task scheduler service is an integrated service to supply the whole function of noise mapping. The user only needs to invoke this single service to start the calculation process.

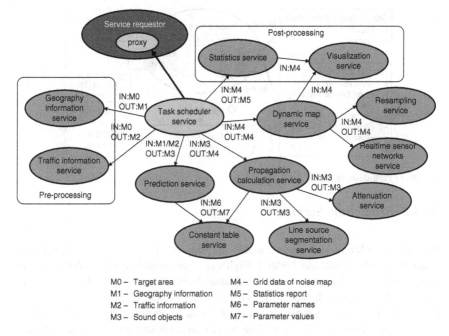

M0 –   Target area   M4 –   Grid data of noise map
M1 –   Geography information   M5 –   Statistics report
M2 –   Traffic information   M6 –   Parameter names
M3 –   Sound objects   M7 –   Parameter values

Fig. 20.2   Hierarchical services structure for noise mapping

20.3   Services for Noise Mapping

20.3.1   Task Scheduler Service

Just like a hinge, the task scheduler service plays an important role in our platform.
In the pre-processing stage (shown in Fig. 20.2), the geography and traffic information will be imported and the noise mapping task will be created in the task
scheduler service. In post-processing, the task scheduler service supplies result
data to the statistics service so that the policy makers can get meaningful information from the noise mapping results.

To handle a large size traffic noise mapping calculation task, the total project is
first subdivided into subtasks with rectangle tiles that fit together and then saved to
database. Then the task scheduler service plays as a service requestor to invoke the
service proxy and send the subtask information to the noise propagation calculation service provider. After that, the service provider loads independently one part
of the project limited by one of the rectangle tiles, and the subtasks can be calculated in parallel with several service providers. The task scheduler automatically
organizes and manages the required service proxy.

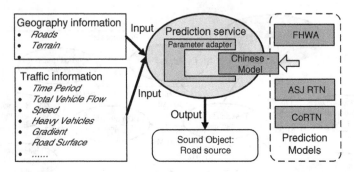

Fig. 20.3 Prediction service

20.3.2 Prediction Service

Nowadays, different prediction models are employed to build the urban traffic noise map, which include Federal Highway Administration (FHWA) model in United States, Calculation of Road Traffic Noise (CoRTN) model in Britain, Acoustical Society of Japan (ASJ) RTN-Model in Japan and Chinese model etc. Our prediction service supplies a parameter adapter to match different prediction models, as shown in Fig. 20.3. The match mechanism for prediction models implies that the service space may include more than one prediction service, the services implement different prediction models but supply the same parameter input or output interface. The input information includes geography information and traffic information (shown in Fig. 20.3), and the output of the prediction service is the road source which is implemented as a sound object. The service requestor does not need to know the implement details of the prediction model in service invoking. Sometimes they even do not need to worry about which model has been employed in the chosen service.

20.3.3 Noise Propagation Calculation Service

In the noise propagation calculation service, all of the noise propagation attenuation terms will be calculated from the method outlined in ISO 9613-2 [7], which include geometrical divergence, atmospheric absorption, diffraction, ground effect and so on. Sometimes, the calculation of the attenuation terms has to employ the geometry topology algorithm, for instance, the reflections effect calculation and the diffraction attenuation caused by barriers depend on the geometry calculation of the reflection sound beam paths and the direct sound beam paths. Due to that, the noise propagation calculation package includes two parts: acoustics model and geometry algorithm, as shown in Fig. 20.4. The noise propagation calculation package will be wrapped as a SORCER service to become net objects which are always ready to be called by service requestors.

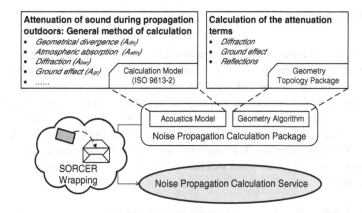

Fig. 20.4 Noise propagation calculation service wrapping

Fig. 20.5 Traffic noise map
of a demonstration area in
Beijing

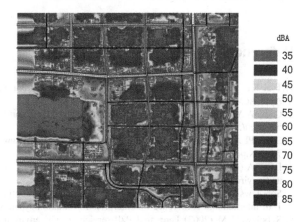

20.4 Platform Application

Most services shown in Fig. 20.2 have been implemented in our platform.
Figure 20.5 shows the demonstration of the prediction service and noise propagation calculation service in a real traffic noise mapping application. Real geography information and traffic information of the demonstration area are imported to drive the noise propagation calculation. In this example, a demonstration area (12 km^2 in Beijing city) noise map is generated using our platform.

Calculation configurations of this demonstration task include: (1) grid size: 20 m; (2) search radius: 1200 m; (3) grid height: 54 m; (4) amount of buildings: 15674; (5) amount of roads: 314; (6) amount of subtasks: 4; (7) calculation time: approximately 6.5 h.

20.5 Conclusions

The SOA based loosely-coupled platform can supply a flexible mechanism to integrate different useful services in noise mapping calculation. The whole solving process, consisting of the task scheduler service, prediction service and noise propagation calculation service, can import and manage traffic data and generate good-quality calculation solutions in a reasonable period of time. The real traffic noise mapping project is introduced to demonstrate the services and the platform. Since traffic noise mapping in a very big size area will cause tremendous cost of calculation time, our future work will focus on efficiency improvement for services in our platform.

Acknowledgments This research is supported by the National Natural Science Foundation of China (No.51175033) and Funding Project for Human Resources Development in Institutions of Higher Education of Beijing, China (PHR201107110).

References

1. Tsai KT, Lin MD, Chen YH (2009) Noise mapping in urban environments: a Taiwan study. Appl Acoust 70(7):964–972
2. CadnaA Webtutorial. Available at http://www.datakustik.com/en/cadnaa-webtutorial/cadnaa-tutorial0/. Accessed 15 June 2012
3. SoundPLAN Update information 7.0. Available at http://www.soundplan.eu/upload/Update_7.0_EN.pdf. Accessed 15 June 2012
4. DEFRA (2001) Towards a national ambient noise strategy. A consultation paper from the air and environmental quality division
5. Sobolewski M (2008) SORCER: computing and metacomputing intergrid. In: Proceedings of 10th international conference on enterprise information systems (ICEIS 2008), pp 74–85
6. Sobolewski M (2002) Federated P2P services in CE environments, advances in concurrent engineering. A.A. Balkema Publishers, pp 13–22
7. ISO 9613-2.(1996) Acoustics—attenuation of sound during propagation outdoors—Part 2: General method of calculation

Chapter 21
A Modified Particle Filter for Dynamic Multipath Mitigation in GPS Receivers

Yun Zhao, Xiaonan Xue and Tingfei Zhang

Abstract To the aim of mitigating the multipath effect in dynamic Global Positioning System (GPS) applications, an approach based on the channel dynamic model and the modified particle filtering technique is proposed, and the corresponding algorithm is integrated into GPS receiver tracking loops. The particle filtering mechanism builds upon the multipath channel measurements, and an increase in the number of correlator channel is required compared with conventional GPS receivers. A partical filter that employs the modified resampling algorithm based on an adaptive filter and the Recursive Least Square (RLS) algorithm is designed for the dynamic estimation of the multipath channel. Then the code and carrier phase receiver tracking errors are compensated by removing the estimated multipath components from the correlators' outputs. To demonstrate the capabilities of the proposed approach, this technique is integrated into a GPS software receiver connected to a navigation satellite signal simulator, thus simulations under the controlled dynamic multipath scenarios can be carried out. Simulation results show that in a dynamic and fairly severe multipath environment, the proposed approach achieves simultaneously instantaneous accurate multipath channel estimation, and significant multipath tracking errors reduction in both code delay and carrier phase.

Keywords GPS · Dynamic multipath mitigation · Modified particle filtering · Adaptive filtering · RLS algorithm

Y. Zhao (✉) · X. Xue · T. Zhang
School of Electronic and Information Engineering, Beihang University,
100191 Beijing, China
e-mail: yunhao@buaa.edu.cn

W. Lu et al. (eds.), *Proceedings of the 2012 International Conference on Information Technology and Software Engineering*, Lecture Notes in Electrical Engineering 211, DOI: 10.1007/978-3-642-34522-7_21, © Springer-Verlag Berlin Heidelberg 2013

21.1 Introduction

Despite continuing improvements in GPS receivers, multipath signal propagation has remained an unsolved problem [1]. Since a conventional receiver provides no inherent discrimination against the multipath signals, the reception of additional signal replica due to reflections causes a bias error in the code delay tracking loop, and also affects the carrier phase tracking loop. When employing 1-chip (correlator spacing) wide standard delay lock loop, multipath can introduce a ranging error up to a hundred of meters into a GPS L1 receiver [2]. And the resulting differential carrier phase estimation error can be orders of magnitude higher compared to the case of no multipath in precision applications [3].

So far receiver-based approaches to GPS multipath mitigation have obtained significant progress, notable among them are modified tracking channel and multipath estimation techniques. Modified tracking channel methods, such as Strobe Correlator [4] or Pulse Aperture Correlator [5], achieve the modified delay-lock discriminator function shape for multipath error reduction. The advantages of this family of methods are that they are relatively simple and able to work in real-time. Nevertheless, these methods can only reduce code multipath error to a limited extent. Multipath estimation methods, such as Multipath Estimation Delay Lock Loop (MEDLL) [6] or Multipath Mitigation Technique (MMT) [7], estimate the unknown parameters of the multipath signal model for multipath error compensation. They apply the maximum-likelihood estimation theory and can mitigate code and carrier multipath errors, however suitable for quasi-static multipath scenarios only.

For dynamic multipath estimation, the sequential Bayesian estimation methods are required. Furthermore only filters that are capable to deal with nonlinearities are suitable. The particle filtering methods for multipath mitigation in GPS receivers has been addressed in a few of literature. For example, in [8] a sequential Monte Carlo method, i.e. the particle filtering, was applied to the multipath mitigation, and a method of the signal compression to reduce the computational complexity is employed. In [9], a particle filtering algorithm was presented to track the satellite signals in the presence of multipath. However these particle filtering approaches employed the conventional particles resampling algorithm, which introduces a problem, i.e. the loss of particles' diversity, and leads to degrading the accuracy of state estimation.

In this paper, the sequential Bayesian theory is applied to the channel processing of GPS receivers, and a dynamic multipath mitigation method based on the modified particle filtering to improve diversity of particles in the resampling step is proposed. This modified method uses an adaptive filter structure and the real-time RLS adaptive algorithm. Then a multipath compensator at the receiver tracking channel level is designed to compensate multipath tracking errors in both code delay and carrier phase.

Fig. 21.1 Correlation
distortion due to multipath

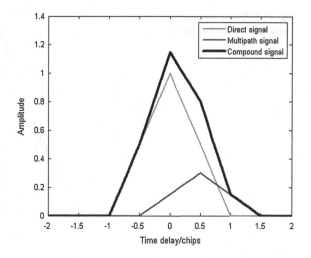

21.2 Sequential Bayesian Approach to Dynamic
Multipath Mitigation

From the a single receiver channel point of view, the multipath propagation
channel corresponding to a navigation satellite can be modeled as

$$y(t) = s(t) \otimes h_c(t) \tag{21.1}$$

where $s(t)$ represents the transmitted satellite signal, $\otimes$ is the convolution operator,
and $h_c(t)$ represents the impulse response of multipath channel that is time-variant
and unknown to the receiver.

After the receiver correlation processing equivalent to the impulse response
function $s(-t)$, the correlator output becomes

$$h_e(t) = y(t) \otimes s(-t) = R_s(t) \otimes h_c(t) \tag{21.2}$$

where $R_s(t)$ is the auto-correlation function of $s(t)$, $h_e(t)$ is the equivalent signal
channel response, i.e. $h_e(t) \approx h_c(t)$, and therefore the multipath channel outputs
can be approximated by the correlation outputs.

In the presence of multipath, as an important effect in the receiver tracking
channel, the ideal triangular correlation function will lose its symmetry. This
distortion of correlation function is illustrated in Fig. 21.1, where only one-path
multipath arrives in the receiver tracking channel, which is just in-phase with the
direct signal. Note that the light thin line represents the original triangular correlation function, the dark thin line the multipath correlation function, and the
thick line is the composite of the two. Whereas for multiple-path multipath scenarios, the correlation function distortion could be very complex.

For conventional receiver tracking loops, the operation of code delay tracking
loop is based on the measurement of the early and late correlator outputs, then the

Fig. 21.2 The distortion
resulting code tracking error

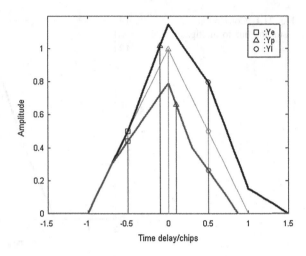

prompt correlation value can be computed [10]. In the case of no multipath (the thin line), one in-phase multipath (the dark thick line) and one out-of-phase multipath (the light thick line), the early, prompt and late correlator outputs are illustrated respectively in Fig. 21.2 (the correlator spacing of 0.5 chip is assumed). It is indicated that the prompt correlation value will coincide with the ideal correlation peak only if $Y_e = Y_l$; the correlation function distorted by multipath, i.e. $Y_e \neq Y_l$, results in an additional code tracking error. Since the carrier phase estimation depends on the in-phase and quadrature-phase components of the prompt correlation, an additional carrier phase tracking error is also introduced.

In this paper, the above characteristic of the multipath channel outputs is utilized in the multipath estimator. In order to obtain the details of the correlation function, a conventional tracking channel is expanded to be consists of a set of correlators that cover the code delay from -1.5 chips to $+1.5$ chips (the multipath effects corresponding to the code delay out of this scope are assumed to be suppressed by the correlator itself) and the correlator spacing is 0.1 chip. In contrast, only a pair of the early and late correlators is employed for a conventional receiver channel. And in order to combat the effect of the correlation peak loss in an actual receiver, a considerably wider pre-correlation bandwidth (e.g. 20 MHz or above) compared to conventional receivers is adopted, which also results in higher sampling frequency.

The proposed method in this paper consists of first sequentially estimating the time-variant multipath channel. This step is followed by achieving a compensator which compensates the multipath channel outputs to the desired outputs of multipath free to the maximum extent possible. And this multipath mitigation technique is integrated into receiver tracking channels.

The sequential Bayesian approach is applied to the dynamic multipath estimation, and the framework of this approach is illustrated in Fig. 21.3. Assuming that the multipath channel is a hidden Markov process, the channel state to be estimated are the sequence (over the temporal index k) $x_k \triangleq \{x_i, i = 0, 1, \ldots\}$ and

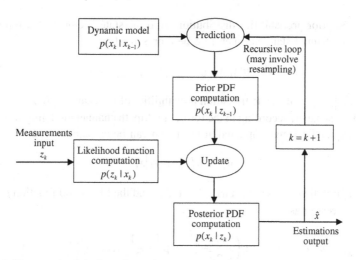

Fig. 21.3 Framework of the Bayesian estimator

the corresponding channel measurements (i.e. the channel outputs) are $z_k \triangleq \{z_i, i = 0, 1, \ldots\}$, for a given posterior PDF at time instance $k - 1$, $p(x_{k-1}|z_{k-1})$, the prior PDF $p(x_k|z_{k-1})$ is calculated based on the state transition PDF $p(x_k|x_{k-1})$ (i.e. the channel dynamic model). And the new posterior PDF $p(x_k|z_k)$ for instance k is obtained by applying Bayes' equation to yielding the normalized product of the likelihood function $p(z_k|x_k)$ and the prior PDF. Once the posterior PDF is calculated, the estimation of the channel parameters can be derived by either maximizing the posterior PDF or solving the expectation. And the latter criterion is adopted, which is equivalent to the minimum mean square error (MMSE) estimation.

21.3 Modified Particle Filtering for Multipath Estimation

In this paper, the particle filtering is used to solve the nonlinear problem in the dynamic multipath estimation. In this approach the posterior PDF at time instance k is represented as a sum form, and is specified by a set of N_p particles given by

$$p(x_k|z_k) \approx \sum_{j=1}^{N_p} w_k^j \cdot \delta(x_k - x_k^j) \qquad (21.3)$$

where each particle with index j has a state x_k^j and has a weight w_k^j. The sum over all particles' weights is 1. If the computation load can bear, N_p is expected large enough.

The state of each particle is drawn randomly from the so-called proposal or importance sampling distribution, one choice for the distribution, which is used here, is the prior probabilities distribution. And the state vector x_k^j that represents the hidden channel state can therefore be represented as

$$x_k^j \sim p(x_k|x_{k-1} = x_{k-1}^j) = p(x_k|x_{k-1}^j) \tag{21.4}$$

where $p(x_k|x_{k-1}^j)$ is the state transition probabilities of the channel process, which is known in this paper, according to the former multipath channel modeling work [11].

The sequential weight updated at each step can be calculated from

$$w_k^j = w_{k-1}^j \cdot p(z_k|x_k^j) \tag{21.5}$$

where the initial weights are set as $w_0^j = 1/N_p$, and the likelihood function $p(z_k|x_k^j)$ can be expressed as

$$p(z_k|x_k^j) = p(z_k|s_k = s_k^j) = \left(\frac{1}{\sqrt{2\pi}\sigma}\right)^L \cdot \exp\left\{-\frac{1}{2\sigma^2}\left(z_k - s_k^j\right)^H\left(z_k - s_k^j\right)\right\} \tag{21.6}$$

where $s(\cdot)$ represents the signal hypothesis that is completely determined the specific channel parameters, i.e. the path delay, amplitude and carrier phase; L is the dimension of the vector z_k or s_k^j.

However the sequence of the received channel outputs z_k is a large vector having the dimension that depends on the sample spacing, and the approximate sequence of much smaller size that depends on the correlator spacing, i.e. the corresponding sequence of the correlation outputs, is adopted in this paper for efficient computation and practical implementation. Actually a further transformation is achieved, since the orthonormal projection of z_k onto a smaller vector space after correlation is not just the correlation outputs. And the transformation matrix can be obtained from a SVD decomposition of the correlation matrix [12] that serves as the transformation of the received channel outputs into the correlation outputs.

Particle filtering algorithms suffer from the so-called degeneracy phenomenon, which states after a certain number of recursive steps, most of particles will have negligible weights. In order to combat this effect, a resampling procedure is introduced. Basically, it consists of discarding particles with low importance weights and replicate particles with high importance weights to keep the total number of particles invariant, then the weights of the particles after resampling is reset to be the initial values. Particles are resampled when the number of the effective particles falls below a specific threshold.

The conventional resampling procedure can decrease the degeneracy phenomenon, but introduces theoretical problems. The resampling leads to the loss of particles' diversity, in other words, the loss of statistical independence, thus degrading the estimation accuracy. Therefore, the modified resampling algorithm is proposed in this paper. This resampling algorithm is achieved by an adaptive filter, which is illustrated in Fig. 21.4. In the adaptive filter for resampling, the time delays of the filter taps represent the multipath delays, the filter taps represent the states of the particles before resampling, and the weights of the particles before

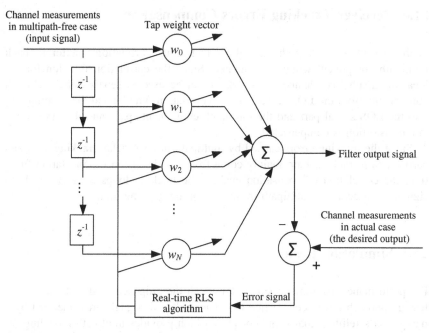

Fig. 21.4 Resampling based on an adaptive filter

resampling are used as the initial weights of the filter taps. In addition, the sequence of the correlation outputs after the projection transformation for the ideal multipath free channel is used as the input signal of the filter, and in the same projection space the channel measurements sequence corresponding to the current multipath channel is used as the desired output signal of the filter. The order of the adaptive filter (i.e. the filter taps) depends on the dimension of the particles. By using adaptive algorithm, when the filter approaches convergence, its tap weights represent the new weights for the particles. After the adaptive filter, the conventional resampling procedure is employed.

The real-time RLS adaptive algorithm [13] is utilized, which is characterized by the forgetting factor and quite suitable for time-variant estimation. The algorithm applied in the channel estimation drives the update of tap weights by minimizing the accumulative square error function given as

$$J(n) = \sum_{i=1}^{n} \lambda^{n-i} e^*(i,n) e(i,n) \qquad (21.7)$$

where λ is the forgetting factor that determines the dependence degree of the algorithm upon the historical data; $e^*(i,n)$ represents the complex conjugate of $e(i,n)$, and $e(i,n)$ is the error computed by using the tap weight vector at time instance n to test the data at time instance i. That the algorithm has converged at time instance n indicates $J(n)$ having reached the minimum value.

21.4 Receiver Tracking Errors Compensation

With the estimated multipath channel parameters, the correlation function for each multipath component would be obtained. Since the correlation function for the ideal multipath free channel is known, it can be used to separate the multipath components from the LOS signal. So the correlation function can be decomposed into the LOS signal part and the multipath components part, and then the correlation distortion is compensated.

Since the tracking errors caused by multipath in code delay tracking loop and carrier phase tracking loop mainly come from the distortion of correlation function, the correlation compensation enables the tracking loops to track the LOS signal, i.e. it achieves multipath mitigation in the tracking loops.

21.5 Simulation Results

For performance assessment, simulations with the proposed modified particle filtering approach have been carried out. The multipath signals are generated by a navigation satellite signal simulator [14], which provides multipath modeling for urban navigation environments [11]. In the simulations, a typical dynamic multipath scenario is specified in which a vehicle carrying a receiver and the antenna mounted on its roof moves round a 30 m circle surrounded by high buildings and at a speed of 20 m/s. Being incorporated with the above multipath mitigation technique, a software receiver [15] processes the signal simulator's generated signals with the non-coherent early minus late delay lock loop (DLL) for code delay tracking and a Costas phase locked loop (PLL) for carrier phase tracking.

Fig. 21.5 The posterior density given by the particles

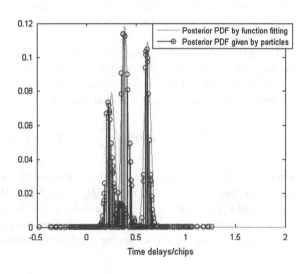

Fig. 21.6 Estimation result of multipath delays

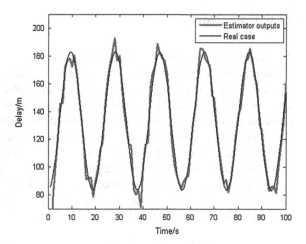

Only GPS L1 signal is involved in the simulations, and the signal's carrier-to-noise-density ratio (C/N$_0$) is set to be 45 dB-Hz.

In the simulation tests, an example of the posterior density obtained from the set of particles is illustrated in Fig. 21.5. As illustrated, the modified particle filter tracks the three strong multipath signals simultaneously. And the resulting estimation performance for the variant time delay of a multipath component is shown in Fig. 21.6. It is indicated that the estimation error can be neglected.

According to the estimated multipath parameters, the correlation function for each multipath component is determined and removed from the actual correlator outputs. The resulting performance for mitigating the tracking errors over the multipath scenario duration is shown in Fig. 21.7, in which the tracking errors after the multipath mitigation are compared to the original multipath tracking errors. Figure 21.7a and b represent the tracking error compensation performance for the code and carrier phase respectively. The normal tracking of the receiver is then recovered, although the specific tracking errors relate to the receiver design.

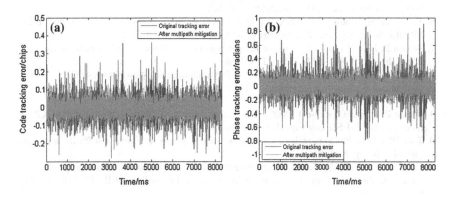

Fig. 21.7 **a** Mitigation result of code error, **b** Mitigation result of phase error

21.6 Conclusions

A receiver-channel based dynamic multipath mitigation approach for the simultaneous estimation of the multipath channel response and compensation of the multipath tracking errors in both the code and the carrier phase loops is proposed in this paper, which is achieved by a modified particle filtering technique. And the modified particles resampling procedure based on an adaptive filter and the real-time RLS algorithm is especially designed for the estimation accuracy improvement.

For evaluation of performance, simulations in which a navigation satellite signal simulator and a GPS software receiver are employed are carried out. Under a dynamic and fairly severe multipath scenario, the proposed approach achieves the accurate multipath channel estimation and the reduction of the multipath tracking errors in both code delay and carrier phase.

Acknowledgments The research work in this paper is supported by National Natural Science Foundation of China (61101075), Pre-research Foundation (9140A24040710HK0126), and the Fundament Research Funds for the Central Universities (YWF-11-02-176).

References

1. Feng X, Wu X, Zhang Z (2012) Multipath mitigation technique based on modifications to GNSS monitor station antennas field. In: China Satellite Navigation Conference (CSNC), pp 655–666
2. Irsigler M, Eissfeller B (2003) Comparison of multipath mitigation techniques with consideration of future signal structures. In: Proceedings of the ION GPS/GNSS 2003, pp 2584–2592
3. Souza E, Monico J et al. (2008) Spectral analysis and low-frequency multipath mitigation for kinematic applications. In: Proceedings of IEEE/ION international symposium on position, location, and navigation, pp 413–417
4. Garin L, Diggelen F, Rousseau J (1996) Strobe and edge correlator multipath mitigation for code. In: Proceedings of ION GPS '96, pp 657–664
5. Jones J, Fenton P, Smith B (2004) Theory and performance of the pulse aperture correlator. http://www.novatel.com/Documents/Papers/PAC.pdf.
6. Townsend B, Fenton P, Van Nee R (1995) L1 carrier phase multipath error reduction using MEDLL technology. In: Proceedings of ION GPS'95, pp 1539–1544
7. Fenton P, Jones J (2005) The theory and performance of NovAtel Inc.'s vision correlate. In: Proceedings of ION GNSS 2005, 2178–2186
8. Lentmaier M, Krach B, Robertson P (2008) Bayesian time delay estimation of GNSS signals in dynamic multipath environment. Int J Navig Observ. Special Issue on Future GNSS Signals, 11 pp (Article ID 372651)
9. Closas P, Prades C, Rubio J (2009) A Bayesian approach to multipath mitigation in GNSS receivers. IEEE J Sel Top Signal Process 3(4):695–706
10. Tsui JB (2006) Fundamentals of global positioning system receivers: a software approach, 2nd edn. Wiley, New York
11. Lu S, Zhao Y (2008) Geometrically based statistical model for multipath propagation of satellite to the earth channel in urban environment. In: Proceedings of ISAPE2008, pp 611–614

12. Lentmaier M, Krach B (2006) Maximum likelihood multipath estimation in comparison with conventional delay lock loops, In: Proceedings of ION GNSS 2006, pp 1741–1751
13. Rappaport T (2002) Wireless communication: principles and practices, 2nd edn. Prentice Hall, New York
14. Zhao Y, Kou Y (2009) Multi-constellation GNSS signal simulator and its software implementation. In: Proceedings of ION GNSS 2009, pp 2213–2219
15. Yang W, Zhao Y (2009) Modeling of GPS multipath signals and receiver testing. J Beijing Univ Aeronaut Astronaut, 35(5):551–554

Chapter 22
Prediction and Early Warning of the Teaching Process Based on CMM Model

Hua Wang, Ningning Chen and Jing Chen

Abstract In this paper, we proposed to apply CMM model in the teaching process, based on analysis of the CMM model. Established a prediction model and warning model, and to directions the feasibility and reliability of the model, combine with the actual data. The results show that colleges and universities to establish the teaching process of CMM-based forecasting and early warning model is feasible, and help colleges and universities to complete the teaching work more scientific, rational and effective use of existing resources.

Keywords CMM model · Teaching process · Prediction model · Warning model

22.1 Introduction

CMM is a framework, it provide an effective improvement via for software organizations to improve the software process capability. CMM provide a stepped, progressive style improvement framework for the software organization process capability, to help software organizations to improve process capability. In the CMM model, there proposed the prevention of system protection and the system concept, can help universities to develop appropriate solutions and strategies for

H. Wang · N. Chen · J. Chen (✉)
Information Engineering Institute, Capital Normal University, No. 56 North Road, 3rd Ring Road West, Haidian District, 100048 Beijing, China
e-mail: chenjing2011cj@163.com

H. Wang
e-mail: wanghua1820@163.com

W. Lu et al. (eds.), *Proceedings of the 2012 International Conference on Information Technology and Software Engineering*, Lecture Notes in Electrical Engineering 211, DOI: 10.1007/978-3-642-34522-7_22, © Springer-Verlag Berlin Heidelberg 2013

the new problems arising in the teaching process in a timely manner; improve their work efficiency; to establish a more scientific, and perfect teaching evaluation system.

22.2 CMM Model and the Teaching Process

In the CMM model, different maturity levels maturity levels consistent with different process capability and process performance prediction, with the maturity level to improve, the software process capability is becoming stronger, process performance will be closer and closer to the desired objectives, process performance prediction is more accurate. Prevention capacity is very crucial in the teaching process, to raise the level of the students' ability is a gradual process, to quantify the ability indicators of students in various stages during teaching. To formulate the standard scores, and monitor, In the monitoring process to predict the development trend of the teaching work, when the predicted outcome indicators did not meet the requirements then there will be a early warning, and pointed out the direction of adjustment, to guide teachers and students to make corresponding adjustments in teaching and learning process in a timely manner. The process improve the ideological is designed to meet the original intention of the school teaching assessment, can help schools to make timely and full discovery of the problem in the teaching process, timely verify the adjustment of teaching methods is valid, So greatly shorten the cycle of the groped to practice, to improve the teaching efficiency, and really do the teaching and the reform progress in step.

To introduction the CMM model is the teaching process evaluation, and use the prediction and prevention ideas to alerts the forecasting and early warning for the teaching process; Processing the data by application of the corresponding algorithm for the different characteristics of the data, Improve the visibility of the teaching evaluation system, the effectiveness of the teaching evaluation level; accordance with the model generation process the tracking system of teaching evaluation, to feedback the analysis results and other to the user. We design a teaching process tracking model based on CMM model thinking, shown in Fig. 22.1.

22.3 The Achieve of Student Achievement Prediction Module

To combination of teaching tracking model with taking into account the conditions of the simulation software, we use BP neural network to predict student achievement data. Firstly, to analyze student achievement data, according to the data analysis to establishment the BP neural network model, And combined with the error analysis shows that the reliability of the model.

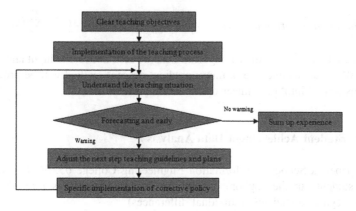

Fig. 22.1 The flowchart of teaching process tracking model based on the CMM

22.3.1 BP Neural Network

Back Propagation (BP) algorithm, is composition by the forward propagation and error back propagation process [1, 2]. Input information to pass through the input layer to the middle layer, inside the middle layer is generally designed for single hidden layer or hidden layer to complete the transformation of information processing, finally, the information passed by the hidden layer to output layer, for the information processing, such a forward propagation learning process is complete, This the information processing results can be output to the outside world through output layer. When this output with the expected output does not match, algorithm will enter the repercussions of error propagation stage. Then error pass by the output layer, layers of the weight correction by the error gradient descent, layer by layer back-propagation to the hidden layer and input layer. This work has been circulating, layers of the weight to continuous adjustment, this process is the training process of neural network learning, the stop condition of the learning process is the network output error can be accepted or designer has been set in advance the number of training learning [3].

If there is M layer, the M layer only contains the output node [4], the first layer is input nodes, then the BP algorithm is:

- select the initial weights W.
- repeat the following process until convergence:

(1) *for k is from 1 to N*

- Calculate the forward process, the value of O_{ik}, netjk and $\hat{y}_k$.
- Calculate the response process to reverse calculation every layers from M to 2

(2) *for the same node, $j \in M$, calculate δ_{jk}, Calculated by the follow formula,*

$$\delta_{jk} = \frac{\partial E_k}{\partial \hat{y}_k}\frac{\partial \hat{y}_k}{\partial net_{jk}} = -\left(y_k - \hat{y}_k\right)f'\left(net_{jk}\right)$$

(3) *the weights correction,* $Wij = Wij - \mu \frac{\partial E}{\partial W_{ij}}$, $\mu > 0$, and $\frac{\partial E}{\partial W_{ij}} = \sum_{k}^{N} \frac{\partial E_k}{\partial W_{ij}}$.

By the introduction of the BP algorithm can be seen above, the input and output of the BP model sample, the ordinary gradient descent method will be processed and transformed into a nonlinear optimization problem.

22.3.1.1 Student Achievement Data Analysis *k*

In this paper, a School of Information Engineering College 05, 06, 07, 08 four grades students in the sophomore year on a course results as reference data (without regard to students' individual differences).

We got a detailed analysis with statistical non-parametric tests on the raw data of the students overall performance. We using two methods Kolmogorov–Smirnov test (D test) and the Shapiro–Wilk test (W test) to test, using SPSS to calculate the results shown in Fig. 22.2.

Figure 22.2 shows the D test and the W test has a significant level of Sig. are very small, less than 0.05, so you can determine the distribution is non-normal distribution. Using SPSS to draw the histogram for the results of normality tests, shown in Fig. 22.3.

We can visually see from Fig. 22.3, the peak tend to the right side of the normal curve of the long tail extended to the left, therefore, can determine the overall distribution of student achievement is not normal, but a negative skewed distribution.

Thus the function distribution based on student achievement, so it can direct MATLAB on BP Neural Network Model.

22.3.1.2 The Establishment and Achieve of the BP Neural Network Model Based on Data Analysis

According to the above student achievement data distribution, for the BP neural network learning characteristics, using 05–07 grade students' performance to predict the 08 student achievement, Concrete steps to establish the learning process as follows:

Semester	Kolmogorov–Smirnov[a]			Shapiro–Wilk		
	Statistics	df	Sig.	Statistics	df	Sig.
05 Score	0.079	612	0.000	0.926	612	0.000
06 Score	0.098	612	0.000	0.869	612	0.000
07 Score	0.076	612	0.000	0.876	612	0.000
08 Score	0.110	612	0.000	0.774	612	0.000
a. Lilliefors Significant level correction						

Fig. 22.2 Student achievement normality test

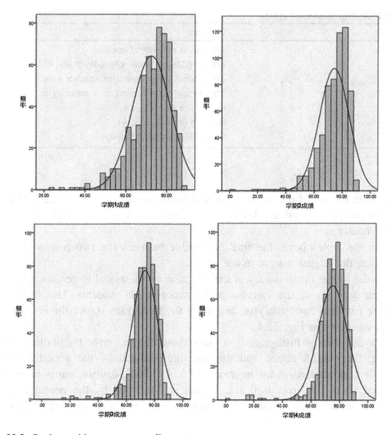

Fig. 22.3 Student achievement normality test

- The neurons initial weights W_{ij} of Randomized given by the hidden layer and input layer.
- From the given sample input X_i calculate the actual output of the hidden layer Y_j.
- To calculate the weights V_{jr} between the output layer and hidden layer, made the R-th neuron of the output layer to be the object, to establish the equation by given output target as the equation of the polynomial value.
- Repeat the third step to calculate the weights of neurons of output layer, In order to output layer weight matrix with random fixed value of the weights between the hidden layer and input layer is equal to the final training of the neural network weight matrix.
- Operate through a computer algorithm.

Meaning of the symbols encountered in the above steps is shown in Table 22.1.

First use the 05, 06, 07 level of student achievement to predict the 08 students achievement through the MATLAB code computing, then compared the forecast

Table 22.1 Explanation of symbols

Symbol	Illustrate
W_{ij}	The initial weights of neurons
V_{ji}	The weights between output layer and hidden layer
x_i	The student achievement of number $i(i = 1, 2, ..., n)$
y_j	The student achievement of number $j(j = 1, 2, ..., n)$
v_a	Grade a (a = 1, 2, 3, 4)
u_b	Grade b (b = 1, 2, 3, 4)
h	Students' learning efficiency

results with the actual results, the compare results is shown in Table 22.2. (Due to the data sample is relatively large, so this interception of the middle part of the data comparison.)

From the table above, the fractional value between the two results are little difference, the largest margin in ten points.

In order to test the accuracy of the neural network model to predict, we made the error analysis of the forecast performance of 08 students. Use MATLAB software for data error analysis, and draw the histogram shows the error distribution, as shown in Fig. 22.4.

Error distribution histogram it is clear show that the error distribution of the training, the correct effect, and the test three aspects of the neural network, Basically concentrated in the interval [−7.374, 7.804], distribution is more concentrated about the error is 0.215. Which is illustrated by the neural network prediction model error is small, prediction accuracy is high, can complete normal forecast.

Table 22.2 Students predict results and actual performance comparison table

Student no	05	06	07	08	08 Forecast results
1	79	74	74	76	76.966
2	75	73	80	74	79.844
3	62	59	68	68	71.069
4	82	83	76	80	81.605
5	76	83	77	83	79.997
51	78	82	79	82	81.745
52	73	70	75	81	76.597
53	76	82	68	77	76.904
54	73	69	74	79	75.604
55	52	20	70	73	79.595
100	69	76	72	75	74.343
101	59	75	72	78	72.313
102	67	79	70	78	75.271
103	80	87	77	76	28.688
104	67	81	70	77	75.729

Fig. 22.4 Error distribution histogram

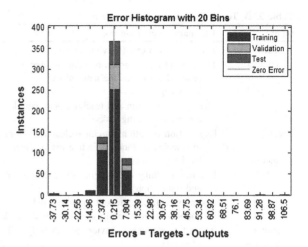

22.4 The Realization of Indicator Warning Module

In this paper, the teacher warning to be the example, first use the function in MATLAB, to establishment of early warning model based on BP neural network. Training the model in the existing data, through the analysis of training results shows the feasibility and reliability of the model.

22.4.1 BP Neural Network

Teaching quality assessment can be regarded as the input (the quality of teaching evaluation) to the output (the results of the final evaluation of teaching quality), non-linear mapping. To establish a three layer (input layer—hidden layer—the output layer) BP neural network model based on the theorem *Kolmogorov*.

First, determine the number of neurons of the input layer. As shown in Table 22.3 teachers indicator system consists of ten evaluation elements, Therefore, these ten indicators of elements as the input, the number of input layer is *n = 10*.

Second, determine the number of neurons of the output layer. In the evaluation process there are three levels involved: excellent, good, and generally, so the number of the output layer neurons is m = 3, and set the input is excellent, output is (0 0 1), input is good, output is (0 1 0), input is generally, output is (0 1 1).

Again, make sure the network hidden layers. We selected the three-layer BP network based on the theorem *Kolmogorov*.

Finally, to determine the hidden layer neuron numbers. The number of hidden layer neurons can be according to the formula: $r = \sqrt{n + m} + l$ (r, m, n were

Table 22.3 Teacher evaluation index system

Index	The main observation point	Good	Well	Common	Bad
Teaching content	The conception exactly, view clearly	–	–	–	–
	The content has a certain breadth and depth, properly introduce the new subject knowledge	–	–	–	–
	Meet the curriculum and teaching plan, could complete teaching tasks	–	–	–	–
Teaching process and methods	Explanation smooth hierarchical clearly attention to teaching methods, effective use of diverse teaching methods	–	–	–	–
	Inspiring teaching encouraging students to think and innovation	–	–	–	–
	Operation will help student to understand the course content carefully correcting homework	–	–	–	–
Teaching implement	Respecting students behavior appropriately full of energy	–	–	–	–
	Fully prepared for classes not free sessions and stop	–	–	–	–
	Strict classroom management practices	–	–	–	–
	Should patient and answer problems from student like to share with student	–	–	–	–

hidden layer and input layer, output layer and l is the number as an integer between 1–9) By calculating $r = 12$.

22.4.2 Analysis of the Feasibility of the Model

- Data processing: After the early warning normalized evaluation results data on ten indicators of the 112 students of a certain teacher, this will not only improve the convergence speed of the network, and strengthen the network sensitivity and fit. Figure 22.5 shows the normalized part of the sample set.

序号	x_1	x_2	x_3	x_4	x_5	x_6	x_7	x_8	x_9	x_{10}
1	0.725	1.000	0.541	0.490	0.245	0.755	0.205	0.000	0.296	0.990
2	0.966	0.926	0.698	0.611	0.00	1.000	0.336	0.349	0.416	0.993
3	0.787	1.000	0.639	0.648	0.271	0.762	0.000	0.549	0.410	0.705
⋮	⋮	⋮	⋮	⋮	⋮	⋮	⋮	⋮	⋮	⋮
110	1.000	0.720	0.398	0.258	0	0.925	0.559	0.226	0.301	0.699
111	0.932	0.985	0.432	0.462	0.303	0.932	0.076	0	0.447	1.000
112	1.000	0.733	0.622	0.533	0.244	0.889	0.144	0.111	0	0.989

Fig. 22.5 Part of the sample set of data preprocessing

Fig. 22.6 Network training
error curve

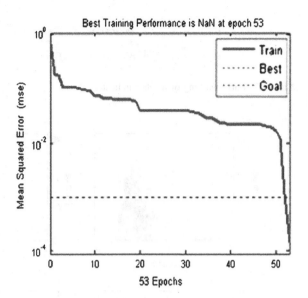

• Training and error analysis of the model: Use 30 training samples to training
  Learning set. In the model, the transfer function of input layer to hidden layer
  we using the function of tansig, hidden layer to output layer we use the function
  of purelin, Target training error is goal = 0.0001, Maximum number of training
  steps is epochs = 1000, The training function is trainbr, it can help improve
  network generalization. After 53 times of training, the network error sum of
  squares and mse reached the error goal requirements. Figure 22.6 shows the
  training error with the change of training times, It can be seen from the figure
  that the network after 53 iterations to achieve the required accuracy and the time
  is very short [5]. This shows that the established network model is reasonable
  and feasible.

22.5 Experimental Verification

We has a experiment with the actual data of a university, through the early
warning module got that teachers need to be adjusted on two indicators: "teaching
stimulating and encouraging students to think and Innovation "and" patiently
answered the student's problem, happy to work with student exchanges". As
shown in Fig. 22.7.

In 2007, the school to strengthen the communication between teachers and
students, launched a series of exchange activities outside the classroom, such as
teachers' seminars, received actual effect is more obvious. In 07, 08 the student
performance has improved significantly (shown in Figs. 22.8 and 22.9).

| Enlightening | 2.0 |
| AC answers | 1.0 |

Fig. 22.7 Early warning of teacher indicators

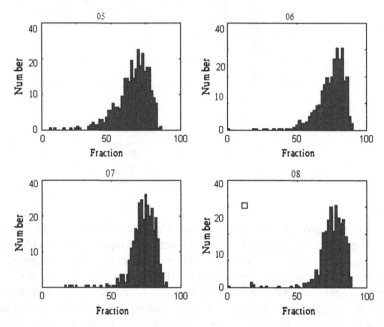

Fig. 22.8 The distribution map of each stage of the student achievement

Sections of student achievement scores in the distribution and intensity can obviously be seen from Fig. 22.8, for example, can be seen from the 08 student achievement is relatively high intensity of about 80 points, in the interval (0, 50) the number is very rare. For more intuitive description the changes in student achievement, we made the distribution shown in Fig. 22.9.

After the analysis of Figs. 22.8 and 22.9, the situation of student achievement is more uncertain. The average score of 07 and 08 students are kept in between [75, 82], Volatility is relatively small, Stable distribution. On the whole, the overall situation of the students is going to the good trend of development. From the side shows that the results forecast and indicators for early warning function of the system is basically to meet the requirements, the establishment of the teaching process tracking model based on CMM can help colleges and universities to improve the teaching evaluation system to improve the teaching level.

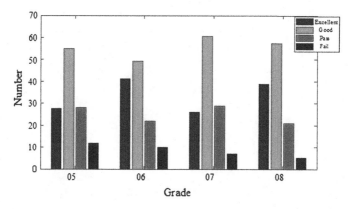

Fig. 22.9 Grade distribution histogram

22.6 Conclusion

In this paper, we use MATBAL software with BP neural network, constructed the forecasting and early warning of the teaching process model based on CMM. The model can help schools to know the development trend of student achievement; Found that the problems in the teaching process then to adjust in a timely manner, thereby improving the quality of teaching level, and ensure the quality of personnel training. The results showed that: the forecasting and early warning model of teaching process based on CMM is scientific and rational, and operability.

References

1. Feng Z (2010) Assessment prediction methods of mathematical modeling. Inform Technol 9:107–108 (in Chinese)
2. Qingbo S (2009) Artificial neural network design evaluation in vocational students graduated. E-commerce 10:87–88 (in Chinese)
3. Meng L (2007) Multi-scale gabor filter and the BP neural network-based text detection algorithm. Northeast Normal University, Changchun (in Chinese)
4. Qingqing W (2005) Based on artificial neural networks portfolio of consumer prediction, 9th edn. Coastal Enterprises and Technology 9:30–33 (in Chinese)
5. Lina Z (2011) Prediction model based on the results of the BP algorithm. 2nd edn. Shenyang Normal University (Natural Science), Shenyang 2:226–229 (in Chinese)

Chapter 23
A Method for Range Estimation Based on Image Processing

Qinghai He, Lianglong Da and Guojun Xu

Abstract Striations image generated in target localization algorithm using a guide source (GTL algorithm) is always blurred and indistinct because of noise pollution. Range estimation can not be realized. In order to achieve the distance accurate localization in the low signal to noise (SNR), image de-noising method is proposed. After de-noising, radon transform has been used. Wavelet threshold de-noising method is proposed in this paper. Because the hard and soft threshold functions have disadvantages, a new method of threshold function is introduced. The simulation results show that the distance localization efficiency of the GTL algorithm has been improved by using the wavelet de-noising method.

Keywords GTL algorithm · Low signal to noise · Wavelet threshold de-noising · Range estimation

23.1 Introduction

The underwater acoustic source object localization is always to be a difficult problem in acoustic subject because of ocean environment can be time-varying. A new localization method—target localization algorithm using a guide source (GTL algorithm) has been proposed by Aaron [1], in which underwater acoustic physics, signal processing and image processing techniques are combined. Under this approach a vertical array receives two time-separated broadband signals, one from a source at a known location and one from an objective source at an unknown

Q. He (✉) · L. Da · G. Xu
Navy Submarine Academy, Qingdao, China
e-mail: 1985hqh@163.com

W. Lu et al. (eds.), *Proceedings of the 2012 International Conference on Information Technology and Software Engineering*, Lecture Notes in Electrical Engineering 211, DOI: 10.1007/978-3-642-34522-7_23, © Springer-Verlag Berlin Heidelberg 2013

location. An interference striations image is generated by these two signals. The range of the unknown objective source can be calculated by image processing technique such as Radon transform [2]. A good localization efficiency is obtained when no noise pollution.

However, signals received by vertical receivers are always polluted by noise, so the sound field interference striations image is blurred and indistinct, range estimation can not be realized. Image processing techniques developed very rapidly these years are taken into GTL algorithm, striations image has been de-noised, and the signal-to-noise ratio is increased, then by use of the Radon transform, the range of objective source can be obtained.

The focus of this paper is derivation of GTL algorithm when received signals are polluted by noise. Based on the characteristics of striations, the wavelet threshold de-noising method [3–6] has been proposed in order to estimate target range. The simulation results show that this method can resolve the wrong localization problem when signals are polluted. The range of objective source can be estimated efficiently by GTL algorithm even when the signal-to-noise ratios of two sound sources are very low.

23.2 GTL Algorithm in Noise Pollution Situation

A vertical array which spans sufficient waveguide depth is used to receive the signals of objective source and guide source, then through proper arithmetic processing to estimate the range of objective source. Kraken model [7] has been used in this paper when sound field are calculated to simulate the algorithm.

As illustrated in Fig. 23.1, the vertical array spans the sufficient waveguide depth, the location of objective source is (z_o, r_o), and the location of guide source is (z_g, r_g).

For the moment it is assumed that the objective source, the guide source, and the receiving vertical array all lie in the same vertical plane in a waveguide of constant depth, and that the vertical array is not tilted. In the frequency domain, the field received from the guide source and objective source can be written as:

$$\mathbf{P}_g(\omega, r_g) = \mathbf{U}_\omega \mathbf{S}_g + \eta_g \tag{23.1}$$

$$\mathbf{P}_o(\omega, r_o) = \mathbf{U}_\omega \mathbf{S}_o + \eta_o \tag{23.2}$$

Fig. 23.1 Locations of sources and vertical array

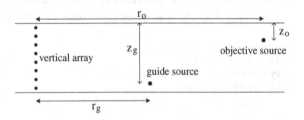

Here $\mathbf{U}_\omega$ is $N \times L$ matrix, N is total amount of array element, L is normal-mode numbers, and the element of mode functions is $\psi_l(z_n)$, means the eigenfunction of mode l at a depth z_n. $\mathbf{S}_g$, $\mathbf{S}_o$ are $L \times 1$ matrix, the element of them are $\frac{ie^{-i\pi/4}}{\rho(z_g)\sqrt{8\pi r_g k_l}}e^{-\alpha_l r_g + ik_l r_g}\psi_l(z_g)$ and $\frac{ie^{-i\pi/4}}{\rho(z_o)\sqrt{8\pi r_o k_l}}e^{-\alpha_l r_o + ik_l r_o}\psi_l(z_o)$, respectively. k_l and α_l are the horizontal wave numbers and attenuation coefficients of mode ψ_l at radial frequency ω. η_g and η_o are embedded noise, which is relative to signal frequency and array element depth. The simulation of this paper is on the assumption that they are white Gaussian noise and same in the same depth and frequency.

In the frequency domain the normalized virtual receiver output is defined as:

$$V(\omega) = \mathbf{S}_g^T \mathbf{U}_\omega^T \mathbf{U}_\omega \mathbf{S}_o + \eta \tag{23.3}$$

Here superscript T means transpose.

When the array spans sufficient waveguide depth, based on the orthogonal identity of normal-mode, $\mathbf{U}_\omega^T \mathbf{U}_\omega = \mathbf{I}$, $\mathbf{I}$ is L dimension identity matrix, $V(\omega)$ can be written as:

$$V(\omega) = \mathbf{S}_g^T \mathbf{S}_o + \eta \tag{23.4}$$

This expression is similar to that of a receiver placed at the guide source location. Multiplying Eq. (23.4) by its complex conjugate yields the acoustic intensity of the objective source at the virtual receiver:

$$I_V = N^2 \sum_l \sum_m e^{-(r_g + r_o)(\alpha_l + \alpha_m)} A_l A_m cos\left[(r_o - r_g)\chi_{lm}(\omega)\right] + \eta' \tag{23.5}$$

Here η' is embedded noise item.

When the guide and objective sources are now mismatched in frequency, with ω_s representing the relative frequency shift between the two signal samples, the orthonormality condition can still be used, and the following expression for the intensity I_V is obtained:

$$I_V(\omega, \omega_s) = N^2 \sum_l \sum_m e^{-(r_g + r_o)(\alpha_l + \alpha_m)} A_l A_m$$
$$\bullet cos\left[r_o\chi_{lm}(\omega) + r_g\chi_{lm}(\omega + \omega_s)\right] + \eta' \tag{23.6}$$

Here

$$A_i = \left[\psi_i(z_g)\psi_i(z_o)\right]/|k_i|, \quad \chi_{lm}(\omega) = k_l(\omega) - k_m(\omega) \tag{23.7}$$

In Eqs. (23.5) and (23.6), N is a normalization constant that is independent of mode number or frequency. From Eq. (23.6), interference striations image generated from $I_V(\omega, \omega_s)$ can be processed by Radon transform, the implementation of GTL algorithm in noise pollution situation is obtained.

Fig. 23.2 Radon transform

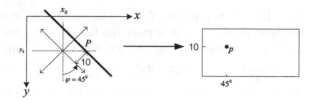

23.3 Radon Transform

The virtual aperture output consists of nearly straight intensity contours, all rotated at an angle φ with respect to the vertical. A natural computational method for estimating this angle is the Radon transform, which performs line integrals across an image along different rotation angles and different offsets from the image center.

The Radon processor is illustrated as Fig. 23.2. A line in original image (line P) has been transformed to a point (p), the light and shade of the point means the integral value of the line. The output is plotted as a function of rotation angle φ and offset distance p. A line lying at an angle φ with respect to the vertical axis and passing a minimum distance of p units away from the image center will be mapped into a point at the coordinates (p, φ).

The formulation of Radon transform can be written as:

$$\Re(p, \varphi, P(x,y)) = \int_{-\infty}^{\infty} P \times (p\cos\varphi + t\sin\varphi, p\sin\varphi + t\cos\varphi)dt\big|_{x,y} \quad (23.8)$$

Instead of summing along the vertical axis, computing the standard deviation appears to be more effective in identifying the striations. The standard deviation operation provides a rough measure of the contrast between the minimum and maximum outputs along the p axis for a given φ value.

23.4 Wavelet Threshold De-Noising Method

Wavelet has good localizing quality at time domain and frequency domain simultaneously and the characteristic of multi-resolution ratio analysis, so it can fulfill all kinds of wave–filtering needs such as low-pass, high-pass, sink wave, random noise de-noising. Compare with traditional wave-filtering methods, wavelet has incomparable advantage. Wavelet has become an effective means of signal analysis.

Image de-noising is a technique which can wipe off the noise based on preserving image edge and other characters. Image de-noising with wavelet analysis has been flourishing. With the characters of multi-scales and de-relevance, wavelet analysis is better than typical methods in magnetic resonance image de-noising of Gauss noise. Especially the Wavelet threshold de-noising is widely used for its simple computation. In wavelet domain it is one of the most effective de-noising ways.

The wavelet threshold de-noising method is non-line treatment, wavelet coefficients are compressed in wavelet domain in order to attain de-noising purpose. The theories premise is on the hypothesis that the wavelet coefficients of the image submit to broad sense Gauss distribution, and the bigger absolute amplitude values of wavelet coefficients mainly are from the signal transformation, but the smaller absolute amplitude values of wavelet coefficients mainly are from the noise transformation, so a threshold can be set to delete noise coefficients, then the purpose of de-noising has been gotten.

The two problems are most important in wavelet threshold de-noising method: threshold and threshold functions.

If the threshold is too small, noise also exist in signal or image after been de-noised; if the threshold is too big, important image information will be filtered out to cause deviation. Global threshold put forward by Donoho is very simple to calculate, and superior to smooth signal which embedded in white Gaussian noise. It has been applied extensively.

$$T = \sigma\sqrt{2\log N} \qquad (23.9)$$

where N is the length of the image, σ is the standard deviation of noise. In this paper, Donoho threshold is used.

Then make sure the threshold function which embodies the different processing strategy to the wavelet coefficient, and different estimate method. Hard and soft threshold function are often applied.

Hard threshold function is given by

$$\hat{W}_{j,k} = \begin{cases} W_{j,k} & |W_{j,k}| \geq \delta \\ 0 & |W_{j,k}| < \delta \end{cases} \qquad (23.10)$$

where $W_{j,k}$ is wavelet coefficient, $\hat{W}_{j,k}$ is estimated wavelet coefficient, δ is de-noising threshold.

Soft threshold function is given by

$$\hat{W}_{j,k} = \begin{cases} sign(W_{j,k}) \cdot (|W_{j,k}| - \delta) & |W_{j,k}| > \delta \\ 0 & |W_{j,k}| < \delta \end{cases} \qquad (23.11)$$

In this paper, a new compromise threshold method that improves performance is introduced, based on the standard compromise threshold method, yet more flexible and easier to treat mathematically. Compared with traditional wavelet compromise methods, the new approach avoids the discontinuity of the hard threshold method and also decreases the fixed bias between the estimated wavelet coefficients and the decomposed wavelet coefficients of the soft threshold method.

The new compromise threshold function can be written as

$$\hat{W}_{j,k} = \begin{cases} sign(W_{j,k}) \cdot (|W_{j,k}| - \alpha \cdot \delta) & |W_{j,k}| \geq \delta \\ 0 & |W_{j,k}| < \delta \end{cases} \qquad (23.12)$$

where α is a random constant, $0 < \alpha \leq 1$, it can be chosen based on the efficiency of de-noising.

Because this paper just use of the fringe characteristic, the image can be set to binary numeric values. The formulation which is presented by this paper is

$$g'(x,y) = sign(g(x,y) - a \cdot f_{mean}(x,y)) \qquad (23.13)$$

where $g(x,y)$ represents the image after wavelet de-noising, $f_{mean}(x,y)$ represents the mean value of image before de-noising, $g'(x,y)$ represents the binary image. a can be chosen in the interval of 0.2–1 based on the efficiency.

23.5 Performance Simulation

Here parts of data from the South China Sea acoustic experiment are analyzed to validate the effect of wavelet compromise threshold de-noising method. The sketch map of the experiment is illustrated as Fig. 23.3.

Acoustic data of three time points have been chosen to validate the algorithm. The range of this three explosion sources to the receiver array are 10000 m (point A), 14500 m (point B), 19300 m (point C). Two of them are chosen to be guide source and objective source, the striations image and final estimated range are obtained by use of GTL algorithm.

The explosion souse of point B is chosen to be guide source, point A is chosen to be objective source, result of GTL algorithm is illustrated as Fig. 23.4.

Table 23.1 shows the de-noising results of three different situations. Signals received by vertical array are embedded in noise in ocean environment, so big deviation will be generated in GTL algorithm when the range of objective source

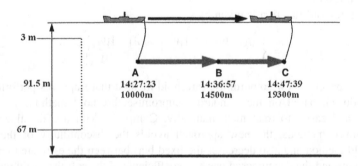

Fig. 23.3 Sketch map of South China Sea acoustic experiment

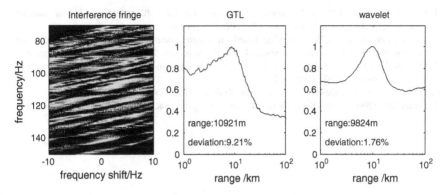

Fig. 23.4 Striations image and result of GTL algorithm

Table 23.1 De-noising effect of compromise method

Guide source	Objective source	GTL (%)	Wavelet (%)
B	A	9.21	1.76
A	B	8.06	0.03
A	C	7.65	0.39

is estimated. Because of this, de-noising method is needed. In wavelet domain compromise threshold de-noising is one of the most effective ways. Localization precision can be satisfied by this method.

23.6 Conclusion

GTL algorithm has been invalidated when embedded in noise. A resolving method based on image processing is proposed in this paper. In the first, striations image has been de-noised; after that extracting technique of characteristics is used to estimate object range. Wavelet compromise threshold de-noising method has been applied. The ocean acoustic data processing results show the good effect of compromise method.

References

1. Thode AM (2000) Source ranging with minimal environmental information using a virtual receiver and waveguide invariant theory. J Acoust Soc Am 108:P1582–1594
2. Wu T, Yuan S, Chen J, Li W (2008) Simulation analysis of new algorithm for LFM signal detection. J Syst Simul 20(9):P2395–2397 (in Chinese)

3. Guo X, Yang H (2008) An improved compromise for soft/hard thresholds in wavelet de-noising. CAAI Trans Intell Syst 3(3):P222–225 (in Chinese)
4. Lan C, Ouyang L (2009) One kind based on improvement soft and hard threshold value compromised method de-noising research. Sci Technol Eng 9(18):P5515–5517 (in Chinese)
5. Donoho DL, Johnstone IM (1995) Adapting to unknown smoothness via wavelet shrinkage. J Am Stat Assoc 12(90):1200–1224
6. Donoho DL (1995) De-noising by soft-thresholding. IEEE Trans IT 41(3):613–627
7. Porter MB (2001) The KRAKEN normal mode program. Saclant Undersea Research Centre, Italy

Chapter 24
A Terrain Model Generation Method Based on 2D Plan Laser Scanner for Micro UAV Autonomous Flight

Jiang Wu, Qianru Li, Miaozhuang He and Feng Zhang

Abstract Simple, real-time and reliable autonomous navigation and location method is crucial for the autonomous micro UAVs flying continuously in complex environment, such as unknown mountain or city areas. A new method of using onboard two-dimensional (2D) laser scanning sensor, GPS and inertial navigation device to establish the navigation terrain data model for the micro UAV autonomous continues flight is proposed, and then the autonomous navigation and location method in unknown environment is introduced. Terrain model generation method based on 2D plan laser scanning is presented. Scanning data fusion processing and filtering algorithms are proposed. Simulation results demonstrate the feasibility of the proposed method and algorithms. The experimental result shows that the improved algorithms will provide more efficient and effective integrating ability for future UAVs autonomous flight and control in the unknown environment.

Keywords UAV · Terrain model · Autonomous

24.1 Introduction

Micro UAVs are more usually used in the complex environment such as mountain areas and cities. They are forced with threats brought by lots of obstacles and the possibility of the invalidation of exterior signal sources such as GPS. The micro UAV itself has limited airborne capability. However, they can only carry low-cost,

J. Wu (✉) · Q. Li · M. He · F. Zhang
Science and Technology on Aircraft Control Laboratory,
Beihang University, Beijing 100191, China
e-mail: wujiang@buaa.edu.cn

W. Lu et al. (eds.), *Proceedings of the 2012 International Conference on Information Technology and Software Engineering*, Lecture Notes in Electrical Engineering 211, DOI: 10.1007/978-3-642-34522-7_24, © Springer-Verlag Berlin Heidelberg 2013

low-power mission device, so the computing capability of the onboard device is limited. Simple, real-time and reliable autonomous navigation and location method is necessary to fly in such complex environment. Autonomous flight needs the micro UAV to be equipped with the ability of perceiving the surrounded environment and avoiding obstacles.

This paper introduced the method with the airborne laser scanning sensor, GPS and inertial devices to generate navigation terrain data model according to the ground surface data scanned by the laser scanner. The method supports the autonomous navigation and location during the flight of UAVs. In the process of flying, laser scanning sensor scans the ground bellow and then makes terrain matching.

24.2 The Generation Method of Digital Terrain Model Based on 2D Plan Laser Scanning Sensor

24.2.1 The Scheme of Terrain Data Generation

Our solution uses laser scanning sensor as the airborne sensor combined with GPS and the inertial navigation. According the planning of the scanning area, UAV flies along the points set of route at the given height. The onboard laser scanning sensor is a 2D scanner, so the scanning result of its each scan frame is a points set of 170 degree scan line. The UAV is simultaneously equipped with GPS and Inertial navigation component which can provide the fusion of position and flight attitude for the terrain scan data.

As is shown in Fig. 24.1, UAV records the data of each frame, the present location data of the GPS and the attitude data of the inertial navigation. When the flight is finished, we can get the original scan data and the flight data of the flight area. By processing with the algorithms proposed in this paper, the digital terrain model (standard elevation terrain model) will be obtained.

24.2.2 Obtain and Process of the Terrain Data

The data obtained by laser scan sensor, and the information of the attitude and location of the plane platform needs to be processed to normalized terrain model data. Figure 24.2 shows the data processing method.

The basic data obtained by the scanner, can be fused with the position and attitude of the UAV platform to generate the global standard coordinate value of each scan point. By splicing the data of the every scanning band area, we can get the non-standardized terrain data.

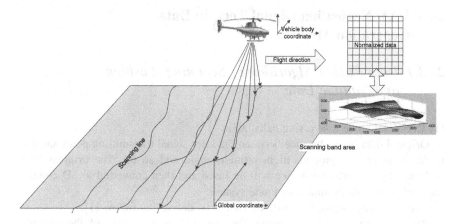

Fig. 24.1 The method of terrain data model generation

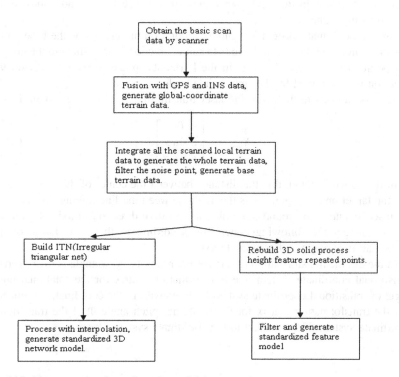

Fig. 24.2 The processing flow of terrain model data

24.3 UAV Navigation Digital Terrain Data Generation Method

24.3.1 Data Fusion Algorithm of Scanning, Position and Attitude Data

(1) Coordinate date conversing calculation

Original data is the distance between the laser signal transmitting point and the target point on the ground, flight attitude angle and so on. The original data collected by the airborne device will be fused and then converted to 3D coordinates of the actual ground coordinate system.

The necessary coordinate systems should be defined as follow [1].

Aircraft body coordinate system Sb: origin O is the center of the aircraft; coordinate system is solidly fixed with body of the UAV. X axis is in the plane's symmetry panel, in parallel with designed axis and points to the head of the plane. Y axis is vertical to the UAV symmetry panel and is pointing to the plane's right direction. Z axis is in the UAV symmetry panel, vertical to X and points to the bottom of the plane.

Ground coordinate system Sg: choose a point on the ground as the base point. X is in the horizontal plane and points to some direction. Z is vertical to the ground and point to the geocentric. Y is in the horizontal plane, vertical to X and the direction is determined by the right-handed rule.

The coordinates in the Sb of the laser transmitting point on the ground is

$$X_{body} = \begin{bmatrix} 0 \\ d\sin\alpha \\ d\cos\alpha \end{bmatrix} \qquad (24.1)$$

In the above formula, d is the distance between the center of the laser scanner and the target on the ground. α is the angle between the line linking the center of the laser scanner and ground target and the positive direction of axis of Z in Sb.

We can get the following conclusion according to the interrelation of the plane's attitude angle and coordinate axis:

In the Sg, the transformation matrix for the rotational yaw angle φ to convert to transitional coordinate system, the transformation matrix for the rotational pitch angle of transitional coordinate system S1 to convert to the coordinate system S2, and the transformation matrix for the rotational pitch angle Φ of the transitional coordinate system S2 to convert to the coordinate system Sb are

$$S_\psi = \begin{pmatrix} \cos\psi & \sin\psi & 0 \\ -\sin\psi & \cos\psi & 0 \\ 0 & 0 & 1 \end{pmatrix}, S_\theta = \begin{pmatrix} \cos\theta & 0 & -\sin\theta \\ 0 & 1 & 0 \\ \sin\theta & 0 & \cos\theta \end{pmatrix},$$

$$S_\phi = \begin{pmatrix} 1 & 0 & 0 \\ 0 & \cos\phi & \sin\phi \\ 0 & -\sin\phi & \cos\phi \end{pmatrix} \tag{24.2}$$

So the transformation matrix form ground coordinate system to plane body coordinate system is

$$S_{\theta\psi\phi} = S_\theta S_\psi S_\phi$$
$$= \begin{pmatrix} \cos\theta\cos\psi & \cos\theta\sin\psi & -\sin\theta \\ \sin\theta\cos\psi\sin\phi - \sin\psi\cos\phi & \sin\theta\sin\psi\sin\phi + \cos\psi\cos\phi & \cos\theta\sin\phi \\ \sin\theta\cos\psi\cos\phi + \sin\psi\sin\phi & \sin\theta\sin\psi\cos\phi - \cos\psi\sin\phi & \cos\theta\cos\phi \end{pmatrix} \tag{24.3}$$

Accordingly, the conversion between the ground laser transmitting point and the plane's body satisfies the relation blow:

$$X_{earth} = S_{\theta\psi\phi}^{-1} X_{body} \tag{24.4}$$

Among the formula above, θ is the pitch angle, φ is the yaw angle, Φ is the roll angle. X_{earth} is the laser transmitting point's coordinates in the actual group coordinate system.

(2) Get the global three-dimensional coordinate data of each scan point.

As the direction of the axis of Z used in the computing is opposite to that used in reality generally, so some processing must be done. If

$$X_{earth} = \begin{bmatrix} x_\varepsilon \\ y_\varepsilon \\ z_\varepsilon \end{bmatrix} \tag{24.5}$$

then the plane's coordinates measured by GPS Xp, the coordinates of the laser transmitting point in the actual group coordinate system Xr are

$$X_p = \begin{bmatrix} x_o \\ y_o \\ z_o \end{bmatrix}, X_r = \begin{bmatrix} x_\varepsilon \\ y_\varepsilon \\ -z_\varepsilon \end{bmatrix} + X_p \tag{24.6}$$

With the real-time data measured by the airborne device d, α, θ, ψ, ϕ, X_p, we can get the ground point's actual group coordinates:

Fig. 24.3 Specificated
digital elevation model
construction method

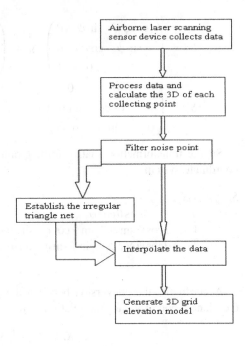

$$X_r = \begin{pmatrix} 1 & 0 & 0 \\ 0 & 1 & 0 \\ 0 & 0 & -1 \end{pmatrix}$$

$$\begin{pmatrix} \cos\theta\cos\psi & \cos\theta\sin\psi & -\sin\theta \\ \sin\theta\cos\psi\sin\phi - \sin\psi\cos\phi & \sin\theta\sin\psi\sin\phi + \cos\psi\cos\phi & \cos\theta\sin\phi \\ \sin\theta\cos\psi\cos\phi + \sin\psi\sin\phi & \sin\theta\sin\psi\cos\phi - \cos\psi\sin\phi & \cos\theta\cos\phi \end{pmatrix}$$

$$\begin{bmatrix} 0 \\ d\sin\alpha \\ d\cos\alpha \end{bmatrix} + \begin{bmatrix} x_o \\ y_o \\ x_o \end{bmatrix}$$

$$(24.7)$$

24.3.2 Data Modeling Process Method

With the processing method of modeling shown in the Fig. 24.3, the data collected during each time of flight would generate normalized terrain data.

The digital elevation model (DEM) is the data set composed of the plane coordinates (X,Y) and the regular grid points within a certain range: the 3D vector finite sequence which represents the terrain of the area of D [2, 3].

$$\{V_i = (X_i, Y_i, Z_i), i = 1, 2, \ldots, n\} \tag{24.8}$$

(X_i, Y_i) is the UAV body coordinates. Z_i is the elevation corresponds to (X_i, Y_i). When the plane coordinates of each vector in the sequence arrange regularly, the UAV body coordinates (X_i, Y_i) can be omitted, in this way DEM is simplified to one-dimensional vector sequence.

In this paper, the algorithm of generate DEM model is to establish TIN by scanning data contour line and elevation points at first, and then using linear or nonlinear interpolation to build DEM.

24.4 Terrain Model Data Processing Algorithms

24.4.1 Point-by-Point Interpolation Algorithm on Conditions of Blocking

The basic idea is that when we get ground data by plane scan laser sensor, divide the whole area according to a certain principle, and then interpolate the different type of blocks using different ways to realize better real-time performance and flexibility.

The description of the algorithm is as below:

Step 1: Using a rectangle to cover the whole area measured this time.

Step 2: Block the area, the basis of blocking is the location in the rectangle of the point.

Step 3: If the terrain of a small region is relatively complex, further division should be made. For example, we can divide region A to four smaller regions: 1,2,3,4. Moreover, considering the border, if a point distributes on the border merely belongs to a single area, it belongs to this area. Otherwise, if a point distributes on the common border of several adjacent areas, it will be arranged according to the principle which is from above to below and from left to right.

Step 4: After blocking process, most relatively simple terrain only need linear processing in relative area, but a small part of very complex terrain should be divided successively and we should get the terrain data of each block to process them with linear interpolation.

Step 5: Generate bigger blocks by processing results of each flight measurement.

24.4.2 Noise Data Point Filtering Algorithm

Filtering discrete noise data will not influence the coordinate calculation [4, 5], however it will influence the ultimate interpolation.

Comparing all kinds of methods, we proposed a simplified filtering method which is based on elevation mutation, called "elevation simplified filtering algorithm" as blow:

Step 1: Calculate the number n of the surrounded points the distance between which and the point is shorter than k_1 (the artificial set distance).

Step 2: Judge the size of n, if $n < k_2$ (artificial set number), then the point should be identified as discrete point, or else omit the point.

Step 3: According to repeated practical test and setting different k_1 and K_2, we can examine the ultimate test result and choose the suitable k_1 and K_2.

The main advantage of the method is that the idea is clear and the realization of the program is relatively simple. And by setting the threshold, the controllability of the algorithm is very strong.

The main calculation in the algorithm is distance calculation, which makes the volume not too large.

24.4.3 Data Interpolation Processing

After the original terrain model data is obtained, the required normalized standard terrain model data can be generated. DEM linear interpolation [6, 7], is used to get the approximately continuous process data, which means using the mathematical analytic method to process and compute the discrete data.

Linear interpolation is to use the three points that are nearest from the interpolation point to determine a plane, then according to the plane, make interpolation to obtain elevation values of the point. Its function is:

$$Z = a_0 + a_1 x + a_2 y \tag{24.9}$$

Based on the three known points $p_1(x_1, y_1, z_1)$, $p_2(x_2, y_2, z_2)$, $p_3(x_3, y_3, z_3)$, we can get the value of the parameters α_0, α_1, α_2.

The calculation formula is as follows:

$$\begin{bmatrix} \alpha_0 \\ \alpha_1 \\ \alpha_2 \end{bmatrix} = \begin{pmatrix} 1 & x_1 & y_1 \\ 1 & x_2 & y_2 \\ 1 & x_3 & y_3 \end{pmatrix}^{-1} \begin{bmatrix} z_1 \\ z_2 \\ z_3 \end{bmatrix} \tag{24.10}$$

Calculating the parameters, we can get the value of the elevation C:

$$Z_c = \alpha_0 + \alpha_1 x_c + \alpha_2 y_c \tag{24.11}$$

The interpolation effect is shown in Fig. 24.4

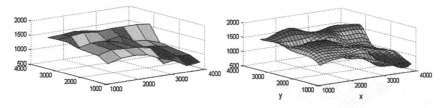

Fig. 24.4 Effect of interpolation data

Fig. 24.5 Simulation terrain map

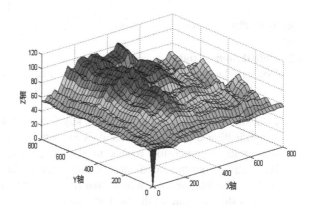

24.5 Simulation and Analysis

In this paper we used some actual flight test data, and expanded it in MATLAB as the simulation model as is shown in Fig. 25.5. The UAV collected data of the simulation terrain model in the process of collecting data points, and processed these simulation data point to construct digital elevation model.

Due to the imitation data collection from the UAV, it is necessary to set the plane trajectories and laser scanning angle. Considering that it is from the simulation data model we get the data of points, so the laser scanning angle is limited, because it cannot be too large.

Collect data in the two directions in Fig. 26.6:

(1) If the aircraft flies along the linear Y = 0, flight level Z = 400;
(2) If the UAV flies along the linear Y = 800t, Z = 400.

The processing method of scanning from multiple directions is the same with that of scanning from two directions.

(1) **The data input**

Since it is impossible to collect all data points in one flight, it is necessary to input the data of each time of flight. In light of this, it is necessary to input and store the data of each time orderly.

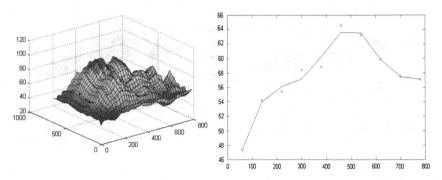

Fig. 24.6 Effect of processed data model

(2) **Calculation of data**

Convert the raw data into the three-dimensional coordinates in the actual coordinate system according to the above method.

(3) **Data storage mode**

Data storage mode can be one of the key factors that influence the algorithm simplification or the improvement of algorithm efficiency. In this paper, we use multiple dimension matrix to realize peritoneal storage of the data. Respectively put the coordinates of each point in the prior 3 dimension of the matrix. The four dimension of the matrix should be used as a flag bit, which is used to store a value to differentiate areas.

Use the number that presents some one-dimension array in the matrix as a flag bit and set different condition to store the points satisfying different condition in different regions.

(4) **The generation of data**

The main job after data storage is to find out the target point among all the stored point and then to interpolate the point which need interpolation process using the searched target point.

The main judging quality to find the target point is the point-to-point plane distance. Firstly, we should get the area of the target point according to the coordinate range of x and y. Secondly, chooses one or several storage areas. Thirdly, filter out the target point among the areas.

After getting the elevation value of all the interpolation point, the needed integral digital elevation model can be obtained.

24.6 Conclusions

The method and algorithms of establishing the navigation terrain data model using laser scanner are discussed in this paper. A new method of using the onboard 2D laser scanning sensor, GPS and inertial navigation device to establish the navigation terrain data model for the micro UAV autonomous continues flight, and then the autonomous navigation and location in unknown environment is introduced. Terrain model generation method based on 2D plan laser scanning is presented. Scanning data fusion processing and filtering algorithms are proposed. Simulation environment is built in Matlab, using the terrain data extended by the actual flight data. The simulation results show that the method and algorithms can efficiently, accurately generate the required specified standard model, which can support small unmanned aerial vehicle to realize the autonomous navigation. The validated method can not only be applied to small UAV in outdoor terrain autonomous flight, but also can be used for small UAV's autonomous flight based on terrain matching. It can provide accuracy for UAV navigation and positioning in spite of the depletion of the GPS navigation data of the terrain.

Acknowledgments The work described in this paper is partially supported by the National Natural Science Foundation of China (61175109).

References

1. Wu S, Fei Y (2005) Flight control system. Beihang university press, Beijing, pp 75–79 (in Chinese)
2. Wu L, Shi W (2005) Principles and algorithms of geographic information systems. Science Press, Beijing, pp 127–131 (in Chinese)
3. Li Y (2009) Research of DEM generation and visualization based on triangulation. Central South University, Changsha, pp 57–63 (in Chinese)
4. Xiang Y, Liu Y (2004) A terrain matching study based on airborne laser scanning altimetry. Tactical missile technology, vol 2, pp 42–46
5. Feng Q (2004) The research on new terrain elevation matching approaches and their applicability. National university of defense technology, Changsha, pp 43–47
6. Lawson CL (1997) A software for C surface interpolation. In: Rice JR (ed) Mathematical software III. Academic Press, New York, pp 235–241
7. Meng H, Wang Q (2010) The algorithm of multi-path terrain contour matching based on laser radar. Comput Simul 27(2):69–71

Chapter 25
The Research on Performances of Dual Receivers Positioning System

Jun Cheng, Huijing Dou, Qian Lei and Wenxue Li

Abstract Passive geolocation of communication emitters provides great benefits to military and civilian surveillance and security operations. Measurement combination for stationary emitters based on Time Difference of Arrival (TDOA) and Frequency Difference of Arrival (FDOA) may be obtained by sensors mounted on mobile platforms, for example, on a pair of Unmanned Aerial Vehicles (UAVs). This paper relies on joint TDOA/FDOA estimation algorithm. Then we put forward a kind of method by adjusting the receiver direction to improve the precision of localization. The results of the simulation show that the method can improve precision of the positioning 2–10 times.

Keywords Passive localization · Double-star positioning system · Time differences of arrival (TDOA) · Frequency differences of arrival (FDOA) · Geometric dilution of precision (GDOP)

25.1 Introduction

With the rapid development of electronic technology, the requirements for real-time positioning and the accuracy positioning are increasing. In the field of military electronic countermeasures, target positioning technology directly affects the

J. Cheng (✉) · H. Dou · Q. Lei · W. Li
School of Electronic Information and Control Engineering, Beijing University
of Technology, 100 Ping Le Yuan, Chao Yang District 100124 Beijing, China
e-mail: 493946972@qq.com

H. Dou
e-mail: dhuijing@bjut.edu.cn

W. Lu et al. (eds.), *Proceedings of the 2012 International Conference on Information Technology and Software Engineering*, Lecture Notes in Electrical Engineering 211, DOI: 10.1007/978-3-642-34522-7_25, © Springer-Verlag Berlin Heidelberg 2013

detection of enemy position and the hidden of our detectors, the field has also been the focus of the national military researching.

Emitter location estimation has been proved to be a widely applicable technique in many fields. Specifically, we consider the scenario that a group of airborne sensors try to passively estimate the location of a non-cooperative radio frequency (RF) emitter on a battlefield. In recent interest, those sensors are placed on small and slow moving Unmanned Aerial Vehicles (UAVs). At each time instance, the UAVs fly at certain velocities within the reachable velocity range. We consider that the sensors employ Time Differences of Arrival (TDOA) and Frequency Differences of Arrival (FDOA) to estimate the geolocation of the emitter, in which case, UAVs must be paired to estimate those values. For simplicity, we will not explore the effect of optimal sensor selection and pairing, rather we simply consider that the UAVs are paired arbitrarily [1, 2].

Location and tracking of maneuvering targets is one of the important goals of passive location system. Positioning technology of TDOA get the target position by comparing the arrival time of target signal which is collected by several detectors. But the drawback is that it has the time lag blur and there is some difficulty for high frequency and maneuvering targets positioning; Positioning technology of FDOA get the target position by use of Doppler frequency drift, which engendered by target relative movement to the detectors. This method characterized by high positioning precision and fast detection of maneuvering target [3].

The model of positioning system is illustrated in Fig. 25.1. Using double-star positioning system modeling, this paper analyzed the influence of detector factors on the positioning precision. Under this condition, through simulation, we can predict the location of the target source, and improve positioning precision by quantitative adjustment of the detector's direction.

Fig. 25.1 Geometrical model for dual-receiver positioning

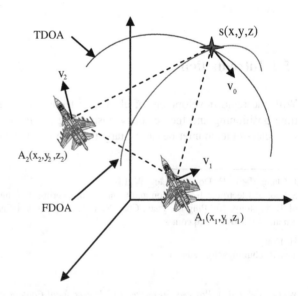

The paper is organized as follows. Problem statement is presented in Sect. 25.2. The influence of positioning accuracy which generated by the relative trend of the TDOA and FODA contour is analyzed in Sect. 25.3. Sections 25.4 and 25.5 present the result of simulation and conclusions.

25.2 Positioning Principle

Because the distances of emitters to two detectors are different, there will be time difference of arrival between signals from emitters. Simultaneously, the radial velocities of the two detectors relative to emitters differ from each other, signals from emitters will result in different Doppler frequencies for each detector. The key part of the dual receivers positioning technology is to calculate the values of TDOA and FDOA, using them to simulate the equivalent curve of TDOA and FDOA in the three-dimensional space, the intersection of two curves is the possible region of the emitter [4, 5].

Supposing the position of receivers are $A_1(x_i, y_i, z_i), (i = 1, 2)$, which velocities are $v_i = (v_{xi}, v_{yi}, v_{zi}), (i = 1, 2)$; the position of the radiant is $S(x, y, z)$, which velocity is $v_0 = (v_x, v_y, v_z)$. TDOA is Δt, FDOA is f_d, and c is the speed of light. TDOA and FDOA are defined as follows [6]:

$$\Delta t = (r_2 - r_1)/c \qquad (25.1)$$

$$f_d = \frac{f_0}{c}\left(\frac{v_{r2}}{r_2} - \frac{v_{r1}}{r_1}\right) \qquad (25.2)$$

where r_1, r_2 are the distance from the emitter to the carrier aircraft 1 and carrier aircraft 2 respectively, v_{r1}/r_1, v_{r2}/r_2 are the radial relative velocity of the emitter to the carrier aircraft 1 and carrier aircraft 2 respectively. c equals to 3×10^8 m/s, f_0 is the frequency of emitter. Generally, f_0 is unknown, but it can be measured by ground equipment, it also can be replaced by the received signal frequency. In addition:

$$r_1 = \sqrt{(x - x_1)^2 + (y - y_1)^2 + (z - z_1)^2} \qquad (25.3)$$

$$r_2 = \sqrt{(x - x_2)^2 + (y - y_2)^2 + (z - z_2)^2} \qquad (25.4)$$

$$v_{r1} = (v_0 - v_1) \cdot r_1 = (v_x - v_{x1})(x - x_1) + (v_y - v_{y1})(y - y_1) + (v_z - v_{z1})(z - z_1) \qquad (25.5)$$

$$v_{r2} = (v_0 - v_2) \cdot r_2 = (v_x - v_{x2})(x - x_2) + (v_y - v_{y2})(y - y_2) + (v_z - v_{z2})(z - z_2) \qquad (25.6)$$

Fig. 25.2 TDOA equivalent curve

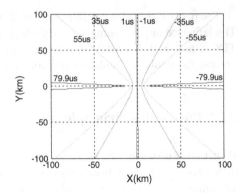

Fig. 25.3 When the carriers speed at $v_1 = v_2 = (0.180)$ m/s, the FDOA equivalent curves

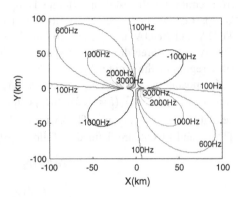

As for moving emitter in three-dimensional space, if we assume that the height and speed of radiation source have known, then it can be achieved the positioning of radiation sources by one single measurement on TDOA and FDOA [7]. The paper gives two-dimensional positioning curve of TDOA/FDOA of the two-plane which are in the horizontal. Supposing that the target is fixed, we can get the two-dimensional positioning equations of TDOA and FDOA, according to the definition of TDOA and FDOA [8, 9]:

$$\Delta t = \left[\sqrt{(x - x_2)^2 + (y - y_2)^2} - \sqrt{(x - x_1)^2 + (y - y_1)^2} \right] \Big/ c \qquad (25.7)$$

$$f_d = \frac{f_0}{c} \cdot \left[\frac{v_{x1}(x - x_1) + v_{y1}(y - y_1)}{\sqrt{(x - x_1)^2 + (y - y_1)^2}} - \frac{v_{x2}(x - x_2) + v_{y2}(y - y_2)}{\sqrt{(x - x_2)^2 + (y - y_2)^2}} \right] \qquad (25.8)$$

Assuming the receivers have a distance of 24 km, then the maximum TDOA would be 80 μs. TDOA equivalent curve is shown in Fig. 25.2, which determined by (25.7), the curve of TDOA are ±1 μs, ±35 μs, ±55 μs, ±79.9 μs.

We assume that the distance of two carrier aircrafts is 24 km, the speed of carrier aircraft is $v_1 = v_2 = (0.180)$ m/s, the frequency of emitter is 10×10^9 Hz.

According to (25.8), we can get the each of FDOA equivalent curve when the frequencies are -1000, 100, 600, 1000 2000 and $3000\,\text{Hz}$. Figure 25.3 shows the result of FDOA curve.

25.3 Analysis

For the double-star positioning system using TDOA and FDOA contour intersection to estimate the emitter location, so the relation of the TDOA and FDOA contour curve is perpendicular or parallel intersecting, which would have a great effect on the positioning precision [5].

According to Fig. 25.4, it can be seen that when the FDOA has a small change, the intersection of the FDOA contour with the TDOA contour changed from a to a_0. However, when TDOA has a small change, the intersection changed from a to a_1. Both of the cases, it would lead to the positioning region expand. As a result, it makes the positioning precision decreased.

From Fig. 25.5, it can be seen that when the FDOA has a small change, the intersection of the FDOA contour with the TDOA contour changed from b to b_0; When TDOA has a small change, the intersection of the FDOA contour with the TDOA contour changes from b to b_1. Because changes of position in both cases are relatively lower, so the positioning error region become narrow, which increased the positioning precision.

We can get the equations by differential deformation for the Eqs. (25.7), and (25 8):

$$
\begin{aligned}
(c_{x2} - c_{x1})dx &+ (c_{y2} - c_{y1})dy + (c_{z2} - c_{z1})dz = \lambda \cdot df_d \\
&+ (c_{x2}dx2 - c_{x1}dx1) + (c_{y2}dy2 - c_{y1}dy1) + (c_{z2}dz2 - c_{z1}dz1) \\
&- (g_{x2} - g_{x1})dv_x - (g_{y2} - g_{y1})dv_y - (g_{z2} - g_{z1})dv_z + (g_{x2}dv_{x2} - g_{x1}dv_{x1}) \\
&+ (g_{y2}dv_{y2} - g_{y1}dv_{y1}) + (g_{z2}dv_{z2} - g_{z1}dv_{z1})
\end{aligned}
\tag{25.9}
$$

Fig. 25.4 Approximate parallel TDOA and FDOA contour intersected

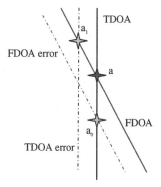

Fig. 25.5 Approximate
vertical TDOA and FDOA
contour intersected

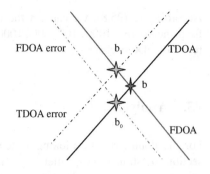

$$(g_{x2} - g_{x1})dx + (g_{y2} - g_{y1})dy + (g_{z2} - g_{z1})dz$$
$$= c \cdot d\Delta t + (g_{x2}dx2 - g_{x1}dx1) + (g_{y2}dy2 - g_{y1}dy1) \qquad (25.10)$$
$$+ (g_{z2}dz2 - g_{z1}dz1)$$

in which $g_{si} = (s - s_i)/r_i$, $c_{si} = 1/r_i \cdot (v_s - v_{s_i} - g_{si} \cdot v_{ri}/r_i)$, $i = 1, 2$.

Equations (25.9) and (25.10) are organized into a matrix form as follows:

$$Cdu = dz - U_1ds_1 + U_2ds_2 - Vdv_0 - V_1dv_1 + V_2dv_2 \qquad (25.11)$$

$$U_1 = \begin{bmatrix} c_{x1} & c_{y1} & c_{z1} \\ g_{x1} & g_{y1} & g_{z1} \end{bmatrix}, \quad U_2 = \begin{bmatrix} c_{x2} & c_{y2} & c_{z2} \\ g_{x2} & g_{y2} & g_{z2} \end{bmatrix},$$

$$V_1 = \begin{bmatrix} g_{x1} & g_{y1} & g_{z1} \\ 0 & 0 & 0 \end{bmatrix}, \quad V_2 = \begin{bmatrix} g_{x2} & g_{y2} & g_{z2} \\ 0 & 0 & 0 \end{bmatrix},$$

$$U = U_2 - U_1, \quad V = V_2 - V_1,$$

Fig. 25.6 GDOP equivalent
curve

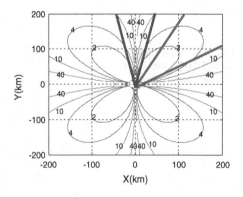

Fig. 25.7 GDOP in three-dimensional space

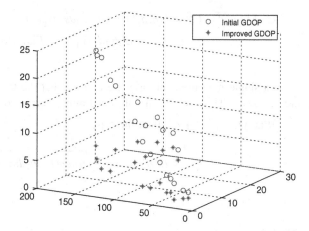

Fig. 25.8 GDOP in the YOZ plane projection

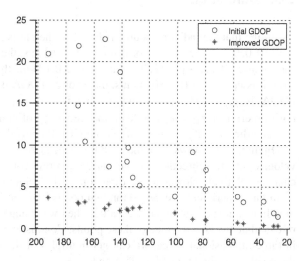

$$dz = \begin{bmatrix} \lambda \cdot df_d \\ c \cdot d\Delta t \end{bmatrix}, \quad du = \begin{bmatrix} dx \\ dy \\ dz \end{bmatrix}, \quad ds_1 = \begin{bmatrix} dx_1 \\ dy_1 \\ dz_1 \end{bmatrix}, \quad ds_2 = \begin{bmatrix} dx_2 \\ dy_2 \\ dz_2 \end{bmatrix},$$

$$dv_i = \begin{bmatrix} dvx_i \\ dvy_i \\ dvz_i \end{bmatrix} \text{ in which } i = 0, 1, 2.$$

Supposing that dz, ds_1, ds_2, dv_0, dv_1, dv_2 of the Eq. (25.5) are independent of each other, we can have obtained mathematical expectation after matrix transformations:

$$C \cdot E[dudu^T] \cdot C^T = E[dzdz^T] + U_1 \cdot E[ds_1ds_1^T] \cdot U_1^T + U_2 \cdot E[ds_2ds_2^T] \cdot U_2^T$$
$$+ V_1 E[dv_1d_1^T]V_1^T + V_2 E[dv_2d_2^T]V_2^T + VE[dv_0d_0^T]V^T$$

$$(25.12)$$

In a single measurement case, we assume that the target altitude and velocity are known. The definition of positioning error of radiation sources is $GDOP(x, y) = \sqrt{\sigma_x^2 + \sigma_y^2}$, then there is,

$$GDOP(x, y) = \sqrt{trace(E[du_1du_1^T])} \qquad (25.13)$$

25.4 Simulation

Assuming that the radiation source is fixed, the height is $z = 10\,\text{km}$, the velocity is $v_0 = (0, 0, 0)\,\text{m/s}$, velocity error is $\sigma_{v0} = (0, 0, 0)\,\text{m/s}$, the initial coordinates of the carrier aircraft are $A_1(-12, 0, 6)\,\text{km}$, $A_2(12, 0, 6)\,\text{km}$, the velocity of the carrier aircraft is $v_1 = v_2 = (0, 180, 0)\,\text{m/s}$, the error of TDOA is $\sigma_{\Delta t} = 10\,\text{ns}$, the error of FDOA is $\sigma_{f_d} = 1\,\text{Hz}$, the velocity error is $\sigma_{v1} = \sigma_{v2} = (0.1, 0.1, 0.1)\,\text{m/s}$, the position error is $\sigma_{A1} = \sigma_{A2} = 20\,\text{m}$, the frequency of emitter is $f_0 = 10 \times 10^9\,\text{Hz}$.

According to (25.13), we can get the GDOP equivalent curve as:

Figure. 25.6 shows that the GDOP changes rapidly in the direction of the velocity and the direction of the carrier aircraft connection; However, GDOP changes relatively slower in the direction of the velocity was 45 ° or 135 °.

In this experiment, we get 20 random points in the area surrounded by the bold blue line and calculate its GDOP value. Then we change the direction of receiver, re-calculate the GDOP value of these points. Contrast the two sets of GDOP values in three-dimensional space, we can get multiples of the method optimization and the results are shown in Figs. 25.7 and 25.8.

25.5 Conclusions

According to Fig. 25.7, we can be adjusted to the carrier aircraft direction $\pm 45°$ in the original direction when the target is located in the direction of the velocity or located within $15°$ difference of connection direction of the carrier aircraft. The targeted area is switched from the enclosed area by the bold blue line into the enclosed area by the bold red line. According to the simulation, Fig. 25.8 shows that the method can improve positioning precision 2–10 times.

By adjustment the positioning carrier aircraft direction, we can make the original region, which is unstable positioning area, is converted to the new stable positioning area. So we can reach the purpose of improving positioning accuracy of the target area.

References

1. Ren R, Fowler ML, Wu NE (2009) Finding optimal trajectory points for TDOA/FDOA geolocation sensors. In: Information sciences and systems, CISS 2009, pp 817–822
2. Musicki D, Koch W (2008) Geolocation using TDOA and FDOA measurements. In: Information fusion, 11th international conference, pp 1–8
3. Ho KC, Chan YT (1997) Geolocation of a known altitude object from TDOA and FDOA measurements. IEEE Trans AES 33:770–783
4. Hu LZ (2004) Passive location. National Defence Industry Press, Beijing, pp 150–203 (in Chinese)
5. Feng TJ (2008) Joint TDOA and FDOA positioning performance research of dual receivers. National Defense University of Electronic Science and Technology, pp 22–32 (in Chinese)
6. Pan Q (2005) Study on AOA and joint location method of TDOA and FDOA in passive location systems. Xidian university, Xi' an, pp 23–15 (in Chinese)
7. Schau HC, Robinson AZ (1987) Passive source localization employing intersecting spherical surfaces from time of arrival differences. IEEE Trans Acoust Speech Signal Process ASSP-35(8):1223–1225
8. Wu SL, Zhao YS, Luo JQ (2007) Performance analysis of dual-satellite joint FDOA and TDOA location system. Aerospace Shanghai, pp 47–50 (in Chinese)
9. Guo XS, Wan Q, Liu X (2006) Digital map aided joint TDOA-FDOA localization using double-star. Comput Eng Appl 23:11–13 (in Chinese)

Chapter 26
Precise Fundamental Matrix Estimation Based on Inlier Distribution Constraint

Yan Zhen, Xuejun Liu and Meizhen Wang

Abstract The fundamental matrix is an effective tool to analyze epipolar geometry relationship between two-view images and plays an important role in computer vision. Traditional RANSAC method selects the biggest consensus set of inliers to estimate fundamental matrix. No previous methods have considered whether such a choice really is the best. In this paper, a new algorithm for fundamental matrix estimation by considering the inliers distribution is proposed. It takes the traditional RANSAC method as the basic framework and selects these sets which contain a large number of inliers to construct a candidate set. Then calculate the density of the inlier distribution and the mean of the epipolar distance of the inlier sets in the candidate set. At last choose the optimum one as the inlier set to estimate the fundamental matrix. Through experiment comparison with previous methods on a large number of simulated and real image data show that the proposed algorithm can achieve a more precise result.

Keywords Computer vision · Fundamental matrix · Epipolar geometry · Inlier set

26.1 Introduction

The fundamental matrix describes the relationship between two images of the same scene taken from two different viewpoints, namely, the epipolar geometry. The epipolar constraint is the only geometric information could available from two uncalibrated images [1]. Therefore, precise estimation of fundamental matrix is

Y. Zhen (✉) · X. Liu · M. Wang
Key Laboratory of Virtual Geographic Environment, Ministry of Education, Nanjing Normal University, Nanjing, China
e-mail: zhenyan0824@163.com

W. Lu et al. (eds.), *Proceedings of the 2012 International Conference on Information Technology and Software Engineering*, Lecture Notes in Electrical Engineering 211, DOI: 10.1007/978-3-642-34522-7_26, © Springer-Verlag Berlin Heidelberg 2013

one of the most crucial steps in many computer vision applications such as 3D reconstruction, visual navigation, stereo vision and motion segmentation [2, 3].

The fundamental matrix is most of the time evaluated from point correspondences. However, the point correspondences inevitable contain noise and outliers, thus affect the precise of the fundamental matrix. Noise calls for estimating fundamental matrix over the largest possible set of correspondences but outliers make it awkward. In recent years, it has been done a lot of work on how to accurately and robustly estimate fundamental matrix. From these studies, it showed that the main difficulty of fundamental matrix estimation is how to quick and accurately eliminate the outliers. The robust algorithms are used to solve this problem. These methods are based on random selecting the points, so the quality of the sampling has a direct impact on the precise of the fundamental matrix. Previous studies showed that the evenly distribution can better represent the variation of the image due to camera motion. So it is important to select a better inlier set for a more precise fundamental matrix. However, only a few studies have taken into account the distribution of the inlier set when estimating the fundamental matrix [4, 5].

Various properties and calculation methods for the fundamental matrix have been studies in the last two decades. They can be roughly divided into three different approaches: the linear, the iterative and the robust [6]. The linear methods [6, 7] estimate the fundamental matrix by using seven or eight corresponding points. With more than eight points, a least-squares technique is used. The advantages of the linear methods are its simplicity for implementation and computational efficiency, but they are very sensitive to noise. In order to obtain a better result, the iterative and robust algorithms have to be considered. The iterative approach [1, 3] has been proposed to minimize the sum of geometric distances between the points and the corresponding epipolar lines, or the gradient-weighted epipolar errors. Although iterative method is direct relation to a meaningful geometric measure and the result is more accurate than linear method, it time consuming and cannot cope with potential outliers. The third one are the robust methods, they can alleviate the effect of outliers to the fundamental matrix estimation. The three representative robust methods are M-Estimators, LMedS and RANSAC [8, 9]. Robust methods can deal with the noise and false point correspondences, but they require much more computational time and they still have their limitations. In addition, in recent years, the genetic algorithm was introduced to the fundamental matrix estimation [10, 11]. This could improve the accuracy of the result, but the genetic algorithm is time consuming and thus result the algorithm need more time.

This paper present a novel method to estimate the fundamental matrix, it based on the RANSAC method and consider the inlier set distribution. Traditional RANSAC method selects the biggest consensus set of inliers to estimate fundamental matrix, no previous methods have consider whether such a choice really is the best. In our algorithm, we select these inlier sets that contain a large number of inliers to construct a candidate set. Then calculate the mean of the epipolar distances and the density of the inlier sets in the candidate set. Finally choose the minimum mean of the epipolar distances which need to meet the condition that it distribution should better than the one that has the largest number of inliers. After selecting the proper inlier set, we use the M-Estimators method to estimate the fundamental matrix.

The rest of this paper is organized as follows. Section 26.2 introduce the epipolar geometry and review the traditional algorithms for fundamental matrix estimation. Section 26.3 we introduce the density of the inlier set and the strategy of the proper inlier set selection. In Sect. 26.4, we describe the proposed algorithm for fundamental matrix estimation. Some experiment results for synthetic and real scenes are given in Sect. 26.5. Finally, the conclusion is described in the last section.

26.2 Point Density and Proper Inlier Set Selection

26.2.1 Point Density

Previous studies show that the evenly distributed point set is effective for the fundamental matrix estimation [4, 5]. This is mainly due to the fundamental matrix contains the relative orientation and position between two cameras, so the inlier set should reflect the variation of the images. Seo and Hong et al. proposed that the standard deviation of the point density in sub-regions and an entire image can be used to evaluate whether the inlier set is evenly distributed [5]. According the number of the inliers, the image is divided into several uniform sub-regions by Eq. (26.1).

$$W_s = W/int\left(\sqrt{N}\right), \ H_s = H/int\left(\sqrt{N}\right) \tag{26.1}$$

where W_s and H_s denote the width and the height of the sub-region, N is the number of the inliers, W and H are the width and height of the image. After divided the image into sub-regions, then calculate the number of the sub-regions and the inliers in each sub-regions, respectively using N_s and P_{si} denote it. At last, compute the standard deviation of the point density by Eq. (26.2)

$$\sigma_p = \sqrt{\frac{1}{N_s}\sum_{i=1}^{N_s}\left(P_{si} - \frac{N}{N_s}\right)^2} \tag{26.2}$$

26.2.2 Proper Inlier Set Selection

The traditional RANSAC method selects the biggest consensus set of inliers to estimate the fundamental matrix. But this selection scheme always does not guarantee the result is the best one. During the experiment, we found that

Table 26.1 The results under different noise levels and different percentages of mismatched

Method (a, b)	RANSAC			Proposed method		
	Mean error	Point density	Inliers	Mean error	Point density	Inliers
(0.0, 0 %)	0.000	0.970	125	0.000	0.970	125
(0.5, 0 %)	0.613	0.940	124	0.594	0.928	117
(0.5, 30 %)	0.555	1.090	80	0.555	1.090	80
(0.5, 45 %)	3.020	0.877	53	3.020	0.877	53
(0.5, 55 %)	11.135	1.330	43	5.653	1.246	38
(1.5, 0 %)	1.150	1.000	100	1.150	1.000	100
(1.5, 30 %)	1.375	1.077	71	1.239	0.909	67
(1.5, 45 %)	2.141	0.848	64	2.141	0.848	64
(1.5, 55 %)	10.418	1.076	52	7.201	1.050	49

sometimes using these inlier sets which are contain less number of inliers than the largest one could obtain better results. So, if the proper inlier selected satisfy the following two conditions: the first condition is that its standard deviation of the point density should not larger than the one which has the largest number of inliers; the other condition is that the average geometry distance should be the minimum one, we can achieve a more precise estimation of the fundamental matrix.

In order to show whether this hypothesis is correct, we use the simulated data which are provided by Armangue and Salvi [6] to test it. The simulated data contains 125 pairs of points. We added the random noise and the percentage of mismatched data in it. Using the vector (a, b) to denote the noise is a Gaussian distribution $N(0, a)$ and the percentage of the mismatched data is b. After sometimes of random sampling, we choose these sets which should contain large number of inliers. Among these sets, the largest number should have 10 % more points than the one which has the least numbers. Then calculate the fundamental matrix and the average geometry distance. At last select the inlier set which should satisfy above conditions. Table 26.1 shows the experiment results.

From Table 26.1 we can see that, there are a total of nine groups of data, except the one which contain no noise and mismatched data, due to all points in this group are inliers, so the selected set contains all the points. Among the other eight groups, only 50 % of the results choose the largest number of consensus as the proper inlier set, the rest 50 % select the other set as the proper inlier set. Both the density and the average distance are better than the traditional selection. So we can conclude that select the proper inlier set can obtain a more precise result.

26.3 Proposed Fundamental Matrix Estimation Algorithm

Because using the traditional RANSAC algorithm always does not guarantee the result is the best one, we propose a new algorithm to solve this problem. Due to the point density has an important influence on the fundamental estimation, so the proposed algorithm considers these factors when selecting the inlier set. The basic idea of the proposed algorithm is as follows: at first randomly selecting some subsets to estimate the fundamental matrix and statistical the number of inliers. Then choose some sets which have large number of inliers to calculate the point density. The range of the candidate set can be determined by the number of the inliers, in the range, the largest number of inliers should have 10 % more points than the least one. Then select inlier set use the strategy that was proposed above. At last use the M-Estimators method to estimate the fundamental matrix based on the selected inlier set.

The complete procedure of the proposed method is summarized as follow:

(1) Select a random sample of eight point correspondences and estimate the fundamental matrix by using the normalized eight-points algorithm. Then compute the distance of point to its epipolar line for each point correspondence and statistical the number of inliers, at the same time record the average distance.

(2) Repeat (26.1) for K times and store fundamental matrix, the number of inliers and the average distance.

$$K = \log(1 - P)/\log(1 - (1 - \varepsilon)^{\gamma}) \tag{26.3}$$

where P is the probability that these points are the inliers in sampling γ points at K times, ε is the ratio of the outlier to the entire set.

(3) Select some inlier sets to construct a candidate inlier set.

(4) Compute the standard deviation of point density of the selected inlier sets.

(5) Select the inlier set by using the method that proposed above as the proper inlier set.

(6) Re-estimate the fundamental matrix from the proper inlier set by using the M-Estimators algorithm.

26.4 Experimental Results and Discussion

In this section, we show some experimental results of the proposed method. We compare it with the results in the survey by Armangue and Salvi [6]. The test data that used in our method are also provided by them, it includes synthesis data and real image data.

First of all, Table 26.2 gives the result of the experiment on the simulation data. From the table we can see that except the proposed algorithm, the LMedS method can provide better result than others. But compared with our method, the result that obtained by our method are better than the LMedS algorithm. So, we can conclude that our proposed method can provide precise fundamental matrix under different levels of noise and different percentages of mismatched.

Table 26.2 Average distances under different noise and percentage of mismatched (unit: pixel)

(a, b) Methods	(0.0, 0 %)	(0.0, 10 %)	(0.5, 0 %)	(0.5, 10 %)	(1.0, 0 %)	(1.0, 10 %)
Seven points	14.250	25.370	163.839	140.932	65.121	128.919
Eigenvalue minimization	0.000	17.124	0.538	19.262	1.065	21.264
Gradients eigen	0.000	18.224	0.554	19.409	1.071	18.730
FNS	0.000	17.124	0.538	22.302	1.065	18.374
CFNS	0.000	16.978	0.543	22.262	1.066	19.638
LMedS	0.000	0.000	0.538	0.586	1.065	1.052
RANSAC	0.000	16.457	0.538	18.942	1.065	14.076
Our method	0.000	0.000	0.506	0.509	0.796	0.825

Table 26.3 Average distances of the real images (unit: pixel)

Scenes Methods	Urban	Underwater	Robot	Kitchen
Seven points	51.633	97.977	119.439	16.956
Eigenvalue minimization	0.440	1.725	4.080	2.623
Gradients eigen	0.446	1.581	4.787	1.901
FNS	0.437	1.599	4.080	2.623
CFNS	0.437	1.609	3.199	1.892
LMedS	0.319	0.847	1.559	0.545
RANSAC	0.440	1.725	3.855	2.623
Our method	0.290	0.538	0.340	0.395

Fig. 26.1 The epipolar lines of the inliers computed by the proposed method for real images

We choose four real images to test our algorithm. The average distances of the four data sets are summarized in Table 26.3. Figure 26.1 gives the epipolar lines of the point correspondences computed from the fundamental matrix estimated by the proposed algorithm. It is obvious from Table 26.3 that our method outperforms the others.

From the experiment results of the simulate data sets and the real images sets, we can conclude that the proposed algorithm can select the proper inlier set to estimate the fundamental matrix and the precise of the result is better than the other algorithms.

26.5 Conclusions

In this paper, we proposed a precise fundamental matrix estimation algorithm. The proposed algorithm takes into account the average distance of the points to its epipolar lines and the distribution of the inlier set to select the proper inlier set. The traditional RANSAC algorithm choose the set that has the biggest number of inliers to estimate the fundamental matrix, but the experimental results show that this select strategy does not always guarantee a precise solution. Compared with the traditional RANSAC algorithm, our algorithm select the inlier set is better than the traditional one. Experimental results on synthetic and real images show that our algorithm can obtain a more precise fundamental matrix. This method can be used in the further work such as camera calibration and 3D scene reconstruction.

Acknowledgments This research has been supported by Natural Science Foundation of the Jiangsu Higher Education Institutions of China (No.10KJA420025), National Science and Technology Support Program References (2012BAH35B02) and Jiangsu colleges and universities superiority discipline construction project subsidization project.

References

1. Hartley R, Zisserman A (2003) Multiple view geometry in computer vision. Cambridge University Press, Cambridge
2. Luong Q, Faugeras O (1996) The fundamental matrix: theory, algorithms, and stability analysis. Int J Comput Vision 17(1):43–75
3. Zhang Z (1998) Determining the epipolar geometry and its uncertainty: a review. Int J Comput Vision 27(2):161–195
4. Choukroun A, Charvillat V (2003) Bucketing techniques in robust regression for computer vision. In: Proceedings of SCIA 2003. Lecture Notes in Computer Science, Goteborg, vol 2749, pp 609–616
5. Jk Seo, Hk Hong et al (2004) Two quantitative measures of inlier distributions for precise fundamental matrix estimation. Pattern Recogn Lett 25:733–741
6. Armangué X, Salvi J (2003) Overall view regarding fundamental matrix estimation. Image Vis Comput 21:205–220

7. Hartley R (1995) In defense of the 8-point algorithm. In: Proceedings of the 8th international conference on computer vision, pp 1064–1070
8. Stewart CV (1999) Robust parameter estimation in computer vision. SIAM Rev 41:513–537
9. Torr PHS, Murray DW (1997) The development and comparison of robust methods for estimating the fundamental matrix. Int J Comput Vision 24:271–300
10. Tang CY, Chen RS et al (2005) Using orthogonal genetic algorithms to estimate fundamental matrices. In: 18th IPPR conference on computer vision, graphics and image processing, pp 1847–1854
11. Hu MX, Karen MM et al (2008) Epipolar geometry estimation based on evolutionary agents. Pattern Recogn 41(2):575–591

Chapter 27
State of Charge Estimation Based on a Composite Method for Power Lithium Battery

Danming Zhang and Yan Zhou

Abstract The state of change (SOC) is used to describe the remaining capacity of battery and its accuracy is very important for power battery. In this paper, according to the composite method, the dynamic system model is established, combining with the ampere hour integral method revised by the compensating factor and the equivalent circuit model. After that, the system state equation and observation equation is introduced. At the same time, the Kalman filtering achieves the minimum error of SOC estimation value. The SIMULINK tool is used to establish the mathematical model of dynamic system. The simulation results show that the composite method can monitor the battery SOC in real-time. Its accuracy can keep the error within 4 %, which is good practical value in the estimate of power battery SOC under the complex operating condition.

Keywords SOC · Dynamic system · Kalman filter · Lithium battery

27.1 Introduction

Power lithium battery is a key to the electric vehicle. The state of change (SOC) reflects the remaining capacity of battery. So accurate estimating the SOC value is vital to the battery management system, and it is also one of the important basis for control the EV. Due to the electrochemical properties of battery is very complicated. It shows highly nonlinear in the process of charging and discharging. And

D. Zhang · Y. Zhou (✉)
School of Electrical and Electronic Engineering, Hubei University of Technology,
430068 Wuhan, People's Republic of China
e-mail: kingkongcassie@163.com

W. Lu et al. (eds.), *Proceedings of the 2012 International Conference on Information Technology and Software Engineering*, Lecture Notes in Electrical Engineering 211, DOI: 10.1007/978-3-642-34522-7_27, © Springer-Verlag Berlin Heidelberg 2013

the influences of current, temperature and charge–discharge cycle make higher difficulty to accurately estimate SOC value. In order to improve the accuracy of estimation, the previous papers took into account the compensation of the charge–discharge efficiency, temperature, aging and other factors in the model algorithm [1]. Nevertheless, a single model to describe the cell dynamic characteristics is rather difficulty and some errors. So the battery SOC estimation has become the difficulty to the battery management system [2].

The traditional SOC estimation methods, such as ampere hour integral method, the open circuit voltage method and impedance method, have their own short-comings. So the researchers pay more attentions on the new methods to estimate SOC value.

The mathematical method to complex dynamic system model is effective, and also can revise the error in a certain degree. Based on the principle of Kalman filtering [3], it combines with Ah integral method and open circuit voltage method to establish filtering system, so as to realize the composite estimation method.

27.2 The Principle of Composite Method

The composite method of SOC estimation mainly embodied in two aspects: firstly, estimation method relies on the accurate dynamic cell model; secondly, it can be applied to real-time estimation the SOC value. The compound method based on Kalman filtering is appropriate for relative complex condition, and can more fully simulate the power battery operating characteristics. A dynamic model to estimate SOC value is proposed.

27.2.1 Ampere-hour Integral Method

Ah integral method estimates the battery SOC through the accumulation power in charge or discharge. It is one of the most simple and commonly used methods at present. The formula of Ah integral method is:

$$SOC(t) = SOC(t_0) - \int_{t_0}^{t} \eta \frac{i(t)}{C} dt \qquad (27.1)$$

where SOC (t_0) is the battery SOC value of initial state, C is the rated capacity, η is the correction coefficient about the temperature, the discharge rate and the number of cycles.

The ampere-hour method estimates SOC value. It is an easy and stable algorithm. The defect is needed to calibrate SOC initial value; and η is not constant under the different discharge conditions; there has a certain error in high temperature and current fluctuation severe situation [4].

27.2.2 Open Circuit Voltage Method

Open circuit voltage method under a certain condition uses the relationship between the SOC and OCV. The dynamic SOC estimation accuracy depends on the power cell model. To establish the mathematical model of the lithium cell requires identifying the parameters, and then building the relationship of equivalent circuit model. The formula of the OCV is:

$$U_{oc} = K_0 - Ri - K_1 x_k + {K_2}/{x_k} + K_3 \ln(x_k) + K_4 \ln(1 - x_k) \qquad (27.2)$$

where U_{oc} is the battery terminal voltage of one cell, x_k is value in different conditions of the SOC, and R is the battery internal resistance (differed values in different charging and discharging status and different SOC). K_1 is the polarization effect of equivalent resistance. K_2, K_3 and K_4 is the model matching parameters [5].

This method needs a rest time in measuring the OCV to ensure the SOC value accurately. So it does not apply to real-time estimation for electric vehicle.

27.2.3 The Principle of Kalman Filtering Method

Kalman filtering method is introduced into the system state space model [5, 6]. The State equation describes the state and variation; it gives the mathematical model of the changing of state transition in adjacent time. The measurement equation describes the information of the measurement state, usually containing observation noise.

Kalman filtering problem is to find the optimal estimation of the system state, based on the obtained information from the measurement equation.

For a discrete time process of state variable, the system state equation is:

$$x_k = Ax_{k-1} + Bu_{k-1} + \omega_k \qquad (27.3)$$

Definition of system measurement equation is:

$$y_k = Cx_k + v_k \qquad (27.4)$$

where the SOC value is the system state variable x_k, the vector u_k is the input, including the factors, such as the power battery current, temperature and discharge ratio. And the vector y_k is the measuring value.

The optimal estimation is the core part of the Kalman filter algorithm, which is revised by the difference between the measured and predicted measurement y_k. So the quantity of state x_k is closer to the real value in this system. And optimal estimate equals to the prior estimation value and algorithm correction [7].

To illustrate this optimal estimation, consider the linear discrete-time system block diagram in Fig. 27.1.

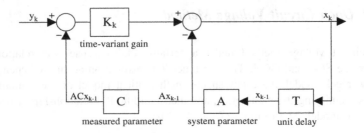

Fig. 27.1 The principle of optimal estimation block diagram

27.3 The Framework of Model

What this work does is taken of Ah integral equation as the system state equation and (27.2) of equivalent circuit equation as measurement equation [8].

1. According to the SOC estimation value at $K - 1$ time, update the SOC prior estimation at the time K by (27.5);
2. According to the prior estimation of SOC, update the prior voltage estimation at time K by (27.6);
3. The formula (27.7) is equation of the algorithm correction, which is the product of filter gain Kk and prediction error. The prediction error is the difference between the measurement value of terminal voltage and its prior voltage estimation at time K.
4. According to the vectors of formulas (27.5–27.7), updating formula (27.8), it can obtain the SOC estimation value at time K and output this value.

Output value at time K, and take it as the initial estimation at time $K + 1$, we can get the SOC prior estimate at time $K + 1$. Through this circle from prediction to update, it can get every moment for SOC filter estimation value [9].

$$x_{k|k-1} = x_{k-1|k-1} - \eta \frac{i(t)}{C} \Delta t \tag{27.5}$$

$$y_{k|k-1} = K_0 - Ri - K_1 x_{k|k-1} + K_2/_{x_{k|k-1}} + K_3 \ln(x_{k|k-1}) + K_4 \ln(1 - x_{k|k-1}) \tag{27.6}$$

$$correct = K_k \times (y_k - y_{k|k-1}) \tag{27.7}$$

$$x_{k|k} = x_{k|k-1} + K_k \times (y_k - y_{k|k-1}) \tag{27.8}$$

where $x_{k-1|k-1}$ is the SOC estimation, $x_{k|k-1}$ is the SOC priori estimation at time K, y_k and $y_{k|k-1}$ are the terminal voltage and the prior voltage estimation at time K, u_{k-1} is the input at time $K - 1$. w_k and v_k are the incentive noise and observation noise. They are both normal distribution of white noise.

The composite algorithm updates the SOC estimation value, and at the same time, takes the minimum error covariance of the system state as the best standards to correct the SOC estimation value [10].

Formula 27.9 is the Kalman filter gain matrix K_k, whose role is to make the system's estimation error covariance minimum.

$$K_k = \frac{C_k \times P_{k|k-1}}{C_k \times P_{k|k-1} \times C_k^T} \tag{27.9}$$

Formula 27.10 is the measured value matrix:

$$C_k = \frac{\partial y_{k|k-1}}{\partial x} = \frac{K_2}{x_{k|k-1}^2} - K_1 + \frac{K_3}{x_{k|k-1}} - \frac{K_4}{1 - x_{k|k-1}} \tag{27.10}$$

Formula 27.11 is the prior estimation covariance matrix:

$$P_{k|k-1} = AP_{k-1|k-1}A^T + Q \tag{27.11}$$

Formula 27.12 is the optimal filtering error covariance update:

$$P_{k|k} = P_{k|k-1} \times (1 - C_k K_k) \tag{27.12}$$

27.4 Simulation and Results

The SIMULINK tool is used for the simulation. The mathematical model is established, on the basis of the composite method. The structure diagram of the model is shown in Fig. 27.2. During the simulation, it simulates the process of discharge with 1C pulse rate, and the discharge current waveform is shown in Fig. 27.3.

Figure 27.4 is the voltage of the storage battery varies with time. After 600 s, the battery terminal voltage is stabilized, and fluctuates within a certain range. For the storage battery maintains at a stable voltage state.

Figure 27.5 shows the difference of SOC value between the composite method and the single Ah integral. Comparing the data, it finds that the composite method based on Kalman filtering method is more accurate in real-time estimating cell SOC value.

Figure 27.6 shows the SOC relative error by the composite method. It display the maximum relative error about 4 %. This may be the reason that the relationship between the OCV and SOC is not very clear in discharged interim at that time, and so the error is larger [11].

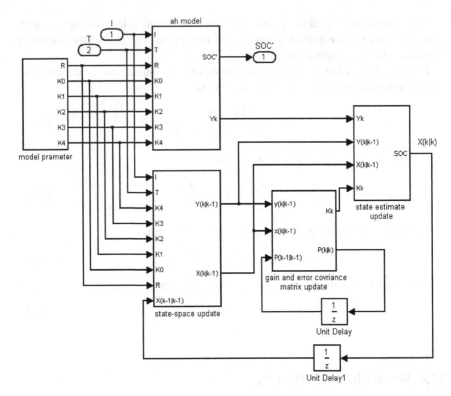

Fig. 27.2 The SOC estimation model based on composite method

Fig. 27.3 The waveform of
discharge current

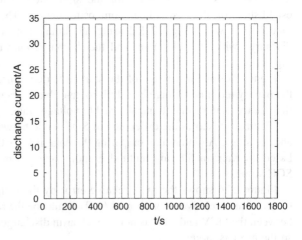

Fig. 27.4 The terminal
voltage of the cell

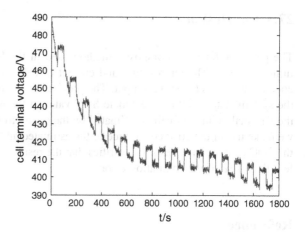

Fig. 27.5 The comparison of
the two estimation methods

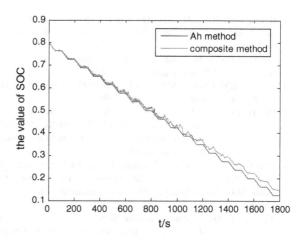

Fig. 27.6 The relative error
of SOC estimation value

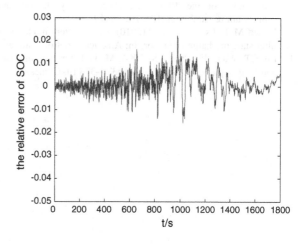

27.5 Conclusion

The paper outlines the composite method used in the SOC estimation of power lithium battery. The temperature and current of cell, as well as theirs correction coefficients are as the system input. The previous moment estimation of SOC is as the system state quantity to estimate SOC value at the next moment. Meanwhile, the terminal voltage of cell is estimated by the open-circuit voltage method. Thus, we make use of the error covariance of the estimated and measured value to revise the SOC estimation. It tests and verifies that the result of simulation experiment is less than 4 % of the estimation error.

References

1. Huang WH, Han XD, Chen QS, Lin CT (2007). A study on SOC estimation algorithm and battery management system for electric vehicle. Automotive Engineering 29(3):198–202 (in Chinese)
2. Piller S, Perrin M, Jossen A (2001) Methods for state-of-charge determination and their applications. J Power Sources 96:113–120
3. Salameh ZM, Casacca MA, Lynch WA (1992). A mathematical model for lead-acid batteries. IEEE Trans Energy Convers 7(1):93–98
4. Do DV, Forgez C, Benkara KEK, Friedrich G (2009) Impedance observer for a Li-Ion battery using Kalman filter. IEEE Trans Veh Technol 58(8):3930–3937
5. Li C (2007) Study on parameter identification and SOC estimation of Ni/MH battery for EV. Tianjin University, Tianjin (in Chinese)
6. Plett GL (2004) Extended Kalman filtering for battery management systems of LiPB-based HEV battery packs Part 3. State and parameter estimation. Power Sour 134(2):277–292
7. Bozic SM (1984) Digital filtering and Kalman filtering. 2nd edn. Science Press, Beijing (in Chinese)
8. Plett GL (2004) Extended Kalman filtering for battery management systems of LiPB-based HEV battery packs Part 2. Modeling and identification, Power Sources 134(2):262–276
9. Plett GL (2002) LiPB dynamic cell models for Kalman-filter SOC estimation. In: Proceedings of the 19th international battery, hybrid and fuel cell electric vehicle symposium & exhibition (EVS19), pp 19–23
10. Knauff M, Dafis C, Niebur D (2010) A new battery model for use with an extended Kalman filter state of charge estimator. In: American control conference (ACC), pp 1991–1996
11. Lin CT, Wang JP, Chen QS (2004) Methods for state of charge estimation of EV batteries and their application. Battery 34(5):376–378 (in Chinese)

Chapter 28
The Research on Algorithm of Determining LR-Visibility in a Simple Polygon

Lijuan Wang, Qi Wei, Yuan Shi and Dandan He

Abstract LR-visibility in a simple polygon plays an important role in many geometric problems, such as two-guard and polygon search problems. The study on which has important theoretical significance and practical value in computational geometry. Based on the characteristics of the simple polygons, analyzing the relationship between the number of non-redundant components and LR-visibility, combined with the necessary and sufficient conditions to determine whether a simple polygon is LR-visible or not, this paper puts forward an algorithm for computing the number of non-redundant components. According to this algorithm and the necessary and sufficient conditions, we can determine whether a simple polygon is LR-visible or not. Particularly, we realize the algorithm with C++ program. The experiment result shows that the algorithm is correct and practicable.

Keywords Simple polygon · LR-visibility · Non-redundant component

L. Wang (✉) · Q. Wei
School of Information Science and Technology, Dalian Maritime University,
1# Linghai Road, 116026 Dalian, China
e-mail: znhy.wang@163.com

Q. Wei
e-mail: 87284143@qq.com

L. Wang · Q. Wei · Y. Shi · D. He
Department of Information and Science, Dalian Institute of Science and Technology, Dalian
Lvshun Economic Development Zone Port Road 999-26, 116052 Dalian, China
e-mail: 20088041@qq.com

D. He
e-mail: 346705850@qq.com

W. Lu et al. (eds.), *Proceedings of the 2012 International Conference on Information Technology and Software Engineering*, Lecture Notes in Electrical Engineering 211, DOI: 10.1007/978-3-642-34522-7_28, © Springer-Verlag Berlin Heidelberg 2013

28.1 Introduction

Characterizing, recognizing and computing visibility polygons under various criteria are central issues in visibility problem in computational geometry and related application areas [1]. The notion of visibility in a polygon from an internal segment arose when Avis and Toussaint considered variations of the following art gallery problem: to place minimum number of stationary guards in an art gallery so that, together they can see every point in the interior of the gallery. In formal setting, the art gallery can be viewed as a simple polygon and guards as some points in the polygon. In fact, many practical problems can be abstracted into the model of a simple polygon, such as installing the monitoring system in banks, post office and some other public places, the two guards patrolling a block, and dynamic target searching, which can be solved by the research achievement of LR-visibility in computational geometry. Therefore, the research on LR-visibility has great theoretical and practical significance.

In this paper, we mainly study the algorithm of determine whether a simple polygon is LR- visible or not. Based on the theory and the characteristics of LR-visible polygon, we put forward an algorithm for computing the number of non-redundant components for given simple polygons, then according to the algorithm and the necessary and sufficient conditions of LR-visible polygon, we can determine whether a simple polygon is LR-visible or not.

28.2 Preliminary

28.2.1 The Problem Description of LR-Visibility and Related Concepts

Let P denote a simple polygon with n vertices, i.e., P has neither self-intersections nor holes.

If all the interior angles of P are less than $180°$, then it's called a convex polygon, otherwise a concave polygon [1]. The interior angles are greater than $180°$ in a concave polygon are called reflex vertices, for example, r_1 is a reflex vertex in the concave polygon as shown in Fig. 28.1. Because the reflex vertices will block the light of some points on the edge of simple polygon, it is necessary to divide the polygons.

Any two points s and t on P divide the boundary of P into two sub-chains, which we call L and R, for left and right chains. The LR-visibility question asks whether each point of L is visible from a point of R, and whether each point of R is visible from a point of L. If the answer is yes, we say P is LR-visible with respect

Fig. 28.1 An example of a
concave polygon

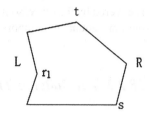

Fig. 28.2 Immediately
preceding and succeeding,
forward, backward ray shots
and components

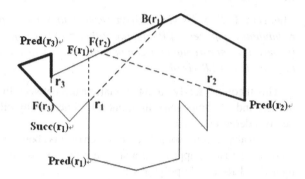

to s and t. If there exists a pair of points on P such that P is LR-visible with respect
to them, we simply say P is LR-visible [2]. The simple polygon shown in Fig. 28.1
is LR-visible.

For a vertex r of the polygon P, let Pred(r) denote the vertex immediately
preceding r clockwise, and Succ(r) the vertex immediately succeeding r clockwise.
An important definition for reflex vertices is that of ray shots: the backward ray
shot from a reflex vertex r, denoted by B(r), and the forward ray shot F(r) is the
first point hit by the bullet shot at r in the direction from Pred(r) to r. In the
Fig. 28.2, Pred(r_1) is the vertex immediately proceeding and Succ(r_1) is the vertex
immediately succeeding, F(r_1) is the forward ray shot of r_1 and B(r_1) is the
backward ray shot of it.

Let u,v denote two boundary points of P, and let P[u,v] and P(u,v) denote the
closed and open clockwise chains of P from u to v, respectively. We define
P[r,B(r)] and P[F(r),r] as the backward component and forward component of the
reflex vertex r, respectively. The point r is referred to as the defining vertex of its
backward or forward component. Two kinds of components which are redundant
component and non-redundant component can be constructed by each reflect
vertex. A component is said to be non-redundant if it does not contain any other
component, no matter which is the forward or backward component [3]. For
example, the components P[F(r_2),r_2] and P[F(r_3),r_3] shown in Fig. 28.2 are non-
redundant, while the component P[r_1,B(r_1)] is redundant because it contains
component P[F(r_3),r_3]. In the two components consisted of each reflex vertex, one

is covered by the other, so it is the redundant component. This paper only discusses the non-redundant components.

28.2.2 The Judging Theorem of LR-visible Polygon

Das and Heffernan first gave the theorem to determine whether a simple polygon is LR-visible in [3].

Theorem 1 *P is LR-visible with respect to s and t if and only if each non-redundant component of P contains either s or t, which contains neitherotherwise, if there is a non-redundant component s nor t in the polygon, then the simple polygon is not LR-visible.*

This theorem clearly gave the relationship between the LR-visible polygon and non-redundant components in it, but it is conceptually difficult and too complex to be considered practical.

Tan et al. presented some latest research results about the LR-visible polygon in [4].

If one situation appears in a simple polygon P as the following two Lemmas, then P is LR- visible polygon.

Lemma 1 *A polygon P is not LR-visible if (N1) it has three pairwise disjoint components.*

Lemma 2 *A polygon P is not LR-visible if (N2) it has k non-redundant components such that each of them exactly intersects with k' other components, where $k \geq 5$ and $k' \leq k-3$.*

Theorem 2 *A polygon P is LR-visible if and only if neither N1 nor N2 applies.*

It can be seen from that the composition and quantity of non-redundant component in a simple polygon P have a close relation with its visibility. If we can compute the number of non-redundant component in the simple polygon, and then according to the above necessary and sufficient conditions of LR-visible polygon, we can determine whether a simple polygon is LR-visible or not. This paper mainly focuses on how to compute the number of non-redundant.

28.3 The Method of Computing the Number of Non-Redundant Component

This paper presents an algorithm on how to compute the number of non-redundant component. The idea of the algorithm is as follows. We first compute two supersets of non-redundant backward and forward components, and then extract the exact set of non-redundant components from them [2]. Finally we can obtain the set of proper components by merging components, and then determine whether neither N1 nor N2 applies. In the case that P is LR-visible, we can also report a pair(s,t) such that P is LR-visible with respect to s and t.

28.3.1 The Algorithm of Solving the Non-Redundant Backward Components

The basic idea of algorithm computing the non-redundant components is to put all components mapping to three components by the necessary and sufficient conditions of LR-visible polygon. First, find out a non-redundant component denoted by A, then traverse all non- redundant components of definition vertex in A. Next, look for the non-redundant component denoted by B whose definition vertex is close to the left endpoint of A and disjoint with A. If no non-redundant component B exists, then we report that P is LR-visible. Thus, only if traverse all non-redundant components of definition vertex not in A, we can compute the superset of non-redundant components, otherwise, traverse all non- redundant components in B, next find a non-redundant component denoted by C whose definition vertex is close to the right endpoint of A and disjoint with A. If no component C exists, then stop the algorithm, otherwise, judge whether C is intersect with B, if they are disjoint each other, then P is not LR- visible, otherwise, then compute all the non-redundant components of definition vertex in C. Thus, we can compute the redundant components set.

Algorithm1: Component-computation

Input: A simple polygon P.

Output: A superset of non-redundant backward components of P.

1. Find the first non-redundant component, say, $P[r, B(r)]$. Then, compute all the "non-redundant" components with their defining vertices in $P[r, B(r)]$.
2. Find the reflex $w \in P(B(r), r)$, immediately preceding r, such that the component $P[w, B(w)]$ is non-redundant and disjoint from $P[r, B(r)]$. If no vertex w exists, then terminate the algorithm after all the "non- redundant" components with their defining vertices in $P[B(r), r]$ are computed. Otherwise, compute all the "non- redundant" components with their defining vertices in $P[w, B(w)]$.
3. Compute the vertex $z \in P(B(w), w)$, immediately succeeding $B(r)$, such that $P[z, B(z)]$ is non-redundant. If no vertex z exists, terminate the algorithm. Otherwise, check whether $P[z, B(z)]$ is disjoint from $P[w,B(w)$ and $P[r,B(r)]$. If yes, then N1 applies and report that P is not LR-visible. Otherwise, compute all the "non- redundant" components with their defining vertices in $P[z,B(z)]$.

Fig. 28.3 A simple polygon
denoted by P

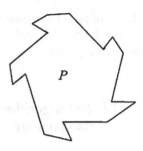

28.3.2 Algorithm Realization

In order to compute the non-redundant number of a simple polygon, let's input a
group of node data, and connect two adjacent nodes clockwise direction to get a
simple polygon. First, traverse all the vertices. Then find out reflex vertices by
the nature of vector fork product, and put them into array r[]. Thus, we can get
the array r[] in which all the reflex vertices. Next, find the B(r) according to the
backward ray, that is to look for the all backward ray shots, then we put them into
array br[] and get the array br[] in which backward ray shots. After getting the
backward components by the r[] and br[], we can get a structure array of the
backward components. Finally, traverse all the backward components, and delete
them according to the character of redundant components, then count the number
of non-redundant components and output them.

A symmetric procedure does the same for the forward components, denoted
by A2. Here we don't descript it in detail.

28.3.3 Algorithm of Component-Merging

If two left endpoints or two right endpoints in a simple polygon are adjacent on the
boundary, then their components intersect each other. Hence, we can use the
intersection of such two components, called the proper component, to represent
them. We call the clockwise first and second endpoints of proper component the
left and the right endpoints, respectively. The method above to merge the components is called component-merging. We can obtain the non-redundant component sets denoted by T by the algorithm1 and algorithm 2, then we can merge two
components into one by component-merging algorithm denoted by algorithm 3,
repeatedly performs the operation of merging, until all endpoints of the resulting
(proper) components are alternate on the boundary of P, thus, we can obtain the
non-redundant and disjoint components.

Fig. 28.4 Non-component and proper component. **a** Non-component. **b** Proper component

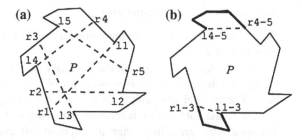

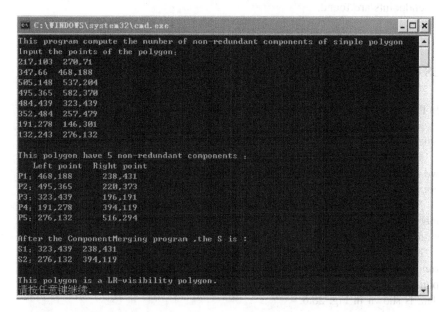

Fig. 28.5 The running result (a LR-visible polygon)

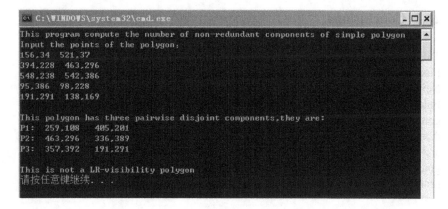

Fig. 28.6 The running result (not a LR-visible polygon)

Algorithm 3: Component-merging

1. Order the endpoints of all non-components of T by a simple scan on the boundary of P.
2. Make a clockwise traversal on the boundary of P to find the two components C_i, C_j such that either their left endpoints, or their right endpoints, are adjacent on P. Then we delete C_i and C_j from T, insert the proper component $C' = C_j \cap C_i$ into T, and continue to traverse the boundary of P from the breaking point.
3. Terminate this procedure when no adjacent left endpoints or adjacent right endpoints are found.

28.4 Recognizing LR-Visibility Polygons

In this paper, we realize the above algorithms with C++ program. Furthermore, we choose the two simple polygons as test data, and apply N1 and N2 to judge whether the given polygon is LR-visible or not.

Test case is as follows. For a given simple polygon P shown in Fig. 28.3, first, we can get all the non-components (see Fig. 28.4a) by A1 and A2 of component-computation.

Next, we can get proper components (see Fig. 28.4b) by the A3 of component-merging. Finally, we can determine P is LR-visible according to the necessary and sufficient conditions. The running result of program is shown in Fig. 28.5.

If three disjoint non-redundant components are found when the algorithm is running, then the polygon is not LR-visible and output the non-redundant components, at the same time, stop the algorithm. The running results of another test data is shown in Fig. 28.6.

28.5 Conclusions

This paper mainly studies on the algorithm whether a polygon is LR-visible or not. First, the related knowledge and concept about LR-visible polygon is introduced. Next, Characterization and the theorem judging LR-visible polygon are anglicized. Finally, an algorithm of computing non-redundant components in a simple polygon is presented and realized with C++ program. Particularly, two groups of test data are applied to test the algorithm. The result shows that the algorithm is correct and efficient. Our algorithm for characterizing and recognizing LR-visible polygons can be used to simplify the existing solutions of some polygon search problems [5–7].

Acknowledgments This work is supported by National Natural Science Foundation of China (No. 61173034) and the General Project of Liaoning Province Science and Research (No. L2012487).

References

1. de Berg M, van Kreveld M, Overmars M et al (1997) Computational geometry: algorithm and applications, 2nd edn. Springer, Berlin
2. Tan X, Zhang J, Jiang B (2010) Simple characterization of LR-visibility polygons. In: 9th international conference, CGGA 2010, Dalian, China
3. Das G, Heffernan PJ, Narasimhan G (1997) LR-visibility in polygons. Comp Geom Theory Appl 7(1):37–57
4. Suzuki I, Yamashita M (1992) Searching for mobile intruders in a polygonal region. SIA- M J Comp 21(5):863–888
5. Heffernan PJ (1996) An optimal algorithm for the two-guard problem. Int J Comput Geom Appl 6(1):15–44
6. Tan X (2008) A unified and efficient solution to the room search problem. Comput Geom Theory Appl 40(1):45–60
7. Tan X (2009) Searching a polygonal region by a boundary searcher. J Comput Sci Technol 24:505–516

Chapter 29
Empirical Mode Decomposition of Long-term Solar Flare Activity

Lin-hua Deng and Song Feng

Abstract The periodic analyses of solar flare activity have been carried out by different authors for about 30 years. In this study we used two new methods to investigate the periodic behavior of solar flare activity separately for the total disk, and the northern and southern hemispheres of the Sun. Solar flare activity can be decomposed into three components: the first is the rotation signal which is understood to be mainly caused by large magnetic structure; the second is an annual-variation and quasi-biennial oscillation signal, however, the origin of which is not known up to now; the third is the inter-solar-cycle signal which is inferred to be caused by emergence of magnetic field at active regions within the photosphere.

Keywords Computing physics · Nonlinearity · Solar flares

29.1 Introduction

The periodic variation of solar activity has been observed with a wide range of time scales varying from minutes to decades. The most prominent oscillations are the 27-day rotational periodicity (short-term fluctuation) and 11-year periodicity

L. Deng
National Astronomical Observatories/Yunnan Observatory, Chinese Academy of Sciences, 650011 Kunming, China

L. Deng
Graduate University of Chinese Academy of Sciences, 100049 Beijing, China

S. Feng (✉)
Computer Technology Application Key Lab of Yunnan Province, Kunming University of Science and Technology, 650500 Kunming, China
e-mail: kgfs@sohu.com

W. Lu et al. (eds.), *Proceedings of the 2012 International Conference on Information Technology and Software Engineering*, Lecture Notes in Electrical Engineering 211, DOI: 10.1007/978-3-642-34522-7_29, © Springer-Verlag Berlin Heidelberg 2013

(long-term variation). The former is related to the modulation imposed on the solar flux at the Earth by solar rotation and the latter reflects the emergence of magnetic field at active regions within the photosphere. The regime between 27 days and 11 years has been called "mid-range" periods [1]. Since a 153-day periodicity in -ray and soft X-ray flare occurrences was discovered [2], a search for additional possible mid-range periodicities in solar activity has become a hot issue in the field of solar physics. In recent years many researchers have investigated mid-range periodicities using various solar activity indicators, and some important period-icities, 51 days, 73–78 days, 150–153 days, 1.3–1.7 years, 2–3 years and nearly 5 years, in different solar features are found.

It is obvious that the Sun displays dissipative nonlinear behavior. Linear analysis approaches, such as Fast Fourier Transform (FFT), may generate artifacts when they are applied to analyze real-world processes. Therefore, nonlinear analysis approaches should be adopted to study the nonlinear behavior of solar activity. Currently, many advanced nonlinear analysis approaches, such as those involving Empirical Mode Decomposition (EMD) and Morlet Wavelet Transform (MWT), are widely used to study the nonlinear behavior of time series. They have been demonstrated to have unprecedented prowess in revealing hidden physical meanings in data [3–9].

The aim of this paper is to perform a detailed analysis to detect mid-term peri-odicities in monthly counts of solar flare activity during the period January 1966 to December 2008. The layout of this paper is as follows. Shown in Sect. 29.2 are the data used and the approaches employed in this work. The results and discussions are revealed in Sect. 29.3. Finally, the main conclusions are shown in Sect. 29.4.

29.2 Data and Methods of Analysis

29.2.1 Data

It is well known that flare index can be used to describe the solar flare activity, therefore, the data of flare index in the northern hemisphere, southern hemispheres and total solar disk are used to investigate their periodicities in present paper. The flare index is calculated by Atac and Ozguc from Bogazici University Kandilli Observatory, and can be downloaded from the web site (ftp://ftp.ngdc.noaa.gov/ STP/SOLAR_DATA/SOLAR_FLARES). Flare index is roughly proportional to the total energy emitted by a flare. A detailed definition of the flare index can be found in [10]. The flare index permits a measure of the short-lived activity of the Sun and allows us to study short- and long-term periodic variations.

Figure 29.1 shows solar flare activity in the northern hemisphere, southern hemispheres and total solar disk, respectively, for the time interval from January 1966 to December 2008. The period analyzed in the present paper fully covers four solar cycle 20 to 23.

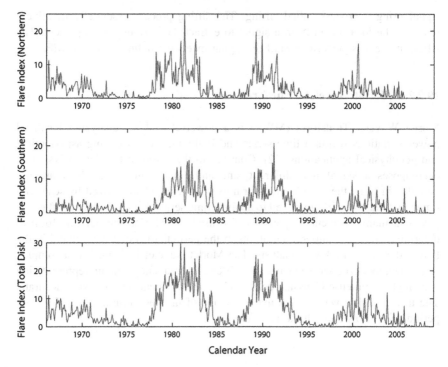

Fig. 29.1 Monthly counts of solar flare activity in the northern hemisphere (*top panel*), southern hemisphere (*middle panel*), and solar total disk (*bottom panel*), respectively, for the time interval from January 1966 to December 2008

29.2.2 Methods

First, we use EMD method to decompose solar flare activity into six IMFs and a resulting trend. And then, Morlet wavelet transform is utilized to study periodicity in the first six IMFs.

29.2.2.1 Empirical Mode Decomposition

Empirical Mode Decomposition (EMD) is a nonlinear time–frequency analysis method [11]. It is an algorithm which decomposes an input signal into a finite set of intrinsic mode functions (IMFs), which are the intrinsic oscillating periodicities of the original signal. These IMFs are extracted from the data themselves, and they are not restricted to have constant phases or amplitudes. Essentially EMD is an empirical algorithm which decomposes a signal, which can be non-stationary and nonlinear, into a finite set of IMFs. These IMFs are defined to be functions which are symmetric about their local mean value, and whose number of extreme and zero crossings are equal or differ at most by one. These IMFs are extracted from a signal using a process called sifting. The sifting process essentially iteratively removes the local mean from a signal to extract the various cycles present. The sifting process is performed until the signal meets the definition of an IMF.

29.2.2.2 Morlet Wavelet Transform

Morlet Wavelet Transform (MWT) is a powerful tool for analyzing localized power variations within a time series and is finding ever-widening astronomical and geophysical applications [12]. Contrary to the classical Fourier analysis that decomposes a signal into different sine and cosine functions which are not bounded in time, the wavelet transform uses wavelets characterized by scale and time position. It can be employed to analyze time series that contain non-stationary power at many different frequencies. We used the Morlet wavelet transform to determine possible temporal variations in the periodicities that were found in the flare index from the EMD analysis. The Morlet wavelet is defined as a complex sine wave, localized with a Gaussian window. Its frequency domain representation is a single symmetric Gaussian peak, and frequency localization is very accurate. The use of such a wavelet has the advantage of incorporating a wave of a clear period, as well as being finite in extent.

29.3 Results and Discussions

Figure 29.2 shows the results of application of the EMD method to solar flare activity in the total disk, and the northern and southern hemispheres of the Sun. These three time series are decomposed into six IMFs and the resulting trend. The code of MWT analysis, which is provided by [12], is utilized to study periodicity in first six IMFs of solar flare activity. The trend is excluded because the limited length of the data used gives no period to the trend at present.

Figure 29.3 shows the Morlet wavelet power spectra of the first six IMFs and their corresponding 95 % confidence level of solar flare activity, respectively, for the northern hemisphere, southern hemisphere and total disk. Table 29.1 gives the main periods in the first six IMFs, which are significant at the 95 % confidence level.

The periods, 0.2206 years (about 81 days), 0.2967 years (about 108 days), 0.5771 and 0.5594 years (about 211 days), 0.6734 and 0.6664 years (about 243 days), 0.7762 years (about 283 days), are inferred to be the 3-, 4-, 8-, 9- and 11-multiple harmonics of the period of around 27–29 days, which is approximately the solar rotation period. There are only those periods in IMFs 1 to 2, which are related to the rotation cycle, thus IMFs 1–2 are called the rotation-variation signal of solar flare activity. Bai (2003) pointed out that the mid-range periodicities covering 35–600 days may be integral multiples of 25–35 days. The periods of 1.524, 1.267 and 1.624 years correspond to the periodical annual variations, and IMF 3 are called annual-variation signal of solar flare activity. The periods of 2.394, 2.707, 2.827 and

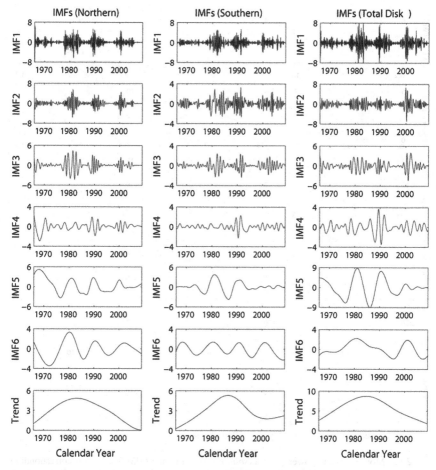

Fig. 29.2 IMFs of solar flare activity, respectively, for the northern hemisphere (*left panel*), southern hemisphere (*middle panel*) and total disk (*right panel*)

3.856 years, which are all around 2–3 years, correspond to the so-called quasi-biennial oscillation. Thus IMFs 3–4 are called the annual-variation and quasi-biennial oscillation signal. There is no doubt that the periods of 10.76, 10.67 and 10.72 years are related to the so-called 11-year Schwabe cycle. The periods of 21.51 and 21.47 years are inferred to be related with the magnetic cycle. However, the MWT method suffers from edge artifacts because the wavelet is not completely localized in time. The span of the data used here is only 43 years, the periods larger than 16 years are so severely affected by the cone of influence that they are unreliable. That is to say, the periods of 21.51 and 21.47 years are not reliable. Therefore, IMFs 1 to 2, IMFs 3–4, and IMFs 5–6, respectively, are related with the rotation-variation signal, the annual-variation and quasi-biennial oscillation signal and the inter-solar-cycle signal.

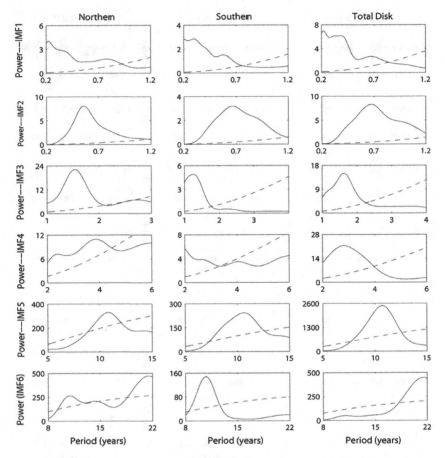

Fig. 29.3 Morlet wavelet power spectra (*solid lines*) of the first 6 IMFs and their corresponding 95 % confidence level (*dashed lines*) of solar flare activity, respectively, for the northern hemisphere, southern hemisphere and total disk

Table 29.1 Periods (in years) in the first 6 IMFs of solar flare activity, respectively, for the northern hemisphere, southern hemisphere and total disk

	IMF1	IMF2	IMF3	IMF4	IMF5	IMF6
Northern	0.2206	0.5594	1.524	2.394	10.76	10.94
(in years)	0.7762			3.856		21.51
Southern	0.2967	0.6664	1.267	2.701	10.67	10.76
(in years)	0.5771					
Total disk	0.2206	0.6734	1.624	2.827	10.72	
(in years)	0.6734					21.47

29.4 Conclusions

Extensive analyses have been done to detect the midrange periodicities for the monthly counts of solar flare activity separately for the total solar disk and the northern and southern hemispheres. Several mid-term periodicities have been detected by EMD and MWT methods. Apart from the 11-year Schwabe cycle which is obvious significance and is found in all three time series with 95 % significance level, we obtained the following prominent periods: around 22-year magnetic cycle, 1.3–1.7 years annual variation signal, around 2–3 years quasi-biennial oscillation, and 0.22 to 0.77 years periods (integral multiples of rotation period).

In summary, we have identified quasi-periods in the data of solar flare activity. Our analyses have revealed the following results:

1. The 11-year Schwabe cycle exists in all three time series, as expected.
2. A number of periodicities detected in solar flare activity are very close to the periodicities observed in other solar activities.
3. The EMD and MWT techniques for the periodic analysis of astronomical and geophysical time series is fairly useful.

Acknowledgments This work is supported by the National Natural Science Foundation of China (NSFC) under grant number 11003041, and the Chinese Academy of Sciences.

References

1. Bai T (2003) Periodicities in solar flare occurrence analysis of cycles 19–23. Astrophys J 591:406
2. Rieger E, Share GH, Forrest DJ, Kanbach G, Reppin C, Chupp EL (1984) A 154-day periodicity in the occurrence of hard solar flares? Nature 312:623
3. Deng LH, Qu ZQ, Wang KR, Li XB (2012) Phase asynchrony between coronal index and sunspot numbers. Adv Space Res. doi:10.1016/j.asr.2012.07.017
4. Deng LH, Qu ZQ, Yan XL, Wang KR (2012) Phase analysis of sunspot group numbers on both solar hemispheres. Rese Astron Astrophys (in press)
5. Xie JL, Shi XJ, Xu JC (2012) Temporal variation of hemispheric solar rotation. Res Astron Astrophys 12(2):187
6. Gao PX, Liang HF, Zhu WW (2011) Periodicity of flare index revisited using the Hilbert–Huang transform method. New Astron 16:147
7. Gao PX, Xie JL, Liang HF (2012) Periodicity in the most violent solar eruptions: recent observations of coronal mass ejections and flares revisited. Res Astron Astrophys 12(3):322
8. Li KJ, Qiu J, Su TW, Gao PX (2005) Sunspot unit area a new parameter to describe long-term solar variability. Astrophys J 621:L81
9. Li KJ, Shi XJ, Liang HF, Zhan LS, Xie JL, Feng W (2011) Variations of solar rotation and sunspot activity. Astrophys J 730:49
10. Ozguc A, Atac T, Rybak J (2003) Temporal variability of the flare index (1966–2001). Sol Phys 214:375

11. Huang NE, Shen Z, Long S, Wu M, Shih H, Zheng Q, Yen N, Tung C, Liu H (1998) The empirica mode decomposition and the Hilbert spectrum for non- linear and non-stationary time series analysis. Proc R Soc Lond 454:903

12. Torrence C, Compo GP (1998) A practical guide to wavelet analysis. Bull Am Meteorol Soc 79:61

Chapter 30
Multiple Pitch Estimation Based on Modified Harmonic Product Spectrum

Xuemei Chen and Ruolun Liu

Abstract This paper proposes the modified harmonic product spectrum method for the multiple pitch estimation of polyphonic music using the harmonic spectrum structure. It also introduces the competition mechanism to improve the accuracy rate. The harmonic components energy distribution was reconsidered, and the first nine partials are then found prominent. Based on a large collection of polyphonic music samples, the proposed method shows the great performance over different types of western instruments.

Keywords Multiple pitch · HPS · HSS · Music separation

30.1 Introduction

The Multiple Pitch Estimation (MPE) plays an important role in the music separation, automatic transcription, melody extraction, and many other applications, particularly in music separation. Despite the fact that more and more people devote to the MPE research, it is still remain a challenging problem. The main difficulty comes from the complex and similar Harmonic Spectrum Structure (HSS) of different instruments. Only through the common properties of different instruments, can the improvement be made. This paper proposes a method for doing this on the single-channel audio signal.

After Noll proposed the Harmonic Product Spectrum (HPS) method to estimate the pitch of speech [1], probably only Master and Ding [2, 3] followed his idea and

X. Chen · R. Liu (✉)
Mechanical Electronics & Information Engineering School, Shandong University at Weihai, 180 Wenhua West, Weihai 264209 Shandong, China
e-mail: ruolun.liu@sdu.edu.cn

W. Lu et al. (eds.), *Proceedings of the 2012 International Conference on Information Technology and Software Engineering*, Lecture Notes in Electrical Engineering 211, DOI: 10.1007/978-3-642-34522-7_30, © Springer-Verlag Berlin Heidelberg 2013

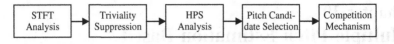

Fig. 30.1 The overview of the MHPS system

used HPS directly into cepstra, without checking its foundation HSS. On the other hand, a lot of different methods have been proposed for the MPE of polyphonic music using the HSS in the different manners. For example, Klapuri proposed an iterative spectrum smoothing and subtraction algorithm using the smoothness of HSS [4, 5], and Yeh and Robel proposed a method based on harmonicity, spectral smoothness, and synchronous amplitude evolution within a single source [6, 7]. There are many other authors proposed the methods based on filter bank. Meddis and Hewitt utilized a multichannel auditory filter bank [8], Tolonen and Karjalainen developed the multichannel method by using the two channel auditory filter bank to calculate the ESACF, which improves the calculation efficiency [9]. Some other algorithms are based on either the probability statistical adaption of waveform models [10, 11], or the specmurt analysis [12], or the harmonics temporal structure clustering [13]. Although these methods achieve higher accuracy rate, the balance between the higher accuracy rate and lower computation cost is remain a challenging problem that need to be solved.

30.2 System Overview

The Modified HPS (MHPS) method provides a frame-based system for the MPE of polyphonic music. As shown by Fig. 30.1, the system depends on mainly the HSS, which is expressed by the spectral peaks selected from short-time Fourier transform. These spectral peaks are the representatives of the components generated from the harmonic sources, and they give a direct access to analyze the underling pitches. Though the HPS analysis part is not so suitable for music, together with the other parts, it makes the system more suitable for real time application such as automatic music transcription, source separation, etc.

30.3 Feasibility Analysis

The different HSSs of different instruments share the common backbone to some degree, i.e. the energy of lower partial is higher than that of the higher partial. The law of the concrete Harmonic Components Energy Distribution (HCED) is still unrevealed. Ibanez [14] modeled the common HSS as a vector $H = [1, 0.5, 0.4, 0.3, 0.2, 0.1, 0.05, 0.02, 0.01]$. Zhou also believes that the energy of every music note is mainly distributed over the first ten partials [15].

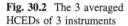

Fig. 30.2 The 3 averaged HCEDs of 3 instruments

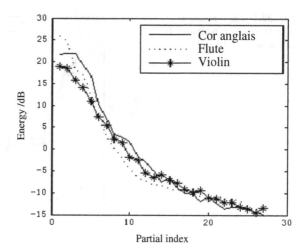

Using the MIDI note index, h, the fundamental frequency and corresponding the m-th partial frequency of a MIDI note are $f_h^\theta = 440 \times 2^{(h-69)/12}$ and $f_h^m = (m+1)f_h^\theta$. Consider the frequencies of the partials within index $m \le 9$, besides that the frequencies of the 1st, 3th, and 7th partials are exactly the fundamentals of notes $(h + 12)$, $(h + 24)$, and $(h + 36)$ respectively, the frequencies of the 2nd, 4th, 5th, 6th, 8th, and 9th partials are also very close to the fundamentals of notes $(h + 19)$, $(h + 28)$, $(h + 31)$, $(h + 34)$, $(h + 38)$, and $(h + 40)$ respectively. Though the overlapping is not always present in polyphonic music, it is indeed possible that fundamentals and partials of different notes overlap together.

To prove the conjecture above, the monophonic and polyphonic music are tested. The monophonic set consisted of 46 samples from cor anglais, flute, and violin in the three octaves from 196 to 523.25 Hz. The polyphonic set is the random mixture of the monophonic samples. Based on the 15 monophonic cor anglais samples, if the mixtures are of 2–6 notes, the volumes of the corresponding polyphonic set are 14, 91, 364, 1001, and 2002 samples.

Three monophonic sets and 5 polyphonic sets are used for HCED tests. As shown by the Fig. 30.2, the 3 averaged HCEDs of the 3 instruments are roughly the same. When the cor anglais A4 is randomly mixed up with 1 to 5 other cor anglais notes, the HCEDs of the mixtures are also relatively stable, as shown by Fig. 30.3.

The Figs. 30.2, and 30.3 show that: the HCEDs of monophonic and polyphonic sample sets have a degressive trend; for the monophonic sample, only the first nine partials have the power higher than 0 dB; for the polyphonic sample, only the first 7 partials stand above 0 dB. For the polyphonic mixture of other instruments, the similar phenomena can also be seen. In general, harmonics of lower index possess the majority of the note energy; the HCED shape is roughly the same no matter how severely the overtones overlap together.

Fig. 30.3 The 6 averaged
HCEDs of the 6 mixture sets
of cor anglais A4

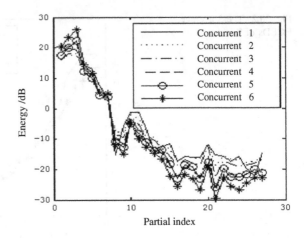

Partial index

30.4 Proposed Method

There are always some unwanted trivial partials of higher index in the STFT,
which degrade the performance of the HPS. A relative threshold γ will suppress
these trivial components as shown below, where $Y(t, f)$ is the magnitude of the
STFT of $y(t)$. A Hamming window is applied to the STFT.

$$\tilde{Y}(t, f) = \begin{cases} Y(t,f), & Y(t,f) > \gamma Y_{\max}(t, f) \\ 0, & \text{otherwise} \end{cases} \tag{30.1}$$

Considering the properties of HSS, up to the M harmonics, the HPS, V, of $\tilde{Y}$ can
be used to select the pitch candidate by another threshold, λ.

$$V(t, f) = \prod_{m=1}^{M} \tilde{Y}(t, mf) \tag{30.2}$$

$$\tilde{V}(t, f_P) = \begin{cases} V(t, f_P), & V(t, f_P) > \lambda V_{\max}(t, f_P) \\ 0, & \text{otherwise} \end{cases} \tag{30.3}$$

where f_P is the peak frequency of the HPS of the trivial suppressed STFT $\tilde{Y}$. The
frequencies of candidate peaks, $\tilde{V}$, are the pitch candidates.

The pitch candidates are evaluated further for tagging with real pitch (RP) and
uncertain pitch (UP). This competition mechanism consists of four steps:

Step 1: The real and uncertain pitches, f_{RP} and f_{UP}, are selected by checking the
candidate peak with a prominence threshold, α.

$$\begin{cases} f_{RP} = f_P, & \tilde{V}(t, f_P) > \alpha \tilde{V}_{\max}(t, f_P) \\ f_{UP} = f_P, & \tilde{V}(t, f_P) \leq \alpha \tilde{V}_{\max}(t, f_P) \end{cases} \tag{30.4}$$

Step 2: Check the first N harmonics of each uncertain pitch. If all the N harmonics have nonzero peaks, this f_{UP} will be reconsidered as real pitch and denoted as f_{RUP}. Otherwise, forwarded the f_{UP} into the next step and denote it as f_{SP}.

Step 3: According to the definition below and 2 thresholds, β_1 and β_2,

$$S(t, f) = \sum_{n=1}^{N} \tilde{Y}(t, nf) \tag{30.5}$$

if $S(t, f_{SP}) > \beta_1 S_{\max}(t, f_{RP})$ and $\tilde{Y}(t, f_{SP}) > \beta_2 \tilde{Y}_{\max}(t, f_{RP})$ as well, this f_{SP} will be reconsidered as a real pitch and denoted as f_{RSP}. Otherwise, reject the spurious pitch. The double thresholds also eliminate the half-pitch estimation.

Step 4: Denote the collection of $\{f_{RP}, f_{RUP}, f_{RSP}\}$ as the real pitch, f_R. According to the relationship between MIDI index and pitch frequency given in Sect. 30.3, convert the time–frequency representation, $S(t, f_R)$, into piano-roll display.

30.5 Experiment Results

The parameters used in the experiments are: the frame length, 0.93 ms; the overlap length, 0.46 ms; the number of harmonics in HPS, $M = 5$; the number of harmonics in Competition Mechanism, $N = 9$; $\gamma = 0.02$; $\lambda = 5E - 5$; $\alpha = 0.3$; $\beta_1 = 0.5$, $\beta_2 = 0.6$.

A. Sinusoid Test A chord (A3, C4, E4, G4) of the common HSS given in Sect. 30.3 by the vector H is generated first. The harmonic phase of each tone is randomly assigned. The MPE results are given in Fig. 30.4. Apparently besides the four prominent peaks, there are spurious peaks at A0, C3, and C4 in HPS. Whereas, MHPS produces a clear spectrum of exactly 4 correct pitches.

B. Random Chord Test The cor anglais mixture of A#3, B3, A4, A#4, B4, and C5 is selected. The 2nd advantage of the MHPS is clearly shown in Fig. 30.5. The MHPS indicates not only the position, but also the energy of each real pitch. While the HPS gives many spurious pitches, the MHPS shows only the real ones.

This example implies that no matter how the pitches are apart from each other, the MHPS detects well all the pitches accurately, even when there is only one semitone between A4 and A#4.

A large number of polyphonic sets were generated by randomly mixing the recorded 46 monophonic samples of cor anglais, flute, and violin with the pitch between 196.0 and 523.3 Hz. Two accuracy rates are provided. According to the MIREX 2012 [16], the precision rate is the portion of the correct pitches over all the pitches retrieved. The recall rate is the ratio of the correct pitches to all the ground truth pitches. The correct estimation is defined within an absolute deviation less than 3 % from the reference pitch. One thousand randomly selected mixtures were tested. As indicates by the accuracy rates shown in Fig. 30.6, higher accuracy can be reached for the mixture of less notes; the lowest accuracy of the 6 notes mixture is higher than 81 %.

Fig. 30.4 The MPE of sinusoid chord (A3, C4, E4, G4). Both results are normalized, but the HPS result is added by 1 after normalization

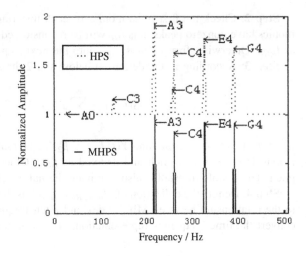

Fig. 30.5 The MPE of random chord (A#3, B3, A4, A#4, B4, C5). Both results are normalized, but the HPS result is added by 1 after normalization

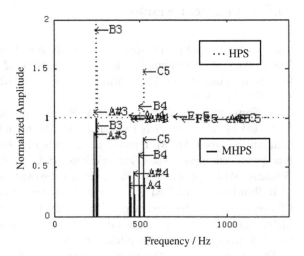

C. Music Clip Test To view the concrete performance of the MHPS, a multiple pitch music segment is tested. The pitch estimation is displayed on a time–frequency plane in this test to ease the comparison to the MIDI indicator. The clip is a segment of the 41st study of "Kreutzer 42 studies for violin solo". The code of the MIDI test reference is provided by Ken Schutte on the website of http:// www.kenschutte.com/midi.

As shown in Fig. 30.7, the result of MHPS is quite similar to the MIDI reference, which means the accuracy of MHPS is quite high. The MHPS generates a pitch distribution frame by frame without knowing the number of pitches in advance.

Fig. 30.6 The accuracy rates over 1000 polyphonic tests. Precision Rate: *black bars*; Recall Rate: *white bars*

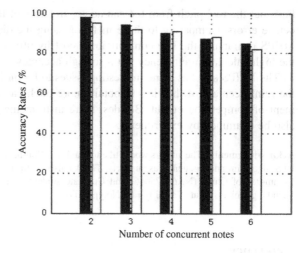

Fig. 30.7 The MPE result of a violin solo segment

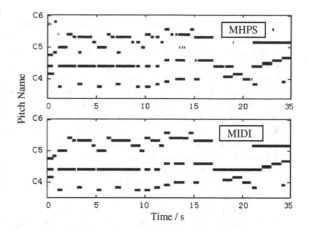

In addition, the computational cost is also encouraging. With a Intel® Core™2 Duo 2.93 GHz processor and 2 GB memory, the time of analyzing an 24.8 s CD quality clip takes only 3 s.

30.6 Conclusion

In this paper, the properties of HSS are re-examined by the experiments on the large number of sample sets. Since music has wider spectrum than that of speech, HPS suffers badly in MPE without modification. Through triviality suppression and peak picking, the HSS is somehow reinforced for the better selection of pitch candidates. The competition mechanism, as the extension of the HSS property, finds out the real pitch from the candidates in terms of less half-pitch and double octave errors. Comparing to those methods using the discrete wavelet transform, MHPS guarantees the low computational cost by utilizing STFT. It has not only the high calculation efficiency but also high accuracy rate.

The MHPS still has some interesting issues to be further studied. For example, the reinforcement of the HSS to obtain more pitch candidates, and the enhancement of competition output. Besides, more instruments of different types should also be examined by experiments.

Acknowledgments The authors would like to thank Dr. Noll for his earnest discussion about the HPS algorithm and his generous supports. Thanks also go to the National Science Foundation Committee of China (No.61075066) and Graduate student research innovation foundation of Shandong University at Weihai (Grant No.yjs11037).

References

1. Noll M (1969). Pitch determination of human speech by the harmonic product spectrum, the harmonic sum spectrum, and a maximum likelihood estimate. In: Proceedings of the symposium on computer processing communications, pp 779–797
2. Master A (2000) Speech spectrum modeling from multiple sources. Master's thesis, Cambridge University, Engineering, Dept., Cambridge, England
3. Ding H, Qian B, Li YP, Tang ZM (2006) A method combining LPC-based cepstrum and harmonic product spectrum for pitch detection. In: Proceeding of the international conference on intelligent information hiding and multimedia signal processing 2006
4. Klapuri A (2003) Multiple fundamental frequency estimation based on harmonicity and spectral smoothness. IEEE Trans Speech Audio Process 11(6):804–815
5. Klapuri A (2008) Multipitch analysis of polyphonic music and speech signals using an auditory model. IEEE Trans Audio, Speech, LangProcess 16(2):255–266
6. Yeh C, Roebel A, Rodet X (2005) Multiple fundamental frequency estimation of poly-phonic music signals. In: Proceedings of IEEE, international conference on acoustics, speech signal process (ICASSP'05), Philadelphia, 2005, vol 3, pp III-225–III-228
7. Yeh C, Roebel A,Rodet X (2010) Multiple fundamental frequency estimation and polyphonic inference of polyphonic music signals. IEEE Trans Audio, Speech, Lang Process 18(6):1116–1126
8. Meddis R, Hewitt MJ (1992) Modeling the identification of concurrent vowels with different fundamental frequencies. J Acoust Soc Amer 91:233–245
9. Tolonen T, Karjalainen M (2000) A computationally efficient multipitch analysis model. IEEE Trans Speech Audio Process 8(6):708–716
10. Davy M, Godsill S, Idier J (2006) Bayesian analysis of polyphonic western tonal music. J Acoust Soc Amer 119(4):2498–2517
11. Duan ZY, Pardo B, Zhang CS (2010) Multiple fundamental frequency estimation by modeling spectral peaks and non-peak regions. IEEE Trans Audio, Speech, Lang Process 18(8):2121–2133
12. Saito S, Kameoka H, Nishimoto T, Sagayama S (2008) Specmurt analysis of polyphonic music signals. IEEE Trans Audio, Speech, Lang Process 16(3):639–650
13. Kameoka H, Nishimoto T, Sagayama S (2007) A multipitch analyzer based on harmonic temporal structure clustering. IEEE Trans Audio, Speech, Lang Process 15(3):982–994
14. Ibanez AP (2010) Computationally efficient methods for polyphonic music transcription. Ph.D. dissertation, Univ. Alicante, San Vicente del Raspeig, Spain

15. Zhou RH, Reiss JD, Mattavelli M, Zoia G (2009) A computationally efficient method for polyphonic pitch estimation. EURASIP J Adv Signal Process. doi:10.1155/2009/729494 11 pp
16. Multiple Fundamental Frequency Estimation & Tracking, MIREX 2012. [Online]. Avaliable: http://www.music-ir.org/mirex/wiki/2012/

Chapter 31
Semi-Physical Research for INS/GPS Integrated Navigation

Guangxin Li and Jiabin Chen

Abstract Inertial navigation system (INS) has a fatal flaw that positioning accuracy deteriorates with time due to possible inherent sensor errors. In order to improve the accuracy and reliability of navigation, INS/GPS system integrated with position and velocity is proposed. Core to integrated navigation systems is the concept of fusing noisy observations from GPS, Inertial Measurement Units (IMU), and other available sensors. Unscented Kalman Filter (UKF) is a filtering algorithm suitable for combining the sensor measurements with predictions coming from nonlinear models of vehicle motion. The filter has the advantages of high accuracy and reliability, and it doesn't need to linearize the nonlinear model. A semi-physical experiment research platform is used to demonstrate the results. The results significantly demonstrate the superiority of the integrated navigation and the performance of UKF-based navigation system is superior to that of the system based traditional Kalman filter on accuracy and reliability.

Keywords INS/GPS · UKF · Kalman filter · Semi-physical research

31.1 Introduction

Inertial navigation system (INS) has the ability to achieve the task of positioning and orientation latently in three-dimensional space worldwide under all-weather conditions. However, INS has a fatal flaw that the positioning error will be

G. Li (✉) · J. Chen
College of Automation, Beijing Institute of Techonology, No. 5 ZhongGuanCun Road, HaiDian, Beijing, China
e-mail: addeh123@163.com

W. Lu et al. (eds.), *Proceedings of the 2012 International Conference on Information Technology and Software Engineering*, Lecture Notes in Electrical Engineering 211, DOI: 10.1007/978-3-642-34522-7_31, © Springer-Verlag Berlin Heidelberg 2013

accumulating over time. Hence, it is difficult to separately complete the task of long time precision navigation.

In contrast, global positioning system (GPS) is able to provide higher accuracy three-dimensional position, velocity information with a consistent and acceptable accuracy when there is a direct line of sight to four of more satellites and its positioning error doesn't accumulated over time.

So presumably, INS and GPS navigation system have exactly complementary performances. The two systems are often paired together in a complimentary fashion so that their drawbacks are minimized or eliminated. It is worldwide recognized that integrating the two subsystems together to form integrated navigation is the best solution [1].

The combination methods of INS and GPS generally can be divided into three ways, loose combination, tight combination and ultra-tight combination. Loose combination integrates the INS and GPS's independently navigation results together through a feed-forward complementary Kalman filter. The flow chart is shown as Fig. 31.1 [2].

Core to integrated navigation systems is the concept of fusing noisy observations from GPS, Inertial Measurement Units (IMU), and other available sensors [3].

Commonly, INS/GPS integrated navigation system uses linear error equation which is derived on the assumption that attitude error angle is a small-angle. In this condition, we generally process it using traditional Kalman filtering. However, when IMU has poor accuracy or carrier move with large angular movement, attitude out of alignment angle will be large, so the nonlinear cannot be ignored [4]. The result of filtering will probably diverge if continually use the traditional Kalman filtering.

Extended Kalman filter (EKF) is generally used to handle nonlinear systems and has been applied successfully. In the EKF, the system state distribution and all relevant noise densities are approximated by Gaussian random variables (GRV), which are then propagated analytically through a first-order linearization of the nonlinear system. This can introduce large errors in the true posterior mean and covariance of the transformed GRV, which may lead to sub-optimal performance and sometimes divergence of the filter [5].

Fig. 31.1 True trajectory used for simulation experiments

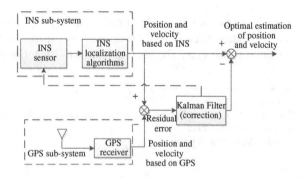

In order to improve the filtering effect of nonlinear problems, Julier [6] proposed unscented Kalman filter (UKF). Implementation of the UKF is often substantially easier and requires no analytic derivation or Jacobi as in the EKF. UKF methods have proven to be far superior to standard EKF based estimation approaches in the areas of nonlinear state estimation [3].

31.2 INS Error Model

The growth of errors in a full three-dimensional navigation system is examined. Probably the most popular INS error model is the psi-angle model [7].

31.2.1 Navigation Parameters Error Model

$$
\begin{aligned}
\delta\dot{\mathbf{V}}^n =&\, \mathbf{f}^n \times \boldsymbol{\phi}^n + \mathbf{C}_b^n \mathbf{f}^b + \delta\mathbf{V}^n \times (2\omega_{ie}^n + \omega_{en}^n) \\
&+ V^n \times (2\delta\omega_{ie}^n + \delta\omega_{en}^n) + \nabla^n
\end{aligned}
\tag{31.1}
$$

$$
\delta\dot{\mathbf{P}} = \delta\mathbf{V}
\tag{31.2}
$$

$$
\dot{\boldsymbol{\phi}} - \omega_{in}^n \times \boldsymbol{\phi} + \delta\omega_{in}^n - \mathbf{C}_b^n \omega_{ib}^b - \boldsymbol{\varepsilon}^n
\tag{31.3}
$$

31.2.2 IMU Error Model

31.2.2.1 Bias Repeatability Error

This offset is not completely fixed. The compensation for it is just the average value. The repeatability error is a zero-mean random constant.

$$
\dot{\varepsilon}_b = 0, \quad \dot{\nabla}_b = 0
\tag{31.4}
$$

where ε_b is the bias repeatability error of gyro; ∇_b is the bias repeatability error of accelerometer.

31.2.2.2 Bias Stability Error

Inertial instruments have the rest error changing with time. It is often described as a first order Markov process.

$$\dot{\varepsilon}_r = -1/\tau_g \cdot \varepsilon_r + \mathbf{W}_g, \quad \dot{\nabla}_r = -1/\tau_a \cdot \nabla_r + \mathbf{W}_a \tag{31.5}$$

where ε_r is the bias stability error of gyro; ∇_r is the bias stability error of accelerometer; τ_g, τ_a are the relevant time of the first order Markov process; $\mathbf{W}_g, \mathbf{W}_a$ are zero-mean white noises.

31.3 System Equations

31.3.1 State Equation

According to the mechanical layout and the error equation, the state equation of the INS/GPS integrated navigation system is established.

$$\dot{\mathbf{x}}(t) = f(\mathbf{x}(t), \mathbf{u}(t), t) + \mathbf{w}(t) \tag{31.6}$$

where $f(\cdot)$ is nonlinear continuous function; $\mathbf{x}$ is the state vector of system.
$\mathbf{x} = [\theta, \gamma, \psi, \delta V_E, \delta V_N, \delta V_U, \delta L, \delta \lambda, \delta h, \varepsilon_x^b, \varepsilon_y^b, \varepsilon_z^b, \nabla_x^b, \nabla_y^b, \nabla_z^b]^T$ where θ, γ and ψ are the pitch, roll and yaw errors, δV_E, δV_N and δV_U are the east, north and up velocity errors, δL, $\delta \lambda$ and δh are the latitude, longitude and altitude errors, $\mathbf{w} = [\mathbf{0}_{1 \times 9}, w_{gx}^b, w_{gy}^b, w_{gz}^b, w_{ax}^b, w_{ay}^b, w_{az}^b]^T$ where $w_{gx}^b, w_{gy}^b, w_{gz}^b, w_{ax}^b, w_{ay}^b$, and w_{az}^b are zero-mean white noises in body frame.

31.3.2 Observation Equation

Selecting the differences of velocity and position between INS and GPS as observations establishes the measurement equation.

$$\mathbf{z}(t) = h(\mathbf{x}(t), t) + \mathbf{v}(t) \tag{31.7}$$

where $h(\cdot)$ is linear function; $\mathbf{v}$ is the noises of observations and R_k is theirs variance matrix. $\mathbf{z} = [V_E^I - V_E^G, V_N^I - V_N^G, V_U^I - V_U^G, L^I - L^G, \lambda^I - \lambda^G, h^I - h^G]^T$.
Because $h(\cdot)$ is linear function, so $h = H$. $H = [\mathbf{0}_{6 \times 3}, \mathbf{I}_{6 \times 6}, \mathbf{0}_{6 \times 6}]$.

31.3.3 Discretization

In order to achieve the calculation on the navigation computer, we must discretize the state equation of system [8].

$$\mathbf{x}_{k+1} = F(\mathbf{x}_k, \mathbf{u}_k, t_k) + \mathbf{w}_k \tag{31.8}$$

where $F(\cdot)$ is a nonlinear discrete function; $\mathbf{w}_k$ is system noise, and Q_k is its variance matrix.

31.4 The Unscented Kalman Filter

The UKF algorithm is summarized as follows [9].

31.4.1 Initialization

$$\begin{aligned} \hat{x}_0^+ &= E(x_0) \\ P_0^+ &= E[(x_0 - \hat{x}_0^+)(x_0 - \hat{x}_0^+)^T] \end{aligned} \tag{31.9}$$

31.4.2 Time Update

$$\begin{aligned} x_{k-1}^0 &= \hat{x}_{k-1}^+ \\ x_{k-1}^i &= \hat{x}_{k-1}^+ + \tilde{x}^{(i)} \quad i = 1, \cdots, 2n \\ \tilde{x}^{(i)} &= \left(\sqrt{(n+\kappa)P_{k-1}^+} \right)_i^T \quad i = 1, \cdots, n \\ \tilde{x}^{(n+i)} &= -\left(\sqrt{(n+\kappa)P_{k-1}^+} \right)_i^T \quad i = 1, \cdots, n \end{aligned} \tag{31.10}$$

$$\hat{x}_k^{(i)} = f(\hat{x}_{k-1}^i, u_k, t_k) \tag{31.11}$$

$$\hat{x}_k^- = \sum_{i=0}^{2n} W_m^{(i)} \hat{x}_k^{(i)} \tag{31.12}$$

where $W_m^{(0)} = \frac{\kappa}{n+\kappa}$, $W_m^{(i)} = \frac{\kappa}{2(n+\kappa)}$ $i = 1, \ldots, 2n$

$$P_k^- = \sum_{i=0}^{2n} W_c^{(i)} (\hat{x}_k^{(i)} - \hat{x}_k^-)(\hat{x}_k^{(i)} - \hat{x}_k^-)^T + Q_{k-1} \tag{31.13}$$

where $W_c^{(0)} = \frac{\kappa}{n+k} + (1 - \alpha^2 + \beta)$, $W_c^{(i)} = \frac{\kappa}{2(n+k)}$ $i = 1, \ldots, 2n$, and $\kappa = \alpha^2 (n + \lambda) - n$

The parameter α determines the spread of sigma points around the given state. The parameter β is used to incorporate the prior knowledge about the distribution of the state space variables. The parameter λ is a secondary constant controlling higher order effects.

31.4.3 Measurement Update

$$\hat{y}_k^{(i)} = h(\hat{x}_k^{(i)}, t_k) \tag{31.14}$$

$$\hat{y}_k = \sum_{i=0}^{2n} W_m^{(i)} \hat{y}_k^{(i)} \tag{31.15}$$

$$P_y = \sum_{i=0}^{2n} W_c^{(i)} (\hat{y}_k^{(i)} - \hat{y}_k)(\hat{y}_k^{(i)} - \hat{y}_k)^T \tag{31.16}$$

The measurement update of the state estimate can be performed using the normal Kalman filter equations:

$$\begin{aligned} K_k &= P_{xy} P_y^{-1} \\ \hat{x}_k^+ &= \hat{x}_k^- + K_k(y_k - \hat{y}_k) \\ P_k^+ &= P_k^- - K_k P_y K_k^T \end{aligned} \tag{31.17}$$

31.5 Simulation Results

For this paper, the iMAR FSAS[-E] IMU was used. It was integrated with the NovAtel OEM4 GPS receiver. The iMAR IMU and the NovAtel GPS were integrated using an off-the shelf assembly. The specifications of the IMU can be found in Table 31.1 [10].

Table 31.1 IMU specifications

Specifications	IMU FSAS[-E]	
Update rate	200 Hz	
	Gyroscope	Accelerometer
Range	450°/s	± 5 g
Bias	0.75°/h	1 mg
Scale factor	<0.03 %	<0.1 %
Random walk	0.1°/$\sqrt{h}$	50 µg/$\sqrt{h}$

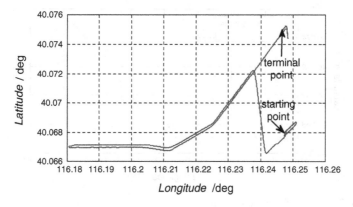

Fig. 31.2 True trajectory used for simulation experiments

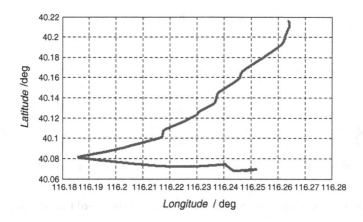

Fig. 31.3 Trajectory calculated by INS only

A road trajectory test was carried out using the above-described setup. As shown in Fig. 31.2.

The experiment is broken up into two parts. The first part is the navigation solution which does not utilize the Kalman filter and the GPS positional corrections. The second part will include these so the limitation of the IMU and benefits of the Kalman filter and GPS can be seen (Fig. 31.3).

Although the trajectories in Fig. 31.4 coincide well with that in Fig. 31.2, the navigation performance of Kalman filter and UKF is different.

Figure 31.5 shows the results of this experiment for both the Kalman filter and UKF. Table 31.2 compares the average root-mean-square (RMS) estimation errors for four different state estimators. The UKF is able to reduce the east and north direction velocity estimation errors by about 80 % and the east and north direction position estimation errors by about 60 %.

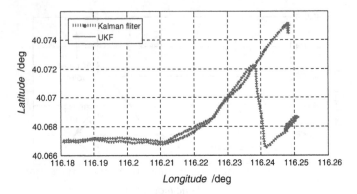

Fig. 31.4 Trajectory of INS/GPS system

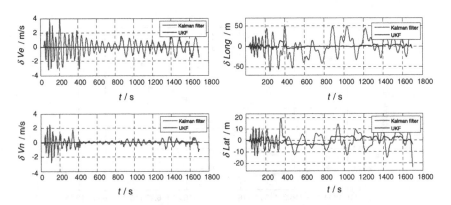

Fig. 31.5 Velocity and position errors of Kalman filter and UKF based INS/GPS system

Table 31.2 Average RMS error

Algorithm	Average RMS error			
	East position (m)	North position (m)	East velocity (m/s)	North velocity (m/s)
Kalman filter	23.26	7.53	1.78	0.89
UKF	8.68	3.12	0.34	0.15

31.6 Conclusions

In this paper we compared the navigation performance of INS system with INS/GPS integrated system. The integrated system provides superior performance over the single INS. Meanwhile, we also compared the navigation performance of Kalman filter based and UKF based integrated systems. The results clearly indicate the superior performance of UKF in processing nonlinear system. Using UKF for INS/GPS integrated navigation system has good theoretical research and engineering reference value.

References

1. Qin YY et al (1998) Kalman filter and the principle for integrated navigation, 1st edn. Northwest Ploytechnical University Press, Xi'an (in Chinese)
2. Xie G (2009) Principles of GPS and receiver design, 1st edn. Publishing House of Electronics Industry, Beijing (in Chinese)
3. van der Merwe R et al (2004) Sigma-point Kalman filters for nonlinear estimation and sensor fusion: applications to integrated navigation. Collection of technical papers—AIAA guidance, navigation, and control conference, vol 3, pp 1735–1764
4. Li BL et al (2009) Application of RBAUKF algorithm to SINS/GPS integrated navigation. Ship electronic engineering 29(9):67–71 (in Chinese)
5. van der Merwe R, Wan EA (2006) Sigma-point Kalman filters for integrated navigation. In: 60th annual meeting of the institute of navigation, vol 1, pp 641–654
6. Julier SJ, Uhlmann JK (1997) A new extension of the Kalman filter to nonlinear system. In: Proceedings of the SPIE—the international society for optical engineering, vol 3, pp 182–193
7. Goshen-Meskin D, Bar-Itzhack IY (1992) Unified approach to inertial navigation system error modeling J Guid Control Dyn 15(3):648–653
8. Yang B et al (2007) Application of UKF in direct method of Kalman filter for INS/GPS. Chinese J Sens Actuators 20(4):842–846 (in Chinese)
9. Simon D (2006) Optimal state estimation, 1st edn. Wiley, New York
10. NovAtel Inc (2010) Span-SE^{TM} user manual, 6th edn. NovAtel Inc., Calgary

Chapter 32
The Demand Forecasting Method for Repairable Spare Parts Based on Availability

Lianwu Zhang, Fanggeng Zhao, Jiangsheng Sun and Xiaoyan Shi

Abstract Demand forecasting is an important basis of spare parts management. A demand forecasting method for weapon repairable spare parts based on availability, in which the demand of parts with different demand pattern are estimated by different means, was proposed in the paper. The parameter in the method was determined by experiments, and computational results verified the validity of our method.

Keywords Demand forecasting · Repairable spare parts · Availability · Croston method · Exponential smoothing

32.1 Introduction

Spare parts are important material basis of equipment support, and they are significant factors to keep and resume the battle effectiveness of weapon equipment. In practice, most of spare parts are repairable. Hence, accurate demand forecasting of repairable spare parts can improve the efficiency and benefit of maintenance support to a great extent.

In recent years, literatures about spare parts are mainly focused on the inventory control models. However, without accurate demand forecasting, the inventory models can not performed well [1]. In this paper, a forecasting method for

L. Zhang (✉) · J. Sun
Machine Technology Research Institute, 050000 Shijiazhuang, People's Republic of China
e-mail: zhaofanggeng@yahoo.com.cn

F. Zhao · X. Shi
Bengbu Automobile Petty Officer School, 233011 Bengbu, People's Republic of China

W. Lu et al. (eds.), *Proceedings of the 2012 International Conference on Information Technology and Software Engineering*, Lecture Notes in Electrical Engineering 211, DOI: 10.1007/978-3-642-34522-7_32, © Springer-Verlag Berlin Heidelberg 2013

repairable spare parts demand based on availability, in which the total equipment rather than a single part is considered, was proposed. In the proposed method, the demand forecasting and inventory control problem are combined to provide an effective tool for equipment support people.

The remainder of this paper is organized as follows. Section 32.2 simply summarizes the literatures of demand forecasting methods for spare parts. Section 32.3 describes the demand forecasting method based on availability, and the results of computational tests are given in Sect. 32.4. Finally, Sect. 32.5 draws the conclusions.

32.2 Related Researches

We restrict ourselves in this review to demand forecasting for weapon spare parts. Since 1950s, Rand Corporation began to research the demand forecasting problem for weapon spare parts. Among the early researches, the most representative achievement was due to Feeney and Sherbrooke [2]. In their research, they proposed the Multi-Echelon Technique for Recoverable Item Control (METRIC), and the model can not only be used to forecast the demand of spare part, but also combined the demand forecasting and inventory control problem.

Since then, there was no influential research on demand forecasting for weapon spare parts in the following 10 years. In 1980, Muckstadt [3] formulated the demand process of spare parts as a non-stationary Poisson distribution. In 1994, Adams [4] researched the weighted regressive method for the demand forecasting of repairable spare parts, and obtained a better results than those by eight-quarter moving average method that was used in US Air Force. Melendez [5] analyzed the performance of exponential smoothing, moving average, auto regressive and linear regressive models, and the first two methods are found to be more precise. Unlu [6] proposed an integrated method named "focus forecasting". In "focus forecasting", several forecasting models, including moving average, weighted moving average, exponential smoothing, auto regressive and so on, are applied to historical data, and the one with the least error will be selected to forecasting the future demand of spare parts. In 2004, Sherbrooke [1] summarized more than 10 forecasting methods that performed well in the practice of US army, and found the best one by experiments to forecasting the future demand of repairable spare parts.

Recently, the demand forecasting of spare parts gradually becomes a hot topic of domestic research, and many demand forecasting measures, such as support vector machines [7], grey theory [8], and the Bayesian method [9], have been developed. However, most of the methods mentioned above aim at single item, while weapon equipments consist of many items. In practice, we often need determine the quantity of purchase for all items under a given budget constraint in the light of demand forecasting. Apparently, these forecasting methods aimed at single item are not convenient for the equipment support decision. Hence, we proposed a demand forecasting method for repairable spare parts based on system availability.

32.3 The Demand Forecasting Method Based on Availability

In Sherbrooke's research, although the forecasting methods are based on the availability of equipment system, a same method is used to all spare parts, and most of the methods are based on exponential smoothing. As we know, exponential smoothing is a very robust forecast method that is able to adapt quickly to changes of demand. However, Croston [10] has shown that it do not perform well for intermittent demand. In fact, there are many spare parts of weapon equipment have a demand pattern with lots of zero values, and other spare parts have a relatively smooth demand pattern. Therefore, applying a same forecasting method as that in [2] to all spare parts may not a good choice. Based on the idea mentioned above, we tries to apply different forecasting method to repairable spare parts with different demand pattern. In our method, the repairable spare parts of weapon equipment are divided into intermittent pattern and smooth pattern, and the category method can refer to the paper of Williams [11]. For spare parts with intermittent pattern, an improved Croston method [12] is utilized to forecasting the demand, and the exponential smoothing method is used for spare parts with smooth pattern.

32.3.1 The Improved Croston Method for Intermittent Demand

Croston argues that for intermittent demand, exponential smoothing does not perform well. Hence he proposed a new method, named Croston method, to provide a more accurate forecasting of the demand by applying exponential smoothing separately to the intervals between nonzero demands and their sizes. Let $\hat{k}_t$ denote the smoothed estimate of the mean interval in period t between nonzero demands, k_t be the time interval since the last nonzero demand at the beginning of period t, $\hat{s}_t$ represent the smoothed estimate of a nonzero demand in period t, and d_t be the actual demand in period t. Croston method works as follows:

$$\hat{s}_{t+1} = \begin{cases} \hat{s}_t & \text{if } d_t = 0 \\ (1-\alpha)\hat{s}_t + \alpha d_t & \text{if } d_t > 0 \end{cases}, \tag{32.1}$$

and

$$\hat{k}_{t+1} = \begin{cases} \hat{k}_t & \text{if } d_t = 0 \\ (1-\alpha)\hat{k}_t + \alpha k_t & \text{if } d_t > 0 \end{cases} \tag{32.2}$$

where α is smoothing constant between 0 and 1. Let $\hat{x}_{t+1}$ denote the forecasted demand in period t, and the Croston forecast is

$$\hat{x}_{t+1} = \frac{\hat{s}_{t+1}}{\hat{k}_{t+1}}. \tag{32.3}$$

Although the Croston method performed better than exponential smoothing for intermittent demand, it is positively biased [12]. To approximately correct for the bias, Syntetos and Boylan [12] propose to deflate the Croston forecast by a factor $1-\alpha/2$. Consequently, the improved Croston method is

$$\hat{x}_{t+1} = \left(1 - \frac{\alpha}{2}\right)\frac{\hat{s}_{t+1}}{\hat{k}_{t+1}}. \tag{32.4}$$

32.3.2 The Exponential Smoothing Method for Smooth Demand

Exponential smoothing (ES) is a widely used time-series method, using historical data to obtain a smoothed value for the series. This smoothed value is then extrapolated to become the forecast for the future value of the series. ES method applies an unequal set of weights that decrease exponentially with time to past data, which means the more recent the data value, the greater its weighting. Let $\hat{x}_t$ denote the forecasted demand in period t, d_t represent the actual demand in period t, the forecasted demand in period $t+1$ is

$$\hat{x}_{t+1} = (1-\alpha)\hat{x}_t + \alpha \cdot d_t, \tag{32.5}$$

where α is a smoothing constant between 0 and 1.

When a trend exists, this method will consider the trend as well as the series average, and ignore the trend that will cause the forecast to underestimate or to overestimate actual demand, depending on whether the trend is increasing or decreasing.

32.3.3 The Computation of System Availability

The availability, A, is the expected percent of the equipment fleet that is not down for any spare parts. And A can be computed as the following expression:

$$A = 100\prod_{i=1}^{I}\left\{1 - EBO_i(s_i)/(NZ_i)\right\}^{Z_i}, \tag{32.6}$$

where l is the total number of spare parts in the equipment, N is the number of equipment in the system, s_i is the stock level of part i, Z_i is the number of occurrences on an equipment of part i, $EBO_i(s_i)$ is the expected backorder of part i when the stock level of part i is s_i, and $EBO_i(s_i)$ is given by the following formula:

$$EBO_i(s_i) = \sum_{x=s_i+1}^{\infty} (x - s_i) \cdot P_i(x) = \sum_{x=s_i+1}^{\infty} x \cdot P_i(x) - s_i \cdot \sum_{x=s_i+1}^{\infty} P_i(x), \quad (32.7)$$

where $P_i(x)$ represents the probability for the number of demand for part i.

32.3.4 The Forecasting Procedure

In the two forecasting methods, there is a smoothing constant α, which will surely affect the accuracy of forecast, need to be determined. To select an appropriate value for α, we designed the forecasting procedure as follows:

(I)   Utilizing the historical demand data from period $T-4$ to $T-1$, the Croston method and ES method with different α values are used to forecast the demands in period T for parts with intermittent and smooth demand pattern, respectively;

(II) Compute the forecasting availability and the stock level for every part in period T according to forecasting results;

(III) Using the actual demands of period T, evaluate the operational effect of each stock strategy obtained in (II), and get the emulational availability, named attained availability, of each stock strategy;

(IV) Apply the forecasting methods with the best α value to forecast the demands in period $T + 1$, and compute corresponding stock level for every part under the constraint of total budget.

In the procedure, the value of α is tested starting from 0.05 and going to 0.45 with increments of 0.05, that is, $\alpha_j = \{0.05, 0.1, 0.15, ..., 0.45\}$. The purpose of evaluating the forecasting methods under different values of α is to find the value of α that can obtain the largest attained availability and the highest precision. Hence, the evaluation criteria is

$$\alpha = \arg \max_{j} \{AR_j - |AF_j - AR_j|\},$$

where j is the serial number of tested parameter value α_j, AF_j denotes the forecasting availability under parameter α_j, and AR_j represents the attained availability under parameter α_j. The flowchart of forecasting method is given in Fig. 32.1.

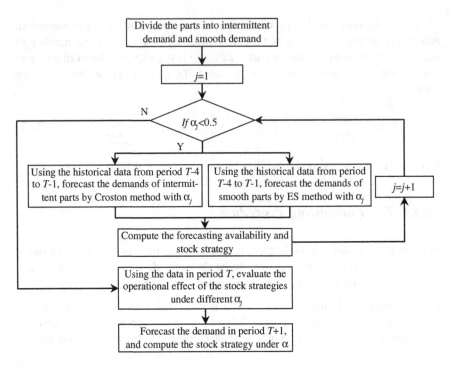

Fig. 32.1 Flowchart of the proposed forecasting method

32.4 Forecasting Results and Discussion

32.4.1 Historical Data

The experimental data used in this study are historical demand data of spare parts consist in a kind of self-propelled artillery equipped in an armored unit during the past 5 years. In the experiments, the data of ten repairable spare parts are considered. The historical demand of the parts and other parameters needed in forecasting are given in Table 32.1. In addition, the invest budget is assumed to be the total cost of spare parts needed in 2011.

32.4.2 Experimental Results and Analysis

Using the historical data showed in Table 32.1, the forecasting experiments were performed under different α values. The forecasting results for 2011 are presented in Table 32.2. To illustrate the validity of our method, the forecasting results that obtained either by exponential smoothing or by Croston method are given in the

Table 32.1 Historical data and parameters

Period	2007	2008	2009	2010	2011	Cost	Z_i	Average repair time (years)
Part 1	0	0	1	1	0	742	1	0.02
Part 2	0	0	1	0	1	1,156	1	0.03
Part 3	1	0	0	2	0	2,659	8	0.05
Part 4	6	6	5	4	7	3,264	24	0.01
Part 5	0	0	1	0	0	4,310	12	0.005
Part 6	1	1	0	2	1	1,296	1	0.05
Part 7	0	1	0	0	1	3,317	1	0.1
Part 8	1	0	1	1	0	2,101	1	0.08
Part 9	3	5	4	3	5	1,085	4	0.05
Part 10	2	2	0	3	3	2,518	1	0.03

Table 32.2 Comparison of forecasting results for 2011

α	Forecasting availability (%)	Attained availability (%)
0.05	87.92	88.95
0.10	91.28	93.35
0.15	94.01	95.83
0.20	93.55	95.72
0.25	94.83	95.36
0.30	92.69	94.18
0.35	90.90	93.33
0.40	87.36	88.17
0.45	88.82	90.13
ES method	87.11	88.29
Croston method	89.67	90.58

last two line of the table. From Table 32.2, we can see that the proposed method provided the best forecasting results when $\alpha = 0.25$, and the results under most of α values are better than those of ES and Croston methods. Hence, we can safely draw the conclusion that our method is more suitable for repairable spare parts of weapon equipment than ES and Croston methods.

According to the procedure of our forecasting method, the demands of repairable spare parts in 2012 are estimated on the condition of $\alpha = 0.25$, and the forecasting results are showed in Table 32.3. By the proposed forecasting method, we can not only get the forecasting availability of equipment system, but also know how to assign the inventory of the repairable spare parts. Therefore, the method would be a useful tool for manager of weapon spare parts.

Table 32.3 Forecasting results for 2012

Parts	Part 1	Part 2	Part 3	Part 4	Part 5	Part 6	Part 7	Part 8	Part 9	Part 10
Stock strategy	1	0	1	6	0	1	1	1	4	3
Forecasting availability	95.10 %									

32.5 Conclusions

In this paper, the demand forecasting method for weapon repairable spare parts based on availability was proposed. In the method, the demands of parts with intermittent pattern are forecasted by the Croston method, while the demands of parts with smooth pattern are forecasted by the ES method. The historical demand data of parts on the self-propelled artillery were utilized to test our method, and the optimal value of smooth constant in the method was determined through experiments. Forecasting results show that our method outperformed both the Croston and ES methods, and the proposed method is a convenient inventory decision tool for spare parts managers.

References

1. Sherbrooke C (2004) Optimal inventory modeling of systems: multi-echelon techniques. Kluwer Academic Publishers, New York
2. Feeney GJ, Sherbrooke C (1965) An objective bayes approach for inventory decisions. Rand Corporation, Santa Monica
3. Muckstadt JA (1980) Comparative adequacy of steady-state versus dynamic models for calculating stockage requirements. Rand Corporation, Santa Monica
4. Adams JL, Abell JB, Issacson KE (1994) Modeling and forecasting the demand for aircraft recoverable spare parts. Rand Corporation, Santa Monica
5. Melendez DA (1998) A forecasting approach to improve logistics planning in the Colombian. Air University, Alabama
6. Unlu NT (2001) Improving the Turkish navy requirements determination process: an assessment of demand forecasting methods for weapon system items. Naval Postgraduate School, Monterey
7. Liu YW, Xing GP, Pan ZL (2009) Research on the forecasting methods of intermittent spare part consumption. Def Sci Technol 30(5):59 (in Chinese)
8. Liu Y, Ren DK (2011) Research on prediction model for intermittent demand spare parts based on grey theory. J Sichuan Ord 32(4):27 (in Chinese)
9. Chen FT, Zuo HF (2011) Research and application of aero-spare based on Bayesian method. J Civil Aviat Univ Chin 29(2):13 (in Chinese)
10. Croston JD (1972) Forecasting and stock control for intermittent demands. Oper Res Quart 23(2):289
11. Williams TM (1984) Stock control with sporadic and slow-moving demand. J Oper Res Soc 35(5):939
12. Syntetos AA, Boylan JE (2001) On the bias of intermittent demand estimates. Int J Prod Econ 71(2):457

Chapter 33
Service Efficiency Evaluation of Distribution Facilities in Comprehensive Passenger Transport Hub

Zhe Zhang, Changxu Ji, Maojing Jin, Qian Li, Lifen Yun, Long Gao, Hong Lan and Ling Huang

Abstract Comprehensive passenger transport hub (CPTH) is the point of different transport modes of the transportation network and is also the distribution center of a large number of passengers. The service efficiency of distribution facilities in CPTH is one of the key factors that influences the distribution efficiency of the Hub. The service efficiency evaluation of distribution facilities in CPTH can help managers find and correct the disadvantages of distribution facilities to improve the distribution efficiency of the hub and satisfy the requirement of passengers-convenient transfer and the expectation of CPTH managers-balanced utilization of facilities. Based on factor analyze of service reliability and ADC model, the paper builds the ADC service efficiency evaluation model of distribution facilities in CPTH and uses that to estimate the service efficiency comprehensively. It verifies the practicability of ADC model in the service efficiency evaluation of distribution facilities in CPTH and it will be helpful for the improvement of distribution service of CPTH.

Keywords CPTH · Service efficiency evaluation · ADC model

Z. Zhang · C. Ji (✉) · Q. Li · L. Yun · L. Gao
State Key Laboratory of Rail Traffic Control and Safety, Beijing Jiaotong University,
100044 Beijing, China
e-mail: chxji@bjtu.edu.cn

M. Jin · H. Lan · L. Huang
The High Technology Research and Development Center, Ministry of Science
and Technology, 100044 Beijing, People's Republic of China
e-mail: lh@htrdc.com

W. Lu et al. (eds.), *Proceedings of the 2012 International Conference on Information Technology and Software Engineering*, Lecture Notes in Electrical Engineering 211, DOI: 10.1007/978-3-642-34522-7_33, © Springer-Verlag Berlin Heidelberg 2013

33.1 Introduction

It is very important for passengers in CPTH that distribution facilities can provide reliable distribution service. They have certain expectations such as shorter queue time, shorter walking distance, more clear walking for facilities service after passengers arrived at CPTH [1].

For CPTH managers, it is also important for passenger distribution that the utilization level of service facilities can be in ideal condition [2]. Because of the inconformity of facility service time, a large number of passengers will be concentrated at some facilities while other facilities are in idle state. It will cause the overweight or low utilization level of service facilities, thus affecting the distribution effectiveness of CPTH system.

Thus it can be seen that improving the service efficiency of distribution facilities in CPTH not only can guarantee convenient transfer, but also can improve distribution efficiency and strengthen the competeveness of CPTH [3]. So, the service efficiency of distribution facilities in CPTH can be identified as the ability of service facilities to finish passenger distribution and provide service for passengers in CPTH in cycle operation of CPTH system.

33.2 ADC Evaluation Model of Service Efficiency of Distribution Facilities in CPTH

33.2.1 ADC Service Efficiency Evaluation Model

The system efficiency evaluation ADC model is a mature efficiency evaluation model of system which is put forward by WSEIAC. This model agrees that system efficiency is the degree of satisfying a series of specific task requirements for system, and it is the function of system availability, dependability and capability.

So the expression of ADC model is $E = ADC$, E ($E = [e_1, e_2, \ldots, e_n]^T$) is the index vector of system efficiency; A is the measurement of availability at the beginning of task execution and reflects the degree of preparation. $A = [a_1, a_2, \ldots, a_n]$. a_i ($i = 1, 2, \ldots, n$) is the probability of mission system being in the state i, i is the possible state number of system availability; D is reliability matrix and says the probability of finishing the required function in use, because the system has n possible states, the reliability matrix D is a $n \times n$ matrix and can be expressed as:

$$D = \begin{pmatrix} d_{11} & \cdots & d_{1n} \\ \vdots & \ddots & \vdots \\ d_{n1} & \cdots & d_{nn} \end{pmatrix} \tag{33.1}$$

In the formula: d_{ij} $(i = 1, 2, \ldots, n; j = 1, 2, \ldots, n)$ is the possibility of mission system being in the state i while system is in state j during expected task time; C is the ability of system operation or quality factors and represents the ability of achieving task goal in available state of system. So system capability is an n × m matrix.

$$C = \begin{pmatrix} c_{11} & \cdots & c_{1m} \\ \vdots & \ddots & \vdots \\ c_{n1} & \cdots & c_{nm} \end{pmatrix} \tag{33.2}$$

c_{ij} $(i = 1, 2, \ldots, n: j = 1, 2, \ldots, m)$ is the probability of finishing the j task in the state i, it depends on the design capacity of system in the condition of right and high efficiency operation [4].

The service efficiency of distribution facilities in CPTH is service facilities' ability to satisfy service reliability in the normal condition. In the formula E = ADC, A represents the probability of distribution service facilities being available. D represents the service reliability of facility operation; it is the probability of achieving the expected service quality in operation. C represents the ability of service facilities in CPTH, it is quality factors. E is the comprehensive capacity showed by system availability and reliability in the respect of service quality, its value range is determined according to the number of A, C and D matrix elements. When A is 1, D is 1 × n line vector, C is n × 1 column vector, and E is an unambiguous numerical value. The full marks of each quality factors is set as 100, when there are n quality factors corresponding to n reliability and the reliability is 1, system efficiency is 100n.

33.2.2 Establishment and Calculation of the Evaluation Indexes

According to the different function and service form, the facilities in CPTH can be divided into four kinds [5]: facilities for walking (pedestrian passage, stair, escalator, and slope), service facilities with delay (apparatus, brake machine, wicket), signage system, service facilities accommodating passengers (waiting hall, outbound hall). The evaluation indexes are built and calculated based on different kinds of facilities.

33.2.2.1 Reliability of Average Occupied Area of Passengers in Channel

The average occupied area of passengers in channel will decrease along with the increasing number of passengers, thus walking strides will be reduced and passengers will slow down. So the time of occupying channel will increase, the carrying capacity will be reduced. The reliability of occupied area of passengers in channel is the probability of the real average occupied area being larger than the limit. The formula can be expressed as:

$$R_{oac} = 1 - P(s_{ra} \leq \alpha s_{ta}) \tag{33.3}$$

In the formula:

R_{oac} The reliability of average occupied area of passengers in channel;
s_{ra} The real average occupied area;
s_{ta} The theoretical average occupied area;
α The correction factor for different kinds of channel.

33.2.2.2 Reliability of Transfer Distance

Generally speaking, the furthest distance that passengers can accept is 500 m [6], so the reliability of transfer distance can be expressed as:

$$R_{wd} = \frac{N_{\leq 500}}{N} \tag{33.4}$$

In the formula:

R_{wd} The reliability of transfer distance;
$N_{\leq 500}$ The number of passengers whose transfer distance is less than 500 m;
N The number of passengers in channel.

33.2.2.3 Reliability of Service Time of Facilities

When the service frequency of facilities is high and yet the work efficiency is low, passengers will be waiting in line before the facility. In this case, the facility in channel will become the bottleneck of reducing walking efficiency of passengers, and then affect the carrying capacity. The reliability of service time of facilities in channel is passengers' requirements for the service ability of facilities. So this reliability can be expressed as the probability that the real time spent in passing the facility is longer than the theoretical time. The formula can be expressed as:

$$R_{stc} = P(t_s \leq \beta t_{s0}) \tag{33.5}$$

In the formula:

R_{stc} The reliability of service time of facilities in channel;

t_s The real time spent in passing the facilities;

t_{s0} The theoretical time spent in passing the facilities;

β The correction factor for different kinds of facilities.

33.2.2.4 Reliability of Signage System

The homologous sign should be set up for guiding passenger to pass in and out of channel. If the signage system in channel cannot indicate the right travel direction to passengers, it is necessary for passengers to slow down or stop to distinguish the right travel direction, thus the distribution speed of passengers will be reduced, and then the carrying capacity will also be reduced. So the reliability of signage system is passengers' requirements for the accuracy and integrity of signage system.

The percentage of people who were not lost and did not ask CPTH managers for route information can be used for expressing the reliability of signage system. The formula can be expressed as:

$$R_{oss} = 1 - \frac{q_L}{q} \tag{33.6}$$

In the formula:

R_{oss} The reliability of signage system;

q_L The daily number of people who are lost and ask CPTH managers for route information on average;

q The daily number of people in CPTH on average.

33.2.2.5 Reliability of Average Occupied Area of Passengers in Service Facilities Accommodating Passengers

This reliability can be used for expressing requirements for the size of personal space of passengers, it is the probability of the real average occupied area being larger than the area that can be accepted by passengers in the psychological aspect. Its formula can be expressed as:

$$R_{aoa} = 1 - P\left(p_i \leq p_{i0}\right) \tag{33.7}$$

In the formula:

R_{aoa} The reliability of average occupied area of passengers.
p_i The real average occupied area.
p_{i0} The area that can be accepted by passengers in the psychological aspect.

33.3 Case Study Analysis

Xizhimen subway station is chose as the case, ADC model is used for the service efficiency evaluation of distribution facilities in Xizhimen.

33.3.1 Numerical Calculation of Reliability and Evaluation Index

(1) A represent the probability of distribution service facilities being available, its number is 1, it is believed that the system is in perfect condition. Four quality factors corresponding to four numbers of reliability are adopted. So, $E \in (0\ 500)$.
(2) Observational data is used for calculating the random event probability which is empirical probability and the number of reliability. The reliability matrix D can be expressed as:

$$D = [D_1\, D_2\, D_3\, D_4\, D_5] = [R_{oac}\, R_{wd}\, R_{stc}\, R_{oss}\, R_{aoa}] \qquad (33.8)$$

The theoretical occupied area of channel in Xizhimen during peak time is $0.91\ m^2/p$ based on investigation and analysis. The probability that the real average occupied area is larger than the number is 0.57 according to the actual survey data, $R_{oac} = 0.57$.

The percentage of passengers whose transfer distance is less than 500 m is 0.68 during peak time. $R_{wd} = 0.68$

The theoretical waiting time of booking hall is 3.8 min in the peak period, the probability that the waiting time is less than 3.8 min is 0.92. $R_{stc} = 0.92$.

The average daily number of passengers in Xizhimen is 0.87 million and the daily number of people who are lost and ask CPTH managers for route information on average is 1000 according to the actual survey data. $R_{oss} \approx 1$.

The average occupied area of waiting area during peak time is $0.14\ m^2/p$, the percentage of the area being larger than $0.14\ m^2/p$ in numerous surveys is 0.6. $R_{aoa} = 0.6$.

Table 33.1 Index of quality grade

Grade of evaluation standard	A	B	C	D	E
Average occupied area of passengers in channel (m^2/p)	≥ 12.077	≥ 3.716	≥ 2.230	≥ 1.394	≤ 1.394
Furthest transfer distance (m)	0–100	100–200	200–350	350–500	≥ 500
Waiting time (min)	≤ 2.0	2.0–5.0	5.0–8.0	8.0–12.0	≥ 12.0
Average occupied area of passengers in waiting area (m^2/p)	≥ 1.0	0.65–1.0	0.3–0.65	0.2–0.3	≤ 0.2
Percentage of lost people and people asking route questions	0–0.1	0.1–0.2	0.2–0.3	0.3–0.4	≥ 0.4
Index	[90,100]	[80,90]	[70,80]	[60,70]	[0,60]

(3) The number of quality index is determined according to the evaluation criterion (see Table 33.1), and it is the number of C matrix $C = [C_1\,C_2\,C_3\,C_4\,C_5]^T$

C_1: The theoretical occupied area of channel in Xizhimen is 0.91 m^2/p, the grade of evaluation standard is E, the index is 43 by using interpolation.

C_2: The furthest transfer distance of channel is 500 m (the vertical distance should be doubled), the index is 60.

C_3: The theoretical waiting time of booking hall is 3.8 min in the peak period, the index is 86.

C_4: The percentage of people who are lost and ask CPTH managers for route information is near zero, the index can be 100.

C_5: The average occupied area of waiting area is 0.14 m^2/p during peak time, the index is 42.

33.3.2 Evaluation and Analysis of Service Efficiency

According to the formula E = ADC, the service efficiency of distribution facilities is calculated.

$$E = R_{oac} \times C_1 + R_{wd} \times C_2 + R_{stc} \times C_3 + R_{oss} \times C_4 + R_{aoa} \times C_5$$
$$= 0.57 \times 43 + 0.68 \times 60 + 0.92 \times 86 + 1 \times 100 + 0.6 \times 42 = 269.63 \tag{33.9}$$

So the facility service reliability of Xizhimen subway station is at failing grade during peak time. The congestion problem of channel and waiting area and the long transfer distance are the main reasons.

33.3.2.1 Congestion of Channel and Waiting Area

The number of passengers that Xizhimen subway station attracts is very large for that the subway station is the center place of working and consumption. The average occupied area of passengers in waiting area is only 0.14 m^2/p, the number that our country announces is 0.2 m^2/p. So the shortage of area becomes the reason that causes congestion of channel and waiting room.

33.3.2.2 Long Transfer Distance

It can be found that the transfer distance between line 13 and line 2 and 4 is further than 500 m [7] based on the on-site investigation, and multiple walking up and down stairs are needed in the transfer process. The time of passenger distribution increases, and then the service efficiency is reduced.

33.4 Conclusion

System reliability is closely related with the system efficiency, this paper confirms the applicability of the classic system efficiency model ADC model in the service effectiveness evaluation of distribution facilities in CPTH. The facility service reliability of Xizhimen is at failing grade during peak time by analyzing the service efficiency whose reason is the congestion problem of channel and waiting room and the long transfer distance.

Acknowledgments This research was supported by the National Natural Science Foundation of China (Nos. 71171015); the State Key Laboratory of Rail Traffic Control and Safety (Contract No. RCS2011ZT002), Beijing Jiaotong University; the Fundamental Research Funds for the Central Universities (Contract No. T12JB00110).

References

1. Perk VA, Foreman C (2003) Florida metropolitan planning organization reports on transit capacity and quality of service: first-year evaluation. Transp Res Rec 1841:128–134
2. Kuo MS, Liang GS (2011) Combining VIKOR with GRA techniques to evaluate service quality of airports under fuzzy environment. Expert Syst Appl 38(3):1304–1312
3. Yang H, Bell MGH, Meng Q (2000) Modeling the capacity and level of service of urban transportation networks. Transp Res Part B 34(3):255–275
4. Zhang CC, Zhu XQ (2009) Service reliability estimation of public transit system based on ADC model. Technol Econ Areas Commun 1(11):56–59

5. Ren JX, Ji CX (2010) Study on the bottlenecks identification methods of distributed network in comprehensive passenger hub. In: 2010 international conference on management science and engineering, pp 105–109
6. Li Q (2011) Analysis and modeling of the distribution service network of comprehensive passenger transportation hub. Beijing Jiaotong University, Beijing (in Chinese)
7. Li JW, Ji CX (2012). Research on passenger mustering and evacuation efficiency evaluation of comprehensive passenger hub. Beijing Jiaotong University, Beijing (in Chinese)

Chapter 34
Analysis and Modeling of the Distribution Control Strategy of Comprehensive Passenger Transportation Hub

Lifen Yun, Changxu Ji, Maojing Jin, Qian Li, Long Gao, Zhe Zhang, Hong Lan and Ling Huang

Abstract The design of differentiation control strategy can effectively improve the operational efficiency of distributed service network of comprehensive passenger transportation hub (CPTH), reflect the "people-oriented" concept of comprehensive traffic service and decide the urban comprehensive transportation network performance bring into play. According to whether the stage of polymerization state is normal, the paper establishes the bi-level programming model of the control strategy by use of the Stackelberg game and designs algorithm by use of genetic algorithm. The research object is distribution service network. By the research on the differentiation of polymerization state of hub feature, the establishment of model and algorithm design, it can provide an idea for the design and realization of high—performance distributed services network.

Keywords CPTH · Stackelberg game theory · Control strategy · Bi-level Programming

L. Yun · C. Ji (✉) · Q. Li · L. Gao · Z. Zhang
State Key Laboratory of Rail Traffic Control and Safety, Beijing Jiaotong University, 100044 Beijing, China
e-mail: chxji@bjtu.edu.cn

M. Jin · H. Lan · L. Huang
Ministry of Science and Technology, The high Technology Research and Development Center, 100044 Beijing, China
e-mail: jin@htrdc.com

W. Lu et al. (eds.), *Proceedings of the 2012 International Conference on Information Technology and Software Engineering*, Lecture Notes in Electrical Engineering 211, DOI: 10.1007/978-3-642-34522-7_34, © Springer-Verlag Berlin Heidelberg 2013

34.1 Introduction

With the rapid development of the city's comprehensive transportation network, the CPTH is increasingly becoming a distribution center for a variety of modes of transportation and large-scale passenger flow. The service level and efficiency of CPTH directly determines the performance of urban traffic network bring into play. The differentiated control strategy of distribution network can effectively improve the efficiency of the distribution service of CPTH, reflect the "people-oriented" concept of transport services and provide better service for the traveling passengers.

The CPTH, whose main feature is the interchange convergence of varieties of transportation modes, is the necessary link for passenger travel process. The main function of CPTH is the transfer between multiple modes of transportation or lines. The existing literature is study on the perspective of the macro-hub location, meso-hub transfer, micro-passenger behavior, to improve the transfer efficiency of the hub. The analysis of Macro-location is evaluation and optimization of the CPTH from the level of integrated transport function. New comprehensive service level investigation method, combined with comprehensive consideration of the urban road network capacity, to coordinate public transportation passenger flow and relieve the public transport network congestion [1, 2]. The overall function system of a large hub, such as geographic position and entry construct location, is planned and designed to optimize the service level that is perceived by the passengers in the integrated transport network [3]. Meso-hub transfer analysis is generally focused on measure evaluating and optimizing the transfer efficiency. The simulation model is used to simulate the flow of passenger within the hub to find the bottleneck of traffic behavior which can be reduced to improve passenger flow transfer efficiency [4]. Considered the hub capacity, comfort, attitude of service personnel, security and other factors of the fuzzy environment, the level of airport service evaluation model is established by using VIKOR and GRA to optimize the transfer efficiency and service [5]. Passenger behavior microscopic analysis focused on the group behavior analysis. Helbing et al. illustrated the complexity characteristics of the passenger traffic flow through the chaos and nonlinear dynamic characteristics of group behavior [6, 7] analysis and proposed the "social force" model [8]. With deep research of passenger behavior, passenger perceived service measure and management gradually get the attention, but concentrate in the internal decision-making management and service of high value-added airport hub. Taiwan's CKS International Airport, using 0–1 integer scientific decision-making program model, analyzed the inefficient problem of airport security facilities and flights shared, and proposed countermeasures to improve the level of service [9]; can also start from the configuration management of the airport staff, the complexity of the strategic, tactical, operational three levels of passenger service systems, the deployment level model [10]. At present, China's distribution service network of CPTH has been basically formed by the coupling elements of distribution facilities, passenger organizations processes and guidance service measures with the characteristics of network, three-dimensional, dynamic [11]. Therefore, the research trend is the structure and integrity analysis of distribution service network. The "people-oriented" differences in control strategy design optimization as a scientific issue which involves transport planning, management, control theory and other multi-disciplinary, has also become the research focus and difficulty of transportation science.

The paper establishes the bi-level programming model of the control strategy by use of the Stackelberg game and designs algorithm. The research object is service network. The division base of stage is the polymerization state of the distributed service network status. It can provide the scientific basis for design and implementation of high—performance distributed service network.

34.2 Analysis of Distribution Service Network Status

In this paper, k denoted the number of state description parameters; n_i ($i = 1, 2, \ldots, k$) denotes the input value of ith parameter. Based on the concept of polymerization state, an input value of parameter n_i is regarded as one point of k-dimension space. All the parameter values of hub can form one possible state of this space, regarded as one polymerization state. The polymerization state is formed by all the point in the $n_1 + n_2 + \cdots + n_k = \omega$ plane of k-dimension space.

34.2.1 Hub Service Network State Description

34.2.1.1 Feature Parameter of Passenger

The feature of comprehensive transportation passenger can be described from meso and micro level. Meso-level describes the relationship between the flux, density and speed of passengers. Micro-level describes the individual characteristics of passenger, such as space occupied characteristic and movement characteristic. The space occupied characteristic parameters is used to describe the status that individual occupies the walk space, such as height, body width, body thickness (the maximum from chest to back), the minimum distance between passenger and obstacle. The movement characteristic parameter is used to describe the movement behavior of individual in the movement, such as the pedestrian path choice and pedestrian walk track.

34.2.1.2 Feature Parameter of Infrastructure

Based on the physical characteristic of distributed service network infrastructure, it can be simplified as network topology structure which is formed by node, link and

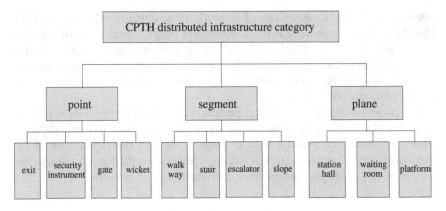

Fig. 34.1 The classification of distribution facilities of CPTH

district, which called "Point"-like facilities, "segment"-like facilities and the "face"-like facilities. The parameters of every infrastructure include the physical attributes, spatial attributes, linking attributes, capacity and utilization. It is shown in Fig. 34.1.

34.2.1.3 Feature Parameter of Environment

The parameters of the environment characteristics within the hub can be described from the perspective of the passenger feel, mainly including air quality, noise pollution. For example, air quality parameters can be divided into whether the main ingredients in the air reach the appropriate standard, smoke and other harmful substances whether over standard and so on.

34.2.2 Criteria of Polymerization State Differentiation for the Classification

The criterion of differentiation division is confirmed according to the digital description of the polymerization state of hub distribution services network and the differentiation control strategy is taken according to the different region.

34.2.2.1 Confirm the Basic Polymerization State

The polymerization state is formed by all the point in the $n_1 + n_2 + \cdots + n_k = \omega$ plane of k-dimension space. The polymerization state should be formulated based on the basic polymerization state. On this basis, setting a control parameter calls the capacity scaling factor, denoted by β. Finally the description of polymerization

Fig. 34.2 The description of
floating section state

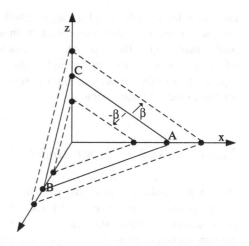

state is the basis of cross-section parameter value in the floating range β. Based on
the design standards of hub, the state can be calculated which is composed of the
hub input parameter value, called the basic polymerization state.

34.2.2.2 Capacity Scaling Factor

After the basic polymerization state is determined, according to the different times
in different hub status, a control parameter called capacity scaling factor β can be
set to make the polymerization state description has a certain degree of flexibility
and more correspond to the realistic situation. The description of floating section
state is shown in Fig. 34.2.

34.2.3 Differentiation Control Strategy

When the hub distribution network polymerization state is under the flexibility basic
polymerization state, it can be thought that the hub is in a normal state (normal) and
the universal control strategy can be used. If there is special circumstance, some
abnormal input values should be distinguished and emergency control strategy
should be used. Thereby it can form the differentiation control strategies.

34.3 Differences in Control Strategy Model

When an input value of polymerization state is out of the normal fluctuation range,
such as the occurrence of natural disasters, social unrest and human accidents, the
highest and only control strategy goal is to protect public life and property safety

and minimize casualties and damage caused by emergencies. Due to the insufficient information and development situation with high degree uncertainty, various public places have the dedicated emergency response strategy to do the most effective control in the limited period of time. Due to the emergency disposal is the separate part of the research contents in security, this paper mainly focuses on the normal universal control strategy.

34.3.1 Stackelberg Game Model

Due to the public nature of the passenger hub, the game between the hub for passenger traffic management and passenger groups should be taken into account in the design of control strategies. Firstly, the mechanism of interaction between the hub management which is the performer in the process of hub control strategy implementation and passenger groups which are the service objects is analyzed. Secondly, the complex relationships of facts and feedback, contrary to and reunification between them are analyzed. Finally, the universal model of the service distribution network control strategy is established.

If there are N passengers, H_i is the strategy pace of passenger i, h_i is the ith strategy in H_i, $h = (h_1, h_2, \ldots, h_N)$ is the strategy profile, $Z_i(h) = Z_i(h_1, h_2, \ldots, h_N)$ is the utility function of strategy profile $h = (h_1, h_2, \ldots, h_N)$ which the passenger selects. The game process can be defined $\Lambda = \{H_1, H_2, \ldots, H_N, Z_1, Z_2, \ldots Z_N\}$, Z_i is the utility function.

If manager makes the optimal use of hub resources as the goal in the game, then it becomes one of the game players. Assume that the traffic managers know people's route choice behavior clearly, they can take better strategy considering people's response. Due to managers in the active position, they can pre-select strategy and generate the implementation program of information guidance. In contrast passengers in the passive position, they can learned the manager's guidance information, and then choose the path. Stackelberg game between managers and passengers is shown in Fig. 34.3. This is an inequality in two games. Meanwhile, the managers can know the passenger's strategy choice and the passenger's response will be brought into the games. So this is an iterative multi- stage game called Stackelberg game.

Achieve the balanced condition is:

$$\max_{g \in G} Z_g(g, h^*(g)) \tag{34.1}$$

$$h^*(g) = \max_{h \in H} Z_h(g, h) \tag{34.2}$$

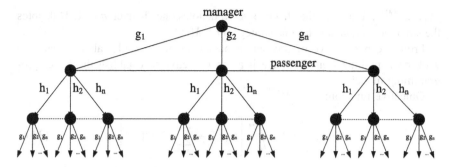

Fig. 34.3 Stackelberg game between managers and passengers

34.3.2 Normal Control Strategy Model

According to the idea of the Stackelberg game, the normal control strategy model is established by using the bi-level program model.

The BPR function is that U.S. Highway Administration through traffic survey on a large number of road sections and regression analysis obtained a formula, which reflects the relationship between travel time and traffic flux on the same road section. In CPTH, the macroscopic properties of travelers' stream are similar to road traffic flow, so BPR function is used as the function of travelers running time.

$$t_a = t_a^0 \left[1 + \alpha \left(\frac{x_a}{c_{amax}} \right)^{\beta} \right] \tag{34.3}$$

Here, $t_a(x_a)$ denotes the travelers running time in channel a; t_a^0 denotes the travelers running time as no flux in channel a; x_a denotes the travelers flux in channel a; c_{amax} denotes the traffic capacity of channel a; α and β denote the impact parameters of running time.

From the perspective of manager of passenger hub, the ultimate goal of manager is to make the optimal performance of the whole hub. So make the total cost of system to minimize as the measure of its performance indicators, in order to establish the upper programming model.

Objective function:

$$\min W(y) = \sum_{a \in A} t_a(x_a) x_a(y_a) \tag{34.4}$$

Constraint condition:

$$y_a^m = 0 \text{ or } 1, \ \forall m \in M, a \in A \tag{34.5}$$

Here, y denotes the strategy profile of all the channels, $y = (y_1, y_2, \ldots, y_a, \ldots, y_{(A)})$; y_a denotes the strategy profile of channel a, $y_a = (y_a^1, y_a^2, \ldots,$

$y_a^m, \ldots, y_a^{(M)}$); A denotes the channels set; a denotes one channel, $a \in A$; M denotes the strategies set; m denotes one strategy, $m \in M$.

From the perspective of traveler of passenger hub, traveler always wants to walk cost minimization. So make it as an objective to establish the lower programming model.

Objective function:

$$\min Q(x) = \sum_{a \in A} \int_0^{x_a} \left[t_a(x_a) - \sum_{m \in M} y_a^m u^m(x_a) \right] dx \qquad (34.6)$$

Constraint condition:

$$\sum_R f_R^w = q^w, \ \forall w \in W \qquad (34.7)$$

$$f_k^w \geq 0, \ \forall k \in K^w, \ \forall w \in W \qquad (34.8)$$

$$x_a = \sum_w \sum_k f_k^w \delta_{ak}^w, \ \forall a \in A \qquad (34.9)$$

Here, W denotes the O-D pairs set, w denotes one O-D pair, $w \in W$; q^w denotes the flux of O-D pair w; K^w denotes the traveler lines set of O-D pair w, k denotes one traveler line, $k \in K^w$; $u^m(x_a)$ denotes the utility function of strategy m; f_k^w denotes the flux of traveler line k of O-D pair w.

34.4 Algorithm Design for Differences in Control Strategy Model

The bi-level programming problem is an NP-hard problem of non-convexity and the solution is extremely difficult. The genetic algorithm (GA) is an adaptive probabilistic search algorithm of global optimization based on the natural selection mechanism and genetic variation mechanism, not only successfully used in solving industrial engineering, artificial intelligence, automatic control of complex issues but also applied to solve the bi-level programming problem.

The genetic algorithm is used to solve the bi-level programming model of the comprehensive transportation strategy in this paper. The specific solution steps are as follow.

Step 1: Initialize. Confirm the genetic algorithm crossover method which is used to create the offspring from the parents selected in the pairing process and mutation probability which is used to confirm the number of chromosomes to mutation, population size M and maximum number of iterations T, the reasonable fitness function and the termination condition.

Step 2: Generate the initial population. Based on the confirmed encoding method, it randomly generated M individuals as the initial population.

Step 3: Put individuals in the population into the lower planning to do UE traffic distribution and then calculate the upper objective function.

Step 4: Perform selection. In this process the selection rate is used to decide how many chromosomes to keep according to the fitness function.

Step 5: Perform crossover operations of genetic algorithm to make the population size to be M.

Step 6: Perform mutation operations of genetic algorithm to decide how many chromosomes to mutate. Then the next generation is formed.

Step 7: Termination condition judgment. If the iteration $t \leq T$, go to step three; otherwise, go to step eight.

Step 8: Algorithm terminate. The optimal solution is output.

34.5 Conclusion

The analysis and modeling of differentiated control strategy of distribution network of CPTH, is scientific issue which involves transport planning, management, control theory and other multi-disciplinary. The aggregation state of differentiation stage is determined by the analysis of the status of comprehensive transportation distribution service network. For the difference of the normal and emergency, this paper established the bi-level programming model of the control strategy by use of the Stackelberg game and designed algorithm. The inadequacies of the model are the lack of instance validation and further study on calibrating model parameters and algorithm application.

Acknowledgments This research was supported by the National Natural Science Foundation of China (Nos. 71171015); the State Key Laboratory of Rail Traffic Control and Safety (Contract No. RCS2011ZT002), Beijing Jiaotong University; the Fundamental Research Funds for the Central Universities (Contract No. T12JB00110).

References

1. Yang H, Bell MGH, Meng Q (2000) Modeling the capacity and level of service of urban transportation networks. Transp Res Part B 34(3):255–275
2. Perk VA, Foreman C (2003) Florida metropolitan planning organization reports on transit capacity and quality of service: first-year evaluation. Transp Res Rec 1841(1):128–134
3. Barros AG, Wirasinghe SC (2002) Optimal terminal configurations for new large aircraft operations. Transp Res Part A 37(4):315–331
4. Lin YD, Trani AA (2000) Airport automated people mover systems: analysis with a hybrid computer simulation model. Transp Res Rec 1703:45–57
5. Kuo MS, Liang GS (2011) Combining VIKOR with GRA techniques to evaluate service quality of airports under fuzzy environment. Expert Syst Appl 38(3):1304–1312
6. Helbing D, Molnar P, Farkas IJ, Bolay K (2001) Self-organizing pedestrian movement. Environ Plan B Plan Design 28(3):361–383

7. Helbing D (2004) Collective phenomena and states in traffic and self-driven many-particle systems. Comput Mater Sci 30(1–2):180–187
8. Helbing D, Buzna L, Johansson A, Werner T (2005) Self-organized pedestrian crowd dynamics: experiments, salutations, and design solutions. Transp Sci 39(l):1–24
9. Yan SY, Tang CH, Chen MJ (2004) A model and a solution algorithm for airport common use check-in counter assignments. Transp Res Part A 38(2):101–125
10. Stolletz R (2010) Operational workforce planning for check-in counters at airports. Transp Res Part E 46(3):414–425
11. Li Q (2011) Analysis and modeling of the distribution service network of comprehensive passenger transportation hub. Beijing Jiaotong University, Beijing (in Chinese)

Chapter 35
Research on the Internal Environment Evaluation Method of Comprehensive Passenger Transportation Hub

Long Gao, Changxu Ji, Maojing Jin, Qian Li, Lifen Yun, Zhe Zhang, Hong Lan and Ling Huang

Abstract On the basis of the existing theories and achievements, this paper analyzes and researches the internal environment evaluation method of comprehensive passenger transportation hub (CPTH). Firstly, summarizes the essential elements of the internal environment based on the special characteristics of CPTH, and builds the internal environment comprehensive evaluation index system. Then, selects the information entropy theory as the internal environment evaluation method, and sets up evaluation model. Finally, selects Beijing South Railway Station and Beijing West Railway Station as the case, it can be learned that carbon dioxide concentration, air smell, lighting coefficient and indoor health are the largest contributions to the evaluation results. What's more, this paper puts forward the optimization measures and countermeasures to enhance passenger comfort level and reflect the people-oriented concept of comprehensive traffic service.

Keywords CPTH · Internal environment evaluation · Information entropy theory · People-oriented concept

L. Gao · C. Ji (✉) · Q. Li · L. Yun · Z. Zhang
State Key Laboratory of Rail Traffic Control and Safety, Beijing Jiaotong University, 100044 Beijing, China
e-mail: chxji@bjtu.edu.com

M. Jin · H. Lan · L. Huang
The High Technology Research and Development Center, Ministry of Science and Technology, 100044 Beijing, People's Republic of China
e-mail: jin@htrdc.com

W. Lu et al. (eds.), *Proceedings of the 2012 International Conference on Information Technology and Software Engineering*, Lecture Notes in Electrical Engineering 211, DOI: 10.1007/978-3-642-34522-7_35, © Springer-Verlag Berlin Heidelberg 2013

35.1 Introduction

With the improvement of people's living standard, passenger requirements to travel environment are increasing, and therefore building a high-quality travel environment has become an important link for advocating green transportation and reflecting the people-oriented in today's society. As a key node and large-scale passenger distribution center in the travel process [1], the CPTH holds a crucial position. The internal environment quality of CPTH makes a direct impact on the passenger's health and travel safety. For this reason, in order to enhance passenger's travel comfort level by improving the internal environment quality, it is very essential and urgent to evaluate the internal environment of CPTH.

As an important branch of the environmental science, environmental evaluation is developing from single factor and index to comprehensive evaluation. Currently, the study on indoor environment evaluation is mainly focused on the air quality, and on this basis, several evaluation methods such as FCE index method, subjective and objective index method, indoor environment quality (IEQ) comprehensive evaluation method and so on are proposed. Monika Frontczak clarifies the essential elements of the internal environment which affect resident comfort level [2]. Zhou Quan obtains the key research contents of the indoor environment evaluation by comparing the different indoor environment evaluation index systems [3]. Chung and Zhang Jian both use indoor environment standards to evaluate the environment quality of elderly health center and library, then propose improvement measures [4, 5]. Karthikeyan evaluates the work environment quality by taking advantage of total environmental quality index (TEQI) [6]. What's more, Wang Ke and Guo Jinping regard indoor air quality as well as sound, light, heat as the research object, and choose entropy theory to evaluate the entire indoor environment [7]. In summary, the theoretical results of the indoor environment evaluation are mainly concentrated in the ordinary places such as indoor living condition, work units and library, there is a lack of evaluation research on the internal environment of CPTH.

This paper puts forward a set of complete evaluation method, so as to provide scientific basis and theoretical reference for hub design, operation and management.

35.2 Theoretical Basis

As we know, when passenger enters into the hub, most of the time is spent in the station hall for departure. Therefore, in this paper, the research scope of internal environment is the station hall environment.

According to the special characteristics of CPTH, the internal environment is divided into seven aspects which include crowded degree, heat-humidity environment, air environment, sound environment, light environment, color

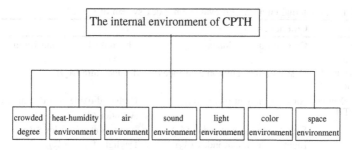

Fig. 35.1 Essential elements of the internal environment

environment, space environment. The internal environment evaluation of CPTH should be carried out from these aspects. Essential elements of the internal environment are shown in Fig. 35.1.

35.3 Model Building

35.3.1 Evaluation Index System

35.3.1.1 The Principle of Selecting Evaluation Index

In order to obtain the true, objective and reasonable evaluation result, should select appropriate evaluation index and build proper evaluation index system. The following principles must be observed, including systematicness, scientificalness, comparability, operability, qualitative and quantitative combination.

35.3.1.2 Evaluation Index System Building

In this section, according to the hierarchical structure which includes object layer, criterion layer and index layer, the internal environment evaluation index system of CPTH is proposed. The internal environment evaluation index system of CPTH is shown in Table 35.1.

The calculation description of each index is listed as follows.

(1) crowded degree index (A_1)

$$A_{11} = S/H_{max} \tag{35.1}$$

Here, A_{11} denotes the theoretical per capita waiting area; S denotes the station hall area, m^2; H_{Max} denotes the maximum passenger number of CPTH. Then, the score standard of crowded degree is shown in Table 35.2.

Table 35.1 The internal environment evaluation index system of CPTH

Object layer	Criterion layer	Index layer
The original internal environment evaluation index system of CPTH	Crowded degree index (A_1)	Theoretical per capita waiting area (A_{11})
	Heat-humidity environment index (A_2)	Temperature (A_{21})
	Air environment index (A_3)	Carbon dioxide concentration (A_{31})
		Air odor (A_{32})
	Sound environment index (A_4)	Equivalent sound level (A_{41})
	Light environment index (A_5)	Daylight factor (A_{51})
		Illuminance level (A_{52})
	Color environment index (A_6)	Colour satisfaction (A_{61})
	Space environment index (A_7)	Spatial layout (A_{71})
		Indoor health (A_{72})

Table 35.2 The score standard of crowded degree

Level	Per capita waiting area (A_{11})	Score (F_1)
A	≥ 3.46	0
B	1.60–3.46	2
C	0.98–1.60	4
D	0.51–0.98	6
E	0.15–0.51	8
F	≤ 0.15	10

Here, F_1 denotes the score of crowded degree

(2) heat-humidity environment index (A_2)

  (a) temperature (A_{21})

   According to the *PMV-PPD* method, the score of temperature is listed as follows.

$$F_{21} = 10 * PPD = 10 * \left(100 - 95e^{\left[-\left(0.03353PMV^4 + 0.2179PMV^2\right)\right]}\right) \qquad (35.2)$$

Here, F_{21} denotes the score of temperature; *PPD* denotes predicted dissatisfied percent; *PMV* denotes the sense of the most people in the environment.

(3) air environment index (A_3)

  (a) carbon dioxide concentration (A_{31})

$$A_{31} = \varphi_0 e^{\frac{-kq_0}{V}} + \frac{k\varphi_0 q_0 + 0.0168 \times H_t}{kq_0}\left(1 - e^{\frac{-kq_0 t}{V}}\right) \qquad (35.3)$$

Here, A_{31} denotes the carbon dioxide concentration; φ_0 denotes carbon dioxide concentration outside, 0.03–0.04 %; k denotes blending factor, $k = 0.9$; q_0 denotes air volume, m^3/h; V denotes volume of the station hall, m^3; H_t denotes

Table 34.3 The score standard of carbon dioxide concentration

Level	Carbon dioxide concentration (A_{31})	Score (F_{31})
A	0.03 % (300 ppm)–0.07 % (700 ppm)	0
B	0.07 % (700 ppm)–0.10 % (1000 ppm)	2
C	0.10 % (1000 ppm)–0.15 % (2000 ppm)	4
D	0.15 % (2000 ppm)–0.50 % (5000 ppm)	6
E	0.50 % (5000 ppm)–1.00 % (10000 ppm)	8
F	>1.00 % (10000 ppm)	10

Here, F_{31} denotes the score of carbon dioxide concentration

the passenger number of CPTH in the time t.

Then, the score standard of carbon dioxide concentration is shown in Table 35.3.

(b) air odor (A_{32})

According to the relevant provisions, the air odor level of the station hall is divided into five grades, the score (F_{32}) follows by 0, 3, 5, 7, 10.

(4) sound environment index (A_4)

$$A_{41} = 10 \times \lg\left(\frac{1}{n}\sum_{i=1}^{n} 10^{0.1L_{Ai}}\right) \tag{35.4}$$

Here, A_{41} denotes equivalent sound level; L_{Ai} denotes sound level of the Ith sample, dB; n denotes the total number of samples.

$$F_{41} = 10 \times PDN = 43.5 \int_{-\infty}^{L_A} \exp\left(-\left(\frac{x - 58.6}{13}\right)^2\right) dx \tag{35.5}$$

Here, F_{41} denotes the score of equivalent sound level; PDN denotes dissatisfied percent of noise, x denotes integration variable.

(5) light environment index (A_5)

(a) daylight factor (A_{51})

$$A_{51} = \sum_{i=1}^{n} (a_i \times b_i) \Big/ (A \times B) \tag{6}$$

Here, A_{51} denotes daylight factor; a_i, b_i respectively denotes length and width of the Ith glass, m; A, B respectively denotes length and width of the flooring, m; n denotes the total number of indoor glass, $i = 1, 2, 3, \ldots\ldots, n$.

Table 35.4 The score standard of daylight factor

Level	Daylight factor (A_{51})	Score (F_{51})
A	>2/3	0
B	1/3.5–2/3	3
C	1/5–1/3.5	5
D	1/6–1/5	7
E	<1/6	10

Table 35.5 The score standard of illuminance level

Level	Illuminance level (A_{52})	Score (F_{52})
A	200–500	0
B	100–200; 500–600	3
C	60–100; 600–700	5
D	20–60; 700–800	7
E	<20; >800	10

Then, the score standard of daylight factor is shown in Table 35.4.

(b) illuminance level (A_{52})

Illuminance level can be measured by illuminometer. The score standard of illuminance level is shown in Table 35.5.

(6) color environment index (A_6)

According to the subjective evaluation, the color environment level of the station hall is divided into five grades, the score (F_{61}) follows by 0, 3, 5, 7, 10.

(7) space environment index (A_7)

Space environment index mainly includes spatial layout and indoor health. By the use of subjective evaluation, each index level is divided into five grades, each score follows by 0, 3, 5, 7, 10.

35.3.2 Evaluation Method and Model

According to analyzing the score diversity of the same index in the different hubs, each index weight can be determined by using the information entropy evaluation method, and then the contribution value of each index can be obtained. Assumed that the number of hubs which need to be evaluated is m, and the number of evaluation indexes to each hub is n. Therefore, the index matrix is listed as follows.

$$X = \begin{pmatrix} x_{11} & \cdots & x_{1n} \\ \vdots & \ddots & \vdots \\ x_{m1} & \cdots & x_{mn} \end{pmatrix} \tag{35.7}$$

$$D_j = 1 - H_j \tag{35.8}$$

Here, D_j denotes the diversity of the same index; H_j denotes the relative strength entropy of X_j

$$W_j = D_j \bigg/ \sum_{i=1}^{n} D_j \tag{35.9}$$

Here, W_j denotes the Jth entropy weight.

Finally, the comprehensive evaluation result of each hub is listed as follows.

$$R = XW_j^T, (j = 1, 2, \ldots, n) \tag{35.10}$$

$$R = (R_1, R_2, \ldots, R_m) \tag{35.11}$$

Here, R_i denotes the comprehensive evaluation result of the Ith hub. Lower number of R_i indicates that the internal environment quality of corresponding hub is better, on the contrary, the internal environment quality of corresponding hub is worse.

35.4 Case Study

In this section, selecting Beijing south railway station and Beijing west railway station as an example. The basic data is obtained through field research. By substituting the basic data into the formulas which are listed in the chapter three, the calculated result and score of each evaluation index is shown in Table 35.6

According to the scores of the Table 35.6, by using the entropy model, the index matrix is listed as follows.

$$X = \begin{array}{c} \begin{matrix} A_{11} & A_{21} & A_{31} & A_{32} & A_{41} & A_{51} & A_{52} & A_{61} & A_{71} & A_{72} \end{matrix} \\ \begin{bmatrix} 2 & 1.06 & 1.657 & 1 & 9.134 & 1.90 & 2.42 & 3 & 2 & 1 \\ 4 & 1.62 & 5.105 & 9 & 8.487 & 9.34 & 5.05 & 7 & 3 & 9 \end{bmatrix} \begin{matrix} \text{south} \\ \text{west} \end{matrix} \end{array} \tag{35.12}$$

Next, the entropy weight matrix of each index is calculated as follows.

$$W = \{W_j\}$$
$$= [0.0418\ 0.0162\ 0.1005\ 0.2714\ 0.0005\ 0.1761\ 0.0467\ 0.0607\ 0.0148\ 0.2714]$$
$$(j = 1, 2, \cdots, 10)$$

$$\tag{35.13}$$

Table 35.6 The calculated result and score of each evaluation index

Index	Result	Score	Result	Score
Theoretical per capita waiting area (A_{11})	2.21	2	1.35	4
Temperature (A_{21})	10.59 %	1.06	16.21 %	1.62
Carbon dioxide concentration (A_{31})	0.063 %	1.657	0.128 %	5.105
Air odor (A_{32})	1	1	9	9
Equivalent sound level (A_{41})	71	9.134	68	8.487
Daylight factor (A_{51})	0.426	1.90	0.174	9.34
Illuminance level (A_{52})	229	2.42	99	5.05
Colour satisfaction (A_{61})	3	3	7	7
Spatial layout (A_{71})	2	2	3	3
Indoor health (A_{72})	1	1	9	9

Finally, the comprehensive evaluation results of two hubs are as follows.

$$R = X \times W^T$$
$$= \begin{bmatrix} 2 & 1.06 & 1.657 & 1 & 9.134 & 1.90 & 2 & 3 & 2 & 1 \\ 4 & 1.62 & 5.105 & 9 & 8.487 & 9.34 & 7 & 7 & 3 & 9 \end{bmatrix}$$
$$\times [0.0418 \quad 0.0162 \quad 0.1005 \quad 0.2714 \quad 0.0005 \quad 0.1761 \quad 0.0467 \quad 0.0607 \quad 0.0148 \quad 0.2714]^T$$
$$= \begin{bmatrix} 1.4737 \\ 7.9448 \end{bmatrix}$$

$$(35.14)$$

Namely, $Rsouth = 1.4737$, $Rwest = 7.9448$.

From the final evaluation results, it can be obtained that the internal environment quality of Beijing south railway station is better than Beijing west railway station, and with the big differences. What' more, it also can be learned that the carbon dioxide concentration, air smell, lighting coefficient and indoor health are the largest contributions to the evaluation results. Therefore, in order to improve the internal environment for enhancing passenger's comfort level, should focus on improving the situation of these four aspects.

35.5 Conclusion

This article puts forward information entropy theory as the internal environment evaluation method of CPTH and sets up the evaluation model, and on this basis, finds out the evaluation index which has the largest contribution to the evaluation result. Finally, puts forward the optimization measures and countermeasures to improve the internal environment for enhancing passenger's comfort level and reflecting the people-oriented concept of comprehensive traffic service. Besides, puts forward a set of complete evaluation method, so as to provide scientific basis and theoretical reference for hub design, operation and management.

Acknowledgments   This research was supported by the National Natural Science Foundation of China (Nos. 71171015); the State Key Laboratory of Rail Traffic Control and Safety (Contract No. RCS2011ZT002), Beijing Jiaotong University; the Fundamental Research Funds for the Central Universities (Contract No. T12JB00110).

References

1. Li Q (2011) Analysis and modeling of the distribution service network of comprehensive passenger transportation hub. Beijing Jiaotong University, Beijing (in Chinese)
2. Frontczak M, Wargocki P (2011) Literature survey on how different factors influence human comfort in indoor environments. Build Environ 46:922–937
3. Zhou Q (2010) Study in assessment of the indoor environment of Guangzhou sport venues. South Archit 5:34–37 (in Chinese)
4. Chung PR (2011) The inquisitional research of indoor environmental quality in Taiwan aging-care-institutions. IEEE Computer Society, pp 1816-1819
5. Zhang J (2004) The appraisement of library's interior environment. J Chengdu Univ (Nat Sci) 23(3):44–49 (in Chinese)
6. Karthikeyan J (2007) Total environmental quality index as a tool for assessment of work environment a case study of industrial units. Progress in environmental science and technology, pp 328–331
7. Wang K, Guo JP (2007) Indoor environment evaluation based on entropy weight theory. China Safety Sci J 17(11):167–171 (in Chinese)

Chapter 36
Research of National Historic City Dynamic Monitoring by Remote Sensing: A Case Study of Kashgar Historic Urban Area

Jianbo Tang and Wensheng Zhou

Abstract Historic Cities in China are facing dual pressures both city construction and tourism development. Monitoring the human factor using RS monitoring technology, the changes can be found and the cause of changes can be analyzed. Taking the Kashgar Historic Urban Area for example, using the 2002, 2005 and 2009 three high-resolution remote sensing images, the information of the Kashgar Historic Urban Area changes has been extracted; the reasons for these changes have been analyzed. The result shows that the original historic features of the Kashgar Historic Urban Area have been maintained. Urban infrastructure construction and public space has made great progress. Human settlements have been greatly improved.

Keywords National historic city · GIS · Remote sensing monitoring · Kashgar historic urban area

36.1 Introduction

In February 1982, the concept of 'Historic City' was officially proposed. According to Law of the People's Republic of China on the Protection of Cultural Relics, the Historic City is referred to as 'cultural relic's especially rich city, with a great historical cultural value and the revolutionary significance. Up to now, China has released 3 batches of 117 national Historic Cities. At present, the factors

J. Tang · W. Zhou (✉)
School of Architecture, Tsinghua University, 100084 Beijing, China
e-mail: zwsbj@163.com

J. Tang
e-mail: virgotang@126.com

W. Lu et al. (eds.), *Proceedings of the 2012 International Conference on Information Technology and Software Engineering*, Lecture Notes in Electrical Engineering 211, DOI: 10.1007/978-3-642-34522-7_36, © Springer-Verlag Berlin Heidelberg 2013

affecting the Historic City are the urban development and tourism development [1], therefore, monitoring these two factors is critical to the protection of Historic City. At present, the remote sensing technology has extensive and in-depth used for land resources monitoring [2], environmental monitoring [3], global change monitoring [4], etc. In the field of heritage conservation, due to the complexity of heritage formation, some remote sensing monitoring projects have been carried out, such as the National Scenic Area monitoring and the Great Sites monitoring. Under the auspices of the Minister of Housing and Urban–Rural Development, the National Historic City, Towns and Villages monitoring have already begun, but face a series of technical problems, the traditional visual interpretation of contrast monitoring with the problem of low automation, low efficiency and capital-intensive. Using object-oriented classification of remote sensing technology, through the comparison of remote sensing image, the changes of historical cities can be quickly found and monitoring results can provide decision support and law enforcement.

36.2 Historic City Monitoring Contents Analysis

The protection of the Historic City is based on conservation planning. The 'code of conservation planning of historic cities' (GB50357-2005) in regulation, the protection content of the Historic City is: the Historic City pattern and style; Closely related to the history and culture of the natural topography, river systems, scenic, ancient and famous trees; Reflecting the historic style of buildings, blocks, towns and villages; Units of cultural relics protection at all levels; Folk essence, Traditional crafts, the traditional culture, etc. [5]. Therefore, the Historic City monitoring content of is also the above. In Chap. 4 the regulations provide protection measures, the Historic City affecting factors can be extracted from these measures. In summary, the main monitoring contents of the Historic City have four aspects:

- The constituent elements of the Historic City monitoring;
- Development and construction activities monitoring;
- Tourism activities monitoring;
- Environmental monitoring.

36.3 Historic City RS Monitoring Key Technologies

36.3.1 Remote Sensing Image Selection

Remote sensing images selection based on spectral characteristics, space features and texture features of the monitoring object, and the spatial resolution, time resolution and spectral resolution three aspects also be considered. The Historical City has the urban fabric and historic space, land cover on the performance of buildings, streets, green spaces, plazas, water, agricultural land and open space, etc. In the historical city remote sensing monitoring, usually choose R, G, B color band and full-color band. Some specific feature extraction also needs to select the infrared band to get the best band combination. Usually, multi-phase images need the same band combination. In addition, other remote sensing data, such as DEM, radar image and remote sensing thematic map, the land use map, can be used as auxiliary data in the remote sensing monitoring and those maps can play an important role.

36.3.2 Object-Oriented Classification

The essence of object-oriented remote sensing image classification method is targeted at the smallest unit of classification or detection. Multi-scale image segmentation, supervised classification and classification rules are the key to object-oriented classification techniques. They determine the accuracy of object-oriented image classification.

- Multi-scale image segmentation
  Remote sensing image segmentation is the basis for objective measurement and the image surface features classification, and also is the first step to achieve the automatic image target extraction [6]. The target of multi-scale image segmentation is to set up a certain threshold value to images.
- Supervised classification
  Supervised classification is pre-determined remote sensing image sample classification techniques. It is the process of using determined classification samples to identify other unknown pixel category.
- Classification rules
  Using attribute expression to describe every rule, these rules can be recognized by the computer. The same type of surface features can be described by different rules, such as buildings, which can be residential buildings, industrial buildings, recreational buildings, etc. The description rules are not the same, there need more than one rule to describe each future through a number of attributes description.

36.3.3 Change Detection

Remote sensing technologies based on dynamic monitoring change detection methods, there are five, respectively is image difference method, image ratio method, the principal component transformation, vegetation index method and the post-classification comparison method [7]. The first four kinds of methods can usually be known as the post-comparison classification method. The post-comparison classification method is carried out between the mutual comparison between the pixel values of image objects, or a certain type of pixels, the principal component, make sure the change pixel, and then to classify these changed pixels, so as to determine the change information. Post-classification comparison method is multi-phase image classification processing first, determine each phase of remote sensing images or interest regional surface features cover types, through classification information overlay comparison to determine change information. No matter use which kinds of change detection method, there need to experience the change detection and classification of two steps, just monitoring steps have different, could detect changes after classification, also could classify after detecting changes. The time and spatial resolution of remote sensing images determines the change detection method.

36.4 Kashgar Historic Urban Area Remote Sensing Monitoring

36.4.1 Image Changes Detection

The Kashgar Historic City located in southwestern Xinjiang is only China's Islamic culture features city block, dating back more than 2100 years of history. In 1986, Kashgar became a National Historic City. The scope of monitoring in the Kashgar Historic Urban Area is based on the conservation planning, including the Kashgar old city and Gaotai residential area. Selecting three dynamic monitoring images of the Kashgar Historic Urban Area, on November 14, 2002, March 7, 2005 and October 18, 2009 (referred to as the image according to the year of images, for example, the image on November 14, 2002 referred to as the 2002.). Using the extraction methods of object-oriented image features, we got three remote sensing images classification results of the Kashgar Historic Urban Area (Figs. 36.1, 36.2 and 36.3).

After three phases of the Kashgar historic city of remote sensing classified, the classification results overlaid to detect changes in the same spatial location. Spatial distribution and area of classified surface features were compared to get the changes between the phase of 2002 and 2005 (Fig. 36.4) and the phase of 2005 and 2009 (Fig. 36.5).

36.4.2 Monitoring Analysis

36.4.2.1 Historic Urban Area Dynamic Changes Information Analysis

By analyzing the seven years from 2002 to 2009, the feature type of transformation and change occurred. After calculating the features area and rate in three phase

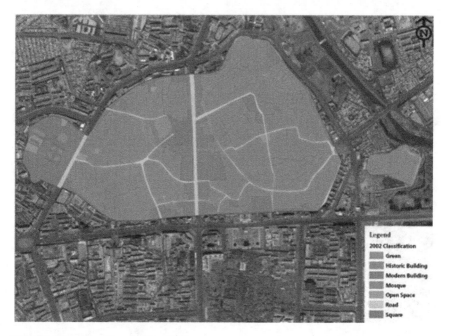

Fig. 36.1 Classification result for 2002

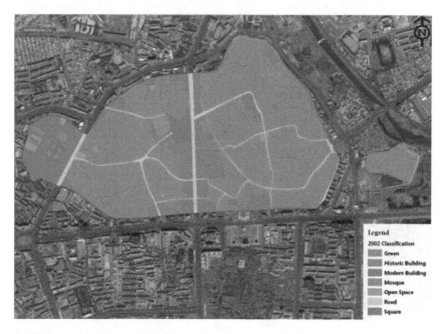

Fig. 36.2 Classification result for 2005

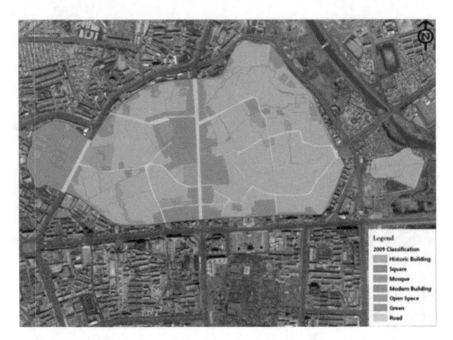

Fig. 36.3 Classification result for 2009

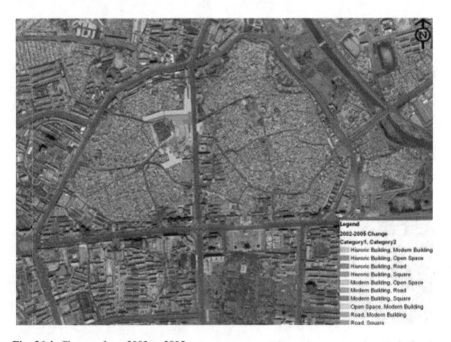

Fig. 36.4 Changes from 2002 to 2005

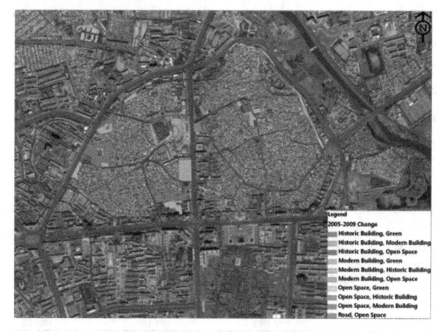

Fig. 36.5 Changes from 2005 to 2009

images classification (Table 36.1), In the Kashgar Historic Urban Area, change information indicates that, roads area proportion is maintained at about 7.4 %, the Square proportion is 2 % in 2005, an increase in the proportion of open space, reach to 5.4 % in 2009, historic building area decreased from 68.4 % in 2002 to 61.9 % in 2009, the proportion of green area in 2009 is 2.4 %, the mosque area did not change, to the modern building, there is a slight increase in 7 years, the average growth rate is 0.2 %.

36.4.2.2 Historic Urban Area Change Rate Analysis

The change rate reflects change magnitude and speed of the various features of in the historic urban area, the average annual change rate reflects a change in trend. The positive change rate reflects an increase speed of the feature area; the negative change rate reflects reduce speed of the feature area. The change rate formula is:

$$K_T = \frac{T_2 - T_1}{T_1} \times 100\%$$

The average change rate formula is:

$$K = \frac{K_T}{t}$$

Table 36.1 Kashgar historic urban area of three images of remote sensing monitoring area changes (units: square meters)

Category	Phase 2002	Proportion (%)	Phase 2005	Proportion (%)	Phase 2009	Proportion (%)
Road	101625.72	7.45	101919.03	7.48	101684.61	7.46
Square	20213.85	1.48	27388.10	2.01	27388.10	2.01
Open space	18088.43	1.32	24997.47	1.83	73523.86	5.39
Historic building	932933.31	68.43	902797.68	66.22	843928.42	61.90
Green	28561.46	2.10	28561.46	2.10	33455.16	2.45
Mosque	1633.97	0.12	1633.97	0.12	1633.97	0.12
Modern building	260224.67	19.09	275983.69	20.24	281667.28	20.66

Table 36.2 The change rate of the Kashgar historic urban area analysis

Category	2002–2005		2005–2009		2002–2009	
	Change rate (%)	Average annual change rate (%)	Change rate (%)	Average annual change rate (%)	Change rate (%)	Average annual change rate (%)
Road	0.29	0.10	−0.23	−0.06	0.06	0.01
Square	35.49	11.83	0.00	0.00	35.49	5.07
Open space	38.20	12.73	194.12	48.53	306.47	43.78
Historic building	−3.23	−1.08	−6.52	−1.63	−9.54	−1.36
Green	0.00	0.00	17.13	4.28	17.13	2.45
Mosque	0.00	0.00	0.00	0.00	0.00	0.00
Modern building	6.06	2.02	2.060	0.52	8.24	1.18

K_T is the change rate of feature in a certain period of time, T_2 and T_1 are the future area in the beginning and end of the monitoring period. K is the average annual change rate. Table 36.2 shows the change rate of the Kashgar Historic Urban Area.

From the 2002 to 2009 period, the Table 36.2 reflects the historic buildings are subject to a certain threat in the process of the Kashgar Historic Urban Area urbanization. But the increase rate is still not affecting the style of the Kashgar historic city. There is also has a certain increase in the historical urban area open space. These open spaces may become modern architecture in the future, there need a further monitoring. Green, mosques and roads are almost no change, and the square area increased a little. It was reflecting the Kashgar Historical City public facilities improved.

36.5 Conclusions

This work studies the National Historic City remote sensing monitoring method and taking the Kashgar Historic Urban Area as an example. Selecting three high-resolution remote sensing images to monitor the Kashgar Historic Urban Area, the changes on the remote sensing images of 7 years from 2002 to 2009 were analyzed, and analyze the reasons for the changes, get the following conclusions:

- The phase and spatial resolution determine the change detection methods. When the phase and spatial resolution are the same, both the post-comparison classification and the post-classification method can be used to monitor the change. It is better to use the post-comparison classification method when faces different phase and different spatial resolution image;
- To the Historic City remote sensing monitoring, it is necessary to conduct a detailed distinction between 'transformations' and 'change', in the same time choose an appropriate change detection results category. To the uncertainty classification, there need more field investigation, and it help to objective analysis the reason of changes;
- Remote sensing monitoring can be used in the Historic City development and construction activities and other issues from a macro perspective, but in the micro-level of the micro-environment and heritage of the monomer structure in the Historic City, as well as the tourist perceptions related to social investigation and heritage economic aspects of monitoring are 'powerless'. Therefore, remote sensing monitoring should combine with other monitoring measures; it will be better to play the role of supervision and management of the Historic City.

Acknowledgments This work is supported by national Nature Science Foundation of China (No.50978153 and No.51178236).

References

1. Ruan Y, Qiu B (2007) To prevent the historical and cultural city "development destruction". Xinhua Daily (in Chinese)
2. Zhang B, Peng Z (2012) Review of remote sensing techniques in land resource investigation and monitoring development in China. West Resour 2012(1):135–136 (in Chinese)
3. Ji H, Zhao B (2008) Summarization of remote sensing techniques on environmental monitoring. Environ Sci Surv 2:21–24 (in Chinese)
4. Wang H, Liu Y (2009) Application of remote sensing technology to global environment change. Environ Sci Manag 1:156–161 (in Chinese)
5. GB50357-2005 The 'code of conservation planning of historic cities' in regulation. (in Chinese)
6. Fu Z, Hu J (2006) The methods of image segmentation on application and analysis of remote sensing images. Remote Sens Technol Appl 5:456–462 (in Chinese)
7. Wu F, Liu R et al (2007) Technology for remote sensing change detection and its application. Geospatial Inf 4:57–60 (in Chinese)

Chapter 37
Comparison Research of Reconstruction Algorithms About Airborne Electromagnetic Response Data

Dawei Yin, Jun Lin and Kaiguang Zhu

Abstract In the field of mineral exploration, airborne electromagnetic method is developing important action. Airborne electromagnetic response data obtained by airborne electromagnetic method presents changing trend of attenuation exponential summation, and which has abundant but redundant information character. In order to fast reconstructing airborne electromagnetic response data, Prony Method and Matrix Pencil Method are applied and eigenvector extraction and reconstruction precision of these two methods are comparatively analyzed in this paper. Research results indicate that, eigenvectors extracted by these two methods reflect intrinsic attribution of underground geological body. To non-noise airborne electromagnetic response data, better reconstruction precision realized by these two methods is presented. To including noise airborne electromagnetic response data, when signal to noise ratio gradually decreases from 20 to 0 dB, reconstruction precision of Prony Method rapidly descends, but that of Matrix Pencil Method merely slight fluctuates. Therefore, the latter is more effective to reconstruct airborne electromagnetic response data in complex electromagnetic environment.

Keywords Attenuation exponential summation · Prony method · Matrix pencil method · Reconstruction

D. Yin · J. Lin · K. Zhu (✉)
College of Instrumentation and Electrical Engineering, Jilin University,
No. 938, The West Chaoyang Road, Changchun, China
e-mail: zhukaiguang@jlu.edu.cn

D. Yin
e-mail: effortman0434@163.com

J. Lin
e-mail: lin_jun@jlu.edu.cn

W. Lu et al. (eds.), *Proceedings of the 2012 International Conference on Information Technology and Software Engineering*, Lecture Notes in Electrical Engineering 211, DOI: 10.1007/978-3-642-34522-7_37, © Springer-Verlag Berlin Heidelberg 2013

37.1 Introduction

Airborne electromagnetic method is the method of searching mineral or solving some geology problems, which is dependent on airplane or other aircraft platform and electromagnetic induction principle, and acquires space, time or frequency feature of anomalous electromagnetic field of underground geological body excited by airborne electromagnetic exploration instruments.

At present, airborne electromagnetic method on time domain is paid more attention because of its advantages, such as rapid survey velocity, lower cost, better passing attribution, use for the sea field exploration and so on. Meanwhile, a great deal of data processing and explanation methods aiming to airborne electromagnetic response data have been quickly developed [1, 2]. Because airborne electromagnetic response data acquired by airborne mineral exploration has huge quantity, complex calculation, and obvious influence to rapid processing explanation on exploration field, one important premise of building forward and inversion model and result analysis are to how to realize rapid pre-process of mass data. Reference [3] indicates that, step electromagnetic response of any isolate conductor can be presented as the sum of exponential. Reference [4] emphasizes that, one necessary procedure of some rapid explanation method is that time domain electromagnetic response data can be decomposed into a group of exponential basis function. In Ref. [5], practical applications of plural E exponential summation function in different electromagnetic field abroad are cited. Consequently, based on attenuation exponential summation model and eigenvector extraction, geometrical attribute and physical property of target geological body can be represented by analyzing airborne electromagnetic response data.

Prony method and matrix pencil method are both generally applied exponential function type of eigenvector extraction methods [6, 7]. In this paper, reconstruction and eigenvector extraction of airborne electromagnetic response data are done in the condition of non-noise and including noise using these two methods. The research provides useful theoretical support for later inversion of the earth model.

37.2 Algorithm Analysis

37.2.1 Prony Method

In 1879, physicist Prony in France put forward well-known Prony method for solving data approximation of gas state equation. In essence, based on auto regressive model or auto regressive moving average model, Prony method extracts pole information from equal time interval instantaneous data, and uses least-squares problem to estimate frequency, amplitude and phase of given signal [8].

Considering a continuous signal y(t), then Prony model can be constructed as,

$$\hat{y}(t) = \sum_{i=1}^{n} B_i e^{\lambda_i t} \tag{37.1}$$

In Eq. (37.1), to time pole $\lambda_i \in C$ ($\lambda_i \neq \lambda_j$, when $i \neq j$), $B_i \in C$ is corresponding residue, our target is acquiring the value of pole, residue and n to ensure the equation approximating with y(t) by the least square form. Because signal y(t) is sampled in some certain sample circle less than Nyquist, Eq. (37.1) can be expressed by discrete time form.

$$\hat{y}(kt) = \sum_{i=1}^{n} B_i z_i^k, k = 0, \ldots \ldots, N - 1 \tag{37.2}$$

where $z_i = e^{\lambda_i T}$ represents the pole of discrete time. If eigen-equation $\hat{y}$ can be expressed as,

$$d(z) = 1 - (a_1 z^{-1} + \ldots + a_n z^{-n}) \tag{37.3}$$

Then, $\hat{y}$ satisfies auto regressive series,

$$\hat{y}(kT) = a_1 \hat{y}((k-1)T) + \ldots + a_n \hat{y}((k-n)T) \tag{37.4}$$

Thus, unknown parameters pole, residue and n value can be solved by three steps as follows.

(1) y is substituted for $\hat{y}$ in Eq. (37.4), and then the equation is solved to get coefficient a. This is so called linear prediction problem.
(2) By factor multiplying expression, λ_i and discrete time pole in Eq. (37.3) can be solved.
(3) For solving residue, Eq. (37.2) is compiled and constructed as Vandermonde matrix by substituting y for $\hat{y}$. The solution is called as Vandermonde problem.

Because mathematics solution is very definite above three steps, detailed realization course don't discuss in the paper.

37.2.2 Matrix Pencil Method

Matrix pencil method was found by Sakar in 1980. Basic principle of this method is that, firstly, two special matrices based on tested data are constructed, secondly, generalized eigenvalues including solution information can be solved according to matrix relation. Consequently, solving attenuation exponential signal parameter problem will be converted into solving generalized characteristic value problem of matrix pencil [9, 10, 11].

Suppose electromagnetic response data sampled in practice is known,

$$y(k\delta t) \approx \sum_{i=1}^{M} R_i z_i^k, (k = 0, 1, \ldots, N - 1) \qquad (37.5)$$

Based on $y(k\delta t)$, two special matrices, Y_1 and Y_2 can be built. Next, combining Y_1 and Y_2, one can construct an $(N - L) \times (L + 1)$ Hankel matrix.

$$Y = \begin{bmatrix} y(0) & y(1) & \cdots & y(L) \\ y(1) & y(2) & \cdots & y(L+1) \\ \cdot & \cdot & \cdot & \cdot \\ y(N-L-1) & y(N-L) & \cdot & y(N-1) \end{bmatrix}_{(N-L)\times(L+1)} \qquad (37.6)$$

L in the formula (37.6) is referred to as pencil parameter. It is very important for eliminating noise in data to rightly choose L.

Subsequently, SVD decomposition is carried out about the matrix Y, then

$$[Y] = [U]\left[\sum\right][V]^H \qquad (37.7)$$

where U and V are unitary matrices. Σ is a diagonal matrix constructed by the singular values of Y, and each value of which corresponds with that of Y.

By use of the arrangement property of diagonal matrix singular values from big to small after singular values decomposition, pole number M can be sure by the ratio between each singular value and maximum singular value in the condition of appointed signal to noise ratio.

After M is sure, the damped matrix V can be reconstructed into matrix V' containing only M dominant right-singular vectors. Considering this change, matrices Y_1 and Y_2 will also be reconstructed, rewritten as $Y_1 = U \sum' V_1^T$ and $Y_2 = U \sum' V_2^T$, where V_1 is obtained from V' with the last row of V' deleted; V_2 is obtained by removing the first row of V'. It is obvious that, the eigenvalues of the matrix $Y_1^+ Y_2 - \lambda I$ are equivalent to that of the matrix $[V_1^T]^+ [V_2^T]^+ - \lambda I$, which can be easily solved by use of classical eigenvalue algorithms. One can see that this methodology for z_i provides minimum variance in the presence of noise. After M and z_i are solved, residue R_i may be got by least square method.

In summary, matrix pencil method can be realized by four steps, discrete sampling electromagnetic response data, constructing Hankel matrix, descending rank, determining the number and value of pole, gaining residue by use of the least-squares method.

37.3 Application Analysis

Based on airborne electromagnetic response data sampling system developed by Jilin University, airborne electromagnetic response data in application analysis is acquired. This sampling system is compose of transmitter, receiver and concentric coil. Transmitting current is 200 A, the diameter of transmitter coil is 15 m, the diameter of receiver coil is 1.2 m.

37.3.1 Reconstructing Precision Comparison of Two Methods in the Ideal Non-Noise Circumstance

In the ideal non-noise circumstance, airborne electromagnetic response data is sampled and reconstructed by Prony method and matrix pencil method separately, the comparison between original curve and reconstructing curve corresponding to different pole number are shown in Fig. 37.1. With the increment of available pole number, reconstruction precision of these two methods are both improved gradually. To Prony method, reconstruction precision of pole number P = 4 is 5.2 %, and reconstruction precision of pole number P = 5 is up to 9.17×10^{-12} %. The result indicates that, reconstructing curve formed by a few of poles can precisely approximate original curve. To matrix pencil method, reconstruction precision of pole number M = 6 is 5.4 %, reconstruction precision of pole number M = 8 is 0.08 %, a better reconstructing curve can be gained in M = 8.

Algorithm analysis indicates that, based on polynomial calculation, Prony method firstly solves matrix equation to gain polynomial coefficients, and then solves corresponding poles by the roots of this polynomial. In the ideal non-noise circumstance, 4 rank model may be used enough to precisely approximate original curve. To matrix pencil method, the changing range of pole number should satisfy

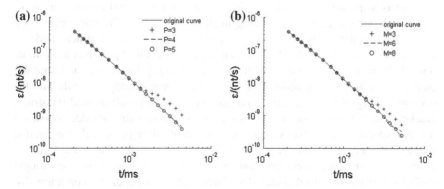

Fig. 37.1 Reconstruction precision comparison of two methods in the ideal non-noise circumstance. **a** Prony method. **b** Matrix pencil method

M < N/2-1, in the paper, pole number M corresponding to 20 sampling dots should be among 1–8. Because different pole represents characteristic information of airborne electromagnetic response data to different extent, a few of pole number merely represent part original data information. Therefore, reconstruction precision using three poles is less than that using eight poles.

Either Prony method or matrix pencil method can realize exact reconstruction to original curve by a few of eigenvectors like poles in the ideal non-noise circumstance. Further, eigenvector actually represents inherent attribution of underground geological body excited by outside electromagnetic field.

37.3.2 Reconstructing Precision Comparison of Two Methods in Including Noise Circumstance

At present, airborne electromagnetic response data sampled often includes various noises because corresponding exploration instruments are always surrounded by complex electromagnetic circumstance. How does noises confused in the response data be stripped, and resume inherent attribution of eigenvectors extracted from response data, it is the important reason to check out these two methods validity.

In the paper, for creating complex electromagnetic circumstance, Gaussian white noise with available zero value is mixed into the ideal airborne electromagnetic response data. The capacity of eliminating noise and reconstruction in the condition of different signal to noise ratio are compared between Prony method and matrix pencil method, it is shown in Fig. 37.2. To Prony method, during signal to noise ratio changing from 20 to 0 dB, relative root mean square error descends from 33.61 % of 20 dB to 142.25 % of 0 dB, and reconstruction capacity is evidently weakened. To matrix pencil method, relative root mean square error descends from 0.23 % of 20 dB to 7.81% of 0 dB, noise disturbance isn't obvious, and reconstruction capacity is steadily kept.

From the self character of algorithm, Prony method solves pole from two steps, the first is acquiring coefficients by linear predict, the second is acquiring roots from character equation. In including noise circumstance, airborne electromagnetic response data is illness, and which is used directly to construct matrix to acquire pole in Prony method. This course causes acquired pole including more noise information, the accuracy of the pole is seriously influenced, and approximating precision of corresponding reconstructing curve quickly descends with the decrease of signal to noise ratio. Contrastively, matrix pencil method constructs Hankel matrix from airborne electromagnetic response data, and decomposes it into two special matrix pencils, then, the problem of solving pole will be converted into the problem of solving generalized eigenvalue. For eliminating noise disturbance, singular value decomposition and matrix descending rank are brought during solving generalized eigenvalue. These measures better weaken noise disturbance to pole.

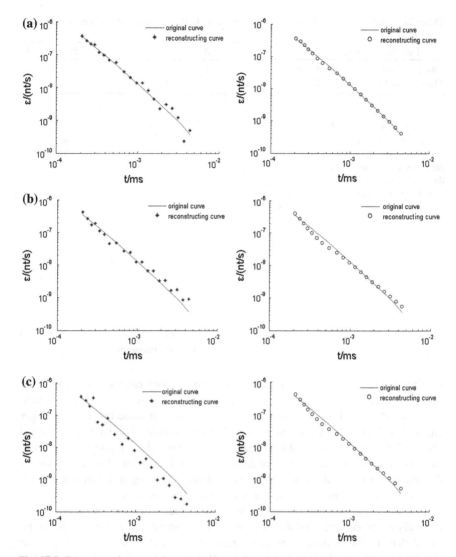

Fig. 37.2 Reconstruction precision comparison of two methods in the condition of different signal to noise ratio. **a** Signal to noise ratio is 20 dB. **b** Signal to noise ratio is 10 dB. **c** Signal to noise ratio is 0 dB (*left side* Prony method; *right side* Matrix pencil method)

Moreover, it can be found from Table 37.1 that, available pole number of Prony method and matrix pencil method gradually descends with decrease of signal to noise ratio. Algorithm analysis reveals that, in including noise circumstance, Prony method constructs L rank polynomial, and produces M single roots as poles, the rest of L-M roots is produced by noise and have no significance. So, bigger noise is, smaller M number are, and fewer available pole number are. Contrastively, to matrix pencil method, after SVD decomposition of Hankel matrix is finished, pole

Table 37.1 Pole number comparison of two methods in the condition of different of signal to noise ratio

Signal to noise ratio (dB)	0	10	30	50	70
Prony method available pole number	2	2	3	4	5
Matrix pencil method available pole number	1	1	3	4	8

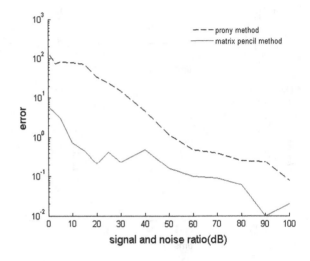

Fig. 37.3 Comparison of root mean square error of curve reconstruction precision of two methods in the condition of different of signal to noise ratio

number can be acquired by comparing the ratio between each singular value and the maximum singular value among diagonal matrix and setting lowest limitation of threshold value. Pole corresponding to bigger singular value possesses stronger capacity of resisting noise disturbance, which includes relatively pure signal information. Pole corresponding to smaller singular value is polluted by noise, validity of signal information is weakened or even disappears. With continuously descending of signal to noise ratio, pole including pure signal information gradually decreases, so, available pole number gradually decrease.

In Fig. 37.3 root mean square error of curve reconstruction precision of two methods in the condition of different signal to noise ratio is compared. It can be found that, Prony method gains better reconstruction effect after signal to noise ratio is more than 40 dB, but matrix pencil method can always keep up better reconstruction precision in the larger changing range of signal to noise ratio. Hence, matrix pencil method has more practical application to deal with including noise airborne electromagnetic response data.

37.4 Conclusion

Prony method and matrix pencil method are both effective methods to solve curve reconstruction problem of attenuation exponential summation model. However, owing to noise disturbance, to Prony method, processing capacity of including noise airborne electromagnetic response data is weak. But, to matrix pencil method, by particular matrix decomposition and descending rank theory, which decreases noise disturbance of signal information to the certain extent, guarantees smaller curve reconstruction error in bigger signal to noise ratio changing range. Thus, compared with Prony method, matrix pencil method possesses obvious advantage to reconstruct airborne electromagnetic response data in complex electromagnetic circumstance.

References

1. Lei D, Hu X-Y, Zhang S-F (2006) Development status geo of airborne ectromagnetic. Contrib Geol Min Resour Res 21:40–53 (in Chinese)
2. Zhao G-Z, Chen X-B, Tang J (2007) Advanced geo-electromagnetic methods in China. Prog Geophys 22:1171–1180 (in Chinese)
3. Stolz EM, Macnae J (1998) Evaluation EM waveforms by singular-value decomposition of exponential basis functions. Geophysics 63:64–74
4. Chen J, Macnae JC (1998) Automatic estimation of EM parameters in Tau-Domain. Explor Geophys 29:170–174
5. Sarkar TK, Pereira O (1995) Using the matrix pencil method to estimate the parameters of a sum of complex exponentials. IEEE Antennas Propag Mag 37:48–55
6. Cai X-H, Zhou Y-Q (2009) Prony method based on time-domain averaging approached to interharmonics detecting. Meas Contr Technol 28:27–30 (in Chinese)
7. Wang S, Guan X, Wang D et al (2007) Application of matrix pencil method for estimating natural resonances of scatters. Electron Lett 43:1–2
8. Trudnowski DJ, Johnson JM, Hauer JF (1999) Making prony analysis more accurate using multiple signals. IEEE Trans Power Syst 14:226–231
9. Hua Y, Sarkar TK (1990) Matrix pencil method for estimating parameters of exponentially damped/undamped sinusoids in noise. IEEE Trans Acoust Speech Signal Process 38:814–824
10. Liu D-H, Zhang Y-S, Chen Z-J et al (2006) Extraction of UWB radar target feature based on ESPRIT matrix pencil algorithm. Syst Eng Electron 28:1655–1658 (in Chinese)
11. Yang X-C, Wang Y-P, Qi Q-C (1997) New method of digital signal processing. J Tsinghua Univ 37:93–96 (in Chinese)

Chapter 38
Gamma Model-Based Target HRRP Rejection

Daiying Zhou, Rong Wang, Chundan Zheng, Jinzhou Su and Xiaozhong Liu

Abstract Target rejection using high resolution range profile (HRRP) means reject the unknown target which not belongs to any class of the database while maintaining a high accuracy in recognition. In radar automatic target recognition (RATR), lacking complete training database is a main problem in unknown target rejection. In this paper, a novel method which generates training samples based on Gamma model is proposed. The paper firstly analyzed the statistical characteristics of echoes of range cells. Then it derived the parameters estimation process of Gamma model. Compared with uniform distributed model, the proposed method can achieve better rejection performance. The experimental results of measured data demonstrate its effectiveness.

Keywords Unknown target rejection · HRRP · Gamma model · Uniform distributed model

38.1 Introduction

A high resolution range profile (HRRP) is the amplitude of the coherent summations of the complex time returns from target scatters in each range resolution cell [1]. Because it contains abundant target structure signatures, target recognition using HRRP has received intensive research in the field of radar automatic target recognition (RATR) [2]. When deal with the classification of target using HRRP,

D. Zhou · R. Wang (✉) · C. Zheng · J. Su · X. Liu
Department of EE, University of Electronic Science and Technology of China,
Chengdu, People's Republic of China
e-mail: lotus611@126.com

W. Lu et al. (eds.), *Proceedings of the 2012 International Conference on Information Technology and Software Engineering*, Lecture Notes in Electrical Engineering 211, DOI: 10.1007/978-3-642-34522-7_38, © Springer-Verlag Berlin Heidelberg 2013

it is need to consider how to reject the unknown target which not belongs to any class of the database while maintaining a high accuracy in recognition.

Reference [3] proposed a refuse recognition threshold of target to solve this problem; [4] used one-class classifier, i.e. support vector data description (SVDD) [5] to reject the unknown radar HRRP of plane. Both of the above methods only require the training dataset of the known target. However, it is difficult for them to obtain good rejection performance because no prior information of the unknown target is used. Reference [6] proposed a way to generate the training HRRP samples of unknown target based on uniform distributed model. However, the assumption of uniform distribution had neither analyzed the HRRP statistical characteristics nor used prior information.

To solve this problem, a novel method which generates training samples based on Gamma model is proposed. This paper is organized as follows. In Sect. 38.2, the statistical characteristics of echoes of three kinds of range cells are analyzed. In Sect. 38.3, Gamma model is proposed for HRRP generation and estimation procedure of the parameters is derived. In Sect. 38.4, two experiments based on measured data are conducted. In the final section, the conclusions are made.

38.2 Statistical Characteristics of the Echoes of Range Cells

Generally, microwave radar's wavelength is far smaller than the targets. Thus, the electromagnetism characteristics of the targets can be described by a discrete set of scattering centers. According to Ref. [7], the scattering center model can be simply expressed by

$$\psi(f) = \sum_{k=1}^{N} a_k \exp(j2\pi f \tau_k) = I + jQ \tag{38.1}$$

where f is the radar operating frequency, N is the numbers of the scattering centers, τ_k corresponds to the arrival time of the echoes of the kth scattering center, a_k is a constant, I and Q are the in-phase and quadrature component of complex echo respectively.

According to the scattering centers model theory, the scatter distribution in a range cell can be divided into three kinds.

1. The first kind of range cell: There are many small scattering centers but no predominant scattering centers. According to Ref. [8], the in-phase and quadrature component of the complex echo of this type of range cell will follow the Gaussian distribution with zero mean. Its amplitude will follow the Rayleigh distribution. The probability density function (pdf) of Rayleigh distribution is

$$P_{Rayleigh}(x) = \begin{cases} \dfrac{x}{\sigma^2} \exp\left(-\dfrac{x^2}{2\sigma^2}\right), & x > 0 \\ 0, & x \le 0 \end{cases} \qquad (38.2)$$

where σ is the scale parameter.

2. The second kind of range cell: There are many small scattering centers but only one predominant scattering center. Similar to the first type, the in-phase and quadrature component of the complex echo of this type of cell are assumed to follow Gaussian distribution. Its amplitude will follow Rice distribution amplitude [8]. The pdf of Rice distribution is

$$P_{Rice}(x) = \begin{cases} \dfrac{x}{\sigma^2} \exp\left(-\dfrac{x^2 + |v|^2}{2\sigma^2}\right) I_0\left(\dfrac{x \cdot |v|}{\sigma^2}\right), & x > 0 \\ 0, & x \le 0 \end{cases} \qquad (38.3)$$

where σ is the scale parameter, v is the non-centrality parameter, and $I_0(\cdot)$ is the modified Bessel function of zero order

3. The third kind of range cell: There are numerous small scattering centers and several predominant scattering centers. If there are only two predominant scattering centers in a range cell, the pdf of the echo amplitude will have two peaks. If there are more than two predominant scattering centers in one range cell, the statistical characteristic can be approximately described by a multi-modal distribution [9].

38.3 Statistical Model for HRRP Generation

38.3.1 Model Selection

As aforementioned in Sect. 38.2, the echoes of the first and second kind of range cells follow Rayleigh and Rice distribution respectively based on the assumption that a large number of scattering centers exist. However, the number of scattering centers per range cell is decreasing with the resolution increasing. Therefore, the Rayleigh and Rice distribution tend to fail in high resolution condition. For the third kind of range cell, the echoes follow a multimodal distribution. The form and component number of the distribution are hard to be determined. Thus, a more flexible distribution should be selected for the generation model.

This paper selects Gamma distribution with the following reasons. First, the variables of Gamma distribution are greater than zero which is the same with the value of echoes per range cell. Second, the two parameters of Gamma distribution

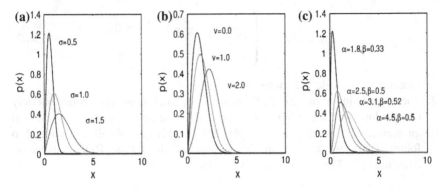

Fig. 38.1 The pdfs of some rayleigh, rice and gamma variates. **a** Rayleigh distribution. **b** Rice distribution. **c** Gamma distribution

can be changed, which make Gamma be a flexible enough distribution [8]. Third, the pdfs of Gamma distribution are quite similar to those of Rayleigh and Rice distribution, just as shown in Fig. 38.1.

38.3.2 Parameter Estimation

This section aims to estimate the parameters of Gamma distribution.

If the pdf of random variable X is

$$f(x; \alpha, \beta) = \begin{cases} \dfrac{1}{\beta^\alpha \Gamma(\alpha)} x^{\alpha-1} e^{-\frac{x}{\beta}}, & x \geq 0 \\ 0, & x < 0 \end{cases} \tag{38.4}$$

where α is the shape parameter and β is the scale parameter. Then X follows Gamma distribution, which is denoted by $X \sim \Gamma(\alpha, \beta)$.

Given a set of observed samples $x_1, x_2, \ldots, x_n$ of which each component is independent and follows Gamma distribution. According to the Maximum Likelihood Estimation, the likelihood function is

$$L(x_1, \ldots, x_n; \alpha, \beta) = \prod_{i=1}^{n} \frac{1}{\beta^\alpha \Gamma(\alpha)} x_i^{\alpha-1} e^{-\frac{x_i}{\beta}}$$

$$= [\Gamma(\alpha)]^{-n} \beta^{-n\alpha} \left[\prod_{i=1}^{n} x_i \right]^{\alpha-1} e^{-\frac{1}{\beta} \sum_{i=1}^{n} x_i} \tag{38.5}$$

Take the logarithm of (38.5) at both sides, get the logarithmic likelihood function is

$$\ln L(x_1, \ldots, x_n; \alpha, \beta) = -n \ln \Gamma(\alpha) - n\alpha \ln \beta + (\alpha - 1) \sum_{i=1}^{n} \ln x_i - \frac{1}{\beta} \sum_{i=1}^{n} x_i \quad (38.6)$$

Set (38.6) equals to zero, get the equations are

$$\begin{cases} f_1(\alpha, \beta) = \dfrac{\partial \ln L(x_1, \ldots, x_n; \alpha, \beta)}{\partial \alpha} = -n\psi(\alpha) - n \ln \beta + \sum_{i=1}^{n} \ln x_i = 0 \\[4mm] f_2(\alpha, \beta) = \dfrac{\partial \ln L(x_1, \ldots, x_n; \alpha, \beta)}{\partial \beta} = -n\dfrac{\alpha}{\beta} + \dfrac{1}{\beta^2} \sum_{i=1}^{n} x_i = 0 \end{cases} \quad (38.7)$$

where

$$\psi(x) = \frac{d[\ln \Gamma(x)]}{dx} \quad (38.8)$$

Use a simple gradient searching scheme (e.g., steepest descent method or Newton method) to (38.7) can obtain the ML value of α and β, denoted by $\hat{\alpha}$ and $\hat{\beta}$, then HRRP can be generated by assuming it follow the Gamma distribution with shape parameter $\hat{\alpha}$ and scale parameter $\hat{\beta}$.

38.4 Experimental Results and Discussion

38.4.1 Experimental Data

The results presented here are based on measured airplane data coming from C-band radar. The measured data are segmented and each segment has 260 HRRPs. The second segments of Yark-42, the forth segments of Cessna Citation S/II and the forth segments of An-26 are chosen as experimental data. The corresponding information about the airplanes is shown in Table 38.1.

According to the analysis is Sect. 38.3, Gamma distribution is used to model for the echoes of rang cells. Figure 38.2 shows the approximated pdfs of three experimental aircrafts' echoes through histogram method and Gamma distribution. Obviously, Gamma distribution can fit the echoes of three kinds of aircrafts well. This also proves that statistical model based on Gamma distribution approximate to the real statistical characteristics.

Table 38.1 Parameters of planes in the ISAR experiment

Airplane	Length (m)	Width (m)	Height (m)
An-26	23.80	29.20	9.83
Yark-42	36.38	34.88	9.83
Cessna citation S/II	14.40	15.90	4.57

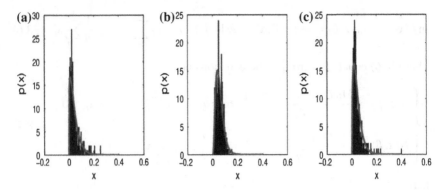

Fig. 38.2 Approximated pdfs of three experimental aircrafts echoes: the *bar* represents the approximation of a pdf via histogram method; the *solid line* represents the approximation of a pdf via the Gamma distribution. **a** A resolution cell of Yak-42. **b** A resolution cell of Cessna Citation S/II. **c** A resolution cell of An-26

38.4.2 Experimental Setting

In this paper, Area under the ROC Curve (AUC) [10] is chosen as performance evaluation criteria. The reason why not use accuracy is that the cost of an unknown target being wrongly classified as a known target is much higher than that of a known target being wrongly classified as an unknown target. Since higher value of AUC means better performance, we chose 0.9 as a threshold. If the value of AUC is higher than 0.9, it means the experiment has received a good performance.

In experiment, one experimental aircraft is assumed as unknown target while the other two are considered as known target. For simplicity, the number of measured data represents the quantity of prior information. The first 10, 26, 52, 104, 156, 208, 260 of measured HRRPs are taken to generate 260 training samples. For unknown target, the generated data is used for training and the measured data is used for testing. For known targets, the measured data of each aircrafts are divided into to two equal parts: one for training, the other for testing.

38.4.3 Experimental Results

Two experiments are conducted on measured data to show the effectiveness of the proposed method. In the proposed method, binary classifier (support vector machine) SVM is used for classification. The first experiment compares the results of uniform distributed model and Gamma model under the same condition. The value of AUC under different statistical models and prior information has been shown in Tables 38.2 and 38.3.

Table 38.2 The value of AUC under uniform distribution and different prior information

HRRP	An-26	Yark-4	Cessna citation S/II
10	0.6309	0.9052	0.9112
26	0.6111	0.9250	0.2310
52	0.5853	0.9371	0.2436
104	0.5898	0.9293	0.2100
156	0.5908	0.9363	0.2440
208	0.9084	0.9292	0.2221
260	0.9967	0.9336	0.2646

Table 38.3 The value of AUC under Gamma distribution and different prior information

HRRP	An-26	Yark-4	Cessna citation S/II
10	0.7726	0.9270	0.9834
26	0.6802	0.9220	0.9618
52	0.7125	0.9388	0.9788
104	0.8745	0.9403	0.9837
156	0.8635	0.9507	0.9900
208	0.9538	0.9599	0.9834
260	0.9841	0.9260	0.9827

It can be seen that no matter which one is the unknown plane, the performance of Gamma distribution is always better than that of uniform. Under uniform distribution, when Cessna Citation S/II is the unknown plane, the value of AUC declines with more prior information. This proves that the echoes of range cells do not follow uniform distribution. Besides, the proposed method can still get good performance when little prior information is used.

38.5 Conclusions

This paper discusses the method combining recognition and rejection techniques when dealing with radar target using HRRP. Since lacking complete training dataset is a main problem in unknown target rejection, Gamma model is proposed in this paper for HRRP generation. By doing experiments on three kinds of aircrafts, the results show that the rejection performance of Gamma distribution is better than that of uniform distribution. Besides, the proposed method is still effective when little prior information is used. The experimental results of measured data demonstrate that the proposed method can be used for radar HRRP rejection effectively.

References

1. Li HJ, Yang SH (1993) Using rang profiles as feature vectors to identify aerospace objects. IEEE Trans Antennas Propag 41(3):261–268
2. Du L, Liu HW, Bao Z (2005). Radar HRRP target recognition based on higher order spectra. IEEE Trans Signal Processing 53(7)
3. Liao K, Fu JS, Yang WL (2010) A refuse-recognition method for radar HRRP target recognition based on Mahalanobis distance. In: Proceedings of the IEEE ICCASM, pp 503–506
4. Li Q, Li B (2011) Plane HRRP rejection based on SVDD technology. In: Proceedings of the IEEE APSAR, pp 1–4
5. Tax D, Duin R (2004) Support vector data description. Mach Learn 54:45–66
6. Chai J, Liu HW, Bao Z (2010) Application of a weighted KNN classifier for HRRP out-of-database target rejection. Syst Eng Electron 32(4):718–723 (in Chinese)
7. Jiang WL, Tang BY, Xu KB, Ke YA (1998) Modeling of high frequency inverse scatterings and estimation of parameters. Acta Electronica Sinica 26(3):70–74 (in Chinese)
8. Evans M, Hastings N, Peacock B (1993) Statistical distributions seconded. Wiley, New York
9. Du L, Liu HW, Bao Z (2006) A two-distribution compounded statistical model for radar HRRP target recognition. IEEE Trans Signal Process 54(6):2226–2238
10. Huang J, Ling CX (2003) Comparing naive Bayes, decision trees, and SVM with AUC and accuracy. In: Proceedings of the IEEE ICDM, pp 553–556

Chapter 39
Application of Fuzzy Chance Constrained Programming in Research on Travel Intention of Passengers Within Comprehensive Transportation Corridor

Yanhong Li, Xiaonian Sun, Zhenzhou Yuan and Xianguang Wang

Abstract The six aspects of supply property aiming at public transportation that passengers take into consideration are security, comfortableness, convenience, rapidity, punctuality and economical efficiency. Starting from those aspects, calculation method and means of expression can be given and model for fuzzy chance constrained programming which serves as a solution for individual passenger intention can be set up. Then, fuzzy simulative genetic algorithm is adopted for the model. Theoretically, the research findings obtained form an integrated system for solving the issue of passengers' travel intention.

Keywords Fuzzy chance constrained programming · Genetic algorithm · Transportation engineering · Comprehensive transportation corridor · Passengers' travel intention

39.1 Introduction

Transportation corridor is a strip of area that bears traffic flow in the same direction which serves as the link for main traffic sources within certain areas. Generally speaking, it consists of several parallel lines applied to different transportation modes with powerful traffic capacity and flexibility for satisfying multiple

Y. Li (✉) · X. Sun · X. Wang
China Academy of Transportation Sciences, No. 240 of Huixinli, Chaoyang District, Beijing, China
e-mail: lisa813328@163.com

Y. Li · Z. Yuan
Beijing Jiaotong University, No. 3 of Shangyuan Residence, Haidian District, Beijing, China
e-mail: zzyuan@bjtu.edu.cn

W. Lu et al. (eds.), *Proceedings of the 2012 International Conference on Information Technology and Software Engineering*, Lecture Notes in Electrical Engineering 211, DOI: 10.1007/978-3-642-34522-7_39, © Springer-Verlag Berlin Heidelberg 2013

transportation needs. Passengers' travel intention means the requirements from the Passengers for selecting transportation modes with certain properties which includes requirements concerned about security, rapidity and comfortableness.

International related researches are as follows: Chen [1] investigated the relationships between service quality, perceived value, satisfaction, and behavioural intentions for air passengers through a structural equation model (SEM). Park et al. [2] researched on improving our understanding of air passengers' decision-making processes by testing a conceptual model that considers service expectation, service perception, service value, passenger satisfaction, airline image, and behavioural intentions simultaneously. Lyons et al. [3] explored an alternative perspective on travel time and it seek to examine the notion that travel time, rather than being wasted, can and does possess a positive utility. Park et al. [4] investigated how perceived price, airline service quality, perceived value; passenger satisfaction and airline image determine passengers' future behavioural intentions. Bamberg et al. [5] examined the logic of the proposition that past behaviour is the best predictor of later behaviour.

Main domestic research methods adopted about individual passenger's travel intention can be categorized into two kinds: one is qualitative analytical method based on surveys among passengers see references [6–8] and the other is disaggregate logit model based on random utility theory of econometrics see references [9–11].

But the above-mentioned methods are mainly worked out through research on urban transportation and they haven't advantages over long distance comprehensive transportation corridors. Viewing from the perspective of behavioural theory, internal urban transportation is "Low-Grade Involvement Purchasing Behaviour" to majority Passengers. Advantages and disadvantages will not be pondered by passengers before trips while habit is the dominant factor that decides passengers' choice behaviour; as for trips within the comprehensive transportation corridor, especially those with time-consuming long distance, it is named "high-grade involvement purchasing behaviour". Before trips, passengers would probe deeper into relevant information and carefully compare all kinds of properties, advantages and disadvantages of different transportation modes and make the final decision. Therefore, it is necessary to conduct research on Passengers' travel intention within the scope of comprehensive transportation corridor. Firstly, research towards individual passenger's travel intention is conducted in the article. Then further discussion on group passengers' travel intention is conducted. Finally, an integrated research system of great significance to passenger traffic market design on travel intention of comprehensive transportation corridor is formed.

39.2 Individual Passenger's Travel Intention

Individual passenger's travel intention means selecting different transportation modes possessed with certain properties. A common psychological need the passengers share is to travel safely, rapidly and comfortably. In fact, choice on travel modes is strictly restricted by income budget and travel times. As a result, the transportation mode expected may not practical. Therefore, it is necessary to study travel intentions of passengers within the restrictions.

As far as passengers concerned, it is ideal to choose the transportation mode that is most close to their own travel intention. The six aspects of supply properties for passenger traffic modes are taken into consideration for the passengers. They are security, comfortable, convenience, rapidity, punctuality and economic efficiency. And the more property one traffic mode owns the better. To passengers, it is obvious that the six properties are related internally. On condition that other technical factors remain unchanged, security and rapidity are correlated. The more it gains speed, the less it gets secured; Comfortableness and convenience correlated with rapidity as well. The longer the passengers stay in transportation vehicles the less comfortable they would feel; the faster each link of passenger traffic is, the more comfortable the passengers would feel; Comfortableness and convenience are correlated with economic efficiency. It is obvious that the lower the economic efficiency which equals to the higher the ticket is the more comfortable and comfortable the passengers would feel. Based on the inherent relationships, the article analyzes passengers' travel needs as well as travel intentions.

39.3 Fuzzy Chance Constrained Programming Model

39.3.1 Assumed Conditions

There are four assumed conditions. Firstly, feeling is fuzzy. And then weight factor is random. The third is that requirements from passengers towards certain properties might be uncertain. Finally, target function can be expressed through possibility form.

39.3.2 Establishment of Fuzzy Chance Constrained Programming Model

39.3.2.1 Decision Variables

Decision variables are factors that passengers should take into consideration when travelling. It includes security, comfortableness, convenience, rapidity, punctuality, economic efficiency and so on. In the model discussed in the article, directly measured factors can be expressed by travel speed rapidly; deviation of time on schedule stands for punctuality; Actual expenditure decides economic efficiency; as for other indirectly measured factors: security indicator, comfortableness indicator, convenience indicator are all set and be valued between the interval [0, 1], 0 stands for the worst and 1 stands for the best. The vector form of decision variable is

$X = (\tilde{x}_1, \tilde{x}_2, \tilde{x}_3, \tilde{x}_4, \tilde{x}_5, \tilde{x}_6)$. In it, $\tilde{x}_1 \sim \tilde{x}_6$ stand for security indicator, comfortableness indicator, convenience indicator, speed, time deviation on schedule and ticket price. According to the analysis, all the decision variables are fuzzy and fall into the category of subordinate function. The analyses are as follows:

(1) Security Indicator

No passengers would choose any kinds of insecure transportation modes. Being indispensible, security is a factor of great significance that affects passengers' choices on transportation modes. Once security is lost, other properties of a transportation mode become meaningless. Security indicator relates with speed and some other factors in certain transportation modes. Influences exerted from speed to security indicator should be taken into consideration. The concept speed itself is clear but the domain (named $\tilde{x}_4$) of speed discussed in the article is fuzzy. Secure domain formed out of security indicators can constitute a subordinate function. A clear $f_1(\tilde{x}_4)$ mapping from speed to "security" can be drawn out. It suggests that speed value with the maximum degree of membership along the speed domain of discourse should be selected and thus security indicators concerned about fuzzy speed can be obtained.

Security not only relates with speed but also other random factors. Therefore a fuzzy variable $\tilde{x}_7 \in [0, 1]$ should be introduced that illustrates other factors (such as natural disasters, weather and passenger numbers) besides speed exert influence over security. Suppose that these two factors form the overall safe value via linear relation, and then the following formula can be worked out:

$$\tilde{x}_1 = \tilde{\omega}_{11}\tilde{x}_7 + \tilde{\omega}_{12}f_{11}(\tilde{x}_4) \tag{39.1}$$

In this formula, $\tilde{\omega}_{11}$ and $\tilde{\omega}_{12}$ are fuzzy coefficients which represent respectively weights of the two parts consisted of factors that affect security. They comply with certain kind of fuzzy distribution and can be determined through expertise and empirical approach.

(2) Comfortableness Indicator

Comfortableness is one of the service characteristics that modern passengers pursue towards transportation. It includes the stability of vehicle operation, the comfortableness of seats and the convenience degree for passengers to eat meals, to go to the washroom and to do activities during the trip. It relates with per capita space and vibration acceleration of vehicles during traveling.

Comfortableness correlates with speed and economic efficiency. Analyzing in the same way just as security indicator does, a mapping $f_{21}(\tilde{x}_4)$ should be drawn out according to the value of speed $\tilde{x}_4$ and security indicator $\tilde{x}_2$. The mapping $f_{21}(\tilde{x}_4)$ stands for comfortableness indicator values decided by speed and the relevant range is $[0, 1]$; based on the same theory, economic efficiency $\tilde{x}_6$ is no longer exact but forms a domain of exact values. Having the range of $[0, 1]$, $f_{22}(\tilde{x}_6)$ mapping that consists of economic efficiency $\tilde{x}_6$ and comfortableness indicator demonstrates comfortableness indicator $\tilde{x}_2$ values that decided by economic efficiency.

For the fact that comfortableness doesn't decide by speed and economic efficiency only, so another fuzzy variable which shows that part of values that are out of the control of speed and economic efficiency should be introduced. Suppose that these three parts form the overall comfortableness indicator via linear relation. Then the following formula can be figured out:

$$\tilde{x}_2 = \tilde{\omega}_{21}\tilde{x}_8 + \tilde{\omega}_{22}f_{21}(\tilde{x}_4) + \tilde{\omega}_{23}f_{22}(\tilde{x}_6) \tag{39.2}$$

In this formula, $\tilde{\omega}_{21}$, $\tilde{\omega}_{22}$, $\tilde{\omega}_{23}$ are fuzzy coefficients which represent respectively effects of the above-mentioned three parts upon comfortableness. The three coefficients comply with a certain kind of fuzzy distribution.

(3) Convenience Indicator

For the fact that travel connecting time has been taken into consideration, transferring frequency and time put aside for waiting are mainly discussed here for describing the convenience property.

Analyzing convenience just the same way as that of comfortableness. A mapping $f_{31}(\tilde{x}_4)$ is drawn out by speed $\tilde{x}_4$ and convenience indicator $\tilde{x}_3$. The mapping $f_{31}(\tilde{x}_4)$ shows values of convenience indicator decided by speed and its range is $[0, 1]$. Another mapping $f_{32}(\tilde{x}_6)$ is drawn out by economic efficiency $\tilde{x}_6$ and convenience indicator $\tilde{x}_3$. Mapping $f_{32}(\tilde{x}_6)$ shows values of comfortableness indicator decided solely by economic efficiency and its range is $[0, 1]$.

Convenience is decided by some other factors as well. The following formula can be worked out after introducing another fuzzy variable which represents values decided by the other factors:

$$\tilde{x}_3 = \tilde{\omega}_{31}\tilde{x}_9 + \tilde{\omega}_{32}f_{31}(\tilde{x}_4) + \tilde{\omega}_{33}f_{32}(\tilde{x}_6) \tag{39.3}$$

In this formula, $\tilde{\omega}_{31}$, $\tilde{\omega}_{32}$, $\tilde{\omega}_{33}$ are fuzzy coefficients and show weights composed of convenience indicator.

(4) Rapidity Indicator

Rapidity is one of the main factors that affect passengers' choice on transportation modes. Rapidity reflects time-related properties of the trip as well as travel efficiency. Indicators that describe rapidity include speed and time. As far as passengers are concerned, the most direct reflection is time and time is used for weighing travel efficiency. For passengers, the total travel time is made up of operation time of vehicles and connecting time of urban transportation (if urban transportation should be taken into consideration). Connecting time for urban transportation should include connecting time from one side of the transportation corridor to the other, which includes connecting time for passengers to reach stations and connecting time for passengers to reach their destinations.

Speed here means rapidity. Manifested as a concept about 80 km/h, speed here is no longer an exact value but a fuzzy one. Speed is positive proportionally to economic efficiency. Speed is not decided by economic efficiency solely. Generally speaking, the higher the speed of the passengers' transportation mode is, the higher the ticket price would be. But besides ticket price there are some other factors that decide speed. Those above-mentioned factors are represented uniformly by $\tilde{x}_{10}$. Another mapping $f_{41}(\tilde{x}_6)$ is drawn out according to economic efficiency $\tilde{x}_6$ and rapidity indicators $\tilde{x}_4$. Mapping $f_{41}(\tilde{x}_6)$ represents rapidity indicator values that decided by ticket price and its range is $[0, 1]$. And the following formula can be worked out:

$$\tilde{x}_4 = \tilde{\omega}_{41}\tilde{x}_{10} + \tilde{\omega}_{42}f_{41}(\tilde{x}_6) \tag{39.4}$$

Suppose that the maximum speed of the transportation mode passenger has selected can reach is V_{max}, and the range of $\tilde{x}_{10}$ and $f_{41}(\tilde{x}_6)$ is from 0 to V_{max}. Complying with a certain kind of fuzzy distribution, $\tilde{\omega}_{41}$ and $\tilde{\omega}_{42}$ are fuzzy coefficients which represent the constitution of rapidity indicator.

(5) Punctuality Indicator

With the development of the society and quickened pace of living pace, the awareness of time as well as intention of planning are strengthened which required elevated punctuality awareness towards transportation service. Passengers are willing to choose those kinds of vehicles with high punctuality in avoidance of the possibility of delay and its consequent time loss accompanied with traveling ahead of schedule.

Represented by time deviation on schedule, punctuality is generally unique which related with some other factors towards quality of characteristic traffic transportation. As mentioned above, in the eyes of passengers, the concept of time deviation on schedule is not clear. Punctuality indicator is restricted by the maximum time deviation that the passengers can stand. Z_{max} is used here to indicate the biggest time deviation value.

(6) Economic Efficiency Indicator

With the development of the society and quickened pace of living pace, the awareness of time as well as intention of planning are strengthened which required elevated punctuality awareness towards transportation service. Passengers are willing to choose those kinds of vehicles with high punctuality in avoidance of the possibility of delay and its consequent time loss accompanied with traveling ahead of schedule.

Vehicles are necessary for a trip which designed to realize spatial displacement from the beginning to the end. The premise for a passenger to enjoy transportation service is payment of corresponding fees. How much does a kind of transportation mode cost is an important factor when selecting vehicles. When considering economic efficiency, passengers would indirectly consider connecting expenditures with ticket price of the transportation mode as a major reference.

Economic efficiency is represented by ticket price, which is a fuzzy concept to passengers as well. The exact value of ticket price isn't attached too much importance. Restricted by passengers' traveling budget, ticket price is represented by P_{max} here.

39.3.2.2 Constraint Conditions of the Model

Various conditions would pose constraint to passengers who adopt comprehensive transportation corridor. But to sum up, it is requirements from the six properties of characteristic traffic quality that really matter. In Fuzzy Chance Constrained Programming, passenger's goal would not be definite because of the existence of random and fuzzy factors. Passenger's goal is a form that can be expressed. That is to say requirements from the passengers to the properties is the ownership of all the six properties or partial of them within certain possible level α that is larger or smaller than $\tilde{b}$ within the fuzzy number interval $[\tilde{b}_{i1}, \tilde{b}_{i2}]$. Goal constraint and divided factor constraint are shown as follows:

Goal Constraint:

$$Pos\left\{\begin{array}{l} c_1 u_1(\tilde{x}_1) + c_2 u_2(\tilde{x}_2) + c_3 u_3(\tilde{x}_3) \\ +c_4 u_4(\tilde{x}_4) + c_5 u_5(\tilde{x}_5) + c_6 u_6(\tilde{x}_6) \geq U \end{array}\right\} \geq \beta \tag{39.5}$$

Security Indicator:

$$Pos\{\tilde{x}_1 \geq \tilde{b}_1\} \geq \alpha_1 \tag{39.6}$$

Comfortableness Indicator:

$$Pos\{\tilde{b}_{21} \leq \tilde{x}_2 \leq \tilde{b}_{22}\} \geq \alpha_2 \tag{39.7}$$

Convenience Indicator:

$$Pos\{\tilde{b}_{31} \leq \tilde{x}_3 \leq \tilde{b}_{32}\} \geq \alpha_3 \tag{39.8}$$

Rapidity Indicator:

$$Pos\{\tilde{b}_{41} \leq \tilde{x}_4 \leq \tilde{b}_{42}\} \geq \alpha_4 \tag{39.9}$$

Punctuality Indicator:

$$Pos\{\tilde{x}_5 \leq \tilde{b}_5\} \geq \alpha_5 \tag{39.10}$$

Economic Efficiency Indicator:

$$Pos\{\tilde{x}_6 \leq \tilde{b}_6\} \geq \alpha_6 \tag{39.11}$$

Related with ticket price, comfortableness, convenience and rapidity are set within a certain interval. It is obviously that the higher the ticket price is, the better those properties would be. Passengers can select those transportation modes which satisfy their individual need so as to avoid overpriced travelling expenditures.

39.3.2.3 Target Function of the Model

Related with ticket price, comfortableness, convenience and rapidity are set within a certain interval. It is obviously that the higher the ticket price is, the better those properties would be. Passengers can select those transportation modes which satisfy their individual need so as to avoid overpriced traveling expenditures.

From what has mentioned above, the target function of passengers is the maximization of total utility which equals to the maximization of service level Max U

Based on comprehensive analyses mentioned above, fuzzy chance constrained programming for passengers' travel intention is:

$$\max U \tag{39.12}$$

$$s.t$$

$$Pos\left\{ \begin{array}{l} c_1 u_1(\tilde{x}_1) + c_2 u_2(\tilde{x}_2) + c_3 u_3(\tilde{x}_3) + c_4 u_4(\tilde{x}_4) \\ + c_5 u_5(\tilde{x}_5) + c_6 u_6(\tilde{x}_6) \geq U \end{array} \right\} \geq \beta \tag{39.13}$$

$$Pos\left\{ \tilde{\omega}_{11}\tilde{x}_7 + \omega_{12}f_{11}(\tilde{x}_4) \geq \tilde{b}_1 \right\} \geq \alpha_1 \tag{39.14}$$

$$Pos\left\{ \tilde{b}_{21} \leq \tilde{\omega}_{21}\tilde{x}_8 + \tilde{\omega}_{22}f_{21}(\tilde{x}_4) + \omega_{23}f_{22}(\tilde{x}_6) \leq \tilde{b}_{22} \right\} \geq \alpha_2 \tag{39.15}$$

$$Pos\left\{ \tilde{b}_{31} \leq \tilde{\omega}_{31}\tilde{x}_9 + \tilde{\omega}_{32}f_{31}(\tilde{x}_4) + \omega_{33}f_{32}(\tilde{x}_6) \leq \tilde{b}_{32} \right\} \geq \alpha_3 \tag{39.16}$$

$$Pos\left\{ \tilde{b}_{41} \leq \tilde{\omega}_{41}\tilde{x}_{10} + \tilde{\omega}_{42}f_{41}(\tilde{x}_6) \leq \tilde{b}_{42} \right\} \geq \alpha_4 \tag{39.17}$$

$$Pos\left\{ \tilde{\omega}_{51}\tilde{x}_5 \leq \tilde{b}_5 \right\} \geq \alpha_5 \tag{39.18}$$

$$Pos\left\{ \tilde{\omega}_{61}\tilde{x}_6 \leq \tilde{b}_6 \right\} \geq \alpha_6 \tag{39.19}$$

$$\tilde{x}_1, \tilde{x}_2, \tilde{x}_3, \tilde{x}_7, \tilde{x}_8, \tilde{x}_9 \in [0,1], \tilde{x}_4, \tilde{x}_{10} \in [0, V_{max}], \tilde{x}_5 \in [0, Z_{max}], \tilde{x}_6 \in [0, P_{max}]$$

In those equations, $u_i(\tilde{x}_i)$ and c_i is utility function and weight respectively for each factor and $i = 1, 2, 3, 4, 5, 6$. The decision variables are $(\tilde{x}_7, \tilde{x}_8, \tilde{x}_9, \tilde{x}_{10}, \tilde{x}_5, \tilde{x}_6)$.

39.4 Genetic Algorithm Based on Fuzzy Simulation

Fuzzy chance constrained programming can be worked out with the combination of computer simulation method and genetic algorithm. Falls into the category of the most optimal heuristic method, genetic algorithm is a method of seeking optimization through simulating natural evolution process with favourable efficiency and astringency. Genetic algorithm is used as a basic method here to solve this kind of fuzzy chance constrained programming issue for optimization. Computer simulation technology is adopted in genetic algorithm when testing constraint conditions and calculating the value of target function.

39.4.1 Genetic Algorithm Based on Fuzzy Simulation

Figure 39.1

Fig. 39.1 Procedures of conducting genetic algorithm on the basis of fuzzy simulation

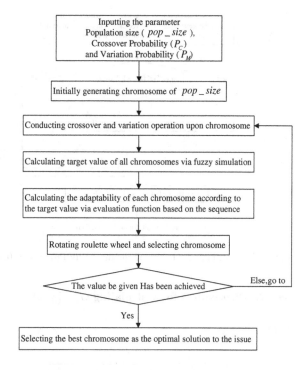

39.4.2 Checkout Procedure Based on Fuzzy Simulation Technique

Fuzzy simulation technique can be used to tell whether the following inequality is correct. And it can work out the possibility of the below-mentioned fuzzy event as well.

$$Pos\{g_i(\varepsilon) \leq 0, i = 1, \ldots, k\} \geq \alpha$$

$$G = \{g_i(\varepsilon) \leq 0, i = 1, \ldots \ldots, k\}$$

And the maximum value of U can be worked out which makes it possible that $Pos\{g(\varepsilon) \geq U\} \geq \beta$.

39.4.2.1 Procedures for Testifying the Inequality
$Pos\{g_i(\varepsilon) \le 0, i = 1, \ldots\ldots, k\} \ge \alpha$

Figure 39.2

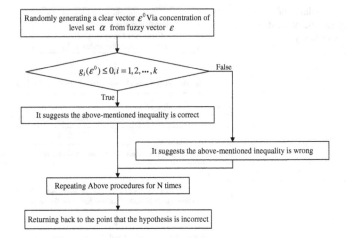

Fig. 39.2 Procedures for testifying the inequality $Pos\{g_i(\varepsilon) \le 0, i = 1, \ldots, k\} \ge \alpha$

39.4.2.2 Procedures for Calculating $G = \{g_i(\varepsilon) \le 0, i = 1, \ldots\ldots, k\}$

Figure 39.3

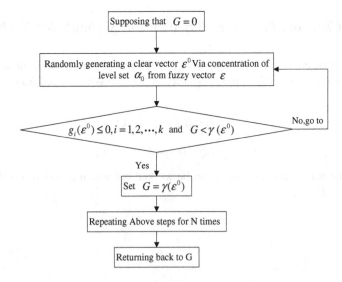

Fig. 39.3 Procedures for calculating $G = \{g_i(\varepsilon) \le 0, i = 1, \ldots, k\}$

39.4.2.3 Procedures for Figuring Out $Pos\{g(\varepsilon) \geq U\} \geq \beta$

Figure 39.4

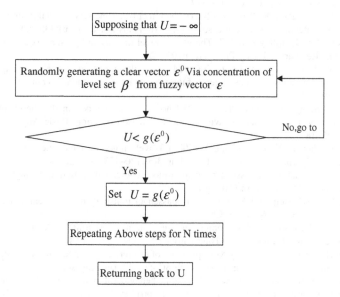

Fig. 39.4 Procedures for figuring out $Pos\{g(\varepsilon) \geq U\} \geq \beta$

39.5 Conclusion

Firstly, the six aspects of supply properties possessed by passenger transportation modes that the passengers take into consideration are discussed in the article. The six aspects are security, convenience, rapidity, punctuality and economic efficiency. Then, calculation method and expression method of each indicator are given. Finally, fuzzy chance constrained programming method is established for working out passengers' travel intention and fuzzy simulation genetic algorithm is designed for testifying the model. The research findings form an integrated system for understanding passengers' travel intentions. But it should be noted that research on passengers' travel intention of choosing among comprehensive transportation modes is conducted in the perspective of theoretical model. How to demarcate parameters of the model and how to apply the above-mentioned model into practical project are main research directions for the author in the future.

Acknowledgments This work was sponsored by Technology Project of Guangdong Transportation Department under Grant No 2011-02-071 and National Basic Research Program of China (No. 2012CB725403). The authors deeply appreciate the supports. The authors are also very grateful for the constructive suggestions and critical comments of the anonymous reviewers.

References

1. Chen C-F (2008) Investigating structural relationships between service quality, perceived value, satisfaction, and behavioral intentions for air passengers: evidence from Taiwan. Trans Res Part A Policy Pract 42(4):709–717
2. Park J-W, Robertson R, Wu C-L (2004) The effect of airline service quality on passengers' behavioral intentions: a Korean case study. J Air Trans Manag 10(6):435–439
3. Lyons G, Jain J, Holley D (2007) The use of travel time by rail passengers in Great Britain (J). Trans Res Part A Policy Pract 41(1):107–120
4. Park J-W, Robertson R, Wu C-L (2006) Modeling the impact of airline service quality and marketing variables on passengers' future behavioral intentions. Trans Plan Technol 29(5):359–381
5. Bamberg S, Ajzen I, Schmidt P (2003) Choice of travel mode in the theory of planned behavior: the roles of past behavior, habit, and reasoned action. Basic Appl Soc Psychol 25(3):175–187
6. Peng H, Chen K, Wang J, Wang Y (2005) Travel choice characteristics of transportation corridor of Europe-Asia. J Traffic Trans Eng 3(5):120–123. (in Chinese)
7. Li Q (2006) Analysis of passenger transport mode choice within Beijing-Shanghai Corridor. Compr Trans (4):65–68. (in Chinese)
8. Liang Q (2003) Beijing-Tianjin inter-city passenger transport market research and analysis. Railw Trans Econ 4:26–27. (in Chinese)
9. Luo X, Li D, Gao S (2006) Comprehensive route-mode sharing model for intersectional passenger traffic. J Southw Jiao Tong Univ 41(5): 554–559. (in Chinese)
10. Zhang H, Ren G, Wang W (2008) Application of discrete choice model in trip mode structure forecasting. J Trans Syst Eng Inform Tech 8(5):44–49. (in Chinese)
11. Dingyu S, Xuming G (1992) Researches on the behavioural model of travellers' mode choice between highway and railway in a transport corridor. J China Railw Soc 14:58—63. (in Chinese)

Chapter 40
Active Vibration Isolation System to Improve Free Space Optics Communication

Asan G. A. Muthalif, Khairiah K. Turahim and Syazwani Ab. Rahim

Abstract A Free Space Optics (FSO) link consists of a transmitter and a receiver telescope which requires a continuous alignment for successful transmission of data. However due to certain factors, misalignment could occur between the transmitter and receiver telescope which later interrupts data transmission. One of the factors that contribute to this misalignment is unwanted vibration at the transmitter or receiver. This paper outlines the design and implementation of an active vibration isolation system prototype to tackle the problem of misalignment caused by vibration for an FSO communication. A prototype is fabricated and a control system is implemented with an objective to suppress vibration coming to the top plate where the transmitter or receiver will be placed. By applying an LQR controller to the system, a reduction of 25.8 % of plate displacement and 49.2 % of amplitude of frequency is achieved at excitation frequency of 12 Hz.

Keywords FSO · LabVIEW · LQR · Active vibration isolation

A. G. A. Muthalif (✉) · K. K. Turahim · S. Ab. Rahim
Faculty of Engineering, Department of Mechatronics Engineering, International Islamic University Malaysia, Jalan Gombak, 53100 Kuala Lumpur, Malaysia
e-mail: asan@iium.edu.my

K. K. Turahim
e-mail: khairiah.turahim@gmail.com

S. Ab. Rahim
e-mail: syazwani_0103@yahoo.com

W. Lu et al. (eds.), *Proceedings of the 2012 International Conference on Information Technology and Software Engineering*, Lecture Notes in Electrical Engineering 211, DOI: 10.1007/978-3-642-34522-7_40, © Springer-Verlag Berlin Heidelberg 2013

40.1 Introduction

Free-space optics (FSO) communication is a technology that uses air as its medium of transmission. The transmission process using FSO is relatively simple. It only needs a laser transmitter and receiver. Each FSO system uses a high-power optical source such as laser and a telescope that transmits light through the atmosphere to another telescope which acts as a receiver. An FSO link refers to a pair of FSO telescope, each aiming a laser beam to the other. Hence, one telescope has dual capability to act as a laser transmitter as well as a receiver [1]. In most cases, these telescopes are installed on top of buildings for free space communication.

For an FSO link to successfully transmit data, it requires a continuous alignment between the transmitter and receiver. Misalignment happens due to movement of the transmitter and receiver from the common line of sight and which causes a decrease in the received signal intensity, which eventually increases the bit error probability (BEP) [2]. One of the key challenges with FSO systems is maintaining the alignment of transmitter and receiver. Buildings are constantly subjected to various sources of motion due to thermal expansion, wind sway and vibration. Therefore an FSO link mounted on top of buildings is also exposed to this motion.

The mounting environment is among the factors that contribute to the misalignment of the FSO link. Usually, a transmitter and receiver are mounted on rooftops or on top of a high-rise building. Here, vibration sources usually come from nearby equipments such as elevators and ventilation units [3]. Misalignment is also a consequent from deformation of the mount due to temperature changes and uneven heating by the sun and human activities such as walking and shutting doors [4]. Nature also causes the misalignment of the FSO link such as weak earthquake and wind, especially when the equipment is placed on tall buildings. Many high-rise buildings sway under the influence of dynamic wind loads in different directions, subjected to twist due to torsion by wind. The horizontal movement of the building due to these effects can vary from 1/200 to 1/800 of the building height. Building sway is a random process that affects system performance since it is a source of pointing error at the beam steering stage [5]. Common vibration sources with their respective frequency and amplitude values are shown in Table 40.1. From above discussion, it is therefore crucial to have an active vibration isolation (AVI) system in order to isolate FSO transmission devices from unwanted vibration and thus improve the performance.

40.2 Overview of Active Vibration Isolation

Vibration isolation is the process of isolating an item, such as a piece of equipment from sources of vibration. Despite application differences, the concept of vibration isolation is the same across the board. There are three major control approaches to overcome vibration problems which are passive, active and semi-active [6].

Table 40.1 Common vibration sources (www.cvimelletsgriot.com)

Source	Frequency (Hz)	Amplitude (in.)
Air compressors	4–20	10^{-2}
Handling equipment	5–40	10^{-3}
Pumps	5–25	10^{-3}
Building services	7–40	10^{-4}
Foot traffic	0.55–6	10^{-5}
Acoustics	100–10,000	10^{-2} to 10^{-4}
Air currents	Labs can vary depending on class	Not applicable
Punch presses	Up to 20	10^{-2} to 10^{-5}
Transformers	50–400	10^{-4} to 10^{-5}
Elevators	Up to 40	10^{-3} to 10^{-5}
Building motion	46/height in meters horizontal	10^{-1}
Building pressure waves	1–5	10^{-5}
Railroads	5–20	±0.15 g
Highway traffic	5–100	±0.001 g

The most commonly applied vibration control technique is the use of passive technologies. The majority of these applications are based on passive damping using viscoelastic materials. Passive vibration isolation systems generally consist of a spring and a damper which does not respond to changes in environmental conditions.

Active vibration isolation system consists of a spring, a feedback circuit which includes a piezoelectric accelerometer, a controller, and an electromagnetic transducer. The acceleration or vibration is processed by the control circuit which allows the system to adjust itself in response to various excitations. For this reason active vibration isolation systems are considered as more effective at suppressing vibrations than ordinary passive vibration isolation or ordinary damping.

A semi-active system combines features of a passive system and an active system. Semi-active control devices are essentially passive devices where properties can be adjusted in real time [7].

40.3 Mathematical Model of Active Vibration Isolation

A mathematical model of the active vibration isolation system is constructed by referring to the diagram in Fig. 40.1. It consists of a top plate, m_1 where the transmitter or receiver telescope will be placed, and a base plate, m_2 which rests on a table that can be modeled as a spring, k_2 and damper, c_2. The system will be excited by vibration coming from the ground, and this vibration will be transferred to base plate, m_2 and top plate, m_1. k_1, c_1 and f_c are the spring constant, damping coefficient of isolation system, and force exerted by the actuator respectively.

By applying Newton's Second Law to m_1 and m_2, the equation of motion of m_1 and m_2 are

Fig. 40.1 Physical model of the active vibration isolation system

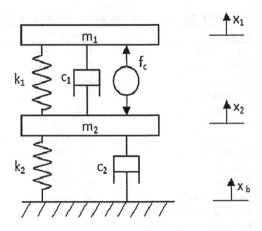

$$m_1\ddot{x}_1 38; = -k(x_1 - x_2) - c_1(\dot{x}_1 - \dot{x}_2) - f_c$$
$$m_2\ddot{x}_2 38; = -k(x_1 - x_2) + c_1(\dot{x}_1 - \dot{x}_2) + f_c - k_2(x_2 - x_b) - c_2(\dot{x}_2 - \dot{x}_b)$$

(40.1)

Based on Eq. (40.1), the state space form becomes

$$\dot{x} = Ax + Bu \qquad y = Cx + Du$$

(40.2)

where the matrices of A, B, C and D are:

$$A = \begin{bmatrix} 0 & 0 & 1 & 0 \\ 0 & 0 & 0 & 1 \\ -\dfrac{k_1}{m_1} & \dfrac{k_1}{m_1} & -\dfrac{c_1}{m_1} & \dfrac{c_1}{m_1} \\ \dfrac{k_1}{m_2} & \dfrac{-(k_1 + k_2)}{m_2} & \dfrac{c_1}{m_2} & \dfrac{-(c_1 + c_2)}{m_2} \end{bmatrix},$$

(40.3)

$$C = \begin{bmatrix} 1 & 0 & 0 & 0 \end{bmatrix},$$

The A, B, C and D matrices are used in simulation studies of the active vibration isolation system to observe the effectiveness before developing the physical prototype.

40.4 Development of an Active Vibration Isolation System Test Rig

The active vibration isolation system consists of an active vibration isolation test rig and an excitation mechanism. Figure 40.2 shows the active vibration isolation test rig which consists of three square aluminum plates with dimension of 30 cm × 30 cm that act as, top plate, m_1, base plate, m_2 and ground. Four stainless

Fig. 40.2 Hardware setup of active vibration isolation system

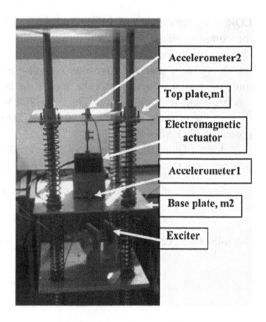

steel rods are placed at each corner to hold the three plates. Linear bearings are fixed into the three square aluminum plates so they are free to move up and down when excited by the excitation mechanism. Springs are put in between the three plates for support and to provide equal distances between them.

Excitation mechanism consists of a DC motor and a small cylindrical-shaped aluminum mass. The purpose of the aluminum mass is to make the excitation system imbalance so that the base plate will move up and down continuously.

The main purpose of using an active vibration isolation system is to reduce vibration at the top plate, where the transmitter or receiver will be placed. To achieve this, an electromagnetic actuator is placed between the top plate, m_1 and base plate, m_2. Two accelerometers are used in the development of this active vibration isolation system test rig. One accelerometer is placed on the top plate, m_1 to provide displacement reading of the plate. Another accelerometer is placed on the base plate, m_2. Accelerometer readings from the top plate and base plate will be sent to controller and later, the output signal is send to the actuator for vibration control; by cancelling the motion and maintaining displacement of m_1 to near zero. This process repeats continuously for the active vibration isolation system.

40.5 Implementation of LQR Controller

A Linear Quadratic Regulator (LQR) controller is implemented in the system to isolate vibration from reaching the top plate, m_1. The main advantage of LQR is at high frequency range, it behaves like a first order system. Another advantage of

LQR is its capability to deliberately locate all the plant poles in given regions of the complex plane. A properly derived gain K, in which Q and R are suitably chosen, guarantees closed loop stability. Some other advantages of LQR includes the ability to be used for three axes control, ease of application for multiple-input multiple-output systems, and the ability to be modified to work for full-state feedback and state estimation. The controller is created in LabVIEW and passed through the system using a data acquisition (DAQ) system. The DAQ used for this project is NI USB 4431.

A Linear Quadratic regulator (LQR) controller can be described by considering a linear time invariant (LTI) system given by its state space model

$$\dot{x}(t)38; = Ax\ (t) + Bu\ (t)$$
$$y(t)38; = cx\ (t) + Du\ (t) \tag{40.4}$$

the following performance index for the optimal controller design is introduced:

$$J = \int_0^\infty \left(x^T Q x + u^T R u\right) dt \tag{40.5}$$

where Q and R are weighting matrices for the state variables and the input variables respectively. Then, the LQR problem can be solved using a linear state feedback with a constant gain matrix, i.e.

$$u(t) = -Kx(t),\ K = -R^{-1}B^T P \tag{40.6}$$

where P is the solution of Algebraic Ricatti Equation (ARE) [8]. Clearly, the closed-loop system is simply

$$[(A - BK), B, C, D] \tag{40.7}$$

A block diagram is first designed in LabVIEW to obtain values of optimal gain, K, through simulation. The two matrices Q (an n × n matrix) and R (an m × m matrix). Depending on how these design parameters are selected, the closed-loop system will exhibit different response. By selecting large value of Q or keeping J small, the state x(t) will have smaller value. On the other hand, selecting R to have large value requires the control input u(t) to have small value in order to minimize the values of J. In other words, larger values of Q generally resulted in the poles of the closed-loop system matrix $A_c = (A - BK)$ being further left in the s-plane so the state decays faster to zero. On the other hand, larger R means that less control effort is required, so the poles decay slower, resulting in larger values of the state x(t). Using heuristic method, optimal values of Q and R matrices, are found to be Q = diag [50000 3000 5000 32] and R = 0.01. The value of optimal gain K is $K = [-1503.6\ 1507.04 -703.71 -10.84]$. A LabVIEW block diagram for LQR controller is constructed according to the flowchart given in Fig. 40.3. Since LQR is a full state feedback controller, both accelerometer1 and accelerometer2 are fully utilized to obtain all the states of the system.

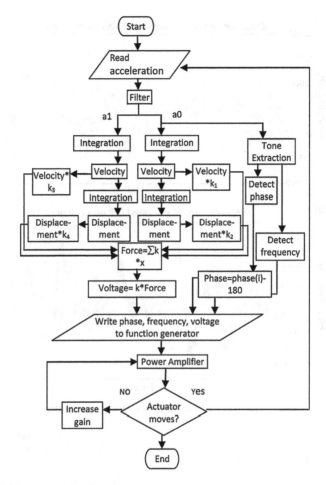

Fig. 40.3 LQR programming flowchart

Acceleration output from accelerometer2 is integrated twice; first integration is to obtain velocity of the top plate which is state x_1 and the second integration is to obtain displacement of the top plate which is state x_2. The same is done for acceleration output from accelerometer1 to obtain velocity and displacement which is state x_3 and state x_4 respectively. The states x_1, x_2, x_3 and x_4 are later multiplied with the optimal gains, **K** values obtained earlier.

After multiplying the states with their corresponding **K** values, all states are summed up to obtain the value of force required to control the system. The required magnitude of the force is inserted into calibration equation of the electromagnetic actuator.

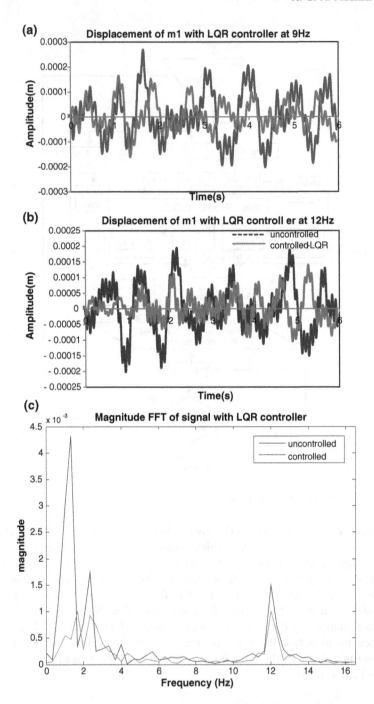

Fig. 40.4 **a** Graph of displacement of m_1 versus time at 12 Hz. **b** Graph of displacement of m_1 versus time at 9 Hz. **c** Frequency response plot

40.6 Results

Graphs for amplitude of displacement for top plate, m_1 versus time and its frequency response are plotted as illustrated in Fig. 40.4a, b, c, using LQR controller at frequency 9 and 12 Hz respectively. Ideally, the graphs are supposed to give a harmonic signal output, but due to hardware or mechanical limitations such as imperfect manufacturing of hardware, bearing friction, unsuitable spring stiffness and improper fixture of springs to the body, distorted harmonic outputs are produced. The springs are not rigidly connected to the body of the hardware and therefore vibration is not fully transferred to the top plate, m_1. Another factor comes from the exciter in which it did not provide a perfect harmonic excitation to the system. These limitations can be improved in the future. Even though the system does not show a harmonic signal, it can be observed in most part of the graph that amplitude of displacement of the top plate, m_1 has lower magnitude using controller rather than without controller.

Table 40.2 shows the reduction in amplitude of displacement and amplitude of frequency. The results show a reduction of 36.8 % in amplitude of displacement and 24.5 % in amplitude of frequency at excitation frequency of 9 Hz. At excitation frequency of 12 Hz, a reduction of 25.8 % in amplitude of displacement and 49.2 % in amplitude of frequency is achieved using LQR controller. When the system is excited by vibration at 9 Hz, the maximum amplitude of displacement at top plate, m_1 is reduced more than at excitation frequency of 12 Hz. However, at excitation frequency of 12 Hz, the average amplitude of frequency is reduced more than at excitation frequency of 9 Hz. This shows that at both excitation frequencies, the system gives similar reduction in amplitude of displacement and amplitude of frequency.

Table 40.2 Summary of results

	Maximum amplitude of displacement (mm)	Average magnitude of frequency (area under the graph)
Uncontrolled (9 Hz)	0.268	0.0139
Controlled-LQR (9 Hz)	0.169	0.0105
Reduction (%)	36.8	24.5
Uncontrolled (12 Hz)	0.203	0.0126
Controlled-LQR (12 Hz)	0.151	0.0064
Reduction (%)	25.8	49.2

40.7 Conclusion

The active vibration isolation system prototype is developed and an LQR controller is implemented in the system to isolate it from vibration. The system is tested using two different excitation frequencies, 9 and 12 Hz. At excitation frequency of 9 Hz, reduction in amplitude of displacement is 36.8 % and reduction in amplitude of frequency is 24.5 %. At excitation frequency of 12 Hz, reduction of 25.8 % can be seen in amplitude of displacement of the plate and a reduction of 49.2 % in amplitude of frequency. The system can be further improved by minimizing the mechanical limitations due to hardware imperfection in order to produce better vibration transmission in the system. Furthermore, the excitation system can also be improved by using a mechanism that is able to provide a perfect sinusoidal input to the system so that analysis can be done with better accuracy.

References

1. Kim et al (1998) Wireless optical transmission of fast ethernet, FDDI, ATM, and ESCON protocol data using the TerraLink laser communication system. Opt Eng 37(12):3143–3155
2. Arnon S (2003) Effects of atmospheric turbulence and building sway on optical wireless-communication systems. Opt Lett 28(2):129–131
3. Jeganathan M, Ionov P (2000) Multi-gigabits-per-second optical wireless communications. http://www.freespaceoptic.com/WhitePapers/Jeganathan%20%20(Optical%20Crossing).pdf. Accessed May 2010
4. Bloom S, Korevaar E, Schuster J, Willebrand H (2003) Understanding the performance of free-space optics [Invited]. J Opt Netw 2(6):178–200
5. Kedar D, Arnon S (2003) Urban optical wireless communication networks: the main challenges and possible solutions. IEEE Commun Mag 42(5):2–7
6. Tantanawat T, Li Z, Kota S (2004) Application of compliant mechanisms to active vibration isolation systems. In: Proceedings of DETC 2004, international design engineering technical conference, 28 Sept–2 Oct 2004, Salt Lake City, UT, USA
7. Preumont A (2002) Vibration control of active structures: an introduction. Kluwer Academic Publishers, Dordrecht
8. Gopal M (2009) Digital control and state variable method. Tata Mc Graw Hill, New Delhi
9. Fundamentals of Vibration Isolation. CVI Melles Griot (2009). https://www.cvimellesgriot. com/Products/Documents/TechnicalGuide/Fundamentals-Vibration-Isolation.pdf. Accessed May 2010
10. Gani A, Salami MJE (2002) A LabVIEW based data acquisition system for vibration monitoring and analysis. Student conference on research and development, pp 62–65

Chapter 41
The Design and Implementation of a Multi-Source Information Wide Area Adaptive Switching Equipment

Hang Zheng

Abstract Aiming at the government's demands of extensive social information when organizing disaster rescue and dealing with emergency, a multi-source information wide area adaptive switching equipment was implemented which was highly efficient and multipurpose. The device can provide functions like information format conversion, communicating protocol and physical port adaption, concurrent execution control, and so on. It can solve the problems of collecting and utilizing multisource information, in the domains of message format, communication protocol and port type, and implement the transparent and highly efficient transmission of different kinds of user messages in heterogeneous network environment, meanwhile, in order to collect and utilize all kinds of useful information and message channel extensively. The device can improve the government's command ability to use information-based system, such as emergency mobile command communication system, as well as providing communication technology support.

Keywords Information format conversion · Communication protocol adaption · Physical port adaption · Multi-source information collection

---

H. Zheng (✉)
Beijing University of Posts and Telecommunications HongFu Campus, Zhenggezhuang, Bei Qijia zhen Changping district 102209 Beijing, China
e-mail: zhcam1003@sina.com

W. Lu et al. (eds.), *Proceedings of the 2012 International Conference on Information Technology and Software Engineering*, Lecture Notes in Electrical Engineering 211, DOI: 10.1007/978-3-642-34522-7_41, © Springer-Verlag Berlin Heidelberg 2013

41.1 Introduction

China is a country with frequently natural calamities, such as the earthquake, mountain torrents, debris flow, inundation, and fire etc., which cause enormous damage on people's lives and production. With the rapid development of technology, Internet has been spread to local governments, enterprise and public institutions, even to the majority of families, however, there are various different information channels in society, if local governments at all levels can take fully advantages of messages in organizing rescues and handling emergencies, they can master disasters and emergencies more promptly, exactly and comprehensively, as a consequence, it will improve the effectiveness of dealing with emergencies and control to avoid expanding situations, as well as alleviating calamity losses. On June, 28th, 2012, a severe debris flow erupted in NingNan country, sichuan province. Because the officers caught disaster warming message in time, more than 500 villagers evacuated successfully, on the contrary, those who working in a constructed building, nearly 14 workers were dead because of lacking warming message, and 26 people disappeared.

Nowadays, there are still many problems for local governments to deal with emergencies with various social information, such as, the diversity and largely differentiation of message format, the poor interconnecting ability between various systems, etc. It is the flexible conversion, highly efficient transmission and comprehensive utility of various information that constricts governments' ability to handle emergencies with information-based system.

In this passage, based on characteristics and application needs of various information, we design and implement a highly efficient and multipurpose device—multisource information wide-area adaptive and switching equipment [1, 2], after deeply studying the multisource-message self-adaptive format conversion, wide-range adaptive exchange and other techniques. This device can automatically manage to adapt and convert users' message format [3], communication protocol [4, 5], physical port type [6], and shield the difference of them between different devices, in this condition, it can achieve assorted messages' transparent and highly efficient transmission, meanwhile, furnish ability to manage communicating parameter configuration and channel quality, as well as monitoring device running status, as a consequence, extensive messages transmit in a rapid and accurate way to governments' emergencies response commanding system and help to handle rescue and emergencies.

41.2 System Components

The device is a comprehensive communication exchange platform integrated software and hardware, which is developed by embedded technology. The appearance of the device is shown as Fig. 41.1.

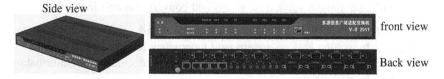

Fig. 41.1 The appearance of device

The equipment adopts a 19-inch chassis with height of 1U, and there are several state indicator lights on the front panel, mainly including lights of battery, 32-way card, four-way card, V35 interface, E1 interface and Ethernet interface, which can display the working state of each component of device. On the back panel, the equipment offers battery, configuration plot and various communication interface. The device adopts the design of double-power hot backup, which can shift to another battery automatically after one was broken, thus ensuring the system functioning properly. Besides, it provides four 10/100 M adaptive Ethernet interface, four-way E1 interface, four V.35/V.24 synchronous and asynchronous settable serial interface; and it also furnishes two expanded slots that can insert two communication expansion cards concurrently; when inserting 32-way card, its serial interface can expand by matched communication expanded chassis and DB62 cable, that is, each chassis provide 16-way serial interface.

There are assorted information processing and system management software, which can manage hardware driver, message format conversion, communication protocol adaption, channel monitoring, and so on.

41.3 System Function

In the wide area transmission of information, the device can automatically manage to adapt and convert users' message format, communication protocol, physical port type, and shield the difference of them between different devices, meanwhile, it can achieve assorted messages' transparent and highly efficient transmission, and furnish ability to manage communicating parameter configuration and channel quality, as well as monitoring device running status.

41.3.1 Information Format Conversion

The device can achieve to convert assorted user message format, and concurrently convert one kind of format of inputting data to other various kinds message to output, thereby integrated conducting and distributing the multisource messages flexible.

Currently, equipment support to access and convert message including:

1. The surveillance video, acoustic image, words and conference information acquired by equipments on government emergency response command car.
2. The surveillance video, acoustic image, words and conference information acquired by pedestrians.
3. The surveillance video, acoustic image, words and conference information acquired by local government or other enterprises.
4. Message provided by other information devices in locale, like PC, camera, mobile phone, DV, avi graph, monitor and so on.
5. Meteorological information offered by nearly meteorological station.
6. Information from rescue plane.
7. Spot monitoring information by ground robot. (wireless accessible)
8. Spot monitoring information on air platform. (wireless accessible)
9. Spot monitoring information by aquatic platform. (wireless accessible)

In addition, the system can provide support to add other format conversion based on embedded programming technology, according actual demands.

41.3.2 Communication Protocol Adaption

The equipment provides support to several communication protocols to adapt automatically, mainly including UDP, TCP, HDLC, ATM, BSC and others. As mentioned above, device can receive and manage data sent by various protocols from external system, and also transmit processed data in proper protocol due to requirements.

41.3.3 Physical Port Adaption

Device contains multiple physical ports, and provides automatic retransmission data between them, besides, it also offers connection between various ports and protocols. Moreover, it furnishes ports with ability to retransmit data, such as Ethernet port, V.35 interface, V.24 asynchronize interface, V.24 synchronize interface, and so on.

41.3.4 Cyclic Redundancy Check and Format Error Correction

The device can judge whether data is wrong or not by CRC, and filtrate the wrong data, thus avoiding system resource loss, improving system performance and decreasing the probabilities of system errors. According to the preset checking rules of correctness of message format, the equipment can check data format and filtrate wrong data, as a consequence, it only sends out correct data.

41.3.5 Device Management and State Monitor

The equipment provides external configuration management software, and interact it with internal related function module invoking interface to manage communicating parameter configuration and channel quality, as well as monitoring device running status.

41.4 System Design

41.4.1 Hardware System Design

Adopting three-layer hardware system architecture of 'main board + core board + expanded board', device's main hardware architecture is made up with main board, core processing board and expanded function board, which assembling layout is shown as Fig. 41.2 and logic constitution is seen as Fig. 41.3.

Main boards provides bus driver, clock processing and basic Ethernet interface, E1 interface, synchronize and asynchronize settable serial port, and expanded communication slot, besides, it also offers double battery backup power supply, which lay a foundation for system's unremitting working and function expansion. The kernel of core processing board is Motorola MPC double kernel architecture (CPU + CPM), which uses embedded Linux operating system efficiently, real-time and preemptive kernel, and it is also deployed with the components like Flash, RAM, crystal oscillator, Bus interface adapter, moreover, it implements equipment working management, message processing, data storage and many other core functions. Expanded function board is made to satisfy customers' needs to flexible add message processing board, which can do related message processing and transmission. This architecture is separated into three parts: basic supporting platform, core processing unit, function expansion unit, so, it is convenient to uniformly manage and use equipment resources, and it also support expansion and maintenance functions.

Fig. 41.2 Hardware assembling layout

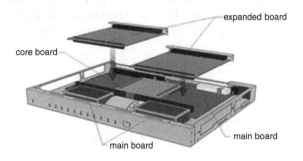

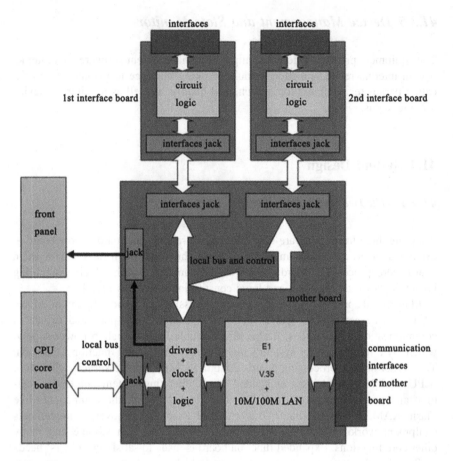

Fig. 41.3 Hardware logic constitution

Due to demand, equipment can expand the number of serial ports by adding external expanded communication chassis to satisfy the need of multi-channel transmission. The communication expansion chassis works in a power supply way without batteries, it provides 16 expanded serial ports, which connect with main board by inserting 16-way synchronize and asynchronize settable serial port expanded card or 32-way asynchronize serial port expanded card, shown in Fig. 41.4.

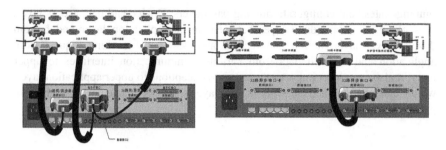

Fig. 41.4 The connection of device by communication expanded chassis port

41.4.2 Software System Design

41.4.2.1 Software System Architecture

The software of device adopts multilayer system architecture, which is made up of kernel (device driver layer), device (data access layer) and application (data processing layer), as shown in Fig. 41.5.

The kernel and device driver layer, implements to drive hardware device and manage access. Gateway application and data process layer, implements to convert information format, handle and retransmit data, monitor hardware and software

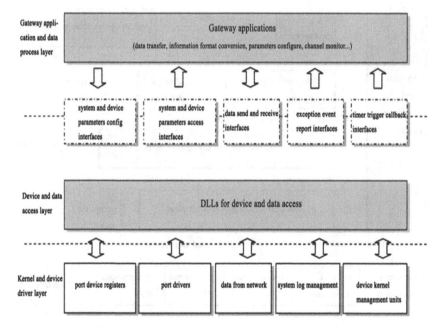

Fig. 41.5 Device software architecture

running states, and configurate running parameters. Device and data access layer, is working as intermediate layer between upper application layer and bottom device driver layer, and it can receive and deal with revoking request from application and transmit data from various communication interfaces to upper layer, it also can report important events and exceptions to upper application layer, which can abstract and simplify upper layer's access management to bottom physical equipments.

41.4.2.2 Software Function Module Design

Based on multilayer architecture, the equipment's function software achieves the function of message format conversion, data receiving and retransmitting, channel detection, parameter configuration management, exception handling, log management, communication protocol, and board or interface driver. All software can coordinate with each other by pre-set processing logic relationship. The software composition and main information relationship is shown as Fig. 41.6.

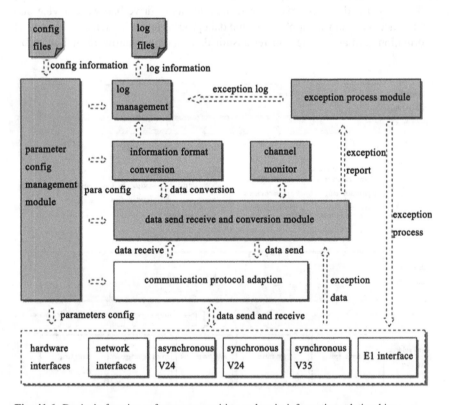

Fig. 41.6 Device's function software composition and main information relationships

The parameter configuration module is responsible for leading parameter configuration files to acquire various parameter and take advantages of 'system(device parameter), state configuration interface' to set parameters to software and hardware module, thus ensuring device's proper running. The data receiving and retransmitting module uses 'systematic data receive and transmit interface' to receive the external data provided by device and transmit data to external system, it also provides receipted data to message format conversion module to convert format, and it can receive the converted and processed data to transmit to external system due to parameter configuration, besides, it uses 'exception incident report interface' to grasp exception report data and send it to exception handling module, moreover, it provides received data to channel detection module, in order to evaluate channel quality. The exception handling module is in charge of taking over exception message report provided by data reception and retransmission module, according to the exception, it can response to relief system proper function and send it to log management module. The message format module can convert formats and provide converted data to data conversion and retransmission module to send externally. The log management can take the exception report from exception handling module and store them in log files according to prescribed format. The channel detection module is able to analyze and count processed data from data reception and transmission module, and generating performance evaluation report. The communication protocol is responsible for receiving and retransmitting data by prescribed protocol. The board or interface driver can achieve to detect hardware device, parameter configuration, and data reception and transmission.

Apart from this, the equipment can also provide management software, run on external PC. According to port configuration and device connection, it interactively implements the ability to manage parameter configuration, monitor data reception and transmission, and detect the status of channel quality and device operation, and so on.

41.4.2.3 Concurrent Execution Control Design

Because of various IO communication interfaces, the device can interact with the matched management software, it must possess a good ability to concurrent execution control design.

In order to dealing with concurrent execution control, device's bottom communication driver uses multi-thread design of threading communication interface, each interface deal with one thread. The upper application layer and communication driver can interact data by callback mechanism [7], when communication interface receives data, it report to upper layer by callback function, and the upper layer application process also reads data from communication driver by callback function. In order to truncate the execution time of callback function and avoid receiving data obstruct, the upper layer application process stores received data, which is read by callback function, in the queue of prearranged cache, then reads and processes the data from cache by processing thread. This scheme is a kind of 'producer–consumer' model: the producer is the procedure from the external data intriguing bottom communication driver to completing information process based on callback mechanism, the consumer is data processing thread that is provided by upper layer application process, and the connection between 'producer' and 'consumer' is data cache. The 'producer' stores data into cache and inform 'consumer' by semaphore, and the 'consumer' checks cache after execution of each data processing cycle, if there are still unprocessed data, it will continue to read and process until the cache is empty, then the 'consumer' will be hung up until occurring new signal light. According to this mechanism, the device can achieve to process the concurrent arrived data in a sequenced and serial way.

Data cache employs two-side ring like queue design, the bottom communication driver will always put newly received data to that end of ring like queue, when upper application process always uses data from top of queue, thus improving the efficiency and security of concurrent execution.

41.5 System Application

The equipment could satisfy the following demands:

1. Differentiated devices with various communication channel, protocols and message format can connect to and communicate with each other.
2. The efficient and transparent wide-range transmission of multisource message of various information systems in heterogeneous network environment.
3. Providing various transmission method as well as transparent and smooth shift control for user information system, expanding transmission channel, adding redundancy of transmission line, improving transmitting ability.
4. Expanding external node number of user information system, improving share degree of user information resources.

41.6 Conclusion

According to the multisource information wide-area adaptive and switching equipment in this passage, the governments' emergency command system can solve the problems of collecting and distributing multisource information, caused by various message formats, communication protocols and port types, and implement the transparent and highly efficient transmission of different kinds of user messages in heterogeneous network environment, meanwhile, collect and utilize all kinds of useful information and message channel extensively for government to organizing rescue and handling emergencies, improve the ability to command and provide flexible information exchange technique.

References

1. Zhang W, Yang L, Cheng S (2009) The router switch application cases tutorial. China Machine Press, Beijing (in Chinese)
2. Yang S-P, Zhang Y (2010) Hardware design and realization of miscellaneous ethernet switch simulation teaching system. J Beijing Technol Bus Univ (Nat Sci Edn) 28(2):50 (in Chinese)
3. Yao X, Wang H, Lu N, Deng W, Lou X (2006) Multimedia file format converting principle and implementation based on windows platform. Computer Systems & Applications, 3rd (in Chinese)
4. Comer D (2006) Internetworking with TCP/IP: principles, protocols, and architecture, 1st edn. Prentice Hall, New Delhi
5. Forouzan BA (2011) TCP/IP protocol suite, 4th edn. Tsinghua University Press, Beijing (in Chinese)
6. Volker (2012) Serial port [EB/OL]. http://en.wikipedia.org/wiki/Serial_port. Accessed 6 July 2012
7. Chen J (2003) Asynchronous message transfer-callback mechanism, [EB/OL]. http://www.ibm.com/developerworks/cn/linux/l-callback/. Accessed 1 Mar 2003 (in Chinese)

References

Part II
Computing Intelligence

Chapter 42
Solving Fuzzy Job Shop Scheduling Problem Based on Interval Number Theory

Chuan He, Dishan Qiu and Hao Guo

Abstract This article discusses the job shop scheduling problem with fuzzy processing time and fuzzy deadline by using interval number theory, which is an efficient method to denote imprecise parameter. Firstly, we convert the original problem to constraint satisfaction problem (CSP) with the assumption that agreement index (AI) is a main optimization objective. Then, the particle swarm optimization (PSO) is merged with genetic algorithm (GA), i.e., an improved particle swarm optimization (IPSO) being used to solve the problem. Finally, the effectiveness of this algorithm is verified by large number of experiments.

Keywords Fuzzy job shop · Scheduling · IPSO algorithm · Interval number

42.1 Introduction

Over the past decades, intensive researches have been conducted aiming at various applications of job shop scheduling problem (JSSP), for instance production planning and control. The typical assumption of JSSP is: there are a set of N jobs and a set of M machines or work nodes. Each job consists of a specific operation set which expresses a distinct processing route that has already been fixed and known in advance. All machines are available at time zero, and preemption is forbidden in work process. Most of all, the processing time of each operation has been given clearly. However, owing to the time-based-competition, the impact of

C. He (✉) · D. Qiu · H. Guo
Science and Technology on Information Systems Engineering Laboratory, Nation
University of defense technology, Changsha, China
e-mail: chuanhe@nudt.edu.cn

W. Lu et al. (eds.), *Proceedings of the 2012 International Conference on Information Technology and Software Engineering*, Lecture Notes in Electrical Engineering 211, DOI: 10.1007/978-3-642-34522-7_42, © Springer-Verlag Berlin Heidelberg 2013

uncertain factors cannot be ignored [1]. The conventional JSSP is not suitable in many cases due to various kinds of vagueness existing in real-world scheduling problems [2]. To meet the requirements of applications, many theses have applied the JSSP in uncertain environment, i.e., fuzzy job shop scheduling problem (FJSSP) [3].

The conventional optimization objectives of JSSP is to reduce tardiness (or Make span) or maximize the utilization of each machine [4, 5]. Generally speaking, many objectives are conflicting, which means it is impossible to optimize all the objectives. Bilkay and others [6] had ever proposed a delay cost concept during the decision-making to minimize the total penalty for the completion delay of the operations, which is one of the most important objectives. Sakawa and Kubota [7] provided a multi-objective FJSSP with fuzzy processing time, which is to maximize the agreement index (AI) and optimize the maximum fuzzy completion time.

In current research, stochastic method and fuzzy set theory are proposed to handle imprecise variables in FJSSP. Sakawa and Mori [8] have developed a novel concept of similarity among individuals, which is an effective solution to measure fuzzy parameters. Meanwhile, Lei [3], Canbolat and Gundogar [9] have established kinds of membership functions (e.g. triangle, trapezoid, and rectangle membership functions) to represent uncertain processing time. Furthermore, Wu and others [10] had applied the fuzzy ranking method and fuzzy procedure into FJSSP to compare the priority of fuzzy variables, which is an effective method to yield scheduling planning.

In this research, interval numbers are adopted to represent fuzzy parameters and a novel ranking method towards interval numbers is proposed. After that, we analyze the constraint conditions of FJJSP and convert it into constraint satisfaction problem with the maximum AI as an optimization objective. The IPSO algorithm is used to yield solutions and the experiment results have proved a good performance of the proposed algorithm.

42.2 Problems and Formulation

42.2.1 Interval Number Theory

Definition 1 [11] We use R to denote a real number set, and for any $a_i^-, a_i^+ \in R$ we refer to the close interval $a_i = \left[a_i^-, a_i^+\right]$ as an interval number when $a_i^- \leq a_i^+$. Especially in case of $a_i^- = a_i^+$, a_i is degenerated as a real number.

By Definition 1, for a discrete interval number a_i, the point values of a_i^- and a_i^+ must be known exactly. Generally speaking, the actual value of a_i is a real number in the close interval $[a_i^-, a_i^+]$, and subject to a special probability distribution (or a membership function).

Definition 2 Suppose X is the actual value of a_i, and x is a discrete variable in $\left[a_i^-, a_i^+\right]$. Then the probability of $X \leq x$ is $F_i(x) = \int_{a_i^-}^x f_i(X)dX$, where $F_i(x)$ and $f_i(x)$ are referred to as the probability distribution function and probability density function respectively.

At present, conventional ranking methods only suitable for interval numbers of special types, for instance, triangle interval number, uniform interval number, and trapezoid interval number [12]. Therefore, the definition of fuzzy binary ordering relation is proposed to determine the priority of any fuzzy variables.

Definition 3 Suppose '$\prec$', '$\succ$' and '$=$' are the fuzzy binary ordering relations for a nonempty interval number set I, and they are referred to as partial order in case the following conditions are satisfied:

(1) Reflexivity: $a_i = a_i, \forall a_i \in I$;
(2) Antisymmetry: If $a_j \succ a_i$, then $a_i \prec a_j, \forall a_i, a_j \in I$;
(3) Transitivity: If $a_i \prec a_j$ and $a_j \prec a_k$, then $a_i \prec a_k, \forall a_i, a_j, a_k \in I$.

Definition 4 If a_i and a_j have been related to probability density functions $f_i(x)$ and $f_j(x)$ respectively, the probability reliability of the partial order '$\succ$', '$\prec$' between a_i and a_j are:

$$P\left(a_i \succ a_j\right) = \iint\limits_{x \geq y} f_i(x)f_j(y)dxdy,$$

$$P\left(a_i \prec a_j\right) = \iint\limits_{x \leq y} f_i(x)f_j(y)dxdy. \tag{42.1}$$

Definition 5 For any two interval numbers a_i, a_j, if $P\left(a_i \succ a_j\right) > 0.5$, we set $a_i \succ a_j$; if $P(a_i \succ a_j) < 0.5$' we set $a_i \prec a_j$; if $P\left(a_i \succ a_j\right) = 0.5$, we set $a_i = a_j$.

The summation and maximum operations are used to solve the FJSSP, therefore, we define aggregate and maximization below:

Definition 6 For discrete interval numbers a_i and a_j, aggregate operation $\oplus$ is given as follows:

$$\tilde{a}_i \oplus \tilde{a}_j = \left[a_i^- + a_j^-, a_i^+ + a_j^+\right]. \tag{42.2}$$

42.2.2 Problem Discussion

The $n \times m$ FJSSP can be described as follows: The scheduling system consists of a job set $\{J_1, J_2, \ldots, J_n\}$ and a machine set $\{M_1, M_2, \ldots, M_m\}$. There are exist precedence constraints, therefore for each job J_i is composed of several operations $\{O_{i1}, O_{i2},..., O_{in}\}$. In the meantime, owing to the constraints of executable, each operation O_{ij} requires uninterrupted and exclusive special machine in its whole processing time. Additionally, deadline of each job has to be considered in the thesis. Other constraints in JSSP are also suitable for FJSSP. We summarize main notations being used in this thesis for your reference as follows:

n	The amount of jobs in scheduling system;
m	The amount of operations in scheduling system;
$T = [t_{ij}]_{n \times m}$	The processing time matrix, where t_{ij} denotes the processing time of O_{ij};
$W = [w_{ij}]_{n \times m}$	The execution machine matrix, where w_{ij} denotes processing machine of O_{ij};
$W = \{d_1, d_2,...,d_n\}$	The deadline vector, where d_i denotes the deadline of job_i;
$X = [x_{ij}]_{n \times m}$	The priority execution matrix, where x_{ij} is an integer in $[1, mn]$ to denote the priority execution ranking of O_{ij};
$TB = [tb_{ij}]_{n \times m}$	The beginning time matrix, where tb_{ij} denotes the beginning time of O_{ij};
$TE = [te_{ij}]_{n \times m}$	The end time matrix, where te_{ij} denotes the completion time of O_{ij};

The solution of FJSSP is the process of matching job tasks and machine resources being connected with time and space. We have confronted with two issues, i.e., assigning each operation to an appropriate machine and also ranking the sequence for all operations. There are several strict constraints must be followed:

(1) Each machine can only execute one job once at the same time, and the jobs assigned to the same machines should be executed in order;
(2) Each job has a unique priority of execution, i.e., any two jobs have different execution order;
(3) Only one operation of a job can be executed at one time and the times of executions should no more than one;
(4) All operations of a job should be executed in order, and the completion time is determined by the last operation;
(5) Each operation is assigned to the fixed machine in advance, and the working time is no less than the required time;
(6) Preemptive is not allowed; therefore the operation will be retained until completion.

Deadline is one of the most important factors and the scheduling planning must take it in consideration, namely, the operations must be completed in their due time. Therefore, the degree of agreement has been set up as an optimization objective in our thesis.

Definition 7 Agreement index (AI) is the expected value of those jobs which have been completed prior to deadline. It is approximated as follows:

$$AI = \sum_{i=1}^{n} \mu(te_{im}, d_i),$$

$$\mu(a_i, a_j) = \int_{a_i^-}^{a_i^+} f_i(x)F_j(x)\, dx.$$

(42.3)

where $f_i(x)$ is the probability density function of a_i; $F_i(x)$ is the probability distribution function of a_j.

Based on the constraints described previously, FJSSP can be converted into constraint satisfaction problem (CSP), and the CSP model is given as:

$$\text{Max } z = AI$$

$$s.t. \begin{cases} te_{ij} \prec tb_{ij}, & \text{if } (x_{ij} < x_{kj}) \wedge (w_{ij} = w_{kj}), \\ x_{ij} \neq x_{kl}, & \text{if } (i \neq k) \vee (j \neq l), \\ (te_{ij} \prec tb_{il}) \wedge (tb_{ij} \prec te_{il}), & \text{if } j < l, \\ x_{ij} < x_{il}, & \text{if } j < l, \\ te_{ij} \succ tb_{ij} \oplus t_{ij}, \\ (te_{ij} \prec tb_{il}) \vee (tb_{ij} \succ te_{il}), & \text{if } w_{ij} = w_{il}, \\ i, k \in [1, n], j, l \in [1, m]. \end{cases}$$

(42.4)

where AI is the optimization objective of CSP model, and Eq. (42.4) corresponds with the mentioned six constraints.

42.3 Algorithm Designing

42.3.1 The Architecture of Algorithm

The IPSO algorithm has been employed to find the solution of the present combinatorial optimization problem. The efficiency of IPSO algorithm is reflected in its fast search ability. However, the convergent speed depends substantially on initial swarm and tends to integrate into local optimization. Consequently, we hereby combine PSO with genetic algorithm (GA) and heuristic algorithms, and then a novel improved PSO (IPSO) is generated as Algorithm 1.

Algorithm 1: The pseudocode of IPSO

```
1: PSOn ← PSOPopulation; GlobalOpt ← NULL; PartOpt ← NULL;
2: HeuristicOperation(); /* initialize swarm by heuristic algorithm */
3: CalculateSwarmAI(); /* evaluate the AI of each particle in swarm */
4: While termination condition is not satisfied do
5:     Update(GlobalOpt, PartOpt); /* save the best individual of swarm */
6:     MoveOperation();
7:     CalculateSwarmAI();
8:     If particle swarm is evolve then /* the swarm is evolution */
9:         ChooseOperation();
10:        CrossoverOperation();
11:    Else
12:        MutationOperation();
13:    End if
14: End while
```

42.3.2 Heuristic Algorithm

To improve the search efficiency of scheduling method, three heuristic algorithms are proposed and applied to produce the initialized elitism particles.

42.3.2.1 EDF Algorithm

The earliest deadline first (EDF) algorithm mainly picks up each job according to corresponding deadline in non-descending order. In particular, since deadline is a fuzzy variable, we sort the jobs with the partial order of due time and arrange the scheduling prior sequence based on the ranking result.

42.3.2.2 SPTF/LPTF Algorithm

The shortest/longest processing time first (SPTF/LPTF) algorithm priority is used to calculate the process time of each job and select the job which consumes the minimum/maximum process time for executing object.

42.3.2.3 LNDF Algorithm

The largest nearby degree first (LNDF) algorithm will select the job which has the nearest processing time to its deadline. The degree of closeness for job_i can be defined as:

$$Var_i = \mu\left(\sum_{j=1}^{m} t_{ij}, d_i\right) \tag{42.5}$$

42.3.3 Algorithm Representation

In the thesis, we encode particles with job numbers, and the chromosome denotes the executing priority sequence of operations. For an $n \times m$ FJSSP, the $n \times m$ length chromosome is established. Each gene represents a special operation, which is expressed in a gene no more than m. The moving vector is designed to implement moving operation, and a chromosome is realized by ranking its moving vector in non-descending order. The chromosome is transferred into a decision matrix in encoding process, and then we can calculate the beginning time and completion time of each operation according to the processing route. The decoding method of particle is designed as Algorithm 2.

Algorithm 1 : The pseudocode of heuristic algorithm
1 : $\forall i \in [1, n], Idle_i \leftarrow 0; /*$ initialize idle times of each machine $*/$
2 : **For** $k \leftarrow 1$ to $n \times m$, find $x_{ij} = k$ **do**
3 : $g \leftarrow w_{ij}; /*$ acquire the node of machine$*/$
4 : **IF** $j = 1$ **then**/ $*$it is the first operation $*/$
5 : $tb_{ij} \leftarrow Idle_g; /*$ the beginning time $*/$
6 : **Else**
7 : $tb_{ij} \leftarrow \max\{Idle_g, te_{i(j-1)}\};$
8 : **End if**
9 : $te_{ij} \leftarrow tb_{ij} \oplus t_{ij}; /*$ the end time $*/$
10 : $Idle_g \leftarrow te_{ij};$
11 : **End for**

42.4 Computation Experiments

In this section, a simulation program is manipulated in Matlab2007 on a personal computer with Pentium IV 3.06GHZ CPU. To test the efficiency of IPSO, we compare it with GA and PSO in twelve benchmark problems (e.g. LA01, LA07,

Table 42.1 Summary results of the different algorithms

Problems	GA		PSO		IPSO	
	AI	CPU time (s)	AI	CPU time (s)	AI	CPU time (s)
LA01(10 × 5)	9.84	1.04	9.09	2.17	9.84	2.19
LA07(15 × 5)	14.10	2.59	13.39	4.10	14.10	4.21
LA11(20 × 5)	16.01	4.09	14.56	6.43	15.45	7.08
LA19(10 × 10)	9.72	1.05	9.24	2.01	9.72	2.12
LA21(15 × 10)	14.74	3.86	14.90	7.47	14.90	7.65
LA27(20 × 10)	11.79	3.57	11.22	5.26	12.08	5.33
YN1(20 × 20)	19.69	16.61	18.57	6.21	19.83	6.56
YN2(20 × 20)	16.21	16.55	15.94	6.12	16.28	6.52
YN3(20 × 20)	19.28	14.83	19.63	3.81	19.63	4.00
SWV06(20 × 10)	13.78	17.93	14.24	23.37	14.24	25.19
SWV08(20 × 15)	17.88	6.51	16.65	7.23	17.88	7.44

LA11, LA19, LA21, LA27, SWV06, SWV08, SWV10, YN1, YN2 and YN3) and the GA and PSO also adopt the same parameters in IPSO. Given the variables in twelve benchmark problems are certain values, we use triangle interval numbers and trapezoid interval numbers to realize the fuzzy disposition of processing time and deadline respectively.

From Table 42.1, we can find out obviously that the IPSO algorithm has eight solutions better than GA. There are four equations, and only one of them is worse than GA. At the same time, only three solutions of IPSO have the same values as PSO, but the CPU time is 5.25 % longer than PSO since the mutation operation are involved in the IPSO. This experiment shows that IPSO can avert early convergence and also search for more optimal solutions, which means high efficiency could be achieved.

42.5 Conclusion

In the thesis, FJSSP with fuzzy processing time and fuzzy deadline has been analyzed. We covert the FJSSP to CSP by defining fuzzy priority rules, in addition, IPSO algorithm is proposed to solve the problem. Heuristic algorithms are combined with the PSO algorithms to improve the search ability of the latter issue. The experiment results have proved the effectiveness of the methods being employed.

References

1. Chen D, Liu F, Luh PB (1997) Scheduling job shops with uncertainties. In: Proceedings of the 36th conference on decision and control PCDCDZ, San Diego pp 3556–3561
2. Mohammad SM, Pahlavani A (2009) A Fuzzy multi-objective programming for scheduling of weighted jobs on a single machine. Int J Adv Manuf Technol 45(1–2):122–139

3. Lei DM (2010) Solving fuzzy job shop scheduling problems using random key genetic algorithm. Int J Adv Manuf Technol 49(1–4):253–262

4. Mohammad SM, Parviz F (2007) Flexible job shop scheduling with tabu search algorithms. Int J Adv Manuf Technol 32(5–6):563–570

5. Chen JS (2006) Single-machine scheduling with flexible and periodic maintenance. J Oper Res Soc 57(6):703–710

6. Bilkay O, Anlagan O, Kilic SE (2004) Job shop scheduling using fuzzy logic. Int J Adv Manuf Technol 23(7–8):606–619

7. Sakawa M, Kubota R (2000) Fuzzy programming for multiobjective job shop scheduling with fuzzy processing time and fuzzy duedate through genetic algorithms. Eur J Oper Res 120(2):393–407

8. Sakawa M, Mori T (1999) An efficient genetic algorithm for job shop scheduling problems with fuzzy processing time and fuzzy due date. Comput Ind Eng 36(2):325–341

9. Canbolat YB, Gundogar E (2004) Fuzzy priority rule for job shop scheduling. J Intell Manuf 15(4):527–533

10. Wu CS, Li DC, Tsai TI (2006) Applying the fuzzy ranking method to the shifting bottleneck procedure to solve scheduling problems of uncertainty. Int J Adv Manuf Technol 31(1–2):98–106

11. Sengupta PTK (2000) On comparing interval number. Eur J Oper Res 127(1):28–43

12. Feng TL (2002) Fuzzy job-shop scheduling based on ranking level interval-valued fuzzy numbers. IEEE Trans Fuzzy Syst 10(4):510–522

Chapter 43
Tags Recommending Based on Social Graph

Benyang Xu and Hongming Zhu

Abstract As fast development of social network, UGC (user generated content) has played a very important role in "Web 2.0". However most of UGC is non-structured data, which is hard to be used by search engine or user recommending system. Social mining is the way to make UGC accessible. But UGC are trivial, noisy, sparse, causing social mining methods inefficient. In this paper, we propose a tag recommending approach based on social graph. Social graphic recommending can reduce mining depending on UGC, thus be able to generate high quality tags. Our most contribution is to combine social graph with LDA algorithm to find users' latent common interest, thus extract tags. We did experiment on real data crawled from Sina Weibo. The evaluation showed that our approach archived much better precision and recall than baseline methods.

Keywords Social mining · Tags recommendation · LDA · Social graph

43.1 Introduction

Social network sites (SNSs), such as Facebook, Twitter, Sina Weibo has attracted millions of users since introduced. SNSs is playing a very important role in "Web 2.0" with countless of UGC are generated. However, the lack of centralized

B. Xu (✉) · H. Zhu
School of Software Enginering, Tongji University Jading Campus, Caoan Rd 4800
201804 Shanghai, China
e-mail: xubenyang@gmail.com

H. Zhu
e-mail: hongming.zhu@gmail.com

W. Lu et al. (eds.), *Proceedings of the 2012 International Conference on Information*   403
Technology and Software Engineering, Lecture Notes in Electrical Engineering 211,
DOI: 10.1007/978-3-642-34522-7_43, © Springer-Verlag Berlin Heidelberg 2013

organizing and well-structured makes UGC become a very big challenge to mine the latent value in the contents. Make it hard to analyze the social networks [1].

To solve the problem, tagging is an effective way to encode interests and characters in the contents and users. Tags play a very important role in tag-based social interest discovery [2], making UGC accessible by search engines, recommending system and advertising systems. Social Tagging [3, 4] has emerged as an effective way to alleviate some of these challenges. Many methods and studies have focused on tag generation and recommending. There are two general approaches to generate tags for items:

1. *Social Tagging System* allows users to create and manage tags of social items. This idea is simple: users can select any meaningful tags or keywords to encode the characteristic attributes of items.
2. *Automatic Tag Recommendation* has been proposed in multiple studies [5–8]. Given an item, the task of automated tag recommendation is to suggest several most relevant tags to the contents using machine learning algorithms.

However, all these approaches have their own defects. For manually tags, since they are not restricted to a certain vocabulary, users can pick any tags they prefer to describe the resource. So these tags can be inconsistent, trivial, or false, duo to the users' personal terminology, depending too much on the users' choice [10]. For automatic-generated tags, most approaches assume the pre-existing tags or the text description of the items. As a result, we do not expect these approaches could still perform well while applied to social sites or systems, that does not built around tags and text description.

This paper aims to improve quality of tag recommendation, overcoming the problem of automatic tag recommending approaches, which depending too much on presenting of text and pre-existing tags. To archive this, we use LDA with social graph together to infer tags on a large scale of group. Social graph implies people are connected by common interest. People with common interest will group together automatically which is called clustering, we can see that in Fig. 43.1. Our approach try to learn user's common interest instead of analyze the basic text description of the user. This will be more accurate and precise to generate high quality tags.

The rest of this paper is organized as follow. In Sect. 43.2 we introduce LDA algorithm and then present our approach. Next we will show our experiments on real data from Sina Weibo and compare it with our baseline approaches in Sect. 43.3. In Sect. 43.4, we conclude this paper.

43.2 Tags Recommendation

In this section, we introduce LDA first, and then explain our approach how to extract tags by adapting LDA and follower graph together.

Fig. 43.1 Users are clustering with common interests on social sites

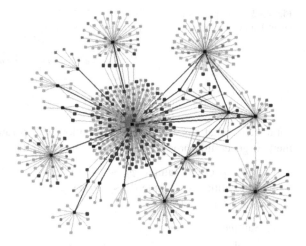

43.2.1 Latent Dirichlet Allocation

Latent Dirichlet Allocation is a probabilistic latent topic model introduced by Blei in 2003 [9]. The general idea of LDA is based on the assume that a person writing a document with certain topics in mind. When wring a document, first pick some topics for the document, and then pick words from vocabulary that with a certain probability about that topic. By repeating this step, a document finally is generated with a mixture of topics, representing by a collection of words. Here, LDA do not care the order of the words, so the probabilities of different words with different orders are treated the same, known as "Bag-of-Words" [11].

In this model, topic is the latent variable added. With topic, LDA helps to explain the similarity of words by grouping them into different topics. The modeling process of LDA can be described finding a mixture of topics for each resource. If there are T number of topics specified, and probability of the ith word w_i can be formalized as following:

$$p(w_i|d) = \sum_{j=1}^{z} p(w_i|z_j)p(z_j|d) \tag{43.1}$$

where w_i represents the ith word in vocabulary. d represents the document. z_j represents the latent topic for ith word. $P(w_i|d)$ is the probability of ith word in the given document d, with latent topic variable z_j. $P(t_i|z_j)$ is the probability of ith word in topic z_j. $p(z_j|d)$ is the probability of picking a word in topic in document d. LDA use latent topic variables to link words and documents. Figure 43.2 shows the plate graph representation of LDA.

The probability of latent topics $p(z|d)$ follows a multinomial distribution with parameter θ that has a Dirichlet distribution with parameter α as it prior. The probability of a word in a topic $p(w|z)$ follows a multinomial distribution with

Fig. 43.2 Plate graph of
latent Dirichlet allocation

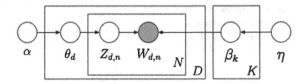

parameter φ that has a Dirichlet distribution with parameter β. With this notion, the text generation process can be explained as follow:

1. For all aspects k, sample $\varphi_k \sim Dir(\beta)$
2. For all entities e, sample $\theta_e \sim Dir(\alpha)$
3. For each term-slot in d_e

    a. Sample an aspect $z_j \sim Mult(\theta_e)$
    b. Sample a term $w_i = w \sim Mult(\varphi_{zj})$

Then parameter Θ and Φ can be learned by many infer methods, such as EM algorithm and Gibbs sampling method. Compared to EM, Gibbs sampling can guarantee a better convergence. Here we choose Gibbs sampling as the training method for LDA. It iterates multiple times over each word w_i in document, and samples a new topic j for the word based on the core probability method $P(z_j|t_i, t_{-i}, z_{-j})$, until the LDA model parameters converge.

$$P(z_j|t_i, t_{-i}, z_{-j}) \propto \frac{n_{j|e,-i} + \alpha}{|d_{e,-i}| + \alpha|K|} * \frac{n_{w|j,-i}}{n \cdot |j, -i|} \qquad (43.2)$$

where $n_{j|e,-i}$ is the number of times aspect j is observed for entity e, $n_{w|j,-i}$ is the number of times word w is sampled from aspect j, $|d_{e,-i}|$ is number of word occurs associated with e, and $n_{.|j,-i}$ is the total number of words generated from aspect j. After learning the Dirichlet distribution Θ and Φ. The posterior probabilities $p(w|z)$ and $p(z|d)$ can be figured out.

43.2.2 Tags Recommendation Based on Social Graph

In this paper, we focus on micro blogging service which is one-directional site, so the social graph is the follower graph. As we can see from Fig. 43.1, people on social sites are clustering with the same common interest [13]. And some other studies have focused on taking advantages of social networks [1, 12]. Our approach does not try to recommend tags on the text description of users, we take the latent advantage of social graph. The general purpose of a user willing to follow somebody is because they share the common interests. So our approach add "common interest" as the latent variable in social graph, and concretely involves two steps to generate tags for a user:

1. Learn users' interest probability distribution.
2. Recommend tags from interest probability distribution

43.2.2.1 Use LDA to Learn User's Interest

As we introduced in Sect. 43.2.1, LDA is a topic model method mostly used to do text categorizing or tag extraction on documents. With the same idea, we take LDA on social graph to infer the probability of user distribution. While LDA adopt "word > topic > document" pattern to generate documents. In social graph, we can treat each follower as "words" in LDA, treat common interests as "topics", treat the followed user as the "document". So the follower graph can be generated with pattern: "follower > common interest > followed-user". If there are M number of common interests are given, the probability of ith user ui follow the target user as follow:

$$P(u_i|u) = \sum_{j=1}^{M} P(u_i|I_j)P(I_j|u) \tag{43.3}$$

Similar with original LDA, u_i represents the ith user. $P(u_i|u)$ indicates the probability that u_i will follow u. I_j is the latent variable representing ith interest. $P(u_i|I_j)$ represents the probability that I_j is ui's interest. While $P(I_j|u)$ represents the probability that I_j is the followed user's interest. Then we can learn the user's interest distribution, with the same approach we introduced in Sect. 43.2.1.

43.2.2.2 From Interest to Tags

After learning the users' interest distribution, then we can use this to extract the actual tags of users, with representing with form of words. So the probability of word ti can the the tag of u can be formalized as follow:

$$P(t|u) = \sum_{j=1}^{M} P(t|I_j)P(I_j|u) \tag{43.4}$$

$$P(t|I_j) = \sum_{i=1}^{N} P(t|u_i)P(u_i|I_j) \tag{43.5}$$

where $p(t|u)$ is the probability of word t_j be the tag of user. $P(t|I_j)$ means the probability of word t_i is interest I_j. So we can break $P(t|I_j)$ into $P(t|u_i)$ and $P(u_i|I_j)$. Because $P(I_j|u)$ and $P(u_i|I_j)$ has learnt during process in Sect. 43.2.2.1, so these are known variables. Then what we must focus on is to learn $P(t|u_i)$, which is the probability of a word be tag of a user.

It seems a recursive routine that we have to figure out $p(t|u_i)$ first in order to get $p(t|u)$. However we can define $p(t|u_i)$ as the "basic tag" probability distribution of all the followers, which not including the followed user's probability $p(t|u)$. So $p(t|u_i)$ is absolute different with $p(t|u)$, we can other approaches to generate "basic tags" for followers. Then use above formulas get followed user's tag. And in this paper, we adopt method introduced in *Latent dirichlet allocation for tag recommendation* [8] to generate basic tags of followers.

43.3 Experiments

In this section, we will illustrate the efficacy of our approach with experiments on real data that crawled from Sina Weibo. It shows that our approach outperforms with all the baseline methods. We will discuss the experiment in detail.

43.3.1 Datasets

We chose data from Sina Weibo, which is the most popular micro blogging service in China. You can follow anyone you like, such as you favorite movies starts, singers. And also you can be followed by anyone found of you. In our experiments, we made a crawler to crawl through the network based on then open platform of Sina Weibo. In order to get the text associated with each user, we collected each user's tweets from April to October in 2012.

43.3.2 Baselines

We chose two classic tag recommendation methods: TFIDF and LDA-Tag Recommendation.

1. *TFIDF* is a simple method to obtain tags from text associated with entities. It treats such text as documents and the use TFIDF method to score all the words, then choose most rating words as the tags for entities.
2. *LDA-Tag Recommendation* treats each tweets of user as different documents [8]. Then use LDA to infer topics-user probabilities and words-topics probabilities. So tags can also be generated with most rating words.

43.3.3 Evaluation

In this experiment, we set 100 as the number of interests of user. The performance of different algorithms is evaluated by the average fraction of wins. There are two views to present the results: followers count and tweets count. From followers count view, we separated users into 8 groups with followers count [0–100], [100–1000], etc. This grouping is to test the performance of algorithm on different popularities. From tweets count view, we separated users into 7 groups with tweets

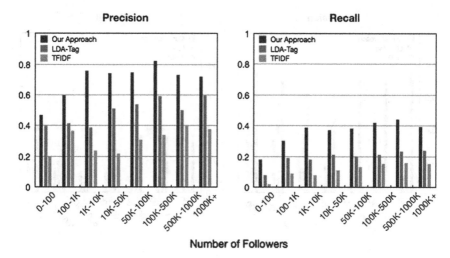

Fig. 43.3 Precision and recall grouped by number of followers

count [0–100], [100–200], etc. This grouping is to test the performance on different frequencies of user on social sites. Then we randomly select 50 users from each group as samples.

Then we showed our result to two annotators for each approach. The annotators are asked to pick the approach with the best tags-set. For each group, we report the average fraction of wins. Figure 43.3 present the precision and recall grouped by followers count for each approach. Figure 43.4 present the precision and recall grouped by tweets count.

It is clear that our approach outperforms all the baseline approaches as expected. However, there is a fall of precision when the count of followers is greater than 500 K in Fig. 43.3. Because it is not easy to determine the actual interest attracted to be followed for users with too much followers. Someone followed the user may just because his friends followed him or the user is so famous that to be followed without obvious interest in common. Figure 43.4 shows us that there is no much difference while taking our approach on different tweet count, while baseline approaches become more precise as the count increasing. It is because our approach is based on the social graph not the text of user, so it's much more stable when the quality of text itself is unpredictable.

43.4 Conclusion

In this paper, we investigate the use of Latent Dirichlet Allocation on social graph to recommend tags. After experimenting, it turns out that our approach outperformances TFIDF and LDA-Tag Recommendation approaches. Our approach not

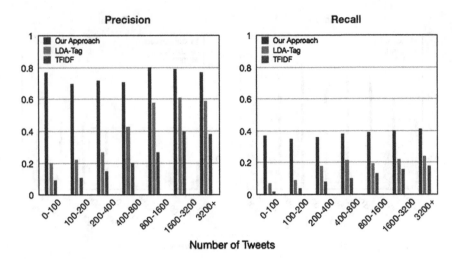

Fig. 43.4 Precision and recall grouped by number of tweets

only recommends more precise and appropriate tags for users, but also works more stably on the range of text qualities. The most contribution of this paper is to combine the latent value of social graph with LDA, archiving better tags recommending.

References

1. Scott J (1988) Social network analysis. Sociology 22:109. doi:10.1177/0038038588022001007
2. Li X, Guo L, Zhao YE (2008) Tag-based social interest discovery. In: Proceeding of the 17th international conference on World Wide Web (WWW'08), pp 675–684
3. Golder S, Huberman BA (2005) The structure of collaborative tagging systems. J Inf Sci 32(2):198–208
4. Marlow C, Naaman M, Boyd D, Davis M (2006) Ht06, taggingpaper, taxonomy, flickr, academic article, to read. In Proceedings of ACM HYPERTEXT'06
5. Basile P, Gendarmi D, Lanubile F, Semeraro G (2007) Recommending smart tags in a social bookmarking system. In: Bridging the gap between Semantic Web and Web 2.0 (SemNet 2007)
6. Matsuo Y, Ishizuka M (2002) Keyword extraction from a document using word co-occurrence statistical information. Trans Jpn Soc Artif Intell 17(3):217–223
7. Jäschke R, Marinho L, Hotho A, Schmidt-Thieme L, Stumme G (2007) Tag recommendations in folksonomies. In: Proceedings of PKDD 2007
8. Krestel R, Frakhauser P, Nejdl W (2009) Latent dirichlet allocation for tag recommendation. In: Proceedings of the third ACM conference on recommender systems, pp 61–68
9. Blei DM, Ng AY, Jordan MI (2003) Latent dirichlet allocation. J Mach Learn Res 3:993–1022
10. Golder S, Huberman BA (2006) Usage patterns of collaborative tagging systems. J Inf Sci 32(2):198–208

11. Wallach HM (2006) Topic modeling: beyond bag-of-words. In: Proceedings of the 23rd international conference on Machine learning (ICML '06), pp 977–984
12. Roth M, Ben-David A, Flysher G et al (2010) Suggesting friends using the implicit social graph. In: Proceedings of the 16th ACM SIGKDD international conference on knowledge discovery and data mining, pp 233–242
13. Viegas FB, Donath J (2004) Social network visualization: can we go beyond the graph? In: Proceedings of the computer supported collaborative work conference (CSCW'04)

Chapter 44
GPS Location History Data Mining and Anomalous Detection: The Scenario of Bar-Headed Geese Migration

Ze Luo, Yan Xiong, Baoping Yan, Diann J. Prosser
and John Y. Takekawa

Abstract It is important to discover common movement sequences and uncommon behaviors during the migration of wild birds. In this paper, we propose a new approach to analyze the GPS location history data of migratory birds. The stopover sites are first extracted from the location history data of birds, and their movement sequences are generated automatically. Then, a consistency calculation method is introduced for calculating the movement sequence consistency degrees among the birds. The common movement sequences and uncommon behaviors can be recognized on the basis of consistency. We conducted experiments on the data collected from bar-headed geese captured in the Qinghai Lake region. The experiment results indicate the correctness of our approach.

Keywords Location history mining · Anomalous detection · Bar-headed goose

---

An erratum to this chapter is available at 10.1007/978-3-642-34522-7_106.

Z. Luo (✉) · Y. Xiong · B. Yan
Computer Network Information Center, Chinese Academy of Sciences,
100190 Beijing, China
e-mail: luoze@cnic.cn

D. J. Prosser
U.S. Geological Survey, Patuxent Wildlife Research Center, Beltsville, MD 20705, USA
e-mail: dprosser@usgs.gov

J. Y. Takekawa
U.S. Geological Survey, Western Ecological Research Center, Vallejo, CA 94592, USA
e-mail: john_takekawa@usgs.gov

W. Lu et al. (eds.), *Proceedings of the 2012 International Conference on Information Technology and Software Engineering*, Lecture Notes in Electrical Engineering 211, DOI: 10.1007/978-3-642-34522-7_44, © Springer-Verlag Berlin Heidelberg 2013

44.1 Introduction

The global positioning system (GPS) has been adopted by ornithologists to track the migration of wild birds over a wide area [1, 2]. The resulting migration data is very meaningful for ornithologists to understand the behavior of migratory birds. Meanwhile, the rapid growth of location history data with a high spatial temporal resolution offers a new challenge for data analysis [3].

Consider movement data analysis of humans and wild birds; the former is mainly focused on providing location-based services, such as advertising and tourism routes recommendations [4, 5], whereas the latter is emphasized on discovering migration behaviors and patterns [6, 7], which would be significant for studying the spread of avian influenza, wildlife conservation and other ecological research [8, 9].

44.2 Preliminary

We first clarify several basic concepts used in this paper.

Point: A point is a GPS record, including a specific timestamp t, latitude lat and longitude lng.

Trajectory: A trajectory is a discrete point set generated by a bird during a certain period and ordered by the timestamps. The trajectory is denoted as $\{p_1, p_2, \cdots, p_n\}$, where $p_i \cdot t < p_{i+1} \cdot t$ for $1 \leq i < n$.

Stopover Site: A stopover site is a geographic region where a wild bird stayed over a time threshold th within a distance threshold dt. It can be characterized by the set of points $\{p_1, p_2, \cdots p_k\}$, in which $p_{k+1} \cdot t - p_1 \cdot t > th$ and for any $1 \leq i, j \leq k$, the distance between p_i and p_j less than dt. It has four attributes: latitude lat, longitude lng, arriving time $arvT$ and leaving time $levT$, where $lat = \frac{1}{k} \sum_{i=1}^{k} p_i \cdot lat, lng = \frac{1}{k} \sum_{i=1}^{k} p_i \cdot lng, arvT = p_1 \cdot t, levT = p_k \cdot t$.

44.3 Location History Data Processing

44.3.1 Stopover Site Extraction

Let AP denotes arrival point. DP denotes departure point. $dist(AP, DP)$ denotes the distance between any two points between AP and DP. $interval(AP, DP)$ denotes the interval between AP and DP. Take the movement trajectory obtained from the GPS location history database, the time interval threshold th and the distance threshold dt as input. We describe the algorithm for extracting stopover sites of an individual as follows:

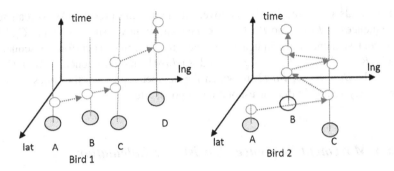

Fig. 44.1 Movement sequence representations

(1) Set the first point in the trajectory as *AP*, set the second point in the trajectory as *DP*, sequentially scan the trajectory

(2) If *dist*(*AP*, *DP*) is great than *dt*

   (a) If *interval*(*AP*, *DP*) is great than *th*, then we find a stopover site between *AP* and *DP*, assign to each stopover site a unique identifier, compute its center location, and record its arrival time and departure time. Set *DP* as new *AP* and the next point on the trajectory as *DP*, go to step (2)

   (b) If *interval*(*AP*, *DP*) is not great than *th*, the points between *AP* and *DP* cannot form a stopover site. Set *DP* as new *AP* and the next point on the trajectory as *DP*, go to step (2)

(3) If *dist*(*AP*, *DP*) is not great than *dt*

   (a) The points between *AP* and *DP* are in the same area, set the next point on the trajectory as new *DP* to extend the points belong the same area, go to (2)

(4) Sequentially scan the trajectory until to the last point.

After the extraction of each individual's stopover sites, we generate the minimum convex hull for each stopover site by Graham scan algorithm. We merge iteratively the stopover sites which have an overlap geographically until all of them are uncrossed. A unique identifier is assigned to each merged stopover site in the result set.

44.3.2 Movement Sequence Extraction

The movement sequence of each bird can be represented as a series of stopover sites and their consecutive occurrence number. Figure 44.1 demonstrates how a sequence is extracted from each individual's GPS data. In Fig. 44.1, the ellipse on the geographical plane denotes the stopover site, and the node with the green ring linked by a dashed line denotes an occurrence of a bird in the stopover site in different time intervals generated by the stopover site extraction process. As we can see, the sequences of *Bird*1 and *Bird*2 share the same stopover sites (*A*, *B* and *C*). The movement sequences are indicated by the green arrows. Therefore, a sequence $<A(1), B(1), C(2), D(2)>$ is generated for *Bird*1 and a sequence $<A(1), C(1), B(1), C(1), B(2)>$ for *Bird*2, in which the number represents the times the bird successively visited in the corresponding stopover site.

44.3.3 Movement Sequence Consistency Calculation

Movement sequence consistency represents the similarity between two movement sequences. It can be calculated as follows: First, extract consistent sequence between any two birds. Then calculate the consistency score by consistency calculation method. The final result can be represented as a $M \times M$ matrix s for M birds, in which the element $s[i][j]$ represents the consistency score between $Bird_i$ and $Bird_j$.

The consistent sequence of *Bird*1 and *Bird*2 is the subsequence with the maximal length shared by movement sequences of *Bird*1 and *Bird*2. For example, the consistent sequence shared by two movement sequences $<A(1) \rightarrow B(1) \rightarrow C(2) \rightarrow D(2)>$ and $<A(1) \rightarrow C(1) \rightarrow B(1) \rightarrow C(1) \rightarrow B(2)>$ is $<A(1) \rightarrow B(1) \rightarrow C(1)>$, as shown in Fig. 44.2.

For any two birds $b1$ and $b2$, the consistency calculation algorithm can be described as follows:

(1) Determine the maximal shared movement sequence. Scan sequentially the shorter sequence as outer loop and scan sequentially the longer sequence as inner loop to compare the identifier of stopover sites on the two trajectories.

   (a) If two identifiers are same, we find a shared stopover site and add to the shared movement sequence. The short sequence moves to next stopover site on the trajectory.
   (b) If two identifiers are different, the longer sequence moves to next stopover site on the trajectory. If the longer sequence reaches its end, the shorter sequence move to next stopover site and the longer sequence start from the last found shared stopover site again.

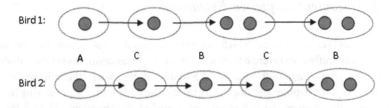

Fig. 44.2 Maximal shared movement sequence

(c) When the shorter sequence reaches its end, step (1) ends, return the maximal shared movement sequence.

(2) Calculate the Levenshtein distance between the maximal shared movement sequence and the two original movement sequences, denoted as $ld1$ and $ld2$.

(3) Calculate the consistency score of bird $b1$ and bird $b2$ as $s[b1][b2] = \left(1 - \frac{ld1}{|b1|}\right) \times 100$, while $s[b2][b1] = \left(1 - \frac{ld2}{|b2|}\right) \times 100$, where $|bi|$ denotes the length of bird bi movement sequence.

Finally, we compute the consistency score between any two birds and get the consistency score matrix.

44.4 Experimental Evaluation

44.4.1 Experiment Dataset

The data used in our work was collected from 29 bar-headed geese captured in the Qinghai Lake region, China. Fourteen of them were captured from March 25 to 31, 2007 and the others were captured from March 28–April 3, 2008. Each bird was equipped with a 45 g solar-powered portable transmitter terminal. Transmitter signals were received either by Argos data system or GPS.

The example GPS location history data is shown in Table 44.1. There are 231,424 total data records starting on March 25, 2007 and ending on June 4, 2009. If a bird had locations for longer than one year we divided that individual's data into one year segments, resulting in 33 migratory trajectories.

44.4.2 Experimental Results

The algorithms were implemented in MATLAB. According to the discussion with ornithologists, we set th as 30 days and dt as 80 km and obtain 10 stopover sites that are located either in India, China or Mongolia. The results are shown in Fig. 44.3, in which the red polygons indicate the convex hulls of stopover sites and the yellow balloons stand for the centers of the stopover sites. Each colored line represents a movement sequence and the width of it is proportional to the number of birds that follow it.

Table 44.1 GPS location history data record example

Animal	Record_id	Datatime	Latitude	Longitude	Lc94
BH07_67586	930784	2007-08-23 06:44:40	34.752	98.183	LG
BH07_67586	930785	2007-08-23 09:00:00	34.758	98.157	LG

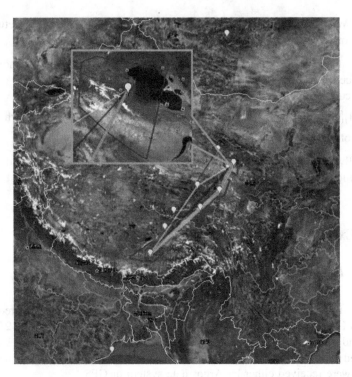

Fig. 44.3 Stopover sites and migration pathways

The consistency result generated by Gephi is shown in Fig. 44.4, in which each node stands for a bird, and an edge represents the existence of consistency between the two birds. Nodes with the same movement sequence form strongly connected sub-graphs, such as the green circular sub-graphs in the left and right side of Fig. 44.4. If a node is connected to a strongly connected sub-graph, it suggests that its movement sequence is a subsequence of other nodes in the sub-graph or in turn. If a node is isolated or has few connections to the others, it indicates that this bird's migration behavior differs from the others.

From Figs. 44.3 and 44.4, we can see that the majority of the 33 movement sequences have common characteristics. 24 birds have full-year data, in which 23 migrate southwestward from Qinghai Lake in summer. 58 % (14 out of 24) birds stayed in the Qinghai Lake during spring and summer, passed the Eling Lake and Zaling Lake or Golmud city, and move southwest to the Lhasa in Tibet for wintering. 8 % (2 of 24) birds have the same migration sequence but they stayed for wintering in Naqu, Tibet. 13 % (3 of 24) birds stayed in the Qinghai Lake for breeding, but moved to the Eling Lake and Zaling Lake for wintering. The remaining 20 % (5 of 24) birds didn't follow a common sequence. From above, we can find that most bar-headed geese breed in the Qinghai Lake, and wintered in east or north Tibet. The common movement sequence is breeding in the Qinghai

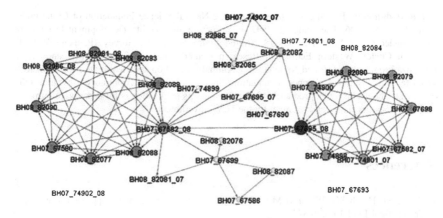

Fig. 44.4 Consistency results of 33 movement sequences

Lake, stopping over in the Eling Lake and Zaling Lake, and wintering in the Lhasa. The result is consistent with the observation and experiments in [6].

Five birds are isolated in Fig. 44.4. When examining their movement sequences, we find that their migration sequences are obviously different from the common sequence. Two birds (No. BH07_74902_08, No. BH08_82084) bred in Hala Lake in the northwest of the Qinghai Lake. One bird (No. BH07_67693) moved to the Arkhangai, Mongolia instead of staying in the Qinghai Lake in the 2007 breed season. One bird (No. BH08_82081) stayed in the Qinghai Lake in 2008, but moved to the Bhitarkanika National Forest Park in India for wintering. One bird (No. BH07_74901) bred in Qinghai Lake and went to the wintering site in the Lhasa in 2007, but in 2008 summer, it stayed in the Yushu County, Qinghai, and wintered in Naqu.

44.5 Conclusions and Future Work

In this paper, we propose a new approach provides the foundation discovery of migration behaviors and patterns of migratory birds by the processes of the stopover sites detection, movement sequence extraction, and sequence consistency calculation. The common sequence and uncommon behaviors can be discovered effectively by visualizing the results.

Our approach does not consider the absolute time factor which is important for analyzing the sequence similarity in some applications. Furthermore, the accuracy of the result is dependent on the choice of the time and distance threshold parameters. In the future, we intend to extend our analysis to other species in the Qinghai Lake to identify the cross migration paths among different species.

Acknowledgments Funding was provided by the Natural Science Foundation of China under Grant No. 90912006; The National R&D Infrastructure and Facility Development Program of China under Grant No.BSDN2009-18; United States Geological Survey (Patuxent Wildlife Research Center, Western Ecological Research Center, Alaska Science Center, and Avian Influenza Program); the United Nations FAO, Animal Production and Health Division, EMPRES Wildlife Unit; National Science Foundation Small Grants for Exploratory Research (No. 0713027). The use of trade, product, or firm names in this publication is for descriptive purposes only and does not imply endorsement by the U.S. Government.

References

1. Cooke SJ, Hinch SG, Wikelski M (2004) Biotelemetry: a mechanistic approach to ecology. Trends Ecol Evol 19:334–343
2. Tomkiewicz SM, Fuller MR et al (2010) Global positioning system and associated technologies in animal behavior and ecological research. Phil Trans R Soc B 365:2163–2176. doi:10.1098/rstb.2010.0090
3. Smouse PE, Focardi S, Moorcroft PR (2010) Stochastic modeling of animal movement. Phil Trans R Soc B 365:2201–2211
4. Li Q, Zheng Y et al (2008) Mining user similarity based on location history. In: GIS '08 Proceedings of the 16th ACM SIGSPATIAL international conference on advances in geographic information systems. doi: 10.1145/1463434.1463477
5. Zheng Y, Zhang L et al (2011) Recommending friends and locations based on individual location history. ACM Trans Web 5(1), Article 5
6. Tang M, Zhou Y et al (2011) Exploring the wild birds' migration data for the disease spread study of H5N1: A clustering and association approach. Knowl Inf Syst 27:227–251
7. Carneiro C, Alp A et al (2008) Advanced data mining method for discovering regions and trajectories of moving objects: "Ciconiaciconia"Scenario. In: Proceedings of AGILE, pp 201–224
8. Cui P, Luo Z et al (2011) Bird migration and risk for H5N1 transmission into Qinghai Lake, China. Vector-Borne Zoonotic Dis 11(2):567–576
9. Sabir B et al (2008) Seasonal movements and migration of Palla's Gulls La-rusIchthyaetus from Qinghai Lake, China. Forktail 24:100–107

Chapter 45
Wave-Front Correction Based on Improved Particle Swarm Optimization

Huizhen Yang and Yaoqiu Li

Abstract Particle Swarm Optimization (PSO) is faster than Genetic Algorithm while GA obtains global convergence more easily than PSO in application of wave-front correction. Basic PSO is improved by using of selection, crossover, and mutation operator of GA. An adaptive optics (AO) system based on improved PSO (IPSO) is simulated to correct the distorted wave-front. The system is composed of a 61-element deformable mirror (DM) and an imaging system. IPSO is used to generate control signals for actuators of DM according to the information of imaging system. We investigate the effectiveness and the convergence speed of IPSO using two different distorted wave-fronts by comparing PSO, GA and IPSO. Simulation results show IPSO obtains the rapid convergence of PSO and the global convergence of GA, which justifies the method we offer in application of wave-front correction.

Keywords Particle swarm optimization · Genetic algorithm · Adaptive optics system · Wave-front correction

45.1 Introduction

More and more researchers on control of adaptive optics (AO) system without a wave-front sensor are attaching importance to model-free optimization technique because of its simpleness in system architecture and adaptability to the complicated conditions. A common strategy in AO system is to consider the performance

H. Yang (✉) · Y. Li
Department of Electronic and Engineering, Huaihai Institute of Technology,
No. 59, Cangwu Road, Xinpu District, Lianyungang, Jiangsu Province, China
e-mail: yanghz526@126.com

W. Lu et al. (eds.), *Proceedings of the 2012 International Conference on Information Technology and Software Engineering*, Lecture Notes in Electrical Engineering 211, DOI: 10.1007/978-3-642-34522-7_45, © Springer-Verlag Berlin Heidelberg 2013

metric as a function of the control parameters and then use certain optimization algorithm to improve the performance metric [1]. Some stochastic algorithms, such as Stochastic Parallel Gradient Descent (SPGD) [2, 3], Genetic Algorithm (GA) [4], Simulated Annealing (SA) [5] and Algorithm of Pattern Extraction (Alopex) [6] are often used as the control algorithm of AO system recently. Particle Swarm Optimization (PSO) is a population-based on heuristic global optimization technology introduced by Kennedy and Eberhart in [7]. It has been used extensively in science, engineering, and commercial applications. Generally, PSO is faster than GA while GA obtains global convergence more easily than PSO in application of wave-front correction. In this paper, we use improved PSO (IPSO) as the control algorithm to generate driving signals for actuators of DM. The effectiveness and convergence speed of AO system based on IPSO will be verified through two different distorted wave-fronts. The AO system model, IPSO and simulative results are presented and discussed as follows.

45.2 AO System Based on Improved PSO

45.2.1 The Model of AO System

The AO system model is shown in Fig. 45.1. The AO system mainly includes a 61-element DM to correct the wave-front aberrations $\varphi(r)$, an imaging system to record the focal spot, a performance metric analyzer to calculate the system performance metric J from the data of focal spot, and the stochastic parallel optimization algorithm to produce control signals $u = \{u_1, u_2, \ldots, u_{61}\}$ for the 61-element DM according to changes of the performance metric J, where $u(r)$ is the compensation phase, $\phi(r) = \varphi(r) + u(r)$ is the residual phase, $\varphi(r)$ and $u(r)$ are continuous functions ($r = \{x, y\}$ is a vector in the plane orthogonal to the optical axes). In this paper, we use IPSO as the control algorithm to drive the actuators of DM and the performance metric J is the fitness function in PSO.

Fig. 45.1 Block diagram of simulation

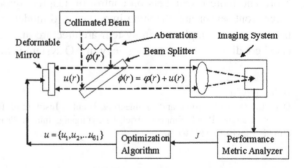

Fig. 45.2 Distribution of actuators location of 61-element deformable mirror

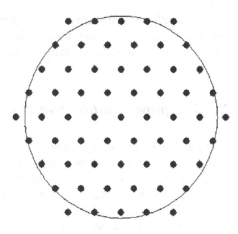

45.2.2 Specifications of 61-Element DM and Considerations for the Performance Metric (Fitness Function)

The phase compensation $u(r)$, introduced by the deformable mirror, can be combined linearly with response functions of actuators:

$$u(r) = \sum_{j=1}^{61} u_j S_j(r) \tag{45.1}$$

where u_j is the control signal and $S_j(r)$ is the response function of the $j'th$ actuator. On the basis of real measurements, we know the response function of 61-element deformable mirror actuators is Gaussian distribution approximately [8]:

$$S_j(r) = S_j(x,y) = \exp\left\{\ln\omega\left[\sqrt{(x-x_j)^2+(y-y_j)^2}/d\right]^\alpha\right\} \tag{45.2}$$

where (x_j, y_j) is the location of the $j'th$ actuator, ω is the coupling value between actuators and is set to 0.08, d is the distance between actuators, and α is the Gaussian index and is set to 2. Figure 45.2 gives the location distribution of 61-element DM actuators. The circled line in the figure denotes the effective aperture and the layout of all actuators is triangular.

We use the Mean Radius (MR) as the system performance metric optimized by the control algorithms. The calculation formula of MR is below:

$$MR = \frac{\int |r - \bar{r}|I(r)d^2(r)}{\int I(r)d^2(r)}, \quad \bar{r} = \frac{\int rI(r)d^2(r)}{\int I(r)d^2r} \tag{45.3}$$

where $\bar{r}$ is the intensity distribution centroid. MR can be easily measured either by a single photo-detector with a special mask attached to it or by post-processing a matrix detector output. This measure appears to be the most attractive one for it gives straightforward mathematical meaning to the idea of energy spread, it is nonparametric, and it accounts for the whole intensity distribution. The smaller the MR value, the smaller the aberration level of wave-front.

45.2.3 Improved Particle Swarm Optimization

Stochastic optimization algorithms have become important for control of AO system without a wave-front sensor in recent years. The control parameters, driving signals of actuators of DM, of AO system are multi-dimensional and the number of dimension usually depends on the number of actuators of DM. The dimension of particle is 61 in our simulation model.

In a PSO process, a swarm of particles, each of which representing a potential solution to an optimization problem, navigates through the search space. The particles are initially distributed randomly over the search space with a random velocity and the goal is to converge to the global optimum of a function or a system. Each particle keeps track of its position in the search space and its best solution so far achieved. This is the personal best value (the so-called *pbest* in [7]) and the PSO process also keeps track of the global best solution so far achieved by the swarm with its particle index (the so called *gbest* in [7]). GA is a kind of evolutionary computation, which represents a class of stochastic search and optimization algorithms that use a Darwinian evolutionary model, adopts the concept of survival of the fittest in evolution to find the best solution to some multivariable problem, and includes mainly three kinds of operation in every generation: selection, crossover, and mutation. GA works with a population of candidate solutions and randomly alters the solutions over a sequence of generations according to evolutionary operations of competitive selection, crossover, and mutation.

Generally, PSO is faster than GA while GA obtains global convergence more easily than PSO in application of wave-front correction. In this paper, we improve basic PSO by using of selection, crossover, and mutation operator of GA and call this kind of PSO as IPSO. The conceptual diagram of IPSO is shown in Fig. 45.3. Particles are processed by selection, crossover and mutation operation before the velocitys and the positions are updated, which maybe increase computation of algorithm but can speed the algorithm.

Fig. 45.3 The improved PSO conceptual diagram

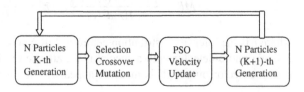

45.3 Simulation Results and Analysis

45.3.1 Descriptions of Wave-Front Aberrations to be Corrected

To investigate the effectiveness and the convergence speed of AO system based on IPSO, we use two different distorted wave-fronts. Distorted wave-fronts are generated using the method proposed by Roddier, which makes use of a Zernike expansion of randomly weighted Karhunen–Loeve functions, to simulate atmospherically distorted wave-fronts [9]. The wave-fronts to be corrected are given in Figs. 45.4a and 45.6a respectively. To estimate correction capability, we also record another metrics, Strehl Ratio (SR), which is defined as the ratio of the maximum intensities of the distorted point spread function and the diffraction-limited point spread function. In optical application the SR has a value between 0 and 1 where a SR of 1 would be a perfect wave-front. Additionally, the standard deviation (SD) is used to evaluate the convergence of AO system, calculated as follows:

$$SD = \frac{<(J - <J>)^2>^{1/2}}{<J>} \tag{45.4}$$

We perform the adaptation process over the two distorted wave-fronts 100 repetitions and results are averaged. The averaged fitness function, the corresponding averaged SR and the SD of the fitness function are the recorded simulation results.

45.3.2 Correction of the First Randomly Generated Distorted Wave-Front

Restoration results of the first randomly generated distorted wave-front are given in Figs. 45.4 and 45.6. Figure 45.4 shows adaptive curves of the averaged fitness

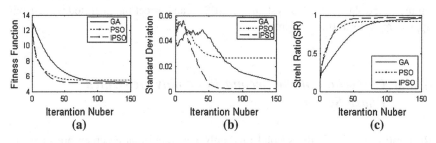

Fig. 45.4 Averaged curve of fitness function (**a**), the corresponding standard deviation curve (**b**) and SR curves (**c**) during 100 iterations by GA, PSO and IPSO respectively

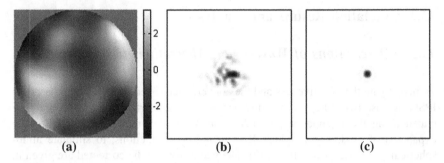

Fig. 45.5 The first generated randomly wave-front (**a**) (the scale of colorbar is *rad*), imaging before correction (**b**) and after correction (**c**)

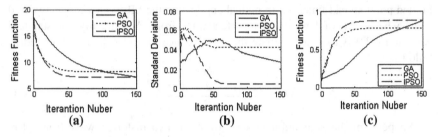

Fig. 45.6 Averaged curve of fitness function (**a**), the corresponding standard deviation curve (**b**) and SR curve (**c**) during 100 iterations by GA, PSO and IPSO respectively

function, the SD of fitness function and the averaged SR by GA, PSO and IPSO respectively.

From Fig. 45.4a, c, we can see the fitness function decreases from 13 to 5.1 and the SR increases from 0.18 to 0.97 after about 150 generations by GA and IPSO while PSO converges to 5.5 and 0.91. PSO and IPSO obviously converge more rapidly than GA. Figure 45.4b indicates the AO system with IPSO has better convergence property than GA and PSO because the standard deviation of 100 repetitions from different stochastic starts by IPSO is much smaller than that by PSO and GA. The original wave-front is given in Fig. 45.5a and imaging of original wave-front and residual wave-front by IPSO are given in Fig. 45.5b, c. Figure 45.5c shows the AO system with IPSO can correct the distorted wave-front approximate to diffraction limit.

45.3.3 Correction of the Second Randomly Generated Phase Screen

Restoration results of the second randomly generated phase screen are given in Figs. 45.6 and 45.7. Figure 45.6 shows adaptive curves of the averaged fitness

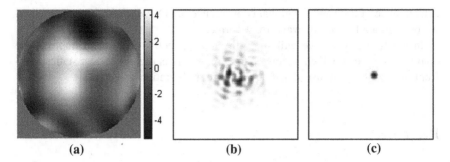

Fig. 45.7 The second generated randomly wave-front (**a**) (the scale of colorbar is *rad*), imaging before correction (**b**) and after correction (**c**)

function, the averaged SR and the SD of fitness function by GA, PSO and IPSO respectively.

From Fig. 45.6a and c, we can see the fitness function decreases from 18.4 to 7.1 and the SR increases from 0.09 to 0.88 after about 150 generations by GA and IPSO while PSO converges to 8.2 and 0.77. PSO and IPSO obviously converge more rapidly than GA. Convergence property of Fig. 45.6 is similar to that of Fig. 45.4. The original wave-front is given in Fig. 45.7a and the imaging of original wave-front and residual wave-front are given in Fig. 45.7b, c.

Noticeably, the aberration level of the second phase screen is bigger than the first phase screen from Fig. 45.7a, b. Comparing values of SR in Figs. 45.4c and 45.6c, we can find the correction capability decrease as the aberration level increases. One reason is that searching the optimum may become difficult, the other reason maybe attribute to the deformable capability of DM.

45.4 Conclusions and Future Work

Stochastic optimization algorithms have become important for control of AO system without a wave-front sensor in recent years. The control parameters, driving signals of actuators of DM, of AO system are multi-dimensional and the number of dimension usually depends on the number of actuators of DM. Particle Swarm Optimization (PSO) is faster than Genetic Algorithm while GA obtains global convergence more easily than PSO in application of wave-front correction. Basic PSO is improved by using of selection, crossover, and mutation operator of GA. An adaptive optics (AO) system is simulated to correct the distorted wave-front. The system is composed of a 61-element deformable mirror (DM) and an imaging system. IPSO is used to generate control signals for actuators of DM according to the information of imaging system. We investigate the effectiveness and the convergence speed of IPSO using two different distorted wave-fronts by comparing PSO, GA and IPSO. Simulation results show IPSO combines the rapid convergence of PSO and the global convergence of GA, which justifies the method we offer in application of wave-front correction.

In the future work, we will study the more effective method to improve the convergence speed, which guarantee that it not only is used to correct static wave-front aberrations, but also dynamic wave-front aberrations.

References

1. Muller RA, Buffington A (1974) Real-time correction of atmospherically degraded telescope images through image sharpening. J Opt Am A 64:1200–1210
2. Weyrauch T, Vorontsov MA, Gary W et al (2011) Experimental demonstration of coherent beam combining over a 7 km propagation path. Opt Let 36(22):4455–4457
3. Yang HZ, Li XY, Gong CL et al (2009) Restoration of turbulence-degraded extended object using the stochastic parallel gradient descent algorithm: numerical simulation. Opt Express 17(5):3052–3062
4. Yang P, Ao MW, Liu Y, Xu B, Jiang WH (2007) Intracavity transverse modes controlled by a genetic algorithm based on zernike mode coefficients. Opt Express 15(25):17051–17062
5. Zommer S, Ribak EN, Lipson SG et al (2006) Simulated annealing in ocular adaptive optics. Opt Lett 31(7):1–3
6. Yang HZ, Li XY (2011) Comparison of several stochastic parallel optimization algorithms for adaptive optics system without a wavefront sensor. Opt Laser Technol 43(3):630–635
7. Kennedy J, Eberhart RC (1995) Particle swarm optimization. In: Proceeding of IEEE international conference on neural networks IV, IEEE, pp 1942–1948
8. Jiang WH, Ling N, Rao XJ (1991) Fitting capability of deformable mirror. In: Proceedings of SPIE 1542, pp 130–137
9. Roddier N (1990) Atmospheric wavefront simulation using Zernike polynomials. Opt Eng 9(10):1174–1180

Chapter 46
Data Scheduling Strategy in P2P VoD System Based on Adaptive Genetic Algorithm

Ya Zhou, Yunping Dai, Guimin Huang, Pingshan Liu
and Xuanfeng Li

Abstract In Peer-to-Peer (P2P) Video-on-Demand (VoD) systems, data scheduling strategy is critical to make the most use of nodes in P2P network, and it also helps optimizing the time consuming of data scheduling and startup delay as well as the utilization of neighbors' uplink bandwidth. But it is a challenging task to design an efficiently scheduling strategy. On one hand, the scheduling strategy should balance the need of segments between one requesting node and the whole system; On the other hand, the problem of scheduling segment transmission is a NP-hard problem due to the dynamic characteristics of P2P network. To resolve those problems we propose a scheduling strategy based on adaptive genetic algorithm (AGA). The scheduling strategy is based on segments' emergency degree, supply and demand ratio and regional position to select the needed segments to schedule in a scheduling cycle. Then through the AGA to select the suitable supply nodes to transmit segments. Experiment results show that our proposed algorithm outperforms the RANDOM and Hill-climbing in terms of reducing the time consuming of each data scheduling, startup delay, and making the most use of the network uplink bandwidth.

Keywords Peer-to-peer · Video-on-demand · Data scheduling · Adaptive genetic algorithm · Segment selection

Y. Zhou (✉) · Y. Dai (✉) · G. Huang · P. Liu · X. Li
Research Center on Data Science and Social Computing, Guilin University of Electronic Technology, No 1, Jinji Road, Qixing Area, Guilin City, Guang Xi, China
e-mail: ccyzhou@guet.edu.cn

Y. Dai
e-mail: 610300039@qq.com

W. Lu et al. (eds.), *Proceedings of the 2012 International Conference on Information Technology and Software Engineering*, Lecture Notes in Electrical Engineering 211, DOI: 10.1007/978-3-642-34522-7_46, © Springer-Verlag Berlin Heidelberg 2013

46.1 Introduction

In recent years, Peer-to-Peer (P2P) technology has become increasingly popular, and leads to the rapid development of P2P VoD systems which achieve some noteworthy breakthroughs. Nowadays there are some successful commercial applications, such as: PPLive, QQLive and QVOD.

In P2P VoD systems, a video is usually partitioned into segments with equal size. The segments are transmitted from multiple source nodes to a requesting node. Then, the requesting node caches the requested segments and advertises those segments to the system. All those operations are determined by the scheduling strategy which is run on the requesting node. In addition, the data scheduling also imposes time constraints on segment transmission. If segments arrive at the requesting node after the playback deadline, the segments are essentially useless. So data scheduling is a main factor that impacts the user perceived visual quality and also may cause the playback failure [1].

In order to reduce the time consuming of each data scheduling and the startup delay, improve the utilization of neighbors' uplink bandwidth and make most use of the network nodes, we design an efficient data scheduling strategy for P2P VoD systems in this paper. The strategy is based on segments' emergency degree, supply and demand ratio and regional position to select the needed segments to schedule in a scheduling cycle, then through the adaptive genetic algorithm to select the suitable supply nodes to transmit segments.

The remaining parts of this paper are structured as follows. In Sect. 46.2, we discuss the related works. In Sect. 46.3, we introduce the system architecture and the data scheduling processes. Then, we focus on describing implementation of AGA scheduling in Sect. 46.4. In Sect. 46.5, several experiments are done to evaluate the performance of AGA scheduling strategy. Finally, Sect. 46.6 gives the conclusion and future work.

46.2 Related Works

Nowadays, a lot of data scheduling strategies have been proposed and used in many commercial P2P streaming systems. A measurement study on PPLive reports that users suffer from long startup delays and playback lags, and suggests that better segment scheduling algorithms are required [1]. Sequential scheduling [2], Random scheduling [3], and Rarest First scheduling [4] are most used, but they do not consider the demand of other peers, which need to use the segments that are received from source nodes and advertise to the network, so the network nodes can not be most utilized. The author of [5] considers the supply and demand of other peers and greatly improves the throughput of the network, but he does not consider the service performance of each peer, so this strategy can not guarantee the quality of service. The author of [6] uses the Genetic Algorithm in data scheduling and it greatly reduces the time of scheduling, but the author assumes that each resource node has all of the data segments, so it is not suitable for the actual system. Also the algorithm easily leads to local optimum and premature convergence, so it may not find the optimal solution. The author of [7] converts the original data scheduling problem to a problem of finding a maximum match on the corresponding bipartite graph, and then assigns data packets to neighbor nodes according to the maximum match. However, the computational complexity of this method is not suitable for real-time systems.

The authors of [8] propose a weighted round-robin algorithm based on source nodes' bandwidth. In their algorithm, the number of segments assigned to each source node is proportional to its bandwidth. In other words, source nodes with higher bandwidth will be assigned more segments than those with lower ones. The authors of [9] propose to assign each segment to the source node that will deliver it the earliest. But all these algorithms do not provide any performance guarantees on user perceived visual quality and may not perform well in on-demand streaming systems [10].

46.3 Description of Data Scheduling Problem

46.3.1 System Architecture

The architecture of the P2P VOD system designed by us is shown in Fig. 46.1. We apply a tracker server and a media server. The media server contains the entire videos which are divided into segments. Each segment is of equal size and has a unique segment ID. Every peer will contact the tracker sever to join the P2P network, the tracker stores the IP address of all peers in the system and the information of super peers when they join in the system. Each super peer is always online and has a public network address. And it manages the information of peers which have the specific media resources. The normal peer which has a globally unique identifier can play the media, buffer the data segments and publish media segments.

When a new peer joins in the system, it works as follows:

(1) The peer registers to the tracker server, and sends a message including IP address and port to tracker server. The peer also informs the tracker server of resources the peer itself caches, and then the tracker sever returns some super peers which manage these resources.
(2) The peer notifies the cache resource information to the super peers returned by tracker server.
(3) When one peer requests a media to play, the peer first sends the request to the tracker server to ask that which super peers manage the media resource. Then the tracker server returns a set of super peers.

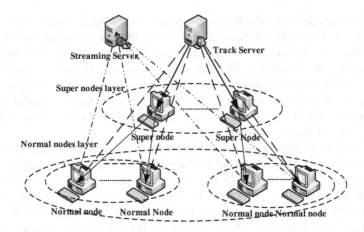

Fig. 46.1 System architecture of P2P VoD

(4) The requesting peer queries the super peers about the media resource, and then the super peers return the peers who have the media resource, and the peers which are in the same or nearby regional location with requesting peers have priority to be return.

(5) The requesting peer establishes a connection with each peer returned by super peers. Peers connected with the requesting peer are called neighbors. Then the requesting peer exchanges the buffer map (BM) information with its neighbors and sends request to its neighbors.

(6) After receiving the data segments from its neighbors, the requesting peer caches and plays the media. The requesting peer informs the super peers that it has the resource segments when it receives the first data segment of this resource.

46.3.2 Evaluation Model of Source Node Selection

The aim of using scheduling algorithm is to schedule the special data segments as little time as possible and make best use of resource nodes in network. Sending time of each data segment can be described in Eq. (46.1):

$$T_{i,j} = SSize_i / EBw_{j,k} \qquad (46.1)$$

where $SSize_i$ is the size of each segment. Since the network delay and the burden of each node should be considered, so we introduce a modification function to modify the time consuming of data scheduling. The modification function of scheduling cycle m is shown as follows:

$$T_m = \sum_{j=1}^{n} \left(TL_j + \left(S_{i,j} - 1 \right) TW_j \right) \qquad (46.2)$$

In the formula (46.2), n is the number of source nodes taking part in this scheduling cycle; TL_j is the delay time from source node j to requesting node. $S_{i,j}$ is the number of data segments those are scheduled in the node j in i cycle; TW_j is the waiting time of one scheduling request in queue on the peer j.

Therefore, we set $TW_{a_{i,j}}^m$ as the time used to schedule the data segments in cycle m, which equals the sending time of each data segment, $T_{i,j}$, plus the modification value, T_m, the equation is expressed as follows:

$$T_{a_{i,j}}^m = \sum_{i=1}^{n} T_{i,j} + T_m \qquad (46.3)$$

The object of using scheduling algorithm is to find out the minimum $T_{a_{i,j}}^m$, but the availability of the data segments in the network and the bandwidth of each peer are uncertain, so it is essentially an NP complete problem [11]. In the next section, the AGA is used to solve this problem.

46.4 Implementation of Adaptive Genetic Algorithm

46.4.1 Segment Selection

In our P2P VoD system, videos are divided into segments with equal size. To describe the play order, every segment is assigned a number (start from zero). Each peer has all or part of the media content and maintains a BM shown in Fig. 46.2.

The BM is used to represent the available information of segments. The BM is consisted of some bits, and each bit is corresponding with a segment. If BM $[i][j] = 1$, it means that peer i has the segment j; otherwise, peer i has no segment j. The requesting node exchanges BM and playback point with its neighbor peers, so it knows which data segments are available and needed by neighbor peers. In the strategy of our paper, an emergency window and a foreseeing window are defined in Fig. 46.2. They start from the playback point. The size of foreseeing window is larger than the size of emergency window. On the one hand, in order to guarantee the quality of service, the data segments which are not cached in emergency window must be scheduled immediately. On the other hand, in order to meet the needs of other neighbor peers and take most use of the peers in the network, the non-cached data segments behind the emergency window are selected to be scheduled according to their ratio of supply and demand. The requesting peer uses a value function to evaluate the usability value of each non-cache data segments behind the emergency window, the data segment with a higher usability value means that it is more useful for the other neighbors. A certain number of pre-fetching data segments are selected

Fig. 46.2 Information of
buffer map

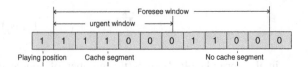

according to the usability value. The neighbors' foreseeing window is defined to predict whether the data segments are needed by neighbors in the near future. We assume that a data segment will be soon scheduled by a neighbor peer if the segment is in the neighbor's foreseeing window. The need degree of each data segment can be calculated by formula (46.4).

$$D_i = \sum_{j=1}^{n-m} C_{i,j} + \sum_{j=n-m+1}^{n} \lambda C_{i,j}, (0 < \lambda < 1) \qquad (46.4)$$

In formula (46.4), the value $C_{i,j}$ represents how urgently the segment i is for the neighbor j. If the segment is not in neighbor's foreseeing window, the value $C_{i,j}$ is zero. $\sum_{j=1}^{n-m} C_{i,j}$ is the sum of urgency value of data segment i needed by the neighbors which are in the same regional location with the requesting peer, $\sum_{j=n-m+1}^{n} \lambda C_{i,j}$ is the sum of urgency value of data segment i needed by the neighbors which are not in the same regional location with the requesting peer. The usability value, V_i of each segment can be calculated by requesting peer using formula (46.5). R_i is the number of replicas of data segment i among its neighbors.

$$V_i = D_i/R_i \qquad (46.5)$$

Finally, we sort the data segments according to their usability value and select some segments with higher usability value to be pre-scheduled.

46.4.2 AGA Scheduling

In the previous section, we describe which data segments should be choose to be scheduled. In this section, we will introduce the AGA based on the mechanism of natural selection and genetics to determine which peer is selected to transmit the special data segment.

- **A. Chromosome Encodings**

The first step to apply AGA to data scheduling problem in P2P VOD system is encoding. We design an encoding for our problem as follows.

First, we sort the data segments which are scheduled in this cycle according to their index number from small to large in the queue and count the BM information of neighbors, so we get a two-dimensional array which is not equal in length to store information and shown in formula (46.6).

$$A_{(n,s_n)} = \Big\{ \big(a_{(1,1)}, a_{(1,2)}\}...a_{(1,s_1)}\big)\big(a_{(2,1)}, a_{(2,2)}...a_{(2,s_2)}\big),$$

$$...\big(a_{(i,1)}, a_{(i,2)}...a_{(i,j)}...a_{(i,s_2)}\big)...\big(a_{(n,1)}, a_{(n,2)}...a_{(n,s_n)}\big) \Big\} \qquad (46.6)$$

Here, i denotes the serial number of data blocks in the queue; j represents the index of the owner of the ith data segment in the queue. S_i represents the total owners number of the ith data segment in the queue. $a_{i,j}$ represents the jth owner of the ith segment in the queue. For example, $a_{(3,8)} = 5$ represents that the peer with ID number 5 is the 8th owner of the 3th data segment in queue. As the scheduling order in one cycle is not important, therefore, the owner index of each data segment in the two-dimensional array is encoded, and the encoded sequence corresponds to the order of data segments in the queue. For example, if a peer wants to schedule data segments from 1 to 6, and the Chromosome encoding is $\{1, 3, 4, 3, 6, 7\}$ which represents the segment 1 is scheduled from owner $a_{(1,1)}$, the segment 2 is scheduled from owner $a_{(2,3)}$ and it is similarly to remain segments.

- **B. Population Initialization**

After selecting the data segments to be scheduled in one cycle, we sort them based on the sequence of each data segment. Then we select the owner index of each data segment randomly to spawn N_{pop} chromosomes by the way discussed in section A.

- **C. Fitness Function and Evaluation**

The AGA does not use external information during the search process, and only use the fitness value of each individual in the population. The fitness value is evaluated by a fitness function which we discussed in the Sect. 46.3. The associated fitness value is the total time that is spent on scheduling all segments in one cycle.

- **D. Selection Methods**

In this paper, we adopt the elite selection strategy. The idea of the strategy is to copy the best individual (called elite individual) of the group directly to the next generation during the evolutionary process.

- **E. Crossover Operation**

The main purpose of crossover operation in data scheduling is to generate a new scheduling coding individual by combining features of two selected scheduling coding parents. In this operation, pairs of scheduling coding individuals are selected at random from the current population and then single point crossover operation is done according to the crossover ratio. What plays a central role is the crossover ratio p_c. Here the adaptive p_c is adopted. Formula (46.7) is used to calculate the crossover ratio.

Fig. 46.3 Example of crossover operation

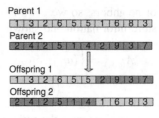

Fig. 46.4 Example of mutation operation

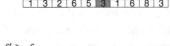

$$p_c = \begin{cases} 0.9 - \dfrac{0.3\left(f'-f_{avg}\right)}{f_{max}-f_{avg}}, & f' \geq f_{avg} \\ 0.9, & f' < f_{avg} \end{cases} \qquad (46.7)$$

Here f_{avg} is the average fitness value of each generation; f' is the maximum fitness value of the two individuals which will cross with each other. f_{max} is the biggest fitness value in each generation of data scheduling. A crossover operation example is shown in Fig. 46.3.

- **F. Mutation Operation**

Just like evolution in nature, chromosomes also should take a mutation operation after the crossover operation. Its main function is to ensure that the AGA has local random search capabilities, maintains the diversity of population and prevents the emergence of non-mature convergence. Here the adaptive mutation ratio p_m is used and shown as follows:

$$p_m = \begin{cases} 0.1 - \dfrac{0.09(f_{max}-f)}{f_{max}-f_{avg}}, & f \geq f_{avg} \\ 0.1, & f < f_{avg} \end{cases} \qquad (46.8)$$

Here f represents the value of individual fitness. A mutation operation is shown in Fig. 46.4.

- **G. Stopping Condition**

The evolution stops if the total number of iterations reaches a predefined number of iterations [12]. In this paper, we define the number 50.

46.5 Simulation and Evaluation

We use simulations to evaluate the performance of scheduling strategy. We assume that each resource node has a certain number of neighbors, and each neighbor node has some segments of data. The requesting peer starts to watch

Fig. 46.5 Time consuming
of data scheduling

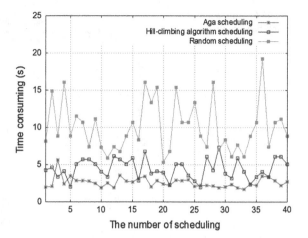

video from the beginning. We set the delay time from the neighbor nodes to the requesting node ranging from 30 to 100 ms randomly. The uplink bandwidth of neighbor nodes allocated to the requesting node is randomly set between 30 and 1,000 Kbps. The waiting time of processing the next request is randomly set between 50 and 100 ms. The simulation does not consider the segment loss. The media file is divided into segments, and the size of each segment is 32 KB. We assume that the total number of segments of the media resource is 2,000, we schedule 50 segments data in each scheduling cycle, so the total cycles of scheduling is 40.

In the experiment of the time consuming of data scheduling, the scheduling strategy based on AGA not only considers the priority of the data segments to be selected in one scheduling cycle, but also allows for the factors such as capacity and bandwidth of the neighbor nodes. In the experiment, we respectively use three kinds of scheduling strategy which are AGA, hill-climbing algorithm scheduling and random scheduling algorithm to generate three scheduling time sets. The results are shown as Fig. 46.5. The vertical axis represents the number of scheduling cycle, the vertical axis represents the time consuming of each scheduling cycle.

From the Fig. 46.5, we can see that the time consuming of data scheduling of random scheduling algorithm is longer and has a wide fluctuation in scale, while the time consuming of data scheduling of scheduling strategy based on AGA is significantly shorter and scheduling time has a very small fluctuation. The hill-climbing algorithm scheduling is better than random scheduling, but it is a local search algorithm, so the result is not better than the AGA.

In addition, we simulate the utilization of the uplink bandwidth. The utilization of the uplink bandwidth is the total bandwidth that the source nodes assign to the requesting node to transmit data content. The utilization of uplink bandwidth is continuously calculated with the number of neighbor nodes increasing. The result is shown in Fig. 46.6, Where the horizontal axis represents the number of neighbor

Fig. 46.6 Utilization of
uplink bandwidth

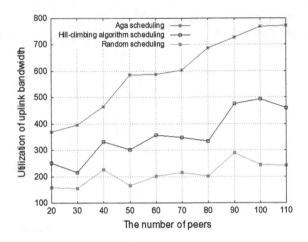

Fig. 46.7 Comparison of
startup delay

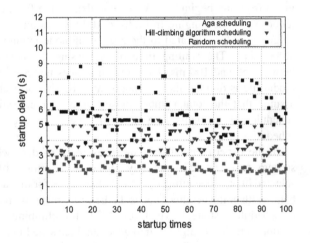

nodes, the vertical axis indicates the size of uplink bandwidth that utilized by
requesting peer.

Figure 46.6 shows that the actual uplink bandwidth utilization raise greatly with
the number of neighbor nodes increasing in the scheduling strategy based on AGA,
so the AGA scheduling can quickly increase the number of the data segment
backup in network and improve the performance of system. While the actual
utilization of uplink bandwidth increase slowly with the number of neighbor nodes
increasing in random scheduling strategy and hill-climbing algorithm scheduling
strategy.

Figure 46.7 shows the effect of three scheduling algorithms on the startup
delay. Here the startup delay is defined as duration of requesting peer accepting
first 30 segments. We all took startup operations for 100 times under three data
scheduling strategy respectively and recorded the delay time every time. The

horizontal axis represents the startup times, the vertical axis indicates the startup delay.

From the Fig. 46.7, we can see that the startup delay of random scheduling algorithm is longer and has a wide fluctuation in scale, while the startup delay of scheduling strategy based on AGA floats up and down in value 2.5 s. It is the best of three scheduling algorithms. Since the hill-climbing algorithm scheduling is a local search algorithm, so the startup delay is longer than the AGA.

46.6 Conclusions and Future Work

In this paper, a scheduling strategy based on AGA is proposed. The scheduling strategy not only considers the segments' urgency and the ratio of segments' supply and demand, but also takes account of the factor of regional location to select the segments which is needed to schedule in a scheduling cycle. After the scheduling strategy selected the needed segments to schedule, it utilizes the AGA to select the suitable source nodes to transmit the selected segments. Finally, the simulation experiments are done to show that our scheduling strategy can reduce the time consuming of each data scheduling and startup delay, make the most use of the network uplink bandwidth, increase the number of data segments backup in the network rapidly and improve the service performance of the system greatly.

In our future work, we will study more details about AGA scheduling strategy in actual systems and how to retransmit the data segments in the case of segments loss.

Acknowledgements This work was supported by the National Natural Science Foundation of China (No. 61063038), the Foundation of Key Laboratory of Guangxi Trusted Software (No. kx201114), and the Foundation of Key Laboratory of Guangxi Wireless Broadband Communication and Signal Processing (No. 11108).

References

1. Hei X, liang C, liang J, Liu Y, Ross K (2007) A measurement study of a large-scale P2P IPTV system. IEEE Trans Multimed 9(3):405–414
2. Zhang X, Liu J, Li B, Yum TSP (2005) CoolStreaming/DONet: a data-driven overlay network for live media streaming. IEEE INFO COM, Miami
3. Venkataraman V, Yoshida K (2006) Chunkyspread: heterogeneous unstructured tree-based peer-to-peer multicast. IEEE International Conference on Network Protocols(ICNP)
4. Locher T (2007) Push-to-pull peer-to-peer live streaming. 21st international symposium on distributed computing (DISC). pp 388–402
5. Fang S-C (2008) A supply-and-demand based scheme for peer-to-Peer video-on-demand system
6. Huang G, Li C, Zhou Y, Bin C (2011) Data scheduling strategy in P2P VoD system based on genetic algorithm. 2011 third international conference on multimedia information networking and security

7. Wu J, Peng Y, Liu F (2011) Transmission scheduling in data-driven peer-to-peer streaming towards optimal throughput. 2011 IEEE international conference on networking, architecture, and storage
8. Agarwal V, Rejaie R (2005) Adaptive multi-source streaming in heterogeneous peer-to-peer networks. SPIE/ACM multimedia computing and networking, San Jose, pp 13–15
9. Kowalski G, Hefeeda M (2009) Empirical analysis of multi-sender segment transmission algorithms in peer-to-peer streaming. IEEE international symposium multimedia (ISM'09), San Diego, CA, pp 243–250
10. Annapureddy S, Guha S, Gkantsidis C, Rodriguez P (2007) Is high-quality VoD feasible using P2P swarming? World Wide Web Conference (www'07), Banff, AB, Canada, pp 903–912
11. Brucker P, Jurisch B, Sievers B (1994) A branch and bound algorithm for job-shop scheduling problem. DiscrAppl Math 49:105–127
12. Srinivas M, Patnaik LM (1994) Genetic algorithms: a survey. IEEE Comput 27:617–626

Chapter 47
Detecting Items in Text Using Large-Scale Knowledge Base

Dianhui Hou, Jiuming Huang, Yunyi Xu, Siyu Jiang and Bin Zhou

Abstract Varieties of text mining applications utilize knowledge bases to understand the semantic of documents. Current knowledge bases are open and very large. Detecting what items in the knowledge base exist in the documents is the first step of the utilization. Existing multiple string matching algorithms cannot be applied to the item detection because of the long lengthes of knowledge items and the large scales of knowledge bases. This paper proposes a novel approach SW-Tree by improving the classical AC-Trie algorithm to achieve higher performance. The approach takes advantage of the specific goal of knowledge item detection and the data features of knowledge bases. Experiments on real data set show that the proposed approach is significantly faster than the baseline approach.

Keywords AC-Trie · Item detection · Knowledge base

47.1 Introduction

Detecting knowledge items in the texts by knowledge bases plays an important role in the applications of knowledge bases. Knowledge bases such as FreeBase [1], DBpedia [2], TrueKnowledge [3], etc. are more and more mature nowadays.

D. Hou (✉) · J. Huang · S. Jiang
PLA Unit 73111, Xiamen, China
e-mail: 34795631@qq.com

Y. Xu
Xiamen Tongrong Software Technology Co., Ltd, Xiamen, China
e-mail: xuyunyi@xmtongrong.com

B. Zhou
College of Computer, National University of Defense Technology, Changsha, China
e-mail: binzhou@nudt.edu.cn

W. Lu et al. (eds.), *Proceedings of the 2012 International Conference on Information Technology and Software Engineering*, Lecture Notes in Electrical Engineering 211, DOI: 10.1007/978-3-642-34522-7_47, © Springer-Verlag Berlin Heidelberg 2013

Applications including named entity recognition, information extraction and document understanding take advantage of the knowledge bases. One of the key processes for applying knowledge base to various applications is to detect what knowledge exists in the target text. Usually, a knowledge base is represented by a set of strings and the relationship among them. Thus, the first step of knowledge detection is to know what substrings in the input text belong to the knowledge base. Given a knowledge base and an input text, the goal of this paper is to search all meaningful matches with a higher performance than traditional technologies.

However, the knowledge bases are rapidly growing and the size is very large. Meanwhile, we focus on free-form input text. Thus, the existing single string matching technologies such as Boyer-Moore [4], Knuth-Morris-Pratt [5] and Rabin-Karp [6] are not suitable because they should check every item (pattern) in the knowledge bases, although they can handle single item in a linear complexity.

Multiple string matching algorithms such as Aho-Corasick (also named AC-Trie) [7], Wu-Manber [8] and variants are more effective for our goal. Considering a knowledge base as a dictionary which is a set of strings, the technologies check all items in dictionary simultaneously for the input text. The worst complexities are within the size of all substrings of the input text. Especially, the AC-Trie scans the text only once. That is, it doesn't need to backtrack to previous characters in the text stream.

In the scenario of knowledge items detection, we only need to extract the substring which matches exactly on the word level. That is, items in the knowledge base which exist in the input text with either non-blank suffix or prefix are not what we want. For instance, say "men's clothing" is an item in the knowledge base and the document contains "women's clothing", considering the document contains "men's clothing" makes no sense or even wrong. Thus, our goal is different from the traditional multiple pattern matching.

In this paper, we firstly develop a naive approach based on the AC-Trie for knowledge items detection, and then propose a novel approach SW-Tree which prunes the building and searching processes of AC-Trie through taking advantage of the features of knowledge bases. The proposed approach is faster than the naive approach theoretically. Finally, we test the baseline algorithm and our approach on a real data set to validate the effect of our approach.

The rest of the paper is organized as follows. Section 47.2 formally defines some preliminaries and the task of the paper. Section 47.3 introduces the main idea of traditional AC-Trie and a naive approach based on the AC-Trie. Section 47.4 gives the theoretical deduction of our pruning approach and then presents our algorithms. Section 47.5 presents the experimental results.

47.2 Problem Definition

Knowledge item detection is to retrieve all items which exist both in the knowledge base and the input text. We formally define the concepts and notions of knowledge base and the task in this section.

We discuss the problem under the practice that the size of alphabet is finite. A word is a sequence of symbols in the alphabet, and an item is a sequence of words separated by some special symbols. For convenience, we use to represent the separating symbol between words. As mentioned, a knowledge base is a set of items and a document is a sequence of words. Formally, above concepts are defined as follows.

Definition 1 Let $\sum$ be the alphabet, and $|\sum|$ is the size of $\sum$, which is finite. Define a word $w = a_1 \triangle a_2 \triangle \ldots \triangle a_k$ where $k = |w|$ is the length of the word and $a_i \in \sum, 1 \leq i \leq k$. Similarly, an item e is a sequence of words over W where W be the set of words, and $|e| = \sum_{i=1}^{k} + k - 1$ where k is the word number of e. A document is also a sequence of words with a longer length usually. Let E be the item set, a knowledge base $B \in E^*$, where E^* E is the power set of E.

Our goal is to search the input document to find out all items in the knowledge base. Definition 2 defines the task formally.

Definition 2 (Knowledge Item Detection): Given a knowledge base B and a document d, the task of item detection is to find out the item set $S = \{e | suffix(e) = \Delta \wedge prefix(e) = \Delta, e \in B \cup d\}$. Where $suffix(e)$ and $prefix(e)$ mean the suffix symbol and prefix symbol of string e respectively.

The problem is that both the size of knowledge base and the number of documents are very large. With limited memory and computing capability, checking all combinations of words in documents and items in knowledge base is unacceptable. We use the AC-Trie to implement a naive approach for the task in the linear complexity and use it as our baseline approach.

47.3 Naive Approach Based on AC-Trie

The AC-Trie checks what strings in knowledge base exist in the given document simultaneously. The complexity of the algorithm is linear in the length of the items plus the length of the given document plus the number of output matches. Note that it finds out all substrings of the document which are also items of the knowledge base. However, many substrings are not cared in our scenario (we will illuminate this in the following).

The AC-Trie algorithm firstly constructs a tree data structure accompanied by a finite state machine over a finite set of strings (the knowledge base). And then for an input text (a document), it scans the text with walking on the tree to find potential substring and utilize the finite state machine to avoid backtracking.

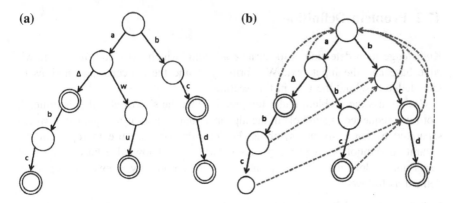

Fig. 47.1 Examples of traditional Trie and AC-Trie: **a** An example of traditional Trie **b** An example of AC-Trie

Essentially, the data structure of AC-Trie is a prefix tree with additional fail-pointer on the nodes. A trie (prefix tree) is an order data structure. The root node is associated with the empty string. Each link between nodes is associated with a symbol. For each node, the path from root node to it represents a string.

As an example, Fig. 47.1a shows the trie for string set of "a", "abc", "abc", "bcd". The nodes whose corresponding strings belong to the knowledge base are assigned with an output label. In our examples, we label an additional cycle on each output node. The children of a parent node are sorted in the alphabet order. For a single item x, such a tree can look up if it contains x as fast as $O(|x|)$. However, for a set of items, say E, searching will cost as high as $O\left(\sum_{e \in E} |e|\right)$. The AC-Trie adds an additional link (named fail-pointer) to each node. A fail-pointer links from the node representing a string (e.g. abc) to the node corresponding to the longest proper suffix (e.g. bc if it exists, else c if that exists, else the root). Figure 47.1b illustrates above examples. Recalling each output node corresponds to an item, for an output node x, all of the items which are substrings of x can be enumerated by following the fail-pointer of x. It then uses the trie at runtime, moving along the input and keeping the longest match, using the suffix links to make sure that computation is linear. For every node that is in the knowledge base and every link along the knowledge base suffix linked list, an output is generated. When meets a node which doesn't contain matching symbol, it doesn't need to backtrack to previous symbols in the string but jump to the node pointed by fail-point in the tree which corresponds to the longest substring-item of the checking item. Therefore, the AC-Trie only needs to scan the input document one time basically. We only concern the exact matched items in the documents on the word level. That is, items in the knowledge base which exist in the document with either non-separating-symbol suffix or prefix are not what we want. For instance, say "men's clothing" is an item in the knowledge base, if the document contains "women's clothing", considering the document contains "men's clothing" makes no sense or even wrong.

As a result, we can simply filter the output strings of AC-Trie to get the correct results. That is, for each output string, we check if its prefix symbol and suffix symbol are blanks or not to determine whether it is an item. Obviously, say the output string set is C, the additional filter process takes additional $|C|$ times scanning the document beyond the basic AC-Trie algorithm.

47.4 Simultaneous Word Tree

In this section, we propose our improved approach (namely SW-Tree) to detect knowledge items. SW-Tree prunes the building process and searching process of AC-Trie algorithm by Theorem 1 (as described in Sect. 4.2). Associated by a new tree structure, our building and searching algorithms work more efficient than the naive approach.

47.4.1 Properties of Large-Scale Knowledge Base

Knowledge bases such as FreeBase, are different from traditional dictionaries in many aspects. As we know, the sizes of traditional dictionaries are not very large and the lengths of strings in the dictionaries basically don't exceed three words. However, knowledge bases contain many long items, and the sizes of them are very large and increasing.

Property 1 (Large scale of Knowledge Bases) The knowledge bases are in large scale. That is, the numbers of knowledge bases' items are very large. See the schema of FreeBase as an example.

Beside the large scale property of knowledge base, knowledge bases usually contain many long strings. The suffix relationship among items in the knowledge base occurs frequently. If we construct an AC-Trie for a knowledge base, due to the large scale property and the frequent suffix relationship, the movements along fail-pointers will occur very frequently.

Property 2 (Density of Knowledge Bases' AC-Trie) The AC-Trie for a knowledge base contains a lot of fail-pointers which don't point to the root node.

47.4.2 AC-Trie Improved SW-Tree

The scale and sparse properties of knowledge base demand faster building speed and searching speed. In terms of properties discussed above, we propose the

Theorem 1 for pruning the processes of AC-Trie. And then develop the algorithms based on the theorem.

For convenience, the root node of the AC-Trie is denoted by root, the separate symbols between words by letting $u \xrightarrow{child} v$, be that node v is a child node of node u, $u \xrightarrow{child} v$ be that the fail-pointer of u points to node v. Furthermore, define the symbol function and the string function as follows:

Definition 3 (Symbol Function) Let x be a node, define function $\sigma(x)$ as the symbol of the link connecting x and the parent node of x.

Definition 4 (String Function) Let x, z be nodes and $x \xrightarrow{fail} z$, define function $str(x; z)$ as the occurrences of strings which are retrieved by walking from x to z.

Theorem 1 *Let x, y, z be nodes in the AC-Trie, $x \xrightarrow{child} y$ and $x \xrightarrow{fail} z$, if $\sigma(x) \neq \Delta \wedge z = root$, say $y \xrightarrow{fail} u$, then str(y, u) should be filtered for word-level matched.*

Proof As defined, a given document is a sequence of symbols, say $\{c_1, c_2, \ldots, c_k\}$, where $c_i \in \sum, 1 \leq i \leq k$. The AC-Trie algorithm walks on the Trie tree according to the input sequence. That is, each specific symbol in the sequence, say c_i, is mapped to a unique node in the Trie. Suppose the algorithm moves to node y when checks the position i, and the depth of y is $d(y)$, then the string corresponding to y is the symbol sequence of path from root node to y. The algorithm moves from y to u only when there is not any child of y can match $c_i + 1$. And as discussed, the corresponding string of u is the longest suffix string for the corresponding string of y. That is, the corresponding string of u is associated by $\{c_{i-d(u)+1}, \ldots, c_i\}$ in the document. If $z = root$, in terms of the definition of fail-pointer, u must be a child of root. Thus, the corresponding string of u is $\{c_i\}$.

If the succeed checking doesn't jump to fail-pointer node, the potential matched item must be the substring starts at position i. Because of $\sigma(x) \neq \Delta$ and $\sigma(x) = c_{i-1}, c_{i-1} \leq \Delta$. Thus, the prefix symbol of potential matched item, which is $\{c_i, \ldots\}$ is not a separate symbol. In this case, the potential matched item should be filtered in our scenario.

On the other hand, if a succeed symbol, say c_j, where $j > i$, doesn't exist on the children of the node corresponding to c_{j-1}, the algorithm will jump to the fail-pointer of c_j. Thus, the start position of potential matched substring is greater than i because the parent node of u is root node. Thus, $str(y, u)$ is not an item in the knowledge base.■

Algorithm 1 Building process of SW-Tree

Input: The built basic prefix tree
Output: The corresponding SW-Tree

    $nodes \leftarrow \emptyset$

    for $nd \in children(root)$ **do**

        FailToRoot(nd , $newNodes$ **)**

    end for

    while $nodes \neq \emptyset$ **do**

        $newNodes \leftarrow \emptyset$

        for $nd \in nodes$ **do**

            if $\sigma(nd.parent) \neq_\triangle \wedge nd.parent.fail = root$ **then**

                FailToRoot(nd , $newNodes$ **)**

                Continue

            end if

            $r \leftarrow nd.parent.fail$

            while $r \neq \varepsilon \wedge$ (r contains transition with $\sigma(nd)$) **do**

                $r \leftarrow r.fail$

            end while

            if $nd = \varepsilon$ **then** $nd.fail \leftarrow root$

                else $nd.fail \leftarrow x$, $x \in children(r) \wedge \sigma(x) = \sigma(nd)$

            Add children(nd) to $newNodes$

        end for

        $nodes \leftarrow newNodes$

    end while

Procedure FailToRoot($node$, $nlist$ **)**

    $node.fail \leftarrow root$

    for $nd \in children(node)$ **do**

        if $\sigma(nd) =_\triangle$ **then** Add nd to $nlist$

        else FailToRoot(nd , $nlist$ **)**

    end for

We prune the traditional AC-Trie algorithm based on Theorem 1 and properties mentioned above to achieve a higher performance. The Property 2 implies that the fail-pointers of many nodes point to root node. According to Theorem 1, for the nodes whose corresponding symbols are not separates and fail-pointer point to root node, we can change the fail-pointers of their children to point to root node, while on traditional Trie they point to the children of root node which have the same symbols. Note that, this change is iterative. Taking Fig. 47.2 as an example, since node 8 satisfies the theorem conditions, we change its fail-pointer to point to the root node. And then node 9 which is the child of node 8 will satisfy the theorem conditions too, so we also change its fail-pointer to the root node. Algorithm 1 shows the building process of our approach and Algorithm 2 shows the searching process. As a reference, we use function $children(x)$ to represent the child set of node x and define ε as null pointer.

Algorithm 2 Searching process of SW-Tree

Input: A document d and a built SW-Tree
Output: Matched item set R
　　$ptr \leftarrow \varepsilon$
　while $index < length(d)$ **do**
　　　if $ptr \neq \varepsilon \wedge ptr.fail = root \wedge \sigma(ptr) \neq_\triangle$ **then**
　　　　while $d[index] \neq_\triangle$ **do**
　　　　　$index \leftarrow index + 1$
　　　　end while
　　　end if
　　　$t \leftarrow \varepsilon$
　　　while $t = \varepsilon$ **do**
　　　　$t \leftarrow x,\ x \in children(ptr) \wedge \sigma(x) = d[index]$
　　　　if $ptr = root$ **then Break**
　　　　if $t = \varepsilon$ **then** $ptr \leftarrow ptr.fail$
　　　end while
　　　if $t \neq \varepsilon$ **then** $ptr \leftarrow t$
　　　if $d[index] =_\triangle$ **then**
　　　　Add string corresponding to ptr to R
　　　　$y \leftarrow ptr$
　　　　while $y.fail \neq \varepsilon$ **do**
　　　　　Add string corresponding to y to R
　　　　　$y \leftarrow y.fail$
　　　　end while
　　　end if
　　　$index \leftarrow index + 1$
　end while

Our approach has the following advantages: Building process is faster. For a node (e.g. node 8 in Fig. 47.2) satisfies the conditions of Theorem, we can easily set its fail-pointer to point to the root node without searching the children of the fail-pointer target node of its parent node (which is the root node in the example shown in the figure).

Searching process is faster. As we known, the traditional AC-Trie outputs all matched substring without checking whether the prefix and the suffix of the matched strings. Therefore, there might be a quadratic number of matches. As a

Fig. 47.2 An example of simultaneous word tree

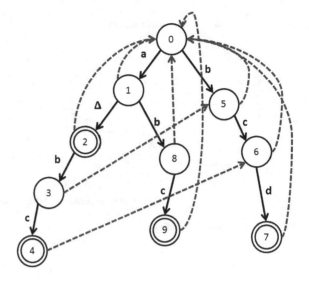

worst example, if every substring matches (e.g. dictionary $= a, aa, aaa, aaaa$ and input string is *aaaa*), the matched strings are as many as $n \times (n-1)/2$ (where n is the length of the input document). Validating of the large number of matched strings takes a lot of time. Especially, the knowledge bases contain abundant items that leads to the outputs of traditional AC-Trie contain a lot of useless strings in our context. By our approach, the outputs are all exact word-level matched items. That is why our approach will be faster.

47.5 Experiments

We implement the baseline approach and our approach uses the same develop tool and the same memory control mechanism, and then test the approaches on the same data set and the same computer to compare their overhead.

The data sets used in this paper are a set of Web documents whose size is 1 million and a subset of instances in FreeBase [1]. The size of the item set is 3 millions. The maximum long items in the item set are as long as 200 characters and the average item length is 29.

Using the naive approach as the baseline algorithm, we validate the correctness of our approach and compare the overhead over the entire web documents. Figure 47.3 shows the time cost of building process on different data scale. And we present the time cost of searching process against the size of knowledge base in Fig. 47.4. Our approach is significantly faster than baseline approach, especially when the size of knowledge base is large. Furthermore, as shown in Fig. 47.4, the performance of searching process is stable.

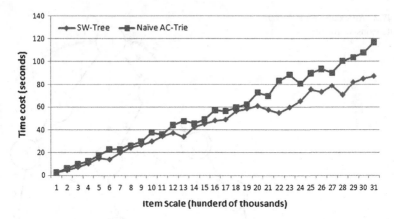

Fig. 47.3 Overhead of building process

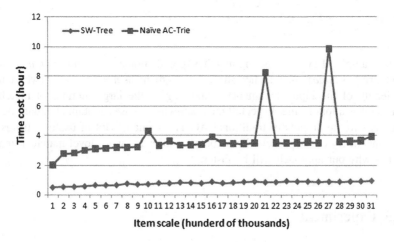

Fig. 47.4 Overhead of searching process

Acknowledgments The work in this paper is supported by National Natural Science Foundation of China under the grant 60873204 and 60933005. It is also partially supported by the National 242 program under the grant 2009A90.

References

1. Bollacker K, Evans C, Paritosh P, Sturge T, Taylor J (2008) Freebase: a collaboratively created graph database for structuring human knowledge. In: Proceedings of the 2008 ACM SIGMOD international conference on management of data. ACM, pp 1247–1250
2. Auer S, Bizer C, Kobilarov G, Lehmann J, Cyganiak R, Ives Z (2007) Dbpedia: a nucleus for a web of open data. In: The Semantic Web, pp 722–735

3. Tunstall-Pedoe W, http://www.trueknowledge.com/
4. Boyer R, Moore J (1977) A fast string searching algorithm. Commun ACM 20(10):762–772
5. Knuth DE, Morris Jr, Pratt VR (1977) Fast pattern matching in strings. SIAM J Comput 6(2):323–350
6. Karp RM, Rabin MO (1987) Efficient randomized pattern-matching algorithms. IBM J Res Dev 31:249
7. Aho A, Corasick M (1975) Efficient string matching: an aid to bibliographic search. Commun ACM 18(6):333–340
8. Wu S, Manber U (1994) A fast algorithm for multi-pattern searching. Technical Report TR-94-17, University of Arizona

Chapter 48
Q-Gram Variation for EBOM

Hongbo Fan and Nianmin Yao

Abstract EBOM is one of the fastest exact single pattern string matching algorithms for short patterns and large alphabet. It is a 2-grams BOM type algorithm. However, only 2-grams is not enough in many case. EBOM is hardly to extend to q-grams because the space complexity of q-grams is exponential. In this article, we presented a q-grams method for BOM which just add one state and applied it on EBOM. Therefore, we presented BOMq algorithm. Experimental results indicated that BOMq is faster than other known algorithms for long patterns and random text of alphabet size 16 on our platform.

Keywords String matching · Q-grams · BOM · Loop unrolling · Design of algorithms

48.1 Introduction

String matching is a fundamental problem in computer science that has been widely used in most fields of text or symbol processing, such as network security, computational biology, and information retrieval [1].

Exact single pattern string matching is the basis of the whole string matching field. It means seeking all the occurrences of a pattern $P = P[0, \ldots, m - 1]$ of length m in a text $T = T[0, \ldots, n - 1]$ of length n over the same alphabet Σ of length σ. In this paper, we concentrate on practical exact single pattern string matching. All algorithms involved in this paper are for searching an exact pattern.

H. Fan · N. Yao (✉)
Department of Computer Science and Technology, Harbin Engineering University,
Harbin, China
e-mail: yaonianmin@hrbeu.edu.cn

H. Fan
e-mail: 270677673@qq.com

W. Lu et al. (eds.), *Proceedings of the 2012 International Conference on Information Technology and Software Engineering*, Lecture Notes in Electrical Engineering 211, DOI: 10.1007/978-3-642-34522-7_48, © Springer-Verlag Berlin Heidelberg 2013

Exact single pattern string matching has been extensively studied and numerous strategies and algorithms have been designed to solve it. To date, the literature [2, 3] is the most comprehensive survey, and it gave a performance comparison of 85 algorithms which covers most of known algorithms as of May 2010. This performance comparison shows that EBOM [4] is faster than other known algorithms for short pattern and large alphabet.

The q-grams technique is an important accelerating technique on pipeline processors. To date, many of the current fast algorithms use q-grams. However, EBOM just a 2-grams algorithms, which may be not enough for some matching conditions. And EBOM is hardly extended to q-grams because the space complexity is exponential for q-grams.

In this article, we presented a q-grams method for EBOM which the space complexity does not increase. And based on the method, we presented the BOMq serial algorithms (EBOM with q-grams). The experimental results shown that BOMq is faster than EBOM in many case, especially for long patterns with alphabet size is 16, BOMq is faster than other known algorithm on our platform.

48.2 Preliminaries

Let the substring of text in the sliding window be W. If $W = XYZ$, all of X, Y and Z are factors of W ($X, Y, Z \in fac(W)$) and Z is a suffix of W ($Z \in suf(W)$).

FO [5, 6] is a DFA and it is one of the simplest factor automata to recognize the set of factors of string. FO is a 5-tuple $\{Q, \Sigma, I, F, \delta\}$, consisting of a set of states, an alphabet, an initial state, a set of final states and a $Q \times \Sigma \rightarrow Q$ transition function respectively. It is acyclic and all states are final. It has $m + 1$ states and a linear number of transitions ($2m - 1$ at most). The most outstanding feature of FO is *weak factor recognition*, which means that a negative answer is always correct when testing whether a string is a factor. Practically, if a string $S \in suf(W)$ is inputted backward to FO for the reversal of P (P^{rv}) and FO rejects this input, $S^{rv} \notin fac(P^{rv})$ and then $S \notin fac(P)$. An example of FO for $P =$ "baabbba" is shown in Fig. 48.1.

Many string matching solutions use FO and they are called BOM [7] type algorithms. BOM type algorithms use the factor method. In the factor method, text characters in the sliding window are inputted to FO for P^{rv} backward until FO rejects the input or the whole window has been accepted. Let the string that has been read be U. If FO rejects U, this window is mismatched and it can safely jump $m - |U| + 1$ characters to let the window jump over U. If the whole window has been accepted, string matching occurs in this window and then the window would slide one character.

Fig. 48.1 Factor oracle for $P =$ "baabbba"

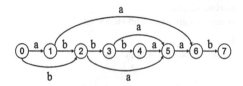

In q-grams, q consecutive characters are processed as a single character in Σ^q. For example, the string "Hello" is processed as "Hel-ell-llo" for 3-grams. This can make the alphabet perceived by the algorithm larger. Because a fairly large alphabet leads to a low rate of branch prediction failure and a high probability of jump, q-grams can greatly enhance the performance. Another benefit of q-grams is that q-grams solutions are more flexible than original one. Generally speaking, smaller alphabets or longer patterns demand bigger q. When an opportune q-grams method is applied, BOM type algorithms should be remarkably faster than ones without the q-grams method.

EBOM is an efficient 2-grams variant of BOM. It records the results of the first two transitions of FO for any pairs of characters in a function $\lambda : (\Sigma \times \Sigma) \rightarrow Q \cup \perp$, which $\perp$ is undefined state, to obtain these results just in one step of calculations, which $\perp$ is the undefined state. The function λ is implemented in a 2-dimensional table with $O(\sigma^2)$ space and it is defined as shown below.

$$for \ \forall \alpha, \beta \in \Sigma, \quad \lambda(\alpha, \beta) = \begin{cases} \perp, & if \ \delta(I, \ \alpha) = \perp \\ \delta(\delta(I, \alpha), \ \beta), & otherwise \end{cases}$$

It is difficult to extend this 2-grams method to q-grams straightforward because this q-grams function λ is a q-dimensional table with $O(\sigma^q)$ exponential space, e.g. 64 MB/3-grams or 16 GB/4-grams is used by λ on ASCII.

EBOM simplifies the matching process of BOM by reducing some unnecessary branches. The code of EBOM is listed as Code.1. cur is the current state in FO.

EBOM (P, T, m, n)
//building phase of FO
create m+1 states; $S[0] \leftarrow -1$;for $i \in [0, \ldots, m + 1], j \in \Sigma$ do $\{\delta(i,j) \leftarrow \perp;\}$
for $cur \in [0, \ldots, m - 1]$ **do**
$\{\sigma \leftarrow P[m - 1 - cur]; \ \delta(cur, \ \sigma) \leftarrow cur + 1; \ k \leftarrow S[cur];$
while $k > -1$ **and** $\delta(k, \ \sigma) = \perp$ **do** $\{\delta(k, \ \sigma) \leftarrow cur + 1; \ k \leftarrow S[k];\}$
if $k = -1$ **then** $c \leftarrow 0$; **else** $c \leftarrow \delta(k, \ \sigma)$; $S[cur + 1] \leftarrow c;\}$
//end of building phase of FO
for $\alpha, \beta \in \Sigma$ **do**//*building the function* λ
$\{cur \leftarrow \delta(I, \ \alpha);$ **if** $cur = \perp$ **then** $\lambda(a,b) \leftarrow \perp$; **else** $\lambda(a,b) \leftarrow \delta(cur,b);\}$
$T[n \ldots n + m - 1] \leftarrow P;pos \leftarrow m - 1;$
while $pos < n$ **do**
$\{cur \leftarrow \lambda(T[pos], T[pos - 1]);$
while $cur = \perp$ **do**
$\{pos \leftarrow pos + m - 1;cur \leftarrow \lambda(T[pos], T[pos - 1]);\}$//*fast loop*
$pos1 \leftarrow pos - 2;$
while $cur \neq \perp$ **do** $\{cur \leftarrow \delta(cur, T[pos1]);pos1 \leftarrow pos1 - 1;\}$//*match loop*
if $pos1 < pos - m + 1$ **then** $\{Report \ a \ match \ finding; \ pos1 \leftarrow pos1 + 1;\}$
$pos \leftarrow pos1 + m;\}$

Code.1. The EBOM algorithm

48.3 Q-Grams Methods

In this section, we propose an easy and common method to realize q-grams on factor automata.

For any factor DFA $\mathcal{A}$, if $\delta(q,c) = \perp (q \in Q, c \in \Sigma)$, we name this transition as a $\perp - trans$. q_S ($\mathcal{A}$) is defined as the current state after the string S has been inputted backward. If there are $\perp - trans$ in DFA, q-grams is not allowed because the transition from undefined state lead to illegal access. Therefore, if we define a state to accept all of $\perp - trans$, illegal access will not happen and q-grams can be applied.

Definition 1 For a factor automaton $\mathcal{A}$, add a new state $\Re$ ($\Re \notin F$), set the target of all $\perp - trans$ be $\Re$ and $\delta(\Re, c) \to \Re$ for $\forall c \in \Sigma$. The result DFA is named $\mathcal{U}\mathcal{A}$ (Unrolling Automaton).

If a string S is input to $\mathcal{A}$ and $\mathcal{U}\mathcal{A}$, there are two possible outcomes as follows:

1. $q_S(\mathcal{A}) \in Q(\mathcal{A})$. Thus $cur \neq \perp$ during S input. Since the only difference between transitions of $\mathcal{A}$ and $\mathcal{U}\mathcal{A}$ are about $\perp - trans$, $q_S(\mathcal{U}\mathcal{A}) = q_S(\mathcal{A})$ and $F(\mathcal{U}\mathcal{A}) = F(\mathcal{A})$. Hence, if S is accepted by $\mathcal{A}$ is equivalent to S is accepted by $\mathcal{U}\mathcal{A}$.
2. For $\forall V \in suf(S)$ such that $cur = \perp$ after V is inputted backward to the automaton $\mathcal{A}$, S is rejected by $\mathcal{A}$. Meanwhile, $q_V (\mathcal{U}\mathcal{A}) = \Re$ according to the definition of $\mathcal{U}\mathcal{A}$ and then no matter what follow up in the input to $\mathcal{U}\mathcal{A}$, $cur = \Re$ in $\mathcal{U}\mathcal{A}$. Hence, $q_S (\mathcal{U}\mathcal{A}) = \Re \notin F$ and S is rejected by $\mathcal{U}\mathcal{A}$.

Therefore, $\mathcal{U}\mathcal{A}$ is an equivalence automaton with $\mathcal{A}$. Because all transitions have been defined and illegal access does not happen no matter what characters are inputted, $\mathcal{U}\mathcal{A}$ supports q-grams. And $\mathcal{U}\mathcal{A}$ just increases one more state to $\mathcal{A}$ and does not change the building time complexity.

We applied the above method to FO and presented $Unrolling\ Factor\ Oracle$ which is build as Code.2. An example of $Unrolling\ Factor\ Oracle$ is shown as Fig. 48.2. The state $\Re$ is the $m + 1$ state in our implementation.

```
//Build Unrolling Factor Oracle (P, m)
    create  m + 2  states;  S  [0]← −1;  for  i  ∈ [0,...,m + 1],  j  ∈ Σ  do
{δ(i,j) ← m + 1;}
    for cur ∈ [0, ..., m − 1] do
    {σ ← P[m − 1 − cur]; δ(cur, σ) ← cur + 1; k ← S [cur];
    while k >−1 and δ(k, σ) = m + 1 do {δ(k, σ) ← cur + 1;k ← S [k];}
    if (k =−1) then c ←0; else c ← δ(k, σ);S [cur +1]←c;}
```

Code.2. Buliding the Unrolling Factor Oracle

Fig. 48.2 The unrolling factor oracle for the reversal of "baabbba"

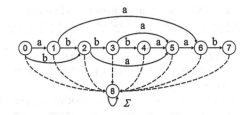

Let *Unrolling Factor Oracle* be applied to EBOM, a new serial of q-grams algorithms named BOMq is gained. An example for $q = 3$ is shown as Code.3.

BOM3 (P, T, m, n)
$\delta \leftarrow$ *Preprocessing Unrolling Factor Oracle* (P, m);
for $\alpha, \beta \in \Sigma$ **do** $\{\lambda (\alpha, \beta) \leftarrow \delta(\delta(I, \alpha), \beta);\}$
$T[n \ldots n + m - 1] \leftarrow P; pos \leftarrow m - 1$;
while $pos < n - m$ **do**
$\{cur \leftarrow \delta(\lambda(T[pos], T[pos - 1]), T[pos - 2])$;
while $cur > m$ **do**//*fast loop*
$\{pos \leftarrow pos + m - 2; cur \leftarrow \delta(\lambda(T[pos], T[pos - 1]), T[pos - 2]);\}$
$pos1 \leftarrow pos - m; pos \leftarrow pos - 3$;
do $\{cur \leftarrow \delta(cur, T[pos]); pos \leftarrow pos - 1;\}$ **while** $cur \leq m$; //*match loop*
if $pos < pos1$ **then** $\{Report\ find\ a\ match;\ pos \leftarrow pos + 1;\}$
$pos \leftarrow pos + m + 1;\}$

Code.3. The BOM3 algorithm

48.4 Experiments Results

To show the performance of BOMq algorithms, we do the following comparative experiment based on SMART [6], which is the implement of article [1–3]:

The platform is Intel i7-2600k@3.4Ghz/Z68/8GB DDR3 RAM/Ubuntu 10.04LTS 64-bit desktop edition/g++4.4.5 with −O3 optimize parameter. We tested under the four 20 MB length random texts with alphabet size is 2,16,64,254 respectively, which the random function was the lib function of g++, rand(), and tested under the DNA sequence E.coli, English text Bible.txt, and natural language samples text world192.txt, which above three texts are from SMART. For each matching condition, the 100 patterns in each pattern set were picked from the 100 prior random selected and non-overlapping positions of the text, and the average matching speed was recorded as the final result which the highest and the lowest 20 % results were ignored. The text had been read in memory to avoid the impact of disk and before each time of matching, a big table had been read sequentially to empty the Cache. Only the matching phase was timed by RDTSC[1] (±30 CPU

---

[1] http://en.wikipedia.org/wiki/Time_Stamp_Counter

Table 48.1 The optimal parameter and average matching speed for the fastest four type algorithms on random text of alphabet size 16, which unit is MB/s

$m = 2$		$m = 4$		$m = 8$	
1 EBOM [4]	1337.0	EBOM	3197.8	SBNDM2_2i32	5534.9
2 TVSBSw6 [11]	1224.1	SBNDM2_2bi32[9]	3019.6	EBOM	5333.0
3 GSB2bi32 [12]	1151.4	GSB2bi32	2926.7	GSB2b2i32	5255.9
4 UFNDM2i32 [9]	1072.8	FSBNDMq_q3f0i32[12]	2364.6	BOM3	4795.5
$m = 16$		$m = 32$		$m = 64$	
1 BOM3	9147.7	BOM3	12370.7	BOM3	14331.8
2 FSBNDMq_q3f1i32	8530.8	SBNDM4bi32	12182.7	SBNDM4bi32	14302.5
3 SBNDM2_2i32	8208.5	FSBNDMqb_q4f0i32	10833.7	FSBNDMw4a64	13335.7
4 EBOM	7903.8	BOM4	10520.9	UFNDM4a64	13266.4
$m = 128$		$m = 254$			
1 BOM3	15333.0	BOM3	21263.0		
2 QF3_5i32[8]	14660.3	BOM4	19189.9		
3 BOM4	14597.2	QF3_5i32	18550.9		
4 TVSBSw6	14006.3	EBOM	15968.6		

ticks). In the experiment, the CPU frequency was locked by cpufrequtils[2]; the network and the unrelated background service are closed to ensure the processor utilization was below to 3 %. This experiment environment is similar with the environment of the article [2, 3], but we used −O3 parameter with auto branch prediction and only timed matching phase, which are more suit for the study habits of the string matching field.

SMART has given the implements of 85 known algorithms, which covered most known algorithms as of May 2010. This experiment continued the work of SMART, complemented the FSO [7], BXS [8], QF [8], Q-Hash_4096 [8], SBNDMqb [9], BSDMq [10], FSBNDM-wk [11], SBNDM-wk [11], FS-wk [11], TVSBS-wk [11], FSBNDMq [12], FSBNDMqb [12], GSB2 [12], GSB2b [12] etc, which are newer algorithms not be included by SMART. All bit parallel solutions are implemented with the 32-bit edition (i32) and the 64-bit edition (a64) and both of them are tested. And just some of parameters of the solutions are listed in SMART, this experiment complemented the unlisted parameters. For example, only 3 conditions of Hashq ($q = 3,5,8$) were listed in SMART, we complemented the solutions of $q = 4,6,7$ etc. If an algorithm with different parameters are called different algorithms, there was more than 300 algorithms are compared, these algorithms covered most of known algorithms. The experiment results indicated that although BOMq is faster than EBOM in many case, and BOMq is faster than other known algorithms only for the random text of alphabet size 16. Due to length constraints we only list the optimize parameter and its average matching speed for

---

[2] http://wiki.archlinux.org/index.php/Cpufrequtils

the fastest 4 type algorithms (if some algorithms are only inconsistent with parameter such as q value of q-grams, and they are presented in one article, they are called a type algorithm) for random text of alphabet size 16 in Table 48.1.

It is shown in Table 48.1 that BOM3 is faster than other known algorithms for long pattern on random text of alphabet size 16.

48.5 Conclusion

In this article, we presented a q-grams method for factor automata, which just adds one state, and we applied it to EBOM. Therefore, we presented the BOMq serial algorithm. The Experimental results shown that BOMq, especially BOM3, is faster than other known algorithms for long patterns and random text of alphabet size 16 on our platform.

Acknowledgments This paper is supported by the National Natural Science Foundation of China under Grant No.61073047; Fundamental Research Funds for the Central Universities: HEUCFT1007, HEUCF100607, HEUCFT1202, Harbin Special funds for Technological Innovation Talents: 2012RFLXG023. Thanks for funding.

References

1. Navarro G, Raffinot M (2002) Flexible pattern matching in strings—practical on-line search algorithms for texts and biological sequences. Cambridge University Press, New York
2. Faro S, Lecroq T (2010) The exact string matching problem: a comprehensive experimental evaluation [DB/OL]. Computing research repository (12th July 2012). http://arxiv.org/pdf/1012.2547
3. Faro S, Lecroq T (2013) The exact online string matching problem: a review of the most recent results [J/OL]. ACM Comput Surv (12th July 2012). http://www-igm.univ-mlv.fr/~lecroq/articles/acmsurv2013.pdf
4. Faro S, Lecroq T (2009) Efficient variants of the backward-oracle-matching algorithm. Int J Found Comp Sci 20(6):967–984. doi:10.1142/S0129054109006991
5. Crochemore M, Ilie L, Seid-Hilmi E (2007) The structure of factor oracles. Int J Found Comp Sci 18(4):781–797. doi:10.1.1.68.4038
6. Allauzen C, Crochemore M, Raffinot M (1999) Factor oracle: a new structure for pattern matching. In: LNCS 1725: Proceedings of SOFSEM'99, theory and practice of informatics, Springer, Berlin, pp 291–306
7. Fredriksson K, Grabowski S (2005) Practical and optimal string matching. In: LNCS 3772: The 12th symposium on string processing and information retrieval, SPIRE 2005, Springer, Berlin, pp 376–387
8. Durian B, Peltola H, Salmela L et al (2010) Bit-parallel search algorithms for long patterns. In: LNCS 6049: The 9th international symposium on experimental algorithms, SEA2010, Springer, Berlin, pp 129–140
9. Durian B, Holub J, Peltola H et al (2009) Tuning BNDM with q-grams. In: Proceedings of the 11th workshop on algorithm engineering and Experiments, ALENEX 2009. SIAM, New York, pp 29–37

10. Faro S, Lecroq T (2012) A fast suffix automata based algorithm for exact online string matching. In: LNCS 7276: The 17th international conference on implementation and application of automata, CIAA 2012, Springer, Berlin, pp 149–158
11. Faro S, Lecroq T (2012) A multiple sliding windows approach to speed up string matching algorithms. In: LNCS 7276: The 11th international symposium on experimental algorithms, SEA 2012. Springer, Berlin, pp 172–183
12. Peltola H, Tarhio J (2011) Variations of forward-SBNDM. 16th prague stringology conference, PSC2011, Czech Technical University, Prague, pp 3–14

Chapter 49
Research on FOPI Controller for Current Loop of PMSM Servo System

Youbin Zhang and Youguo Pi

Abstract A fractional order proportional integral (FOPI) controller for the current loop of permanent magnet synchronous motor (PMSM) servo system is presented. Oustaloup filter is used to realization the FOPI controller and a tuning method is also given. A comparison between the FOPI and the integer order proportional integral (IOPI) has done, and the study of the robustness of the FOPI has done too. Simulation and experiment results prove the FOPI outperforms the IOPI on control characteristics and the FOPI has strong robustness.

Keywords FOPI controller · PMSM servo system · Current loop · Tuning · Robustness

49.1 Introduction

The permanent magnet synchronous motor (PMSM) servo system is applied more and more widely in automation equipment such as CNC machine tools, industry robots and so on. The PMSM servo system based on vector control is usually a three-loop control structure which consists of current loop, speed loop and position

Y. Zhang (✉) · Y. Pi
College of Automation Science and Engineering, South China University of Technology, Guangzhou, 510640 Guangdong, China
e-mail: 0668zyb@163.com

Y. Pi
e-mail: 454164001@qq.com

Y. Zhang
Department of Automation, Guangdong University of Petrochemical Technology, Maoming, 525000 Guangdong, China

W. Lu et al. (eds.), *Proceedings of the 2012 International Conference on Information Technology and Software Engineering*, Lecture Notes in Electrical Engineering 211, DOI: 10.1007/978-3-642-34522-7_49, © Springer-Verlag Berlin Heidelberg 2013

461

loop [1]. As the innermost of the three-loop structure, the current loop reforms the current object, and accelerates current (torque) response process. It has a very important significance to the dynamic performance of the system.

As the order of integration and differential is integer, the classic PID is called integer order PID (IOPID) controller which is different from the fractional order PID controller (FOPID) when the order of integration and differential is fractional. The IOPID control strategy has the advantages of simple principle, convenient using and technology easy to master, so it has been widely used in various industrial fields. In the traditional design of current loop, the inductance and resistance of plant are considered as lumped parameter components and be approximated as linear. The current regulator uses the principle of compensation to reform the object for achieving good control performance [2]. In fact, the inductance and resistance of plant is time variation nonlinear in high performance servo system, the IOPD is difficult to meet the needs of the control system.

Between varying the order of differential and integral and varying the coefficient of PID, the former is easier to vary the system frequency response characteristic [3]. In recent years, as the promotion of IOPID, the FOPID has got more and more attentions and applications [4]. The FOPID has two freedoms that are more than the IOPID: the order of differential and integral, so the FOPID has larger regulation range and it can be designed for robust control systems [5].

FOPID controller will be designed for current loop of PMSM servo system to reduce the influences caused by the PMSM parameters variation. Thereby it will achieve better control performance.

We analyze the characteristics of fractional PID based on the theory of the fractional calculus, then a fractional order proportion integral (FOPI) controller is designed for the current loop of PMSM servo system by using the Oustaloup filter to finish digital realization and using Graphic method based on phase-frequency response characteristic to realize the parameter tuning, and the controller performance is researched by simulation and experiment.

49.2 Fractional Order PID Controller and Oustaloup Filter

FOPID controller can be written as $PI^\lambda D^\mu$. Its transfer form is shown as Eq. (49.1). As $PI^\lambda D^\mu$ is more than IOPID two freedoms λ and μ, $PI^\lambda D^\mu$ can provide more new possibilities to the system for getting better performance [6].

$$G(s) = K_p + K_i s^\lambda + K_d s^\mu (\lambda < 0, \mu > 0) \tag{49.1}$$

where K_p is the proportional coefficient, K_i is the integral coefficient, K_d is the differential coefficient, λ is the integral order, μ is the differential order and $\mu > 0$. They can be any real number.

If $\lambda = 1$ and $\mu = 1$, Eq. (49.1) is for IOPID. It means IOPID is a special case of $PI^\lambda D^\mu$. If $K_d = 0$, then it becomes the FOPI, it can be written as PI^λ.

49.3 The Design for Current Loop of PMSM Servo System

The current loop simplified dynamic structure is shown as Fig. 49.1 [1].

In Fig. 49.1, the ACR is the regulator of current loop. We chose the PI^λ controller as ACR. For convenience, the gain of plant K and the gain of controller K_c can combine as $K_p = K_c K$. So the plant $P(s)$ is as Eq. (49.2) and the controller $G(s)$ is as Eq. (49.3)

$$P(s) = \frac{K}{(T_1 s + 1)(T_2 s + 1)} \tag{49.2}$$

where $T_1 = 0.0048$ s, $T_2 = 0.00016$ s, $K = 96$.

$$G(s) = K_p(1 + K_i s^\lambda) \quad (\lambda < 0) \tag{49.3}$$

We use the tuning method that the given gain crossover frequency and phase margin are achieved to ensure the PI^λ. Its basic idea is according to the performance needs of the control system [7], and three equations will be obtained as Eqs. (49.6)–(49.8), and then the parameters will be solved. The detailed steps are given as follow:

When the controller transform is $C(s)$ and the plant transform is $P(s)$, the open-loop transform is that $G(s) = C(s)P(s)$. we can obtain

(i) gain crossover frequency specification.

$$20 \lg|G(\omega_c)| = 20 \lg|C(\omega_c)P(\omega_c)| = 0\,\text{dB} \tag{49.4}$$

(ii) phase margin specification.

$$\arg[C(\omega_c)P(\omega_c)] = -\pi + \phi_m \tag{49.5}$$

(iii) robustness to variation in the gain of the plant.

$$\frac{d}{d\omega} \arg[C(\omega_c)P(\omega_c)]\bigg|_{\omega=\omega_c} = 0 \tag{49.6}$$

where ω_c is cut-off frequency, ϕ_m is phase margin.

The phase Bode plot is flat at the gain crossover frequency; it means the system is more robust to gain variation and the overshoots of the response are almost the same;

For plant and controller, there are

$$|P(j\omega)| = \frac{K}{\sqrt{(T_1\omega)^2 + 1} \cdot \sqrt{(T_2\omega)^2 + 1}} \tag{49.7}$$

$$\arg[P(j\omega)] = -\arctan(T_1\omega) - \arctan(T_2\omega) \tag{49.8}$$

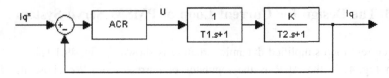

Fig. 49.1 Current loop dynamic structure of PMSM

$$|C(\omega)| = \left| K_p\left[\left(1 + K_i\omega^\lambda \cos\frac{\lambda\pi}{2} + jK_i\omega^\lambda \sin\frac{\lambda\pi}{2}\right)\right]\right|$$
$$= K_p\sqrt{\left(1 + K_i\omega^\lambda \cos\frac{\lambda\pi}{2}\right)^2 + \left(K_i\omega^\lambda \sin\frac{\lambda\pi}{2}\right)^2} \tag{49.9}$$

$$\arg[C(\omega)] = \arctan\frac{K_i\omega^\lambda \sin\frac{\lambda\pi}{2} + K_i\omega^\lambda \sin\frac{\lambda\pi}{2}}{K_p + (K_i\omega^\lambda \cos\frac{\lambda\pi}{2} + K_i\omega^\lambda \cos\frac{\lambda\pi}{2})} \tag{49.10}$$

On the condition that $\omega_c = 3000\,\text{rad/s}$ and $\phi_m = 70°$, according to Eqs. (49.4)–(49.6), we can obtain follow equations:

$$|C(\omega_c)P(\omega_c)| = \frac{K_p\sqrt{[(1 + K_i\omega_c^\lambda \cos\frac{\lambda\pi}{2})]^2 + (K_i\omega_c^\lambda \sin\frac{\lambda\pi}{2})^2}}{\sqrt{(T_1\omega_c)^2 + 1} \cdot \sqrt{(T_2\omega_c)^2 + 1}} = 1 \tag{49.11}$$

$$K_p = \sqrt{\frac{[(T_1\omega_c)^2 + 1][(T_2\omega_c)^2 + 1]}{[(1 + K_i\omega_c^\lambda \cos\frac{\lambda\pi}{2})]^2 + (K_i\omega_c^\lambda \sin\frac{\lambda\pi}{2})^2}} \tag{49.12}$$

$$\arg[G_c(\omega_c)P(\omega_c)] = \arctan\left(\frac{K_i\omega_c^\lambda \sin\frac{\lambda\pi}{2}}{1 + K_i\omega_c^\lambda \cos\frac{\lambda\pi}{2}}\right) - \arctan(T_2\omega_c) - \arctan(T_1\omega_c)$$
$$= -\pi + \phi_m \tag{49.13}$$

$$\frac{d}{d\omega}\arg[C(\omega)P(\omega)]\bigg|_{\omega=\omega_c} = \frac{d}{d\omega}\left[\arctan\frac{K_i\omega^\lambda \sin(\lambda\pi/2)}{1 + K_i\omega^\lambda \cos(\lambda\pi/2)} - \arctan(\omega T_1) - \arctan(\omega T_2)\right]\bigg|_{\omega=\omega_c} = 0 \tag{49.14}$$

From Eq. (49.13), the relation of K_i and λ is,

$$K_i = \frac{M}{\omega_c^\lambda \sin\frac{\lambda\pi}{2} - M\omega_c^\lambda \cos\frac{\lambda\pi}{2}} \tag{49.15}$$

where $M = \tan[\arctan(T_2\omega_c) + \arctan(T_1\omega_c) - \pi + \phi_m]$.

Fig. 49.2 Relation curve of K_i and λ

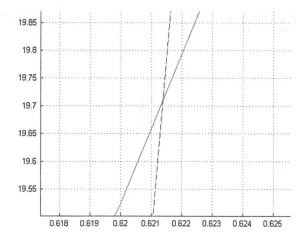

From Eq. (49.14), the relation of K_i and λ can be obtained as Eq. (49.16).

$$A\omega^{2\lambda}K_i^2 + BK_i + A = 0 \qquad (49.16)$$

where

$$\left.\begin{aligned}
A &= \frac{T_1}{1 + (\omega_c T_1)^2} + \frac{T_2}{1 + (\omega_c T_2)^2} \\
B &= 2A\omega^{\lambda}\cos(\lambda\pi/2) - \omega^{\lambda-1}\lambda\sin(\lambda\pi/2) \\
K_i &= \frac{-B \pm \sqrt{B^2 - 4A^2\omega^{2\lambda}}}{2A\omega^{2\lambda}}
\end{aligned}\right\} \qquad (49.17)$$

From Eqs. (49.15) and (49.16), K_i and λ can be worked out, and then K_p can be worked out if K_i and λ substituted into Eq. (49.12). However, it will be very difficult to work out K_i and λ by analysis method. Fortunately, a graphical method can be used as a practical and simple way to get K_i and λ. we draw the curves matching with Eqs. (49.15) and (49.16) in Fig. 49.2.

Then the results are the point of intersection of the two curves. According to Fig. 49.2, we take $K_i = 19.71$, $\lambda = -0.62$, and we get $K_p = 14.81$ by substituting K_i and λ into Eq. (49.12). So $K_c = K_p/K = 14.81/96 = 0.154$, and the controller is $C(s) = 0.154\,(1 + 19.71s^{-0.62}) = 0.154 + 3.04s^{-0.62}$.

49.4 Simulation and Experiment Research

We use Oustaloup filter to approximate the fractional calculus [7].

In MATLAB, we build a FOPI control simulation module. For comparing with the integer order PI (IOPI), we build an IOPI control simulation module also. The

Fig. 49.3 Step response of
current loop

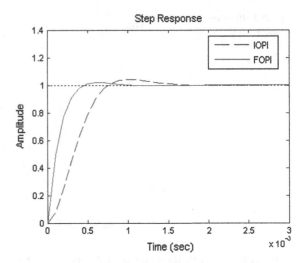

parameters of IOPI controller are got by ITEA method and its transfer form is
(0.00069 s + 0.15)/0.0046 s.

The step response waveforms of IOPI and FOPI are shown in Fig. 49.3.

Figure 49.3 shows that on the rise time, adjust time and overshoots, the performances of FOPI controller are better than that of IOPI controller, and on the current follower performance, the FOPI controller is superior to IOPI controller.

In fact, the current loop parameters are time variant. To research the robustness of FOPI and to contrast the IOPI controller with FOPI controller, we study the step responses of resistance variation and inductance variation and the simulation experiment results are shown in Fig. 49.4.

Figure 49.4a shows that in the IOPI control system, the overshoot is varied from 3.69 to 5 %and the setting time is varied from 1.27 to 1.43 ms with resistance varying in ±10 %, and the overshoot is varied from 3.76 to 5.18 % and the setting time is varied from 1.23 to 1.49 ms with inductance varying in ±10 %. However, with the same condition, the control performances are almost not varied in the FOPI control system. These indicate that the influence on FOPI is much smaller than that on IOPI with plant parameters variation in wide range. The simulation experimental results indicate that the FOPI controller has strong robustness.

In experiment, we use the FOPI controller as the current loop regulator of PMSM servo system which is based on vector control. On the condition that position loop is opened and speed loop is closed, by the graphical interface of DSP simulation software CCS2000, we obtain the q axis current response waveform which affects by speed controller output value, namely the current closed-loop given signal. To compare with IOPI controller, we also experiment with IOPI controller. The parameters of controllers are same to simulation module. The waveforms are shown in Figs. 49.5 and 49.6. The upper is given current value and the lower part is current response waveform. Y-coordinate unit is per unit. X-coordinate unit is seconds (s).

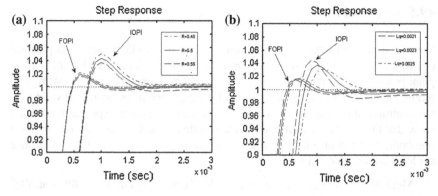

Fig. 49.4 Step response of plant parameter variation. **a** With resistance variation (±10 %). **b** With induction variation (±10 %)

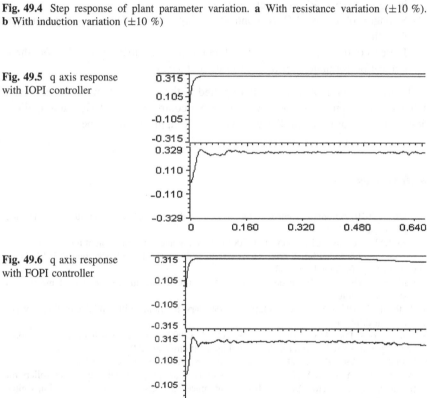

Fig. 49.5 q axis response with IOPI controller

Fig. 49.6 q axis response with FOPI controller

The experiment results indicate that FOPI controller can make current response faster, overshoot smaller, setting time shorter. The current loop output can be a very good follower of a given value. It achieves the current control requirements. It proved that the fractional order proportional integral controller can be used for practical application in the servo control system, and good control effect can be got.

49.5 Conclusion

We introduce the fractional proportional integral into PMSM current loop as the controller, for the FOPI controller can reduces the influence that be affected by plant parameters variation and meets the high performances of servo system. The tuning method that is based on crossover frequency and phase margin is valid, and the controller have very good control effect. Simulation and experimental results show that FOPI is better than IOPI to adapt to time variant system. As current loop regulator, FOPI controller has some advantages as follow that IOPI controller couldn't comparable with.

(1) More flexibility. Because the order of FOPI can freely choose, FOPI controller is bigger than IOPI on selecting range.
(2) Stronger robustness. FOPID controller is not sensitive for the plant parameters variation.
(3) Better control performance. FOPI controller is superior to IOPI on three control performances in fast, accurate and steady.

To sum up, the FOPID controller applied to the servo system current loop can achieve better control performances. In servo control system design and application, fractional order controller will have broad application prospects.

References

1. Chen B (2010) Automatic control system of electric drive. Mechanical Industry Press, Beijing (in Chinese)
2. Peng KM, Chen BM, Cheng GY et al (2005) Modeling and compensation of nonlinearities and friction in a micro hard disk drive servo system with nonlinear feedback control. IEEE Trans Control Syst Technol 13(5):708–721
3. Barbosa R, Duarte F, Machado TJ (2002) A fractional calculus perspective of mechanical systems modeling
4. Podlubny I (1997) Numerical solution of ordinary fractional differential equations by the fractional difference method
5. Vinagre BM, Podlubny I, Hernandez A, Feliu V (2000) Some approximations of fractional order operators used in control theory and applications 2000(03)
6. Podlubny I (1999) Fractional differential equations. Academic Press, San Diego
7. Wang C, Lou Y, Chen Y (2009) Tuning fractional order proportional integral controllers for fractional order systems. In: 47th IEEE conference on decision and control, Guilin, China, pp 17–19

Chapter 50
Optimization Design of Operating Parameters for Hydrogen Cyanide Conversion Rate Based on an Improved Particle Swarm Optimization and BP Neural Network

Yuantao Zhang and Taifu Li

Abstract An optimal design method of operating parameters in hydrogen cyanide (HCN) production process is presented. Firstly the soft sensor model of HCN conversion rate is established by BP neural network. Then considering the practical constraints of operating parameters and taking the maximum HCN conversion rate as objective function, an improved particle swarm optimization (IPSO) algorithm is introduced to optimize the operating parameters, which takes into account the dynamic inertia weight and the particle average position to avoid falling into local optimum and accelerate the convergence. Simulation results with actual production data show that, compared with genetic algorithm (GA) optimization, this method can obtain the optimal operating parameters of the HCN production process.

Keywords Particle swarm optimization · BP neural network · HCN conversion rate · Operating parameters optimization · Soft sensing model

50.1 Introduction

Hydrogen cyanide (HCN) is a colorless transparent toxic liquid with a bitter almond flavor. It is widely used in the electroplating industry, mining industry, cabin and warehouse smoked rodent control, manufacturing all kinds of resin

Y. Zhang (✉) · T. Li
School of Electrical and Information Engineering, Chongqing University of Science and Technology, 401331 Chongqing, China
e-mail: zyt998@tom.com

T. Li
e-mail: litaifuemail@qq.com

W. Lu et al. (eds.), *Proceedings of the 2012 International Conference on Information Technology and Software Engineering*, Lecture Notes in Electrical Engineering 211, DOI: 10.1007/978-3-642-34522-7_50, © Springer-Verlag Berlin Heidelberg 2013

monomers such as methyl acrylate resin and other industries. Furthermore HCN can generate a lot of derivatives, which have important uses in the field of pharmaceuticals, pesticides, fuel, light-sensitive chemicals, and engineering materials. Therefore HCN market demand is broad. Nowadays most of the production of HCN comes from the direct production, while the rest comes from the byproduct of acrylonitrile. But direct method HCN conversion rate is usually low (60–70 %). Therefore, the use of advanced computational intelligence techniques to study imminent HCN conversion rate increases. However, the current research literature in this respect at home and abroad is rare. Neural network can establish the object mathematical model without considering the exact process by its strong nonlinear approximation ability, it is widely used in the modeling of complex chemical processes [1–3]. Particle swarm optimization (PSO), which comes from simulating birds foraging in the process of migration and clustering behavior, is a global random search algorithm based on swarm intelligence. PSO can be used to solve a large number of nonlinear, nondifferentiable and multi-peak complex optimization problems [4, 5]. In this paper, BP neural network is used for establishing the soft sensor model of HCN conversion rate firstly, then taking the maximum HCN conversion rate as objective function, an improved PSO algorithm is presented to optimize the operating parameters. The research results can provide a new way of thinking to improve HCN conversion rate in actual production process.

50.2 HCN Conversion Rate Soft Sensing Model Based on BP Network

The direct method is also called Andrussow method by using methane, ammonia gas and oxygen as the main raw material. It is an ammonia oxidation with the raw material mixture passing through the wire mesh-like catalyst bed made of platinum iridium alloy in the conditions of atmospheric pressure and 1000 °C above. Literature [6] indicates that three-layer BP neural network can be realized arbitrarily complex nonlinear mapping as long as enough hidden nodes. That is to say it can approximate function with arbitrary precision to achieve a very curve fitting. Therefore we use three-layer BP neural network to establish HCN production process firstly. Comprehensively analyzing of the HCN production process, the nine operating parameters of HCN (the settings of the control system, shown in Table 50.1) is chosen as the input variables of BP neural network and the output is HCN conversion rate. The nodes of hidden containing layer are 5, the transfer function of hidden layer nodes is Tausig function and the transfer function of output layer nodes is Logsig function.

The BP neural network training samples come from 3411 groups of HCN real-time production data in Chongqing Unisplendour Chemical Plant, in which 3241 groups are selected randomly as network training and the rest of 170 groups are selected as predictive test. Firstly HCN production data are preprocessed, including

Table 50.1 Operation parameters of HCN

Ammonia gas compensation pressure	Natural gas compensation pressure	Air compensation pressure	Ammonia gas compensation temperature	Drum pressure
P_{AG}	P_{NG}	P_A	T_{AG}	P_D
Reactor outlet temperature	Ammonia gas compensation flow	Natural gas/ Ammonia gas	Air/Ammonia gas	
T_{RO}	F_{AG}	NGTAG	ATAG	

Table 50.2 Actual production data of HCN

Operating parameters	Group 1	Group 2	Group 3	...	Group 3410	Group 3411
$T_{AG}(^\circ C)$	31.6	31.3	31.5	...	31.8	32.1
$F_{AG}(kgf/cm^3)$	601	598	601	...	599	600
NGTAG	1.1430	1.1505	1.1464	...	1.1385	1.1333
ATAG	6.2013	6.2140	6.2096	...	6.2971	6.2933
$P_{AG}(MPa)$	2.00	2.02	2.00	...	1.99	2.00
$P_{NG}(MPa)$	1.99	1.99	1.99	...	1.99	2.00
$P_A(MPa)$	2.00	2.01	2.00	...	1.99	1.99
$P_D(MPa)$	2.77	2.53	2.67	...	2.92	2.85
$T_{RO}(^\circ C)$	79	78	79	...	79	79
α	71.787	71.952	71.886	...	71.402	71.336

gross error elimination, 3σ method and five-spot triple smoothing algorithm. The preprocessed data are shown as Table 50.2, where α denotes HCN conversion rate.

Figure 50.1 shows the predicted HCN conversion rate by trained BP neural network and Fig. 50.2 shows the error between prediction output and desired output. The prediction performance indicators are as follows: mean absolute deviation (MAD) is 1.1248, mean square error (MSE) is 2.4826, mean forecast error (MFE) is 0.0327 and mean absolute percentage error (MAPE) is 1.5938.

50.3 IPSO Algorithm

Particle swarm optimization (PSO) algorithm is a new evolution of computing technology based on social group behavior. The basic idea of PSO algorithm is derived from study on the behavior of birds prey. In PSO, each iteration of the particle updates itself by tracking personal optimal position and group optimal position until now. Therefore, this algorithm is an efficient parallel search algorithm, which can be used to solve a large number of nonlinear, nondifferentiable, and multi-peak complex optimization problems. The basic PSO algorithm can be described as follows:

Fig. 50.1 Prediction output

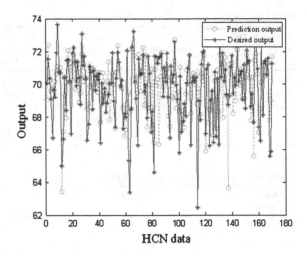

Fig. 50.2 Prediction error

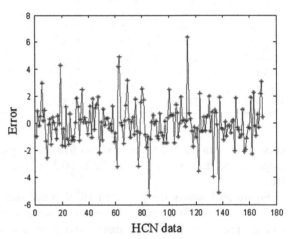

Assume m particles compose a group in D-dimensional target search space, where the ith particle is expressed as a D-dimensional vector $x_i = (x_{i1}, x_{i2}, \cdots x_{iD})$, that is the potential solution. The best previous position of any particle is recorded and represented as *pbest*. The best particle among all particles is called as *gbest*. The flight velocity denoted by $v_i = (v_{i1}, v_{i2}, \cdots v_{iD})$ is also a D-dimensional vector. The position and velocity of particles are updated according to the following equations.

$$v_{id}(t+1) = \omega v_{id}(t) + c_1 r_1 [pbest_{id}(t) - x_{id}(t)] + c_2 r_2 [gbest_d(t) - x_{id}(t)] \quad (50.1)$$

$$x_{id}(t+1) = x_{id}(t) + v_{id}(t+1) \quad (50.2)$$

where $i = 1, 2, \cdots, m, d = 1, 2, \cdots, D$, ω is inertia weight which decides the impact of particle present speed to next generation. c_1 and c_2 are acceleration coefficients with positive values. The relative sizes of c_1 and c_2 reflect the relative importance of p_i and p_g in evolution. r_1 and r_2 are random numbers between 0 and 1. $v_{id} \in [-v_d^{\min}, v_d^{\max}]$, $x_{id} \in [-x_d^{\min}, x_d^{\max}]$, $v_d^{\min}$, $v_d^{\max}$, $x_d^{\min}$ and $x_d^{\max}$ represent actual bounds.

Suitable selection of inertia weight provides a balance between global and local explorations, thus requiring less iteration on average to find a sufficiently optimal solution. As originally developed, often decreases linearly from 0.9 to 0.4 during a run. The inertia weight is set according to the following equation [7].

$$\omega = \omega_{start} - (\omega_{start} - \omega_{end}) * k / G_{\max} \tag{50.3}$$

where ω_{start} is initial inertia weight, ω_{end} is inertia weight iterated to maximum number, k is the number of iterations, $G_{\max}$ is the maximum number of iterations.

As we known, each particle only uses individual optimum and group optimum information in basic PSO algorithm. Considering the sharing of information in group is the result of an evolutionary, the idea of group average position is presented to avoid group into a local optimum and accelerate the convergence.

Supposing that a particle swarm is composed of m particles, then the positions of m particles can be denoted as $[P_1 \; P_2 \; \cdots P_m]$, and the average position of m particles is

$$Pmean = \sum_{i=1}^{m} \frac{P_i}{m} \tag{50.4}$$

Therefore the velocity update equation of IPSO algorithm is

$$
\begin{aligned}
v_{id}(t+1) = {} & \omega v_{id}(t) + c_1 r_1 [pbest_{id}(t) - x_{id}(t)] + c_2 r_2 [gbest_d(t) - x_{id}(t)] \\
& + c_3 r_3 [pmean_d(t) - x_{id}(t)]
\end{aligned}
\tag{50.5}
$$

where c_3 is a positive constant, r_3 is a uniform random number between 0 and 1, ω is shown as Eq. (50.3). The position update equation of IPSO algorithm is equal to basic PSO algorithm as Eq. (50.2).

It can be seen from Eq. (50.5) that each particle in IPSO draws lessons form the experience of other particles and uses more information to decide its own behavior. In other words, each particle is on longer search between group optimum and individual optimum, but in group optimum, group average position and individual optimum. IPSO algorithm still retains particle swarm global best position, and furthermore, it can speed up the convergence rate, while group average position is used for avoiding the group into a local optimum.

50.4 Operating Parameters Optimization of HCN Conversion Rate

Choosing the maximum HCN conversion rate as fitness function, GA and IPSO are used for optimizing the operating parameters respectively and the results are shown in Table 50.2; Figs. 50.3 and 50.4. In IPSO, evolutionary generations

Fig. 50.3 Fitness curve of
GA

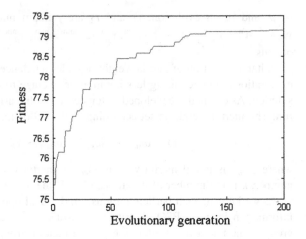

Fig. 50.4 Fitness curve of
IPSO

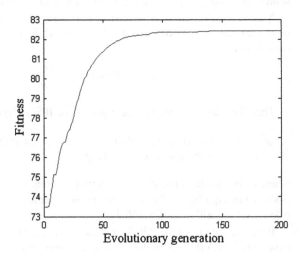

are 200, population numbers are 80, acceleration coefficients $c_1 = c_2 = 1.5$, $c_3 = 1.2$, inertia weight $\omega = 0.9 - 0.5 * k/70$. In GA, crossover probability is 0.4, mutation probability is 0.2, evolutionary generations and population numbers are the same as IPSO. The actual constraint ranges of operating parameters are also shown in Table 50.3.

The simulation results show that the optimization performance of IPSO is better than GA. IPSO has a faster convergence rate and stronger extremum optimization ability. In Figs. 50.3 and 50.4, GA evolves to 188 generation to converge to 79.1282, while IPSO only evolves to 141 generation to converge to 82.4150. The optimized operating parameters are shown in Table 50.2.

Table 50.3 Constraint ranges and optimization results of HCN operating parameters

Optimized result	P_{AG}	P_{NG}	P_A	T_{AG}	P_D	T_{RO}	F_{AG}	$NGTAG$	$ATAG$
Constraint ranges	1.98–2.02	1.99–2.01	1.97–2.11	18.77–43.68	2.11–3.08	77–81.17	462.82–708.08	1.12–1.17	6.11–6.37
GA									
$\alpha = 79.1282$	2.0072	2.0037	1.9933	41.6411	2.9939	78.6458	565.4187	1.1220	6.2970
IPSO	2.0118	2.0102	1.9979	43.6829	2.7013	79.6965	551.0604	1.1201	6.3763
$\alpha = 82.4150$									

50.5 Conclusion

According to the fact that direct method HCN conversion rate is low in Chongqing Unisplendour Chemical Plant, in this paper, firstly the soft sending model of HCN conversion rate is established by BP neural network, and then the operating parameters of HCN production process are optimized by GA and IPSO respectively to achieve extremum optimization. IPSO takes into account the dynamic inertia weight and the particle average position to avoid falling into local optimum and accelerate the convergence. The simulation results show that the optimization performance of IPSO is better than GA. Furthermore, the optimized operating parameters have been used in practical production to improve HCN conversion rate indeed, therefore this paper has a certain academic value and engineering significance.

Acknowledgments The authors would like to appreciate the support of Chongqing Educational Committee Science and Technology Research Project (KJ121407) and Chongqing University of Science and Technology Intramural Scientific Foundation (CK2011B11).

References

1. Wu M, Xu CH, She JH, Cao WH (2012) Neural-network-based integrated model for predicting burn-through point in lead-zinc sintering process. J Process Control 22(5):925–934
2. Shakil M, Elshafei M, Habib MA, Maleki FA (2009) Soft sensor for NOx and O2 using dynamic neural networks. Comput Electr Eng 35(4):578–586
3. Tian XM, Wang Q, Deng XG (2011) Soft sensing based on wavelet neural networks with momentum. J Chem Ind Eng 62(8):2238–2242 (in Chinese)
4. Gao S, Zhang ZY, Cao CG (2010) Multiplicate particle swarm optimization algorithm. J Comput 5(1):150–157
5. Yang TQ (2011) A multi-objective PSO algorithm for energy-efficient scheduling. Adv Mater Res 143–144:663–667
6. Hassoun MH (1995) Fundamentals of artificial neural networks. The MIT Press, Cambridge
7. Kennedy J, Eberhart R (1995) Particle swarm optimization. In: Proceedings of the IEEE international conference on neural networks. Perth, pp 1942–1948

Chapter 51
Q-Grams Suffix Type Single Pattern String Matching Algorithms

Zhiwei Zhang, Lijun Liu, Hongbo Fan and Qingsong Huang

Abstract String Matching is one of the most basic problems in computer science. This paper presented a general research method for calculating the jump distance of q-grams bad-char rule which is named figure example method for q-grams suffix type algorithms. Using this method, we applied q-grams on TVSBS and gained TVSBSq. And by fully utilizing the information of characters in the sliding window, we presented a serial of algorithms called FQ-Hash. Experimental results indicated that above algorithms is faster than TVSBS and they are faster than other known algorithms in some cases on our platform.

Keywords String matching · Text searching · Exact single pattern · Algorithm design · Figure example method · Suffix matching

Z. Zhang · H. Fan · Q. Huang (✉)
Department of Computer Science, Kunming University of Science and Technology, Kunming, China
e-mail: kmustailab@hotmail.com

Z. Zhang · H. Fan · Q. Huang
Yunnan Key Laboratory Of Computer Technology Applications,
Kunming University of Science and Technology, Kunming, China

L. Liu
Department of Biomedical Engineering,
Kunming University of Science and Technology, Kunming, China
e-mail: cloneiq@126.com

W. Lu et al. (eds.), *Proceedings of the 2012 International Conference on Information Technology and Software Engineering*, Lecture Notes in Electrical Engineering 211, DOI: 10.1007/978-3-642-34522-7_51, © Springer-Verlag Berlin Heidelberg 2013

51.1 Introduction

String matching is one of basic problems in computer science. It has been widely used in many important fields, such as network security, information processing, and computational biology. The exact single pattern string matching is the foundation of other variety of string matching problems, and it is used most widely [1]. Hence, the study of the exact single pattern string matching is significantly important. We concentrate on practical exact single pattern string matching. The algorithms without special definitions involved in this paper are for exact single pattern string matching algorithm.

According to the jumping mechanism, the known algorithms can be classified as prefix matching, suffix matching and substring matching, most of algorithms are belong to suffix matching.

The q-grams technique is an important accelerating technique on pipeline processors. To date, many of the current fast algorithms use q-grams. Generally speaking, smaller alphabets or longer patterns demand bigger q. However there are no general research methods for q-grams suffix matching and it is hard to gain the jump distance of q-grams unrolling more than two characters. It causes a serious impact on research.

In this paper, we proposed a general research method called Figure Example Method for q-grams suffix matching algorithms, and also proposed the algorithms TVSBSq and FQ-Hash which based on the algorithm TVSBS. The experimental results indicated that TVSBSq and FQ-Hash have a much better performance when they dealing with extremely short pattern on small alphabet.

51.2 Preliminaries

For given alphabet $\Sigma(|\Sigma| = \sigma)$, Σ^* is the Kleene closure for Σ, and for given text string $T = t_0 t_1 \ldots t_{n-1}$ and pattern string $P = p_0 p_1 \ldots p_{n-1} (P, T \in \Sigma^*)$, the exact single pattern string matching problem is the problem of calculating the set of $O = \{pos | P[j] = T[pos+j], \forall 0 \le j \le m, 0 \le pos \le n-m\}$. Most of algorithms are implemented with sliding window of the same length with the pattern. The sliding window slides from left to right along the text. Report the matching window position while the text in the window is equal to the pattern. Let $S, X, Y, Z \in \Sigma^*$ if $S = XYZ$, then X is a prefix of S, Z is a suffix of S, and X, Y, Z are all substrings of S. The substring from $S[i]$ to $S[j]$ of S is called $S[i \ldots j]$.

In q-grams, q consecutive characters are processed as a single character. For example, the string "Hello" is processed as "Hel-ell-llo" for 3-grams. This can make the alphabet perceived by the algorithm larger. Because a fairly large alphabet leads to a low rate of branch prediction failure, a high probability of jump and a large average jump distance, q-grams can greatly enhance the performance. But q-grams can increase the use of space and it can reduce the maximal jump distance.

Most of the BM type algorithms use bad-char rule as the main jumping mechanism. And most algorithms, such as BR, Q-Hash, Wu-Manber, TVSBS etc., uses the bad grouped characters rule(or called as bad string rule) instead of using the bad character regulation to enhance the performance of small character sets by adopting the q-grams mechanism.

TVSBS is one of the 2-grams BM algorithms. In the searching phase, the string in the window is compared with the pattern and jump according to the following two characters after the window by the 2-grams bad string rule, which the compare order is the last character of the window, the first character of the window and other characters compared backward.

In the pre-processing phase of the algorithm, the jumping distance of each pair of character in $\Sigma \times \Sigma$ is pre-computed and these results are stored in a 2-dimension shift table. To reduce the occurrence space of the shift table, TVSBS uses a hash method which hash function is $hash(a,b)=(a<<5)+b$, which leads the space reduced from 256 to 32 KB after the hash method introduced. The code of algorithm TVSBS show as Code.1 following:

Code.1 algorithm TVSBS

```
TVSBS (P, T, m, n){
1. Σ' ← [0,((σ−1) << 5)+σ−1]; for a ∈ Σ' do shift[a] ← m+2;
2. for a ∈ Σ do shift[(a << 5)+P[0]] ← m+1;
3. for j ← 0 to m−2 do shift[(P[j] << 5)+P[j+1]] ← m−j;
4. for b ∈ Σ do shift[(P[m−1] << 5)+b] ← 1; pos ← m−1;
   c ← P[m−1]; d ← P[0];
5. while pos < n do
6. {if T[pos] = c and T[pos−m+1] = d then
7.   {if P[1...m−2] match T[pos−m+2...pos−1]  then Report ( pos−m+1);}
8.   pos ← pos+shift[(T[pos+1] << 5)+T[pos+2]];}}
```

2-grams should be not enough for small alphabet. To improve the performance of algorithms for small alphabet, most of fast algorithms use q-grams which $q \geq 2$. If the q-grams method is applied to TVSBS, it would show better performance. However, there is no an easy way to calculate the jump distance of q-grams bad-string rule. Meanwhile, the character information on jump read into the TVSBS window without any help, resulting in a larger waste.

51.3 The q-Grams Method for Suffix Matching Algorithm

It is hard to describe the jump method by language when the q-grams method is applied on bad-string rule. For that purpose, we proposed a general research method for computing the jump distance of q-grams bad-string rule, which is called the figure example method, in this section. This method is brief, clear, general and it can be translated directly into the pre-processing code of the algorithms.

Definition 1 For the q-grams bad-string rule, the location of the q consecutive characters should be read is not fixed for different algorithms. Call the window for the position of these q characters is determining word window. And call the length of the overlapping part between the determining word window and the sliding window is q_1, call the length of the non-overlapping part is q_2, which $q_1 + q_2 = q$.

Normally, $q_1 > 0$ for original BM type algorithm to determine whether string matching occurs in the sliding window by the shift distance of bad-char rule. If some other jump method introduced, therefore, q_1 is tolerated equal or less than zero. For example, $q_1 = 0$ for Quick Search serial algorithm by a na matching before bad-char rule jump and $q_1 < 0$ for FJS or SBNDM-BMH etc. by the KMP matching or BNDM matching before bad-char rule jump.

In fact, suffix matching algorithms using the bad-char (bad-string) method can be described with the parameters of q_1, q_2 and jump method before the bad-char (bad-string) method.

For an algorithm, let the minimum jump distance of the sliding window is $shift_{min}$ and the maximum jump distance is $shift_{max}$. There is a following characteristic in the string matching fields.

If the jump distance of a current jumping strategy can reach s, than the sliding window jump any distance from $shift_{min}$ to s can ensure that the sliding window may not miss the position matches the pattern. That is means the method to jump any distance from $shift_{min}$ to s can realize the string matching currently.

Therefore, if there are a number of jump categories for a determining word window and there is one category is current at least, let the jump distance of the category i be $shift_i$, to jump $\min(\{shift_i\})$ is always currently.

Thus, we can acquire a general research method to compute the jump distance for q-grams bad-string rule based on above characteristic. And this method can be described as the following:

1. Give the parameters of m, q_1, q_2, Here, we can set m is five without losing of the generality. And draw the border of each window according to above parameters.
2. Compute $shift_{min}$ and $shift_{max}$ of q-grams.
3. List each situation that the jump distance of the sliding window is between $shift_{min}$ and $shift_{max}$. Indicate the position of each character in every sliding window in the figure.
4. List the determining conditions that the sliding window can slide here by adopting the Top-Down strategy. If the determining word window is included in the sliding window after slide, which is the substring $P[i \ldots i + q - 1]$ is in the determining word window, the value of correction of jump distance x should be calculated for $shift = m - i + x$ based on the figure. Generally $x = q_1$.

The result figure is the figure example of the given parameters q_1, q_2. For example, let $q_1 = 0$ and $q_2 = 3$ which is just the 3-grams extended TVSBS bad-

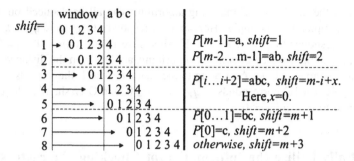

Fig. 51.1 The figure example for 3-grams TVSBS

string rule. Because the Quick Search mechanism has been used in, $shift_{min} = 1$ and $shift_{max} = m + 3$ while all of characters in the determining word window are not appeared in the pattern. Hence, the figure example for this case is shown as the Fig. 51.1.

The jump distance increasing strictly from top to down in the figure example, and all probable jump situations have been included. If all determining conditions and corresponding jumping distances form the figure example are listed down-top in the pre-processing phase, and then for $\forall U \in \Sigma^q$, its result jumping distance is the minimum jump distance of every jumping mechanisms corresponded, that is a calculating method of the jump distance of the q-grams bad-string rule is obtained.

Because of the tremendous space usage of the table *shift*, so we also introduced the hash mechanism to reduce the table space usage. Here, we refer to the Hash mechanism of TVSBS, and define the hash method as the following: $hash(a, b, c) = a + (b \ll 4) + (c \ll 8)$. Consequently, we got the algorithm TVSBS of 3-grams, named TVSBS3, which code shows as Code.2.

Code.2 algorithm TVSBS3

```
TVSBS3 (P, T, m, n){
1. for  a ∈ [0,σ−1+((σ−1) << 4)+((σ−1) << 8)]  do shift[a] ← m+3 ;
2. for  ab ∈ [0,σ−1+((σ−1) << 4)]  do shift[ab + (P[0] << 8)] ← m+2 ;
3. for  a ∈ Σ  do shift[a + (P[0] << 4) + (P[1] << 8)] ← m+1 ;
4. for  j ← 0 to m−3  do shift[P[j] + (P[j+1] << 4) + (P[j+2] << 8)] ← m−j;
5. for  c ∈ Σ  do shift[P[m−2] + (P[m−1] << 4) + (c << 8)] ← 2 ;
6. for  bc ∈ [0,σ−1+(σ−1) << 4]  do shift[P[m−1] + (bc << 4)] ← 1 ;
7. pos ← m−1 ; m1 ← m−1; T[n...n+m−1] ← P ; CW ← (P[m−1] << 8) + P[0] ;
8. while true do
9. {if (T[pos] << 8) + T[pos−m+1] = CW  then
10.   {if  T[pos−m+2...pos−1] match (backward) P[1...m−2]  then
11.     {if  pos < n  then Report; else return;}}
12.       pos ← pos + shift[T[pos+1] + (T[pos+2] << 4) +(T[pos+3] << 8)] ;}}
```

Most of the known suffix matching algorithms can all be deduced out by the Figure Example. For example, Horspool corresponds to $q_1 = 1$, $q_2 = 0$, Quick Search corresponds to $q_1 = 0$, $q_2 = 1$, TVSBS corresponds to $q_1 = 0$, $q_2 = 2$. And besides, the jump distance of some of algorithms are less than the distance gained by figure example method. According to the characteristic 1, they are also correct. For example, BMH2 corresponds to $q_1 = 2$, $q_2 = 0$, and Q-Hash, Wu-Manber etc. correspond to $q_1 = q$, $q_2 = 0$.

51.4 Fully Utilize the Information of Checking Characters Within the Window

In TVSBS, the information of characters within the window is not utilized for increasing the jump distance which causes wasting. In this section, we presented a mechanism that the determining window is cross the sliding window border. In this mechanism, the information of the characters in the sliding window is still utilized for calculation of jump distance which assures the jump as far as possible.

If the overlapping part of the sliding window and the determining word window match the corresponding suffix of the pattern, this sliding window may match the pattern and the whole sliding windows should be matched. To quick determine these situations, the jump distance of these situations can be set a negative number, which the absolute value is the jump distance of q-grams bad-string rule which is calculated by the figure example method. Therefore, the jump distance can be gained quickly form the shift table.

The Figure examples for $q_1 = 1$, $q_2 = 1$ and $q_1 = 2$, $q_2 = 1$ are just shown as Figs. 51.2 and 51.3. Because of the tremendous table space usage of *shift*, so we also adopted the hash mechanism to decrease the space of the shift table. We selected hash functions are as follows: For $U = ab$, $hash(a, b) = (a \ll 8) + b$, and for $U = abc$, $hash(a, b, c) = a + (b \ll 4) + (c \ll 8)$.

Since the forward method like FSBNDM [2] and q-grams and hash methods are applied, we named this algorithm that the determining window strides across the border of the sliding window as FQ-Hash $q_1\_q_2$. According to the figure example shown in Fig. 51.2, the implementation of the algorithm FQ-Hash1_1 is shown as

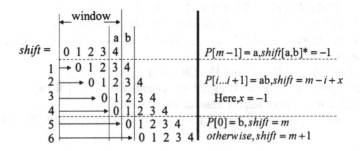

Fig. 51.2 The figure example for FQ-Hash1_1

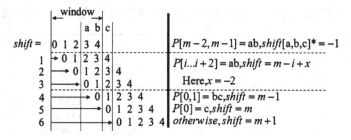

Fig. 51.3 The figure example for FQ-Hash2_1

Table 51.1 Average matching speed against pattern length on English text (MBps)

Bible.txt	2	4	8	16	32	64
Shift-And	341.8	338.0	339.2	341.9	340.8	N/A
SBNDMqb	472.4(2b)	886.8(2 + 2b)	1542.2(2 + 2b)	2536(4b)	3010(6b)	N/A
BXS	367.0(1)	431.6(1)	698.0(4)	1629(4)	2621(5)	3025(5)
QF	N/A	540.4(2,7)	1053.6(2,6)	1927(3,4)	2819(4,3)	3220(4,3)
EBOM	428.1	1124.3	1568.1	2071	2299	2683
SEBOM	429.4	1135.4	1629.3	2185.9	2414.3	2852.1
Q-Hash	N/A	307.3(3)	851.6(3)	1819(3)	2794(3)	3047(3)
SQ-Hash	N/A	333.3(3)	924.9(3)	1952(3)	2863(3)	3100(3)
TVSBS	420.3	655.1	909.0	1441	2272	2820
TVSBSq	488.1(3)	703.4(2)	982.1(2)	1615(2)	2378(2)	2828(2)
FQHash	449.9(1_1)	787.9(1_1)	1213.5(2_1)	2068(2_1)	2795(2_1)	3086(2_1)

Code.3, in which, Σ' indicates the size of the shift table. And other FQ-Hash algorithms can be gained quickly from the figure example method.

Code.3 The implementation of algorithm FQ-Hash1_1

```
FQ-Hash1_1(P, T, m, n){
1. for j ∈ [0,((σ−1)<<8)+σ−1] do shift[j]←m+1;
2. for a ∈ Σ do shift[(a<<8)+P[0]]←m;
3. for j←0 to m−2 do shift[(P[j]<<8)+P[j+1]]←m−j−1;
4. for b ∈ Σ do shift[(P[m−1]<<8)+b]←−1×shift[(P[m−1]<<8)+b];
5. T[n...n+m−1]←P; pos←m−1;
6. while pos<n do
7. { s←shift[(T[pos]<<8)+T[pos+1]];
8. if s<0 then
9. { if T[pos−m+1...pos] match P then Report(pos-m+1);
pos←pos−s; continue;}
10. pos←pos+s;}}
```

Table 51.2 Average matching speed against pattern length on DNA sequence (MBps)

E.coli	2	4	8	16	32	64
Shift-And	341.2	341.2	341.2	341.8	341.3	N/A
SBNDMqb	336.7(2b)	549.6(2b)	1149.0(4b)	2164.7(4b)	2980.6(6b)	N/A
BXS	165.5(1)	217.0(1)	417.7(1)	994.3(4)	1933.3(5)	2306.2(5)
QF	N/A	303.1(3,3)	730.8(3,3)	1620.7(4,3)	2594.4(4,3)	3115.2(5,3)
EBOM	305.4	452.0	558.1	780.0	1289.1	2072.3
SEBOM	309.2	471.3	602.7	898.1	1513.0	2361.7
Q-Hash	N/A	291.5(3)	800.2(3)	1563.4(3)	2594.5(4)	2946.5(4)
SQ-Hash	N/A	313.3(3)	854.1(3)	1627.0(3)	2699.5(4)	2980.7(4)
TVSBS	239.5	302.8	487.7	660.7	559.3	1224.5
TVSBSq	302.4(2)	387.4(2)	611.9 (2)	781.7(2)	1010.7(3)	2114.2(3)
FQHash	298.8(2_1)	585.8(2_1)	1064.9(2_1)	1773.1(2_1)	2649.4(2_1)	2968.0(3_1)

51.5 Experimental Results

To show the performance of the mentioned algorithms, the following comparative experiments have been done. The experimental platform is AMD® Phenom® FX-5000 4-core@2.2GHz/2G DDR2 800 RAM/AMD 785G/UBUNTU 10.10 32bit/ g++4.4.5 (optimized by –O3, with the branch prediction default). We tested under the DNA sequence *E.coli*, English test Bible.txt, and natural language samples text world192.txt, which above three texts are from the Large Canterbury Corpus [3]. For each matching condition, the 100 patterns in each pattern set were picked from the 100 prior random selected and non-overlapping positions of the text, and the average matching speed was recorded as the final result which the highest and the lowest 20 % results were ignored. The text had been read into memory to avoid the impact of disk. Only the matching phase was timed by RDTSC[1] (±30 CPU ticks). In this experiment, the CPU frequency was locked by cpufrequtils,[2] the network and the unrelated daemon background services are closed to ensure the processor utilization was below to 3 %. The comparative algorithms of this experiment includes Shift-and [4], SBNDMqb [5], Q-Hash [2], SQ-Hash [6], EBOM [2], SEBOM [7], BXS [8], QF [8], TVSBS. Those algorithms which described as the Ref. [9] have a much higher performance based on the extreme short pattern. The concrete experimental data list from Tables 51.1 to 51.3 together with the most optimal q of algorithm performance.

Experimental results indicate that the performance of algorithm presented in this paper is faster than TVSBS in many cases. Furthermore, under the three situations that is DNA character set, the pattern of length is 4, and the patter length of English or natural text is 2, the performance of the algorithms this paper proposed are higher than the other compared algorithms on our platform.

---

[1] http://en.wikipedia.org/wiki/Time_Stamp_Counter

[2] http://wiki.archlinux.org/index.php/Cpufrequtils

Table 51.3 Average matching speed against pattern length on natural language text (MBps)

World192	2	4	8	16	32	64
Shift-And	341.6	340.6	341.4	341.8	341.4	N/A
SBNDMqb	491.7(2b)	950.6(2+2b)	1784.7(2+2b)	2502.5(2+2b)	2926.3(2+2b)	N/A
BXS	467.2(1)	573.7 (1)	780.0(1)	1621.9(4)	2632.2(5)	3005.0(5)
QF	N/A	574.7(2,6)	1169.5 (2,7)	1829.8(3,4)	2633.9(3,4)	3126.8(4,3)
EBOM	452.6	1242.0	2039.9	2380.1	2693.9	2960.8
SEBOM	450.9	1250.7	2098.7	2468.0	2783.9	3060.0
Q-Hash	N/A	309.9(3)	860.4(3)	1733.4(3)	2774.3(3)	2997.1(3)
SQ-Hash	N/A	336.9(3)	936.9(3)	1858.7(3)	2853.8(3)	3024.1(3)
TVSBS	462.5	710.4	1093.6	1601.7	2713.9	3002.7
TVSBSq	496.6(2)	710.5(2)	1100.9(2)	1781.3(2)	2631.3(2)	2909.6 (2)
FQHash	502.8(1_1)	854.9(1_1)	1365.7(1_1)	2116.9(1_1)	2956.2(1_1)	3100.8(1_1)

51.6 Conclusion

This paper proposed a general research method, figure example method, for computing the jump distance of the q-grams suffix matching algorithm. The figure example method is simple, clear, general and it can be translated directly into algorithm pre-processing code. By applying q-grams on TVSBS, an improved algorithm of TVSBS was presented, which is named TVSBSq.

And by fully utilizing the information of checking characters within the window, the serial q-grams suffix type algorithms are presented named FQ-Hash that the determining window strides across the border of the sliding window. Experimental results indicated that the algorithm is fast for very short pattern on our platform.

Acknowledgments This paper is supported by the Yunnan Province Social Development Science and Technology Project of China (NO.2010CA016) and the Innovation Fund for Technology Based Firms of China (NO. 10C26215305130). Thanks for the funding.

References

1. Navarro G, Raffinot M (2002) Flexible pattern matching in strings—practical on-line search algorithms for texts and biological sequences [M]. Cambridge University Press, New York
2. Faro S, Lecroq T (2008) Efficient variants of the backward- oracle-matching algorithm [C]. In: Proceedings of the Prague stringology conference 2008. Czech Technical University in Prague, Czech Republic, pp 146–160
3. The large canterbury corpus [OL. Last check: Oct 3, 2011].http://corpus.canterbury.ac.Nz/descriptions/
4. Baeza-Yates R, Gonnet GH (1992) A new approach to text searching [J]. Commun ACM 35(10):74–82
5. Durian B, Holub J, Peltola H et al (2009) Tuning BNDM with q-grams [C]. ALENEX 2009, SIAM, New York, pp 29–37
6. Fan H, Yao N, Ma H (2011) A practical and average optimal string matching algorithm based on Lecroq [C]. ICICSE'10, IEEE CPS. Washington, DC, pp 57–63

7. Fan H, Yao N, Ma H (2010) Fast variants of the backward-oracle-marching algorithm [C]. ICICSE'09 IEEE Computer Society, Washington DC, pp 56–59
8. Durian B, Peltola H, Salmela L et al (2010) Bit-parallel search algorithms for long patterns [G]. LNCS 6049: SEA2010. Springer, Berlin, pp 129–140
9. Faro S, Lecroq T (2010) The exact string matching problem: a comprehensive experimental evaluation [C]. CoRR 2010. http://arxiv.org/pdf/1012.2547

Chapter 52
Fast Multi-Pattern String Matching Algorithms Based on Q-Grams Bit-Parallelism Filter and Hash

Peng Yang, Lijun Liu, Hongbo Fan and Qingsong Huang

Abstract Multi-pattern string matching has become the performance bottleneck of many important application fields. In this article, a q-grams method for BNDM type algorithms named Uq-grams which simulates the bit mask table for higher q value with unrolling the bit mask table for the bit mask table for lower q value was presented. By adopting the Uq-grams and the hash method on the one of the fastest multi-pattern string matching algorithm BG, a serial of algorithms named BGqus are presented. Experimental results indicated that BGqus is faster than BG in most of case, and it can support gigabyte applications for very large-scale matching on large alphabet.

Keywords Algorithm design · Multi-pattern string matching · Bit-parallelism filter · Hash · BG · Q-grams

52.1 Introduction

String matching is a fundamental problem in computer science. It has been widely used in most fields of text or symbol processing, such as network security, computational biology, and information retrieval [1]. Especially in the main research

P. Yang · H. Fan · Q. Huang (✉)
Department of Computer Science, Kunming University of Science and Technology,
Yunnan Key Laboratory of Computer Technology Applications, Kunming, China
e-mail: kmustailab@hotmail.com

L. Liu
Department of Biomedical Engineering, Kunming University of Science and Technology,
Kunming, China
e-mail: cloneiq@126.com

W. Lu et al. (eds.), *Proceedings of the 2012 International Conference on Information Technology and Software Engineering*, Lecture Notes in Electrical Engineering 211, DOI: 10.1007/978-3-642-34522-7_52, © Springer-Verlag Berlin Heidelberg 2013

fields of our team which are the large-scale information retrieval and the mass medical information processing, poor performance of string matching caused a serious impact on our research.

For the given alphabet Σ of size σ, Σ^* is the closures of Σ, and for the given text string $T = t_0 t_1 \ldots t_{n-1} \in \Sigma^*$ and the set of patterns $P = \{P_1, P_2 \ldots P_{r-1}\}$, which $\forall P_i = p_0 p_1 \ldots p_{mi-1} \in \Sigma^*$ and mi is the length of P_i, the multi-patterns string matching is the problem of calculating the set:

$$O = \{pos | \exists k, \ P_k[j] = T[pos+j], \ 0 \leq k < r, \ 0 \leq j < mi, \ 0 \leq pos < n\}.$$

To date, the multi-pattern string matching has become a performance bottleneck of many application fields, such as network and content security, intrusion detection, information retrieval and filtering etc. For example, in the well-known open source IDS software, snort, more than 70 % computing time is for the multi-pattern string matching [2]. With the fast developing of these fields, the requirement for the performance of the multi-pattern string matching is endless, which demand the research the fast multi-pattern string matching. In this article, we concentrate on practical multi-pattern string matching.

In the literature [3], three fast algorithms named BG, SOG and HG are presented by applying the method of q-grams bit-parallelism filter on SBNDM [4], Shift-Or [5], and Horspool [6] respectively. The filter method can quickly filter out most of positions can not match a pattern in the pattern set P. Therefore, the slow multi-pattern string processing is avoided for these positions in searching phase. Introducing the filter method can obviously increase the performance of algorithms. Experimental results indicated that BG is one of the fastest multi-pattern known algorithms.

The q-grams technique is an important accelerating technique on pipeline processors. To date, many of the current fast algorithms use q-grams. In q-grams, q consecutive characters are processed as a single character. For example, the string "Hello" is processed as "Hel-ell-llo" for 3-grams, each continuous q characters is called a q-gram. This can make the alphabet perceived by the algorithm larger. Because a fairly large alphabet leads to a low rate of branch prediction failure and a high probability of jump, q-grams can greatly enhance the performance. Another benefit of q-grams is q-grams solutions are more flexible than the original one.

Large-scale matching needs big q to gain enough low the branch prediction failure rate. Although BG is a q-grams algorithm, it is hard to support big q because of exponential space of the bit vector table. And for large-scale multi-pattern, the cost of memory access has become the bottleneck of performance, reducing the space occupied is the important accelerating way.

In this article, we presented a new q-grams method for BNDM type algorithm named Uq-grams that is a method to realize q-grams for higher q value with the q-grams bit vector table for lower q value. And we introduced the hash method into the q-grams bit vector table, which reduce the space of the table further. Therefore, we presented a serial multi-pattern string matching algorithms named

BGqus. Experimental results indicated that BGqus is faster than BG in most of case, and it can support gigabit applications even for very large-scale matching and large alphabet.

52.2 BG Algorithm

SBNDM is the fundamental algorithm of BG. SBNDM uses a bit-parallelism method to simulate the NFA which can recognize all of substring of pattern. It uses the factor method to jump among the text. In the factor method, text characters in the sliding window of the same length with the pattern that is sliding along the text are inputted backward until the inputted string not a factor (substring) of pattern or the whole window are inputted. Let the string that has been read be U. If U is not a substring of the pattern, the string matching may not occur in this window and the window can safely jump $m - |U| + 1$ characters to let the window over U. If the whole window has been accepted, a string matching is found and after that the window slides one character because the substring of length m of the pattern is just equal to the pattern.

To realize reorganization of all substring of a string, SBNDM pre-computes a bit vector table B by associating each character with a bit mask expressing its occurrences in the reversal of pattern. Therefore, with the bit-parallel Shift-and technique [5] the algorithm maintains a state vector D, which has 1 in each position where a substring of the pattern stats such that the substring is a suffix of the processed text window. If and only if D is zero after a suffix of the window has been inputted, the inputted string is not a factor of the pattern.

Let the pattern set P is {pattern, filters}, the BG algorithm can be described as follows:

If the q-grams method is not applied, BG processes the pattern set as $P' = \{\{p, f\}, \{a, i\}, \{t, l\}, \{t\}, \{e\}, \{r\}, \{n, s\}\}$ and deals with the multi-pattern matching as an extended single pattern string matching with classes of characters firstly for that the extended pattern is P', which the classes of characters are means that each position in pattern corresponding a set of characters. If the substring of text in the current sliding window can not match the extended pattern P', this substring can not match any pattern in the pattern set P. Therefore, the sliding window can quickly jump over the current position to avoid the slow multi-pattern string matching processing and the extended single pattern string matching can be a filter for multi-pattern matching.

BG uses the extended SBNDM algorithm with classes of characters as the method of extended single pattern string matching. The extended SBNDM with classes of characters is similar with the original SBNDM. The difference just is that extended SBNDM sets the i-th bit of the bit mask for characters belong to the character set of the m-1-i position of extend pattern is 1, and SBNDM set the i-th bit for the bit mask of character $P[m - 1 - i]$ is 1. The matching method of extended SBNDM is same with the matching method of SBNDM. If a sliding windows has been inputted backward and the bit vector D is still not zero, there is a extended string matching, and a multi-pattern string matching processing should be done to determine whether there is a sting matching of a pattern in the set of P. In the multi-pattern string matching phase, any current multi-pattern string matching method is allowed and the difference of performance is little when the filter method can filter out most of positions may not match.

For large-scale matching, the characters in the set corresponding to a position in extended pattern P' have become more and more and it may include most of characters in the alphabet, which deteriorate the performance seriously. To improve the filter capability, q-grams is a good method. The q-grams can exponential enlarge the alphabet perceived by the algorithm. For example, for 2-grams, the pattern set P can be processed as the extended pattern $P'_2 = \{\{pa, fi\}, \{at, il\}, \{tt, lt\}, \{te\}, \{er\}, \{rn, rs\}\}$. At this time, the proportion of the 2-grams characters in the character set of a position of extended pattern is decreased in 2-grams alphabet, which avoids the deterioration to some degree.

Since any multi-pattern method is allowed after the extended pattern matching found, we selected the TRIE structure for multi-pattern matching instead of the RKBT multi-pattern matching method used in original BG. Experimental results indicated that using TRIE is faster for most of cases on our platform. The code of 2-grams BG with TRIE multi-pattern matching is listed as Code.1.

Code.1 2-grams BG with TRIE multi-pattern matching

```
//2-grams BG with Trie (P, T, m, n, r)
//preprocessing
newstate ← 0; pos ← −1;
for i ← 0 to r−1 do
{ m ← | P_i |; a_0 a_1...a_{m-1} ← P_i^{rv}; cur ← 0; j ← 0; k ← 1;
    while g(cur,a_j) ≠⊥ and j < m do { cur ← g(cur,a_j); j ← j+1;}
    while j < m do
    { newstate ← newstate +1; g(cur,a_j) ← newstate; cur ← newstate; j ← j+1;
}
    output[cur] ← output[cur] ∪ a_0 a_1...a_{m-1};
    for j ← m−1 to 1 do
    { B[(P_i[j] << 8)+ P_i[j−1]] ← B[(P_i[j] << 8)+ P_i[j−1]] | k; k ← k <<1;}}
//matching
while pos < n − m do
{ D ←~ 0; j ← m−1;
do { D ← D & B[(T[pos + j +1] << 8) + T[pos + j]]; D ← D <<1; j ← j−1;
}while D ≠ 0 and j ≠ 0;
if D ≠ 0 then
    { cur ← 0;
    for i ← 1 to m and cur ≠⊥ do { cur ← δ(cur,T[pos + i]);}
    if cur ≠⊥ then Report find matches of output[cur];}
pos ← pos +1+ j ;}
```

The q value impacts the performance greatly for q-grams algorithms. Smaller alphabet, longer patterns or larger scale leads to low branch prediction failure rate and low capability of filter. In these cases, it demands bigger q to gain high performance. However, the space occurrence is increased exponential and it can not support big q. To decrease the space and enhance the memory access performance, a variant of BG that only build the bit mask for the lowest 6 bit of all characters has been presented to in [3], which reduce the space from $4\sigma^q$ bytes to 4×64^q bytes. This has not solved the problem that that space is too big completely and BG can not support bigger q still after this method introduced.

52.3 Uq-Grams Mechanism

In this section, a new q-grams method for BNDM type algorithm named Uq-grams (unrolling q-grams) is presented. This method can simulate the q-grams bit mask table for bigger q with the table for lower q, which reduces the branch prediction failure rate furthermore without increase the space occurrence.

According to the definition of SBNDM bit vector, there is the following property:

For a 3-gram $t_{pos}t_{pos-1}t_{pos-2}$, and let the table B is the bit vector table of SBNDM, if let the 2-grams bit vector table B_2 is defined as $B_2[t_{pos}t_{pos-1}] = (B[t_{pos}] \ll 1) \& B[t_{pos-1}]$, the 3-grams bit vector $B_3[t_{pos}t_{pos-1}t_{pos-2}] = (B[t_{pos}] \ll 2) \& (B[t_{pos-1}] \ll 1) \& B[t_{pos-2}] = (((B[t_{pos}] \ll 1) \& B[t_{pos-1}]) \ll 1) \& ((B[t_{pos-1}] \ll 1) \& B[t_{pos-2}]) = (B_2[t_{pos}t_{pos-1}] \ll 1) \& B_2[t_{pos-1}t_{pos-2}]$. Therefore, the 3-grams bit mask table can be simulated by 2 unrolling of the 2-grams bit mask table for reducing the branch prediction failure rate. Generally, the k unrolling of the q-grams bit mask table can simulate the $k + q - 1$ grams bit mask table. And if the result of bit vector D is zero after the k unrolling in q-grams BG, the sliding window can jump $m - (q + u - 1) + 1 = m - q - u + 2$ characters by the factor method.

52.4 Hash Method

Because the bit vector table B of BG space occupied is still very big, to reduce the space occurrence of the bit mask table furthermore, we introduced the hash method. We use the such hash method can be fast calculated as follows, although the results are not very uniform:

Let the operations to solve calculating the position in the 3-grams bit mask table of the string $P_i[j - 2 .. j]$ is $(P_i[j] \ll 2 \times s) + (P_i[j - 1] \ll s) + P_i[j - 2]$ instead of the operation $(P_i[j] \ll 16) + (P_i[j - 1] \ll 8) + P_i[j - 2]$ in original BG.

After introducing of the Uq-grams method and above hash method, the result algorithm based on BG is named BGqus (BG with q-grams, u Unrolling and s-bit shift hash method). An example of BGqus for $q = 3$, $u = 2$ and $s = 5$ is listed as Code.2.

Code.2 BGqus Algorithms for q=3, u=2, s=5

```
// BGqGuUsS for q=3,u=2,s=5 (P, T, m, n)
//preprocessing
newstate ← 0; q ← 3; u ← 2; s ← 5;
for i ← 0 to r−1 do
{ m ←| P_i |; a_0 a_1 ...a_{m−1} ← P_i^{rv}; cur ← 0; j ← 0; k ← 1;
   while g(cur, a_j) ≠⊥ and j < m do { cur ← g(cur, a_j); j ← j+1;}
   while j < m do
   { newstate ← newstate+1; g(cur, a_j) ← newstate;
   cur ← newstate; j ← j+1;}
   output[cur] ← output[cur] ∪ a_0 a_1 ...a_{m−1};
   for j ← m−1 to q−1 do
   { B[(P_i[j] << (2*s)) + (P_i[j−1] << s) + P_i[j−2]] |= k; k ← k <<1;}}
//matching
pos ← m−1; T[n...n+m−1] ← P_0; edge ← n−m+q−1;
while pos ≤ edge do
{ D ← B[(T[pos] << (2*s)) + (T[pos−1] << s) + T[pos−2]]
     & B[(T[pos−1] << (2*s)) + (T[pos−2] << s) + T[pos−3]];
   while D = 0 do
   { pos ← pos+m−q−u+2;
   D ← B[(T[pos] << (2*s)) + (T[pos−1] << s) + T[pos−2]]
        & B[(T[pos−1] << (2*s)) + (T[pos−2] << s) + T[pos−3]];}
   j ← m−q−u+1; pos ← pos−u;
   D ← (D <<1) & B[(T[pos] << (2*s)) + (T[pos−1] << s) + T[pos−2]];
   while D ≠ 0 and j ≠ 0 do
   { pos ← pos−1; j ← j−1;
   D ← (D <<1) & B[(T[pos] << (2*s)) + (T[pos−1] << s) + T[pos−2]];}
   if j = 0 then
   { cur ← 0; pos ← pos+1;
   for i ← 0 to m−1 and cur ≠⊥ do cur ← g[cur][T[pos−q+1+i]];
   if cur ≠⊥ then Report find matches of output[cur]; }
   pos ← pos+m−q+1;}
```

52.5 Experiments Results

To show the performance of BGqus algorithms, we do the following comparative experiment with AAC [7], Set BOM [8] and the serial algorithms of BG:

Table 52.1 The optimal parameter and average matching speed for the fastest four type algorithm on random text of alphabet size 2, which unit is MB/s

rand2	m = 8				m = 24			
r=	10	100	1000	10000	10	100	1000	10000
AAC	285.2	143.0	120.5	120.5	246.7	101.3	14.9	9.6
SetBOM	78.4	18.2	12.6	10.3	253.1	82.6	14.4	5.8
BGqGxB	31.4(3,6)	16.6(1)	18.8(1)	18.9(1)	127.9(3,6)	8.7 (1)	3.2 (1)	1.2(1)
BGqGuUsS	75.7	15.9	16.0	15.8	278.2	7.0	2.9	1.2
	(5,3,2)	(4,5,1)	(4,5,1)	(4,5,1)	(5,3,1)	(2,4)	(2,4)	(2,4)

Table 52.2 The optimal parameter and average matching speed for the fastest four type algorithm on random text of alphabet size 16, which unit is MB/s

rand16	m = 8				m = 24			
r=	10	100	1000	10000	10	100	1000	10000
AAC	276.3	192.6	56.4	10.6	275.6	184.5	40.3	16.1
SetBOM	604.6	348.8	79.2	33.8	1124.1	656.0	223.9	93.5
BGqGxB	516.1(2)	334.2(3,6)	154.(3,6)	8.5(3,6)	1264.3(2)	863.6(3,6)	511.5(3,6)	17.4(3,6)
BGqGuUsS	1677.0	937.3	367.8	141.1	2939.5	2475.5	1218.0	386.8
	(2,2)	(3,2,5)	(3,2,5)	(4,2,5)	(3,2,3)	(3,2,5)	(4,3,3)	(5,3,3)

Table 52.3 The optimal parameter and average matching speed for the fastest four type algorithm on random text of alphabet size 64, which unit is MB/s

rand64	m = 8				m = 24			
r=	10	100	1000	10000	10	100	1000	10000
AAC	289.5	196.1	65.2	10.4	274.1	198.9	55.9	18.9
SetBOM	896.2	648.2	147.5	94.4	1622.9	888.8	339.8	134.4
BGqGxB	888.3	794.7	410.3	224.0	1829.7	1386.3	892.2	354.7
	(2)	(2,6)	(2)	(3,6)	(2)	(2,6)	(2)	(3,6)
BGqGuUsS	2151.0	2161.7	1162.1	442.0	2754.7	2572.0	1995.0	521.8
	(2,2)	(2,2)	(3,2,4)	(3,2,5)	(2,2)	(2,2)	(3,2,4)	(3,3,5)

Table 52.4 The optimal parameter and average matching speed for the fastest four type algorithm on DNA sequence, which unit is MB/s

dna	m = 8				m = 24			
r=	10	100	1000	10000	10	100	1000	10000
AAC	270.1	138.4	43.8	10.8	267.3	133.4	16.8	11.6
SetBOM	238.0	94.6	23.8	3.2	624.7	260.8	56.3	23.8
BGqGxB	180.5(3,6)	30.7(3,6)	11.1(1)	4.9(3,6)	552.6(3,6)	92.3(3,6)	5.7(1)	3.5(1)
BGqGuUsS	384.1	148.8	21.6	5.2	1414.0	675.5	125.7	3.3
	(3,2,3)	(5,1,3)	(5,3,3)	(5,3,2)	(5,3,1)	(5,3,2)	(5,3,3)	(2,5)

Table 52.5 The optimal parameter and average matching speed for the fastest four type algorithm on English text, which unit is MB/s

bible	m = 8				m = 24			
r=	10	100	1000	10000	10	100	1000	10000
AAC	275.6	183.8	61.8	27.6	274.4	179.2	27.7	11.6
SetBOM	377.5	151.6	27.8	7.9	826.2	361.4	61.0	16.4
BGqGxB	348.8(2)	140.3(3,6)	33.1(3,6)	8.5(3,6)	903.5(2)	509.8(2)	156.4(3,6)	6.6(3,6)
BGqGuUsS	738.6	227.7	53.5	12.0	1830.9	799.7	263.0	31.9
	(3,2,2)	(3,2,3)	(5,1,3)	(5,3,3)	(3,3,2)	(3,5,3)	(5,3,2)	(5,3,3)

Table 52.6 The optimal parameter and average matching speed for the fastest four type algorithm on natural language, which unit is MB/s

world192	m = 8				m = 24			
r=	10	100	1000	10000	10	100	1000	10000
AAC	277.2	206.4	59.1	27.1	273.9	195.2	26.5	13.7
SetBOM	402.9	174.8	24.2	5.8	855.3	324.1	23.4	3.5
BGqGxB	395.1(2)	170.3(2)	47.9(3,6)	9.2(3,6)	932.1 (2)	517.7 (2)	86.7 (3,6)	7.0(3,6)
BGqGuUsS	821.8	291.6	61.0	12.0	1690.5	692.6	105.5	9.3
	(2,2)	(3,2,3)	(4,2,3)	(4,4,3)	(3,2,2)	(3,3,3)	(3,3,3)	(4,4,3)

The platform is AMD Fx-5000 4-core@2.2Ghz/785G/2GB DDR2 RAM/Ubuntu 10.04LTS 64-bit desktop edition/g++4.4.5 with −O3 optimize parameter. We tested under the three 20 MB length random texts with alphabet size is 2,16,64 respectively, which the random function was the lib function of g++, rand(), and tested under the DNA sequence *E.coli*, English test Bible.txt, and natural language samples text world192.txt, which above three texts are from SMART [9]. For each matching condition, the pattern set were picked from the 400 prior random selected and non-overlapping substring of the text with the same length, and the average matching speed was recorded as the final result. The text had been read in memory to avoid the impact of disk and before each time of matching, a big table had been read sequentially to empty the Cache. Only the matching phase was timed by RDTSC[1] (±30 CPU ticks). In this experiment, the CPU frequency was locked by cpufrequtils[2]; the network and the unrelated background service are closed to ensure the processor utilization was below to 3 %.

The experimental results of the optimal parameter and the average matching speed which unit is MB/s are shown from Tables 52.1 to 52.6.

For small alphabet and large-scale matching, because string matching occurs at most of positions of text, the filter method is ineffective. Then AAC is the fastest algorithm in comparative algorithms because of its liner worst time complexity.

---

[1] http://en.wikipedia.org/wiki/Time_Stamp_Counter

[2] http://wiki.archlinux.org/index.php/Cpufrequtils

And in other cases, BGqus is always the fastest one and faster than other algorithms of times on our platform.

Especially for alphabet size 64 and pattern length 8, even for the scale 10000 patterns, BGqus can reach 3.5 Gbps performance. Since it is point out that the alphabet size of the equivalent character set of random network flow is about 64 [3], BGqus give the possible way to achieve the network security and information filtering on current computer for Gigabyte network.

52.6 Conclusion

In this article, a q-grams method for BNDM type algorithms named Uq-grams which simulates the bit mask table for higher q value with unrolling the bit mask table for the bit mask table for lower q value was presented. By adopting the Uq-grams and the hash method on the bit-parallelism filter algorithm BG, a serial of algorithms named BGqus are presented. The experimental results indicated that BGqus is obviously faster than BG for large alphabet. In some cases the performance of BGqus is times of the performance of BG. BGqus give the possible way to achieve the network security and information filtering on current computer for Gigabyte network.

Acknowledgments This paper is supported by the Yunnan Province Social Development Science and Technology Project of China (NO.2010CA016) and the Innovation Fund for Technology Based Firms of China (NO. 10C26215305130). Thanks for the funding.

References

1. Navarro G, Raffinot M (2002) Flexible pattern matching in strings—practical on-line search algorithms for texts and biological sequences. Cambridge University Press, New York
2. Calder B, Tuch N, Sherwood T, Varghese G (2004) Deterministic memory-efficient string matching algorithms for intrusion detection. IEEE INFOCOM, 2004
3. Salmela L (2009) Improved algorithms for string searching problems Ph.d. thesis. Helsinki University, Helsinki
4. Peltola H, Tarhio J (2003) Alternative algorithms for bit-parallel string matching. In: Proceedings of the 10th international symposium on string processing and information retrieval SPIRE'03, Manaus, Brazil, vol 2857 of LNCS, 2003. Springer, Berlin, pp 80–94
5. Baeza-Yates R, Gonnet GH (1992) A new approach to text searching. Commun ACM 35(10):74–82
6. Horspool RN (1980) Practical fast searching in strings. Softw Pract Exp 10(6):501–506
7. Aho AV, Corasick MJ (1975) Efficient string matching: an aid to bibliographic search. Commun ACM 18:333–340
8. Allauzen C, Crochemore M, Raffinot M (2001) Efficient experimental string matching by weak factor recognition. In: Proceedings of the 12th annual symposium on combinatorial pattern matching, vol 2089 of LNCS, Springer, Berlin, pp 51–72
9. http://www.dmi.unict.it/~faro/smart/[OL,2012/6/25]

Chapter 53
An Improved Memetic Algorithm and its Application in Multi-Constrained Test Paper Generation

Zhihao Wang and Xiangwei Zheng

Abstract In order to improve the quality of intelligent test paper generation, an improved Memetic Algorithm (MA) is proposed as the strategy for intelligent test paper generation in this paper, which is based on Particle Swarm Optimizer (PSO) and Simulated Annealing (SA) (referred to as PMemetic). PMemetic takes PSO as the global search strategy while SA as the local search strategy. The mathematical models corresponding to the constraints for test paper generation and difficulty distribution functions and test paper generation model of PMemetic are established. The experimental analysis indicates that the method is effective, feasible and practical for test paper generation.

Keywords Intelligent test paper generation · Memetic algorithm · Particle swarm optimization · Local search strategy · Simulated annealing algorithm

53.1 Introduction

With the development of computer assisted instruction (CAI), the research and application of test database is more extensive. However, intelligently extracting test questions is difficult in the research of intelligent test database. Using a certain

Z. Wang (✉)
School of Information Science and Engineering, Shandong Normal University
Shandong Provincial Key Laboratory for Distributed Computer Software
Novel Technology, Jinan, China
e-mail: hy861125@126.com

X. Zheng (✉)
School of Information Science and Engineering, Shandong Normal University, Jinan, China
e-mail: xwzhengcn@gmail.com

W. Lu et al. (eds.), *Proceedings of the 2012 International Conference on Information Technology and Software Engineering*, Lecture Notes in Electrical Engineering 211, DOI: 10.1007/978-3-642-34522-7_53, © Springer-Verlag Berlin Heidelberg 2013

strategy to extract the test questions that meet the requirements from a large test database is related to the factors including chapter distribution, average level of difficulty, type and score distribution of the test questions. Intelligent extraction of test questions is a multi-objective optimization problem. In recent years, some researchers try to use intelligent algorithms in the research of test paper generation, and have made some valuable results. Based on PSO [1] and SA, the MA [2] is applied in this paper to optimally solve the above problem.

The remainder of this paper is organized as follows. Section 53.2 details the mathematical model of intelligent test paper generation. Section 53.3 describes the intelligent algorithm to extract questions. Section 53.4 presents the experimental analysis and the application of multi-constrained intelligent algorithm to extract questions based on MA. Section 53.5 concludes the paper and points out future work.

53.2 Mathematical Model of Test Paper Generation

In the generation process of test paper, the requirements, namely the constraints of the multi-objective optimization problem of intelligent test paper generation, mainly include the following six items: total score, difficulty distribution, mastery requirements, chapter distribution of knowledge points, distribution of question types, total estimated answer time. These constraints can be computed from the attribute values of the test questions. The test papers may be represented by target matrix P; the line represents test questions; the column represents attributes of the questions. Suppose a test paper has m questions and each question has n attributes, then P is an $m \times n$ matrix shown, and column vector represents the constraints, with their respective target attribute being score, difficulty, mastery degree, chapter, question type, total estimated answer time. These target attributes should satisfy the following constraints [3], where a_{ij} is the jth attribute value of the ith subject, $i = 1,2,...,m$, $j = 1,2,...,n$. Total score of test paper is defined as $pc = \sum_{i=1}^{m} a_{i1}$. Difficulty coefficient of test paper is defined as $d = \sum_{i=1}^{m} \frac{a_{i1}a_{i2}}{pc}$. Score of questions with mastery requirement being z is $p_z = \sum_{i=1}^{m} c_{1i}a_{i1}$ where

$$c_{1i} = \begin{cases} 1, & a_{i3} = z \\ 0, & a_{i3} \neq z \end{cases}.$$ The scores of questions with mastery requirement being z can be set themselves. Score of questions with knowledge point being K is

$$p_K = \sum_{i=1}^{m} c_{4i}a_{i1} \text{ where } c_{4i} = \begin{cases} 1, & a_{i4} = K \\ 0, & a_{i4} \neq K \end{cases}.$$ Scores of questions with type being

Q is $p_Q = \sum_{i=1}^{m} c_{5i}a_{i1}$ where $c_{5i} = \begin{cases} 1, & a_{i5} = Q \\ 0, & a_{i5} \neq Q \end{cases}$. Total estimated answer time is

$t = \sum_{i=1}^{m} a_{i6}$, where difficulty constraint presents a curve distribution [4]. Suppose pc_i represents scores of the questions in each difficulty level, for $\sum_{i=1}^{v} s_i = pc$, scores of the questions in each difficulty level, for $\sum_{i=1}^{v} s_i = pc$, wherein v is the sum of difficulty levels, difficulty coefficients 0–0.2 for easier level, 0.2–0.4 for easy level, 0.4–0.6 for medium level, 0.6–0.8 for less difficult level, 0.8–1 for difficult level. In order to conveniently specify difficulty curve distribution, this article selects Poisson distribution of discrete random variables as the model of difficulty curve distribution. Formula of Poisson distribution is shown as $P(x = k) = \frac{\lambda^k}{k!}e^{-\lambda}$.

53.3 An Improved MA Used to Extract Questions

MA is a hot research topic in the field of evolutionary computing in recent years, which is a guiding idea for the design of an algorithm. This article presents an improved MA (named as PMemetic) which takes PSO as global search strategy and SA as local search strategy to solve this multi-objective optimization problem of intelligent question extraction.

53.3.1 MA

At present, MA has become a general term for a class of algorithms combining population-based global search methods with local search methods [5]. Compared with simple evolutionary algorithms, MA can often achieve the solutions having higher accuracy with less computational cost [6], and have obvious advantages in solving complex, high-dimension, large-scale, multi-objective problems. MA is described as the following:

(1) Determine global search strategy;
(2) Determine local search strategy;
(3) Initialization of the population, either random initialization, or artificial improvement of individuals in the population with prior knowledge of the optimization problems;
(4) Perform global search on the population according to the selected global search strategy;
(5) Perform local search on some individuals according to local search strategy;
(6) Update the population;
(7) Determine whether the ending conditions are satisfied. Terminate if the conditions are satisfied, otherwise return to step (4).

53.3.2 PSO

PSO algorithm is inspired by artificial life and social psychology, and originates in the simulation of a simplified society model. The basic concept thereof comes from study of cluster phenomena of bird or fish. It demonstrates great charm in the application of various problems such as power system, pattern recognition, image processing and machine learning [7]. The motion equation of the ith particle in the dth dimensional space in PSO algorithm can be described by a set of differential equations, such as shown in formulae (53.1), (53.2).

$$v_{id} = \omega \times v_{id} + c_1 \times rand_1 \times (p_{id} - x_{id}) + c_2 \times rand_2 \times (p_{gd} - x_{id}) \qquad (53.1)$$

$$x_{id} = x_{id} + v_{id} \qquad (53.2)$$

where ω is inertia weight; c_1 and c_2 are acceleration constants; $rand_1$ and $rand_2$ are random functions between [0,1]; x_{id} and v_{id} respectively represent the position and velocity component of the particle in dth dimensional space; p_{id} is the historical best position *pbest* of particle individual has experienced; p_{gd} is the best position *gbest* of the population.

53.3.3 SA

SA is a random optimization algorithm based on Monte Carlo strategy for iterative solution, which is inspired by the annealing process of solid substances. The basic theory of the algorithm is similar to physical annealing process, uses Metropolis criterion to accept a lower solution, and have the ability to avoid local optimum. Metropolis criterion is that if the function is $f(S)$, the current solution is $f(S1)$, the new solution is $f(S2)$, the increment $df = f(S2) - f(S1)$. The Metropolis criterion is shown as formula (53.3). If df is lower than 0, accept the new solution with the probability 1; otherwise accept the new solution with probability $exp\,(-\Delta T/kT)$.

$$p = \begin{cases} 1 & df < 0 \\ \exp\left(-\frac{df}{T}\right) & df \geq 0 \end{cases} \qquad (53.3)$$

53.3.4 PMemetic-Based Test Paper Generation

Based on MA framework, this article puts forward a MA based on improved PSO and SA (PMemetic), and its detailed steps are as follows:

(1) Initialize the particle population and set the size of the population, the dimension of parameters, inertia weight, acceleration coefficients, the maximum allowable number of iterations or adaptive value error limit, constant maximum algebra, initial position and velocity of each particle, etc. Set the parameters of the SA: set a sufficiently large initial temperature T, make $T = T_0$, and determine the number of iterations at each T, namely the chain length L of Metropolis. Randomly extract n sets of test papers (n particles)

from the test database with each has m questions (m-dimensional vector), each dimension corresponds to one test question and encode with attribute value of the question.

(2) Compute the fitness value of the particle.
(3) Update individual historical best position and the global optimal position of the particles.
(4) Implement SA:

   (a) Generate a new solution *gbest"* under random disturbance of the current global best position *gbest*, compute the increment $df = f(gbest")-f(gbest)$ of *gbest"*, wherein *f(gbest)* is the cost function of *gbest*;
   (b) If $df < 0$, accept *gbest"* to be the new global optimal position, that is *gbest* = *gbest"*; otherwise compute acceptance probability of *gbest"* $\exp(-\Delta t/kT)$, that is randomly generating uniformly distributed random function *rand* on (0,1) interval; if $\exp(-\Delta t/kT) > rand$, also accept *gbest"* as the new global optimal position, *gbest* = *gbest"*; otherwise retain *gbest*;
   (c) If the new solution *gbest"* in a plurality of continuous Metropolis chains fails to be accepted or reach the preset ending temperature, the SA ends, otherwise go to step (a).

(5) Determine whether the ending conditions are satisfied, terminate if the conditions are satisfied, and otherwise continue.
(6) Update the particle velocity and position according to the formulae (53.1) and (53.2), and return to step (2).

53.3.5 Fitness Function

When the parameters are initialized, the estimated answer time, distribution of question types and requirement of test paper scores are planned in detail and the particles are generated according to the requirements, so the objective function can be built as follows with just consideration of the distribution of difficulty, chapters and mastery requirements. Suppose the scores of questions with different difficulty levels in the generated test papers are represented with pc_i (*i* represents the level of difficulty), the scores corresponding to different difficulty levels computed in accordance with the difficulty distribution curve are represented by k_i, the error allowed by the difficulty levels is e_i, and w_i represents the weight of the *i*th indicator, reflecting the strength of the constraints, then the evaluation function of the test paper difficulty distribution can be represented as formula (53.4).

$$f_1 = \sum_{i=1}^{n} w_i g_i, \quad g_i = \begin{cases} 0 & |pc_i - k_i| \le e_i \\ |pc_i - k_i| - e_i & |pc_i - k_i| > e_i \end{cases} \quad (53.4)$$

The generated papers get closer to the distribution requirements of the difficulty if f_1 is lower. The evaluation function of distribution of chapters and mastery requirements can also use a similar method, which can be represented as formula (53.5), where m is the total number of the test questions; $l_{ij}^{p_k}$ is the percentage of the knowledge points with the mastery requirement being j in Chapter i; l_k represents

$$f_2 = \sum_{i=1}^{m} \left(\sum_{i=1}^{m} l_{ij}^{p_k} / \sum_{k=1}^{m} l_k \right) \tag{53.5}$$

the score of the kth question.

53.4 Experimental Analysis

53.4.1 Problem Description and Parameter Setting

The algorithm is achieved through Matlab2011b programming, with the test platform of a PC equipped with Pentium IV2.61GHZ and Win XP system and a memory of 1 GB.

Database of the course "Operating System" includes 500 practice tests, and they are respectively given the attribute values based on requirements and stored in the test database. Randomly extract 50 distinct questions to compose a test paper to satisfy the constraints. Figures 53.1 and 53.2 show fitness evolutions of using two methods to extract questions for solution. Table 53.1 gives a set of optimal circumstances of generating test papers in the course of the "Operating System". The experimental results show that for the solution of the model of test paper generation based on PMemetic, the optimal test paper generation scheme is achieved with the number of iterations being 20, the smallest error of difficulty distribution being 0.032 (objective optimization function), the objective function value of the

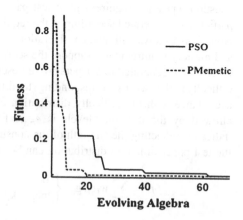

Fig. 53.1 Comparison of difficulty distribution of test paper generation based on PSO and PMemetic

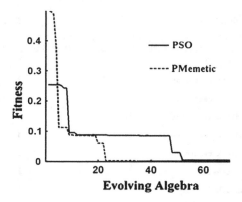

Fig. 53.2 Distribution of chapter and mastery requirement of test paper generation based on PSO and PMemetic

Table 53.1 Optimal test paper generation with PMemetic

Score	Chapter	Question type	Knowledge point	Difficulty coefficient
4	3	Essay question	Critical resource	0.36
2	4	Multiple choice	Processes scheduling	0.28
4	5	Blank-filling	Spooling system	0.41
5	6	Blank-filling	Virtual memory	0.53
3	1	Essay question	Characteristics of the OS	0.36
15	4	Program question	Deadlock avoidance	0.56
6	4	Essay question	Scheduling algorithm	0.41
5	7	Blank-filling	Disk scheduling	0.68
2	8	Multiple choice	Semaphore value	0.71
2	1	Blank-filling	Basic types of OS	0.29
3	8	Multiple choice	Disk scheduling	0.32
3	7	Multiple choice	Deadlock rescinding	0.55
4	2	Essay question	Program executed in the order of features	0.32
5	4	Blank-filling	The reason to cause deadlock	0.12
3	4	Blank-filling	Deadlock necessary conditions	0.39
4	5	Multiple choice	Dynamic partition algorithm	0.42
4	2	Multiple choice	The definition of the process	0.20
3	8	Blank-filling	The junction of the file directory	0.57
3	2	Blank-filling	Program concurrent execution features	0.28
3	6	Multiple choice	Page-replacement algorithms	0.61
5	7	Blank-filling	Buffer pool	0.34
2	2	Multiple choice	The definition of the process	0.20

distribution of chapters and mastery requirements being up to 0.043. For the solution of the model of test paper generation based on PSO algorithm, with the number of iterations being 63, the smallest error of difficulty distribution being

Question type	Question	▲ Score	Difficulty Coefficient
Essay Question	Basic types of OS	4	0.29
Blank Filling	buffer pool	3	0.34
Multiple Choice	characteristics of	2	0.36
Multiple Choice	critical resource	2	0.36
Blank Filling	deadlock avoidance	3	0.56
Essay Question	deadlock necessary conditions	4	0.39
Multiple Choice	deadlock rescinding	2	0.55
Multiple Choice	disk scheduling	2	0.68
Multiple Choice	disk scheduling	2	0.32
Essay Question	dynamic partition algorithm	4	0.42
Blank Filling	page-replacement algorithms	3	0.61
Multiple Choice	processes scheduling	2	0.28
Programme Qu...	program concurrent execution features	15	0.28
Blank Filling	Program executed in the order of features	3	0.32
Blank Filling	scheduling algorithm	3	0.41
Blank Filling	semaphore value	3	0.71
Multiple Choice	Spooling system	2	0.41
Blank Filling	the definition of the process	3	0.2
Blank Filling	the junction of the file directory	3	0.57
Multiple Choice	the reason cousing deadlock	2	0.33
Blank Filling	the reason cousing deadlock	3	0.12
Essay Question	virtual memory	4	0.53

Fig. 53.3 "Operating System" intelligent test paper generation

0.0602, the objective function value of the distribution of chapters and mastery requirements being up to 0.0541, the achieved scheme is not the best for test paper generation, but the suboptimal solution for test question extraction.

53.4.2 The Application Examples of Multi-constrained Intelligent Algorithm to Extract Questions Based on Memetic Algorithm

The system uses the multi-constrained intelligent algorithm to extract questions based on MA which intelligently extract the questions from the test database according to certain conditions. The test database preserves the attribute information of the questions, such as subject, total score, and difficulty level, answer time, etc. Take "Operating System" course as an example for intelligent test paper generation, and the results are shown in Fig. 53.3.

53.5 Conclusion

Intelligent test paper generation is the key process for intelligent examination system. Since PSO has the disadvantages of being easily trapped into local optimum and prematurity, this paper applies PMemetic which is based on improved PSO and SA to intelligently generating test paper. Experiments show that the test papers generated based on PMemetic are significantly feasible than the papers obtained by PSO. The feasibility, effectiveness and practicality of PMemetic have been verified. PMemetic is applied to the intelligent test paper generation system and achieves good results, also lays the foundation for the subsequent analysis and research.

References

1. Kennedy J, Eberhart RC (1942–1948) Particle swarm optimization. In: Proceedings of the international conference on neural networks. IEEE Press, Perth
2. Krasnogor N, Smith JE (2005) A tutorial for competent memetic algorithms: model, taxonomy and design issues. IEEE Trans Evol Comput 9(5):474–488
3. Zhou W (2006) An application of an improved genetic algorithm to composing, a test paper based on knowledge points. J Shandong Norm Univ (Nat Sci) 21(3):39–42
4. Rao L, Wang X (1990) Educational statistics. Nanjing University Press, Nanjing
5. Liu B, Wang L, Jin YH (2007) An effective PSO-based memetic algorithm for flow shop scheduling. IEEE Trans Syst Man Cybern Part B Cybern 37(1):18–27
6. Peter M, Bernd F (1998) Memetic algorithms and the fitness landscape of the graph Bi partitioning problem. PPSN VLNCS, pp 765–774
7. Kennedy J, Eberhart RC, Shi Y (2001) Swarm intelligence. Elsevier Science Press, Singapore, pp 202–210

Chapter 54
A Short Term Load Forecasting Based on Bagging-ELM Algorithm

Ru-zhi Xu, Xiao-feng Geng and Fan-ya Zhou

Abstract Focused on Load forecasting for electric power plan, a novel prediction model, which was based on machine learning, was established. We propose Bagging algorithm optimized Extreme Learning Machine (ELM) prediction model with the fast learning ability of ELM and weight altering of Bagging to increase the prediction accuracy. Finally, it is applied on short term load forecasting problem verified by the EUNITE load forecasting datasets. Compared with winning algorithm of EUNITE competition, Bagging-ELM prediction model has a better performance on prediction accuracy.

Keywords Short term load forecasting · Regression · Bagging · ELM · EUNITE

54.1 Introduction

Power System load forecasting usually analyses the historical data, explores the intrinsic relationship between things and predicts the load altering trend based on the current demand for electricity and the same period electricity consumption associated with electricity, economic, social, meteorological and other factors. Because electricity energy is not easy to store, it is hoped that this kind of energy

R. Xu (✉) · X. Geng · F. Zhou
North China Electric Power University, Changping District, 102206 Beijing, China
e-mail: xuruzhi@ncepu.edu.cn

X. Geng
e-mail: gxfantasy@163.com

F. Zhou
e-mail: zanzarahfanya@hotmail.com

W. Lu et al. (eds.), *Proceedings of the 2012 International Conference on Information Technology and Software Engineering*, Lecture Notes in Electrical Engineering 211, DOI: 10.1007/978-3-642-34522-7_54, © Springer-Verlag Berlin Heidelberg 2013

can be minimized the losses at any time. Hence, it is significant to establish a prediction model which has good performance on accuracy and speed to this problem.

Recently, various using intelligent algorithm to prediction methods are emerging, including neural networks [1–3], expert systems [4, 5], support vector machine [6–11]. These methods represent the forefront of the power system load forecasting.

However, the intelligent algorithms mentioned before have some drawbacks. The main drawback of the expert systems is that they are incapable of learning anything from the environment. Also, the rules must be explicitly stated and stored in advance. It is poor in adaptability. Neural network models can be very complex computationally and a lot of training sample to be applied successfully, and their iterative training procedures usually are slow to converge. The major drawback of SVM is its high computational burden for the constrained optimization.

In this paper, the prediction model based on Bagging optimized Extreme Learning Machine (ELM) is proposed. ELM has a strong learning ability and fast convergence capability associated with Bagging voting to avoid the bad generalization performance when using single algorithm. The experimental results verify that is prediction model has good performance on dealing with load forecasting problem.

The rest of the paper is organized as follows. Section 54.1 introduces ELM algorithm briefly. In Sect. 54.2, Bagging algorithm is illustrated and the compound prediction model is proposed. The experimental results are used to evaluate this prediction model which has better performance than the winning algorithm of EUNITE competition in Sect. 54.3. Finally, our conclusions and future work are presented in Sect. 54.4.

54.2 Extreme Learning Machine

ELM [12–14] is proposed by G.-B. Huang. It is rigorously proved that the input weights and hidden layer biases of (Single-hidden Layer Feed forward Neural Network) SLFNs can be randomly assigned if the activation functions in the hidden layer are infinitely differentiable. After the input weights and hidden layer biases are chosen randomly, SLFNs can be simply considered as a linear system and the output weights of SLFNs can be analytically determined through simple generalized inverse operation of the hidden layer output matrices. ELM's learning velocity can be thousands of times faster than traditional feedforward network learning algorithms like BP algorithm while obtaining better generalization performance (Fig. 54.1).

Given a standard SLFN with N arbitrary distinct samples (x_i, t_i) where $x_i = [x_{i1}, x_{i2}, \ldots, x_{in}]^T \in \mathbb{R}^n$, $t_i = [t_{i1}, t_{i2}, \ldots, t_{im}]^T \in \mathbb{R}^m$, N hidden nodes and activation function $g(x)$:

Fig. 54.1 Illustration of SLFN

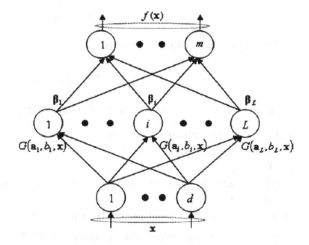

$$\sum_{i=1}^{\tilde{N}} \beta_i g_i(x_j) = \sum_{i=1}^{\tilde{N}} \beta_i g(a_i \cdot x_j + b_i) = t_j, j = 1, \ldots, N \qquad (54.1)$$

where, $a_i = [a_{i1}, a_{i2}, \ldots, a_{in}]^T$ is input weight of the ith hidden layer; b_i is ith hidden nodes bias. $\beta_i = [\beta_{i1}, \beta_{i2}, \ldots, \beta_{im}]^T$ is the output weight of i th hidden layer; $a_i \cdot x_j$ denotes inner product of a_i and x_j. Activaction $g(x)$ can be Sigmoid, Sin and RBF.

$$\mathbf{H}\beta = \mathbf{T} \qquad (54.2)$$

where,

where, $\mathbf{H}(a_1, \ldots, a_{\tilde{N}}, b_1, \ldots, b_{\tilde{N}}, x_1, \ldots, x_N)$

$$= \begin{bmatrix} g(a_1 \cdot x_1 + b_1) & \cdots & g(a_{\tilde{N}} \cdot x_1 + b_{\tilde{N}}) \\ \vdots & \cdots & \vdots \\ g(a_1 \cdot x_N + b_1) & \cdots & g(a_{\tilde{N}} \cdot x_N + b_{\tilde{N}}) \end{bmatrix}_{N \times \tilde{N}}$$

$$\beta = \begin{bmatrix} \beta_1^T \\ \vdots \\ \beta_{\tilde{N}}^T \end{bmatrix}_{\tilde{N} \times m} \qquad T = \begin{bmatrix} t_1^T \\ \vdots \\ t_N^T \end{bmatrix}_{N \times m}$$

H is the hidden layer output matrix of N samples. β is the weight vector connecting ith hidden neuron and output neurons.

The smallest norm least squares solution of the above linear system is:

$$\hat{\beta} = H^+ T \qquad (54.3)$$

where $H^\dagger$ is the Moore–Penrose generalized inverse of matrix H.

$$Y = H\hat{\beta} = HH^+T \qquad (54.4)$$

The error matrix can be described as:

$$\|e\|^2 = \|Y - T\|^2 = \left\|HH^\dagger T - T\right\|^2 \qquad (54.5)$$

Hence, the ELM algorithm can be denoted as following.

Step1: Input the training sample set $N = \{(xi, yi) | xi \in R^d, t_i \in R^m, i = 1, \ldots, N\}$, the hidden layer number L and the hidden layer transfer function $G(a_i, b_j, x)$, $j = 1, \ldots, L$;

Step2: Randomly generate the hidden layer parameters: $(aj, bj), aj \in R^d$, $b_j \in R, j = 1, \ldots, N$;

Step 3: Calculate the output matrix $\mathbf{H}$ of hidden layer;

Step 4: Calculate the output weight vector $\hat{\beta} = \mathbf{H}^\dagger \mathbf{T}$;

Step 5: Output the ELM network.

54.3 Bagging Algorithm

In fact ELM is also a kind of neural network. The drawback of neural network is analyzed previously. To solve this problem, the Bagging algorithm is used to improve the prediction accuracy.

The basic idea of Bagging [15] is given a weak learning algorithm and a training data set which is learned by weak learning algorithm. Taking an account to low accuracy of single weak learning algorithm, it can be handled by the sequence of prediction function which is obtained through voting to the output of repetitive using this algorithm and picking the one which gets a plurality.

It is random to draw 1/2 samples from the training data set on each turn to obtain an ELM regression network. Multiple ELM regression network can be generalized by the same way. A sequence of prediction function φ_1, φ_2, $\ldots \varphi_T$ is obtained after training in order to get the most voted function ψ. The Bagging-ELM regression structure is shown in Fig. 54.2.

54.4 Experiment

The experimental data is from EUNITE competition load forecasting dataset, which is provided by East-Slovakia Power Distribution Company, including load data every 30 min, maximum daily load, daily mean temperature and holiday information. The experimental environment is on the condition of Intel Core i5 CPU 2.4 GHz, 4 GB RAM; The EUNITE data is described in Table 54.1.

Fig. 54.2 The bagging-ELM processing

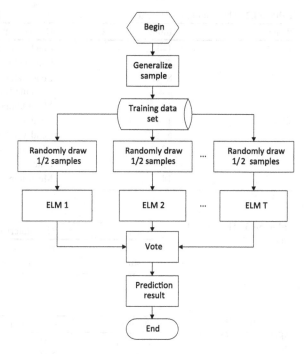

Table 54.1 Specification of datasets

Attributes	Time interval	Number
Load data every 30 min	1997.1.1–1999.1.31	36528
Maximum daily load	1997.1.1–1999.1.31	761
Daily mean temperature	1997.1.1–1999.1.31	761
Holiday information	1997–1999	45

It is significant to normalize the data which is the processing of mapping the data into the interval [0, 1] with the formula (54.6) when the input is obtained. If there exists a certain data which varies widely comparing to the other data, in the training process, this kind of data usually has highly effect on output which would cover up the contribution of other data. So, the normalizing process is independent.

$$\hat{x} = \frac{x - x_{\min}}{x_{\max} - x_{\min}} \tag{54.6}$$

The Mean Absolute Percentage Error (MAPE) is an important prediction accuracy criterion.

$$MAPE(X_i) = \frac{1}{l} \sum_{i=1}^{l} \left| \frac{a_i - p_i}{a_i} \right| \tag{54.7}$$

Table 54.2 The sample construction

Name	Input	Description
S1	1–4	Load value of current time during 2 h
	5–7	Load value of same time during 3 days
	8–11	Load value of same time before last four same type data
	12	Mean temperature of current day
S2	1–4	Load value of current time during 2 h
	5–11	Load value of same time during 3 days
	12	Whether it is a public vacation
	13	Date
	14	Mean temperature

Table 54.3 The EUNITE data

Name	Time interval	Number
Training	1997.1.1–1998.12.31	34897
Testing	1999.1.1–19991.31	1441

Table 54.4 The experimental results of samples

Date	MAPE (S1) %	MAPE (S2) %
1999.1.1	1.51	2.73
1999.1.2	2.11	2.23
1999.1.3	2.15	2.34
1999.1.4	1.61	1.91
1999.1.5	1.94	1.92
1999.1.6	2.00	3.78
1999.1.7	1.59	2.55

where l is the number of samples; a_i is the ith true value of testing sample; p_i is the ith prediction value of testing sample.

54.4.1 Sample Selection

There exists two different ways of sample selection S1 and S2 which are shown in Table 54.2.

The EUNITE data is plotted as training data and testing data which is given as Table 54.3. As it is shown in Table 54.4, the prediction result about the first 7 days of 1999.1 based on S1 and S2 is given after 100 repeated experiments. The experimental result denotes that S1 is better than S2 which means the sample of feature selection based on the same data is better than the one based approximate data.

Table 54.5 The experiment sample set

Name	Time interval	Number
Training set	1997.1.1–1998.12.31	730
Testing set	1999.1.1–1999.1.31	31

Fig. 54.3 The experimental results of maximum load forecasting prediction

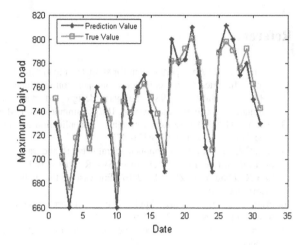

Table 54.6 The compare of experimental results

Name	MAPE(%)
ELM	5.48
Bagging-ELM	1.52
EUNITE winner [16]	1.95

54.4.2 Maximum Daily Load Prediction

In this experiment, the sample is constructed as the way of S1. The data plotted is shown in Table 54.5. As it is shown in Fig. 54.3 and Table 54.6, the MAPE of ELM after weighted by Bagging algorithm decreases from 5.48 to 1.52 % which means the accuracy increases and the result is better than EUNITE winner's result.

54.5 Conclusion

In this paper, we have proposed Bagging-ELM prediction algorithm solving load forecasting problem. With strong learning ability and fast convergence capability, ELM is weighted by Bagging algorithm which is testified by experiment that compound prediction model can efficiently process the nonlinear problem and avoid the poor performance on generalization by single algorithm. Experiment results verify that the proposed Bagging-ELM can achieve a high accuracy on load forecasting problem. In the future work, we will conduct the experiments and consummate the prediction algorithm to improve usage efficiency and apply in different problems.

References

1. Chen D (1991) An expert system for short-term load forecasting. Advances in power system control. In: International conference on operation and management, pp 330–334
2. Rahman S, Baba M (1989) Software design and evaluation of a microcomputer-based automated load forecasting system. IEEE Summer Power Meet Portland Or 1989:782–788
3. Hsu YY (1992) Fuzzy expert systems: an application to short-term load forecasting. IEEE Proc Transm Distrib 139(6):471–477
4. Kim C-I, Yu I-K (2002) Kohonen neural network and transform based approach to short-term load forecasting. Elect Elecr Power Syst Res 63(3):169–176
5. Luo X, Zhou Y-H, Zhou H (2007) Forecasting the daily load based on ANN. In: Control theory and application, pp 1–4
6. Francis E, Tay H (2001) Application of support vector machines in financial time series forecasting. Omega 29:232–239
7. Chen B-J (2001) Load forecasting using support vector machines. A study on EUNITE competition
8. Ruping S (2001) Incremental learning with support vector machines. In: Proceedings IEEE international conference on ICDM 2001, pp 641–642
9. Cauwenberghs G, Poggio T (2000) Incremental and decremental learning with support vector machine. NIPS. MIT Press, Cambridge, pp 409–415
10. Ma J, Theiler J (2003) Accurate on-line support vector regression. Neural Comput 15(11):2683–2703
11. Karasuyama M, Takeuchi I (2009) Multiple incremental decremental learning of support vector machines. In: 23rd annual conference on neural information processing systems (NIPS 2009), MIT Press, Vancouver, pp 1048–1059
12. Huang G-B, Hou H, Ding X, Hang R (2010) Extreme learning machine for regression and multi-classification. In: IEEE transactions on pattern analysis and machine intelligence, pp 513–529
13. Huang G-B, Zhu Q-Y, Siew C-K (2004) Extreme leaning machine: a new learning scheme of feedforward neural networks. In: Proceedings of international joint conference on neural networks (ICNN2004), vol 2, pp 985–990
14. Huang G-B, Zhu Q-Y, Siew C-K (2006) Extreme learning machine: theory and applications. Neurocomputing 70:489–501
15. Breiman L (1996) Bagging predictors. Mach Learn 24(2):123–140
16. http://neuron.tuke.sk/competition/index.php

Chapter 55
Information Extraction Based on Event Driven from Template Web Pages

Xiuhong Zhang and Zhe Gong

Abstract In order to acquire real-time information related to catastrophic events in emergency field, e.g., place, time, population casualties, etc. This paper puts forward a kind of template used for filtering Webpage noise. At the same time, studying on how to make the Bootstrapping algorithm applied to the emergency field and extract information from Web pages based on event driven to expand the scope of information extraction while ensure the information of real-time. Experiment results demonstrate that compared with the traditional Web information extraction ways, this method which achieve high accuracy and efficiency in Web information extraction, to a great extent, can meet the requirement of real-time and be successfully applied in the emergency field.

Keywords Emergency field · Information extraction · Event driven · Web template · Bootstrapping algorithm

55.1 Introduction

In recent years, as the Internet scale surges and the network information transmission advantage appears, Web information has become the attention of governments at all levels and departments. Especially in the emergency field, there is "information delay" and "information failure" problem, extracting real-time

X. Zhang (✉)
School of Computer, BeiHang University, XueYuan Road No.37, HaiDian District, Beijing, China
e-mail: tracyz0928@163.com

Z. Gong
Beijing Institute of Spacecraft Environment Engineering, China Academy of Space Technology, XueYuan Road No.37, HaiDian District, Beijing, China

W. Lu et al. (eds.), *Proceedings of the 2012 International Conference on Information Technology and Software Engineering*, Lecture Notes in Electrical Engineering 211, DOI: 10.1007/978-3-642-34522-7_55, © Springer-Verlag Berlin Heidelberg 2013

catastrophic information related to the disaster event from Web pages, for example, places, time, population casualties, etc., so as to provide basis for decision making in the emergency field. In addition, professionals can obtain the information of public opinion, have a comprehensive grasp of public opinion dynamic and make the right public opinion guides.

Web information extraction is different from common text extraction, this is because that information on the Internet mostly comes out in the form of Web page, and the structure of Web page itself is constantly changing, namely, Web information extraction is a kind of text information extraction with variable structure. The existing methods of Web information extraction mainly include the method based on statistical theory, visual feature, DOM tree structure and Web template, the last two are widely used. Although the method based on DOM tree structure has higher degree of automation than the one based on Web template, but the applicable scope and complexity of the algorithm based on Web template is superior to the former, and this method avoids the repetitive computation on similar Web pages, summarizes unified extraction templates for similar page, greatly improves the efficiency of Web information extraction through the intervention of people. To sum up, the current Web information extraction method is still not completely mature.

One of the research emphases in the Web information extraction is how to improve the accuracy of topic information extraction. Because most of Web pages fill with floating ads, website navigation and other Web pages noise not related to the catastrophic information, it is difficult to extract the higher topic related information. This paper proposes the event driven Web information extraction method based on the template, which is combining with event characteristics and for the purpose of extracting places, time, population casualties and other real-time catastrophic information. With the intervention of people, this method make up the defect of the low detailed degree and low efficiency of automatic machine recognition method, so as to meet the demand of Web information extraction efficiency and accuracy in the emergency field. In addition, by constructing and updating disaster keyword setin real-time, the method further improves the degree and accuracy of Web information extraction.

There are many Web information extraction methods at home and abroad now [1, 2]. Main methods are as follows. Web-Page Blocking makes use of Web page marks to put parts of Web page [3], expresses the Web page block as characteristic vector, and identify subject content block according to the orderly mark set. Although the method can extract information based on the same structure in the same website, but detailed degree of information is not high, not extract the catastrophic information based on the emergency field needs, and at the same time the accuracy is lower; A novel method based on template uses detect template to extract data from Web pages automatically [4], and has the very high accuracy while tend to "list page" type of Web page without considering user needs. The way to using machine learning to automatically generate template and extracting the information [5, 6] is also put forward. And the accuracy of extraction information is higher, but if the goal is to extract information which includes the title, users, published time and other detailed information, the frequent learning leads to decline in efficiency. The methods mentioned above are not preferred the relevance of event, while the extraction method based on event frame [7] considers the relevance of event, can extract more detailed information of event and the efficiency is higher, but it is too dependent on the event frame, so if the frame is not complete, it will affect the accuracy of Web information extraction.

This paper uses the event driven method based on the Web template to extract Web information, which is not only overcome the "information delay" and "information failure" difficult, but also has the characteristics of method based on template that balancing filtering Web page noise with information extraction efficiency, achieves the goal of accurate and efficient extraction related to disaster event, and according to the defined data model to realize information storage, provides convenience for related departments to carry out research on disaster relief.

55.2 Problem Definition

In this paper, we first give related definitions as follows.

- Definition 1 (HTML parsing). HTML document is controlled by tags and text content, its parse is a process during which HTML document will be converted into a DOM tree, and tags are the tree nodes. After the parsing, the handle of the HTML document equals with the operation of the DOM tree. For example, in Fig. 55.1, the left is a simple HTML document and the right side of a DOM tree.

In this paper, HTML parser uses its tag classes including Link Tag, Image Tag, Form Tag and Table Tag to generate DOM tree by receiving URL. It is easily process all types of tags when extracting information, because HTML parser has kinds of different tag classes and different tags will be transferred to corresponding tag class. What's more, an instance of the class will be return to a list and each element will be introduced into it. Through the instance can access start position, end position and content of the current tag. At the same time, we can also visit its father tag and all sub-tags, then using method to clean all HTML information in the tag.

- Definition 2 (template). A template T of a set of Web pages is a regular expression over an alphabet $\sum = M \cup A \cup D \cup K$, where

M   is the set of template tag, including both the HTML start tags and end tags.
A   is the set of attribute that descript the template tags. An attribute, which is defined with a value, is a part of a template tag.
D   is the set of data fields. In most cases, a data field corresponds to a column of a table in relational database.
K   is the set of keyword which can be described as event driven factor in this paper. During extracting Web information, Bootstrapping algorithm will be applied to update keyword set.

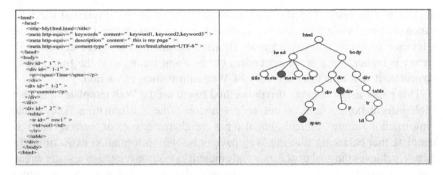

Fig. 55.1 Model of HTML document and DOM tree

55.3 Description of Our Approach

55.3.1 Overview

In this paper, we design a new Web information extraction structure, to meet the real-time requirement of emergency event field, in Fig. 55.2.

As shown in above figure, it is mainly made up of HTML parser, template generator, information extraction and information storage, where

- HTML parser is used to convert and parse document into DOM tree.
- Template generator is used to generate template which consist of tags selected with the intervention of people and keyword set related to the characteristic of emergency event.
- Information extraction module is used to extract information from template Web page, and the result data will be dealt with data model.
- Information storage is used to store the event information in the database.

The implementation procedure of the structure is described as follows. Firstly, filtering the noise in the Web pages by template, then applying Bootstrapping algorithm to update keyword set, which improve the accuracy and coverage of information extraction related to disaster events. Therefore this structure can meet the accuracy, recall rate and efficiency of information extraction about emergency event.

55.3.2 Structuring Template

In this paper, we use HTML tags to label the position of the information, including title, time, abstract, content which are related to the emergency event. The model of template, called Web_Template, is expressed by a four-tuple as follows.

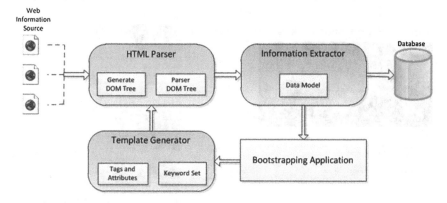

Fig. 55.2 Structure of Web information extraction

$$Web\_Template = \{(template_{id}, template_{name}, keyWords, webInfo)\} \quad (55.1)$$

The $template_{id}$, in Formula (55.1), represents the unique identity of the template, while $template_{name}$ is the name of the template, keyWords means keyword set in the emergency field, where $keyWords \in KeyWords$

$$KeyWords = \{key_{id}, key_{value}\} \quad (55.2)$$

Above Formula (55.2), *KeyWords* contains two parts, one is key_{id} which represents the unique identity of keyword, the other is key_{value} which is the value of the keyword.

In Formula (55.1), the last property called *webInfo*, which means the configuration information of website, where $webInfo \in WebInfo$.

$$WebInfo = \{coreWeb, generalWeb\} \quad (55.3)$$

Above Formula (55.3), *WebInfo* includes two sources of information, one is *coreWeb* which provides information of the important Web, the other is *generalWeb* which has information of the general Web, all of them inherit from *Web* below.

$$Web = \{URL_{id}, URL_{value}\} \quad (55.4)$$

$$generalWeb = \{URL_{id}, URL_{value}\} \quad (55.5)$$

$$coreWeb = \left\{ \begin{array}{ccc} URL_{id}, & URL_{name}, & URL_{value} \\ tag_{name}, & tag_{attname}, & tag_{value} \end{array} \right\} \quad (55.6)$$

Above Formula (55.4, 55.5), *Web* has two basic properties, the one is URL_{id} which represents the unique identity of the *URL*, the other is URL_{value} which means the value of the *URL*. Additional, *CoreWeb*, in Formula (55.6), has its own properties, including URL_{name} which is the name of the *URL*, tag_{name} which is the

Fig. 55.3 Application of Web template

name of the HTML tags, $tag_{attname}$ which is the attribute name of the HTML tags in *CoreWeb*, and tag_{value} which means the value of $tag_{attname}$.

For example, Fig. 55.3 shows an instance where the upper left part is the original Web page and the right lower one is the result filtered by the template.

55.3.3 Generating Keywordset

In this paper, Bootstrapping algorithm is used to update keyword set in the emergency field. During extracting Web information, the update of keyword set will drive the procedure to continue, until the content of the keyword set no longer changes, the current Web information extraction will be stopped. First give some related definitions.

- *keyword* is learnt from a larger number of real Web pages by machine learning, such as time, location, death, damage, etc.
- *s_keyWord* is used in the beginning of automatic learning.
- *w_keyWord* is the candidate word of emergency field from Web pages.

- $x\_keyWord$ is the important word of emergency field which obtain higher evaluation.
- $new\_keyWord$ is selected from $w\_keyWords$ which meet the evaluate conditions and formula.

The application of Bootstrapping algorithm in emergency field described as follows.

1. Begin. Select $s\_keyWord$ to start the information extraction, $s\_keyWord \in s\_KeyWords$, $keyWord \rightarrow x\_keyWord$.
2. Structure $w\_KeyWords$.
3. Evaluating and Selecting $new\_keyWord$.

   - The first evaluation. For each $w\_KeyWord \in w\_KeyWords$, if it meet the conditions $F_w \geq F_{\min}$ and $\frac{F_{wx}}{F_w} \geq R_{\min}$, then add $w\_KeyWord$ into $w_1\_KeyWords$ where w does not belong to disable word, F_w is the sentence number of $w\_keyWord$ in all extracted Web pages, F_{wx} is the sentence number of $x\_KeyWord$ where $x\_keyWord \in w\_keyWords \cap x\_keyword \in x\_KeyWords$, F_{min} is the minimum value of frequency, R_{min} is the threshold value of minimum support, the value of F_{min} and R_{min} pointed with intervention of people.
   - The second evaluation. For each $w_1\_KeyWord \in w_1 KeyWords$, if it meet the formula $m_w = Log_2 F_{wx} \times \frac{F_{wx}}{F_w}$ where m_w is the value of the second evaluation, the higher the value, the more impossible of $w_1\_KeyWord$ is the keyword, m_{min} is the value of minimum standard, if it meet $m_w \geq m_{min}$ add it into the $w\_KeyWords$, generally, $m_{\min} = \log_2 5 \times (0.5 + loopNum \times 0.005)$, $loop Num$ is the times of study.
   - Select $new\_keyWord$, for each m_w, if it meet $m_w > m_{\min}$. $new\_keyWord \in new\_KeyWords$, $KeyWords = KeyWords \cup new\_KeyWords$.
   - Select $new\_x\_keyWord$ by two or three, for each $new\_KeyWord$, if it has the value of the best. $new\_x\_keyWord \in new\_x\_KeyWords$.

4. If $new\_KeyWords$ is null, stop.
5. $x\_KeyWords = x\_KeyWords \cup new\_x\_KeyWords$, jump to step 2.

55.3.4 Extracting Information

In order to meet the real-time requirement of emergency field, we take the following method to extraction information, then according to

Step 1   Initiating event, then starting threads.
Step 2   for each $coreWeb$, $URLlist \leftarrow Extracting\ related\ URL$ in the $coreWeb$ homepage.
Step 3   for each $URL \in URLlist$

Step 4   if *URL* belongs to the current *coreWeb*, then extracting its text based on the template, otherwise, adding it into the *generalWeb* list.

Step 5   *SearchResult* ← *SearchInfo* × *DataModel*, is the data stored in the database, *SearchInfo* is the information related to the event.

Step 6   end for

Step 7   end for

Step 8   Application Boot strapping algorithm to update keyword set in the template.

Step 9   If the keyword set update, jump to the step 2, otherwise, exit the procedure.

55.4 Experiments

In the following machine environment detects algorithm accuracy, recall rate and efficiency. Experimental computer is the Intel Core i5 CPU processor, running under 32-bit Windows operating system, and CPU main frequency is 2.80 GHZ, memory is 4.00 GB. The Web information extraction method realized in the paper aims at extracting earthquake event information from Xinhua website, people website, sohu website and sina website, and the test results is shown in Table 55.1.

Considering precision, the recall rate and efficiency in system evaluation, they are defined as follows.

$$precision = \frac{m}{n} \qquad (55.7)$$

$$recall = \frac{m}{k} \qquad (55.8)$$

$$efficiency = \frac{t}{n} \qquad (55.9)$$

Above Formulas (55.7–55.9), n refers to the extraction number of events, m refers to the correct extraction number of events, k refers to the number of actual events and t refers to the time taken in the extraction process.

The result in the table above reveals the event driven Web information extraction method based on Web template and features in emergency field used in this system can get satisfactory results, and the system performance is optimal.

Table 55.1 Result of event-driven Web information extraction method

URL	Precision (%)	Recall rate (%)	Efficiency (ms/page)
www.xinhuanet.com	91.8	86.5	135
www.people.com.cn	92.5	83.6	110
www.sohu.com	93.3	89.4	100
www.sina.com	93.6	87.8	105

55.5 Conclusion and Future Work

This paper puts forward the event driven Web information extraction method based on template, has the following features. (1) Web information extraction is driven by disaster event during the whole information extraction processing, which improves information extraction of real-time; (2) Configuring Web templates based on the characteristics of disaster events in the emergency field and filtering Web page noise improve the information extraction accuracy and efficiency; (3) Making Bootstrapping algorithm applied to the Web information extraction and updating keyword set after each round of information extraction improve the information coverage in the next round of extraction.

The experimental results show that this method not only has higher accuracy, recall rate and efficiency in event-related Web information extraction, but also can automatically update keyword set, solve the emergency field problem, "information delay" and "information failure", so as to meet the real-time needs of emergency field, and extract the time, place, abstract, content and other detailed information from Web pages to provide decision basis for carrying out disaster relief. This method has successfully applied in emergency field for extracting catastrophic information.

So far, some problems exist in this method, for example, extracting information in different website need to configure the HTML tags information in the Web template before executing the information extraction. So how to configure website information for emergency field through the machine learning automatically and achieving the complete automation extraction will become a study emphasis in further research.

References

1. Wang JY, Lochovsky FH (2002) Data-rich section extraction from HTML pages. IEEE Computer Society Press, Singapore, pp 313–322
2. Feng H, Liu B, Liu Y (2005) A framework for extracting the content and analysis for the Web pages with the position coordinates tree. Tsinghua Sci Technol 45(s1):1767–1771
3. Yin XL, Li M (2007) An automatic extraction algorithm of Web pages topical information based on blocks. J HuaZhong Univ Sci Technol (Nature Science Edition) 35(10):39–41
4. Yang SH, Lin HL, Han YB (2008) Automatic data extraction from template_generated Web pages. J Softw 19(2):209–223
5. Zheng CS, Fu Y, Yu L (2009) Template-based information automatic extraction of Web. Appl Res Comput 26(2):570–573 (in Chinese)
6. Ou JW, Dong SB, Cai B (2005) Topic information extraction from template Web pages. Tsinghua Sci Technol 45(s1):1743–1747 (in Chinese)
7. Liang H, Cheng QX, Wu PB (2005) Information extraction system based on event frame. J Chin Inf Process 20(2):40–46 (in Chinese)

Chapter 56
An Improved Simulated Annealing Algorithm for Traveling Salesman Problem

Yong Wang, De Tian and Yuhua Li

Abstract Traveling salesman problem (TSP) is one of the well-known NP-Complete problems. The simulated annealing algorithm is improved with the four vertices and three lines inequality to search the optimal Hamiltonian circuit or near optimal Hamiltonian circuit. The four vertices and three lines inequality is considered as the heuristic information to change the local Hamiltonian paths into the local optimal Hamiltonian paths. The local optimal Hamiltonian circuits are generated with the basic simulated algorithm firstly, and the local Hamiltonian paths in them are changed into the local optimal Hamiltonian paths with the four vertices and three lines inequality, and then the shorter local optimal Hamiltonian circuits are obtained. The algorithm of the improved simulated annealing is designed and tested with several TSP instances. The experimental results show that the shorter local optimal Hamiltonian circuits are found than those searched with the basic simulated annealing algorithm under the same preconditions.

Keywords Traveling salesman problem · Simulated annealing · Four vertices and three lines inequality · Algorithm

56.1 Introduction

Traveling salesman problem (TSP) aims to find the optimal Hamiltonian circuit (OHC) in a tourist map. It has been proven to be one of the NP-Complete problems. The number of the Hamiltonian circuits (HC) increases exponentially

Y. Wang (✉) · D. Tian · Y. Li
School of Renewable Energy, North China Electric Power University, No.2 Beinong
Road, Hui Longguan, Changping district, 102206 Beijing, China
e-mail: wangyyong100@163.com

W. Lu et al. (eds.), *Proceedings of the 2012 International Conference on Information Technology and Software Engineering*, Lecture Notes in Electrical Engineering 211, DOI: 10.1007/978-3-642-34522-7_56, © Springer-Verlag Berlin Heidelberg 2013

proportion to the number of the cities in the map [1] (given the cities are connected by the routes). The TSP has been widely studied in the fields of combinatorial mathematics, graph theory and computer science due to its theoretical and practical values as it is resolved within a reasonable computation time.

The algorithms for TSP can be categorized into three types which are the exact algorithms, the approximate algorithms and the intelligent algorithms. With the exact algorithms, the OHC is ensured to be found whereas they are not appropriate to cope with the large scale TSP. These algorithms include the traditional graph search algorithms [2], linear programming methods [3] and dynamic programming methods [4]. The experiments illustrated that the better exact algorithms are feasible to resolve the TSP with less than 1,000 cities [5] with powerful computers. If the TSP scale becomes larger, the computation time is too long. The approximate algorithms can not guarantee to find the OHC. However, they play an important role for TSP because the time complexity is polynomial but not exponential. When the local improvement rules or heuristic information are added to the exact algorithms, the exact algorithms turn into the approximate algorithms. The approximate algorithms for TSP include minimum spanning tree algorithms [6], the subset cover algorithms [7] etc. The k-opt ($k = 2, 3, 4, 5$) algorithms and the LK or LKH algorithms are the competitive algorithms for TSP [5]. It is reported that these algorithms are robust to tackle the large TSP with thousands of cities, even with more than 3,000,000 cities [8]. The researchers also claimed that the tours quality can not be evaluated because the OHCs of these instances are not known.

In the end of last century, the intelligent algorithms become more and more mature, and TSP is taken as one of the best platforms to test their performance. Almost all of the intelligent algorithms, such as the artificial neural network [9], the genetic algorithms [10], the simulated annealing (SA) algorithm [11], the ant colony optimization algorithm [12], the particle swarm optimization algorithm [13] and the consultant-guided search algorithm [14] etc., are applied to TSP. The intelligent algorithms evolve to the best solutions based on the evolutionary principles, which are the global optimization rules different from the local improvement rules used by the approximate algorithms. The evolutionary principles are generally represented with the statistical formulae. The near optimal solutions are usually found, and the intelligent algorithms are always being improved to obtain the better solutions. The memetic algorithms are the integration of the intelligent algorithms and the local improvement rules, which utilize the advantages of the two kinds of algorithms for the large scale of TSP [4].

The SA algorithm is one of the efficient methods for the optimization problems. The evolutionary principle is the cooling schedule, which is convenient to be implemented. In addition, the SA algorithm has no much demand for the initial solutions. Although it has many merits, it is always criticized for its bad performance and slow convergence when it is applied to the complex TSP. The basic simulated annealing (BSA) is improved by several researchers for TSP. Liu introduced the SA integrated with the Tabu search to detect the better solutions. The temperature is reduced adaptively with a temperature control function [11].

Based on most edges of the best circuit linked by neighbor cities, the probabilistic neighborhood model was introduced by Li et al. [15] and merge into the optimization process of the SA algorithm. The SA algorithm is also integrated with the other intelligent algorithms [16] to utilize their advantages together.

To accelerate the convergence of BSA and obtain the shorter HCs, the four vertices and three lines inequality is merged into the optimization process of the BSA. Four point conditions for symmetrical TSP was summarized by Vladimir [17]. The four vertices and three lines inequality is the extension of one of the four point conditions. It is the constraint of the local optimal Hamiltonian paths and can be applied to the asymmetrical TSP. After the local optimal Hamiltonian circuits are generated with the BSA, the four vertices and three lines inequality is applied to the local Hamiltonian paths in the local OHCs. After the local Hamiltonian paths are transformed into the local optimal Hamiltonian paths, the shorter local OHCs are obtained. The computation process is executed until the OHC or near OHC is found. The improved simulated annealing (ISA) algorithm is tested with TSP instances and compared with the BSA. The results show that the shorter local OHCs are found with the ISA and the convergence is also accelerated.

56.2 Mathematical Model of TSP

The objective of TSP is to find the OHC from the weighted graph (WG). The cities and routes in the tourist map correspond to the vertices and edges in the WG, respectively. The length of the OHC is shortest among all of the HCs. For graph G including n vertices, it is represented as G = <V, E>, where V = <$v_1, v_2,..., v_n$> are the vertices sets and E = <$e_{1\times2}, e_{1\times3},..., e_{(n-1)\times n}$> are the edges sets. v_i ($1 \leq i \leq n$) is the vertex and $e_{i\times j}$ ($1 \leq i, j \leq n$) is the edge linking the two vertices v_i and v_j. Graph G is represented as the adjacent matrix A(G) = $\{a_{i\times j}\}$ ($1 \leq i$, $j \leq n$), where $a_{i\times j}$=1 if (v_i, v_j) ∈ E(G) and v_i and v_j are adjacent in the graph G. Otherwise, $a_{i\times j}$=0. If the edges are assigned with weights W = <$w_{1\times2}, w_{1\times3},...,$ $w_{(n-1)\times n}$>, the graph G becomes one WG. The weight $w_{i\times j}$ is often taken as distance, cost etc. for various kinds of TSP.

Given the HC including n vertices, it is represented as HC^{n+1}=($v_1, v_2, v_3,..., v_n,$ v_1). The HC includes all of the vertices in the WG once and only once unless it is the head and end vertices. The head and end vertices are the same vertex to form the HC. The middle vertices locate between the them. Given $l_{i\times j}$ is the distance between the two adjacent vertices v_i and v_j in the HC, the mathematical model of the Euclidean TSP is given as formula (56.1).

$$\left.\begin{array}{c} L_{min} = \min(L(HC)) = \min \sum_{i,j=1}^{n} l_{i\times j} \\ \text{s.t.} \quad v_i \neq v_j \text{ and } e_{i\times j} \in E(HC) \end{array}\right\} \qquad (56.1)$$

where $L(HC)$ is the length of the HC, $e_{i\times j}(1 \leq i, j \leq n)$ is the edge linking the two adjacent vertices v_i and v_j in the HC.

The HC is composed of the local Hamiltonian paths (LHP) and the OHC includes the local optimal Hamiltonian paths (LOHP). For an arbitrary LOHP in the OHC, its two end vertices are determined in general, and its length is the minimum among those of the LHPs including the same vertices. The LHP or LOHP including i vertices is represented as LHP^i or $LOHP^i = (v_1, v_2, v_3, ..., v_i)$. For the symmetrical TSP, LHP^is $(v_1, v_2, v_3, ..., v_i)$ and $(v_i, v_{i-1}, ..., v_2, v_1)$ are identical.

56.3 The Improved Simulated Annealing

The ISA algorithm contains the BSA algorithm and the four vertices and three lines inequality. The framework of the ISA for TSP is given in Table 56.1.

The main steps in Table 56.1 are described as follows. Step 1 is to generate the initial HC. The numbers represent the n vertices are chosen randomly to form the initial HC, such as HC = (2, 1, 4, 3, 5, 2). There are two computation loops in the ISA algorithm. The outer loop is controlled by the appointed end temperature in step 2, and the inner loop depends on the assigned maximum iterations in step 3.

The next HC' is generated at step 6. Firstly, two different cities in the previous HC are selected randomly and exchanged, and the next HC' is generated. For example, 1 and 3 in the HC = (2, 1, 4, 3, 5, 2) are selected and exchanged, then

Table 56.1 The procedure of the ISA algorithm

Step	The contents of ISA algorithm
1	Generate an initial HC and compute its length L.
2	Set the initial temperature $T:=T_0$ and the end temperature $T:=T_E$.
3	Set the maximum iterations of the inner loop $N:= N_c$ and iteration index $t:=1$.
4	While (*temperature bigger than T_E*)
5	While (*iterations less than N_c*)
6	Generate the next HC' with the previous HC.
7	Compute the length L' of the HC' and $\Delta L:=L-L'$.
8	If ($\Delta L > 0$)
9	Replace the HC by the HC' and $t:=t+1$.
10	Else
11	If ($exp(\Delta L/T) >$ rand())
12	*Apply the four vertices and three lines inequality.*
13	Replace the HC by the HC' and $t:=t+1$.
14	Else
15	Discard the HC' and $t:=t+1$.
16	End
17	Update the temperature $T:=kT$.
18	End

HC' $= (2, 3, 4, 1, 5, 2)$ is generated. If the HC' is longer than the HC, a LHP in the HC' is selected randomly and the vertices in the LHP are reversed. For example, LHP $= (3, 4, 1, 5)$ in the HC' is chosen and reverse, the HC' $= (2, 5, 1, 4, 3, 2)$ is produced. The two operations to generate the HC' are executed once in one computation cycle. The next HC' is maintained if it meets the conditions at step 8 or step 11. Otherwise, it is discarded at step 15.

exp denotes the base of the natural system of logarithms and the value is assigned as 2.71828. The four vertices and three lines inequality can be imposed on the HC' once it is generated. In the ISA algorithm, it is placed at step 12 to change the HC' into shorter HC'. The principle of four vertices and three lines inequality is illustrated in Fig. 56.1.

Given the HC exists in the WG, two different HCs including n vertices are shown in Fig. 56.1a and b, and the HC in Fig. 56.1a is the OHC. One of the LOHP^{4}s in Fig. 56.1a is LOHP$^4 = (v_{i-1}, v_i, v_j, v_{j+1})$ $(2 \leq i \leq n, 1 \leq j \leq n - 1)$. The LHP$^4 = (v_{i-1}, v_j, v_i, v_{j+1})$ in Fig. 56.1b includes the same four vertices v_{i-1}, v_j, v_i, v_{j+1}. Given the two dashed paths LHP^{n-4}s are identical except the LOHP^4 and LHP^4, the length of the two LHP^{n-4}s are equal and they are noted as L_{rest} in Fig. 56.1a and b. For the LOHP^4 and LHP^4, $l_{i \times j}$ is the length of the edge $e_{i \times j}$. Two pairs of three edges $e_{(i-1) \times i}, e_{i \times j}, e_{j \times (j+1)}$ and $e_{(i-1) \times j}, e_{j \times i}, e_{i \times (j+1)}$ link the four vertices $v_{i-1}, v_i, v_j, v_{j+1}$ in LOHP^4 and LHP^4. The length of the LOHP^4 is computed as $l_{(i-1) \times i} + l_{i \times j} + l_{j \times (j+1)}$ and the length of the LHP^4 is computed as $l_{(i-1) \times j} + l_{j \times i} + l_{i \times (j+1)}$. The length of the OHC is shorter than or equal to the length of the HC, and the four vertices and three lines inequality holds. Any arbitrary LOHP^4 in the OHC conforms to the four vertices and three lines inequality. It is the heuristic information to change the LHP into the LOHP, and the shorter HCs will be obtained.

$$l_{(i-1) \times i} + l_{i \times j} + l_{j \times (j+1)} \leq l_{(i-1) \times j} + l_{j \times i} + l_{i \times (j+1)} \tag{56.2}$$

Because the OHC is composed of the LOHPs, the OHC is also taken as the combinations of n LOHP^{4}s. The function of four vertices and three lines inequality is to transform the LHP^{4}s into the LOHP^{4}s to generate the shorter HCs.

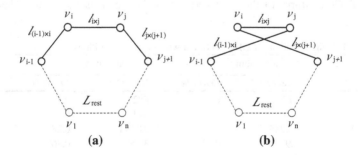

Fig. 56.1 The illustration of the four vertices and three lines inequality

Table 56.2 The parameters of the improved SA algorithm

Initial temperature T_0	End temperature T_E	Maximum cycle of inner loop N_c	Factor of temperature decrement k
Citynum × 15	0.0001	Citynum × 500	0.99

When the inner loop is completed at step 16, the temperature is updated at step 17. k is the factor of temperature decrement, and it is less than 1 to ensure the temperature become smaller and smaller. The ISA converges to the OHC or near OHC once the temperature T is equal to or less than T_E.

56.4 Illustrative Examples

The TSP instances are downloaded from the website: www2.iwr.uni-heidelberg.de/groups/comopt/software/TSPLIB95/tsp/. These TSP instances are used to illustrate the performance of the ISA. The ISA algorithm is coded with C++ language and runs on the Lenovo computer with processor 2.3 GHz and inner memory 2 GB. The BSA algorithm is also coded and executed on the same computer for comparisons. The parameters of SA algorithm are set as those in Table 56.2. The initial HCs are generated at random. For different TSP instances, the initial temperature and computation cycle of inner loop are set as different.

The experiments are tried for the selected four TSP instances, and the length of the OHCs or near OHCs generated with the two algorithms is shown in Table 56.3. The integer parts of the results are maintained and the decimal parts are neglected. The length of the OHC is computed with the real number of the city coordinates according to the given OHC. They are larger than those of the length computed with the integers of the city coordinates. The error of the near OHCs to the OHC is defined as $Error = (L(HC) - L(OHC))/L(OHC) \times 100\%$. For the experiments of the TSP instances, the errors of the near OHCs are computed and given in Table 56.3.

In view of the computation results, it is found that the shorter HCs are computed with the ISA algorithm. With the BSA algorithm, most of the LHPs in the local OHCs conform to the four vertices and three lines inequality whereas a

Table 56.3 Length of the near OHCs detected with the two algorithms

TSP instances	ISA algorithm		BSA algorithm		OHC
	Near OHC	Error/ %	Near OHC	Error/ %	
St70	677	0	682	0.74	677
Eil76	544	0	544	0	544
KorA100	21,285	0	21,344	0.28	21,285
TSP225	3,933	0.33	3,950	0.76	3,920
A280	2,627	1.5	2,637	1.9	2,586

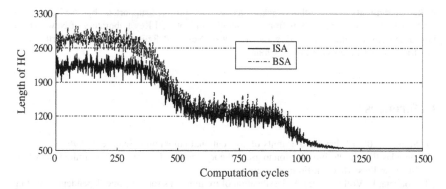

Fig. 56.2 The change processes of the HCs generated with the ISA and BSA algorithms

smaller number of LHPs do not. When these LHPs are adjusted with the four vertices and three lines inequality, the shorter local OHCs are obtained. However, the performance of the ISA is determined by the BSA. The four vertices and three lines inequality is useful when the LHPs in the local OHCs violate it. It is also found that the parameters of the SA algorithm play an important role to affect the quality of the local OHCs. When the parameters are changed slightly, the different near OHCs are generated.

For the Eil76, the changes process of the HCs detected with the ISA and BSA algorithms are illustrated in Fig. 56.2. The x-coordinate is the number of the generated HCs in the computation process. Before the 1,500th HC, the two algorithms converge to the near OHCs. The y-coordinate is the length of the HCs. Before they converge to the same near OHCs, the ISA algorithm always finds the shorter HCs. The optimization processes of the other cases have the similar change.

56.5 Conclusion

The ISA method is introduced for TSP. It is the integration of the BSA algorithm and the four vertices and three lines inequality. The four vertices and three lines inequality is convenient to apply to the HCs and the shorter local OHCs are generated. The performance of the ISA algorithm is mainly determined by its parameters. In view of the experimental results, the ISA algorithm always detects the shorter local OHCs than those searched with the BSA algorithm at the same iterative computation time before they converge to the same OHC or near OHC. The convergence rate of the ISA algorithm is faster than that of the BSA algorithm. The future work is to enhance the methods to find the next better HC' at step 6 in Table 56.1, and the more appropriate position to apply the four vertices and three lines will also be tried.

Acknowledgments The authors acknowledge the project supported by NSFC (Grant No.51205129). The work benefits from the facilities of National Key Laboratory of New Energy Power System and the Beijing Key Laboratory of New and Renewable Energy, North China Electric Power University, Beijing, China.

References

1. Seife C (2005) What are the limits of conventional computing. Science 309:96
2. Douglas BW (2006) Introduction to graph theory. Pearson Education Asia Limited and China Machine Press (Section Edition), Beijing
3. Gouveia, L, Voβ S (1995) A classification of formulations for the (time-dependent) traveling salesman problem. Eur J Oper Res 83(1):69–82
4. Bontoux B, Artigues C, Feillet D (2010) A memetic algorithm with a large neighborhood crossover operator for the generalized traveling salesman problem. Comput Oper Res 37(11):1844–1852
5. Helsgaun K (2012). An effective implementation of the Lin-Kernighan traveling salesman heuristic. Available: www2.iwr.uni-heidelberg.de/groups/comopt/software/TSPLIB95/tsp/
6. Borradaile G, Kiein P, Mathieu C (2009) An O(n log n) approximation scheme for Steiner tree in planar graphs. ACM Trans Algorithm 5(3):1–33
7. Jia LJ, Lin GL, Noubir G et al (2005) Universal approximations for TSP, Steiner tree, and set cover. 37th annual ACM symposium on theory of computing, STOC 2005, 22–24 May, Baltimore, MD, pp 386–395
8. Johnson DS, McGeoch LA (2004) The traveling salesman problem and its variations, combinatorial optimization, vol 12. Springer Press, London, pp 445–487
9. Ghaziri H, Osman IH (2003) A neural network algorithm for the traveling salesman problem with backhauls. Comput Ind Eng 44(2):267–281
10. Liu YH (2010) Different initial solution generators in genetic algorithms for solving the probabilistic traveling salesman problem. Appl Math Comput 216(1):125–137
11. Liu Y, Xiong SW, Liu HB (2009) Hybrid simulated annealing algorithm based on adaptive cooling schedule for TSP. In: Proceedings of the first ACM/SIGEVO summit on genetic and evolutionary computation, GEC'09, 12–14 June, Shanghai, pp 895–898
12. Dorigo M, Birattari M, Stützle T (2006) Ant colony optimization. IEEE Comput Intell Mag 1(4):28–39
13. Chen WN, Zhang J et al (2010) A novel set-based particle swarm optimization method for discrete optimization problems. IEEE Trans Evol Comput 14(2):278–300
14. Iordache S (2010) Consultant-guided search-a new metaheuristic for combinatorial optimization problems. In: Proceedings of the 12th annual conference companion on genetic and evolutionary computation, GECCO'10, 7–11 July, Portland, pp 225–232
15. Li Y, Zhou AM, Zhang GX (2011) Simulated annealing with probabilistic neighborhood for traveling salesman problems. In: 2011 seventh international conference on natural computation, ICNC 2011, 26–28 July, Shanghai, pp 1565–1569
16. Liu B, Meng PS (2009) Simulated annealing-based ant colony algorithm for traveling salesman problems. J Huazhong Univ Sci Technol (Nat Sci Ed) 37(11):26–30 (in Chinese)
17. Deineko V, Klinz B, Woeginger G (2006) Four point conditions and exponential neighborhoods for symmetric TSP. In: Proceedings of the seventeenth annual ACM-SIAM symposium on discrete algorithm, SODA 2006, 22–26 Jan, Miami, pp 544–553

Chapter 57
The Selection of Information Diffusion Monitoring Nodes in Directed Online Social Networks

Yongcheng Li, Shuguang Huang, Chaoran Fan and Guozheng Yang

Abstract In order to effectively monitor the information diffusion in online social network, we focus on the selecting monitoring nodes in the directed OSN. Simulation based monitoring capabilities of every node can be obtained by simulating the independent cascades derived from each node. It shows that the monitoring capability of the nodes depending more on the D-core index than on the K-core index and the out-degree value. Thereby, through a combination of D-coreindex and out-degree value, this paper proposes a new node centrality method called monitoring center, proving that it can effectively identify the monitoring capability of node.

Keywords Information diffusion models · Node centrality · Diffusion monitoring

57.1 Introduction

The problem of diffusion in network is always hot in network spreading dynamics. There are many realistic problems in this area such as the early research on the spread of infectious diseases, rumor spreading, and the spread of computer viruses and "viral marketing" research based on "reputation spread" in recent years, etc. Recently, as more and more people use Online Social Networks (OSN) as a way of information dissemination and communication, it makes research on large-scale social network information diffusion, diffusion models and diffusion prediction

Y. Li (✉) · S. Huang · C. Fan · G. Yang
Department of Network Engineering, Electronic Engineering Institute, 460 Huangshan Rd, Hefei, Anhui, P. R. China
e-mail: Liyc_1986@163.com

W. Lu et al. (eds.), *Proceedings of the 2012 International Conference on Information Technology and Software Engineering*, Lecture Notes in Electrical Engineering 211, DOI: 10.1007/978-3-642-34522-7_57, © Springer-Verlag Berlin Heidelberg 2013

possible. OSN can provide real social network data [1, 2], and massive real diffusion data [3, 4]. However, many researches focused on the way of selecting influential node for obtaining a larger diffusion result. But the problem of how to select effective nodes to monitor diffusion is still rarely, and it is very important for epidemic monitoring, public opinion monitoring and so on.

In this paper, we focus on the problem of information diffusion monitoring in directed OSN. We propose D-core index and its algorithm, and the experiment confirms its importance on the information diffusion monitoring. Then, we propose a new node centrality method which can effectively identify the monitoring capability of nodes.

57.2 Monitoring Maximization Problems

Network monitoring is to select nodes for discovering the diffusion in the network by monitoring the status of nodes. Real social networks owning a large number of nodes, monitoring of all nodes in the network is not feasible considering both the consumption of resources and the time measurement, therefore, how to obtain maximum effect with limited resources is worth studying.

Our goal is to maximum the scope of the monitoring, namely choosing the nodes that can monitor more information diffusion, while the goal that finding diffusion earlier isn't our concern. Generally speaking, the information diffusion can be categorized into single-source spread and multi-source spread by the number of spreading source. For a clear analysis, this paper assumes that the information is single-source spread. Similar to the node influential study of K-set nodes [5] and most influential node [6], the choice of the monitoring node can be divided into selecting a specified number node-set makes monitoring best and identify the monitoring capability of each node, that is, given the rank of monitoring capability of each node.

We assume that a social network $G(V, E)$ has node-set $V = (v_i | i = 1, 2, 3 \ldots n)$, the diffusion originated from v_i makes node-set P_i ($P_i \subseteq V$) become active, if the node $v_j \in P_i$, then $v_i \in M_j$ and M_j ($M_j \subseteq V$) represents the node-set that can be monitored by v_j, we use $|M_j|$ represents the number of nodes in M_j, then $|M_j| - 1$ represents the number of nodes those can be monitored by v_j. Therefore, the Monitoring Maximization Problem (MMP) can be solved by identifying $|M_j|$ of nodes, and ranking nodes by their monitoring capabilities.

57.3 Information Diffusion Models

According to the dissemination of different objects, researchers have proposed different diffusion models, for example, the SIR and SIS models for the spread of the disease [7] and the extended SIR rumor diffusion model [8]. However, the background of this paper is being the diffusion of information in OSN, so we have to choose the appropriate diffusion model. The difference between the disease spread and information diffusion is that the recovering status does not exist in the latter. Common information diffusion model are the Cascades Model (CM) and the Threshold Model(TM) [9] rooted in the fields of communication. The cascade model mainly considers the different probability of the nodes' impact to their neighbor nodes, and the threshold model mainly considers the different nodes with different activation threshold. In the simulation of this paper, we used the Independent Cascade Model (ICM) [10] which is most widely used in CM. Below we describe the independent cascade process of information in directed OSN.

57.3.1 ICM and Simulation Method

There are a lot of directed networks in the current OSN, for example, the Twitter network based on concern relationship and the Epinions network based on trust relationships, etc. The information dissemination among nodes in the network is often associated with edge directions (such as information always flows from followee to follower). Therefore, the independent cascade process of information in directed OSN is described as follows.

First of all, the network node has two types according to the status of whether the nodes know information: one for Active Node if node knows the information; node which doesn't knows the information is called Inactive Node. At the time t_0, suppose there is only one active node, then this node is the spreading source. In this paper, we assume that the direction of dissemination of information is opposite along the edge. Once the node v is activated at time t, then v has only one opportunity to activate its inactive neighbors (pointing to v) w with the probability $p_{v,w}$. If the node is activated by multiple nodes, the order is arbitrary. Once the node w is activated, then w becomes the Active Node and the process repeats at time $t + 1$. Spread will stop when no new node in the network is activated.

According to the task of MMP, we can set each node as spreading source, and then we can get the results $P_1, P_2 \ldots P_n$ after each spreads. The monitoring node-set $M_1, M_2 \ldots M_n$ corresponds to each node can be obtained by collecting nodes contained in P_1, $P_2 \ldots P_n$ respectively. The simulate rank R_0 could be got according to nodes' monitoring capability, we can get the distances between R_0 and the other methods R_x. However, there are two questions in the simulation.

In the ICM, the activation probability p should be determined before executing. The values can be different or same. We use the same value, 0.01, 0.02, 0.05, respectively (too large or too small p value may decrease the sensitivity).

The results node-set P_i of the same node may be different after two diffusions, so we need to repeat many times for every node to reduce the effects of probability to diffusion results. Here, we assume that S is the number of repetitions and $|M_i^m|$ is the monitoring capability of node i in the mth repeated, and then the average monitoring capability $|M_i^\infty|$ of node i is:

$$|M_i^\infty| = \frac{1}{S}\sum_{m=1}^{s}(|M_i^m - 1|) \tag{57.1}$$

57.3.2 Network Data Set

We used two real-world OSNs as the basic network for diffusion.

The Epinions network comes from Epinions.com website which is a general product review site, each user can post a review on any product and other users would rate the review with trust or distrust. So a directed network of reviewers connected with trust relationships can be created. The edge direction represents the direction of trust [11]. It contains 75,879 nodes and 508,837 edges.

The Slashdot0902 network comes from Slashdot.org website which is a site features user-submitted and editor-evaluated current primarily technology oriented news, In 2002, Slashdot introduced the Slashdot Zoo which allows users to tag each other as "friends" or "foes". We used the data obtained in February 2009 [12]. It contains 82,168 nodes and 948,464 edges.

57.4 D-Core Index

The node in network center is considered to have higher influence and monitoring capability. Therefore, researchers have proposed a lot of centrality algorithms based on different criteria. Degree centrality is a naive method to get node centrality, in our dissemination mode, we can use the out-degree (higher value represents concerning more nodes) to rank the node monitoring capability. However, the degree centrality can only say that the number of nodes connected to itself but the exact response the location of network. K-core index is an important criterion of measuring the node location, which can be obtained by k-shell decomposition to graph and expressed as Ks, higher Ks values of the node means close to the network core, whereas the node closest to the periphery of the network. Nodes near the network core have higher influence than nodes near the network periphery [13], and can earlier find dissemination [14] in network. However, K-core index is primarily for undirected graphs, the edge direction is often be ignored in directed graphs ($k = k_{in} + k_{out}$) [15]. An improved method for directed graphs called D-core decomposition, represented by $DC_{k,l}(D)$, where k and l respectively represents their in-degree and out-degree [16]. Therefore, based on D-core decomposition, we propose a method to compute D-core index $D(\alpha)s$ of nodes, and $\alpha \in \{in, out\}$. The difference with k-shell decomposition is when a node is deleted, only one class of degree can be considered (in-degree or out-degree).

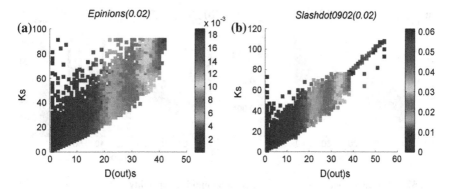

Fig. 57.1 Effects of *ks* and *D(out)s* on monitoring capability

We use Monitoring Coverage Density (MCD) $\rho(\Upsilon)$ to represent the monitoring capability of a set Υ of nodes, where $|\Upsilon|$ the number of node-set, n is the number of nodes in network.

$$\rho(\Upsilon) = \frac{1}{|\Upsilon|} \sum_{i \in \Upsilon} (\frac{|M_i^\infty|}{n-1}) \qquad (57.2)$$

First, in order to compare effects of the K-core index and the D-core index, we computed the distribution of $\rho(Ks, D(out)s)$, Fig. 57.1 shows the experimental results of two datasets with p = 0.02 (similar results with p = 0.01 and p = 0.05), where the horizontal axis indicates $D(out)s$, and the vertical axis indicates Ks, the color bar indicates ρ (the closer the red, said the higher MCD, the closer the blue, the lower). So we can draw two conclusions: (57.1) for a fixed Ks, there is a wide spread of ρ values. In particular, there are many node located at the core of the network but don't follow others that are poor monitor; (57.2) for a fixed $D(out)s$, ρ is approximately independent of the Ks of the nodes. This result shows that node monitoring capabilities are more depend on the value of $D(out)s$ than Ks value.

Further, we compared effects of the out-degree and the D-core index, Fig. 57.2 also shows the experimental results of two datasets with p = 0.02, unlike Fig. 57.1, the vertical axis represents the out-degree, similar to the above results can be obtained from this figure, that is for a fixed $D(out)s$, the ρ value is close to each other, but for a fixed out-degree, ρ value has a great scope. These results shows that node monitoring capabilities are more depend on the value of $D(out)s$ than out-degree value.

57.5 Monitoring Center *Mc*

The experiment result in section four shows that $D(out)s$ has an important impact on node's monitoring capability, however, $D(out)s$ only gives the level of monitoring capability. In order to further distinguish those which have the same $D(out)s$

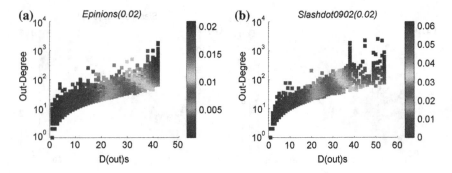

Fig. 57.2 Effects of out-degree and $D(out)s$ on monitoring capability

value of nodes, we propose a new method to compute the node centrality through a combination of $D(out)s$ and out-degree called monitoring centrality, represented by Mc, calculated as: $Mc = \lg(outDegree) \times D(out)s$.

In order to compare monitoring centrality and other methods, we compute the distances between each rank of centrality algorithms and rank R_0. However, there are a lot of low-connected nodes in real OSN, Therefore, the top-k position in pairs list are within our consideration. The improved Kendall's τ rank correlation coefficient can be used to solve these top-k lists similarity problem [17], and it normalized to interval $[-1, 1]$, In the case of maximum similarity between two rankings, $\tau = 1$ (rankings are identical). In the case of maximum dissimilarity, $\tau = -1$(one ranking is reverse of the other).

We compare the centrality of degree, out-degree, in-degree, PageRank, Authority, Hub, and monitoring, by computing the Kendall's τ and those with R_0 at the range of rank Top100 to Top1000. Figure 57.3a shows the result of Epinion network with p = 0.02, we found that with all the values of Top-K, the result of Mc method being closer to R_0 than any other methods. Figure 57.3b shows the result of Slashdot0902

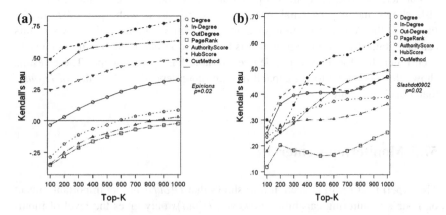

Fig. 57.3 The Kendall's Taus derived from difference methods

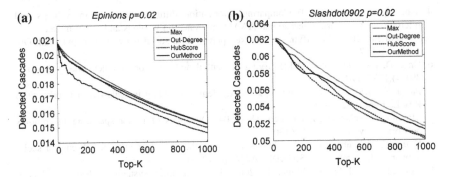

Fig. 57.4 MCD derived from difference methods

network also with p = 0.02, except for Top-K = 200 and Top-K = 300, *Mc* also got results more closely to R_0 than all other methods.

In order to further confirm the efficiency of monitoring centrality, we computed the MCD of the Top-K nodes with higher values from Kendall's τ algorithm. As shown in Fig. 57.4, the Max curve is the MCD of R_0. Figure 57.4a shows the result of Epinion network with p = 0.02, we can find that the presented monitoring centrality in this paper being higher than Hub centrality and out-degree centrality, Fig. 57.4b shows the result of Slashdot0902 network with the same probability, consistent with the results of Fig. 57.3, our monitoring centrality method has lower MCD within only 100 and 300, but in most cases our method is superior to other methods.

57.6 Conclusions

Inspired by the impact of K-core index to the influence of node, this paper confirms that the D-core index is important for information diffusion monitoring in directed OSN. Furthermore, considering both the value of $D(out)s$ and it's out-degree, we propose a new method computing *Mc* value, finding that the simulation results are more closer to the real ones using *Mc* to rank nodes.

References

1. Java A, Song X et al (2007) Why we twitter: understanding microblogging usage and communities. The 9th WebKDD and 1st SNA-KDD 2007 workshop on Web mining and social network analysis, ACM, pp 56–65
2. Backstrom L, Boldi P, Rosa M et al (2011) Four degrees of separation. Arxiv Preprint arXiv:1111.4570
3. Zhou Z, Bandari R et al (2010) Information resonance on Twitter: watching Iran. In: Proceedings of the first workshop on social media analytics, ACM, pp 123–131

4. Yang J, Counts S (2010) Comparing information diffusion structure in weblogs and microblogs. The fourth international AAAI conference on weblogs and social media
5. Borgatti SP (2006) Identifying sets of key players in a social network. Comput Math Org Theor 12(1):21–34
6. Chen D, Lü L et al (2012) Identifying influential nodes in complex networks. Physica A 391(4):1777–1787
7. Pastor-Satorras R, Vespingnani A (2001) Epidemic spreading in scale-free networks. Phys Rev Lett 86(4):3200–3203
8. Moreno Y, Nekovee M, Pacheco AF (2004) Dynamics of rumor spreading in complex networks. Phys Rev E 69:066130
9. Kempe D, Kleinberg J et al (2003) Maximizing the spread of influence through a social network. The ninth ACM SIGKDD, ACM, pp 137–146
10. Goldenberg J, Libai B, Muller E (2001) Using complex systems analysis to advance marketing theory development. Acad Market Sci Rev
11. Richardson M, Agrawal R, Domingos P (2003) Trust management for THE semantic Web. ISWC
12. Leskovec J, Lang K, Dasgupta A, Mahoney M (2009) Community structure in large networks: natural cluster sizes and the absence of large well-defined clusters. Internet Math 6(1):29–123
13. Kitsak M, Gallos LK et al (2010) Identification of influential spreaders in complex networks. Nat Phys 6(11):888–893
14. Christakis NA, Fowler JH (2010) Social network sensors for early detection of contagious outbreaks. PLoS ONE 5(9):e12948
15. Borge-Holthoefer J, Moreno Y (2011) Absence of influential spreaders in rumor dynamics. Arxiv preprint, arXiv:1112.2239
16. Giatsidis C, Thilikos DM et al (2011) D-cores: measuring collaboration of directed graphs based on degeneracy. ICDM2011, pp 201–210
17. Fagin R, Kumar R et al (2003) Comparing top k lists. The fourteenth annual ACM-SIAM symposium on discrete algorithms, society for industrial and applied mathematics, pp 28–36

Chapter 58
A Correcting Method for Article Error in English Essays of Chinese Students Based on Hybrid Features Classification

Ya Zhou, Xiaojuan Wang, Guimin Huang, Xiaolan Zeng
and Xiangyan Zeng

Abstract This paper presents a method for automatic article identification and correction in writing by Chinese learners of English. We train on one million noun phrases extracted from a corpus of published textbooks. In extracting features, we use the n-grams for local context features in the form of words and part of speech tags and the parse tree for syntactic features which is more linguistically sophisticated. At the same time, this paper raises a new approach based on mutual information and the contribution for training and classification. Performance of this new approach shows both effectiveness and efficiency, and the results are a significant improvement on the previous best results.

Keywords Article correction · Parser · N-grams · Feature classification

This work is supported by the Research Foundation of Humanity and Social Science of Ministry of Education of China (No. 11YJAZH131) as well as the Project Foundation of Science Research and Technical Development of Guilin (No. 20120104-4).

Y. Zhou (✉) · X. Wang (✉) · G. Huang · X. Zeng · X. Zeng
Research Center on Data Science and Social Computing, Guilin University of Electronic Technology, No. 1, Jinji Road, Qixing Area, Guilin City, Guang Xi, China
e-mail: ccyzhou@guet.edu.cn

X. Wang
e-mail: wxj0125@163.com

W. Lu et al. (eds.), *Proceedings of the 2012 International Conference on Information Technology and Software Engineering*, Lecture Notes in Electrical Engineering 211, DOI: 10.1007/978-3-642-34522-7_58, © Springer-Verlag Berlin Heidelberg 2013

58.1 Introduction

In recent years, non-native speakers of English, who outnumber their native counterparts [1], increasingly need to communicate in this lingua franca of the world. At present, the number of Chinese English learners in the world is the largest. Many students learn in English-as-a-Second-Language (ESL) courses at secondary schools and universities. For ESL learners, one of the most difficult problem is the use of *a* (or *an*), *the*, or *0* (*zero* or *null*) article at the beginning of a noun phrase. Many languages don't have any articles, so foreign language learners often have difficulty choosing appropriate English article and tend to underuse them [2]. In a set of 150 essays from the Test of English as a Foreign Language (TOEFL), written by native speakers of Chinese, Japanese and Russian, one article error was produced on average for every 16 noun phrases, or once every three or four sentences [2].

An English noun phrase (NP) may contain a determiner, such as *this, that, a, an* or *the*, which specifies the reference of its head. The two most common of these determiners, *a/an* and *the*, are also known as articles. Broadly speaking, *the* indicates that the head refers to someone or something that is uniquely defined; *a/an*, or the absence of any articles, indicates that it is a general concept.

The goal of our work is to use a method that provides feedback to the Chinese students and others when they choose an article (*a instead of the, or vice versa*), fail to use an article when one is required, or use an article when there should be none. Meanwhile, determining correct article usage is valuable for more than just second language learning. It is crucially important for high quality machine translation (MT), as well as for text summarization, text generation, and a host of other applications ranging from optical character recognition to text-to-speech devices for the disabled [3, 4].

In this paper, we train on up to one million noun phrases (NPs) extracted from a corpus of published text and use a new feature classification algorithm. The system uses local context features in the form of words and part of speech tags and linguistic features from the parser tree to compute the probability that the NP will have *a/an*, *the*, or *0* article.

58.2 Related Work

Although in the past there has been some research on article choice in the first language (L1) writing for applications such as generation and machine translation output, work to date on automatic error detection in the second language (L2) writing has been fairly limited.

In one of the earliest studies, decision trees are used to pick either *a/an* or *the* for NPs extracted from the Wall Street Journal. Its motivation was to improve the output of a Japanese to English translation system. There are over 30,000 features in the trees. By classifying the more frequent head nouns with the trees and guessing *the* for the rest, the overall accuracy is 78 %.

A memory-based learning approach is applied in Minnen [4] to choose between *a/an, the* and *null*. Their features are drawn from the Penn Treebank, such as the NP head and its part-of-speech (POS) and functional tags, the category and functional tags of the constituent embedding the NP, and other determiners in the NP. Additional features are drawn from a Japanese-to-English translation system, such as the countability preference and semantic class of the NP head. The best result is 83.6 % in terms of accuracy.

John Lee' study [5] applies the log-linear model to automatically restore missing articles based on features of the noun phrase. It shows that the model yields competitive results in article generation and describes methods to adjust the model with respect to the initial quality of the sentence. The best results are 20.5 % article error rate (insertions, deletions and substitutions) for sentences where 30 % of the articles have been dropped, and 38.5 % for those where 70 % of the articles have been dropped.

Han et al. [2, 6] describes the performance of a maximum entropy classifier to select among *a/an, the*, or *zero* article for noun phrases, based on a set of features extracted from the local context of each. When the classifier was trained on 6 million noun phrases, the accuracy rate for classification is about 87.99 %.

Finally, Turner and Charniak [7], utilize a language model based on a statistical parser for Penn Tree Bank data. Gamon et al. [8] use a complex system including a decision tree and a language model for both preposition and determiner errors, while Yi et al. [9] propose a web count-based system to correct determiner errors (P 62 %, R 41 %).

In this paper, we use a new model for article selection. The work presented here displays some similarities to the papers mentioned above in its use of a maximum entropy classifier and a set of features. However, our feature set is more linguistically sophisticated in that it relies on a full syntactic analysis of the data. It includes some semantic components which we believe play a role in correcting class assignment.

58.3 Features

58.3.1 Training Corpus

The different language environment where students were brought up might expose them to different usage and a more varied array of word senses and lead to the diversity of corpus, which poses a greater challenge for any statistical classifier.

This paper focuses on correcting article errors of Chinese students in their writing of College English Test (CET). It is precisely for this reason that we have chosen a multi-source dataset to build a model for students' essays. We have used text from a diverse corpus of English, it consists of all the texts in the English textbooks from kindergarten to graduate school and New Concept English 1–4. Corpus is a collection of approximately 23,000 text files, about 300 million words in all, basically consisting of words and phrases in the CET 4–6 writing. We have trained on much larger sets than earlier studies, up to one million NPs, in the hope that greater lexical coverage in training will support better performance in testing.

58.3.2 Feature Sets

In building feature sets, the first thing needs to be done is to disambiguate the clause with maximum entropy classifier. This paper needs to take the syntactic structure of sentences into account, so the Penn Treebank Tags label set for the word part of speech tagging is used. After pre-procession of split sentence and speech tags, we began to extract the features of the article.

In many state-of-the-art systems that use the classification approach, features are extracted only from the local context, such as a window of n preceding and subsequent words. This window does not always include the most relevant context. We investigate the use of linguistic features so as to exploit words drawn from longer distances.

Features are drawn from two sources: the n-grams of the article and the parse tree of the sentence. Thirteen categories of syntactic and semantic features are extracted from each base NP. Take the sentence "This morning there was a terrible storm in the city." as an example. From its parse tree, part of which is shown in Fig. 58.1, the following features are extracted for the base NP "a terrible storm":

Parse tree features include head, head POS, noun type, parent, non-article determiner. Head is the root form of the head of the NP. It is determined using the rules in Collins' paper [10]. Head POS is the POS tag of the NP head. Noun type judges countability of the head, if head is an uncountable noun it is uncountable, otherwise it is countable. Parent is the category of the parent node of the NP. Non-article determiner is a determiner other than *a* or *the* in the NP.

N-gram features include **words before head, words after head, POS of words before head, POS of words after head, words before NP, words after NP, POS of words before NP, POS of words after NP. Words before head** refers to words inside the NP that precede the head, excluding determiners, and the next three

Fig. 58.1 The parse tree of the sentence, this morning there was a terrible storm in the city

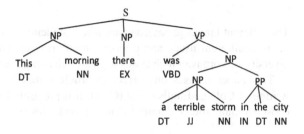

Table 58.1 Article feature set for NP "a terrible storm" on the tree

Type	Feature	Feature value
Parse tree features	Head	Storm
	Head POS	NN
	Noun type	Countable
	Parent	NP
	Non-article determiner	Null
N-gram features	Words before head	Terrible
	Words after head	Null
	POS of words before head	JJ
	POS of words after head	Null
	Words before NP	There, was
	Words after NP	In, the
	POS of words before NP	EX, VBD
	POS of words after NP	IN, DT

share similar feature. **Words before NP** means the two words preceding the base NP but this feature can be null, and the last three share similar feature.

Finally, the label is the article in the original sentence. For this NP, the label is "a"; in other NPs the label could be "the" or "null". Table 58.1 shows the whole features of this NP.

58.4   A Correcting Model for Article Error

58.4.1   Feature Extraction

In this paper, we use the method of mutual information for feature extraction. Mutual information is used to measure the relevance of the two events, so the definition of the following formula is used to calculate the characteristics of context and the current word.

$$Information(f, a_i) = \log\left\{\frac{p(f, a_i)}{p(f)p(a_i)}\right\} \approx \log\left\{\frac{count(f, a_i) \times sum}{count(f) \times count(a_i)}\right\} \quad (58.1)$$

In the formula, f is the article's context features, a_i denotes the current article, $p(f, a_i)$ is the co-occurrence probability of f and a_i, and $p(f)$ and $p(a_i)$ represent feature and the probability of the current article. We know that the probability function of certain type of language event $p(*)$ is usually unknown, so the mutual information of f and a_i is calculated by using the relative frequency and maximum likelihood estimation method. And the $count(*)$ represents the frequency of the words in the training corpus, sum identifies the total number of words in the training corpus. Church et al., by studying the mutual information, reached the following conclusions:

(1) If $Information(f, a_i) > 0$, it indicates that the context feature and the article is clear and credible relationship, and the relationship between the two bindings is enhanced with the increase in the value of $Information(*)$.

(2) If $Information(f, a_i) = 0$, it indicates that the combination of feature and the article does not have a clear and credible relationship.

(3) If $Information(f, a_i) < 0$, it shows that there is a negative correlation between the feature and the article and they have a weak combination, the possibility of co-occurrence is very low, and the relationship between the two bindings weakens with the reduction of the value of $Information(*)$.

In the article checking, if the correlation of the feature and article is less than a given threshold, then they rarely mix together in the writing, so it is likely to be an article mistake, the need for article correction.

58.4.2 Weights

When we calculate the weights of the features, we should consider the contribution of the feature to the weight, that is, computing a feature's important degree for the article. It measures a discriminant validity of the feature f relative to the article a_i, and this contribution information with the mutual information together determine the weight feature relative to the center of the word.

$$Weight(f, a_i) = Information(f, a_i) \times Contribution(f, a_i)$$

$$\text{where: } Contribution(f, a_i) = \frac{count(f, a_i)}{\sum_{i=1}^{n} count(f, a_i)} \qquad (58.2)$$

$count(f, a_i)$ is a co-occurrence frequency feature f and article a_i, $\sum_{i=1}^{n} count(f, a_i)$ indicates the sum co-occurrences frequency of the feature f and all articles. If this feature f with the article has a high frequency of co-occurrence and has a low one with others of the article confusion set, then the contribution of this feature is great to this article, which means that using this feature to distinguish this article is better than focusing on other articles of the confusion set. On the contrary, if the co-occurrence frequency of this feature f with the article is very low and it is very high with other articles, the contribution is small.

58.4.3 A Correcting Model

In the training phase, through the feature extraction and weight calculation, we get the feature weight data of all articles. In the correction phase, we use these training data to calculate the score of the articles. $F_{article}$ is a set of contextual features of articles extracted from the current sentence.

$$Score(a_i) = \sum_{f_j \in F_{article}} \beta_j \cdot Weight(f_j, a_i)$$

$$\beta_j = \begin{cases} 0 & \text{feature } f_j \text{ includes in the feature set of article } a_i \\ 1 & \text{feature } f_j \text{ doesn't include in the feature set of article } a_i \end{cases} \quad (58.3)$$

In checking the articles, we first calculate the score of the current article $a_{current}$. Then we calculate the scores of other articles of the confusion set, and take out the article $a_{optimal}$ with the maximum score. When it satisfies the following formula (58.4), the best article is obtained from executing article error correction by parallel replacement and substituting the article with the maximum score for the current article. The setting of the threshold value is determined by the experiment.

$$\frac{Score(a_{optimal})}{Score(a_{current})} > threshold \quad (58.4)$$

58.5 Experiments for Correcting Model

In the corpus, the most common article was the zero article (62.83 % of all NPs), followed by *the* (24.99 %), and *a/an* (12.18 %). Testing data are selected from Chinese students' CET 4–6 compositions, totaling 80 articles, 600 sentences, and we remove or modify the article before the NP according to the type of error. The overall distribution of article deletions, insertions and substitutions (Table 58.2) shows that deletion is the overwhelming type of error.

In this paper, there are two categories of feature sets, n-gram feature set and parse tree feature set. Therefore, three training sets, with increasingly richer feature sets, were created: $Train_{n-gram}$: This set uses the n-gram features; $Train_{parse}$: This set uses the parse features; $Train_{entire}$: This set uses our full set of features. During the training phase, we trained models on the above-mentioned three feature sets. In the testing phase, classifier uses three models to compute the score of articles, and these models are applied in the test data correction of an article for each NP. Table 58.3 shows the accuracy rates.

Table 58.2 Relative frequencies of deletions, insertions and substitutions of articles

Type	Error	Percent (%)	Example
Deletions	a → null	39.9	She is [a → null] friend of mine
	the → null	30.7	
Insertions	null → the	14.3	[null → The] failure is the mother of success
	null → a	4.1	
Substitutions	a → the	7.9	I go home [the → a] month
	the → a	3.1	

The notation [<crr> → <err>] will be used to indicate that the correct word, <crr>, is mistakenly replaced with the word <err> by the non-native speaker

Table 58.3 The accuracy rates of article correction use different feature sets

Feature set	Precision (%)
$Train_{entire}$	88.0
$Train_{parse}$	82.5
$Train_{n-gram}$	77.8

Table 58.4 The final article correction accuracy

Type	Deletions		Insertions		Substitutions	
Error types	a/a → null	the → null	null → a/an	null → the	a/an → the	the → a/an
Sentences	100	100	100	100	100	100
Errors total	27	31	30	33	25	27
Correction	24	26	26	27	23	25
Precision (%)	88.9	83.97	86.67	84.85	92.00	92.59
Average (%)	88					

We use the above definition of the classification model to test three types of errors of the article. The threshold is determined by experiments. The experiment shows that the greater the value of *threshold* is, the higher the accuracy rate is; and the accuracy rate can reach more than 92 % when *threshold* is greater than 3. But at the same time, there are a lot of errors undetected, leading to low recall rate. When *threshold* is less than 2, 85 % of the errors will be found and corrected, but the accuracy rate drops to 80 %. After measuring many experimental results, *threshold* is set to be 2.5 in order to balance precision and recall rate. Table 58.4 shows the final article error correction results.

58.6 Conclusions and Future Work

In this paper, the combination method of the n-gram model and syntax tree is used to extract features and a new training and classification method is used to train on noun phrases in a very large corpus, which contributes to the good results of the article correction.

The main advantage of this approach is that it is fully automated and does not require additional lexical or knowledge resources. At the same time, this training method on the correction of the preposition and part of speech confusion is instructive and meaningful. Its main deficiency is a lack of effective solutions to the specific reference of *the* article, which results in the low error correction rate of the definite article *the*. The analysis of the expansion of the scope of the sentence, adding more sophisticated contextual features, including referent information and WordNet feature, should improve system performance, but there will still be many subtleties of article usage that are beyond the classifiers capabilities. Despite this, this method could still solve article correction and other problems in English grammar; it will prove to be a valuable tool for language instruction and necessary to the further development studies, in order to achieve higher error correction efficiency.

Acknowledgments We would first like to thank teachers who guide this grammar error correction project and provide the corpus. We also acknowledge the peers in our research track for their valuable pointers and guidance during the project period.

References

1. Ronowicz E, Yallop C (2005) English: one language, different cultures. Continuum International Publishing Group, London, p 26
2. Lee JSY (2009) Automatic correction of grammatical errors in non-native English text. Ph D thesis, MIT, p 15
3. Han N-R, Chodorow M, Leacock C (2004) Detecting errors in English article usage with a maximum entropy classifier trained on a large, diverse corpus. In: Proceedings of the LREC, pp 1625–1628
4. Minnen G, Bond F, Copestake A (2000) Memory-based learning for article generation. In: Proceedings of the 4th conference on computational language learning and the 2nd learning language in logic workshop, pp 43–48
5. Lee J (2004) Automatic article restoration. In: Proceedings of the HLT-NAACL, pp 31–36
6. Han N-R, Chodorow M, Leacock C (2006) Detecting errors in English article usage by non-native speakers. Nat Lang Eng 12(2):115–129
7. Turner J, Charniak E (2007) Language modeling for determiner selection. The conference of the North American chapter of the association for computational linguistics; companion volume, short papers, pp 177–180
8. Gamon M, Gao J, Brockett C, Alexander K (2008) Using contextual speller techniques and language modeling for ESL error correction. In: Proceedings of IJCNLP, pp 449–456
9. Ying X, Gao J, Dolan WB (2008) A web-based English proofing system for ESL users. In: Proceedings of IJCNLP, pp 619–624
10. Collins M (2003) Head-driven statistical models for natural language parsing. Comput Linguist 29(4):589–637

Chapter 59
Adaptive Determining for Optimal Cluster Number of K-Means Clustering Algorithm

Jiankai Sun, Zhong Li, Fengyuan Zou and Yunchu Yang

Abstract The clustering accuracy of K-means algorithm highly depends on the initial number of clusters and it takes a long time when dealing with the large sample data with high dimension. To solve these problems, this paper proposes a method to reduce the dimensionality for high dimensional data by multidimensional scaling transformation and designs a measure which can effectively evaluate the quality of nuclear clustering algorithm. Furthermore, an adaptive method to determine the optimal cluster number is presented. It firstly predicts the initial cluster number in a low-dimensional space by the tree clustering. Then, the optimal cluster number is gotten by the adaptive algorithm. Experiments show that this method has higher accuracy and stability.

Keywords Optimal cluster number · Kernel cluster · Multidimensional scaling transformation · Dimensionality reduction

59.1 Introduction

Cluster analysis, also called as unsupervised learning, can divide the sample into several clusters without training. Its principle is to make the data correlation within groups higher than between groups. Therefore, it becomes a very active research topic in data mining and other related fields [1].

K-means cluster algorithm is a widely used iterative descent clustering algorithm. However, there are some shortcomings: (1) K-means algorithm has

J. Sun · Z. Li (✉) · F. Zou · Y. Yang
Department of Mathematical Sciences, Zhejiang Sci-Tech University,
310018 Hangzhou, China
e-mail: lizhong@zstu.edu.cn

W. Lu et al. (eds.), *Proceedings of the 2012 International Conference on Information Technology and Software Engineering*, Lecture Notes in Electrical Engineering 211, DOI: 10.1007/978-3-642-34522-7_59, © Springer-Verlag Berlin Heidelberg 2013

good clustering effect for the data with circular or similar circular distribution, but it has poor result for the non-circular distribution data. (2) The quality of the K-means clustering results depends on the selection of the initial center and the initial cluster number. So far, many improved methods have been presented to solve these shortcomings. In order to determine the better initial cluster centers, Yuan and Zhou [2] used a sampling method to improve the quality of initial central points. Zalik [3] provided a recursive method to determine the best initial cluster centers and made the K-clustering algorithm to achieve the globally optimal convergence. Likas et al. [4, 5] presented the kernel clustering algorithm which is a good solution for the problem that the K-means clustering algorithm cannot deal with the non-circular distribution data. This kernel clustering method uses the Mercer kernel [6] to make the input sample map into a high dimensional feature space and cluster it in a feature space. So, nonlinear sample classification problem can be transformed into a linear classification problem. The kernel function, which is introduced to the clustering algorithm, can improve the sample characteristics optimization and get a more accurate clustering result.

In this paper, we improve the kernel clustering algorithm and design a new measure to evaluate the quality of the clustering result. It can reduce the dissimilarity in the same cluster and increase the dissimilarity between different clusters, so that the clustering results are more accurate. At the same time, the multidimensional scaling transformation is used to reduce the data dimensionality, so as to avoid the 'dimension disaster' and maintain the intrinsic link between the different data. Based on above improvement, an adaptive algorithm to determine the optimal cluster number is finally presented.

59.2 The Kernel K-Means Clustering Algorithm

59.2.1 K-Means Clustering Algorithm

K-means clustering is a well-known hierarchical clustering algorithm. It moves the cluster center through minimizing repeatedly the total measure value among the data of each cluster (e.g., distance or similarity). Assume that $X_i, i = 1, \ldots N$ are the samples and $c_k, k = 1, \ldots, K$ are initial cluster centers. Initial cluster centers can be randomly selected. K-means clustering algorithm is alternately performed as the following

(1) For each sample, find the nearest cluster center point,

$$k = \arg \min_{k \in \{1, \ldots, K\}} d(c_k, X_i), \quad k = 1, \ldots K. \tag{59.1}$$

(2) Compute the mean of each cluster data and make the mean vector as a new cluster center

$$c_k = \frac{1}{n_k} \sum_{j=1}^{n_k} x_j^{(k)}, \quad k = 1, \ldots, K \tag{59.2}$$

where n_k is the k-th cluster contains the number of samples.

Repeat two steps until there are no or few samples whose cluster will change. The shortcoming of the K-means algorithm is that the expected cluster number should be given in advance which is not applicable in some applications. In addition, K-means algorithm is not suitable for a non-circular samples and cannot found clusters with the great size difference. We will present a new adaptive algorithm with the kernel function to solve these problems in the next parts of this paper.

59.2.2 Clustering in the Kernel Space

Recently, the kernel function clustering method with good applicability was presented in order to solve the sample distribution problem. The kernel function clustering algorithm is to transform the sample from the input space into a high-dimensional feature space by a nonlinear mapping method and cluster the sample data in a feature space. The detailed description of the method is as follows.

Assume that the sample data from the input space is $x_k \in R^N$, $k = 1, 2, \ldots l$, the nonlinear mapping function is ϕ and the data in the high-dimensional feature space (H) is $\phi(x_1), \phi(x_2), \ldots, \phi(x_l)$. Now, we can use the Mercer kernel to express the dot product from the input space as Eq. (59.3)

$$K(x_i, x_j) = (\phi(x_i) \cdot \phi(x_j)). \tag{59.3}$$

So we get a kernel matrix $K_{ij} = k(x_i, x_j)$. In the feature space, Euclidean distance can be expressed as

$$d(x_i, x_j) = \|\phi(x_i) - \phi(x_j)\|$$
$$= \sqrt{(\phi(x_i), \phi(x_i)) - 2 \cdot (\phi(x_i), \phi(x_j)) + (\phi(x_j), \phi(x_j))}. \tag{59.4}$$

Generally, the nonlinear function is unknown, but the distance expression in the original input space can be transformed into Eq. (59.5) according to (59.3) and (59.4)

$$d(x_i, x_j) = \sqrt{k(x_i, x_i) - 2k(x_i, x_j) + k(x_j, x_j)}. \tag{59.5}$$

We define the expression as the measure function of the cluster similarity. The final clustering criterion is to minimize the following objective function.

$$J = \min \sum_{i=1}^{c} \sum_{j=1}^{k} \|x_j - a_i\|^2, \tag{59.6}$$

where c is the number of cluster and a_i is the center of the i-th cluster.

Based on Eqs. (59.6) and (59.4), the kernel clustering algorithm can be described as follows

Algorithm 1 Kernel clustering algorithm

Step 1   Determine the cluster number c, $2 \leq c \leq l$ and standardize the sample data set.

Step 2   Select the kernel function and parameter and determine initial cluster centers w_i.

Step 3   Update the cluster centers w_i according to the criterion of minimizing the objective function J.

Step 4   If w_i is no longer to change, then finish the algorithm. Otherwise, turn to step 3.

59.2.3 Clustering Validity Index Based on Similarity Measurement Kernel Function

From algorithm 1, we can see the importance of the kernel matrix K for the kernel function clustering. Each matrix element defines the inner product of two samples in a feature space and also defines their similarity because the kernel clustering algorithm provides a natural similarity measure. We take the Gaussian kernel function (59.7) as an example

$$K(x_i, x_j) = \exp\left(\frac{-\|x_i - x_j\|^2}{2\sigma^2}\right). \tag{59.7}$$

When $\sigma \to 0$, the diagonal elements of the kernel matrix are all equal to 1, and the non-diagonal elements are close to zero. In this case, a sample is only similar to itself and not similar to other samples. So each sample was divided into one cluster. When $\sigma \to \infty$, the result is opposite, all samples were divided in the same cluster. All elements of the kernel matrix are equal to 1 and all samples belong to one cluster.

Generally, given a proper σ, the diagonal elements of the kernel matrix belong to [0, 1]. The value of the kernel matrix element can measure the sample similarity. The kernel matrix reflects the inherent clustering structure of the data set. The kernel matrix K provides all information about evaluating the clustering quality and validity.

From above discussion, we know that the kernel matrix element K_{ij} can measure the sample similarity. However, K_{ij} reflects the similarity only between two samples. In order to describe the similarity among all samples in a cluster, the cluster average similarity S_{within} is defined as

$$S_{\text{within}} = \frac{1}{N_i - 1} \sum_{k=1}^{N_i} K_{kj}, \tag{59.8}$$

where N_i is the number of the i-th cluster and K_{ij} is the similarity of the sample i, j.

Similarly, we define a variable to describe the average similarity $S_{between}$ between the i-th sample and all samples in a different cluster by

$$S_{between} = \frac{1}{N - N_i} \sum_{k=1}^{N-N_i} K_{kj}.$$ (59.9)

Here, we propose a new method to determine the number of the K-means algorithm. Firstly, we establish the effective index of the kernel function of clustering algorithm based on the similarity measure. A good clustering algorithm is divided as far as possible to reflect the internal structure of the data set and make the sample in a cluster as similar as possible. Namely, it requires that S_{within} is as large as possible and $S_{between}$ is as small as possible. Combining these two aspects, we define the cluster validity index as

$$V(K; W, c) = \frac{\sum\limits_{i=1}^{c} S_{between}}{\sum\limits_{i=1}^{c} S_{within}}.$$ (59.10)

Therefore, the smaller $V(K; W, c)$, the higher cluster similarity; the bigger cluster difference and the better clustering result.

59.2.4 Multidimensional Scaling Transformation Dimensionality Reduction

In the data mining, high-dimensional data appears more and more frequently. At present, the dimensionality reduction of high dimension data becomes the research focus of the data analysis. Multidimensional scaling transformation is the method of data representation in the space of a small dimension. It can be as much as possible to retain the similarity of the original data structure. Compared with the factor analysis, it is an iterative approach. Compared with the principal component analysis, it has a greater range of applications because it is not necessary to give some assumed conditions for the distance scale used to measure similarity.

The basic idea of multidimensional scaling transformation is to use an iterative approach which tries to locate the feature vector in the reduced dimensional space, and make the distance and dissimilarities among them to be preserved as much as possible. For this reason, it needs to constantly reduce the squared error P as

$$P = \sum_{i,j} [d^*(x_i, x_j) - f(d(x_i, x_j))]^2.$$ (59.11)

Here, x_i, x_j are a random pair of samples, $d(x_i, x_j)$ is the original difference between x_i and x_j, $d^*(x_i, x_j)$ is the difference of low-dimensional space after transformation, f is a monotonic transformation function.

59.3 Adaptive Kernel Clustering Algorithm

K-means clustering algorithm needs to give the number of the cluster in advance, but this is not practical in some applications. At the same time, the quality of K-means clustering results depend on the selection of the cluster number K. If initial clustering number is good, the clustering result will be better. Otherwise, the clustering result may appear error.

Here, we present an adaptive method for determining the optimal number of clusters. First, the multidimensional scaling transformation is used to reduce the dimension of the data set, and the initial number c of the cluster can be gotten by using the tree clustering. Then the clustering process is done iteratively based on the validity of the new evaluation until the optimal number of clusters is obtained. Finally, the optimal clustering result is achieved after the clustering.

The process of K-means adaptive iterative algorithm is described as follows

Step 1   Reduce the dimensionality of the data set using the multidimensional scaling
Step 2   Use the tree clustering to get the cluster number c in the reduced space
Step 3   According to the cluster number c, get the clustering matrix W_C using K-means algorithm
Step 4   Compute $V(K; W, c)$ according to K and W_C
Step 5   Compare $V(K; W, c)$ and $V(K; W, c - 1)$. If $V(K; W, c) \geq V(K; W, c - 1)$, go to step6; otherwise, $c = c + 1$ and go to step 2
Step 6   Select $V(K; W, c)$ with smallest c and take the label matrix W as the final clustering results

59.4 Experimental Results

In order to test the effectiveness of our new algorithm and evaluating index, five standard data sets in UCI database were used in this section. The test includes three parts: the first part is to test the influence of the cluster number on the clustering result; the second one is to test the performance of the cluster number obtained by the adaptive algorithm and the third part is to test the stability of the clustering algorithm and we finally do a comparison with other algorithms.

In experiment 1, the data was used from Iris standard database. We do the clustering by choosing different cluster number. The clustering results are shown in Figs. 59.1, 59.2, and 59.3 and the clustering analysis is compared in Table 59.1. From the Table 59.1, we find that a suitable K is important to the results of the K-means clustering algorithm.

In experiment 2, four standard data sets (Iris, Glass, Wine, and BUPA) from the UCI database were used. First, we use a tree clustering algorithm to do a preliminary prediction for one Iris data set (shown in Fig. 59.4), and then find the best

Fig. 59.1 Iris data set
(k = 2)

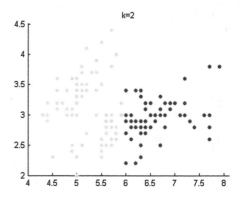

Fig. 59.2 Iris data set
(k = 3)

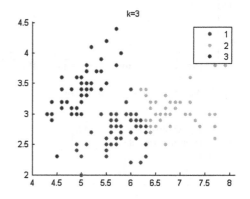

Fig. 59.3 Iris data set
(k = 4)

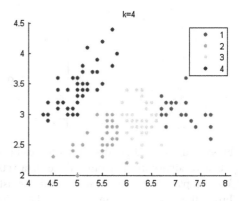

Table 59.1 The comparison results of experiment 1

K value	Wrong cluster number	The clustering accuracy (%)
K = 2	12	80
K = 3	30	92
K = 4	46	69.4

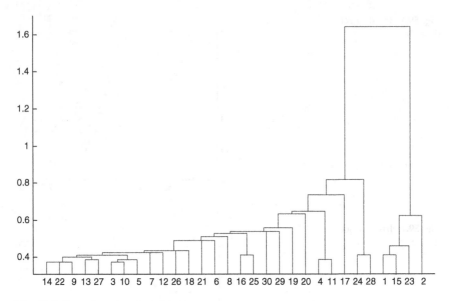

Fig. 59.4 Tree clustering about Iris set

Fig. 59.5 Adaptive algorithm on the Iris data clustering

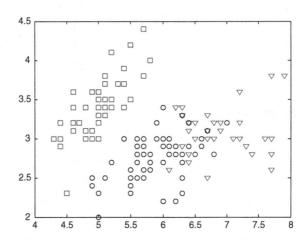

cluster number and get the clustering results (shown in Fig. 59.5) according to the adaptive algorithm. For other three data sets, similar clustering process is done. We compare the results with some other clustering method, as show in Table 59.2. From this table, we can see that the adaptive algorithm has good ability to determine the optimum cluster number. Furthermore, it can not only improve the computational efficiency, but avoid the problem that cannot effectively deal with large data set.

In experiment 3, we do the clustering analysis for some clustering algorithms using Iris, Glass, Wine, Lonosphere four standard datasets. Because all clustering algorithms may produce random results, we repeat 10 times clustering for each

Table 59.2 The comparison result of experiment 2

Data Set	Sample number	Property number	Real cluster number	The accuracy of different algorithm			
				Vpc [7]	Xie-beni [8]	Girolami [9]	Our method
Iris	150	4	3	2, 3	2, 3	3–6	2, 3
Glass	214	9	6	2	5	3–7	6
Wine	178	13	3	2	3	3	3
BUPA	345	6	2	2	2	2,3	2

Table 59.3 The result of experiment 3

Data Sets	Sample number	Property number	Real cluster number	The accuracy of different algorithm		
				K-means (%)	MGKM (%) [10]	Our method (%)
Iris	150	4	3	85.3	87.6	90.2
Glass	214	9	6	73.8	80.3	82.6
Wine	178	13	3	52.1	59.7	61.9
Ionosphere	351	34	2	70.8	82.4	86.4

data set and set the average for the comparison standard. Table 59.3 gives the experiment comparison result. We find our method achieves the more accurate clustering result.

59.5 Conclusions

In this paper, we present an adaptive kernel function K-means clustering algorithm to determine the optimal cluster number. Meanwhile, the effective evaluating index was presented to reflect the sample similarity in a cluster and the sample difference between two clusters from the statistics analysis. In our algorithm, multidimensional scaling dimension reduction method also used to reduce the computational complexity and retain the internal correlative information among data.

Acknowledgments This research was supported from the National Natural Science Foundation of China (No. 60903143 and 51075421); Natural Science Foundation of Zhejiang Province of China (No. Y1110504); Qianjiang Talent Project of Zhejiang Province of China (No. QJD0902006); Science and Technology Project of Zhejiang Province of China (No. 2012C21035); Project of National Research Center for College Teaching of China (No. 2009IM010400-1-11) and Project of Zhejiang Provincial Research Center of Clothing Engineering Technology.

References

1. Tzortzis GF, Likas AC (2009) The global kernel k-means algorithm for cluster in feature space. IEEE Trans Neural Netw 20(7):1181–1194
2. Yuan F, Zhou ZY (2007) K-means clustering algorithm with meliorated initial center. Comput Eng 33(3):65–66
3. Zalik KR (2008) An efficient k-means clustering algorithm. Pattern Recogn Lett 29(9): 1385–1391
4. Likas AC, Vlassis M, Verbeek JJ (2003) The global k-means clustering algorithm. Pattern Recogn 36:451–461
5. Tzortzis GF, Likas AC (2008) The global kernel k-means clustering algorithm. In: Proceedings of IEEE international joint conference on neural networks, pp 1977–1984
6. Mercer J (1909) Functions of positive and negative type and their connection with the theory of integral equations. In: Philosophical transactions of the Royal Society of London, pp 415–446
7. Bezdek JC, Pal NR (1998) Some new index of cluster validity. IEEE Trans Syst Man Cybern 28(3):301–315
8. Xie XL, Beni G (1991) A validity measure for fuzzy clustering. IEEE Trans Pattern Anal Mach Intell 13(8):841–847
9. Girolami M (2002) Mercer Kernel-based clustering in feature space. IEEE Trans Neural Netw 13(3):780–784
10. Bagirov AM (2008) Modified global k-means algorithm for minimum sum-of-squares clustering problems. Pattern Recogn 41(10):3192–3199

Chapter 60
A Linked Data-Based Approach
for Personalized Multimedia Retrieval

Dehai Zhang, Tianlong Song, Tianming Liu, Jun He
and Qing Kang

Abstract With the development of the Semantic Web, more and more multimedia datasets are represented as RDF format and become part of the Linked Data, which provide a fundamentally new venue for personalized content-based multimedia information retrieval on the Web of Data. In this paper, we propose a personalized multimedia retrieval approach which is performed by comparing RDF-based user profiles with multimedia dataset in Linked Open Data. The experimental results show that the proposed approach can effectively return multimedia resources with respect to the user's interests.

Keywords Linked data · Personalized multimedia information retrieval · User profile

D. Zhang (✉) · T. Song · J. He
School of Software, Yunnan University, No.52 North Cuihu Road, Kunming City, China
e-mail: dhzhang@ynu.edu.cn

T. Song
e-mail: songtianlong@gmail.com

J. He
e-mail: hejun@ynnic.gov.cn

T. Liu
Computer Science Dept, University of Georgia, Atlanta, United States
e-mail: tliu@uga.edu

Q. Kang
Computer Yunan Aidi Technology Co., Ltd, Kunming, China
e-mail: Kangqing595@162.com

W. Lu et al. (eds.), *Proceedings of the 2012 International Conference on Information Technology and Software Engineering*, Lecture Notes in Electrical Engineering 211, DOI: 10.1007/978-3-642-34522-7_60, © Springer-Verlag Berlin Heidelberg 2013

60.1 Introduction

With the explosion of the multimedia information on the Web, people's requirement for multimedia information retrieval (MIR) is strongly growing. However, it
is difficult to describe the semantics of multimedia information, since people are
used to exploit high-level semantic concepts to retrieve information [1]. In general,
the current technologies of MIR can only handle low-level features of multimedia
content, like grey scale, texture of images or key frames of video [2], which creates
a wide gap between low-level features and high-level semantic concepts [3]. This
semantic gap makes MIR a major problem for research.

In recent years, the Web has evolved from a global information space of linked
documents to Linked Data [4], which have been adopted by an increasing number
of data providers over the last few years. According to the statistics of ESW wiki,[1]
the Web of Data consists of 4.7 billion RDF triples, which are interlinked by
around 142 million RDF links by May 2009.

Technically, Linked Data uses RDF [5] to make typed statements that link
arbitrary things in the world. For these reasons, the Linked Data opens up new
possibilities for personalized multimedia information retrieval. In this paper, we
present an approach for personalized multimedia information retrieval based on
Linked Data, which use a novel RDF graph based matching algorithm to extract
the semantics of the user profiles defined as RDF graphs and the multimedia
dataset provided in Linked Open Data. The approach can use high-level semantic
concepts of multimedia to search data, while avoiding complex computing in MIR.

60.2 Related Works

Recently, some researches based on multimedia, computer vision and AI related to
MIR have been received high citations [6]. An image retrieval method based on
relevance feedback [7] is a research hotspot in image retrieval field, it works out
pretty good, but the complexity of this method is as high as pattern recognition and
AI technology. Sebe and Tian [8] has an approach for personalized MIR, but it not
an implemented approach, and the technologies it involved also complex.

There are numerous of organizations working on the publication of Linked
Data. Linking Open Data (LOD) provides a platform in order to link all RDF
datasets on the web [9]. Multimedia Ontologies [10] implies that fragments should
be defined before multimedia being used in semantic annotations. Music Ontology
[11] provides a framework for the temporal annotation of audio signals. Henry [12]
aggregates music processing workflows available on the Web and applies them on
audio signals to dynamically derive temporal segmentations and interlink these

---

[1] http://esw.w3.org/topic/TaskForces/CommunityProjects/LinkingOpenData/DataSets/Link
Statistics

different segments with Web identifiers for music-related concepts. Linked Movie Database (LinkedMDB) [13] contains hundreds of millions RDF triples through the properties (like actors, director, country, etc.).

Ferragina and Gulli [14] implement an open source and personalized search engine based on web-snippet hierarchical clustering using given variable length query statement to perform searching. The keywords-based search engines as we known today (like Google [15]) exploit user's personalized requirements by analyzing web-browsing history. But keywords-based information retrieval is hard to reflecting personalized information. A graph-based query can enables the IR process with additional semantics. Kasneci et al. [16] present a semantic search engine NAGA. It extracts information from several sources on the web and support graph-based query, but user has to learn all the relations linked two entities and a specific query language.

60.3 The Approach

60.3.1 User Profile

A user profile can be used to describe the personalized information of individuals. It contains basic information of individuals like name, gender, height, weight etc. or social information of individuals like career, specialty, title etc., as well as hobby information such as favorite movies, music, food etc.

For demonstration purposes of our method, we build two static examples of user profiles using the Andrew's and Amy's user information. For illustration, the Andrew's user profile has been represented in RDF graph, as showed in Fig. 60.1.

60.3.2 The Process of Personalized Multimedia Retrieval

The personalized multimedia retrieval process is shown in Fig. 60.2, and described as follows:

Step 1 Utilize the keywords inputted to find the labels which contain the keywords in the dataset, then use SPARQL with particular properties to address the subjects of the labels, and iterate this process until find the films' URIs. After filtering, we will get an interlinking network filtered with keywords.

Step 2 Traverse the interlinking network using films' main URI until the nodes are labels. After this stage, a set of RDF graphs waiting to be matched with user profile will be generated.

Step 3 Match user profile to the set of RDF graphs, and then calculate the similarity to determine the matching extent, finally return a ranked list according to the similarity.

Step 4 Return the URIs (HTTP URIs) of resources so it can be accessed.

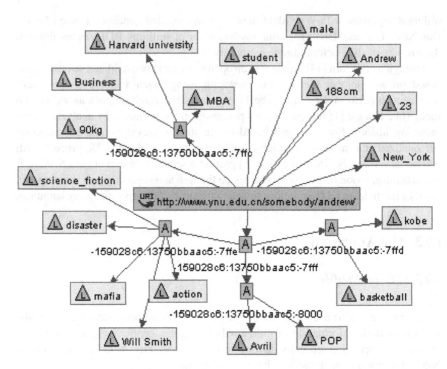

Fig. 60.1 A RDF graph for an example of a user profile

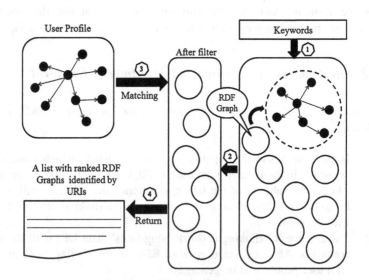

Fig. 60.2 Schematic diagram for method of personalized multimedia retrieval

60.3.3 Similarity Matching Based on RDF Graph Matching

The nature of RDF graph similarity calculating is the core algorithm in our approach. There are still some effective related graph matching algorithms, such as Similarity Flooding [17], which relies on the intuition that elements of two distinct models are similar when their adjacent elements are similar. Moreover, Zhu et al. [18] integrates similarities between nodes and similarities between arcs to construct similarity between graphs. But these algorithms cannot be used in our method directly, because the real RDF graphs has its own characteristics that many nodes in RDF graphs are URIs.

Consequently, our RDF graph matching algorithm takes the linguistic similarity and structural similarity of triples in RDF graph into account. In order to measure the features in RDF graphs.

The formula to calculate similarity of two graphs is as follows:

$$Sim(G_U, G_R) = \frac{\sum_{i=1}^{n} [Sim_{statement}(s_R^i, s_U^{i\_max}) \times Deg(s_R^i)]}{\sum_{i=1}^{n} Deg(s_R^i)} \tag{60.1}$$

where G_U is the RDF graph of user profile, and G_R is the RDF graph which describes the multimedia resource, $Sim_{statement}(s_R^i, s_U^{i\_max})$ is the similarity between triple (also called statement) i in G_R (represented by s_R^i) and the triple in G_U that has maximum similarity with triple i in G_R (represented by $s_U^{i\_max}$), and the $Deg(s_R^i)$ is the degree of s_R^i which as the weight of triple in graph.

We denote the similarity between statements use $Sim_{Statement}(t^u, t^r)$ that defined in formula (60.2), where t^u is the statement comes from user profile and t^r comes from the multimedia RDF graph.

$$Sim_{Statement}(t^u, t^r) = \theta \times Sim_{Triple}(t^u, t^r) + \gamma \times Sim_{Structural}(t^u, t^r)$$
$$(\theta + \gamma = 1) \tag{60.2}$$

The $Sim_{Triple}(t^u, t^r)$ and $Sim_{Structural}(t^u, t^r)$ are labels similarities and structural similarity between t^u and t^r respectively, θ and γ are references of weights.

For the purpose of reducing computation complexity, we take a triple as the smallest element when calculate the similarity. The similarity between two triple is defined as follows:

$$Sim_{Triple}(s_R^i, s_U^j) = \frac{Sim_{label}(s_R, s_U) + Sim_{label}(p_R, p_U) + Sim_{label}(o_R, o_U)}{3} \tag{60.3}$$

where $Sim_{label}(s_R, s_U)$, $Sim_{label}(p_R, p_U)$ and $Sim_{label}(o_R, o_U)$ is the linguistic or string similarity of the subjects, properties and objects in multimedia resource and user profile.

Fig. 60.3 The upper set and
lower set of a statement

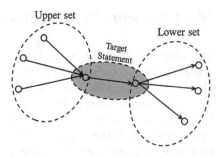

For calculating the linguistic similarity between triples, we use WordNet [19] to measure the semantic distance between words in two nodes or arcs in RDF graph. For those strings of labels do not exist in WordNet, Levenshtein [20] algorithm is used to calculate the string distance of the labels.

The structural similarity between statements is the weighted sum of upper set similarity and lower set (shown in Fig. 60.3) similarity of the distinct statements.

$$Sim_{Structural}(t^u, t^r) = \alpha \times Sim_{upper}(t^u, t^r) + \beta \times Sim_{lower}(t^u, t^r)$$
$$(\alpha + \beta = 1) \tag{60.4}$$

The upper set similarity between t^u and t^r is defined as follows:

$$Sim_{upper}(t^u, t^r) = \frac{\sum_{j=1}^{k} \max(Sim_{1j}, Sim_{2j}, Sim_{3j}, \ldots, Sim_{dj})}{k} \tag{60.5}$$

where the Sim_{dj} presents the similarity between the two corresponding statements in user profile and target graph.

The lower set similarity can be defined in the same way, and denoted by $Sim_{lower}(t^u, t^r)$.

60.4 Evaluation and Discussions

We use "Will Smith" as keywords filtered out 20 movies from LinkedMDB related to Will Smith, and convert them into RDF graphs then compare with user profiles.

Figure 60.4 show Andrew and Amy's matching results by line chart. In the charts, the black highlighted dots represent those movies Andrew or Amy could possibly interested in and those gray highlighted ones represent there is a slim chance for Andrew or Amy loves it. The rest of them present the movies they may not prefer.

According to the figures and statistics, we can see that the result for Amy is what she expected, but Andrew's is not that good. The reason is not all the movies

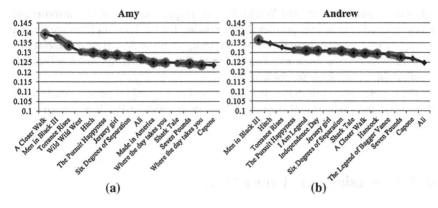

Fig. 60.4 Line chart of films ranking for Amy (**a**) and Andrew (**b**) by RDF graph similarity

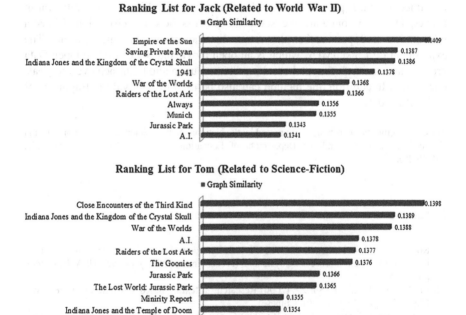

Fig. 60.5 Ranking lists for Jack and Tom

in LinkedMDB dataset is tagged with genre. But the ranking list still contains all the films that user expected. We also found if the more information had been described in a movie, the better the result will be, and the easier to be distinguished from one and another. We can conclude the ranking for both Andrew and Amy are personalized.

Figure 60.5 shows another ranking experiment related to keywords "Steven Spielberg's films". The lists were filtered by Jack's and Tom's favorite movie subjects (Science-Fiction and World War II, respectively), and this information was generated in their user profiles. In the ranking list for Tom, all films are related to subject of "science-fiction". In list for Jack, all films described the subject of "World War II" had been returned in top 6. We hold that the ranking lists are satisfied the expectation for Jack and Tom.

The experiment result shows our framework can be used for personalized movie retrieval in the LinkedMDB dataset, providing an efficient PMIR approach w.r.t. user's interests.

60.5 Conclusions and Future Work

In our framework, the process of retrieval multimedia data which is annotated with Linked Data principle avoided the complex recognitions for low-level features of multimedia data. It provides a new idea that personalized information retrieval in Linked Data environment. We show the process how to retrieval multimedia information and personalize the return lists according the user profile. The experiment on LinkedMDB which is an open movie dataset of Linked Open Data project, and the experimental results indicate our method can achieve the goals effectively. In addition, the method can also be used to retrieval the fragments of multimedia data.

Acknowledgments This work is supported by the National Natural Science Foundation of China (Grant No. 61263043) and the Department of Education of Yunnan Province (Grant No. 2011Z020).

References

1. Rowley H, Baluja S, Kanade K (1996) Human Face detection in visual scenes. In: Advances in neural information processing systems 8 (Proceedings of NIPS), Denver, USA, Nov 1996, pp 875–881
2. Li QY, Hu H, Shi ZP, Shi ZZ (2006) Research on texture-based semantic image retrieval. Chin J Comput 29(1):116 (in Chinese)
3. Lew M, Sebe N, Djeraba C, Jain R (2006) Content-based multimedia information retrieval: state-of-the-art and challenges. ACM Trans Multimed Comput Commun Appl 2(1):1–19
4. Berners-Lee T (2006) Linked data, design issues. http://www.w3.org/DesignIssues/LinkedDa-ta.html, 27 July 2006
5. Klyne G, Carroll JJ (2004) Resource description framework (RDF): concepts and abstract: syntax. The World Wide Web Consortium (W3C)
6. Datta R, Joshi D, Li J, Wang JZ (2008) Image retrieval: ideas, influences, and trends of the new age. ACM Comput Surv 40(2):1–60 (Article 5)
7. Gondra I (2008) Personalized content-based image retrieval. In IGI Glob 2008:261–287
8. Sebe N, Tian Q (2007) Personalized multimedia retrieval: the new trend? MIR'2007, 28–29 Sept, Augsburg, Germany

9. Bizer C, Heath T, Ayers D, Raimond Y (2007) Interlinking open data on the Web (poster). In: 4th European semantic Web conference (ESWC2007), pp 802–815

10. Arndt R, Troncy R, Staab S, Hardman L, Vacura M (2007) COMM: designing a well-founded multimedia ontology for the Web. In: 6th international semantic Web conference (ISWC'07), Busan, Korea, pp 30–43

11. Raimond Y, Abdallah S, Sandler M, Giasson F (2007) The music ontology. In: 8th international conference on music information retrieval (ISMIR'07), Vienna, Austria, pp 417–422

12. Raimond Y, Sandler M (2008) A Web of musical information. In: 9th international conference on music information retrieval (ISMIR'08), Philadelphia, USA

13. Hassanzadeh O, Consens MP (2009) Linked movie data base. In: Proceedings of the WWW 2009 workshop on linked data on the Web (LDOW2009)

14. Ferragina P, Gulli A (2005). A personalized search engine based on Web-snippet hierarchical clustering. In: International World Wide Web conference committee (IW3C2) 10–14 May, Chiba, Japan

15. Sherman C (2005) Google personalized search leaves Google labs. Search engine Watch.com. 10 Nov 2005

16. Kasneci G, Suchanek FM, Ifrim G, Ramanath M, Weikum G (2008) Naga: searching and ranking knowledge. In: ICDE 2008

17. Melnik S, Garcia-Molina H, Rahm E (2002) Similarity flooding: a versatile graph matching algorithm. In: Proceedings of the 18th international conference on data engineering (ICDE). San Jose. CA

18. Zhu H, Zhong J, Li J, Yu Y (2002). An approach for semantic search by matching RDF graphs. In: Proceedings of the fifteenth international Florida artificial intelligence research society conference, Pensacola Beach, Florida, 14–16 May, pp 450–454

19. Fellbaum C (1998) WordNet: an electronic lexical database (language, speech, and communication). The MIT Press, Cambridge

20. Levenshtein IV (1966) Binary codes capable of correcting deletions insertions and reversals [J]. Cybern Control Theor 10(8):707–710

Chapter 61
A Genetic Algorithm for Multiple Mobile Data Collectors' Path Planning in WSNs

Zhuowei Shen and Min Cao

Abstract In mobile data collector (MDC)-based wireless sensor networks, we need to design paths for MDCs for better data collection. In this paper, we use predictable mobility pattern and apply a heuristic algorithm to design paths of MDCs. The algorithm aims to make the time cost by MDCs covering the whole network as short as possible. The algorithm is taken by two steps. Firstly, choose the stop points, and then, construct the paths. Both steps are computed using genetic algorithm (GA). In choosing stop points algorithm, improved stochastic tournament selection is adopted to deal with restraints and special fitness is used to enhance differentiation of solutions. An asexual reproduction based GA with 2-opt optimization mechanism is used to construct MDCs' paths. As experiments show, the algorithm proposed in this paper performs better than greedy algorithm.

Keywords Wireless sensor network · Mobile data collector · Path planning · Genetic algorithm

61.1 Introduction

In mobile data collector (MDC)—based WSNs, there exists several MDCs' mobility patterns, such as random mobility [1], predictable mobility [2, 3] and controlled mobility [4]. Among them, predictable mobility is widely used. With this pattern, path planning of the MDCs has become a key factor to improve the performance of data collecting.

Z. Shen (✉) · M. Cao
Key Lab of Computer Network and Information Integration, MOE, School of Computer and Engineering, Southeast University, Nanjing, China
e-mail: zwshen@seu.edu.cn

W. Lu et al. (eds.), *Proceedings of the 2012 International Conference on Information Technology and Software Engineering*, Lecture Notes in Electrical Engineering 211, DOI: 10.1007/978-3-642-34522-7_61, © Springer-Verlag Berlin Heidelberg 2013

A two-step method proposed in [4] is used to design path for a single mobile base station. The first step is choosing stop points; the second step is solving Travelling Salesman Problem (TSP) with greedy algorithm [5] comes up with an optimized Genetic Algorithm (GA) for TSP. The second step will evolve into Multiple Travelling Salesman Problem (MTSP) while multiple MDCs exist [6] proposed a GA with asexual crossover to solve MTSP.

In this paper we propose an algorithm for path planning of multiple MDCs, which falls to the predictable mobility pattern. The algorithm is taken by two steps. The algorithm of first step is similar to the method in [7]. Moreover, fitness function and selection are optimized to deal with restrains of the problem. The algorithm of second step is based on [6]. Meanwhile, 2-opt method is adopted. The algorithm aims to make the MDCs cover the whole WSN as soon as possible.

The rest of this paper is organized as follows. The problem description and the algorithm's designing detail are shown in Sect. 61.2. Then the algorithm's performance is evaluated in Sect. 61.3. Finally we conclude the paper in Sect. 61.4.

61.2 Multiple MDCs' Path Planning in WSNs

61.2.1 Problem Description

There are n fixed sensors randomly deployed in an area. And m MDCs, with speed of V and communication radius of R, are sent to collect data. The MDCs all leave from sink and return to sink after they communicate with the rest $n-1$ sensors.

This problem is divided into two sub-problems, that is, choosing stop points and constructing moving paths. The corresponding algorithms for these two sub-problems are named choosing stop points (CSP) algorithm and constructing path (CTP) algorithm.

61.2.1.1 Choosing Stop Points

The positions where MDCs must move to and stay are called stop points. Pick out p ($p \leq n$) sensors as the stop points. The chosen stop points should match following conditions.

- Stop points are chosen from the fixed sensors.
- Sink node is a stop point.
- MDCs can reach all sensors if they communicate with sensors within k-hop their communication ranges at each stop point.

Under the circumstance, the number of stop points is supposed to be as small as possible.

61.2.1.2 Constructing MDCs' Paths

We sent m MDCs to reverse the p stop points chosen by the first step. T_i stands for the time cost by the MDC d_i to finish travelling its path. The evaluation criterion of this step is shown as (61.1).

$$T = \text{Max}_{i=1}^{m} T_i \qquad (61.1)$$

These two sub-problems resemble cover set problem and MTSP respectively. Due to their NP-hardness, we solve both sub-problems with GA [8].

61.2.2 Simple Genetic Algorithm

The flow chart of Simple Genetic Algorithm (SGA) is illustrated in Fig. 61.1.

GA generates solutions to optimization problems using techniques inspired by natural evolution, such as mutation, selection, and crossover. The algorithm we proposed is based on SGA with elitist preservation [9]. We adjust the presentation, fitness function and genetic operators for various problems.

61.2.3 Choosing Stop Points Algorithm

61.2.3.1 Representation and Fitness Function

The traditional binary string representation is adopted. Thus a solution is represented as (61.2). The length of binary string is the number of fixed sensors.

$$X = \{x_1, x_2, \ldots, x_n\}, \quad x_i = \begin{cases} 1, & s_i \text{ is chosen as a stop point} \\ 0, & \text{otherwise} \end{cases} \qquad (61.2)$$

Fig. 61.1 Flow chart of SGA

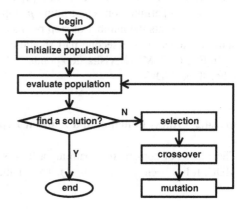

The fitness function is given by (61.3). The fitness consists of an integer and a decimal. The integer shows the number of stop points while the decimal expresses the average distance from the stop points to the sink node.

$$\text{minf}(X) = \sum_{i=1}^{n} x_i + \alpha \times \frac{\sum_{x_i=1} \text{dis}(s_1, s_i)}{\sum_{i=1}^{n} x_i} \tag{61.3}$$

Considering each MDC starts its trip from sink and finally returns to sink, if two solutions have the same number of stop points, the one with smaller average distance is regarded as the better solution.

61.2.3.2 Genetic Operators

Stochastic tournament selection with tournament size of two is adopted in CSP algorithm. And we customize the method of comparing fitness as follows.

- If both solutions are feasible, select the one which has smaller fitness.
- If both solutions are non-feasible, select the one which violate the restrain lighter. Restrain is defined as the number of uncovered sensors.
- If one solution is feasible while the other is not. Consider the non-feasible solution's violation firstly. If the violation is bearable, select the one which has smaller fitness. Otherwise, select the feasible solution.

Single point crossover is performed with 90 % probability. And bitwise bit-flipping with 30 % probability is selected as mutation.

61.2.4 Constructing Path Algorithm

61.2.4.1 Chromosome Presentation

The two-part chromosome technique [6] is selected. The first part of the chromosome is a permutation representing p stop points. The second part is of length m and represents the number of stop points assigned to each of the m MDCs. The sum of integers in the second part should equal p.

In Fig. 61.2, MDC1 visits stop points 1, 2, 5, 14, 6, 1 in order and so on for the other three MDCs.

61.2.4.2 Fitness Function and Asexual Reproduction

The fitness of constructing path algorithm is the time cost by the latest returned MDC. It has been shown in (61.1). The smaller the solution's fitness is, the better.

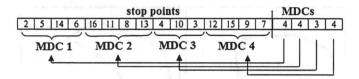

Fig. 61.2 Two-part chromosome representation for 16 stop points and 4 MDCs

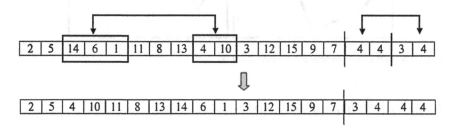

Fig. 61.3 Illustration of asexual reproduction

We swap the gene segments of a chromosome to produce offspring. The operation is described in Fig. 61.3. This asexual reproduction scheme ensures that the newly created chromosomes do not violate the constraints caused by the two-part chromosome representation.

The asexual reproduction may not supply enough mutate strength. We use optimizing schemes to provide reproduction a good starting point. The optimizing schemes are described as below:

1. Optimization of the first part of chromosome

As each MDC's path is randomly generated, there is a high probability that the MDC make some detours. We use 2-opt algorithm to rearrange the order the of stop points each MDC visits. Though the optimizing operation can improve performance, overusing it may result in premature of algorithm. So the optimization should be used with caution.

2. Optimization of the second part of chromosome

This optimization performs after the gene reversion of the second part of chromosome. The chromosomes of a population can be described as $\{A(A_1 \mid A_2),$ $B, C, \ldots\}$. A represents a chromosome consists of its first part A_1 and second part A_2 and so on for B, C.

A new second part A_2' is created by reversing gene segments. Matching all second parts of the population with A_1, we get pairings $\{(A_1 \mid A_2'), (A_1 \mid A_2), (A_1 \mid B_2), \ldots\}$. Compute each pairing's fitness and replace A with the pairing which has the smallest fitness. The solution space is expanded by this way.

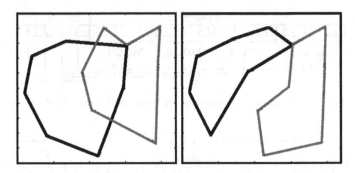

Fig. 61.4 *Left* greedy optimization, *right* 2-opt method

61.3 Experiments and Analysis

Figure 61.4 presents an example result of taking either greedy optimization or 2-opt method into constructing path algorithm. 13 stop points and 2MDCs are deployed. 2-opt method shorten the longest tour length for MDCs to 454.9 m compared with 476.5 m obtained by greedy optimization. It follows that 2-opt optimization is effective in constructing path algorithm.

Experiments below were conducted on a square with edge length 200. A hundred fixed sensors are deployed randomly. We first get the stop points by greedy algorithm and CSP we proposed separately. The greedy strategy is repeating selecting the sensor which covers the most uncovered sensors as the stop point, until all sensors are covered. Results are given in Fig. 61.5. We can see that CSP gets less stop points.

When 16 stop points are given, we construct MDCs' paths by GA and greedy solution separately. The greedy solutions were determined by rotating through all the MDCs in a round-robin fashion, assigning the closest unvisited stop points to each MDC in turn, and continuing on until all the stop points are assigned. The speed of a MDC is 10 m/s and a MDC stays 5 s at each stop point. Figure 61.6 shows that GA proposed by us leads to less time cost. And more MDCs can also reduce the time cost computed by GA. As when the number of MDCs increases from 2 to 4, the time cost decreases significantly. We deploy 4 MDCs in the next experiment.

The last experiment applies CSP algorithm to choose stop points and then construct MDCs' paths via constructing path algorithm. The contrast group is using greedy algorithm to solve both sub-problems. The statistics are given in Fig. 61.7. In short, the algorithm we proposed behaves better.

Fig. 61.5 Result comparison
of choosing stop points

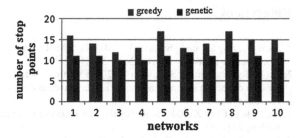

Fig. 61.6 More MDCs lead
to less time for covering the
WSN

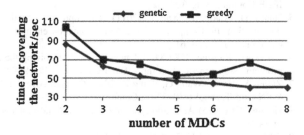

Fig. 61.7 Final results
comparison

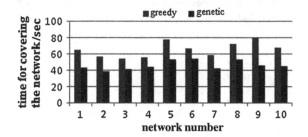

61.4 Conclusion

In this paper, we propose a two-step genetic algorithm for multiple MDCs' path
planning. New features are applied to SGA, for example, in CSP algorithm, customized stochastic tournament selection is introduced to deal with constraint and
special fitness function is designed for convenient detailed comparison; in CTP
algorithm, 2-opt algorithm is used to optimize asexual GA.

As experiments shown, the algorithm we proposed performs better than greedy
algorithm. However, the work still can be improved. For example, the position of a
stop point can be not only one position of fixed sensors, but also anywhere in the
area.

Acknowledgments This paper is supported by the Natural Science Foundation of China (Grant
No. 60903163) and Aviation Science Foundation (Grant No. 20101969010).

References

1. Shah RC, Roy S, Jain S, Brunette W (2003) Data MULEs modeling a three-tier architecture for sparse sensor networks. Ad Hoc Netw 30–41
2. Jea D, Somasundara A, Srivastava M (2005) Multiple controlled mobile elements (data mules) for data collection in sensor networks. Lecture notes in computer science, vol 3560, Springer, Heidelberg, pp 244–257
3. Xu J, He L, Chen Z (2008) Reducing the path length of a mobile BS in WSNs. Future BioMed Inf Eng 271–274
4. Ekici E, Gu Y, Bozadag D (2006) Mobility-based communication in wireless sensor networks. IEEE Commun Mag 6:56–62
5. Huafu D, Xiaolu L, Xue L (2011) An improved genetic algorithm for combinatorial optimization. In: Computer science and automation engineering (CSAE) IEEE international conference, 1, pp 58–61
6. Carter AE, Ragsdale CT (2006) A new approach to solving the multiple traveling salesperson problem using genetic algorithms. Eur J Oper Res 175:246–257
7. Zhong Y, He W, Wang G, Wang Z (2011) Optimal coverage based on genetic algorithm in WSNs. Inf Technol 6:18–23 (in Chinese)
8. Holland JH (1975) Adaptation in natural and artificial systems. The University of Michigan Press, Ann Arbor
9. Eiben AE, Aarts EH, Van Hee KM (1991) Global convergence of genetic algorithms: an infinite Markov chain analysis. In: Schwefel HP, Manner R (eds) Paraleel problem solving from nature. Springer, Berlin, pp 4–12

Chapter 62
Statistics Analysis of the Structural Stress Process Based on the Wavelet Neural Network

Lihong Gao, Shenquan Liu, Jing Huang and Chuanliangzi Liu

Abstract Aiming to the structure reliability analysis, a large amount of structural loading distribution data are required. In general the simulation or real test are used to get these data. But in fact large machine structure with low fault rate is often unable to collect necessary statistic data. The new developing machine also has not large amount of statistical data due to no precedent of use. And moreover the numerical simulation is very enormous for human and time consumption, which its results need be tested and verified. Considering the advantages and disadvantages of the real test and simulation, statistical analysis of loading process is developed based on the wavelet neural network (WNN), to gain the stress mean and standard deviation, and as well as their respective coefficient. Through the application to the stress statistical analysis of the four-bar arm frame crane, the results show that the measured stress data as samples to train WNN can further ensure actual prediction. It is very high efficiency to predict the loading distribution data using the trained WNN. The stress mean and standard deviation required by the reliability analysis can be obtained. Its results can also meet the requirements of the project.

Keywords Wavelet neural network (WNN) · Stress statistical analysis · Stress mean coefficient (SSC) · Stress standard deviation coefficient (SSDC)

L. Gao (✉) · S. Liu · J. Huang
Department of Mechanical Engineering, Taiyuan Institute of Technology,
030008 Taiyuan, China
e-mail: glh0610@sina.com

L. Gao
School of Mechanical and Electronic Engineering, Lanzhou University of Technology,
730050 Lanzhou, China

C. Liu
School of Mechanical Engineering, Taiyuan University of Science and Technology,
030024 Taiyuan, China

W. Lu et al. (eds.), *Proceedings of the 2012 International Conference on Information Technology and Software Engineering*, Lecture Notes in Electrical Engineering 211, DOI: 10.1007/978-3-642-34522-7_62, © Springer-Verlag Berlin Heidelberg 2013

62.1 Introduction

In structural reliability analysis a lot of structure loading distribution data is required, but it is very difficult to obtain these data. In general the simulation or real test is used to get these data [1]. If a kind of method is only used, either one is insufficient. The hypothesis conditions for simulation make the data too ideal.

At the same time the simulation model is different for those of different objects and different application purposes. The mathematical model is often very complex for building model and solving, or even not to get. There are many difficulties to obtain the data in real test. Firstly the more discrete the different objects data is, the larger workload data processing is. Secondly it is very large for human and material consumption to get test data. Thirdly the test data is affected by the scene conditions and work arrangement.

In this paper, combining with the advantages of two methods, the structural loading process analysis is developed based on the Wavelet Neural Network (WNN). WNN is a feed forward network which is provided on the basis of a breakthrough in wavelet analysis research in recent years [2], it uses the wavelet function and scale function forming neurons, and then making the wavelet and neural network merged [3]. Because the WNN combines the time–frequency localization properties of the wavelet transform with the traditional neural network self-learning ability, it has better approximation and error tolerance [4]. Nonlinear wavelet is taken as the incentive function, forming the neurons. Combing the advantages with Wavelet and neural network, WNN model is built.

The data of structural load distribution are obtained based on WNN. It is very helpful to the structural reliability analysis. WNN is used for the simulation calculation section. With the calculation comparison, the optimal network structural parameters can be determined, such as the learning rate, error coefficient, the number of samples, the relationship of the amount of sample and the number of hidden layer. The main arm-frame for the four-bar arm crane is looked as the studying object. The crane work level is set to the fixed value. The grab operation is taken as a typical working condition and has no rotation. According to the feature extraction, the crane's lifting capacity, working radius, the lifting speed are chosen as the major factors to establish the WNN trained samples. The crane's lifting capacity, amplitude and lifting speed are looked as the input nodes, the mean and variance of the stress is looked as the output nodes. The samples can be used for simulation to get more data samples. So the incomplete data of real test are perfect. Using learning network can efficiently predict the mean coefficient and standard deviation coefficient of the stress for each measuring point. The measured data are used as samples to train the neural network, which can further ensure the authenticity of the prediction. It is efficiency using WNN to predict. And the processing method is very simple.

62.2 Wavelet Neural Network

WNN uses the nonlinear wavelet function or scale function instead of the BP network Sigmoid function, the signal is realized passing through the selected wavelet linear superposition [5]. The signal $s(t)$ is fitted by the Wavelet base $\psi_{a,b}(t)$.

$$\hat{s}(t) = \sum_{j=1}^{H} w_j \psi \left| \frac{t - b_j}{a_j} \right| \tag{62.1}$$

where, $\hat{s}(t)$ is the fitting signal; w_j, b_j, a_j is respectively weight value, wavelet translation factor and scaling factor; H is the wavelet base number. The Morlet mother wavelet [5] is shown as below

$$\psi(t) = \cos(1.75t) e^{-\frac{t^2}{2}} \tag{62.2}$$

In practical application, three layer neural network is usually adopted. Suppose the input nodes of network for M, a total number of samples for P and the output nodes of samples for N. Then the output for the pth sample and the nth node is shown as below [6].

$$y_n^p = f \left(\sum_{i=1}^{H} w_{ik} \psi \left(\frac{\sum_{j=1}^{P} w_{ji} p_j - b_i}{a_i} \right) + b_n \right) \tag{62.3}$$

where, M represents the node number of the input layer, H for the node number of the hidden layer, namely wavelet neuron number, w_{ji} represents the weight between the jth unit for the input layer and the ith unit for the hidden layer, w_{ik} represents the weight between the ith unit for the hidden layer and the kth unit for the output layer, a_i, b_i is respectively the scale factor and shift factor for the ith unit of the hidden layer, w_{ji}, w_{ik}, a_i, b_i can be optimized with the error back-propagation method [7].

In the Fig. 62.1 the input nodes for arm frame structure are the lifting capacity, the working radius and the lifting speed; the output nodes are the mean coefficient and standard deviation coefficient for each measuring point stress. Provided that the hidden layer nodes are eight. A part of the computation results are used as the input and output value for network training. At the same time in order to verify the accuracy of the network, another part of the calculation results are used for network authentication.

Fig. 62.1 Self-adaptive
wavelet neural network

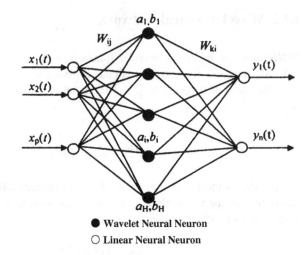

● Wavelet Neural Neuron
○ Linear Neural Neuron

62.3 Measurement and Prediction Analysis of the Structural Stress Distribution Parameters

62.3.1 Analysis of Measured Structural Stress Distribution Parameter

According to the stress characteristic and the actual operation situation of the arm-frame structure, the crane's working cycle for the actual situation is firstly to adjust the instrument to zero at the minimum amplitude, and then to test the luffing movement, no-load decline, capture bulk material and heavy lifting to the minimum amplitude direction load amplitude, unloading operation, and finally the circulation ends.

Measuring point layout is shown at A–A section in Fig. 62.2, which provided with four strain gauges. From the arm-frame root to its front, the distribution piece of the left upper corner is the measurement point 1, the distribution piece of the right upper corner is the measurement point 2, the distribution piece of the right lower corner is the measurement point 3, the distribution piece of the left lower corner is the measurement point 4. According to the test results of the four points, the analysis results for the maximum stress can be obtained for structural reliability calculation, and individual stress results can also be obtained using the statistical results of the three points.

In general, the stress amplitude distributions of heavy machinery structure with the frequent intermittent operation obey to the normal distribution [8]. Because the length is confined, the distribution test is no longer done here. According to the experimental results and the reflected situation from Figs. 62.3 and 62.4, the stress mean fluctuation for the lifting capacity, lifting speed, amplitude is small during the entire cycle, the standard deviation is also the smaller. The results show the

Fig. 62.2 Structural chart for
10t Portal crane

measured condition choice is ideal, the stress process is the smooth ergodic process, and its amplitude distributions submit to the normal distribution. In the practical test, the arm-frame is required to return to the minimum amplitude after each cycle ends. Although in actual test there are some errors, the error can be ignored because it is very small.

Every measuring point needs a neural network, so it needs to construct the four neural network. In order to improve the efficiency and stability of network training, the parameters need do dimensionless processing. The lifting capacity index indicates weight divided by the rated capacity, the rated starting weight of the actual machine is 2 tons; amplitude index are expressed as measure amplitude divided by the maximum amplitude value, the maximum range of the actual machine is 11 m; the lifting speed index indicates the measured lifting speed data divided by the rated hoisting speed, the rated lifting speed of the measured machine is $0.5 \, \mathrm{m \, s^{-1}}$; the coefficients of stress mean and standard deviation for each measuring point are Figs. 62.3 and 62.4 data divided by the structural allowable stress as 170 MPa.

Fig. 62.3 Stress mean
curves of each test point

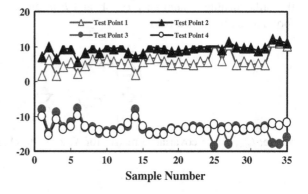

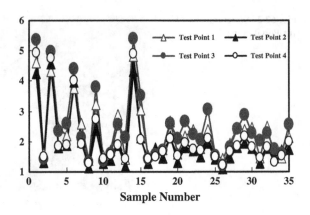

Fig. 62.4 Stress standard deviation curve of each test point

62.3.2 Pretreatment and Prediction Algorithm of the Wavelet Network Training Samples

62.3.2.1 Pretreatment of the Wavelet Network Training Samples

According to the Karhunen–Loeve (K-L) transformation principle, the network training sample pretreatment is realized. Suppose a observed vector $X = (x_1, x_2, \ldots, x_n)$, which is composed of the coordinate representation for n arbitrary independent base vectors. If $t_1, t_2, \ldots t_n$ is n base vectors, and matrices $T = (t_1, t_2, \ldots t_n)$, then X can be expressed as [9]

$$X = YT = \sum_{i=1}^{n} y_i t_i \qquad (62.4)$$

where, Y is the new feature vector required to transform. If the m items $(m < n)$ is to approximate, then $\hat{X} = \sum_{i=1}^{m} y_i t_i + \sum_{i=m+1}^{n} b_i t_i$.

To make the mean square value of the error Δx the minimum, it should satisfy the orthogonality condition: $t_i^T t_i = 1$, and b meets $b_i = E(y_i) = E(X)t_i^T$. So the formula can be gained below

$$
\begin{aligned}
E(\|\Delta X\|^2) &= \sum_{i=m+1}^{n} t_i^T E\{[X - E(X)][X - E(X)]^T\} t_i \\
&= \sum_{i=m+1}^{n} t_i^T C_{ovx} t_i = \sum_{i=m+1}^{n} \lambda_i
\end{aligned}
\qquad (62.5)
$$

where, C_{ovx} is the covariance matrix for X, λ_i as ith characteristic value for C_{ovx}.

Therefore, the mean square error of ΔX is minimum. Namely the smaller the sum of λ_i for $m + 1$ item, the mean square error is smaller. In the practical use, λ_i need to be normalized getting the new eigenvalue λ_i^*.

$$\lambda_i^* = \frac{\lambda_i}{\sum\limits_{i=1}^{n} \lambda_i} \quad (i = 1, 2, \ldots, n) \tag{62.6}$$

Queuing λ_i^*, and then a valve value δ is set. if $i > L$, $\lambda_i^* < \delta$. The remaining λ_i^* ($i=$ L+1,...,n) and the corresponding eigenvectors can be omitted. Without losing the main features, the sample vectors reduce from n dimension to L dimension. Thereby the sample pretreatment is completed.

62.3.2.2 Prediction Algorithm of the WNN Training Samples

After network learning and training end, the weight matrix W_1, W_2 and deviation matrix B_1, B_2 for each network neuron can determine the character of the network. Thus, the fixed network layers, the fixed neuron number for each layer and the fixed weights and bias values between the neurons constitute a fixed dedicated network, it can predict the learning and training issues.

Set P as input variables matrix, ONE is a matrix 1 for the 1 row and N columns, N is the number of columns for the matrix $W_1 \times P$, then $z = W_1 \cdot P + B_1 \cdot ONE$, $A_1 = f(z)$.

$$A_n = W_n \cdot A_{n-1} + B_n \cdot ONE_{n-1} \tag{62.7}$$

where, $f(z)$ is the wavelet function.

The stress mean μ and the stress sample variance σ from $m + 1$th to nth can directly be gotten by the network predicting as shown in Eq. (62.8) [10].

$$\mu = \frac{\sum\limits_{i=m+1}^{n} \mu_i}{n}, \sigma = \sqrt{\frac{n}{n-1} \sum\limits_{i=m+1}^{n} (\mu_i - \mu)^2} \tag{62.8}$$

Then according to the probability sampling distribution theory, the prediction results and the measured results can be made comprehensive. Namely the total distribution parameters of the structural stress for the measured and the WNN simulation will be obtained.

62.4 Example Analysis

The main arm-frame of the four-bar arm crane is taken as the research objects, the level of the work is set to the determined value. Provided that the grabbing operation is chosen as the working conditions, the whole machine has no rotation.

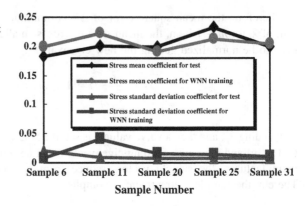

Fig. 62.5 Comparison of WNN training results and test samples for test 1

So lifting and derricking mechanism is at work. Due to grabbing the cargo weight relatively small, the crane load amplitude distribution is more accord with the normal distribution. Because a crane is used for the real test, all sizes of the crane arm structure are fixed. So only the stress causal relationship with the lifting capacity, the amplitude and the lifting speed need be recorded in the measurement. In more general, 6, 11, 20, 25 and 31 serial samples are randomly select as the test sample after network training, the other samples are chosen as training samples, which learning rate is 0.01 and the accuracy of convergence is 0.001. Take for an example of test 1, the comparison of neural network training results and testing samples for test 1 is shown in Fig. 62.5.

From Fig. 62.5, the maximum prediction error of the stress mean coefficient and the standard deviation coefficient for the test 1 is respectively 10.4 and 317 %. Similarly the maximum prediction error of the stress mean coefficient and the standard deviation coefficient for the test 2 is respectively 10.8 and 44 %; the maximum prediction error of the stress mean coefficient and the standard deviation coefficient for test 3 is respectively 12.7 and 360 %; the maximum prediction error of the stress mean coefficient and the standard deviation coefficient for test 4 are respectively 10.1 and 300 %. So the predicting results of stress mean coefficient is

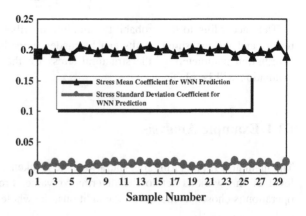

Fig. 62.6 The results of WNN predicting 30 samples for test 1

Table 62.1 Mean and standard deviation of the structural stress process

Test point	SMC	SSDC	SM (MPa)	SSD (MPa)
1	0.1986	0.0151	33.7580	2.5642
2	0.2212	0.0104	37.6051	1.7703
3	−0.2742	0.0067	−46.6134	1.1452
4	−0.2741	0.0143	−46.5993	2.431

quite acceptable. The error of the standard deviation coefficient is too big since the value itself is too small. But according to the sample distribution principle, it will not affect the distribution estimation of the overall parameter, so the error size is not important. It can play a advantageous role to engineering analysis.

According to the data presented, 60 samples or more will make the research object with the more stable characteristics estimation. In this paper 65 samples are selected. Because the test has 35 samples, the neural network prediction will use 30 samples. The prediction results as an example of test 1 is smooth and the smaller error (about 4.069 %), which are shown in Fig. 62.6. According to the sampling distribution theory, the mean and standard deviation of the structural stress process will be obtained as shown in Table 62.1.

62.5 Conclusions

The advantages of the measurement and simulation have been combined to gain the necessary structural load distribution data. WNN is used for simulation. Through network calculation and comparison, the optimal network structural parameters such as the learning rate, control precision, the number of samples are determined. The main arm frame of the four-bar crane is looked as the object in the experiment. According to the feature extraction, the lifting capacity, the lifting speed, and the working radius are chosen as the major factors. The training samples and the optimal network parameters were established. And the simulation of the structural stress process was realized by the measured data.

The structural stress process measurement planning is discussed from the aspects of the measuring point arrangement and the stress parameters distribution. With application to the crane arm-frame structure, the coefficient of the stress mean and standard deviation for each point can be gained. The results show the simulation data can be acceptable for engineering analysis. And then the structural stress statistical parameters were obtained. So the test data and the data predicted by WNN will be enough for the structural reliability analysis, and it can also satisfy the engineering requirement.

References

1. Liu QP, Yu XL, Feng QK (2003) Fault diagnosis using wavelet neural networks. Neural Process Lett 18(2):7115–7123
2. Zhou B, Shi AG, Cai F, Zhang YS (2004) Wavelet neural network for nonlinear time series analysis. Lect Notes Comput Sci 3174:165–192
3. Chen YH, Yang B, Dong JW (2006) Time-series prediction using a local linear wavelet neural network. Neurocomputing 69(6):449–465
4. Awad M (2010) Chaotic time series prediction using wavelet neural network. J Aritif Intell 3(3):73–80
5. Chen XY, Shan XM, Wu XQ (2011) Improved wavelet neural network and its matlab simulation. J Inn Mong Uni Natl (Nat Sci) 4:33–37
6. Sharma A, Agarwal S (2012) Temperature prediction using wavelet neural network research. J Inf Technol 4:22–30
7. Li Y, Zhong SS, Zhang Y (2007) Research and simulation of a continuous wavelet process neural network. Caai Trans Intell Syst 6:112–116
8. Hu XH, Chen L (2009) Wavelet neural network research and applications based on genetic algorithm. J Northwest Univ Technol 29(2):38–42
9. Wang L, Zhang JR, Jin PF (2010) Strength prediction of corrode reinforcing steel based on wavelet neural network. J Highw Transp Res Dev 27(3):69–74
10. Wang TH, Ge YP, Yu FS (2003) Appliation of wavelet neural networks for nonlinear function approximation. Southwest Inst Nat Sci 29(1):38–40 (in chinese)

Chapter 63
Evolving Activation Dynamics in Feedforward Neural Networks

Yu Chen and James A. Reggia

Abstract A feedforward neural network has many basic elements, such as its topology, connection weights, biases, and activation functions, and an extensive literature has explored how to optimize these elements using evolutionary algorithms. However, most of this literature has focused on how to evolve the connection weights or the topological structure, while the activation functions are usually preset, uniform, and held constant during evolution. Here we explore the implications of allowing the activation functions associated with individual hidden and output nodes to evolve simultaneously while evolving connection weights and biases. Computational experiments done using challenging benchmark problems show that simultaneously evolving activation functions is both more effective and more efficient than evolving weights alone. We conclude that including variation of activation functions in the evolutionary process can significantly improve neuroevolution.

Keywords Feedforward neural networks · Activation functions · Evolutionary algorithms

Y. Chen (✉)
College of Computer Science, Sichuan University, Chengdu, China
e-mail: yuchen@scu.edu.cn

J. A. Reggia
Department of Computer Science, University of Maryland, College Park, MD, USA
e-mail: reggia@cs.umd.edu

W. Lu et al. (eds.), *Proceedings of the 2012 International Conference on Information Technology and Software Engineering*, Lecture Notes in Electrical Engineering 211, DOI: 10.1007/978-3-642-34522-7_63, © Springer-Verlag Berlin Heidelberg 2013

63.1 Introduction

During the last two decades, feedforward neural networks (FNN) have achieved great success in a wide range of fields. Error back-propagation (BP) [1] is the most widely used algorithm for training such networks, but BP has two main drawbacks: slow convergence speed, and the possibility of becoming stuck in a local minimum of the error landscape. In typical BP applications, the same activation function (e.g., logistic or tanh sigmoid) is usually adopted uniformly for all nodes, at least throughout each layer. Furthermore, these activation functions are restricted to those that are continuous and differentiable, even though any bounded function could be a reasonable candidate for use.

An alternative approach to training FNN has been to evolve their architecture and/or weight values, and there is now an extensive literature in this area. A detailed review about evolving neural networks (neuroevolution) can be found in literature [2]. Most of this literature has focused on how to evolve the connection weights or the topological structure during training, while the activation functions used are preset, uniform, and held constant during evolution. However, a few studies have examined also evolving activation functions, at least in a limited sense. For example, in one study the topological structure, activation functions and connection weights were evolved at the same time [3], but only sigmoid and/or Gaussian functions were allowed for hidden layer nodes (output node activation functions were fixed as sigmoid functions and not evolved). Other work has evolved activation functions for hidden nodes [4, 5], but altered weights using a conjugate gradient algorithm [6] and used an unusual cascade mechanism based on multiplicative and/or additive compositions of hidden layer node activities for computing the network output values. This cascade mechanism can work effectively. However, it faces some limitations: (1) the structure of the cascade between the hidden layer and the output layer can be complex and require substantial computation, especially when there are many nodes in the network; (2) adopting a cascade of activation functions in the output layer would introduce more connection weights in the cascade mechanism, and this would easy lead to more computation; and (3) this approach still needs to adopt gradient computations to adjust the connection weights.

In this paper, we explore the evolution of weights, biases and activation rules simultaneously. Unlike past work, we allow each hidden and output node to take on its own specific activation rule (rather than restricting all nodes in a layer to have the same activation function), and we consider a broader range of possible activation functions, including some that have not been applied significantly in past neural nets (e.g., trigonometric functions). Since no use is made of gradient descent, non-continuous activation functions (e.g., step function) are also used. Computational experiments are used to explore the effectiveness of this approach.

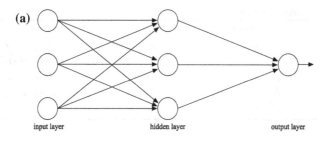

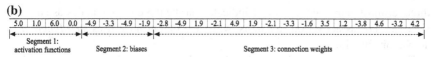

Fig. 63.1 a The structure of an example feedforward neural network as used in this study (networks used were usually much larger than that pictured here for illustrative purposes). **b** The corresponding chromosome for this network, where each box represents one gene. See text for further details

63.2 Methods

In this study, we used a fixed, single-layer feedforward neural network architecture typical of those used with basic error backpropagation, as illustrated in Fig. 63.1. There are four sets of parameters associated with this network: weights w_{ji} between input nodes i and hidden nodes j, weights v_{kj} between hidden nodes j and output nodes k, biases b_{hj} of hidden nodes j, and biases b_{ok} of output nodes k. Also, there is a function f_{hj} associated with each hidden node j, and a function f_{ok} associated with each output node k.

An individual neural network is encoded as a single linear chromosome that is divided into three segments, each segment composed of a sequence of real-valued "genes". This is illustrated in Fig. 63.1b for the network in Fig. 63.1a. Segment 1 consists of the activation function identifiers for hidden and output nodes, in that order. While these are real-valued, they are treated as integer indices for different functions. Thus, in Fig. 63.1b, functions f_5, f_1, and f_6 were used by the three hidden nodes, while f_0 was used by the output node. Segment 2 consists of the biases of hidden and output nodes, given in the same order as the functions. Thus the three leftmost entries in Segment 2 indicate hidden unit biases, while the rightmost entry is the bias of the output node. Segment 3 is all of the connection weights. The nine leftmost entries in Segment 3 are input to hidden connection weights, while the last three entries are hidden to output connection weights. All biases and connection weights are represented as real-valued numbers of restricted range.

Activation functions that can be used by hidden and output nodes are listed in Table 63.1. All of these functions are bounded, and all have similar values or have a similar variation tendency within the domain $[-1, +1]$. Thus, in Fig. 63.1b, the

Table 63.1 Activation functions

Step function	$f_0 = step(x)$	cos	$f_6 = \cos(x)$
sec	$f_1 = 2e^x/(1 + e^{2x})$	tansigmoid	$f_7 = 2/(1 + e^{-2x}) - 1$
gaussian	$f_2 = e^{-x^2/2}$	arctan	$f_8 = a\tan(x).2/\pi$
sigmoid	$f_3 = 1/(1 + e^{-x})$	tanh	$f_9 = (e^{2x} - 1)/(e^{2x} + 1)$
1- sigmoid	$f_4 = 1/(1 + e^x)$	F_{10}	$f_{10} = 1/\sqrt{1 + x^2}$
sin	$f_5 = \sin(x)$		

three leftmost entries in Segment 1 indicate that the three hidden nodes use the *sin*, *sech*, and *cos* as activation functions, while the output node uses *step function* as activation function.

The evolutionary algorithm used in this study, a fairly typical genetic algorithm, is outlined in Table 63.2. Termination criteria are that either a pre-specified fitness level is achieved or a pre-specified maximum number of generations have occurred.

The genetic operators used in the algorithm work as follows: (1) *Selection*: in each generation, individuals are selected for reproduction based on their fitness using roulette wheel sampling. A slightly modified version of elitism is used. The best individual in the previous generation is identified, and two copies are carried forward into the next generation. One copy is carried forward unchanged (as with traditional elitism), but the other is used for further genetic manipulations. This procedure is followed to guarantee that not only is the best individual always carried forward, but that it is also always used in recombination operation. (2) *Recombination*: both one-point and two-point recombinations are used. Crossover points are always selected randomly. With one-point recombination, the genes after the crossover point can be viewed as exchanged, while with two-point recombination, the genes between the two crossover points are exchanged. (3) *Mutation*: all genes are mutated with probability p_m. If the i-th gene is selected for mutation by this preset mutation probability, there are two cases for what happens. For the first case, with probability 0.95, a new gene value is generated and assigned using the same method as with population initialization. For the second case, with probability 0.05, the i-th gene is replaced with the random selected j-th gene's value in the same segments.

Table 63.2 The evolutionary algorithm

Initialize population
Until termination criteria met *do*:
    Calculate fitness of each decoded chromosome
    Apply fitness-based reproduction
    Perform genetic operations
      – Mutation
      – Recombination
      – Inversion
Return the best individual

(4) *Inversion*: two inversion points are randomly chosen, and then the genes between these two points are reversed in order. The inversion points are restricted to both be within the same segment of the chromosome. This operation may be viewed as a macro-mutation.

During each generation, the fitness of each individual chromosome is evaluated according to the following steps: (1) Decode the structure of the FNN from each chromosome, including the activation function of each node, the bias of hidden and output nodes, and all connection weights. (2) Calculate the output value of the FNN for each of the input data patterns. (3) Calculate the error E of the network using $E = 0.5 \times \sum_{i=1}^{n_p} \sum_{j=1}^{n_o} \left(T_{ij} - O_{ij}\right)^2$, where n_p is the number of input patterns, n_o is the number of nodes in the output layer, and T_{ij} (O_{ij}) is the target (output) value with input pattern i for the j-th output node. (4) If E is less than a preset target value p, let $E = 0$ (p is the preset error precision). (5) The fitness of each individual chromosome is evaluated using *fitness* $= 1/(1 + E)$.

63.3 Experimental Methods

To evaluate and analyze the effects of evolving activation functions as well as weights and biases, we performed evolutionary runs using two popular benchmark problems: n-bit odd parity problems and n-bit symmetry problems of varying sizes n. Both the n-bit odd parity problem and the n-bit symmetry problem are widely used and very challenging benchmark problems, and both of them are difficult to tackle using traditional evolution of weights/biases alone and/or error backpropagation, especially as n increases in size.

We focused on comparing the performance between evolving feedforward neural nets when only the connection weights and biases are evolved (control condition) versus when activation functions were also simultaneously evolved (experimental condition). In the control condition, activation functions were preset and fixed. Our evolutionary software was implemented in Java.

In each computational experiment, both experimental and control runs are performed 200 times independently. In each run, the maximum number of generations was limited to 100,000. A run was classified as successful if the fitness of the chromosome reached 1, which encodes the best-evolved network (or the total error of network is less than a preset error precision value). In each experiment, the success rate was recorded, which is the percent of successful outcomes in the 200 independent runs. Further, based on successful runs only, the minimum generation (Min), the maximum generation (Max), the average generation (Mean), and the standard deviation (SD) were also recorded. Simulation parameter values are given in Table 63.3. As seen in Table 63.3, we used tansigmoid (f_7) and sigmoid (f_3) activation functions for hidden and output nodes, respectively, in the control evolutionary runs and the error back propagation runs. These specific functions were selected as they are very widely used in the literature.

Table 63.3 Parameter values used in computational experiments

Parameters	Odd Parity problem		Symmetry problem	
	Control	Experiment	Control	Experiment
Mutation rate	0.088	0.088	0.044	0.044
One-point/two-point crossover rate	0.3	0.3	0.3	0.3
Inversion rate	0.1	0.1	0.1	0.1
Population size	50	50	100	100
Bias/weight range	$(-5, +5)$	$(-5, +5)$	$(-5, +5)$	$(-5, +5)$
Function for hidden layer	f_7	$f_0\text{-}f_{10}$	f_7	$f_0\text{-}f_{10}$
Function for output layer	f_3	$f_0\text{-}f_6$	f_3	$f_0\text{-}f_6$
Topology of FNN	$n\text{-}n\text{-}1$	$n\text{-}n\text{-}1$	$n\text{-}2\text{-}1$	$n\text{-}2\text{-}1$

63.4 Results

63.4.1 n-Bit Odd Parity Problems

The n-bit odd parity problem has been one of the most popular benchmarks in evaluating neural network training algorithms [7]. This problem includes the well-known, non-linearly separable XOR problem when $n = 2$. In this set of tests, we compared experimental and control evolutionary processes on problems of from 2 inputs to 13 inputs in size.

From Table 63.4, it can be seen that the success rate of evolution of just weights and biases diminishes to zero, while surprisingly it remains 100 % if activation functions are also evolved. While the number of generations required for success increases with larger problems, the efficiency of the evolutionary process remains quite reasonable.

63.4.2 n-Bit Symmetry Problems

The symmetry problem is another challenging benchmark problem [1, 8]. In this set of tests, we compared experimental and control evolutionary processes on problems of from 5 inputs to 10 inputs in size. Table 63.5 gives the results of evolutionary runs with/without evolution of activation functions.

As seen in Table 63.5, both the efficiency and the success rate of evolution including activation functions are better. However, our experimental results show that this class of problems is very difficult for evolution of just weights and biases.

Table 63.4 Results with n-bit odd parity problem, $p = 0.001$

		Success rate (%)	Min	Max	Mean (SD)
2-bit	Control	100	1	302	57.72(40.25)
	Experiment	100	1	47	10.92(9.64)
3-bit	Control	100	15	2,014	390.04(307.05)
	Experiment	100	1	203	34.24(32.21)
4-bit	Control	70.5	1,304	96,908	19151.09(21178.45)
	Experiment	100	2	453	57.12(59.83)
5-bit	Control	45	19,415	98,926	58513.77(20970.5)
	Experiment	100	2	596	81.76(89.32)
6-bit	Control	0	–	–	–
	Experiment	100	21	2,464	153.36(206.11)
7-bit	Control	0	–	–	–
	Experiment	100	11	1,316	232.66(198.16)
8-bit	Control	0	–	–	–
	Experiment	100	49	1,357	356.73(276.39)
9-bit	Control	0	–	–	–
	Experiment	100	93	4,972	546.02(517.81)
10-bit	Control	0	–	–	–
	Experiment	100	147	3,589	800.35(519.64)
13-bit	Control	0	–	–	–
	Experiment	100	547	34,937	4740.7(5440.24)

Table 63.5 Results with n-bit symmetry problem, $p = 0.01$

		Success rate (%)	Min	Max	Mean (SD)
5-bit	Control	100	301	42,056	2254.23(5353.99)
	Experiment	100	25	7,047	252.66(544.66)
6-bit	Control	0	–	–	–
	Experiment	100	71	47,219	1287.2(4669.42)
7-bit	Control	0	–	–	–
	Experiment	100	159	36,958	1343.38(3008.48)
8-bit	Control	0	–	–	–
	Experiment	89.5	280	96,093	11053.04(18257.88)
9-bit	Control	0	–	–	–
	Experiment	79	592	89,881	11419.63(18468.98)
10-bit	Control	0	–	–	–
	Experiment	51	1,030	87,254	16132.9(19167.17)

63.5 Conclusions

We conclude that incorporating variation of activation functions in a neuroevo-
lutionary process can very significantly improve the results obtained, at least on
some well known and challenging benchmark problems. In addition, further work
is needed to explore the generality of such results with other network architectures
and application problems.

Acknowledgments This work was partially supported by the Young Faculty Foundation of Sichuan University under grant No. QN2011-2 and the National Natural Science Foundation of China under grant No. 61173099.

References

1. Rumelhart D, Hinton G, Williams R (1986) Learning representations by back-propagating errors. Nature 323:533–536
2. Yao Xin (1999) Evolving artificial neural networks. Proc IEEE 87(9):1423–1447
3. Liu Y, Yao X (1996) Evolutionary design of artificial neural networks with different nodes. In: Proceedings of IEEE international conference on evolutionary computation, pp 670–675
4. Iyoda EM, Von Zuben FJ (1999) Evolutionary hybrid composition of activation functions in feedforward neural networks. International joint conference on neural networks, vol 6, pp 4048–4053
5. Iyoda EM, Von Zuben FJ (2002) Hybrid neural networks: an evolutionary approach with local search. Integr Comput Aided Eng 9(1):57–72
6. Bazaraa MS, Sheraly HD, Shetty C (1992) Nonlinear programming: theory and algorithms, 2nd edn. Wiley, New York
7. Liu Derong, Hohil Myron E, Smith Stanley H (2002) N-bit parity neural networks: new solutions based on linear programming. Neurocomputing 48:477–488
8. Chabuk T, Reggia JA (2010) Causally-guided evolutionary computation for adapting weights. The fourth international conference on neural, parallel scientific computations

Chapter 64
Multi-Objective Model and Optimization for Airport Gate Assignment Problem

Dongxuan Wei and Changyou Liu

Abstract Airport gates are scarce and expensive resources in air transportation. Assigning aircraft to gate must consider the profits of airport, airlines and passengers. Based on the passengers' satisfaction and the efficiency and effectiveness of airport and airline, a multi-objective model was established, and then GATS algorithm combining genetic algorithms with tabu search was given to optimize it. The adaptive weight approach was adopted to evaluate the fitness of each individual, and the crowded-comparison operator was used to guide the selection process and the update of Pareto set. The numerical simulation and comparison of algorithms illustrated the validity of model and effectiveness of algorithm. Those can provide theory and methods supports for airport ground control.

Keywords Gate assignment · Multi-objective optimization · Genetic algorithm · Adaptive weight approach

64.1 Introduction

With the development of air transport traffic, the number of flights has grown rapidly, and the complexity of airport management has increased significantly. For example, the Beijing Capital International Airport has three runways, three terminals, and more than 300 gates to service 1,500 aircrafts in each day. Flight delays or accidents

D. Wei (✉)
Highway School, Chang'an University, Southern Middle Section
of the Second Circular Road, Xi'an, China
e-mail: dxwei@chd.edu.cn

C. Liu
College of Air Traffic Management, Civil Aviation University of China, Tianjin, China

W. Lu et al. (eds.), *Proceedings of the 2012 International Conference on Information Technology and Software Engineering*, Lecture Notes in Electrical Engineering 211, DOI: 10.1007/978-3-642-34522-7_64, © Springer-Verlag Berlin Heidelberg 2013

might happen if operation will not be handled well, and domino effect might happen to influence the whole operation of airport. The airport gate assignment problem (AGAP) is one of the most complicated and important issues in the daily operations of airport. The objective of the task is assigning each flight (aircraft) to an available gate while maximizing both conveniences to passengers and the operational efficiency of airport. The classical AGAP is a combinatorial optimization problem with NP-hard. Researchers have carried out extensive studies to help airport authorities more effectively assigning flights to gates. Mathematical programming techniques have been used to formulate the AGAP, such as 0–1 linear programming [1] and branch and bound and linear programming relaxation [2]. However, the problem can not be solved within polynomial time by mathematical programming approach when the scale is large for its NP-hard. And then, various meta-heuristics, especially Tabu Search (TS) [3–5] and Genetic Algorithms (GA) [6–8] and Ant Colony Collaborative Algorithms [9], were developed to get optimal or near optimal solutions. In addition, multi-runway airport gate assignment and a model aimed at reducing the time travelers spent in the airport flight area were developed respectively in [10, 11].

There are two optimization objectives in traditional researches. The first is minimizing the overall walking distances or connection times required for passengers to catch their connection flights [2–4, 7]. Another objective usually considered is maximizing the robust of gate assignment to make it insensitive to variations in flight schedules [6, 12, 13]. Clearly, the objective of gate assignment operations may vary for different airports. In this paper, a new multi-objective model is presented by considering three objectives including the robust of gate assignment, the satisfaction of passengers and the match rate of types of aircraft-to-gate. Combination algorithm using GA based on adaptive weight approach and TS is proposed to efficiently solve large-scale problem in practice.

64.2 Problem Analyzing and Modeling

64.2.1 Constraints

The AGAP can be considered as a case of the constraint resource assignment problem where the gates are resources and flights are consumers. The problem involves a set of arriving and departing flights during the operational stage (1 day or a few hours), and a set of gates which have to be assigned. The information of AGAP should be considered involves the daily flight schedules, the density and the quantity of flights and turn-round time, the layout of gates, the aircraft type associated with each flight, etc. Let N and M are the numbers of flights and gates, respectively. All flights can be classified into three types: departure, arriving and transferring flights. The transferring flights are always formed as flight pairs, and one pair flight is assigned to a same gate. The operation process of a pair transferring flight includes landing, taxi-in, turn-round, taxi-out and departure. All flights have starting and ending time to use a gate. All flights are sorted according the starting time to use gate, and $A = \{ a_1, a_2, \ldots a_N \}$ is used to denote the flights set. The information of each flight is schedule and the number of arriving, departing and transferring passengers. The serial number of airport is used to illustrate the gate set $G = \{ g_1, g_2, \ldots g_M \}$. Gate information includes the relation distance between other gate and check-in counter and the baggage claim area. The capacity of gates can satisfy the requirement of all flights, and gate shortage condition while peak hour can not be considered in this paper. The constraints are commonly required in a feasible gate assignment as follows:

(1) Every flight must be assigned to one and only one gate.
(2) No two aircraft may be assigned to the same gate when their turn-round times overlap. The occupying of gate for flight is exclusive in time and space. A gate can not be available for other aircraft until it is released again while it is occupied by one aircraft. Every aircraft has one flight next/later it at the same gate at the most according to this constraint.
(3) The idle time period between two continuous flights assigned to a same gate should be greater than a security time. The safety time can absorb the stochastic flight delays, and ensure the safety of operations including aircraft, vehicles and workers. This security constraint is equivalent to the occupied time is extend.
(4) Aircraft-gate size compatibility. Size compatibility of the aircraft and gate as well as gate's access to government inspection service are also important. A small aircraft can be assigned to a big gate, but a large aircraft can not be assigned to a small gate. A large gate has the flexibility to accommodate various size of aircraft where as a small gate is more limited. Some references could not consider this constraint, and gates are assumed to be homogenous. The constraints can be formulated as follows:

$$\sum_{k=1}^{M} y_{ik} = 1, \forall i \in N \tag{64.1}$$

$$y_{jk} \geq \sum_{i=1}^{N} z_{ijk}, \forall j \in N, \forall k \in M \tag{64.2}$$

$$y_{ik} \geq \sum_{j=1}^{N} z_{ijk}, \forall i \in N, \forall k \in M \tag{64.3}$$

$$(E_i - D_j)z_{ijk} \geq \alpha, \forall i, j \in N, \forall k \in M \tag{64.4}$$

$$(U_k - V_i)y_{ik} \geq 0, \forall i \in N, \forall k \in M \tag{64.5}$$

$$y_{ik}, z_{ijk} \in \{0, 1\}, U_k, V_i \in \{1, 2\} \tag{64.6}$$

Constraint (64.1) denotes that every flight must be assigned to one and only one gate. $y_{ik} = 1$ if and only if flight i is assigned to gate k. Constraint (64.2) ensures every flight has one immediately proceeding flight at most. Constraint (64.3) specifies every flight has one immediately succeeding flight at most. $z_{ijk} = 1$ if and only if flight i and flight j are both assigned to gate k, and flight i is the immediately proceeding flight of j, else $z_{ijk} = 0$. Formulation (64.4) specifies each idle time must be greater than the security idle time α. Constraint (64.5) denotes the type matching of aircraft-to-gate. U_k and V_i are the type of gate and aircraft, respectively. Small aircraft and gate is denoted by 1, and large is 2. (64.6) denotes variables values.

64.2.2 Objectives

In this paper, three objectives are considered including the robust of gate assignment, the satisfaction of passengers and the match rate of types of aircraft-to-gate.

(1) Maximizing the robust of gate assignment. Flight delays are very common in air transport. Uncertain changes of flight schedule, due to severe weather conditions, equipment failures, etc., may disrupt the initial assignments and increase the difficulty of maintaining smooth station operations. So the static gate assignment should be robust to handle the stochastic disturbance. Reference [6] denotes the nature of robustness is minimizing dispersion of idle time periods for static flight-to-gate assignment, and then this function is adopted to achieve the objective in this paper. The optimization of objective 1 can get balance of all gates use. For each assignment solution, each flight i would be one immediately preceding idle time S_i before it, and every gate has one idle time S_k before closing. So the total of idle time is $N + K$. Formulation (64.7) and (64.8) define the first and last idle time of each gate, and (64.9) states the others idle times. E_i and D_i is the arriving and departure time flight i to gate respectively, and C_k is the closure time of gate k.

$$S_k = C_k - D_i, i = \max(i), i \in \{i|y_{ik} = 1\} \tag{64.7}$$

$$S_i = E_i - D_j, i, j = 1, \cdots, N, z_{ijk} = 1 \tag{64.8}$$

$$S_i = E_i - B_k, i = \min(i), i \in (i|y_{ik} = 1) \tag{64.9}$$

For a set of flights with fixed arrival and departure time, the total available time of gates and the ground time of flights are constant. The dispersion of idle time periods for static flight-to-gate assignment can be formulated as follow:

$$F_1 = \sum_{i=1}^{N} S_i^2 + \sum_{k=1}^{M} S_k^2 \tag{64.10}$$

(2) Minimizing the total walking distance of passengers. The satisfaction level of passengers is a major evaluation of airport operation. Many literatures handled the AGAP by considering this objective. Suppose flight i is assigned to gate k, and flight j to gate l, T_{kl} denotes the distance between gate k and l, and P_{ij} is the passenger number transferring from the flight i to flight j. The objective function can be formulated as:

$$F_2 = \sum_{i=1}^{N} \sum_{j=1}^{N} \sum_{k=1}^{M+1} \sum_{l=1}^{M+1} P_{ij} T_{kl} y_{ik} y_{jl} \qquad (64.11)$$

(3) Degree of aircraft-gate size matching. In order to improve operation efficiency and economic performance of airport, aircraft should be assigned to a gate whose size is same to it as far as possible. The others two objectives are both minimization problem, so this objective is transferred to degree of aircraft-gate size no-matching. Let q_i is binary variable, and $q_i = 1$ while the aircraft type is not equal to the type of assigned gate, otherwise $q_i = 0$. The objective function is:

$$F_3 = \frac{1}{N} \sum_{i=1}^{N} q_i \times 100\% \qquad (64.12)$$

64.3 Algorithm Design

Genetic Algorithms as powerful and broadly applicable stochastic search and optimization techniques [14, 15], are perhaps the most widely know types of Evolutionary Computation methods today. As a novel approach to multi-objective optimization problem, GAs has received considerable attention. NSGA-II [14] has high-performance in multiple optimization Evolutionary Algorithms, which can find much better spread of solutions and better convergence near the true Pareto-optimal front in most problems. However, NSGA-II adopts a fast non-dominated sorting approach to define the fitness of individuals. The comparison is carried on a population with double size, and has long run time. In this paper, GATS algorithm is proposed to solve the model. Adaptive weight approach is proposed to evaluate those three incomparable objectives, and diversity preservation of NSGA-II is adopted to update the Pareto set and select new population.

64.3.1 Adaptive Weight Approach

There are three optimization objectives in the model, and which have different order of magnitude and are incommensurability and conflict. Adaptive Weight Genetic Algorithm utilizes some useful information from the current population to readjust weights to obtain a search pressure toward a positive ideal point [15]. Multi-objective optimization problem with q objective functions can be represented:

$$\min F(x) = (F_1(x), F_2(x), \ldots F_q(x)) \tag{64.13}$$

For the examined solutions at each generation, two extreme points were defined: $F^{\min} = (F_1^{\min}, F_2^{\min}, F_3^{\min})$, $F^{\max} = (F_1^{\max}, F_2^{\max}, F_3^{\max})$, where $F_i^{\max}$ and $F_i^{\min}$ are the maximal and minimal values for the ith objective in the population. Two extreme points will update at each generation, and $F^{\min}$ will approach positive ideal point. The adaptive weight for objective i can be calculated as $w_i = \frac{1}{F_i^{\max} - F_i^{\min}}$. And then, the adaptive weighted-sum objective function is then given by:

$$F(x) = \sum_{i=1}^{q} \frac{F_i - F_i^{\min}}{F_i^{\max} - F_i^{\min}} \tag{64.14}$$

The function value of individual x can be adopted as fitness value to evaluate it.

64.3.2 Representation

An N-digit integer string was used as a chromosome, where the value at the jth digit represents the gate number assigned for the flight j. The assignment of large aircrafts must be assured for a large gate has the flexibility to accommodate various sizes of aircraft where a small gate can not service to large aircraft. All flights are classified several types according to the size. Supposing there are two types aircrafts, the set of large aircraft is A_B, and the set of small aircraft is A_s. At first, assigning gate for each flight of A_B, and the steps are as follows:

Step 1: Assign gates to flight according to arriving time. Set $i = 1$ and gate condition is original state.

Step 2: Search available gates in big gates for flight i. Supposing the available gates set is G_i.

Step 3: Assign stochastically one gate from G_i to the flight i. And then gate condition changes.

Step 4: If all flights have been assigned, turn to step 5, else, let $i = i + 1$ and turn to step 2.

Step 5: Output the solution and the gate condition.

Secondly, assigning gates for small flights of A_s based on the assignment of A_B by the same method. Small flights can insert into the interval of two big flights while satisfying all constraints.

64.3.3 Pareto Set Preservation and Selection

The best Pareto set $\hat{P}(t)$ will be preserved and updated during the process iteration of GAs. Suppose the maximum size of $\hat{P}(t)$ is λ, all the members of Pareto set will be preserved in $\hat{P}(t)$ if the size of Pareto set is smaller than λ. In general, the count of solutions in the Pareto set would be larger than λ, we choose the best solutions from the Pareto set using the crowded-comparison approach [11]. This method can enhance convergence speed and better spread of solutions near the true Pareto-optimal fronts. Elitists are selected stochastically from $\hat{P}(t)$ according to elitist selection probability and join the population to carry genetic operators. Elitist selection probability is decided by the population size and λ. For the sake of clarify, we suppose $\varphi(\phi < \lambda)$ elitist individuals are chosen, and then, the selection operator need select $\delta - \phi$ individuals from last population where δ is the size of population. Roulette wheel approach is used by selection operation. Crossover and mutation will operate on the new population $P(t)$.

64.3.4 Crossover

One-cut point Crossover is adopted by the nature of AGAP in the paper. Crossover and mutation are common GA operators. Crossover Operates on two chromosomes at a time and generating offspring by combining both chromosomes' features. The first step is getting two parents randomly from $P(t)$. Secondly, a random point k is produced where $k < N$. Then exchange the right parts of two parents to generate offspring.

Those two offspring chromosomes may be infeasible, so a checking and modifying process is promoted as follows. For the child chromosome f whose cut point is k. Because those genes before it are feasible, checking will begin from gene $k + 1$. For the gene $k + 1$ (flight $k + 1$): getting the present condition of gates firstly. Secondly, checking its gene is feasible or not; yes then turning to next gene, if not, reassigning for it and the condition of gates changed, then turning to next gene.

64.3.5 Mutation

As is well known, the mutation operator is used by GAs to keep the diversity of the population high by modifying genes of some chromosomes. Because of various of constraints, general mutation operators can not be used in this problem. Tabu Search is a mathematical optimization method which enhances the performance of a local search method by using memory structures. In this paper, some individuals are changed their modules by TS to exploit solution space as widely as possible and retard premature convergence of GAs. Two neighborhood exchange operation are proposed in the TS mutation. (1) $a \leftrightarrow b$: select flight a at firstly, and then selecting flight b which has overlap time with a. Those two flights exchange their gates. (2) $a \leftrightarrow \phi$: flight a exchange genes with a dummy flight, in other words, flight a is inserted an unoccupied gate during the turn-round time of flight a. The purpose of mutation is changing the module of individual, and then the iteration time may equal the half of flight number.

64.4 Experimental Results

The experimental data were obtained from 1 day schedule of one terminal in Beijing Capital International Airport. There are 117 flights and 23 gates during 8:00 to 18:00, where 35 large aircrafts and 82 small aircrafts. 23 gates have been considered where the quantity of large gates is 15 and small is eight. The distances between gates and check-in/baggage claim area are denoted by the related distances, and the initial gates are assumed empty. The parameters of model are set as Table 64.1.

In order to compare the performance of two algorithms, GATS and standard GA, each algorithm is implemented 10 times, and the results are shown in Table 64.2. The optimization percentages of each objective are got by comparing with the positive ideal point in global where $F^{\min} = (763229, 2514628, 0.1538)$. From the result we find that, GATS can get better solutions than GA. Both algorithms can not get better optimization percentage for $F2$ and $F3$, and the optimization difference is not marked for $F3$. The reason is considering the usage balance for all gates, and the value of safety time is much close confinement. By the nature of the objective function $F2$, much more aircrafts will be absorbed to a few attractive gates while it is optimized alone. The busiest gate will service eight flights while another gate only service one flight. The near-optimum solution value of $F2 = 2514628$, but the assignment robustness is very weak while $F1 = 1082164$. It is not obviously suitable for real-time use.

For the third objective, some small flights must be scheduled in large gates for there are much more small flights while less small gates at the terminal. Those small gates will be much busier than others if $F3$ is optimized alone. The distribution of idle times is shown in Fig. 64.1. There are 94 idle time periods while the first and the last idle times of each gate can not be calculated. From the statistics

Table 64.1 The parameters of algorithm

Parameter	Value	Parameter	Value
Population size	50	Mutation probability	0.05
The size of best Pareto set	10	TS generation	60
Selection probability	0.7	Maximum generation	2000
Crossover probability	0.7	The safety time	30 min

Table 64.2 Comparison of algorithms GATS and GA

	GATS			GA		
	F1	F2	F3	F1	F2	F3
1	845343	3514415	0.2821	925353	3743555	0.2991
2	828367	3309535	0.3333	879309	3818835	0.2991
3	778109	3392675	0.3077	892215	3745455	0.2906
4	802497	3325875	0.3248	810939	3249975	0.3333
5	795997	3476135	0.2906	811219	3358075	0.3077
6	811705	3322955	0.3162	778061	3302375	0.3248
7	800711	3404895	0.2906	788539	3275015	0.3333
8	817551	3355095	0.2991	825565	3263895	0.3248
9	782613	3447875	0.2991	793087	3312375	0.3162
10	805537	3326915	0.3162	814309	3295115	0.3162
Average	806843	3387637	0.3060	831860	3436467	0.3145
Optimization percentages (%)	105.7	134.7	198.9	109	136.7	204.5

Fig. 64.1 Idle times distribution

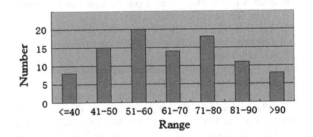

we can find that the most idle time periods concentrate in 50–80 min, which can absorb minor flight delays in real-time. The assignment solution which considers three objectives can satisfy the requirement of airport operation.

64.5 Conclusion

The assignment of civil airport gate is a complex interactive process while considering the usage of airport resources, the convenience of passengers and the airlines operating efficiency, etc. A multi-objective model is proposed, and GATS with adaptive weight approach is used to solve the problem. The global search is implemented by maintaining potential Pareto solutions at each generation. The TS mutation operator is adopted to retard premature. The experiment tests show the model and algorithms can help airport authorities to handle the gate assignment problem. The gate resource over-constraint and some special constraints could not be considered in the paper. Future research will focus on those aspects.

Acknowledgments This work is supported by National Nature Science Foundation under Grant: 60979007, 60736045, and the Special Fund for Basic Scientific Research of Central Colleges, Chang'an University, CHD2009JC081.

References

1. Bihr R (1990) A conceptual solution to the aircraft gate assignment problem using 0, 1 linear programming. Comput Ind Eng 19(1–4):280–284
2. Babic O (1984) Aircraft stand assignment to minimize walking. J Transp Eng 110(1):55–66
3. Xu J-F, Glenn B (2001) The airport gate assignment problem: mathematical model and a tabu search algorithm. In: Proceedings of the 34th Hawaii international conference on system sciences, IEEE, Hawaii, pp 102–111
4. Ding H, Lim A, Rodrigues B et al (2004) Aircraft and gate scheduling optimization at airports. In: Proceedings of the 37th Hawaii international conference on system sciences, IEEE, Hawaii, pp 74–81
5. Wang L, Liu C-Y, Tu F-S (2006) Optimized assignment of civil airport gate. J Nanjing Univ Aeronaut Astronaut 38(4):433–437 (in Chinese)
6. Bolat A (2001) Models and a genetic algorithm for static aircraft-gate assignment problem. J Oper Res Soc 152(4):1107–1120
7. Wei D-X, Liu C-Y (2007) Optimizing gate assignment at airport based on genetic-tabu algorithm. In: Proceedings of IEEE conference on intelligent control and logistics, Jinan, pp 1135–1140
8. Liu C-Y, Guo N (2011) Research on gate assignment for aircraft based on operational safety. China Saf Sci J 21(12):108–114 (in Chinese)
9. Ding J-L, Li X-L, Li Q-F (2011) A stands assignment model based on ant colony collaborative algorithms of graph's weight. Comput Eng Sci 33(9):151–156 (in Chinese)
10. Yin J-N, Hu M-H, Zhao Z (2010) Simulation model and algorithm of multi-runway airport gate assignment. J Traffic Transp Eng 10(5):71–76 (in Chinese)
11. Feng C, Hu M-H, Zhao Z (2012) A new optimization model of airport gate assignment. J Transp Syst Eng Inf Technol 12(1):131–138 (in Chinese)
12. Yan S-Y, Huo C (2001) Optimization of multiple objective gate assignments. Transp Res A 35(5):413–432
13. Lim A, Wang F (2005) Robust airport gate assignment. In: Proceedings of 17th international conference on tools with artificial intelligence, IEEE Press
14. Deb K, Agrawal S, Amrit P (2002) A fast and elitist multi-objective genetic algorithm: NSGA—II. IEEE Trans Evolut Comput 6(2):182–197
15. Mitsuo G, Cheng R-W (2004) Genetic algorithms and engineering optimization. Tsinghua University Press, Beijing (in Chinese)

Chapter 65
A Simulation- and Metaheuristic-Based Approach for Inventory Optimization of Complex Distribution Systems

Dianjun Fang and Cong Li

Abstract In today's dynamic market numerous dynamic influencing factors have seriously aggravates the difficulties of inventory planning of the complex distribution systems. This paper proposes a simulation- and metaheuristic-based approach for the optimization of the inventory policies in complex distribution systems. The initial multi-echelon inventory policies are handed over to a simulation model, which is capable of modeling complexity and uncertainties of the distribution network and simulating them under respective scenarios. Through comprehensively analyzing the KPIs (logistic service level and logistic costs) of this set of multi-echelon inventory policies, their levels of robustness can be clearly ascertained. Based on the simulation results, a metaheuristic-based optimizer regenerates improved (more robust) multi-echelon inventory policies, which are once again comprehensively and precisely evaluated through simulation. This closed feedback loop forms a simulation optimization process that enables the autonomous evolution of multi-echelon inventory policies of complex distribution systems.

Keywords Distribution system · Simulation · Metaheuristic · Evolutionary algorithms · Inventory policies

D. Fang
Sino-German College for Graduate Study, Tongji University, Shanghai, China
e-mail: fang.dianjun@cdhk.tongji.edu.cn

C. Li (✉)
Fraunhofer Institute for Material Flow and Logistics, Dortmund, Germany
e-mail: Cong.Li@iml.fraunhofer.de

W. Lu et al. (eds.), *Proceedings of the 2012 International Conference on Information Technology and Software Engineering*, Lecture Notes in Electrical Engineering 211, DOI: 10.1007/978-3-642-34522-7_65, © Springer-Verlag Berlin Heidelberg 2013

608   D. Fang and C. Li

65.1 Introduction

In today's dynamic market, distribution networks are always finding themselves in a continuously changing environment. Numerous driving forces of changes come not only from outside such as volatile customer demand, shortened product life cycle and individualized customer wishes [16]; but also from inside, like short-of-stock, delay or suspension [19]. These mutually overlapping and interacting factors cause turbulent changes in the environment that distribution networks are facing and impose strong pressures for adaptation on every level of distribution networks [5]. Consequently, today's distribution networks are highly expected to be adaptive or robust, which means that they will not leave the specified (optimal) logistic cost and logistic service level corridor even under the changing conditions [14].

Inventory is one important type of configuration parameter of distribution networks. On the one hand, as "an aggregate resource that spans and connects all nodes" in distribution networks, inventory serves as an important means to "separate or buffer one location in the distribution channel from another and the discontinuity of customer demand from available inventories", so that the customers' wishes of time, location, quantity, quality and price can be fulfilled [18]. On the other hand, large amounts of resources including capital, labor and space, are tied up in holding the inventories [2, 15, 18, 23], which takes up a significant proportions of the logistics costs [19]. It is imperative to carefully conduct the inventory planning so that optimal inventory policies can be made out. However due to the turbulent changes in today's dynamic market, the behaviors and status of the distribution network are completely unforeseeable and incomprehensible [13], which has largely aggravated the mismatch between supply and demand. Correspondingly, the optimized inventory policies are strongly expected to be able to withstand these dynamic influences. The inventory policies should be robust enough to cope with various uncertainties and dynamics.

65.2 State-of-the-Art Approaches for Optimization of Inventory Policies

Traditional approaches for optimized inventory policies are mostly based on simplified deterministic single- or multi-echelon inventory models, which have provided a deep insight into the mechanism of inventory controls throughout the distribution network [2, 21]. But they are no longer capable of delivering the desired results or even greatly deteriorate the performance of the complex distribution networks in today's dynamic environment, leading to either low logistic service level or high logistic costs [11].

Besides the traditional analytical approaches, another type of approaches for analyzing complex distribution systems is simulation, which is increasingly utilized with the rapid development of information technology [4, 13]. Apart from the traditional view that simulation serves only as "a descriptive tool in the modeling and analysis of a wide variety of complex real systems", recent advancement in optimization approach and computing technology make it "a prescriptive tool in support decision making" [20]. In Barton's work, the simulation-based optimization is defined as "repeated analysis of the simulation model with different values of design parameters, in an attempt to identify best simulated system performance" [3]. In other words, the optimal (or sub-optimal) design parameters of the real system are "determined by the simulation optimization process, rather than in an ad hoc manner based on qualitative insights gained from exercising the simulation model" [3]. It seems pretty simple to understand, however, a wide variety of difficulties have arisen when applying a simulation-based optimization process in practice. First of all, there typically exist a large numbers of different types of parameters that are subject to optimization. For this kind of problems, the optimization itself is not an easy task. Moreover, although simulation can be regarded as a "function" that evaluates the performance of a set of alternatives in a simulation optimization process [1], little is known about the explicit form of this function. Thus, the effort of accelerating convergence speed or finding an improving direction often ends in vain. Consequently, a great number of alternatives have to be simulated before favorable ones are obtained, which implies great computational effort.

All the mentioned analytical, simulation and simulation-based optimization approaches on inventory policies for distribution networks have failed to solve the difficulties resulting from the inherent complexity, volatile customer demand and multi-objective optimization of the complex distribution systems. To overcome these challenges, a new simulation- and metaheuristic-based approach is introduced in this paper.

65.3 Introduction of the Simulation- and Metaheuristic-Based Approach

Based on the above analysis, a new integrated approach is developed which is composed of two closely interrelated components: a simulation-based evaluation of the multi-echelon inventory policies under the context of dynamics and uncertainty, and a metaheuristic-based optimizer that improves these multi-echelon inventory policies on the basis of simulation results. The schematic diagram of this integrated approach is illustrated in Fig. 65.1.

The integrated approach starts with generation of an initial generation of multi-echelon inventory policies, which will be handed over to a simulation model. The professional simulation tool OTD-NET, developed by Fraunhofer-Institut für

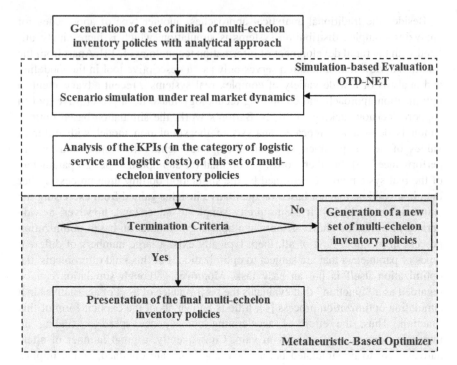

Fig. 65.1 A new integrated approach to robust multi-echelon inventory policies for distribution networks

Materialfluss und Logistik (IML), is applied, which is capable of modeling complexity and uncertainties of the distribution network and simulating them under respective scenarios (i.e. market dynamics). Through comprehensively analyzing the KPIs (in the category of logistic service and logistic costs) of this set of multi-echelon inventory policies, their levels of robustness can be clearly ascertained.

Based on these results, a metaheuristic-based optimizer regenerates improved (more robust) multi-echelon inventory policies, which are once again comprehensively evaluated through simulation. This closed feedback loop forms a simulation optimization process that enables the autonomous evolution of multi-echelon inventory policies. The iteration continues until given termination criteria are finally satisfied. Since each multi-echelon inventory policy has been carefully tested under real dynamics, the robustness level of the resulting multi-echelon inventory policies can be determined. In other words, under these multi-echelon inventory policies, the distribution network can maintain a specified optimality (or sub-optimality) in spite of dynamic influencing factors.

65.4 Metaheuristic-Based Optimizer of Multi-Echelon Inventory Policies for Distribution Networks

The metaheuristic-based optimizer is designed on the basis of a special evolutionary algorithm NSGA-II, which is one of the most widely used multi-objective evolutionary algorithms [12, 22]. Prior to the optimization process, the fundamental input parameters must be assigned, which include population size POP_SIZE, crossover rate CRO_RATE (probability of crossover), mutation rate MUT_RATE (probability of mutation) and termination criteria (e.g. maximum generations MAX_GEN). Then, the number of generation genNo is set to be zero, and two set of individuals are initialized, which are called population P(genNo) (individual set) and archive A(genNo) (elite set) respectively. For the main iteration process, the population and archive of the current generation are firstly combined into a new set, of which the Pareto rank and crowding distance are assigned or calculated for each individual. Based on these two criteria, a new elite set A(genNo+1) is created. Within this new elite set, a mating pool is formed through different selection methods (e.g. binary tournament selection) and a new population P(genNo+1) is generated through crossover and mutation from the mating pool. This iterative process will be continuously repeated until given termination criteria are satisfied.

With regard to the optimization of multi-echelon inventory policies, there exist two types of parameters in this metaheuristic-based optimizer. One is the running parameters, which are used during the optimization process; the other is the termination parameters, which are employed to stop the optimization process. In an evolutionary algorithm, running parameters usually include population size, crossover rate and mutation rate, while the frequently used termination parameters are target fitness value and maximum generation. However, not all of these parameters have to appear in a single algorithm, which are determined in accordance with the distinct requirements of a problem. Conventional evolutionary algorithms usually transform a multi-objective optimization problem into a single-objective one and then evaluate the fitness of individuals according to this objective function. In contrast, NSGA-II tries to simultaneously assess individuals in all dimensions without any artificial alteration or distortion, which defines two criteria for evaluating individual: quality (absolute fitness) and distribution (relative fitness) [22].

In this multi-echelon inventory policy problem, there are two incommensurable and conflicting objectives. Inventory costs are measured in monetary unit and are the lower the better, whereas fill rate is evaluated as percentage and is the higher the better. Since it is impossible to compare two multi-echelon inventory policies directly, the concepts of Pareto rank and crowding distance are employed to assess different multi-echelon inventory policies.

After the mating pool has been formed, a new set of multi-echelon inventory policies (i.e. population) can be generated. Each time two individuals are selected randomly without replacement from the mating pool to perform crossover and mutation. There are numerous kinds of approaches to conduct crossover and mutation. In this research the simulated binary crossover (SBX) and polynomial mutation [8] are applied according to the standard NSGA-II. In this customized evolutionary algorithm, the procedures of polynomial mutation have been embedded into SBX crossover to reduce the probability of mutation and thus stabilize the optimization process.

SBX crossover is aimed to simulate the sharing centroid property, which originally exists in the case of binary code crossover, after a real code crossover [6]. An important variable called spread factor β_i is used to determine the amount of the change of the difference between two i-th genes that is caused by crossover, i.e. [6].

$$\beta_i = \left| \frac{c_i^1 - c_i^2}{p_i^1 - p_i^2} \right| \tag{65.1}$$

where c_i^1 and c_i^2 are i-th genes of the two children while p_i^2 and p_i^2 are those of the two parents respectively. If $\beta_i < 1$, the operator is called a contracting crossover; if $\beta_i > 1$, it is called an expanding crossover; and if $\beta_i = 1$, it is called a stationary crossover [22]. Since the stationary crossover is expected to occur frequently whereas the contracting or expanding crossover should appear only with a relatively low probability, they proposed a probability density function for the random variable β_i as below [22]

$$P(\beta_i) = \begin{cases} 0.5(n+1)\beta_i^n & \beta_i \leq 1 \\ 0.5(n+1)\beta_i^{\frac{1}{n+2}} & \beta_i > 1 \end{cases} \tag{65.2}$$

where n is a control parameter. In this probability distribution, the larger n is, the higher probability β_i has of being close to 1 [22].

To generate the random number β_i that follows the above probability density function, the most frequently used method is the inverse transformation that generates it from a uniformly distributed random number $u_i \sim U(0, 1)$, i.e. [22]

$$\beta_i = \begin{cases} (2u_i)^{\frac{1}{n+1}} & u_i \leq 0.5 \\ [2(1-u_i)]^{-\frac{1}{n+1}} & u_i > 0.5 \end{cases} \tag{65.3}$$

Correspondingly, the i-th genes of these two children is given by [22]

$$c_i^1 = 0.5(p_i^1 + p_i^2) + 0.5\beta_i(p_i^1 - p_i^2) \tag{65.4}$$

$$c_i^2 = 0.5(p_i^1 + p_i^2) + 0.5\beta_i(p_i^1 - p_i^2) \tag{65.5}$$

The polynomial mutation is based on the polynomial distribution, of which the mean equals to the current value and the variance is a function of the distribution control parameter n [7]. To carry out mutation, a perturbance factor δ_i is defined to measure the amount of change in the i-th gene, i.e. [22]

$$\delta_i = \frac{c_i - p_i}{\Delta_{max}} \tag{65.6}$$

where c_i and p_i are the i-th gene of the child and parent, and Δ_{max} is the largest permissible perturbance of the i-th gene.

The perturbance factor δ_i follows a polynomial distribution, which is given by Deb and Goyal [7].

$$P(\delta_i) = 0.5(n+1)(1 - |\delta_i|)^n \tag{65.7}$$

where n is a control parameter and $\delta_i \in [-1, 1]$. Moreover, the larger n is, the higher probability δ_i has of being close to 0 [22]. The random variable δ_i can be generated with the similar inverse transformation as the spread factor β_i in SBX crossover, i.e. [22]

$$\delta_i = \begin{cases} (2u_i)^{\frac{1}{n+1}} - 1 & u_i \le 0.5 \\ 1 - [2(1 - u_i)]^{\frac{1}{n+1}} & u_i > 0.5 \end{cases} \tag{65.8}$$

Then, the mutated value of the i-th gene is given as below [22]

$$c_i = p_i + \delta_i * \Delta_{max} \tag{65.9}$$

Besides, the positive and negative perturbance factor are defined in the dissertation

Positive perturbance factor:

$$[\delta_i]^+ = \begin{cases} 1 - (2u_i)^{\frac{1}{n+1}} & u_i \le 0.5 \\ 1 - [2(1 - u_i)]^{\frac{1}{n+1}} & u_i > 0.5 \end{cases} \tag{65.10}$$

Negative perturbance factor:

$$[\delta_i]^- = \begin{cases} (2u_i)^{\frac{1}{n+1}} - 1 & u_i \le 0.5 \\ [2(1 - u_i)]^{\frac{1}{n+1}} - 1 & u_i > 0.5 \end{cases} \tag{65.11}$$

The metaheuristic-based optimizer is developed to work in together with the simulation module, so that a simulation optimization process can be carried out. Since the metaheuristic-based optimizer is designed on the basis of a special evolutionary algorithm NSGA-II, the main task of the implementation is to enable the autonomous evolution of multi-echelon inventory policies according to their robustness levels that are evaluated through simulation.

65.5 Case Study

In the exemplary distribution network, finished products are produced in one German plant and sold in selected 14 European markets. For the confidential reason, the plant name and its location are kept anonymous. To deliver the products to end customers, a European distribution center (EDC) and 14 regional distribution centers (RDCs) have been constructed. The plant makes out production plan according to its forecast data and manages production accordingly (build-to-stock, BTS). The followed-up distribution process, on the contrary, is triggered by actual replenishment (build-to-order, BTO). More specifically, the deliveries from the plant to EDC are triggered by orders from EDC while those from EDC to RDCs are triggered by orders from different RDCs, which are considered to face directly the end customers. Respective forecast scenarios are used to reflect the volatility of the markets (see Fig. 65.2 for example of Article I).

The new integrated approach is applied in the exemplary distribution network. The evolutionary process of multi-echelon inventory policies is demonstrated in Fig. 65.3. Here, the accepted corridor of inventory costs is specified between 500 and 700 monetary units, that is to say, the optimized multi-echelon inventory policies should only be accepted when the resulting inventory costs of the distribution network have not left this corridor. It can be seen that the multi-echelon inventory policies after 50th generations (diamond shaped symbol in Fig. 65.3) have brought about remarkably better performance than those after 10th generations (square shaped symbol in Fig. 65.3), which implies that the logistic service level (i.e. fill rate) and the logistic costs (i.e. inventory costs) of the distribution network are simultaneously enhanced. The improvement obtained from the 50th generation to 90th generation (triangle shaped symbol in Fig. 65.3), however, is not that distinguish. This can be explained by the fact that as the multi-echelon inventory policies become increasingly robust, little room is left for improvement. From another perspective, this phenomenon has also demonstrated that the metaheuristic-based optimizer can find out highly qualified multi-echelon inventory policies in relatively short computational time, i.e. it is quite efficient. The quality of the initial generation of multi-echelon inventory policies is irrelevant for the simulation- and metaheuristic-based approach.

Fig. 65.2 Daily demand of article I aggregated over all 14 markets

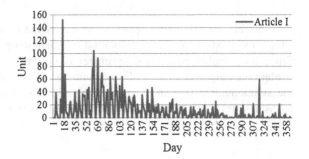

Fig. 65.3 Simulation results of the initially and finally optimized multi-echelon inventory policies

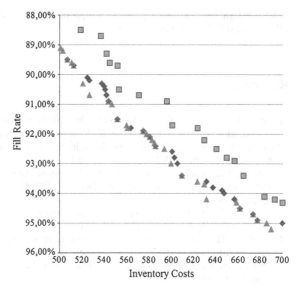

Optimized Multi-Echelon Inventory Policies after 10th Generation
♦ Optimized Multi-Echelon Inventory Policies after 50th Generation
▲ Optimized Multi-Echelon Inventory Policies after 90th Generation

65.6 Conclusions

Due to the inherent complexity and external dynamics of a distribution network in today's dynamic market, the traditional approaches have failed to propose robust multi-echelon inventory policies that can lead to high logistic service with low logistic costs under market dynamics. In this paper an integrated approach for deriving robust multi-echelon inventory policies for distribution networks has been developed, which integrates a simulation-based evaluation of multi-echelon inventory policies with a metaheuristic-based optimizer together. To evaluate the robustness level of these inventory policies under market dynamics, the initial multi-echelon inventory policies are handed over to an OTD-NET simulation model. Based on the simulation results, i.e. the robustness level of the proposed multi-echelon inventory policies, a metaheuristic-based optimizer is developed to regenerate improved (more robust) multi-echelon inventory policies, which are once again automatically evaluated through simulation. Instead of a single optimal multi-echelon inventory policy, multiple Pareto optimal multi-echelon inventory polices are proposed, which is quite beneficial to the practical decision making. This integrated approach has been applied to an industrial case, in which a set of robust multi-echelon inventory polices are proposed. These optimized multi-echelon inventory policies maintain a specified optimality (or sub-optimality) despite anticipated market dynamics and are quite superior to existing approaches.

Acknowledgments The research has been supported by German DFG (project: MMeAS – KU 619/18-1) and China Scholarship Council.

References

1. April J, Glover F, Kelly JP, Laguna M (2003) Practical introduction to simulation optimization. In: Proceedings of the 2003 winter simulation conference, vol 1, pp 71–78
2. Axsäter S (2006) Inventory control, 2nd edn. International series in operations research & management science 90. Springer, New York
3. Barton RR, Meckesheimer M (2006) Metamodel-based simulation optimization. In: Henderson SG, Nelson BL (eds) Handbooks in OR & MS, vol 13, Elsevier, New York, pp 535–574
4. Chopra S, Meindl P (2010) Supply chain management: strategy, planning, and operation, 4th edn. Pearson, Boston, pp 85–121, 263–344
5. Cisek R, Habicht C, Neise P (2002) Gestaltung wandlungsfähiger Produktionssysteme. Zeitschrift für wirtschaftlichen Fabrikbetrieb 97:441–445
6. Deb K, Agrawal RB (1995) Simulated binary crossover for continuous search space. Comp Syst 9:115–148
7. Deb K, Goyal MA (1996) Combined genetic adaptive search (GeneAS) for engineering design. Comp Sci Inform 26:30–45
8. Deb K, Pratap A, Agarwal S, Meyarivan T (2002) A fast and elitist multiobjective genetic algorithm: NSGA-II. IEEE Trans Evol Comput 6(2):182–197
9. Fu MC, Glover FW, April J (2005) Simulation optimization: a review, new developments, and applications. In: Proceedings of the 2005 winter simulation conference, pp 83–95
10. Glover F, Kelly JP, Laguna M (1996) New advances and applications of combining simulation and optimization. In: Proceedings of the 28th conference on winter simulation, pp 144–152
11. Klingebiel K, Li C (2011) Optimized multi-echelon inventory policies in robust distribution networks. In: Proceedings 25th European conference on modelling and simulation, pp 573–579
12. Konak A, Coit DW, Smith AE (2006) Multi-objective optimization using genetic algorithms: a tutorial. Reliab Eng Syst Safe 91(9):992–1007
13. Kuhn A, Hellingrath B (2002) Supply chain management: Optimierte Zusammenarbeit in der Wertschöpfungskette. Engineering. Springer, Berlin, pp 1–35, 87–124, 213–228
14. Kuhn A, Klingebiel K, Schmidt A, Luft N (2011) Modellgestütztes Planen und kollaboratives Experimentieren für robuste Distributionssysteme. Tagungsband des 24. HAB-Forschungsseminars der Hochschulgruppe für Arbeits- und Betriebsorganisation
15. Mangan J, Lalwani C, Butcher T (2010) Global logistics and supply chain management. Wiley, Chichester
16. Nyhuis P, Reinhart G, Abele E (eds) Wandlungsfähige Produktionssysteme: Heute die Industrie von morgen gestalten. PZH Produktionstechnisches Zentrum, Garbsen, pp 20–28
17. Ólafsson S (2006) Metaheuristics. In: Henderson SG, Nelson BL (eds) Handbooks in OR & MS, vol 13, Elsevier, Amsterdam, pp 535–574
18. Ross DF (1996) Distribution: planning and control. Chapman & Hall materials management/ logistics series. Chapman & Hall, New York, pp 4–23, 213–237, 388–412
19. Rushton A, Oxley J, Croucher P (2002) The handbook of logistics and distribution management, 2nd edn. Reprinted. Kogan Page, London, pp 3–10, 35–48, 73–82, 181–197, 200–213
20. Tekin E, Sabuncuoglu I (2004) Simulation optimization: a comprehensive review on theory and applications. IIE Trans 36(11):1067–1081

21. Tempelmeier H (2006) Inventory management in supply networks: problems, models, solutions. Books on Demand, Norderstedt
22. Yu X, Gen M (2010) Introduction to evolutionary algorithms. Decision engineering. Springer, London
23. Zipkin PH (2000) Foundations of inventory management. McGraw-Hill, Boston

Chapter 66
A Novel Algorithm for Text Classification Based on KNN and Chaotic Binary Particle Swarm Optimization

Hui Xu, Shoudong Lu and Shixiang Zhou

Abstract The main problem of chinese text classification is the high dimensional feature space. A novel algorithm for text classification based on KNN and chaotic particle swarm optimization is proposed. The algorithm utilizes chaotic particle swarm algorithm to traverse the feature space of training set and selects feature subspace, then utilizes KNN algorithm to classify text in feature subspace. In the particle swarm's iterative process, chaotic map is used to guide swarms for chaotic search. It makes the algorithm out of local optimum, and expands the ability of finding global optimal solution. Experimental results show that the novel algorithm for chinese text classification is effective, the classification accuracy and recall rate are better than KNN algorithm.

Keywords Binary particle swarm · Chaos · KNN · Text classification

66.1 Introduction

Text classification is a process of automatically classifying text content into one or more predefined categories. With rapid growth of online text message in Internet, text classification process and organization have become one of primary technologies in domain of processing and organization of text data. Automatic text

H. Xu (✉) · S. Lu
School of Information and Statistics, Guangxi University of Finance and Economics, Nanning, 530003 Guangxi, China
e-mail: xhui28@163.com

S. Zhou
College of Science, Shandong University of Technology, Zibo, Shandong, China

W. Lu et al. (eds.), *Proceedings of the 2012 International Conference on Information Technology and Software Engineering*, Lecture Notes in Electrical Engineering 211, DOI: 10.1007/978-3-642-34522-7_66, © Springer-Verlag Berlin Heidelberg 2013

classification has been applied in web page classification, topic identification, real-time documents sorting, information retrieval, search engine, e-mail classification, and information filtering etc. In recent years, researchers proposed a variety of text classification algorithm [1] such as: Support Vector Machine (SVM), K-Nearest Neighbor (KNN), Artificial Neural Networks, Naïve Bayes probabilistic Classifier, and Decision Trees.

The major difficulty of text classification is the high dimension of feature space and the sparsity of text vector [2]. Determining how to reduce dimension without loss of classification performance is the most important issue in text classification. Therefore, this paper proposes a novel text classification algorithm, it uses binary chaotic particle swarm optimization (CBPSO) algorithm to select optimal feature items as feature subspace in training text set, and implements KNN classification.

66.2 Chinese Text Preprocessing

The process of text classification includes text preprocessing, classifier design and evaluation. Since chinese text is natural language text that has almost no structure, it is difficult for computer to understand directly it. Thus, for chinese text classification, the first task is chinese preprocessing, that is, classification algorithms convert chinese text to structured digital format. This process includes key technologies such as chinese word segmentation, word frequency, text vector representation, text feature selection, creating vector space model (VSM). Secondly, it determines the category of text. It often uses statistical methods or machine learning methods to design a classifier, the classifier will be used to assign new texts to one or more categories.

66.2.1 Chinese Word Segmentation

Chinese word segmentation is the first step in chinese text prepressing. Chinese text is cut into a series of phrases. In this paper, we use ICTCLAS components developed by Dr. Zhang Huaping for chinese word segmentation, POS tagging, and use stop words table to remove stop words and low frequency phrases in training set, and retain nouns and verbs as a collection of original features items.

66.2.2 Text Vector Representation

Text is generally represented by VSM. After chinese word segmentation, each text is represented by feature vector which is composed of feature item's weight, immediately, text D_i is expressed as the weight vector $(w_{i1}, w_{i2}, ..., w_{iM})$, where w_{ik}

is the weight of feature items t_k in text D_i, it is calculated by term frequency-inverse document frequency (TF-IDF) Eq. (66.1), so $w_{ik} \in [0,1]$.

$$
w_{ik} = \frac{tf_{ik} \times \log(N/n_k + 0.01)}{\sqrt{\sum\limits_{t_k \in D_i} [tf_{ik} \times \log(N/n_k + 0.01)]^2}}
\tag{66.1}
$$

where tf_{ik} is term frequency of feature items t_k in training text D_i, n_k is the number of texts that contain feature items t_k in training text set, N is the total number of texts in training text set, M is the number of feature items.

TF-IDF formula is used to assess the importance degree of feature items in text. It represents that the weight of items appearing in text is proportional to the number of times, but it is inversely proportional to the number of text which contain this feature item in training set. Equation (66.1) shows that if the number of feature items which appears in a text is very high, and rarely appears in other texts, then this feature item will well express classification ability.

66.2.3 Text Similarity

Similarity of text D_i and D_j is defined as:

$$
sim(D_i, D_j) = \sum_{k=1}^{M} w_{ik} \times w_{jk} \bigg/ \sqrt{\left(\sum_{k=1}^{M} w_{ik}^2\right)\left(\sum_{k=1}^{M} w_{jk}^2\right)}
\tag{66.2}
$$

66.2.4 Text Feature Selection

After comparing the effect of above feature selection algorithm in English text, Yang and Pedersen [3] proposed the conclusion: χ^2 statistical method had best performance, highest classification accuracy, followed by IG method, DF, IG, and CHI method had roughly the same effect, MI method was the worst. Dai et al. [4] compared the performance of these four feature selection methods in Chinese texts, experiments showed that DF was better than other three methods, MI method had unstable performance when using SVM and KNN classifier.

χ^2 statistic measures the associated level between feature item t_i and category C_j. χ^2 is more greater, the associated level is more larger between feature items t_i and category C_j, and category information is more larger. χ^2 statistic is expressed as Eq. (66.3) [3]:

$$\chi^2(t_i, C_j) = \frac{N(AD - BC)^2}{(A + C)(B + D)(A + B)(C + D)} \tag{66.3}$$

where N is the total number of training text set, A is the number of texts which contain ti in class C_j, B is the number of texts which contain t_i in other class, C is the number of texts which don't contain ti in class C_j, D indicates the number of texts which donot contain t_i in other class.

For each pair of C_j and t_i, $\chi^2(t_i, C_j)$ is calculated. For each category, feature items are sorted according to their χ^2 statistic in descending order. According to the total number of items, the number of texts of each category, and the total number of texts in training set, the number of selected feature items is determined, then feature items with higher χ^2 value are selected, and the dimension is reduced.

66.3 Chaos Binary Particle Swarm Optimization

66.3.1 Binary Particle Swarm Optimization

Binary particle swarm optimization (BPSO) [5] was used to solve combinatorial optimization problems. In binary space, particles consist of P-particles in d-dimensional space, each particle's position consists of a series of binary bits, the position of ith particle is represented as vector $X_i = (x_{i1}, x_{i2}, ..., x_{id})$, where x_{ij} is binary bit value 0 or 1, 1 represents selecting the appropriate feature, 0 represents not selecting the appropriate feature. The speed of ith particle is represented as vector, $V_i = (v_{i1}, v_{i2}, ..., v_{id})$. Initial velocity is random decimal which ranges in $[0,1]$. Particle's speed limits in $[V_{min}, V_{max}]$. Vector $Pb_i = (p_{i1}, p_{i2}, ..., p_{id})$ represents ith particle best position searched for so far. The best position of all particles, known as global best position, is denoted by $Gb = (g_1, g_2, ..., g_d)$. In BPSO algorithm, when each iteration, each particle's velocity and position are computed according to Eqs. (66.4), (66.5), (66.6), (66.7). Then it assesses each particle's optimal fitness value **pbest** and global optimal fitness value **gbest**.

$$v_{ij}^{t+1} = wv_{ij}^t + c_1 r_1 (p_{ij} - x_{ij}^t) + c_2 r_2 (g_j - x_{ij}^t) \tag{66.4}$$

$$v_{ij}^{t+1} = \begin{cases} v_{max}, & v_{ij}^{t+1} > v_{max} \\ v_{min}, & v_{ij}^{t+1} < v_{min} \end{cases} \tag{66.5}$$

$$s(v_{ij}^{t+1}) = \frac{1}{1 + e^{-v_{ij}^{t+1}}} \tag{66.6}$$

$$x_{ij}^{t+1} = \begin{cases} 1, & rand < s(v_{ij}^{t+1}) \\ 0, & rand \geq s(v_{ij}^{t+1}) \end{cases} \tag{66.7}$$

In Eq. (66.4), w is inertia weight, c_1, c_2 are speed factors, $rand$, r_1, r_2 are random decimal in [0,1]; v_{ij}^t is the speed that ith particle updated before and v_{ij}^{t+1} is the speed that ith particle updated after; x_{ij}^t and x_{ij}^{t+1} are the positions that around ith particle updated before and after. Equation (66.5) limits that speed values of ith particle are in $[V_{min}, V_{max}]$. Equation (66.6) determines the probability of particle location update. Equation (66.7) determines particles updated in next iteration. If $s(v_{ij}^{t+1})$ is greater than random decimal decimal between 0 and 1, then x_{ij}^{t+1} is set to 1, that is, choosing jth feature as a feature updated in next iteration; otherwise x_{ij}^{t+1} is set to 0.

66.3.2 Inertia Weight Chaotic Map

In BPSO algorithm, inertia weight controls global search and local search capabilities of particle swarm, large inertia weight is conducive to global search, while small inertia weight is conducive to local search. Inertia weight w is a critical factor of convergence of problem solving process, it greatly affects BPSO's search process. Thus it affects classification accuracy. As BPSO algorithm is easy to fall into local optimum, resulting in prematurely convergence. Chaotic map is introduced to BPSO algorithm to form a chaotic binary particle swarm optimization (CBPSO) algorithm. CBPSO algorithm overcomes prematurely convergence, ensures to search global optimum, and ensures the search speed. It makes more better performance of classification algorithms.

In each iteration of BPSO algorithm, chaotic maps is used to determine inertia weight value. Inertia weight value is calculated by Eq. (66.8) of Logistic map [6]:

$$w(t+1) = u \times w(t) \times (1 - (w(t)), \qquad t = 0, 1, 2, \ldots \qquad (66.8)$$

where $w(t)$ is chaotic sequence, it's in $(0,1)$, u is control parameter, when $3.571448 \leq u \leq 4$, Logistic map is in a chaotic state. In particular, $u = 4$, it is in complete chaos. When inertia weight is close to 1, CBPSO enhances global optimal search capabilities. When inertia weight is close to 0, CBPSO enhances local optimal search capabilities.

66.4 Text Classification Algorithm Based on CBPSO and KNN

The basic idea of the proposed new algorithm is that when CBPSO algorithm iterates, it results P particles. According to each particle's position in feature space set, it selects corresponding feature items to form subset of feature items, then KNN text classification is implemented for test texts in these subset of feature items, and gets P groups results. Each group has K neighbors. The algorithm compares fitness value of all particles, and gets the current best particle, that is most similar current global optimal K neighbors. After CBPSO continuously iterative, it ultimately finds K nearest neighbor text which have the highest fitness, then in accordance with KNN classifier method, test text is calculated and determined it's text category.

66.4.1 Particle Structure

Each particle's position is represented as binary bit strings $X_i = (x_{i1}, x_{i2}, ..., X_{id})$, it represents feature subset of the selected feature space, where d is the feature space dimension of training text set after feature selection, x_{ij} is 0 or 1, 1 represents selected feature, 0 represents not selected feature. Particle's velocity vector is a d-dimensional vector, its components is calculated by above Eqs. (66.4), (66.5).

66.4.2 The Particle's Fitness Function

Each particle's fitness is calculated by the evaluation criteria F_1 of KNN text classification effectiveness. F_1 is defined as Eq. (66.9):

$$F_1 = 2pr/(p + r) \tag{66.9}$$

where p is classification accuracy and r is recall. F_1 is the harmonic mean of p and r, it is closer to the smaller of two values. Therefore, only p and r are very high, F_1 value is very high. F_1 value is greater, the quality of classification is better.

66.4.3 Text Classification Algorithm Based CBPSO and KNN

Text classification based on CBPSO and KNN is the following steps:

Input: training text set D, test text X, total number of training documents N, the number of nearest neighbor text K, the total number of feature items F, the number of particles P, the particle's velocity limits in $[V_{min}, V_{max}]$, the maximum number of iterations $MAXIter$.

Output: K nearest neighbors with F_1 optimal values, and the category of test text.

Step 1. For each document in training set, it does chinese word segmentation, removes stop words, calculates term frequency and documents frequency of words.

Step 2. Using χ^2 statistics feature selection method to select feature items of training set, reduces dimension of text feature space, and establishs VSM model of training set.

Step 3. For X, it does chinese word segmentation, calculates each feature item's TF-IDF value, and establishs VSM vector of X.

Step 4. Initialize particle swarm. It generates P particles, randomizes their location X_i and speed V_i. best particle's position $pbest_i$, best global position $gbest$, each positions of particle is set to 0 or 1,the speed is random number in (0,1), the current iteration times $t = 0$.

Step 5. FOR $i = 1$ to P

a. Evaluating the fitness of ith particle, $F(X_i)$. Where KNN method is used to select K nearest neighbors, then it calculates classification evaluation standard F_1 value, and selects the particle with highest F_1 value as the global optimal particle.

b. Calculating inertia weight chaotic sequence.

c. Updating the particle's velocity and position, and the speed is limited in $[V_{min}, V_{max}]$.

d. Calculating the optimal position $pbest_i$ of ith particle and global best position $gbest$ of particle swarm.

END

Step 6. $t = t + 1$

Step 7. Checking termination condition is met, if met, then goto step 8; otherwise goto step 5.

Step 8. According to K neighbors corresponding to $gbest$, it calculates category of X, outputs category of X.

66.5 Experimental Results and Analysis

66.5.1 Experimental Data Sets

The experimental data has been retrieved from Sogou Laboratory, chinese text classification corpus, the corpus is divided into nine categories, each category has 1990 documents. For each category, 300 documents are randomly selected as a set of documents, total of 2700 documents.

Table 66.1 The result of KNN algorithm and CBPSO-KNN algorithm comparison

Class	KNN			CBPSO-KNN		
	Precision (%)	Recall (%)	F1	Precision (%)	Recall (%)	F1
Health	93.49	74.67	83.03	90.58	86.16	88.31
Education	71.69	75.33	73.46	82.46	88.29	85.28
Sports	93.43	89.64	91.50	94.57	93.33	93.95
Recruitment	63.49	78.67	70.27	79.57	81.53	80.54
Culture	74.57	60.00	66.50	77.30	71.98	74.55
Tourism	80.79	82.67	81.72	86.74	84.00	85.35
Finance	82.55	84.67	83.59	83.16	89.05	86.00
Military	84.55	89.35	86.88	86.53	93.33	89.80
IT	77.40	69.33	73.15	85.49	76.59	80.80
Average	80.22	78.26	78.90	85.16	84.92	84.95

66.5.2 Experimental Design and Results

Text classification uses classification accuracy, recall and F_1 to assess classification performance of each category. To illustrate the proposed algorithm's classification performance, it is compared to traditional KNN text classification algorithms. Experimental environment is Windows XP, memory 2 GB, CPU is Core I3 2.13 GHz. We use C# 2005 multi-thread programming techniques and fivefold cross-validation approach. BPSO-KNN algorithm's parameters $c_1 = c_2 = 2$, particle number $P = 30$, minimum and maximum particle's velocity are respectively set to $-2, 2$. Initial value of chaotic sequence is $u_0 = 0.48$, the maximum number of iterations is 100. Two algorithm's parameters K are respectively set to 30, 45, 60, 80, 100. Experimental results show that when K is 60, F_1 is optimal. Table 66.1 shows experimental results, where the total number of feature items is 2000, $K = 60$.

In order to verify classification effect of different dimensions, feature dimensions are set to 500, 1000, 2000, 3000, 4000, 5000. F_1 distribution of experiment shows in Fig. 66.1. For CBPSO-KNN algorithm, when the dimension is 2000, F_1 changes most significant. When feature's dimension is greater than 2000, F_1 changes little. Results show that the dimension is not larger, better the classification, but increases computation time.

By analysing experimental results of Table 66.1 and Fig. 66.1, for different feature dimension, the proposed CBPSO-KNN algorithm is compared to traditional KNN algorithm, experimental results show that, for most categories, CBPSO-KNN algorithm is better than KNN algorithm in terms of classification accuracy, recall and F_1. In terms of the average classification performance, the former is better than the latter.

Fig. 66.1 Impact of feature dimension to F_1

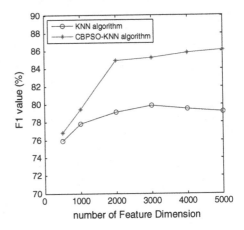

66.6 Conclusion

This paper presents a text classification algorithm (CBPSO-KNN) which combines CBPSO and KNN text classification algorithm. It uses chaotic maps to produce inertia weight chaotic sequence of particle swarm. The algorithm randomly selects feature items of training set by CBPSO, generats a number of feature subset, and builds KNN classifier in these features subset, then CBPSO algorithm finds optimal K-nearest neighbor text category. The algorithm uses Sogou chinese corpus for experiment. Simulation results show that the proposed CBPSO-KNN classification algorithm is effective, it reduces dimension of feature space, and improves the accuracy of text classification.

References

1. Sebastiani F (2002) Machine learning in automated text categorization. J ACM Comput Surv 34:1–47
2. Tan S, Wang Y, Cheng X (2008) An efficient feature ranking measure for text categorization. In: Proceedings of the 2008 ACM symposium on applied computing (SAC'08), Fortaleza, Ceará, Brazil, pp 407–413
3. Yang Y, Pedersen JP (1997). A comparative study on feature selection in text categorization. In: 14th international conference on machine learning, pp 412–420
4. Dai L-L, Huang H-Y, Chen Z-X (2004). Chinese text categorization comparative study of feature extraction method. J Chin Inf Process 18:26–32 (in Chinese)
5. Kennedy J, Eberhart RC (1997) A discrete binary version of the particle swarm algorithm. In: IEEE proceedings of the IEEE international conference on systems, man, and cybernetics, pp 4104–4108
6. Chuang L-Y, Yang C-H, Li J-C (2011) Chaotic maps based on binary particle swarm optimization for feature selection. J Appl Soft Comput 11:239–248

Chapter 67
Clustering and Recommendation of Scientific Documentation Based on the Topic Model

Bin Liao, Weihua Wang and Chunmei Jia

Abstract In this paper, we propose a novel and efficient method for topic modeling and clustering of scientific documentation. It is a technology of content-based filtering and aims to find the same topics. Incorporating topic features will enhance the accuracy of document clustering methods. Based on the clustering results, we use the method of calculating similarity of scientific documentation to get the related documentation consistent with the content. The ranking of recommendation is according to the value of similarity of documentation. Clustering results are evaluated by F-measure. Empirical study on real-world datasets shows that the LDA's performance is better than PLSA's in the document clustering. Meantime, we find the proper number of topics in document representation.

Keywords Scientific documentation · Recommendation · LDA · Cluster

67.1 Introduction

Searching scientific documentation is an effective way for us to acquire knowledge and skills. Users get feedback webpages, when searching papers on search tools such as CNKI or Google Scholar. The result not only includes abstract, information of author and published information but also recommends a number of related papers on the terms of retrieving paper. The related papers of recommendation are from the three main sources: sometimes the related papers share the

B. Liao · W. Wang (✉) · C. Jia
Electrical and Electronic Engineering School, North China Electric Power University,
No 2 Beinong Road, Beijing, Changping District, China
e-mail: wangweihua@ncic.ac.cn

W. Lu et al. (eds.), *Proceedings of the 2012 International Conference on Information Technology and Software Engineering*, Lecture Notes in Electrical Engineering 211, DOI: 10.1007/978-3-642-34522-7_67, © Springer-Verlag Berlin Heidelberg 2013

same words in their titles, sometimes they hold the same keywords, or are from references. Those results are inseparable from the retrieving paper which is convenient for users to acquire related knowledge and expand our horizons in the field. Although the three above-mentioned ways can mostly cover scope of related papers, the result is not based on the content of the paper which is the most important thing. The content is the main part of paper certainly, so ignoring the content makes the recommended information incomplete. In many cases users focus on information of the top five which are considered to be the most relevant, the recommended sequence in the paper is also important. Users select information difficultly only relaying solely on appearance of keywords to determine accurately the recommended order. In reality some inconsistencies papers on the titles or keywords, but very close to their research and discussion the contents of these recommended information to be omitted, on the recommendation of the integrity of information left a regret.

Clustering of document is a classic problem in text mining, which overcomes the defect of tradition information retrieval [1]. That a good clustering method can quickly and efficiently with the assistance of the computer division of the document types is convenient browsing and navigation for users. By clustering the text document, the documents sharing the same topic are grouped together. Different from classification, clustering is a way of unsupervised leaning which is less human intervention and higher level of automation. An outstanding algorithm of clustering not only easily indicates the topic but also the differences of each others. A perfect document representation and an outstanding algorithm of clustering are two significant things which decide the quality of clustering result [2].

In this paper, we propose a novel and efficient method for topic modelling and clustering of scientific documents. It is a technology of content-based filtering and aims to find the same topics. Using technology of clustering greatly reduce computation of similarity among papers. Based on the clustering results, we use the similarity method of calculation of scientific documents to get documents consistent with the content. The ranking of recommendation is according to value of similarity of documents. Our framework contains three layers to complete the design goal. The first layer is for document representation of topic model which is based on latent dirichlet allocation (LDA) model. The second layer is for document clustering which is on the basis of K-means cluster algorithm. The third layer is to calculate the values of similarity of documents based on LDA model.

The following section is involving about the related works and Sect. 67.3 about proposed works based on the three layers. Section 67.4 gives the result of experiment. Section 67.5 concludes the paper and discusses about the future work.

67.2 Related Works

Proper and excellent document representation is good beginning of text mining. Vector Space Model (VSM) as a typical model of bag of words is a commonly and widely used in document representation for clustering and classification. VSM is seen as a matrix of document collection and a feature vector represents single document. Weight of vector hold a variety of reorientation such as term frequency (TF) and term frequency-inverse document frequency (TF-IDF). TF-IDF fully take the value into account together in a single document and multi-document sets. In large set of documents vector holds thousands of dimensions, which makes matrix high sparsity. Probabilistic Latent Semantic Analysis (PLSA) [3] and LDA [4] which are two main probabilistic topic models complete the target of mapping the term-document representation to a lower-dimensional latent semantic space and treat the document as a mixture of topics. The two algorithms aim to analyze the words of original texts to discover the topics that run through them, how those topics are connected to each other. Also they do not require any prior annotations or labeling of documents.

PLSA and LDA are both deformation of VSM in low-dimension and the value of dimension could be determined by people. In PLSA an LDA, the conditional probability between terms and documents is modeled as a latent variable. Sometimes LDA which assumes that a document's topic distribution has a Dirichlet prior and that this simplifying assumption improves the Bayesian inference process shows better performance than PLSA. Another advantage of LDA is that it allows us to interpret each topic by looking at the words with a high probability of selection in that topic [5].

In [6], the dimensionality reduction via PLSA and LDA results in document clusters of almost the same quality as those obtained by using original feature vectors. And the result suggests that no difference between them for dimensionality reduction in clustering. In [7], experimental results have shown the effectiveness of the framework in clustering documents according to their mixtures of topics, and have highlighted the advantages offered by employing state-of-the-art topic model and their combination with the Bhattacharya distance.

In [8], Google Inc. generates recommendations using three approaches: collaborative filtering using MinHash clustering, PLSA and covisitation counts. Their approach is content agnostic and consequently domain independent, making it easily adaptable for other application and languages with minimal effort. In [9], after documents clustering based on LDA, a modified iterative PageRank algorithm ranked the research papers in a topic which assign an authoritative score to each paper based on the citation network.

67.3 Our Approach

In this section, we describe the proposed method in detail. As mentioned in introduction, the method is divided into three layers in Fig. 67.1, which is also treated as a linear model combing with many different algorithms for recommendations.

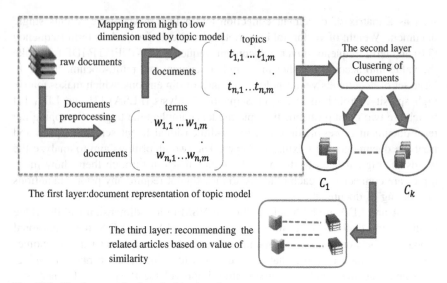

Fig. 67.1 The framework of method in three layers

67.3.1 Document Representation

The format of most scientific documents is PDF which is structured and hard to be processed by computer. *Pdf2txt*[1] is a good tool for converting pdf to txt. In the document preprocessing phrase, the paragraphs and sentences are segmented to isolated words. Through porter stemming[2] algorithm and be filtered by stopwords vocabulary, the document is represented as the format of term and TF. Let $D = \{d_1, d_2, \ldots, d_m\}$ is a set of documents. Let $W = \{w_1, w_2, \ldots, w_n\}$ is the vocabulary of terms in the set of documents, and the size of vocabulary is n.

When constructing the matrix of document collection, the weight of vector is the value of TF-IDF. Although porter stemming and stopwords filtering effectively decrease the scale of vocabulary size, the dimensionality is still high. Further using value of TF-IDF removes the words which are popular in document collection. We select a proper threshold of TF-IDF to accomplish the target of dimensionality continually. Let θ is the threshold and denotes that the percent of terms with TF-IDF. Within the scope of θ, the terms is dismissed.

$$TF - IDF(d_m, w_n) = TF(d_m, w_n) \bullet \log\left(\frac{|D|}{df(w_n)}\right) \qquad (67.1)$$

We get the VSM of documents collection and the terms are isolated and not related with each others. But those words are closely linked and the combination of

---

[1] http://www.foolabs.com/xpdf/download.html

[2] http://tartarus.org/martin/PorterStemmer/

words constitutes the semantic information. Next we apply the LDA to mine the potential semantic information among words. After associated words coming together to form the topic, the vector of document is denoted by the fixed topics. Let $d = \{t_1, t_2, \ldots, t_k\}$ is representation of topics of document. Based on LDA, we draw the probability distribution among the topics and each document. We could clearly determine the topic of document belongs by the feature value.

The weights of document vector based on LDA are clearly show the topics which the document belongs to. Using technique of clustering automatically divides the corpus into sub-section which holds the same topics. Then, a clustering method, K-means, is performed on the vector space of document collection.

67.3.2 Document Clustering

In the phase of document representation, the topics are constituted by the collection of words. For example the *computer* topic has words about software, hardware, network with high probability. The center points of each cluster are shown by topics as same as the documents.

Algorithm 1. Documents with multiple topics clustering

Input: document collection representation based on LDA: $D = \{d_1, d_2, \ldots, d_m\}$, specified clustering value of k.

Output: clustering collection of document $C = \{c_1, c_2, \ldots, c_m\}$

1. Calculate Euclidean distance $d(d_i, d_j)$ in the document collection D, find the two vectors which hold the farthest distance in collection, make the two as initial cluster-points p_1, p_2 and delete them from collection D.

2. Find the vector which is the farthest distance with p_1 and p_2 in D, make it as p_3, and delete it from D.

3. Repeat the step 2 and find out the rest initial cluster-points $P = \{p_1, p_2, \ldots, p_k\}$

4. Calculate the Euclidean distance of every document point with cluster-points and each document is assigned to the nearest cluster.

5. Calculate mean value of cluster as new cluster-point

6. Repeat step 3 and step 5 until each cluster centroid is no longer change or reach a specified number of iterations.

67.3.3 Similarity Measure

Clustering finds out the documents which hold similar contents. We could not exhibit the all result of clustering because we recommend targeted information for every document. In sub-sections we calculate the similarity of each document with the other documents. In this proposed work, cosine similarity measure is the similarity used.

$$sim(d_1, d_2) = \cos\theta = \frac{d_1 \bullet d_2}{|d_1| \bullet |d_2|} = \frac{\sum (t_{1,i} \bullet t_{2,i})}{\sqrt{\sum t_{1,i}^2 \bullet \sum t_{2,i}^2}} \qquad (67.2)$$

67.4 Experiment and Results

67.4.1 Datasets and Method of Evaluation

The recommended information is based on accurate result of clustering, and to show the accuracy of our algorithm and evaluate the experiment we prepare two test datasets. The first set is from Sougou laboratory[3] and the second set is from 20_newsgroups.[4] The set of SogouCS contains 18 channels such as Olympic games, sports, IT, the domestic and the international from Sohu News during January 2008 to June. The 20_newsgroups dataset is a collection of approximately 20,000 newsgroup documents, partitioned (nearly) evenly across 20 different newsgroups. In our experiment, we select four sorts to verify the accuracy of clustering.

We use F-measure to evaluate the quality of document clustering based on topic model. It combines the precision and recall of test datasets to compute the accuracy. The F-measure can be denoted as a weighted average of the precision and recall where F-measure is range from 1 to 0. Furthermore 1 is the best value and 0 reaches the worst. The recall and precision of the cluster for each given class are calculated.

$$F - measure(clustering) = \frac{2}{k} \bullet \sum_{i=1}^{k} \frac{precision(i) \bullet recall(i)}{precision(i) + recall(i)} \qquad (67.3)$$

The number of topics determines the size of document dimension based on topic model and will also impact the accuracy of clustering. We also adopt two topic models involving LDA and PLSA to calculated F-measure in those datasets. Figure 67.2 shows that LDA performs better than PLSA and with the number of topic increasing, the accuracy of clustering have an improvement. In comprehensive consideration of the number of clustering and the class of topic model, we take topic's value of 30 and LDA in subsequent experiments. In table, the value of θ mentioned in Sect. 67.3.2 is to filter the usual words in dataset and the result shows that θ range from 5 to 10 % effectively increase the F-measure (Table 67.1).

---

[3] http://www.sogou.com/labs/resources.html

[4] http://kdd.ics.uci.edu/databases/20newsgroups/20newsgroups.html

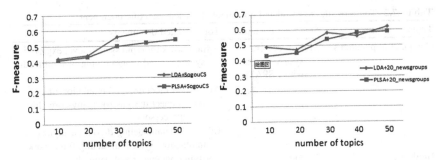

Fig. 67.2 Clustering performance by varying the clustering size on SogouCS and 20_newspapers

Table 67.1 F-measure on different value of θ

Dataset	θ	F-measure
SogouCS	0	0.56
	5 %	0.6
	10 %	0.61
20_newsgroups	0	0.58
	5 %	0.62
	10 %	0.62

Fig. 67.3 The value of RSS by varying the clustering size

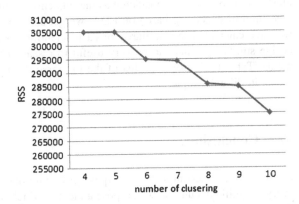

67.4.2 Result

To fulfill the final target of finding out the related documents for every scientific document, the previous steps which make each cluster corresponding to a topic have laid a good foundation. We have crawled 20,000 scientific documents' abstracts from ACM. Different from those two datasets, the scientific document collection don't have fixed number of class. So we want to guess the reasonable value and get the optimal number of clustering. We use value of RSS (residual sum of squares) to achive. Figure 67.3 shows that ranging from 4 to 10 the number of

Table 67.2 Top three the most related documents for each scientific document

Topic	Scientific document	Top 3 related documents
Computer applications	Multi-processor system design with ESPAM	A framework for rapid system-level exploration, synthesis, and programming of multimedia MP-SoCs
		Automated modeling and emulation of interconnect designs for many-core chip multiprocessors
		EWD: A metamodeling driven customizable multi-MoC system modeling framework
Hardware	A model for distributed systems based on graph rewriting	Verifying parameterized networks
		Accelerating multi-party scheduling for transaction-level modeling
		Caisson: a hardware description language for secure information flow
Theory of computation	Compositional verification of concurrent systems using Petri-net-based condensation rules	Modeling time in computing: A taxonomy and a comparative survey
		Software model checking
		Using formal specifications to support testing

clustering is 6 which is considered as the inflection point. Upon implementing the algorithm of clustering based on LDA, we get six sub-sections. For each cluster, we have calculated the similarity of each scientific document with the others by cosine similarity. This can be very useful to researchers studying a given documents. Table 67.2 shows the list of the top three documents for retrieving documents in different topic.

67.5 Conclusions

In this paper, to accomplish the purpose of finding out the related documents for every scientific document, we propose a method which derives topics and clusters those documents. Through experiment, we find out the most appropriate document representation and number of topic to get optimal result. In practical application, we extend the traditional method and the users could get more information.

Our future enhancement is the clustering algorithm to bring more precise divisions. The documents which are in the cluster boundary find out the related not only in the divided cluster but also in neighboring clusters. A better similarity measure is needed to improve the accuracy.

References

1. Manning CD, Raghavan P, Schütze H (2008) Introduction to information retrieval, Cambridge University Press, Cambridge
2. Rong X, Liang K, Yan Z, Min W (2011) CDW: a text clustering model for diverse versions discovery. In: FSKD 2011, pp 1113–1117
3. Hofmann T (1999) Probabilistic latent sematic analysis. Uncertainty in artificial intellogence
4. Blei DM, Ng AY, Jordan MI (2003) Latent dirichlet allocation. J Mach Learn Res 3:993–1022
5. Blei DM Introduction to probablilistic topic models, http://www.cs.princeton.edu/~blei/topicmodeling.html
6. Masada T, Kiyasu S, Miyahara S (2008) Comparing LDA with pLSI as a dimensionality reduction method in document clustering. In: LKR 2008, pp 13–26
7. Ponti G, Tagarelli A (2009) Topic-based hard clustering of documents using generative models. In: ISMIS 2009, pp 231–240
8. Das A, Datar M, Garg A, Rajaram S (2007) Google news personalization: scalable online collaborative filtering. In: WWW 2007, pp 271–280
9. Shubankar K, Singh A, Pudi V (2011) A frequent keyword-set based algorithm for topic modeling and clustering of research papers. In: DMO 2011, pp 96–102

Chapter 68
The Application of Hybrid Immune Algorithm in Distributed Generation Distribution Planning

Chun Li and Xiaoliu Shen

Abstract This paper focuses on how to determine the location and the constant volume of distributed generation. Firstly, we establish the multi-objective distributed generation planning model for the minimum network loss, minimum average deviation of the node voltage and the minimum total investment cost. Then the hybrid immune algorithm (HIA) is used in the optimization computing of distributed power distribution planning. In order to improve the convergence speed, the clonal selection algorithm has been modified to adjust the circumstance. Also the PSO algorithm is introduced in the calculation of high-frequency variation. The improved algorithm overcomes the problem that the calculation of the latter part is easy to fall into local convergence. The case study applies the HIA to IEEE 33 nodes test system, the simulation result shows that the HIA is effective and feasible in the problem of distributed generation distribution planning.

Keywords Hybrid immune algorithm · PSO · Distributed generation · Multi-objective optimization

68.1 Introduction

In recent years, along with the implementation of smart grid strategy, distributed generation has been recognized worldwide. Market penetration is still very low, but the field is undergoing rapid growth. Therefore, actively studying the distributed energy development model in the smart grid environment is of great

C. Li (✉) · X. Shen
North China Electric Power University, Beijing, China
e-mail: yxlichun@126.com

W. Lu et al. (eds.), *Proceedings of the 2012 International Conference on Information Technology and Software Engineering*, Lecture Notes in Electrical Engineering 211, DOI: 10.1007/978-3-642-34522-7_68, © Springer-Verlag Berlin Heidelberg 2013

significance for the future large-scale development of distributed energy and eases the energy crisis [1].

The combination of main power grids and distributed power generation is recognized as the most important way which is able to save the investment, reduce energy consumption and improve power system reliability and flexibility [1]. When a large number of distributed generations in the planning scheme, a large number of random changes in the power system appears, and improves the complexity of the system [2]. To address this issue, in this paper, the improved clonal selection algorithm is applied to optimize the distribution network, trying to establish a comprehensive, robust distribution network system.

68.2 Distributed Generations

Distributed generation (DG) is a small unit which is dispersed installed on the user side, both independent of the public grid directly provide electrical power for the around user, and access to distribution networks with the public grid to provide users with small generators of electricity [3]. These small units include fuel cells, small gas turbine or gas turbine and fuel cell hybrid device.

DG plays the role of load shifting and load balancing. It can compensate for the lack of security and stability of large power grids, avoid large-scale power outage, and provide users with more secure and stable supply of electricity [3].

68.3 Mathematical Model of Distributed Power Distribution Planning

In the distribution network planning, according the decision variables can be divided into two types, one is the single planning and another is coordinated planning [2]. Single planning is to optimize the installation location and capacity of distributed generation equipment in the condition of the feeder lines and substation configuration does not change; the coordinated planning is for global optimization planning, and includes the feeder lines. This paper focuses on the former.

68.3.1 Multi-Goal Programming Objective Function

In this paper, we focus on the distributed power distribution planning problem, mainly to consider economy and security. Ultimately, we establish the multi-objective model for the objectives of the network minimum network loss, minimum average deviation of the node voltage and the minimum total investment cost [4]. The objective function of the total investment cost φ is as follows:

$$\min \varphi = \sum_{i=1}^{n_{DG}} (C_{i1} + C_{i2}) P_{DGi} \tag{68.1}$$

In the formula, n_{DG} is the number of distributed generation equipment installed; P_{DGi} is the DG rated capacity installed in the node i; C_1, C_2 were distributed device unit capacity of node i overall equipment costs and installation costs.

The objective function of the network minimum loss is as follows:

$$\min P_{loss} = \sum_{i=1}^{N} R_i (P_i^2 + Q_i^2) / |U_i|^2 \tag{68.2}$$

P_{loss} is the loss of active network; N is the number of slip; R_i is the slip resistance; P_i, Q_i, U_i, respectively, for node i active power, reactive power and voltage.

The objective function of the average deviation is as follows, U_i^* is the rated voltage of the node i:

$$\min U_{ad} = \frac{1}{N} \sum_{i=1}^{N} |U_i - U_i^*| \tag{68.3}$$

68.3.2 Constraint Conditions

The Equality constraints are the distributed generation access with the grid system power balance equation:

$$\begin{cases} P_{Gi} + P_{Di} - P_{Li} = U_i \sum_{j=1}^{N} U_j (G_{ij} \cos \delta_{ij} + B_{ij} \sin \delta_{ij}) \\ Q_{Gi} + Q_{Di} - Q_{Li} = U_i \sum_{j=1}^{N} U_j (G_{ij} \sin \delta_{ij} - B_{ij} \cos \delta_{ij}) \end{cases} \tag{68.4}$$

$$\begin{cases} |U_i|^{\min} \leq |U_i| \leq |U_i|^{\max} \\ |I_i| \leq |I_i|^{\max} \\ P_{DGi}^{\min} \leq P_{DGi} \leq P_{DGi}^{\max} \\ \sum_{i=1}^{n_{DG}} P_{DGi} \leq \alpha \sum_{i=1}^{N} P_{LDi} \end{cases} \tag{68.5}$$

In this formula, P_{Gi}, Q_{Gi} is the injected generator active power and reactive power of i; P_{Di}, Q_{Di} is injected distributed generation; P_{Li}, Q_{Li} is the active power and reactive power; U_i and U_j are the voltage of the first node i and the end node j.

The inequality constraints include: the node voltage upper and lower limits, and the distributed power generation capacity, the maximum limit of the slip power.

68.3.3 Transform the Multiple Objectives into Single Objective

For the reunification of the dimension of each sub-goal, we introduced the general linear piecewise function to represent the fuzzy membership function for each sub-goal [5].

$$\mu_i = \begin{cases} 1, (f_i \leq f_i^*) \\ \dfrac{f_i^- - f_i}{f_i^- - f_i^*}, (f_i^* \leq f_i \leq f_i^-) \\ 0, (f_i \geq f_i^-) \end{cases} \tag{68.6}$$

$$\max\lambda = \min\{\mu_1, \mu_2, \mu_3\} \tag{68.7}$$

In this formula, μ_i is the corresponding sub-goals of the membership; f_i^- is the maximum function value of the corresponding sub-goals; f_i^*, optimized to get the best target for the corresponding sub-goals; n is the value of overall satisfaction.

68.4 Hybrid Immune Algorithm

Artificial immune algorithm is mainly used in the operation mechanism of the artificial immune system to solve practical problems. The clonal selection algorithm in this paper is also based on immune algorithm.

68.4.1 Clonal Selection Algorithm

Clonal selection algorithm simulates the mechanism of biological immune system [6] (Fig. 68.1). Generally we put the objective function to be optimized and constraints as the antigen and the algorithm steps are as follows:

Step 1 Initialization: randomly generated N-antibody corresponds to a possible solution.
Step 2 Classification: N antibody decomposition of m and r antibody composed of two in part A_m, A_r, respectively, into the memory set of antibodies and the rest, the antibodies who can enter the memory set have a higher affinity.
Step 3 Cloning: select the k-affinity antibodies were cloned; the number of clones is proportional to their affinity.
Step 4 Mutation: mutation operation on the cloned antibodies and the mutation rate is inversely proportional to affinity.
Step 5 Reselect: recalculate the affinity of the mutated antibodies to formulate the new memory set.

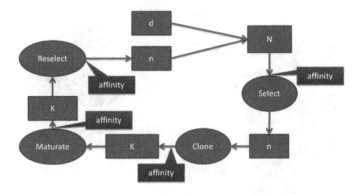

Fig. 68.1 Standard clonal selection algorithm processes

Step 6 Demise: simulated biological clonal selection process 5 % of B cells die a natural death.
Step 7 Check whether it meets the termination condition, if terminate, otherwise go to step 2 into the next iteration.

68.4.2 Improved Clonal Selection Algorithm

The study found that the algorithm has several obvious shortcomings:

1. High-frequency variation rate lack the automatic adjustment feature.
2. The lack of memory bank.
3. Lack of collaboration and communication between the antibodies.

68.4.2.1 Particle Swarm Optimization (PSO)

Compared with the artificial immune algorithm, particle swarm optimization algorithm has a lot to learn from its advantages. The standard particle swarm optimization algorithm solves the optimization problems through the cooperation and competition between particle swarm individual [7]. Each individual in the population referred to as particles, each particle represents the problem to be optimized a possible solution.

Update position and velocity with the following formula:

$$
\begin{cases}
v_1(t+1) = \omega v_1(t) + c_1 R_1(p_1(t) - x_1(t)) + c_2 R_2(p_g(t) - x_1(t)) \\
x_1(t+1) = x_1(t) + v_1(t+1)
\end{cases}
\tag{68.8}
$$

In this formula, ω is the Inertia coefficient, c_1 and c_2 are the acceleration constant; $R_1 \sim U(0, 1)$ and $R_2 \sim U(0, 1)$ are two independent random functions.

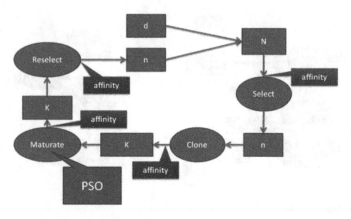

Fig. 68.2 Improved clonal selection algorithm processes

68.4.2.2 Hybrid Immune Algorithm

In this paper, we use the particle swarm optimization to compensate for clonal selection algorithm's shortcomings, such as the long training time, and to reduce the population size; at the same time, we use the clonal selection algorithm's diversity to compensate for the shortcomings of PSO to improve search accuracy.

Through the clonal selection, each antibody has used its own historical information, therefore when introduce the evolution equation of particle swarm optimization algorithm, we should only consider approaching the global optimum, then we use PSO formula which is mentioned above, so that evolution has a more clear direction to improve the convergence rate, while taking advantage of the variation in the immune algorithm and demise the operation to ensure that the diversity of antibodies, both the use of the cloning algorithm to maintain the advantages of antibody diversity, but also advantage of the characteristics of group information sharing in the PSO algorithm (Fig. 68.2).

Consider each antibody as a particle in the particle swarm optimization, at the beginning of the clonal selection algorithm, determine the affinity vector F of random initial population of A_N, then order to do the steps of the clonal selection algorithm, and then update the velocity and position of existing antibody using the PSO algorithm, the limit does not exceed the boundary, and update P_g, the guidance of antibodies to high frequency variation, followed by clonal selection algorithm receptor editing process.

68.4.3 Hybrid Immune Algorithm to Solve the Problem of Distribution

In this paper, in order to solve the planning problem of distributed power distribution in the distribution network, simplifying the problem to determine the distributed

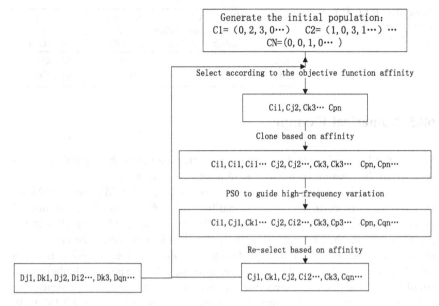

Fig. 68.3 Hybrid immune algorithm processes

power distribution network in the location and capacity. We use real number encoding method to express the location and capacity of distributed power variables, and assume that the distributed power installed in the load node, and one can only install one distributed power. The radial distribution network allows N nodes to install, distributed power building programs use a set of variables $C = \{c_1, c_2 \dots c_n\}$ to represent [1]. The magnitude of c_i, illustrates the construction of distributed power corresponding to the load node i, if $c_i = 0$ indicates the load of node i is not the construction of distributed power; if $c_i = 2$ indicates 20 kVA, and so on.

Using HIA to find the optimal solution, we first need to solve the problem how to initial antibody population. Generally is generated randomly, but the number of such infeasible solutions would be too large, in turn affect the search vegetarian range and convergence speed. Therefore when we generate the initial antibody population must be restrained by some constraints. The first one is the total capacity of the distributed power can not exceed the maximum capacity of planned distribution network to new load, and verify the capacity of each power must be within the rated range. All of the N antibodies should be generated in this way.

In the solution process, the HIA starting from the initial antibody population based on the affinity function, and then selection, cloning, mutation; PSO algorithm is used to achieve the exchange of information between individuals and guidie high frequency variation. The specific process is as follows [5] (Fig. 68.3).

Table 68.1 IEEE 33 node test system	Method	DG access location	DG installation number	Active power loss before the DG (kW)	Active power loss after the DG (kW)
	HIA	30	2	180.918	82.1835
	PSO	30	2	180.778	82.1820

68.5 Numerical Example

We use the IEEE 33 node distribution test system to verify the algorithm. It is a pure radial distribution network; has 33 nodes, 32 branches.

The total active and reactive powers of the load were 298 MW and 129 Mvar. HIA parameter is set to: the number of antibody $M = 60$, the maximum number of iterations to 100, and an accuracy of $d = 0.0001$. Calculated using HIA in the previous section, the first randomly generated 60 solutions within the constraints, to calculate the antigen–antibody affinity according to the objective function (68.7), and iteratively until the termination condition. By the above calculation, the simulation results are as follows: the location of 30 is the best access location of the distributed power, at this time the system active power loss for 82.1820 kW optimized active power loss decreased rate of 54.53 %. In order to verify the effectiveness and superiority of the HIA, the algorithm with the standard PSO calculations were compared the results in the table.

It can be seen from Table 68.1 that the calculated results are basically the same in HIA and PSO, it proves that a HIA for distributed power supply location and constant volume is feasible and effective. The DG's access makes the active power loss is much lower, it is indicate that the DG's access could greatly reduce the active power loss if the location and constant volume is planned reasonably. Shown in Fig. 68.4 for the convergence of two algorithms in the optimization process, in this paper, the HIA have a certain improvement in convergence and adaptability than the standard PSO.

Fig. 68.4 HIA and PSO convergence curve

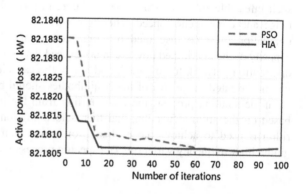

68.6 Conclusion

In the rapid development of smart grid, distributed power generation equipment has begun large-scale applications; an access to a variety of distributed power securely and reliably has important significance [3]. This article is just start on this point; it adopts the multi-objective optimization model of distribution network planning, and uses HIA in distribution planning. HIA mainly uses the clonal selection theory as the mechanism, and considers the PSO algorithm as the guidance for high-frequency variation, which can adjust the direction of the variability during the optimization process; this can improve the computational efficiency of the algorithm and avoid falling into local optimum too early. In order to verify the algorithm, we used the IEEE 33 node test system for simulation and put the results to compare with the standard PSO algorithm; proved its effectiveness and efficiency.

As a preliminary study, this paper only consider distributed power distribution planning problem in a pure environment, although we used multi-objective optimization methods, there still have many influencing factors did not taken into account, and need for the further research.

References

1. Ramachandran B, Srivastava SK, Edrington CS, Cartes DA (2011) An intelligent auction scheme for smart grid market using a hybrid immune algorithm. IEEE Trans Industr Electron 58(10):4603–4612
2. Moslehi K, Kumar R (2010) A reliability perspective of the smart grid. IEEE Trans Smart Grid 1(1):57–65
3. Gu Y, Wang K, Zhang B (2010) Distributed generation technologies and their current applications. Power Syst Clean Energy 26(6):38–43 (in Chinese)
4. Lin H, Liu K (2002) Distributed generation technologies and their current applications. Power Syst Clean Energy 16(2):18–23 (in Chinese)
5. Yang D-D, Jiao L-C, Gong M-G, Yu H (2010) Clone selection algorithm to solve preference multi-objective optimization. J Softw 21(1):14–33 (in Chinese)
6. Li L, Li H, Xie S, Li X (2008) Immune particle swarm optimization algorithms based on clone selection. Comput Sci 35(10):253–256 (in Chinese)
7. Tang J (2010) Principle and application of PSO algorithm. Comput Technol Dev 20(02): 213–216 (in Chinese)

Chapter 69
An Improved Market-Based Auction Algorithm for UAVs Task Assignment Problem

Xin Liu and Ronggang Zhu

Abstract This paper analyzes distributed task assignment for unmanned aerial vehicles (UAVs) using a market-based parallel auction algorithm. This approach includes five steps: choosing tasks into subset, auctioning the task subset, evaluating the bids, assigning tasks to unmanned aerial vehicles and arranging the velocity of each UAV and tasks execution times. Through auctioning several tasks, including coupling and individual tasks, in one time, this method greatly reduces the communication requirements between unmanned aerial vehicles in the process of distributed task assignment, and therefore results in lower risk of being detected and higher real time property. Simulation results show that market-based parallel auction algorithm can efficiently allocate tasks to UAVs.

Keywords Distributed task assignment · UAVs · Market-based parallel auction algorithm

69.1 Introduction

With the development of artificial intelligence (AI) and the application of AI on unmanned aerial vehicles (UAVs), the capability of UAVs' autonomous determination is promoted gradually [1]. In the future, UAV teams may plan and

X. Liu (✉) · R. Zhu (✉)
Science and Technology on Electro-optic Control Laboratory,
25th West Kaixuan Road, Luoyang 471009, China
e-mail: 511065048@qq.com

R. Zhu
e-mail: ZHURG613@sina.com

W. Lu et al. (eds.), *Proceedings of the 2012 International Conference on Information Technology and Software Engineering*, Lecture Notes in Electrical Engineering 211, DOI: 10.1007/978-3-642-34522-7_69, © Springer-Verlag Berlin Heidelberg 2013

execute missions without human feedback. Unmanned Systems Integrated Road-map FY2011-1036 promulgated by the Department of Defense of the United States hopes to make UAV teams has the ability of autonomous collaborative combat before 2017.

Collaborative task assignment is the key technology of UAVs collaboration system [2, 3]. The purpose of collaborative task assignment is to assign a set of cooperative tasks to UAV team and arrange mission sequences and execution times for every UAV in the team. Distributed task assignment based on multi-agent technology can utilize every team member's computation capability and make the system robust and flexible [4]. To achieve the goal of autonomous collaboration, we require the agents to be able to compute a coordinated task strategy and share the available data.

Market-based approach is suitable for distributed task assignment [5]. One of the representative market-based approaches is auction algorithm [6]. Auction algorithm assigns task to UAV which has the greatest superiority through pro-cesses of tender and biding. But the traditional one-by-one auction algorithm has one disadvantage that is only one task will be assigned in one auction process. So the communication demands among UAVs are very huge. For the existence of communication delays, frequent communication will affect the real time property of this approach. At the same time, frequent communication increases the risk of be detected by enemy.

This paper presents an improved market-based auction algorithm to solve the problem of allocating tasks including coupled ones to multiple UAVs. The outline of this paper is as follows. After the introduction, the scenario of collaborative task assignment for UAV team is showed (Sect. 69.2). Section 69.3 describes the improved market-based auction algorithm in detail. After the simulation results, presented in Sects. 69.4 and 69.5 reports the conclusions and future developments.

69.2 Scenarios

Given a list of N_T tasks and a UAV team formed by N_U UAVs, the goal of the task assignment is to find a conflict-free matching of tasks to UAVs that maximizes performance of the whole system. An assignment is said to be conflict-free if each task is assigned to no more than one UAV [7, 8]. Some tasks have close collab-oration requirements that constraint tasks to be carried out simultaneously. Every task has an earliest execution time point ET_j and a latest execution time point LT_j which limit the task to be carried out in the time bounds $[ET_j, LT_j]$. There are N_D dangerous areas defended by ground-to-air missile or antiaircraft artillery in the planning environment across which UAVs are forbidden to fly. The performance of the whole system is assumed to be a sum of local reward values, while each local reward is determined as a function of tasks assigned to each UAV.

The task assignment problem described above can be written as the following program with binary decision variables x_{ij} that indicate whether or not task j is assigned to UAV i:

$$\text{Min} \quad \sum_{i=1}^{N_U} \sum_{j=1}^{N_T} cost_{ij} x_{ij} \tag{69.1}$$

$$\text{Subject to}: \quad \sum_{j=1}^{N_T} x_{ij} \le M_{iT} \tag{69.2}$$

$$\sum_{i=1}^{N_U} x_{ij} \le 1 \tag{69.3}$$

$$t_j \in [ET_j, LT_j] \tag{69.4}$$

$$x_{ij} \in \{0, 1\} \tag{69.5}$$

where $x_{ij} = 1$ if task j is assigned to UAV i and c_{ij} is a nonnegative function of assignment x_{ij}. $cost_{ij}$ is the cost of UAV i to carry out task j includes the length of route UAV i flying to task j location and the risk of being shot down if it cross enemy antiaircraft weapon defense areas. If UAVs are enforced to avoid the threat areas then $cost_{ij}$ is just the length cost. t_j is the estimate time when task j is carried out, which should be in the time window $[ET_j, LT_j]$.

It is assumed in this paper that UAVs in the team are isomorphic, that is when not think about the consumption of fuel each UAV has the same probability of finishing the same task successfully [9].

69.3 Algorithms

Market-based auction algorithm is suitable for distributed multi-agent task assignment scene for it does not require each agent in the team know about the global information. But the auction algorithm is inefficient when the size of task assignment is large because of abundant deals and communication between agents [10]. Another disadvantage of auction algorithm is that coupling constraints between tasks are not taken into account when tasks are allocated.

To satisfy the need of efficient cooperative task assignment, a parallel auction (PA) algorithm is presented. PA algorithm auctions a subset of tasks includes coupling and separated tasks in one time. The decrease of auction times reduces the communication requirements between agents. And it is easy to deal with collaborative demands when coupling tasks are auctioned together. The details of PA algorithm are as follows.

69.3.1 Subset of Tasks

Tasks are picked up and compose a subset of tasks waiting for auction before executing the PA algorithm. Every task which has not be allocated is endued with a priority defined as

$$pri\_T_j = 1 - \frac{LT_j}{\max\limits_{i=1}^{N_T} LT_j} \qquad (69.6)$$

Equation (69.6) reflects the urgency of tasks. The earlier of the latest start time point, the higher of the priority.

The agent who is in charge of the auction picks up the task with highest priority T_k into subset. Then the close coupling tasks of the highest priority task T_k are sent to subset. The number of tasks in the subset N_{ST} should not larger than N_{CU}. N_{CU} is the number of usable UAVs in the team. If $N_{ST} < N_{CU}$, no more than $N_{CU} - N_{ST}$ tasks which have lower priority will be chosen into the subset.

All the tasks in the subset will be auctioned together. Each agent can get no more than one task in one auction process.

69.3.2 Auction

After the subset of tasks is collected, the principal agent sends task information of the subset to all the agents in the team. Team members respectively work out practical scheme for every task in the subset. A scheme bid_{ij} consists of three parts: cap_{ij} showing the capability of agent i to execute task j, $length_{ij}$ computing the length of route through which agent i flies to the position of task j and $[min\_rt_{ij}, max\_rt_{ij}]$ estimating time bound of agent i to execute task j.

$$bid_{ij} = \left\{ cap_{ij}, length_{ij}, \left[min\_rt_{ij}, max\_rt_{ij} \right] \right\} \qquad (69.7)$$

$bid_i = \left\{ bid_{ij} \mid j = 1, 2, \ldots, N_{ST} \right\}$ is the aggregate of agent i's scheme.

To calculate bid_{ij}, the route planning system of the agent i plans a feasible route $route_{ij}$ from the position of the latest task in its task schedule to task j's position and route $route_{jo}$ from the position of task j to the reclaiming airport. We can get $length_{ij}$ and $[min\_rt_{ij}, max\_rt_{ij}]$ via $route_{ij}$ and the velocity range of agent i and get $length_{jo}$ via $route_{jo}$. The capability of agent i fulfilling task j can be defined as

$$cap_{ij} = \begin{cases} 0, & length_{ij} + length_{jo} > rest\_length_i \\ 0, & weapon_j > rest\_weapon_i \\ v\_length_{ij} \times (1 - \beta) + v\_weapon_{ij} \times \beta, & others \end{cases} \qquad (69.8)$$

$$v\_length_{ij} = 1 - \frac{length_{ij} + length_{jo}}{length_i} \tag{69.9}$$

$$v\_weapon_{ij} = 1 - \frac{weapon_j}{rest\_weapon_i} \tag{69.10}$$

where $rest\_length_i$ is the length that agent i can fly by its rest fuel and $rest\_weapon_i$ is the qualities of rest weapons after agent i finishes its task schedule. The more fuel and weapons remain means agents have the higher possibility to execute one task again if the first execution activity is failed.

69.3.3 Evaluate

Every member of the team sends back its bid to the principal agent. The principal agent evaluates all the bids together. The results constitute a $N_{CU} \times N_{ST}$ superiority matrix Sup where Sup_{ij} reflects the superiority of agent i competing with other agents for task j. The measurement equation of Sup_{ij} is

$$Sup_{ij} = \begin{cases} 0, & cap_{ij} = 0 \\ \left[cap_{ij} \times (1 - \rho) + pro\_len_{ij} \times \rho\right] \times ctime_{ij}, & cap_{ij} > 0 \end{cases} \tag{69.11}$$

where

$$pro\_len_{ij} = 1 - \frac{length_{ij}}{\max\limits_{i=1}^{N_U}(length_{ij})} \tag{69.12}$$

and

$$ctime_{ij} = \begin{cases} 0, & min\_rt_{ij} > LT_j \\ 0.5, & max\_rt_{ij} < ET_j \\ 1, & [min\_rt_{ij}, max\_rt_{ij}] \cap [ET_j, LT_j] \notin \varnothing \end{cases} \tag{69.13}$$

pro_len_{ij} is the route length factor that makes the agent i near the position of task j has a high probability of being chosen to execute task j. But it does not mean that the nearest agent has the highest probability to execute the task. For every task has special executing time window $[ET_j, LT_j]$, $min\_rt_{ij} > LT_j$ means even the agent i flies to task position with the highest velocity it cannot arrive the task location before the deadline of the task j and $max\_rt_{ij} < ET_j$ is the case that even the agent i flies to task position with the lowest velocity it will get to the task location before ET_j. $ctime_{ij}$ is a time punishment factor. In the first case above, agent i can not finish task j within the prescriptive time bounds, so $ctime_{ij}$ is set as 0. In the second case agent i has to plan a waiting route and cruise until fit the time requirement. To punish the waste of fuel the time punishment factor is set as 0.5. When $[min\_rt_{ij}, max\_rt_{ij}]$ and

$[ET_j, LT_j]$ have intersection, which means agent i will get to task position between $[ET_j, LT_j]$ by adjusting its flying velocity, $ctime_{ij}$ will be set as 1.

The length of route, time fitness and the capability of agent i performing task j have been taken into account in the computation of Sup_{ij}. Sup_{ij} is a composite result of three factors mentioned above. β is an accommodation coefficient with a range from 0 to 1 which reflects decision-maker's favor. For all the factors in the function have a bound of $[0, 1]$, the magnitude of Sup_{ij} is between 0 and 1.

69.3.4 Assignment

As mentioned in Sect. 69.3.1, each agent only can get no more than one task in one auction and each task can be distributed to one agent. The problem of assigning UAVs to tasks in the subset is defined as

$$\text{Max} \quad \sum_{i=1}^{N_{CU}} \sum_{j=1}^{N_{ST}} Sup_{ij}x_{ij} \tag{69.14}$$

$$\text{Subject to}: \sum_{j=1}^{N_{ST}} x_{ij} \leq 1 \tag{69.15}$$

$$\sum_{i=1}^{N_{CU}} x_{ij} \leq 1 \tag{69.16}$$

$$x_{ij} \in \{0, 1\} \tag{69.17}$$

Hungary algorithm has been designed to solve such problem [11]. But the normal Hungary algorithm can deal with the case that N_{ST} equals to N_{CU}. If $N_{CU} > N_{ST}$, we can set $N_{CU} - N_{ST}$ fictitious tasks and consider superiority of every UAV biding those fictitious tasks as 0.

$$Sup_{ij} = 0, \quad i = 1, 2, \ldots, N_{CU}; j = N_{ST} + 1, \ldots, N_{CU} \tag{69.18}$$

After those fictitious tasks join the subset, the dimension of superiority matrix is $N_{CU} \times N_{CU}$. Then we can get a $N_{CU} \times N_{CU}$ 0-1 matrix R shows the allocation result computed by normal Hungary algorithm. Delete the last $m - n$ lists of R and we will get the final assigning result.

69.3.5   Velocity and Execution Time Arrangement

The above steps insure that tasks can be carried out in special time windows. Then we need to fix the practical execution time point of each task and the flying velocity of each UAV. In this part, the data got from Sect. 3.3 will be useful.

Assume that agent i is assigned to individual task j, we will have two segments of time $[min\_rt_{ij}, max\_rt_{ij}]$ and $[ET_j, LT_j]$. Through evaluation in part C and assignment in part D the situation of $min\_rt_{ij} > LT_j$ is avoided. If $max\_rt_{ij} < ET_j$, ET_j is the time point for agent i to execute task j, and agent i should fly to task position with its lowest velocity V_{min}. In this case a path of waiting route is needed and the length of waiting route is calculated by Eq. (69.19).

$$wlength_{ij} = V_{min} \times (ET_j - min\_rt_{ij}) \tag{69.19}$$

If $[min\_rt_{ij}, max\_rt_{ij}] \cap [ET_j, LT_j] \not\subseteq \varnothing$ and the intersection is $[at_j^{min}, at_j^{max}]$, at_j^{min} will be the execution time of task j and flying velocity of agent i in this section is defined as

$$v_{ij} = \frac{length_{ij}}{at_j^{min} - pretime_i} \tag{69.20}$$

where $pretime_i$ is the estimate time that agent i finish its task sequence.

It is analogous to get the execution times of simultaneous tasks. Generally, simultaneous tasks have the same time windows. Assume that agent k and agent l are assigned to carrying out simultaneous tasks with time window $[ET_m, LT_m]$, $[min\_rt_k, max\_rt_k]$ and $[min\_rt_l, max\_rt_l]$ are the estimating time bounds of agent k and agent l to carry out those simultaneous tasks mentioned above. For the usage of waiting route and waiting time, the latest time that agent k and agent l carry out collaborative tasks can be set to LT_m. ct is defined as $ct = max\{min\_rt_k, min\_rt_l\}$. If $ct \in [ET_m, LT_m]$, the execution time equals to ct, else it equals to ET_m. The computation of waiting length and flying velocity is the same as Eqs. (69.19) and (69.20).

69.4   Simulation Examples

To clarify the scenarios and illustrate the assignment algorithm presented in Sect. 69.3, a simulation example with a problem of size $N_U = 3$ and $N_T = 8$ is presented here. UAVs and task positions are placed in an area 100 km wide and 100 km long. Four detected and some undetected antiaircraft threats with different threaten ranges exist in the planning environment. The parameters of UAVs, tasks and threats are showed in Tables 69.1, 69.2 and 69.3 respectively. Time windows are set to the bounds from the start time point of the assignment process.

Table 69.1 The parameters of UAVs

UAV	Original location (X, Y)/km	Velocity/km/h	Weapon units	Rest length/km
1	(5.00, 15.00)	[80, 150]	3	300
2	(15.00, 5.00)	[80, 150]	3	300
3	(5.00, 5.00)	[80, 150]	4	300

Table 69.2 The parameters of tasks

Task	Location (X, Y)/km	Time window/min	Simultaneous task
1	(50.12, 42.22)	[20, 30]	
2	(32.62, 60.89)	[30, 40]	2
3	(32.62, 60.89)	[30, 40]	3
4	(60.76, 73.77)	[55, 65]	
5	(80.11, 50.99)	[45, 55]	
6	(85.65, 40.76)	[40, 50]	
7	(90.11, 92.90)	[70, 80]	8
8	(90.11, 92.90)	[70,80]	7

Table 69.3 The parameters of threats

Threat	Location (X, Y)/km	Range/km
1	(24, 45)	12
2	(45, 25)	15
3	(64, 50)	12
4	(80, 74)	15
5	(50, 80)	12

We assume that communications between UAVs are perfect, without delay and information losses. One of the team members is chosen as the tasks owner and host auctions. Each UAV has a route planner planning the best flying routes between two positions with sparse A* (SAS) algorithm [12] and task time availability windows are computed based on computing the length of the best flying routes. The progression of the simulation is shown in Fig. 69.1.

Figure 69.1a shows the UAV and task positions at the beginning of the simulation. UAV team is cruising in the battle field. Figure 69.1b shows the first round auction result. Task1, 2 and 3 are chosen into the subset of tasks. After the processes of auction, evaluation and assignment presented in Sect. 69.3, Task1, 2 and 3 are assigned to UAV3, 1 and 2 respectively. The colorized lines are the best flying routes planned by SAS algorithm. Figure 69.1c, d show the second and third round auction result.

The velocity of each UAV in different phases and estimating execution time of each task is computed by method presented in Sect. 69.3.5. The arrangement results are shown in Table 69.4.

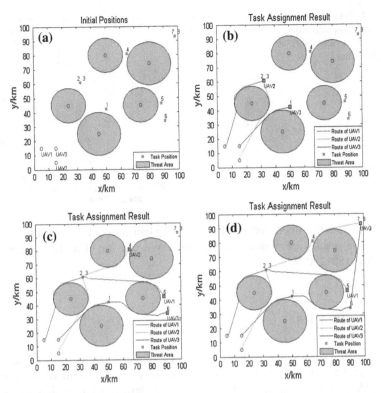

Fig. 69.1 Simulation example. **a** Initial positions. **b** First round auction results. **c** Second round auction results. **d** Third round auction results

Table 69.4 The arrangement of execution times and velocity

UAV	Task	Execution time/min	Velocity/km/h	Length of route/km
1	2	30.0000	118.4850	59.2425
1	5	54.2236	150.0000	60.5589
2	3	30.0000	123.0209	61.5105
2	4	55.0000	92.2935	38.4556
2	8	73.6703	113.7336	35.3906
3	1	20.0000	135.9763	45.3254
3	6	40.0000	130.2465	43.4155
3	7	73.6703	104.3601	58.5639

From the simulation results we can find eight tasks are assigned to three UAVs by three times of auction activities, less than eight times of auction activities of the traditional one-by-one auction algorithm. So the efficiency is promoted nearly 167 %. To calculate the efficiency promoted by parallel auction algorithm, a series of tests was carried out in the same battle scene with 1–20 tasks. 3 UAVs with sufficient fuel and weapons join the tests. Respectively run the traditional auction

Fig. 69.2 Parallel auction algorithm compared with traditional auction algorithm in auction times

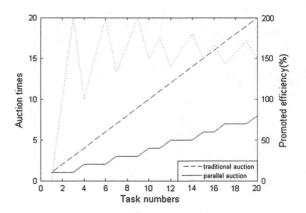

algorithm and the improved parallel auction algorithm and record the auction times. The results are showed in Fig. 69.2. We can see that the efficiency is promoted 150–200 %.

69.5 Summaries

The problem of assigning collaborative and individual mixed tasks to multiple UAVs has been presented. The problem was solved using an improved market-based PA algorithm. This methodology allows the host agent to auction a series of tasks in one time therefore greatly decreasing the number of deals compared to traditional market-based auction algorithm. The reduction in number of auctions results in decrease in communication cost. The simulation results show that PA algorithm presented is realizable and has higher efficiency than traditional auction algorithm.

References

1. Joint Planning and Development Office. NextGen UAS research, development and demonstration roadmap (2012)
2. Shima T, Rasmussen S (2008) UAV cooperative decision and control. Society of Industrial and Applied Mathematics, Philadelphia
3. Liao M, Chen Z (2007) Dynamic target assignment method based on multi-agent decentralized cooperative auction. J Beijing Univ Aeronaut Astronaut 33(2):180–183 w(in Chinese)
4. Long T (2006) Research on distributed task allocation and coordination for multiple UCAVs cooperative mission control. Graduate School of National University of Defense Technology, Changsha (in Chinese)
5. Gao P (2009) Market-based approach to multi-robot task allocation. Central South University, Changsha (in Chinese)

6. Sujit PB, Beard R (2007) Multiple MAV task allocation using distributed auctions. In: AIAA guidance, navigation and control conference and exhibit, Hilton Head. AIAA 2007-6452
7. Yang L, Kreamer W, Adams M et al (2004) Hierarchical planning for large numbers of unmanned vehicles. In: AIAA 1st intelligent systems technical conference, Chicago. AIAA 2004-6246 (in Chinese)
8. Vandermeersch BRR, Chu QP, Mulder JA (2005) Design and implementation of a mission planner for multiple UCAVs in a SEAD mission. In: AIAA guidance, navigation, and control conference and exhibit, San Francisco. AIAA 2005-6480
9. Shaferman V, Shima T (2009) Task assignment and motion planning for multiple UAVs tracking multiple targets in urban environments. In: AIAA guidance, navigation, and control conference, Chicago. AIAA 2009-5778
10. Li Y (2008) Research on coalition and task allocation in multi-agent system. Hefei University of Technology, Hefei (in Chinese)
11. Xu Y, Zhang H (2006) Operational research. Peking University Press, Beijing (in Chinese)
12. Ding M, Zheng C, Zhou C et al (2009) Route planning for unmanned aerial vehicles. Publishing House of Electronics Industry, Beijing (in Chinese)

Chapter 70
Experimental Analysis of Non-Rollbackable Pseudo Random Number in Optimistic Parallel Simulation

Bing Wang, Bo Deng, Lili Chen, Fei Xing and Yiping Yao

Abstract Pseudo-Random Number Generator (PRNG) fulfills the need to generate random variables in discrete event simulation. Particularly, the quality of Pseudo-Random Numbers (PRNs) not only has great impact on the performance, but also directly impacts the correctness of the Parallel Discrete-Event Simulation (PDES). In this paper, experiments have been conducted to study the influence to the quality of random number sequences brought by optimistic parallel simulation. From the preliminary results, we have found out that the random number sequence generated by non-rollbackable PRNG in optimistic parallel simulation passed the uniformity test, but failed in the independence test.

Keywords Parallel discrete-event simulation · Optimistic execution · Pseudo-random number · Experimental analysis

70.1 Introduction

Ensuring the consistency with the sequential execution is one of the core issues in parallel computing. In Parallel Discrete-Event Simulation (PDES) [1], real world problems often involve employing a large amount of pseudo random numbers, so

B. Wang (✉) · B. Deng · L. Chen
Software Division, Beijing Institute of Systems Engineering, 100101 Beijing, People's Republic of China
e-mail: wangbing.nudt@gmail.com

F. Xing · Y. Yao
School of Computer, National University of Defense Technology, 410073 Changsha, People's Republic of China

W. Lu et al. (eds.), *Proceedings of the 2012 International Conference on Information Technology and Software Engineering*, Lecture Notes in Electrical Engineering 211, DOI: 10.1007/978-3-642-34522-7_70, © Springer-Verlag Berlin Heidelberg 2013

the quality of the pseudo-random numbers is of great importance to the performance and correctness of PDES [2].

Repeatability and determinism are the basic motivation to make a Random Number Generator rollbackable in parallel simulation. However, whether to implement state saving for pseudo-random number generators (PRNG) as for state variables in optimistic parallel simulation, is generally regarded as an option left to the users on many mainstream parallel simulation platforms [3, 4]. Furthermore, in performance testing, it is also practical to shutdown the rollback of RNGs to kick out their effect. This is because although rollbackable PRNG in optimistic PDES is a necessary condition for strict repeatability of the simulation result, state saving resulted from the large amount of rollbackable PRNGs involves huge storage overhead. The current main memory access speed and CPU computation speed gap is still large, and for large-scale optimistic parallel simulation system execution, rollbackable PRNG often becomes a serious bottleneck.

Thus, with the knowledge that the crucial need for repeatability and determinism in parallel simulation, we further study the influence to the quality of pseudo random number stream brought by non-rollbackable PRNG in optimistic parallel simulation.

While the study on parallel PRNGs has already been with huge literature [5], the quality of pseudo-random numbers in parallel speculative execution is attracting greater attention. Recently researches focus on the efficiency and correctness of rollbackable PRNG algorithms [6, 7].

Among all the desirable properties a good random-number generator should have, uniformity and independence are among those who have direct impact on the correctness of the simulation results. In this paper, quality of random numbers generated by non-rollbackable PRNG in optimistic parallel simulation is studied. First, PRN sequences are generated from experiments using sequential and optimistic parallel simulation algorithms. Second, the tests for uniformity and independence to the PRN are conducted. Finally, we close the paper with a discussion on the major findings and provide some direction for future work.

70.2 Experiment

70.2.1 Experiment Setup

The setup of model, Simulation Algorithm, Pseudo Random Number Generator, Hardware/Software Platform, Experiments are described in below.

Model. A full connected PHOLD Model [8, 9] is used as the benchmark, the time increment follows a $(0,1)$ uniform distribution, and the size of the PHOLD is 4×4.

Simulation Algorithm. Two types of optimistic time management algorithms are studied for PDES against the sequential discrete event simulation [1], they are Time Warp (TW) [10] and Breathing Time Bucket (BTB) [3], implemented in James II [9].

Pseudo Random Number Generator. Two types of schemes to share the PRNG are respectively deployed, In the first case, all logical processes share a single PRNG, including Java Math.Random and Java SecureRandom. In the other case, each logical process has its own PRNG, including James II Unidistribution and James II MersenneTwister.

Hardware/Software Platform. The simulation experiments run on a workstation with an IntelCoreTM2 Quad Q8200 processor, the frequency of each core is 2.33 GHz, the memory capacity is 2 GB, and the operating system is Windows XP SP3, with JDK version 1.5.0.19. The simulation platform is James II-LP [9], on top of James II [11] with core version 0.821.

Experiment. Run the simulation until 350000 random numbers are recorded. in sequential execution, the Random Numbers are directly written to file, in parallel execution with TW and BTB, only those used in committed event are recorded, the PRNG is not rollbackable. Each experiment is repeated for 5 times, the average value is used.

70.2.2 Testing for Uniformity

Frequency Test [12, p. 12] is a common method to check the level of significance between the theoretical frequency and the empirical frequency.

Define

$$\chi^2 = \frac{k}{N} \sum_{i=1}^{k} \left(N_i - N/k \right)^2 \tag{70.1}$$

where k is the number of subdivisions in [0,1], which is set as k = 100, and χ^2 obeys the $\chi^2(k-1)$ distribution.

In the table of Chi-square statistics, corresponding to a degree of freedom (k−1) = 99 and level of significance $\alpha = 0.05$, t_α has a value of 123.225. It can be found in Table 70.1 that for sequential simulation, PDES with BTB and TW, the values of χ^2 of the generated PRN stream, are all less than t_α. So the assumption that the pseudo random number is evenly distributed for both BTB and TW is acceptable under the significance level of $\alpha = 0.05$.

70.2.3 Testing for Independence

Serial Test [12, p. 12] is used to evaluate the independence of the PRNs. Pair the sequence of PRNs generated by the simulations to two-dimensional points set (with distance e ∈ N): (ξ_1, ξ_{e+1}), (ξ_2, ξ_{e+2}),....,(ξ_N, ξ_{e+N}).

Partition the 2D space [0 ≤ x ≤ 1,0 ≤ y ≤ 1] into k × k grids, and check the difference between number of points in grid n_{ij} and N/k^2, where i,j ∈ N.

Table 70.1 Test for the uniformity of the pseudo random numbers, using frequency test, with different time management algorithms including sequential(seq), BTB and TW)

TM Alg	RNG	Mean	χ^2
Seq	Java Math.Random	0.5001	108.4932
Seq	James II Mersenne Twister	0.5009	104.2635
Seq	Java SecureRandom	0.4991	105.1136
Seq	James II Unidistribution	0.5004	109.6408
BTB	Java Math.Random	0.4997	97.4376
BTB	James II Mersenne Twister	0.4917	93.4233
BTB	Java SecureRandom	0.5017	90.1716
BTB	James II Unidistribution	0.4992	94.1209
TW	Java Math.Random	0.4995	110.5007
TW	James II Mersenne Twister	0.5001	95.1447
TW	Java SecureRandom	0.5001	80.4163
TW	James II Unidistribution	0.4999	108.2869

Java Math.Random and SecureRandom are from Java SDK native, in which all LPs mutually access to a single PRNG, James II MersenneTwister and Unidistribution are from James II native, in which each LP possesses its own PRNG

$$\chi^2 = \sum_{i=1}^{k} \sum_{j=1}^{k} \frac{k^2}{N} \left(n_{ij} - \frac{N}{k^2} \right)^2 \tag{70.2}$$

χ^2 follows a $\chi^2\,((k-1)^2)$ distribution, in which k = 11, e = 10000. Referring to Table 70.2, almost all results from the sequential execution pass the χ^2 test, but all results from the optimistic parallel simulation fail the χ^2 test. This is a 2-dimensional version of the Chi-square test, it is used for testing independence between successive observations. We generate $U_1,...,U_{2n}$; if the assumption that all $U_i(i)$ $(1 \le i \le 2n)$ follow a i.i.d. U(0,1) is true, then the non-overlapping pairs $(U_1,U_2),(U_3,U_4),...,(U_{2n-1},U_{2n})$ should be i.i.d. random vectors uniformly distributed in the square $(0,1)^2$. The procedure is:

- First, divide the square $(0,1)^2$ into n^2 subsquares;
- Second, count how many outcomes fall in each subsquare;
- Third, apply a χ^2 test to the data.

From Table 70.2, it is shown that the non-rollbackable PRNG leads to a significant degradation in the Independence of the generated sequence of PRNs.

70.3 Discussion and Future Work

In this paper, through a series of simulation experiments on a set of PRNG, following conclusion is made based on the preliminary result. On one hand, the hypotheses that the pseudo random numbers generated by non-rollbackable PRNG

Table 70.2 Test for the independence of pseudo random number using serial test. with different time management algorithms (sequential, BTB and TW), $k = 11, e = 10^4$

TM Alg	RNG	χ^2
Seq	Java Math.Random	95.7505
Seq	James II Mersenne Twister	88.4439
Seq	Java SecureRandom	105.11361
Seq	James II Unidistribution	81.5651
BTB	Java Math.Random	1993.1325
BTB	James II Mersenne Twister	2519.4341
BTB	Java SecureRandom	1750.3940
BTB	James II Unidistribution	1563.8511
TW	Java Math.Random	2236.5385
TW	James II Mersenne Twister	2977.9411
TW	Java SecureRandom	2975.2505
TW	James II Unidistribution	2767.5845

is evenly distributed for both BTB and TW is not rejected at the significance level of $\alpha = 0.05$; on the other, non-rollbackable RNG leads to a significant degradation in independence level for the generated pseudo random numbers. The result experimentally validates part of the theoretical result in [13], in which Prof. Tsitsiklis has pointed out that the non-rollbackable PRNG in optimistic parallel simulation would cause a shift in its distribution.

We are aware of the fact that in most cases, it is theoretically impossible and practically unnecessary to make the PRNG "true random". In PDES, it is sufficient for the random number sequence to exactly fulfill the required qualities by the simulation applications. For example, distribution uniformity is often more important than the true random number uniformity [12]. For most parallel simulation, as long as the quality of pseudo-random number sequence fulfill the statistical tests required by the application, the corresponded PRNGs are acceptable technically.

The focus of future research is to systematically conduct the experiments with larger model scale, different hardware platforms, various PRNG algorithms, synchronization protocols with different optimistic levels, and more tests for desirable properties of the Pseudo Random Numbers. In addition, further theoretical and practical efforts should be made on how to relief the quality degeneration of RNs generated by parallel speculative execution.

Acknowledgments This work is partly supported by the China Scholarship Council (Grant No.2007U39612), the National Science Foundation of China (NSFC) (Grant No. 61003075, 61170047). The first authors would like to show his gratitude to Prof. Adelinde M. Uhrmacher, Dr. Jan Himmelspach, Dr. Roland Ewald for some key idea was inspired when he was visiting University of Rostock. The authors would also like to give special thanks to Prof. John N. Tsitsiklis, Prof. Wengan Ma, and Dr. Matthias Jeschke for their continuous input throughout the development of this work.

References

1. Fujimoto RM (2000) Parallel and distributed simulation systems. Wiley, New York
2. Hill DRC (2011) Distribution of random streams in stochastic models in the age of Multi-Core and manycore processors. In: 2011 IEEE workshop on principles of advanced and distributed simulation (PADS)
3. Steinman JS (1991) SPEEDES: Synchronous parallel environment for emulation and discrete event simulation. In: Proceedings of the SCS multiconference on advances in parallel and distributed simulation, pp 95–101
4. Yao Y, Zhang Y (2008) Solution for analytic simulation based on parallel processing. J Syst Simul 20(24):6617–6621 (in Chinese)
5. Srinivasan A, Mascagni M, Ceperley D (2003) Testing parallel random number generators. Parallel Comput 29:69–94
6. Entacher K, Uhl A, Wegenkittl S (1998) Linear and inversive pseudorandom numbers for parallel and distributed simulation. SIGSIM Simul Dig 28:90–97
7. Passerat-Palmbach J, Mazel C, Hill DRC (2011) Pseudo-random number generation on GP-GPU. In: Principles of advanced and distributed simulation (PADS), 2011 IEEE workshop on, IEEE, pp 1–8
8. Fujimoto RM (1990) Performance of time warp under synthetic workloads. In: Proceedings of the SCS multiconference on distributed simulation, pp 23–28
9. Wang B, Himmelspach J, Ewald R, Uhrmacher AM (2009) Experimental analysis of logical process simulation algorithms in James II. In: Rossetti MD, Hill RR, Johansson B, Dunkin A, Ingalls RG (eds) Proceedings of the 2009 winter simulation conference, winter simulation conference, pp 1167–1179
10. Jefferson DR (1985) Virtual time. ACM Trans Program Lang Syst 7(3):404–425
11. Himmelspach J, Ewald R, Uhrmacher AM (2008) A flexible and scalable experimentation layer. In: WSC'08: Proceedings of the 40th conference on winter simulation, winter simulation conference, pp 827–835
12. Ma W (2011) Computational physics. Modern Physics Series. Science Press, Beijing
13. Tsitsiklis JN (1989) On the use of random numbers in asynchronous simulation via rollback. Inf Process Lett 31(3):139–144

Chapter 71
Imbalanced Data Classification Method Based on Clustering and Voting Mechanism

Rui Tang, Yuquan Zhu and Geng Chen

Abstract In order to resolve the poor predictive accuracy problems over minority class, which caused by imbalanced distribution existed in imbalanced data classification, this paper proposes an Imbalanced Data Classification Method Based on Clustering and Voting Mechanism. This method gets various clustered results through clustering, then acquires the final data clusters via voting mechanism, besides, determines sampling ratio from the feature of final data clusters and data inclination. It can guarantee the minority class quantity when compressing data sets. The experimental results show that our method is effective and feasible, besides has high classification accuracy.

Keywords Imbalanced data classification · One-pass clustering algorithm · Voting mechanism · Under-sampling

71.1 Introduction

The imbalance of data distribution is widely existed in the real world, like network intrusion detection, fraud detection, spam identification and disease diagnosis etc., classifying them has become an important research area of data mining and machine learning.

R. Tang (✉) · Y. Zhu
School of Computer Science and Telecommunications Engineering, Jiangsu University, 212013 Zhenjiang, Jiangsu, China
e-mail: 517457284@qq.com

G. Chen
School of Information Science, Nanjing Audit University, 211815 Nanjing, China

W. Lu et al. (eds.), *Proceedings of the 2012 International Conference on Information Technology and Software Engineering*, Lecture Notes in Electrical Engineering 211, DOI: 10.1007/978-3-642-34522-7_71, © Springer-Verlag Berlin Heidelberg 2013

Sampling is a common used method to process imbalanced data sets [1]. It reduces the quantity variance between the plus part and minus part through changing their distribution. Over-sampling and Under-sampling are the two common used ways in sampling. Over-sampling makes data sets distribution more balanced via copying the plus part. There are typical over-sampling algorithms: COG (Local decomposition for rare class analysis) based on local clustering over-sampling, which proposed by Wu et al. Synthetic Minority Over-sampling Technique (SMOTE) algorithm proposed by Chawla, Bowyer et al. [2] SMOTE selects the nearest object S to the plus part, and generates new samples between S and the plus part, this algorithm can avoid over fitting problem in random sampling, besides, keep the minority's decision boundary far away from the majority's. However, it has flaws like hard to determine the ratio of over-sampling and new combined noise, and can cause high frequency error problem, etc. In contrary the former, Under-sampling achieves data balance through decreasing the minus part, simple under-sampling is random under-sampling approach [3], thus, keep the plus quantity unchanged, combines the sampled samples with the plus samples to get a new training set. This method is simple and effective, but it has random sampling blindness and the uncertainty of sampling ratio problem, etc. [4]. Consequently, Yen et al. proposed SBC (under-sampling based on clustering), it determines the sampling ratio parameter through the proportion of the clustered plus and minus clusters, but this algorithm only considered the size of clusters, may result in great difference between sampled data distribution and original data distribution, so it is not quite accurate to predict minority samples.

Due to the limitations of based on clustering sampling methods, this paper presents a imbalanced data classification method based on clustering and voting mechanism, this method gets various clustered results through clustering, then acquires the final data clusters via voting mechanism, besides, determines sampling ratio from the feature of final data clusters and data inclination. It can guarantee the plus quantity when compressing the minus, and preserve the typical plus and minus samples information, so as to retain the distribution features of the original data.

71.2 Imbalanced Data Classification Method Based on Clustering

In order to solve the great separation from original data distribution when using under-sampling, Katia Kermanidis et al. present a method; it can combine one-sided sampling [4] with tomek links [5] to remove minus noise and data redundancy so as to balance the overall data distribution [6]. Yen et al. propose SBC (under-sampling based on clustering) [7]. SBC determines the sampling ratio parameter through the proportion of the clustered plus and minus clusters.

For given training set $S = \{(x_1, y_1),(x_2, y_2),...,(x_{num}, y_{num})\}$, here num is the total number of samples in training set, of which, xi is a d-dimensional eigenvector, class identification $yi \in \{P, N\}$, P means minority class (also named plus class), N means majority class (also named minus class), let $X = \{x_1, x_2, ..., x_{num}\}$.

Definition 1 The summary information of class, is made up of the different frequency information and numeric attribute of mass center among classification attributes, i.e. Summary = $\{<Stat_1, ..., Stat_{mC}, c_{mC+1}, c_{mC+2}, ..., c_{mC+mN}>\}$, here $Stat_i = \{(a, Freq_{C|Di}(a))|a \in C|D_i\}$ is the various frequency value set of $D_i(1 \leq i \leq m_C)$, $C|D_i$ is the projection of D_i on C, $Freq_{C|Di}(a)$ is the frequency of attribute a appears in $C|D_i$, if a is not belong to C|Di, then FreqC|Di(a) = 0; c_j is the mass center of numeric attribute $Dj(mC + 1 \leq j \leq mC + mN)$.

Definition 2 Cluster Summary Information (CSI) is defined as CSI = {n, ClusterID, Summary}, of which, n is the size of cluster, ClasterID is the ID set of object identification number in cluster, i.e. Recording which objects make up this cluster.

Definition 3 The distance of cluster C_1 and C_2 is defined as

$$d(C_1, C_2) = \sqrt{\sum_{i=1}^{m} \frac{dif(c_i^{(1)}, c_i^{(2)})^2}{m}},$$ here $dif(C_i^{(1)}, C_i^{(2)})$ is the variance of C_1 and C_2 on attribute D_i. The value of classification attribute D_i is defined as the average value of the distance between C_1 and C_2 on attribute $D_i(1 \leq i \leq m_C)$.

Definition 4 Let SampleRatio to be the sampling proportion of cluster C, the calculation is as follow:

$$SampleRatio = \begin{cases} e^{t-2}, t > \beta \\ 1, \quad t \leq \beta \end{cases}, \text{ of which, } t = \frac{EX + DX}{R}.$$

Parameter R is the real radius of cluster C, EX is the average distance between every element to the cluster center, DX is the Standard Deviation of the distance between every element to the cluster center, β is the parameter to classify different clusters.

The based on clustering sampling method is an imbalanced data manipulation criteria. It first clusters the training set to get new sample data and then sample the former data to get a classification model. Algorithm 1 is the detail:

Algorithm 1: sampling classification method based on clustering.

Input: training set S, over-sampling ratio n, under-sampling ratio m, the nearest count k, clustering times h, threshold value α of clustering consistency coefficient CI.

Output: classification model H.

(1) Do the feature analysis of training set;
(2) Randomly select the sub-eigenspace F_t of the t times clustering among original eigenspace;
(3) Randomly select k initial cluster centers in dataset X;

(4) Update initial cluster center;
   //in sub-eigenspace F_t, cluster data set X using k-means algorithm to generate cluster member π_t;
(5) Match h clustering members' cluster identifications;
(6) Calculate clustering consistency coefficient CI of the samples among minority class and majority class respectively;
(7) If minority class CI < α;
   Add samples to minority boundary area sample set P-Boundary;
(8) If majority class CI < α;
   Add samples to majority central area sample set N-Safe;
(9) If all class CI < α;
   Add samples to data set NewDataSet;
(10) Over-sample the samples in P-Boundary;
(11) Add new generated samples to NewDataSet;
(12) Under-sample the samples in N-Safe;
(13) Do classification learning to the re-sampled training set NewDataSet;
(14) Generate classification model H.

This algorithm only considered the size of clusters, ignored the data distribution features, may result in great difference between sampled data distribution and original data distribution, so it is not quite accurate to predict minority samples.

71.3 Imbalanced Data Classification Method Based on Clustering and Voting Mechanism

Normally, there are two limitations of clustering sampling methods, one is the great difference between sampled data distribution and original data distribution, the other is the low predict accuracy when processing minority samples. Hence, this paper presents an imbalanced data classification method based on clustering and voting mechanism, this method gets different clustering results through re-using one-pass clustering algorithm to divide data, and determines sampling proportion from the feature of final data clusters and data inclination, to preserve shape features of clusters. In imbalanced data sets, the amount of minus class is far more than plus class, thus minus class will be clustered to high density cluster. Consequently it can guarantee the sufficient amount of plus class because high density clusters will be less sampled, so the final samples can reflect original data distribution well through preserving the typical plus class and minus class samples information.

Let M to be the times or fusion times of re-executing clustering algorithm. co-ass oc[N][N] is the associated matrix between patterns, element co-assoc[j][i] is the times of pair oi, oj be divided into one class among all M different divisions. la[N] is a flag vector, element la[i] is the cluster number of which o_i finally be divided into. And r is clustering threshold value, while r_{Max} and r_{Min} stand for upper and lower limit respectively.

Detail procedures of algorithm are as follows:

Input: data set D, clustering threshold value, flag vector, associated matrix, distance between classes, radius threshold value, classification attribute value, numeric attribute

Output: clustering result

Procedures:

(1) Set all elements of flag vector and associated matrix to zero;
(2) Randomly select several object pairs in data set D;
(3) Calculate average distance between every object pair;
(4) Calculate average distance value of step (2);
(5) Let $r_{Max} = EX$, $r_{Min} = 0.5*EX$;
(6) Randomly select clustering threshold value in given scope $r \in [r_{Min}, r_{Max}]$;
(7) Execute algorithm 1 on data set D to get N_0 classes: $\{C1, C2, ..., C_{N0}\}$;
(8) For any two different objects o_i, o_j in class $C_k(k = 1, ..., N_0)$, add 1 to co-assoc(i,j) and co-assoc(j,i);
(9) Get new k clusters $C = \{C1, C2, ..., Ck\}$;
(10) For every cluster Ci$(1 \leq i \leq k)$, calculate SampleRatio following definition 3;
(11) Do simple randomly sample to Ci according to SampleRatio;
(12) Combine samples of every cluster Ci$(1 \leq i \leq k)$ to generate training set;
(13) Do classification learning to the re-sampled training set NewDataSet;
(14) Generate classification model.

71.4 Experiment Result and Analysis

71.4.1 Evaluation Standard

In order to verify the effectiveness of the method presented by this paper, we use three evaluation indicators: minority accuracy, G-mean and minority F-value. They are as Eqs. (71.1), (71.2) and (71.3). TN and TP are the sample amount of minority class and majority class of true classification respectively, while FN and FP are the sample amount of minority class and majority class of false classification respectively.

$$\text{Accuracy} = \frac{TP + TN}{TP + TN + FP + FN} \tag{71.1}$$

$$\text{G} - \text{mean} = \sqrt{\frac{TP}{(TP + FN)} \cdot \frac{TN}{(FP + FN)}} \tag{71.2}$$

$$\text{F} - \text{value} = (1 + \beta_2) \cdot \text{recall} \cdot \text{precision} / (\beta_2 \cdot \text{recall} + \text{precision}) \tag{71.3}$$

71.4.2 Simulation Experiment

Experiment software is LIBSVM, running on Windows XP OS; all experiments
are implemented by software programming based on Matlab 2009 and LibSVM
toolkit. In order to verify the effectiveness of the method presented by this paper,
select 7 second-class imbalanced data sets in UCI database, Table 71.1 shows the
feature descriptions of experimental data sets.

71.4.2.1 Experiment Result

Tables 71.2, 71.3, and 71.4 list the contrastive results among the algorithm
presented by this paper, simple randomly sample and one roundtrip clustering
sampling according to three evaluation indicator AUC, G-mean and F-value. Bold
text means the best results in our experiment.

71.4.2.2 Experiment Result Analysis

Known from Tables 71.2, 71.3 and 71.4, according to this paper presented algorithm, there are higher values of AUC, G-means and F-value among most
imbalanced data sets, and we can get a better result when records amount are more
than 1000 data sets in contrary to data sets which have less than 1000 records (i.e.
Cancer bell, mushroom, onehr); Considering F-value indicator, when applying to
severe imbalanced data sets (i.e. votes, Yea st-ME2) which they get a plus class
proportion less than 5 %, we can get a better minority classification performance
than other data sets. This is because minus class always be clustered to high
density clusters, then sampling a few of them, and discard a part of minus class to
balance original data sets, so as to improve the imbalanced level of data sets.

Because both under-sampling and simple randomly sampling can cause original
data missing, hence in some data sets, there is a performance reduction. The
algorithm presented by this paper can acquire a better result than simple randomly
sampling, that means the training set sample we get via our algorithm can preserve
the original data distribution features, and make the overall data distribution more

Table 71.1 Data sets feature description

Datasets	Size	Attribute	Min ratio	Min class
Cancer Bell	748	5	0.29	Recurrence events
Mushroom	863	80	0.41	Poisonous
Votes	5140	36	0.03	Disagree
Sick	5800	9	0.16	Sick
Onehr	990	10	0.09	1
Yeast-ME2	1484	9	0.05	Me2
German-credit	1000	24	0.3	Bad

Table 71.2 Experiment result among each data set according to AUG indicator

Datasets	Simple randomly sample	Algorithm presented by this paper	One roundtrip clustering
Cancer Bell	0.53	0.56	**0.61**
Mushroom	**0.68**	0.62	0.54
Votes	0.70	**0.80**	0.72
Sick	0.69	**0.72**	0.58
Onehr	0.65	**0.77**	0.60
Yeast-ME2	0.55	**0.70**	0.69
German-credit	0.48	0.63	**0.70**

Table 71.3 Experiment result among each data set according to G-mean indicator

Datasets	Simple randomly sample	Algorithm presented by this paper	One roundtrip clustering
Cancer Bell	**0.64**	0.35	0.63
Mushroom	0.80	0.69	**0.81**
Votes	0.76	**0.83**	0.80
Sick	**0.92**	0.79	0.68
Onehr	0.50	**0.89**	0.60
Yeast-ME2	0.55	**0.70**	0.69
German-credit	0.53	0.69	**0.72**

Table 71.4 Experiment result among each data set according to F-value indicator

Datasets	Simple randomly sample	Algorithm presented by this paper	One roundtrip clustering
Cancer Bell	0.55	0.60	**0.65**
Mushroom	0.45	0.32	**0.78**
Votes	0.82	**0.91**	0.88
Sick	0.54	**0.89**	0.82
Onehr	0.55	**0.97**	0.90
Yeast-ME2	0.55	**0.70**	0.6
German-credit	**0.85**	0.60	0.70

reasonable. Besides, although time complexity increases, our algorithm definitely has a better classification effect than one roundtrip clustering, especially significantly improved the classification accuracy of minority class.

71.5 Conclusion

Aiming at the imbalanced data distribution problem, this paper presents an imbalanced data classification method based on clustering and voting mechanism. This method gets new data cluster using voting mechanism after clustering, automatically determines sampling proportion and sampling the cluster according to the feature of every cluster, and apply the samples to classification and clustering of imbalanced data sets. The experiment result based on UCI data sets shows that the sampling algorithm presented by this paper preserves minus information well, improves the classification performance. The data classification method which has distinct class and large sample amount can get a better result than sampling method based on clustering. However, there are limitations of this paper presented algorithm, and how to adaptively select a more appropriate parameter β to separate different density clusters is our subsequent research subject.

Acknowledgments This work is supported by Scientific and Technological Enterprise Technological Innovation Fund of Jiangsu (No.BC2012201).

References

1. Wu J, Xiong H, Wu P et al (2007) Local decomposition for rare class analysis. In: Conference on knowledge discovery in data. New York, pp 814–823
2. Chawla NV, Bowyer KW, Hall LO et al (2006) SMOTE: synthetic minority over-sampling technique. J Artif Intell Res 16:321–357
3. Prati RC, Batista GEAPA, Monard MC (2008) A study with class imbalance and random sampling for a decision tree learning system. In: IFIP international federation for information processing. Springer, Boston, pp 131–140
4. Garcìa S, Herrera F (2009) Evolutionary undersampling for classification with imbalanced datasets: proposals and taxonomy. Evolut Comput 17(3):275–306
5. Yang Z, Qiao L, Peng X (2007) Research on data mining method for imbalanced dataset based on improved SMOTE. Acta Electronica Sinica 35(12):22–26
6. Chen S, Guo G, Chen L (2010) Semi-supervised classification based on clustering ensembles. In: Proceedings of the international conference on artificial intelligence and computational intelligence. Shanghai, China, pp 629–638
7. Yen S-J, Lee Y-S (2006) Under-sampling approaches for improving prediction of the minority class in an imbalanced dataset. Lecture notes in control and information sciences. Springer Berlin/Heidelberg, pp 731–740

Chapter 72
The Worst Case Minimized Upper Bound in #2-SAT

Wenxiang Gu and Honglin Wang

Abstract #SAT problem is NP-complete, so the small improvement of #SAT problems at the worst case (such as from $O(c^k)$ to $O((c-\varepsilon)^k)$) will make the efficiency of the algorithm improved in the level of exponent. In this paper, we present a new #2-SAT algorithm based on DPLL regarding the number of clauses as parameter. In order to improve the upper bound, we propose two new transformation rules and make a more elaborate analysis of the constraint graph for choosing better variables to branch. By analyzing, we obtain the new worst case upper bound $O(1.1740^m)$, which is the best result up to now within our knowledge.

Keywords #2-SAT · Worst case · Upper bound on the time complexity · DPLL

72.1 Introduction

#SAT problem is to count the number of satisfying assignments of a given proposition formula in conjunctive normal form (CNF), which is NP-complete, which can not be solved in polynomial time, so it is very important to analyze their computing complexity at the worst case. The subject of this paper is the #2-SAT problem, i.e. Counting models of the proposition formula that every clause in it contains two literals at most. In analyzing the time complexity at the worst case,

W. Gu · H. Wang (✉)
School of Computer Science, Northeast Normal University, 130117 Changchun, China
e-mail: wanghl101@nenu.edu.cn

W. Gu
Department of Basic Subjects Teaching, ChangChun Architecture and Civil Engineering College, 130607 Changchun, China

W. Lu et al. (eds.), *Proceedings of the 2012 International Conference on Information Technology and Software Engineering*, Lecture Notes in Electrical Engineering 211, DOI: 10.1007/978-3-642-34522-7_72, © Springer-Verlag Berlin Heidelberg 2013

researchers usually consider the SAT and #SAT problems from two perspectives: the number of clauses [1, 2] (denoted by m) and the number of variables [3, 4] (denoted by n). At present, in terms of clauses, the best result is $O(1.234^m)$ [2] in SAT, $O(1.1892^m)$ [5] in #2-SAT, $O(1.4142^m)$ [5] in #3-SAT; In terms of variables, the best result is $O(1.473^n)$ [6] in SAT, $O(1.246^n)$ [7] in #2-SAT, (1.6423^n) [8] in #3-SAT. The DPLL-based algorithm is one of the popular #SAT algorithms. The efficiencies of these algorithms depends on the transformation rules for simplifying formula and the choices of the branching variables. In [5, 9], it obtains better results that transform a formula into constraint graph and choose variables to branch through the analysis of the characters of the constraint graph.

In this paper, we present a new DPLL-based algorithm for #2-SAT, and we proposed new transformation rules and new methods of choosing branching variables combining with constraint graph in it. Finally we use the branching tree to analyze the time complexity of the algorithm and improve the worst case upper bound from $O(1.1892^m)$ to $O(1.1740^m)$.

72.2 Preliminaries

In this section, we introduce some essential notations and definitions. $v_i (i = 1,2,3...)$ denotes a boolean variable; x_i is the corresponding positive literal of v_i, and $\neg x_i$ is its negation. $C_i (i = 1,2,3...)$ denotes a clause, which is a disjunction of literals. $F_i (i = 1,2,3...)$ denotes a CNF formula, which is a conjunction of clauses.

The length of a clause is the number of literals it contained. If the length of a clause is k, we define it as K-Clause. 1-Clause is also called unit clause. A satisfying assignment is an assignment to every variable of a propositional formula making it true. #2-SAT is a problem of counting all satisfying assignments of a propositional formula, which only has 2-clause or unit clauses.

Such a 2-SAT formula can be transformed to an undirected graph called constraint graph. Given a formula F over a set V of variables, where $V = \{v_1, v_2,..., v_n\}$, we denote the constraint graph by $< V, E >$ with $E = \{(v_i, v_j)| v_i$ and v_j appear in the same clause of F, and $1 \le i, j \le n\}$. The elements in V and E are called vertexes and edges respectively in the constraint graph. We also make the following notations: $N(v_i) = \{v_j|(v_i, v_j) \in E\}$ denotes the set of the neighbors of v_i; $d(v_i)$ is the cardinality of $N(v_i)$ called the degree of v_i; $d(F) = \max\{d(v_i)| v_i \in V\}$ is the degree of F; $v_i \to v_j$ denotes the shortest path from v_i to v_j. We define the length of the path $| v_i \to v_j |$ as the number of the edges of the path. If there is a path $v_i \to v_j$ with $(v_i, v_j) \in E$, the path is a cycle. If none of the vertexes on the path (or cycle) is adjacent to other vertexes not on the path (or cycle), we called it disjoint path (or cycle). $U(v_i) = \{v_j | v_j \in N(v_i) \wedge (v_k, v_j) \in E \wedge v_k \notin N(v_i) \cup v_i\}$ is a set containing vertexes which are adjacent to v_i and other vertexes not in $N(v_i)$. $L(v_i)$ is the cardinality of $U(v_i)$.

72.3 Algorithms for #2-SAT

In this section, we will introduce the new #2-SAT algorithm, and prove its correctness. First, We conclude our new transformation rules for simplifying formula in the help function $Reduce(F,R)$ (see in Fig. 72.1). Considering a formula $F = (x_1 \wedge x_2)$, when x_1 is true, F is true, but x_2 has not yet been assigned. So we use a set R to record the variables like x_2, and $|R|$ is the cardinality of R. In Fig. 72.1, $F(x)$ denotes the new formula after assigning true to x. $F(x_1/x_2)$ denotes the new formula after replacing x_2 by x_1. It also means $x_2 = x_1$, so even though x_2 has not been assigned at the moment, it doesn't belong to R. $l(C)$ denotes a set containing literals in C. The inputs of the function are a required formula F and an empty set R. After processing the function, the simplify formula F doesn't contain unit clauses by (R1), the two variables that the literals of any clause in F corresponds to are different from that in any other clauses by (R2) and (R3), which are our new rules. So the number of clauses in F is equal to the number of edges in the corresponding constraint graph, which is convenient to choose branching variables by analyzing the constraint graph in the #2-SAT algorithm.

Then, we make a detailed introduction of the new algorithm. The basic idea of #SAT algorithm is as follows: First, choose one or more variable to branch for getting a number of sub-formulas of F. Then, the sub-formulas can be simplified again by transformation rules. This process will execute recursively until identify that every assignment satisfies F or not. Now, introduce two straightforward principles for #SAT based on DPLL. #SAT(F,R) denotes the number of satisfying assignments of F. $V(F)$ denotes the set of variables in F. If $F = F_1 \wedge F_2 \wedge ... \wedge F_n$ with $V(F_i) \cap V(F_j) = \varnothing$ ($i \neq j$), $F_1, F_2, ..., F_n$ are called disjoint components of F.

Theorem 1 [8] *Arbitrarily choose* $v \in V(F)$, *then,* #SAT$(F,R) =$ #SAT$(F(x),R)$ $+$ #SAT$(F(\neg x),R)$.

Function $Reduce(F,R)$

(R1)**if** F has unit clause $\{x\}$, **return** $Reduce(F(x),R)$.

(R2)**if** F has any two clauses C_1 and C_2 with the same variables v_1 and v_2, and x_1(or $\neg x_1) \in l(C_1) \cap l(C_2)$, $x_2 \in l(C_1)$, and $\neg x_2 \in l(C_2)$, **return** $Reduce(F(x_1),R)$(or $Reduce(F(\neg x_1),R)$).

(R3)**if** F has any two clauses C_1 and C_2 with the same variables v_1 and v_2, and both literals are complementary literals in C_1 and C_2, **return** $Reduce(F(x_1/\neg x_2),R)$.

(R4) **if** F is changed in (R1)-(R3), **then** goto (R1), **else return** (F,R).

Fig. 72.1 Help function Reduce(F,R)

Algorithm $MC_2(F,R)$

1. $Reduce(F,R)$

2. if F has an empty clause, **return** 0.

3. if F is empty, **return** $2^{|R|}$.

4. if $F = F_1 \wedge F_2 \wedge \dots \wedge F_k$ and $V(F_i) \cap V(F_j) = \varnothing$, where $1 \leq i < j \leq k$, **return** $2^{|R|} \times MC_2(F_1, \varnothing) \times MC_2(F_2, \varnothing) \times \dots \times MC_2(F_k, \varnothing)$.

5. if $|F| \leq 5$, **return** $E(F,R)$.

6. if $d(F)=2$,

    6.1 if F is a disjoint path, choose v to be a variable that can split F into two paths so that the length of one exceeds the other with no more than 1, **return** $MC_2(F(x),R)+ MC_2(F(\neg x),R)$.

    6.2 if F is a disjoint cycle, choose v arbitrarily, **return** $MC_2(F(x),R)+MC_2(F(\neg x),R)$.

Fig. 72.2 Function $MC_2(F,R)$ for #2-SAT

According to Theorem 1, *if we choose* $v_i, v_j \in V(F)$ *to branch, then* #SAT(F,R) $=$ #SAT$(F(\neg x_i, \neg x_j),R)$ $+$ #SAT$(F(x_i, \neg x_j),R)$ $+$ #SAT$(F(\neg x_i, x_j),R)$ $+$ #SAT$(F(x_i, x_j),R)$.

Theorem 2 [8] *Let* $F_1, F_2, \dots, F_n$ *be disjoint components of* F, *then* #SAT$(F,R) = 2^{|R|} \times$ SAT$(F_1, \varnothing) \times$ #SAT$(F_2, \varnothing) \times \dots \times$ #SAT$(F_n, \varnothing)$.

The #2-SAT algorithm contains four parts: $E(F,R)$, $MC_2(F,R)$, $MC_3(F,R)$ *and* $MC(F,R)$. $E(F,R)$ *is an exhaustive search algorithm for #2-SAT, when* $|F| \leq 5$. $|F|$ *denotes the number of clauses in* F. $MC_2(F,R)$ *is a function containing some cases which can be solved in polynomial time.* $MC_3(F,R)$ *is a function solving the case* $d(F) \leq 3$. $MC(F,R)$ *is the main function solving the case* $d(F) \geq 4$. *If* $d(F) = 1$, $|F| = 1$, *which can be solved in* $E(F,R)$. *The case* $d(F) = 2$ *is solved in* $MC_2(F,R)$ (Fig. 72.2).

The details of $MC_3(F,R)$ can be seen in Fig. 72.3. $V_3(F)$ denotes the set of variables whose degree is 3 in F. Similarly, $V_3(v \rightarrow v^*)$ denotes the set of variables whose degree is 3 on the path $v \rightarrow v^*$. In this algorithm, we first execute $MC_2(F,R)$ to simplify the formula, then deal with the case $d(F) = 3$. The main idea is that consider a variable v with $d(v) = 3$, analyze all cases which it faces of, choose a variable to branch to make $d(v) \leq 2$, and execute this process recursively until $d(F) = 2$. At last, we deal with the formula by $MC_2(F,R)$.

Now, we analyze all cases when $d(F) = 3$. In Fig. 72.4, we draw a picture of the constraint graph corresponding to the eight cases in $MC_3(F,R)$. Because $d(v) = 3$ for $v \in V(F)$, so $N(v) = 3$ and $L(v) \leq 3$. If $L(v) = 0$, F has only three clauses, and $E(F,R)$ is applied. So we only consider three cases: $L(v) = 1$(case 2.1), $L(v) = 2$(case 2.3 and 2.4), and $L(v) = 3$(case 2.2). In case 2.1, introduce a new variable v_1 (see in Fig. 72.4 ① and ②). Because $v_1 \in U(v)$, so $d(v_1) = 3$ (case 2.1.1) or $d(v_1) = 2$ (case 2.1.2). When $L(v) = 2$, we divide it into two cases: $|V_3(F)| = 1$(case 2.3) and $|V_3(F)| \geq 2$(case 2.4). For more efficiency, the case 2.4 is divided into four cases by $|v \rightarrow v^*|$, where $d(v^*) = 3$ and no more the degree of

Algorithm $MC_3(F,R)$

1. $MC_2(F,R)$.

2. if $d(F)=3$, choose v with $d(v)=3$,

   2.1 if $L(v)=1$,where $N(v)=\{v_1,v_2,v_3\}$ and $U(v)=\{v_1\}$

      2.1.1 if $d(v_1)=3$, **return** $MC_3(F(x_1),R) + MC_3(F(\neg x_1),R)$.

      2.1.2 if $d(v_1)=2$, where $N(v_1)=\{v,v_4\}$, **return** $MC_3(F(x_4),R)+ MC_3(F(\neg x_4),R)$.

   2.2 if $L(v)=3$, **return** $MC_3(F(x),R)+ MC_3(F(\neg x),R)$.

   2.3 if $L(v)=2$ and $V_3(F)=\{v\}$, **return** $MC_3(F(x),R)+ MC_3(F(\neg x),R)$.

   2.4 if $|V_3(F)|\geq 2$,and exists $v\to v^*$ with $V_3(v\to v^*)=\{v,v^*\}$

      2.4.1 if $|v\to v^*|=1$,**return** $MC_3(F(x),R)+ MC_3(F(\neg x),R)$.

      2.4.2 if $|v\to v^*|\geq 3$,where $N(v)=\{v_1,v_2,v_3\}$,$N(v^*)=\{v_1^*,v_2^*,v_3^*\}$, $v_2\notin V(v\to v^*)$, $v_2^*\notin V(v\to v^*)$, and $v_2\neq v_2^*$, **return** $MC_3(F(x_2,x_2^*),R) + MC_3(F(\neg x_2, \neg x_2^*),R) + MC_3(F(\neg x_2,x_2^*),R) + MC_3(F(x_2, \neg x_2^*),R)$

      2.4.3 if $|v\to v^*|=2$ and $V_3(F)=\{v, v^*\}$, where $V_3(v\to v^*)=\{v,v_1,v^*\}$, **return** $MC_3(F(x_1),R)+MC_3(F(\neg x_1),R)$.

      2.4.4 if $|V_3(F)|\geq 3$, $|v\to v^*|=2$ and $V_3(v\to v^*)=\{ v, v^* \}$, where $|v\to v'|=2$ and $V_3(v\to v')=\{ v, v^*\}$, **return** $MC_3(F(x',x^*),R) +MC_3(F(\neg x', \neg x^*),R) + MC_3(F(\neg x', x^*),R) +MC_3(F(x', \neg x^*),R)$.

Fig. 72.3 Function $MC_3(F,R)$ for #2-SAT

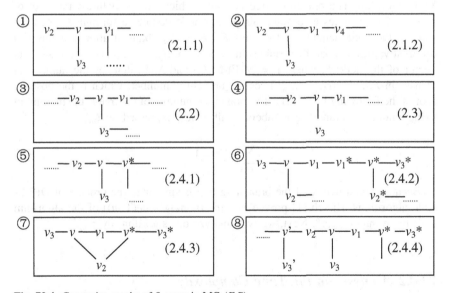

Fig. 72.4 Constraint graphs of 8 cases in $MC_3(F,R)$

any other vertex exceeds 2 except for v and v^*. $|v \to v^*| = 1$ is case 2.4.1, and $|v \to v^*| \geq 3$ is case 2.4.2. When $|v \to v^*| = 2$, we also divide it into two cases: $|V_3(F)| = 2$(case 2.4.3) and $|V_3(F)| \geq 3$(case 2.4.3). The analysis above contains all cases when $d(F) = 3$, so $MC_3(F,R)$ is right.

Algorithm MC(F,R)
1. MC$_2$(F,R)
2. **if** d(F) $\leq$ 3, **return** MC$_3$(F,R).
3. **if** d(F) $\geq$ 4, choose v arbitrarily with d(v) $\geq$ 4, **return** MC($F(x),R$)+ MC($F(\neg x),R$).

Fig. 72.5 Main function MC(F,R) for #2-SAT

The details of the main function MC(F,R) can be seen in Fig. 72.5. In MC(F,R), we also first execute MC$_2$(F,R) to simplify the formula, then choose different methods by judging d(F) $\leq$ 3 or d(F) $\geq$ 4. The main idea is similar to MC$_3$(F,R), i.e. Choose a branching variable v where d(v) $\geq$ 4 originally, and execute this process recursively until d(F) = 3. At last, we deal with the formula by MC$_3$(F,R).

72.4 Complexity Analysis for #2-SAT Algorithms

72.4.1 The Complexity Measure

First, introduce the branching tree used for computing time complexity for the #2-SAT algorithm. The branching tree is a hierarchical tree structure with a set of nodes, which denotes a formula. Suppose a node denotes a formula F, then the sons of the node denote the formulas F_1, F_2,...,F_n obtained after assigning all different values to a part of variables in F. A vector ($r_1,r_2,...,r_n$) is called branching vector of the node F, where $r_i = M(F)$-$M(F_i)$ and $M(F)$ denotes the number of clauses in F. $s = \tau(r_1,r_2,...,r_n)$ is called branching number, which is the positive root of the following Eq. (72.1). The branching number of the tree is the maximum value among the branching numbers of all nodes, expressed by τ_{max}.

$$\sum_{i=1}^{n} s^{-r_i} = 1 \tag{72.1}$$

Because the structure of the branching tree is similar to the process of DPLL-style algorithms, Hirsch [1] proved that the running time($T(m)$) of the algorithm isn't more than $(\tau_{max})^m$. Next, we will analyze our algorithm by τ_{max}.

72.4.2 Analysis on the Time Complexity

Now, we analyze the time complexity of the algorithm in this subsection.

Theorem 3 *Algorithm* MC$_2$(F,R) *runs in polynomial time.*

Proof As we know, case 1, 2, 3 and 5 run in polynomial time. Case 4 does not increase the running time. In case 6.1, choosing x to branch can split the path into two disjoint paths, so the time bounded by recurrence $T(m) \leq 4T(\lceil m/2 \rceil - 2)$, i.e. $T(m) \in O(m^2)$. In case 6.2, F is transformed into a path after assigning a value to v, so the running time $T(m) = O(m^2)$. As above, $MC_2(F,R)$ can run in polynomial time.

Theorem 4 *Algorithm $MC_3(F,R)$ runs in $O(1.1740^m)$ time.*

Proof Based on theorem 3, case 1 runs in polynomial time. Let us analyze the algorithm at following eight cases when $d(F) = 3$.

Case 2.1.1 when v_1 is fixed a value, every clause containing v_1 is removed from F. Then F' is generated with three variables (v_2, v_3 and v) and two edges, which is solved by $E(F,R)$. So, at least $3 + 2 = 5$ clauses are removed, we have the running time $T(m) = 2T(m-5)$, i.e. $O(1.1486^m)$.

Case 2.1.2 Similarly, when v_4 is fixed a value, F' is generated with four variables (v_1, v_2, v_3 and v) and three edges, which is solved by $E(F,R)$. And because if $d(v_4) = 1$, the formula meets case 5 in $MC_2(F,R)$, so $d(v_4) \geq 2$, at least 5 clauses are removed altogether. It follows that $O(1.1486^m)$.

Case 2.2 Suppose when v_4 is fixed a value, v_1 is forced to assign, which will cause the clauses containing v_1 are removed. But when v_4 is fixed the other value, v_1 would not be forced to assign. So the worst case is that when v_4 is fixed one value, v_1, v_2 and v_3 are all forced to assign, and at least 6 clauses are removed. The opposing assignment would reduce 3 clauses. So the running time $T(m) = T(m-3) + T(m-6)$, i.e. $O(1.1740^m)$.

Case 2.3 Because $V_3(F) = \{v\}$, F is transformed into two or more paths after assigning a value to v, which can be solved by $MC_2(F,R)$. For $|F| \geq 5$, at least 5 clauses are removed. It follows that $O(1.1486^m)$.

Case 2.4.1 Similar to case 2.2, the worst case is that when v is fixed one value, at least 6 clauses are removed. The opposing assignment would reduce 3 clauses. So this case also runs in $O(1.1740^m)$.

Case 2.4.2 When v_2 and v_2^* are fixed values, it will generate a disjoint path $v_3 \rightarrow v_3^*$, which can be solved by $MC_2(F,R)$. If $(v_2, v_2^*) \in E$, there is one assignment not satisfying F. So 8 clauses are removed under other three assignments, and the running time is $T(m) = 3T(m-8)$, i.e. $O(1.1472^m)$. But if $(v_2, v_2^*) \notin E$, 9 clauses are removed under other four assignments, and the running time is $T(m) = 4T(m-9)$, i.e. $O(1.1666^m)$, which is the worst case.

Case 2.4.3 When v_1 is fixed value, it will generate a disjoint path $v_3 \rightarrow v_3^*$, which can be solved by $MC_2(F,R)$. Because $|v_3 \rightarrow v_3^*| = 4$, so 6 clauses are removed. The running time is $T(m) = 2T(m-6)$, i.e. $O(1.1225^m)$.

Case 2.4.4 When v' and v^* are fixed values, F' is generated with four variables (v_1, v_2, v_3 and v) and three edges, which is solved by $E(F,R)$. Because $d(v') \geq 2$ and $d(v^*) \geq 2$, so 9 clauses are removed. So this case also runs in $O(1.1666^m)$.

In summary, the upper bound of $MC_3(F,R)$ is $O(1.1740^m)$.

Theorem 5 *Algorithm* $MC(F,R)$ *runs in* $O(1.1740^m)$ *time.*

Proof In $MC_2(F,R)$ algorithm, case 1 runs in polynomial time, and case 2 runs in $O(1.1740^m)$. In case 3, if $d(v) \geq 5$, at least 5 clauses are removed, the running time is $O(1.1486^m)$. If $d(v) = 4$, $U(v) \neq \emptyset$. Because if $U(v) = \emptyset$, the formula can be solved by $E(F,R)$. When v is fixed one value, at least one of v_1, v_2, v_3 and v_4 is forced to assign, and at least 5 clauses are removed. The opposing assignment can reduce 4 clauses. So the running time is $T(m) = T(m\text{-}4) + T(m\text{-}5)$, i.e. $O(1.1673^m)$. In total, $MC(F,R)$ will execute at most in $O(1.1740^m)$.

72.5 Conclusion

This paper proposes a new #2-SAT algorithm based on DPLL, and obtains the worst case upper bound $O(1.1740^m)$ regarding the number of clauses as parameter. The main method of improving efficiency is the elaborate analysis of the constraint graph to choose branching variables. So it is significant to combine DPLL-based algorithm with graph, backdoor and so on for #SAT problems.

Acknowledgments The authors acknowledge the support of the National Natural Science Foundation of China (61070084, 60803102, 60873146) and the Research Fund for the Doctoral Program of Higher (20050183065).

References

1. Hirsch EA (2000) New worst-case upper bounds for SAT. J Autom Reason 24(4):397–420
2. Yamamoto M (2005) An improved $O(1.234^m)$-time deterministic algorithm for SAT. IEIC Tech Rep 105(499):37–42
3. Monien B, Speckenmeyer E (1985) Solving satisfiability in less than 2^n steps. Discret Appl Math 10(3):287–295
4. Brueggemann T, Kern W (2004) An improved local search algorithm for 3-SAT. Theoret Comput Sci 329(1–3):303–313
5. Junping Z, Minghao Y, Chunguang Z (2010) New worst-case upper bound for #2-SAT and #3-SAT with the number of clauses as the parameter. Proceedings of the twenty-fourth AAAI conference on artificial intelligence. AAAI Press, pp 217–222
6. Brueggemann T, Kern W (2004) An improved local search algorithm for 3-SAT. Theoret Comput Sci 329(1–3):303–313
7. Fürer M, Prasad Kasiviswanathan S (2007) Algorithms for counting 2-SAT solutions and colorings with applications. Proceeding of the 3rd int conference on algorithmic aspects in information and management. Springer, New York, pp 47–57
8. Kutzkov K (2007) New upper bound for the #3-SAT problem. Inform Proc Leters 105(1):1–5
9. Dahllöf V, Jonsson P, Wahlström M (2002) Counting satisfying assignments in 2-SAT and 3-SAT. Proceeding 8th international computing and combinatorics conference. Springer, New York, pp 535–543

Chapter 73
A Frequent Concept Lattice Algorithm Based on FP-tree for Mining Association Rules

Wang Hui

Abstract Finding frequent item sets is a very important step in the process of mining association rules. However most of the classical association algorithms are low efficiency in this step. So a new algorithm for finding frequent item sets was proposed. The item sets are found in the concept lattice, and the concept lattice is generated on the basis of FP-tree. During building lattice, all nodes are formatted by the index of items appearing in the frequent-item head table. These nodes are selected by the support threshold. In the Hasse graph of the lattice, the intention of node is frequent item set and the extension of node is support count of this item set. All of these are benefit for generating association rules. The simulation shows the feasibility of the algorithm proposed.

Keywords Data mining · Association rules · Frequent item sets · Concept lattice

73.1 Introduction

The problem for discovering frequent patterns and extracting association rules is the key issues in the data mining field. To solve this problem, the Apriori algorithm was proposed by the Rakesh Agrawal originally [1]. Calculating frequent item sets is always the first step for mining the association rules. However, more candidate item sets will be generated in the calculating process of the Apriori algorithm, and the database will be traversed for many times. This reduced the efficiency of mining

W. Hui (✉)
Information Security Engineering Department, Chinese People's Public Security University, 100038 Beijing, China
e-mail: wanghui0330@gmail.com

W. Lu et al. (eds.), *Proceedings of the 2012 International Conference on Information Technology and Software Engineering*, Lecture Notes in Electrical Engineering 211, DOI: 10.1007/978-3-642-34522-7_73, © Springer-Verlag Berlin Heidelberg 2013

seriously. So many improving algorithms have been proposed in order to reduce the numbers of traversing database during the generating process, e.g. the FP-growth algorithm [2], the concept lattice algorithm [3–5], and so on.

The FP-growth algorithm was proposed by J Han. The candidate item sets will not be generated during the mining process of this algorithm. It only needs twice traversing database at the same time. But in the producing process of FP-tree, the FP-tree's depth depends on the number of items contained in each transaction, and the frequent item sets requires repeatedly generating sub-FP-tree and comparing links. These steps reduce the efficient for searching frequent item sets.

The concept lattice is a powerful tool for data analysis. It reflects the generalization and specialization relationship between concepts. The Hasse graph of the lattice is simple and easy to realize. It is more intuitive to discover association rules based on the Hasse figure. But the efficiency of constructing concept lattice directly determines the applicability of mining association rules. In order to mine associations quickly, the Discover Frequent Concept Lattice Algorithm (DFCLA) based on the FP-tree is proposed in this paper. The DFCLA is used to search the FP-tree by depth-firstly mining. And the advantage of the classic FP-growth algorithm is integrated into the constructing process of concept lattice. Experiments show that the algorithm is intuitive and efficient.

73.2 Related Concepts

In the following, the related concepts and definitions of association rules and concept lattice will be represented.

Definition 1 [6] Let item set $I_1 \subseteq I$, and the support of I_1 in the data set D is expressed as

$$Support(I_1) = \|\{t \in D | I_1 \subseteq t\}\| / \|D\| \qquad (73.1)$$

where, the support is the percentage of affairs in D, which contain I_1.

Definition 2 [6] The confidence of association rule $(I_1 \Rightarrow I_2)$ which is defined in the attribute set I and data set D, is expressed as

$$Confidence(I_1 \Rightarrow I_2) = Support(I_1 \cup I_2) / Support(I_1) \qquad (73.2)$$

where, $I_1, I_2 \subseteq I. I_1 \cap I_2 = \varnothing$. The confidence is the ratio of affairs number which is respectively included in $I_1 \cup I_2$ and I_2.

Definition 3 [6] The Strong Association Rule (SAR) is the association rule which satisfies with *Minsup* (Min-support) and *Minconf* (Min-confidence) in D and I. When SAR is a nonempty set, it is called frequent item sets. If any element of SAR doesn't contained by the others, it is called the maximum frequent item sets.

Definition 4 [7, 8] Giving a background as $T = (D, I, R)$, it is the group with three elements. Where, D is the transaction sets. I is the attribute sets. R is a relation and $R \subseteq D \times I$. If there is only one partial order relation to generate the lattice structure, the background is called as concept lattice.

Definition 5 [7] The node of lattice L is a ordered pairs and expressed as $\langle X, Y \rangle$. Where, X is a collection of transactions and called the extension. Y is the common attribute of all instances in X and called the connotation. Each pair is complete, expressed as

$$X = \alpha(Y) = \{x \in D | \forall y \in Y, xRy\}$$
$$Y = \beta(X) = \{y \in I | \forall x \in X, xRy\}$$
(73.3)

73.3 Mining Association Rules Based on DFCLA

In the process for mining association rules, the rules that satisfy the minimum support threshold are concerned only. According to the lattice space theory of item sets, the subset of frequent item sets is still frequent, and the supersets of non-frequent item set is still non-frequent [6]. Therefore, the maximum frequent item sets need to be concerned only. All of its subsets are still frequent item sets.

On the one hand, the concept lattice of DFCLA is generated on the basis of the FP-tree which is constructed by the classical FP-growth algorithm. Considering the Hasse diagram with the value of the 1 frequent item sets, the layers $L_i(i \geq 2)$ are generated by indexing Htable (Header-table) of the FP-growth algorithm. On the other hand, the nodes are selected by comparing with the minimum support threshold. So each node is frequent. And the connotation of each node is frequent item set. The maximum frequent item sets are composed of the connotations of leaf nodes. At the same time, the Sub-Hasse diagram with frequent node value 1 is not cross each other. And the association rules on Hasse diagram can be directly generated.

73.3.1 Building Process of the Frequent Concept Lattice Hasse Graph

Because only the support count number is required in the generating process of associations, X of the lattice node $\langle X, Y \rangle$ is set as the cardinal of extension. This is more beneficial to associations generating. The constructing process of the frequent concept lattice Hasse diagram is as follows:

Input   transaction database D, minimum support threshold *Minsup − count*.
Output   the Hasse diagram of concept lattice which is corresponding to D.

Step 1   Through scanning the database D once, the 1 frequent item sets are generated. The support count number is recorded. And then, 1 frequent items list T_F is obtained by descending the count number of the frequent items. Let the number of frequent item set with value 1 is N.

Step 2   Considering the Hasse diagram, the root of L_0 layer node is created, which is marked as $\langle \|D\|, \varnothing \rangle$. According to T_F, the L_1 layer is created. Its node is expressed as $\langle \|A_i\|, \{A_i\} \rangle$. Where, $A_i(i \leq N)$ was frequent items with T_F, $\|A_i\|$ is the support count number of A_i.

Step 3   Constructing the Htable and the FP-tree of T_F. Each node of the FP-tree is consisted of node name, node count number, node-link and pointer of parent node [8].

Step 4   According to the Htable's item order, each nodes A_i of FP-tree is respectively executed by depth-first searching, where $(i = 1, 2, \cdots N)$.

Step 5   If N = 0, turn to Step 8 else Step 6.

Step 6   Call function LatticeGen (FP-tree, A_i, Minsup-count).

Step 7   if $A_i = A_{i+1}$, then $N = N - 1$, turn to Step 5. //Layer $L_j(j > 1)$ of Hasse diagram is generated in above steps.

Step 8   Output the Hasse graph corresponding to D and support threshold.

Procedure LatticeGen (FP-tree, A_i, Minsup-count)

(1) begin

(2) if $(A_i.node - link \neq \wedge)$ then // the same name generates same node.

(3) for all the single path $P(A_iP_1, P_2, \cdots P_h)$ do //Same path does not calculate repeatly.

(4) Generate items combination starting as A_i, $\beta = A_i \cdots P_k(k \leq h)$

(5) for each combination β of generated node $\beta \langle X_\beta = P_k.count, Y_\beta = \{\beta\} \rangle$ //The $\alpha \langle X_\alpha = P_k.count, Y_\alpha = \{\alpha\} \rangle$ was the node had been generated.

(6) if $Y_\beta = Y_\alpha$ then $X_\alpha = X_\alpha + X_\beta$, Delete β

(7) endif

(8) endfor

(9) for $(n = 1, n > 0, n + +)$ do

(10) if $X_n < Minsup - count$ then

(11) Delete all the node of the Hasse diagram

(12) endif

(13) endfor

(14) for $(j = 1, j > 0, j ++)$ do

(15) if $Y_\alpha \subseteq Y_\beta$ then // α, β was adjacent layer node

(16) Connect the edge of α, β

(17) endif

(18) end

On the basis of the above processes, the Hasse diagram of the frequent concept lattice is constructed. The frequent item sets with value 1 were considered during the constructing process of FP-tree. For all projects contained by each transaction have been sorted in according with the support number, the related nodes of the Hasse-diagram's L_1 layer appear orderly. Because each nodes of the sub-Hasse diagram with value 1 appear orderly, the lattices are complete. And the above inner nodes are no-repeat, the Sub-Hasse diagram of frequent item sets with value 1 can be generated independently.

73.3.2 Relation Rule Extraction

After generating the Hasse diagram of frequent concept lattice, extracting rules becomes easier. Considering the Hasse diagram and letting the Minimum reliability as *Minconf*, in addition to root node the content of other nodes is frequent item sets. And the extension of the node is the support count number in transaction database D. Then the algorithm of extracting rules as follows:

Input   The Hasse diagram of the frequent concept lattice L (The layer number is k)

Output   Strong association rules (SAR)

Step 1   Each layer nodes $\langle X_i, Y_i \rangle$ and $\langle X_j, Y_j \rangle$ were considered in accordance with the bottom-up principle. if $Y_i \subseteq Y_j$, according to the definition 2, the *Confidence* can be expressed as *Confidence* $= X_j/X_i$.

Step 2   if *Confidence* $\geq$ *Mincof*, the association rules is given as $X_i \Rightarrow X_j - X_i$

73.3.3 Example Verification

In order to verify the effectiveness of the algorithm proposed, the sample database is selected in Ref. [4] and shown in Table 73.1.

As the Ref. [4], the minimum support count number is 2. The Htable and FP-tree of the sample database are shown in Figs. 73.1 and 73.2.

According to DFCLA, the frequent concept lattice Hasse diagram of FP-tree is shown in Fig. 73.2. The information needed for mining associations is as same as

Table 73.1 Sample database

TID	Transaction item sets
1	ABC
2	ACD
3	EFG
4	ABCD
5	A
6	BCD

Fig. 73.1 A frequent tree of the sample

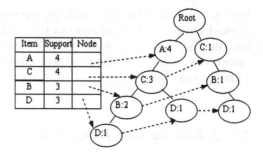

Item	Support	Node
A	4	
C	4	
B	3	
D	3	

Fig. 73.2 Frequent concept lattice Hasse diagram

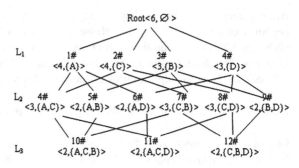

other results that are generated by using the algorithm of Ref. [4] and FP-growth algorithm.

According to DFCLA, the process of generating Hasse diagram can be described as follows. Firstly, during constructing the FP-tree, the root node and L_1 layer is directly generated. Secondly, according to the sequence of frequent items in Htable shown in Fig. 73.1, the remaining layer's nodes are generated independently.

For example, the generating process of the Hasse diagram for item A can be described as follow. Firstly, the sub-tree of item A has two branches and one public path. The branches are ACBD and ACD and the public path is AC. Secondly, according to DFCLA, the ACBD branch's nodes are $\langle 3, \{A, C\}\rangle$, $\langle 2, \{A, B\}\rangle$, $\langle 1, \{A, D\}\rangle$, $\langle 2, \{A, C, B\}\rangle$, $\langle 1, \{A, C, D\}\rangle$, $\langle 1, \{A, B, D\}\rangle$ and $\langle 1, \{A, C, B, D\}\rangle$. The ACD branch's nodes are $\langle 1, \{A, D\}\rangle$, $\langle 1, \{A, C, D\}\rangle$. Finally, merging above nodes according to the minimum support, we can get five nodes. They are $\langle 3, \{A, C\}\rangle$, $\langle 2, \{A, B\}\rangle$, $\langle 2, \{A, D\}\rangle$, $\langle 2, \{A, C, B\}\rangle$, $\langle 2, \{A, C, D\}\rangle$. The connotations of these nodes are frequent item sets needed.

The generating process of the Hasse diagram for other items C, B, D is similar to item A. Considering the frequent items in Htable, their nodes pointing to same item-name need to merge.

After generating Hasse diagram, the comparison of nodes' connotation with direct and indirect relationship will be executed by bottom-up principle. Meantime, through calculating the confidence, we can get the results. If the confidence is greater than the minimum confidence, the strong association rules will be generated. For example, considering the nodes 8# and 11#, if *Mincof* = 50 %, their confidence satisfy the inequality. *Confidence* $=X_{11}/X_8 = 2/3 > 50\%$. The strong association rule $CD \Rightarrow A$ is generated.

73.4 Simulation

To further illustrate the accuracy and effectiveness of the DFCLA, the matlab simulation of DFCLA, FP-Growth and the algorithm in Ref. [4] are done respectively. The mushroom data set of machine learning database UCI (http://archive.ics.uci.edu/ml/) is chosen as the simulation data. There are 8124 transactions and 23 properties. The data set is provided by American University of California.

In the process of simulation, different minimum supports (1, 5, 10, 15, 20 %) are chosen. The test of the processes for generating frequent item sets and all association rules is done by using three algorithms above. The simulation result is shown in Fig. 73.3.

From Fig. 73.3, the following conclusions are got. Firstly, the number of all frequent item sets generated by three algorithms is same. Secondly, when the minimum support is 1 %, the efficiency of generating frequent item sets is same. When the minimum support is less than 1 %, the time spending on constructing tree and lattice is overhead relatively. Thirdly, with the increase of support, the advantage of DFCLA becomes clear gradually. With the frequent item generation, more infrequent items are pruned. This reduces the times of comparison and improves the efficiency obviously.

In addition, we can also get the inclusion relation between frequent item sets. This can be visually reflected by the frequent concept lattice of DFCLA. And the confidence can be directly calculated by associating these nodes. This is convenient to extract the strong association rules.

Fig. 73.3 The simulation results of three algorithms

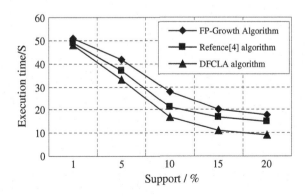

73.5 Conclusion

In this paper, the DFCLA algorithm based on FP-tree was proposed. The algorithm is used to extract association rules. The process for pruning branch is executed synchronously during constructing lattice. Considering the sub-tree corresponding to 1 frequent item, the algorithm reduces the comparing count between the sequence nodes. At the same time, because the Hasse diagram of the frequent concept lattice contains all information for extracting association rules the confidence can be directly calculated. This is more convenient to extract the strong association rules. It is shown that the DFCLA is effective and efficient by simulating and comparing with other algorithm.

References

1. Agrawal R, Imieliński T, Swami A (1993) Mining association rules between sets of items in large databases. In: Lecture notes in proceedings of the 1993 ACM SIGMOD international conference on management of data. New York, pp 207–216
2. Han J, Pei J, Yin Y (2000) Mining frequent patterns without candidate generation. In: Lecture notes in volume 29 of ACM SIGMOD international conference on management of data. New York, pp 1–12
3. Hu K, Lu Y, Shi C (2000) An integrated mining approach for classification and association rule based on concept lattice. J Softw 11(11):1478 (in Chinese)
4. Chen X, Wu Y (2011) Mining associations based on simplified concept lattice by improved algorithm. Appl Res Comput 28(4):1293 (in Chinese)
5. Liu S, Rao T, Sun J (2010) Non-redundant association rules extraction based on improved concept lattice. Comput Eng 36(10):52 (in Chinese)
6. Mao G, Duan L, Wang S et al (2005) Principles and algorithms of data mining. Tsinghua University Press, Bei Jing (in Chinese)
7. Wille R (1982) Restructuring lattice theory: an approach based on hierarchies of concepts. Ordered Sets. Dordrecht, Reidel
8. Vo Bay, Le Bac (2011) Mining minimal non-redundant association rules using frequent itemsets lattice. Int J Intell Syst Technol Appl 10(1):92

Chapter 74
The Research of Embedded Database Hybrid Indexing Mechanism Based on Dynamic Hashing

Huijie Chen and Jianwei Li

Abstract For the sake of improving the retrieval and insertion efficiency of embedded database when dealing with large-scale data, this paper was proposed a hybrid indexing structure based on dynamic hashing and designed a hybrid indexing mechanism combined with the characteristic of extendible hashing, linear hashing and red black tree. After retrieving and inserting large amounts of data, the results show that this hybrid indexing mechanism can make the time complexity of embedded database retrieval and update operation almost to be O(1). At last, the hybrid index mechanism provides for embedded database with real-time index insertion and record querying.

Keywords Embedded database · Hybrid indexing mechanism · Dynamic hashing

74.1 Introduction

With the developing of information and electronic technology recent years, the increasing sharply of information that need to manage by the embedded systems prompted the embedded device requires have more effective data management capabilities. The combination of embedded systems and database technology can greatly enhance the data management capability of embedded devices. Besides, the

H. Chen · J. Li (✉)
School of Computer Science and Technology,
Taiyuan University of Science and Technology,
Taiyuan 030024, China
e-mail: ghhong2004@163.com

H. Chen
e-mail: chenhuijie666@163.com

W. Lu et al. (eds.), *Proceedings of the 2012 International Conference on Information Technology and Software Engineering*, Lecture Notes in Electrical Engineering 211, DOI: 10.1007/978-3-642-34522-7_74, © Springer-Verlag Berlin Heidelberg 2013

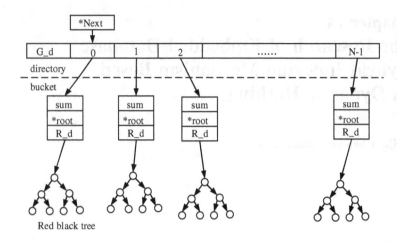

Fig. 74.1 Hybrid indexing structure

index mechanism is an important part of database system and determine largely the database operate performance. Therefore, the design of an efficient indexing mechanism used in embedded environments is essential.

However, most of the existing embedded database may make some real-time operation cannot be guaranteed. It is because of that the embedded database uses the dynamic growth tree structure as their index structure.

In order to solve the problem above mentioned, many hybrid indexing structures, such as Hybrid-TH tree [1], HT trees [2], H-Tail [3] and H-T*tail [4], was designed out. These hybrid index structures are divided into two parts, the upper is the static hash structure, and the lower part of it is the tree structure. However, with the amount of data increasing, this hybrid index structure needs to deepen the tree depth to accommodate the more data. Therefore, the data retrieval and insertion efficiency also will be further decreased.

This paper will present a new dynamic hashing splitting methods taking account of the characteristic of extendible hashing [5] and linear hashing [6], then design a hybrid indexing mechanism combined with red black tree [7]. This mechanism can solve the problem of the embedded database processing efficiency is continuing decrease when dealing with massive data.

74.2 Hybrid Indexing Structure

Hybrid indexing structure is shown in Fig. 74.1.

1. Directory. Figure 74.1 shows that the upper part of the hybrid indexing structure is directory. The directory consists of some directory entries. Directory entry numbers vary from 0 to N−1. The directory entry stored the corresponding bucket addresses. G_d [8] is the global depth of directory that

means that the number of the current directory need at least G_d bit to be coded. Next [9] is a pointer that pointing the directory entry that will be split. The changes rules are as follows:

$$Next = \begin{cases} Next + + & Next! = 2^{G\_d} - 1 \\ 0 & Next == 2^{G\_d} - 1 \end{cases} \tag{74.1}$$

2. Bucket. Figure 74.1 shows that the lower part of the hybrid indexing structure is bucket. The bucket is composed by the total of keyword stored in this buckets, the local depth of this bucket and the pointer to the red black tree root nodes. The local depth [10] means that the trailing bit of every keyword stored in the buckets are same. The relationship between the local depth B_d and global depth is $0 < B\_d \leq G\_d$. If two directories entry are point to one bucket at the same time, the bucket is called with shared bucket.

74.3 Hybrid Indexing Mechanism

The explanation of symbols:
   N: the total number of directory entries in the directory.
   H(x): the hashing function, input x and produce a integer.

- Search Operation

   1. K: get the keyword of record
   2. $M = \lfloor H(k) \rfloor_{G\_d}$. $M = H(k) \% 2^{G\_d}$
   3. get the directory entry number B(K) by the following formula:

$$B(K) = \begin{cases} \lfloor H(K) \rfloor_{(G\_d)} & (M < N) \\ \lfloor H(K) \rfloor_{(G\_d-1)} & (M \geq N) \end{cases} \tag{74.2}$$

   4. Search the nodes of keyword is K in the bucket that id = B(K).

- Insert Operation

   1. K: get the keyword of record
   2. $M = \lfloor H(k) \rfloor_{G\_d}$. $M = H(k) \% 2^{G\_d}$
   3. get the directory entry number B(K) by the formula (74.2).
   4. Insert the record into the bucket that id = B(K). At last check whether the barrel overflow. If do not meet the split conditions, this operation is over, otherwise, do the split operation.

- Split Operation

   Get the local depth B_d of the bucket the corresponding directory entry M that need to split.

1. If the bucket that need to split is not shared bucket, B_d = = G_d

   - j = G_d; G_d ++; the global depth should plus 1.
   - Get the directory entry number that the brother bucket of M. B_M = M|(1 < < j)
   - Expand the directory entry number to B_M.
   - Split the nodes of bucket to M and B_M bucket.
   - The local depth of bucket M and brother bucket B_M should plus 1.
   - The directory entry from N to B_M-1 should pointer to their brother bucket.

2. If the bucket that need to split is shared bucket, B_d < G_d

   - if G_d = B_d + 1

   (a) The smallest directory entry number pointer to bucket M is mini_M = M & ((1 < < B_D) − 1), and its brother bucket is max_M = mini_M|(1 < < B_d)

   (b) If max_M < N, it means the bucket max_M have already in the directory. The bucket M should split the bucket mini_M and bucket max_M. The B_d of mini_M and max_M should plus 1.

   (c) If max_M ≥ N, it means the bucket max_M is not in the directory. Then expand the directory entry number to max_M. The bucket M should split the bucket mini_M and bucket max_M. The depth of both of the bucket should plus 1. The directory entry from B to B_M - 1 should pointer to their brother bucket.

   - if G_d > B_d + 1

   (a) The smallest directory entry number pointer to bucket M is mini_M = M & ((1 < < B_D) − 1), and its brother bucket is max_M = mini_M| (1 < < B_d).

   (b) The bucket M should split the bucket mini_M and bucketmax_M. The depth of both of the bucket should plus 1. The directory entry from B to B_M − 1 should pointer to their brother bucket.

74.4 Simulation

74.4.1 Search Operation

The retrieval operation of the hybrid indexing mechanism is composed by hash operation and search operation in bucket. For the part of Hash, the time-consuming by calculating the location of the bucket can be negligible. These sections mainly discuss the average time trend of search operation in bucket. The time trend of average retrieval shown in Fig. 74.2.

Fig. 74.2 The time trend of average retrieval time

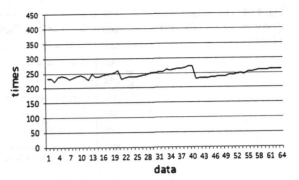

Fig. 74.3 The trend of fill rate

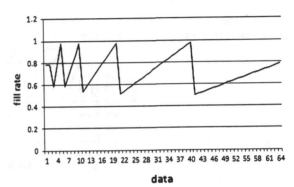

Overall, with the amount of data increasing, the average retrieval time trend tends to parallel. And some periodic fluctuations can see in the figure. The reasons for the retrieval time tends to parallel depends mainly on the tree depth of the red–black tree structure in the lower part of the hybrid index structure. And the bucket depth is strictly limited. For some fluctuations in the growth trend of the retrieval time, it is mainly affected by the bucket fill rate in hybrid index structure. The trend of fill rate is shown in Fig. 74.3 and the fill rate is calculated as follows:

$$\text{fill rate} = \frac{\text{the sum of data}}{\text{the number of bucket} \times \text{bucket volume}} \qquad (74.3)$$

74.4.2 Insert Operation

The Insertion operation of the hybrid indexing mechanism contains Hashing, the operation of insert nodes into the bucket and adjusting. For the part of Hash, the time-consuming by calculating the location of the bucket can be negligible. These sections mainly discuss the average time trend of inserting nodes into the bucket and adjusting.

Fig. 74.4 The average insert
time if the bucket depth have
a limit

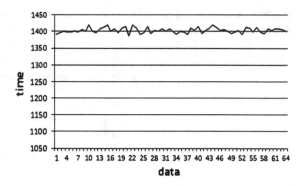

Fig. 74.5 The trend of
average adjustment time

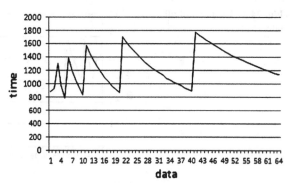

74.4.2.1 The Operation of Insert Nodes into the Bucket

The Insert operation efficiency will be decreased with the tree depth to be deeper. However, if the tree depths have an upper limit, the insert operation efficient will not increase. Figure 74.4 shows the average insert time if the bucket depth have a limit.

74.4.2.2 Adjusting

The adjustment process is composed by the directory expansion and the bucket split. If a bucket is overfilled, it needs to split into two partially filled buckets. The average adjustment time is shown in Fig. 74.5. The average adjusting time is calculated as follows:

$$\text{average adjustment time} = \frac{\text{the total of adjustment time}}{\text{the total of data}} \quad (74.4)$$

The trend of average inserts time shown in Fig. 74.6. The average insertion time is calculated as follows:

$$
\begin{aligned}
\text{the average insertion time} = {} & \text{the average insert a node time} \\
& + \text{the average adjustment time} \quad (74.5)
\end{aligned}
$$

Fig. 74.6 The trend of
average insert time

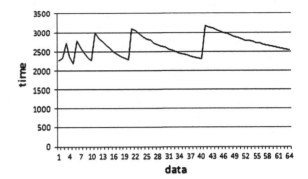

74.5 Conclusions

The experiment shows that the search operation complexity of hybrid indexing mechanism is O(1). The insert operation is affected by the fill rate of bucket and show a periodic fluctuations trend. And the time of insert operation have an upper limit. However, the drawback is that in the normal data insertion process, there will be a certain period of adjustment operations, the insert operations cannot continue during this time. It has to need use other techniques to improve.

Acknowledgments This work is under the support of the "Shanxi Province nature Foundation (No. 2012011027-3)", authors hereby thank them for the financial supports.

References

1. Ryu C, Song E, Jun B, Kim Y-K, Jin S (1998) Hybrid-TH: a hybrid access mechanism for real time main-memory resident database systems. In: Real-time computing system and applications 1998 proceeding, fifth international conference on 1998, pp 303–310
2. Jiali X (2003) H-T: an index mechanism for real-time main memory database systems. Comput Appl Softw 20(6):61–63 (in Chinese)
3. Lin P, Li H, Xu X (2004) Optimization of T-tree index of main memory database in critical application. Comp Eng 30(17):75–76 (in Chinese)
4. Chen J, Zhu W (2009) A new index mechanism fitted for the embedded database. Microcomput inform 25(3–2):84–86 (in Chinese)
5. Fagin R, Nievergelt J (1979) Extendible hashing—a fast access method for dynamic files. ACM Trans Database Syst 4(3):315–344
6. Litwin W (1980) Linear hashing: a new tool for file and table addressing. In: Proceedings of the 6th international conference on very large data bases, Montreal, pp 212–223
7. Hinze R (1999a) Constructing red-black trees. In: Workshop on algorithmic aspects of advanced programming languages, 89–99
8. Rammohanrao K, Lloyd JK (1982) Dynamic hashing schemes. Comput J 25 478–485
9. Rathi A, Lu H (1991) Performance comparison of extendible hashing and linear hashing techniques. ACM Press New York. Doi:10.1145/122045.122048.19-26
10. Larson P (1985) Performance analysis of a single-file version of linear hashing. Comput J 28:319–326

Chapter 75
Question Understanding and Similarity Computation Method Based on Semantic Analysis

Xia Yan

Abstract In order to search the similar questions accurately, this paper provides a question understanding method based on the semantic chunk recognition and the question split. Based on the understanding, a quadruple-based question representation model which represents a question as a quadruple is proposed. Furthermore, in order to deal with the different wording style of different uses in the QA community, a word similarity computation method based on synonymy thesaurus in the question similarity computation is brought up. Thereby, based on the above representation model and algorithm, a question similarity computation method based on the multi-feature fusion is provided. Experimental results show that the proposed model and method are successful, and can effectively improve the performance of similar question searching.

Keywords QA community · Similarity computation · Semantic analysis · Question understanding

75.1 Introduction

In recent years, there appears a new question and answering system—Community Question and Answering System (CQA), which is also referred as Q&A community, cooperative question answering system, and so on, for example, Baidu

X. Yan (✉)
School of Computer Engineering, Shenzhen Institute of Information Technology,
518029 Shenzhen, China
e-mail: yanx@sziit.com.cn64403182@qq.com

W. Lu et al. (eds.), *Proceedings of the 2012 International Conference on Information Technology and Software Engineering*, Lecture Notes in Electrical Engineering 211, DOI: 10.1007/978-3-642-34522-7_75, © Springer-Verlag Berlin Heidelberg 2013

zhidao,[1] Sinaiask[2] and Yahoo! Answers.[3] Compared to the traditional search engine based on keyword matching, in the CQA, users will ask a question and wait for the answers, and other users who know the answer will give directly his answer to this question. So, in the CQA, people can get the answers more quickly, accurately and effectively, and they don't need to browse lots of web pages before they find their needed answer as they usually do in the traditional search engine. And for this reason, CQA develops rapidly, and play important roles in many fields. CQA is now a research focus in the natural language processing.

With the development of CQA, CQA has amassed lots of problems which have been resolved by the users. Question similarity computation is a research focus in the CQA, which can be used to find the similar question. If a user asks a question which has been resolved before (or its similar question), CQA should return the user with the answers immediately based on the similarity computation between the asked question and the questions in the database. Now, researcher usually adopt the traditional Vector Space Model (VSM) to represent a question when computing the question similarity. This may cause many defects. CQA is an open platform, which allows any user to ask the question. Different people have different wording habit and different writing style, which will result in the following issue: the question structures and the words will be complex. So the traditional, single VSM can not deal with these complex issues. In order to understand the question correctly, we propose a question understanding method based on the semantic chunk recognition and question split, and then we propose a quadruple-based question representation model and a multi-feature fusion-based question similarity computation method. The experimental results show that these proposed methods are very successful.

In the following structure of the paper, Sect. 75.2 introduces the related work; Sect. 75.3 gives an emphasis on the question understanding method based on the semantic chunk recognition and the question split; Sect. 75.4 describes in detail the multi-feature fusion-based question similarity computation method; Sect. 75.5 discusses the experiments and result; Sect. 75.6 makes the conclusions.

75.2 Related Works

Researches about CQA have drawn the researcher's attention widely. In 2007, researchers of City University of Hong Kong developed an actuarial Q&A community [1]. Xin [2] used error-driven method in the classification of questions which achieve a good result. Young-In Song [3] adopted language model to represent a question to count the frequence of a question, and then used the result

---

[1] http://zhidao.baidu.com

[2] http://iask.sina.com.cn/

[3] http://answers.yahoo.com/

in the ranking of the questions. About the research of the semantic analysis, Yu [4] recognized the subject and subject focus based on the Minimum Description Length (MDL). Ang [5] carried out research on the answer extraction which is based on the query word and shallow parsing. When searching the similar questions, Fangtao Li [6] proposed to use a page ranking method which is based on the question subject and other semantic information.

AI Lab of the University of Chicago developed a system, referred as FAQ Finder. During the development of this system, researchers do lots of work about the semantic analysis and question similarity computation [7, 8], which are based on queried word matching, syntactic analysis and question subject recognition, and so on. Based on the test of answers, Stoyanchev [9] analyzed the influence of Name Entity on the performance of question retrieving. Chali [10] proposed to use the result of parsing and shallow semantic annotation to analyze the questions. Bunescu [11] proposed a new question iterance method when he searched the similar questions from CQA question database. Wang [12] did some research work on the automatic question extraction based on the parsing result. Li Cai et al. [13] proposed a new question similarity computation method, and they proposed to use the question subject, the query class and other parameter to create a semantic similarity computation method. And the proposed method worked successfully. Faguo [14] improved the keyword-based question model, and proposed to use the synonyms during the similarly computation, and then created a Q&A system.

75.3 Question Understanding Method Based on Semantic Chunk Recognition and Question Split

75.3.1 Semantic Chunk Recognition of the Questions

Question is a special sentence, has the special semantic function, and its expression style is also special. Analyzing the semantic of the question accurately is the basis and prerequisite of the accurate question similarity computation. In this paper, we adopt the semantic analysis method based on the semantic chunk recognition which is proposed by Fan [15]. In this method, the question will be split into five components: (1) question subject, (2) subject focus, (3) restriction information, and (4) query information, (5) other information. In order to better understand these components, we give some examples listed in Table 75.1.

Fan [15] adopted the CRF to recognize the semantic chunk, and devided the query information into 12 classes, which is listed in Table 75.2

Table 75.1 Semantic chunk of questions

Semantic chunk	Definition	Example
Question subject	Subject of the question	For the question: when will East Crystal
Subject focus	The additional information of subject	Electronic list? The subject is "East Crystal Electronic", and the focus is "list"
Restriction information	Restriction to the subject or focus, usually time restriction and location restriction	This year, In Shenzhen, yesterday...
Query information	Query word	What, how, when...
Other information	Words no meaning for the question	Thank you, please...

75.3.2 Question Representation Model Based on the Semantic Chunk Recognition and Question Split

Experimental results show that the above recognition method can effectively recognize the semantic chunk of the questions, and then we can represent a question as a quadruple. During the research, we find that the structures of the questions in the CQA are very complex, which may be a single sentence, but in many other cases, they are usually compound sentences. For example, the question—"*who is the creator of Baidu? When is it founded?*"—is a compound sentence. In detail, this question includes two questions, the former is about "People" class (Table 75.2), and the latter is about the "Time" class. So when we return the similar question for this question, it will include two parts (two questions), one for the former question, and the other for the latter question. Based on these analyses, in order to find the similar question effectively, we propose to split the question firstly, and then create the question representation model. But the compound sentences are complex because of the following issues:

Table 75.2 The classification of query information

Class	Example	Class	Example
Choice	How about appreciation of the RMB?	People	Who is the creator of Baidu?
Definition	What is the meaning of gravitation?	Process	How to decompose indicators of GDP energy intensity reduction?
Contrast	Please compare the cost of living of Beijing and that of Shanghai.	Quantity	What is the altitude of the top of the mountain?
Description	Please discuss the next year's stock market tendency.	Reason	Why these dresses have been marked down?
Entity	Where is the main engine located?	Time	When will East Crystal Electronic list?
Location	Where can I exchange my American money for foreign money?	Yes/No	Whether the meeting will go ahead as planned?

(1) On the one hand, we can also see that the semantic components of the latter question of the above question are in-complete, for example, there is no question subject (the subject of it should be Baidu).

(2) On the other hand, another question—*"what are the main micro-credit company in He Nan? I have never deal with this problem, please help me"*—is also a compound sentence, and can be split into two sentences. But the latter sentence (*"I have never dealt with this problem, please help me"*) is not a question which does not require to answer. But, in the traditional VSM, this information will affect the similarity between two sentences.

So, in order to get effective question representation model, there has to do some further analysis after the question split. We propose to use the Algorithm 1 to create the question representation model, which as follows:

Algorithm 1: Creating question Representation Model

Input: A question: S

Output: the representation of S

Then, the pseudo codes of Algorithm 1 are as follows:

Step 1: Split S into k ($k = 1, 2, 3 \ldots$) sentences: $s_1, s_2, \ldots, s_k$

Step 2: Suppose $s_i (1 \leq i \leq k)$ is the first question. Recognize the semantic chunk of s_i, and get the question subject (*sub*), the subject focus (*foc*), and the restriction information (*res*), the query information (*que*) and the other information.

Step 3: If s_i ($1 \leq i \leq k$) include all the semantic chunk, create the representation model of s_i as a quadruple: $<sub, foc, res, que>$, and each tuple is represented by a VSM. Else:

(1) If s_i has no *sub*, then $s_i(sub) = s_{i-1}(sub)$;
(2) If s_i has no *foc*, then $s_i(foc) = s_{i-1}(foc)$;
(3) If s_i has no *res*, then $s_i(res) = s_{i-1}(res)$;
(4) If s_i has no *que*, then $s_i(que) = s_{i-1}(que)$;

Step 4: Execute step 3 circularly to create the quadruple-based representation model of $s_j(i + 1 \leq j \leq k)$.

It's should be noted that step 3 is a recursive procedure, that is to say, when the semantic chunk of s_i is in-complete, it will use the relative information of s_{i-1}, and when that of s_{i-1} is in-complete, it will use that of s_{i-2}, until s_1.

According to the algorithm, we can create the representation model of the questions, which is based on the quadruples. Let's sum up the procedure: each question will be represented by k quadruples, and the each quadruple include $m(1 \leq m \leq 4)$ VSM. Please note that some semantic chunk may be in-complete, so m will not always be equal to 4.

75.4 Question Similarity Computation Method Based on Multi-feature Fusion

75.4.1 Word Similarity Computation Based on Synonymy Thesaurus

CQA is an open platform, and anyone can ask a question on this platform. Different users have different wording style. For example, the two questions: (1) *When will the teachers' salaries rose?* (2) *When will the schoolteachers' wages be raised?* These two questions are identical in meaning, but the words used in them are different, with the result that the similarity of them will be zero. In order to deal with this issue, we take the word similarity into account during question similarity computation.

Now, researchers usually compute the word similarity based on a certain semantic dictionary, for example, WordNet, HowNet and Synonymy Thesaurus, and so on. In this paper, we compute the word similarity based on the Synonymy Thesaurus which is developed by Information Retrieval Lab of Harbin University of Technology. And we used the method proposed in [16] to compute the word similarity.

75.4.2 Question Similarity Computation Method

As described in Algorithm 1, each question will be split into several simple sentences, and each simple sentence will be represented by quadruples, where each quadruple is a VSM. In order to compute the similarity more accurately, we take the simple sentence as unit when computing the question similarity. Suppose $S1$ and $S2$ are two simple sentences, and can by represented by $S1 = <sub1, foc1, res1, que1>$ and $S2 = <sub2, foc2, res2, que2>$, respectively. Then the similarity between $S1$ and $S2$ are computed based on Formula 75.1:

$$Sim(S1, S2) = (Cos(sub1, sub2) + Cos(foc1, foc2) + Cos(res1, res2)) \\ * SimT(que1, que2) \qquad (75.1)$$

where α, β and γ are adjustable parameters, which indicate the weight of every semantic chunk in the similarity between two questions, and $\alpha + \beta + \gamma = 1$. $Cos(sub1, sub2)$, $Cos(foc1, foc2)$ and $Cos(res1, res2)$ are similarity between subjects, focuses and restrictions of $S1$ and $S2$, respectively. All these three similarities are computed based Cosine, which is shown in Formula (75.2), where x and y are two VSM, w_{xk} and w_{yk} are feature's weight in the VSM, which is computed based on TFIDF (shown in formula (75.3)):

$$\cos(x, y) = \frac{\sum_{k=1}^{n} w_{xk} * w_{yk}}{\sqrt{\sum_{k=1}^{n} w_{xk}^2} * \sqrt{\sum_{k=1}^{n} w_{yk}^2}} \qquad (75.2)$$

$$w_{ij} = \frac{TF_{ij} * \log(N/DF_i + 0.01)}{\sqrt{\sum_{k} [TF_{kj} * \log(N/DF_k + 0.01)]^2}} \qquad (75.3)$$

where TF_{ij} is the term frequency of a word in a singly question, DF_i is document frequency of a word of all the questions.

Please note that we take the word similarity based on Synonymy Thesaurus into account when we use Cosine to compute the similarity between two simple sentences.

In the Formula (75.1), $SimT(que1, que2)$ is the similarity between two query information of two questions. Traditional research regards that the similarity between two different query classes is zero. But it is not always true. For example, the two question: (1) *how does the trend of warrants 580989 today?* (2) *Will warrants 580989 raise today?* The first question belongs to the description class, and the second question belongs to the Yes/No class, but they are very similar. So we propose to use the Formula (4) to compute the similarity between two query information.

$$SimT(que1, que2) = \frac{CSim(que1, que2) * (C(que1) + C(que2))}{2 * C(que1) * C(que2)} \qquad (75.4)$$

where $C(que1)$ and $C(que2)$ are the number of the questions belonging to $que1$ and $que2$ respectively, $CSim(que1, que2)$ is the number of questions which are similar, and at the same time, they belong to $que1$ and $que2$.

After we get the similarity of two simple sentences using Formula (75.1), we adopt the following Formula 75.5 to judge whether the two simple sentences are similar, where θ is a similarity threshold, which is trained using train corpus.

$$\begin{cases} if(Sim(S1, S2) > \theta) & S1 \ and \ S2 \ is \ similar \\ else & S1 \ and \ S2 \ is \ not \ similar \end{cases} \qquad (75.5)$$

75.5 Experiments and Results Analysis

75.5.1 Corpus and Evaluation Metrics

To test the validity of the proposed model and method, we firstly create the train corpus and test corpus. We gather 500 questions manually, where 300 questions are used as the train corpus, and the rest 200 question as test corpus. And then we extract 10 (3 % of them are compound questions) from train corpus and test corpus respectively to act as the user's questions, and the rest 90 % acting as the existing question which are already recorded in the database. The evaluation process is as follows: use the 10 as the question, search the similar question from the rest 90 % question in the database.

During the evaluation, we adopt the precision, recall and F1 score as the evaluation metric, which are computed by the following formulas:

$$precision_i = \frac{c}{m} \tag{75.6}$$

$$recall_i = \frac{c}{n} \tag{75.7}$$

$$F1_i = \frac{2 * precision_i * recall_i}{precision_i + recall_i} \tag{75.8}$$

$precision_i$, $recall_i$ and $F1_i$ are precision, recall and F1 when we use the ith question as the user question to search the question for similar questions. c is the number of the similar questions within the system retrieved questions, m is the number of questions system retrieved, and n is the number of questions which are actually similar with the ith question in the corpus. The system evaluation result is the average of all the 10 % questions evaluation results.

After trained on the train corpus, the proposed method achieve the best performance when $\alpha = 0.5$, $\beta = 0.4$ and $\gamma = 0.1$, $\theta = 0.77$.

75.5.2 Experiments Settings and Results Analysis

We then carry out four experiments to test the performance of the proposed model and method, the settings of which are as follows:

Experiment 1: In this experiment, we use the traditional single VSM to represent a question, and use the Cosine to compute the similarity between two questions

Experiment 2: In this experiment, we first carry out the semantic chunk recognition, and create the quadruple-based based on recognition result. Then use Formula (75.1) to compute the similarity. But we don't take the word similarity into account during the sentence similarity computation.

Table 75.3 Experimental results

Experiments	Precision	Recall	F1
Experiment 1	0.4495	0.4190	0.4337
Experiment 2	0.5647	0.5278	0.5456
Experiment 3	0.6002	0.6375	0.6183
Experiment 4	0.6873	0.7174	0.7020

Experiment 3: In this experiment, we first create the quadruple-based question representation model based on Algorithm 1, and then use Formula (75.1) to compute the similarity. But we don't take the word similarity into account during the sentence similarity computation.

Experiment 4: In this experiment, we first create the quadruple-based question representation model based on Algorithm 1, and then use Formula (75.1) to compute the similarity. At the same time, we take the word similarity into account during the sentence similarity computation.

The experimental results are shown in Table 75.3.

From the experimental results, we can see that the F1 score of experiment 2 is nearly 9 % higher than that of experiment 1, which indicates the representation model based on the semantic chunk is successful. At the same time, from the result of experiment 3, we can see that question split is also an effective work, which improve the performance effectively. Experiment 4 achieves the highest performance of all the four experiments, that is to say, word similarity based on semantic dictionary is also effective in the question similarity computation. From all these experiments, we can see that we must take the characteristic of question within CQA into account during similar questions searching.

75.6 Conclusions

In order to search the similar question accurately, we thoroughly study the question similarity computation method in this paper. We carry out mainly the two tasks.

Firstly, we propose a question representation model based on the semantic chunk recognition and question split. Semantic chunk recognition divides a question into five components, and question split will split a question into several simple sentences. And then a question will be represented by several quadruples. Experimental results show that the proposed model can improve the performance effectively.

Secondly, in order to deal with the informal wording of the question, we adopt the word similarity based on semantic dictionary during the question similarity computation. And then we propose a multi-feature fusion similarity computation method. The experimental results show the proposed similarity method is successful.

Therefore, we can conclude that we must take the characteristics of questions into account during the similarity computation between questions, for example, the question structure, the informal wording, and so on.

References

1. Song W, Feng M, Gu N, Wenyin L (2007) Question similarity calculation for FAQ answering. Third international conference on semantics, knowledge and grid, pp 298–231
2. Xin L, Xuanjing H, Lide W (2008) Combined multiple classifiers based on TBL algorithm and their application in question classification. J Comp Res Dev 45(3):535–541(in Chinese)
3. Young-In Song YCH-CR, Lin C-Y (2008) Question utility: a novel static ranking of question search. In proceeding of AAAI
4. Huizhong Duan C-YL, Cao Y, Yu Y (2008) Searching questions by identifying question topic and question focus. In proceeding of ACL, pp 156–164
5. Ang S, Minghu J, Yifan H, Lin C, Baozong Y (2008) Chinese question answering based on syntax analysis and answer classification. Electronica Sinica 36(5):833–839 (in Chinese)
6. Fangtao Li MH, Tang Y, Zhu X (2009) Answering opinion questions with random walks on graphs. In: Proceedings of the 47th annual meeting of the ACL and the 4th IJCNLP of the AFNLP, PP 737–745
7. Mlynarczyk S, Lytinen S (2005) Faqfinder question answering improvements using question answer matching. In: Proceedings of human language technologies as a challenge for computer science and linguistics. Poznan Poland, pp 33–40
8. Tomuro N (2004) Question terminology and representation for question type classification. J Terminol 10(1):153–168
9. Stoyanchev S, Young Chol Song AL (2008) Phrases in information retrieval for question answering. In: Proceedings of coling, pp 9–16
10. Chali Y, Joty SR (2008) Improving the performance of the random walk model for answering complex questions. In: Proceedings of ACL
11. Bunescu R, Huang Y (2010) A utility-driven approach to question ranking in social QA. Coling, pp 125–133
12. Wang K, Chua T-S (2010) Exploiting salient patterns for question detection and question retrieval in community-based question answering. Coling, pp 1155–1163
13. Cai L, Zhou G, Liu K, Zhao J (2011) Learning the latent topics for question retrieval in community QA. Proceedings of the 5th international joint conference on natural language processing, pp 273–281
14. Faguo Z, Bing-ru Y (2008) New method for sentence similarity computing and its application in question answering system. Comp Eng Appl 44(1):165–167 (in Chinese)
15. Fan S, Zhang Y, Ng WWY, Wang X, Wang X (2008) Semantic chunk annotation for complex questions using conditional random field. Proceedings of the workshop on knowledge and reasoning for answering questions, pp 1–8
16. Jiule T, Wei Z (2010) Words similarity algorithm based on tongyici cilin in semantic web adaptive learning system. J Jilin Univ (Inform Sci Ed), 06:603–605 (in Chinese)

Chapter 76
A Universal Heterogeneous Data Integration Standard and Parse Algorithm in Real-Time Database

Fei Chang, Li Zhu, Jin Liu, Jin Yuan and Xiaoxia Deng

Abstract The online automatic monitoring is a hot topic in the real-time application. Generally, the real-time data could come from different sources with different formats, resulting in difficulty in data parsing. To solve this problem, this paper proposes a Universal Heterogeneous Data Integration Standard (UHDIS) associated with a Parsing Algorithm to data of UHDIS in real time. The UHDIS could reduce the redundant information, leading high compression ability and transmission efficiency. For the parsing algorithm, we propose to parse data by utilizing template, which could map the integrated data of UHDIS to the desired tables in database. Based on this structure, our parsing algorithm could be adapted to different kinds of integrated real time data by adding new templates instead of changing the algorithm, thus has a good universality. We conduct experiments on data from the on-line environment monitoring system. As the experiments show, our approach has a good performance.

F. Chang (✉) · J. Liu
China Academic of Engineering Physics, Computer Application Institute,
Mianyang, Sichuan, China
e-mail: dongfangqiujian@gmail.com

J. Liu
e-mail: jliu@caep.cn.ac

L. Zhu
School of Software Engineering, Xi'an Jiaotong University, Xi'an, China
e-mail: zhuli@xjtu.edu.cn

J. Yuan · X. Deng
School of Computing, National University of Singapore, Singapore, Singapore
e-mail: yuanjin@comp.nus.edu.sg

X. Deng
e-mail: dengxiaoxiaxjtu@gmail.com

W. Lu et al. (eds.), *Proceedings of the 2012 International Conference on Information Technology and Software Engineering*, Lecture Notes in Electrical Engineering 211,
DOI: 10.1007/978-3-642-34522-7_76, © Springer-Verlag Berlin Heidelberg 2013

Keywords Universal heterogeneous data integration standard · Template · Parsing algorithm

76.1 Introduction

Recently, the real-time database technology takes more and more attentions and is widely used in various applications such as Industrial Control and Factory Automation etc. In the real-time data processing, it usually needs to collect different data formats from different devices, and then integrates these heterogeneous data to a uniform format which is suited for data storage in database. Currently, the typical data integrating approach is the OPC protocol, which utilizes the Microsoft COM/DCOM technology to collect and integrate data [1]. The OPC protocol requires the equipment vendors to provide the OPC server, and then the client side could collect and integrate data according to the OPC server [2]. This approach solves the problem of heterogeneous data integration to some extent, but has some shortcomings. First, the OPC protocol uses Microsoft's COM/DCOM technology, thus it is mainly used on Windows OS platform, leading to the low compatibility for other platforms. Second, in the OPC protocol, each device needs to provide the OPC server, and there exist a lot of data-driven programs to deal with different data formats, thus the developing cost is high. To avoid these problems, XML is widely used to heterogeneous data integration [3, 4]. Chirathamjaree et al. [5] proposed to integrate data with a Mediated Integration Architecture, while Liu et al. [6] proposed a grid service framework for heterogeneous data integration. In [7], Liu et al. proposed a middleware-based data integration approach. Although those XML-based approaches achieved some success, they have shortcomings. A notable drawback is the data redundancy problem where enormous useless or repeated symbols exist in the data such as the terminator "< \attribute >". Data redundancy is undoubtedly a major flaw since it occupies a large amount of network resources and disturbs the real-time property [8]. To alleviate the data redundancy problem, in [9], Shi et al. proposed SXML. However, compared to XML, the improvement by SXML is limited when the data size is <1 K. Another feasible approach is to compress data before transmission. In [10], Cheney et al. adopt textual compression algorithm to alleviate the data redundancy problem, however, this approach is time consuming, and only suited for the case with rich computing resource.

In this paper, we focus on monitoring the environmental data in real time. Our system works on Linux OS, with a limited computing resource and short data size (<1 K), therefore, the OPC protocol and the SXML compression algorithms fail in our system. To monitor real time data, we propose a Universal Heterogeneous Data Integration Standard (UHDIS) and its corresponding Parsing Algorithm. As Fig. 76.1 shows, in our system, the heterogeneous data are first collected from different sources by some data acquisition machines (DAMs), and then transferred to a uniform format (integrated data) according to our UHDIS. After that, users

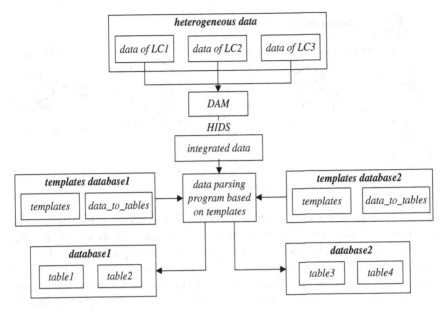

Fig. 76.1 The data processing in our system

provide the "Template" format and the to-be-saved tables in our database, and then our parsing algorithm automatically saves the integrated data into the indicated tables. Here, "Template" is a mapping structure which indicates the corresponding relationship between the attributes of the integrated data and the field of tables. There are two advantages of our approach: First, the integrated data format in UHDIS reduces the redundant information and saves the transmission time, thus it is suitable for real time monitoring. Second, when a new integrated data is added, we just need to add a new template instead of changing the parsing algorithm, thus our parsing algorithm is robust to various applications.

The rest of this paper is organized as follows. The Sect. 76.2 introduces the characteristics of real-time database system and online Environment Monitoring. In Sect. 76.3, we elaborate our Universal Heterogeneous Data Integration Standard, and in Sect. 76.4 we present our Parsing Algorithm. The Sect. 76.5 is the experimental results, followed by the conclusion in Sect. 76.6.

76.2 Related Work

76.2.1 Real-Time Database System

Real-time database system (RTDBS) is a database system. The information and data contained in it has the characteristic of timing or timing display. The correction of the system does not only rely on the logic result, but also rely on

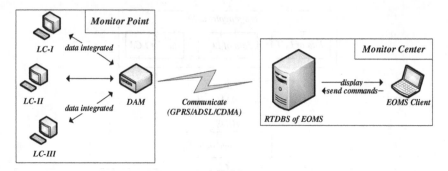

Fig. 76.2 The framework of online environment monitoring

the out-put time of the logic result. RTDBS stressed on both the characteristics of real-time and information handling from the traditional database. It's not the simple combination of the both things on their concepts, technologies and machines [10, 11]. Data in a real-time database are subdivided into two types: sensor data and derived data. Sensor data are data issued from sensors, and derived data are data computed using sensor data [12, 13]. Data from different kind of sensors is not the same format, so integration of heterogeneous sensors' data is an important part in real-time database.

76.2.2 Online Environment Monitoring

Data collection. A monitor center (MC) controls many monitor points (MP) on Online Environment Monitoring (OEM). The relationship between monitor center and monitor points is remote and local (as Fig. 76.2 shown). Every monitor point has many local machines (LM) which monitor different environment factors and collect different kinds of data. Common environment factors include polluted water and waste gas. In fact, it does not need to collect all data of a local machine, just collect part useful data. One solution is that a data acquisition machine (DAM) is used to collect the useful data from different local machines and transfer commands from remote computer (RC) to local machines in each monitor point, and then remote machine connects to the data acquisition machine, reads data and sends commands.

Real-time data requirement. There are diverse level monitors center with different priorities. Different priority monitor center focuses on different kinds of data; the deadline of different data is not the same. E.g. the MC of county is the highest priority because it collects data from DAMs directly; it focuses on real-time data which can reflect the environment status on time. The provincial MC has low priority for reading data from MC of County, it focuses on statistical data. In addition, the data from LM include real-time data, history data, alarm data, equipment status data, and so on.

$$\underbrace{\qquad\qquad Seg_g \qquad\qquad}_{} \qquad \underbrace{\qquad\qquad Seg_l \qquad\qquad}_{}$$

UHDIS: $\overbrace{ST = 32;CN = 2011;\underbrace{DataTime = 04051602}}$ & & $\overbrace{B01 = 100;\underbrace{101:Rtd=1.1,Flag=N}}$

$\qquad\qquad\quad \underset{Att_i}{\uparrow}\ \underset{Val_i}{\uparrow}\quad \underset{Att_g}{\uparrow}\ \underset{Cell_g}{\overset{}{}}\ \underset{Val_g}{\uparrow}\qquad \underset{Att_l}{\uparrow}\ \underset{Val_l}{\uparrow}\quad \underset{Cell_l}{\overset{}{}}\underset{Att_s}{\uparrow}\ \underset{Val_s}{\uparrow}$

XML: `<DATA>`
         `<ST>32</ST><CN>2011</CN><DataTime>04051602</DataTime>`
         `<B01>100</B01><101><Rtd>1.1</Rtd><Flag>N</Flag></101>`
         `</DATA>`

Note:

   ST: Index number for different polluted types such as air pollution, water pollution etc.
   CN: Index number for different data types such as real time data, historical data etc.
   DataTime: The time of data collecting
   B01, 101:Index number for different pollutant elements such as Hq, As etc.
   Flag: The flag of data
   Rtd: Indicate whether the data is real time

Fig. 76.3   Heterogeneous real-time data integrated by UHDIS and XML

76.3   Universal Heterogeneous Data Integration Standard

The data integration by XML has the following drawbacks: (1) high data redundancy; (2) large network bandwidth; (3) long communication delay. These characteristics of XML limit its application in monitoring real-time data. To solve these problems, in this paper, a UHDIS is proposed. In the UHDIS, a data is concatenated by multiple attributes and their values. Figure 76.3 illustrates an integrated data in UHDIS from the online environment monitoring system. In the following, we make some definitions:

   Global attribute (Att_g). This attribute is effective in the whole data such as the attribute "DataTime" in Fig. 76.3.

   Local attribute (Att_l). This attribute is effective in local area of the data. For example, "Rtd" in the string "101:Rtd" represents the amount of the pollution element 101 in the real time, it is effective only in the area of the attribute "101".

   Index attribute (Att_i). All index attributes in the data could be concatenated as a key in the table "data-to-tables" (see Fig. 76.4), which is a mapping structure to help finding the corresponding tables and templates for the data. For example, the template attributes ST and CN could be concatenated as (ST, CN) which is a key in the table "data-to-tables".

   Global cell ($Cell_g$). Global cell is composed of a global attribute and its attribute value.

   Local cell ($Cell_l$). Local cell is composed of a local attribute and its attribute value or multiple local sub attributes and their values. For example, the local cell "B01 = 100" satisfies the former style and the "101-Rtd = 1.1, Flag = N" is the latter style.

   Local cell ($Cell_l$). Local cell is composed of a local attribute and its attribute value or multiple local sub attributes and their values. For example, the local cell "B01 = 100" satisfies the former style and the "101-Rtd = 1.1, Flag = N" is the latter style.

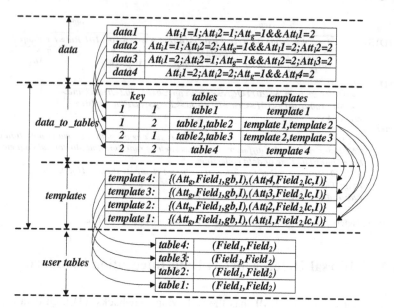

Fig. 76.4 An illustration of tables related to parsing algorithm

Global segment (Seg_g). Global segment is composed of all the global cells.

Local segment (Seg_l). Local segment is composed of all the local cells.

As Fig. 76.3 shown, the integrated data by our UHDIS has smaller bytes than that by the XML approach since the UHDIS does not need the terminator to identify the end of one attribute while the XML needs it. Therefore, our UHIDS provides a good compression performance for real-time data. The formal description of UHDIS is shown in the following grammar.

$$
\begin{aligned}
data &\rightarrow Seg_g \&\&Seg_l \\
Seg_g &\rightarrow Seg_g;Cell_g \backslash Cell_g \\
Seg_l &\rightarrow Cell_l;Seg_l \backslash Seg_l \\
Cell_g &\rightarrow Att_g = Val_g \\
Cell_l &\rightarrow Att_l:Cell_l \backslash Att_l = Val_l \\
Cell_s &\rightarrow Cell_s,Cell_s \backslash Attr_s = Val_s \\
Att_g &\rightarrow a\ string\ definited\ by\ user \\
Val_g &\rightarrow constant \\
Attr_l &\rightarrow a\ string\ definited\ by\ user \\
Val_l &\rightarrow constant \\
Attr_s &\rightarrow a\ string\ definited\ by\ user \\
Val_s &\rightarrow constant
\end{aligned}
$$

76.4 Parsing Algorithm

After data collection, the system needs to parse the data and store the data into the user tables in database. Since users have various requirements, leading to various data formats to be saved, thus our database should provide the corresponding tables to record different data formats. The parsing algorithm performs this task to parse various data formats and saves these data into tables in database. However, the difficulty of implementing the parsing algorithm is the algorithm universality problem that means the algorithm should be adapted to various data formats.

Therefore, in this paper, we propose a template-based data parsing algorithm. In our implementation, there are some tables (see Fig. 76.4) related to our parsing algorithm, In the following, we first introduce these tables, then we explain the detail of our parsing algorithm.

76.4.1 User Table

In the real application for real-time database, the system needs to collect the data as well as to store and display them in real time. As different applications and users need different data formats, the system needs to extract partial attributes from the integrated data to parse and to store; therefore, we create some user tables to save different data formats. For example, the integrated data in Fig. 76.3 will be saved in two user tables as follows:

$$
\begin{aligned}
&table1: (1st\ Field \rightarrow ``DataTime'', 2nd\ Field \rightarrow ``B01'') \\
&table2: (1st\ Field \rightarrow ``DataTime'', 2nd\ Field \rightarrow ``Rtd'', 3rd\ Field \rightarrow ``Flag'')
\end{aligned}
\tag{76.1}
$$

According to this expression, the integrated data is saved into two user tables. The first field in the "table 1" stores the value of the attribute "Datatime", while the second field saves the value of the attribute "B01". In the "table 2", there are 3 fields which save the values of the attributes "Datatime", "Rtd" and "Flag", respectively.

76.4.2 Mapping Integrated Data Into User Tables

Aforementioned, the integrated data may be saved in different tables according to users' requirements, therefore, we should create table "data-to-tables" to save the mapping relationship between the integrated data and the users tables. As illustrated in Fig. 76.4, the "data-to-tables" contains three fields: the first field "key" is comprised of the index attributes of integrated data. The second field "table" saves the names of user tables, if the integrated data relates to multiple tables, these tables are separated by a comma. The last field "template" stores the names of templates. If the templates are more than one, the template names are separated by a comma. In this table "data-to-tables", for an integrated data, we can find the corresponding

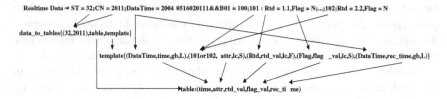

Fig. 76.5 An example of template

user tables and templates through the primary key. The "data-to-tables" table could find the user tables for each integrated data. However, it could not tell the mapping relationship between the attributes of integrated data and the fields in the user tables. As a result, we utilize "template" to identify this mapping relationship. As illustrated in Fig. 76.5, a template is composed of multiple quad-tuples defined in Eq. (76.2). In a quad-tuple, the first item "attribute" is the attribute name in the integrated data, the second item points to a field of the user table, the third and fourth one represents the attribute type and the value type, respectively. With the template, the parsing algorithm could save an integrated data into the user tables correctly.

$$Template = \{Qtuple_1, Qtuple_2, \ldots, Qtuple_m\}$$
$$Qtuple_1 = (Attribute, Field, Scope, Datatype) \tag{76.2}$$

Notes:
attribute: the attribute in an integrated data.
field: field name in user table.
scope: the scope of the attribute including global (gb) and local (lc).
datatype: types of attribute values including Integer (I), Float (F) and String (S) etc.

76.4.3 Algorithm Implementation

In this section, we describe our parsing algorithm. Before that, some tables described above should be created:

(1) Create series of user tables according to users' requirement.
(2) Create a template for each user table accordingly and store it in the table "template".
(3) Choose some global attributes from integrated data as index attribute, and then create the table "data-to-tables".

After all the tables created, we save an integrated data into the user tables by the following steps:

(1) Read the value of index attributes from the integrated data and generate the key.
(2) Find the user tables and the corresponding templates by the key in the table "data-to-tables".
(3) Get the attribute names and values from the integrated data according to the template.
(4) Save the attribute names and values into the user tables.

Algorithm 1 Parsing Algorithm

Input: An integrated data d

Output: The parsed data p

Definition:

   getKeyVal(): get key from an integrated data

   getTemplatesByKey(): get templates by a key

   getMapsOfTemplate(): get all the quad-tuples from a template

   getElementByMaping(): get value of attribute according to map in template

   CellN: the number of cells in an integrated data

Process:

   key = getKeyVal(d);

   templates = getTemplatesByKey(key);

   tpN = length(templates);

   FOR i=1 TO tpN DO

      tuples = getMapsOfTemplate(templates[i]);

      tuN = length(tuples);

      FOR j=1 TO CellN DO

        FOR k=1 TO tuN DO

          IF tuples[k].Scope == gb THEN

            p(i,j,k)=getElementByMaping(Segg,maps[k]);

          END IF

          IF tuples[k].Scope == lc THEN

            p(i,j,k)=getElementByMaping(Celll[j],maps[k]);

          END IF

        END FOR

      END FOR

   END FOR

   RETURN p.

76.5 Experiment Results

76.5.1 Evaluation on Data Compression

In this experiment, we compare the compression ability by our UHDIS to the typical XML approach. The data are collected from the online environment system. We randomly select 10–70 attributes from the data and describe these attributes by UHDIS and XML respectively. The results are shown in Table 76.1. Compared to XML, the data in our UHDIS has been greatly compressed, with an average 0.52 compression ratios which is defined as Eq. (76.3).

$$\text{Compression Ratio} = \frac{\text{UHDIS data length}}{\text{XML data length}} \tag{76.3}$$

This compression ability seems promising; as a result, our UHDIS could integrate heterogeneous data well in real time since the data transmission time is reduced.

76.5.2 Evaluation on Parsing Algorithm

In this experiment, we evaluate the parsing time of our Parsing Algorithm. Aforementioned, when the templates increase, the parsing time becomes longer. In this experiment, we record this change. We use three kinds of data from the online environment monitoring system: Real time data, Historical data and Alarm data. For all the data, the average length is almost the same. We set the template number from 2 to 6 and record the average parsing time on 20000 data, the results are shown as Table 76.2.

The results on Table 76.2 illustrate that the parsing time increases slowly as the templates increase. This change is linear as Fig. 76.6 shown. For these three data (Real-time data, Historical data and Alarm data), we calculate the linear function by the least square approach, and the results are shown as Eq. (76.4) where y is the parsing time and x is the number of template. From Eq. (76.4), we could make the following conclusions: First, the linear expressions are very similar for different data, thus our algorithm is robust to various data formats. Second, when we add a template, the parsing time only increases about 40 ms, thus our algorithm has a good scalability in template number.

$$
\begin{aligned}
y &= 40.550x + 616.6 \text{ for Real-time data} \\
y &= 40.575x + 606.4 \text{ for Historical data} \\
y &= 40.563x + 610.0 \text{ for Alarm data}
\end{aligned}
\tag{76.4}
$$

Table 76.1 Compression ability comparison between UHDIS and XML data

The number of attributes	10	20	30	40	50	60	70
UHDIS data Length byte	213	416	638	867	1023	1182	1458
XML data Length byte	405	813	1236	1656	2016	2257	2811
Compression ratio	0.525	0.511	0.515	0.523	0.507	0.523	0.518

Table 76.2 The parsing time comparison with different number of templates

Template Number	Real time data		Historical data		Alarm data	
	Data length (byte)	Parse Time (ms/20000)	Data length (byte)	Parse Time (ms/20000)	Data length (byte)	Parse Time (ms/20000)
2	980	694.5	997	690.25	986	692.375
3	997	734	981	726.5	986	730.25
4	995	772.5	985	760.25	986	766.375
5	998	827.5	961	820.25	986	823.875
6	993	850.5	989	846.25	986	848.375

Fig. 76.6 The change of parsing time with different numbers of templates

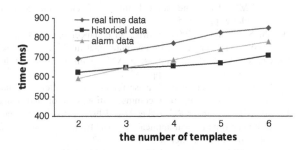

76.6 Conclusion

In this paper, a Universal Heterogeneous Data Integration Standard (UHDIS) and its Parsing Algorithm to integrate realtime data are proposed. The real-time data represented by UHDIS could be compressed well compared to the XML, thus UHDIS is suited for real-time data integration and transmission. In the parsing algorithm, specially designed templates are utilized to automatically parse and save integrated data. Based on the templates, our parsing algorithm could be adapt to various integrated data, thus has a good universality. As the experiments show, our approach has a good performance.

References

1. Jin Q-B, Wang Y-Y (2009) The crossing platform research of OPC data access based on FDT. IEEE 4th international conference on computer science & education, pp 981–985
2. Wu J, Ye M, Feng D et al. (2009) Application of OPC technology in monitoring system of AS/RS.IEEE 10th international conference on computer-aided industrial design & conceptual design, pp 2136–2139
3. Wu X, Yuan Y (2010) XML-based heterogeneous database integration system design and implementation. IEEE 3rd international conference on computer science and information technology (ICCSIT), pp 547–550
4. Xiong F, Xie H, Kuang L (2009) Research and implementation of heterogeneous data integration based on XML.IEEE 9th international conference on electronic measurement & instruments, pp 711–715
5. Chirathamjaree C, Mukviboonchai S (2002) The mediated integration architecture for heterogeneous data integration. IEEE Region 10 conference on computers, communications, control and power engineering, pp 77–80
6. Liu Y, Liu Z, Luo L (2009) Heterogeneous data integration framework based on grid service. IEEE international conference on network infrastructure and digital content, pp 871–874
7. Liu Y, Liu X, Yang L (2010) Analysis and design of heterogeneous bioinformatics database integration system based on middleware. IEEE 2nd international conference on information management and engineering (ICIME), pp 272–275
8. Pankowski T, Pilka T (2008) Dealing with redundancies and dependencies in normalization of XML data. International multiconference on computer science and information technology, pp 543–550
9. Shi S, Zhang R (2009) SXML, an enhancement of XML documents in mobile learning. International conference on computational intelligence and software engineering, pp 1–4
10. Cheney J (2001) Compressing XML with multiplexed hierarchical PM models. Data compression conference, pp 163–172
11. Yu J (2009) Real-time database for enterprise integrated automation system. International colloquium on computing, communication, control, and management, pp 632–635
12. Son SH, Beckinger RC, Baker DA (1997) A distributed realtime database server for high-assurance time-critical applications. The twenty-first annual international computer software and applications conference, pp 362–367
13. Ramamritham K, Son S, DiPippo L (2004) Real-time databases and data services. Real-time systems, pp 179–215

Chapter 77
The Research of Efficient Algorithm to Generate Sudoku Puzzle

Sen Huang, Jin-cai Huang, Qing Chen, Sheng-yun Liu and Yan-jun Liu

Abstract Method to solve a puzzle, evaluation of difficulty level, guaranteeing a single solution and time complexity are the main factors to generate Sudoku puzzles. This paper develops three kinds of Methods to generate a puzzle, namely Randomly Generating Method, Removal Generating Method and Construction Generating Method. Randomly Generating Method can generate simple puzzle with a high efficiency; Removal Generating Method is good at generating medium and difficult puzzles; Construction Generating Method has the latent capacity to generate those quite difficult puzzles. Then the complexity of algorithm is analyzed. Two techniques, Partly Greedy Strategy and Bit Wise Logical Operation, are used to reduce the complexity. Applying the two techniques generate a 9*9 Sudoku, the complexity is improved by 9^2 time theoretically. The algorithm can generate puzzles of high qualification with a high time efficiency, and the difficulty level of the puzzle must meet the requirement.

Keywords Sudoku · Complexity · Partly greedy · Bit wise logical operation

77.1 Introduction

Sudoku means "single number". The puzzle is played on a 9*9 grid and starting with numbers in the range of 1 through 9 given in some cells. One should fill it so that each row, each column and each 3*3 sub-grid contains 1–9 once [1]. The first

S. Huang (✉) · J. Huang · Q. Chen · S. Liu · Y. Liu
Science and Technology on Information System Engineering Laboratory, University of Defense Technology, 410073 Changsha, People's Republic of China
e-mail: huangsen_1987@163.com

W. Lu et al. (eds.), *Proceedings of the 2012 International Conference on Information Technology and Software Engineering*, Lecture Notes in Electrical Engineering 211, DOI: 10.1007/978-3-642-34522-7_77, © Springer-Verlag Berlin Heidelberg 2013

Sudoku Puzzle was published in the U.S., and became popular in Japan in 1986. The attraction of Sudoku is that the rule is simple but the task can be really difficult. The number of valid Sudoku Solution grids for the standard 9*9 grid was calculated by Bertram Felgenhauer in 2005 to the 6670903752021072936960. This number is equal to 9!*72^2*2^7*27704267971.

Generally, All Sudoku puzzles have one and only one solution. Maybe different people solve the puzzle in different methods, but the answer is ultimately the same. The difficulty level of a puzzle can be evaluated by the logical techniques used to solve it. The more advanced techniques used, the more difficult a puzzle is.

77.2 Flow Chart of the Algorithm

In order to have a holistic impression, the flow chart of the algorithm is given first. The algorithm generates puzzles with a single solution until the difficulty of it meet requirement (Fig. 77.1).

77.2.1 About the Solver

There are two methods to solve a puzzle: Logical Deducing Method and Brute Force Searching Method. The characteristics of the two methods are as follows.

Logical Deducing Method [2]: The time efficiency of the method is high. However, because the logical rules are limited and not advanced enough, it is possible that a single solution exists but the method cannot find it. Brute Force Searching Method [3]: By the traversal process, all the possible solutions can be

Fig. 77.1 Tough flow chart of logical consequence model

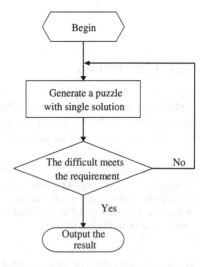

found. However, because of backtracks in the process, the time efficiency of the method is poor. In our algorithm, we combine the two methods to find a single solution effectively. The advantage of the combination is: It guarantees to find the single solution if it exists. Beside, the time efficiency is acceptable. And, there are two sufficient conditions to guarantee a single solution: if a Sudoku puzzle can be solved using logical techniques only, then it has a single solution [4]. Traversal and find all the possible solutions of the puzzle. If only one solution is found after traversal, the puzzle is guaranteed a single solution [5].

77.2.2 About Difficulty Levels

Generally, there are two kinds of evaluation of difficulty levels: it is assumed that when people solve a Sudoku, they use simple logical techniques first; if the simple techniques won't work, they'll try advanced ones. Hence the difficulty level of a puzzle can be represented by the most complex technique applied to solve it [6]. Secondly, the difficulty level should be evaluated by a variable. Grade techniques with points, advanced techniques with more points [7]. Trace the process of solving a puzzle, when a technique is applied, the points of that technique are added to the variable. Superimpose until the puzzle is solved. The bigger the variable is, the more difficult the puzzle is.

77.3 Three Generating Methods

77.3.1 Randomly Generating Method

Generating a Sudoku Puzzle is not an exact science. Here is a basic way to generate a puzzle [2].

Step 1: Place a random number (1–9) into a random grid within the field;
Step 2: Check if there are any immediate violations of Sudoku rules. If not, do it;
Step 3: Repeat steps 1 and 2 until k = K numbers have been placed in the grid;
Step 4: Check if the resulting Sudoku has a unique solution. If it has no solution at all, discard it and start with an empty field and step 1;
Step 5: If it has multiple solutions, repeat steps 1, 2 and 4;
Step 6: If it has exactly one solution, finish.

The value of K has severely impact on performance of the algorithm. If $K < 25$, there is a high probability that the resulting Sudoku has multiple solutions. As a result, the algorithm backtracks a lot and the time efficiency is poor; If $K > 35$, the probability is high to generate a Sudoku with no solution. Hence, the algorithm has to repeat the steps.

Fig. 77.2 Times to generate a sudoku

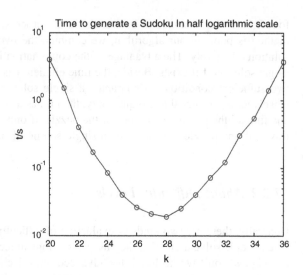

After running the algorithm for many times, it can get such result:

This process takes about 26 ms. It seems that K = 26 is a good choice. When K = 26, about 70 Sudoku puzzles are discarded before a valid one is found (Fig. 77.2).

77.3.2 Removal Generating Method

To generate a single solution puzzle, a nature idea is that: remove some cells of a full-filled puzzle, and the resulting puzzle is guaranteed being soluble. By using some strategies in the process of removing cells, it can control the resulting puzzles develop to the anticipated difficulty level. The process of the method is as follows.

Step 1: Scan the grid from left up to right down and generate a random number for each cell, guaranteeing it satisfies the rules of Sudoku;

Step 2: Choose S cells randomly and remove them, guaranteeing the resulting puzzle has a single solution;

Step 3: Choose a cell in a greedy style from all the removable cells and remove it.

Step 4: Evaluate the difficulty level of the puzzle. If the puzzle is up to the mustard, finish.

Step 5: If no cell in the puzzle is removable, go to Step 2; else go to Step 3.

Greedy: Greedy algorithm is shortsighted. We search some randomly chosen cells to find the one makes the resulting Sudoku the most difficult. **Removable Cells**: If the removal of a cell results in a puzzle with a single solution, the cell is called a "Removable Cell". **Up to the mustard**: A puzzle is up to the mustard when it satisfies the following two conditions:

Fig. 77.3 The relation curve between S and the probability to generate a puzzle with a single solution

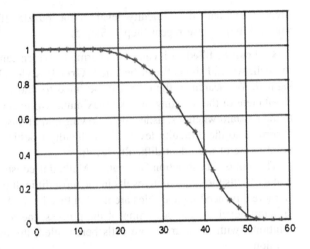

The logical rules used are accordant to the difficulty level. The Difficulty Coefficient of the puzzle is in the point range of accordant difficulty level.

In the procedure, it should choose some cells randomly and remove them before applying greedy chosen process. The reason is to Guarantee the variety of puzzles generated, provide necessary information for the greedy process and guarantee a high probability to get puzzles with a single solution (Fig. 77.3).

It can be seen when $S < 20$, the probability is almost 100 % to generate a puzzle with a single solution. However, if we remove only a few cells, there will not be enough information for the greedy process. In this algorithm, S is assigned 20.

77.3.3 Construction Generating Method

Construction Generating Technique tries to solve the puzzle in the opposite way with Removal Generating Technique. The soul of Construction Generating Technique is: start with a puzzle contains few filled cells; digits are filled into empty cells step by step through heuristic factors, and then a puzzle can be generated finally. If the generated puzzle has a single solution, output the result. The process of the algorithm is as follows.

Step 1: Scan the grid from left up to right down, and generate a random number for each cell, guaranteeing it satisfies the rules of Sudoku;
Step 2: Choose 64 cells randomly and remove them. That is, leave 17 cells in the grid randomly;
Step 3: Try to solve the resulting puzzle;
Step 4: If the puzzle is insoluble, find all the cells that can be filled. Choose a cell in a greedy style, fill a random number (1–9) into it and go to Step 3;

Step 5: Evaluate the difficulty level of the puzzle. If the puzzle is up to the mustard, finish; else repeat Step 1–Step 5.

Cell can be filled: If it can't be determined which candidates should be filled in the cell, we call the cell can be filled. **Greedy style**: Greedy algorithm is shortsighted. We search in the cells can be filled to find the one makes the Difficult Coefficient of the resulting Sudoku maximum. **Up to the mustard**: A puzzle is up to the mustard when it satisfies the following conditions: The logical rules used are accordant to the difficulty level. The Difficulty Coefficient of the puzzle is in the point range of accordant difficulty level;

The aim of Construction Generating Method is constructing the difficult puzzle. It always fills the cell which results in the most difficult puzzle in this method. That is, more advanced logical rules are needed to solve it. This process maximizes the difficulty level. At the beginning of the process, the resulting may have multiple solutions; with more and more cells being filled, the puzzle finally has a single solution.

77.4 Complexity Analysis and Improvements

In the following discussion, n presents the number of cells in a row of the puzzle. Suppose that there are m empty cells, each cell has n candidates, hence there are n^m states in the worst case. However, because of the rules of Sudoku and the usage of Logical Techniques, the actual complexity will be far better. From the analysis of solver based on Logical Techniques and Brute Force Searching Method, time complexity is $O(n^6)$.

(1) Complexity of Randomly Generating Technique
   The procedure can generate 2,000 full grids in a second; hence the complexity of this process is neglected. This technique removes k cells in $O(1)$ time and then finds if there are any removable cells randomly. Hence the time complexity is $O(n^6)$.
(2) Complexity of Removal Generating Techniques
   The time spent to generate a grid without empty cells can be neglected. Every time the greedy process judge if a single solution exists and evaluate the difficulty level, with complexity $O(n^2)$. This process run n^2 times at the most. Besides, the complexity of to solve a puzzle is $O(n^6)$. Hence, the time complexity is $O(n^{10})$.
(3) Complexity of Construction Generating Technique
   The time spent to generate a grid without empty cells can be neglected. In the initial state, there are only a few filled cells. This results in many times of Brute Force Search Technique. Determining whether a puzzle has a single

Table 77.1 Judgment and modification of state

Technique	Implement	Results	Time complexity
Judge if state m contain a candidate a	m and 2^a AND operation	=0, include >0, not included	O(1)
Delete a candidate from state m	m = m|2^a OR operation	–	O(1)
Find common candidates of two states m_1, m_2	m_1 and m_2 AND operation	–	O(1)

Table 77.2 Comparison of complexity before optimization and after optimization

Techniques	Randomly generating	Removal generating	Construction generating
Before	$O(n^6)$	$O(n^{10})$	Worse than $O(n^{10})$
After	$O(n^6)$	$O(n^8)$	Worse than $O(n^8)$

solution is the bottleneck of the algorithm. As a result, in the worst situation, the time complexity is worse than $O(n^{10})$.

In this part, two measures took in our algorithm to improve complexity of the algorithm are introduces. They are Partly Greedy Algorithm and Bitwise Logical Operations.

In the Removal Generating Method, it applies greedy algorithm to some randomly chosen cells instead of all the cells. Time complexity to search for local optimal is optimized from $O(n^2)$ to $O(1)$ (constant time) [8]. Partly greedy improve the speed of execution efficiently. Especially for generating a difficult puzzle, the speed is improved 5 times than without an optimization.

Bitwise logical operations are used to store and operate the state of cells. Suppose the candidates in a cell are a_1, a_2, ..., a_k (k = 1...9, a_i = 1...9, i = 1...k), the state of the cells is $2^{a1} + 2^{a2} + ... + 2^{ak}$. That is, we can use a number to represent all the candidates of the cell. For example, if candidates in a cell are 1, 3, 5, the result of bitwise operation is $2^1 + 2^3 + 2^5 = 42$. Hence, the state of the cell is 42.

By Bitwise Logical Operation, the modification and judgment of the state can be implemented efficiently (shown in Table 77.1).

The comparison of complexity of algorithm before and after optimization is shown in Table 77.2.

77.5 Results Analysis

Using the three methods, program can get the results shown in Table 77.3.

There are seven kinds of difficulty levels, including Easy, Medium, Difficult, Ex-Difficult (ED), Diabolical, Obscene, and Maximum Difficulty Coefficients (Max DC).

Table 77.3 Number of puzzles generated by the three methods in 1 min

Technique	Easy	Medium	Difficult	ED	Diabolical	Obscene	Max DC
Randomly	5,4392	617	121	3	0	0	172
Removal	1,723	1,120	219	64	33	347	375
Construct	94	61	12	1	0	0	168

Table 77.4 Average number of empty cells

Tech level	Average number of empty cells		
	Removal	Randomly	Construction
1	55.47	38.7	46.79
2	56.20	46.1	47.26
3	55.85	48.3	49.14
4	55.76	None	52
5	56.02	None	None
6	56.31	None	None

Table 77.3 shows the number of puzzles of different levels generated in 1 min. It can be seen that: Randomly Generating Technique generates puzzles at a highest speed, while the Construction Generating Technique generates at the lowest speed; Randomly Generating Technique and Construction Generating Technique can hardly generate hard puzzles, while Removal can generate hard puzzles easily; Randomly Generating Technique is good at generating easy puzzles. Removal Generating Technique is good at generating medium and difficult puzzles; The time efficiency of Construction Generating Technique is low. Besides, it can only generate some easy puzzles.

The distribution of numbers and cells is shown in Table 77.4.

It can be seen that: there is no obvious relation between difficulty level of a puzzle and number of empty cells. Puzzles generated by Removal Generating Technique have more empty cells.

Figures 77.4 and 77.5 can be seen that: each digit has almost the same probability to appear in a puzzle, and the distribution of digits in the puzzle is balanced.

Seed analysis results

The program generates two seeds (grid without empty cells, guarantee satisfying constrains of Sudoku) randomly, and applies Removal Generating Technique to generate 5,000 puzzles respectively.

The proportion of puzzles of each level of the two seeds is shown in Fig. 77.6.

It can be seen clearly that puzzles generated by the two seeds are almost the same in the distribution of difficulty level. The algorithm is steady and independent with the seed generated.

Fig. 77.4 Average times each digit appears in 100 puzzles

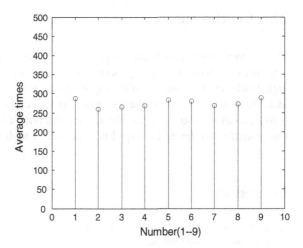

Fig. 77.5 Average times a digit appears in each cell in 100 puzzles

	1	2	3	4	5	6	7	8	9
A	26	36	33	30	33	21	28	30	31
B	27	30	33	34	36	34	34	32	21
C	34	25	35	38	26	28	26	32	28
D	20	27	26	20	28	31	32	33	40
E	24	31	34	36	28	29	30	29	31
F	23	32	30	34	37	38	34	33	32
G	34	27	36	26	31	40	22	32	28
H	39	27	28	29	29	28	30	22	31
I	27	31	31	24	19	35	24	32	31

Fig. 77.6 The distribution of different difficulty levels

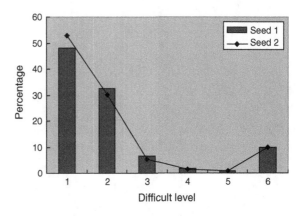

77.6 Conclusions

Three generating methods are proposed in this paper. Each method has its characteristics. The methods can generate puzzles of various difficulty levels with a high efficiency. Complexity of the algorithm is analyzed in detail. Some advanced measures are taken to improve the complexity, such as bitwise logical operations, partly greedy and so on. From the results analysis, it is found that the algorithm can generate puzzles of high qualification with a high time efficiency.

References

1. Sudoku (2007) Wikipedia, the free encyclopedia, (based on Oct 19th 2005 version) http://en.wikipedia.org/wiki/Sudoku
2. A-Crystal-Man Software Studio (2007) Help on iSudoku
3. Yato T, Seta T (2002) Complexity and completeness of finding an-other solution and its application to puzzles. Available at http://www.phil.uu.nl/oostrom/cki20/02-03/japansepuzzles/ASP.pdf
4. Lei L, Shen F-K (2007) Design and implementation of the algorithm about sudoku. Develop research and design techniques
5. Monfroy E, Saubion F, Lambert T (2004) On hybridization of local search and constraint propagation. In: ICLP 2004, number 3132 in LNCS, pp 180–194
6. Green D (2007) Conceptis Sudoku difficulty levels explained. http://www.conceptispuzzles.com/products/sudoku/solution_examples.htm
7. Abnormal Variety of Difficulty Coefficient (2007) http://oddest/nc.hcc.edu.tw/phpBB/viewpotic.php?t-127
8. Jarvis AF, Russell E (2006/2007) Mathematics of Sudoku II. Math Spectr 39:54–58

Chapter 78
Oriented to the Privacy Protection Role Based on Access Control Model and Conflict Studies

Chen Wang, Lianzhong Liu and Lijie Gao

Abstract Nowadays, people pay great attention to the privacy protection, therefore the technology of access control has been widely used, however, the current access control model for privacy protection has some defects, such as the lack of effective means to detect and avoid the conflict. Therefore, based on the analysis of existing models, this paper extended existing oriented to privacy protection RBAC models. We proposed an improved privacy protection model CA-PRBAC, which adds restrictions such as purpose, condition and obligation to original model, so that the new model has function of conflict avoidance; described the permission assignment policies for general resources and sensitive resources in detail, and designed algorithms based on the policies. Therefore, we can detect the conflicts during the privacy protection, and further enhance the privacy protection performance.

Keywords RBAC · Privacy · Privacy protection · Conflict

78.1 Introduction

In recent years, the technology of data mining has been widely used in information systems [1], which made a great contribution to the development of information technology. However, at the same time, data privacy is threatened by this technology. Therefore, privacy protection technology [2] appears to protect data from

C. Wang (✉) · L. Liu · L. Gao
Beijing Key Laboratory of Network Technology, School of Computer Science
and Engineering, Beihang University, Beijing 100191, China
e-mail: abomb007@126.com

W. Lu et al. (eds.), *Proceedings of the 2012 International Conference on Information Technology and Software Engineering*, Lecture Notes in Electrical Engineering 211, DOI: 10.1007/978-3-642-34522-7_78, © Springer-Verlag Berlin Heidelberg 2013

being disclosed during the application process. Access control is one of the methods to protect privacy. Its task is to prevent computer or network resources from unauthorized use and unauthorized access [3]. At present, the role-based access control (RBAC) model [4] has become the mainstream model of access control, and has a good scalability. To cope with different issues, scholars can make different extended models based on RBAC, thus make the models are suitable of related problems.

Based on existing research results, this paper improves the currently existing RBAC model and its extended model for privacy protection. Facing the problem exists in the original model that the model cannot effectively avoid conflict, we proposed an improved model and a method to detect the conflict, in addition, we design an algorithm to avoid the problem. Therefore this paper solves the problem of privacy protection to a certain extent.

78.2 Relate Research on the Privacy Protection

Ravi Sandhu proposed Role-Based Access Control 96 in 1996, after several years' development, the American National Standards Institute (ANSI) published RBAC American National Standards in February 2004. The basic idea of RBAC is to grant permissions to roles rather than directly to grant to principals, the principals gain the permission of access objects by the distribution of roles. RBAC is one of the most successful researches in the field of information security in recent years. RBAC not only can easily support the modeling based on levels, separation of duties, and dependent on constraint, but also has flexibility to support the other access control policies including DAC and MAC. Therefore RBAC has become the preferred model in the multi-domain environment. Many extended RBAC model have appeared after RBAC model was proposed. These models are based on RBAC, and tend to solve specific problems.

Anour and others proposed an extended model which is based on RBAC model. The extended model named PRBAC, sensitive resources section is added to the model for privacy protection in data mining. Users can access different data sets and mine in accordance with its role. The model first introduced the concept of sensitive resources, which can separate the sensitive resources and common resources. However, the model is not perfect. One serious problem is that the conflict during the distribution. In this model, there is no conflict detection and conflict avoidance algorithm, as a result, there are many problems in practical applications [5].

Qun Ni and others proposed an RBAC-based privacy policy. This policy uses purpose, condition and obligation to limit the strategy in permission assignment. However, this policy has no special treatment for sensitive resources, so it is easy for users to cope with the sensitive objects like common objects, resulting in the privacy risks [6].

78.3 Extended RBAC Model for Privacy Protection

78.3.1 PRBAC

In the previous section we mentioned PRBAC model, the model uses access control to protect sensitive resources. This model consists of six parts, namely, users (U), roles (R), session (S), permissions (P), resources (the Obj), sensitive resources (Sobj). Like RBAC, a role can be mapped to multiple permissions, and permissions can be assigned to multiple roles; permission is a symbol to allow access to resources or sensitive resources, and assignment of permissions is a policy to judge whether users can access. However, the model only add sensitive resources section to the basic RBAC model, and no increase in other conditions, as a result, a number of problems in RBAC has not been resolved through this model, such as the conflict.

78.3.2 CA-PRBAC

We propose a solution to the conflict in PRBAC model—Conflict-Avoidance Privacy-Aware Role Based Access Control Model (CA-PRBAC), to improve the existing PRBAC model. The model is shown in Fig. 78.1:

Components in the model are defined as follows:

- User (U): In this model, a corresponding user may be a person.
- Session (S): The activation of one's role in a subset of users need to establish a session.

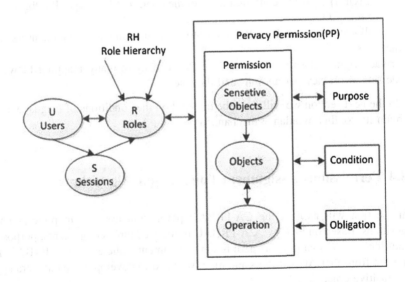

Fig. 78.1 CA-PRBAC model

- Role (R) and the Role Hierarchy (RH): A role correspond a responsibility within the organization. The role hierarchy is used to naturally reflect the relationship between rights and responsibilities of the characters; a high-level role can inherit the permissions of the low-level roles.
- Permission (Pe): Permission allow users to access resources.
- Operation (Op): An executable program, using for users to perform certain functions.
- Object (Obj): Include or receive the information entity, or have system resources can be exhausted (such as documents, video, etc.).
- Sensitive Object (Sobj): Sensitive objects, such objects is part of the objects, but they relate to sensitive data, so they have different access permissions. The objects can be a table or even a row of data.
- Purpose (Pu): The purpose of the operation is to achieve the goal.
- Condition (C): The prerequisite to perform operations, the usual case is a must.
- Obligation (Obl): The follow-up operation must perform after the operations on objects.

Compared with the original PRBAC model, CA-PRBAC model introduces three components: purpose, condition and obligation. The role must state the purpose before the operation, comply with the conditions laid down by the permission assignment, and carry out the corresponding obligations after operation.

Consider each component in CA-PRBAC as a data set, the relationship of components in CA-PRBAC can be defined as follows:

- Permission set $Pe = \{(op, obj) \mid op \in Op, obj \in Obj\}$. If the objects are sensitive objects, Pe set rewritten as $Pe = \{(op, sobj) \mid op \in Op, sobj \in Sobj\}$.
- Privacy permission set $PP = \{(pe, pu, c, obl) \mid pe \in Pe, pu \in Pu, c \in C, obl \in P(Obl)\}$. C is the condition to meet the condition language, P (Obl) is the power set of Obl.
- User allocation $UA \subseteq U \times R$, a many-to-many mapping between the users and the roles.
- Privacy rights allocation $PPA \subseteq R \times PP$, a many-to-many mapping between the sets of privacy permissions and the roles.

In the next section we will describe in detail on the conditions of language, and explain its conflict avoidance mechanism.

78.4 Permissions Assignment Policies and Algorithms

This section will explain the CA-PRBAC permission assignment policies and algorithms. Based on PRBAC, CA-PRBAC introduced three components: purpose, condition, and obligation. So permission assignment policies of CA-PRBAC is different from PRBAC. At the same time, we need to develop a separate strategy for sensitive objects.

78.4.1 Permission Assignment

Do not consider sensitive objects, the permission assignment strategy of CA-PRBAC can be defined as following set:

<R,Op,Obj,Pu,C,Obl>

Among them, R is the role, Op is the operation, Obj is the object, Pu is the purpose, C is the condition, Obl is the obligation.

In addition, C is the condition which meets the condition language. Condition language is defined as follows:

X is defined as a set of context variables; each x belongs to X in the limited domain of possible values, the domain is DX; Each domain has two kinds of relationships operator = and $\neq$. An atom condition (ac) is defined in X as (x opr v), where $x \in X$, $v \in DX$, $opr \in \{=, \neq\}$. When a condition in line with one of the following two situations, its condition can be said to meet the condition language:

(1) An atomic condition is a condition;
(2) If ci and cj are conditions, ci $\cap$ cj is condition.

For example:

(1) StuedntConsent, domain = {yes, no}
(2) AllowTime, domain = {7AM–3PM, 3PM–11PM, 11PM–7AM}

Both correspond with the language conditions.

For example, in school personnel management system, each element in the strategy as follows:

- R = {teacher, principal}
- Op = {read, write}
- Obj = {name, grade, age, sex, tel, email}
- Pu = {register, statistic, research, inform}
- Context variables = {StudentConsent, StudentAge, TeacherConsent, AllowTime}
- Obl = {mark, announce, exit}

When we consider the following policies:

1. "Teachers can access the student's email to inform their message."
2. "In the case of students allowed, principal can access the students' sex for statistics, and notice through the website."

These policies in CA-PRBAC as follows:

P1: (teacher, ((read, email), inform, N/A, ø)))
P2: (principal, ((read, sex), statistic, StudentConsent = YES, announce (ByWebSit-e))

78.4.2 Conflicting Detection

Let us consider the cases under which the permission assignment policies, conflicts arise. For example, the assignment policy 3 is:

"In the case of the teacher allowed, principal can access students' sex for statistics, and notice through the website."

This policy in CA-PRBAC as follows:

P3: (principal, ((read, sex), statistic, TeacherConsent = YES, announce (ByWebSit-e)))

The analysis with P2, these two policies are not in conflict. Conditions in these two policies can be merged to get a new policy P4:

P4: (principal, ((read, sex), statistic, StuedntConsent = YES∧ TeacherConsent = YES, announce (ByWebSite)))

However, let us consider P5:

"In the case of the teacher allowed, principal can access sex students who under 15 years old for statistics, and notice through the website."

P5: (principal, ((read, sex), statistic, StuedntAge = Under15∧ TeacherConsent = YES, announce (ByWebSite)))

The policy which direct merge P5 and P2 is P6:

P6: (principal, ((read, sex), statistic, StuedntConsent = YES∧ StuedntAge = Under-15∧ TeacherConsent = YES, announce (ByWebSite)))

The policy expression means: "In the case of the teacher and the students themselves allowed, principal can access sex students who under 15 years old for statistics, and notice through the website".

Obviously, the policy does not correctly represent the mean of the previous two policies, because the policy does not allow principal to access the sex of the students over age of 15. However, actually when principal attempt to access the sex of the students over age of 15, he does not need teacher's consent, he only need students' consent. This conflict is called the condition conflict.

To avoid this case, we introduce split context variables (SCV) to solve this problem.

SCV is defined as follows:

1. The SCV is related to the data subject information;
2. The value of the SCV can be divided into disjoint data set;
3. The SCV is not used to represent the consent information.

By definition, we can see that StuedntConsent is not SCV, StuedntAge and AllowTime are SCV.

Only when both C1 and C2 do not contain SCV, or they contain SCV but the values are same, they can be safely rewritten as C1∧C2.

Therefore, prior to the combination of P2 and P3 is correct to P4, but the combination of P2 and P5 to P6 is problematic. If we want to correctly express the meaning of the combination of P2 and P5, we need to rewrite P2 to P7:

P7: (principal, ((read, sex), statistic, StuedntAge $\neq$ Under15$\wedge$ StuedntConsent = YES, announce (ByWebSite)))

Together with P5 can correctly express permission assignment policy.

Let us consider when the conditions make conflicts arise. Obviously, the premise of the condition conflict is generated in the case of the same roles, objects, operations and purposes. Another premise of the condition conflict is that the conditions are comparable.

The definition of comparable conditions as follows:

c_i and c_j are conditions in two permissions assignment when there is a common SCV between c_i and c_j, their value sets do not intersect, called not-comparable conditions. Otherwise, we call that c_i and c_j are comparable conditions, written as $c_i \approx c_j$.

For example, c_i is AllowTime = 7AM–3PM, c_j is AllowTime = 10AM–6PM, then c_j and c_j are comparable condition.

For not-comparable conditions, there is no conflict between them. Such as P2 and P3 do not conflict in the previously mentioned examples.

For comparable conditions, we can be divided them into the compatibility conditions and conflict conditions. In the above example, c_i and c_j are compatible, because they have a common intersection of 10AM–3PM; however, if c_i is AllowTime = 7AM–3PM, c_j is AllowTime = 4PM–11PM, c_i and c_j are conflict conditions, because their intersection does not exist.

Therefore, if c_i and c_j are the two comparable conditions, when c_i and c_j exists at least one common context variables and the variable value does not intersect, then c_i and c_j are in conflict, denoted by $c_i \gtrsim c_j$. Otherwise, c_i and c_j are compatible, denoted by $c_i \approx c_j$.

Similarly, when c_i and c_j compatible, we need to consider whether obl_i and obl_j are compatible. Such as assignment policies P8 and P9:

P8: (principal, ((read, sex), statistic, StuedntConsent = YES, announce (By-WebSit-e)))

P9: (principal, ((read, sex), statistic, StuedntConsent = YES, exit))

Clearly, in the case of other conditions are same, the obligations of these two policies conflict. When simultaneously execute these two policies, we will not know the final action: notice through the website or exit directly. Similar to conditions, the conflicts between the obligations defined for $obl_i \gtrsim obl_j$.

As a result, the conflicts of the two permission assignment policies can be defined as follows:

Let $P_i = (r_i, (op_i, obj_i), pu_i, c_i, obl_i)$ and $P_j = (r_j, (op_j, obj_j), pu_j, c_j, obl_j)$ are two assignment policies. When consist with one of the following two conditions, P_i and P_j conflict:

- $(r_i = r_j) \wedge (obj_i = obj_j) \wedge (op_i = op_j) \wedge (pu_i = pu_j) \wedge (c_i \gtrsim c_j)$.
- $(r_i = r_j) \wedge (obj_i = obj_j) \wedge (op_i = op_j) \wedge (pu_i = pu_j) \wedge (c_i \approx c_j) \wedge (obl_i \gtrsim obl_j)$.

78.4.3 Permission Assignment of the Sensitive Objects

When the role attempts to access sensitive objects, the permission assignment policies will change. The policy can be defined as following set:

<R,Op,Obj,Sobj,Pu,C,Obl>

Among them, R is the role, Op is the operation, Obj is the object, Sobj is the sensitive object, Pu is the purpose, C is the condition, Obl is the obligation.

System need to label each sensitive objects, make it be different from general objects. But for attributes, they still belong to the objects; therefore, the conflict detection mechanism mentioned is still applicable.

Each sensitive object is a sub-object of the general object. Therefore, before access to sensitive data, the role must comply with the permissions to access the parent objects.

For example, a system contains personal information objects, and contains four sub-objects name, gender, telephone number, and email. Among them, the telephone and the email are defined as sensitive objects.

Assignment policy can be described as follows:

"In the case of the students allowed, principal can access students' info for statistics, and notice through the website."

In CA-PRBAC the policy as follows:

P10: (headmaster, ((read, info), statistic, StudentConsent = YES, announce (ByWebSite)))

However, because the telephone number and the email are sensitive objects, after the policy enforcement the principal is not allowed to access students' telephone number and email, but only be allowed to access to name and gender. In fact, the policy is equivalent to policy 11:

P11: (principal, ((read, name & sex), statistic, StudentConsent = YES, announce (ByWebSite)))

If the principal needs to access the students' telephone number and email, in other words access sensitive objects, we need to adopt permission assignment policy for sensitive objects:

P12: (principal, ((read, info, tel & email), statistic, StudentConsent = YES, announce (ByWebSite)))

In policy 12, principal can completely access students' personal information.

78.4.4 Conflict Detection Algorithm

Based on previous mentioned permission assignment policies, we designed the CA-PRBAC model-based conflict detection algorithm. The core idea of this algorithm is based on each subset of conditions and obligations in alphabetical order, compare each subset of conditions and obligations respectively. For subsets of obligations, we only need to compare the same sub-set value, if not equal then

Table 78.1 Conflict detection algorithm

Algorithm: Conflict Detection Algorithm
Input: Policy1, Policy 2
Output: Conflict/Not Conflict
Initialization: *Sort Condition 1 of Policy 1 in Alphabetical Order for Sub-conditions*   *Sort Obligation 1 of Policy 1 in Alphabetical Order for Sub-obligations*   *Sort Condition 2 of Policy 2 in Alphabetical Order for Sub-conditions*   *Sort Obligation 2 of Policy 2 in Alphabetical Order for Sub-obligations*   *Result* = Not Conflict

Process:
 For each *Context Variables* of *Condition 1* Do
   For each *Context Variables* of *Condition 2* Do
     If *Context Variable i* of *Condition 1*= = *Context Variables j* of *Condition 2*
       If *Context Variable i* is not *SCV*
         If *Value of Context Variable i* ! = *Value of Context Variable j*
           Result = Conflict;
           Break;
         Else
           i + +; *j* + +;
         End If
       Else If *Context Variable i* is SCV
         If *Value of Context Variable i* && *Value of Context Variable j* = = ⌀
           Result = Conflict;
           Break;
         Else
           i + +; *j* + +;
         End If
       Else
         i + +; *j* + +;
     End If
   End For
 End For
 For each *Context Variables* of *Obligation 1* Do
   For each *Context Variables* of *Obligation 2* Do
     If *Context Variable iof Obligation 1* = = *Context Variables jofObligation 2*
       If *Value of Context Variable i* ! = *Value of Context Variable j*
         Result = Conflict;
         Break;
       Else
         i + +; *j* + +;
       End If
     Else
       i + +; *j* + +;
     End If
   End For
 End For

determine the two obligations conflict; for subsets of the conditions, we need to divided them into two cases: (1) subsets are not split context variables (SCV), we only need to compare the same sub-set value, if not equal then determine the two conditions conflict; (2) subsets are split context variables (SCV), we need to judge whether the value of the same subsets have intersection, if not have then determine the two conditions conflict. Based on these we can propose a conflict detection algorithm for two assignment policies (Table 78.1).

78.4.5 Existing Problem

The model and permission assignment policies still have some problems. One of the most important problem is the emergence of redundancy in the assignment policies. For example, personal information object includes two sub-objects name and sex, let us consider the Policy 13 and Policy 14:

$P13$: (teacher, ((read, info), statistic, StudentConsent = YES, ø))

$P14$: (teacher, ((read, name & sex), statistic, StudentConsent = YES, ø))

The performance of these two policies are: "In the case of the students allowed, teacher can access students' name and sex for statistics". However, since the system cannot identify that name and sex are the only two sub-objects of info, the two policies will be executed at the same time, but in fact they are functionally identical.

78.5 Conclusion

In this paper, we analyzed the existing privacy-oriented RBAC model, and propose an improved model to solve the problems existing in the previous extended RBAC model, by means of introducing components like purpose, condition and obligation; analyzed the reason of conflict in the original model and proposed the solution, to avoid the conflict; retained sensitive objects component and disposed the sensitive objects independently, so that the privacy will not be disclosed. At the same time, we designed algorithms according to permission assignment policies. Finally, we proposed some problems in the model, solving these problems is our future work.

Acknowledgments This work has been supported by Co-Funding Project of Beijing Municipal Education Commission under Grant No. JD100060630.

References

1. Han J, Kamber M (2006) Data mining: concepts and techniques, 2nd edn. Morgan Kaufmann Publishers, San Francisco
2. Verykios VS, Bertino E, Fovino IN, Provenza LP, Saygin Y, Theodoridis Y (2004) State-of-the-art in privacy preserving data mining. ACM SIGMOD Rec 3(1):50–57
3. Sandhu R, Samarati P (1994) Access control: principles and practice. IEEE Commun Mag 32(9):40–48
4. Sandhu R, Coyne E, Feinstein H et al (1996) Role-based access control models. IEEE Comput V29(2):38–47
5. Dafa-Alla AFA, Kim EH, Ryu KH, Heo YJ (2005) PRBAC: An extended role based access control for privacy preserving data mining. In: Proceedings of the fourth annual ACIS international conference on computer and information science
6. Ni Q, Bertino E, Lobo J, Brodie C, Karat C-M, Karat J, Trombeta A (2010) Privacy-aware role-based access control. ACM Trans Inf Syst Secur 13:24:1–24:31

Chapter 79
Simulation and Stability Analysis of SRM Speed Control System Based on Fuzzy Self-Tuning PID

Jialiang Gan and Zhimin Li

Abstract A dynamic simulation model for SRM (switched reluctance motor) speed control system based on fuzzy self-tuning PID is established in the environment of MATLAB/Simulink. Comparing with the result of the SRM speed control system based on conventional PID, the performance of SRM speed control system by fuzzy self-tuning PID control algorithm is obviously better. Stability analysis for the SRM speed control system is carried out by using a new stability criterion for nonlinear time-invariant systems.

Keywords Switched reluctance motor · Fuzzy self-tuning PID control · Speed control system · Simulation · Stability analysis

79.1 Introduction

Switched Reluctance Drive (SRD) is a new speed control system, which avoids both the commutation spark of the DC motor while reversing and complex structure of AC motor with high cost. The SRD with the advantages of speed control of both the DC motor and the AC motor has high output and high energy efficiency. Although its electromagnetic principle and structure are quite simple, the SRD can't get an ideal control result with the conventional PID control algorithm because it is a timing-variable, nonlinear, multivariate system. Fuzzy control is a typical intelligent control, which has a strong adaptability to nonlinear

J. Gan (✉) · Z. Li
School of Computer and Information Science, HuBei Engineering University, Xiaogan 432100, China
e-mail: xgjlgan@163.com

W. Lu et al. (eds.), *Proceedings of the 2012 International Conference on Information Technology and Software Engineering*, Lecture Notes in Electrical Engineering 211, DOI: 10.1007/978-3-642-34522-7_79, © Springer-Verlag Berlin Heidelberg 2013

parameters that changes in the speed control application. In order to improve the performance of switched reluctance motor speed control, the fuzzy algorithm and the PID algorithm are combined to make the fuzzy self-tuning PID control algorithm that has the advantages of both.

79.2 The Mathematical Model of Switched Reluctance Motor System

There are three popular methods to solve the basic equation of the SRM: linearization, quasi linearization and nonlinear linearization. The linearization method simplifies the parameters of the SRM and emphasizes the basic physical characteristics of the SRM [1]. Although the precision of linearization is relatively lower, the relationship between the basic characteristics of the SRM and parameters can be understood with analysis of the approximate analytic expression. The variables of the analytical formula of SRM are solved by the linearization in this paper with the following equations [2].

(1) Circuit equation

$$U_k = R_k i_k + \frac{d\psi_k}{dt} \tag{79.1}$$

(2) Flux equations

$$\psi_k = L_k(\theta_k, i_k) i_k \tag{79.2}$$

(3) Mechanical equation

$$T_e = J \frac{d^2\theta}{dt} + D \frac{d\theta}{dt} + T_L \tag{79.3}$$

Which the angular velocity of the rotor:

$$\frac{d\theta}{dt} = \omega \tag{79.4}$$

(4) Equation of mechanical and electrical contact

$$T_e = \frac{\partial W'_m(\theta, i_1, i_2, \cdots, \theta)}{\partial \theta} \tag{79.5}$$

where U_k: the k-phase motor winding voltage; i_k: the k phase winding current; R_k: the k-phase winding resistance; ψ_k: K phase winding flux. ω: the rotor angular velocity; D: the viscous friction coefficient; J: the moment of inertia; T_L: the load torque.

When the SRM is running, an internal magnetic circuit is highly nonlinear and the electromagnetic relationship is very complex. The SRM is linearly analyzed to explore the motor internal basic electromagnetic relationship. In order to simplify the analysis in the linearization to make the following assumptions in a Linear model: excluding the influence of the magnetic circuit saturation, no matter with the size of the winding inductance and current, ignoring the nonlinear flux edge effects of the magnetic circuit, ignoring core hysteresis and eddy current effects, ignoring all the power loss, with an ideal semiconductor switch, instantaneous switch action, constant speed and voltage of the motor [1–3].

In the Fig. 79.1 an ideal linear model indicates the relationship of the cyclical changes between the stator winding inductance and rotor position angle

The SRM's winding inductance segmented analytical formula based on the linear model is in the Fig. 79.1:

$$L(\theta) = \begin{cases} L_{\min} & 38; (\theta_1 \le \theta < \theta_2) \\ K(\theta - \theta_2) + L_{\min} & 38; (\theta_2 \le \theta < \theta_3) \\ L_{\max} & 38; (\theta_3 \le \theta < \theta_4) \\ L_{\max} - K(\theta - \theta_4) & 38; (\theta_4 \le \theta < \theta_5) \end{cases} \tag{79.6}$$

$$K = \frac{L_{\max} - L_{\min}}{\theta_3 - \theta_1} \tag{79.7}$$

The Eq. (79.5) can be simplified with Eq. (79.6)

$$T_e = \frac{\partial W'_m(\theta, i)}{\partial \theta} \Big|_{i=const} \tag{79.8}$$

$$W_m = W'_m = \frac{1}{2} i \psi = \frac{1}{2} L i^2 \tag{79.9}$$

Fig. 79.1 The relationship between phase inductance and rotor position angle in the linear model

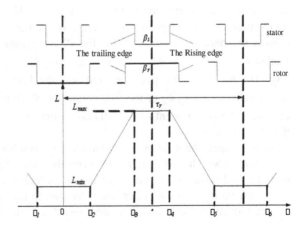

To get the following formula from (79.6), (79.8), (79.9)

$$T_e = \begin{cases} 0 & 38; (\theta_1 \leq \theta < \theta_2) \\ \frac{1}{2} Ki^2 & 38; (\theta_2 \leq \theta < \theta_3) \\ 0 & 38; (\theta_3 \leq \theta < \theta_4) \\ \frac{1}{2} Ki^2 & 38; (\theta_4 \leq \theta < \theta_5) \end{cases} \tag{79.10}$$

79.3 Switched Reluctance Motor Control System Mode

With high reliability, good stability and high adaptability the Conventional PID controller algorithm is simple, easily designed and widely used in process control. In the industrial process control the object of control is complicated and changeable and the interference factor is complex. In order to obtain satisfactory control performance, the PID parameters should be in a situation of a real-time adjustment [4]. Some parameters are constantly changing so there are no specific mathematical models and rules for them. It is feasible and practical choice for the adjustment of the PID parameters to use the fuzzy controller. Not only has the fuzzy-PID controller learned successful practical and operating experience of real-time non-linear adjustment but also got good control performance of the PID controller eventually to make the whole system get the best control results [5]. In this paper the fuzzy algorithm and the PID algorithm are combined to make the fuzzy self-tuning PID control algorithm that gets a good control performance.

79.3.1 Definition of Membership Functions and Control Rules

With the fuzzy self-tuning PID controller the input deviation e of the PID controller and deviation rate of change e_k are entered into the fuzzy controller at the same time. Three correction parameters Δk_p, Δk_i, Δk_d that are obtained by fuzzy logic inference rules respectively are entered into the PID controller to real-timely correct the parameters k_p, k_i, k_d of the PID controller online. The Calculation methods are $k_p = k_p' + \Delta k_p$, $k_i = k_i' + \Delta k_i$ and $k_d = k_d' + \Delta k_d$, which means the Δk_p, Δk_i, Δk_d are respectively entered into the PID control after added by the initial value of k_p', k_i', k_d' of the PID controller. With the methods the parameters can meet the requirement of the PID controller at different time and the control performance is good.

In this paper, the difference e between the given Speed value and the actual

In this paper, the difference e between the given Speed value and the actual output speed value and its rate of change e_c, which are the input variables of the fuzzy self-tuning PID controller, are converted to the range of input variables by the quantification factor and then are converted to the input domain of the fuzzy controller by the corresponding membership functions deviation e, error change rate e_c and fuzzy output Δk_p, Δk_i, Δk_d domain {−6, −5, −4, −3, −2, −1, 0, 1, 2, 3, 4, 5, 6}. The fuzzy sets of the variables are: {Negative big, negative medium, negative small, zero, positive small, positive middle, positive big} named as {NB, NM, NS, ZO, PS, PM, PB}. The membership functions of e, e_c, Δk_p, Δk_i, Δk_d are shown in Fig. 79.2. The rule tables of Δk_p, Δk_i, Δk_d for the fuzzy control are in the Tables 79.1, 79.2, and 79.3.

79.3.2 Quantization Factor and Proportion Factor to be Determine

In the fuzzy self-tuning controller, the quantization factor k_e, k_{ec} and proportion factor k_p, k_i, k_d greatly influence the dynamic performance of the fuzzy control system. Generally, the bigger the k_e is, the more the system overshoot reaches; the less the k_e is, the slower the system changes and the less the static precision is. The k_{ec} Partially influences the dynamic performance of the system and the value of k_p, k_i, k_d directly determine the value of the correction coefficient Δk_p, Δk_i, Δk_d. The quantization factor and the proportion factor are determined by the following equation.

Quantization factor = Value of fuzzy theory domain/Value of the physics domain range

Proportion factor = Value of the physics domain range/Value of fuzzy theory domain

The fuzzy theory domain of the quantization factor k_e, k_{ec} and proportion factor k_p, k_i, k_d is [−6, 6] and the value of fuzzy theory domain is 12, but the physical theory domain's values of the k_e, k_{ec}, k_p, k_i, k_d is different. The quantization factor k_e, k_{ec} and proportion factor k_p, k_i, k_d of fuzzy self-tuning PID controller designed in this paper are determined after repeatedly observations, researches and adjustments. $k_e = 0.006$, $k_{ec} = 0.001$ and $k_p = 0.033$, $k_i = 0.024$, $k_d = 0.166$. The originally settings of parameters of the PID controller are $k_p = 0.05$, $k_i = 3.5$, $k_d = 0.005$.

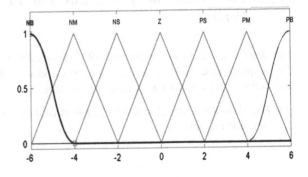

Fig. 79.2 The membership function of e, e_k, Δk_p, Δk_i, Δk_d

Table 79.1 Fuzzy rule table for Δk_p

e_c / e	NB	NM	NS	Z0	PS	PM	PB
NB	PB	PB	PM	PM	PS	ZO	ZO
NM	PB	PB	PM	PS	PS	ZO	NS
NS	PM	PM	PM	PS	ZO	NS	NS
ZO	PM	PM	PS	ZO	NS	NM	NM
PS	PS	PS	ZO	NS	NS	NM	NM
PM	PS	PS	NS	NM	NM	NM	NB
PB	ZO	ZO	NS	NM	NM	NB	NB

Table 79.2 Fuzzy rule table for Δk_d

e_c / e	NB	NM	NS	Z0	PS	PM	PB
NB	NB	NB	NM	NM	NS	ZO	ZO
NM	NB	NB	NM	NS	NS	ZO	ZO
NS	NB	NM	NS	NS	ZO	PS	PS
ZO	NM	NM	NS	ZO	PS	PM	PM
PS	NM	NS	ZO	PS	PS	PM	PB
PM	ZO	ZO	PS	PS	PM	PM	PB
PB	ZO	ZO	PS	PM	PM	PB	PB

Table 79.3 Fuzzy rule table for Δk_d

e_c / e	NB	NM	NS	Z0	PS	PM	PB
NB	PS	NS	NB	NB	NB	NM	PS
NM	PS	NS	NB	NM	NM	NS	ZO
NS	ZO	NS	NM	NM	NS	NS	ZO
ZO	ZO	NS	NS	NS	NS	NS	ZO
PS	ZO	ZO	ZO	ZO	ZO	ZO	ZO
PM	PB	NS	PS	PS	PS	PS	PB
PB	PB	PM	PM	PM	PS	PS	PB

79.3.3 The Simulation of SRM Based on Fuzzy Self-tuning PID Control

The simulation model of the discrete SRM speed control system is constructed and the sampling time Ts is set to 2.5exp (−5) (s) in this paper to ensure there is no distortion to the simulation speed of the system.

(1) The Simulation model of the SRM speed control system based on Fuzzy self-tuning PID control

The SRM speed system uses dual closed-loop controls, which the fuzzy self-tuning PID control algorithm is used in the outer speed loop and the conventional PID control algorithm is used in the inner current loop. The output value of the dual closed-loop fuzzy controller is compared with the output value of the classical PID controller by the pulse width of the phase position signal detected by the position. The result of the comparison controls the IGBT main switch of power converter circuit of to drive the SRM. Refer to the Sect. 79.4 for the detail of the system stability analysis [6]. The Simulation model of the SRM speed control system based on Fuzzy self-tuning PID control is shown in Fig. 79.3.

(2) Fuzzy self-tuning PID module

A simulation model of the speed controller for the fuzzy self-tuning PID control algorithm is built (shown in Fig. 79.4) according to the design principle and steps of the fuzzy self-tuning PID controller introduced in the previous parts. The fuzzy controller actually consists of three sub controllers. Firstly the deviation e and the deviation rate of change e_c are entered into the three sub fuzzy controllers at the same time; secondly the three output values are respectively multiplied with the output values of the three PID controllers to get same dimensions after fuzzification, approximate reasoning and sharp processing; and then the output values are respectively added by the output values of the three PID controllers to get the output value of the PID control after adjustment.

(3) The position detection module

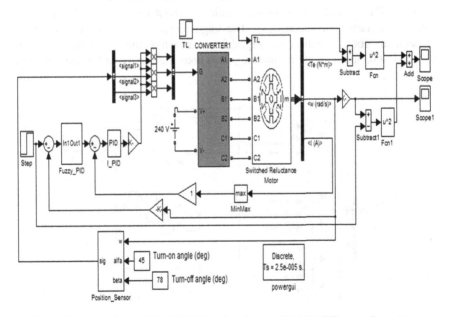

Fig. 79.3 The simulation model of SRM based on fuzzy self-tuning PID control

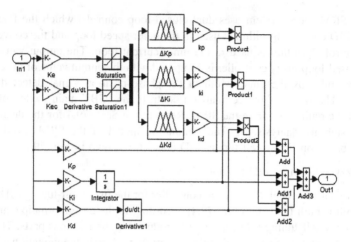

Fig. 79.4 The simulation model of speed for fuzzy self-tuning PID

The speed control system position detection module is shown in Fig. 79.5. Assume that the initial position of a phase stator salient pole and centerline and the rotor groove are at a same centerline, which means the phase inductance value is the smallest, according to the characteristics of the 6/4 pole reluctance motor stator and rotor with the detection of switched reluctance motor angular velocity [7]. The rotor makes centerline of another phase stator salient pole coincides with the centerline of the rotor groove after each 30 degrees rotation, which minimizes the phase inductance. The rotor goes back to the initial state after each 90 degrees rotation. The ω multiplies with the coefficient $180/\pi$ to get an angle which the SRM rotor turns per second [8]. The angle degrees of three phases can be respectively got by the discrete integral functions which the three initial states are 0, −30, −60, and then the position signal is converted into a pulse one. The Alfa

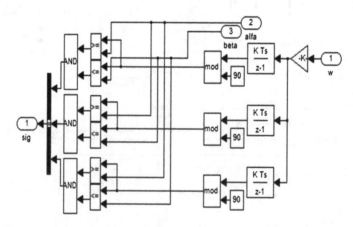

Fig. 79.5 The simulation model of the position detection

and Beta in the Fig. 79.5 are respectively the turn-on angle and turn off angle and set to 45 and 78 degree.

(4) The system settings of the simulation parameters

The switched reluctance motor parameters: Type: 6/4; initial velocity and position: [0 0]; rated power: 60 kw; rotational inertia: 0.05 kg m^2.

79.4 Analysis of Simulation Results

The simulation model is structured in accordance with the Fig. 79.3. The amplitude of step signal is set to 1000, which a given speed is 1000 r/min. The curve in the Fig. 79.6 is the result of the simulation.

The waveforms of the fuzzy self-tuning PID control and conventional PID control are shown in the Fig. 79.7. Not only is the adjusting speed of the SRM speed control system based on fuzzy self-tuning PID control obviously faster than the other one, but its super-harmonic and oscillations also are significantly less.

The Fig. 79.8 shows the changes of the waveforms after a sudden load is applied to the two different systems. System based on the fuzzy self-tuning PID control has a smaller speed drop and shorter recovery time than another one. Therefore, the SRM speed control system based on the fuzzy self-tuning PID control has a better anti-disturbance ability. Specifically, it has a good control performance of the SRM speed control system after a sudden load is applied, which embodies the advantage of the fuzzy self-tuning PID control.

The above simulation diagram indicates that the switched reluctance motor speed control system based on the fuzzy self-tuning PID control has following features: fast response speed, small overshoot, short adjusting time, strong anti-jamming capability etc. The dynamic performance of the system is greatly improved.

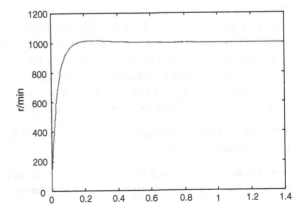

Fig. 79.6 The simulation curve of the speed based on fuzzy self-tuning PID control

Fig. 79.7 The curve of the speed for comparing the Fuzzy self-tuning PID with the conventional PID

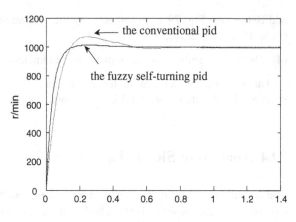

Fig. 79.8 The curve of the speed for comparing the Fuzzy self-tuning PID with the conventional PID when increasing load suddenly

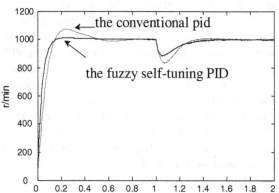

79.5 Analysis of the System Stability

The attribute of stability is the most important for a control system. Unstable system is unable to work. Usually the Lyapunov Second Method is used to determine the stability of nonlinear control systems. However, it is extremely difficult or impossible to construct Lyapunov function for certain nonlinear systems (such as described in this article SRM speed control system). A new stability criterion based on the computer numerical calculation and simulation of nonlinear constant control system is proposed in the literature [5–8]. The criterion selects the square of the system state variables and functions as generalized energy functions, and extends sufficient condition for local stability in the second method of Lyapunov stability theory to the necessary and sufficient one.

Theorem For the non-linear constant system, $\dot{X} = f(X)$ (where $X = [x_1 \ x_2 \ \cdots \ x_n]^{\mathrm{T}}$ that is the state vector).

Assumption 1 The equilibrium of the system is state space origin (if the equilibrium point is not at the origin, then parallel move the equilibrium point to the

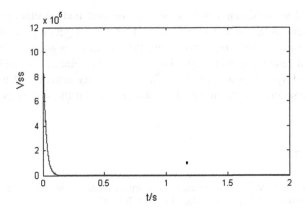

Fig. 79.9 The changing curve of V_{ss} with time

state space origin with the variable substitution coordinate translation can be the equilibrium point level moved to the origin of the state space without affecting the stability of the system).

When $X(t_0) \in B_\varepsilon$ (where B_ε is the neighborhood of radius of the origin of the state space) and $t \geq t_0$, $X(t)$ is bounded.

The sufficient and necessary condition to make the system be locally uniformly asymptotically stable is

$$V_{ss} = \sum_{i=1}^{n} x_i^2 = (x_1^2 + x_2^2 + \cdots + x_n^2) \to 0 \qquad (79.11)$$

which the sum of all the squares of the variables of each state is close to be zero after enough time with the simulation or numerical calculation.

The above stability criterion can be applied to the stability analysis of the SRM speed control system. The control system model is shown in Fig. 79.3. Assume $x_1 = T_{Li} - T_L$, $x_2 = n_i - n$ act as the state variables, $V_{ss} = x_1^2 + x_2^2$, which T_{Li} is a given torque value, T_L is actual torque value, n_i is a given speed value and n is the actual speed value. Figure 79.9 shows the curve of the $V_{ss}(t)$.

In the Fig. 79.9 V_{ss} converges to zero with change of time. According to the stability criterion, The SRM speed control system of the fuzzy self-tuning PID control is uniformly asymptotically stable.

79.6 Conclusions

In this paper the fuzzy self-tuning PID control strategy is studied and introduced into the switched reluctance motor speed control systems. It is compared with the SRM speed control system based on conventional PID control with modeling and simulation. The simulation results show that the switched reluctance motor speed control system using the fuzzy self-tuning PID control gets a good dynamic and static performance. The fuzzy self-tuning PID control is a good choice to control the switched reluctance motor speed control system. Finally, the stability of the speed control system is analyzed with a new stability criterion of the nonlinear time-invariant control system and the result shows that the system is stable.

References

1. Krishnan R (2001) Switched reluctance motor drives: modeling, simulation, analysis, design, and applications. CRC Press, Florida, LLC.USA 2001.10
2. Wu H (2010) Switched reluctance motor system theory and control. China Electric Power Press, Beijing, pp 287–321 (in Chinese)
3. Shi XM, He Z (2008) Fuzzy control and MATLAB simulation. Tsinghua University Press and Beijing Jiaotong University Press, Beijing, pp 223–256 (in Chinese)
4. Cui X, Shi S, Liu Z (2012) Fuzzy PID control system based on adaptive universe for switched reluctance motors. Micromotors (in Chinese)
5. Zeng Z, Xiao Q, Zhu J (2011) Fuzzy neural network PID speed control of switched reluctance motor. In: Proceedings of the CSU-EPSA (in Chinese)
6. Su Y, Wang Y, Cai D (2010) Research of switched reluctance drive system based on fuzzy PID. J Wuhan Univ Technol (in Chinese)
7. Krishnan R, Lee B-S, Vallance P (2000) Integral linear switched reluctance machine based guidance, levitation and propulsion system. In: Proceedings of Maglev 2000 Conference, June 7–10, Rio de Janeiro, pp 281–286
8. Bae HK, Lee BS, Vijayraghavan P, Krishnan R (2000) A linear switched reluctance motor: converter and control. IEEE Trans Ind Appl 36(6):1351–1359

Chapter 80
MPPT Control Method of PV System with PSO Algorithm Based on Minimal Particle Angles

Tianpei Zhou and Wei Sun

Abstract The output of photovoltaic array was affected by the environmental factors such as irradiation and temperature, it was necessary to track the maximum power point of photovoltaic array. Aiming at shortage of the traditional particle swarm optimization algorithm for multi-objective optimization, multi-objective particle swarm optimization algorithm based on minimal particle angles was proposed, the globally optimal particle was updated by comparison of angles between different particles in the objective space; A method of updating locally optimal particles and swarm is presented based on particle densities. The maximum power point tracking method was established and simulated with Matlab/Simulink. Simulation results showed that the algorithm could rapidly and accurately track the maximum power point when the external environmental changed, and ensure the steady state characteristics of PV systems.

Keywords PV array · Maximum power point tracking · Particle swarm optimization algorithm · Minimal particle angles · Particle densities

T. Zhou (✉) · W. Sun (✉)
School of Information and Engineering, China University of Mining and Technology,
Xuzhou 221008, China
e-mail: zhoutianpei_001@163.com

W. Sun
e-mail: sw3883204@163.com

T. Zhou
Xuzhou College of Industrial and Technology, Xuzhou 221140, China

W. Lu et al. (eds.), *Proceedings of the 2012 International Conference on Information Technology and Software Engineering*, Lecture Notes in Electrical Engineering 211, DOI: 10.1007/978-3-642-34522-7_80, © Springer-Verlag Berlin Heidelberg 2013

80.1 Introduction

With the development of society, energy and environmental issues became more and more serious, solar energy, as a renewable energy, had good application prospects. But conversion efficiency of photovoltaic cells was low, and output power has a significant relationship with sunshine intensity and ambient temperature, due to obvious non-linear, the maximum power point tracking (MPPT) circuit was connected between the photovoltaic device and load in order to give full play to the effectiveness of photovoltaic cells [1]. Particle Swarm Optimization algorithm, as an effective optimization tool, has been applied to the maximum power point tracking of solar independent components. But particle swarm optimization algorithm was initially only for single-objective optimization problem, for multi-objective optimization problem that various objectives was likely to be competing, the traditional particle swarm optimization operation became unsatisfactory, which must be improved. In this paper, a strategy for updating the globally optimal particle is brought forward by comparison of angles between different particles in the objective space; A method of updating locally optimal particles and swarm is presented based on particle densities. The research results were applied to the MPPT control of PV systems, and proved the effectiveness and practicality of the algorithm.

80.2 Particle Angles

For two particles x_i, x_j, we define [2]

$$\delta_{ij} = \delta(x_i, x_j) = \arccos \frac{f(x_i) \cdot f(x_j)}{|f(x_i)| \cdot |f(x_j)|} \tag{80.1}$$

as the particles of the objective space for particles x_i, x_j, referred to as particle angles, where, $f(x_i)$, $f(x_j)$, respectively for objective function vector value of particles x_i, x_j.

80.3 Selection of Globally Optimal Particles Based on Minimal Particle Angles

The selection method of globally optimal particle x_i was as follows: Among the target vector space, the angle $\delta(x_i, a_j), j = 1, 2, \ldots, |A|$ of the particle swarm x_i and particle a_j in reserve set A was calculated by formula (80.1), and a_k was found, making $\delta(x_i, a_k) = \min_{j \in \{1,2,\ldots,|A|\}} \delta(x_i, a_j)$, then a_k as globally optimal particles x_i. The algorithm procedure was as follows:

Fig. 80.1 Geometric
explanation of selecting
globally optimal particles

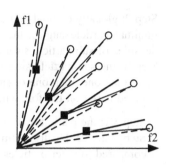

For $i = 1$ to N
  $\min \delta_i = \delta_{i1}, P_g^i = a_1$
  For $j = 2$ to $|A|$
  $\delta_{ij} = \delta(x_i, a_j)$
    If $\delta_{ij} < \min \delta_i$ Then
    $\min \delta_i = \delta_{ij}, P_g^i = a_j$
    EndIf
  EndFor
EndFor

Geometric explanation of selecting globally optimal particles was shown in Fig. 80.1, in which ■ for particles of the reserve set, ○ for particles of the particle swarm. As you can see from Fig. 80.1, the method was actually selecting particle, that the line angle was minimum between particles of the reserve set and particles of the particle swarm, as their globally optimal particles [3].

80.4 Update of Particles and Their Locally and Optimal Particles Based on Particle Densities

In this paper, the updating idea of particles and their locally optimal particles was as follows: if locally optimal particles and their newborn particles were dominant relationship, their locally optimal particles were determined according to the dominant relationship; otherwise, the particle swarm was divided into several sub-particle swarms according to selection of globally optimal particles based on minimal particle angles, particle densities were determined in accordance with the number of particles in each sub-particle swarm, then, the particles and their locally optimal particles were updated in the light of particle densities and the dominant relationship [4]. Based on the above ideas, specific methods of updating particles and their locally optimal particles were achieved, steps were as follows:

Step 1: the locally optimal value $P_i(t)$ of particles $x_i(t)$ was saved to particle swarms, locally optimal value of $P_i(t)$ and $x_i(t + 1)$ was initialized for their own;

Step 2: globally optimal particles of $x_i(t + 1)$ and $P_i(t)$ were selected according to minimal particle angles, the sub-particle swarms were determined, the particle densities of sub-particle swarms were updated;

Step 3: the sub-particle swarms with the largest particle densities were found, if more than one, then one of sub-particle swarms was randomly selected, and was updated based on the following methods;

Step 3.1: the particle $x_r(t)$ was randomly selected from the sub-particle swarms;
Step 3.2: the locally optimal value $P_r(t)$ of particles $x_r(t)$ were dominantly compared to other particles of the sub-particle swarms, if $P_r(t)$ was dominated, former dominated particles and the corresponding locally optimal particles were deleted, otherwise, $x_r(t)$ and $P_r(t)$ were deleted.

80.5 Application

In maximum power point tracking control of photovoltaic system, the potential solution of each optimal problem (namely the maximum power point current) was a "particle" of the search space, all particles had an fitness value that determined by objective function [5]. Specific steps were as follows:

Step 1: the particle swarm was initialized. Particle velocity for zero, locally optimal value for itself, and reserve set was null, the swarm size $N = 100$, the maximum evolution generation $T_{max} = 100$, the maximum particle velocity $v\_max = 2$, c1 = 2, c2 = 2.

Step 2: the newborn particles were evaluated. After initializing various parameters, the fitness value of newborn particles corresponding to the objective function was calculated through formula (80.2), the reserve set was updated through dominantly comparing to locally optimal particles. The objective function for total power function of photovoltaic array, the expression of fitness function as [6]:

$$fit = p = IV = (I_{SC} \times (1 - c_1(e^{\frac{V + \Delta V}{c_2 V_{OC}}} - 1)) + \Delta I) \times V \qquad (80.2)$$

where,

$$c_1 = (1 - \frac{I_{mp}}{I_{SC}})e^{-\frac{V_{mp}}{c_2 V_{oc}}} \qquad (80.3)$$

$$c_2 = (\frac{V_{mp}}{V_{oc}} - 1)/\ln(1 - \frac{I_{mp}}{I_{SC}}) \qquad (80.4)$$

$$\Delta I = \alpha S(T - T_{ref}) + I_{SC}(S - S_{ref}) \qquad (80.5)$$

$$\Delta V = \beta(T - T_{ref}) + R_s \Delta I \qquad (80.6)$$

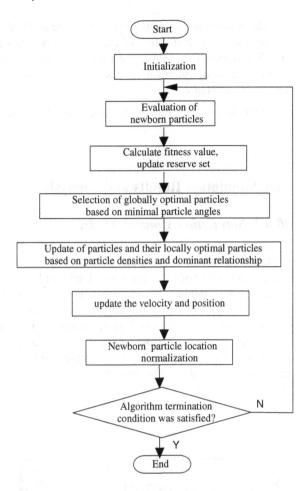

Fig. 80.2 MPPT control algorithm of PSO based on minimal particle angles

where, (1) I_{mp}, V_{mp}: maximum power point current and voltage of the PV array; (2) I_{SC}, V_{OC}: short-circuit current and open-circuit voltage of the PV array; (3) α: temperature coefficient of current change (Amps/°C); (4) β: temperature coefficient of voltage change (V/°C); (5) R_S: the series resistance of solar cells.

Step 3: selection of globally optimal particles, update of particles and their locally optimal particles was respectively completed through using minimal particle angles, particle densities and dominant relationship.

Step 4: for the ith evolutionary particle x_i^t with t generation, its position as matrix P_i^t, globally optimal value as matrix G_i^t, locally optimal value as matrix L_i^t. Therefore, the update formula of particles x_i^t as [7]:

$$V_i^{t+1} = w \times V_i^t + c_1 r_1 \times (L_i^t - P_i^t) + c_2 r_2 \times (G^t - P_i^t) \tag{80.7}$$

$$P_i^{t+1} = P_i^t + V_i^{t+1} \tag{80.8}$$

The position and velocity of particles were updated through the formula (80.7) and (80.8), normalization of the newborn particles position was completed.

Step 5: To determine whether a termination condition was satisfied, if satisfied, the algorithm ceased, optimization was end, the optimal solution was output, otherwise, went to Step 2.

MPPT control algorithm of PSO based on minimal particle angles was shown in Fig. 80.2.

80.6 Simulation Results and Analysis

80.6.1 Simulation Control Model

In Matlab environment, using the Simulink tool, combined with S-function, MPPT simulation module of PV array was established based on the above mathematical model. MPPT simulation module of PV array was shown in Fig. 80.3, where, *sfunpv* for S-function that was used to solve maximum power voltage V_{mp} and current I_{mp} of solar cell in real-time, corresponding any solar radiation, environment temperature. I_{out} for output current of PV array, which may was I_{mp} or the actual array current I_{pv} according to whether the system with MPPT, P_{max} for the maximum power of the PV array [8].

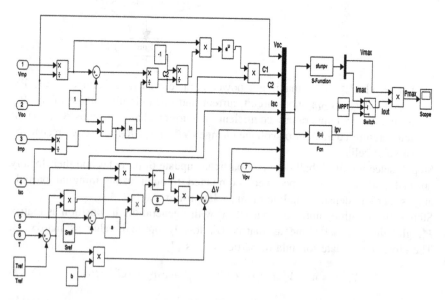

Fig. 80.3 MPPT simulation module of photovoltaic array

Table 80.1 Photovoltaic array parameter table

Parameter	Values
Open circuit voltage (V_{OC})	21.7 V
Maximum power voltage (V_{mp})	17.5 V
Short-circuit current (I_{sc})	3.53 A
Maximum power current (I_{mp})	3.05 A
Series resistance (R_S)	0.0027 Ω
Reference temperature (T_{ref})	25 °C
Reference sunlight intensity (S_{ref})	1000 W/m²
Temperature coefficient of current change α(Amps/°C)	0.0012 I_{sc}
Temperature coefficient of voltage change β (V/°C)	0.005 V_{OC}

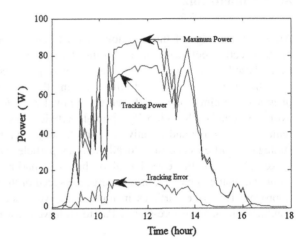

Fig. 80.4 Simulation diagram using traditional PSO algorithm

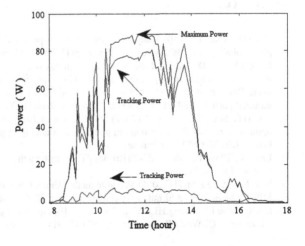

Fig. 80.5 Simulation diagram using PSO algorithm algorithm based on minimal particle angles

80.6.2 Simulation Results

The system was simulated when the simulation parameters of PV array was set parameters in Table 80.1 [9, 10]. Simulation diagram using traditional PSO algorithm and Simulation diagram using PSO algorithm based on minimal particle angles respectively was shown in Figs. 80.4 and 80.5.

It can be seen from the simulation results that power tracking error tracking of Fig. 80.5 was greatly lower than Fig. 80.4, but did not the speed of tracking system, the tracking control quality was effectively improved, the energy loss was reduced, the effectiveness and practicality of algorithm was verified.

80.7 Conclusions

Aiming at shortage of the traditional particle swarm optimization algorithm for multi-objective optimization, multi-objective particle swarm optimization algorithm based on minimal particle angles was proposed. The advantage of the algorithm is mainly reflected in the following three aspects: (1) selection method of globally optimal particles based on minimal particle angles, could effectively avoid the defects that globally optimal particles was too concentrated, did not require the positive and negative of particles objective function value; (2) update strategy of particles and their locally optimal particles was proposed, which could make full use of the effective algorithm information on the basis of the less computational complexity, the convergence speed of the algorithm was effectively improved; (3) make particles in multi-objective space more evenly distributed, conducive to achieve fore-end of Pareto with well-distributed.

References

1. Chen JM, Chen L (2010) Study on maximum power point indirect tracking algorithm of solar photovoltaic power. Water Resour Power 28(1):148 (in Chinese)
2. Jiang ZS, Qin DK (2007) Limit language complexity of elementary cellular automation of Rule 164 examined from particles. J East China Univ Sci Technol 33(4):584 (in Chinese)
3. Gong DW, Zhang Y, Zhang JH (2005) Multi-objective particle swarm optimization based on minimal particle angle. Lect Notes Comput Sci 3644(1):571–580
4. Wu HT, Sun YZ, Meng C (2011) Application of fuzzy controller with particle swarm optimization algorithm to maximum power point tracking of photovoltaic generation system. Proc CSEE 31(6):52 (in Chinese)
5. Liu YL, Zhou H, Cheng Z (2010) MPPT control method of PV system based on PSO. Comput Eng 36(8):265
6. Mao MQ, Yu SJ, Su JH (2005) Versatile matlab simulation model for photovoltaic array with MPPT function. Acta Simulata Systematica Sinica 17(5):1248
7. Liu SQ, Zou LF, Zhang HL, Wang JW (2010) Hydrothermal generation scheduling based on enhanced PSO. Water Resour Power 28(7):153 (in Chinese)

8. Zheng HL, Ge BM, Bi DQ (2010) RT-LAB based real-time simulation of photovoltaic power generation system. Adv Technol Electr Eng Energy 29(4):62 (in Chinese)
9. Zhang C, Guo XY, Chen JM (2011) MPPT control of grid-connected photovoltaic power generation system based on PSCAD. Water Resour Power 29(9):29 (in Chinese)
10. Yang HZ, Jin XM (2006). Research on improved measure of MPPT control and its experiment in a grid-connected photovoltaic system. Adv Technol Electr Eng Energy 25(1):63 (in Chinese)

Chapter 81
Research of Nesting Problem of Difform Parts Based on Optimization Theories

Fengqi Zhang

Abstract Contour feature location algorithm (CFLA) was proposed for solving optimal layout problems, which mainly improved the local optimal capabilities by its own structure characteristics. Using dynamic programming thoughts based on "optimization theories" constructed mathematical model, and illustrated the algorithm's structure in detail. This paper used the global convergence of immune-backtracking genetic algorithm to optimizing the algorithm's parameters further, which greatly improved the global optimal capabilities of CFLA. Many optimal results are put out by the nesting system written under the platform of Visual C++6.0, and prove the algorithm's efficiency for difform parts' nesting problem.

Keywords Contour feature location algorithm · Nesting utilization · Optimization theory · Difform parts · Time complexity

81.1 Introduction

Nesting problem, for the purpose of achieving maximum sheet utilization, is widely used in apparel, mechanical manufacture, paper, automobiles and many other industries. The early layout algorithms were used in solving the regular part's nesting problems, such as the bottom and left (BL) algorithm. As the researching on the nesting problem deeply and widely, heuristic and intelligent

F. Zhang (✉)
The Institute of Mechanical Science and Engineering, Jilin University, Changchun, China
e-mail: zhangfengqi2006@163.com

F. Zhang
Xiamen Golden Dragon Bus Co., Ltd, Xiamen, China

W. Lu et al. (eds.), *Proceedings of the 2012 International Conference on Information Technology and Software Engineering*, Lecture Notes in Electrical Engineering 211, DOI: 10.1007/978-3-642-34522-7_81, © Springer-Verlag Berlin Heidelberg 2013

algorithms are put forward gradually, such as genetic algorithm [1], artificial immune algorithm [2], no-fit polygon (NFP) algorithm [3, 4] and so on, which are widely used to solve the irregular part's nesting problems to making good results. Although many professors and scholars devoted themselves to researching these fields, there are still many problems to be solved.

- Current nesting theories pay more attention to the global layout, while local layout needs to be further improved.
- Layout algorithm does not search for all feasible positions completely, greatly reduces the nesting utilization.
- As the part's shape complexity increases, layout algorithm makes hard to nest parts directly on the sheet without any solutions to decrease the shape complexity.

However, contour feature location algorithm using the methods of comparisons, analysis and information of "matching degree", in virtue of basic operators of translation, rotation and flip, can get the local optimal nesting results. Otherwise, the algorithm not only can converge at optimum in less time complexity, but also obtain higher packing utilization. The algorithm's greatest advantage is that it can nest difform parts directly, which upgrades the nesting utilization 1–5 % compared with other algorithms [5, 6] that nesting parts by its approximate shape.

81.2 Contour Feature Location Algorithm

81.2.1 Establishment of Mathematical Model

For the proposes of using "optimization theories" of the dynamic programming [7, 8] to search for part's optimal nesting position, this paper makes nesting problem as the multi-stage decision-making problems according to the number of parts. Supposing the number of the parts is N, and divides the layout problem into N-level sub-problem, K denotes level variables, the mathematical model of the contour feature location algorithm is shown in Fig. 81.1.

$$0 \leq d_{ik} \leq N_K(x_{ik}), 0 \leq d_{jk} \leq L_K(x_{jk}) \tag{81.1}$$

$$p_{1,N}(x_{i1}, x_{j1}) \in P_{1,N}(x_{i1}, x_{j1}) \tag{81.2}$$

The formula of each optimal strategy:

$$R_{1,N}(x_{i1}, x_{j1}, p_{1,N}) = \sum_{K=1}^{N} R_K(x_{i1}, x_{j1}, d_{i1}, d_{j1}) \tag{81.3}$$

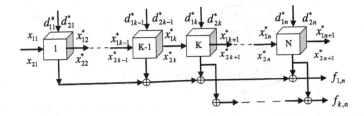

Fig. 81.1 Mathematical model

The formula of otal optimal strategy:

$$f_{1,N} = opt_{\bullet} \underset{p_{1,N} \in P_{1,N}}{R_{1,N}} (x_{i1}, x_{j1}, p_{1,N}) = R_{1,N}(x_{i1}, x_{j1}, p^*_{1,N}) \qquad (81.4)$$

$$p^*_{1,N}(x_{i1}, x_{j1}) = MaxP_{1,N}(x_{i1}, x_{j1}) \qquad (81.5)$$

where x_{ik}, x_{jk} denotes respectively the K-level node of part and sheet contour, $d_k(x_{ik}), d_k(x_{jk})$ denotes decision variable, $N_K(x_{ik}), L_K(x_{jk})$ denotes respectively the K-level total nodes of part and sheet contour. Initial state variables are x_{i1}, x_{j1}, p denotes a strategy, P denotes a set of feasible strategies, P^* denotes the level optimal strategy, f denotes the overall optimal strategy, and R_k denotes each level strategy.

The basic position principle of nesting algorithm is: when the selected node's information of a part matches with the node information of sheet contour presently, the part can position on the sheet. Each level strategy that is good or not uses the "matching function" to evaluate it, defined in formula (81.6).

$$R_K(x_{ik}, x_{jk}, d_{ik}, d_{jk}) = \frac{S_{part}(x_{ik})}{S_{part}(x_{ik}) + S_{wastage}(x_{jk}, d_{jk})} - \eta \times H(x_{ik}, x_{jk}, d_{jk}) \quad (81.6)$$

While $S_{part}(x_{ik})$ denotes K-level part's area, $S_{wastage}(x_{jk}, d_{jk})$ denotes wastage that the part positions on the node of d_{jk} in the K level, $H(x_{ik}, x_{jk}, d_{jk})$ denotes height value after the part positioned, η is the influence coefficient of the height.

81.2.2 Algorithm Structure and Function

Contour feature location algorithm is an algorithm based on the thoughts of region filling and local optimum, whose principle is to fill the concave and convex contours formed by both parts and sheet positioned. The algorithm making full use of attribute information achieves the best profile match, and obtains the local optimal nesting utilization. The contour feature location algorithm consists of 5 modules, of which the main function is briefly described, and the flowchart is shown in Fig. 81.2.

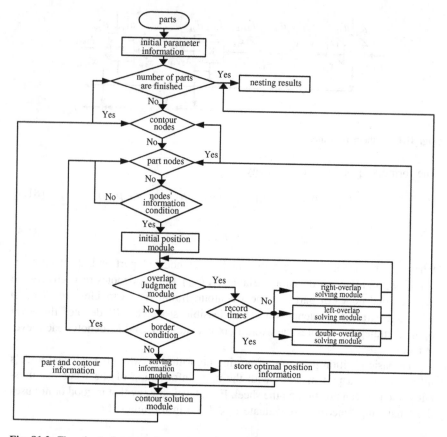

Fig. 81.2 Flowchart of contour feature location algorithm

• Initial position module

This module carries out transformation operators of translation, rotation and flip, and revises data and fault information, improving algorithm's robustness.

• Overlap judgment module

This module determines overlap information between part and sheet contour, and verifies the overlap result, enhancing module's reliability.

• Overlap processing module

This module determines accurately the overlap side, solves the overlap values, and verifies position information.

• Information solution module

This module solves the relative utilization after the part is positioned, stores the optimal values and corresponding information both parts and sheet.

- Profile processing module

This module solves the information of optimal position and sheet's contour node, processes left–right roundabout contour and bilateral node information that influences the convergence rate.

81.2.3 Parameter Optimization

The most important factors influencing nesting utilization mainly include: the population N_0, sample complexity, cycle index N, crossover parameter P_0 and mutation parameter P_m. This paper researches the relationship between nesting utilization and parameters of the population, cycle index, crossover and mutation under the conditions of selecting series of parts, whose sample complexity has common characteristics. The research determinates parameter's selectable range and optimal parameters reversely by time expression.

- The number of population

The number of population affects directly the nesting algorithm's global convergence and search capability. The paper researches the relationship between the population and nesting utilization, when the parameters of cycle index and sample complexity vary, showed in Figs. 81.3 and 81.4. Figure 81.3 reflects the relationship between the population and cycle index. Figure 81.4 reflects the relationship between the population and sample complexity.

From the Figs. 81.3 and 81.4, when the value of the population N_0 is under 12, nesting utilization increases fleetly with the number of population, when the population is between 12 and 22, nesting utilization increases slowly with the number of population, when the population is above 22, nesting algorithm

Fig. 81.3 Cycle index varies

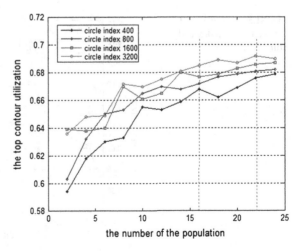

Fig. 81.4 Sample
complexity varies

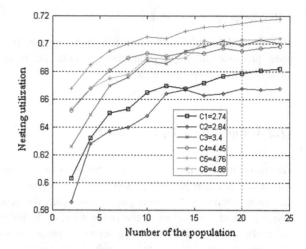

converges stably on a high nesting utilization and get a good nesting result no
matter how the cycle index and sample complexity change. So the optimal value of
population is $N_0 \geq 22$.

- Cycle index

The cycle index affects the global and local search characteristics of the nesting
algorithm. This paper researches the relationship between cycle index and nesting
utilization, when the parameters of the population and sample complexity vary,
shown in Fig. 81.5.

From the Fig. 81.5, when the value of cycle index is under 5000, nesting
utilization increases fleetly with the number of cycle index, when the cycle index is
between 5000 and 10000, nesting utilization increases slowly with the number of

Fig. 81.5 The relationship
between cycle index and
utilization

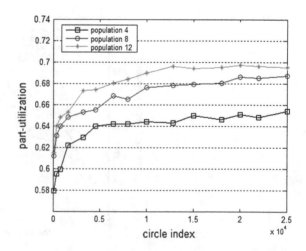

Table 81.1 The relationship between cycle index and sample complexity

Sample complexity	2.74	2.84	3.4	4.45	4.76	4.88	5.76	6.28	6.52
Utilization	0.68	0.668	0.701	0.693	0.718	0.702	0.692	0.73	0.72
Cycle index	1200	2000	2600	3000	3200	3400	3500	3400	3500

cycle index, when the cycle index is above 10000, nesting utilization converges on a good value.

As we know, the number of population is less than optimal value of 22 in Fig. 81.5, so this paper researches relationship between cycle index and sample complexity when the value of the population is above 22, showed in Table 81.1.

It could be concluded that when the value of cycle index is above 3500, the nesting algorithm can get a optimal layout result whatever the part complexity is complex or not. So the optimal value of cycle index is $N \geq 3500$.

- Parameter of crossover and mutation

To ensure that the population has well global and local search characteristics, the algorithm should select mutually matching parameter values both crossover and mutation. This paper researches the relationship between utilization and parameters of crossover and mutation, when the parameters of the population and cycle index vary, shown in Figs. 81.6 and 81.7. Figure 81.6, the curve of blue, green, red, sky-blue means respectively that the number of population is 16, 8, 8 and 4, and the value of cycle index is 1600, 800, 400, 100. Figure 81.7, the curve of blue, green and red means respectively that the number of population is 16, 8, 8, and the value of cycle index corresponding to respectively be 1600, 800, 400.

From the Figs. 81.6 and 81.7, when the values of crossover and mutation are $P_o = 0.8$, $P_m = 0.09$, the nesting algorithm not only has good convergence and robustness, but also achieves a good layout result. So the optimal values are $P_o = 0.8$, $P_m = 0.09$.

Fig. 81.6 The relationship between crossover and nesting utilization

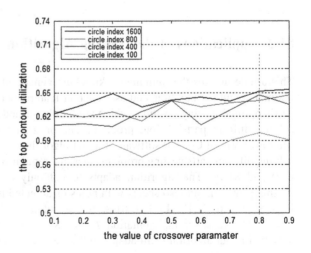

Fig. 81.7 The relationship
between mutation and nesting
utilization

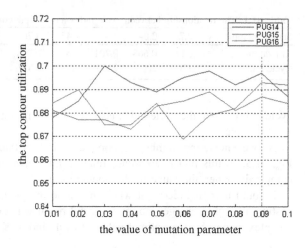

- Optimal parameter selection

Through deeply researching and analyzing nesting algorithm, this paper draws the time estimation formula shown in Eq. (81.7). According to it, the parameters or times can be solved by inputting each side of parameter's value of the equation, achieving the best match between the parameters' selection and nesting algorithm. There is no doubt that the optimal parameters will greatly improve the algorithm's layout utilization.

$$y = 1.15x_f + \frac{0.075}{4} \cdot 2^k \cdot x_z - 2.5 \tag{81.7}$$

where y denotes nesting time, x_f denotes sample complexity, x_z denotes the population. Cycle index is expressed as $N = 2^k \times 100, (k = 0, 1, 2 \ldots)$, thereunto, 2^k is the value of the equation.

81.3 Applications of the Nesting Algorithm

This article utilizes the immune-backtracking genetic algorithm to get the global optimal layout permutation, and uses contour feature location algorithm to achieve part's optimal nesting position, which are totally termed as the nesting system for solving difform parts' layout problem. The programs are completed under the Microsoft Visual C++6.0 software. Layout algorithm can get higher utilization in solving difform parts nesting problem, so as the regular parts showed in Figs. 81.8, 81.9 and 81.10. The algorithm adapts to not only regular and irregular sheet nesting problem, but also sheets with holes or defects inside, results are shown in Figs. 81.9 and 81.10. In Fig. 81.8, the population $N_0 = 22$, the cycle index $N = 3000$, crossover and mutation $P_o = 0.8$, $P_m = 0.09$, nesting utilization is 0.7795. Layout algorithm still adapts to the sheet with defects (the blue region) as

Fig. 81.8 Result of regular sheet

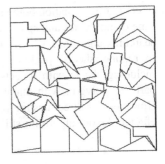

Fig. 81.9 Result of defective sheet

Fig. 81.10 Result with circular parts

Fig. 81.9, the utilization is 0.8026. Otherwise, the algorithm can carry out the random polygon parts' layout problems, so as the circular and arc parts showed in Fig. 81.10, the utilization is 0.7924.

81.4 Conclusions

On the point of solving irregular parts' nesting problem, the contour feature location algorithm can get higher packing utilization compared to others' nesting algorithm. It not only can quickly carry out the optimal nesting by making full use of contour information both parts and sheet, but also greatly reduce the algorithm's time complexities and spare complexities. The algorithm is a heuristic intelligence searching algorithm, which can directly deal with irregular parts nesting. It adapts to regular sheets' packing problem, and can do well with irregular sheets', including sheets with defects too. Otherwise, the algorithm transforms circular parts to polygon with suitable vertices according to the value of part's area. However, for direct nesting of the spline curve shape and circular parts, the more efficient layout algorithm still need to be further studied.

References

1. Soke A, Bingul Z (2006) Hybrid genetic algorithm and simulated annealing for two-dimensional non-guillotine rectangular packing problems. Eng Appl Artif Intell 19(5):557–567
2. Liang L, Ye J (2008) A solution of irregular parts nesting problem based on immune genetic algorithm. In: Proceedings of the 2008 international symposium on computational intelligence and design, ISCID 2008, vol 1, pp 217–220
3. Bennell JA, Dowsland KA, Dowsland William B (2001) The irregular cutting-stock problem—a new procedure for deriving the no-fit polygon. Comput Oper Res 28(3):271–287
4. Yu MT, Lin TY, Hung C (2009) Active-set sequential quadratic programming method with compact neighborhood algorithm for the multi-polygon mass production cutting-stock problem with rotatable polygons. Int J Prod Econ 121(1):148–161
5. Riff MC, Bonaire X, Neveu B (2009) A revision of recent approaches for two-dimensional strip-packing problems. Eng Appl Artif Intell 22(4–5):823–827
6. Liang L, Ye J, Wei D (2008) Application of improved ant colony system algorithm in optimization of irregular parts nesting. In: Proceedings—4th international conference on natural computation, ICNC 2008, vol 7, pp 507–510
7. Cintra GF, Miyazawa FK, Wakabayashi Y, Xavier EC (2008) Algorithms for two-dimensional cutting stock and strip packing problems using dynamic programming and column generation. Eur J Oper Res 191(1):61–85
8. Lazarev A, Werner F (2009) A graphical realization of the dynamic programming method for solving NP-hard combinatorial problems. Comput Math Appl 58(4):619–631

Chapter 82
The Prediction of Short-term Traffic Flow Based on the Niche Genetic Algorithm and BP Neural Network

Chuan-xiang Ren, Cheng-bao Wang, Chang-chang Yin, Meng Chen and Xu Shan

Abstract The paper analyses the prediction model of BP neural Network and the principles of niche genetic algorithm prediction, then sets up the neural network algorithm based on the niche genetic algorithm. The paper also sets up the short-term traffic flow based on the BP neural network, designs the BP neural network algorithm based on the prediction model of the short-term traffic flow. Good results are obtained and the effectiveness of the algorithm is verified.

Keywords The genetic algorithm · BP neural network · Niche genetic algorithm · The prediction of short-term traffic flow

82.1 Introduction

Since the 1960s, scholar began to apply mathematics, computer as well as other related areas of mature theories and models to short-term traffic flow forecasting field. Error Back Propagation (BP) neural network model is one of the most widely apply algorithm in Short-term traffic field. BP neural network doesn't need the existed model, complex nonlinear systems can be identified only by learning.

C. Ren (✉) · C. Wang · C. Yin · M. Chen
Institute of Traffic Information, Shandong University of Science and Technology, Qingdao, Shandong Province, China
e-mail: ren_chx@sina.com

X. Shan
Electronic and Information Engineering, Beijing Jiao Tong University, Beijing, China
e-mail: shanxu9198@126.com

W. Lu et al. (eds.), *Proceedings of the 2012 International Conference on Information Technology and Software Engineering*, Lecture Notes in Electrical Engineering 211, DOI: 10.1007/978-3-642-34522-7_82, © Springer-Verlag Berlin Heidelberg 2013

Transport system is a very large and complex system, so BP neural network can be suitable for transportation field. However it still has some formidable problems, for example easily trapped into local minima, weaker applicability and other problems [1]. Niche Genetic Algorithm (NGA) is an intelligent optimization method which has inherently implicit parallelism and better ability of global optimizing, adopts probability optimizing method and can automatically optimize as well as doesn't need previously established rules [2]. In the paper, use the advantages of niche genetic algorithm for global optimization, and then combine NGA and BP neural network algorithm, build the BP neural network algorithm based on niche genetic algorithm then apply to predict short-term traffic flow [3].

82.2 Neural Network Algorithm Based on Niche Genetic Algorithm

82.2.1 Artificial Neural Network Algorithm

The artificial neural network is constitute by cell which is similar to neurons and weighted connections between units arc, each node units have a threshold parameter. Neural network training through study various types of samples repeatedly, it continue to adjust the connection weights on the threshold parameter of node and the internal state of the neuron. When the neural network weights and thresholds achieve a certain steady state, neural network be able to correctly reflect the mapping relationship between input sample and output parameters, finally achieve the purpose of training to learn.

However, due to the BP neural network model uses stationary conversion function, the deficiency result in network exist the problem of local minima, slow rate of convergence, difficult to achieve online adjustment and so forth [4].

82.2.2 Niche Genetic Algorithm

The genetic algorithm starts from a population of the solution, and the population is consist of the encoding individuals. The approximate solution which has the smaller and smaller error can be got through the evolution of every generation [5]. Introduced niche technique which based on crowding mechanism into genetic algorithm constitute niche genetic algorithm can avoid high fitness value individual breed fast and filled the entire group so that lose the diversity of solution in later evolution. Therefore niche genetic algorithm keep the diversity of solution better as well as has highly global searching ability and convergence speed [6].

82.2.3 BP Neural Network Based on Niche Genetic Algorithm

The BP neural network algorithm based on niche genetic algorithm calculation steps are as follows:

(1) Determine the fitness function formula and parameters: number population M, crossover probability p_c and mutation probability p_m and so on.
(2) Initialize population p_0, randomly generate M feasible solutions to compose the initial population.
(3) Calculate fitness value of the individual in the population and arrange in ascending order. Memory former N individual ($N < M$).
(4) Selection operation. Use roulette method in group selection operation.
(5) In accordance with the crossover probability p_0 to conduct cross operation.
(6) In accordance with the mutation probability p_m to conduct mutation operation.
(7) Niche crowding out operation: Merge together M individual in (6) and N individual then get a contain $M + N$ individual new population and then calculation hamming distance between every two individual x_i and x_j among the $M + N$ individual:

$$\left\| x_i - x_j \right\| = \sqrt{\sum_{k=1}^{k=M} (x_{ik} - x_{jk})^2} (i = 1, 2 \ldots M + N - 1; j = i + 1, i + 2 \ldots M + N)$$

$$(82.1)$$

While $\left\| x_i - x_j \right\| < L$, compare the individual fitness of x_i and x_j then punish the fitness higher individual.

(8) Get new population and calculate the optimum solution, determine whether to meet the termination condition, if the stopping condition is met, then out put the optimal solution and terminate genetic algorithm, else return to step (4).
(9) Substitute genetic algorithm optimal solution into BP neural network, and further optimize the solution until obtain the optimal solution.

82.3 Traffic Flow Forecasting Model

Apply the BP neural network based on niche genetic algorithms to traffic flow forecasting and the simulation experiment is done. The acquisition time is 24 h. Treat traffic data which is collected preliminary every 5 min as a unit then normalize these data. Build forecasting model based on the niche genetic algorithm and BP neural network.

Fig. 82.1 BP neural network
traffic flow forecasting model

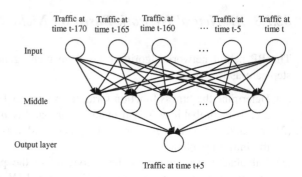

82.3.1 BP Neural Network Design

In the simulation experiment, in order to improve the accuracy of the network fit, through experience and several attempts select the number of input layer neuron nodes is 35, the number of output layer neurons node is 1 and the hidden layer neurons number is 30, BP neural network prediction model is shown in Fig. 82.1.

82.3.2 Genetic Algorithm Design

82.3.2.1 Encoded Mode

In the encoding process, the weight of nodes between input layer and middle layer, the middle layer and output layer, the threshold value of the middle layer and output layer node are encoded into one individual of the population. The individual length L = N × P + P × M + P + M (N is the number of input nodes, P is the number of hidden nodes, M is the number of output nodes), so the encoding length in the experiment is L = 35 × 30 + 30 × 1 + 30 + 1 = 1111.

82.3.2.2 Fitness Function

The niche Genetic Algorithm formula is follows:

$$F(X) = 1/f(X) \tag{82.2}$$

where, $f(X) = \sum \sum |d^p - o^p|$, and d^p, o^p respectively means the desired output and actual output of the output node in the p-times training sample. In the fitness function the greater objective function value stands for better individual's fitness value.

82.3.2.3 Selection Operator

The Monte Carlo method is used in the selection operator. For example, the fitness of individual X_i is f_i, and its probability of being selected is follows:

$$p_i = f(X_i) / \sum_{i=1}^{n} f(X_i) \qquad (82.3)$$

82.3.2.4 Crossover and Mutation Operator

Select one point crossover method as crossover operation, mutation operation employs uniform mutation operation.

82.4 Simulation and Result Analysis

Set the NGA parameter, the population size is 200, crossover probability Pc is 0.9, mutation probability Pm is 0.05 and generation number is 100 after many test simulations. Also the BP neural network learning efficiency is selected as 0.05, error accuracy is 1×10^{-3}, and the iteration number is 1000. The Matlab program language is used in the simulation and then gets the simulation results. Figure 82.2 shows the comparison of BP neural network based on NGA and standard BP

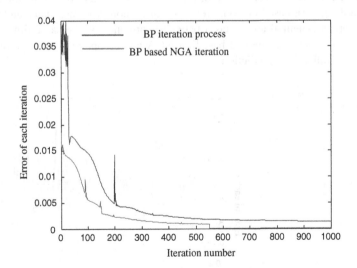

Fig. 82.2 The iterative process of BP neural network based NGA and standard BP neural network Iteration number

Fig. 82.3 Convergence
process of GA and NGA

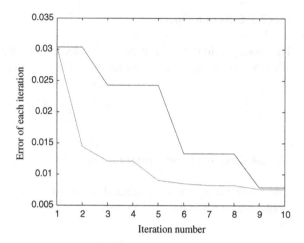

neural network iterative process. The Fig. 82.3 shows the convergence process of
GA and NGA and Fig. 82.4 shows the Error of BP based NGA and BP method.

Figure 82.2 shows that after NGA initial optimization the BP neural network
converges faster and then gets the solution which is satisfied the error precision.
On the contrary, standard BP neural network optimization converse slowly and
fails to get a solution which meets the accuracy requirements in the 1000 iteration
process. Figure 82.3 shows the Niche genetic algorithm is better than the standard
genetic algorithm in the solving speed. Figure 82.4 means the final solution from
the algorithm of BP neural network method based on NGA has smaller error than
standard BP neural network method. Figures 82.2 and 82.4 proved the method of
BP neural network based on NGA reflects reality more accurate than standard BP
neural network method and it has a better performance, at the same time proved
the BP neural network method based on NGA can be applied to the problem of
short-term traffic flow prediction.

Fig. 82.4 Error of BP based
NGA and BP method

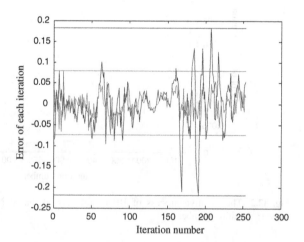

82.5 Conclusion

The paper researched the short-term traffic flow forecasting model and method. Because the BP neural network algorithm has disadvantage of easily trapping into local minima, and slow convergence speed, so the niche genetic algorithm is introduced into the BP neural network algorithm and build the combined NGA and BP neural network algorithm, then design short-term traffic flow forecasting model. Introduced niche technique which based on crowding mechanism into genetic algorithm, constitute niche genetic algorithm can avoid high fitness value individual breed fast and filled the entire group so that lose the diversity of solution in later evolution of genetic algorithm. The simulation is done and the results show combined niche genetic and BP neural network can conquer the problems of standard BP neural network and Genetic algorithm, and can get the optimal solution more faster than stand BP network, at the same time the niche genetic algorithm is combined also enhanced the neural network's ability of acclimatization to some extent, so the method can be applied to short-term traffic flow forecasting.

Acknowledgments The research is supported by the Graduate science and technology innovation fund, Shandong University of Science and Technology (No. YCA120426) and supported by The Scientific Research Foundation for the Excellent Middle-Aged and Youth Scientists of Shandong Province (No.BS2012DX031) and supported by National Nature Science Foundation (No.61273197).

References

1. Wang Z, Huang Z (2003) Analysis and evaluation of short term traffic flow prediction model. Syst Eng 21(6):98–100 (in Chinese)
2. Gong X, Tang S (2003) Short-term traffic flow prediction and incident detection algorithm based on non-parametric regression. China J Highway 2004 3:82–85 (in Chinese)
3. Chen G, Wang X (2001) Genetic algorithms and application. Posts and Telecommunications Press, Beijing, pp 105–106 (in Chinese)
4. Holland JH (1992) Adaptation in nature and artificial systems. vol 2003, issue 1, MIT Press, Cambridge, [D]pp 66–67
5. Chen H, Grant Muller S (2000) Use of sequential learning for short-term traffic flow forecasting. Transport Res 7(6):11–13 (in Chinese)
6. Manoel CN (2009) Online-SVR for short-term traffic flow prediction under typical and atypical traffic conditions. Expert Syst Appl 2009(36):6164–6173

Chapter 83
An Algorithm Based on Predicate Path Graph for Mining Multidimensional Association Rules

Hengmin Zhu and Qing Li

Abstract Multidimensional association rules is more common in association rule mining. For a shortcoming that current multidimensional association mining algorithms need to scan database many times, this paper presents an association rule mining algorithm, Ex-Apriori, based on the predicate path graph. The algorithm can produce the predicate path graph by scanning database only once, and dig out the frequent pattern based on the frequent predicate path graph. Hence it avoids the shortcoming of scanning database many times. The experiment shows that compared with the classical association rule mining algorithm Apriori, Ex-Apriori algorithm has a significant improvement in time efficiency.

Keywords Association mining · Multidimensional association rules · Predicate path graph

83.1 Introduction

The concept of association rules was proposed by Agrawal first in 1993 [1], it is an important direction in data mining. The most famous association mining algorithm is Apriori algorithm and its extensions [1, 2], which is an iterative searching process, and it needs to scan the database many times to find out the frequent patterns of every layer. Low time efficiency is an obvious shortcoming when Apriori is applied in large-scale database.

H. Zhu (✉) · Q. Li
College of Economics and Management, Nanjing University of Posts
and Telecommunications, Nanjing 210046, China
e-mail: hengminzhu@163.com

W. Lu et al. (eds.), *Proceedings of the 2012 International Conference on Information Technology and Software Engineering*, Lecture Notes in Electrical Engineering 211, DOI: 10.1007/978-3-642-34522-7_83, © Springer-Verlag Berlin Heidelberg 2013

At present, a lot of association rule mining algorithms are for mining single dimensional association rules which contains only one predicate appearing repeatedly. Compared with the single dimensional rules, the multidimensional association rules involving two or more predicates are more general. Although some algorithms for mining single dimensional association rules can be extended for multidimensional rules, they're low efficiency when applied to large-scale database. It's an important task of association mining to study an efficient mining algorithm of the multidimensional association rule. The relevant research works are as following: Fu and Kamber presented an association rule mining algorithm guided by meta-rules, in which a rule template was used to describe the expected rules form. In order to find all of the multidimensional association rules, it needs to define too many rule templates [3, 4]. Shen [5] proposed a multidimensional association rule mining algorithm based on the combination of ant algorithm and genetic algorithm, which needs to set many parameters, and its result is unstable. So it cannot guarantee that all the frequent itemsets can be found out. Gunopulos [6] proved that it is a NP-complete problem to judge whether a database exists the frequent itemsets with at least t attributes and support σ. Therefore, reducing the database traverse times is the main way to improve the efficiency of the algorithm for mining frequent itemsets. In order to reduce the database traversal times, Liu [7] proposed a multidimensional mining association rule algorithm named MPG based on frequent pattern graph, and Xu [8] proposed a fast algorithm named MDFM. These two algorithms need scanning the database only once to construct the data graph of MPG or the list structure of MDFM, but it's necessary to accumulate the record identification which is corresponding with the data items of node in the data graph or the list structure. Furthermore, the support of patterns is evaluated by calculating the intersection of the sets of record identification. In summary, the existing multidimensional association rule mining algorithms need to traverse the database many times or calculate the intersection of the sets of record identification, which affects space and time efficiency of the algorithms in a certain extent.

For the shortcoming that multidimensional association mining algorithms need to scan the database many times, an efficient association rules mining algorithm based on predicate path graph is presented. The algorithm produces a predicate path graph by scanning the database once, based on which the algorithm can dig out the frequent patterns without repeatedly traversing the database or calculating the intersection of the sets of record identification time after time. The algorithm significantly improves time efficiency of association rules mining.

83.2 Description and Construction of Predicate Path Graph

To reduce the scanning times in database when evaluating the candidate itemsets and consequently improve time efficiency of the association mining algorithm, the concept of predicates path is presented in this paper. Each record in the database corresponds to a predicate path. Taking predicate path as a unit and counting the number of the records in database which corresponds to a same predicate path, the frequency of each path or common predicates in different paths can be calculated, and then the frequent patterns of the database can be obtained.

83.2.1 Basic Concepts

The schema of data table D is described as the attributes set $A = \{A_1, A_2, ..., A_m\}$, A_i is a discrete attribute, and its domain is denoted as Dom (A_i). Each record is denoted as T $(t_{1j}, t_{2j},..., t_{mj})$, in which the predicate term t_{ij} means the value of record T in attribute A_i, and $t_{ij} \in$ Dom (A_i).

Definition 1 *Predicate Path* A <attribute,value> pair in database can be called a predicate. A certain arrangement P of attributes is designated arbitrarily, according to which the <attribute,value> pairs of each record in the database corresponds to a predicate path.

Definition 2 *Frequency of Predicate Path* If there are n records in the database corresponding to a predicate path r, then the frequency of r is n, denoted as num (r) = n.

Definition 3 *Same-named Predicates* If there exists $n(n \geq 2)$ predicates which have the same <attribute,value> pair and are in n different predicate paths, then these n predicates are called as same-named predicates.

Definition 4 *Predicate Path Graph Predi-G (V, E, N)* A predicate path graph can be denoted as **Predi-G (V, E, N)**, and V is the set of all the predicates in table D, being divided into m sub-sets according to the attributes, that is, $\cup V_i = V$, where V_i only includes the predicates whose attribute are A_i; E is the directed arc set of two adjacent predicates in the same record, that is $E = \{ <v_i, v_j > \mid v_i \in V_i, v_j \in V_j$, where v_i and v_j are adjacent in the same record}; N is the directed arc set of same-named predicates, that is $N = \{ <v_i^m, v_i^n > \mid v_i^m = v_i^n = v_i$, and v_i^m, v_i^n are in the different predicate paths}.

Each data node of the predicate path graph corresponds to a predicate. The structure of the data node is shown in Fig. 83.1, in which the pointer road_before points to the prepositive predicate of data node in the same predicate path, and the pointer samePredi_next points to its subsequent predicate in the list of same-named predicates, t_{ij} is the value of this predicate, and num is its frequency.

Fig. 83.1 The structure of data node in predicate path graph

Suppose that there are four attributes $A_i(1 \leq i \leq 4)$ in the sample database D and all six records as follows: $T_1 = (t_{11}, t_{21}, t_{31}, t_{41})$, $T_2 = (t_{12}, t_{21}, t_{31}, t_{41})$, $T_3 = (t_{11}, t_{21}, t_{31}, t_{41})$, $T_4 = (t_{13}, t_{22}, t_{31}, t_{41})$, $T_5 = (t_{11}, t_{22}, t_{31}, t_{42})$, $T_6 = (t_{13}, t_{23}, t_{32}, t_{42})$. Then the predicate path graph can be constructed as Fig. 83.2.

Definition 5 *Frequent Predicate Path Graph* If each predicate v_i in the predicate path graph Predi-G (V, E, N) is frequent, that means the frequency sum of all the same-named predicates of v_i is greater than or equal to the minimum support, then we called it as frequent predicate path graph.

The main steps to generate a frequent predicate path graph are as follows: first, to count the frequency of each predicate in the predicate path graph, and then determine whether it is frequent; second, to delete the predicate v_i from the paths if v_i is not frequent, and to increase a directed arc from the after of v_i to the before of it to ensure the connectivity of the path.

For example, for the predicate path graph shown in Fig. 83.2, let that the minimum support min_sup = 2/N (N is the total number of records in the database), then we can get the frequent predicate path graph shown in Fig. 83.3.

Theorem 1 In the frequent predicate path graph, let $\sup(t_{ia}, \ldots, t_{jb})$ denote the support of the pattern $(t_{ia}, \ldots, t_{jb})$, then $\sup(t_{ia}, \ldots, t_{jb}) = \frac{1}{N} \sum\limits_{t_{ia}, \ldots, t_{jb} \in r_k}^{r_k exists} num(r_k)$, where N is the total number of records, and r_k is the path including the pattern $(t_{ia}, \ldots, t_{jb})$

Proof As the definition of pattern support as we know, $\sup(t_{ia}, \ldots, t_{jb})$ = the number of the records which including the pattern $(t_{ia}, \ldots, t_{jb})$/N. By definition 1, we know that each record corresponds to one and only one predicate path. The corresponding relationship of the record and the path is discussed in two cases: ①If the record T and the predicate path r is one-to-one, then num (r) = 1; ②If n records correspond to the same predicate path r, according to definition 2, num (r) = n. Let

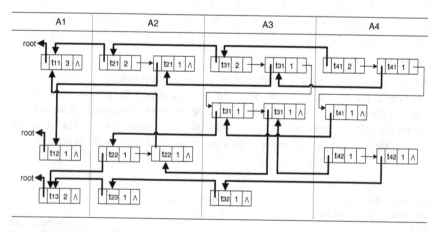

Fig. 83.2 An example of predicate path graph

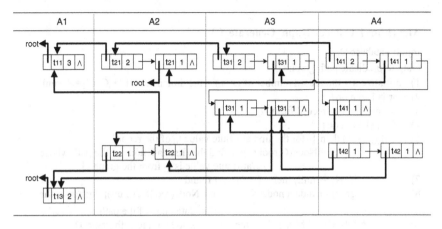

Fig. 83.3 Frequent predicate path graph

the record set D which contains the pattern $(t_{ia}, \ldots, t_{jb})$ corresponds to m predicate paths in the predicate path graph, then we can divide D into m subsets to make all the records of each subset D_i correspond to the same predicate path r_i. Let $|D_i|$ denote the number of records in D_i, then the number of the records which including the pattern $(t_{ia}, \ldots, t_{jb}) = |D_1| + \ldots + |D_m| = \text{num}(r_1) + \ldots + \text{num}(r_m)$, so theorem 1 is established.

Theorem 1 indicates that we can evaluate pattern support by calculating the frequency of predicate path in frequent predicate path graph, which improves time efficiency of mining multidimensional rules without repeatedly traversing the database or calculating the intersection of the sets of record identification time after time.

83.2.2 Construction Algorithm of Predicate Path Graph

The construction of predicate path graph is to read records in the database one by one, and based on which to search the existing path or re-construct a new predicate path. The whole construction process needs to scan the database only one time. The main steps are shown in algorithm 1.1.

Algorithm 1.1 PrediGraph_Generate（ ）

Input: database D.

Output: predicate path graph G.

1) Initialize n = the record number of D , m = the dimension of D ,G=N_1=N_2=null;
2) for i=1 to n do{
3)   to read the i-th record from D;
4)   for j=1 to m do{
5)   if (j == 1) then {//for the first attribute value t_{i1} of the record
6) N_1=FindNode(G,root,t_{i1}); // find the first data node of the path whose
                                    //attribute value is t_{i1} from the graph G
7)   if (N_1 ==null) then   {   //if not found
8)   to generate a data node N_1=GenDataNode(root,t_{i1},1,null); //generate the
                                    //first data node of the path
9)   AddNode (G,N_1); } //add the first data node to the path graph D
10)   else AddNum(G,N_1);   } //if success to find N1, it just needs to adjust
                                    // the frequency of the data node
11)   else {   //for the other attribute values t_{ij} of the record
12) N_2=FindNode(G,N_1,t_{ij}); //find the data node whose prepositive
                                    // node is N_1 and attribute value is t_{ij}
13)   if (N_2 ==null) then { //if not found
14)   to generate a data node N_2=GenDataNode(N_1,t_{ij},1,null); //generate data
                                    // node N_2
15)   AddNodeToList(G,N_2); } //add N_2 to the corresponding same-named
                                    //predicate list in the path graph G
16)   else AddNum(G,N_2); //if success to find N_2, it just needs to
                                    //adjust the frequency of the data node
17) N_1=N_2; } //take N_2 as a prepositive node to update N_1
18)   j=j+1;}
19) i=i+1;}
20) return G.

In the algorithm 1.1, step (5–10) creates the head node of the predicate path or
updates the frequency of the existing node by reading the first attribute value of the
record; step (11–17) creates the rest nodes of the predicate path according to the
other attribute values of the record, or updates the frequency of the existing nodes.

83.3 Multidimensional Association Rule Mining Algorithm Ex-Apriori Based on the Predicate Path Graph

According to the concept of predicate path graph and related theories, this paper
improves the classical association mining algorithm Apriori, and proposes a
multidimensional association rule mining algorithm Ex-Apriori based on the
predicate path graph.

As the basic ideas of Apriori, the Ex-Apriori algorithm also produces candidate itemsets and frequent itemsets at different levels. The improved place is that Apriori evaluates the support of the candidate itemsets by scanning database, while Ex-Apriori completes the support evaluation by calculating the frequency of predicate path. The main steps of Ex-Apriori are shown in Algorithm 1.2.

Algorithm 1.2 Ex-Apriori ( )

Input: database D, minimum support min_sup;

Output: frequent itemsets at all levels L ;

1) initialize $L=\varnothing$, k=1;

2) to construct predicate path graph G with PrediGraph_Generate algorithm;

3) to generate frequent predicate path graph PG by removing the infrequent predicate from G;

4) all the predicates in the PG compose frequent 1-itemsets L_1;

5) repeat

6) k=k+1;

6) C_k= GenCandidate(L_{k-1}) ;

7) for each candidate item c_{kj} in C_k do {

8) $sup(c_{kj}) = \dfrac{1}{N} \sum\limits_{c_{kj} \in r_i}^{r_i exists} num(r_i)$;

9) if $sup(c_{kj}) \geq$ min_sup then $L_k = L_k \cup \{c_{kj}\}$; }

10) if $L_k \neq \varnothing$ then $L=L \cup L_k$; }

11) until $L_k=\varnothing$;

12) return L.

Ex-Apriori completes the support evaluation of candidate sets based on the frequent predicate path graph, and it only needs to traverse the database one time for the construction of predicate path graph without storing and calculating the intersection of the sets of record identification, which remarkably improves mining efficiency of the algorithm.

83.4 Experimental Result

In order to test the time performance of Ex-Apriori, we use the development tool Visual C++6.0 to implement Ex-Apriori and Apriori. Experimental data is the mushroom database of UCI ML Repository from World Wide Web with URL: http://archive.ics.uci.edu/ml. The database has 23 attributes and 8124 records. Experiments are done on the computer with 3 GHZ Pentium CPU, 2 GB memory and Windows XP OS. Experiment compares the time efficiency of two algorithms for the whole database at different minimum support threshold. The result is shown in Fig. 83.4. The execution time of Ex-Apriori is 2–3 times faster than that of

Fig. 83.4 Execution time of
two algorithms at different
minimum support

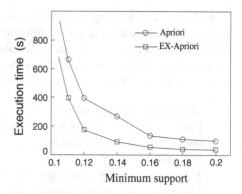

Apriori at each support threshold. Since the bigger size of frequent itemsets are
generated when minimum support closes to 0.1, the execution time of two algorithms at minimum support 0.1 is much more than that at the others.

83.5 Conclusion

This paper presents a multidimensional association rule mining algorithm
Ex-Apriori based on the theory of predicate path graph. The algorithm constructs
the predicate path graph first by scanning database once, and evaluates the candidate itemsets based on the frequent predicate path graph without scanning the
database many times. Experiments show that, compared with the classical association rule mining algorithm Apriori, Ex-Apriori has a significant improvement in
time efficiency for mining multidimensional association rule.

Acknowledgments This paper is supported by the Ministry of education projects for Humanities
and Social Sciences (No.10YJC870052) and the project supported by the National Natural
Science Foundation of China (No.71271120 and 70972083).

References

1. Agrawal R, Imielinski T, Swami A (1993) Mining association rules between sets of items in
   large databases. In: Proceedings of 1993 ACM-SIGMOD international conference on
   management of data (SIGMOD'93). ACM Press, New York, pp 207–216
2. Agrawal R, Srikant R (1994) Fast algorithms for mining association rules. In: Proceedings of
   the 20th international conference on very large data bases (VLDB'94). Morgan Kaufmann, San
   Francisco, pp 487–499
3. Fu Y, Han J (1995) Meta-rule-guided mining of association rules in relational databases. In:
   Proceedings of the 1st international workshop on integration of knowledge discovery with
   deductive and object-oriented databases, pp 39–46

4. Kamber M, Han J, Chiang J (1997) Metarule-guided mining of multi-dimensional association rules using data cubes. In: Proceedings of 1997 international conference on knowledge discovery and data mining. AAAI Press, Menlo Park, pp 207–210
5. Shen G, Qin Z (2006) New multidimensional association rule mining algorithm. Mini-Micro Syst 27:291–294 (in Chinese)
6. Gunopulos D, Khardon R, Mannila H et al (2003) Discovering all most specific sentences. ACM Trans Database Syst 28:140–174
7. Liu B, Pan J (2007) Research of algorithms based on a frequent pattern graph for mining multidimensional association rules. Electron J 35:1612–1616 (in Chinese)
8. Xu W, Wang R (2006) A fast algorithm of mining multidimensional association rules frequently. In: Proceedings of the fifth international conference on machine learning and cybernetics, Dalian, pp 13–16

Chapter 84
Manifold Learning Technique for Remote Sensing Image Classification

Kang Liu and Xu Qian

Abstract In many remote sensing image classification tasks, labels are usually expensive and the unlabeled samples are abundant. To reduce the cost on collecting labels, it is crucial to predict which unlabeled samples are the most informative. Active learning technique seeks to interactively construct a smaller and optimal training set that is the most informative and useful for the classifier. However, most of previous approaches try to discover the discriminant structure of the sample space, whereas the geometrical structure is not well respected. In this paper, we propose a novel active learning algorithm which is performed in the sample manifold space. Using the notion of the Laplacian of the graph, we then compute a low-dimensional representation of the sample set that optimally preserves local neighborhood information in a certain sense. By minimizing the expected error with respect to the optimal classifier, we can select the most representative and discriminative samples for labeling. The effectiveness of the proposed method is evaluated by comparing it with other active learning techniques existing in the literature. Experimental results on dataset confirmed the effectiveness of the proposed technique.

Keywords Active learning · Manifold learning · Graph Laplacian · Hyperspectral imagery · Machine learning

K. Liu · X. Qian
School of Mechanical Electronic and Information Engineering, China University
of Mining and Technology, Beijing, Beijing, China

K. Liu (✉) · X. Qian
Room 707A, Science and Technology Building, China University
of Mining and Technology, Beijing, School Road NO.11, Haidian District,
100083 Beijing, China
e-mail: liukang1112@gmail.com

W. Lu et al. (eds.), *Proceedings of the 2012 International Conference on Information
Technology and Software Engineering*, Lecture Notes in Electrical Engineering 211,
DOI: 10.1007/978-3-642-34522-7_84, © Springer-Verlag Berlin Heidelberg 2013

84.1 Introduction

Recent advances in remote sensing technology have made remote sensing image, such as hyperspectral imagery, with hundreds of narrow contiguous bands more widely available. Thus, the image can reveal subtle differences in the spectral of land cover classes which appear similar when viewed by previous sensors [1]. Because of the very high dimensionality of the image, supervised methods need to collect a large set of labeled samples to estimate parameters for classifiers. But, it is very expensive and time consuming to obtain labeled samples. Therefore, defining an efficient training set is the most delicate phase for the success of remote sensing image classification. There is need for a procedure that builds training set as small as possible and selects samples that are important for the quality of the prediction. This kind of procedure is known in the machine learning literature as active learning. In the active learning framework, it aims at building efficient training sets by iteratively improving the performance through sampling. Active learning becomes effective when confronted to problems dealing with large amounts of sample. Nonetheless, applications in remote sensing are rare [2].

The focus of this paper is on remote sensing image classification using few labeled samples. There are two popular groups of active learning algorithms in machine learning literature. One group of algorithms select the most uncertain sample based on the distance to the decision hyperplanes with SVM. The closer to the decision boundary a sample is, the more uncertainty its classification is. In [3], Tuia et al. presented two batch-mode active learning techniques for multiclass remote sensing image classification problems. Another group chooses the representative sample which can optimize expected measures. In statistics, the problem of selecting samples to label is typically referred to as experimental design [4]. The research of optimal experimental design (OED) is concerned with the design of experiments which are expected to minimize variance of classification model. The classic optimal experimental design techniques consist of A-optimal design, D-optimal design, and E-optimal design in which they select samples to minimize the confidence region for the model parameters. Recently, Yu et al. [5] has proposed Transductive Experimental Design (TED) with both sequential and convex optimization. The TED technique selects sample to minimize the average predictive variance of the labeled function on pre-defined dataset which yielded impressive results on experiments.

However, above algorithms only consider the labeled sample, but ignore unlabeled sample. Recently, many researchers have considered the manifold learning which the sample is drawn from sampling a probability distribution that near to a sub-manifold of the ambient space. In order to exploit the underlying manifold structure, many manifold learning algorithms have been proposed, such as Locally Linear Embedding (LLE) [6], ISOMAP [7], and Laplacian Eigenmap [8]. The most important part of the manifold learning is locally invariant [9], it shows that the nearby samples have the similar labels.

In this paper, we proposed a new active learning algorithm for remote sensing image classification which benefits from recent progresses on optimal experimental design. Unlike traditional experimental design techniques, the loss function of our algorithm is defined on both labeled and unlabeled samples. It is essentially based on a graph-based learning algorithm that introduce a locality preserving into the standard least square error based loss function. The new loss function aims to find a classifier that is locally as smooth as possible. According to the defined function, we can select the representative samples to user for labeling.

The rest of the paper is organized as follows: in Sect. 84.2, we provide a brief review of the related work. Our manifold learning algorithm is introduced in Sect. 84.3. The experimental results are presented in Sect. 84.4. Finally, we provide the concluding remarks and suggestions for future work in Sect. 84.5.

84.2 Related Work

84.2.1 Active Learning

A general active learner can be modeled as a quintuple (G, Q, S, L, and U) [10]. G is a classifier, which is trained on the labeled samples in the training set L. Q is a query function used to select the most informative samples from an unlabeled sample pool U. S is a supervisor who can assign the true class label to the selected samples from U. Initially, the training set L has few labeled samples to train the classifier G. After that, the query function Q is used to select a set of samples from the unlabeled pool U, and the supervisor S assigns a class label to each of them. Then, these new labeled samples are included into L, and the classifier G is retrained using the updated training set. The closed loop of querying and retraining continues for some predefined iterations or until a stop criterion is satisfied.

84.2.2 Optimal Experimental Design

Optimal Experimental Design considers learning a linear function:

$$y = \mathbf{w}^T \mathbf{x} + \varepsilon \tag{84.1}$$

where y is the observation, $\mathbf{x}$ is the independent variable, $\mathbf{w}$ is the weight vector, and ε is observation error ($\varepsilon \sim N(0, \sigma^2)$). Suppose we have a set of labeled samples $(\mathbf{z}_1, y_1), \cdots, (\mathbf{z}_k, y_k)$, where y_i is the label of $\mathbf{z}_i$. Thus, the maximum likelihood estimate for the weight vector ($\mathbf{w}$) is obtained by minimizing the sum squared error

$$SSE(\mathbf{w}) = \sum_{i=1}^{k} \left(\mathbf{w}^T \mathbf{z}_i - y_i \right)^2 \tag{84.2}$$

Let $Z = (\mathbf{z}_1, \mathbf{z}_2, \ldots \mathbf{z}_k)^T$ and $\mathbf{y} = (y_1, y_2, \ldots y_k)^T$. The optimal solution is

$$\hat{\mathbf{w}} = \left(ZZ^T\right)^{-1} Z\mathbf{y} \tag{84.3}$$

It can be proved that $\hat{\mathbf{w}}$ has a zero mean and a covariance matrix given by $\sigma^2 H_{sse}^{-1}$, where H_{sse} is the Hessian of $SSE(\mathbf{w})$.

$$H_{sse} = \left(\frac{\partial^2 SSE(\mathbf{w})}{\partial \mathbf{w}^2}\right) = \left(\sum_{i=1}^{k} \mathbf{z}_i \mathbf{z}_i^T\right) = ZZ^T \tag{84.4}$$

The optimal experimental design formulates the optimization problem by minimizing some measurement of estimation error derived from H_{sse}^{-1}. The three usual measures are the trace of H_{sse}^{-1}, determinant of H_{sse}^{-1}, and maximum eigenvalue of H_{sse}^{-1}. Many works on OED can be found in [5, 11, 12].

84.3 Manifold Active Learning Algorithm

84.3.1 Manifold Regularized I-optimal Experimental Design

Traditional experimental design makes use of only labeled samples, while neglecting the large amount of unlabeled samples. Laplacian Regularized Least Squares makes use of both labeled and unlabeled samples to explore the intrinsic geometry structure among the samples [13]. It satisfies the locally invariant idea, which assumes that if two samples $\mathbf{x}_i$ and $\mathbf{x}_j$ are sufficiently close to each other, then their labels $f(\mathbf{x}_i)$ and $f(\mathbf{x}_j)$ are close as well [14]. Suppose there are k samples from m samples are labeled. Let W be a similarity matrix. Thus, the new loss function is defined as follows

$$RRS(\mathbf{w}) = \sum_{i=1}^{k} \left(f(\mathbf{z}_i) - y_i\right)^2 + \lambda \sum_{i,j=1}^{m} \left(f(\mathbf{x}_i) - f(\mathbf{x}_j)\right)^2 W_{ij} + \beta \|\mathbf{w}\|^2 \tag{84.5}$$

where $\lambda \geq 0$ and $\beta \geq 0$ are the regularization parameters. y_i is the label of $\mathbf{z}_i$. In the loss function, the symmetric weights W_{ij} incurs a heavy penalty when neighboring samples are mapped far apart.

In order to model the manifold structure, we construct a nearest neighbor graph G. For each sample $\mathbf{x}_i$, we find its nearest neighbors and put an weight between $\mathbf{x}_i$ and its neighbors. There are many choices of the similarity matrix. A common definition is as follows

$$W_{ij} = \begin{cases} \exp\left(-\dfrac{\|\mathbf{x}_i - \mathbf{x}_j\|^2}{\sigma^2}\right) & \mathbf{x}_i \in N(\mathbf{x}_j) \ or \ \mathbf{x}_j \in N(\mathbf{x}_i) \\ 0 \end{cases} \tag{84.6}$$

By using the similarity matrix, the graph Laplacian is defined as $L = D - W$ where D is a diagonal degree matrix, it is given by $D_{ii} = \sum_j W_{ij}$. It reflects the intrinsic geometry of the samples. Therefore, the optimal solution of (84.5) is given as follows

$$\hat{\mathbf{w}} = \left(ZZ^T + \lambda XLX^T + \beta I\right)^{-1} Z\mathbf{y} \tag{84.7}$$

Let $S = (ZZ^T + \lambda XLX^T + \beta I)$, the covariance matrix of $\hat{\mathbf{w}}$ is

$$\begin{aligned} \mathrm{cov}(\hat{\mathbf{w}}) &= S^{-1} Z\,\mathrm{cov}(\mathbf{y})Z^T S^{-1} \\ &= \sigma^2 S^{-1} ZZ^T S^{-1} \\ &= \sigma^2 S^{-1}\left(S - \lambda XLX^T - \beta I\right)S^{-1} \\ &\approx \sigma^2\left(ZZ^T + \lambda XLX^T + \beta I\right)^{-1} \end{aligned} \tag{84.8}$$

where I is an $n \times n$ identity matrix.

According to previous discussion, the Laplacian regularized least square has made use of both labeled and unlabeled sample to estimate a linear fitting function that considering the intrinsic geometrical structure among the samples. A optimal design is to choose a subset $Z \subseteq X$ which simultaneously minimizes the confidence region for $\hat{\mathbf{w}}$ and the predictive variance of $f(\mathbf{x})$. The most important design in application is I-optimality, in which the average predictive variance is minimized. Here, we consider a test set $V = \{\mathbf{v}_1, \ldots \mathbf{v}_l\}$ besides candidates in $X = \{\mathbf{x}_1, \ldots \mathbf{x}_m\}$. Given a test sample $\mathbf{v}$, its prediction value is $f(\mathbf{v}) = \hat{\mathbf{w}}^T\mathbf{v}$ with variance $Var(f(\mathbf{v})) = \mathbf{v}^T\mathrm{cov}(\hat{\mathbf{w}})\mathbf{v}$. Therefore, the average predictive variance on V is

$$\begin{aligned} &\frac{1}{l}\sum_{i=1}^{l} \mathbf{v}_i^T \mathrm{cov}(\hat{\mathbf{w}})\mathbf{v}_i \\ &\approx \frac{\sigma^2}{l}\sum_{i=1}^{l} \mathbf{v}_i^T\left(ZZ^T + \lambda XLX^T + \beta I\right)^{-1}\mathbf{v}_i \\ &= \frac{\sigma^2}{l} Tr\left(V^T\left(ZZ^T + \lambda XLX^T + \beta I\right)^{-1}V\right) \end{aligned} \tag{84.9}$$

Then, the key problem of active learning is to find a subset $Z \subseteq X$ to minimize equitation (84.9). By introducing m indicator variables $\{\alpha_i\}_{i=1}^{m} \in \{0, 1\}$ where α_i indicates whether or not to select sample $\mathbf{x}_i$, finding a subset to minimize above equation is equivalent to the following optimization problem

$$\min \quad Tr\left(V^T\left(\textstyle\sum_{i=1}^m \alpha_i \mathbf{x}_i \mathbf{x}_i^T + \lambda XLX^T + \beta I\right)^{-1}V\right)$$
$$\text{s.t.} \quad \{\alpha_i\}_{i=1}^m \in \{0,1\}, \quad \textstyle\sum_{i=1}^m \alpha_i = k \tag{84.10}$$

where the variables are $\{\alpha_i\}_{i=1}^m$ and k is the number of samples to be selected. To simplify the presentation, we use vector $\boldsymbol{\alpha} = [\alpha_1, \cdots \alpha_m]$ to denote all the variables. The variable vector $\boldsymbol{\alpha}$ is sparse and has only k non-zero entries.

However, the optimization of Eq. (84.10) is NP-hard. Thus, we relax the integer constraints on α_i and take real non-negative values. Therefore, the value of α_i shows how significantly $\mathbf{x}_i$ contributes to the minimization in (84.10). By minimizing the l_1-norm that is a popular method in regression of $\boldsymbol{\alpha}$, the sparseness of $\boldsymbol{\alpha}$ can be controlled efficiently [15].

Following the convention of optimization, we use $\boldsymbol{\alpha} \succeq 0$ to denote that all the elements in $\boldsymbol{\alpha}$ should be non-negative. Based on that, the l_1-norm of $\boldsymbol{\alpha}$, i.e., $\|\boldsymbol{\alpha}\|_1$ is equal to $\mathbf{1}^T\boldsymbol{\alpha}$, where $\mathbf{1}$ is a column vector containing all ones. Thus, the optimal problem of Eq. (84.10) becomes

$$\min \quad Tr\left(V^T\left(\textstyle\sum_{i=1}^m \alpha_i \mathbf{x}_i \mathbf{x}_i^T + \lambda XLX^T + \beta I\right)^{-1}V\right) + \gamma \mathbf{1}^T\boldsymbol{\alpha}$$
$$\text{s.t.} \quad\quad\quad\quad\quad\quad\quad\quad \boldsymbol{\alpha} \succeq 0 \tag{84.11}$$

where the variable is $\boldsymbol{\alpha} \in \mathbb{R}^m$, and $\gamma \geq 0$ is the trade-off parameter for sparse.

84.3.2 Optimization Scheme

Semi-definite programming (SDP) has been the most important mathematical development in mathematical programming. It has been successfully used to solve the traditional convex constrained optimization and in such diverse domains as control theory and combinatorial optimization.

Here, we describe the SDP technique briefly. Given a symmetric matrix X, it is partitioned as follows

$$X = \begin{pmatrix} A & B \\ B^T & C \end{pmatrix}$$

If A is invertible, the matrix $S = C - B^T A^{-1} B$ is called the Schur complement of A in X. Schur complement theorem shows that, if A is positive definite, then X is positive semi-definite if and only if S is positive semi-definite.

By using a new variable $P \in \mathbb{R}^{l \times l}$, the optimization problem (84.11) can be equivalently rewrote as follows

$$\min \quad Tr(P) + \gamma \mathbf{1}^T\boldsymbol{\alpha}$$
$$\text{s.t.} \quad P \succeq_{s_i^l} V^T\left(\textstyle\sum_{i=1}^m \alpha_i \mathbf{x}_i \mathbf{x}_i^T + \lambda XLX^T + \beta I\right)^{-1}V \tag{84.12}$$
$$\boldsymbol{\alpha} \succeq 0$$

where S_l^+ denotes the set of symmetric positive semi-definite $l \times l$ matrices, which is called positive semi-definite cone in the field of optimization. The associated generalized inequality $\succeq_{s_l^+}$ is the usual matrix inequality: $A \succeq_{s_l^+} B$ means $A - B$ is a positive semi-definite matrix.

According to the Schur complement theorem, the optimization problem (84.12) can be equivalent to the following semi-definite programming

$$
\begin{aligned}
\min \quad & Tr(P) + \gamma \mathbf{1}^T \boldsymbol{\alpha} \\
s.t. \quad & \begin{pmatrix} \left(\sum_{i=1}^m \alpha_i \mathbf{x}_i \mathbf{x}_i^T + \lambda X L X^T + \beta I \right)^{-1} & V \\ V^T & P \end{pmatrix} \succeq_{S_{n+l}^+} 0 \\
& \boldsymbol{\alpha} \succeq 0
\end{aligned} \tag{84.13}
$$

As explained previously, $A \succeq_{s_{n+l}^+} 0$ means A is a positive semi-definite $(n + l) \times (n + l)$ matrix. We can get the optimal solution $\boldsymbol{\alpha}^*$ by using interior-point methods and then select k samples with the largest significant indicators (α_i^*) for user to label. Once we select the most representative samples, any classification algorithms can be applied to do pattern classification.

84.4 Experiments

84.4.1 Simple Two Moons Example

In this simple example, the effectiveness of the proposed method is evaluated by comparing it with Transductive Experimental Design (TED) which is also experimental design technique. The difference between them is whether the geometric structure among the samples is considered (Fig. 84.1).

As we can see from the figure, all the samples selected by TED are from one side of the dataset, while proposed technique selects both sides of the dataset.

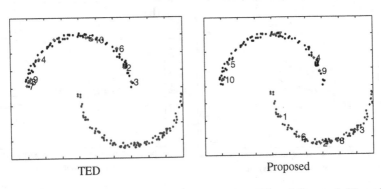

| TED | Proposed |

Fig. 84.1 Sample selection by active learning algorithms TED and Proposed. The selected samples are marked as numbers

Therefore, the samples selected by the proposed method can better represent the original data set.

84.4.2 Hyperspectral Dataset

The data set is Hyperspectral image. It is a 220-bands AVIRIS image taken over Indiana's Indian Pine test site in June 1992. The image is 145 × 145 pixels, contains 16 classes representing different crops, and a total of 10366 labeled pixels. This image is a classical benchmark to validate model accuracy and constitutes a very challenging classification problem because of the strong mixture of the class signatures. Twenty water absorption channels were removed prior to analysis. In the experiment, classes with less than 100 labeled pixels were removed, resulting thus in a 13 classes classification problem with 10266 labeled pixels. Among the available labeled pixels, 7000 were used for the training and candidate sets. Each experiment starts with pixels (ten per class). As for the previous image, the remaining 3266 pixels have been used to test the generalization capabilities.

To assess the effectiveness of the proposed technique, we compared it with three other methods: (1) the random sampling (RS); (2) the margin sampling (MS); (3) the multiclass-level uncertainty (MCLU). For the hyperspectral data set, initially only 130 labeled samples were included in the training set and 20 samples were selected at each iteration of active learning. The whole process was iterated until the satisfied result achieved. The active learning process runs 20 trials to reduce the random effect on the results. Figure 84.2 shows the average overall classification accuracies and error reduction provided by different methods versus the number of samples included in the training set at different iterations for the hyperspectral data

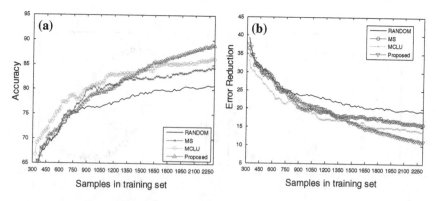

Fig. 84.2 **a** The classification accuracy and **b** error reduction over 20 trials runs provided by the proposed, the MCLU, the MS, and the RS methods for the hyperspectral data set

set. From the figure, we can see that the proposed active learning method always resulted in higher classification accuracy than the other methods.

From above figures, we can see that the accuracy of the proposed method is lower than the other methods in the previous iteration. It is because that the samples selected from the pool were not enough to reflect the intrinsic geometry of the whole sample space. Therefore, for the classifiers, the selection was biased. However, after some iteration, when the selected samples reached 1450, the accuracy of the proposed active learning technique increased faster than the others. Although the proposed method needed more samples to converge, at the end of iteration, it resulted in higher classification accuracy than the other techniques. Furthermore, for hyperspectral data set, the proposed technique yielded an accuracy of 89.169 % with only 2200 labeled samples, while the full pool as training set which is consist of 7000 samples. It is worth noting that the proposed technique is effective. From the Fig. 84.2b, we can see that, in previous iteration, the MCLU method decreased fastest because of selecting the more informative samples than the others. But the error reduction of the proposed method decreased faster since 1600 samples in the training set.

Figure 84.3a and b shows the average classification accuracy gain obtained by the proposed and the other two active learning algorithms. From the analysis of these figures, we can conclude that, in the previous steps, the samples of the proposed technique selected for the classifiers are not all from the uncertain zone, thus, the accuracy gain is less than the other techniques. However, since the training data set reached 1450, the proposed method can efficiently reflect the intrinsic geometry of the sample space, the accuracy gain increased more than the others until convergence. It is worth noting that, even if the increase of accuracy is limited on the considered data set, we have improvements at all iterations of the active learning process.

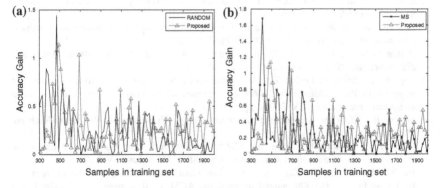

Fig. 84.3 The classification accuracy gain over 20 trials runs provided by the proposed, the MS, and the RS methods for the hyperspectral data set

84.5 Conclusion

In this paper, unlike the other active learning algorithms which explore data-independent structure of the sample space, we have presented a novel active learning technique for solving classification problem with manifold structure. To empirically assess the effectiveness of the proposed method, we compared it with other three active learning techniques using hyperspectral remote sensing image data set. In this comparison, we observed that the proposed method provided higher accuracy than those achieved by some of the most effective techniques presented in the literature. As the computational complexity of the proposed method, it is not suitable for large scale data sets. In the future development, we may apply clustering algorithms to select the most representative samples during the pre-processing phase.

Acknowledgments This work was supported in part by National Natural Science Foundation of China under Grant 70701013 and China Postdoctoral Science Foundation under Grant 2011M500035 and Research Fund for the Doctoral Program of Higher Education of China under Grant 20110023110002.

References

1. Pearlman JS, Berry PS, Segal CC, Shapanski J, Beiso D, Carman SL (2003) Hyperion: a space-based imaging spectrometer. IEEE Trans Geosci Remote Sens 41(6):1160–1173
2. Rajan S, Ghosh J, Crawford MM (2008) An active learning approach to hyperspectral data classification. IEEE Trans Geosci Remote Sens 46(4):1231–1242
3. Tuia D, Ratle F, Pacifici F, Kanevski MF, Emery WJ (2009) Active learning methods for remote sensing image classification. IEEE Trans Geosci Remote Sens 47(7):2218–2232
4. Atkinson C, Donev AN (2007) Optimum experimental designs, with SAS. Oxford University Press, Oxford
5. Yu K, Bi J, Tresp V (2006) Active learning via transductive experimental design. In: Proceedings of the 23rd international conference on machine learning, Pittsburgh
6. Roweis S, Saul L (2000) Nonlinear dimensionality reduction by locally linear embedding. Science 290(5500):2323–2326
7. Tenenbaum J, de Silva V, Langford J (2000) A global geometric framework for nonlinear dimensionality reduction. Science 290(5500):2319–2323
8. Belkin M, Niyogi P (2001) Laplacian eigenmaps and spectral techniques for embedding and clustering. Adv Neural Inf Process Syst 14:585–591
9. Hadsell R, Chopra S, LeCun Y (2006) Dimensionality reduction by learning an invariant mapping. In: Proceedings of the 2006 IEEE computer society conference on computer vision and pattern recognition (CVPR'06), pp 1735–1742
10. Settles B (2010) Active learning literature survey. University of Wisconsin-Madison, Madison, CS Technical Report 1648
11. Flaherty P, Jordan MI, Arkin AP (2005) Robust design of biological experiments. In: Advances in neural information processing systems, Vancouver, vol 18
12. He X, Min W, Cai D, Zhou K (2007) Laplacian optimal design for image retrieval. In: Proceedings of the 30th annual international ACM SIGIR conference on research and development in information retrieval (SIGIR'07)

13. Belkin M, Niyogi P, Sindhwani V (2006) Manifold regularization: a geometric framework for learning from labeled and unlabeled examples. J Mach Learn Res 7:2399–2434
14. He X (2010) Laplacian regularized D-optimal design for active learning and its application to image retrieval. IEEE Trans Image Process 19(1):254–263
15. Boyd S, Vandenberghe L (2004) Convex optimization. Cambridge University Press, Cambridge

Chapter 85
Complex Vehicle Scheduling Optimization Problem Based on Improved Ant Colony Algorithm

Yong Zeng, Dacheng Liu and Xiangyu Hou

Abstract As to a kind of complex vehicle scheduling problem (CVSP) with loading and unloading and task combination, a dynamic expense coefficient model according to the actual load is built, and in ant colony algorithm the coding method is changed from based on site to based on operating. It makes the algorithm designing and programming easier. In the local operation routing search the corresponding heuristics algorithm is designed. By programming and calculating, an example proves the algorithm is effectual.

Keywords Vehicle scheduling optimization · Ant colony algorithm · Dynamic expense coefficient · Loading and unloading staggered

85.1 Introduction

In daily activities logistics companies may have to face such a kind of distribution problems: the distribution activity relates to many tasks; the quantity of each task does not exceed the capacity of the vehicle, and each has its own loading spot and unloading spot; the goods can be loaded together. CVSP is a well-known combinatorial optimization problem and is also a focal problem of distribution management. Many different approaches have been developed to attempt to solve the CVSP. Since the vehicle routing problem (VRP) is an NP-hard problem [1],

Y. Zeng (✉) · D. Liu · X. Hou
Department of Industrial Engineering, Tsinghua University, Beijing 100084, China
e-mail: zengyong7505@163.com

W. Lu et al. (eds.), *Proceedings of the 2012 International Conference on Information Technology and Software Engineering*, Lecture Notes in Electrical Engineering 211, DOI: 10.1007/978-3-642-34522-7_85, © Springer-Verlag Berlin Heidelberg 2013

as Toth and Vigo [2] reported, no exact algorithm can consistently solve RVP-instances with more than 50 customers; thus, heuristic algorithms or biological evolutionary algorithms such as genetic algorithm (GA), neural network (NN), ant colony algorithm (ACA) are considered as a reasonable choice in finding solutions for large-scale instances [3–7]. Aiming at the particularity of the problem, this paper intends to use improved ant colony algorithm (IACA) to solve CVSP better.

85.2 Problem Description

The problem can be described as follows: There are l tasks $(r = 1,...,l)$; the goods quantity of task r is $g_r(r = 1,...,l)$; the loading spot is R_s^r and the unloading spot is R_t^r, correspondingly the operating time in the spot is T_s^r and T_t^r respectively. All goods are to be transported by vn vehicles from logistics enterprise's parking yard; all vehicles are the same and the rated load capacity is q; the working time t_k does not exceed T and the travel distance S_k does not exceed S; the vehicle should be in the parking spot after task. The tasks can and should be combined so that fewer vehicles are to be utilized. Determine the value of vn, each vehicle's tasks and routing optimally.

If each g_r meets the condition $0.5q < g_r \leq q(r = 1,...,l)$, a vehicle can't load several tasks at the same time, and the tasks can only be executed one by one. If there is g_r meeting the condition $g_r \leq 0.5q$, some tasks can be combined, and unloading and loading are staggered to some vehicle in some spots.

85.3 Model Building

Assume that the spot i is $0, 1,..., n$, in which the parking spot's number is 0. Define variables y_{kr} and x_{ijk},

$$y_{kr} = \begin{cases} 1 & \text{task } r \text{ belongs to vehicle } k \\ 0 & \text{otherwise} \end{cases},$$

$$x_{ijk} = \begin{cases} 1 & \text{vehicle } k \text{ travels from } i \text{ to } j \text{ directly} \\ 0 & \text{otherwise} \end{cases}.$$

85.3.1 Dynamic Expense Coefficient Model

Function $c(q_{ijk}, d_{ij})$ reflects the transport expense from spot i to spot j directly. The dynamic expense coefficient calculation model is designed as follows:

$$c(q_{ijk}, d_{ij}) = \begin{cases} c_0 + c_1 d_{0j} & q_{ijk} = 0; i = 0; j = 1, \ldots, n & (1.1) \\ c_1 d_{ij} & q_{ijk} = 0; i \neq 0; j = 0, 1, \ldots, n & (1.2) \\ (c_1 + \alpha q_{ijk}) d_{ij} & q_{ijk} \neq 0; i, j = 1, \ldots, n & (1.3) \end{cases} \quad (85.1)$$

In (85.1), q_{ijk} is the actual load of vehicle k from spot i to spot j; d_{ij} is the distance between i and j; c_0 is the fixed expense of dispatching a vehicle; c_1 is the expense coefficient of no-load mileage; αq_{ijk} is the increased expense coefficient because of load; α is the conversion coefficient from load to expense.

Equation (1.1) represents the expense of vehicle from parking area to loading spot, including fixed expense and no-load expense. Equation (1.2) represents the no-load expense of vehicle from i to j. Equation (1.3) represents the load expense.

Different value of c_0, c_1, α determines a different routing optimization strategy.

- If the value of c_0 is larger, the strategy is to reduce the number of vehicle as possible.
- If c_1 is larger, the strategy is to minimize the no-load mileage.
- If α is larger, the strategy is to reduce the circuitous mileage as far as possible when the vehicle is weight-bearing.

Under the constraint of vehicle capacity, working time and distance, this paper is to minimize the no-load mileage and the invalid turnover on the basis of minimizing the number of vehicles.

85.3.2 Mathematical Model of CVSP

A mathematical model of CVSP is created as follows:

$$\min z = \sum_i \sum_j \sum_k C(q_{ijk}, d_{ij}) x_{ijk} \tag{85.2}$$

$$s.t. \quad q_{ijk} \leq q \quad i, j = 0, 1, \ldots, n; \forall k \tag{85.3}$$

$$\sum_r (T'_s y_{kr}) + \sum_r (T'_l y_{kr}) + \sum_i \sum_i (t_{ij} x_{ijk}) \leq T \quad \forall k \tag{85.4}$$

$$\sum_i \sum_j (d_{ij} x_{ijk}) \leq S \quad \forall k \tag{85.5}$$

$$\sum_k y_{kr} = 1 \quad \forall r \tag{85.6}$$

$$\sum_i \sum_k^k x_{0ik} = vn \tag{85.7}$$

$$\sum_i^i \sum_k^k x_{0ik} - \sum_j \sum_k x_{j0k} = 0 \tag{85.8}$$

$$x_{ijk} = 0 \; or \; 1 \qquad i,j = 0, 1, \ldots, n; \forall k \tag{85.9}$$

$$y_{kr} = 0 \; or \; 1 \qquad \forall k, r \tag{85.10}$$

Equation (85.2) is the objective function, (85.3) shows that the quantity of goods delivered must not exceed the vehicle capacity, (85.4) is the constraint of working time, (85.5) expresses the total length of each route has a limit, (85.6) denotes one task can only be executed by one vehicle, (85.7) all vehicle should start from the parking area, (85.8) all vehicle should come back to the parking area after task, (85.9) and (85.10) are the constraints of value of the variables.

85.4 Algorithm Design

85.4.1 ACA Introduction

ACA is put forward by researchers who are inspired by real ant colony behavior [8]. After a lot of detailed observation, the expert of bionics found that the ants transmit information between individuals through hormone. Ants leave the hormone on the path and can sense the substance and are guided to the motion direction. Therefore, the collective behaviors of ant colony will show a positive feedback phenomenon. The more ants walk on the path, the latter chooses the path in greater probability.

85.4.2 IACA Design

This problem is very different from the typical TSP:

- There may be loading and unloading at the same spot, so the ant need pass through it several times.
- Different tasks need to be assembled, resulting in the path is not direct from the loading point to its corresponding unloading point.
- Under the constraints of mileage and time, the ants must be back to parking area and start again.
- Under the constraint of carrying capacity, ant's next step is determined by the tasks together with the constraints of time and mileage.

Therefore, in order to express every step clearly (spots arrived at, tasks performed, loading or (and) unloading) in the algorithm, loading and unloading of all tasks are numbered. There are l tasks, so the operating number is $2l$, together with the 0 number of the parking yard, the number is $2l + 1$. In the algorithm Ants pass through each operating in turn, and a number sequence forms (At the same time the spatial path is decided). Because the ant should return parking area in the middle of path, the maximum amount of operating of completing one cycle is $3l$ times (when go back to spot 0 after every task).

In order to simulate the actual behavior of ants, assume m is the amount of ants in the colony; $c_{ij}(i, j = 0, 1, 2, ..., 2l)$ is the expense from operating i to operating j; $\tau_{ij}(nc)$ indicates the residual amount of information on the path ij after the program runs nc times. In the initial $\tau_{ij}(0) = C$ (C is a constant), the amount of information on the paths is equal. Ant k ($k = 1, 2, ..., m$) decides its direction according to the amount of information on the path (task sequence and place sequence). $p_{ij}^k(t)$ is the probability of transferring from operating i to operating j at the time t.

$$p_{ij}^k(t) = \begin{cases} \tau_{ij}^\alpha(nc)\eta_{ij}^\beta(t) \Big/ \displaystyle\sum_{j \in allowed(k)} \tau_{ij}^\alpha(nc)\eta_{ij}^\beta(t), & j \in allowed(k) \\ 0, & otherwise \end{cases} \quad (85.11)$$

In (85.11), $allowed(k)$ represents the operating that is allowed to be chosen by ant k in next step, it can only be down-operating (unloading) whose up-operating has been passed through, or up-operating (loading) not passed; $now(k)$ records the operating that has been passed in present trip by ant k; $before(k)$ records the operating that has been gone through in before trip by ant k; $next(k)$ records the operating that need to be passed in next trip by ant k; $\eta_{ij}(t)$ is the expectation degree from operating i transferring to j at time t, which is determined through specific heuristic algorithm: If the operating j is the up-operating not passed, weather the task can be added into the path depends on the constraints; If it can be added, the expectation degree is higher when the increased expense is lower after local order is listed; If it can't be added, it is recorded in $next(k)$; If j is the down-operating whose up-operating is passed by ant k, j is the operating which must be passed. The order of several down-operating is only local and can be decided by the method of travelling through. α, β express the different function of information accumulated and heuristic factor in the path selection.

Assume parameter ρ is the residual degree of information, after $3l$ times the ant finishes one cycle and the amount of information on the path is adjusted.

$$\tau_{ij}(nc + 1) = \rho \cdot \tau_{ij}(nc) + \Delta\tau_{ij}, \Delta\tau_{ij} = \sum_{k=1}^m \tau_{ij}^k. \quad (85.12)$$

In (85.12), $\Delta\tau_{ij}^k$ is the amount of information on the path ij that is left by ant k in present cycle. $\Delta\tau_{ij}$ is the amount of information on the path ij that is left in present cycle.

$$\Delta \tau_{ij}^k = \begin{cases} Q/C_k, & \text{ant } k \text{ passes through path } ij \text{ in present cycle} \\ 0, & \text{otherwise} \end{cases} . \qquad (85.13)$$

In (85.13), Q is a constant, C_k is the total cost of ant k in present cycle.

The value of parameter m, α, β, ρ, C, Q is determined at last after constantly comparing and adjusting and experimenting on the computer based on existing research results. The condition of stopping running can be the fixed times of cycle or the state of evolutionary trend when it is not apparent.

85.4.3 Designing Step of Algorithm

Based on the algorithm principle, the step of the improved ant colony algorithm is designed as follows:

Step (1): Initialization. Each parameter is assigned initial value; if there is nothing improved after max times continuous cycle, exit; the count of cycle $nc = 0$; m ants are placed in the parking yard, and randomly select the up-operating of l tasks; $now(k)$ records the initial up-operating of ant k, and determine $allowed(k)$ and $next(k)$; time $t = 1$.

Step (2): If $jilu =$ max, the best path is found, the result is listed and exit; if $jilu <$ max, go Step (3).

Step (3): According to $allowed(k)$, calculate $p_{ij}^k(t)$ of ant k, select the next operating j, and add it to $now(k)$, $t = t + 1$, and modify $allowed(k)$ and $next(k)$ at the same time. If $allowed(k)$ is empty, it means the end of the trip, ant k back to the yard; if $next(k)$ also is empty, it means that all tasks have been implemented. If $next(k)$ is not empty, the ant backs to the yard and once again starts to execute the task (the first operating can be determined at random when no information data, or determined according to the information amount of path). Repeat this step until all ants have completed all tasks. $nc = nc + 1$.

Step (4): Calculate C_k, $\Delta \tau_{ij}^k$, $\Delta \tau_{ij}$, $\tau_{ij}(nc)$, update the present optimal path and the information amount on each path. If the optimal path is updated, $jilu = 0$; if not updated, $jilu = jilu + 1$.

Step (5): All ants proceed from the parking spot and select the initial up-operating of probability depending on the information amount, update $now(k)$, $allowed(k)$ and $next(k)$; time $t = 1$. Go to Step (2).

From the output, the final optimized operating path and the corresponding expense can be obtained, and further the task order, spatial path and the amount of vehicles (that is the time of ants backing to yard) can be obtained.

85.5 An Example

In order to validate the effectiveness of the IACA designed in this paper, a specific instance of vehicle scheduling optimization is analyzed.

Table 85.1 Details of distribution tasks

Task r	1	2	3	4	5	6	7	8	9									
Weight	0.9	3.9	4	2.2	2.7	1	3.7	2.5	2.1									
From i to j	$2 \to 10$	$3 \to 4$	$3 \to 6$	$4 \to 5$	$5 \to 11$	$7 \to 5$	$8 \to 12$	$9 \to 1$	$12 \to 8$									
Operating No.	1	2	3	4	5	6	7	8	9	10	11	12	13	14	15	16	17	18

Table 85.2 Number and coordinates of spots of parking, loading and unloading

Spot No.	0	1	2	3	4	5	6	7	8	9	10	11	12
Abscissa	35	5	22	15	7	27	25	33	49	40	42	52	75
Ordinate	23	4	8	23	61	70	42	13	6	21	40	38	40

Table 85.3 The comparison of experiment result

Experiment algorithm	Average success rate (%)	Average total cost	Average search time (s)
Genetic algorithm	17	33,095	35.3
Basic ant colony algorithm	27	29,265	27.6
Improved ant colony algorithm	39	26,545	17.4

There are 9 tasks and $r = 1,\ldots, 9$; $q = 5$(tons), the speed is 50 km/h, $T = 6$(h); $T_s^r = T_t^r = 20$min; $S = 200$ km; $c_0 = 200$ yuan/vehicle, $c_1 = 10$ yuan/km, $\alpha = 20$ yuan/tonne km; the straight-line distance between spots is obtained with the coordinates. Other information is shown in Tables 85.1 and 85.2.

Through running the program on the computer and improving the value of parameters, ultimately $m = 100$, $\alpha = 1$, $\beta = 5$, $\rho = 0.5$, C = 0, $Q = 1000$, and the optimal total cost is 22,555 yuan. The operating sequence is 0-13-14-17-18-0-11-3-4-7-8-12-9-10-0-15-1-16-5-6-2-0, so the spot sequence is 0-8-12-8-0-7-3-4-5-11-0-9-2-1-3-6-10-0 and the task sequence is 0-7-9-0-6-2-4-5-0-8-1-3-0.

The optimal proposal as follows: $vn = 3$. The first route is $0 \to 8 \to 12 \to 8 \to 0$ including task 7, 9; the mileage is 129.6 km; the corresponding load is 0, 3.7, 2.1, 0; the working time is 3.93 h. The second route is $0 \to 7 \to 3 \to 4 \to 5 \to 11 \to 0$ including task 6, 2, 4, 5; the mileage is 154.8 km; the corresponding load is 0, 1, 4.9, 3.2, 2.7, 0; the working time is 5.76 h. The third route is $0 \to 9 \to 2 \to 1 \to 3 \to 6 \to 10 \to 0$ including task 8, 1, 3; the mileage is 123.6 km; the corresponding load is 0, 2.5, 3.4, 0.9, 4.9, 0.9, 0; the working time is 4.47 h.

By comparing with genetic algorithm or basic ant colony algorithm, we can find the one designed in this article has higher search efficiency and can get better results as shown in Table 85.3.

85.6 Conclusion

Of course, at present ACA still lack a solid mathematical foundation and a rigorous analysis method. The value of parameters is determined through experiments or relying on experience, the relevant theory still have not put forward. All these need further study. To CVSP it is difficult to design efficient and accurate algorithms, and it is necessary and more realistic to look for approximate algorithms.

References

1. Laporte G (1992) The vehicle routing problem: an overview of exact and approximate algorithms. Eur J Oper Res 59:345–358
2. Toth P, Vigo D (2002) The vehicle routing problem. SIAM monographs on discrete mathematics and applications. SIAM, Philadelphia
3. Li J (1995) Vehicle routing problem with non-full load of less freight quantity. J Southwest Jiaotong Univ 3(1):41–50 (in Chinese)
4. Mosheiov G (1998) Vehicle routing with pick-up and delivery: tour-partitioning heuristics. Comput Ind Eng 34(3):669–684
5. Li J (1996) A heuristic for vehicle routing with time windows. Syst Eng 14(5):45–50 (in Chinese)
6. Xie B, Li J, Guo Y (2000) Genetic algorithm for vehicle scheduling problem of non-full loads with time windows. J Syst Eng 13(3):290–294 (in Chinese)
7. Zeng Y, Yin X (2007) The application of Tabu search in physical distribution capacitated vehicle routing optimization problem. In: International conference on transportation engineering (ICTE). ASCE, pp 2560–2565
8. Colorni A, Dorigo M, Maniezzo V (1991) Distributed optimization by ant colonies. In: Proceedings of the first European conference on artificial life. Elsevier Publishing, Paris, France, pp 134–142

Chapter 86
The Spacecraft Diagnostics Expert System Based-on the Flexible Knowledge Modeling

Hongzheng Fang, Jian Sun, Liming Han and Haobo Yang

Abstract The knowledge representation of spacecraft has many forms, leading to the establishment of the spacecraft fault knowledge base imperfect. This paper proposed a method of the spacecraft flexible knowledge modeling, making the internal conversion between different kinds of knowledge, such as model, case and rule using the unified knowledge modeling platform. Besides, an integrated diagnostic inference method is proposed. Furthermore, a spacecraft power system diagnostic expert system is implemented. The method and expert system has been applied and verified in the process of the spacecraft operation and maintenance, and has strong practical significance in the field of the spacecraft engineering.

Keywords Flexible knowledge · Diagnostics · Expert system · Knowledge

86.1 Introduction

For the spacecraft fault diagnosis system, the diagnostic inference engine capabilities and the correctness and completeness of the knowledge base directly determine the accuracy and efficiency of the spacecraft fault diagnosis. Especially the spacecraft failure knowledge base is a core component of the fault diagnosis system, if the lack of knowledge in database or knowledge error, whatever the

H. Fang (✉) · J. Sun · L. Han · H. Yang
Beijing Key Laboratory of High-speed Transport Intelligent Diagnostic and Health
Management, 100041 Beijing, China
e-mail: hongzhengf@163.com

H. Fang · J. Sun · L. Han · H. Yang
Beijing Aerospace Measure and Control Corp. Ltd, 100041 Beijing, China

W. Lu et al. (eds.), *Proceedings of the 2012 International Conference on Information Technology and Software Engineering*, Lecture Notes in Electrical Engineering 211, DOI: 10.1007/978-3-642-34522-7_86, © Springer-Verlag Berlin Heidelberg 2013

diagnosis inference engine cannot arrive at a correct diagnosis conclusions. Therefore establishing reliable and complete fault knowledge is very important.

There are some related references. Jet Propulsion Laboratory (JPL) developed diagnostic expert system, SHINE, which is a high speed inference system based on the rules [1]. Besides, the JPL has also developed fault diagnostic software, BEAM, which can learn the normal behavior of the system and make an independent diagnostic for the system failure [2]. The Stennis Research Center diagnosed the J-2X rocket engine failure using the fault tree [3]. The Ames Research Center for NASA developed the diagnosis software Livingstone, which build based on the qualitative behavioral models, and has been used for the Deep Space 1 and other spacecrafts [4, 5]. In 2003 ARC researched the HyDE system, using the mixed model describing the system dynamics [6]. However, the flexible knowledge representations are still need to be researched in-depth.

86.2 The Spacecraft Flexible Knowledge Modeling Technology

86.2.1 Models Knowledge Modeling Method

The spacecraft model knowledge representation can make full use of the system structure to avoid the experience knowledge difficult from the specialist. The most important problems of the spacecraft diagnosis model, includes the depth of the domain knowledge, the organization of the domain knowledge, etc. Domain knowledge reflects the description depth of the diagnosis object, using the physical structure to describe the system is the most direct description method, and is also the most deep description method; using the behavior structure to describe the system is quite shallow description method. According to the complex system diagnosis knowledge level and depth characteristics, the system model can be divided into three categories: the deepest is the structural description category, the structure model of system can provide the most detailed representation of the elements and relationship; secondly deep is behavior description, which reflects the system engineering process or dynamic process; the depth of the causal description is close to the experience knowledge. As shown in Fig. 86.1.

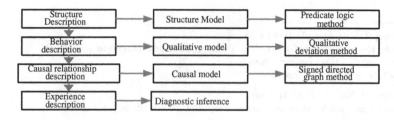

Fig. 86.1 The spacecraft system model classification

Fig. 86.2 The structure of the case library based on the object-oriented knowledge representation

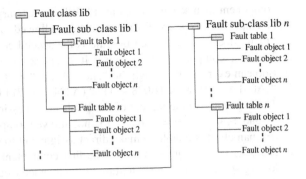

86.2.2 Cases Knowledge Modeling Method

The object-oriented case representation is adopted here to express the field object static characteristics, behavior characteristics and restraint, expert experience. The method is started from the fault class (fault class can have its super class), the fault class can have their own fault subclasses, and a subclass can have their own fault object (here is actually a failure cases). Taking the fault object as the center, the properties of the fault object, the dynamic behavior characteristics, the related domain knowledge and data processing methods and other relevant knowledge can be encapsulated in the expression fault object structure, thus constructing the object-oriented case representation.

Corresponding to the structure of the object-oriented case representation, we can design the related hierarchical structure of the fault case base. The first step is to establish a fault class layer (which is the first layer of the fault hierarchical structure); Secondly, the fault class can have its fault subclasses, and the space fault classification is made according to the failure mode (which is the second layer of the fault hierarchical structure); the fault subclasses layer can have a lot of objects belong to the object (which is the failure case). The corresponding fault attribute and the operation of the fault case will be included in the fault objects. Therefore, we can organize the fault case base according to such a hierarchical structure, as shown in Fig. 86.2.

86.2.3 Rules Knowledge Modeling Method

According to the analysis of the requirement of the spacecraft monitoring diagnosis, we constructed the architecture and grammar of the knowledge representation based on the rules, mainly including:

1. The composition and form of the knowledge. The rule is mainly composed of the rules statement, the rules statement is mainly composed of the rules key word, first component and the second components. The main form is: "if first

component then second component". When necessary, the first component can be empty, but the second component is not allowed to be empty. If the keyword "then" does not exist, then the rule is the second component.

2. The first component of the rules. It is an expression combined by several Boolean expression through the "and" (& &) "or" (| |) logic operator, such as "(A001 > = 9) & & (B078 < 1)" "(A324 = = 7) | | (A301 < 7)" and so on. The connector in the middle of the Boolean expressions is relational operators (< and >, < =, > = = =, etc.). It is not allowed to appear assignment operator (=), namely it is unable to make direct assignment to parameter, or the validity check of the rule appears error. The first component mainly includes the following several ways: the condition of the telemetry parameter; the condition of the instructions; the condition of the ground equipment; time and so on.

3. The second component of the rules. It is usually composed of expectation expressions and related instructions composition. Relevant instruction includes parameter or the error limit of the function. The second component mainly includes the following several ways: expected range; expectation values; expect changes in law; variable assignment, etc.

4. The owner of the rules. The keyword "this" can replace the owner of the rules, and the owner can be omitted the owner, so that the rules are easy to copy.

The representation of the rule is the production rule. According to the different area and scope, the classification of the rules includes fault detection rules, fault location rule and system rules.

86.2.4 Flexible Knowledge Modeling Method

Domain knowledge reflects the description depth of the diagnosis object, using the physical structure to describe the system, it is the most direct description method, and is also the most deep description method; using the behavior structure to describe the system is quite shallow description method. According to the complex system diagnosis knowledge level and depth characteristics, the system model can be divided into three categories: the most deep is the structural description category, the structure model of system can provide the most detailed representation of the elements and relationship; secondly deep is behavior description, the behavior model reflects the system engineering process or dynamic process, for complex system can only provide the qualitative behavior model; the depth of the causal description is close to the experience knowledge. As shown in Fig. 86.3.

Fig. 86.3 Spacecraft fault knowledge hierarchical relationships

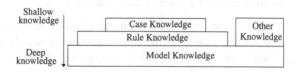

From the above analysis, we can conclude that spacecraft fault knowledge base contains deep fault knowledge, the more fault diagnosis conclusion of the higher accuracy. The deeper fault knowledge for the spacecraft fault knowledge base, the higher accuracy for the fault diagnosis conclusion. But in reality world, all kinds of fault knowledge acquisition is in a different way, leading to the fact that the deep knowledge of the actual fault knowledge base is far less than shallow knowledge (as shown in Fig. 86.4), namely the majority of the diagnosis knowledge for case knowledge and rule knowledge.

If the spacecraft fault knowledge base adopts single kind of the fault knowledge representation, it will cause the diagnosis results are not accurate because of the shortage of the single fault knowledge. If the spacecraft fault knowledge base uses the many kinds of fault knowledge representation, and it is only a simple coordination of the different fault knowledge representation of knowledge, it also cannot achieve the full use of the knowledge. Aiming at the imbalance of the different types of spacecraft fault knowledge quantity, in order to make full use of all kinds of fault knowledge, we put forward the spacecraft fault flexible knowledge modeling method, as shown in Fig. 86.5.

Flexible knowledge modeling. It means that the knowledge base has a unified knowledge modeling interface. In the knowledge base internal, through the knowledge association, transformation and learning between the different knowledge representation forms, the knowledge base can be more quickly adapt to the changes of all kinds of knowledge representation and various knowledge acquisition mode. At the same time, the redundancy useless knowledge can be eliminated in the knowledge base.

Flexible knowledge transformation. In order to improve the benefit of knowledge base in the process of the fault diagnosis reasoning, for fault knowledge base of commonly used three different representation of knowledge transformation between knowledge, in order to improve the deep knowledge quantity. The representations of knowledge in the fault knowledge base need to be transformed between knowledge to improve the deep knowledge quantity. The knowledge transformation between different knowledge representations includes three parts: knowledge learning, knowledge validation and knowledge check. The knowledge learning is to get more universality and deeper knowledge by shallow knowledge through learning method; the knowledge validation means that the deep knowledge through learning can be used as universality knowledge in shallow knowledge for validation; the knowledge check means that the same layer knowledge can be checked at any time to ensure the correctness and reliability according to the change of knowledge.

Fig. 86.4 Distribution of the amount knowledge based on the different knowledge representation

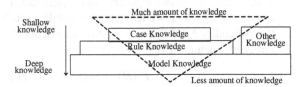

Fig. 86.5 Spacecraft fault
knowledge flexible modeling

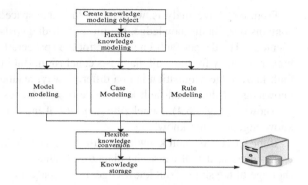

86.3 Multi-mode Integrated Diagnostic Reasoning

According to the different theoretical basis, the uncertainty reasoning can be
divided into many kinds of methods; here the method of credibility is taken. In the
uncertainty reasoning model based on the credibility, the knowledge is represented
with the production rule, the general form is

$$if \ E \ then \ H \ (F_c(H, E)) \tag{86.1}$$

In (86.1), E is the evidence of production, used for pointed out that the production
conditions available; H is a group of conclusion, used for pointed out the conclusion
should be when E condition is met; $F_c(H,E)$ is the credibility of the knowledge, called
credibility factor or rule intensity, is in the range between 0 and 1, and reflecting the
contact strength between the premise and the conclusion, its value is directly related
to the trade-offs of the reasoning conclusions. The meaning of (86.1) is: if the
evidence E is met, we have the possibility of $F_c(E)$ to draw the conclusion H.

In this model, the evidence is also represented by the credibility factor. There is
two sources of the evidence credibility $F_c(E)$: for the initial data, the credibility
value is provided by the users who puts forward the evidence; for the conclusion
previously concluded as the evidence of the current reasoning, the credibility value
of the drawn conclusion can be calculated by the uncertainty transfer algorithm.

The result of reasoning is influenced by the error of the telemetry data in a great
extent. When the data error rate is high, normal data may be submerged. Therefore
we need to analyze a coefficient of credible data on telemetry data. This confidence
factor will be involved in the reasoning as the coefficient of the factual information. According to this credibility, eventually the credibility of the conclusions can
be drawn. The credibility transfer algorithm includes the following two conditions:

1. The credibility transfer algorithm of a single fact. If the number of the support
   conclusion fact is only one, and the credibility $F_c(E)$ of the known facts E, and
   the credibility $F_c(H,E)$ of the factual knowledge "*if E then H*", and the credibility of conclusion H is

$$F_c(H) = F_c(E) \times F_c(H, E) \tag{86.2}$$

2. The credibility transfer algorithm of the combination facts. If known facts have multiple form a combination fact E

$$E = E_1 \wedge E_2 \wedge E_3 \ldots \wedge E_n \tag{86.3}$$

And the credibility $F_c(E_i)$ of every known fact, the weight coefficient $P(Ei)$ of each fact in this combination of facts, and the credibility $F_c(H,E)$ of the factual knowledge "*if E then H*", then the credibility of the conclusion H is

$$F_c(H) = \frac{\sum_{i=1}^{n} f_c(E_i) \times P(E_i)}{\sum_{i=1}^{n} P(E_i)} \times F_c(H,E) \tag{86.4}$$

Combined with the received telemetry data, remote control instruction and environmental events, the spacecraft fault diagnostic expert system can use the inference methods at the same time, as shown in Fig. 86.6.

The integrated diagnosis inference engine includes a spacecraft inference engine and a user interface. Through the user interface, experts can build diagnostic knowledge base. Users can browse the diagnosis results and query the case base.

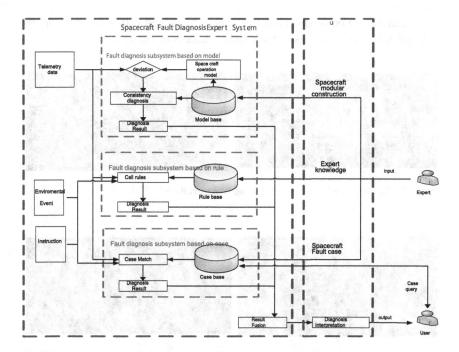

Fig. 86.6 Multi-mode fault diagnosis reasoning general structure diagram

The core of the integrated fault inference engine includes three subsystems: the fault diagnosis subsystem based on the model, rules and case. According to the telemetry data, instruction and events, these subsystems can diagnose on the spacecraft on-orbit based on the model, case and rule engine. Finally the diagnosis results are fused by the inference engine to get the final fault diagnosis results.

86.4 The Spacecraft Diagnostics Expert System

Based on the above methods, taking the power system as a background, a spacecraft diagnosis expert system based on the flexible knowledge modeling and multi-mode integrated diagnostic reasoning is developed. In the spacecraft fault knowledge flexible modeling platform, the rules knowledge, case knowledge, model knowledge for the spacecraft subsystem and components can be modeled. We can also implement the flexible conversion between different kinds of the knowledge representation methods. As shown in Fig. 86.7.

According to the telemetry data, instruction, environmental events, the diagnosis expert system can trigger the three kinds of the inference engine to give the diagnosis results, as shown in Fig. 86.8.

We took 3 years' telemetry data, instruction, events of power system of a satellite to test the efficiency of different diagnosis methods. As shown in Table 86.1.

We can see the omission number of integrated method is 0. It accords with the high reliability requirements in the running process of the spacecraft.

Fig. 86.7 The model and rules knowledge modeling interface

Fig. 86.8 The diagnosis results interface

Table 86.1 The result of different diagnosis methods

Method	Num of actual fault or abnormal	Num of correct results	Num of omission	Num of false alarm
Model-based	16	14	2	1
Case-based	16	15	1	2
Rule-based	16	15	1	1
Integrated	16	16	0	1

86.5 Conclusion

This paper proposed a spacecraft flexible fault knowledge modeling method to make the internal conversion between different kinds of knowledge. On the basis of that, the integrated diagnostic inference method is also proposed. The method and expert system has been applied and verified in the process of the spacecraft operation and management and achieved good results.

References

1. Riedesel J (1989) A survey of fault diagnosis technology. In: Proceedings of the 24th intersociety energy conversion engineering conference, pp 183–188
2. Barrett A (2005) Model compilation for real-time planning and diagnosis with feedback. In: International proceedings of conference on artificial intelligence, pp 1195–1200
3. Allan JV, Tom B, Robort L, Donald LS (2004) Development of an information fusion system for engine diagnostics and health management, NASA
4. Hayden S, Sweet A (2004) Livingstone model-based diagnosis of earth-observing one. In: AIAA 1st intelligent system technical conference, pp 1–11
5. Bajwa A, Sweet A (2003) The Livingstone model of a main propulsion system. In: IEEE aerospace conference, pp 2_869–2_876
6. Narasimhan S, Brownston L (2007) HyDe-a general framework for stochastic and hybrid model-based diagnosis. In: 18th international workshop on principles of diagnosis, pp 162–169

Chapter 87
The Modern City Central Business District Evolution Simulation

Lianpeng Zhu, Shuming Jiang, Shijie Xu and Jinfeng Miao

Abstract In recent years, with the development of world economy and urbanization speed increase, the research on CBD [1] by countries researchers' attention. This paper proposed based on double evolutionary CBD evolution simulation model thought, from the social evolution model and the spatial evolution model two levels were introduced, and through the simulation experiment is simulated verification.

Keywords Central Business District · Double evolutionary

87.1 Introduction

Along with the economic globalization and the global industrial transfer upgrade, the construction and development of domestic CBD in recent years is in the ascendant. CBD is the English abbreviations of "Central Business District", which is usually translated into Business District or the Central Business District. The concept began in the early 1920s western industrial developed countries, has been 80 years of research history.

CBD is the agglomeration of modern urban core function, a city of the most vigorous economic area, and also a urban development level of symbolic area.

L. Zhu (✉) · S. Jiang · S. Xu
Information Research Institute, Shandong Academy of Sciences,
Jinan Keyuan Road Num. 19, Shandong, China
e-mail: zlp8961@163.com

J. Miao
Jining Entry-Exit Inspection and Quarantine Bureau, Xiamen, China
e-mail: mjf_mjf@163.com

W. Lu et al. (eds.), *Proceedings of the 2012 International Conference on Information Technology and Software Engineering*, Lecture Notes in Electrical Engineering 211, DOI: 10.1007/978-3-642-34522-7_87, © Springer-Verlag Berlin Heidelberg 2013

823

Therefore constructing CBD is the desire of the governments at all levels and target. The research of CBD is related to not only the law of urban development, but also the city planning layout, therefore, whether the model of CBD's space structure is reasonable, not only affects the city of every internal factors of the configuration benefits, but also related to the urban internal concentration benefit and to the city of the hinterland of attraction and radiation.

87.2 Based on Double Evolutionary CBD Evolution Simulation Model

CBD evolution [2] is a complex system, including the original cellular automata simulation CBD external environment "space evolution" subsystem and using MAS simulation enterprise business behavior of "social evolution" subsystem, Synchronous evolution, the mutual influence of both two subsystems make up the complex system (Fig. 87.1).

87.2.1 CBD Social (Enterprise) Evolution System Model

The enterprise's own development and enterprise subjective business interactive behavior, formed the CBD social evolution [3] subsystem, and exerts a subtle influence on promoting the evolution of the CBD, development. In other words, the central business district CBD is the formation of a large number of service main body of spatial agglomeration result, the business centre of the city formation and evolution process in fact are comprehensive of a series behaviors such as the service main body generation, migration, parking, profit, and a series of comprehensive behavior.

Fig. 87.1 Based on double evolutionary CBD evolution simulation model

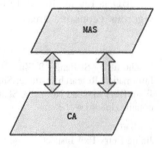

87.2.1.1 Subject Description

(1) Body state

Survival or death, the subject in the state of survival under will exert all kinds of behavior, when conditions of existence can't satisfy the death.

(2) Subject scope of perception

Subject to perceived environmental change of the maximum range, the subject carries out its business activities in its perception within the scope of the area.

(3) The Main Operating Costs

Definition with the first i patch (original cell) location as the center, the subject i cognitive range for radius area defined as regional i.

$$cost_r = cl + ct \tag{87.1}$$

$$cl = pl \cdot \left(1 + g_i^{at}\right) \cdot p_\varepsilon + (1 - p_\varepsilon) \cdot pl \tag{87.2}$$

$$ct = k \cdot (x_i - a_i)^2 + b \tag{87.3}$$

Among them, $cost_r$ is the enterprise operation cost; cl is land price cost; ct is traffic cost; pl is Basic land price (initial datum land price); g_i^{at} is regional i business atmosphere; p_ε is regional i enterprise occupancy rate; x_i is regional I enterprise quantity; a_i is the bearing capacity of the regional I (maximum enterprise capacity); b is traffic cost lower limit.

(4) Subject Transfer Cost

In the CBD industrial concentration lead to business activities "inseparable sex", "precipitation cost", the new location of industrial agglomeration of greatly increased "resting," cost, and cause the commercial institutions in the location selection existing in a lot of inertia. So the enterprise in determining the migration, in the original operation cost an additional part based on transfer cost, cost transfer cost and location of the business relations and industry cluster of related, define enterprise migration cost for:

$$cost_m = g_i^- \cdot income \tag{87.4}$$

Among them, g_i^- is the enterprise area i business atmosphere; Δt is enterprises in the position of the stop duration (algebra); income is t − 1 h enterprise income.

(5) Subject migration rules

In the business process, according to its revenue and expenditure comparison with certain probability, main body chooses whether migration, migration rules are as follows:

$$p_m = income/(cost_r + cost_m)$$

$$A_{migration}, p_m \in [0, 1]$$

$$A_{remain}, \text{otherwise} \tag{87.5}$$

Among them, the p for transfer probability; $A_{migration}$ is enterprise Agent migration behavior, A_{remain} is enterprise Agent parking behavior. When $p_m \in [0,1]$, the enterprise Agent to probability p to commercial atmosphere better regional migration; When $p > 1$, it shows that the enterprise Agent income is greater than the operation cost, the normal operation then can, take resident in situ strategy.

(6) The New Subject Produce Rules

If the subject can't get enterprise Agent service main body of the market space, the spending power will show wheel accumulation, when spending power reaches a certain threshold value, will create new enterprise Agent service main body (Fig. 87.2).

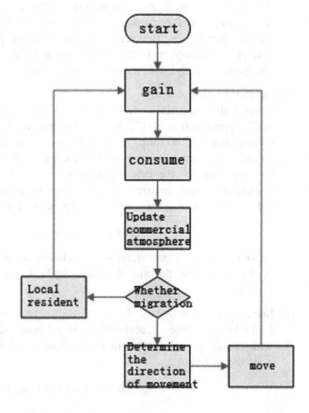

Fig. 87.2 Main body behavior process description

87.2.2 CBD Space (Environment) Evolution System Model

87.2.2.1 Environment Description

(1) Regional Commercial Atmosphere

Service main body gathered by the formation of the commercial atmosphere [4] in the traditional thinking often consider various economics under the action of the original theory, urban economic system running generated a result, but in reality the development of commercial center exist some "Matthew effect", for consumers, business atmosphere is one kind of consumer behavior attract factors, real life people tend to be more inclined to people bustling, commercial breath rich environment consumption shopping; For service main body is concerned, commercial atmosphere can become a business advantage, this advantage can, in turn, strengthen the cohesion of the commercial center, and at the same time, in many cases, commercial atmosphere will directly be service main body the basis of selection of space. Define an area i business atmosphere g_i^- for:

$$g_i^{at} = count^{neighbor}(agent)/count(agent) \qquad (87.6)$$

Among them, $count^{neighbor}$ (patches) for Patch i (original cell i) and its neighbors in the total number of enterprises; count(agent) is all the number of enterprises in the world.

(2) Regional Consumption Ability

Spending power properties are used to characterize the reality city region (tile) is the demand for goods and services and consumption ability in model of operation for each round will be produced, and then through the enterprise Agent profit behavior is consumption, model assumption initial state spending power distribution is uniform, if consumption ability can't get consumption will be accumulated to model operation the next round.

$$cs_i = pcs \cdot \left(1 + \lambda g_i^{at}\right) \qquad (87.7)$$

Among them, cs_i is the area I consumption ability; pcs for the initial reference consumption ability; g_i is regional i commercial atmosphere; λ is adjustment coefficient.

(3) Shoring of Foundation

Enterprise's supportive foundation, mainly refers to the enterprise operation necessary conditions, i.e. superior convenient geographic location (commercial atmosphere), such as city's neighboring by sea or rivers, having natural deepwater port, and advanced communication facilities and urban traffic, all of these can reduce business costs, improve income level.

$$b_i(r) = \mu g_i^{at} / cost_r \qquad (87.8)$$

Among them, $b_i(r)$ is the area i foundation support measure; g_i is Regional i business atmosphere; $cost_r$ is Regional i comprehensive operation cost; μ is Adjustment coefficient.

(4) Market Demand

Enterprise's economic environment (market), mainly refers to the commercial function of the market demand scale and critical degree, etc. In the commercial activity, the customer contact is obviously the most important factor, geographically, short distance to commercial service demand market is an obvious priority conditions. Area in the hinterland of economic scale, economic growth fast, economic system healthy and active, and cities equipped with free economic environment, are also helpful to reduce business cost and to improve the income level. The comprehensive consideration of the market demand growth speed and the overall size of the given the market demand index, describe the region of the world GDP in the proportion of GDP, defined as follows:

$$e_i(r) = \left(1 + \left(cs_i^t - cs_i^{t-1}\right)/cs_i^t\right) \cdot cs_i^t / cs^t \qquad (87.9)$$

Among them, $e_i(r)$ is the area i market demand index; $cs_i^t - cs_i^{t-1}$ were the first generation of regional i t and t − 1 generation of market demand, consumption demand); cs is the whole world market demand (consumer demand).

(5) Enterprise aggregation intensity

Enterprise gathering strength mainly refers to the existing business industry industrial cluster and specialization degree. Here it refers to the scale of the enterprise size, integrity and developed degree. A large number of financial, trading services gathered together, and large quantity of high quality means the money supply, developed supporting service, will make the cash flow, information flow between and in the center, and in the center, the flow is convenient, thus making the CBD be able to more efficient way to provide business services. An enterprise may also enjoy the scale economy and specialized economy aspects of benefit, but can also effectively reduce the risk companied with the opportunity. A regional gathering strength are defined as follows, describe the number of enterprises in the unit area:

$$s_i^r = count(agent)/count(patches) \qquad (87.10)$$

Among them, $S_i(r)$ is the area i gathering strength, count(agent) is this area enterprise total, count(patches) is this area overall size (Fig. 87.3).

Fig. 87.3 Original cell
behavior process description

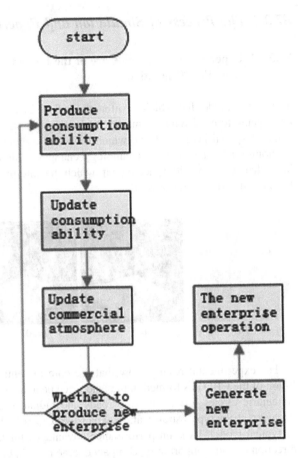

87.3 The Simulation Experiment

87.3.1 The Simulation Tool

This project uses NetLogo [5] as a simulation experiment development platform. NetLogo is used to natural and social phenomena which are simulation programmable modeling environment. It is made up of Wilensk, which was launched in 1999, the connection learning and computer modeling center (CCL) is responsible for sustainable development. NetLogo is especially suitable for over time to the evolution of complex system modeling. The researchers can send out instruction to hundreds of thousands of independent operation of the "main body" (agent) instruction. This makes exploration on the micro level and macro model of the behavior of the individual the connection between the possible, these macro model is composed of many interaction between individual emerged.

87.3.2 The Process of Simulation and Experiment

87.3.2.1 Experiment One: The Core of the Layout of the CBD Space form Evolution Simulation

The layout mode that which is often showed in CBD core focus structure is the centripetal force driving primarily business agglomeration development at the stage of spatial layout pattern, which reflects the industrialization process, scale economy and transportation technology changes. This experiment mainly simulates changes in the city space layout, which the enterprise gathered brought about by the industrial spatial layout.

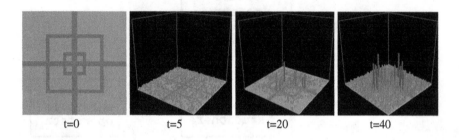

t=0   t=5   t=20   t=40

The experimental results show that the core in centralized structure, the evolution of the CBD has formed in the land price peak area as the core, cross shaft or concentric circles form, plus ring roads and radiate road as the basic skeleton, "spheres of the type" stratification expansion, China is the business space growth of typical model. Its main performance advantages for the development of CBD direction of equal opportunity, compact degree is high, boundary clear, finalize the design sex good, CBD center position is outstanding, may obtain higher concentration efficiency.

87.3.2.2 Experiment Two, the Axis of the Layout of the CBD Space form Evolution Simulation

Axis layout by the traffic is along with potential to the high efficiency, at the same time, both sides of the CBD may be affected by terrain limits, growth process is mainly along the traffic system of the main axis direction, and develop into strip development form.

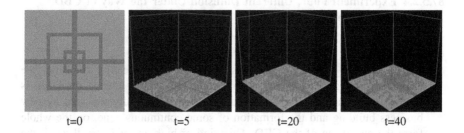

t=0	t=5	t=20	t=40

The experimental results show that the axis layout by modern means of transport for material conditions, through the establishment of large capacity traffic line to help the expansion of the CBD, it can alleviate crowded contradictions and pressure caused by the urban block expansion; it also an effective way to solve the new CBD and in the center of city traffic contact. To achieve the city space adjustment and the need to protect the historical cultural view, with urban design as the backing, along the city main development axis do axial extension, not only have the city space outstanding value, but also for the strengthening of the axis, itself also get strengthened in the new location attraction and cohesion.

87.3.2.3 Experiment Three, Waterfront of the Layout of the CBD Space form Evolution Simulation

In the business activities to upgrade gathered in the process, the city waterfront domain gradually becomes the most vigorous areas, including a large number of beautiful environment and convenient traffic land, which is in line with CBD location selection elements conditions, broad shoreline and water space can be improve the urban commercial space environment quality to provide rare natural conditions [6].

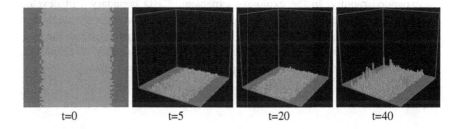

t=0	t=5	t=20	t=40

87.3.2.4 Experiment Four, Different Diffusion Under the Way of CBD Simulation

(1) Spread

CBD evolution process is the most common way. Steady expansion, the change of boundary is small and irregular, the overall change produced is limited, only making CBD surrounding building gradually replaced by new business building and the formation of some continuous zone, on the whole form the expansion of the CBD. This kind of high-end industry through the replacement of function into the development process of CBD in essence is a kind of old city renewal behavior, but on the whole is behaved for CBD the spread of steady expansion. The picture below is known that the CBD in the process of development, is a steady spread of the process, and continues to spread.

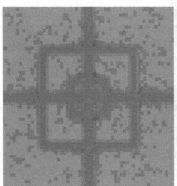   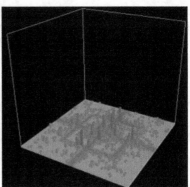

Spread type diffusion plan   Spread type diffusion 3 d map

(2) Explosive Diffusion

Under the governmental dominance and social push force, the CBD has expanded rapidly. In the explosive expansion, CBD boundary will develop along the particular direction to peripheral propulsion, the thorough non business purpose area and will not CBD blocks the same package into the area, even though continuous time is very short, but the boundary of propulsion depth is very big, and promote the prosperity of the whole area.

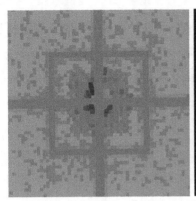 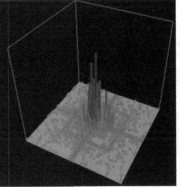

Explosive diffusion plan   Explosive diffusion 3 d map

Experiments show that, with certain policy support the government offered, the development of CBD will go toward the direction of the policy support for rapid asymmetric development. Since the CBD to economic development play a positive role, they don't have to wait for long time to let its slowly form, can be in it for the development trend of certain promote and guide, strive for in the short term formation is full of vitality and attraction of the CBD. From this perspective, the construction of CBD and with a planned economy color.

87.4 Conclusion

CBD evolution system is a kind of typical complex adaptive system, because it involves many complex behavior main bodies, which the traditional methods for CBD research (such as mathematics method) is difficult to describe and solve effectively. With the complex adaptive system theory as the foundation, this project mixed the bottom of the multi-agent modeling method and the original cell automata theory organic, and establishes a double evolution model with subject and the environment in the evolution, which effectively simulates the CBD the formation and development of the evolutionary process. The simulation to the evolution of CBD can analysis its development mechanism and affecting factors from a higher and macro level, so as to make it better applied in the human society phenomenon of economic research.

References

1. Ning J, Wang H, Guo S, Liu B (2010) First international conference on pervasive computing signal processing and applications, 17–19 Sept 2010, pp 352–356 (in Chinese)
2. Tabandeh S, Michalska H (2009) IEEE congress on evolutionary computation, 2009 CEC'09. 18–21 May 2009, pp 2948–2955

3. Chaharbaghi K, Willis R (1998) Eng Manag J pp 251–256
4. Wong W, Laurenson L, Livesey RG, Troup AP (1988) J Vac Sci Technol A Vac Surf Films: 1183–1186
5. Longbin J, Chunxiao Z (2009) Ninth international conference on hybrid intelligent systems, HIS '09 12–14 August 2009, pp 49–53 (in Chinese)
6. Atmar W (1994) IEEE transactions on neural networks, January 1994. AICS Res. Inc., University Park, pp 130–147

Chapter 88
DDR: A Multidimensional Case Retrieval Optimization Algorithm

Jing-Bin Wang and Xuan Hu

Abstract Ontology-based case retrieval system, the efficiency of case retrieval will increase as the number of cases continue to lower. In this paper, a multi-dimensional case retrieval optimization algorithm, the algorithm through the multi-dimensional case dimensionality reduction into clusters of two-dimensional space, using a two-dimensional spatial clustering to represent a collection of case, and this two-dimensional spatial clustering to establish the R-tree spatial index, by the two retrieval methods to the multidimensional case retrieval. Proved that the method not only improves the accuracy of case retrieval, but also greatly improve the efficiency of case retrieval.

Keywords Case retrieval · R-tree index · Relative point · Relative vector

88.1 Introduction

Case-Based Reasoning (CBR) is a solution of similar problems in the past with results to establish a case library, the new case obtain a similar solution cases in the case base to adapt to the current strategy, which is an important field of artificial intelligence reasoning method [1, 2]. System of case-based reasoning, case retrieval efficiency related to the efficiency of the entire system, is the case

J.-B. Wang · X. Hu (✉)
College of Mathematics and Computer Science, Fuzhou University,
Fuzhou 350001, Fujian, China
e-mail: 43806652@qq.com

J.-B. Wang
e-mail: wjbcc@263.net

W. Lu et al. (eds.), *Proceedings of the 2012 International Conference on Information Technology and Software Engineering*, Lecture Notes in Electrical Engineering 211, DOI: 10.1007/978-3-642-34522-7_88, © Springer-Verlag Berlin Heidelberg 2013

retrieval efficiency of case retrieval results [3]. Growing system use case library will make the gradual reduction in the efficiency of case retrieval, this phenomenon is known as swamp phenomenon [4]. In every case in the previous case retrieval than similarity are demand once traversal, that every retrieval are the full match search queries gradually grow to a certain size will reduce the efficiency of this in the case base. Huan-tong [5, 6] in view of this situation, a clustering algorithm is applied to the maintenance of the case base. Zheng [7] proposed a K-Means clustering algorithm. Changzheng [8], the feature weighting C-means clustering algorithm (WF-C-means) and clustering-based case retrieval program to create the index, due to C-means clustering algorithm to adjust the weights of all attributes are included in the difference in the definition of the difference in the definition adopted by the retrieval and new cases similar case is very precise and objective. Li [9] proposed an improved k-means clustering case retrieval algorithm to solve the clustering error due to noise, to evaluate the ability of cases by collecting user feedback and Case energy force as the rules of the selected sample cases.

The paper proposes a multi-dimensional case optimization algorithm the DRR: First point to the case of multidimensional space in the case base through dimensionality reduction calculation, the two-dimensional spatial clustering, and re-established the two-dimensional space clustering R-tree index; fault by dimensionality reduction calculation, the current failure of the two-dimensional representation; through the R-tree index lookup can help us to quickly locate the current failure of the two-dimensional clustering where then KNN algorithm in two dimensional spatial clustering multidimensional case, find the closest current fault near multidimensional Case.

88.2 Multidimensional Case Retrieval Optimization: DRR Algorithm: DRR

88.2.1 Case Dimension Reduction

In case-based reasoning system, set the case library $CS = (c_1, c_2, c_3,...c_n)$ a nonempty finite set composed by the n-th case, $\exists c_i$ $(0 \leq i \leq n)c_i \in CS_0$

The case of CS is usually based on the feature vector representation. Can be set case $c = (f_1, f_2,...f_i...f_m)$ is a nonempty finite set, where $f_i(1 \leq i \leq m)$ is a feature item of c, characterized term is used to describe the case a property.

Definition 1 $\forall a,b$ $a,b \in CS$ then the case space distance between two points for the Euler distance R_{ab}

$$R_{ab} = \sqrt{\sum (a_i - b_i)^2}(1 \leq i \leq m)$$

Fig. 88.1 Case spatial point
dimensionality reduction

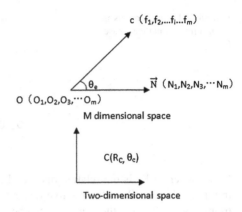

Definition 2 $\forall a,b\ a,b \in CS$, then the angle between the two vector case space for θ_{ab}.

$$\theta_{ab} = \cos^{-1} \frac{\sum a_i * b_i}{\|a\| * \|b\|}\ (1 \leq i \leq m)$$

Assuming an m-dimensional global reference point O $(O_1,O_2,O_3,....O_m)$, a global reference vector $\vec{N}(N_1,N_2,N_3,...N_m)$. According to definition 1 and definition 2, we calculate the relative distance of the case point c and O in the case space R_{co} (This simplified denoted as R_c), the angle between the case point c and vector $\vec{N}$ the reference angle θ_{co} (This simplified referred to as θ_c), then m dimensional case point c can be expressed in a two-dimensional spatial point C(R_c, θ_c), as shown in Fig. 88.1.

Space points in the m-dimensional case, there will be the same as the number of the global reference point O $(O_1,O_2,O_3,...O_m)$ the relative distance, and with the global reference vector $\vec{N}$ $(N_1,N_2,N_3,...N_m)$ having the same folder corner points, thus obtaining the case of a two dimensional clustering. We define:

Definition 3   Let a point D(R_d, θ_d) in a two-dimensional space S, represents a set of points $(d_1,d_2,...d_i...d_n)$. $d_i \in CS$, the two-dimensional space of where d_i Represents both the D(R_d,θ_d).

Definition 4   Target case e($e_1,e_2,e_3,...e_m$), the representation in the two-dimensional space is E(R_e, θ_e). $\forall a(a_1,a_2,a_i...a_m)$ a $\in$ CS; the representation in the two-dimensional space is A(R_a, θ_a). If E(R_e,θ_e) and A(R_a, θ_a) is closest in the ltwo-dimensional space S, then the Case point A is the most similar point of the target case e in the case space CS.

Proof According to Fig. 88.2, in the space CS in the m-dimensional case by the reference point O $(O_1, O_2, O_3,....O_m)$, the fault case point e $(e_1,e_2,e_3,...e_m)$, similar case point a$(a_1,a_2,a_i...a_m)$ of a plane defined by three points forming a triangle $\triangle$

Fig. 88.2 The case points in
the m-dimensional case base
CS

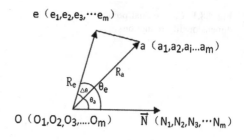

OAE. Wherein R_e is the relative distance between the e and O (the length of the triangle sides θ_e), R_a is the relative distance between A and O (the length of the triangle sides θ_a), and the angle $\triangle\theta$ can be with the angle between a and the angle $\vec{N}$ between the e subtraction can be obtained, $\triangle\theta = |\theta_a - \theta_e|$.

In order to prove the case point a is similar to the fault case e that calculate the minimum Euler distance R_{ea} of the case point e with the case point a in the space CS (triangle edges ea's length).

By the law of cosines can be obtained in the case of m-dimensional space CS

$$R_{ea} = \sqrt{R_e^2 + R_a^2 - 2R_a R_e \cos\triangle\theta}$$

$$\Rightarrow R_{ea} = \sqrt{R_e^2 + R_a^2 - 2R_a R_e + 2R_a R_e - 2R_a R_e \cos\triangle\theta}$$

$$\Rightarrow R_{ea} = \sqrt{(R_a - R_e)^2 - 2R_a R_e(1 - \cos\triangle\theta)}$$

$$\Rightarrow \lim_{\substack{R_a \to R_e \\ \triangle\theta \to 0}} \sqrt{(R_a - R_e)^2 - 2R_a R_e(1 - \cos\triangle\theta)}$$

The derivation of the formula can be obtained If the R_e of the current fault e infinitely approaching the R_a of point a in case library, and the angle between the e and a infinitely close to 0 (θ_e infinitely close to θ_a), in the two-dimensional space representation of S is $E(R_e, \theta_e)$ and $A(R_a, \theta_a)$ two points infinitely close, then limit R_{ea} will infinitely close to 0, that is, to prove the highest degree of similarity between the e and a in the case base CS.

88.2.2 Indexing R-Tree

Definition 5 Point $D(R_d, \theta_d)$ is a point in a two-dimensional space S, the minimum bounding MBR of point D is M_d, wherein M_d to $(R_d - \triangle r, \theta_d - \triangle\theta)$, $(R_d + \triangle r, \theta_d + \triangle\theta)$ for the two pairs of corner points of the rectangular range.

Point $D(R_d,\theta_d)$ in the R-Tree index is represented as a leaf node $D'(ID, M_d)$, where ID is the case point identification ID, M_d is a the minimum outsourcing rectangle of the point D, all the space point to the establishment of the R-tree index.

88.2.3 Case Initial Search

Definition 6   Current fault e $(e_1,e_2,e_3.....e_m)$, expressed in two-dimensional space S $E(R_e, \theta_d)$, and the scope of the query point E rectangular the M_{se} based $(R_e,-\triangle sr, \theta_e -\triangle s\theta)$, $(R_e + \triangle sr, \theta_e +\triangle s\theta)$ for the two pairs of diagonal points, wherein $\triangle sr$, $\triangle s\theta$ as the point E in the scope of the query, the query higher rectangular greater the accuracy of the query. Set a two-dimensional space S in the case of point set D, represented as R tree M_d, M_d and M_{se} intersect, then the case point set D is a similar set of points of the point E in a two-dimensional space S, whereby the query intermediate nodes Result set $R(R_1,R_2,R_3...R_n)$.

The assumption that the junction point of the R-tree index is T, a new look up on current fault $e(e_1,e_2,e_3.....e_m)$, find the highest similarity to the case of the case e algorithm described as follows:

(1) The calculation of e with a global reference point $O(O_1,O_2,O_3,...O_m)$ of the relative distance R_e, calculating the angle θ_d of the global reference vector $\vec{N}$ $(N_1,N_2,N_3,...N_m)$ and case e in the two-dimensional, so the mapping point in the space S is E (Re, e).
(2) Calculation the query range rectangular M_{se} of $E(R_e, \theta_e)$ in the R-tree index.
(3) If T is not a leaf node then check M_{se} whether intersect with M_t intersect then recursively check E intersects T sub-node, if the disjoint abandon find the node.
(4) If the T is a leaf node, it is determined whether all records in the T intersects with the M_{se}. So that we can find the record of the intersection of all the E in R-tree, and find along the branches of the tree down to find, and not to traverse the tree in each record.
(5) To find all the intermediate results set R $(R_1,R_2,R_3...R_n)$ M_{se} intersect.

Fig. 88.3 Intermediate result
set of case retrieval

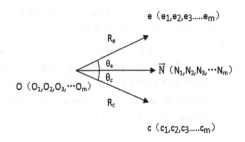

88.2.4 Case Filter

Filter the intermediate result set R to calculate e $(e_1, e_2, e_3 \ldots e_m)$ and intermediate result concentrate all cases the similarity, and get the highest similarity case points.

The intermediate result set R may be the case in Fig. 88.3:

At this time, for the case c, the $R_e - \triangle sr > = R_c <= R_e + \triangle sr, \theta_e - \triangle s\theta > = \theta_e <= \theta_e + \triangle s\theta$, case c is a case point in the intermediate result set R, but the case c is not similar to the case of the fault case e, dimension reduction and lead to the concentration of the two-dimensional space point case point difference becomes smaller, thus redundant case point intermediate result set will be similar to the case c, when the needs of the middle result set to be filtered, and calculating $e(e_1, e_2, e_3 \ldots e_m)$ and intermediate result on the similarity of all cases, and the highest similarity to the case of point.

In this paper, the K-nearest neighbor (K-Nearest Neighbor Algorithm KNN) algorithm to calculate the similarity. It will be the case of feature vectors as points in a high-dimensional space, and then looking for a match with the current failure point in the problem space, will exceed the similarity threshold case is returned to the user, the general process is described as follows:

Input to be retrieved the fault case e output case object which similar to the case e. Results set R have k cases, each case by m attributes described, that $x_i = \{x_{i1}, x_{i2}, \ldots, x_{ij}, \ldots, x_{im}\}$, $i = 1, 2, \ldots, k$; $j = 1, 2, \ldots, m$, calculated case x_i with the current fault e of between the Euclidean distance $d(x_i, e)$:

$$d(x_i, e) = \sqrt{\sum (x_{ij} - e_j)^2} (1 \leq j \leq m)$$

Based on this, it is easy to know the similarity between the existing cases xi with the current fault case e:

$$SIM(x_i, e) = 1 - d(x_i, e)$$

88.2.5 Case Studies and R-Tree Index Correction

For new case e $(e_1, e_2, e_3 \ldots e_m)$, if the case base CS exists the case c $(c_1, c_2, c_3 \ldots c_m)$, and $c_i = e_i$ $(1 \leq i \leq m)$, then say that the new case in the case library already exists, no new case with index correction.

If there is more than is required for the new case, Case Study:

(1) New case e is inserted into the case base CS.
(2) Calculation of the relative distance R_e of the new case e with the global reference point O, the angle θ_c between the case e and the global reference vector $\vec{N}$, the m-dimensional case point e can be expressed as two-dimensional spatial point $E(R_e, \theta_e)$.

(3) In two-dimensional space S for the new point E(R_e, θ_c), determine the point in space already exists, if there is illustrated in this cluster already exists, and is just a new clustering increasing identification ID; case point if there is no point in the space, a new clustering points, you need to re-adjust the R-tree index.

88.3 Experiment

We conducted a number of experiments in order to verify the validity of the DRR algorithm, the DRR algorithm and the traditional retrieval method based on rough set K-means algorithm [8] to compare the case base using a fault diagnosis system data, test case data were 30000, 50000, 80000, 100000, 200000, 300000, 500000. Algorithm by eclipses, JVM maximum memory 512 m.

88.3.1 Parameter Settings

The case spatial dimension m = 10, the reference point O ($O_1, O_2, O_3, \ldots O_m$) is 0 (0,0,0,..., 0), the reference vector $\vec{N}$ (1,0,0,...0), the two-dimensional space point outsourcing rectangular size as $\triangle$ R = 1, $\triangle\theta$ = 1, the case similarity threshold value of 0.9, the query of the current failure rectangular range as $\triangle$ sr = 60 $\triangle$ sθ = 30.

88.3.2 Experimental Results and Analysis

88.3.2.1 Precision Experiments

The standard set of test cases has been given experiment (i.e query case base test case similarity is greater than the number of cases of 0.9), the query results closer to the standard result set is to illustrate the higher accuracy of the query. The experimental results shown in Table 88.1. As can be seen from Table 88.1, the K-means algorithm is more sensitive to the noise data when the data set of the query 50000, thereby affecting the accuracy caused by the clustering of the deviation due to the noise data. Noise data for the results of a query of the DRR algorithm is almost no effect, and the DRR algorithm result set high accuracy, stability to be higher than the K-means algorithm.

Table 88.1 Precision experiments

Case library size	Standard result set	K-means		DRR	
		Result	Accuracy (%)	Result	Accuracy (%)
30000	237	216	91.13	236	99.57
50000	410	308	75.12	405	98.78
80000	662	641	96.82	656	99.09
100000	829	807	97.34	817	98.55
200000	1630	1434	87.97	1606	98.52
300000	2585	2235	86.46	2547	98.64

Table 88.2 Comparison table of the efficiency of several algorithms

Case library size	Traditional algorithm (ms)	K-means (ms)	DRR (ms)
50000	29.33	15	11
80000	31.78	16	13
100000	37	16	15
200000	67.67	51.67	36.67
300000	93.33	73.25	53
500000	Memory overflow	Memory overflow	235

Fig. 88.4 Query results of the histogram

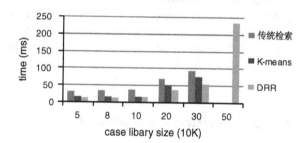

88.3.2.2 Query Efficiency Experiments

Our in 6 case data set of three algorithms query efficiency comparative experiments, the results as shown in Table 88.2 and Fig. 88.4.

Traditional retrieval methods every time all the data read memory query compared with the gradual growth of case space data, the time of the query data also gradually growth occurs when the data reaches a certain number of memory overflow. K-means and DRR algorithm to read data in the case base, indexing, each query are index-based query, so efficiency will be relatively fast indexing K-means based on the data of the entire case base, when the data reaches a certain amount of time will run out of memory; the DRR algorithm, dimensionality reduction means of two-dimensional clustering of the records in the case base, after for 2D clustering results establish the R-tree index, so that in memory R-tree index space is much smaller than the index of the K-means algorithm. Datasets great when DRR algorithm can still achieve inquiries, not only does not appear out of memory and a good solution to the K-means algorithm search efficiency degradation caused by the sample points is too large, large data amount of case the retrieval efficiency of the library.

88.4 Conclusion

In this paper, a multi-case retrieval optimization algorithm DRR algorithm, the algorithm by clustering, two retrieval of dimensionality reduction method, not only speed up the retrieval efficiency, and the case of two-dimensional clustering is based on unrelated business, to avoid the classification errors caused by manual sorting, while avoiding the degradation caused due to the sample point is too large, the search efficiency, and to improve the case library retrieval efficiency of the large amount of data. The next step will algorithm to further improve weight impact on the clustering of feature items considering the case, in order to improve the accuracy and efficiency of case retrieval.

References

1. Aamodt A, Plaza E (1892) Case—based reasoning: Foundational issues, methodological variations, and system approaches. AI Communications 1994 7(1):39–59
2. Clerk Maxwell J (1892) A treatise on electricity and magnetism, vol. 2, 3rd edn. Clarendon, Oxford, pp 68–73
3. Yin—Shan G, Qiang H, Yan Z et al. (2003) Case-base maintenance based on representative selection for I-NN algorithm 2003 international conference on machine learning and cybemetics. pp 2421–2425 (in Chinese)
4. Derere L (2000) Case-based reasoning: diagnosis of faults in complex systems through reuse of experience. proceedings of international test conference, pp 77–105
5. Huantong G, Mingjun X, Xiang Z, Qingsheng C (2005) Research on application of clustering algorithm in CBM. Comp Eng 31(12):166–168
6. Yorozu Y, Hirano M, Oka K, Tagawa Y (1982) Electron spectroscopy studies on magneto-optical media and plastic substrate interface. IEEE Transl J Magn Jpn 2:740–741, Aug 1987. [Digests 9th annual conference magnetics Japan, p 301] (in Chinese)
7. Zheng F (2008) A rough-based k-means clustering algorithm. Computer engineering and applications 44(20):141–142 (in Chinese)
8. Changzheng L, Dong D (2010) Case indexing and retrieval based on clustering algorithm of weighted feature C-MEANS. Comp Appl Softw 27(2):111–114 (in Chinese)
9. Li Q, Huilin J (2011) Case retrieval algorithm based on k-means clustering. Comp Eng Appl 47(4):185–187 (in Chinese)

Chapter 89
Method to Increase Diversity in the Artificial Immune System

Jing Xie, Yaobin Hu, Huiling Zhu and Yulin Wang

Abstract For Artificial Immune System optimization process, this paper studies how to maintain the diversity of Monoclonal antibodies. After recognizing and forecasting the flutter fault frequently occurring when CA6140 horizontal lathe is used to machine the work pieces with a slim shaft by virtue of AIS system, an algorithm simulating the surname inheritance through setting family marks is proposed based on the traditional Clone Selection Algorithm. This algorithm can effectively enrich the current algorithms, avoid the repetitive computation caused by too fast constriction of antibodies during evolution, and accordingly effectively raise algorithm efficiency.

Keywords Artificial Immune System · Clone algorithm · Inheritance algorithms

89.1 Introduction

People never give up developing artificial intelligence in all ages [1]. They have proposed the artificial neural network model through studying and simulating the biological cranial neuroid network, and developed the model greatly.

In addition, the artificial immune system (called as AIS, too) proposed based on the immunological network theory proposed by Jerne [2] become a hot spot in the artificial intelligence field. In 1986, Farmer et al. proposed the dynamic model of the immune system based on the immunologic network theory, and probed into the relationship between the immune system and other artificial intelligence methods,

J. Xie (✉) · Y. Hu · H. Zhu · Y. Wang
School of Mechanical Engineering, University of South China, Hengyang, China
e-mail: xiejing168@163.com

W. Lu et al. (eds.), *Proceedings of the 2012 International Conference on Information Technology and Software Engineering*, Lecture Notes in Electrical Engineering 211, DOI: 10.1007/978-3-642-34522-7_89, © Springer-Verlag Berlin Heidelberg 2013

and started studying the artificial immune system. Later, the artificial immune system becomes more and more developed, which reflects mainly in the negative selection algorithm proposed by Forrest in 1996 for detecting computer viruses [3], the RLAIS algorithms proposed by Timmis in 2000 [4], the Clone Selection Algorithm proposed by De Castro in 2002 [5], the aiNet [6], etc. These algorithms were proposed by fully drawing lessons from the biological immune method of the immune cells, like B-cells and T-cells in the immune system [7], lay a foundation for the artificial immune system, and have born many application fruits especially in computer virus prevention field, etc. However, as for the Smart Diagnosis of the mechanical equipment, the study target is more complex, and the requirement for AIS system is different.

At present, the study and application of AIS focuses on data clustering, but AIS, especially the Clone Selection Algorithm is featured by flexible application and wide applicability, which means they are very applicable for global optimization. Traditional intelligent algorithms, like the BP algorithm of the artificial neural network, are often subjected to local extremum, which can be relieved by AIS. Considering the above, the paper presents the study on how to keep the diversity of antibodies during AIS development, and presents a method that enriches algorithms and effectively avoids premature constriction and repetitive computation by setting family identifications and simulating surname inheritance based on the traditional Clone Selection Algorithm. This method speeds up the computation.

89.2 Clone Selection Algorithm and Improvement

As the study goes on, the Clone Selection Algorithm also undergoes continuous development. The flow of the Clone Selection Algorithm [8] proposed by De Castro is shown as below:

(1) Generate a candidate scheme set $S(P)$, which is the sum of the subset of memory cells (M) and residual groups (P_r), $(P = P_r + M)$;
(2) Determine n best individuals P_n in the group P based on the affinity extent;
(3) Clone (copy) the N best individuals to generate a clone group C;
(4) Put the clone group C under mutation operation with the mutation probability in inverse proportion to the affinity of the antibodies. Then generate a mature antibody group C^*;
(5) Reselect improved individuals from the group C^* to form a memory cell set, and some of the members of the set P may be replaced by the improved ones of the group C^*;
(6) Replace d low-affinity antibodies in the group to maintain the diversity of antibodies.

Similar to the classical genetic algorithm proved by Rbdolph, it can be proved that the algorithm constriction is based on probability if the best individual of every population does not participate in the hybridization and mutation. So, when

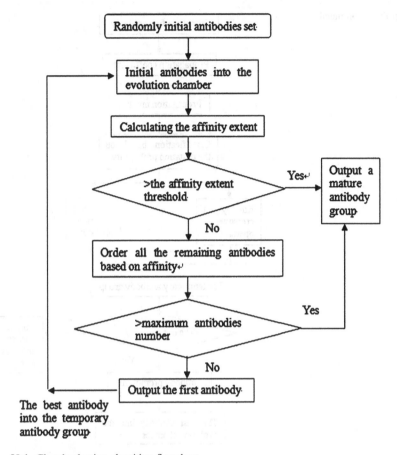

Fig. 89.1 Clonal selection algorithm flowchart

the Clone Selection Algorithm is employed, the best antibodies are always reserved. In order to reserve the diversity of antibodies, a mutation operator is employed for the temporary clone group C that is put under mutation operation, and a crossover operator is always employed for the gene interchange of the individuals of the temporary clone group C. The Fig. 89.1 shows the flow of the Clonal Selection Algorithm.

In this paper, the improvement for the Clone Selection Algorithm is to further raise antibody diversity by adding genetic marker bits to the temporary antibody group during the evolution for the purpose of raise algorithm global search and efficiency. The details of this are shown as below:

(1) Provide family identifications as per generation order when generating an initial antibody group;
(2) When employ a mutation operator, the antibody family marker is used for newly generated antibodies;

Fig. 89.1 continued

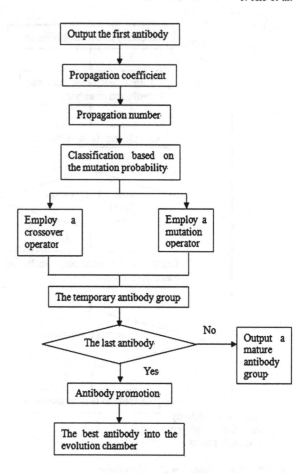

(3) When employ a crossover operator, all the family markers of the actively employed antibodies are succeeded to newly generated antibodies;

(4) Order the members of each family based on affinity as per family identifications at first when ordering temporary antibody groups;

(5) Put the best antibodies from each family into the temporary antibody group (namely the evolution chamber), and discard surplus temporary antibodies as per the set maximum concentration;

(6) After removal, order all the remaining antibodies based on affinity, and then inject them into the evolution chamber.

Mainly through setting marker bits, this method is to raise ergodicity and algorithm efficiency by avoiding the large amount of useless computation caused by the premature constriction of antibodies at local extremum point. The concentration is defined as the ratio of a whole family to the temporary antibody group. In order to verify the algorithm, this paper develops the analysis according to the training process of the vibration data during the machining course of CA6140 horizontal lathe.

89.3 Experimental Results

During the experiment, AIS system was used to identify and forecast the flutter fault occurring frequently when the lathe machines a workpiece with a slim shaft, and the vibration signals of the lathe in the x, y and z directions were acquired respectively, and the signal energy in each frequency domain was normalized to act as eigenvalue. The following Fig. 89.2 shows the constriction results of the training of the antibodies with family markers and those without family markers respectively based on evolutionary generation.

When use the abscissa to represent the evolutionary generation, adopting the surname inheritance algorithm can delay the constriction of antibodies, which is caused by keeping antibody diversity. However, because some over concentrated antibodies are discarded, the algorithm' speed becomes much higher. In the following table, the maximum affinity and training duration (set 50 families) figured out by using the surname inheritance algorithm under various concentrations, the same specimens and the same other parameters.

According to the Table 89.1, although the maximum becomes a little lower after adopting the surname inheritance algorithm, the falling amplitude may be neglected. However, when the surname inheritance algorithm is not adopted, the average duration is 6.11 s, and the duration at concentration peak (0.4) is 5.49 s; after the surname inheritance algorithm is adopted, the duration at the concentration peak (0.1) sharply cuts down to 3.47 s. Similarly, according to the distribution of the 50 evolutionary antibodies in the temporary antibody chamber, we can see that such algorithm raises antibody diversity.

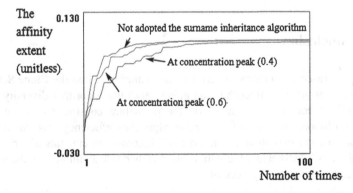

Fig. 89.2 Convergence results of the antibodies with family markers and those without family markers respectively

Table 89.1 The maximum affinity and training duration (set 50 families) by adopted/not adopted the surname inheritance algorithm

	1st	2nd	3rd
Not adopted/the affinity extent	0.090377	0.090346	0.090335
Not adopted/time(s)	6.000	7.516	6.438
At concentration (0.8)/the affinity extent	0.090332	0.090334	0.090338
At concentration (0.8)/time(s)	5.688	6.141	6.156
At concentration (0.6)/the affinity extent	0.090343	0.090316	0.090271
At concentration (0.6)/time(s)	5.25	6.14	4.828
At concentration (0.4) the affinity extent	0.090313	0.090308	0.090323
At concentration (0.4)/time(s)	5.047	3.484	4.672
At concentration (0.2)/the affinity extent	0.090318	0.090327	0.090249
At concentration (0.2)/time(s)	3.031	3.563	3.156
At concentration (0.1)/the affinity extent	0.090336	0.090331	0.090328
At concentration (0.1)/time(s)	3.078	2.921	2.89
	4th	5th	6th
Not adopted/the affinity extent	0.090323	0.090340	0.090346
Not adopted/time(s)	5.484	6.438	6.86
At concentration (0.8)/the affinity extent	0.090345	0.090343	0.090339
At concentration (0.8)/time(s)	6.188	6.64	5.187
At concentration (0.6)/the affinity extent	0.090335	0.090314	0.090312
At concentration (0.6)/time(s)	6.109	5.453	5.578
At concentration (0.4) the affinity extent	0.090336	0.090336	0.090338
At concentration (0.4)/time(s)	3.656	5.39	4.86
At concentration (0.2)/the affinity extent	0.090340	0.090291	0.090336
At concentration (0.2)/time(s)	3.594	3.579	3.063
At concentration (0.1)/the affinity extent	0.090309	0.090323	0.090311
At concentration (0.1)/time(s)	2.75	3.328	2.984

The evolutional antibodies gotten by using such algorithm can correctly recognize the lathe fault.

89.4 Conclusion

The paper presents a surname inheritance algorithm based on the Clone Selection Algorithm. Using such algorithm can effectively raise algorithm diversity, avoid the repetitive computation caused by the premature constriction of antibodies during evolution, and accordingly raise algorithm efficiency. As an auxiliary algorithm for the evolution of the artificial immune system, this algorithm can bring obvious effects when the evolution chamber size is limited or the optimal value needs not to be very accurate.

References

1. Forrest S, Hofmeyr S, Somayaji A (1996) A sense of self for UNIX processes. IEEE Symposium Security and Privacy, Oakland, pp 120–128
2. Cai ZX, Gong T (2004) Advance in research on immune algorithms, Cont Dec 19(8):841–846 (in Chinese)
3. Zhang WJ, Wang X, Wu XY (2011) Fault diagnosis method for gun-launched missile based on negative-selection algorithm of AIS. J Acad Arm Force Eng 25(6):53–55 (in Chinese)
4. Timmis J, Neal M (2002) A resource limited artificial immune systems for data analysis [J]. Knowl Based Syst 14(3):121–130
5. Ma CH, Zhong Y (2011) Dynamic adaptive immune clone selection algorithm by applying population division. Comp Eng Appl 47(30):29–31(in Chinese)
6. Geng LC, Wu YD (2010) Remote sensing image retrieval algorithm based in aiNet model artificial immune network computer engineering and application. Comp Eng Appl 46(7):226–228 (in Chinese)
7. Wang BX, Zhang ZH (2011) Tracking control of the controlled system based on immune network model. Inform Control, 40(5):664–668 (in Chinese)
8. Fan Aj, Pan ZQ (2012) Algorithm of artificial immune network based on multiple memory antibody clonal Selection. Comp Simulat 29(2):102–104 (in Chinese)

Chapter 90
Research on Contextual Design in Human–Computer Interaction Under the Framework of Activity Theory

Xiaoxiao Cao, Lijue Wang and Shijian Luo

Abstract To further explore the importance and research value of context in Human–Computer Interaction (HCI) design, a research on Contextual Design (CD) under the Framework of Activity Theory (AT) was proposed. CD was divided it into three stages, which were contextual data exploring, contextual model building and contextual design converting. This paper proposed the process of CD under the framework of AT, and explained how to apply it in HCI design by a case named "Cycler". An experiment was conducted to evaluate the usability of the prototype, and to verify the effectiveness and practicality of contextual design process under the framework of AT.

Keywords Activity theory · Contextual design · Context model · HCI

90.1 Introduction

As a new interdisciplinary discipline, Human–Computer Interaction (HCI) is a composite, which has its own methodology and practice. A method, which is widely used nowadays in HCI called, Scenario-Based Design [1]. The method

X. Cao (✉)
Department of Industrial Design, College of Computer Science and Technology, Zhejiang University, Room 318, Caoguangbiao, No. 38 Zheda, Hangzhou 310027, China
e-mail: caoxiaoxiao@live.com

L. Wang
Texun Office Building, No.701, Jianghui Road, Binjiang District, Hangzhou 310052, China
e-mail: wanglijue.id@gmail.com

S. Luo
Department of Industrial Design, Zhejiang University, Hangzhou 310027, China
e-mail: sjluo@zju.edu.cn

W. Lu et al. (eds.), *Proceedings of the 2012 International Conference on Information Technology and Software Engineering*, Lecture Notes in Electrical Engineering 211, DOI: 10.1007/978-3-642-34522-7_90, © Springer-Verlag Berlin Heidelberg 2013

provides designers with an efficiency mean of communication and design. It helps designers to fully realize users' purpose, so that they can express and actualize project objective correctly [2].

Activity Theory (AT) is a philosophy investigating human affairs. The core thought is that People's minds come from practical activities, so inner mind and the activities outside have the same structure. That is to say, research on people's activity can also help the research on people's mind.

In this paper, we did research on users' cognizance, activity, attitude, etc. based on the content and framework of AT, and proposed the process of Contextual Design (CD) under the Framework of AT. It was used to guide the HCI design, and to improve user experience and usability at the same time. As devices are made into network and information is ecological, the improvement is becoming increasingly important. Afterwards, we took an application called "Cycler" as an example to validate the process of CD.

90.2 Literatures Review

90.2.1 Human–Computer Interaction

HCI is a discipline, which designs a computer-based system and evaluates whether it is easy for human to used. It not only includes the interface, but also all the interaction between human and computer. Nowadays, people tend to use computer, cellphone and other devices to communicate and cooperate with others. Depaula (2003) proposed that HCI should also include social elements to adapt to current situation [3].

Usability is an important evaluation approach for HCI. It is defined by ISO09241-11 as the validity, efficiency and satisfaction of specific users when doing specific task under particular Usage-Situation. Nielsen divided usability into five attributes, which were leamability, efficiency, memorability, errors and satisfaction [4]. Usability evaluation pays more attention on reached parameters during a series of users' operations.

Folmer, Bosch (2004) and other pundit indicated that there were two big downsides in usability engineering [5, 6]. "(1) Most usability problems and usages would not be found out until the post-test. Redesign would largely increase the cost. (2) Traditional usability analyses did not include long time and dynamic usability during the using system processes."

Preece et al. (2002) pointed out that "in HCI design, the users' activities during the interaction with the product must be considered. Only by the observation to the activities could we understand the using context of users and discover potential users, and could we clearly define the real target the system needed to reach. Thus, the target of HCI should not only be the creation of highly usability product, but also should note the feelings and experience of users, and combined the activities of the users as well."

90.2.2 Activity Theory

AT is a psychology theoretical system established by A. Leontyev who is a main delegacy of the cultural historical school of USSR. Today, AT has become a multidisciplinary and international theory. Researches on AT expand to fields such as information science, social, education, etc.

As shown in the Fig. 90.1, Engestrom's activity theory model includes six elements, namely object, subject, Mediating artefact, community, division of labour and rules. Object refers to the executor of the activities, can be individuals, groups or teams. Subject is manipulated by Object. Mediating artefact is the psychological or physical media during the subject transformation. Community consists of several individuals and groups, sharing with subject and constructing self in order to distinguish with the other communities; Division of labour is the horizontal and vertical allocation of tasks, rights and status of members in community; Rules are regulations constraining the activities, laws, policies and the potential social norms, membership etc. [7]. Besides, these six elements combining with each other constitute four small triangles, namely production, exchange, distribution and consumption.

The most common way AT is used in HCI is analytic method with the framework of AT. The secondary common one is activity checklist, posed by Kaptelinin (1999). The purpose of activity checklist is to refine the activity elements in HCI to become analysis tools that can be used practically.

Additionally, Kuutti [8] described a matrix for computer supported cooperative work (CSCW). The relevant scholars point out that the above analysis tools derived from AT are relatively new. That is to say, these methods need to be further validated and improved in the future study. Besides, new methods are also need to be proposed to apply the AT into practical design and evaluation.

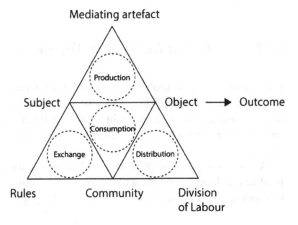

Fig. 90.1 The framework of AT

90.2.3 Contextual Design

The earlier case using scenarios method is the voice messaging system developed by IBM for Los Angeles Olympic Games, and thereafter, scenarios method appears in various forms in the software development [9]. Sato et al. [10] proposed contextual visualization methods of interactive system design. It made modular contextual as its mechanism, in order to integrate different expression formats in a common information platform with designed information framework. Articulated that scenario, trigger factors, and the impact on the users through the combinations of modular contextual models. Luo et al. [11] proposed the knowledge system of the user experience design (UED), dividing UED into three dimensions, namely problem context, solving context and results context. That constructed the UED scenario dimension involved in the process.

User-centered design emphasizes on user scenarios research. User experience is difficult to obtain quantitatively, so user context is often built [12]. By simulating scenario, designers can obtain the same or similar user experience, and that contribute to design. A series of effective design tools have already been established in user context. The most typical one is storyboard. It builds user context by way of storytelling, in order to identify problems and find design solutions [13]. Usually a storyboard contains four elements: people, products, events, and background.

The CD proposed by Beyer and Holzblatt [14] perfectly defined user-centered design process, providing a structured method that includes collecting user data on site, explaining and then integrating. After that, a prototype product or service concept is created, and then comes with the final user test and concept perfecting. The core idea of CD is user study to learn their tendencies, desire and motivation. Because these are all invisible, the only way is field survey. Holzblatt and Beyer proposed a contextual design process, which includes contextual query, report interpretation, model classified analysis, design vision, storyboarding, using environmental design, paper prototypes, and detailed design. In that theory, users' work models are divided into five categories, which are flow model, sequence model, artifact model, cultural model and the physical model.

90.2.4 Contextual Design and Activity Theory

Lacking of a scenario analysis framework for reference makes it hard for designers to stay in their zone quickly, and also the contextual elements often difficult to capture because of it. Kaptelinin (1999) pointed out that AT could provide a theoretical framework used to describe the structure and user activity of the scenario analysis.

As is shown in Fig. 90.2 that, AT analysis the relationships among users, products and environments with its theoretical framework and activity level, but CD mainly with on site visits. Therefore, the paper argues that CD and AT are

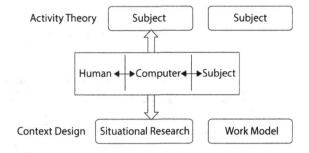

Fig. 90.2 The matching picture of CD and AT

essentially based on the exploration of the context. What makes them different is that AT provides theoretical frameworks predictability.

Under the framework of AT, this paper proposed that context refers to the various elements and their dynamic inter-relationship of an activity system. It is close to the definition of Nardi [15]: Scene contains user, context and the tasks user is doing or to do. Based on the study of real activities, some description should be added. Glancing at prospect of the future, contemplate how technology can better support the activities of the people.

Based on these studies, this paper considered that the knowledge and perspectives of AT could be introduced as a theoretical support in CD used in HCI.

90.3 Method

90.3.1 Contextual Information Exploration

Contextual information Collecting methods include natural observation, deep tracking, contextual consult, focus groups interview and questionnaires, etc. When browsing the original and transcription of contextual information, we want find out different themes and tendencies of the content, so as to recognize the relationship of the observation. That is to say, we need to recognize that some of the contextual information can be grouped into specific categories, then marked them out with a suitable label. Today, context is till a general concept in the field of design. If not clearly understood or classified, it is difficult to conduct research thoroughly and effectively. According to various elements of the AT, five contextual classifications of user activity can be mapped: personal context, task context, environmental context, spatio-temporal context, and social context [16]. What shown in Fig. 90.3 is the description of the context composition based on some concepts in AT. The five classifications on the top come from the analysis of activity elements and contextual knowledge under the framework of AT.

After specifying the five principle of AT (object-oriented, internalization and externalization, activity level structure, intermediaries and development), and combining specific context of interactive system, or the target technologies to be

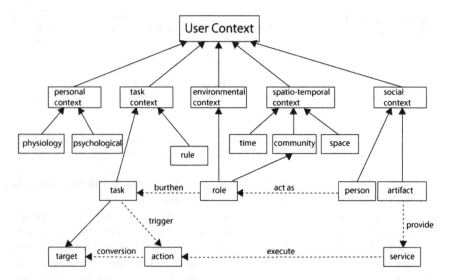

Fig. 90.3 The contextual composition based on AT

designed or evaluated, a so-called activities checklist can be compiled. The activity checklist consists of four parts of assessments content roughly: Means/goals (embody activity hierarchy principle); The social level and the physical level of the environment (embody the object-oriented principle); Learning, cognition, and clarity (embody the principle of internalization and exteriorization); Development (embody the principle of development).

90.3.2 Contextual Model Building

The model is widely used in design and development, allowing us to better understand, discuss or visualize the expression of complex structures and relationships. So the authors abstract the research result form the stage of exploratory contextual information into the users' contextual model. Contextual model is quiet a powerful tool in CD.

When certain types of contextual information are more complex, we can describe them with layered contextual model, and obtain the integration of hierarchical model base on it. That allows better analysis of contextual information.

The five classes of users working model based on CD is workflow model, sequence model, artifact model, cultural model, and physical model [17].

It is not easy to find a new design point if designers stay only in a hierarchical contextual model. Integrated contextual model can be obtained by the Superposition of hierarchical contextual model, as shown in Fig. 90.4. By this way, user context can be better understood, and new points can be formed at the same time. Often hidden problems will also be fleshed out easily, providing inspiration or basis for further design.

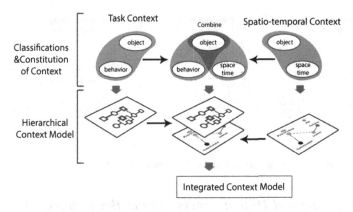

Fig. 90.4 The attaining of integrated context model

90.3.3 Contextual Design Transformation

Although the Scenario-based characters are not real, they are based on the observed behavior and motivation of real people. They are comprehensive prototypes formed based on actual user behavior data, representing real persons in the whole design process. User behavior patterns are observed in the study phase, and are modeled at the creation stage. Then characters are formed [18]. CD holds the view that only the characters created through contextual research are real and effective.

To export the scene, contextual model should be described and analyzed from various aspect with the contextual model created before. In the process of building integrated contextual model, information should be fully excavated, translated and interpreted. Based on the characters, scene can be deduced. The scene can be expressed with storyboards and context etc. Scene building should be open, and also can be improved with the development of system interaction. It will be better if can be modified, updated and recreated easily.

After defining the needs with characters and context in preceding paragraphs, the whole structure of the system can be defined with user environment design. That also means to plan for an overall architecture with users' needs reasonably. Therefore, the user environment design is an important step from requirements to design.

In the phase of user environment design, focus areas and the relationship between them are presented by the users' workflow and system structure. Focus areas represents task types that the users are doing, every of them have a specific purpose and a supporting function. Each focus area can describe how it helps users to work, and how it connects to the other focus areas. User environment design can integrate the focus areas with correlation between them. Redundant system functions should be removed, so that the purpose of each focus area can be more clearly. User environment design concerned about the consistency of user actions, thus ensuring effective user experience.

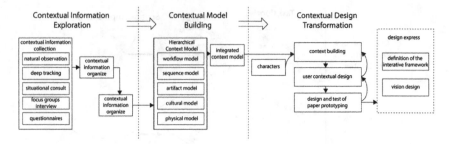

Fig. 90.5 Contextual design process under the framework of AT

90.3.4 Contextual Design Process Under the Framework of Activity Theory

This paper proposes a Contextual Design process under the Framework of AT, to better support the user-centered design. It can be apply to the products, services, and other HCI systems. The process is shown in Fig. 90.5.

90.4 Case Study

Hangzhou is the first city promoting the public bicycle rental system. The "Unattended, Self-service, rent-return incorporated" intelligent public bicycle service system largely alleviate the traffic pressure. The travel can be divided into Rigid Travel and Flexible Travel. Rigid Travel is daily repeat, while Flexible Travel (including shopping, visiting friends, etc.) cannot be rigidly in a same way. The choice of travel way is related to many factors in Flexible Travel. In this paper, people who often travel with public bicycle are regarded as the target user group. And an application will be design after research on their flexible travel.

90.4.1 Exploratory Experiment of Contextual Information

Purpose: collect the target users' contextual information for the use of public bicycle rental system.

Method: deep tracking, contextual consult, focus groups interview and questionnaires, etc.

Subjects: natural observation and questionnaire: the user of public bicycle rental system in Hangzhou; deep tracking, contextual consult: 12 public bicycle users aged from 18 to 34 years old, own or once used smart phones. 7 males and 5 females.

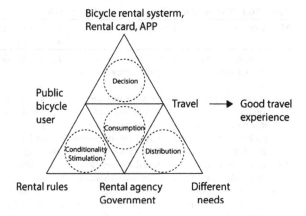

Fig. 90.6 The analysis of travelling by public bicycle in the framework of AT

Procedure:

(1) Use natural observation to observe, photograph and record the users of public bicycle in Hangzhou.
(2) Conduct a survey about the public travel in 116 subjects from different fields in Hangzhou. The result will be analyzed mainly with Excel.
(3) With deep tracking and contextual consult method, the users' contextual information will be analyzed. Try to organize and analyze the contextual information with the Framework of AT and activity checklist.

Results and Analysis: the questionnaire result showed that in the 116 questionnaires, 51 % users of public bicycle users were students educated above college, 33 % were officer, 29 % of them travelled mainly with bicycle, and 60 % with bus. The collected contextual information was classified with contextual consult. This paper made a description of the travel with public bicycle under the Framework of AT, which was shown in Fig. 90.6. The collected contextual information was further analyzed with activity checklist shown in Table 90.1.

90.4.2 Contextual Model Building and Contextual Design Transformation

Contextual Model Building: the task context is relatively complex in bicycle rental process. As is shown in Fig. 90.7, it is built with sequence model.

Among all kinds of contextual information, location is a very important factor affecting the use of public bicycle. Figure 90.8 shows the physical model of public bicycles. The model describes two ways to use the public bicycles: One is designed for closer destinations and the destination is generally quite familiar to users; another is designed for destinations with a bus station nearby. The users seldom ride public bicycle in a distant destination because they are not familiar

Table 90.1 The checklist of travel with public bicycle

Means/targets	Environment	Learning, cognition, and clarity	Development
User student, officer *Main target* travel in city *Sub-target* security, economy, convenience, comfort, and accurateness *The conflict between the targets* advantage of public bicycle, such as suitable for short-distance, flexible, not affected by peak period etc. Shortage of bicycle, such as low speed, physical strength costs, constrained by weather and road etc., hard to find the rental station etc.	*Target technology* public bicycle rental service *Other tools* bus card (car rental card), phone navigator, rental station, online distribution maps for rental station etc. *Environmental social/ physical level* bicycle rental points should build adjacent to the bus station Competition for bicycles or park places. Consideration of social interaction by using public bicycle	*Knowledge of target technology in environment* the state of the bicycle rental points, such as scale, remaining parking points *Thinking* recall the location of rental points; route planning *Activities* looking for rental points, renting and returning *External* presents the distribution of rental points *Internality* results provided by query system affect the route choice	1. Consideration of the possible use at all stages traveling with bicycle 2. Users can get high-level target after using this application 3. Public bicycle rental system may impact the structure of users' behavior

with the surrounding environment. They prefer mobile navigation or asking directions to find the corresponding bus station.

In addition, we build a culture model of the target group, as is shown in Fig. 90.9. The main social relations of students and young white-collar workers are family, friends, colleagues or classmates. We can find how social factors affect users' travel activities and deep-seated motivation.

Persona creation: we create persona considering the market and contextual information, as is shown in Fig. 90.10.

Integrated contextual model is generated from hierarchical contextual models. Figure 90.11 shows the integration model generated from spatio-temporal context and task context.

We define the Structure of Cycler application with characters and contextual model, and design it with user environment.

90.4.3 Interface Design of System Prototype

Cycler is a query application for public bicycles in handheld mobile devices, mainly for young people from 20 to 35 years old. In design process of Cycler, four key function interfaces were design: bike stations, directions, milestone and settings (Figs. 90.12, 90.13, 90.14, 90.15).

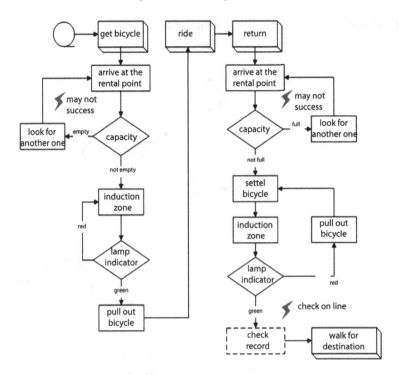

Fig. 90.7 Series model of renting/returning public bicycle

90.4.4 Design Test

Purpose: verify the effectiveness of CD in HCI under the Framework of AT. Learn the satisfaction of use about the application.

Experimental materials: the aforementioned interface is the test object. Test the prototype with iPhone.

Subjects: 6 Undergraduate or postgraduate in Zhejiang University, which consist of 7 males and 9 females, aged 21 to 34 years old.

Procedure: test with interviews and questionnaires. Set typical tasks for the users to complete. After complete, evaluate the interaction design of Cycler (easy or not, action efficient, interactive mode, compatibility of hardware and software, task correctness etc.) Give overall satisfaction.

Results: it was found in the test that, because of the big difference between the interaction of prototype interface and the operation of actual phone application, there were many discrepancies in the result of the experiment. It could not fully explain the actual availability of the application. So a detailed analysis will not be preceded here. The Statistics of user satisfaction is shown in Table 90.2. From the analysis results of user's operation satisfaction, there were 4 from 5 tasks got more than 4 points in satisfaction. That is to say, user satisfaction is basically good.

Fig. 90.8 Physical model

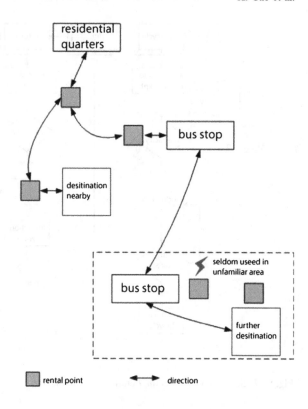

rental point   ◀▬▶ direction

Fig. 90.9 Culture model of
the target group

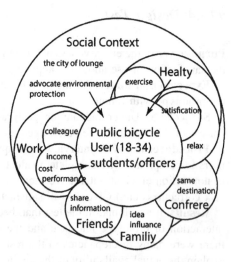

Lin Shan

"Hope that I can make full use of public bicycle rental system even in the unfamiliar area of the city!"

Technical attributes and appeal:
Electronic device:
Phone HTC G3, mainly used to make calls, send SMS and Weibo, navigation. Sony laptop, mainly used to study, see movies, surfing internet and play computer games.

Technical appeal:
Receptive to Technology, but not keen to follow the ease of use and the attractive appearance; like all kinds of gadgets

Personal Information:
Age: 26
Sex: female
Education: postgraduate
Job: student
Income: 3000 Yuan
Hobby: shopping, movies and Weibo.
Character: outgoing, independent and assertive.

The use of public bicycle:
Travel around the campus; close to nature, Low-carbon and environmentally friendly; free, convenient and unrestricted.

Lifestyle:
Have many classmates and friends, play and learn, feel comfortable. Pressures are mainly from studies and economy. Set the knowledge and achievements as life goals. Willing to accept new things, highly sensitive to them and have good ability to accept and learn everything.

Story:
Lin Shan is a girl from Sichuan. 5 years ago she went to Zhejiang University, study Environmental Engineering. Now she is studying for a master's degree. College life is full and colorful for her. On weekends she'd like to go shopping, see movies, go hiking, visit West Lake or enjoy the nature in Taizi Bay. She also joined the dance class and Japanese class. She loves the city Hangzhou. Several years ago the public bicycle rental system began to test run. She rents bikes occasionally when she needs to go out. And she also has an own bike. She'd like to ride her own bike in the campus. She feels so good when she travel in the beautiful city.

Fig. 90.10   Persona

Fig. 90.11   Integration model generated from spatio-temporal context and task context

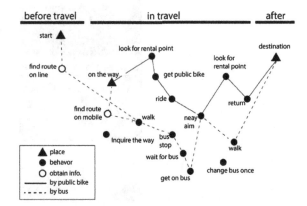

Fig. 90.12   The bicycle stations interface

Fig. 90.13 The milestones
interface

Fig. 90.14 The milestones
interface

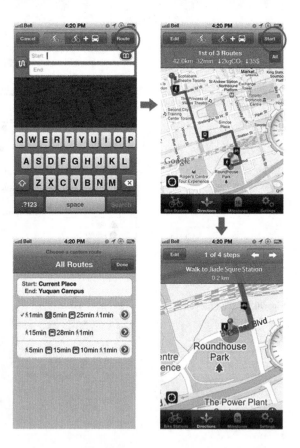

Fig. 90.15 The setting interface of cycler

Table 90.2 The statistics of user satisfaction

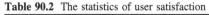

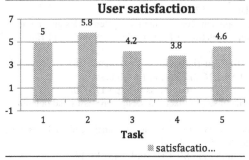

90.5 Conclusions

This paper is an applied research of the contextual design process in HCI. It is also a research and design practice that introduces AT into CD.

It is an exploratory theoretical research used to guide the design practice. It proposed a CD under the Framework of AT. Theory of psychology, sociology and other disciplines are increasingly often introduced into the field of design. This paper is one of such attempts. The research found in the practice process that analytical framework and principles of AT could help the designers to analyze user's activities more systematically. However, the AT is highly theoretical, it should be flexible used in the specific design. We will strive to solve the usability problem of AT in contextual analysis in future research, to ensure that the final design can support the users' activities well.

References

1. Carroll JM (2000) Making use: scenario-based design of human-computer interactions. MIT Press, Cambridge
2. Wang D, Zhang G (2006) Pen-based user interface with scenarios tree. J Computer-Aided Design Comput Graph 18(8):1276–1280 (in Chinese)
3. Depaula R (2003) A new era in human computer interaction: the challenges of technology as a social proxy. In: Proceedings of the Latin American conference on human-computer interaction, pp 219–222
4. Nielsen J (1994) Usability engineering. Academic Press, Burlington
5. Folmer E, Bosch J (2004) Architecting for usability: a survey. J Syst Softw 70:61–78
6. Curve UX (2011) A method for evaluating long-term user experience. Interact Comput. doi:10.1016/j.intcom.2011.06.005
7. Lv J, Liu M, Shi L (2007) An inquiry into evolutionary skeleton and application of activity theory. Mod Educ Technol 17(1):8-14 (in Chinese)
8. Kuutti K, Arvonen T (1992) Identifying CSCW applications by means of activity theory concepts: a case example. In: Proceedings of the 1998 ACM conference on computer-supported collaborative work, pp 233–240. Toronto, Ontario, Canada, 1–4 November
9. Gould JD (1988).How to design usable systems. Handbook of human–computer interaction. Elsevier Science Publishers, Amsterdam, pp 757–789
10. SATO K (2004) Context-sensitive approach for interactive systems design: modular scenario-based methods for context representation. J Physiologic Anthropol Appl Hum Sci 23(6):277–281
11. Luo S, Zhu S, Ying F, Zhang J (2010) Scenario-based user experience design in mobile phone interface. Comput Integr Manuf Syst 16(2):239–248 (in Chinese)
12. Shedroff N (2001) Experience design 1. Waite Group Press, US, pp 174–202
13. Delarge CA (2004) Storytelling as a critical success factor in design processes and outcomes. Design Manag Rev 2:76–79
14. Beyer H, Holtzblatt K (1998) Contextual design: defining customer- centered systems. Morgan Kaufmann, San Francisco. ISBN 1-55860-411-1
15. Nardi BA (1992) The use of scenarios in design. SIGCHI Bull 24(3):13–14
16. Kofod-Petersen A, Cassens J (2006) Using activity theory to model context awareness. Lect Notes Artif Intell 3946:1–17
17. Holtzblatt K (2001).Contextual design: experience in real life. In: Mensch and Computer 2001
18. Cooper A et al (2008). About Face 3—the essentials of interaction design. Publishing House of Electronics Beijing, p 18

Chapter 91
Multi-Objective Particle Swarm Optimization Based on Self-Update and Grid Strategy

Jianguo Wang, Wenjing Liu, Wenxing Zhang and Bin Yang

Abstract A multi-objective particle swarm optimization based on self-update and grid strategy was proposed for improving the function of Pareto set. The method chooses *pBest* with self-update strategy, uses grid method as the selection mode of *gBest*. It is tested to compare with the performance of the optimal solution's evaluation and selection. The results show that algorithm has gained better convergence with even distributing and diversity of Pareto set.

Keywords Particle swarm algorithm · Multi-objective optimization · Grid method · Pareto set

91.1 Introduction

Multi-objective optimization problem is hot issue in the development areas of scientific practice, engineering system design, social production and economic. There are conflicts among those goals, which will to be optimized. If one of those goals has been optimized, and led to other goals degradation. So we must take consider with every sub-goal and gain a group of solution set for achieve the optimization of general goal.

Particle swarm optimization (PSO) is a relatively recent heuristic inspired by the choreography of a bird flock. PSO has been found to be successful in a wide variety of optimization tasks, but until recently it had not been extended to deal

J. Wang · W. Liu (✉) · W. Zhang · B. Yang
Mechanical Engineering School, University of Science and Technology Inner Mongolia,
Baotou 014010, Inner Mongolia, China
e-mail: yes_eternal@126.com

W. Lu et al. (eds.), *Proceedings of the 2012 International Conference on Information Technology and Software Engineering*, Lecture Notes in Electrical Engineering 211, DOI: 10.1007/978-3-642-34522-7_91, © Springer-Verlag Berlin Heidelberg 2013

with multi-objectives. PSO seems particularly suitable for multi-objective optimization mainly because of the high speed of convergence that the algorithm presents for single objective optimization.

C.A introduced the conception of external repository into PSO to maintain diversity [1]; D.M Lei proposed the MOPSO with Pareto through archive maintaining and *gBest* being combined [2]; S.M improved the speed of operation and the diversity of solution by readjust the size of external archive [3]; A.B.J proposed the optimize strategy of select *gBest* from the division, which is the external set of dominate one particle [4]; W.J.G put forward by using update on individual strategies of the optimal value of the selected [5]; K.B put forward the method of the distance from the crowded external file maintenance and further increase the diversity of the algorithm [6]; E.Z proposed SPEA2 by the methods of maintenance archive to choose the global optimal value [7]; K.J took grid algorithm to update and maintain the archive [8], from the above documents we can see, in the term of improving itself performance, some take the combined approach with other algorithms, some use the approach of update external archive, but there is no researcher enhance the solution performance through update *gBest*. In this paper, we propose a proposal, called "Multi-objective Particle Swarm Optimization Based on Self-Update and Grid Strategy", which has gained better convergence with even distributing and diversity of Pareto set.

91.2 Multi-Objective Optimization

A multi-objective optimization problem is of the form [9]:

$$Min \ y = f(x) = [f_1(x), f_2(x), \ldots, f_n(x)], s.t \quad x \in s = [x|g_j(x) \leq 0, j = 1, 2, \ldots, p],$$

where x is called decision vector, s decision space, y objective vector and $g_j(x)$ is the j_{th} constraint. The following three concepts are of importance:

(1) Pareto dominance: A solution x^0 is said to dominate (Pareto optimal) another x^1 (denoted $x^0 < x^1$) if: $\forall i \in \{1, \ldots m\} : f_i(x^0) \leq f_i(x^1) \wedge (\exists k \in \{1, \ldots, m\} : f_k(x^0) < f_k(x^1))$;
(2) Pareto optimal: a solution x^0 is said to dominate (Pareto optimal) if and only if: $\neg \exists x^1 \in S : x^1 > x^0$;
(3) Pareto optimal set: The set P_s of all Pareto optimal solutions: $P_s = \{x^0 | \neg \exists x^1 \in S : x^1 > x^0\}$.

91.3 Performance Metrics

To measure performances of our approach against these three heuristics we chose three metrics [10]. Based on those notions, we adopted one metric to evaluate each of three aspects previously indicated:

(1) Spacing (SP): It measures how well distributed the solutions in the non-dominated set found are:

$$SP = \sqrt{\frac{1}{n-1} \sum_{i=1}^{n} (\bar{d} - d_i)} \qquad (91.1)$$

where $d_i = \min_{j=1,2,\ldots,n} (\sum_{k=1}^{M} |f_k^i - f_k^j|)$, $i,j = 1,\ldots,n$, $\bar{d}$ is the mean for all d_i, and n is the number of non-dominated vectors found so far. This metric is the standard of diversity, and the value is the smaller the better.

(2) Generational Distance (GD): It finds the average distance of the non-dominated set of solutions found from the Pareto optimal set:

$$GD = \frac{\sqrt{\sum_{i=1}^{n} d_i^2}}{n} \qquad (91.2)$$

where d_i is the Euclidean Distance between solution i from the set of n non-dominated solutions found and the closest element from the Pareto optimal set (in research space). This metric on behalf of convergence and a smaller value indicates more proximity.

(3) Error Ratio (ER): This metric is to indicate the percentage of solutions that are not members of the true Pareto optimal set:

$$ER = \frac{\sum_{i=1}^{n} e_i}{n} \qquad (91.3)$$

where n is the number of vectors in the current set of non-dominated vectors available; $e_i = 0$ if vector i is a member of the Pareto optimal set, and $e_i = 1$ otherwise. This metric addresses the third issue from the list previously provided.

91.4 Multi-Objective Particle Swarm Optimization Based on Self-Update and Grid Strategy

This optimization method takes self-update strategy as the method of selecting *pBest*, takes grid method to select *gBest*. Firstly, we gain the initial *pBest* set and evaluate all particles' fitness values; secondly, take a part of the *pBest* set which is corresponding to the former small fitness values as the true candidate *pBest*, and others are abandoned; finally, take one *pBest* from candidate set randomly as the current *pBest* for position updating. In the process of select *pBest* from each iteration, the diversity of archives and *pBest* set has been improved through the boost from a large number of different candidate particles simultaneously. This method is different from other methods. It's not sleet particle with minimum fitness as *gBest*, but takes the other method. Firstly, calculate density information of every grid; and then, determine one grid; finally, select *gBest* from that grid. In the paper, choose the grid with minimum density information. The algorithm of MOPSO is the following:

Step 1: Initialize the population P, the External Archive A, the inertia weight w, the accelerate factor $c1$, $c2$, the current iteration t and maximum iterations T_{max};
Step 2: Set $t = t + 1$, loop;
Step 3: Evaluate fitness value, Update archive A and $SU(self - update)$;
Step 4: Establish a grid among A, then put a better particle into grid and calculate the position of particles;
Step 5: Find out the grid of the lest density, and select the best particle as $gBest$ to Guide other particle the next direction of flight;
Step 6: On the basis of self-update strategy, select *pBest* from SU;
Step 7: Update x and v;
Step 8: If it meets the condition export; unless return to Step 2.

91.5 Experimental

In order to allow a quantitative assessment of the performance of a multi-objective optimization algorithm, two test functions were taken from the specialized literature to compare our approach.

The first test function was proposed by Schaffer [11], the acceleration factors $c1 = c2 = 0.5$; the inertia weight change from $w_{ini} = 0.9$ to $w_{end} = 0.4$ by linear decrease, and $-12 \leq V_{max} \leq 12$ is search space. Our second test function was proposed by Kursawe [12], the acceleration factors from $c_{1ini} = 0.9$ to $c_{1end} = 0.2$ by linear decrease, however, from $c_{2ini} = 0.2$ to $c_{2end} = 0.9$ by linear increase; the inertia weight change from $w_{1ini} = 0.9$ to $w_{1end} = 0.5$ by linear decrease and take $-10 \leq V_{max} \leq 10$ as search space. The number of grid is $M = 4$, the population is

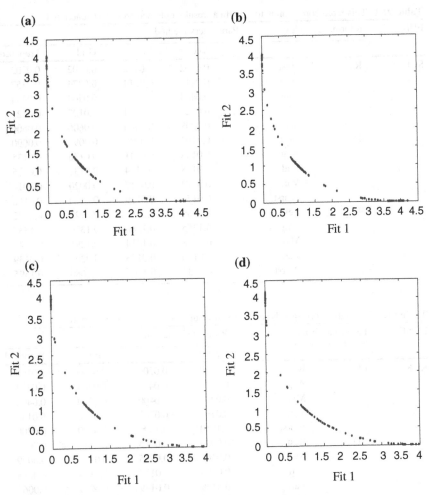

Fig. 91.1 This graphical results were obtained from test function 1.**a** Vector assessment method,**b** SU-MOPSO,**c** grid algorithm,**d** proposed algorithm

100 particles, the maximize iteration is 100, and we report the results obtained from performing 30 independent runs of each algorithm compared.

Test function 1:

M in $f_1(x) = x^2$, Min $f_2(x) = (x - 2)^2$, where $x \in [-5, 7]$.

The followed Fig. 91.1 was obtained by those methods from test function 1. In this paper, the proposed algorithm has got the absolute advantage, especially convergence and diversity. From the Table 91.1, we can know that convergence and diversity has been improved 4.26 and 3.90 % separately. The results show that comparable results to our method.

Table 91.1 This table corresponds to statistical results obtained from test function 1

FUNC	Performance index		Parameters method			
			Vector	SU	Grid	Proposed
SCH	ER	Best	0.0202	0.0202	0.0202	0.0202
		Avg	0.0418	0.0314	0.0374	0.0357
		Mid	0.0404	0.0404	0.0404	0.0354
		Var.	0.0124	0.0104	0.0107	0.0121
		Worst.	0.0808	0.0606	0.0606	0.0606
	GD	Best	0.0102	0.0090	0.0094	0.0090
		Avg	0.0138	0.0141	0.0136	0.0135
		Mid	0.0138	0.0144	0.0131	0.0136
		Var.	0.0012	0.0017	0.0020	0.0014
		Worst.	0.0176	0.0179	0.0170	0.0162
	SP	Best	0.0909	0.0883	0.0927	0.0882
		Avg	0.1355	0.1386	0.1336	0.1332
		Mid	0.1358	0.1414	0.1291	0.1343
		Var.	0.0120	0.0173	0.0201	0.0139
		Worst.	0.1732	0.1767	0.1680	0.1595

Table 91.2 This table corresponds to statistical results obtained from test function 2

FUNC	Performance index		Parameters method			
			Vector	SU	Grid	Proposed
KUR	ER	Best	0.0200	0.0200	0.0100	0.0100
		Avg	0.0420	0.0440	0.0343	0.0373
		Mid	0.0400	0.0400	0.0300	0.0400
		Var.	0.0163	0.0203	0.0176	0.0141
		Worst.	0.1010	0.1000	0.0700	0.0700
	GD	Best	0.0020	0.0016	0.0014	0.0002
		Avg	0.0166	0.0155	0.0122	0.0099
		Mid	0.0104	0.0102	0.0114	0.0098
		Var.	0.0149	0.0149	0.0059	0.0068
		Worst.	0.0715	0.0762	0.0250	0.0373
	SP	Best	0.0204	0.0297	0.0134	0.0022
		Avg	0.1649	0.1539	0.1216	0.0986
		Mid	0.1029	0.1081	0.1133	0.0970
		Var.	0.1483	0.1487	0.0588	0.0673
		Worst.	0.7139	0.7613	0.2497	0.3710

Test Function 2:

$$Min\ f_1(x) = \sum_{i=1}^{n-1}(-10\exp(-0.2\sqrt{(x_i^2 + x_{i+1}^2)}))Min\ f_2(x) = \sum_{i=1}^{n}(|x_i|^{0.8}+5\sin(x_i)^3),$$

where $x_1, x_2, x_3 \in [-5, 5]$.

It can be seen from the Table 91.2, the convergence of the proposed method is proposed to improve the average 18.18 %, diversity increased by 18.11 %, and the stability of the algorithm has been improved.

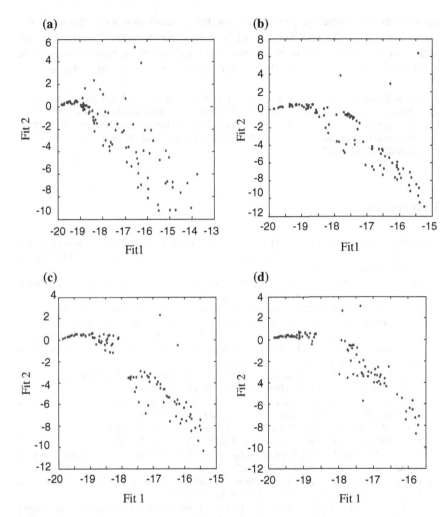

Fig. 91.2 This graphical results were obtained from test function 2. **a** Vector assessment method, **b** SU-MOPSO, **c** grid algorithm, **d** proposed algorithm

The followed figures were obtained by those methods from test function 2, which show comparable results to our method (Fig. 91.2).

91.6 Conclusion

This paper puts forward to update strategy for the foundation, and the grid was applied to the global optimal value of the multi-objective particle swarm optimization algorithm, update process through the change of the values of the global optimal selection strategy. Numerical experiment result shows that the suggested method improves the MOPSO algorithm of each performance. Due to the complexity of the algorithm is to make operation time growth, so how to improve the efficiency of the algorithm and the future research needs to be part of the problem.

Acknowledgments This research is supported in part by the Natural Science of Foundation Inner Mongolia (No.2011ZD08), Inner Mongolia High School Research Project (No.JZY11150), Baotou Science and Technology Bureau intellectual Property Development Project (2011Z1006), and Intramural Foundation of Inner Mongolia University of Science and Technology (No.2009NC032 and No.2010NC032).

References

1. Carlos A, Maximino S (2002) MOPSO: a proposal for multiple objective particle swarm optimization. In: Congress on evolutionary computation, vol 1. Piscataway, IEEE Service Center, pp 1051–1056
2. Lei D, Wu Z (2006) Multi-objective particle swarm optimal with pareto repository. Pattern Recognit Artif Intell 19(4):475–480 (in Chinese)
3. Mostaghim S, Teich J (2003) The role of ε-dominance in multi objective particle swarm optimization methods. http://www.lania.mx/~ccoello/EMOO/. Accessed May 2003
4. Alvarez J, Everson R, Fieldsend J (2005) AMOPSO algorithm based exclusively on Pareto dominance concepts. In: The 3rd international conference on evolutionary multi-criterion optimization, Guanajuato, LNCS, pp 459–473
5. Wang J, Liu W (2011) Multi-objective particle swarm optimization algorithm based on self-update strategy. Am J Eng Technol Res 11(9):98–104 (in Chinese)
6. Kalyanmoy D, Amrit P, Sameer A et al (2002) A fast and elitist multi-objective genetic algorithms NSG-II. IEEE Trans Evolut Comput (S1089-778x) 6(2):82–197
7. Eckart Z, Marco L, Lothar T (2001) SPEA2: improving the strength Pareto evolutionary algorithm. http://www.lania.mx/~ccoello/EMOO/. Accessed May 2001
8. Knowles J, Corne D (2000) Approximating the non-dominated front using the Pareto archive evolutionary strategy. Evolut Comput 8(2):149–172
9. Meng H (2005) Multi-objective evolutionary algorithms and their applications. Ph.D. Xi'an University of Technology, China, pp 15–37 (in Chinese)
10. Zitzler E, Deb K, Thiele L (2000) Comparison of multi-objective evolutionary algorithms: empirical results. Evolut Comput 8(2):173–195
11. Schaffer J (1985) Multiple objective optimization with vector evaluated genetic algorithms. In: The first international conference on genetic algorithms, Lawrence Erlbaum
12. Kursawe F (1991) A variant of evolution strategies for vector optimization. Problem solving from nature vol 496. Springer, Berlin, pp 193–197

Chapter 92
Research on the Prediction of the Machining Quality of Maintenance Parts of Vehicle Equipment Based on LS-SVM

Qiaoyun Wu, Gang Chang and Huaijun Zhang

Abstract The sample size of machining quality of maintenance parts of vehicle equipment is so small that the prediction of machining quality based on neural network can cause the problems such as over-fitting, low generalization ability and local minima. The paper proposed a prediction model of machining quality of maintenance parts of vehicle equipment based on LS-SVM and compared the performance of the model with other common models. The experiments confirmed the efficiency of the model to provide a feasible solution for the control of the machining quality of maintenance parts of vehicle equipment.

Keywords Least Square · Support vector machine · Maintenance parts · Prediction of the quality

92.1 Introduction

Maintenance parts are the material basis of the maintenance of vehicle equipment. The machining quality of maintenance parts directly affects the quality of maintenance of vehicle equipment. To improve the quality of maintenance parts is vital to extend the life of the vehicle equipment and improve the intact rate of vehicle equipment [1]. The factors influencing the machining quality of maintenance parts

Q. Wu (✉) · H. Zhang
Department of Equipment Support, Military Transportation University, Dongjuzi 1#,
Chenlin road, Hedong district, Tianjin, China
e-mail: 1208552210@qq.com

G. Chang
Department of Military Transportation, Military Transportation University, Dongjuzi
1#,Chenlin road, Hedong district, Tianjin, China

W. Lu et al. (eds.), *Proceedings of the 2012 International Conference on Information Technology and Software Engineering*, Lecture Notes in Electrical Engineering 211, DOI: 10.1007/978-3-642-34522-7_92, © Springer-Verlag Berlin Heidelberg 2013

include processing, transportation, staff, storage method, inventory environment and equipment. The machining of spare parts is the most direct and the most fundamental factor [2]. Therefore, quality control in advance based on prediction in the machining is the key to improve the quality of maintenance spares.

The quality-prediction model is important to quality control. The traditional prediction methods such as expert systems, inference learning, and fuzzy theory are based on statistics theoretically [3]. According to the law of large number, the statistical laws can be expressed accurately only when the number of training samples nearly infinite. The machining of the maintenance spares of military vehicle equipment maintenance belongs to low-volume and high-variety production. Therefore, these theoretically good prediction methods are difficult to have outstanding performance in practical applications. There are some problems such as over-fitting, low generalization ability and local minimum in some cases [4]. In addition, the machining process is a complex dynamic process with the characteristics such as multi-input, multi-output, nonlinear and time-delay. The relation between the error data of the production of the maintenance parts is hard to be expressed by the traditional prediction model [5].

Artificial Neural Network (ANN) technology has been more common used in prediction as a new kind of intelligent prediction method because of its strong self-learning, fault-tolerant, non-linear and parallel-distributed processing capabilities. It can handle noisy data and incomplete data [6]. It can get more accurate prediction results than traditional mathematical prediction model. However, it also has congenital disadvantages such as be easy to fall into local minima and weak generalization ability for small sample data and is hard to apply in the prediction of the machining quality of the maintenance spares of military vehicle equipment maintenance [7]. The birth of statistical learning theory (SLV) and support vector machine (SVM) have opened up a new way to solve this problem.

SVM is based on the structural risk minimization criteria and its topology is determined by support vector to overcome many shortcomings of the ANN prediction and traditional statistical prediction method. It solves the problems such as high-dimensional, local minima and the small sample data preferably [8]. Especially, SVM showed high generalization capability in the small sample data. It could describe the complex machining process without precise mathematical model and more data [9, 10]. It makes it possible to high-precision prediction of the machining quality of the maintenance spares of military vehicle equipment maintenance [11]. Least squares support vector machine (LS-SVM) is a new extension of the standard SVM that replace inequality constraints of the standard SVM with equality constraints, viz. convert the planning problem into solving linear equations. The replacement further reduces the computational complexity and speed up the solving speed in the same time while keeps the SVM learning ability. In the paper, LS-SVM model is used to predict the machining quality of the outer ring of the bearing of military vehicle and its prediction accuracy is compared with traditional prediction model. The experiment showed the prediction model of machining quality of the maintenance parts of the military vehicle equipment has practicality and rationality.

92.2 LS-SVM

The SVMs were proposed by Vapnik [8]. Generally speaking, SVM is to minimize the structural risk instead of the usual empirical risk by minimizing an upper bound of the generalization error and it obtains an excellent generalization performance. Moreover, SVM is especially suitable for solving problems with small sample size and has already been used for classification, regression and time series prediction.

The SVM regression function is formulated as:

$$y = f(x) = \omega \bullet \phi(x) + b \tag{92.1}$$

where $\phi(x)$ is nonlinear mapped from the input space X. The coefficients ω and b are estimated by minimizing

$$R(C) = C \frac{1}{N} \sum_{i=1}^{N} L_\varepsilon(f(x_i), y_i) + \frac{1}{2} \|\omega\|^2 \tag{92.2}$$

$$L_\varepsilon(f(x_i), y_i) = \text{Max}(0, |f(x_i) - y_i| - \varepsilon) \tag{92.3}$$

where both C and ε are user-determined parameters, x_i represents the input value at period i, y_i represents the prediction value at period i. Additionally, the first term in Eq. (92.2) denotes the empirical error, the second term represents the function flatness and the C is used as the trade-off between the empirical error and the model flatness. Introducing the positive slack variables ζ_i and ζ_i^*, which represent the distance from the actual values to the corresponding boundary values of ε-tube. Equation (92.2) is transformed to the following constrained formation:

$$R(w, \zeta, \zeta^*) = \frac{1}{2} \omega \omega^T + C \sum_{i=1}^{N} (\zeta_i + \zeta_i^*)$$

$$s.t. \begin{cases} \omega \bullet \phi(x_i) + b_i - y_i \leq \varepsilon + \zeta_i^* \\ y_i - \omega \bullet \phi(x_i) - b_i \leq \varepsilon + \zeta_i \\ \zeta_i^*, \zeta_i \geq 0 \\ i = 1, 2, \cdots, N. \end{cases} \tag{92.4}$$

Finally, introducing Lagrangian multipliers, the optimization formulation can be transformed into a dual form:

$$Max\, R(\alpha_i - \alpha_i^*) = \sum_{i=1}^{N} y_i(\alpha_i^* - \alpha_i) - \varepsilon \sum_{i=1}^{N}(\alpha_i + \alpha_i^*)$$
$$- \frac{1}{2}\sum_{i,j=1}^{N}(\alpha_i^* - \alpha_i)(\alpha_j^* - \alpha_j)K(x_i, x_j)$$

$$s.t. \begin{cases} \sum_{i=1}^{N}(\alpha_i^* - \alpha_i) = 0 \\ 0 \leq \alpha_i, \alpha_i^* \leq C\, i = 1, 2, \cdots, N \end{cases}$$

The Lagrange multipliers α_i^*, α_i are calculated and an optimal weight vector of the regression hyperplane is expressed as:

$$w^* = \sum_{i=1}^{N}(\alpha_i - \alpha_i^*)K(x_i, x) \tag{92.5}$$

Hence, the solution is expressed as:

$$f(x) = \sum_{i=1}^{N}(\alpha_i - \alpha_i^*)K(x_i, x) + b \tag{92.6}$$

The kernel function $K(x_i, x_j) = \varphi(x_i) \bullet \varphi(x_j)$ satisfies the Mercer's conditions and performs the non-linear mapping. Those sample points that appear with non-zero coefficients in Eq. (92.3) are called support vectors (SV). Kernel function can be a Gaussian function, a polynomial function, or a sigmoid function etc. The Gaussian kernel function

$$K(x_i, x_j) = \exp\left(-\frac{\|x_i - x_j\|}{2\sigma^2}\right) \tag{92.7}$$

is used in our SVR model because Gaussian kernels tend to give good performance under general smoothness assumptions.

LS-SVM is least squares version of SVM. LS-SVM reformulates the minimization problem of SVM as:

$$\min \frac{1}{2}\omega^T\omega + \frac{1}{2}\gamma\sum_{i=1}^{N}\xi_i^2, \tag{92.8}$$
$$s.t. y_i = \omega^T\phi(x_i) + b + \xi_i, \, i = 1, 2, \dots, N,$$

where γ is tuning parameter and positive real number. Introducing Lagrangian function:

$$L(\omega, b, \xi, a) = \frac{1}{2}\omega^T\omega + \gamma\sum_{i=1}^{N}\xi_i^2 - \sum_{i=1}^{N}a_i[\omega\phi(x_i) + b + \xi_i - y_i] \tag{92.9}$$

where $a_i, (i = 1 \ldots, N)$ are Lagrange multipliers.

The optimal $a_i(i = 1 \ldots, N)$ and b can be got according to KKT condition:

$$\begin{cases} \dfrac{\partial L}{\partial \omega} = 0 \rightarrow \omega = \sum_{i=1}^{N} a_i \phi(x_i) \\[2ex] \dfrac{\partial L}{\partial b} = 0 \rightarrow \sum_{i=1}^{N} a_i = 0 \\[2ex] \dfrac{\partial L}{\partial \xi} = 0 \rightarrow a_i = \gamma \xi \\[2ex] \dfrac{\partial L}{\partial a} = 0 \rightarrow \omega \phi(x_i) + b + \xi - y_i = 0 \end{cases} \tag{92.10}$$

After the optimal a and b are got, LS-SVM can be used to predict the value using the equation:

$$y(x) = \sum_{i=1}^{N} a_i \psi(x_i, x) + b \tag{92.11}$$

92.3 Model Implementation and Experiment Results

Because maintenance organizations organize maintenance parts of equipment vehicle according to the number of vehicle maintenance machining, the amount of machining of each batch is so small that it is difficult to provide large samples. We chose an error data sequence of processing of WD615 cylinder bore showed in Table 92.1 as the testing data. In the Table 92.1, the error data sequence of semi-automatic machining of cylinder bore is given and the tolerance of the cylinder is $92^{+0.45}_{+0.30}$ and $\Delta D_{\max}$ represents the maximum deviation of the measured bore.

To verify the performance of LS-SVM, we compare it with polynomial model, back propagation neural network (BP neural network). The LS-SVM prediction

Table 92.1 Error data sequence of processing of WD615 cylinder bore

Number of workpiece	1	2	3	4	5	6	7	8	9	10	11	12	13	14	15
$\Delta D_{\max}$	0.36	0.38	0.40	0.38	0.39	0.43	0.42	0.45	0.38	0.37	0.41	0.40	0.40	0.41	0.39
No. of workpiece	16	17	18	19	20	21	22	23	24	25					
$\Delta D_{\max}$	0.38	0.42	0.42	0.44	0.42	0.40	0.43	0.42	0.44	0.45					

Table 92.2 MRE of polynomial model, BP neural network and LS-SVM

Model	MSE
Polynomial model	3.1×10^{-4}
BP neural network	2.3×10^{-4}
LS-SVM	0.9×10^{-5}

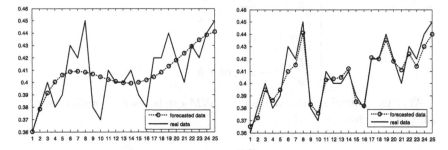

Fig. 92.1 Predicted processing error by polynomial model and BP neural network VS real processing error

Fig. 92.2 Predicted processing error by polynomial model VS real processing error

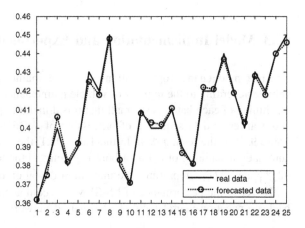

model was built based on the first 20 data and the last five data are used to verify the performance of the model by comparing the real data with predicted data.

The order of polynomial model is set as 4. The learning rate α of BP neural network is set as 0.1 and training steps is set as 10000. The amount of hidden neuron of BP neural network is set as 6. The tuning parameter γ is set as 500. The mean square error (MSE) defined as Eq. (92.13) is chosen as performance evaluation criteria.

$$MSE = \frac{1}{N} \sum_{i=1}^{N} (d_i - z_i)^2 \tag{92.13}$$

where N is the number of workpiece, d_i is real error of the ith cylinder bore, and z_i is the prediction error of the ith cylinder bore.

The MSE of each prediction model is listed in Table 92.2. Figure 92.1 shows the predicted error by use of polynomial model, BP neural network model and the real error of 25 workpieces. Figure 92.2 shows the predicted error by use of LS-SVM model and the real error of 25 workpieces.

According to the MSE value and figures, it can be included that LS-SVM model has higher prediction accuracy than BP neural network and Polynomial model.

92.4 Conclusion

In the paper, a small-batch quality-prediction model based on LS-SVM is proposed to predict the machining quality of maintenance parts of military vehicle equipment. The experiment shows that LS-SVM is suitable for the machining quality prediction. On the one hand, LS-SVM can handle small-sample machine learning. On the one hand, quality prediction model proposed technology for smart core, on the other hand, it converts the quadratic programming problem into linear equations and has faster modeling process than the standard support vector machines. Therefore, it should be suitable for online quality intelligent prediction.

References

1. Cao JX (2011) Quality control of spare parts for equipment repair shop. Equip Qual 2(1):26–27 (in Chinese)
2. Wu QY, Zhang XT (2010) Research on vehicle equipment maintenance quality based on SPC. The First Military Equipment Wheeled Vehicle Forum, 214–216. (in Chinese)
3. Shewhart M (1992) Interpreting statistical process control charts using machine learning and expert system techniques. In: Proceedings of the IEEE 1992 national aerospace and electronics conference
4. Huang XY, Zhang ZH, Hu XB (2005) The theory and application of modern intelligent algorithm. Science Press, Beijing (in Chinese)
5. Zhang LN (1998) Research on machining error and predicting model. Acta Metrologica Sinica 19(3):183–188 (in Chinese)
6. Zhang WQ (2009) Evaluation of product model design based on BP neural network. Comput Eng Des 30(24):5715–5717 (in Chinese)
7. Zhang XG (2000) About statistical learning theory and support vector machines. ACTA Automatic Sinica 26(1):32–44 (in Chinese)
8. Vapnik VN (1998) Statistical leaning theory. Wiley, New York
9. Vapnik VN (2000) Essence of statistical learning theory. Tsinghua University Press, Beijing
10. Cristianini N, Schawe-Taylor J (2000) An introduction to support vector machines. Cambridge England University Press, Cambridge
11. Jiang L, Liu J (2005) Support vector machines based method for machining error prediction model. Modul Mach Tool Autom Manuf Tech 8:13–15 (in Chinese)

Chapter 93
A Personification and Genetic Combinational Algorithm for the Placement Problem of Digital Microfluidics-Based Biochips

Jingsong Yang, Zhenjing Yao, Yanxing Song and Chuncheng Zuo

Abstract A new algorithm based on the combination of personification and genetic algorithm is established for the placement of digital microfluidic biochips, in which, the personification heuristic algorithm is used to control the packing process, while the genetic algorithm is designed to be used in multi-objective placement results optimizing. As an example, the process of microfluidic module physical placement in multiplexed in vitro diagnostics on human physiological fluids is simulated. The experiment results show that personification and genetic combinational algorithm can achieve better results in multi-objective optimization, compare to the parallel recombinative simulated annealing algorithm.

Keywords Personification heuristic algorithm · Genetic algorithm · Digital microfluidics-based biochips · Placement

93.1 Introduction

Digital microfluidics-based biochips, which are widely used in more and more different fields, such as analytical chemistry, clinic diagnosis, biology manufactory, environmental monitor, and military [1–3]. As biochips are adopted for complex procedures in molecular biology, the design complexity of digital

J. Yang (✉) · Z. Yao · Y. Song
Institute of Disaster Prevention, Sanhe 605201, China
e-mail: yangjingsong@cidp.edu.cn

C. Zuo
College of Mechanical Science and Engineering, Jilin University, Changchun 130022, China
e-mail: zuocc@jlu.edu.cn

W. Lu et al. (eds.), *Proceedings of the 2012 International Conference on Information Technology and Software Engineering*, Lecture Notes in Electrical Engineering 211, DOI: 10.1007/978-3-642-34522-7_93, © Springer-Verlag Berlin Heidelberg 2013

microfluidics-based biochips is expected to increase due to the need of multiple and concurrent assays on a biochip. The international technology roadmap for semiconductors (ITRS) clearly points out that the integration of electro-biological devices is one of the major challenges of system integration beyond 2009. The placement of digital microfluidics-based biochips is one of the key points in the chip design, through which the physical position of each biochemical analysis operation can be found with the smallest biochip area and the shortest completion. The algorithm for the placement has been paid great attention by different groups. Su and Chakrabarty presented a unified synthesis and placement flow based on parallel recombinative simulated annealing. They used the list-scheduling algorithm for scheduling and a greedy placement algorithm for physical placement [4–6]. The placement is somehow not very compacted and cannot meet all design specifications. While the T-tree formulation developed by Yuh etc. from Taiwan University [7, 8] shows better results with a tree-based topological representation, but the completion time is not so good due to the large amount of calculations needed and that is time-consuming.

The placement of digital microfluidics-based chip is an optimization of multi-objectives. In this article, we combine personification heuristic algorithm with genetic algorithm to solve the placement problem. The results showed a better biochip area and shorter completion time, compare to the parallel recombinative simulated annealing algorithm and T-tree.

93.2 The Placement of Microfluidic-Based Biochips

The procedure of the placement of microfluidic-based biochips is shown as Fig. 93.1. There are three inputs to the placement problem. The first one is the sequencing graph $G = \{V, E\}$ that represents the protocol of a bioassay, where $V = \{v_1, v_2, \ldots, v_m\}$ represents a set of m assay operations and $E = \{(v_i, v_j), 1 \leq i, j \leq m\}$ denotes the data dependencies between two assay operations; i.e., the *precedence constraints*. We may need at most one storage unit for each edge in G to store the intermediate data between two data-dependent operations. The second one is the microfluidic module library that contains the basic modules for biochips. Each basic module is characterized by its functionality (i.e., mix, dilution, etc.) and parameters (i.e., width, height, and operation duration). The third one is the design specification, that is, the resource constraints.

The placement of modules on the microfluidic array can be modeled as a 3-D packing problem. Each microfluidic module is represented by a 3-D box, the base of which denotes the rectangular area of the module and the height denotes the time-span of its operation. The microfluidic biochip placement can now be viewed as the problem of packing these boxes to minimize the total base area, while avoiding overlaps.

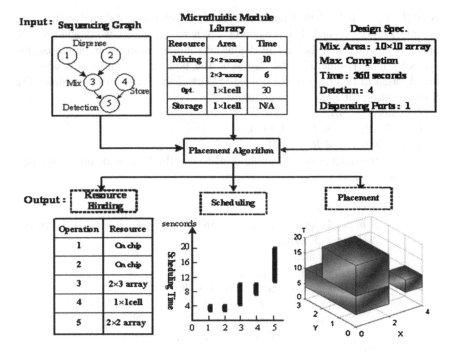

Fig. 93.1 Overview of the placement problem of biochips

93.3 Design of the Personification Heuristic Genetic Algorithm

Personification heuristic algorithm is formulated based on the simulation of natural optimization law, which has some advantages of solving the optimization of the 3-D packing problems, especially when for the large-scale problems with great complexity. In order to obtain a more compact placement layout, we combine the personification heuristic algorithm with the genetic algorithm. Personification heuristic algorithm is used to control the placement of the modules, and then optimize the placement results of the multiple objectives by genetic algorithm in order to achieve the goal of smallest microfluidic array area and shortest completion time. The key points of genetic algorithm are the design of encoding and the selection of the fitness function.

93.3.1 Personification Heuristic Algorithm

As we know, the efficiency of personification heuristic application was firstly proved on the three-dimensional packing problem [9]. 3 D-placement algorithm process is given, the algorithm input is an orderly digital microfluidic module set

$B = \{b_1, b_2,..., b_n\}$, where T represents scheduling end time of digital microfluidic module, I represents orderly place point set. When I is updated, we should keep the order of I elements. If the current digital microfluidic module can be placed, the symbol $flag = 1$, otherwise the $flag = 0$. The time of placement is t, which is mainly used to find the t moment need to start of the layout of the module. The flow of placement algorithm is as follows:

3D-*placement* (B).

$I = \{(0,0,0)\}$, $L_y = L_x = 0$, $t = 0$;

for $t = 0$ to T, and B not null

   $\{n = $ the number of scheduling digital microfluidic module on t moment;

    for $i = 1$ to n

     $\{flag = 0$;

       for $(x, y, z) \in I$

         if b_i can be placed at (x, y, z), and $x + l_i' \le L_x$, $y + w_i' \le L_y$, then

           $\{flag = 1$, exit;$\}$

         if $flag = 0$, then

           if $L_x = 0$ or $L_x = L$, then

             if b_i can be placed at $(0, L_y)$, then

               $\{x = 0$, $y = L_y$, $flag = 1$, $L_y = L_y + w_i'$, $L_x = l_i'$;$\}$

             else if $L_y < L$, then

               $\{L_y = L$, $L_x = L$, $i = i - 1$;$\}$

         else

            $\{$for $(x, y, z) \in I$ and $x = L_x$, $y = 0$

             if b_i can be placed at (x, y, z) and $y + w_i' \le L_y$, then

               $\{flag = 1$, $L_x = L_x + l_i'$, exit;$\}$

             if $flag = 0$, then

               $\{L_x = L$, $i = i - 1$;$\}\}$

        if $flag = 1$, then

         $\{$place b_i at (x, y, z), $I = I/\{(x, y, z)\}$, translate b_i along the x and y coordinate in decrease order, keep the translation coordinates (x', y', z'), $I = I \cup \{(x' + l_i', y', z'), (x', y' + w_i', z');\}\}$

   add one to z coordinate and $z \in I$;

   delete the already layout node form B;

   move forward the back node.$\}$

93.3.2 Design of Encoding

The encoding of genetic algorithm in this paper consists of three parts for the resources binding, scheduling and placement, respectively, which determine the start time and end time of each operation, perform the distribution and placement for the operations needed on the microfluidic arrays, such as mixing operations, storage operations, dilution operations and observation. Each chromosome consists of $k + m + n$ genes, and each gene $g(i) \in (0,1)(i \in (1, k + m + n))$ represents the priority of the operation, where k represents the number of resources binding, m represents the number of total operations, n represents the number of operations need to be placed, which means the digital microfluidic module with higher priority will be placed firstly in the queue.

93.3.3 Fitness Function

In order to evaluate the quality of the placement layout, the optimization of two parameters need to be considered, the smaller area of the microfluidic arrays and the shorter completion time. This is a typical multi-objective optimization issue. In this article, the adaptation values are obtained through the adaptive weights method, in which the weights are adjusted according to the adaptation of current generation to acquire the searching ability of positive direction, and the valuable information of current population is used to readjust the weights in each generation. The selective power of this method is in between of fixed-weight method and the random weight method. For a given chromosome x, the fitness function of self-adaptive weight is as follows:

$$f(x) = -w_1 A(x) - w_2 T(x) \tag{93.1}$$

$$w_1 = \frac{1}{A_{\max} - A_{\min}} \tag{93.2}$$

$$w_2 = \frac{1}{T_{\max} - T_{\min}} \tag{93.3}$$

where $A(x)$ and $T(x)$ denote the area of microfluidic array with a given chromosome x and the total completion time; $A_{\max}$ and $A_{\min}$ are the maximum and minimum values of the placement layout area of current population; $T_{\max}$ and $T_{\min}$ are the maximum and minimum values of the completion time of all operations in current population.

93.3.4 The Procedure of Personification Heuristic Genetic Algorithm

The main steps of the personification heuristic genetic algorithm are as follows:

(1) Initialization of genetic parameters: set the initial population size as PopSize; hereditary generation as G_n; crossover probablity as P_c; the ratio of chromosomes copied directly to next generation as TOP; the ratio of new individuals generated randomly as BOT;

(2)   To generate PopSize initial possible solution with the priority-based encoding method, set $k = 1$ (k is the initial searching number);

(3)   To decode each chromosome: perform the heuristic decoding for the first k genes to determine the area of microfluidic array and completion time; sort the first $k + 1$ to $k + m + 1$ genes to determine the scheduling order and calculate the start time, end time of each operation and the total time spent $T(x)$ by all the operations under the conditions of resource constraint; place all the operations under the scheduling order used the personification heuristic algorithm to obtain the placement coordinates and the area of each operation $A(x)$.

(4)   To calculate the weight of self-fitness w_1, w_2, convert the target value of the current population into the fitness function value, and sort the chromosomes in descending order according to the fitness function value, save the best fitness function value into $f(x)$, and the best chromosome into Placement;

(5)   To judge the ending condition, if the condition met, go to step (11) (the ending condition here is $k \leq G_n$; if not, go to the next step;

(6)   To generate new individuals under the crossover probability Pc, the quantity of new individuals is PopSize × (1-TOP-BOT);

(7)   To generate PopSize × BOT new individuals according the coding principle randomly;

(8)   To perform Topological sort and evaluation for the new individuals generated;

(9)   To sort the PopSize × TOP chromosomes of the generation k together with the new ones by Fitness function value in increasing order, save the best into the Placement, and save the fitness value into Placefunction;

(10)   Set $k = k + 1$, go to step (5);

(11)   Output the optimized Placement, algorithm ended.

93.4 Results and Discussion

In order to evaluate the performance of the personification heuristic genetic algorithm (PHGA), a simulation experiment based on the multiplexed in vitro diagnostics was carried out under the environment of Visual C++ as described in Ref. [5] with the algorithm formulated here.

For the multiplexed in-virto diagnostics, we used the same design specifications (resource constraint) as Su and Chakrabarty [5]. We assumed that there is one reservoir/dispensing port for each type of samples and reagents and one optical detector for each enzymatic assay. First, we assumed that no defective cells exist. Table 93.1 summarizes the result of the multiplexed in vitro diagnostics. Comparing with those obtained in Ref. [5], in which the Parallel recombinative simulated annealing algorithm (PRSA) were used in the three experiments, the results

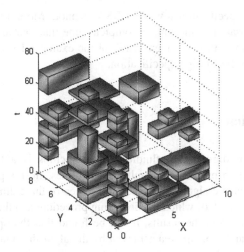

Fig. 93.2 The 3D view of the placement result of the example 1 with the $9 \times 9 \times 100$ design specification

Table 93.1 Comparison Experimental result

Description	Design Spec.	PRSA		PHGA	
		Basal area (cm)	Complete time (s)	Basal area (cm)	Complete time (s)
Example 1: S_1, S_2, S_3 and S_4 are assayed with A_1, A_2, A_3 and A_4	$9 \times 9 \times 100$	9×9	98	9×8	74
	$8 \times 8 \times 120$	10×9	117	7×5	102
	$7 \times 7 \times 140$	9×9	126	4×5	106
Example 2: S_1, S_2 and S_3 are assayed with A_1, A_2, A_3 and A_4	$8 \times 8 \times 100$	8×8	98	7×5	71
	$7 \times 7 \times 120$	7×9	112	4×5	83
	$6 \times 6 \times 140$	7×8	150	4×5	77
Example 3: S_1, S_2 and S_3 are assayed with A_1, A_2 and A_3	$7 \times 7 \times 80$	7×7	79	6×6	48
	$6 \times 6 \times 100$	6×8	93	5×5	58
	$5 \times 5 \times 120$	5×8	120	4×5	54

by personification heuristic genetic algorithm (PHGA) show great advantage in completion time and the biochip area. Column 1 lists the type of samples and reagents used in each example: S_1: blood plasma, S_2: blood serum, S_3: emiction, S_4: saliva; A_1: glucose inspection, A_2: lactic acid salt inspection, A_3: pyruvic acid salt inspection, A_4: glutamine inspection. For each example, we applied three different design specifications, as listed in column 2. For instance, an experiment with the scale of $9 \times 9 \times 100$ means the maximum values of the bottom coordinate projection of x and y are 9, and the longest completion time of the experiment is 100 s. We report the resulting area (centimeter) and completion time (in seconds) used the algorithm PRSA and PHGA. As shown in this table, PHGA can meet all design specifications while PRSA cannot. More importantly, PRSA requires larger basal area and longer complete time than our algorithm.

Figure 93.2 shows the placement result of the example 1 shown in Table 93.1 with the 9 × 9 × 100 design specification.

93.5 Conclusion

The placement of digital microfluidics-based biochips is a three dimensional packing optimization problem for multiple objectives. In this paper, a personification heuristic genetic algorithm based on the idea of three dimensional packing problems is formulated, of which the designing procedure and the CAD simulation are also provided. From the results, it can be found that the optimization of the completion time and biochip area achieved by the algorithm make the foundation of the studies on placement of defect-tolerant digital microfluidic biochips established, and in the meantime, the algorithm can also be used in many other three dimensional packing problem.

Acknowledgments   This work was funded by Special Fund of Fundamental Scientific Research Business Expense for Higher School of Central Government (Projects for creation teams) Grant No. **ZY20110104**.

References

1. Hull H (2003) Smallpox and bioterrorism, Public-health responses. Lab Clin Med 142(4): 221–228
2. Zeng XF, Yue RF, Wu JG et al. (2006) Creating liquid droplets by electrowetting-based actuation for digital microfluidics-biochips. Sci China Tech Sci 36(1):105–112. (in Chinese)
3. Yang JS, Zuo CC, Lian J et al. (2007) Droplet scheduling algorithm for digital microfluidics-based biochips. Journal of Jilin University (Engineering and technology edition) 37(6): 1380–1385. (in Chinese)
4. Srinivasan V, Pamula VK, Fair RB (2004) An integrated digital microfluidic lab-on-a-chip for clinical diagnostics on human physiological fluids. Lab Chip 4(4):310–315
5. Su F, Chakrabarty K (2006) Module placement for fault-tolerant microfluidics-based biochips. ACM Trans Des Autom Electr Syst 11(3):682–710
6. Su F, Chakrabarty K (2005) Unified high-level synthesis and module placement for defect-tolerant microfluidic biochips. 42nd design automation conference
7. Yuh PH, Yang CL, Chang YW (2006) Placement of digital microfluidic biochips using the T-tree formulation. 43rd design automation conference, ACM, San Francisco, pp 24–28
8. Yuh PH, Yang CL, Chang YW. Placement of defect-tolerant digital microfluidic biochips using the T-tree formulation
9. Zhang DF, Wei LJ, Chen QS et al. (2007) A combinational heuristic algorithm for the three-dimensional packing problem. J Softw 18(9):2083–2089 (in Chinese)

Chapter 94
Incremental Update Algorithm of the Skyline Cube Over Label Security Database

Pengxin Ban

Abstract Skyline cube pre-computes and materializes all the skyline query results to improve the response speed of skyline queries. It contains a large amount of data that cause the update complicated. And it is especially costly when the entire cube needs to be recalculated just because a small amount of source data is changed. In order to improve the update efficiency of label skyline cube over label security database, two incremental update algorithms for insertion and deletion, which update the label skyline cube based on existing cube, are proposed. The algorithms traverse the affected labels in a bottom-up way and use containment relationship of point set derived from domination relationship of labels to share calculations between labels. The experimental results show that the algorithms significantly improve update efficiency.

Keywords Skyline · Security database · Label · Label skyline cube · Incremental update

94.1 Introduction

Skyline [1] query has significant value in the application of multi-objective decision-making. For example, when selecting online stores, online shoppers often concern about two aspects: low prices of commodity and less negative feedback from other net friends. If a store A is not worse than store B in all directions (both are better in these two aspects or one is better and the other is the same), then A is

P. Ban (✉)
School of Computer Science and Technology, Huazhong University of Science and Technology, 1037 Luoyu Road, Wuhan, China
e-mail: bpx@hust.edu.cn

W. Lu et al. (eds.), *Proceedings of the 2012 International Conference on Information Technology and Software Engineering*, Lecture Notes in Electrical Engineering 211, DOI: 10.1007/978-3-642-34522-7_94, © Springer-Verlag Berlin Heidelberg 2013

893

"better than" B. Obviously, only those online stores that no others are "better than" are worth online shoppers' consideration. How to find those worth considering stores belongs to skyline query problem.

With the popularity of skyline, different skyline query occurs frequently, and rapid response is required in higher real-time occasion. So skyline cube concept is proposed. A skyline cube is a collection of multiple skyline queries results. It precomputes and materializes all possible skyline query results, and then any skyline query can be answered immediately by getting the result from the cube directly without calculating, therefore the response speed of skyline queries is enhanced.

The cube contains a large amount of data. When a small amount of the source data changes, all or part of the query results containing in this cube would be invalid, so the cube needs to be updated accordingly. Recalculate the whole cube is too expensive undoubtedly. So how to reduce the cost of updating the cube is a task worth attention.

The existing research on skyline often assumes that different users face the same data set, and skyline query is on this basis. Actually in some instances, for the need of data security and privacy protection, the data set that different credibility users can access should be differentiated. Security database uses labels to distinguish data sensitivity and user credibility, and both users and tuples in the table are labelled. Only when the user's label dominates a tuple's label, can the tuple be read by the user. This feature makes that during the skyline query, users with different labels would access different data sets, which causes that the processing object of skyline query and the results different. Label skyline cube is a cube over security database, composed of skyline query results from all different labels of users. Current research on the skyline cube update is for non-secure database, and it cannot be directly applied to label skyline cube. Therefore the update of label skyline cube is a new topic.

Main contribution in this paper is: we put forward incremental update algorithms for label skyline cube which update the cube based on existing cube. The algorithms traverse the affected labels in a bottom-up way and use containment relationship of point set derived from label domination to share calculations between labels, therefore effectively reduces the cost of cube update. We also analyze the performance of the proposed algorithms through experiments.

94.2 Related Works

Skyline concept [1] has been focused by many of the researchers in the world today, since it was put forward. The classical algorithm contains BNL [1], D & C [1], SFS [2], NN [3], and BBS [4] and so on. Currently the scope of the study has been extended to unconventional database, such as [5] which studied the skyline for the multi-tenant database. Based on the single skyline study, [6] presented skyline cube concept composed of multiple skylines. Since then, some skyline cube variants have been proposed, such as k-dominant cube [7], grouping skyline cube [8, 9] studied the problems for skyline cube update under certain conditions.

However, none of these studies are oriented to security database. They can boil down to the problem of different dimensions of skyline or skyline cube for the same identity of user. Label skyline cube considers the case of many different status users, and has major differences with other skyline cubes, resulting in that the study results of existing cube update can not be directly used in this cube.

94.3 Preliminaries

The notations to be used in subsequent discussion are summarized in Table 94.1.

94.3.1 Mandatory Access Control via Label

A simplified label security control model used in this paper is described as follows.

Table 94.1 Notations

Notation	Definition
l, l_i, l'	A level
Ψ	A level series
m	$|\Psi|$
C_i	A category
Ω	A set of all categories
n	$|\Omega|$
S, S_1, S_2	A subset of Ω
L, L_1, L_2, L'	A label
Lp	The label of tuple p
$\Gamma, \Gamma', \Gamma''$	A set of labels
$L_1 \geq L_2$	L_1 dominates L_2
p, q, t	A point (namely a tuple)
$D, F, G, T, P, Q,$ R	A set of points (namely a set of tuples, or a table)
$p \prec q$	p dominates q
$\Delta(D)$	Skyline of D
$U(R, L)$	All tuples which can be read by user who labelled as L in table R
$L \propto P$	Add a new label column labeled L to P, and the original label column of P degenerated into a normal data column
$LS(R, L)$	Skyline of $U(R, L)$
$LSCUBE$ $(\Psi,$ $\Omega, R)$	Label skyline cube on Ψ, Ω, R

Definition 1 *Label.* We assume that $\Psi = \{l_i \mid 1 \le i \le m, \text{ if } i \le j, \text{ then } l_i \le l_j\}$ is a totally ordered set, and represents a level series. $\Omega = \{C_i \mid 1 \le i \le n\}$ is a set of elements (each of them is called a category for short as follows), which are independent of each other, unordered, and nonhierarchical. One label is a two-tuple group $L = (l, S)$, in which $l \in \Psi$ represents level, $S \in 2^{\Omega}$ (the power set of Ω which composed of all subsets in Ω) represents category set. The set of all possible labels is $\Gamma = \{(l, S) \mid l \in \Psi \wedge S \in 2^{\Omega}\}$.

Definition 2 *Dominate.* Given two labels $L_1 = (l, S_1)$, $L_2 = (l', S_2)$, it calls that L_1 dominates L_2 (or L_2 is dominated by L_1) and denotes as $L_1 \ge L_2$ (or $L_2 \le L_1$), only when $l \ge l'$ and $S_1 \supseteq S_2$.

Property 1 $l \ge l'$ and $|S_1| \ge |S_2|$ is necessary for label $L_1 = (l, S_1)$ to dominate label $L_2 = (l', S_2)$.

In security database, users and the tuples in table are labeled with labels, respectively called *user label* and *tuple label*. A label column is added in the table to store tuple labels. User reads the tuple of the table following the MAC (mandatory access control) rules: if and only if a user's user label dominates a tuple's tuple label, can the user read the tuple.

94.3.2 Skyline

Definition 3 *Point domination* [1]. Given two tuple of the labelled tuple set (or called point set) $D, p, q \in D$. We call p point dominating q, and record as $p \prec q$, if and only if the value of p is not greater than q in any non-labelled columns, and at least smaller than the value of q in someone non-labelled column. Point domination is also named as domination if it is not confused with definition 2.

Definition 4 *Skyline* [1]. The set of points that are not dominated by any other points in the points set of D is called the skyline of D, and denotes as $\Delta(D)$. The points in $\Delta(D)$ are called skyline points. Skyline query is to find the skyline of the table (or tuple set/point set).

Property 2 $\forall p \in F \subseteq G$, if $p \notin \Delta(F)$, then $p \notin \Delta(G)$.

Property 3 Assuming $T = \Delta(T)$, if it is existed that $q \in T$ making $p \prec q$ available, then $p \in \Delta(T \cup \{p\})$.

94.3.3 Label Skyline Cube

Definition 5 *L-dominated view.* All tuples which can be read by the user who labelled as $L \in \Gamma$ in table R makes up the L-domination view of R, denotes as $U(R, L)$.

Definition 6 *L-label skyline.* For any $L \in \Gamma$, we define L-label skyline of table R as $LS(R, L) = \Delta(U(R, L))$.

Definition 7 *Label skyline cube.* Given Ψ, Ω and R as described above, we assume that P is any subset of R, containing label columns. $L \propto P$ denotes adding a new label column labeled L to P, and the original label column degenerated into a normal data column. Label skyline cube is defined as

$$\text{LSCUBE}\,(\Psi, \Omega, R) = \bigcup\nolimits_{L \in \Gamma} (L \propto LS(R, L)).$$

94.4 Incremental Update of the Skyline Cube

94.4.1 Incremental Update Strategy

The idea of incremental update is to take full advantage of existing results for label skyline cube, and update the affected part on this basis, avoiding the enormous cost brought from global recalculation. Several strategies are described below.

1. Using containment relationship of point set derived from label dominance relationship.

   When label $L_1 \leq L_2$, according to MAC read access rules, we can get point set $U(R, L_1) \subseteq U(R, L_2)$. When the containment relationship exists between point sets, there is a certain relationship of the skyline in those sets. In fact, property 2 shows that non-skyline point of F as a subset of G is also the non-skyline point of G, so the non-skyline points in $U(R, L_1)$ is also the non-skyline points in $U(R, L_2)$. So, when one point is not in label skyline of L_1, we can omit the detection of whether the point is in label skyline of L_2.

2. Using features of skyline point set.

   Label skyline cube store multiple query results of skyline, namely the skyline point sets. This kind of point set is different from the general point set, as it has some features useful. For example with property 3, when a new point p is added to points set of T, if p could dominate one point of previous T, then we know that p can become the skyline point of the new points set $T \cup \{p\}$, without making domination detection with other points of T. It means that we can quickly judge that the point is a skyline point, saving a lot of time for detection.

3. Arrange the process order in a bottom-up turn, according to the domination relationship of label.

Label skyline cube contains skyline results of all labels, and when updating, in principle we need to process all labels. But actually, we just need to consider the labels which can dominate the label of insertion or deletion point (other label skyline is not affected by this insertion or deletion point). The processing order for those labels is worth consideration. According to property 1, it is more reasonable to handle, in a bottom-up turn that the label levels from low to high and the category set scale from small to large. This could guarantee those labels that have the ability to dominate other labels being handled after the dominated labels, thus we could get the opportunity to use the results of handled labels.

4. When dealing with a label, incidentally process the one that dominate the label.

When dealing with a label, if you encounter a test result which could be applied to other labels that dominate it, you can incidentally process the other labels together, and will no longer do the similar detection in the future.

94.4.2 Incremental Update Algorithm

According to the above incremental update strategies, we put forward the label skyline cube update algorithm for insertion named *BUI* (bottom-up insertion) in Table 94.2, and label skyline cube update algorithm for deletion named *BUD* (bottom-up deletion) in Table 94.3.

The 2nd row represents that only those labels dominating L_p need to be disposed. 3–5th rows deal with these labels in the bottom-up turn. 7th row lets Γ'' to be the set of labels which dominate the current label. When 12th row test that the insertion point p is not the label skyline point of current label, property 2 could conclude that it is not those label skyline points in labels of Γ'', so the labels in Γ'' shall not need to be processed in the future (their related skyline is not affected), and then 14th row would delete Γ'' from Γ'. After 18th row, following the property 3, simply detects the inserted point p is the label skyline point of current label, 21st row removes the original skyline point dominated by p. Not only in the current label skyline should it be removed, but also in other labels of Γ'' it is dealt in passing, in accordance with the strategy of Sect. 94.4.1. Finally, based on the previous judgment, 24th row determine whether to add p as the current skyline point. In the algorithm, the variable "flag" uses the value of 0, 1, 2 to respectively represent the three cases of q dominating p, p dominating q, no dominance relationship between p and q.

BUD algorithm has many similarities with BUI algorithm. 9th row judges that the deletion point is not in original skyline points of current label, and then those skylines related to labels in Γ'' would not be affected by whether the point is removed, so in the 11th line Γ'' would be removed from Γ'. During 14–21th rows,

Table 94.2 Bottom-up insertion algorithm

Algorithm 1: *BUI Algorithm.*

Input : Ψ, Ω, label skyline cube C, table R, the tuple to be inserted p (label is Lp).

Output: Updated label skyline cube C'.

Process:

1. $C' = C$;

2. $\Gamma' = \{(l, S) | l \in \Psi \wedge S \in 2^{\Omega} \wedge (l, S) \geq Lp\}$;

3. For $i=1$ to $|\Psi|$ Do

4.   For $k=0$ to $|\Omega|$ Do

5.   For each $L = (l_i, S) \in \Gamma' \wedge |S| = k$ Do

6.   {

7. $\Gamma'' = \{ L' | L' \in \Gamma' \wedge L' \geq L\}$;

8. $T = \{t | (L \propto \{t\}) \subseteq C' \}$;

9.   flag=0;

10.   For each $q \in T$ Do

11.   {

12.   IF (flag==0) IF $(q \prec p)$

13.   {

14. $\Gamma' = \Gamma' - \Gamma''$;

15.   flag=2;

16.   Break;

17.   }

18.   IF $(p \prec q)$

19.   {

20.   flag=1;

21.   For each $L' \in \Gamma''$ Do $C' = C' - (L' \propto \{q\})$;

22.   }

23.   }

24.   IF (flag<2) $C' = C' \cup (L \propto \{p\})$;

25.   }

---

it handles the deletion point which is in original skyline points of current label. 14th row deletes an original skyline point. 15th row would identify the points set Q, in which the points may become the new skyline point, after testing and filtration by the 16–20th rows, the points would be put into the result by the 21st row.

Table 94.3 Bottom-up deletion algorithm

Algorithm 2: *BUD Algorithm.*

Input: Ψ, Ω, label skyline cube C, table R, the tuple to be deleted p (label is Lp).

Output: Updated label Skyline cube C'.

Process:

1. $C'=C$;

2. $\Gamma'=\{(l,S)|l \in \Psi \wedge S \in 2^{\Omega} \wedge (l,S) \geq Lp\}$;

3.   For $i=1$ to $|\Psi|$ Do

4.   For $k=0$ to $|\Omega|$ Do

5.   For each $L=(l_i,S) \in \Gamma' \wedge |S|=k$ Do

6.   {

7. $\Gamma''=\{ L' \mid L' \in \Gamma' \wedge L' \geq L\}$;

8. $T=\{t|(L \propto \{t\}) \subseteq C'\}$;

9.   IF $(p \notin T)$

10.   {

11. $\Gamma'=\Gamma'-\Gamma''$;

12.   Continue; //goto line 5.

13.   }

14. $C'=C'-(L \propto \{p\})$;

15. $Q=\{q|q \in U(R,L)-T \wedge p \prec q\}$;

16.   For each $q \in Q$ Do

17.   {

18.   IF (exist $t \in T-\{p\}$ meet $t \prec q$) $Q=Q-\{q\}$;

19.   }

20. $Q=\Delta(Q)$;

21. $C'=C' \cup (L \propto Q)$;

22.   }

94.5 Experimental Evaluation

This section shows the experimental verification for the incremental update algorithm BUI and BUD. Experimental environment is that Intel 1.2 GHz CPU, 2 GB memory, 300 GB hard drive notebook. We realize the algorithms through VC++ programming on Windows XP. We apply random data set generator specifically for skyline query [1] to generate multidimensional point sets of anti-related distribution, and add a label column for each point set, containing information of levels and category set with random values. The dimension number of non-label column is set to 5 in this experimental. For the same point set, firstly we continuously delete 10 random points, and make the corresponding cube update time when delete a point on average as BUD spent time; then in turn insert that 10 deleted-points, make the

Fig. 94.1 Update time of different point set scale

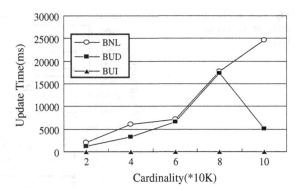

corresponding cube update time when insert a point on average as BUI spent time. Currently there is no other update algorithm of label skyline cube, we used BNL [1] algorithm to recalculate the corresponding label (namely, Lp in algorithm 1 and 2) skyline for inserted or deleted point, and take the average time spent by each point of these 10 point for comparison (marked BNL in latter figure). The following sets $|\Psi| = m$, $|\Omega| = n$, and sets the scale for point set to c.

1. Different point set scale comparison.

Figure 94.1 shows the experimental results when $m = 10$, $n = 3$ and $c = 20,000$–$100,000$. You can see in this experiment, BUI algorithm takes very little cost; BUD cost is greatly affected by the deletion point label (namely Lp). When its level is lower, the scale of category set is smaller, the number of the label which could dominate it is relevantly more, and the updated cost accordingly greater. We select delete points randomly, thus the update cost has some fluctuation.

Figure 94.1 shows that BUD algorithm is generally better than BNL, and indicates that incremental update algorithm could adapt to the size change of point set

2. Different label level and category number comparison.

All possible label number is $m \times 2^n$. We will separately examine the effect of different m, n in the following.

Figure 94.2 shows the experimental results of $c = 20,000$, $n = 3$ and $m = 2$–10. Figure 94.3 shows the experimental results for $c = 20,000$, $m = 10$ and $n = 1$–5.

Both Figs. 94.2 and 94.3 show that the update time of BUI expenses is very little. As the increase of label number, the update time of BUD algorithm takes increasing. This is because the number of label that could dominate the label of deleted point increases.

Note that, the BNL in each diagram updates only one label skyline, actually the label (algorithm 1, 2, in the 2nd row of all Γ' labels) of cube affected by the

Fig. 94.2 Update time of different number of label levels

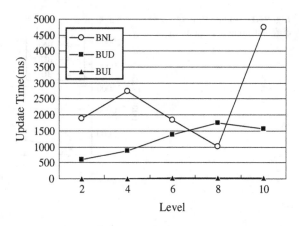

Fig. 94.3 Update time of different number of label categories

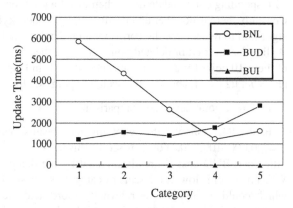

insertion, deletion algorithm are generally far more than one. If all labels are respectively processed by BNL algorithm, the cost would have orders of magnitude increase. Although the incremental update algorithms process multiple labels, the case that their cost is double that of BNL is not much in Figs. 94.1, 94.2, and 94.3.

The experimental results show that the incremental update algorithms BUI and BUD for label skyline cube is effective.

94.6 Conclusion

For the feature of label skyline cube, this paper puts forward incremental update algorithms which makes full use of existing cube to efficiently complete the update of label skyline cube in real time and avoid the enormous overhead of completely recalculate the skyline of affected labels. The experiments show that the proposed algorithm is effective. The update of label skyline cube remains to be researched further. For example, judged by results, compared to the insertion algorithm, the deletion algorithm still has room for optimization. In addition, we can consider to use the trigger mechanisms to achieve the automatically update of cube if the source table changes.

References

1. Borzsonyi S, Kossmann D, Stoeker K (2001) The skyline operator. In: Georgakopoulos D, Buchmann A (eds) Proceedings of the 17th international conference on data engineering, 2–6 April 2001, Heidelberg, Germany. IEEE Computer Society, Portland, pp 421–430
2. Chomicki J, Godfrey P, Gryz J et al (2003) Skyline with presorting. In: Proceedings of the 19th international conference on data engineering (ICDE), Los Alamitos, CA, USA. IEEE Computer Society, Washington, USA, pp 717–719
3. Kossmann D, Ramsak F, Rost S (2002) Shooting stars in the sky: an online algorithm for skyline queries. In: Proceedings of the 28th international conference on very large data bases (VLDB 2002), 20–23 Aug 2002, Hong Kong, China. Morgan Kaufmann, San Francisco, USA, pp 275–286
4. Papadias D, Tao Y, Fu G et al (2005) Progressive skyline computation in database systems. ACM Trans Database Syst 30(1):41–82
5. Sun S, Huang Z, Li P (2011) Skyline computation over multi-tenant database system. J Frontiers Comput Sci Technol 5(4):289–304 (in Chinese)
6. Yuan Y, Lin X, Liu Q et al (2005) Efficient computation of the skyline cube. In: Böhm K, Jensen CS, Haas LM, et al. (eds) Proceedings of the 31st international conference on very large data bases, Trondheim, Norway, 30 Aug–2 Sept 2005. New York ACM, pp 241–252
7. Dong L, Liu G, Cui X et al (2009) Sharing-based algorithm to find the k-dominant skyline cube. Mini-micro Syst 30(6):1072–1076 (in Chinese)
8. Yiu M, Lo E, Yung D (2012) Measuring the sky: on computing data cubes via skylining the measures. IEEE Trans Knowl Data Eng 24(3):492–505
9. Tang J, Liu G, Xi J et al (2010) Algorithms for finding multi-k-dominant skyline under renewed environment. J Yanshan Univ 34(1):61–66 (in Chinese)

Chapter 95
Improved MPPT Method Applied to PV System

Wenchao Li, Yuchao Sun, Xin Li, Xiaopeng Sha, Zhiquan Li
and Yiying Du

Abstract This paper considers the maximum power point tracking (MPPT) problem of the photovoltaic array, an improved method (the application of genetic algorithms to optimize the fuzzy controller) is presented based on fuzzy control. The simulation results are shown in different external environment conditions. It can be concluded that the proposed method can quickly track the maximum power point of photovoltaic arrays, and also reduce the maximum power point oscillation energy loss. Therefore, the energy conversion efficiency of photovoltaic power generation system is improved.

Keywords Maximum power point tracking (MPPT) · Photovoltaic · Fuzzy control · Genetic algorithm

95.1 Introduction

At present, as the growing energy crisis and environmental issues, it has become a global concern for effective and rational use of existing resources. The photovoltaic power generation is a broad prospect of green energy, and has become the

W. Li (✉)
School of Control and Engineering, Northeastern University at Qinhuangdao,
Qinhuangdao 066004, People's Republic of China

Y. Sun · X. Sha · Z. Li · Y. Du
Institute of Electrical Engineering, Yanshan University, Qinhuangdao 066004,
People's Republic of China

X. Li
Control and Simulating Center, School of Astronautics, Harbin Institute of Technology,
Harbin 150080, People's Republic of China

W. Lu et al. (eds.), *Proceedings of the 2012 International Conference on Information Technology and Software Engineering*, Lecture Notes in Electrical Engineering 211, DOI: 10.1007/978-3-642-34522-7_95, © Springer-Verlag Berlin Heidelberg 2013

hotspot of domestic and international academic and industrial research. The bottleneck problem of the photovoltaic cell research is the low efficiency of photoelectric conversion. In order to solve this problem, an effective measurement of maximum power point tracking Maximum Power Point Tracking (MPPT) is employed to improve the efficiency of the PV system [1–3]. This approach allows to maximize the power output of photovoltaic cells in load and environmental conditions.

Traditional MPPT control methods include the constant voltage method, perturbation and observation method and the incremental conductance method and so on [4]. But in practical application, there are various shortcomings for different methods. Recently, control based on smart technology becomes a common method [5]. In this paper, the fuzzy control technique is applied to the MPPT control, and genetic algorithms are used to optimize the fuzzy controller, which can further improve the performance of the MPPT controller. Simulation results show that this method can effectively improve the system's ability to respond with changes of the external environment and reduce the oscillations around the maximum power point.

95.2 Characteristics of Photovoltaic Cells

The relations between current and voltage of photovoltaic cell output is given by

$$I = I_S - I_0 \left\{ \exp\left[\frac{q}{AKT} V\right] - 1 \right\} \tag{95.1}$$

where, I is photovoltaic cell output current, I_s is short circuit current, I_0 is the reverse saturation current, q is charge constant, A is p-n junction coefficient of semiconductor devices in Photovoltaic cells, K is Boltzman constant, T is absolute temperature, and V is the output voltage of Photovoltaic cell.

Photovoltaic cell is neither a constant voltage source, nor the constant current source, but a non-linear DC power supply. Its output current is approximately constant in the most range of the work. However, when it's up to the open circuit voltage, the current sharply declines. From Fig. 95.1a and b, maximum output power of the PV array varies with the sunlight intensity and temperature. Therefore, it is necessary to control maximum power point tracking of photovoltaic arrays so that the array can obtain maximum power output under any conditions [6].

95.3 Fuzzy Controller Design

The Fuzzy inference system [7] is shown in Fig. 95.2. Mamdani fuzzy inference method is used and the defuzzification is utilized as the method in the area center of gravity.

Fig. 95.1 PV curves with the external environment variation. **a** Curve of solar radiation intensity. **b** Curve of the temperature changes

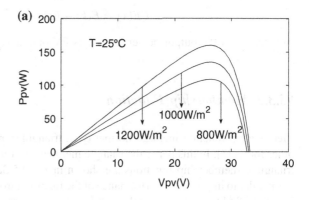

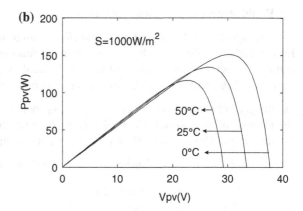

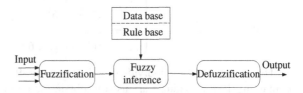

Fig. 95.2 Fuzzy inference system

95.3.1 Input and Output of Fuzzy Controller

The two inputs of the fuzzy controller are the error E and error change CE. The error E and error change CE have been defined in formula (95.2) and (95.3), and the output is duty cycle change of switching device in the MPPT circuit.

$$E(k) = \frac{P_{pv}(k) - P_{pv}(k-1)}{v_{pv}(k) - v_{pv}(k-1)} \tag{95.2}$$

$$CE(k) = E(k) - E(k-1) \qquad (95.3)$$

where, P_{pv} is PV output power and v_{pv} is PV output voltage.

95.3.2 Membership Function

Membership function includes normal type, triangular, rectangular, Gaussian and other forms [8]. In this paper the triangle membership function is used. Traditional triangular membership functions are shown in Fig. 95.3a.

In order to improve the performance of the fuzzy controller, the genetic algorithm is used to find the optimal membership function. Specific steps are as follows:

(1) Establishment of the initial population

Two inputs $E(k)$, $CE(k)$ and an output dD are used in fuzzy controller design. Each variable are described by five membership functions. The group includes a certain number of individuals, and each individual is composed of three chromosomes: $E(k)$, $CE(k)$ and dD, which is described as follows:

(a) the gene of chromosome $E(k)$: A_1, A_2, A_3, A_4 are changing in the interval $(0, 1)$.
(b) the gene of chromosome $CE(k)$: B_1, B_2, B_3, B_4 are changing in the interval $(0, 1)$.
(c) the gene of chromosome dD: C_1, C_2, C_3, C_4 are changing in the interval $(0, 1)$.

The respective relationships between each gene and x_i, y_i, z_i are denoted by

$$\begin{cases} x_1 = & (A_4 + A_3) \times (-20) \\ x_2 = & A_3 \times (-20) \\ x_3 = & A_1 \times 20 \\ x_4 = & (A_1 + A_2) \times 20 \end{cases} \qquad \begin{cases} y_1 = & (B_4 + B_3) \times (-20) \\ y_2 = & B_3 \times (-20) \\ y_3 = & B_1 \times 20 \\ y_4 = & (B_1 + B_2) \times 20 \end{cases}$$

$$\begin{cases} z_1 = & (C_4 + C_3) \times (-6) \\ z_2 = & C_3 \times (-6) \\ z_3 = & C_1 \times 6 \\ z_4 = & (C_1 + C_2) \times 6 \end{cases}$$

The schematic of the individual is shown in Fig. 95.4. In this paper, the groups containing 100 individuals are used to obtain the optimal solution.

(2) Applying the following fitness function to select:

$$J = \int_0^{t_f} (P_{max} - P)^2 dt$$

where, P is the ideal power and P_{max} is the maximum output power of the module under standard conditions. The ways to produce the next generations are as follows:

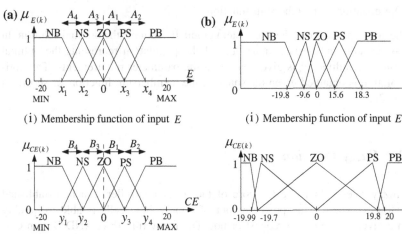

(i) Membership function of input E (i) Membership function of input E

(ii) Membership function of input CE (ii) Membership function of input CE

(iii) Membership function of input dD (iii) Membership function of input dD

Fig. 95.3 The membership functions of fuzzy input and output variables. **a** Traditional membership function. **b** Optimized membership function

Fig. 95.4 Description of an individual

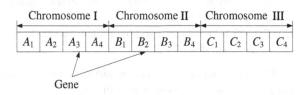

Gene

(1) The crossover operator: the continuous variables of a crossover probability are equal to 1 and the distribution of index n = 5.

(2) Variation: the use of continuous variables, the probability $P_m = 1/N_g = 1/12$, and distribution of index n = 5.

(3) Implementation of the restructuring: the optimal strategy. Parent population and offspring population are put together, selecting the best N individuals into new populations.

(4) Termination conditions: Computation is terminated when the largest genetic generation is up to 60, then the fitness function achieves the minimum.

(3) Optimization of membership function

The above process enables the system gradually achieve the optimal solution. In the last generation, the best individual of the population represents the optimal solution. The individual is given based on the parameter requirements. The optimal solution is obtained given the shape of the membership function, as shown in Fig. 95.3b.

95.3.3 Fuzzy Decision

The fuzzy rules, which are the core of the fuzzy controller, can be established according to whether the power output of photovoltaic cells is able to quickly reach a given scope of the request or not. The fuzzy rule IF A AND B then C is used [9], and the final fuzzy rules are shown in Table 95.1.

95.4 Simulation and Results Analysis

Figure 95.5 shows the simulation system block diagram. The system consists of photovoltaic modules, DC/DC converter, and the fuzzy logic controller. Simulations are employed by Matlab/Simulink [10], and under the standard state that the temperature $T = 25\ °C$, light intensity $R = 1000\ W/m^2$, the photovoltaic cell output power waveform is shown in Fig. 95.6.

Further test of the system performance are shown in the following steps

(1) $R = 1000\ W/m^2$ is constant and temperature slowly roses from 25 to 30 °C at the time of 0.05–0.15 s.
(2) $T = 25\ °C$ is constant and light intensity slowly rise from 1000 to 1200 W/m^2 at the time of 0.05–0.15 s.

With the external environment variation, the waveform of the output power of the photovoltaic cells is shown in Fig. 95.7.

The simulation results show that the optimized fuzzy MPPT controller possesses excellent performance. As can be seen in Fig. 95.6, the output power of photovoltaic cells can be stabilized at maximum power point in the 5 ms. Meanwhile, the steady-state tracking accuracy is up to 99.9 % and steady state accuracy is close to 100 % under standard conditions. It can be seen from Fig. 95.7 that the photovoltaic cells can quickly and accurately track the alternation as the external environment varies. The law is compliance with the output characteristics of photovoltaic cells and the new maximum power point can be obtained with very high tracking accuracy.

Table 95.1 Fuzzy control rule table

E	CE				
	NB	NS	ZO	PS	PB
NB	ZO	ZO	PB	PB	PB
NS	ZO	ZO	PS	PS	PS
ZO	PS	ZO	ZO	ZO	NS
PS	NS	NS	NS	ZO	ZO
PB	NB	NB	NB	ZO	ZO

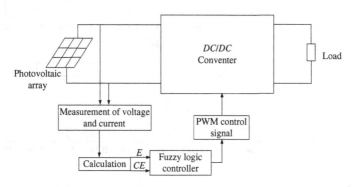

Fig. 95.5 Basic block diagram of the system

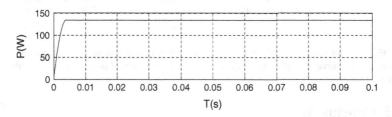

Fig. 95.6 Output power waveform in the standard state

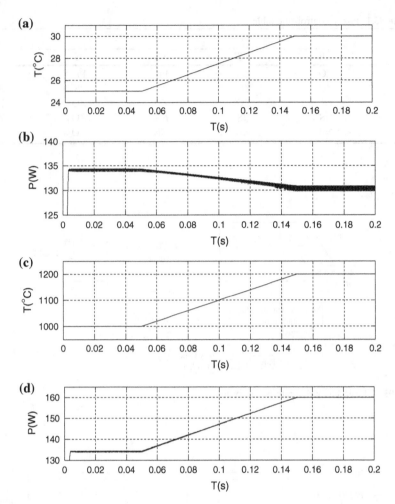

Fig. 95.7 Output power waveform with external environment change. **a** Temperature curve. **b** Temperature curve. **c** Light intensity curve. **d** The battery output power waveform with light intensity change

95.5 Conclusions

In order to improve the conversion efficiency of PV systems under different temperatures and light intensities, the fuzzy control is applied in the MPPT of photovoltaic cells. Firstly, the MPPT controller based on fuzzy logic control technology is designed. In order to improve the performance of the controller, the genetic algorithm is used to obtain the optimal membership function. Then, we test the optimized fuzzy MPPT controller under different conditions of temperatures and light intensities. Optimized controller shows the expected tracking performance, and has a high control accuracy and stability.

References

1. Salas V, Olias E, Barrado A, Lazaro A (2006) Review of the maximum power point tracking algorithms for stand-alone photovoltaic systems. Sol Energy Mater Sol Cells 90:1555–1578
2. Kim TY, Ahn HG, SK Park et al (2001) A novel maximum power point tracking control for photovoltaic power system under rapidly changing solar radiation. In: Proceedings of IEEE conference on international symposium on industrial electronics, Pusan, pp 1011–1014
3. Esram T, Chapman PL (2007) Comparison of photovoltaic array maximum power point tracking methods. IEEE Trans Energy Convers 22(2):439–449
4. Mutoh N, Ohno M, Inoue Takayoshi (2006) A method for MPPT control while searching for parameters corresponding to weather conditions for PV generation systems. IEEE Trans Industr Electron 4:1055–1056
5. Tariq A, Jamil Asghar MS (2005) Development of an analog maximum power point tracker for photovoltaic panel. IEEE Power Electron Drives Syst (1):251–255
6. Shmilovitz D (2005) Photovoltaic maximum power point tracking employing load parameters. In: IEEE international symposium on industrial electronics, Dubrovnik, Piscataway, IEEE, pp 1037–1039
7. Ben Salah C, Chaaben M, Ben Ammar M (2008) Multi-criteria fuzzy algorithm for energy management of a domestic photovoltaic panel. Renewable Energy 33:993–1001
8. Zhang C, He X (2005) Maximum power point tracking by using asymmetric fuzzy control combined with PID for photovoltaic energy generation system. Trans China Electrotech Soc 20(10):72–76
9. Hua C, Lin J (2004) A modified tracking algorithm for maximum power tracking of solar array. Energy Convers Manage 45:911–925
10. Mao M, Yu S, Su J (2005) Versatile matlab simulation model for photovoltaic array with MPPT function. Acta Simulata Systematica Sinica 17(5):1248–1251

Chapter 96
Character Recognition Based on Genetic Algorithm and Neural Network

Xin-Yan Cao, Hong-Li Yu and Ying-Yong Zou

Abstract Aiming at the complexity and limitations of traditional character recognition design method, an algorithm combined with genetic algorithms and neural network is proposed. Using this method, the advantages genetic algorithm which global optimal solution or a very good performance suboptimal solutions can easily be obtained is fully utilized. The shortcomings of neural network model such as slow convergence speed, entrapment in local optimum, unstable network structure etc. are solved. Combined neural network and genetic algorithm is to make full use of the advantages of both, so that the new algorithms both neural network learning capability and robustness, but also a strong genetic algorithms global random search capability, the neural network has self-evolutionary, adaptive capacity, so as to construct evolutionary neural network. The actual application in character recognition results show that, compared with the traditional method, this model has a strong feasibility and effectiveness.

Keywords Character recognition · Neural network · Genetic algorithm · Digital image processing

X.-Y. Cao (✉) · Y.-Y. Zou
College of Electronic Information Engineering, University of Changchun, Changchun, Jilin Province, China
e-mail: ccdxcaoxinyan@yahoo.com.cn

X.-Y. Cao · Y.-Y. Zou
School of Communication Engineering, Jilin University, Changchun, Jilin Province, China

H.-L. Yu · Y.-Y. Zou
Scientific Research Administrative Department, University of Changchun, Changchun, Jilin Province, China
e-mail: hongliyu@126.com

W. Lu et al. (eds.), *Proceedings of the 2012 International Conference on Information Technology and Software Engineering*, Lecture Notes in Electrical Engineering 211, DOI: 10.1007/978-3-642-34522-7_96, © Springer-Verlag Berlin Heidelberg 2013

96.1 Introduction

The neural network is a parallel distributed processor has a large number of connections. It has the ability to acquire knowledge and problem-solving through learning. The characteristics of the mode can be effectively extracted through trained network. The existing heuristic pattern recognition system can not be a good solution to the invariant detection, adaptive, abstract or summary can be solved [1]. But the BP neural network training is slow. It is easy to fall into the shortcomings of weak local minima and the global search ability. However, the genetic algorithm is easy to get the global optimal solution or the good performance of the suboptimal solutions. To combine neural networks and genetic algorithms, you can make full use of the advantages of both, so that the learning ability and robustness of the new algorithm is a neural network and genetic algorithm a strong global random search capabilities, making the neural network has self-evolutionary, adaptive capacity, to construct evolutionary neural network. Basic genetic algorithm to optimize the production of the initial population is random, often resulting in adaptation to spend large individual appears. With the selection, crossover and mutation operation, due to the presence of large individual, thereby increasing the probability that the individual is selected to copy, thus causing many of the offspring of the individual's ancestors are large individuals, this is the genetic algorithm, premature convergence phenomenon [2]. At this time, individuals tend to be concentrated in a region of the search space, so easily lead to convergence to a local extreme point, or if the problem exists more than one extreme point can only be searched part of the extreme points. In order to ensure the global convergence of the genetic algorithm to prevent the occurrence of premature convergence phenomenon, it must maintain individual diversity in the population, to avoid high-adapt to the degree of individual loss. Niche technology provides a new way to solve this problem. Niche genetic algorithm can guarantee to maintain a relatively stable population diversity in the evolutionary process, in large measure to improve the ability of global optimization of the basic genetic algorithm, to avoid falling into local optimal solutions.

In this paper, the combination of niche genetic optimization algorithm and neural network is applied to the identification of mathematical symbols, not only to overcome the genetic algorithm does not have the global convergence and artificial neural network is easily trapped into local minimum point defects, but also make full use of their respective advantages. This method to extract characters complementary characteristics of the coarse grid, the projection characteristics, cross-sectional characteristics and structural characteristics, and these four features constitute the feature vector input of BP neural network fusion classification. Using a genetic algorithm optimized artificial neural network weights and thresholds, and then use the trained NGA-BP network identification of

Fig. 96.1 Image
normalization

mathematical symbols. The experimental results show that: the method has higher recognition rate and reliability.

96.2 Handwritten Digit Symbol Image Preprocessing

Handwritten mathematical symbol recognition, the character will be written on paper, by photoelectric scanning analog signals, analog to digital conversion with a gray value digital signal input into the computer. The shaped distortion, smear, broken pens, cross-linked will be caused because paper thickness, whiteness, smoothness, ink shades, printing or writing quality and other factors [3]. In addition, due to the differential rate of input devices, linearity, quantization process will generate noise, so pretreatment prior to character recognition [4]. The pretreatment generally include normalization, binarization, denoising, and refinement.

Character normalization is to eliminate the character dot matrix on the size of the deviation, to identify the characters have the same size and shape, in order to facilitate the feature extraction and recognition. Image after size normalization and position normalization is illustrated in Fig. 96.1. Character binary is that digital gray scale image processing into a binary image to reduce the data storage capacity, reducing the complexity of subsequent processing. Image binarization before and after comparison is illustrated in Fig. 96.2. The purpose of the character of denoising is to remove isolated noise, interference, smooth stroke edge. Effect diagram of median filtering is illustrated in Fig. 96.3. Refinement in order to approximate the shape of the original region, consists of a simple curve graphics. Refine the text image not only retains the original text the vast majority of features, feature extraction, and storage than the original text value of the lattice is much less, reducing the processing workload. The character refinement image is illustrated in Fig. 96.4.

Fig. 96.2 Image binarization

Fig. 96.3 Effect diagram of
median filtering

Fig. 96.4 Character
refinement

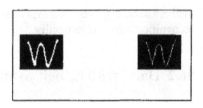

96.3 Character Feature Extraction

Character features are extracted using a combination of methods of statistical characteristics and structural features to obtain additional target identification information, and help to improve the positive recognition rate and reliability of the system.

96.3.1 Cross-Cut Features

Through the analysis of the characters, the main features of the character concentrated in the middle part of the picture, and the middle of the gesture changes most of the site, if you want to accurately identify the symbols, it is necessary to maximize the extraction of symbols can distinguish between the characteristics. In this paper a non-uniform cross-sectional feature extraction approach has been adopted, more to the picture the more dense central method to extract the cross-sectional characteristics. The specific method is refined image lattice horizontal divided into four parts: Images were taken, line 8, line 12, line 16, line 20, line 24 and 8, column 12, 16, 20, 24 as a characteristic extraction line, its the horizontal scan can be five transverse cross-sectional and five longitudinal cross-sectional, as the eigenvectors of the cross-sectional characteristics.

96.3.2 Projection Characteristics

The number of black pixels and the number of black pixels of each row, each column using image projection statistics in order to better reflect the pixel distribution. In this paper, a method of combining the vertical projection and horizontal projection, vertical projection and horizontal projection of the refined image, to form a feature vector based on the projection method.

96.3.3 Structural of Feature

The main extract some special points in the symbols skeleton graphics, such as endpoints, discount points, trigeminal point, quad point.

96.3.4 Coarse Grid Characteristics

First, the square lattice (32 × 32) divided into 16 small cell, each cell are (8 × 8) lattice. Each cell, from left to right, top to bottom, progressive scan, statistical points laterally within each cell is '1' appears.

96.4 Character Feature Extraction

96.4.1 Determine the Network Layers

Although in some cases, with two hidden layer neural network may bring additional benefits, but the increase in the number of hidden layer makes the network more complex, increase the computing workload and will require more samples number, so that the network's training cycle is longer [5]. Symbols identify the problem, with one hidden layer neural network has enough.

96.4.2 Input and Output Mode

The role of the buffer memory from the input layer, it receives the external input data, the number of nodes depends on the dimension of the input vector, after a symbolic feature extraction, with the feature vector as input of neural network. This article will include numbers and letters, including the commonly used 112 mathematical symbols for the study, each symbol corresponds to the feature vector length of 93, each type of symbol training for 20 groups, so the input feature matrix [2240 * 93].

The output layer nodes depends on two aspects of the output data type and indicates that the type size of the data required. Too much because the number of characters using 8 binary coding method to encode the symbol [00000000], for every increase of 1, corresponding to a mathematical symbol. When the input–output model to determine the input layer and output layer of BP network corresponding to the number of neurons along OK, the input layer neurons, 93 output layer neuron number is 8.

96.4.3 BP Network Learning Rates and Learning Algorithms

Large learning rate may lead to system instability and lead to longer training time is too small learning rate, learning rate selected is generally in the range of 0.01–0.8. In this paper Select the learning rate is 0.05 and BP neural network learning algorithm is the momentum BP algorithm.

96.4.4 Activation Function

In order to improve the range of the input vector, and make the range of the output vector within the desired (0, 1) range, select tansig function as the activation function of hidden layer neurons, select logsig function as the output layer neuron activation function.

$$\text{Tansig function:} f(x) = \frac{1 - \exp(-x)}{1 + \exp(-x)} \tag{96.1}$$

$$\text{Logsig function:} f(x) = \frac{1}{1 + \exp(-x)} \tag{96.2}$$

96.4.5 Hidden Layer Nodes

The number of hidden layer nodes affects the accuracy of the network's training model [6]. Number of hidden nodes depends on the complexity of the law contains a select number of samples the number and size of the sample noise and sample. Implied more layer nodes, the stronger the model approximation ability, but too much of hidden nodes increases the estimation error of the model, while in the case of a limited number of samples are also prone to over fitting phenomenon, reduce network generalization ability; of hidden nodes is too small, will lead to lack of network learning ability. Therefore, considering the number of iterations and the network generalization, select the hidden layer nodes. First, according to the empirical formula 96.3, calculate the implicit layer node number of rough estimates, the initial number of hidden nodes in the range of 10–20. Select the hidden layer nodes in order to better determine the network structure, between 10 and 20.

$$H = \sqrt{m + n} + a \tag{96.3}$$

where H is the hidden layer nodes, m is the input layer nodes, n is the output layer nodes, a is a constant between 1 and 10.

Feature extraction sample as the training set, 9–20 network training of the hidden layer nodes, and then another part of the sample as the test set, the trained

Table 96.1 The NGA-BP and BP model convergence comprehensive tables

Training methods	Average convergence steps	The number of non-convergence
NGA-BP model	27643.2	5
BP model	36472.6	14

Table 96.2 Recognition results statistical table

Test methods	Correctly recognition	Error recognition	Recognition rate (%)
NGA-BP model	906	94	90.6
BP model	784	216	78.4

network to test and found that when the hidden layer nodes between 16 and 20, the network convergence steps, considering the convergence speed and recognition rate, the hidden layer nodes is determined to be 20.

96.5 Training and Recognition of the Network Model

After the NGA-BP mathematical symbol recognition model is established, the network training starts and comparative analysis of training results with the original BP model (Table 96.1).

Statistics in the table show that for the same training methods, the convergence rate of the two network training have great differences. NGA-BP algorithm improves the convergence speed and convergence stability. The NGA-BP network model established in this paper the data samples for training and recognition, the recognition results are shown in Table 96.2.

Figure 96.5 is the convergence curve of the NGA-BP algorithm, Fig. 96.6 is the convergence curve of the BP algorithm.

Fig. 96.5 NGA-BP algorithm

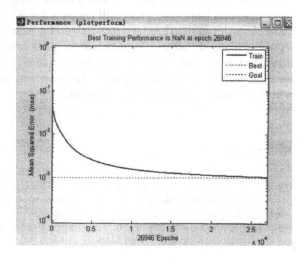

Fig. 96.6 BP algorithm

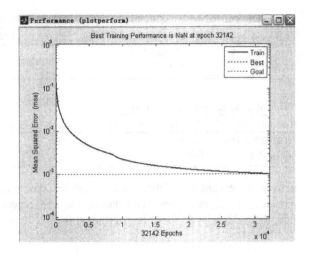

Experiments show that the convergence rate of the NGA-BP network model was 21.7 % higher than the original BP model. The NGA-BP network model of recognition rate is 12.2 % higher than the original BP model. Visible, the overall performance of the NGA-BP network model is superior to the BP neural network model to improve the recognition accuracy of the mathematical symbols.

96.6 Conclusion

The genetic algorithm is highly efficient, parallel, strong robustness and adaptive advantages, can solve complex optimization problems. The artificial neural network with adaptive self-organization, strong learning, association and fault tolerance, can be a good solution to uncertain and ambiguous, complex information processing problems. This paper will combine the advantages of both, and overcome through improved niche genetic algorithm neural network convergence is slow and likely to fall into local minimum point defects, and genetic algorithm may occur in the population is unevenly distributed premature convergence into local minima defects effectively solve the uncertain, ambiguous, complex handwritten mathematical character recognition.

References

1. Liu Z, Sugisaka M (1999) A genetic algorithm approach used to generate the network structures[C]. In: Proceedings of the 1999 IEEE/RSJ international conference on intelligent robots and system, Kyongju, SouthKorea, vol 1, pp 763–768
2. Li M, Li S, Kou J (1999) Effective method of preventing premature of genetic algorithm [J]. Trans Tianjin Univ 5(l):31–35 (in Chinese)

3. Yu T, Tang YY (1999) The feature extraction of Chinese character based on contour information [J]. ICDAR vol 99. pp 637-640, Sept 1999
4. Cao J Ahmadi M, Shridhar M (1995) Recongnition of handwritten numerals with multiple feature and multistage classifier [J]. Pattern Recognit 28(2):153–160 (in Chinese)
5. Fan JS, Tao Q, Fang TJ (2000) Genetic algorithm optimizes neural network based on structure risk minimization [C]. In: Proceedings of 3rd word congress on intelligent control and automation, pp 948–952, June 28–July 2
6. Srinvivas M, Patnail LM (1994) Adaptive probabilities of crossover and mutation in genetic algorithms [J]. IEEE Trans Syst Man Cybern 24(4):656–667

Chapter 97
Simulation of Sliding Mode Control for Artillery Velocity Servo System

Shu An, Zhengchun Liu and Fengbiao Yang

Abstract In order to enhance aiming and tracking accuracy of the artillery, a method of classical control with sliding mode control is proposed on the basis of dual closed loops velocity servo system in this paper. Conventional PI control is used in current loop and sliding mode control is designed in speed loop of artillery speed servo system. Because pure sliding mode control can result static error under load disturbance, load external disturbance current observer is put forward using feed-forward to compensate the static error from external disturbance. The matlab simulation demonstrates that in artillery velocity servo system the sliding mode control strategy based on current observer is superior to conventional PI control strategy and is able to meet the requirements of artillery equipment for overshoot depression and quick response.

Keywords Sliding mode control · Artillery velocity servo system · Current observer · Matlab simulation

97.1 Introduction

Currently, conventional dual closed loop PI controller is widely adopted in artillery velocity servo system. With the high performance of modernized equipment, the aiming and tracking accuracy of artillery are further improved, which are hardly satisfied by PI controller. Sliding mode control (SMC), as one strategy of

S. An (✉) · Z. Liu · F. Yang
Department of Vehicle and Electrical Engineering, Ordnance Engineering College,
Shijiazhuang 050003, People's Republic of China
e-mail: bluetree05@sohu.com

W. Lu et al. (eds.), *Proceedings of the 2012 International Conference on Information Technology and Software Engineering*, Lecture Notes in Electrical Engineering 211, DOI: 10.1007/978-3-642-34522-7_97, © Springer-Verlag Berlin Heidelberg 2013

variable structure control system, has complete robustness for variable parameter, uncertain models. Therefore, its application in velocity servo system is desirable.

This paper capitalizes on traditional current and speed dual closed loops of system by keeping its inter loop while applying SMC to its outer loop. The defect is that under certain external disturbance, especially loading, pure SMC system shows obvious steady state error, failing in reaching the inquired performance index [1]. The commonly-used solution to this problem is in series connection to a link of integral compensation after SMC [2–4]. Although this scheme has been successfully applied in many projects, its great limitation can not be neglected, in which the system model of the control object is required to be the controllable normalized form without any zero. Additionally, because of the link of integral compensation, the output change intensity of sliding mode controller is lowered, which to great extent weakens the strong robustness of SMC. Therefore load external disturbance current observer is put forward using feed-forward to compensate the static error from external disturbance in the paper. The sliding mode controller is further designed in velocity servo system, and the matlab simulation between this controller and PI controller proves that the former performs better than the latter. And the superiority is more conspicuous to meet the requirement of superpower artillery servo system for no overshoot.

97.2 Composition of Artillery Velocity Servo System

Artillery velocity servo system adopts speed and current dual closed loop system, in which the inter loop is for current to ensure the fastest dynamic response and also avoid overpower starting current; the outer loop is for speed loop to eliminate the influence of external disturbance on electric motor that belongs to brushless DC motor (BLDCM). The artillery velocity servo system is illustrated in Fig. 97.1.

In combination with Fig. 97.1 and the dynamic structure of BLDCM math model in [5], the dynamic structure of artillery speed servo system can be shown in Fig. 97.2.

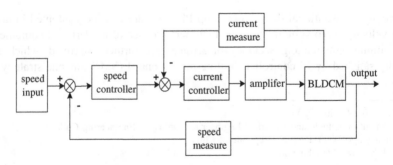

Fig. 97.1 Artillery velocity servo system

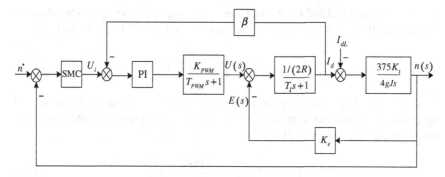

Fig. 97.2 Dynamic structure of BLDCM dual loop system

In Fig. 97.2 SMC is the speed controller, with sliding mode control; PI is the current controller, with PI control; $\frac{K_{PWM}}{T_{PWM}s+1}$ is transfer function of the pulse-width modulation (PWM) power amplifier, and combined with the closed feedback loop of $E(s)$ opposing electromotive force, it forms the BLDCM math model, in which β is the current feedback radio.

97.3 Design of Sliding Mode Controller

97.3.1 Design of Load Current Observer

In artillery velocity servo system, the load torque tends to change continuously in a slow and steady way. Therefore, this type of load is deemed as step type "constant" load, and $\dot{d} = 0$ is used for its math model.

Usually, the state equation with disturbance is shown as (97.1):

$$\begin{cases} \dot{x} = Ax + Bu + Dd \\ y = Cx \end{cases} \tag{97.1}$$

And the external disturbance equation is:

$$\dot{d} = 0 \tag{97.2}$$

In (97.1), $x \in R^{n \times 1}$ is state vector; $y \in R^{p \times 1}$ is output vector; $u \in R^{m \times 1}$ is control vector; $x \in R^{n \times 1}$, $A \in R^{n \times n}$, $B \in R^{n \times m}$, $D \in R^{n \times 1}$ and $C \in R^{p \times n}$ are constant external disturbance vectors. Further (97.1) and (97.2) can be integrated into an augmented system, shown in (97.3):

$$\begin{cases} \begin{bmatrix} \dot{x} \\ \dot{d} \end{bmatrix} = \begin{bmatrix} A & D \\ 0 & 0 \end{bmatrix} \begin{bmatrix} x \\ d \end{bmatrix} + \begin{bmatrix} B \\ 0 \end{bmatrix} u \\ y = \begin{bmatrix} C & 0 \end{bmatrix} \begin{bmatrix} x \\ d \end{bmatrix} \end{cases} \tag{97.3}$$

The necessary and sufficient condition of this augmented system to be observed is that Eq. (97.1) can be observed, and meanwhile Eq. (97.4) is satisfied.

$$rank \begin{bmatrix} A & D \\ C & 0 \end{bmatrix} = n + 1 \tag{97.4}$$

If PI-controlled inter loop is treated as typical I system with the use of approximate adjustment in projects [6], while the outer loop adopts SMC, the inter loop can be simplified as follows:

$$(I_d(s) - I_{dL}(s)) \times \frac{375K_t}{4gJs} = n(s) \tag{97.5}$$

$$I_d(s)(2T_i s + 1) = \frac{U_i(s)}{\beta} \tag{97.6}$$

From (97.5) and (97.6), it follows that

$$\begin{cases} \dot{n} = \frac{375K_t}{4gJ}(I_d - I_{dL}) \\ \dot{I}_d = -\frac{1}{2T_i}I_d + \frac{1}{2T_i\beta}U_i \end{cases} \tag{97.7}$$

In (97.7), n is speed; I_{dc} is armature current; I_{dL} is load current; U_i is current loop controlled input; K_t is torque constant; K_e is voltage constant and T_i is current loop equivalent inertia constant. When the system is set as: $x = \begin{bmatrix} n & I_d \end{bmatrix}^T$ and the load disturbance $d = I_{dL}$, in which n and I_d can be observed, if $C = I$, then $y = Cx = \begin{bmatrix} n & I_d \end{bmatrix}^T$. In this way (97.7) can be modified as follows:

$$\dot{x} = \begin{bmatrix} 0 & \frac{375K_t}{4gJ} \\ 0 & -\frac{1}{2T_i} \end{bmatrix} x + \begin{bmatrix} 0 \\ \frac{1}{2T_i\beta} \end{bmatrix} U_i + \begin{bmatrix} -\frac{375K_t}{4gJ} \\ 0 \end{bmatrix} d \tag{97.8}$$

$$y = \begin{bmatrix} 1 & 0 \\ 0 & 1 \end{bmatrix} x \tag{97.9}$$

Obviously, $rankC = 2$(full rank); Eqs. (97.8) and (97.9) can be fully observed, and the augment system is shown in (97.10):

$$\begin{bmatrix} A & D \\ C & 0 \end{bmatrix} = \begin{bmatrix} 0 & \frac{375K_t}{4gJ} & -\frac{375K_t}{4gJ} \\ 0 & -\frac{1}{2T_i} & 0 \\ 1 & 0 & 0 \\ 0 & 1 & 0 \end{bmatrix} \tag{97.10}$$

Fig. 97.3 Load current observer

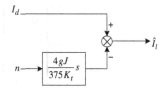

In (97.10), the 1st, 3rd and 4th row vectors are linear independence, so we get $rank\begin{bmatrix} A & D \\ C & 0 \end{bmatrix} = 3$ (full rank). Also the augment system can be observed and the load current observer is existent, as shown in Fig. 97.3.

97.3.2 Design of Sliding Mode Controller

If I_{dl} is replaced by the observed value $\hat{I}_l$, x_1 and x_2 are set as $x_1 = n^* - n$, $x_2 = I_d - \hat{I}_l$, while n^* is the given value of speed, with $\cdot\hat{I}_l = 0$ and $\dot{n}^* = 0$, then the state equation of the velocity system is:

$$\begin{cases} \dot{x}_1 = -\dot{n} = -\frac{375K_t}{4gJ}x_2 \\ \dot{x}_2 = \dot{I}_d = -\frac{x_2}{2T_i} + u^{\bullet} \end{cases} \tag{97.11}$$

In (97.11), $u^{\bullet} = \frac{1}{2T_i}\left(\frac{1}{\beta}U_i - \hat{I}_l\right)$. According to the variable structure control theory, when SMC uses proportion switching control, the logical equation and sliding mode switching equation are respectively (97.12) and (97.13):

$$u^{\bullet} = \varphi_1 x_1 + \varphi_2 x_2 \tag{97.12}$$

$$s(x) = cx_1 + x_2 \tag{97.13}$$

As deduced, the necessary and sufficient conditions of the system sliding mode movement to exist and converge in the original point are:

a. $s(x)\dot{s}(x) < 0$ (97.14)

b. The characteristic value of $cx_1 + x_2 = 0$ is under zero (97.15)

Proof:

$$s(x)\dot{s}(x) = s(x)(c\dot{x}_1 + \dot{x}_2)$$
$$= \varphi_1 x_1 s(x) + \left(\varphi_2 - \frac{375K_t c}{4gJ} - \frac{1}{2T_i}\right)x_2 s(x) < 0$$

$$\text{If}\begin{cases} \varphi_1 = \begin{cases} \alpha_1 < 0 & x_1 s(x) > 0 \\ \beta_1 > 0 & x_1 s(x) < 0 \end{cases} \\ \varphi_2 = \begin{cases} \alpha_2 < \left(\frac{375K_t c}{4gJ} + \frac{1}{2T_i} \right) & x_2 s(x) > 0 \\ \beta_2 > \left(\frac{375K_t c}{4gJ} + \frac{1}{2T_i} \right) & x_2 s(x) < 0 \end{cases} \end{cases} \tag{97.16}$$

Then condition (a) is satisfied. Substituting (97.11) into (97.15), it follows that $cx_1 - \frac{4gJ}{375K_t} \dot{x}_1 = 0$, with $\lambda = \frac{375K_t c}{4gJ}$ as its characteristic root. If $c < 0$, then $\lambda < 0$, with the sliding mode converging in the original point. And the lower the value of λ is, the faster the system is, but the precondition is that λ is above $-\frac{1}{2T_i}$, the characteristic value of current equivalent regular link.

What follows the above is $\lambda = \frac{375K_t c}{4gJ} = -\frac{1}{2T_i}$, then

$$c = -\frac{2gJ}{375K_t T_i} \tag{97.17}$$

Substituting $u^\bullet$ in Eq. (97.11) into (97.12), it follows that

$$u_i = \varphi_1' x_1 + \varphi_2' x_2 + \beta \hat{I}_l \tag{97.18}$$

Then Eq. (97.16) becomes :

$$\begin{cases} \varphi_1' = \begin{cases} \alpha_1 < 0 & x_1 s(x) > 0 \\ \beta_1 > 0 & x_1 s(x) < 0 \end{cases} \\ \varphi_2' = \begin{cases} \alpha_2 < 0 & x_2 s(x) > 0 \\ \beta_2 > 0 & x_2 s(x) < 0 \end{cases} \end{cases} \tag{97.19}$$

By combining equivalent control and switching control in sliding mode equation [7], we get $u = u_{eq} + u_i$, where u_{eq}, the equivalent control, keeps the system state in sliding mode while u_i, the switching control, compels the system state to slip on the sliding mode.

In this system, $A = \begin{bmatrix} 0 & -\frac{375K_t}{4gJ} \\ 0 & -\frac{1}{2T_i} \end{bmatrix}$, $b = \begin{bmatrix} 0 \\ 1 \end{bmatrix}$, $c = \begin{bmatrix} \frac{2gJ}{375K_t T_i} & 1 \end{bmatrix}$, if u_{eq} is set as

$u_{eq} = -[cb]^{-1} cAx$, then its u_{eq} can be calculated.

Ordinarily, as the starting and braking current of the electric motor can not surpass the rated value, the current-loop input u is limited, which is the reason why a clipper is added in the whole process to permit the maximum current u_{im}^*. To ensure the quick start and improve the dynamic response of the system, there is constraint condition on φ_1' and φ_2', that is when the movement trail of the system phase plane first arrives at the sliding mode switching line, φ_1' and φ_2' must maintain the maximum current, and the output of the sliding mode controller is u_{im}^*. Then, if the external disturbance is set as 0, $\varphi_1' x_1 + \varphi_2' x_2 \geq u_i^m$, and $cx_1 + x_2 = 0$, $x_2 = u_{im}^*$, it can be proved that:

$$\frac{-\beta_1}{c} + \beta_2 \geq 1 \tag{97.20}$$

$$\text{Accordingly,} \frac{-\alpha_1}{c} + \alpha_2 \geq 1 \qquad (97.21)$$

Based on the approximate treatment of the inter loop, the dynamic structure of system math model, with current observer, is shown in Fig. 97.4.

97.4 Simulation Analysis

In this part, the matlab simulation is conducted based on the system structure shown in Fig. 97.4. The relevant parameters of each component are listed as follows.

The brushless DC motor: $K_t = 0.11\,\text{N} \cdot \text{m/A}$, $K_e = 0.012\,\text{V/rpm}$,

$$R_a = 0.02\,\Omega, J = 7.3 \times 10^{-4}\,\text{kg} \cdot \text{m}^2, GD^2 = 4\,\text{gJ}$$

The drive amplification circuit of the dual closed loop system: $K_{\text{PWM}} = 9$, $T_{\text{PWM}} = 0.1 \times 10^{-3}$ s, $\alpha = 1$, $\beta = 0.05$.

The current loop PI controller: $K_p = 0.6$, $K_i = 20$.

The speed loop sliding mode controller: $c = 15$, $\alpha_1 = -22.5$, $\alpha_2 = -0.3$, $\beta_1 = 55$, $\beta_2 = 6.5$.

According to the simulation, Figs. 97.5 and 97.6 are respectively the current and speed when PI control and sliding mode control are started under no load; Figs. 97.7 and 97.8 are respectively the response curve when the system, disturbed by two times current at 0.6 s, works with rated load.

The following conclusion can be drawn from the simulation results: (1) A comparison between Figs. 97.5 and 97.6 shows that when the system is controlled by PI, there is relatively high starting current and overshoot in speed response; when the system is controlled by SMC, there is obvious decrease in starting current and the rev is in good line with the step input without overshoot. (2) A comparison between Figs. 97.7 and 97.8 shows that SMC system has small curve

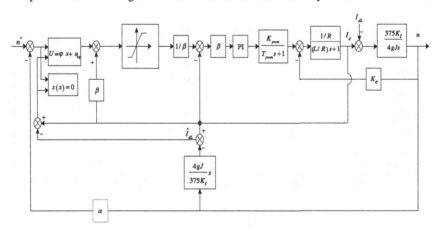

Fig. 97.4 Dynamic structure of BLDCM velocity servo system with SMC

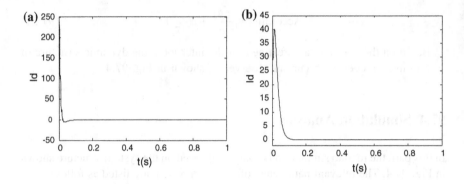

Fig. 97.5 No-load starting current. **a** PI control, **b** sliding mode control

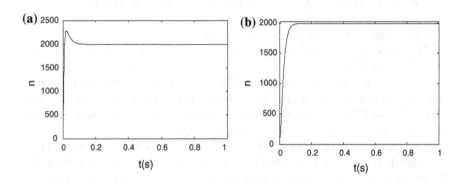

Fig. 97.6 No-load starting speed. **a** PI control, **b** sliding mode control

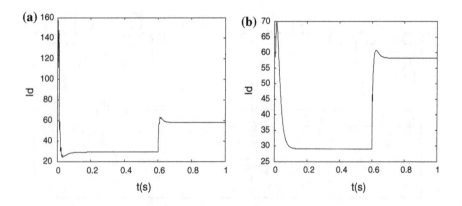

Fig. 97.7 Current added 1 time rated load at 0.6 s. **a** PI control, **b** sliding mode control

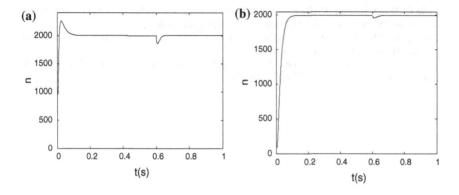

Fig. 97.8 Speed added 1 time rated load at 0.6 s after start. **a** PI control, **b** sliding mode control

wave and its speed can get back to the steady state quickly without static error when added one time disturbance.

Therefore, the controller designed in this paper has achieved comparatively desirable effect in terms at overshoot depression, response speed-up and fast start.

97.5 Conclusion

Aiming at the special requirement of artillery equipment for servo system, artillery velocity servo system with SMC is designed and load disturbance current observer, using feed-forward to compensate the static error generated by external disturbance is proposed in the paper. By establishing the sliding mode speed adjuster with load current observer, it further makes the matlab simulation of the designed system together with the comparison with PI speed adjuster. The simulation demonstrates that the sliding mode controller is superior to PI controller in dynamic response performance, with low starting current without overshoot, and has small speed rebound to recover stability in a short time under shock load, all of which are able to meet the requirements of artillery equipment for overshoot depression and quick response.

References

1. Liu J (2005) MATLAB simulation for sliding mode control. QingHua University Press, Beijing (in Chinese)
2. Seshagiri S, Khalil H (2002) On introducing integral action in sliding mode control. In: Proceedings of the 41st IEEE conference on decision and control, vol 2, pp 1473–1478
3. Zhang F, Tian K (2012) Sliding-mode variable structure control of the high precision antenna servo system. Manufact Autom 34(3):43–45 (in Chinese)
4. Fan L, Yang L (2010) Adaptive fuzzy integral sliding mode control for electrical servo system. Proc CSU-EPSA 22(2):27–31 (in Chinese)

5. Liu G, Wang Z, Fang JC (2008) The control technology and application of permanet magnet brushless DC motors. China Machine Press, Beijing (in Chinese)
6. Hong N (2010) Modeling and simulation of power electronics and machines control system. China Machine Press, Beijing (in Chinese)
7. An S, Yang X (2010) Research on fuzzy sliding changeable structure control of brushless DC motor. Comput Simul 27(4):172–175 (in Chinese)

Chapter 98
Attitude Control System Research of Unmanned Airship

Bo Tian, Song Wang, Wang Guo and Juan Li

Abstract This paper describes the attitude control technology for unmanned airships, and presents a structure of attitude control system including feedback of angular position and feedback of angular rate. Then, attitude estimation algorithm based on MIMU and Kalman filter is focused on. In order to improve attitude information performance, an adaptive Kalman filter is designed on the basis of Radial Basis Function Neural Networks (RBFNN), which adjusting filter gain matrix and observation noise matrix on-line. Thus, the accuracy of attitude control for unmanned airships is ensured. Finally, ground and flight test results verify the validity of the algorithm.

Keywords Unmanned airship · Attitude control · MIMU · Kalman filter · RBFNN

98.1 Introduction

Minitype unmanned airship has the advantages of excellent security, lower cost, big payload, little noise, light pollution, take-off and landing vertically and air hovering, no need of special landing site and runway, etc. Gradually, it has become

B. Tian · S. Wang (✉) · W. Guo
UAV Research Institute, Beihang University, Beijing, China
e-mail: wsongking@126.com

J. Li
Institute of Tracking and Telecommunication Technology, Beijing, China
e-mail: helj2000@sina.com

W. Lu et al. (eds.), *Proceedings of the 2012 International Conference on Information Technology and Software Engineering*, Lecture Notes in Electrical Engineering 211, DOI: 10.1007/978-3-642-34522-7_98, © Springer-Verlag Berlin Heidelberg 2013

the favor of many users of the industry, and been widely used in air remote sensing, security, news broadcast, communication relay, power lines, etc. [1].

To the minitype unmanned airship, the attitude control is the key to steady flight, and necessary measure to improve the antidisturbance. And the attitude control depends on real-time, accurate and reliable posture measurement, so the attitude control technology researched in this paper contains both the structure of the controller and the obtain of the attitude information.

Because of the excessive volume power consumption and the overtop cost, the traditional posture information source such as inertial navigation and vertical gyro can't be widely used in minitype unmanned airship. So suitable attitude measuring scheme becomes one of the focal and difficult points of minitype unmanned airship studies. Along with the development of microelectronic technology, micro inertial measurement unit (MIMU), combined by micro gyro and micro accelerometer, has been widely used in the minitype unmanned spacecraft because of its characteristics of low cost, small volume, low energy consumption, etc. [2–4]. Data fusion by MIMU can get the attitude information of the carrier, but there exist some limitations at present [4–6]. The gyroscope can provide instant dynamic angle change, but due to the influence of its inherent characteristics, the temperature and integral process, it will produce drift error with the extension of working time. Although the accelerometer can provide static angle accurately, it is vulnerable to the interference of carrier mobility and environmental noise, and the data is volatile [4, 7].

This paper puts forward a kind of attitude control technology applicable to minitype unmanned airship, to improve the accuracy of posture measurement information through adapting Kalman filter algorithm, and on this basis to realize the attitude control to minitype unmanned airship, finally the feasibility and effectiveness of this design can be verified through a series of ground and flight test.

98.2 Structure of Attitude Control for Small Unmanned Airship

Unmanned airship is a complex nonlinear system. Various factors in the process of flight cause its difficult solving of dynamics and kinematics model, and difficult to realize precise control. And the vertical-horizontal and horizontal-lateral coupling of the conventional airship is rather severe. If the controller design is unreasonable, the flight stability will be reduced greatly.

This article aims to build minitype unmanned airship attitude control system through the attitude control loop (angle position feedback) and stabilization loop (angular rate feed-back), and posture controller uses the classical PID controller [8]. Due to the character that airship dynamic always haves larger lag, stabilization loop plays an important role in the attitude control system. The experiments show that if stabilization loop is weakened or cancelled, the attitude control results will have obvious concussion phenomenon. The refresh cycles of attitude control loop and stabilization loop are all 30 ms, control structure diagram as shown in Fig. 98.1.

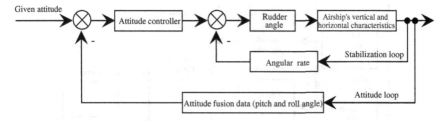

Fig. 98.1 Attitude control structure of unmanned airship

Figure 98.1 also shows that attitude fusion data plays an important role in the whole control system. If attitude fusion data is not accurate and even has measurement error, it will lead to control unstably or divergently, so later in this paper will focus on the method of accessing attitude information.

98.3 Posture Estimate Based on MIMU and Kalman Filter

MIMU includes a 3-axis MEMS gyroscope and a 3-axis MEMS accelerometer. The angular rate information output by gyro can get carrier attitude though integral (strap-down solution). This attitude information has excellent dynamic performance and short-term precision, and is not affected by carrier mobile acceleration. But due to the low precision of MEMS, posture error accumulates quickly over time. Accelerometer can determine the attitude angle through the size of perception gravity acceleration g in its measurement shaft. This attitude information has excellent and long term stability, but can be influenced seriously by the carrier mobile acceleration. In the basis of the angular rate gyro information setting up the state transition matrix, and in the basis of accelerometer information setting up the system observation matrix, constructing and extending Kalman filter to fuse the above data, can get a posture estimate that both static drift and dynamic characteristics are preferable. As shown in Fig. 98.2 [4, 9–11].

Kalman filter is a filter algorithm of the optimal estimate that is widely used in random signal state parameters, which takes the minimum mean square error as the optimum criterion of estimate, uses continuous observations to modify the parameter matrix, and expects to get the system state estimation.

Kalman state equation and observation equation are as follows:

$$X(k + 1) = \phi(k)X(k) + G(k)W(k) \tag{98.1}$$

$$Y(k) = H(k)X(k) + V(k) \tag{98.2}$$

Among them, $X(k) \in R^{n \times 1}$ is target state vector, $Y(k) \in R^{m \times 1}$ is quantity sequencing list, $W(k) \in R^{p \times 1}$ is state noise, $V(k) \in R^{m \times 1}$ is measurement noise; state noise and measurement noise are the irrelevant gaussian white noise

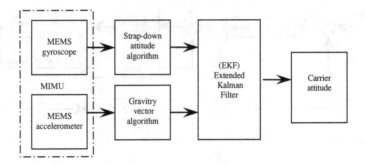

Fig. 98.2 Posture estimate based on MIMU and Kalman filter

sequence, and their respective covariance matrix are $Q(k)$ and $R(k)$; $\varphi(k) \in R^{n \times n}$, $G(k) \in R^{n \times p}$ and $H(k) \in R^{m \times n}$ are the state transition matrix, noise input matrix and observation matrix.

In the design of this paper, System state variable $X(k) = (q_0 \ q_1 \ q_2 \ q_3 \ b_0 \ b_1 \ b_2)^T$, among them q_0, q_1, q_2, q_3 are the quaternion of system state variable in the process of posture computation; b_0, b_1, b_2 are drifts of roll rate gyro, elevation angle rate gyro, and yaw angular rate gyro; system observed quantity is $Y(k) = [\theta_a(k) \ \phi_a(k)\varphi_a(k)]^T$. Among them, $\theta_a(k)$, $\phi_a(k)$ are the pitching angle and revolving angle calculating through the accelerometer to gravitational field through for the measurement of the gravitational field; $\varphi_a(k)$ is the yaw angle based on geomagnetic information, provided by magnetic compass.

Hypothesis the statistic characteristics of measurement noise and state noise are:

$$E[W(k)] = 0 \quad E[W(k)W^T(j)] = Q(k)$$
$$E[V(k)] = 0 \quad E[V(k)V^T(j)] = R(k)$$

And the original state X_0 is independent of $W(k)$ and $V(k)$, namely

$$E[X_0 W^T(k)] = 0 \quad E[X_0 V^T(k)] = 0$$

Thus can get the state estimation:

$$\hat{X}(k) = \hat{X}(k/k-1) + K(k)\lfloor Y(k) - H(k)\hat{X}(k/k-1)\rfloor \tag{98.3}$$

Here, one-step predictive state:

$$\hat{X}(k/k-1) = \phi(k, k-1)\hat{X}(k-1)$$

Filter gain matrix:

$$K(k) = P(k/k-1)H^T(k)[H(k)P(k/k-1)H^T(k) + R(k)]^{-1}$$

Prediction error variance array:

$$P(k/k - 1) = \phi(k, k - 1)P(k - 1)\phi^T(k, k - 1)$$
$$+ G(k, k - 1)Q(k - 1)G^T(k, k - 1)$$

Estimate error variance array:

$$P(k) = P(k/k - 1) - K(k)H(k)P(k/k - 1)$$

In the process of attitude estimation, there are two calculation loops: gain (K) calculation loop and filter (X) calculation loop. Among them, the gain calculation loop is independent, and the filter calculation loop depends on the gain calculation loop. The results of gain calculation loop directly influence the effect of attitude estimation. This paper later will construct adaptive Kalman filter, adjust gain calculation loop online according to the mobile condition of carrier, and thus estimate the optimal angle value.

98.4 The Adaptive Kalman Filter Algorithm

The traditional posture estimation algorithm based on the low cost MIMU and Kalman filter is seriously disturbed by external things (carrier mobility, engine vibration, etc.), and it is difficult to provide exact solutions [4, 9]. Therefore, based on the current state of the carrier movement and the neural net-work, this paper adjusts the Kalman filter parameters online, and improves the information fusion accuracy.

Conventional Kalman filter algorithm highly dependents on the systematic and accurate mathematical model, supposes that the system noise and measurement noise are zero mean white gaussian noise of known statistical characteristic, but when the priori noise statistical characteristic is not estimated accurately, the performance of Kalman filter will be degraded, and even diffused. Therefore, we, through a large number of actual flight data, train RBFNN neural network to adjust the Kalman filter gain matrix and measure matrix noise online, making the filter, based on the error information between the attitude measured value and estimated value, adjusts the filter parameters at real-time to abate the influence that measurement noise which is led by the environment changes brings to the overall attitude fusion accuracy, and improve the environment adaptability of unmanned airship attitude control system. At the same time, it also can effectively eliminate the existing outliers in the sensor data, making filtering results more stable. The input of RBFNN is the sum of squares of the current new rate $Z(k/k - 1)$, GPS location second difference decomposition value, and carrier triaxial accelerometer measurement value, while the output is the adjustment factor of gain matrix and measure noise matrix. In order to get a better training result, we use the minimum square difference method to train the center value and weight of neural network.

Improved adaptive Kalman filter algorithm is as follows:

$$\hat{X}(k) = \hat{X}(k/k - 1) + \overset{\bullet}{K}(k)\, Z(k/k - 1) \qquad (98.4)$$

Here,

$$\hat{X}(k/k - 1) = \phi(k - 1)\hat{X}(k - 1)$$

$$Z(k/k - 1) = Y(k) - H(k)\hat{X}(k/k - 1)$$

$$\overset{\bullet}{K}(k) = w_1 P(k/k - 1)H^T(k)\left[H(k)P(k/k - 1)H^T(k) + R(k)\right]^{-1}$$

Among them,

$$P(k/k - 1) = \phi(k - 1)P(k - 1)\phi^T(k - 1) + G(k - 1)Q(k - 1)G^T(k - 1)$$

$$R(k) = w_2 R(k - 1) + (1 - w_2)[(I - H(k)\,K(k\overset{\bullet}{-}1))\,Z(k/k - 1)Z(k/k - 1)^T$$

$$\bullet\,(I - H(k)\,K(k\overset{\bullet}{-}1)) + H(k)P(k)H(k)^T]$$

$$P(k) = P(k/k - 1) - K(k)H(k)P(k/k - 1)$$

w_1, w_2 are the outputs of three layer RBFNN neural network, and are used to adjust the K value and measurement noise. Through the adjustment of K value, the influence that outliers bring to the attitude filter can be reduced. Through the adjustment to measured noise, the adaptability of the system to the environment can be improved.

98.5 Validation Test

Figure 98.3 shows the ground dynamic test data of un-manned airship attitude measuring algorithm. To reflect the necessity and advantage of this design-adaptive Kalman filter, four comparing data curves have been made, sampling frequency for 100 Hz.

Curve A is a attitude angle getting through the measurements made by the accelerometer to gravity field. In order to simulate the carrier mobile, in the first half of the sampling data, seven group outliers were joined artificially. Among them, the first six groups are isolated-type outliers, and the last group is spot type outliers, last time around 1 s.

Curve B is the attitude angle getting through the strap-down solution by angular rate gyro.

Curve C is the attitude angle getting by the angular rate gyro and accelerometer through the conventional Kalman filter.

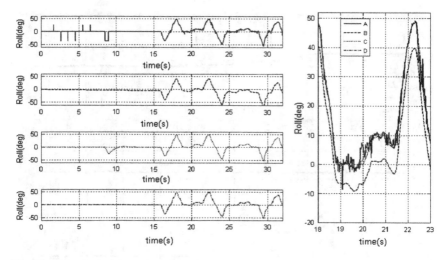

Fig. 98.3 The ground dynamic test curve

Curve D is the attitude angle getting by the angular rate gyro and accelerometer through the adaptive Kalman filter.

Curve A shows that when the accelerometer is in statistic situation, it can get more precise attitude of the carrier, while volatile seriously in dynamic circumstances. It is easy to appear outliers under the influence of carrier mobile. Curve B shows that the angular rate gyro strap-down attitude can response the dynamic changes of carrier excellently, and the data is level and smooth, but it has a long term drift due to their own limitation on accuracy. Curve C shows that conventional Kalman filter can fuse the static stability and angular rate gyro excellently, and get an attitude with better stability and dynamic. What's more, the ability of isolated outliers is also relatively strong, but to spot type outliers, the handles effect is not good, and the attitude appears quite large fluctuations. Curve D shows that in this paper the design, based on the adaptive Kalman filter attitude estimates, does not only have the stability, dynamic, and the anti-isolated type outliers of ability of conventional Kalman filter posture attitude, but also have a very good effect on spot type outliers.

Figure 98.4 shows the attitude control rendering in the real flight process of a minitype unmanned airship. The airship only has the elevator and rudder, and the roll is not controlled. In the attitude remote control mode, the given target pitch angle changes from 10 to 0°, and the target heading maintains at 120°. By the Fig. 98.4 we can see that the unmanned airship attitude control is stable, and the attitude control precision is about 1°, heading control precision about 3°.

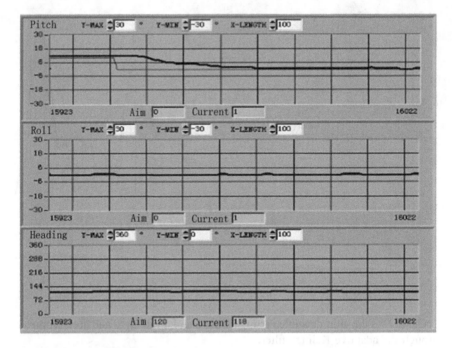

Fig. 98.4 The attitude control results

98.6 The Conclusion

This paper introduces the design of the attitude control system solutions of minitype unmanned airship, including the attitude control structure and posture measurement method which is based on adaptive Kalman filter. Tests and simulations show that the attitude control precision of attitude control system scheme is about 1°, and this can meet the use needs of conventional minitype airship, besides the cost is lower.

Assuredly, the attitude control system is just an important base of minitype unmanned autonomous airship flights; we also design the control algorithm of independent flights based on the attitude control system. The airline flight test shows that the effect of independent airline flight with attitude control is obviously superior to the independent airline flight without attitude control.

Acknowledgments The correlational studies of this paper were completed with the help of national high technology research and development program (Program 863), the subject number is 2008AA121802.

References

1. Rao J, Gong Z, Luo J, Xie S (2005) Unmanned airships for emergency management. In: Proceeding of the 2005 IEEE international workshop on safety, security and rescue robotics, Kobe, pp 125–130
2. Metni N, Pflimlin J-M, Hamel T, Souères P (2006) Attitude and gyro bias estimation for a VTOL UAV. Control Eng Pract 14(12):1511–1520
3. Wendel J, Meister O, Schlaile C et al (2006) An integrated GPS/MEMS-IMU navigation system for an autonomous helicopter. Aerosp Sci Technol 10(6):527–533
4. Wang S, Tian B, Zhan Y, Li Z (2011) Based on the modified EKF attitude estimate of minitype airship. High Technol Commun 21(6):612–618 (in Chinese)
5. Hong SK (2003) Fuzzy logic based closed-loop strap-down attitude system for unmanned aerial vehicle (UAV). Sens Actuators A Phys 107(2):109–118
6. Rodrigo MV, Carlos H (1999) Preliminary design of a low speed, long endurance remote piloted vehicles for civil applications. Aircr Des (2):167–182
7. De La Parra S, Angel J (2005) Low cost navigation system for UAV. Aerosp Sci Technol 9:504–516
8. Zhang M (1994) The flight control system. Aviation Industry Press, Beijing, pp 12–92 (in Chinese)
9. Li P, Wang TM, Liang JH et al (2007) An attitude estimate approach using MEMS sensors for small UAVs. In: 2006 IEEE international conference on industrial informatics, INDIN'06, Singapore, pp 1113–1117
10. Xiao Y (2001) The modeling of aviation spacecraft movement—the theory basis of flight dynamics. The Press of Beijing University of Aeronautics and Astronautics, Beijing, 2003.6-138, vol 29(4), pp 42–45 (in Chinese)
11. Chai W, Hou Y (2001) The attitude algorithm of strap-down inertial navigation system. Mod Def Technol 29(4):42–45 (in Chinese)

Chapter 99
The Identification of Main Contradictory Information

Rui Zhao, Yongquan Yu and Tao Zeng

Abstract After characteristics of contradictory information and its presentation have been studied, another important thing must be considered that how to find the main contradictory information to enhance the efficiency of solving a contradictory problem. The present article therefore defined a contradictory degree to express the incompatible level of a pair of contradictory information and constructed a new coordinates system called average angle plane coordinates to describe it. In the coordinates system, all contradictory degrees can be marked and connected forming a contradictory information field, which provides a good tool for differentiating primary and secondary contradictory information. These basic studies are the foundation of intelligent processing of contradictory problems.

Keywords Identification · Contradictory information · Average angle plane coordinates

99.1 Introduction

Contradictory problem is conflicting or incompatible [1]. Its solution is the concentrated expression of human intelligence and is one of the core problems of artificial intelligence. The key to solve a contradictory problem using computers is to define or formulate the problem correctly. So constructing an appropriate model is necessary. Extenics is therefore established. Formalizing research on contradictory

R. Zhao (✉) · Y. Yu · T. Zeng
College of Computer Science, Guangdong University of Technology,
510006 Guangzhou, China
e-mail: zhaorui118204@163.com

W. Lu et al. (eds.), *Proceedings of the 2012 International Conference on Information Technology and Software Engineering*, Lecture Notes in Electrical Engineering 211, DOI: 10.1007/978-3-642-34522-7_99, © Springer-Verlag Berlin Heidelberg 2013

problem has been completed by now. But many problems are still stopping on the stage of depending on human intelligence. In this age of the information, intelligent processing about contradictory problem has been an urging subject. So there is a need for further research on contradictory problem using information processing technology.

By far, lots of mature theories and methods have been established to solve accurate and fuzzy information [2], while the study of contradictory information is just beginning. In the article [3], characteristics of contradictory information and its presentation have been researched. But related researches about measuring of contradictory information status and the identification of main contradictory information are always lacking. This paper will research these problems.

99.2 Extension Theory

Extension theory [4] is mainly used to solve contradictory problem. The kernel of extenics is basic-element theory and extension set theory.

Basic-element is the logic cell of the extension including the matter-element, affair-element, and relation-element. An ordering triple can be used to describe it [5].

$$B = (O, C, V) = \begin{bmatrix} O, & c_1, & v_1 \\ & c_2, & v_2 \\ & \dots & \dots \\ & c_n & v_n \end{bmatrix} \tag{99.1}$$

where, o denotes an object (matter, affair or relation). $c_i(i = 1.2, \ldots, n)$ denote the characteristics of the object, and $v_i(i = 1.2, \ldots, n)$ are the values of these characteristics.

Extension set is the most important concept in the theory of extenics. Extension set provides a new mathematical tool of recognition and classification.

Definition 1 Let U be the universe of discourse, K be a mapping from U to a real number field I, then $\tilde{A} = \{(u, y) | u \in U, y = K(u)\}$ is called an extension set of U, $y = K(u)$ is the dependent function of $\tilde{A}$, and $K(u)$ is the dependent degree of u about $\tilde{A}$ [6].

$$A = \{u | u \in U, K(u) \geq 0\} \tag{99.2}$$

$$\tilde{A} = \{u | u \in U, K(u) \leq 0\} \tag{99.3}$$

$$J_0 = \{u | u \in U, K(u) = 0\} \tag{99.4}$$

These are called respectively the positive fields, negative field and zero boundary. Positive number expresses the degree that a given object u possesses the property. Negative number expresses the degree that u doesn't possess the property. Zero boundary implies $u \in A$ and $u \notin A$. There are three kinds of transformation of $\tilde{A}$ on U, namely, the transformation Tu of elements, the transformation TK of dependent function and the transformation TU of the universe of discourse.

99.3 Contradictory Problems and Contradictory Information

A problem consists of goals and conditions, and can be described as $P = G * C$. If the goal can not be achieved under the condition, the problem is a contradictory problem. In the contradictory problem, conditions and goals form a contradictory body. The contradictory body can be described as a matter-element M.

$$M = \begin{bmatrix} B & c & v_c \\ & g & v_g \end{bmatrix}$$ (99.5)

where, B denotes the contradictory body. c and g denote the characteristic of conditions and goals respectively, and v_c and v_g are the values of these characteristics.

Definition 2 The difference between v_c and v_g can said to be contradictory degree, and denoted by N.

$$N = \left| \frac{v_g - v_c}{\max(v_g, v_c)} \right|$$ (99.6)

In the contradictory problem, as we know $0 < N < 1$, the value of N shows the incompatible degree of the contradictory body about the pair contradictory characteristics.

Definition 3 If use a basic-element to describe contradictory body and its characteristics corresponding contradictory degree, then the basic-element can said to be contradictory information basic-element model of contradictory problems, or contradictory information for short.

The contradictory information can be described as follows.

$$CI = \begin{bmatrix} B & c & v_c \\ & g & v_g \\ & N & v_N \end{bmatrix}$$ (99.7)

Contradictory information is the crux of the problem, which represents the characteristics and essence of contradictory problems. In general contradictory problems, a contradictory body can have multiple pairs of contradictory characteristics. Each pair of contradictory characteristics forms a contradiction. Therefore in a contradictory body containing many contradictions, many pairs of contradictory information exist.

Definition 4 In a contradictory body, all contradiction pairs constitute a group contradictory information basic-element, which can be called the contradictory information set.

Definition 5 In a contradictory information set, some contradictory information plays a dominant and decisive role on processing of the contradictory problem. They can said to be the main contradictory information.

Looking for the main contradictory information is the key to solve contradictory problems quickly.

99.4 Main Contradictory Information

99.4.1 Average Angle Plane Coordinates

Definition 6 A contradictory information set contains n contradictions and every contradiction has a contradictory degree, there are n contradictory degrees in all. Given an origin o in a plane and using n axes to average the plane, the angle between any two axes is 360°/n. We call the coordinates system average angle plane coordinates.

When a contradictory information set contains three contradictions, average angle plane coordinates show as in the Fig. 99.1a, in which $N_i(i = 1, 2, 3)$ are contradictory degrees. Suppose a contradictory information set contains 6 contradictions, then average angle plane coordinates have 6 coordinate axes, and the angle between any two axes is 60°. Each axis is arranged in the plane according to the contradiction order number by clockwise from 0, as shown as in Fig. 99.1b.

Some main functions of average angle plane coordinates are described as follows.

1. Use a coordinate graph to describe the contradictory information set.

There are many traditional methods to describe a set, such as the formula method, enumeration method, symbolic method or graphic method. This is a novel representation.

2. Can show current contradictory state of any contradictory information.

In the average angle plane coordinates system, contradictory degree of any contradictory information is marked on the corresponding coordinate axes, which makes current contradictory state about all contradictory information is known easily.

3. Can show dynamic changes of contradictory state about the contradictory information set.

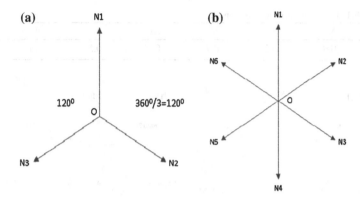

Fig. 99.1 **a** Contain three contradictions, **b** contain six contradictions

If record down the new state in the average angle plane coordinates system with change of contradictory degree. We can observe the whole change process of the contradictory state while dealing with the contradictory problems.

4. Can show the elimination process of a contradiction.

In the process of contradictory problems, the removing of a contradiction means coordinate axes layout renews. Coordinate axes decreasing ceaselessly reflects continuously removing process and result of contradictions.

99.4.2 Contradictory Information Field

Definition 7 In the angle plane coordinates system, marks every contradictory degree of the contradictory information set on the corresponding coordinate axes, and connects all the contradictory degree by a straight line forming a reflecting contradictory degrees situation vector map. This map shows static distribution about all contradictory degrees in the angular plane, and can be called the static contradictory information field, contradictory information field for short, denoted as F_N.

Contradictory information field is constructed on the angle plane coordinates, while contradictory information field is not the simple mark-up about contradictory degrees, but a vector field effectively reflecting the overall contradictory information "tension" of the contradictory problem. Contradictory information field can show the dispersion of a contradictory information set, and can display dynamic changes about elimination of contradiction. Contradictory information field not only provides a kind of effective tool for differentiating primary and secondary contradictory information, but also enhances the visibility about contradictory problem process.

Table 99.1 Contradictory information sct

N_1	N_2	N_3	N_4	N_5	N_6	N_7	N_8
0.5	0.9	0.3	0.7	0.2	0.5	0.6	0.7

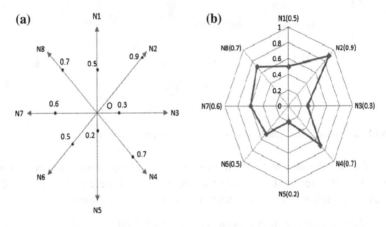

Fig. 99.2 **a** Contradictory degree mark-up, **b** contradictory information field F_N

For example, suppose there is a contradictory information set containing 8 contradictions. Their contradictory degrees are given in Table 99.1.

These contradictory degrees can be described in the average angle plane coordinates as Fig. 99.2a. If use some lines connect these separate coordinate dots, a contradictory information field of the contradictory information set is formed, as shown as Fig. 99.2b.

99.4.3 The Identification of Main Contradictory Information

When dealing with a complex contradictory problem, the identification of the primary and secondary contradictory information is very crucial. It will improve the efficiency of solving the problem. Contradictory information field can effectively show the level of separation and division of contradictory information. For given contradictory information fields, by setting a specific threshold, can separate all the contradictory information in a contradictory information set, resulting in two different levels of contradictory information subset, in one which contains the primary contradictory information.

For example, suppose there is a contradictory information field F_N.

$$F_N = (N_1 \perp N_2 \perp N_3 \perp N_4 \perp N_5 \perp N_6 \perp N_7 \perp N_8) \tag{99.8}$$

Fig. 99.3 Contradictory information field F_N

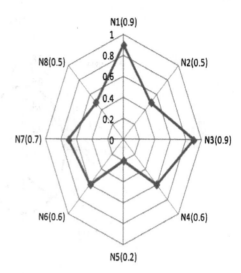

where $N_i (i = 1, \ldots, 8)$ denote contradictory degrees in the contradictory information set, and $\perp$ as a same field symbol, represents relevant contradictory information being at the same contradictory information field.

If a group of contradictory degrees are as follows:

$$N_1 = 0.9, N_2 = 0.5, N_3 = 0.9, N_4 = 0.6, N_5 = 0.2, N_6 = 0.6, N_7 = 0.7, N_8 = 0.5 \tag{99.9}$$

Then the contradictory information field can be described as:

$$F_N = (0.9 \perp 0.5 \perp 0.9 \perp 0.6 \perp 0.2 \perp 0.6 \perp 0.7 \perp 0.5) \tag{99.10}$$

The contradictory information field is shown as in Figure. 99.3.

Given a threshold H ($H = 0.55$), we can draw a dotted line arc with H as the radius in the contradictory information field. The dotted line arc divides the field into two parts, one part in the arcs, and another part out of the arcs, as shown as in Fig. 99.4.

Using H threshold to separate contradictory information field can be described as follows:

$$F_N \backslash H = F_{N_1} | F_{N_2} \tag{99.11}$$

where, $\backslash$ is a separating operation symbol; $|$ is a coexistence of operation symbol; F_{N_1} and F_{N_2} denote two new contradictory information fields after separation.

$$F_{N_1} = (N_1 \perp N_3 \perp N_4 \perp N_6 \perp N_7) = (0.9 \perp 0.9 \perp 0.6 \perp 0.6 \perp 0.7) \tag{99.12}$$

$$F_{N_2} = (N_2 \perp N_5 \perp N_8) = (0.5 \perp 0.2 \perp 0.5) \tag{99.13}$$

After separation, the two new contradictory information fields, F_{N_1} and F_{N_2} are shown as in Fig. 99.5.

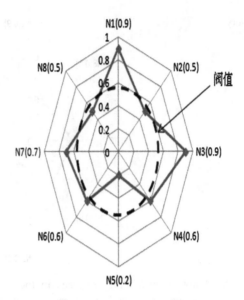

Fig. 99.4 Contradictory information field F_N under separate threshold H

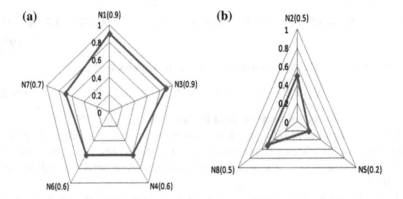

Fig. 99.5 **a** F_{N_1}, **b** F_{N_2}

99.5 Conclusions

It is one of the core issues to find the main contradictory information when solving a contradictory problem. Take a new coordinates system as a tool, characteristics of contradictory information are described and marked with contradictory degree. The study brings a suitable and efficient way to differentiate primary and secondary contradictory information, and which supplies the foundation for the further study about intelligent processing contradictory problem.

Acknowledgments The authors are grateful to National Natural Science Foundation of China (60272089) and Science Foundation of Guangdong University of Technology for decisive support.

References

1. Poulin D, St.-Vincent P, Bratley P (1993) Contradiction and confirmation. In: Proceedings of 4th international conference on database and expert systems applications, pp 502–513
2. Zadeh LA (1979) Fuzzy sets and information granularity, advances in fuzzy set theory and applications. Amsterdam, North-Holland, pp 3–18
3. Zeng T, Wang C, Yu Y (2009) Characteristics of contradictory information and its presentation. ICSPS 123:394–397
4. Cai W (1999) Extension theory and its application. Chin Sci Bull 44(17):1538–1548 (in Chinese)
5. Yang C, Cai W (2008) The extension engineering. Science Press, Beijing, pp 18–24 (in Chinese)
6. Cai W (1983) Extension set and non-compatible problem. Sci Explor 3(1):83–97 (in Chinese)

Chapter 100
A Semi-Supervised Network Traffic Classification Method Based on Incremental Learning

Pinghong Li, Yong Wang and Xiaoling Tao

Abstract In order to solve low accuracy, time consumption and limited application range in traditional network traffic classification, a semi-supervised network traffic classification method based on incremental learning is proposed. During training Support Vector Machine (SVM), it takes full advantage of a large number of unlabeled samples and a small amount of labeled samples to modify the classifiers. By utilizing incremental learning technology to void unnecessary repetition training, improve the situation of original classifiers' low accuracy and time-consuming when new samples are added. Combined with the Synergies of multiple classifiers, this paper proposes an improved Tri-training method to train multiple classifiers, overcoming the strict limitation of traditional Co-verification for classification methods and sample types. Experiments' results show that the proposed algorithm has excellent accuracy and speed in traffic classification.

Keywords Traffic classification · Support vector machine · Semi-supervised · Incremental learning · Tri-training

100.1 Introduction

Network traffic is an important carrier of recording, reflecting the network status and user activities, it plays an increasingly important role in effective network management. Network traffic classification [1] classifies the two-way TCP or UDP

P. Li (✉) · Y. Wang · X. Tao
Guilin University of Electronic Technology, NO.1 Jin-ji Road, Qixing District, Guilin, Guangxi, China
e-mail: lipinghong0601@163.com

W. Lu et al. (eds.), *Proceedings of the 2012 International Conference on Information Technology and Software Engineering*, Lecture Notes in Electrical Engineering 211, DOI: 10.1007/978-3-642-34522-7_100, © Springer-Verlag Berlin Heidelberg 2013

stream generated by network communication according to the types of network applications (such as WWW, FTP, MAIL, P2P) in the Internet based on TCP/IP protocol.

Recently, applying machine learning method to classify and identify network applications is a research hotspot. There are two traditional strategies in machine learning [2], that's supervised learning and unsupervised learning. Supervised learning methods, such as Bayesian methods, Decision tree methods, are high detection rates, but require that the sample data is correctly marked in advance and they are unable to find the unknown category samples. Unsupervised learning methods, such as Clustering method, group samples according to the data similarity. They don't need labeled data, but only model unlabeled data, detection accuracy is low.

Semi-supervised learning can take full advantage of a large number of unlabeled samples and a small amount of labeled samples. It makes up for the shortage of supervised learning and unsupervised learning. In this paper, a novel Least Area-SVM (LA-SVM) traffic classification algorithm is proposed, and we use improved Tri-training method to train classifiers collaboratively based on semi-supervised learning, the method makes the most of incremental learning in the classification efficiency and collaborative training techniques in accuracy, which improves network traffic classification performance.

100.2 SVM and Incremental Learning

100.2.1 SVM

SVM is an efficient and general machine learning algorithm based on Statistical Learning Theory (SLT). It's goal is to separate two classes by Constructing an objective function. Compared with conventional machine learning methods, SVM has many advantages [3]. (1) Global optimal solution. (2) Good Generalization performance. (3) Kernel skills application. (4) Good robustness [3, 4].

For the classification problems, if sample set is $\{X_i, Y_i\}$, $i = 1,...,l$. $X_i \in R^n$, $Y_i \in \{-1, +1\}$, Maximizing the distance of the hyper plane with the nearest samples to ensure the classification accuracy. If the classification problem is nonlinear, the input space is mapped into high dimensional feature space by using kernel functions. When and only if each support vector a satisfies the KKT conditions, $a = [a_1, a_2, ..., a_l]$ is the optimal solution. The KKT conditions as formula (100.1)

$$\begin{cases} a_i = 0 \Rightarrow f(x_i) \geq 1 \ or \ f(x_i) \leq -1 \\ 0 < a_i < C \Rightarrow f(x_i) = 1 \ or \ f(x_i) = -1 \\ a_i = C \Rightarrow -1 \leq f(x_i) \leq 1 \end{cases} \qquad (100.1)$$

where a is Lagrange multiplier, when a > 0, the corresponding samples are called Support vector. C is the regularization parameter.

100.2.2 Incremental Learning

With the development of modern technologies, the ever-growing network traffic information is increasingly large, it is very difficult to obtain a complete training data set at an early stage. This requires the classifiers can continuously improve the learning accuracy with the accumulation of data samples, so the incremental learning is very important.

For standard SVM Incremental learning algorithm, it takes support vector set obtained from last training as historical learning results instead of training samples during the training of SVM. Batch SVM [5] incremental learning method divides new samples into several disjoint subsets, and gets the final results by constructing new support vector set and classification hyper plane Sequence, but these serial incremental learning strategies can not reduce the time complexity of the classification process [6]. The two typical incremental learning algorithms do not fully consider the initial samples and new samples which may be converted to support vector data, leading to some useful historical data to be eliminated early and affecting the classification accuracy.

100.3 Semi-Supervised Learning and Co-Training

Co-training is a kind of semi-supervised learning paradigm that was proposed by Blum and Mitchell first [7]. It assumes that attributes can be split into two sufficient and redundant views. Tow independent classifiers are trained with the labeled data. Then each classifier labels unlabeled data with samples of high confidence that are selected from unlabeled data, and puts them into the labeled training set in the other classifier.

As most data can't meet fully redundancy conditions of views, Goldman and Zhou proposed an improved Co-training algorithm [8]. It no longer requires the problem itself has fully redundant views, but 10 times cross-validation to determine unlabeled samples' confidence. Its disadvantage is time-consuming. Zhou proposed Tri-training algorithm [9] for solving the problem. It uses three classifiers and doesn't require the data be described with sufficient and redundant views, but its auxiliary classifiers may produce noise samples. In addition, Deng [10] proposed adaptive data editing algorithm based on Tri-training and proved it's fast and easy to extend for common data.

100.4 SVM Network Traffic Classification with Incremental Learning and Improved Tri-Training

100.4.1 Changes of Support Vectors After Adding New Samples

Zhou [11] proved new samples which meet KKT conditions will not change support vector sets, while new samples against KKT conditions do. Wang [12] proved if there are new samples against the KKT conditions, non-support vectors in original samples may be converted to support vectors. It can be concluded that: the classifier's performance depends mainly on samples in new samples against the KKT conditions, support vector set in original samples and non-support vectors which may be converted to support vectors in original samples.

In this paper, Fig. 100.1 gives the illustration on Changes of support vectors after adding new samples. A1, A2, A3, A4 are support vectors in original samples, B1, B2, B3, B4 are newly added samples, when they are added, the support vectors become C1, C2, C3, C4, B1, B3, A1. Among them, C1, C2, C3, C4 are non-support vectors in original samples, B1, B3 are new samples, A1 is support vector in original samples. This show that support vectors changes when new samples are added. Firstly, non-support vectors C1, C2, C3, C4 in original samples and new samples B1 and B3 become support vectors. Then, although A1, A2, A3, A4 are support vectors in original samples, only A1 becomes new support vector after new samples are added. Therefore, how to ensure support vectors is of importance.

100.4.2 LA-SVM Method

According to the analysis above, for SVM incremental learning in the application of incremental learning, the traditional algorithms mostly not fully consider the initial samples and new samples which can be transformed into support vectors, which results in some useful data are prematurely eliminated and affecting classification accuracy. The starting point of LA-SVM method is finding out non-support vectors which can be transformed into new support vectors in the original sample sets.

Fig. 100.1 Changes of support vectors after adding new samples

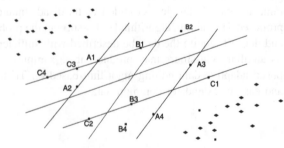

For new samples, LA-SVM method only keeps samples against KKT conditions. For initial samples, LA-SVM method only keeps support vectors, and non-support vectors within $[-1 - u, \ 1 + u]$ (u is Threshold) area from support vectors.

Based on the ideas above, LA-SVM method can be described as: Assume the initial sample set is X_0, the new sample set is X_i, $i = 1,\ldots,$ n, and $X_0 \cap X_i = \Phi$. The purpose is to find new classifier based on $X_0 \cap X_i$ and the corresponding support vector set SV. The specific steps as follows:

Step 1: train initial sample set X_0 to get SVM classifier T_0, Support vector set X_0^{sv} and non- Support vector set X_0^{nsv} of the initial sample.

Step 2: verify samples in X_i to check whether there are samples against the KKT condition, if so, divide X_i into X_i^{sv} (samples that satisfy the KKT condition) and X_i^{nsv} (samples that don't satisfy the KKT condition). If not, jump to step 4.

Step 3: search sample points within $[-1 - u, \ 1 + u]$ away from X_0^{sv}, collect them as set X_a, delete repeated points in X_a, and define the rest points in X_a as X_A.

Step 4: set $X = X_0^{sv} \cup X_A \cup X_i^{nsv}$, get SVM classifier T and support vectors SV by training X.

Step 5: T and SV are what we need.

100.4.3 Semi-Supervised SVM Based on Improved Tri-Training

The improved Tri-training method needs three learners as classifiers. It has no special demand for these classifiers. Let X_0 denote the initial labeled example set, X_u denote the unlabeled. The specific steps as follows:

Step 1: train labeled sample sets by bootstrap sampling to obtain three labeled training sets. By training the three labeled training sets in LA-SVM algorithm to achieve there initial classifiers A, B and C.

Step 2: after the initial training, one of the three classifiers will act as the training target classifier (assume it is A) and the others are auxiliary classifiers (assume they are B and C).

Step 3: B and C are used to classify samples in set X_u, if they have reach a consensus on the label of an unlabeled sample, the sample and the corresponding labels will be gathered together as $X_{a'}$.

Step 4: let $U = X_0 \cup X_{a'}$, retrain classifier A by set U to get $X_{A'}$, and put $X_{a'}$ back to unlabeled set X_u.

Step 5: compare $X_{A'}$ with previous classifier, if there are changes, jump to step 3; if there are no changes, jump to Step 6.

Step 6: Training end. Classifier $X_{A'}$ is what we need.

For improved Semi-supervised Tri-training method, it should be noted that $X_{a'}$ is not as the labeled data and will be put back to unlabeled set X_u in next round. If

$X_{a'}$ is correct prediction, the training target classifier will have additional correct samples. If $X_{a'}$ is wrong prediction, it will get extra nosy samples [10]. The noise will decrease the classifiers' performance, that's why this paper lets $X_{a'}$ as the unlabeled sample in the next round. By this way, it can reduce the classification error rate. The method has no constraint for attribute sets and semi-supervised learning algorithms used in three classifiers. Without cross-validation, therefore it is applicable to a much wider range and more high efficient.

100.5 Experiments

In experiments, we select data set used in paper [13] by Professor Moore, computer department of Cambridge University, this paper called it Moore-set. The Moore-set is the most authoritative network traffic classification test data set, which provides 10 traffic classification data subsets, each subset contains tens of thousands of data. Each stream contains 249 properties, which are composed of the statistical properties such as the port number and network properties such as the average time interval. The last property is classification target attribute, indicating types of the traffic samples, such as the WWW, FTP, P2P and so on. All our experiments run on Windows XP with MATLAB V7.1 and Myeclipse V8.5.0 installed.

100.5.1 Experiments Results

The experiment extracted 10 % of each subset in Moore_set, a total of 37,740 network traffic data. In order to verify the ability of proposed LA-SVM to process labeled and unlabeled samples in the same time under Tri-training. Compare training time and accuracy of standard SVM, Batch SVM and LA-SVM incremental learning under the unlabeled rate from 80 to 25 %. The experimental results are shown in Figs. 100.2 and 100.3. In order to verify the incremental learning ability of proposed LA-SVM under Tri- training, Select 40 % of samples as the initial sample set, divide the rest of the sample into 11 parts and add one part once. Compare training time and accuracy of standard SVM, Batch SVM and LA-SVM incremental learning. The experimental results are shown in Figs. 100.4 and 100.5.

100.5.2 Experiments Analysis

Figures 100.2 and 100.3 indicate the variation tendency of classification accuracy and training time under different unlabeled rates. Figure 100.2 shows that the

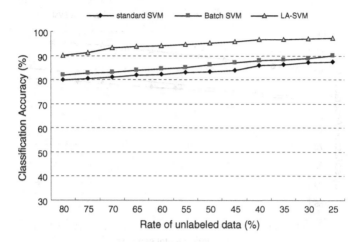

Fig. 100.2 Accuracy under different unlabeled rates

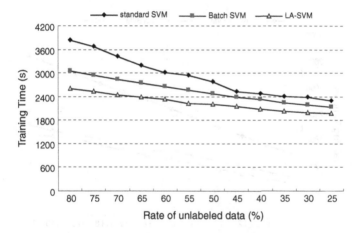

Fig. 100.3 Time under different unlabeled rates

classification accuracy of LA-SVM is better than standard SVM and Batch SVM incremental learning at different stages. The accuracy difference is the maximum under 80–70 % unlabeled rate. But classification accuracy rate of the three methods increase not obviously under 20–30 % unlabeled rate. Figure 100.3 reveals that the training time of LA-SVM costs less than the other two algorithms under different unlabeled rates. That's because LA-SVM incremental learning can

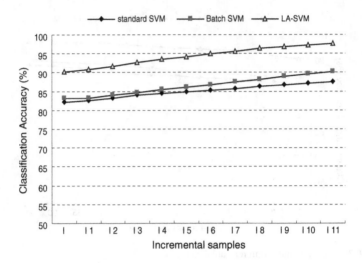

Fig. 100.4 Accuracy with incremental samples

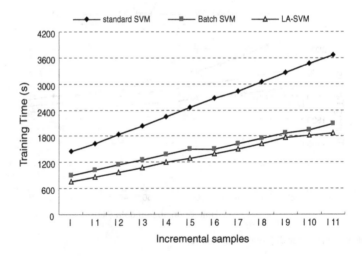

Fig. 100.5 Time with incremental samples

take full advantage of a large number of unlabeled samples and a small amount of labeled samples.

Figures 100.4 and 100.5 indicate the variation tendency of classification accuracy and training time with incremental samples, and we can see that the performance of LA-SVM in classification accuracy and time-consuming are much better than the other two algorithms with new samples are continuously added. The reason in that LA-SVM incremental learning adopts reasonable historical data elimination mechanism, which Consider the influences of Non-support vector in the initial sample set for incremental learning. It achieved high accuracy and efficiency. The experiments show that the LA-SVM algorithm is feasible and effective.

100.6 Conclusion

In this paper, a novel LA-SVM incremental learning algorithm is proposed. Compared with other methods, it fully consider samples in new samples against the KKT conditions, support vector set in original samples and non-support vectors in original samples which may be converted to support vectors. It avoids useful data to be eliminated early. Incremental learning techniques make full use of the results of historical study, significantly reducing training time. Finally, we use improved Tri-training method to train the classifiers. Experiments show that the method proposed has preponderance in network traffic classification accuracy and speed.

The methods of Support Vector Machine and Incremental Learning have bright prospects in the network traffic classification. Recently, researchers proposed some solutions and improved the algorithms from different aspects, but there are still some problems need to study. Firstly, how to collect valuable samples as little as possible. Secondly, how to realize fuzzy SVM incremental learning. Lastly, how to achieve online incremental learning. Due to traffic classification data is large scale, research on incremental learning algorithm with multiple support vector machine classifiers may be a research direction for traffic classification.

References

1. Zhang B, Yang J-H, Wu J-P (2011) Survey and analysis on the internet traffic model. J Softw 22(1):115–131 (in Chinese)
2. Tan PN, Steinbach M, Kumar V (2006) Introduction to data mining. Addison Wesley, Boston
3. Zhu XJ Semi-supervised learning literature survey, Technical Report 1530. Department of Computer Sciences, University of Wisconsin at Madison, Madison, WI, 2007–12
4. Gu C, Zhang S (2011) Network traffic classification based on improved support vector machine. Chin J Sci Instrum 32(7):1507–1513
5. Ratnasamy S, Francis P, Handley M et al (2001) A scalable content-addressable network. ACM SIGCOMM, San Diego
6. Rowstron A, Druschel P (2001) Pastry: scalable, decentralized object location, and routing for large-scale peer-to-peer system. ACM IFIP international conference on distributed systems platforms (Middleware 2001), Heidelberg, 2001
7. Blum A, Mitchell T (1998) Combining labeled and unlabeled data with co-training/ proceedings of the 11th annual conference on computational learning theory, Madison, 1998, pp 92–100
8. Goldman S, Zhon Y (2000) Enhancins supervised learning with unlabeled data/proceedings of the17th IGML. Morffan Kaufmann, San Francisco, GA, pp 327–334

9. Zhou ZH, Li M (2005) Tri-training: exploiting unlabeled data using three classifiers. IEEE Trans Knowl Data Eng 17(11):1529–1541

10. Deng C, Guo M-Z (2007) Tri-training with adaptive data editing. Chin J Comput 30(8):1214–1226 (in Chinese)

11. Zhou W-D, Zhang L, Jiao L-C (2001) An improved principle for measuring generalization performance. Chin J Comput 29(5):590–594 (in Chinese)

12. Wang X-D, Zheng C-Y, Wu C-M, Zhang H-D (2006) New algorithm for SVM-Based incremental learning. J Comput Appl 26(10):2440–2443 (in Chinese)

13. Moore AW, Zuev D (2005) Internet traffic classification using Bayesian analysis techniques. In: Proceedings of the 2005 ACM SIGMETRICS international conference on measurement and modeling of computer systems, pp 50–60

Chapter 101
Tuning the EBOM Algorithm with Suffix Jump

Hongbo Fan and Nianmin Yao

Abstract EBOM is one of the fastest exact single pattern string matching algorithms for short patterns and large alphabet. In this article, a suffix jump method based on the automaton of EBOM (Factor Oracle) is presented. After the suffix jump method applied, an additional jump which the distance is similar with 2-grams bad-char rule is gained and the additional jump distance can be calculated together with the factor method based on Factor Oracle. We combined the suffix jump method with the factor method of EBOM and presented an improved algorithm of EBOM called SufOM2. Experimental results indicated that SufOM2 is very fast for large alphabet and short patterns on our platform.

Keywords String matching · EBOM · BOM · Suffix jump · Design of algorithms

101.1 Introduction

String matching is a fundamental problem in computer science that has been widely used in most of fields for text or symbol processing, such as network security, computational biology, and information retrieval [1].

Exact single pattern string matching is the basis of the whole string matching field. It means seeking all the occurrences of a pattern $P = P[0, \ldots, m-1]$ of

H. Fan · N. Yao (✉)
Department of Computer Science and Technology, Harbin Engineering University,
Harbin, China
e-mail: yaonianmin@hrbeu.edu.cn

H. Fan
e-mail: 270677673@qq.com

W. Lu et al. (eds.), *Proceedings of the 2012 International Conference on Information Technology and Software Engineering*, Lecture Notes in Electrical Engineering 211, DOI: 10.1007/978-3-642-34522-7_101, © Springer-Verlag Berlin Heidelberg 2013

length m in a text $T = T[0, \ldots, n-1]$ of length n over the same alphabet Σ of length σ. In this paper, we concentrate on practical exact single pattern string matching. All algorithms involved in this paper are for searching an exact pattern.

Exact single pattern string matching has been extensively studied and numerous strategies and algorithms have been designed to solve it. To date, the literature [2, 3] is the most comprehensive survey, and it gave a performance comparison of 85 algorithms which covers most known algorithms as of May 2010. This performance comparison shows that EBOM [4] is faster than other known algorithms for short pattern and large alphabet.

According to the jump mechanism, algorithms can be classified as prefix matching, suffix matching, and factor matching. EBOM only uses the factor method to jump over the locations that impossibly match the pattern. However, many algorithms combine more than one mechanism and gain better performance than the one only uses a mechanism such as FJS [5], BNDM-BMH [6]. In this article, we presented a simple way to realize suffix jump on the automaton of EBOM (Factor Oracle or *FO* for short). Then, we combined this method with the factor method and presented SufOM algorithm. It is indicated in experimental results that SufOM is very fast for large alphabet and short patterns on our platform.

101.2 Preliminaries

Let the substring of text in the sliding window be W. If $W = XYZ$, all of X, Y and Z are factors of W ($X, Y, Z \in fac(W)$) and Z is a suffix of W ($Z \in suf(W)$).

FO [7, 8] is a DFA and it is one of the simplest factor automata to recognize the factor set of a string. *FO* is a 5-tuple $\{Q, \Sigma, I, F, \delta\}$, consisting of a set of states, an alphabet, an initial state, a set of final states and a $Q \times \Sigma \rightarrow Q$ transition function respectively. It is acyclic and all states are final. It has $m + 1$ states and a linear number of transitions ($2m-1$ at most). The most outstanding feature of *FO* is *weak factor recognition*, which means that a negative answer is always correct when testing whether a string is a factor. Practically, if a string $S \in suf(W)$ is inputted backward to *FO* for the reversal of P (P^{rv}) and *FO* rejects this input, $S^{rv} \notin fac(P^{rv})$ and then $S \notin fac(P)$. In practical, the wrong recognition is rare. An example of *FO* for $P = $ "baabbba" is shown in Fig. 101.1.

Many string matching solutions use *FO* and they are called BOM [8] type algorithms. BOM type algorithms use the factor method. In the factor method, text

Fig. 101.1 Factor Oracle for $P = $ "baabbba"

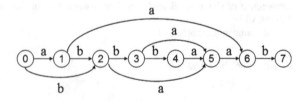

characters in the sliding window are inputted to FO for P^{ry} backward until FO rejects the input or the whole window has been accepted. Let the string that has been read be U. If FO rejects U, this window is mismatched and it can safely jump $m - |U| + 1$ characters to let the window jump over U. If the whole window has been accepted, string matching occurs in this window and then the window would slide one character.

EBOM is an efficient 2-grams variant of BOM. It records the results of the first two transitions of FO for any pairs of characters in a function $\lambda : (\Sigma \times \Sigma) \rightarrow Q \cup \perp$, which $\perp$ is undefined state, to obtain these results just in one step of calculations, which $\perp$ is the undefined state. The function λ is implemented in a 2-dimensional table with $O(\sigma^2)$ space and it is defined as shown below.

$$for\ \forall \alpha, \beta \in \Sigma, \quad \lambda(\alpha, \beta) = \begin{cases} \perp, & if\ \delta(I, \alpha) = \perp \\ \delta(\delta(I, \alpha), \beta), & otherwise \end{cases}$$

EBOM simplifies the matching process of BOM by reducing some unnecessary branches. The code of EBOM is listed as Code. 1. cur is the current state in FO.

EBOM (P, T, m, n)
//building phase of FO
create $m+1$ states; $S[0] \leftarrow -1$; for $i \in [0,...,m+1]$, $j \in \Sigma$ do $\{ \delta(i, j) \leftarrow \perp; \}$
for $cur \in [0...m-1]$ **do**
$\quad \{ \sigma \leftarrow P[m-1-cur]; \ \delta(cur, \sigma) \leftarrow cur+1; \ k \leftarrow S[cur];$
$\quad$ **while** $k > -1$ **and** $\delta(k, \sigma) = \perp$ **do** $\{ \delta(k, \sigma) \leftarrow cur+1; \ k \leftarrow S[k]; \}$
$\quad$ **if** $k = -1$ **then** $c \leftarrow 0$; **else** $c \leftarrow \delta(k, \sigma)$; $S[cur+1] \leftarrow c$; $\}$
//end of the building phase of FO
for $\alpha, \beta \in \Sigma$ **do**
$\quad \{ cur \leftarrow \delta(I, \alpha)$; **if** $cur = \perp$ **then** $\lambda(a,b) \leftarrow \perp$; **else** $\lambda(a,b) \leftarrow \delta(cur,b); \}$
$T[n...n+m-1] \leftarrow P$; $pos \leftarrow m-1$;
while $pos < n$ **do**
$\quad \{ cur \leftarrow \lambda(T[pos], T[pos-1])$;
$\quad$ **while** $cur = \perp$ **do**
$\quad\quad \{ pos \leftarrow pos+m-1$; $cur \leftarrow \lambda(T[pos], T[pos-1]); \}$//fast loop
$\quad pos1 \leftarrow pos-2$;
$\quad$ **while** $cur \neq \perp$ **do** $\{ cur \leftarrow \delta(cur, T[pos1])$; $pos1 \leftarrow pos1-1; \}$ //match loop
$\quad$ **if** $pos1 < pos-m+1$ **then** $\{$Report a match finding; $pos1 \leftarrow pos1+1; \}$
$\quad pos \leftarrow pos1+m; \}$

Code.1 The EBOM algorithm

101.3 Suffix Method on FO

In this section, we propose a q-grams suffix jump method based on the fact that FO is acyclic. Here, $q_S(FO)$ is defined as the current state (written as *cur* too) after the string S has been inputted backward to FO.

Lemma 1 *For any $S \in \Sigma^q$, $q_S(FO) = q$ if and only if S matches the suffix of P of length q.*

Proof According to the build method of the FO for P^{rv}, for $\forall i < m$, $\delta(i, c) \to i + 1$ if and only if $c = P^{rv}[i]$ and $\delta(i, c) > i + 1$ if and only if $c \neq P^{rv}[i]$. Therefore, if $q_S(FO) = q$, for $\forall i \in \{0, 1, \ldots, q - 1\}$, $S^{rv}[i] = P^{rv}[i]$, that is means S matches the suffix of P of length q.

Lemma 2 *For any $S \in \Sigma^q \cap suf(W)$, which W is the string in the sliding window, if $q_S(FO) \neq \bot$, the window can jump $q_S(FO) - q$ characters safely.*

Proof When a character is inputted, the current state should increase 1 at least because FO is acyclic. Thus, after S input, no matter what next $m - q_S(FO) + 1$ characters are inputted, the current state increase $m - q_S(FO) + 1$ at least. Thus, *cur* should be bigger than m because the first state of FO is labeled as 0, and moreover, $cur = \bot$ after any $m - q_S(FO) + 1$ characters inputted. It is means the suffix of W of length $q + m - q_S(FO) + 1$ is not a factor of P. Therefore, the window can jump $m - (q + m - q_S(FO) + 1) + 1 = q_S(FO) - q$ characters according to the factor method. According to lemma 1, if $q_S(FO) \neq \bot$, the minimum value of $q_S(FO)$ is q. Since, the jump distance is always positive when S does not match the suffix of P of length q, and the jump distance is zero only while S matches the suffix of P of length q, this jump is safely.

According to the lemma 1 and lemma 2, we have:

Lemma 3 *Let pos is the position of the last character of the sliding window, if $\lambda(t[pos], t[pos - 1]) = \bot$, the window can jump $m - 1$ characters by the factor method and if $\lambda(t[pos], t[pos - 1]) \neq \bot$, the sliding window can jump $\lambda(t[pos], t[pos - 1]) - 2$ characters, if the window still not jumps that means $t[pos - 1]t[pos]$ is the suffix of the pattern.*

Let $P = $ "baabbba" as the example shown in Fig. 101.1, the jump distances of EBOM, BMH2 [9] 2-grams bad char rule and lemma 3 for any pair characters are listed as Table 101.1.

Table 101.1 The jump distance of EBOM, BMH2 and lemma 3 for $P = $ "baabbba"

	aa	ab	ba	bb
EBOM	0	0	0	0
BMH2	4	3	0	1
Lemma3	4	3	0	1

From Table 101.1, it can be seen that the jump distance of lemma 3 is similar with the jump distance of BMH2 2-grams bad char rule, while EBOM can not jump based on these input. In fact, at most of time, the jump distance of the suffix method on FO is equal to the jump distance of BMH2 2-grams bad char rule in most of cases.

Let the function $poccur \in \Sigma^* \times \Sigma^* \to N$ be defined as: if $U \in fac(P)$, $poccur(U^{rv}, P^{rv}) = min\{|SU|, P^{rv} = SU^{rv}V\}, P, S, U, V \in \Sigma^*$. According to the definition of BMH2 2-grams bad char rule, the jump distance of BMH2 2-grams bad char rule for any $U \in fac(P)$ is $min\{|S|, P^{rv} = SU^{rv}V\} = poccur(U^{rv}, P^{rv}) - |U|$. And it is proofed in [8] that U^{rv} is recognized by FO build for P^{rv} in a state $j \le poccur(U^{rv}, P^{rv})$, and only if U^{rv} is wrong recognized by the other FO for the prefix of P^{rv} of length $poccur(U^{rv}, P^{rv}), j < poccur(U^{rv}, P^{rv})$. Because the wrong reorganization is rare in practice, most of U^{rv} is recognized at the state $poccur(U^{rv}, P^{rv})$. Therefore at most of time, the jump distance of lemma 3 is $poccur(U^{rv}, P^{rv}) - |U|$ which is equal to the jump distance of BMH2 2-grams bad char rule.

Hence, the method of lemma 3 is named the suffix jump method on FO.

Here, we combined the factor method and the suffix jump method and we obtained a new algorithm named SufOM2 (SUFfix jumping Oracle Matching with 2-grams). The implement of SufOM2 is listed in Code.2.

SufOM2 (P, T, m, n)
1. $\delta \leftarrow$ *building Factor Oracle* (P, m);
2. **for** $\alpha, \beta \in \Sigma$ **do**
3. $\{ cur \leftarrow \delta(I, \alpha)$; **if** $cur = \perp$ **then** $\lambda(a,b) \leftarrow \perp$; **else** $\lambda(a,b) \leftarrow \delta(cur,b)$;$\}$
4. $T[n...n+m-1] \leftarrow P$; $pos \leftarrow m-1$;
5. **while** $pos < n-m$ **do**
6. $\{ cur \leftarrow \lambda(T[pos], T[pos-1])$;
7.   **while** $cur > m$ **do**   //inner loop
8. $\{ pos \leftarrow pos+m-2$; $cur \leftarrow \lambda(T[pos], T[pos-1])$;$\}$
9.   **if** $(cur > 2)$ **then**$\{ pos \leftarrow pos+cur-2$; **continue;**$\}$
10. $pos1 \leftarrow pos - m$; $pos \leftarrow pos-2$;
11. **do** $\{ cur \leftarrow \delta(cur, T[pos])$; $pos \leftarrow pos-1$; $\}$ **while** $cur \le m$; //match loop
12. **if** $pos < pos1$ **then** $\{Report find a match; pos \leftarrow pos+1$; $\}$
13. $pos \leftarrow pos+m+1$; $\}$

Code.2 The SufOM2 algorithm

Obviously, in SufOM2, cur has been calculated in the inner loop, and it can be gained immediately when the suffix jump of line 9 is executing. Thus, the suffix method on FO can gain additional jump distance than EBOM. Although both the 2-grams bad char rule and the function λ use a high cost 2-dimensional table lookup operation, the suffix method on FO can share this cost with the factor method on FO, and the average cost for the suffix jump on FO is lower than the

2-grams bad char rule. Therefore, SufOM2 is better than the algorithm simply combines the 2-grams bad char rule and EBOM.

101.4 Experiments Results

To show the performance of SufOM2 algorithms, we do the following comparative experiment based on SMART [10], which is the implement of the article [2, 3]:

The platform is Intel I7-2600 k@3.4Ghz/z68/8 GB DDR3 RAM/Ubuntu 10.04LTS 64-bit desktop edition/g ++4.4.5 with −O3 optimize parameter. We tested under the DNA sequence (*E. coli*), English text (Bible.txt), and natural language samples text (world192.txt), which above three texts are from SMART. For each matching condition, the 100 patterns in each pattern set were picked from the 100 prior random selected and non-overlapping positions of the text, and the average matching speed was recorded as the final result which the highest and the lowest 20 % results were ignored. The text had been read in memory to avoid the impact of disk and before each time of matching, a big table had been read sequentially to empty the Cache. Only the matching phase was timed by RDTSC[1] (±30 CPU ticks). In the experiment, the CPU frequency was locked by cpufrequtils[2]; the network and the unrelated background service are closed to ensure the processor utilization was below to 3 %. This experiment environment is similar with the environment of the article [2, 3], but we used −O3 parameter with auto branch prediction and only timed matching phase, which are more suit for the study habits of the string matching field.

SMART has given the implements of 85 known algorithms, which covered most known algorithms as of May 2010. This experiment continued the work of SMART, complemented the FSO [11], BXS [12], QF [12], Q-Hash_4096 [12], SBNDMqb [13], BSDMq [14], FSBNDM-wk [14], SBNDM-wk [15], FS-wk [15], TVSBS-wk [15], FSBNDMq [16], FSBNDMqb [16], GSB2 [16], GSB2b [16] etc., which are newer algorithms not be included by SMART. All bit parallel solutions are implemented with the 32-bit edition (i32) and the 64-bit edition (a64) and both of them are tested. And just some of parameters of the solutions are listed in SMART, this experiment complemented the unlisted parameters. For example, only 3 conditions of Hashq ($q = 3, 5, 8$) were listed in SMART, we complemented the solutions of $q = 4, 6, 7$ etc. If an algorithm with different parameters are called different algorithms, there was more than 300 algorithms are compared, these algorithms covered most of known algorithms. The experiment results of the optimize parameter and its average matching speed for the fastest four type algorithms (if some algorithms are only inconsistent with parameter such as q value of q-grams, and they are presented in one article, they are called a type

---

[1] http://en.wikipedia.org/wiki/Time_Stamp_Counter
[2] http://wiki.archlinux.org/index.php/Cpufrequtils

Table 101.2 The optimal parameter and average matching speed for the fastest four type algorithms on DNA sequence, which unit is MB/s

	$m = 2$		$m = 4$		$m = 8$	
1	FSO_U61a64 [10]	953.4	UFNDM4_a64 [12]	1380.3	SBNDM4b_i32 [12]	2732.9
2	Shift-Or_i32 [16]	927.9	FAO_U59a64	1061.9	UFNDM4_a64	2466.6
3	Shift-And_i32 [16]	713.0	FSBNDMqq3f0i32[15]	970.8	FSBNDMqbq4f1i32	2397.2
4	**SufOM2**	**687.3**	Shift-Or_i32	928.0	QF_3_5i32 [11]	1485.3
	$m = 16$		$m = 32$		$m = 64$	
1	SBNDM4b_i32	5299.1	SBNDM6b_i32	8758.1	SBNDM6b_a64	12344
2	FSBNDMqq5f1i32	4977.1	FSBNDMqbq6f0i32	8743.8	FSBNDMqbq6f0a64	11503
3	UFNDM6_a64	4460.1	UFNDM6_a64	7969.9	UFNDM6_a64	11193
4	QF_4_3i32	3421.5	QF_5_3i32	6111.9	QF_6_2i32	8878.8

Table 101.3 The optimal parameter and average matching speed for the fastest four type algorithms on English text, which unit is MB/s

	$m = 2$		$m = 4$		$m = 8$	
1	**SufOM2**	**1262.6**	**SufOM2**	**2916.9**	**SufOM2**	**4262.7**
2	EBOM	1214.7	EBOM	2721.2	SBNDM2_2_i32	4198.9
3	TVSBS_w6 [14]	1160.8	SBNDM2_2i32	2658.5	EBOM	3812.9
4	GSB2b_i32 [15]	1067.1	GSB2b_i32	2561.3	GSB2b_i32	3734.1
	$m = 16$		$m = 32$		$m = 64$	
1	SBNDM4b_a32	6437.2	SBNDM4b_a32	9702.5	SBNDM6b_a64	11542
2	FSBNDMq_q5f2i32	5502.1	UFNDM4_i32	8802.5	TVSBS_w6	11350
3	UFNDM4_i32	5257.2	FSBNDMqb_q4f0i32	8468.5	UFNDM6_a64	11169
4	**SufOM2**	**5208.8**	TVSBS_w6	7618.3	BXS5_a64 [11]	10304

Table 101.4 The optimal parameter and average matching speed for the fastest four type algorithms on natural language, which unit is MB/s

	$m = 2$		$m = 4$		$m = 8$	
1	TVSBS_w6	1407.5	**SufOM2**	**3186.2**	**SufOM2**	**5283.4**
2	**SufOM2**	**1324.2**	EBOM	3045.5	SBNDM2_2_i32	5070.8
3	EBOM	1311.0	SBNDM2_2_i32	2975.5	EBOM	4749.9
4	GSB2b_i32	1134.3	GSB2b_i32	2803.1	GSB2b_i32	4608.4
	$m = 16$		$m = 32$		$m = 64$	
1	**SufOM2**	**7683.1**	SBNDM4_i32	9421.2	TVSBS_w8	11957
2	bndm2_2_i32	7445.6	**SufOM2**	**9172.5**	SBNDM4b_a64	11508
3	FSBNDMq_q3f0i32	7140.5	TVSBS_w6	9120.4	UFNDM4_a64	11456
4	EBOM	6539.0	UFNDM4_i32	8873.9	**SufOM2**	**11301**

algorithm) are listed for DNA sequence, English test and the sample of natural language in from Tables 101.2, 101.3, 101.4.

From these table, it can be seen that SufOM2 is very fast for short patterns on large alphabet text and it is slow for small alphabet and long patterns. It is obviously that the 2-grams is not enough for small alphabet and long patterns. We will research the q-grams method of SufOM2 to increase the performance for long patterns in the future works.

101.5 Conclusion

In this article, we presented a suffix jump method on Factor Oracle, and combined this method with the factor method of EBOM. Therefore, an improved algorithm of EBOM, named SufOM2, is presented. The Experimental results indicated that SufOM2 is faster than other known algorithms for large alphabet and short patterns on our platform.

Acknowledgments This paper is supported by the National Natural Science Foundation of China under Grant No.61073047; Fundamental Research Funds for the Central Universities: HEUCFT1007, HEUCF100607, HEUCFT1202, Harbin Special funds for Technological Innovation Talents: 2012RFLXG023. Thanks for funding.

References

1. Navarro G, Raffinot M (2002) Flexible pattern matching in strings—practical on-line search algorithms for texts and biological sequences. Cambridge University Press, New York
2. Faro S, Lecroq T (2010) The exact string matching problem: a comprehensive experimental evaluation [DB/OL]. Comput Res Repos http://arxiv.org/pdf/1012.2547. [2012/7/12]
3. Faro S, Lecroq T (2013) The exact online string matching problem: a review of the most recent results [J/OL]. ACM Comput Surv http://www-igm.univ-mlv.fr/~lecroq/articles/acmsurv2013.pdf. [2012/7/12]
4. Faro S, Lecroq T (2009) Efficient variants of the backward-oracle-matching algorithm. Int J Found Comput Sci 20(6):967–984. doi:10.1142/S0129054109006991
5. Franek F, Jennings CG, Smyth WF (2007) A simple fast hybrid pattern matching algorithm. J Discret Algorithms 5(4):682–695
6. Holub J, Durian B (2005) Fast variants of bit parallel approach to suffix automata, The Second Haifa Annual International Stringology Research Workshop of the Israeli Science Foundation http://www.cri.haifa.ac.il/events/2005/string/presentations/Holub.pdf
7. Crochemore M, Ilie L, Seid-Hilmi E (2007) The structure of factor oracles. Int J Found Comput Sci 18(4):781–797
8. Allauzen C, Crochemore M, Raffinot M (1999) Factor oracle: a new structure for pattern matching. LNCS 1725: Proceedings of SOFSEM'99. Theory and practice of informatics. Berlin, Springer, pp 291–306
9. Kalsi P, Peltola H, Tarhio J (2008) Comparison of exact string matching algorithms for biological sequences. In: Communications in computer and information science 13:

proceedings of the second international conference on bioinformatics research and development, BIRD'08. Springer-Verlag, Berlin, pp 417–426

10. http://www.dmi.unict.it/~faro/smart/ [2012/7/12]

11. Fredriksson K, Grabowski S (2005) Practical and optimal string matching. LNCS 3772: The 12th symposium on string processing and information retrieval, SPIRE 2005. Springer, Berlin, pp 376–387

12. Durian B, Peltola H, Salmela L et al (2010) Bit-parallel search algorithms for long patterns. LNCS 6049: The 9th international symposium on experimental algorithms, SEA 2010. Springer, Berlin, pp 129–140

13. Durian B, Holub J, Peltola H et al (2009) Tuning BNDM with q-grams. In: Proceedings of the 11th workshop on algorithm engineering and experiments, ALENEX 2009. SIAM, New York, pp 29–37

14. Faro S, Lecroq T (2012) A fast suffix automata based algorithm for exact online string matching. LNCS 7276: The 17th international conference on implementation and application of automata, CIAA 2012. Springer, Berlin, pp 149–158

15. Faro S, Lecroq T(2012) A multiple sliding windows approach to speed up string matching algorithms. LNCS 7276: The 11th international symposium on experimental algorithms, SEA 2012. Springer, Berlin, pp 172–183

16. Peltola H, Tarhio J (2011) Variations of forward-SBNDM. In: 16th prague stringology conference, PSC2011. Czech Technical University, Pragure, pp 3–14

Chapter 102
Implement IP Core of the Conversion Between Fixed-point Format and Floating-point Format on FPGA

Jianye Wang, Cang Liu, Peng Jing and Chao Zhou

Abstract Custom floating-point format based on Field Programmable Gate Array (FPGA) [1] offers a good solution for better operating efficiency and full-use of resource in realtime signal processing program designing. The conversion between fixed-point format and floating-point format then becomes the key point in real-time signal processing program designing. Based on Field Programmable Gate Array, the paper introduces an IP core design of the mutual conversion between fixed-point format and floating-point format. In this design, some flexible improvements on several parameters are introduced while using the pipeline technology, and, in the end, a comprehensive simulation is presented through QuartusII software. The result shows that the IP core, compared with document No.5, effectively double the operation speed.

Keywords Floating-point format · Fixed-point format · IP core · Field programmable gate array (FPGA)

102.1 Introduction

Floating-point format provide higher precision and larger dynamic range than the fixed-point format. With the increasing of data accuracy and the speed of realtime signal processing in the field of modern digital signal processing, the traditional DSP processor has been difficult to meet the requirements, implementation of floating-point calculation on FPGA (Field Programmable Gate Array, FPGA) offers a good solution with its high efficiency parallel architecture [2].

J. Wang · C. Liu (✉) · P. Jing · C. Zhou
The Missile Institute of Air Force Engineering University, Shanxi Xian 710051, China
e-mail: 731427586@qq.com

W. Lu et al. (eds.), *Proceedings of the 2012 International Conference on Information Technology and Software Engineering*, Lecture Notes in Electrical Engineering 211, DOI: 10.1007/978-3-642-34522-7_102, © Springer-Verlag Berlin Heidelberg 2013

Because FPGA is mainly with fixed-point in number system and calculation, the mutual conversion between fixed-point format and floating-point format is an indispensable step in implementation of digital signal processing in floating-point format on FPGA. This paper presents an implementation scheme of the IP core that mutual conversion between binary complement (the most popular signed fixed-point format currently) and floating-point format, compared with some existed IP core implementations, this scheme has achieved a higher conversion rate consideration to resource utilization.

102.2 Number System of Floating-Point

Number system of Floating-point follows IEEE standard [3, 4] for the single precision (word length is 32 bits) or double precision (word length is 64 bits) floating-point format in most microprocessors, but the FPGA-based system usually used custom floating-point format [5]. The floating-point format in this IP core design consists of sign bit(s), exponential (e) and unsigned (decimal fraction) normalized mantissa (m), digit number of exponential (e) and unsigned (decimal fraction) normalized mantissa (m) can be set in the IP core, the format is shown in Table 102.1.

This is a format of the binary signed amplitude, "1" does not appear in binary code floats which is hid in the mantissa, digit number of exponential is expressed using "E", algebraic form of the floating-point format is expressed in the following:

$$X = (-1)^S \times 1.m \times 2^{e-Dev} \tag{102.1}$$

$$Dev = 2^{E-1} - 1 \tag{102.2}$$

IEEE 754-1985 standard also defines some processing of useful special value. It is preserved for infinity that "$e = E_{max} = 1 \ldots 1_2$" and "$m = 0$" in the standard, "0" is encoded that "$e = E_{min} = 0$" and "$m = 0$", this paper extends the processing of special value. The representation method for special value of (1, 6, 5) floating-point format is shown in Table 102.2.

102.3 Conversion Fixed-point Numbers to Floating-point Numbers

This design adopts the three-level pipeline structure for achieving a higher conversion rate. First, judgment whether the input fixed-point number is "0" of

Table 102.1 The floating-point format

Sign bit(s)	Exponential (e)	Unsigned normalized mantissa (m)

Table 102.2 The representation method for special value of (1, 6, 5) floating-point format

Sign bit	Format of (1, 6, 5)		Decimal system
0	000000	00000	+0
1	000000	00000	−0
0	111111	00000	+∞
1	111111	00000	−∞

special value in the first stage of the pipeline, we do not need to consider whether the input number is infinity and the sign bit of "0", because the fixed-point number is expressed by binary complement. Second, convert the fixed-point number which is expressed by the format of non-zero binary complement to a format of the binary signed amplitude, that is to say, need to calculate the complement of the fixed-point number if the sign bit is "1" for getting the format of the binary signed amplitude, and the complement of the fixed-point number is itself if the sign bit is "0". A non-standardized mantissa can been obtained if remove the sign bit of the format of the binary signed amplitude. Get the number of leading zeros in the non-standardized mantissa in the second stage of the pipeline, then get exponential and normalized mantissa of the floating-point format through a simple calculation. In this design, the number of leading zeros is determined through FOR_LOOP statement in the PROCESS. Output "0" of the floating-point format if the input fixed-point number is "0" of special value in the third stage of the pipeline, else the sign bit, exponential and normalized mantissa would been connected into the number of floating-point format. Flow charts shown in Fig. 102.1.

In general, in order to get normalized mantissa, get the number of leading zeros first, then mantissa was left shift until the first "1" away from the mantissa register according to the number of leading zeros, this implies that the normalized mantissa has been gotten easily, because the hidden "1" has been away from the mantissa register.In this design, considering the corresponding relationship between the number of leading zeros, non-standardized mantissa and normalized mantissa, connect "0" (the same amount of normalized mantissa) behind the non-stan-dardized mantissa first, then assign to the normalized mantissa register directly which part belongs to normalized mantissa. It is effective saving logic element and improve the conversion rate. Schematic diagram shown in Fig. 102.2.

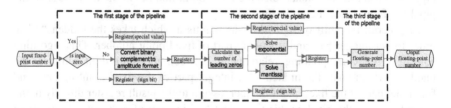

Fig. 102.1 Flow chart of conversion fixed-point numbers to floating-point numbers

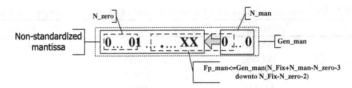

Fig. 102.2 Schematic diagram of getting the normalized mantissa

102.4 Conversion Floating-Point Numbers to Fixed-Point Numbers

Conversion floating-point numbers to fixed-point numbers is more complex than conversion fixed-point numbers to floating-point numbers, mantissa was left shift or right shift according to exponential and deviation which is bigger, in addition, need to consider ± 0 and $\pm \infty$ of special number.

Three-level pipeline structure is adopted in this design for higher conversion rate. First, judgment whether the input floating-point number is special value in the first stage of the pipeline. Second, judgment exponential of non-special value and deviation which is bigger, digit number of left shift the decimal point of the mantissa which takes the hidden "1" can be gat through exponential deduct deviation when exponential is bigger than deviation, and then determine whether the floating-point number is bigger than the maximum value of the fixed-point number refer to the digit number of left shift, output will be the maximum value if the floating-point number is bigger than the maximum value. On the contrary, digit number of right shift the decimal point of the mantissa which takes the hidden "1" can be gat through deviation deduct exponential when deviation is bigger than exponential, output will be the zero if the floating-point number is smaller than the minimum value of the fixed-point number (if the digit number of right shift the decimal point is bigger than the digit number of mantissa then the fixed-point number will be zero). Integer part and fractional part of fixed-point number is got if the floating-point number is in the effective range on the Basis of the corresponding relationship between digit number of shift, the mantissa which takes the hidden "1", digit number of integer part of the fixed-point number and digit number of fractional part of the fixed-point number in the second stage of the pipeline. Generate and standardize the fixed-point number in the third stage of the pipeline. Flow chart shown in Fig. 102.3.

In general, left shift or right shift the mantissa which takes the hidden "1" in order to get integer part and fractional part of fixed-point number. This algorithm considers the corresponding relationship between the shift digit number, the mantissa which takes the hidden "1", integer part of the fixed-point number and fractional part of the fixed-point number, assign to the result register directly in the second stage of the pipeline. First, connect "0" in front of or behind the mantissa register which takes the hidden "1", then assign to the integer register part and the fractional register part of the fixed-point number which part belongs to them, the

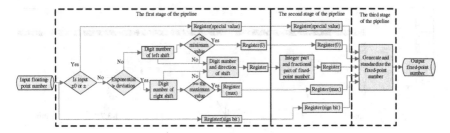

Fig. 102.3 Flow chart of conversion floating-point numbers to fixed-point numbers

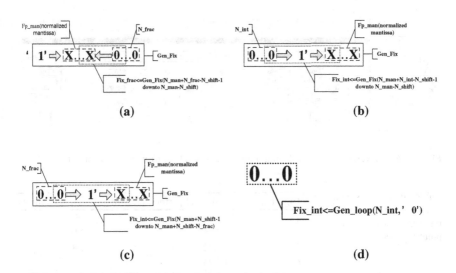

Fig. 102.4 Schematic diagram of getting integer part and fractional part of fixed-point. **a** Left shift the decimal point to get fractional part of the fixed-point. **b** Left shift the decimal point to get integer part of the fixed-point. **c** Right shift the decimal point to get fractional part of the fixed-point. **d** Right shift the decimal point to get integer part of the fixed-point

problem of that digit number is not enough can be solved effectively. The function of Gen_loop(N, 'X') is used in package of user-defined [6], the signal of standard logic vector that the number of "X" is N is generated in this function. It is effective saving logic element and improve the conversion rate that the algorithm is used in this design. Schematic diagram shown in Fig. 102.4.

102.5 Simulation Verification for the IP Core

A vector waveform file is created to simulate the IP core in the Quartus development environment when the design has been accomplished. The input signal covers the special value of ± 0 and $\pm\infty$, the maximum value and the minimum

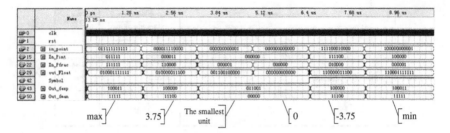

Fig. 102.5 Conversion (1, 5, 6) fixed-point format to (1, 6, 5) floating-point format

Fig. 102.6 Conversion (1, 6, 5) floating-point format to (1, 5, 6) fixed-point format

Table 102.3 The simulation results of conversion fixed-point number to floating-point number

Digit number	Registered performance (MHz)	Logic elements
12	317.86	96
24	235.85	228
32	178.22	296
64	144.28	660

value in the range of fixed-point and the non-special value, etc. The simulation result shows that time sequence is correct. When the format of floating-point is (1, 6, 5) and the format of fixed-point is (1, 5, 6), the simulation result shown in Figs. 102.5 and 102.6.

Three-level pipeline structure is adopted in this design and the relationship between each signal is handled flexibly, the result shows that it has saved logic element and conversion rate has been greatly improved. The format of floating-point is (1, 6, 5), (1, 7, 16), (1, 8, 23) and (1, 11, 52) respectively, the simulation show that the corresponding fixed-point is (1, 5, 6), (1, 11, 12), (1, 15, 16) and (1, 31, 32) in EP2C35F484C6 of Cyclone, the registered performance and the logic elements of conversion floating-point number to fixed-point number and conversion fixed-point number to floating-point number are shown in Tables 102.3 and 102.4.

Traditional algorithm is improved in the design, Tables 102.3 and 102.4 show that the working speed is twice that of 5 references, conversion fixed-point number to floating-point number have used elements less than 5 references, conversion floating-point number to fixed-point number have used elements little more than 5 references.

Table 102.4 The simulation results of conversion floating-point number to fixed-point number	Digit number	Registered performance (MHz)	Logic elements
	12	243.61	163
	24	239.69	243
	32	187.83	537
	64	137.95	831

102.6 Conclusion

This paper investigates mutual conversion between fixed-point format and floating-point format based on FPGA. It reach the target of using less elements to implement higher speed that pipeline technology is used and the relationship between each signal is handled flexibly.

References

1. Wand X, Xiong S, Li Y (2009) The introduction and improvement of EDA technology, 2nd edn. Xi'an Electronic Sience &Technology University Press, Xi'an
2. Kuang J, Mao X, Peng J (2010) An FPGA implementation of signal precision float-point multiplier. Application of Electronic Technique 5:17–19 (in Chinese)
3. IEEE (1985) Standard for binary floating-point arithmetic. IEEE Std 754-1985, pp 1–14
4. IEEE (1981) A proposed standard for binary floating-point arithmetic. IEEE Tran Comput 14(12):51–62, Task P754
5. Meyer-Baese U (2007) Digital signal processing with field programmable gate array, 3rd edn. Springer, Berlin
6. Roth CH Jr, Kurian John L (2004) Digit systems design using VHDL, 2nd edn. Prentice Hall, Upper Saddle River

Chapter 103
A New Method of Self-Adaptive Tracking Based on IMM-CS

Jiesheng Liu, Dengyi Zhang, Zhiyun Zhang and Biyin Zhang

Abstract Tracking the target is hotspot of research in fusion. This paper proposed an improved method for tracking named IMM-CS, which has achieved the aim of tracking by choosing self-adaptively the maneuver frequency and the maximum possible acceleration of target. The numerical experiment shows that this new method could track maneuvering target effectively, improving the precision of the target and having application value.

Keywords Target tracking · CS model · Self-adaptive · Maneuver frequency

103.1 Introduction

The maneuvering target tracking is the hotspot and difficulty in the field of data fusion, which has a wide range of requirements and applications in the defense area of missile defense, air early warning and battlefield surveillance. Now the current statistic model (CS model) proposed by a famous Chinese scholar Zhong Hongren in 1983 has shown strong vitality in the tracking field of maneuvering targets, which is one of the popular methods for tracking of maneuvering targets [1–4]. Because this model possesses solid theoretical foundation and ingenious design, which adopts the non-zero mean value and the revised Rayleigh distribution to characterize the maneuver acceleration characteristics so that it will be

J. Liu · D. Zhang
Computer School, Wuhan University, Wuhan 430072, China

Z. Zhang · B. Zhang (✉)
Wuhan Digital Engineering Institute, Wuhan 430074, China
e-mail: succor_com@sina.com

W. Lu et al. (eds.), *Proceedings of the 2012 International Conference on Information Technology and Software Engineering*, Lecture Notes in Electrical Engineering 211, DOI: 10.1007/978-3-642-34522-7_103, © Springer-Verlag Berlin Heidelberg 2013

more truthful. But there are certain problems in the CS model when it is used to describe the tracking of weak maneuvering target and the value of the acceleration. Reference [5] has proposed an improved CS method, bringing forward that the revised normal distribution should be used to make up the shortcomings of revised Rayleigh distribution. It will solve the problem in tracking weak maneuvering target, but it may cause a significant drop in tracking performance when the target acceleration changes too significantly. Reference [6] self-adaptively regulates the maximum acceleration via the fuzzy reasoning system, so that the status noise covariance of the system can regulate self-adaptively during the tracking process. But it is difficult to control the dependence degree in the fuzzy reasoning system, which may easily cause a sudden change in the system noise estimation. The above methods are aimed to locally solve certain types of target maneuver problem, but it is hard for them to adapt to the target tracking in the complex environments such as high maneuver, weak maneuver and movement at constant speed.

This paper has sufficiently combined the advantages of the CS model and the improved CS model, based on which an improved IMM-CS self-adaptive tracking algorithm is put forward. By controlling the maneuver frequency, three models can be chosen self-adaptively, i.e. weak maneuver, evasion maneuver and atmospheric disturbance, which can solve the tracking problem of complex maneuvering target.

103.2 Current Statistics Model Algorithm and Analysis

103.2.1 Current Statistics Model Algorithm

Based on the Singer Model, Professor Zhou Hongren has put forward the "current" statistic (CS) model of maneuvering targets. In nature this algorithm model is a Singer model [1, 6] with self-adaptive non-zero even acceleration. But different from the approximation even distribution assumption in the Singer model algorithm, the revised Rayleigh distribution is used in this algorithm to describe the statistical characteristics of the maneuver acceleration. The assumed distribution possesses the following advantages: the distribution will change as the even value changes, and the variance is determined by the even value. Therefore, while estimating the target status, this algorithm can also identify the maneuver acceleration mean value, which will revise the acceleration distribution in real time. By feeding the variance back to the filter gain at the next moment, the closed loop self-adaptive tracking will be realized, whose tracking principle runs as follows:

Assuming that the target movement status equation is

$$X(k + 1) = F(k)X(k) + G(k)\bar{a} + V(k) \tag{103.1}$$

where $F(k)$ is the state transition matrix, and $G(k)$ is the input control matrix, i.e.

$$G(k) = \begin{bmatrix} \frac{1}{\alpha}\left(-T + \frac{\alpha T^2}{2} + \frac{1-e^{-\alpha T}}{\alpha}\right) \\ T - \frac{1-e^{-\alpha T}}{\alpha} \\ 1 - e^{-\alpha T} \end{bmatrix} \tag{103.2}$$

$V(k)$ is the discrete time white noise sequence, and

$$Q(k) = E[V(k)V'(k)] = 2\alpha\sigma_a^2 \begin{bmatrix} q_{11} & q_{12} & q_{13} \\ q_{12} & q_{22} & q_{23} \\ q_{13} & q_{23} & q_{33} \end{bmatrix} \tag{103.3}$$

In the formula, α is the autocorrelation time constant, σ_a^2 is maneuver acceleration variance, and $\bar{a}(k)$ is the maneuver acceleration even value, i.e.

$$\sigma_a^2 = \frac{4 - \pi}{\pi}[a_{\max} - \bar{a}(k)]^2 \tag{103.4}$$

$$\bar{a}(k) = \hat{\tilde{x}}(k|k - 1) \tag{103.5}$$

The current statistic model algorithm has already possessed the capability of regulating the progress noise self-adaptively according to the acceleration estimate value at the previous moment, with its more concern on the current statistical characteristics of the target maneuver [7, 8], i.e. when a target is moving at a certain speed, the changing range of the acceleration at its next moment is limited, which can only be inside a certain neighborhood of the current acceleration. Therefore, compared to the Singer model algorithm, the current statistic model algorithm can more realistically reflect the target maneuver range and its intensity changes.

103.2.2 Analysis on CS Model Problems

The thought of the CS model is: when a target is now maneuvering at certain acceleration, its acceleration range at the next moment will be very limited. And moreover, it can only be inside the "current" acceleration range, i.e. the maneuver acceleration should conform to the non-zero even value time correlation process, whose probability density will be described by the revised Rayleigh distribution.

When the target's "current" acceleration is positive, the probability density function is:

$$p_r(a) = \begin{cases} \frac{a_{\max}-a}{\mu^2}\exp\left(-\frac{(a_{\max}-a)^2}{2\mu^2}\right) & 0 < a < a_{\max} \\ 0 & a \geq a_{\max} \end{cases} \tag{103.6}$$

When the target's "current" acceleration is negative, the probability density function is:

$$p_r(a) = \begin{cases} \frac{a - a_{-max}}{\mu^2} \exp\left(-\frac{(a-a_{-max})^2}{2\mu^2}\right) & 0 > a > a_{-max} \\ 0 & a \leq a_{-max} \end{cases} \quad (103.7)$$

From (103.6) we know that

$$\int_0^{a_{max}} a^2 p(a) da = E^2(a) + D(a) \leq a_{max} \int_0^{a_{max}} ap(a) = a_{max} E(a) \quad (103.8)$$

Therefore the current statistic model can only describe the maneuvering target whose acceleration is in the range of $\left[\left(\frac{4-\pi}{4}\right)a_{max}, a_{max}\right]$ and $\left[a_{-max}, \left(\frac{4-\pi}{4}\right)a_{-max}\right]$, which shows the essential reason why it has rather large errors during the tracking of weak maneuvering targets, i.e. the current statistic model cannot describe the weak maneuvering targets within the region of $\left[\left(\frac{4-\pi}{4}\right)a_{-max}, \left(\frac{4-\pi}{4}\right)a_{max}\right]$. Besides, the value selection of a_{max} has a quite large effect on the tracking performance of the CS model. If a_{max} is selected too big, even though it can enlarge the bandwidth of the tracking filter, so as to improve the tracking capability of the maneuvering targets, the steady-state error of the tracking filter will increase at the same time. If a_{max} is selected too small, it will definitely decrease the bandwidth of the tracking filter. Even though it can decrease the steady-state of the tracking filter, it will reduce the tracking capability on maneuvering targets.

103.3 Improved IMM-CS Algorithm

Aiming at the above mentioned problems, this paper combines with the method in Ref. [2] to solve the tracking problem of weak maneuvering target pertinently. And based on this, this paper has proposed the improved IMM-CS algorithm to realize the self-adaptive selection on maneuver frequency α and maximum acceleration a_{max}, which will effectively solve the tracking performance decrease problem caused by the inappropriate selection of a_{max}.

Three kinds of representative CS models are selected in the improved IMM-CS model algorithm, with each kind of model corresponding to one typical maneuver frequency and progress noise, whose specific value runs as follows:

In CS model 1, the maneuver frequency $\alpha_1 = 1$, and the maximum acceleration $a_{max} = 0.1$.
In CS model 2, the maneuver frequency $\alpha_1 = 1/60$, and the maximum acceleration $a_{max} = 20$.
In CS model 3, the maneuver frequency $\alpha_1 = 1/20$, and the maximum acceleration $a_{max} = 60$.

For the given moment k, the state estimate $\hat{X}_i(k|k)$ for the ith model, the status covariance $P_i(k|k)$, the model probability $\mu_i(k)$ and the model transition probability matrix is $\pi = \begin{bmatrix} 0.8 & 0.15 & 0.05 \\ 0.3 & 0.4 & 0.3 \\ 0.05 & 0.15 & 0.8 \end{bmatrix}$, π_{ij} stands for the probability of transition from model i to model j.

The normal process to calculate the target status estimate $\hat{X}(k+1|k+1)$ at the moment $k+1$ runs as follows:

1. Filter

   The status and pre-experiment covariance of each model after one step of predication are respectively:

$$\hat{X}_i(k+1|k) = F_i(k)\hat{X}_i(k|k) + U\bar{a} \tag{103.9}$$

$$P_i(k+1|k) = F_i(k)P_i(k|k)F_i(k)' + Q_i(k) \tag{103.10}$$

   The status estimate and post-experiment covariance of each model after the filtering

$$\hat{X}_i(k+1|k+1) = \hat{X}_i(k+1|k) + K(k+1)\lfloor Z(k) - H(k)\hat{X}_i(k+1|k)\rfloor \tag{103.11}$$

$$P_i(k+1|k+1) = (I - K(k+1)H(k+1))P_i(k+1|k) \tag{103.12}$$

2. The model probability update of the dynamic weight value distribution based on the dependence degree

   Assume that the status difference between the model i and model j at the moment $k+1$ is

$$\Delta X_j(k+1) = X_i(k+1) - X_j(k+1) \tag{103.13}$$

Then the sum of range deviations between model i and other models is

$$d_i(k+1) = \sum_{j \neq i}^{n} sqrt\left(\Delta X_j(t)\Delta X_j(t)'\right) \tag{103.14}$$

According to the range deviation $d_i(k+1)$, deviation mean value $\bar{d}(k+1)$ and variance $\sigma(k+1)$ of each model, the dependence degree obtained between each model and other models is

$$\xi_i(k+1) = \exp\left(-\frac{d_i(k+1) - \bar{d}(k+1)}{\sigma(k+1)}\right) \tag{103.15}$$

Then the dependence relationship between each model and other models can be calculated as

$$\mu_i(k+1) = \xi_i(k+1)/\sum_{j=1}^{n} \xi_j(k+1) \tag{103.16}$$

3. Interactive output

$$\hat{X}(k+1) = \sum_{i=1}^{n} \mu_i \hat{X}_i(k+1|k+1)$$

$P(k+1|k+1)$

$$= \sum_{i=1}^{n} \left(P_i(k+1|k+1) + x_{oi}(k+1|k+1)x_{oi}(k+1|k+1)' \right) \mu_i(k+1)$$

where $x_{oi}(k+1|k+1) = \hat{X}_i(k+1|k+1) - \hat{X}(k+1|k+1)$.

103.4 Simulation Results and Analysis

The simulation environment and parameters are set up according to the Ref. [1], pp. 164 of this paper, i.e. the original position of the target in the Cartesian coordinate system is (120, 2 km), the target velocity is 426 m/s, the course is 270°, the radar precision is 100 m, 0.03°, the radar scan period is 1 s, and the target lasting process is 100 s. And the moment when the target maneuver occurs and the acceleration sizes are shown in Table 103.1:

Figures 103.1 and 103.2 are the results of the Monte Carlo simulation experiment, in which Fig. 103.1 is the simulated scenario, radar measurements and the target moving trajectory tracking with IMM-CS algorithm, and Fig. 103.2 is the positional root mean square error of the IMM-CS model. From Fig. 103.1, we can intuitively see that: IMM-CS algorithm proposed in this paper can perform rather good tracking of weak maneuver at the tracking beginning phase, besides adapting quite well to the tracking of largely maneuvering target with quick switchover for different accelerations.

The Ref. [1] has quite comprehensively compared and simulated the current popular tracking algorithms and their tracking error precisions. This paper investigated the RMS (as shown in Fig. 103.2) of IMM-CS algorithm under the simulated environment of same scenario and the parameter settings with that of Ref. [1]. In Ref. [1], the algorithm with the highest precision under this environment is Jerk Model, whose error is about 60 m, while the algorithm with a big error is the Singer Model, whose error is about 100 m. Under the same simulated

Table 103.1 Target maneuver situation table

Moment of target maneuver	t = 31	t = 38	t = 49	t = 61	t = 65	t = 66	t = 81
Acceleration in X direction	5	−8	10	0	−10	−5	5
Acceleration in Y direction	−10	18	−20	30	−8	0	−10

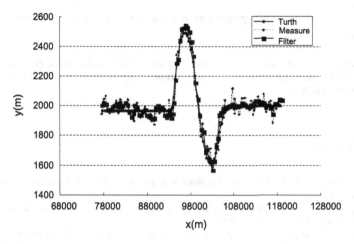

Fig. 103.1 Target moving trajectory diagram

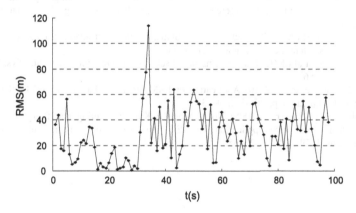

Fig. 103.2 RMS statistics of tracking algorithm

environment, the error of the algorithm proposed in this paper is about 40 m. By comparing Ref. [1] and the tracking RMS effects in Fig. 103.2, the results show that the tracking precision of this algorithm has been greatly improved.

103.5 Conclusion

The numerical value comparison experiments in this paper show that this method has obvious tracking effects, which can not only effectively adapt to the tracking of largely maneuvering target, but also can improve the target tracking precision greatly. Moreover, we have also found out during the experiment that when switching over different tracking models, there are big jitters in the target velocity and course, and the convergence rate is quite slow, which needs further study in the future.

Acknowledgments The work was supported by National Defense Advanced Research of China (No. 51306030201) and National Defense Advanced Research Foundation of China (No. 9140A06040111CB39).

References

1. He Y, Xiu J et al (2009) Radar data processing and application. Electronics Industry Press pp 143–144
2. Wang X, Qin Z et al (2009) Fuzzy self-adaptive tracking algorithm based on Current Statistic Model. War Ind J 33(8):1089–1093
3. Li H, Feng X et al (2004) A new maneuvering target model and its self-adaptive tracking algorithm. Electron Inf J 26(6):966–970
4. Li XR, Jilkov VP (2000) A survey of maneuvering target tracking: dynamic models. In: Proceedings of the SPIE conference on signal and data processing of small target 4048: 212–235
5. Wang S, Ruan H (2011) Revised "Current" Statistic Model self-adaptive tracking algorithm. Electron Inf Countermeas Technol 26(1):34–38
6. Ba H, Zhao Z et al (2002) Maneuvering target self-adaptive tracking algorithm. Syst Simul J 16(6):1181–1186
7. Yang L, Yuan Z et al (2010) Application of IMM algorithm based on model CS in target tracking. Comp Eng Appl 6(33):230–238
8. Abdolreza DT, Nasser S (2008) Novel adaptive Kalman filtering and fuzzy track fusion approach for real time application. In: IEEE conference on industrial electronics and applications. IEEE, US, pp 20–35

Chapter 104
Chinese Text Filtering Based on Domain Keywords Extracted from Wikipedia

Xiang Wang, Hu Li, Yan Jia and SongChang Jin

Abstract Several machine learning and information retrieval algorithms have been used for text filtering. All these methods have a common ground that they need positive and negative examples to build user profile. However, not all applications can get good training documents. In this paper, we present a Wikipedia based method to build user profile without any other training documents. The proposed method extracts keywords of a special category from Wikipedia taxonomy and computes the weights of the extracted keywords based on Wikipedia pages. Experiment results on Chinese news text dataset SogouC show that the proposed method achieves good performance.

Keywords Text filtering · Wikipedia · User profile

104.1 Introduction

With the explosion of electronic documents, Information filtering applications become more and more important because they can automatically send potentially interested information to users. Information filtering systems need to build up a model to represent user's interests. Users can show positive examples and negative examples to Information filtering systems to build the model. We call this model "user profile" or "topic profile". When a new article comes and it's a substantial

X. Wang (✉) · H. Li · Y. Jia · S. Jin
School of Computer, National University of Defense Technology, 410073 Changsha, China
e-mail: xiangwangcn@gmail.com

H. Li
e-mail: lihu201314@163.com

W. Lu et al. (eds.), *Proceedings of the 2012 International Conference on Information Technology and Software Engineering*, Lecture Notes in Electrical Engineering 211, DOI: 10.1007/978-3-642-34522-7_104, © Springer-Verlag Berlin Heidelberg 2013

match to user profile, then Information filtering systems will send the article to the user. Comparing to information classification which classifies documents to many different categories, information filtering is just binary text classification that classifies documents to "relevant" and "not relevant".

TREC conferences introduced the filtering track and attracted many researchers around the world. In TREC batch filtering track, it's assumed that the "user profile" does not change any more once it's constructed and information filtering system does not have to return ranked documents to users.

To best of our knowledge, methods proposed in information filtering need positive and negative examples or training documents to build "user profile". No matter information retrieve algorithms such as Rocchio algorithm or machine learning algorithms such as naive bayes algorithm, k-nearest neighbour methods and support vector machines, they all need positive and negative examples or training documents to build "user profile". In some applications there are no relevance documents to build "user profile". How to build "user profile" becomes a big problem. This paper is trying to build "user profile" from Wikipedia which is the largest free, collaboratively edited, multilingual Internet encyclopedia.

Wikipedia now contains nearly 22 million articles in all linguage. Its articles have been written collaboratively by volunteers around the world. Many researches are based on Wikipedia. Evgeniy Gabrilovich and Shaul Markovitch [1] computed semantic relatedness using Wikipedia and proposed ESA algorithm. David Milne and Ian H. Witten [2] obtain semantic relatedness only using Wikipedia links. Xiaohua Hu et al. [3] used Wikipedia as external knowledge for document clustering. Pu Wang and Carlotta Domeniconi [4] built semantic kernels for text classification using Wikipedia.

We can extract many keywords of a specified category from Wikipedia taxonomy. Every concept (concept can be used as keyword) in Wikipedia has a page to explain it. Then we can calculate weight of these keywords from Wikipedia pages. The weighted keywords then can be used as "user profile". In our method, there are no need positive and negative examples. Our method just learns from the free encyclopedia Wikipedia.

The remaining of the paper is organized as follows. In Sect. 104.2, we give a brief introduction to the related work. In Sect. 104.3, we describe the problems and our methods. Section 104.4 is the experiment study, which compares our methods with traditional VSM based models in a real dataset of SogouC. Section 104.5 concludes this study.

104.2 Related Work

Information retrieval and information filtering were often thought to be two sides of the same coin [5]. Although many underlining issues were similar in information retrieval and information filtering, there were some differences in the design issues and the techniques between them [6]. The main different was that users used "queries" like keywords to get the information they wanted at any time in IR systems but in IF systems "user profile" had to be constructed in the beginning. IF systems were commonly personalized to satisfy long term information needs of users [7]. Text filtering is one of the important research branches of IF. Text filtering is an information seeking process in which documents are selected from a dynamic text stream to satisfy a relatively stable and specific information need.

Text filtering has been studied from two different perspectives. One is from the machine leaning point, and the other from the IR view [8]. In the machine learning community, various methods such as naive Bayes classifiers, k-nearest neighbour methods, support vector machines and neural networks have been used for document filtering. Yang compared these methods with significance analyses [9]. In the information retrieval community, most studies used the Rocchio algorithm as baseline method for their classifiers. The Rocchio algorithm they used in their studies is a weak version. There are several improvements to Rocchio algorithm, such as better term weight, query-zoning, dynamic feedback optimization [10].

In text filtering, the representation of the user information need is referred to as "user profile" or "topic profile". The quality of "user profile" directly influences the performance of text filtering. There were two methods to represent "user profile", one is term-based method and the other is phrase-based method.

The term-based IF systems used terms to represent the "user profiles". This representation is simple and common. The basic term-based IF models used in TREC 2002 were SVM, Rocchio's algorithm, probabilistic models and BM25 [11]. The advantage of term-based mode is good computational performance and the term weighting method has been studied for many decades from the IR and machine learning community. However, term-based method has some disadvantages. First, the relationship among the words can not be reflected in this method. Second, the synonym problem and homonym problem can not be well solved.

Because of the disadvantages of term-based method, phrase-based method was therefore proposed. This method used the phrases as features to overcome the limitations of the semantic ambiguity problem. The simple term-based representation of the profile is usually inadequate, because single words usually cannot discriminate accurately. The main research work in this paper is to use phrases which are extracted from Wikipedia to represent "user profile".

104.3 Build User Profile

In this section, we describe the method used to information filtering. The method includes two stages. The first stage is to construct "user profile" from Wikipedia taxonomy. The second stage is to use this "user profile" to filter documents.

In the first stage, we have to build user model from Wikipedia taxonomy. Wikipedia is a very large knowledge base. It contains nearly 500,000 concepts in Chinese and these concepts are in a category hierarchy. Concepts in Wikipedia are

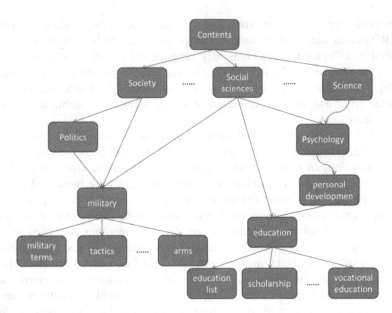

Fig. 104.1 Wikipedia taxonomy

explicitly assigned to one or more categories. The central goal of the category system is to provide navigational links to all Wikipedia pages in a hierarchy of categories to ensure readers can quickly browse and find sets of pages on topics [12]. Wikipedia's category hierarchy forms a graph. Any category may contain subcategories, and it is possible for a category to be a subcategory of more than one "parent" category. Figure 104.1 is abridged general view of the Wikipedia taxonomy.

In Fig. 104.1, we can find concept "military" and "Education" both belong to more than one category and have more than one subcategory. There are three main kinds of category: topic category, set category and set-and-topic category. Topic categories are named after a topic such as category "France" contains articles related to the topic France. Set categories are named after a class (usually in the plural) such as category "Cities in France" contains articles whose subjects are cities in France. Set-and-topic category combine topic category and set category such as category "Voivodeships" of Poland which contains articles about particular voivodeships as well as articles relating to voivodeships in general. But there are some categories that are not explicitly belong to the three main categories. For example, category "Chicago Stags Coaches" is a subcategory of "Natural Sciences". So if we get keywords of a special domain like education from Wikipedia taxonomy, we have to consider the relationships that are not explicit.

In Wikipedia's category hierarchy, the depth can reach up to 15 or higher. We can give an empirical result that when the depth is higher, there is more irrelevant keywords. So if you're trying to actually find pages about a special class, it's necessary to limit the depth of your breadth first search down the graph.

Fig. 104.2 Wikipedia page "Nell Alden Armstrong"

In experiment, we just use depth 2 because the keywords extracted will be very relevance.

In the second stage, we have to compute the weight of keywords extracted from Wikipedia taxonomy. We know that a concept in Wikipedia is explained by a page. Figure 104.2 is a Wikipedia page of "Nell Alden Armstrong". There are words, pictures and so on to explain the concept "Nell Alden Armstrong". We use this explain page to calculate the weight of keywords.

We have to compute the extracted keywords' tf value. We use the following equation to compute it.

$$weight(k_i) = \frac{freq(k_i)}{W} \tag{104.1}$$

where $weight(k_i)$ is the weight of keyword k_i. $freq(k_i)$ is the frequence of k_i in all pages contained in this domain. W is sum of all words' frequence in all pages.

Then we can use this weighted keywords to information filtering. We extracted keywords of category "Education" and "Military" from Wikipedia taxonomy and computed the weights. Table 104.1 shows the top-10 weighted keywords of the two categories.

In this paper we use vector of weighted keywords to represent "user profile". A new document in the incoming stream of information filtering system is token to words and we compute the tfidf value as weight of each word. Then we use consine metric to compute the similarity of the user profile vector and document vector. This is known as vector based model. We call this method "WikiBasedMethod".

Table 104.1 Top-10 weighted keywords of category education and military

Education	Military
Education	Military
Examinee	War
Examination	National defense
Review	Soldier
Score	Politics
Vocational school	Strategy
Examination questions	Military equipment
Test paper	Tactic
Composition	Strategic
Self-study examination	Politics

104.4 Experimental Studies

We do our experiments on a real dataset of SogouC [13]. The SogouC dataset comes from website of "Sohu news". The corpus is arranged manually and partitioned into ten categories: automobile, financial, IT, health, sports, travel, education, career, culture and military. There are totally 80,000 classified news documents. Every category contains 8,000 news documents. The size of the dataset is 221 M. In this experiment, we split all categories' documents in SogouC into two parts: one is used for training and the other is used for testing. Both training and testing sets have 4,000 documents. The baseline method uses training set to learn and both our method and the compared method use the testing sets to evaluate.

Our method described in Sect. 104.3 is compared to a method which is based on vector space model and using training documents to build user profile. This method computes words' tfidf values in training set and uses the resulting vector as "user profile". Then this method calculates the similarity of testing documents and "user profile". If the similarity is larger than the threshold value, then it will be filtered. We call this compared method "TrainDocsBasedMethod".

We firstly compare our method "WikiBasedMethod" with the compared method "TrainDocsBasedMethod" in category "Education". Figures 104.3 and 104.4 show that as the threshold changes, the recall value, precision value and f1 value of method "TrainDocsBasedMethod" and method "WikiBasedMethod" changes. In Fig. 104.3, we can find the point that recall value, precision value and f1 value equal to each other. This is the best value we can get and the value is 0.6485. In Fig. 104.4, we also can find the same point, while the recall value, precision value and f1 value is 0.6508. We can find that our method's precision value, recall value and f1 value nearly the same as the "TrainDocsBasedMethod" method. This means that our method can reach the same result as training documents based method.

Secondly, we compare our method "WikiBasedMethod" with method "TrainDocsBasedMethod" in category military. Figures 104.5 and 104.6 show that as the threshold changes, the recall value, precision value and f1 value of

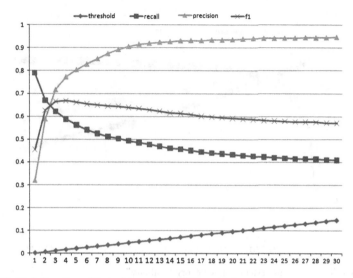

Fig. 104.3 TrainDocsBasedMethod in category "Education"

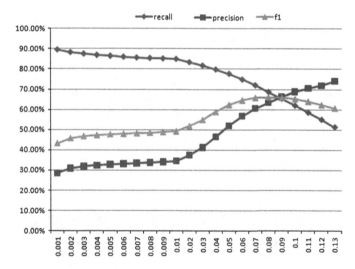

Fig. 104.4 WikiBasedMethod in category "Education"

method "TrainDocsBasedMethod" and method "WikiBasedMethod" changes. In Fig. 104.5, we can find that in "TrainDocsBasedMethod" method when the threshold value is 1.8, the f1 value is the largest one. In the same time, the recall value reaches to 0.8495 and precision value reaches 0.8618. In Fig. 104.6, we can find that in "WikiBasedMethod" method when the threshold is 7.1, the f1 value is the largest one, and the recall value is just 0.8086 and the precision value is

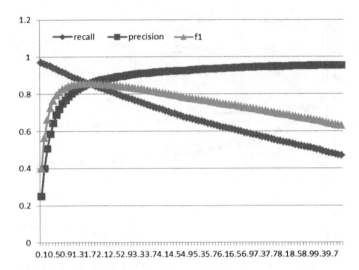

Fig. 104.5 TrainDocsBasedMethod in category "Military"

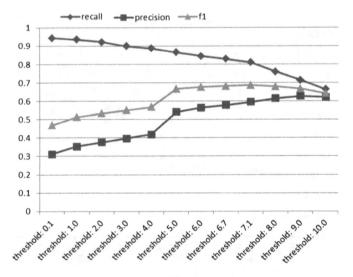

Fig. 104.6 WikiBasedMethod in category "Military"

0.6856. Comparing to "TrainDocsBasedMethod" method, we can find that the precision of our method is smaller, but our method also reach a high recall and precision. We can get the conclusion that in different category, comparing to "TrainDocsBasedMethod" method, our method will get different efficiency.

104.5 Conclusion

Wikipedia contains much semantic knowledge that helps to improve text classification, clustering and filtering. However, most researches before just used Wikipedia as external knowledge to improve semantic. In this paper, we take full advantage of Wikipedia and use it as the source of user profile. Then we don't need positive examples or negative examples to build user profile. Our method is compared to method "TrainDocsBasedMethod" that uses training documents to build user profile. The experimental results on Chinese news text dataset SogouC show that the proposed method achieves good performance. Our method in category Education gets nearly the same results as "TrainDocsBasedMethod". Though the proposed method get lower precision than "TrainDocsBasedMethod", the performance is still very good. This research would be a significant contribution to text filtering for using Wikipedia to build user profile and get good performance. In future, we will try to further study on other categories like sports, automobile and so on.

Acknowledgments This work was supported by Basic Research Program of China (973 Program) under Grant No.2007CB311100, the National Natural Science Foundation of China (No. 61003261), the Key Project of National Natural Science Foundation of China under Grant No. 60933005, NSFC under Grant No. 60873204, "863" under Grant No. 12505, and "863" under Grant No. 2011AA010702.

References

1. Gabrilovich E, Markovitch S (2007) Computing semantic relatedness using Wikipedia-based explicit semantic analysis. In: Proceedings of the 20th international joint conference on artificial intelligence, AAAI Press, Hyderabad, pp 1606–1611
2. Milne D, Witten IH (2008) An effective, low-cost measure of semantic relatedness obtained from Wikipedia links. In: Proceedings of the 23th association for the advancement of artificial intelligence, AAAI Press, Chicago, pp 25–30
3. Hu X, Zhang X, Lu C, Park EK, Zhou X (2009) Exploiting Wikipedia as external knowledge for document clustering. In: KDD'09, 2009
4. Wang P, Domeniconi C (2008) Building semantic kernels for text classification using Wikipedia. In: KDD'08, 2008
5. Belkin NJ, Bruce Croft W (1992) Information filtering and information retrieval: two sides of the same coin? Commun ACM 35(12):29–38
6. Tryfonopoulos C, Koubarakis M, Drougas Y (2009) Information filtering and query indexing for an information retrieval model. ACM Trans Inf Syst 27(2):1–47
7. Zhou X, Li Y, Bruza P, Xu Y, Lau R (2010) A two-stage information filtering based on rough decision rule and pattern mining. J Emerg Technol Web Intell 2(4):326–332
8. Kim Y-H, Hahn S-Y, Zhang B-T (2000) Text filtering by boosting Naive Bayes classifiers. In: Proceedings of SIGIR'00, pp 168–175
9. Yang Y, Liu X (1999) A re-examination of text categorization methods. In: Proceedings of SIGIR'99, pp 42–99

10. Schapire RE, Singer Y, Singhal A (1998) Boosting and Rocchio applied to text filtering. In: Proceedings of SIGIR'98, pp 215–223
11. Robertson SE, Soboroff I (2002) The trec 2002 filtering track report. In: TREC, 2002
12. Wikipedia: categorization. http://en.wikipedia.org/wiki/Wikipedia:Categorization
13. SogouC dataset. http://www.sogou.com/labs/dl/tce.html

Chapter 105
An Evolutionary Semi-Supervised Subtractive Clustering Method by Seeding

Lei Gu

Abstract A semi-supervised subtractive clustering has been proposed recently. However, it performance depends greatly on the choice of the parameters of the mountain function and only proper parameters enable the clustering method to produce a better effect. In this paper, an evolutionary semi-supervised subtractive clustering method by seeding is presented. The novel approach uses the genetic algorithms for tuning the relative parameters of the subtractive clustering by minimizing the Davies Bouldin clustering validity index regarded as the fitness function. To investigate the effectiveness of our approach, several experiments are done three real datasets. Experimental results show that our proposed method can improve the clustering performance significantly compared to other two traditional semi-supervised clustering algorithms.

Keywords Semi-supervised clustering · Subtractive clustering · Genetic algorithms · Seeds

105.1 Introduction

Data clustering, known as one pattern recognition technique, has been used in a wide variety of fields. Clustering is a division of data into homogeneous groups called clusters. Each group consists of objects having the larger similarity between

L. Gu
The Key Laboratory of Embedded System and Service Computing, Ministry of Education, Tongji University, Shanghai 200092, China

L. Gu (✉)
School of Computer Science and Technology, Nanjing University of Posts and Telecommunication, Nanjing 210046, China
e-mail: gulei@njupt.edu.cn

W. Lu et al. (eds.), *Proceedings of the 2012 International Conference on Information Technology and Software Engineering*, Lecture Notes in Electrical Engineering 211, DOI: 10.1007/978-3-642-34522-7_105, © Springer-Verlag Berlin Heidelberg 2013

themselves than objects of other groups [1, 2]. Different measure and criteria of similarity lead to various clustering algorithms such as the c-means [3], fuzzy c-means [4], fuzzy c-mediods [5], partitioning round mediods [6], neural gas [7] and hierarchical algorithms.

The mountain clustering method, proposed by Yager and Filev, is a simple and effective method for estimation of cluster centers [8]. Because the mountain method can lead to the growing computational complexity, an approach known as the subtractive clustering method is suggested by Chiu [9]. Pal and Chakraborty proposed a scheme to tune the accuracy of the prototypes obtained by the mountain and subtractive methods [10]. Kim et al. improved the subtractive method by using the kernel trick and increased the accuracy of the subtractive clustering [11].

A small amount of labeled data is allowed to be applied to aiding and biasing the clustering of unlabeled data in semi-supervised clustering unlike the unsupervised clustering, and so a significant increase in clustering performance can be obtained by the semi-supervised clustering [12]. The popular semi-supervised clustering methods are composed of two categories called the similarity-based and search-based approaches respectively [13]. It is noticeable that semi-supervised kemans clustering by seeding was proposed in [12]. Basu et al. [12] introduced the clustering method viewed as the semi-supervised variants of k-means called Seed-KMeans (SeedKM). SeedKM can apply some labeled data called seeds to the initialization of KM.

One semi-supervised subtractive clustering method by seeding (SeedSCM) has been presented in [14]. The performance of SeedSCM depends heavily on the parameters of the mountain function and these parameters set to the positive constants are inappropriate to selecting or tuning. In this paper, an evolutionary semi-supervised subtractive clustering method by seeding (SeedSCMGA) is proposed. Based on the algorithm described in [15], SeedSCMGA can not only employ the genetic algorithms in tuning the parameters by minimizing the Davies–Boulidin (DB) index [16] as the fitness function.

The remainder of this paper is organized as follows. Section 105.2 reports the SeedSCM and the DB clustering validity index. In Sect. 105.3, the evolutionary semi-supervised subtractive clustering method SeedSCMGA is formulated. Experimental results are shown in Sects. 105.4, and 105.5 gives our conclusions.

105.2 The Previous Works

105.2.1 The SeedSCM

In [14], one semi-supervised subtractive clustering by seeding is presented. This approach also called SeedSCM is inspired by the SeedKM and applies the seed set S with a small scale to help the traditional subtractive clustering. The SeedSCM is outlined as follows [14]:

Step 1   Let k be the number of clusters, and α is a positive constant. Set $t = 1$. Given $X = \{x_1, x_2, \ldots, x_n\}$, S is the seed set and the subset of X.

Step 2   For each data point x_i ($i = 1, 2, \ldots, n$) from X, calculate the mountain function using by Eq. (105.1).

$$M(x_i) = \sum_{j=1}^{n} e^{-\alpha \cdot d(x_i, x_j)} \tag{105.1}$$

where $d(x_i, x_j) = \| x_i - x_j \|^2$ and α is positive constant.

Step 3   Based on Eq. (105.1). Choose the data point $\hat{x}$ whose mountain function is highest as a cluster center.

Step 4   Assign $\hat{x}$ to the same label with one nearest labeled data x^* from the seed set S, but the label of $\hat{x}$ should be different from the labels of other obtained already cluster centers.

Step 5   Let $t = t + 1$. If t is equal to the number of clusters k, then Step 8; otherwise go to Step 6.

Step 6   Remove all data with the same label as x^* from X and S respectively.

Step 7   Remove x^* from X and go to Step 2.

Step 8   End SeedSCM.

However, SeedSCM is sensitive to the parameter α selected and tuned difficultly. Therefore, the genetic algorithms are used for tuning the parameters by minimizing the value of the DB clustering validity index.

105.2.2 The DB Clustering Validity Index

The goodness of clustering can be evaluated by validity indices. The Davies–Bouldin index is a sort of clustering validity indices and a function of the ratio of the sum of within-cluster distance to between-cluster separation. The DB index can be defined by [16]:

$$I_{DB} = \frac{1}{k} \sum_{i=1}^{k} \max_{j, j \neq i} \left\{ \frac{W(U_i) + W(U_j)}{d(U_i, U_j)} \right\} \tag{105.2}$$

where k is the number of clusters, $1 \leq i, j \leq k$ $W(U_i)$ and $d(U_i, U_j)$ are defined as the within ith cluster scatter and the between ith and jth cluster distance respectively. Here the distance can be chosen as the Euclidean metric. When the found clusters have minimum within-cluster scatter and maximum between-class separation, the clustering can minimizes the value of the DB index and is taken as the optimal clustering.

105.3 The Proposed SeedSCMGA

Firstly, the semi-supervised technology by seeding is introduced into one improved unsupervised subtractive clustering presented in [15]. This novel obtained semi-supervised clustering approach is outlined as follows:

Step 1   The generation of seeds is given. Given the number of clusters k and a nonempty set $X = \{x_1, x_2, \ldots, x_n\}$ of all unlabeled data in the d-dimensional space R^d, the clustering algorithms can partition X into k clusters. Let S, called the seed set, be the subset of X and for each x_q ($x_q \in S$), the label be given by means of supervision [12]. We assume that S can be divided into k groups on the basis of data labels and each subgroup should contain at least two labeled data for the implementation of one-class support vector machine. Therefore, we get a k partitioning $\{S_1, S_2, \ldots, S_k\}$ of the seed set S.

Step 2   Let $P = X$, $t = 1$, and the parameters $\theta, \delta \in (0, 1)$.

Step 3   Let m be the number of elements in P. If $\lceil m \cdot \theta \rceil = 0$, then go to Step 10; otherwise for each data point x_i ($i = 1, 2, \cdots, m$) in P, find $\lceil m \cdot \theta \rceil$ nearest points including x_i in the set P to x_i, let the corresponding H^i be a set of these points, and calculate the mountain function of x_i using the following equation:

$$M(x_i) = \sum_{j=1}^{\lceil n \cdot \theta \rceil} e^{-d(x_i, h_j)} \tag{105.3}$$

where $d(x_i, h_j) = \|x_i - h_j\|^2$, and $h_j \in H^i (j = 1, 2, \ldots, \lceil m \cdot \theta \rceil)$.

Step 4   Choose the data point $\hat{x}$ whose mountain function is highest from P as a obtained cluster center.

Step 5   Assign $\hat{x}$ to the same label with one nearest labeled data x^* from the seed set S, but the label of $\hat{x}$ should be different from the labels of other obtained already cluster centers.

Step 6   If t is equal to the number of clusters k, then stop otherwise go to Step 7.

Step 7   Assume that $\hat{H}$ is the set of some nearest points including $\hat{x}$ in P to $\hat{x}$. It noticed that If $t = 1$, then the number of the elements in $\hat{H}$ is equal to $\lceil m \cdot \theta \rceil$, otherwise it is equal to $\lceil m \cdot \delta \rceil$. Remove all points belonging to $\hat{H}$ from P.

Step 8   Let m be the number of elements in P again. If P is empty or $\lceil m \cdot \delta \rceil$, $= 0$, then go to Step 10; otherwise for each data point x_i ($i = 1, 2, \ldots, m$) in the P, find $\lceil m \cdot \delta \rceil$ nearest points including x_i in P to x_i, and let the corresponding H^i be a set of these points again, and calculate the mountain function of x_i via the equation:

$$M(x_i) = \sum_{j=1}^{\lceil m \cdot \delta \rceil} e^{-d(x_i, h_j)} \tag{105.4}$$

where $h_j \in H^i$ $(j = 1, 2, \ldots, \lceil m \cdot \delta \rceil)$.

Step 9   Let $t = t + 1$ and go to Step 4.

Step 10   Obtain k same cluster centers and stop.

Secondly, the seeds should be applied to assigning each data x_i to one class label after k clusters centers are acquired according to the above algorithm flow.

If $x_i \in S$, then x_i is the labelled data; otherwise assign x_i to the uth cluster by the Eqs. (105.5) and (105.6).

$$u = \arg \min_{j=1}^{k} \left(\|x_i - c_j\|^2 \right), \quad if\ \forall x_q \in S,\ \min_{j=1}^{k} \left(\|x_i - c_j\|^2 \right) \leq \|x_i - x_q\|^2 \tag{105.5}$$

$$u = l, \quad if\ \forall j = 1, 2, \ldots, k, \min_{x_q \in S} \left(\|x_i - x_q\|^2 \right) < \|x_i - c_j\|^2 \tag{105.6}$$

where c_j is the jth cluster and the seed x_q belongs to the lth cluster.

Nextly, the value of the DB index can be calculated according to the labels of data points. The less value of the DB index indicates the better clustering here if using the DB index evaluates the above semi-supervised subtractive clustering.

Finally, for the parameters θ and δ the genetic algorithms (GAs) is uses for generating theirs optimal value. In SeeSCMGA, five main operations of GAs will be done as follow:

Encoding	In our encoding scheme, each parameter is encoded using 20 bits in a chromosome. A population size is set to 20 chromosomes.
Fitness evaluation	The value of the corresponding DB index is chosen as the fitness function to be minimized.
Selection	Our selection strategy was the stochastic universal sampling routine. Assuming a population of size N, the new population contains $0.9 N$ individuals from the original population after selection.
Crossover	The single-point crossover routine is used here. The crossover probability used in our experiments was 0.9.
Mutation	The mutation probability used here was 0.02.

Furthermore, here we set the maximum number of generations to 50

105.4 Experimental Results

To demonstrate the effectiveness of the SeedSCMGA, we compared it with two semi-supervised clustering methods, such as SeedSCM and SeedKM, on two UCI real datasets [17], referred to as BUPA and Haberman respectively. The BUPA dataset contains 345 cases with 6-dimensional feature from two classes. The Haberman dataset collects 306 3-dimensional cases belonging to two classes. All experiments were done by Matlab on Windows XP operating system.

Because the parameters of the traditional subtractive clustering method were set to $\alpha = 5.41$ and $\beta = 1.5$ as suggest by Pal and Chakarborty [10], in SSCS, only one parameters α is given the better value that can be selected from the set $\{5.4, 1.5\}$. For SeedSCMGA, SeedKM and SeedSCM, on each dataset, we randomly generated $P\%$ $(P = 3, 4, 5, \ldots, 10)$ of the dataset as seeds. Since true labels are known, clustering accuracies $Q\%$ on unlabeled data, the remaining $(100 - P)\%$ of the dataset, could be quantitatively assessed. Therefore, the clustering accuracies $G\%$ of the whole dataset consisting of unlabeled data and labeled seeds could be calculated by $Q\% \cdot (100 - P)\% + P\%$. To show that SeedSCMGA can have the better clustering performance than the SeedKM and SeedSCM when using a small amount of labeled data, the seed sets with a very small scale are applied to these smi-supervised clustering methods. On each dataset, the SeedSCMGA, SeedSCM and SeedKM were run 20 times for different P $(P = 3, 4, 5, \ldots, 10)$ and we report in Figs. 105.1 and 105.2 the average accuracies $G\%$ of the whole dataset obtained over these 20 runs.

Firstly, In Figs. 105.1 and 105.2, although the SeedKM and SeedSCM can improve the clustering performance on each dataset, we can see that the proposed SeedSCMGA can achieve the best clustering performance compared with them. Secondly, Figs. 105.1 and 105.2 demonstrate that the novel SeedSCMGA outperforms the SeedKM and SeedSCM when a very small amount of seeds is used to aid these semi-supervised clustering.

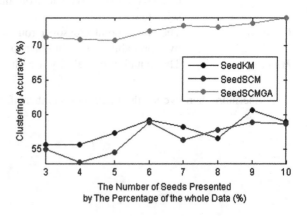

Fig. 105.1 Comparison of clustering accuracies on the Haberman dataset

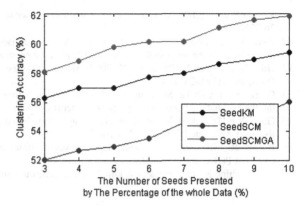

Fig. 105.2 Comparison of clustering accuracies on the BUPA dataset

105.5 Conclusions

In this paper, the presented method called SeedSCMGA applies the genetic algorithms to selecting the parameters of SeedSCMGA and tuning them. Experimental results show that the optimal parameters can lead to the better clustering performance compared with other semi-supervised clustering SeedSCM and SeedKM.

Acknowledgments This research is supported by the Open Foundation of the Key Laboratory of Embedded System and Service Computing, Ministry of Education, Tongji University, China (No.2011-01). This research is also supported by the Scientific Research Foundation of Nanjing University of Posts and Telecommunications (No.NY21 0078).

References

1. Jain AK et al (1999) Data clustering: a review. ACM Comput Surv 31(3):256–323
2. Xu R, Wunsch D (2005) Survey of clustering algorithms. IEEE Trans Neural Netw 16(3):645–678
3. Tou JT, Gonzalez RC (1974) Pattern recognition principles. Addison-Wesley, London
4. Bezdek JC (1981) Pattern recognition with fuzzy objective function algorithms. Plenum Press, New York
5. Krishnapuram R et al (2001) Low complexity fuzzy relational clustering algorithms for web mining. IEEE Trans Fuzzy Syst 9(4):595–607
6. Kaufman L, Rousseeuw PJ (1990) Finding groups in data: an introduction to cluster analysis. Wiley, New York
7. Matinetz TM et al (1993) "Neural-gas" network for vector quantization and its application to time-series prediction. IEEE Trans Neural Netw 4(4):558–568
8. Yager RR, Filev DP (1994) Approximate clustering via the mountain method. IEEE Trans Syst Man Cybern 24(8):1279–1284
9. Chiu SL (1994) Fuzzy model identification based on cluster estimation. J Intell Fuzzy Syst 2:267–278
10. Pal NR, Chakraborty D (2000) Mountain and subtractive clustering method: improvements and generalization. Int J Intell Syst 15:329–341

11. Kim DW et al (2005) A kernel-based subtractive clustering method. Pattern Recogn Lett 26:879–891
12. Basu S, Banerjee A, Mooney RJ (2002) Semi-supervised clustering by seeding. In: Proceedings of the nineteenth international conference on machine learning, pp 27–34
13. Grira N, Crucianu M, Boujemaa N (2008) Active semi-supervised fuzzy clustering. Pattern Recognit 41(5):1834–1844
14. Gu L, Ling LX (2012) Semi-supervised subtractive clustering by seeding. In: Proceedings of the 9th international conference on fuzzy systems and knowledge discovery, pp 738–741
15. Gu L, Wu HZ (2008) A subtractive clustering method based on genetic algorithms. Pattern Recognit Artif Intell 21(6):758–761 (in Chinese)
16. Bezdek JC, Nikhil RP (1998) Some new indexes of cluster validity. IEEE Trans Syst Man Cybernet Part B 28(3):301–315
17. UCI machine learning repository. http://www.ics.uci.edu/~mlearn/MLSummary.html

Chapter 106
Erratum to: GPS Location History Data Mining and Anomalous Detection: The Scenario of Bar-Headed Geese Migration

Yan Xiong, Ze Luo, Baoping Yan, Diann J. Prosser
and John Y. Takekawa

Erratum to:

GPS Location History Data Mining and Anomalous Detection: The Scenario of Bar-Headed Geese Migration, doi:10.1007/978-3-642-34522-7_44.

Page	Item or line	Corrections
413	Chapter 44	Replace the order of authors from Ze Luo, Yan Xiong, Baoping Yan, Diann J. Prosser and John Y. Takekawa by Yan Xiong, Ze Luo, Baoping Yan, Diann J. Prosser and John Y. Takekawa

The online version of the original chapters can be found at doi:10.1007/978-3-642-34522-7_44.

Y. Xiong · Z. Luo (✉) · B. Yan
Computer Network Information Center, Chinese Academy of Sciences,
Beijing 100190, China
e-mail: luoze@cnic.cn

D. J. Prosser
U.S. Geological Survey, Patuxent Wildlife Research Center,
Beltsville, MD 20705, USA
e-mail: dprosser@usgs.gov

J. Y. Takekawa
U.S. Geological Survey, Western Ecological Research Center,
Vallejo, CA 94592, USA
e-mail: john_takekawa@usgs.gov

W. Lu et al. (eds.), *Proceedings of the 2012 International Conference on Information Technology and Software Engineering*, Lecture Notes in Electrical Engineering 211, DOI: 10.1007/978-3-642-34522-7_106, © Springer-Verlag Berlin Heidelberg 2013